AMERICAN LEGAL PROCESS

ASPEN CASEBOOK SERIES

AMERICAN LEGAL PROCESS

BRADLEY SCOTT SHANNON

Professor of Law
Florida Coastal School of Law

Wolters Kluwer

ISBN 978-1-4548-4196-8

Library of Congress Cataloging-in-Publication Data

Shannon, Bradley Scott, author.
  American legal process/Bradley Scott Shannon, Professor of Law, Florida Coastal School of Law.
      pages cm. — (Aspen casebook series)
  ISBN 978-1-4548-4196-8
1. Justice, Administration of—United States. 2. Legislation—United States. 3. Separation of powers—United States. I. Title.
  KF384.S49 2015
  347.73—dc23
2014040732

2014040732

About Wolters Kluwer Law & Business

Wolters Kluwer Law & Business is a leading global provider of intelligent information and digital solutions for legal and business professionals in key specialty areas, and respected educational resources for professors and law students. Wolters Kluwer Law & Business connects legal and business professionals as well as those in the education market with timely, specialized authoritative content and information-enabled solutions to support success through productivity, accuracy and mobility.

Serving customers worldwide, Wolters Kluwer Law & Business products include those under the Aspen Publishers, CCH, Kluwer Law International, Loislaw, ftwilliam.com and MediRegs family of products.

CCH products have been a trusted resource since 1913, and are highly regarded resources for legal, securities, antitrust and trade regulation, government contracting, banking, pension, payroll, employment and labor, and healthcare reimbursement and compliance professionals.

Aspen Publishers products provide essential information to attorneys, business professionals and law students. Written by preeminent authorities, the product line offers analytical and practical information in a range of specialty practice areas from securities law and intellectual property to mergers and acquisitions and pension/benefits. Aspen's trusted legal education resources provide professors and students with high-quality, up-to-date and effective resources for successful instruction and study in all areas of the law.

Kluwer Law International products provide the global business community with reliable international legal information in English. Legal practitioners, corporate counsel and business executives around the world rely on Kluwer Law journals, looseleafs, books, and electronic products for comprehensive information in many areas of international legal practice.

Loislaw is a comprehensive online legal research product providing legal content to law firm practitioners of various specializations. Loislaw provides attorneys with the ability to quickly and efficiently find the necessary legal information they need, when and where they need it, by facilitating access to primary law as well as state-specific law, records, forms and treatises.

ftwilliam.com offers employee benefits professionals the highest quality plan documents (retirement, welfare and non-qualified) and government forms (5500/PBGC, 1099 and IRS) software at highly competitive prices.

MediRegs products provide integrated health care compliance content and software solutions for professionals in healthcare, higher education and life sciences, including professionals in accounting, law and consulting.

Wolters Kluwer Law & Business, a division of Wolters Kluwer, is headquartered in New York. Wolters Kluwer is a market-leading global information services company focused on professionals.

To Ann, who probably never thought she would see this day

Summary of Contents

Contents *xi*

Preface *xix*

Acknowledgments *xxv*

Chapter 1. Introduction to American Legal Process 1

Chapter 2. The Judicial Branch: The Making and Application of Case Law 23

Chapter 3. The Legislative Branch: The Enactment and Interpretation of Statutes 427

Chapter 4. The Executive Branch: Presidential Signing Statements, Executive Orders, Regulations, and the Role of Agencies in the Interpretation of Statutes 671

Table of Cases *759*

Table of Authorities *763*

Table of Constitutional Provisions, Statutes, Rules, Regulations, and Executive Orders *771*

Index *773*

Contents

Preface   *xix*
Acknowledgments   *xxv*

Chapter 1: Introduction to American Legal Process   1

A. Introduction to Legal Process   1

B. Introduction to the American Legal System   2
    1. The Federal System of Government   2
    2. State Systems of Government   2
    3. Sources of Law and the Priority of Authorities   3
    4. A Few Words About Conflicts of Laws   6

C. The Rule of Law   7
    Brian Z. Tamanaha, A Concise Guide to the Rule of Law   7

Chapter 2: The Judicial Branch: The Making and Application of Case Law   23

A. The Functions of Federal Courts   24

B. The Adjudicative Process in Perspective   25
    Henry M. Hart, Jr. & Albert Sacks, The Great Pyramid of
    Legal Order   25
    Lon L. Fuller, The Forms and Limits of Adjudication 27

C. The Role of Formal Logic   44
    Ruggero J. Aldisert, et al., Logic for Law Students: How to
    Think Like a Lawyer   44

D. The Parts of a Judicial Decision   57
    1. Syllabus and Headnotes   59
    Gil Grantmore, The Headnote   59

E. The Various Types of Opinions   **64**
    Sidebar: The Practice in Foreign Judicial Systems   73

F. Holding and Dicta   **74**
    Michael C. Dorf, Dicta and Article III   74
    Sidebar: A Further Word on Case Law Interpretation   82
    Sidebar: A Word About Case Law Terminology   84

G. The Binding Effect of Prior Decisions in Related Proceedings   **85**
    1. Law of the Case   85
        Christianson v. Colt Industries Operating Corp.   86
    2. Rehearing and Rehearing en Banc   92
        Easley v. Reuss   92
        Sidebar: The Doctrine of Judicial Estoppel   94
        Sidebar: The Rooker-Feldman Doctrine   95

H. The Concept of Precedent and the Doctrine of Stare Decisis   **96**
    1. Vertical Stare Decisis Generally   97
        Evan H. Caminker, Why Must Inferior Courts Obey
        Superior Court Precedents?   97
    2. State Law in Federal Courts   101
        Commissioner of Internal Revenue v. Estate of Bosch 101
    3. Federal Law in State Courts   103
        Donald H. Zeigler, Gazing into the Crystal Ball: Reflections on
        the Standards State Judges Should Use to Ascertain Federal Law 103
    4. Deference to Other Federal Courts as to the Law of a State
    Within Its Jurisdiction   105
        Salve Regina College v. Russell   106
        Factors Etc., Inc. v. Pro Arts, Inc.   114
    5. Certification to Another Court   120
        Jonathan Remy Nash, The Uneasy Case for
        Transjurisdictional Adjudication   120
        Jonathan Remy Nash, Examining the Power of Federal Courts
        to Certify Questions of State Law   123
    6. Horizontal Stare Decisis   132
        a. Stare Decisis in Practice   132
        Patterson v. McLean Credit Union   132
        Payne v. Tennessee   134
        Planned Parenthood of Southeastern Pa. v. Casey   138
        Sidebar: English and Civil Law Views of Precedent   151
        b. Horizontal Stare Decisis in the United States Court of Appeals 152
        In re Korean Air Lines Disaster of September 1, 1983 152
        c. Horizontal Stare Decisis in the District Courts   158
        d. Stare Decisis in Theory   159
        Henry M. Hart, Jr. & Albert M. Sacks, Note on the Reasons
        Supporting a General Practice of Adherence to Prior Holdings 159
        Frederick Schauer, Precedent   161

Gary Lawson, Mostly Unconstitutional: The Case Against
Precedent Revisited 179
Michael Stokes Paulsen, Does the Supreme Court's Current
Doctrine of Stare Decisis Require Adherence to the
Supreme Court's Current Doctrine of Stare Decisis? 187
7. Avoiding Precedent 201
8. Overruling by Implication 202
Practice Problem: Overruled by Implication 205
9. The Adoption of Precedent by Newly Created Courts 206
Bonner v. City of Prichard 206

I. Other Aspects of the Doctrine of Stare Decisis 212
1. The Significance (or Insignificance) of Denials of Further Review 212
2. Vacatur 218
United States Bancorp Mortgage Co. v. Bonner Mall Partnership 218
3. The "Unpublished" Decision Problem 225
Anastasoff v. United States 226
Hart v. Massanari 231
Sidebar: Citation Practice in England 244

J. Persuasive Authority 245
Antonin Scalia & Bryan A. Garner, Master the Relative
Weight of Precedents 245
Frederick Schauer, Authority and Authorities 247
Chad Flanders, Toward a Theory of Persuasive Authority 262

K. The Use of Foreign Law 274
Roper v. Simmons 275
Stephen Yeazell, When and How U.S. Courts Should Cite
Foreign Law 279

L. What is a "Hearing"? 285
Perez-Llamas v. Utah Court of Appeals 285
1. The Purpose and Value of Oral Argument 291
Antonin Scalia & Bryan A. Garner, Appreciate the
Importance of Oral Argument, and Know Your Objectives 292

M. The Need to Provide Reasons for the Decision 295
In re Shell Oil Co. 295
Taylor v. McKeithen 296
Frederick Schauer, Giving Reasons 298

N. The Propriety of Sua Sponte Decisions 318
Day v. McDonough 318
Greenlaw v. United States 327
Wood v. Milyard 335
Sidebar: Amicus Curiae Practice 341

O. **Deciding Issues for the First Time on Appeal**   **342**
    Weisgram v. Marley Co.   342

P. **The Retroactive and Prospective Application of Decisions**   **354**
  1. The Problem   354
  2. Basic Concepts   355
    Henry M. Hart, Jr. & Albert M. Sacks, A Further Note on
    the Conflict of Laws in Time   355
    a. A Brief Note on Terminology   356
  3. The Modern Cases   357
    Linkletter v. Walker   357
    Chevron Oil Co. v. Huson   364
    Griffith v. Kentucky   368
    Harper v. Virginia Department of Taxation   373
  4. Possible Constitutional Limitations on the Retroactive
    Application of Decisions   386
    Rogers v. Tennessee   386

Q. **Legislative Versus Judicial Resolution**   **399**
    Sidebar: Legislative Versus Adjudicative Facts and Relative
    Institutional Competence   401

R. **Judicial Impartiality**   **402**
    Cheney v. United States District Court for the District of
    Columbia, No. 03-475, Memorandum of Justice Scalia   402
    Caperton v. A.T. Massey Coal Co., Inc.   412

Chapter 3: The Legislative Branch: The Enactment and Interpretation of Statutes   427

A. **The Legislative Process**   **428**
    John V. Sullivan, Parliamentarian, United States House of
    Representatives, How Our Laws Are Made   429

B. **Statutes as Law**   **445**
    Mary Whisner, The *United States Code*, Prima Facie Evidence,
    and Positive Law   445
    Sidebar: Codes in Civil Law Countries   451
    Practice Problem: The Federal Legislative Process   452
    Sidebar: Treaties   453
    Sidebar: Initiatives and Referenda   454

C. **The Interpretation of Statutes**   **457**
  1. Basic Concepts   457
    Reed Dickerson, "Four Constitutional Assumptions"   457
  2. Historical Development   460
    a. Early Landmarks   461

Heydon's Case	461
Church of the Holy Trinity v. United States	463
Caminetti v. United States	468
United States v. American Trucking Associations, Inc.	475
Henry M. Hart, Jr. & Albert M. Sacks, Note on the Rudiments of Statutory Interpretation	480
b. The Modern Standard	487
Griffin v. Oceanic Contractors, Inc.	488
United States v. Ron Pair Enterprises, Inc.	493
c. A Case Study in Modern Statutory Interpretation	500
Smith v. United States	500
Bailey v. United States	512
Watson v. United States	517
3. Tools of Statutory Interpretation	522
a. The Parts of a Statute	523
b. Statutory Definitions	524
c. The Use of Dictionaries	526
Nix v. Hedden	526
Practice Problem: Dictionaries	531
d. The Use of Canons of Construction	532
William N. Eskridge, Jr. & Philip P. Frickey, Foreword: Law as Equilibrium	533
Practice Problem: Canons of Construction	538
e. Rules of Clear Statement	538
Equal Employment Opportunity Commission v. Arabian American Oil Co.	539
f. Statutory History	545
g. The Use of Legislative History	546
Sidebar: The English Perspective	552
h. Legislative Inaction	553
i. The Rejected Proposal Rule	553
ii. The Acquiescence Rule	555
Henry M. Hart, Jr. & Albert M. Sacks, The Implications of the Failure of Congress to Legislate	555
iii. The Reenactment Rule	557
i. Subsequent Legislative History	559
j. The Interpretation of Borrowed Statutes	560
4. Special Problems in Statutory Interpretation	561
a. The Absurdity Doctrine and the Problem of Scrivener's Errors	562
Green v. Bock Laundry Machine Co.	562
Practice Problem: Sexual Battery in Florida	568
b. Dealing with the Unanticipated: The Problem of New Applications of Old Statutes	569
McBoyle v. United States	569
In re Blanchflower	570

D. **Theories of Statutory Interpretation**   575
  William N. Eskridge, Jr. & Philip P. Frickey, Statutory
  Interpretation as Practical Reasoning   575
  1. Intentionalism vs. Textualism   578
     Henry M. Hart, Jr. & Albert M. Sacks, Why Should Word
     Meanings Be Respected at All?   578
     John F. Manning, Textualism and Legislative Intent   579
  2. Purposivism vs. Textualism   590
     John F. Manning, What Divides Textualists from Purposivists?   590
     Hillel Y. Levin, The Food Stays in the Kitchen: Everything
     I Needed to Know About Statutory Interpretation I Learned
     by the Time I Was Nine   605
     Practice Problem: No Dogs in the Park   613

E. **The Retroactive and Prospective Application of Statutes**   615
  Bradley v. School Board   616
  Bowen v. Georgetown University Hospital   621
  Landgraf v. USI Film Products   623
  Vartelas v. Holder   642
  1. Possible Constitutional Limitations to the Retroactive
     Application of Statutes   650
     Calder v. Bull   650

F. **Statutory and Other Conflicts**   657

G. **The Fate of Unconstitutional Statutes**   659
  Ayotte v. Planned Parenthood   660

H. **May Congress Retroactively Reopen Federal Court Judgments
   With Which It Disagrees?**   666
  Plaut v. Spendthrift Farm, Inc.   666

Chapter 4: The Executive Branch: Presidential Signing Statements, Executive Orders, Regulations, and the Role of Agencies in the Interpretation of Statutes 671

A. **Presidential Signing Statements**   672
  T.J. Halstead, Presidential Signing Statements: Constitutional
  and Institutional Implications   672

B. **Executive Orders and Other Presidential Directives**   685
  Tara L. Branum, President or King? The Use and Abuse of
  Executive Orders in Modern-Day America   685
  Youngstown Sheet & Tube Co. v. Sawyer   686

C. **Administrative Agencies, Regulations, and the Regulatory Process**   **691**
American Bar Association, Section of Administrative Law and
Regulatory Practice   692

D. **The Role of Administrative Agencies in the Interpretation of Statutes**   **700**
1. Historical Beginnings   700
Skidmore v. Swift & Co.   700
2. The Modern Standard   702
Chevron U. S. A. Inc. v. Natural Resources Defense Council, Inc.   702
3. Back to the Future?   706
United States v. Mead Corp.   706
Zuni Public School District v. Department of Education   722
4. The Latest Word   736
City of Arlington v. Federal Communications Commission   736
5. The Effect of Judicial Interpretation on Administrative
Interpretation   741
National Cable & Tel. Assn. v. Brand X Internet Services   742
United States v. Home Concrete & Supply, LLC   750

Table of Cases   *759*
Table of Authorities   *763*
Table of Constitutional Provisions, Statutes, Rules, Regulations,
and Executive Orders   *771*
Index   *773*

Preface

This book is about the American legal process, though not from the perspective of the political scientist, but rather that of the lawyer. It consists of a broad overview of what law is and how law is and should be made and applied. As explained by two leading pioneers in this field:

> Many of the troublesome and most frequently recurring difficulties in the law are not difficulties of the law of contracts, or torts, or property, or civil procedure, or constitutional law, or of any other of the conventional fields of substantive or procedural law. They are difficulties which are intrinsic in the whole enterprise of organizing and maintaining a society which will serve the purposes which societies exist to serve. They pose problems and implicate concepts which appear and reappear in every field of substantive law and in every process of decision—judicial, legislative, administrative, and private.
>
> . . . .
>
> [Such problems and concepts] present themselves in every law course. But teachers distracted by the often too acutely felt need of covering the ground indicated by the subject matter heading of the particular course cannot and do not pause to examine them in their full dimensions. The questions, however, are important to lawyers, and ought to be examined. They can be most economically dealt with in a course which is devoted to *law* and not simply to one of its subordinate branches.[1]

What was true more than 50 years ago when this excerpt was written remains true today. Because of its pervasive nature, "Legal Process" is and always will be an important law school subject—perhaps one of the most important—and a subject deserving of its own place in the curriculum.

Regarding the importance of the subject matter: It is often said that we now live in the age of statutes.[2] As a result, the law school graduates of today should be well adept at making arguments concerning the proper interpretation of statutes, meaning they should understand well the theory underlying this area of the law. Indeed, in a recent interview, Justice Antonin Scalia was asked whether law students today

---

1 HENRY M. HART, JR. & ALBERT M. SACKS, THE LEGAL PROCESS: BASIC PROBLEMS IN THE MAKING AND APPLICATION OF LAW cxxxvii-cxxxviii (William N. Eskridge, Jr. & Philip P. Frickey eds., 1994).
2 *See generally* GUIDO CALABRESI, A COMMON LAW FOR THE AGE OF STATUTES (1982).

"would be better served if they focused more on statutory construction than the case method."[3] Justice Scalia's response:

> Well, I have made that very point on occasions when I speak to law faculties and when I give a lecture at a law school. If they ask me how would I improve the current process of law teaching, I do make the point that what judges do nowadays is very little common law. But what they do almost all the time is that they interpret a text. They almost always have a text in front of them. And yet, at least when I went to law school, we didn't have a single textual course in the first year.
>
> And I think the law schools are changing that. I think that more and more of them are introducing a course on legislation, or on statutory construction, in the first year. I think that's important, not just for what it teaches but for the perspective it gives to the novice lawyer. This is not a world of the common law. It's a world in which textual interpretation is very important.[4]

Many have agreed, and many of the nation's leading law schools now have courses such as Justice Scalia describes. But statutory interpretation is just one aspect of a Legal Process course. Today's law school graduates should know how to work with *case* law as well. For example, they should also have a firm understanding of the distinction between holding and dicta, between binding and persuasive precedent, and whether a recently-decided case applies to their problem. Issues involving these and the other concepts addressed in this book arise in practice almost daily. And yet, no book available today encompasses all of these concepts. Hence, the reason for *this* book.

Regarding the need for a separate course on this subject: Another legal scholar once wrote (hopefully, perhaps): "Law school training enables a lawyer to figure out which laws to look up and how to look them up, and most importantly, what on earth to do with them once they are found."[5] Regrettably, it has been my experience that law school graduates today often do not know what to do with those laws they have found. Rather, most law school graduates today seem almost oblivious to Legal Process-type concepts. Though they might have some vague notions of these ideas, based largely on fleeting references made in other courses or in certain cases, they have no firm understandings along these lines. In large part, the general lack of understanding of these concepts is due to the lack of courses specifically directed toward this subject. (Indeed, unlike more typical subjects like Contracts and Torts, Legal Process—which is variously named Legal Method or Introduction to Law, among others—"ha[s] no common name."[6]) This is regrettable, for when Legal Process-type concepts are raised in other courses, they are done so only haphazardly, in an incomplete form and often by an instructor with little interest or knowledge in this area. But it seems that any subject worth teaching should be taught thoroughly and systematically, and that is another reason for this book. Admittedly, this book represents only an introduction to Legal Process. Not only have some

---

3 A.B.A. J. May 2008, at 38.
4 *Id.*
5 Anthony D'Amato, Introduction to Law and Legal Thinking viii (1996).
6 Richard B. Cappalli, *The Disappearance of Legal Method*, 70 Temp. L. Rev. 393, 438 (1997).

subjects been left unexplored, but those that are explored could be considered in much greater detail. Hopefully, though, the introduction set forth here will prove to be better than nothing.

Yet another reason for writing this book is my hope that practicing lawyers will consider this book something of a reference source. And that raises another point. A concerted effort was made in the writing of this book not only to raise questions, but also to answer them. Just as in Contracts and Torts, there is some settled law in the Legal Process area. The reader should know what that law is. But a firm understanding of the current state of the law does not mean that competing viewpoints have been omitted, or that there is no room for criticism or reform. To the contrary, efforts have been made to include that material as well.

Deciding what to include in this book has been difficult. Legal Process lies at the intersection of a number of areas of law, including administrative law, civil and criminal procedure, conflict of laws, constitutional law, federal courts, jurisprudence, and trial and appellate advocacy. Efforts have been made to confine the discussion to material and topics not typically covered in other courses (though some overlap is probably inevitable, and in a few places, some duplication is certainly possible). In particular, though this book includes a chapter on Executive Branch lawmaking, this book is *not* a substitute for a full course on administrative law. I believe that administrative law remains an important course in its own right and that a course that includes a reasonably thorough treatment of the legislative and judicial processes cannot do sufficient justice to administrative law as well. Some might disagree, just as some might believe that statutory interpretation itself should be taught as a stand-alone course. But in my mind, an introductory course on legislative, executive, and judicial lawmaking makes more sense than either a stand-alone legislation course or a "leg-reg" course with a more thorough (but still far from complete) picture of administrative law. The line has to be drawn somewhere, and that is where it is drawn here. I have also tried to avoid many of the subjects I believe are more appropriately dealt with in a course on jurisprudence. This is not to downplay the importance of the theoretical underpinnings of those doctrines that are included, but in the interest of time and space, something had to give, and I am content to operate at what some have described as the "retail level of statutory and common law interpretation,"[7] and to leave it to others to deal with the "wholesale level of constitutional law" and the "meta-level of jurisprudence."[8] Thus, this book assumes (e.g.) that there is such a thing as law and that one may intelligently build upon that assumption. In any event, I very much look forward to hearing from readers regarding coverage and any other suggestions for improvement.

Though almost any legal system could serve as an object of study, this book concerns the American Legal Process, and primarily federal Legal Process. Of

---

7 William N. Eskridge, Jr. & Philip P. Frickey, *An Historical and Critical Introduction to* The Legal Process, *in* Henry M. Hart, Jr. & Albert M. Sacks, The Legal Process: Basic Problems in the Making and Application of Law cii (William N. Eskridge, Jr. & Philip P. Frickey eds., 1994).
8 *Id.*

course, a thorough understanding of the legal process of one system enables one to profitably compare that with another system, and the reader is invited to investigate how federal Legal Process differs from state Legal Process, and how American Legal Process differs from that of other countries. Indeed, in many places the book provides "Sidebars" highlighting some of the comparative differences.

One dilemma in the teaching of Legal Process is whether to teach the course in the first year of law school or teach it as an upper-level course. On the one hand, I do not know how beginning law students will understand (e.g.) how to read a statute (or even know why they are important) without some systematic instruction on these and related subjects. On the other hand, space in the first-year curriculum is scarce, and students might have a greater appreciation for the materials in this book after having some general exposure to law and legal principles. I do not know which is better; perhaps it depends upon the school. I look forward to hearing about the experiences of others regarding this issue as well.

A note about the materials included in this book: First, the reader should be aware that I have used certain conventions, some perhaps unusual, in the excerpting of the authorities that have been reproduced. All featured authorities and any other quoted material has been taken as precisely as possible from the original source, except for original omissions, alterations, and (in some instances) footnotes, which have been omitted without indication. Accordingly, the reader should be aware that any indications of omissions or alterations represent changes that I have made. I have also omitted some citations to other authorities that I regard as inconsequential, including some that are quoted in the original (though I have tried to retain all original quotation marks). Similarly, and consistent with current scholarly style, I have not indicated omissions of material before or after that which has been quoted. The reader, of course, is welcome (and even encouraged) to view any or all of these authorities in their entirety. Finally, though I was impressed (and largely persuaded) by Frank Tuerkheimer's suggestion that the names of counsel be included in case excerpts (*see A Short Essay on the Editing of Cases in Casebooks*, 58 J. OF LEGAL ED. 531 (2008)), I have not (yet) done so. But again, for those who are interested, such names are easily discoverable.

Finally, a word about the inspiration for this book. While a student at the University of Washington School of Law, I had the privilege of taking a course on Legal Method from Professor James Hardisty. The "text" for the course was a set of unbound materials by Henry M. Hart, Jr., and Albert M. Sacks entitled, *The Legal Process: Basic Problems in the Making and Application of Law* (tentative ed. 1958), which has been described by one legal scholar as "the most influential book not produced in movable type since Gutenberg."[9] Though Hart and Sacks's work was not formally published until fairly recently, it had (and continues to have) a significant impact in a number of areas, including statutory interpretation, at least among

---

9 J.D. Hyman, *Constitutional Jurisprudence and the Teaching of Constitutional Law*, 28 STAN. L. REV. 1271, 1286 n.70 (1976). For a detailed discussion of the philosophical and jurisprudential underpinnings of *The Legal Process*, see Charles Barzun, *The Forgotten Foundation of Hart and Sacks*, 99 VA. L. REV. 1 (2013).

legal academics and certain judges. Indeed, "[a]long with Justice Breyer, Justices Scalia, Kennedy, Souter, and Ginsburg are all alumni of Henry Hart's and Albert Sacks's Harvard Law School courses on 'The Legal Process.'"[10] I am indebted to Professor Hardisty and to his having exposed me to these materials.

Bradley Scott Shannon

Ponte Vedra Beach, Florida
November 2014

---

10 William N. Eskridge, Jr. & Philip P. Frickey, *Foreword: Law as Equilibrium*, 108 HARV. L. REV. 26, 27 (1994).

Acknowledgments

I thank Carol McGeehan at Wolters Kluwer for agreeing to take on this project, and Kathy Langone and Annalisa Rodriguez of The Froebe Group for their editing and other support throughout this process.

I also thank the copyright holders of the following works for graciously granting permission to republish excerpts in this work:

REED DICKERSON, THE INTERPRETATION AND APPLICATION OF STATUTES (1975)

HENRY M. HART, JR. & ALBERT M. SACKS, THE LEGAL PROCESS: BASIC PROBLEMS IN THE MAKING AND APPLICATION OF LAW (William N. Eskridge, Jr. & Philip P. Frickey eds., 1994)

JAMES WM. MOORE, MOORE'S FEDERAL PRACTICE (3d ed. 2008)

ANTONIN SCALIA & BRYAN A. GARNER, MAKING YOUR CASE: THE ART OF PERSUADING JUDGES (2008)

SECTION OF ADMINISTRATIVE LAW AND REGULATORY PRACTICE, AMERICAN BAR ASSOCIATION, A BLACKLETTER STATEMENT OF FEDERAL ADMINISTRATIVE LAW (2004)

NORMAN J. SINGER, STATUTES AND STATUTORY CONSTRUCTION (6th ed. 2002)

Brian Z. Tamanaha, *A Concise Guide to the Rule of Law*, in RELOCATING THE RULE OF LAW (G. Palombella & N. Walker eds., 2009)

CHARLES ALAN WRIGHT ET AL., FEDERAL PRACTICE AND PROCEDURE (various dates)

Ruggero J. Aldisert et al., *Logic for Law Students: How to Think Like a Lawyer*, 69 U. PITT. L. REV. 1 (2007)

Tara L. Branum, *President or King? The Use and Abuse of Executive Orders in Modern-Day America*, 28 J. LEGIS. 1 (2002)

William N. Eskridge, Jr. & Philip P. Frickey, *Foreword: Law as Equilibrium*, 108 HARV. L. REV. 26 (1994)

Chad Flanders, *Toward a Theory of Persuasive Authority*, 62 OKLA. L. REV. 55 (2009)

Lon L. Fuller, *The Forms and Limits of Adjudication*, 92 HARV. L. REV. 353 (1978)

Gil Grantmore, *The Headnote*, 5 GREEN BAG 2D 157 (2002)

Arthur J. Jacobson, *Publishing Dissent*, 62 WASH. & LEE L. REV. 1607 (2005)

Gary Lawson, *Mostly Unconstitutional: The Case Against Precedent Revisited*, 5 AVE
MARIA L. REV. 1 (2007)

Hillel Y. Levin, *The Food Stays in the Kitchen: Everything I Needed to Know About
Statutory Interpretation I Learned by the Time I Was Nine*, 12 GREEN BAG 2D
337 (2009)

John F. Manning, *Textualism and Legislative Intent*, 91 VA. L. REV. 419 (2005)

John F. Manning, *What Divides Textualists from Purposivists?*, 106 COLUM. L. REV.
70 (2006)

Michael Stokes Paulsen, *Does the Supreme Court's Current Doctrine of Stare Decisis
Require Adherence to the Supreme Court's Current Doctrine of Stare Decisis?*, 86
N.C. L. REV. 1165 (2008)

Frederick Schauer, *Precedent*, 39 STAN. L. REV. 571 (1987)

Frederick Schauer, *Giving Reasons*, 47 STAN. L. REV. 633 (1995)

Frederick Schauer, *Authority and Authorities*, 94 VA. L. REV. 1931 (2008)

Mary Whisner, *The United States Code, Prima Facie Evidence, and Positive Law*,
101 LAW LIBR. J. 545 (2009)

Stephen Yeazell, *When and How U.S. Courts Should Cite Foreign Law*, 26 CONST.
COMMENT. 59 (2009)

Donald H. Zeigler, *Gazing into the Crystal Ball: Reflections on the Standards
State Judges Should Use to Ascertain Federal Law*, 40 WM. & MARY L. REV. 1143
(1999)

The Reg Map, ICF INCORPORATED (2003)

What Are Ballot Propositions, Initiatives, and Referendums?, INITIATIVE &
REFERENDUM INSTITUTE AT THE UNIVERSITY OF SOUTHERN CALIFORNIA,
http://iandrinstitute.org

WJP Rule of Law Index 2014, WORLD JUSTICE PROJECT, http://worldjusticeproject.
org/

AMERICAN LEGAL PROCESS

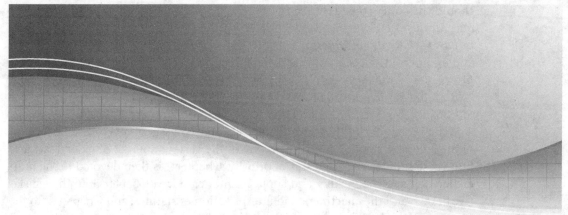

CHAPTER 1

Introduction to American Legal Process

A. INTRODUCTION TO LEGAL PROCESS

This book is about American legal process — not *the* American legal process per se, but rather legal process as a particular area of the law. What is "legal process"? "Legal process" may be defined as the "basic functions of each lawmaking body and its interaction with the others," and includes the "processes by which law is created in the three forums, and later elaborated and applied by courts and agencies." Richard B. Cappalli, *The Disappearance of Legal Method*, 70 TEMP. L. REV. 393, 399 (1997). For example, most people are probably aware that legislatures, administrative agencies, and even courts in some sense "make" law. But how, exactly, do each of these bodies do it? And how does each of these bodies deal with that law made by the others? How *should* they do these things? Knowing the answers to these questions not only has the potential to lead to better lawmaking, but also can affect whether law is made at all, as well as the nature and substance of that law. Perhaps more importantly, knowing these things can also lead to better lawyering.

Consider a more specific example, borrowed from a famous debate between Professors H.L.A. Hart and Lon Fuller. Suppose that a legislative body were to enact a statute prohibiting "vehicles" from a certain park. Does this statute prohibit tricycles? Horses? A non-operative jeep included as part of a war memorial? How should a court, if called upon to resolve disputes along these lines, decide these questions? Aside from the words of the statute itself, what should the court consider? *See* H.L.A. Hart, *Positism and the Separation of Law and Morals*, 71 HARV. L. REV. 593 (1958); Lon L. Fuller, *Positism and Fidelity to Law — A Reply to Professor Hart*, 71 HARV. L. REV. 630 (1958). (For a recent and excellent discussion of this debate, see Frederick Schauer, *A Critical Guide to Vehicles in the Park*, 83 N.Y.U. L. REV. 1109 (2008). *See also* Bernard W. Bell, *"No Motor Vehicles in the Park": Reviving the Hart-Fuller Debate to Introduce Statutory Construction*, 48 J. LEGAL EDUC. 88 (1998).)

The remainder of this introductory chapter consists of a very brief overview of the federal system of government and of the various sources of federal law and how these sources rank in terms of priority. Chapter 2 is then devoted to the judicial branch and the making and application of case law; Chapter 3, to the legislative branch and the enactment and interpretation of statutes; and Chapter 4, to the executive branch and the role of the President and administrative agencies. Each of these chapters will include a general description of the lawmaking process as it relates to that branch and a discussion of many of the more important issues relating to the law thereby created, particularly as it relates to the other branches.

B. INTRODUCTION TO THE AMERICAN LEGAL SYSTEM

1. The Federal System of Government

The Constitution of the United States specifies that there be three main departments or branches of government: the legislative, the executive, and the judicial. Generally speaking, the legislature (Congress) is responsible for enacting statutes and treaties. *See* U.S. CONST. art. I. The executive (primarily through the President) also plays a role in the enactment of statutes and treaties and, with the help of administrative agencies, promulgates regulations and other forms of administrative law. *See* U.S. CONST. art. II. Finally, the judicial branch decides cases. *See* U.S. CONST. art. III. Though each of these branches engage in other forms of lawmaking activities — for example, the judicial branch also is responsible for promulgating its own rules of practice and procedure, and the President issues a broad array of orders and proclamations beyond the more traditional executive orders — it is the above activities that constitute the bulk of these branches' lawmaking work.

A diagram of the government of the United States can be found at the conclusion of this Introduction.

2. State Systems of Government

The various state systems of government tend to be organized more or less like the federal government. Though state sytems of government raise many of the same legal process issues as does the federal system, the focus of this book is on the federal government.

3. Sources of Law and the Priority of Authorities

Obviously, there are many different types or sources of law. It is important for the lawyer to know what those various sources are and the extent to which those sources are considered controlling with respect to the issue presented. It is also important for the lawyer to understand the hierarchical relationship between those sources considered controlling — i.e., in the event two or more sources of law conflict, which sources take priority over the others.

As already discussed, in the United States, there are two primary governmental systems: the federal system, and various state systems. By virtue of the Supremacy Clause of the Constitution of the United States, federal law — perhaps regardless of its nature — takes priority over the law of any state. *See* U.S. CONST. art. VI, cl. 2 ("This Constitution, and the Laws of the United States which shall be made in Pursuance thereof; and all Treaties made, or which shall be made, under the Authority of the United States, shall be the supreme Law of the Land; and the Judges in every State shall be bound thereby, any Thing in the Constitution or Laws of any State to the Contrary notwithstanding."); *M'Culloch v. Maryland*, 17 U.S. 316, 326-27 (1819).

Within the federal system, the *United States Constitution* represents the highest form of authority. As a result, the Constitution takes priority over all other sources of federal law. *See, e.g.*, *Marbury v. Madison*, 5 U.S. (1 Cranch) 137, 180 (1803).

The second highest source of law in the federal system is *statutory law*. As the Supremacy Clause indicates, aside from the Constitution, a federal statute will take priority over any other source of law. *Cf. Rubber Co. v. Goodyear*, 76 U.S. 788, 791 (1869) ("At the place where the letters testamentary were issued the common law relied upon by the appellants was in conflict with the statutory provisions of the State, and was therefore abrogated. It could no more be recognized in the Federal than in the State tribunals."). *Procedural rules* (such as the Federal Rules of Civil Procedure) and *treaties* are also generally considered as operating at the same level as statutes. *See* 28 U.S.C. § 2072(b) (2012) ("All laws in conflict with such rules shall be of no further force or effect after such rules have taken effect."); *Medellin v. Texas*, 552 U.S. 491, 509 n.5 (2008) ("[A] later-in-time federal statute supersedes inconsistent treaty provisions."). *But see* Vesan Kesavan, *The Three Tiers of Federal Law*, 100 NW. U. L. REV. 1479 (2006) (concluding that federal statutory law takes priority over treaties).

Next in the federal hierarchy is *regulatory law*. Though a federal regulation must yield to a federal statute, it will take priority over contrary federal common law.

At the bottom of the federal hierarchy is *federal decisional law* (i.e., case law). This might be surprising to some, given the great attention paid to federal court decisions today. But notice that, in a strict sense anyway, this hierarchical feature of case law applies only to those decisions involving the making of federal common law — decisions that make up only a small fraction of the federal judicial caseload. Most federal judicial decisions involve the interpretation and application of constitutional provisions, statutes, and federal regulations, and once a precedent-setting court decides what one of these other sources means, most scholars believe that a case essentially assumes the level of authority of that source, at least for those bound thereby. Thus (for example), when the Supreme Court of the United States holds that a particular statute means X, it means X, and aside from a later decision overruling that holding, only a further act of Congress may alter that result. *See, e.g.*, C. HUGHES, THE SUPREME COURT OF THE UNITED STATES 230 (1928) ("[A] federal statute finally means what the Court says it means."). This also means that when the Supreme Court interprets a particular provision of the Constitution, the only recourse (again, other than an overruling judicial decision) is to amend the Constitution. Moreover, the Supreme Court has held that federal courts have the power of judicial review — i.e., the ability to declare federal statutes unconstitutional, thus essentially nullifying their effect. *See* (again) *Marbury v. Madison*, 5 U.S. (1 Cranch) 137 (1803).

State governmental systems tend to mirror the federal system. Thus, state constitutions are generally considered the highest source of law within any particular state system, followed by statutes, regulations, and state common law. Again, though, because the federal system is supreme, any source of federal law will take priority over any source of state law, even a state constitution.

The foregoing, *primary* sources of law, where applicable, are considered controlling (or "binding"), in the sense that they must be applied where relevant. But there are also an almost unlimited number of nonbinding secondary sources of law that, though not strictly controlling, often are considered by courts as supplying (or at least supporting) the applicable legal rule in the absence of any binding source of law. And once a legal rule supplied by one of these *secondary* sources is adopted by a precedent-setting court as the rule of decision, that rule becomes binding law for that jurisdiction. A few of the more prominent examples of such secondary sources are discussed below.

Perhaps the most widely used secondary source is *case law from other (nonbinding) jurisdictions*. For example, a court in Idaho, in deciding an issue of common law, might look to the case law of other states (such as Washington) which, though not binding on Idaho courts, might be found persuasive and therefore dispositive.

Another often-used secondary source is the *Restatement*. A "Restatement" is "[o]ne of several influential treatises published by the American Law Institute describing the law in a given area and guiding its development." BLACK'S LAW DICTIONARY 1507 (10th ed. 2014). Undoubtedly, you have encountered (or soon will encounter) Restatements in some of your other law school courses. According to the American Law Institute website, Restatements now exist on the following subjects:

Agency
Conflict of Laws
Contracts
Foreign Relations Law of the United States
Judgments
Landlord and Tenant

Property (including Mortgages and Servitudes)
Restitution
Security
Suretyship and Guaranty
The Law Governing Lawyers
Torts (including Products Liability and Apportionment of Liability)
Trusts
Unfair Competition

New and revised Restatements also are continually being developed. For more on Restatements, see American Law Institute, *About the American Law Institute, available at* http://www.ali.org/doc/thisIsALI.pdf. *See also* Bennett Boskey, *The American Law Institute: A Glimpse at Its Future*, 12 GREEN BAG 2D 255 (2009).

Also commonly used are *uniform and model acts*, both of which are drafted by the National Conference of Commissioners on Uniform State Laws. A "uniform act" (or "law") is "[a]n unofficial law proposed as legislation for all the states to adopt exactly as written, the purpose being to promote greater consistency among the states." BLACK'S LAW DICTIONARY 1763 (10th ed. 2014). By contrast, a "model act" is "[a] statute . . . proposed as guideline legislation for the states to borrow from or adapt to suit their individual needs." *Id.* at 1156. Why the distinction between a uniform act and a model act, and the perceived need for both? As stated in the following excerpt from the "Prefatory Note" accompanying the 1996 Uniform Law Commissioners' Model Punitive Damages Act, 14 UNIFORM LAWS ANNOTATED 315, 315 (2005):

> In 1994 the National Conference of Commissioners on Uniform State Laws established a Drafting Committee on the subject of punitive damages. The scope of the project was limited to one of developing a Model Act, as compared to a Uniform Act. Unlike a Uniform Act, whose principal objective is to obtain immediate uniformity among the States on a particular legal subject, a Model Act may be more of an experimental effort to assist States in developing effective new approaches to a particular problem area of the law. A Model Act may contain more novel approaches, the efficacy of which can only be attained through some trial and error. Although uniformity may prove to be desirable at some point, it is not imperative in the short term. Consequently, for reasons discussed below, the subject of punitive damages was thought to be appropriate for a Model Act.

The website of the Uniform Law Commission (which also contains a current list of such acts) is available at *http://www.uniformlaws.org*. For more on the history of the National Conference of the Commissioners on Uniform State Laws, see James J. White, Ex Proprio Vigore, 89 MICH. L. REV. 2096 (1991). For more on model acts, see Mary Whisner, *There Oughta Be a Law — A Model Law*, 106 LAW LIBR. J. 125 (2014). You should also be aware that there are other sources for such acts besides the National Conference. For a more complete list, see http://lawsource.com/also/usa.cgi?usm.

There are a number of other important and sometimes influential secondary sources besides restatements and uniform and model acts. Perhaps the next most important sources are *treatises*, which are often found persuasive by courts.

Excellent treatises now exist in almost every area of the law. For example, in the area of civil procedure, two well-known treatises are *Federal Practice and Procedure* and *Moore's Federal Practice.*

Scholarly *books* and *articles*, particularly from law school reviews and journals, also sometimes supply the rule for decision.

Other possible secondary sources include *legal encyclopedias* and *dictionaries*, though the number and type of secondary sources being consulted by courts today seems to be growing.

The priority of authorities thus may be generally summarized as follows:

Federal system **(binding where applicable, otherwise persuasive only).**

Constitution
Statutes
Regulations
Case law

State systems **(binding where applicable, otherwise persuasive only).**

Constitution
Statutes
Regulations
Case law

Secondary Authorities **(persuasive).**

For a more detailed introduction to the American legal system, see MARGARET Z. JOHNS & REX R. PERSCHHACHER, THE UNITED STATES LEGAL SYSTEM: AN INTRODUCTION (2002).

4. A Few Words About Conflicts of Laws

Frequently, two or more potentially relevant sources of law will appear to be in conflict. The law has developed mechanisms for dealing with these various conflicts of laws, depending on the nature of the conflict.

Perhaps the most common types of conflicts of laws are what might be called geographic (or geopolitical) conflicts — that is, conflicts between the laws of different sovereigns. Geographic conflicts sometimes arise when a dispute involves domiciliaries of different states or countries, or somehow relates to more than one state or country. These sorts of "classic" conflicts of laws, though important, are typically the subject of a course devoted specifically to that subject.

A second, somewhat related type of conflict of laws can arise as a result of our federal system of government. For example, a federalism-based conflict potentially arises when a state law-based claim is adjudicated in a federal court. Should the federal court apply federal law, or state law? Though federalism-based conflicts of laws typically are covered in a course on civil procedure (if not also in a conflict of laws course), some aspects of this issue will be discussed in Chapter 2.

Another potential conflict of laws might be termed an inter-departmental (or inter-branch) conflict of laws. For example, for some particular issue of federal law, a federal statute might be in conflict with a decision of the Supreme Court. This issue is resolved by consideration of the priority of authorities, discussed above.

Yet another type of conflict occurs when, say, a federal statute seems to conflict with another federal statute, or when a federal court decision cannot be reconciled with another decision by another federal court on the same issue. Such conflicts might be termed intra-branch (or, in some instances, intra-court). Intra-court conflicts, which are resolved under the doctrine of stare decisis, are discussed in Chapter 2. A discussion of the mechanisms for resolving federal statutory conflicts can be found in Chapter 3.

Finally, there exist what might be termed conflicts of laws in time. For example, a statute that otherwise appears relevant might have been enacted after the conduct or event at issue occurred, or even after litigation has been commenced. To what extent, if any, does the statute apply in those situations? Questions such as these concerning temporal conflicts of statutory laws are addressed in Chapter 3. A similar section on the retroactive and prospective application of judicial decisions can be found in Chapter 2.

C. THE RULE OF LAW

It is popular today to talk about whether some particular legal system or practice is consistent with the "rule of law." The notion of the "rule of law" also underlies much of legal process. For example, the rationale for the doctrine of stare decisis (i.e., precedent) largely mirrors rule of law principles, as does the reasoning behind the need for judicial impartiality and even certain aspects of the various theories of statutory interpretation. But what, exactly, does this phrase mean? Consider the following recent summary.

Brian Z. Tamanaha

A CONCISE GUIDE TO THE RULE OF LAW

Relocating the Rule of Law
(G. Palombella & N. Walker eds., 2008)[1]

Discussions among theorists about the "rule of law" are riven by disagreements over what it means, its elements or requirements, its benefits or limitations, whether it is a universal good, and other complex questions. These debates are essential, but they can be confusing to non-specialists who seek to obtain a basic understanding of this important concept. The present chapter will provide an overview of core

---

1. Reproduced with permission from Brian Z. Tamanaha and Neil Walker.

aspects of the rule of law. It is by no means exhaustive on the subject and does not resolve any of the hard questions; it does not address any philosophical or theoretical disputes about the rule of law. Rather, it is a pragmatic guide to the basic issues, oriented to the circumstances and concerns of societies that are working to develop the rule of law. The topics covered are (in order): definition, functions, benefits and elements. Several key points will be made about each subject, followed by a few additional comments on limitations or concerns. After covering these subjects, a brief explanation will be provided for why certain notions often associated with the rule of law have not been included. The overview will then close with a few reasons to be wary of the rule of law. The usefulness of this outline as a guide, it is hoped, will outweigh its oversimplifications and lack of nuance.

I. RULE OF LAW NARROWLY DEFINED

The rule of law, at its core, requires that government officials and citizens be bound by and act consistently with the law. This basic requirement entails a set of minimal characteristics: law must be set forth in advance (be prospective), be made public, be general, be clear, be stable and certain, and be applied to everyone according to its terms. In the absence of these characteristics, the rule of law cannot be satisfied.

This is the "formal" or "thin" definition of the rule of law; more substantive or "thicker" definitions of the rule of law also exist, which include reference to fundamental rights, democracy, and/or criteria of justice or right. The narrow definition is utilized here because it represents a common baseline that all of the competing definitions of the rule of law share, although a number of versions go beyond this minimum. As will be indicated, this version is amenable to a broad range of systems and societies.

II. TWO *FUNCTIONS* OF THE RULE OF LAW, WITH PROBLEMS

A. Restraints on Government Officials

One function of the rule of law is to *impose legal restraints on government officials*, in two different ways: (i) by requiring compliance with existing law; and (ii) by imposing legal limits on law-making power.

Fear of the uncontrolled application of coercion by the sovereign or the government is an ancient and contemporary concern. The rule of law responds to this concern by imposing legal constraints on government officials.

The first type of legal restraint is that *government officials must abide by valid positive laws in force at the time of any given action*. This first restraint has two aspects: government actions must have positive legal authorisation (without which the action is improper); and no government action may contravene a legal prohibition or restriction. Although exceptions or flexibility may exist with respect to the first aspect, the second (prohibitive) aspect is strict. If government officials wish to pursue a course of action that violates existing positive laws, the law must be changed in accordance with ordinary legal procedures *before* the course of action can be pursued.

The fundamental problem with this first type of restraint is enforcement. It requires that the government bind and coerce itself. Hobbes considered this a logical and practical impossibility, remarking that "he that is bound to himself only, is not bound." The solution to this problem lies in the institutionalised separation of government powers, and by distinguishing between the private person and the government office he or she occupies. Government officials hence do not coerce themselves, but rather members of one institutionalised part of the government (prosecutors, courts) hold another part or another official legally accountable.

The second type of legal restraint *imposes restrictions on the law itself, erecting limitations on the law making power of the government.* Under this second type of restraint, certain prohibited actions cannot be legally allowed, even by a legitimate law-making authority. Legal restrictions of this sort rank above and impose control over ordinary law-making. The most familiar versions of this are: (1) constitutionally imposed limits, (2) transnational or international legal limits, (3) human rights limits, and (4) religious or natural law limits. In different ways and senses, these types of law are superior to and impose restraints upon routine law making.

The first two versions share a quality described above in that the limits they impose can be changed by legal bodies, but they are nonetheless distinct in that alterations usually cannot be made in the ordinary course by the government subject to the limitation. Constitutionally imposed limitations and transnational or international legal requirements are often more difficult to modify than ordinary legislation — as when a higher threshold must be overcome or changes must be made by a different law making body. Constitutional amendments, for example, may require a supermajority vote while ordinary legislation requires only a majority vote, or must be made by a special body with a constitutional mandate; changes in transnational or international law rules must be made by transnational or international institutions, and thus are beyond the power of the nation state to alter unilaterally. These heightened hurdles enhance the efficacy of the legal limits.

The third and fourth limits, in contrast, are often perceived to be completely beyond the law making power of state or international law making bodies. Human rights declarations, while embodied in positive laws, are widely thought to pre-exist or exist apart from the documents that recognise them and would thus survive even if the documents were altered or abolished. Natural law principles and religious principles, similarly, are generally thought to exist independent of any human law making agency (although religious authorities have a say in the latter). Owing to this quality, they establish limits on state law that no government or law maker can alter.

Several interrelated problems arise with the second type of legal limitation on government. This type of limitation is frequently controversial because it frustrates the ability of government officials to take actions or achieve objectives. These are the main problems:

(i) In democratic societies, it is criticised for overruling or restricting democratic law making; in authoritarian states, it hampers the ruling authority from using the law to do as it desires. In both cases, when the motivation is sufficiently compelling, there will be attempts to circumvent or ignore the higher legal limits.

(ii) Very difficult questions will arise over the scope, meaning and application of said legal limits, often raising disputable questions of interpretation.

(iii) A crucial matter is the designation of the institution or person with the final say over interpretation — which are often courts, but not necessarily. In theory, the authority to interpret the legal limits should not be vested in the same body as is authorised to pass ordinary laws, for that would potentially vitiate the limitation. When this power is allocated to the courts, and where the clauses being interpreted are open-ended and the decisions have political implications, objections may be raised that the courts are thereby engaged in the judicialisation of politics insofar as their decisions restrict or override political authorities.

(iv) Another crucial issue, parallel to the first type of limit above, is whether the limits imposed by these decisions can be enforced. This problem arises because law sets limits on the government's law making power. When these limits are internal to the system — like constitutionally imposed limits — the institutionalised separation described previously can solve the problem. When the limits are external — as with transnational law, human rights, natural law and religious limits — the cooperation of the government which is thereby limited must be secured, either voluntarily or through the threat of a sanction. Human rights norms and religious norms, in particular, come up against the reality that governments can ignore their dictates with relative impunity.

B. Social Ordering

A second function of the rule of law is to maintain order and coordinate behaviour and transactions among citizens.

This aspect of the rule of law holds that a framework of legal rules governs social behaviour. People must generally behave in a fashion that does not breach legal rules. Transgressions of legal rules or social disruptions — whether treated as criminal or civil (societies draw different lines) — will provoke a response from legal institutions charged with enforcing legal requirements and resolving disputes in accordance with applicable legal norms.

Satisfaction of this second function does not entail that the entire realm of social behaviour must be governed by state legal rules. That is neither possible nor desirable. Multiple normative orders exist within every society, including customary norms, moral norms, religious norms, family norms, norms of social etiquette, workplace norms, norms of business interaction, and so on. Sometimes the norms from these various orders overlap, but often they are different in orientation, extension, scope, penetration and efficacy. The presence, scope and penetration of state law varies between societies and between regions. Some societies or regions are thickly governed by law, where serious disputes are resolved by well developed state legal institutions. In other societies or regions, state law has a marginal or negligible role in social ordering — usually when state law is relatively weak — and disputes are resolved primarily through social institutions. In order to be consistent with the rule of law, the law need not cover everything, but what the law does cover should be largely adhered to by the citizenry.

III. PRIMARY *BENEFITS* FROM THE RULE OF LAW, AND PROBLEMS FLOWING FROM EACH BENEFIT

The rule of law enhances *certainty, predictability, and security* in two contexts: between citizens and the government (vertical), and among citizens (horizontal).

With respect to the government, citizens benefit by knowing in advance the government's likely response to their actions. This is an important aspect of liberty, whereby citizens know the full range of conduct they can engage in without fear of being subjected to government interference or sanction. Any action not prohibited by the law can be undertaken by the citizen without fear. Without this assurance, one always acts at one's peril.

Although such predictability is critical to liberty, it is important to recognise that this benefit in itself does not guarantee to citizens any particular area of free action. The scope of action allowed can be quite narrow or oppressive, yet comply with the rule of law in the "thin" sense defined at the outset.

With respect to fellow citizens, people are able to interact with one another knowing in advance which rules will be applied to their conduct should a problem or dispute occur. Such predictability furthers their ability to make choices and to interact with others. This includes acting with the appropriate (legally established) degree of care and responsibility when dealing with other people or their property, and when engaging in transactions with strangers or acquaintances.

When evaluating the horizontal and vertical benefits just described, it is important to remember that both assume substantial knowledge and foresight about the law on the part of citizens. The reality, however, may be that citizens are poorly informed about the law or give scarce consideration to it before they act.

B. Restriction of Government Discretion

The rule of law *restricts the discretion* of government officials, reducing wilfulness and arbitrariness.

A common worry of citizens is that government officials may be unduly influenced in their government actions by inappropriate considerations — by prejudice, whims, arbitrariness, passion, ill will or a foul disposition, or by any of the many factors that distort human decision making and actions. The rule of law constrains these factors by insisting that government officials act pursuant to and consistent with applicable legal rules. The law operates in two ways to obtain this benefit. First, government officials are required to consult and conform to the law before and during actions. Second, legal rules provide publicly available requirements and standards that can be used to hold government officials accountable both during and after their actions.

The main negative consequence that comes with this second benefit is that under many circumstances it may be useful or necessary for government officials to exercise discretion or make situation-specific judgments. Legal rules are general prescriptions that cannot anticipate every aspect of every situation in advance, and legal rules can become obsolete as social views and circumstances change. The application of existing rules to unanticipated situations or changed circumstances can have harmful or unfair consequences or lead to socially undesirable outcomes. In such contexts, allowing the decision maker to use her expertise, wisdom or judgment may produce better results than insisting that she comply with the legal rules. In some circumstances, moreover, strictly following legal rules in a fashion that produces a winner and a loser can exacerbate conflict, while finding a compromise that bypasses the rules might achieve a consensus. In these and other situations, a strict adherence to the rule of law may be detrimental. Underlying this benefit of the rule of law is the fear of potential abuse at the hands of government officials, but every functional polity must accord some degree of trust and discretion to government officials.

C. Peaceful Social Order

A *peaceful social order* is maintained through legal rules.

A peaceful social order is marked by the absence of routine violence, and by the presence of a substantial degree of physical security and reliable expectations about the conduct of others. These are the minimal conditions necessary for a tolerable social existence.

The relationship between social order and legal rules is extremely complex and variable. It is important to bear in mind that the legal rules in the books do not necessarily correspond to, reflect or maintain the social order (nor is it the case that legal officials and institutions always enforce the rules in the books). In virtually all social contexts, moreover, social norms largely shape and govern daily existence; legal norms may be largely irrelevant to the bulk of routine social conduct. Legal rules can conflict or clash with prevailing social norms. For these reasons, it must not be assumed that law is the main (or even a major) source of social order.

Furthermore, legal rules and institutions can impose an oppressive social order, as occurs in totalitarian societies. Although such societies are not superficially marked by routine violence, and therefore qualify as "peaceful" and ordered, the social order can nonetheless be experienced as intolerably restrictive.

Two problematic situations deserve to be mentioned. When law has been transplanted from elsewhere — either by imposition or through voluntary borrowing — social and legal norms may clash, reflecting different social, cultural and moral world views. A clash may also occur when a society consists of distinct groups (cultural, ethnic or religious), while the law represents only one. In both situations, the norms and values of the law will not match the norms and values of many of the citizens. In a few contexts (often post-colonial), the language of the law is different from the common vernacular of groups within society, which heightens the clash, and gives the law an alien and obscure feel. In many of these situations the law has a weak role in preserving social order.

D. Economic Benefits

Economic development is facilitated by certainty, predictability, and security, for two basic reasons.

As indicated at the outset, the rule of law enhances certainty, predictability and security. In addition to enhancing liberty, it is widely believed that market-based economic systems benefit from these qualities in two different respects, the first related to contracts and the second to property. First, economic actors can better predict in advance the anticipated costs and benefits of prospective transactions, which enables them to make more efficient decisions. One can enter into a contract with some assurances of the consequences that will follow if the other party fails to live up to the terms of the contract. This encourages the creation of contracts with strangers or parties at a distance, which expands the range and frequency of commercial interactions, thus increasing the size of the economic pie.

Second, the protection of property (and persons) conferred by legal rules offers an assurance that the fruits of one's labour will be protected from expropriation by others. This security frees individuals, thus enabling them to allocate the bulk of their efforts to additional productive activity, and to enjoying its benefits, rather than spending time and effort on protecting existing gains.

These economic benefits conferred by the rule of law have been identified in connection with capitalism on local and global levels. One must examine both the law and the relationship between the law and the system of economic exchange in a given situation in order to determine whether and to what extent these claims are borne out. When law and legal institutions are obscure, inefficient, costly or unreliable, commercial transactions and economic development might be inhibited by the legal system, and economic actors may prefer to resort to other institutions in situations of dispute (like private arbitration), thereby avoiding the legal system entirely. In certain contexts, moreover, other mechanisms, such as norms of reciprocity or long term social or business relationships, can effectively provide predictability and security in transactions, thus rendering the law secondary or superfluous.

E. The Fundamental Justice of Equality of Application of the Law

The equality of application of law, an aspect of the rule of law, is a component of fundamental justice. It is widely considered unfair and unjust when the identity or status of a person affects how legal officials apply or interpret the law. No one should be unduly favoured or ill-treated by legal officials. This requirement does not prohibit laws from drawing distinctions between people or groups, as occurs with laws that treat men and women differently, or which impose graduated tax rates; it only requires that the law be applied in accordance with its terms no matter whom it is being applied to (president or citizen, celebrity or common person, rich or poor).

This essential aspect of justice, known as formal equality, can also have negative consequences, especially in situations with substantial social inequalities. Applying laws equally to everyone according to their provisions may have one-sided effects or serve to perpetuate an unjust social order. A law that forbids the rich and poor alike from sleeping on a park bench, for example, may be applied equally to all, but it will have consequences mainly for the poor.

IV.   BASIC *ELEMENTS* IN ESTABLISHING THE RULE OF LAW, AND RELATED PROBLEMS

A. Widely Shared Orientation within Society — among Citizens and Government Officials — that the *Law Does Rule and Should Rule*

In order for the rule of law to exist, people must believe in and be committed to the rule of law. They must take it for granted as a necessary, proper, and existing part of their political-legal system. This attitude is not itself a legal rule. It is a shared political ideal that amounts to a cultural belief. When this cultural belief is pervasive, the rule of law can be resilient, spanning generations and surviving episodes in which the rule of law is flouted by government officials. When this cultural belief is not pervasive, however, the rule of law ends up being either weak or non-existent.

Cultural beliefs are not subject to human control, so it is no easy matter to inculcate belief in the rule of law when it does not already exist. A specific problem is that in many societies the government is distrusted and state law is feared or avoided. This tends to be the case in societies where the law has a long or recent history of enforcing authoritarian rule, or where legal officials are perceived to be corrupt or inept, or where legal professionals are widely distrusted, or where the content or application of the law is seen to be unfair or is identified with particular interests or the elite. In situations where the legal rules and systems have been transplanted from elsewhere, as indicated earlier, many people will not identify with (or even know) the law, so making it much harder to develop a cultural orientation that the law should rule, although this can change over time. Moreover, when society is made up of distinct cultural, religious, or ethnic groups, and the law — either its norms, or the people who monopolise legal positions — is identified with one group but not others, people from the excluded groups may well see the law as a threat, and are unlikely to embrace the notion that the law should rule.

This is an essential element of the rule of law, and it is the hardest to achieve. Above all else, in order for this cultural belief to be viable, people must identify with the law and perceive it as worthy of ruling. General trust in law must be earned, and it takes time to become what is tantamount to a cultural view about law passed on through socialisation.

B. Presence of an Institutionalised, *Independent Judiciary*

An institutionalised, independent judiciary is crucial to both functions of the rule of law: it is an important means for holding government officials to the law (vertical), and for resolving disputes between citizens in accordance with the law (horizontal). Judges individually and as a group must be committed to interpreting and applying the law to everyone (including government officials) according to its terms, fairly and without bias or outside influence.

An independent judiciary is difficult to establish and preserve. At a minimum, it requires the allocation of adequate material resources: functional buildings, competent staff, access to legal resources, reasonable salaries, and job security. Since the courts typically lack direct authority over the police or other enforcement agencies, an essential condition of the independence of the judiciary is that other government officials respect the independence of the judiciary and comply with court rulings. Returning to the first element above, in order for an independent judiciary to exist there must a strong cultural ethic that courts should not be interfered with, and that their legal decisions must be complied with. An independent judiciary also depends upon the existence of a legal profession committed to upholding the law. Judges are recruited from the profession and must be indoctrinated in the values of the rule of law; the profession must also actively support an independent judiciary, and be willing to defend it when threatened.

C. Existence of a *Robust Legal Profession and Legal Tradition* Committed to Upholding the Rule of Law

A well developed legal profession and legal tradition committed to upholding the law is necessary for several reasons: to develop the body of legal rules in a coherent and accessible fashion that helps achieve predictability and certainty in the law; to provide the legal services required to ensure compliance with the law (in vertical and horizontal terms); to help fill the ranks of government legal positions (including regulators, prosecutors, and judges) with the orientation that the law must reign supreme; and to come to the defence of the rule of law when it is under pressure. Without a body of lawyers committed to the law and to the rule of law, there can be no rule of law, for the knowledge, activities, and orientations of lawyers as a group are the social bearers of the law — they are the group whose collective activities directly constitute the law. Building a robust legal profession and legal tradition requires a legal education system that transfers legal knowledge and inculcates legal values in those it trains. Moreover, the system must attract and reproduce people who are committed to the law and to developing legal knowledge.

A potential problem for this element exists in societies where only people from wealthy classes or selected groups have access to legal education or to positions of authority in the legal system, because this raises the risk that they will develop and utilise the law to advance their own interests at the expense of others, introducing distortions and bias into the law. Citizens will perceive the law as unbalanced, which weighs against the first element above, making it harder to develop a general cultural belief that the law should rule.

D. A Further Problem with These Basic Elements

None of the above three elements is easy to establish when it is absent, but the situation is further complicated because each element in various ways depends upon the others. They are distinct and yet intertwined, and each relies upon a myriad of supporting economic, political, and cultural conditions. These are the social, cultural, and institutional underpinnings of the rule of law, and are not entirely subject to human design or control. All of this makes it extraordinarily difficult to put the elements of the rule of law in place, and practically impossible to do so quickly. A lengthy period, perhaps generations, is required to build up a general cultural belief that the law does and should rule, to build up an independent judiciary, and to build up a legal profession and legal tradition committed to upholding the rule of law. The good news is that, when it comes about, this interconnectedness makes the rule of law resilient.

V. WHAT WAS *NOT MENTIONED* AS A CORE ASPECT OF THE RULE OF LAW

A. Democracy

Democracy is a mechanism for selecting political leaders. Many societies use democratic means to determine who has the authority to make law (voting for legislators) and to create valid laws (voting on proposed laws). Democracy also serves as a legitimating ideal which establishes the obligatory force of law: because the people or their representatives create the law (at least in theory), they thereby consent to and are hence bound by it. Nothing within the thin understanding of the rule of law however mandates democratic institutions. Undemocratic systems can satisfy all the conditions set forth in this chapter.

B. Content of the Law

The thin conception of the rule of law does not impose any requirements concerning the content of the law. This openness with respect to content renders the rule of law amenable to all sorts of cultures, societies and political systems. It does not specify the kinds of law a society must have, nor does it indicate any particular limits on the law. It requires only that government officials and citizens be bound by and act in accordance with the law, whatever the law might require. This also means that oppressive or immoral rules can be enacted — for example, imposing slavery, apartheid and religious or caste distinctions — without falling foul of the requirements of the rule of law.

C. Human Rights

The account of the rule of law set out in this chapter does not itself require a regime of human rights. Enforcement of human rights may be an aspect of the rule of law within a given system, as indicated earlier, but all of the elements discussed above can be established without necessarily protecting human rights.

A large number of scholars who write about the rule of law include one or more of these three aspects as integral to the rule of law. These aspects, however, are not essential to a thin understanding of the rule of law. A narrower approach is taken here because it hews to common ground and applies to the broadest range of systems. Many societies do not embrace liberal values, and a number do not embrace democracy. A state and society may develop the thin version of the rule of law without necessarily adopting the political arrangements or values of liberal democracies.

The rule of law is ultimately about government officials and citizens acting in accordance with legal rules. This is an essential idea with a range of implications, but it cannot solve every problem or be the repository of everything valuable.

VI. REASONS TO BE *WARY* OF THE RULE OF LAW

One reason to be wary of the rule of law follows from the preceding discussion that the rule of law does not in itself require democracy, respect for human rights or any particular content in the law. Developing the rule of law does not ensure that the law or legal system is good or deserves obedience. In situations where the law enforces an authoritarian order, where the law imposes an alien or antagonistic set of values on the population, or where the law is used by one group within society to oppress another, the law can be a fearsome weapon. Fidelity to the rule of law in these circumstances serves to enhance legally enforced oppression. It is important to remember that the rule of law is a necessary but not sufficient condition for a fair and just legal system.

A second reason to be wary is that support for the rule of law can shade subtly into (or be wrongly interpreted as) support for the relentless extension of the reach of law into the social, economic and political realms. This spreading insinuation of law — sometimes called the juridification of the life world — does not follow from the rule of law itself. To insist that government officials must act consistently with the law and to say that the population should abide by the law does not suggest that the law must or ought to rule everything. The appropriate reach of the law can only be determined following an examination of the circumstances of each social arena. As the earlier discussion indicated, in various situations the extension or application of legal rules can be detrimental to social relations, and even to the law itself (by fostering rampant disobedience of the law). Specifically, when legal norms or institutions clash with lived social norms or institutions, it is prudent to be cautious in relation to the subjects and functions the law undertakes.

A third reason to be wary of the rule of law is the risk that it may evolve into the rule of judges (or lawyers). An increasing assertiveness by judges in handing down decisions that infringe upon political authorities, especially when interpreting broad clauses like human rights provisions, has been noted in many systems. When this occurs, the judiciary may become the target of political attacks and efforts at political influence, thereby resulting in the politicisation of judicial appointments and judging. The judicialisation of politics hence leads directly to the politicisation of the judiciary, which in turn reduces the autonomy of the judiciary and diminishes the rule of law. A delicate balance is required in which judges strive to abide by the law and render decisions with an awareness of the proper (limited) role of the courts in a broader polity.

The final reason to be wary of the rule of law — or more accurately, wary of *talk* about the rule of law — is that many abuses of the law have been committed by states and government officials who claim to embrace and abide by the rule of law. The rule of law is a powerful legitimating ideal. As such, it provides cover for cynical political leaders who pay lip service to the rule of law while violating it. This behaviour tarnishes the rule of law ideal, as people come to view talk about the rule of law in a cynical light. The only solution to this problem is vigilantly to hold government officials to account for their behaviour in accordance with legal standards, and to not be fooled by false posturing.

Notes and Questions

---

1. A more complete exploration of the issues surrounding the rule of law can be found in Brian Z. Tamanaha, On the Rule of Law: History, Politics, Theory (2004).

2. The American Bar Association has become quite interested in the "rule of law" through its Rule of Law Initiative. According to its website:

   > The ABA Rule of Law Initiative is a public service project of the American Bar Association dedicated to promoting rule of law around the world. The ABA Rule of Law Initiative believes that rule of law promotion is the most effective long-term antidote to the pressing problems facing the world community today, including poverty, economic stagnation, and conflict.

   See http://www.abanet.org/rol/. Interestingly, despite its considerable efforts in this regard, the ABA Rule of Law Initiative does not appear to have a definition of "rule of law."

3. Another organization heavily involved in the promotion of the "rule of law" is the World Justice Project (or "WJP"). The WJP provides the following "working definition" of the "rule of law":

   > The government and its officials and agents as well as individuals and private entities are accountable under the law.
   >
   > The laws are clear, publicized, stable and just; are applied evenly; and protect fundamental rights, including the security of persons and property.
   >
   > The process by which the laws are enacted, administered, and enforced is accessible, fair and efficient.

Justice is delivered timely by competent, ethical, and independent representatives and neutrals who are of sufficient number, have adequate resources, and reflect the makeup of the communities they serve.

About the WJP, http://worldjusticeproject.org/what-rule-law/. The WJP further publishes a "Rule of Law Index." Version 3.0 of the Index "is composed of 10 factors derived from the WJP's universal principles" that are "divided into 49 sub-factors which incorporate essential elements of the rule of law." These factors and sub-factors are as follows:

Factor 1: Constraints on Government Powers

1.1 Government powers are effectively limited by the legislature

1.2 Government powers are effectively limited by the judiciary

1.3 Government powers are effectively limited by independent auditing and review

1.4 Government officials are sanctioned for misconduct

1.5 Government powers are subject to non-governmental checks

1.6 Transition of power is subject to the law

Factor 2: Absence of Corruption

2.1 Government officials in the executive branch do not use public office for private gain

2.2 Government officials in the judicial branch do not use public office for private gain

2.3 Government officials in the police and the military do not use public office for private gain

2.4 Government officials in the legislative branch do not use public office for private gain

Factor 3: Open Government

3.1 The laws are publicized and accessible

3.2 The laws are stable

3.3 Right to petition the government and public participation

3.4 Official information is available on request

Factor 4: Fundamental Rights

4.1 Equal treatment and absence of discrimination

4.2 The right to life and security of the person is effectively guaranteed

4.3 Due process of law and rights of the accused

4.4 Freedom of opinion and expression is effectively guaranteed

4.5 Freedom of belief and religion is effectively guaranteed

4.6 Freedom from arbitrary interference with privacy is effectively guaranteed

4.7 Freedom of assembly and association is effectively guaranteed

4.8 Fundamental labor rights are effectively guaranteed

Factor 5: Order and Security

5.1   Crime is effectively controlled

5.2   Civil conflict is effectively limited

5.3   People do not resort to violence to redress personal grievances

Factor 6: Regulatory Enforcement

6.1   Government regulations are effectively enforced

6.2   Government regulations are applied and enforced without improper influence

6.3   Administrative proceedings are conducted without unreasonable delay

6.4   Due process is respected in administrative proceedings

6.5   The government does not expropriate without lawful process and adequate compensation

Factor 7: Civil Justice

7.1   People can access and afford civil justice

7.2   Civil justice is free of discrimination

7.3   Civil justice is free of corruption

7.4   Civil justice is free of improper government influence

7.5   Civil justice is not subject to unreasonable delay

7.6   Civil justice is effectively enforced

7.7   ADR is accessible, impartial, and effective

Factor 8: Criminal Justice

8.1   Criminal investigation system is effective

8.2   Criminal adjudication system is timely and effective

8.3   Correctional system is effective in reducing criminal behavior

8.4   Criminal system is impartial

8.5   Criminal system is free of corruption

8.6   Criminal system is free of improper government influence

8.7   Due process of law and rights of the accused

Factor 9: Informal Justice

9.1   Informal justice is timely and effective

9.2   Informal justice is impartial and free of improper influence

9.3   Informal justice respects and protects fundamental rights

4. Much more has been written on the rule of law, including Jeremy Waldron, *The Concept and the Rule of Law*, 43 Ga. L. Rev. 1 (2009).

5. As you read the chapters that follow, ask yourself whether the various theories and methodologies espoused advance or impair the rule of law.

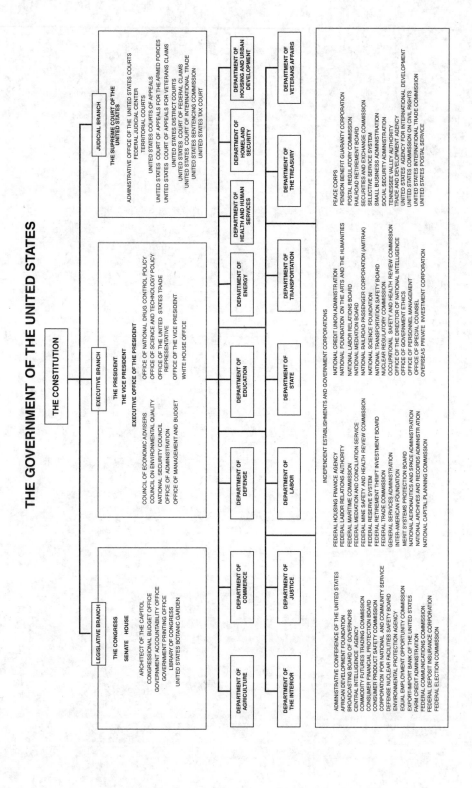

THE GOVERNMENT OF THE UNITED STATES

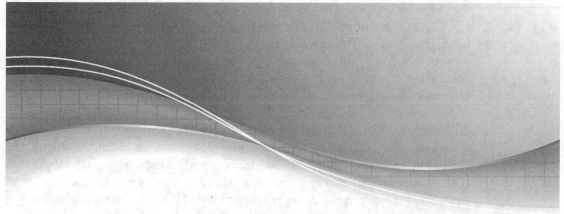

CHAPTER 2

The Judicial Branch: The Making and Application of Case Law

This chapter relates to the development of case law in the federal judicial system. The study of case law is important for a number of reasons. For one thing, common law (i.e., judge-made law), though ranking last in the priority of authorities, still represents a significant source of law. But most case law today probably consists of what might be called *interpretive* case law — i.e., case law in which the court in question is interpreting some higher form of authority (such as a constitutional provision or a statute). And as discussed previously, when a court interprets a higher form of authority, its decision essentially assumes the level of the law being interpreted, at least with respect to those for whom the court's decision is in some sense "binding." Thus, though the reasons for its importance have changed, case law continues to constitute a substantial part of the law in almost every area. Even subjects that purport to involve other sources of law (such as constitutional law) tend to be dominated by case law. The same is true of the interpretation of statutes, which tend not to interpret themselves, but instead require some role for the judiciary. Obviously, this means that in order to understand those other areas of the law, one also needs to understand how case law works more generally.

This chapter will begin with a discussion of the primary functions of federal courts, the adjudicative function and the precedent-setting function. After a discussion of the adjudicative process in perspective, as well as the role of formal logic, the chapter will proceed to a discussion of the different parts of a judicial decision; the various types of opinions in multi-judge courts; and the distinction between holding and dicta. The chapter will then proceed to a discussion of the various ways in which an earlier decision can affect later decisions, the most significant being those related to the concept of precedent. Included in this discussion will be materials relating to the role and purpose of persuasive authority and on the use of foreign law, a topic of growing significance. The chapter will further proceed to discussions of topics that, in some ways, represent challenges to our adversarial system of justice: the perceived need to provide reasons for judicial decisions, and the propriety of sua sponte decision-making and of deciding issues for the first time on appeal. The chapter will then conclude with a discussion of several topics that also play a role in the development and use of case law, including the issue of whether and to what extent a judicial decision should apply to cases in some sense arising prior to the date of that decision; the appropriateness of judicial resolution of disputes vis-à-vis other alternatives; and the need for (and meaning of) judicial impartiality.

A. THE FUNCTIONS OF FEDERAL COURTS

As you probably know, federal courts — and American courts generally — have two primary functions. The first function is to *decide cases*. The second function is to *set precedent*. *See* Bradley Scott Shannon, *The Retroactive and Prospective Application of Judicial Decisions*, 26 HARV. J.L. & PUB. POL'Y 811, 838 (2003).

To perform its decisional, or adjudicative, function, courts "must decide a litigated issue that is otherwise within their jurisdiction and in doing so must give effect to the supreme law of the land." Herbert Wechsler, *The Courts and the Constitution*, 65 COLUM. L. REV. 1001, 1006 (1965).

> In order to carry out these commands, federal courts must do several things. First, they must identify the issue before the court for resolution. Second, they must ascertain the relevant law — the standard by which the conduct or events at issue is to be evaluated. Finally, they must apply that law to the facts relevant to each issue, thereby deciding the case. This [process] is often referred to as the adjudicative process.

Shannon, 26 HARV. J.L. & PUB. POL'Y at 838-39.

The precedent-setting function refers to the fact that the decisions of some courts, in addition to deciding the case before it, also becomes the law that will be used to decide certain other, similar cases that arise in the future.

There is some debate as to which function is the more important. Some have argued, for example, that, at least with respect to the Supreme Court, its most important function is setting precedent. But we will see that trial courts are generally considered as having no ability to set precedent, obviously meaning that, for those courts, the adjudicative function is the more important. And the Supreme Court, of course, also decides cases in the course of setting precedent; indeed, under the Constitution, it could not set precedent any other way. For our purposes, though, it really does not matter which function is the more important. The bottom line is that both functions are important and worthy of study.

B. THE ADJUDICATIVE PROCESS IN PERSPECTIVE

The preceding section discussed the adjudicative process in elemental form as the application of relevant law to relevant fact. Undoubtedly, you will learn more about the mechanics of this process in courses on civil and criminal procedure and in "advocacy"-type courses, such as legal writing. The purpose here is different. The purpose here is to put that process in some perspective. The following excerpt — a landmark in this area — relates to the important (but more fundamental) question of how and why cases get adjudicated at all.

Henry M. Hart, Jr. & Albert Sacks

THE GREAT PYRAMID OF LEGAL ORDER

**The Legal Process: Basic Problems in the Making and Application of Law
(William N. Eskridge, Jr. & Philip P. Frickey eds., 1994)**

The overwhelming proportion of the things which happen and do not happen in American society pass without any later question. Many of these acts and omissions are the result of decisions which people make in the exercise of a private discretion, accorded to them by official recognition of private liberty. Still others are in conformity, conscious or unconscious, with officially formulated arrangements conferring private powers or declaring private duties. The remainder are in violation, likewise conscious or unconscious, of such arrangements.

The billions upon billions of events and non-events which in one or another of these fashions stir no later question may be thought of as forming the bottom layer, or base, of the pyramid about to be described.

The second layer of the pyramid consists of all the trouble cases — the situations in which established general arrangements are claimed to have been violated. It is of the essence of the healthy functioning of any legal order that these instances of trouble in the second layer should be only a very, very minor fraction of the instances of success, or at least of no trouble, in the first.

The third layer is the one with which . . . this prefatory note is attempting to put in perspective. Many of the trouble cases, of course, never do get formally settled. People grumble and perhaps quarrel and then forget about them. But of the remainder which do proceed to a formal and orderly conclusion an astonishingly large proportion are settled privately, without invocation of any official process. . . . [T]hree of the most important of these processes of private settlement [are] agreement and formal release; arbitration; and the decision by private associations of their own internal disputes. . . .

It should be noticed that the process of private settlement and release, in the case of privately enforced arrangements, has a significant parallel in the process of official settlement outside of court, in the case of officially enforced arrangements. Here likewise the trouble cases which do not reach the courts far outnumber those which do.

The fourth layer in the pyramid consists of the cases which are instituted in courts or in other tribunals endowed with powers of formal adjudication. Much the greater proportion of these cases, too, are settled in some fashion or other, and never come to formal judgment.

The fifth layer consists of cases finally disposed of by formal judgment, but which were never actually contested. In every American legal system these cases represent a very large proportion of the cases initially filed. Thus, many criminal cases are terminated by a judgment entered upon a plea of guilty. Many civil cases terminate by default or some form of consent judgment.

The sixth layer thus consists of litigated cases in courts or other tribunals of first instance.

Most litigated cases are not appealed, and in judicial systems having intermediate courts of appeal most appealed cases never reach the court of last resort. The seventh layer in the pyramid includes all the cases which go to some reviewing tribunal. How many sub-layers there are at this level depends, of course, on how many reviewing tribunals are available.

The functions and significance of courts of last resort . . . can be understood only by observing the relationship between their decisions and the various layers of action and decision below.

Notes and Questions

---

1. What is the point (or points) of this excerpt? How does it help one understand the role of adjudication in our society?

2. According to Professors Hart and Sacks, what are the seven layers in the "great pyramid"? Why does any case reach the layer that it does?

We normally think of adjudication as the litigation (or "trying") of a case, or perhaps as the product of a trial or even a dispositive pretrial motion. But what is the *essence* of adjudication? What are its distinctive qualities? How does it compare to other forms of social ordering? And at what point does adjudication become a poor vehicle for resolving disputes and formulating law? Consider, with respect to these questions, the following excerpt, another landmark in the history of legal process.

Lon L. Fuller

THE FORMS AND LIMITS OF ADJUDICATION

92 Harv. L. Rev. 353 (1978)[1]

I. THE PROBLEMS TOWARD WHICH THIS ESSAY IS ADDRESSED

The subject matter of this essay is adjudication in the very broadest sense. As the term is used here it includes a father attempting to assume the role of judge in a dispute between his children over possession of a toy. At the other extreme it embraces the most formal and even awesome exercises of adjudicative power: a Senate trying the impeachment of a President, a Supreme Court sitting in judgment on the powers of the government of which it is a part, an international tribunal deciding a dispute between nations, a faculty of law — in former centuries — undertaking to judge the rival claims of kings and popes, the Congregation of Rites of the Roman Catholic Church hearing the arguments pro and con in a procedure for canonization.

As the term adjudication is used here its application is not restricted to tribunals functioning as part of an established government. It includes adjudicative bodies which owe their powers to the consent of the litigants expressed in an agreement of submission, as in labor relations and in international law. It also includes tribunals that assume adjudicative powers without the sanction either of consent or of superior governmental power, the most notable example being the court that sat in the Nuremberg Trials.

The problems that are the concern of this paper are those suggested by the two terms of the title, the *forms* and *limits* of adjudication. By speaking of the *limits* of adjudication I mean to raise such questions as the following: What kinds of social tasks can properly be assigned to courts and other adjudicative agencies? What are the lines of division that separate such tasks from those that require an exercise of executive power or that must be entrusted to planning boards or public corporations? What tacit assumptions underlie the conviction that certain problems are inherently unsuited for adjudicative disposition and should be left to the legislature? More generally, to borrow the title of a famous article by Roscoe Pound, what are the limits of effective legal action? — bearing in mind that legislative determinations often can only become effective if they are of such a nature that they are suited for judicial interpretation and enforcement.

By the *forms* of adjudication I refer to the ways in which adjudication may be organized and conducted. For example, in labor relations and in international law we encounter a hybrid form called "tripartite arbitration" in which a "public" or "impartial" arbitrator sits flanked by arbitrators appointed by the interested

---

1. Though not published in this form until 1978, after Professor Fuller's death, this article was based on lectures delivered in the late 1950s and early 1960s. *See id.* at 353 (special editor's note).

parties. Such a deviation from the ordinary organization of adjudication presents such questions as: What, if any, are its proper uses? What are its peculiar limits and dangers? Other deviational forms present less subtle questions, such as Judge Bridlegoose's decisions by a throw of the dice. In general the questions posed for consideration are: What are the permissible variations in the forms of adjudication? When has its nature been so altered that we are compelled to speak of an "abuse" or a "perversion" of the adjudicative process?

Questions of the permissible forms and the proper limits of adjudication have probably been under discussion ever since something equivalent to a judicial power first emerged in primitive society. In our own history the Supreme Court at an early date excluded from its jurisdiction certain issues designated as "political." This exclusion could hardly be said to rest on any principle made explicit in the Constitution; it was grounded rather in a conviction that certain problems by their intrinsic nature fall beyond the proper limits of adjudication, though how these problems are to be defined remains even today a subject for debate. In international law one of the most significant issues lies in the concept of "justiciability." Similar problems recur in labor relations, where the proper role of the arbitrator has always been a matter in active dispute.

. . . .

The purpose of this Article is to offer an analysis that may be helpful in answering questions like those posed in the preceding paragraphs. Now it is apparent that any analysis of this sort, transcending as it does so many conventional boundaries, will be meaningless if it does not rest on some concept equivalent to "true adjudication." For if there is no such thing as "true adjudication," then it becomes impossible to distinguish the uses and abuses of adjudication. Yet it is unfortunately also true that any suggestion of a notion like "true adjudication" goes heavily against the grain of modern thought. Today it is a mark of intellectual liberation to realize that there is and can be no such thing as "true science," "true religion," "true education," or "true adjudication." "It is all a matter of definition." The modern professional university philosopher is particularly allergic to anything suggesting the doctrine of essence and takes it as a sure sign of philosophic illiteracy when a writer speaks of "the essence of art" or "the essence of democracy."

Yet we must examine critically the implications of this rejection. Does it imply, for example, that international lawyers are talking nonsense when they discuss the question of what kinds of disputes between nations are suited to decision by tribunal? Are students of labor relations engaged in mere verbal shadowboxing when they ask how an arbitration should be conducted and what sorts of questions arbitrators are fitted to decide? Do those engaged in discussions of this sort deceive themselves in believing that they are engaged in a rational inquiry? Surely if adjudication is subject to a reasoned analysis in a particular context, there is no a priori reason for supposing that the context cannot be expanded so that adjudication becomes the object of a more general analysis.

. . . .

Accordingly I shall have to begin our inquiry with an attempt to define "true adjudication," or adjudication as it might be if the ideals that support it were fully realized. In doing so I shall of necessity be describing something that never fully exists. Yet it is only with the aid of this nonexistent model that we can pass intelligent judgment on the accomplishments of adjudication as it actually is. Indeed, it is only with the aid of that model that we can distinguish adjudication as an existent institution from other social institutions and procedures by which decisions may be reached.

II. THE TWO BASIC FORMS OF SOCIAL ORDERING

It is customary to think of adjudication as a means of settling disputes or controversies. This is, of course, its most obvious aspect. The normal occasion for a resort to adjudication is when parties are at odds with one another, often to such a degree that a breach of social order is threatened.

More fundamentally, however, adjudication should be viewed as a form of social ordering, as a way in which the relations of men to one another are governed and regulated. Even in the absence of any formalized doctrine of stare decisis or res judicata, an adjudicative determination will normally enter in some degree into the litigants' future relations and into the future relations of other parties who see themselves as possible litigants before the same tribunal. Even if there is no statement by the tribunal of the reasons for its decision, some reason will be perceived or guessed at, and the parties will tend to govern their conduct accordingly.

If, then adjudication is a form of social ordering, to understand it fully we must view it in its relation to other forms of social ordering. It is submitted that there are two basic forms of social ordering: *organization by common aims* and *organization by reciprocity*. Without one or the other of these nothing resembling a society can exist.

. . . .

III. ADJUDICATION AS A FORM OF SOCIAL ORDERING

In discussing reciprocity and organization by common aims, I pointed out that these two forms of social ordering present themselves along a scale of varying formal explicitness. To some extent the same thing is true of adjudication. We talk, for example, of "taking our case to the forum of public opinion." Or two men may argue in the presence of a third with a kind of tacit hope that he will decide which is right, but without any explicit submission of their dispute to his arbitrament.

On the very informal level, however, forms of social ordering are too mixed and ambiguous to make comparisons fruitful. It is only when a particular form of ordering explicitly controls a relationship that it can be set off clearly against alternative forms of ordering. For this reason, therefore, I am here employing contract to represent reciprocity in its formal and explicit expression. I shall take elections as the most familiar formalization of organization by common aims.

Adjudication, contract, and elections are three ways of reaching decisions, of settling disputes, of defining men's relations to one another. Now I submit that the characteristic feature of each of these forms of social ordering lies in the manner in which the affected party participates in the decision reached. This may be presented graphically as follows:

Form of Social Ordering	Mode of Participation by the Affected Party
Contract	Negotiation
Elections	Voting
Adjudication	Presentation of proofs and reasoned arguments

It is characteristic of these three ways of ordering men's relations that though they are subject to variation — they present themselves in different "forms" — each contains certain intrinsic demands that must be met if it is to function properly. We may distinguish roughly between "optimum conditions," which would lift a particular form of order to its highest expression, and "essential conditions," without which the form of order ceases to function in any significant sense at all.

With respect to the principle of contract an analysis of optimum and essential conditions would be exceedingly complex and would require an analysis of the requirements of a market economy, of the peculiar qualities of bargaining in situations of oligopoly, etc. We can observe, however, that a regime of contract presupposes the absence of certain kinds of coercion; a contract signed at the point of a gun is hardly in any significant sense a contract at all. However, it will be simpler if we confine our attention here to a comparison of elections with adjudication.

Elections present themselves in many forms, varying from the town meeting to the "ja-nein" plebiscite. Voting can be organized in many ways: simple majority vote . . . and various complicated mixed forms. At the same time, all of these expressions of political democracy have in common that they afford the person affected by the decision which emerges a peculiar form of participation in that decision, namely, some form of voting. The optimum conditions that would give fullest meaning to this participation include an intelligent and fully informed electorate, an active interest by the electorate in the issues, candor in discussing those issues by those participating in public debate — conditions, it is needless to say, that are scarcely ever realized in practice. On the other hand, there are certain essential conditions without which the participation of the voter loses its meaning altogether. These would include that the votes be honestly counted, that the ballot boxes not be "stuffed," that certain types of intimidation be absent, etc.

Now much of this paper will be concerned in carrying through with a similar analysis of the optimum and essential conditions for the functioning of adjudication. This whole analysis will derive from one simple proposition, namely, that the distinguishing characteristic of adjudication lies in the fact that it confers on the affected party a peculiar form of participation in the decision, that of presenting proofs and reasoned arguments for a decision in his favor. Whatever heightens the significance of this participation lifts adjudication toward its optimum expression. Whatever destroys the meaning of that participation destroys the integrity of adjudication itself. Thus, participation through reasoned argument loses its meaning if the arbiter of the dispute is inaccessible to reason because he is insane, has been bribed, or is hopelessly prejudiced. The purpose of this paper is to trace out the somewhat less obvious implications of the proposition that the distinguishing feature of adjudication lies in the mode of participation which it accords to the party affected by the decision.

But first it will be necessary to deal with certain objections that may be raised against my starting point, namely against the proposition that the "essence" of adjudication lies in the mode of participation it accords to the affected party.

IV. ADJUDICATION AND RATIONALITY

It may be said that the essence of adjudication lies not in the manner in which the affected party participates in the decision but in the office of judge. If there is a judge and a chance to appear before him, it is a matter of indifference whether the litigant chooses to present proofs or reasoned arguments. He may, if he sees fit, offer no argument at all, or pitch his appeal entirely on an emotional level, or even indicate his willingness that the judge decide the case by a throw of the dice. It might seem, then, that our analysis should take as its point of departure the office of judge. From this office certain requirements might be deduced, for example, that of impartiality, since a judge to be "truly" such must be impartial. Then, as the next step, if he is to be impartial he must be willing to hear both sides, etc.

The trouble with this is that there are people who are called "judges" holding official positions and expected to be impartial who nevertheless do not participate in an adjudication in any sense directly relevant to the subject of this paper. Judges at an agricultural fair or an art exhibition may serve as examples. Again, a baseball umpire, though he is not called a judge, is expected to make impartial rulings. What distinguishes these functionaries is not that they do not hold governmental office, for the duties of a judge at a livestock fair would scarcely be changed if he were an official of the Department of Agriculture. What distinguishes them from courts, administrative tribunals, and boards of arbitration is that their decisions are not reached within an institutional framework that is intended to assure to the disputants an opportunity for the presentation of proofs and reasoned arguments. The judge of livestock may or may not permit such a presentation; it is not an integral part of his office to permit and to attend to it.

If, on the other hand, we start with the notion of a process of decision in which the affected party's participation consists in an opportunity to present proofs and reasoned arguments, the office of judge or arbitrator and the requirement of impartiality follow as necessary implications. . . .

It may be objected at this point that "reasoned argument" is, after all, not a monopoly of forensic proceedings. A political speech may take the form of reasoned appeal to the electorate; to be sure, it often takes other forms, but the same thing may be said of speeches in court. This objection fails to take account of a conception that underlies the whole analysis being presented here, the conception, namely, of a form of participating in a decision that is institutionally defined and assured.

When I am entering a contract with another person I may present proofs and arguments to him, but there is generally no formal assurance that I will be given this opportunity or that he will listen to my arguments if I make them. (Perhaps the only exception to this generalization lies in the somewhat anomalous legal obligation "to bargain in good faith" in labor relations.) During an election I may actively campaign for one side and may present what I consider to be "reasoned arguments" to the electorate. If I am an effective campaigner this participation in the decision ultimately reached may greatly outweigh in importance the casting of my own single vote. At the same time, it is only the latter form of participation that is the subject of an affirmative institutional guarantee. The protection afforded my right to present arguments to the electorate is almost entirely indirect and negative. The way will be held clear for me, but I shall have to pave it myself. Even if I am given an affirmative right (for example, under the "equal time" rule of the FCC), I am given no formal assurance that anyone will listen to my appeal. The voter who goes to sleep before his television set is surely not subject to the same condemnation as the judge who sleeps through the argument of counsel.

Adjudication is, then, a device which gives formal and institutional expression to the influence of reasoned argument in human affairs. As such it assumes a burden of rationality not borne by any other form of social ordering. A decision which is the product of reasoned argument must be prepared itself to meet the test of reason. We demand of an adjudicative decision a kind of rationality we do not expect of the results of contract or of voting. This higher responsibility toward rationality is at once the strength *and the weakness* of adjudication as a form of social ordering.

In entering contracts, men are of course in some measure guided by rational considerations. The subsistence farmer who has a surfeit of potatoes and only a handful of onions acts reasonably when he trades potatoes for onions. But there is no test of rationality that can be applied to the results of the trade considered in abstraction from the interests of the parties. Indeed, the trade of potatoes for onions, which is a rational act by one trader, might be considered irrational if indulged in by his opposite number, who has a storehouse full of onions and only a bushel of potatoes. If we asked one party to a contract, "Can you defend that contract?" he might answer, "Why, yes. It was good for me and it was good for him." If we then said, "But that is not what we meant. We meant, can you defend it on general grounds?" he might well reply that he did not know what we were talking about. Yet this is precisely the kind of question we normally direct toward the decision of a judge or arbitrator. The results that emerge from adjudication are subject, then, to a standard of rationality that is different from that imposed on the results of an exchange.

I believe that the same observation holds true when adjudication is compared with elections. The key to the difference lies again in the mode in which the affected party participates in a decision. If, as in adjudication, the only mode of participation consists in the opportunity to present proofs and arguments, the purpose of this participation is frustrated, and the whole proceeding becomes a farce, should the decision that emerges make no pretense whatever to rationality. The same cannot be said of the mode of participation called voting. We may assume that the preferences of the voters are ultimately emotional, inarticulate, and not subject to rational defense. At the same time there is a need for social order, and it may be assumed that this need is best met when order rests on the broadest possible base of popular support. On this ground, a negative defense of democracy is possible; the will of the majority controls, not because it is right, but — well, because it *is* the will of the majority. This is surely an impoverished conception of democracy, but it expresses at least one ingredient of any philosophy of democracy, and it suggests a reason why we demand of adjudication a kind of rationality that we do not expect of elections.

This problem can be approached somewhat obliquely from a different direction by asking what is implied by "a right" or by "a claim of right." If I say to someone, "Give me that!" I do not necessarily assert a right. I may be begging for an act of charity, or I may be threatening to take by force something to which I admittedly have no right. On the other hand, if I say, "Give me that, I have a right to it," I necessarily assert the existence of some principle or standard by which my "right" can be tested.

. . . .

VI. THE FORMS OF ADJUDICATION

. . . .

2. Is an Adversary Presentation Necessary to Adjudication?

The Lawyer's Role as Advocate in Open Court

The lawyer appearing as an advocate before a tribunal presents, as persuasively as he can, the facts and the law of the case as seen from the standpoint of his client's interest. It is essential that both the lawyer and the public understand clearly the nature of the role thus discharged. Such an understanding is required not only to appreciate the need for an adversary presentation of issues, but also in order to perceive truly the limits partisan advocacy must impose on itself if it is to remain wholesome and useful.

In a very real sense it may be said that the integrity of the adjudicative process itself depends upon the participation of the advocate. This becomes apparent when we contemplate the nature of the task assumed by any arbiter who attempts to decide a dispute without the aid of partisan advocacy.

Such an arbiter must undertake, not only the role of judge, but that of representative for both of the litigants. Each of these roles must be played to the full without being muted by qualifications derived from the others. When he is developing for each side the most effective statement of its case, the arbiter must put aside his neutrality and permit himself to be moved by a sympathetic identification sufficiently intense to draw from his mind all that it is capable of giving, — in analysis, patience and creative power. When he resumes his neutral position, he must be able to view with distrust the fruits of this identification and be ready to reject the products of his own best mental efforts. The difficulties of this undertaking are obvious. If it is true that a man in his time must play many parts, it is scarcely given to him to play them all at once.

It is small wonder, then, that failure generally attends the attempt to dispense with the distinct roles traditionally implied in adjudication. What generally occurs in practice is that at some early point a familiar pattern will seem to emerge from the evidence; an accustomed label is wanting for the case and, without awaiting further proofs, this label is promptly assigned to it. It is a mistake to suppose that this premature cataloguing must necessarily result from impatience, prejudice, or mental sloth. Often it proceeds from a very understandable desire to bring the hearing into some order and coherence, for without some tentative theory of the case there is no standard of relevance by which testimony may be measured. But what starts as a preliminary diagnosis designed to direct the inquiry tends, quickly and imperceptibly, to become a fixed conclusion, as all that confirms the diagnosis makes a strong imprint on the mind, while all that runs counter to it is received with diverted attention.

An adversary presentation seems the only effective means for combatting this natural human tendency to judge too swiftly in terms of the familiar that which is not yet fully known. The arguments of counsel hold the case, as it were, in suspension between two opposing interpretations of it. While the proper classification of the case is thus kept unresolved, there is time to explore all of its peculiarities and nuances.

These are the contributions made by partisan advocacy during the public hearing of the cause. When we take into account the preparations that must precede the hearing, the essential quality of the advocate's contribution becomes even more apparent. Preceding the hearing, inquiries must be instituted to determine what facts can be proved or seem sufficiently established to warrant a formal test of their truth during the hearing. There must also be a preliminary analysis of the issues, so that the hearing may have form and direction. These preparatory measures are indispensable whether or not the parties involved in the controversy are represented by advocates.

Where that representation is present there is an obvious advantage in the fact that the area of dispute may be greatly reduced by an exchange of written pleadings or by stipulations of counsel. Without the participation of someone who can act responsibly for each of the parties, this essential narrowing of the issues becomes impossible. But here again the true significance of partisan advocacy lies deeper, touching once more the integrity of the adjudicative process itself. It is only through the advocate's participation that the hearing may remain in fact what it purports to be in theory: a public trial of the facts and issues. Each advocate comes to the hearing prepared to present his proofs and arguments, knowing at the same time that his arguments may fail to persuade and that his proofs may be rejected as inadequate. It is a part of his role to absorb these possible disappointments. The deciding tribunal, on the other hand, comes to the hearing uncommitted. It has not represented to the public that any fact can be proved, that any argument is sound, or that any particular way of stating a litigant's case is the most effective expression of its merits.

These, then, are the reasons for believing that partisan advocacy plays a vital and essential role in one of the most fundamental procedures of a democratic society. But if we were to put all of these detailed considerations to one side, we should still be confronted by the fact that, in whatever form adjudication may appear, the experienced judge or arbitrator desires and actively seeks to obtain an adversary presentation of the issues. Only when he has had the benefit of intelligent and vigorous advocacy on both sides can he feel fully confident of his decision.

Viewed in this light, the role of the lawyer as a partisan advocate appears not as a regrettable necessity, but as an indispensable part of a larger ordering of affairs. The institution of advocacy is not a concession to the frailties of human nature, but an expression of human insight in the design of a social framework within which man's capacity for impartial judgment can attain its fullest realization.

When advocacy is thus viewed, it becomes clear by what principle limits must be set to partisanship. The advocate plays his role well when zeal for his client's cause promotes a wise and informed decision of the case. He plays his role badly, and trespasses against the obligations of professional responsibility, when his desire to win leads him to muddy the headwaters of decision, when, instead of lending a needed perspective to the controversy, he distorts and obscures its true nature.

. . . .

3. May the Arbiter Act on His Own Motion in Initiating the Case?

In his *The Nature and Sources of the Law*, John Chipman Gray wrote:

> A judge of an organized body is a man appointed by that body to determine duties and the corresponding rights *upon the application of persons claiming those rights*. It is the fact that such application must be made to him, which distinguishes a judge from an administrative officer. The essence of a judge's office is that he shall be impartial, that he is to sit apart, is not to interfere voluntarily in affairs but is to determine cases which are presented to him. To use the phrase of the English Ecclesiastical courts, the office of the judge must be promoted by some one.

A German socialist critic of "bourgeois law" once caricatured this view by saying that courts are like defective clocks; they have to be shaken to set them going. He, of course, added the point that shaking costs money.

Certainly, it is true that in most of the practical manifestations of adjudication the arbiter's function has to be "promoted" by the litigant and is not initiated by itself. But is this coy quality of waiting to be asked an essential part of adjudication?

It would seem that it is not. Suppose, for example, the collision of two ships under circumstances that suggest that one or both masters were at fault. Suppose a board is given authority to initiate hearings in such a case and to make a determination of fault. Such a board might conduct its hearings after the pattern of court proceedings. Both masters might be accorded counsel and a full opportunity for cross-examination. There would be no impairment of the affected parties' full participation by proofs and reasoned arguments; the integrity of adjudication seems to be preserved.

Yet I think that most of us would consider such a case exceptional and would not be deterred by it from persisting in the belief that the adjudicative process should normally not be initiated by the tribunal itself. There are, I believe, sound reasons for adhering to that belief.

Certainly it is clear that the integrity of adjudication is impaired if the arbiter not only initiates the proceeding but also, in advance of the public hearing, forms theories about what happened and conducts his own factual inquiries. In such a case the arbiter cannot bring to the public hearing an uncommitted mind; the effectiveness of participation through proofs and reasoned arguments is accordingly reduced. Now it is probably true that under most circumstances the mere initiation of proceedings carries with it a certain commitment and often a theory of what occurred. The case of the collision at sea is exceptional because there the facts themselves speak eloquently for the need of some kind of inquiry, so that the initiation of the proceedings implies nothing more than a recognition of this need. In most situations the initiation of proceedings could not have the same neutral quality, as, for example, where the occasion consists simply in the fact that a corporation had gone two years without declaring a dividend.

There is another reason which justifies the common conception that it is not normal for the adjudicative process to be initiated by the deciding tribunal. If we view adjudication in its widest extension, as including not only the work of courts but also that of arbitrators in labor, commerce, and international relations, it is apparent that the overwhelming majority of cases submitted to adjudication involve the assertion of claims founded directly or indirectly on *contract* or *agreement*. It seems clear that a regime of contract (more broadly, a regime of reciprocity) implies that the determination whether to assert a claim must be left to the interested party.

. . . .

The belief that it is not normal for the arbiter himself to initiate the adjudicative process has, then, a two-fold basis. *First*, it is generally impossible to keep even the bare initiation of proceedings untainted by preconceptions about what happened and what its consequences should be. In this sense, initiation of the proceedings by the arbiter impairs the integrity of adjudication by reducing the effectiveness of the litigant's participation through proofs and arguments. *Second*, the great bulk of claims submitted to adjudication are founded directly or indirectly on relationships of reciprocity. In this case, unless the affected party is deceived or ignorant of his rights, the very foundations of the claim asserted dictate that the process of adjudication must be invoked by the claimant.

4. Must the Decision Be Accompanied by a Statement of the Reasons for It?

We tend to think of the judge or arbitrator as one who decides and who gives reasons for his decision. Does the integrity of adjudication require that reasons be given for the decision rendered? I think the answer is, not necessarily. In some fields of labor arbitration (chiefly, I believe, where arbitration is a facility made available without charge by the state) it is the practice to render "blind" awards. The reasons for this practice probably include a belief that reasoned awards are often misinterpreted and "stir up trouble," as well as the circumstance that the arbitrator is so busy he has no time to write opinions. Under the procedures of the American Arbitration Association awards in commercial cases are rendered usually without opinion. (Written opinions are, however, usual in *labor* cases.) Perhaps the special practice in commercial cases has arisen because arbitrators in such cases normally serve without fee and writing opinions is hard work. Perhaps also there is a fear that explanations ineptly phrased by lay arbitrators might open too wide a door to judicial review.

By and large it seems clear that the fairness and effectiveness of adjudication are promoted by reasoned opinions. Without such opinions the parties have to take it on faith that their participation in the decision has been real, that the arbiter has in fact understood and taken into account their proofs and arguments. A less obvious point is that, where a decision enters into some continuing relationship, if no reasons are given the parties will almost inevitably guess at reasons and act accordingly. Here the effectiveness of adjudication is impaired, not only because the results achieved may not be those intended by the arbiter, but also because his freedom of decision in future cases may be curtailed by the growth of practices based on a misinterpretation of decisions previously rendered.

5. May the Arbiter Rest His Decision on Grounds Not Argued by the Parties?

Obviously the bond of participation by the litigant is most secure when the arbiter rests his decision wholly on the proofs and arguments actually presented to him by the parties. In practice, however, it is not always possible to realize this ideal. Even where all of the considerations on which the decision rests were touched on by the parties' arguments, the emphasis may be very different. An issue dealt with only in passing by one of the parties, or perhaps by both, may become the headstone of the arbiter's decision. This may mean not only that, had they foreseen this outcome, the parties would have presented different arguments, but that they might also have introduced evidence on very different factual issues.

If the ideal of a perfect congruence between the arbiter's view of the issues and that of the parties is unattainable, this is no excuse for a failure to work toward an achievement of the closest approximation of it. We need to remind ourselves that if this congruence is utterly absent — if the grounds for the decision fall completely outside the framework of the argument, making all that was discussed or proved at the hearing irrelevant — then the adjudication process has become a sham, for the parties' participation in the decision has lost all meaning. We need to analyze what factors influence the desired congruence and what measures may be taken to promote it.

One circumstance of capital importance is the extent to which a particular process of adjudication takes place in a context of established rules. In branches of the law where the rules have become fairly settled and certain, it may be possible for lawyers to reach agreement easily in defining the crucial issues presented by a particular case. In such an area the risk is slight that the decision will fall outside the frame of reference set by the proofs and arguments. On the other hand, in areas of uncertainty, this risk is greatly increased. There are, to be sure, dangers in a premature crystallization of standards. On the other hand, one of the less obvious dangers of a too long delayed formulation of doctrine lies in the inevitable impairment of the integrity of adjudication that is entailed, for the reality of the parties' participation is reduced when it is impossible to foretell what issues will become relevant in the ultimate disposition of the case.

. . . .

I have mentioned two devices that can help to prevent a lack of fit between the case as argued and the case as decided—the request for a reargument and the tentative decree. Oral argument is also of the greatest importance in this connection, for a written submission is often truly a shot in the dark. In appellate cases it is also important that the judges have studied the record before oral argument, for without this preparation the virtue of the oral argument in defining the crucial issues may be lost.

. . . .

6. Qualifications and Disqualifications of the Arbiter

A full discussion of the questions suggested by this title would lead too far afield for the purposes of this paper. Even a consideration of the comparative efficacy of the various devices intended to guarantee impartiality would require a long chapter.

I shall merely suggest that the problem of securing a properly qualified and impartial arbiter be tried by the same touchstone that has been used throughout—what will preserve the efficacy and meaning of the affected party's participation through proofs and arguments? Obviously, a strong emotional attachment by the arbiter to one of the interests involved in the dispute is destructive of that participation. In practice, however, another kind of "partiality" is much more dangerous. I refer to the situation where the arbiter's experience of life has not embraced the area of the dispute, or, worse still, where he has always viewed that area from some single vantage point. Here a blind spot of which he is quite unconscious may prevent him from getting the point of testimony or argument. By and large I think the decisions of our courts in commercial cases do not represent adjudication at its highest level. The reason is a lack of judicial "feel" for the problems involved.

. . . .

7. Must the Decision Be Retrospective?

In practice both the decisions of courts and the awards of arbitrators are retrospective, both as to their effect on the litigants' rights and their effect as precedents for the decisions of other cases. A paradox is sometimes squeezed from this traditional way of acting, to the effect that courts, in order to avoid the appearance of legislating, cast their legislative enactments in the harshest possible form, making them ex post facto.

The philosophy underlying the retrospective effect of the judicial decision can be stated somewhat as follows: It is not the function of courts to create new aims for society or to impose on society new basic directives. The courts for various reasons analyzed previously are unsuited for this sort of task. Perhaps the most compelling objection to an assumption of any such function lies in the limited participation in the decision by the litigants who (1) represent generally only themselves and (2) participate in the decision only by proofs and arguments addressed to the arbiter. On the other hand, with respect to the generally shared aims and the authoritative directives of a society, the courts do have an important function to perform, that of developing (or even "discovering") case by case what these aims or directives demand for their realization in particular situations of fact. In the discharge of this function, at times the result is so obvious that no one thinks of a "retroactive effect." Theoretically, a court might distinguish between such decisions and those which announce a rule or standard that seems "new," even though it may represent a reasoned conclusion from familiar premises. But if an attempt were made to apply such a distinction pervasively, so that some decisions would be retrospective, some prospective only, the resulting confusion might be much less bearable than the situation that now obtains.

. . . .

8. How Is Adjudication Affected by the Source of the Arbiter's Power?

The power to adjudicate may represent a delegated power of government, as in the case of a judge, or it may derive from the consent of the litigants, as in most forms of arbitration. Are these two basically different "forms" of adjudication? Obviously it has been a tacit assumption of this paper that they are not.

On the other hand, this does not mean that the discharge of the arbiter's function is wholly unaffected by the source of his power. In a summary way we may say that the possible advantages of adjudication supported by governmental authority are: (1) The judge is under less temptation to "compromise" than is the contractually appointed arbitrator. (2) The acceptability of the judge's decision may be enhanced by the fact that he seems to play a subservient role, as one who merely applies rules which he himself did not make.

Among the possible advantages of adjudication which derives its power from a contract of the parties are the following: (1) Being unbacked by state power (or insufficiently backed by it in the case of an ineffective legal sanction), the arbitrator must concern himself directly with the acceptability of the award. He may be at greater pains than a judge to get his facts straight, to state accurately the arguments of the parties, and generally to display in his award a full understanding of the case. (2) Being relatively free from technical rules of procedure, the wise and conscientious arbitrator can shape his procedures upon what he perceives to be the intrinsic demands of effective adjudication. Thus, the "due process" which animates his conduct of the hearing may appear to the parties as something real and not something that has to be taken on faith, as allegedly inhering in technical rules that seem quite arbitrary to the layman.

. . . .

VII. THE LIMITS OF ADJUDICATION

1. Introduction

Attention is now directed to the question, What kinds of tasks are inherently un-suited to adjudication? The test here will be that used throughout. If a given task is assigned to adjudicative treatment, will it be possible to preserve the meaning of the affected party's participation through proofs and arguments?

2. Polycentric Tasks and Adjudication

This section introduces a concept — that of the "polycentric" task — which has been derived from Michael Polanyi's book *The Logic of Liberty*. In approaching that concept it will be well to begin with a few examples.

Some months ago a wealthy lady by the name of Timken died in New York leaving a valuable, but somewhat miscellaneous, collection of paintings to the Metropolitan Museum and the National Gallery "in equal shares," her will indicat-ing no particular appointment. When the will was probated the judge remarked something to the effect that the parties seemed to be confronted with a real prob-lem. The attorney for one of the museums spoke up and said, "We are good friends. We will work it out somehow or other." What makes this problem of effecting an equal division of the paintings a polycentric task? It lies in the fact that the disposi-tion of any single painting has implications for the proper disposition of every other painting. If it gets the Renoir, the Gallery may be less eager for the Cezanne but all the more eager for the Bellows, etc. If the proper apportionment were set for argu-ment, there would be no clear issue to which either side could direct its proofs and contentions. Any judge assigned to hear such an argument would be tempted to assume the role of mediator or to adopt the classical solution: Let the older brother (here the Metropolitan) divide the estate into what he regards as equal shares, let the younger brother (the National Gallery) take his pick.

As a second illustration suppose in a socialist regime it were decided to have all wages and prices set by courts which would proceed after the usual forms of adjudication. It is, I assume, obvious that here is a task that could not successfully be undertaken by the adjudicative method. The point that comes first to mind is that courts move too slowly to keep up with a rapidly changing economic scene. The more fundamental point is that the forms of adjudication cannot encompass and take into account the complex repercussions that may result from any change in prices or wages. A rise in the price of aluminum may affect in varying degrees the demand for, and therefore the proper price of, thirty kinds of steel, twenty kinds of plastics, an infinitude of woods, other metals, etc. Each of these separate effects may have its own complex repercussions in the economy. In such a case it is simply impossible to afford each affected party a meaningful participation through proofs and arguments. It is a matter of capital importance to note that it is not merely a question of the huge number of possibly affected parties, significant as that aspect of the thing may be. A more fundamental point is that each of the various forms that award might take (say, a three-cent increase per pound, a four-cent increase, a five-cent increase, etc.) would have a different set of repercussions and might require in each instance a redefinition of the "parties affected."

We may visualize this kind of situation by thinking of a spider web. A pull on one strand will distribute tensions after a complicated pattern throughout the web as a whole. Doubling the original pull will, in all likelihood, not simply double each of the resulting tensions but will rather create a different complicated pattern of tensions. This would certainly occur, for example, if the doubled pull caused one or more of the weaker strands to snap. This is a "polycentric" situation because it is "many centered" — each crossing of strands is a distinct center for distributing tensions.

Suppose, again, it were decided to assign players on a football team to their positions by the process of adjudication. I assume that we would agree that this is also an unwise application of adjudication. It is not merely a matter of eleven different men being possibly affected; each shift of any one player might have a different set of repercussions on the remaining players: putting Jones in as quarterback would have one set of carryover effects, putting him in as left end, another. Here, again, we are dealing with a situation of interacting points of influence and therefore with a polycentric problem beyond the proper limits of adjudication.

. . . .

It should be carefully noted that a multiplicity of affected persons is not an invariable characteristic of polycentric problems. This is sufficiently illustrated in the case of Mrs. Timken's will. That case also illustrated the fact that rapid changes with time are not an invariable characteristic of such problems. On the other hand, in practice polycentric problems of possible concern to adjudication will normally involve many affected parties and a somewhat fluid state of affairs. Indeed, the last characteristic follows from the simple fact that the more interacting centers there are, the more the likelihood that one of them will be affected by a change in circumstances, and, if the situation is polycentric, this change will communicate itself after a complex pattern to other centers. This insistence on a clear conception of polycentricity may seem to be laboring a point, but clarity of analysis is essential if confusion is to be avoided. For example, if a reward of $1000 is offered for the capture of a criminal and six claimants assert a right to the award, hearing the six-sided controversy may be an awkward affair. The problem does not, however, present any significant polycentric element as that term is used here.

Now, if it is important to see clearly what a polycentric problem is, it is equally important to realize that the distinction involved is often a matter of degree. There are polycentric elements in almost all problems submitted to adjudication. A decision may act as a precedent, often an awkward one, in some situation not foreseen by the arbiter. Again, suppose a court in a suit between one litigant and a railway holds that it is an act of negligence for the railway not to construct an underpass at a particular crossing. There may be nothing to distinguish this crossing from other crossings on the line. As a matter of statistical probability it may be clear that constructing underpasses along the whole line would cost more lives (through accidents in blasting, for example) than would be lost if the only safety measure were the familiar "Stop, Look & Listen" sign. If so, then what seems to be a decision simply declaring the rights and duties of two parties is in fact an inept solution for a polycentric problem, some elements of which cannot be brought before the court in a simple suit by one injured party against a defendant railway. In lesser measure, concealed polycentric elements are probably present in almost all problems resolved by adjudication. It is not, then, a question of distinguishing black from white. It is a question of knowing when the polycentric elements have become so significant and predominant that the proper limits of adjudication have been reached.

In speaking of the covert polycentric elements almost always present in even the most simple-appearing cases, it should be noted that the efficacy of adjudication as a whole is strongly affected by the manner in which the doctrine of stare decisis is applied. If judicial precedents are liberally interpreted and are subject to reformulation and clarification as problems not originally foreseen arise, the judicial process as a whole is enabled to absorb these covert polycentric elements. By considering the process of decision as a collaborative one projected through time, an accommodation of legal doctrine to the complex aspects of a problem can be made as these aspects reveal themselves in successive cases. On the other hand, if a strict or "literal" interpretation is made of precedents, the limits of adjudication must perforce be more strictly drawn, for its power of accommodation has been reduced.

If problems sufficiently polycentric are unsuited to solution by adjudication, how may they in fact be solved? So far as I can see, there are only two suitable methods: *managerial direction* and *contract* (reciprocity).

. . . .

The final question to be addressed is this: When an attempt is made to deal by adjudicative forms with a problem that is essentially polycentric, what happens? As I see it, three things can happen, sometimes all at once. *First*, the adjudicative solution may fail. Unexpected repercussions make the decision unworkable; it is ignored, withdrawn, or modified, sometimes repeatedly. *Second*, the purported arbiter ignores judicial proprieties — he "tries out" various solutions in posthearing conferences, consults parties not represented at the hearings, guesses at facts not proved and not properly matters for anything like judicial notice. *Third*, instead of accommodating his procedures to the nature of the problem he confronts, he may reformulate the problem so as to make it amenable to solution through adjudicative procedures.

. . . .

In closing this discussion on polycentricity, it will be well to caution against two possible misunderstandings. The suggestion that polycentric problems are often solved by a kind of "managerial intuition" should not be taken to imply that it is an invariable characteristic of polycentric problems that they resist rational solution. . . .

Finally, the fact that an adjudicative decision affects and enters into a polycentric relationship does not of itself mean that the adjudicative tribunal is moving out of its proper sphere. On the contrary, there is no better illustration of a polycentric relationship than an economic market, and yet the laying down of rules that will make a market function properly is one for which adjudication is generally well suited. The working out of our common law of contracts case by case has proceeded through adjudication, yet the basic principle underlying the rules thus developed is that they should promote the free exchange of goods in a polycentric market. The court gets into difficulty, not when it lays down rules about contracting, but when it attempts to write contracts.

Notes and Questions

1. According to Professor Fuller, what is the defining characteristic of adjudication? How does it differ from contracts and elections (i.e., the other major forms of social ordering)? Do you agree?

2. In his discussion of the "forms" of adjudication, Professor Fuller discusses a number of possible characteristics of adjudication in its highest form, including (a) an adversary presentation; (b) the initiation of the case by a party, rather than by the court; (c) an explanation of the reasoning behind the court's decision; (d) a decision based on grounds argued by one of the parties; (e) a properly qualified and unbiased judge; (f) a decision that is applied retroactively — i.e., to the parties in that case and to all other, similarly situated persons; and (g) an arbiter whose power derives from the government. As to which of these characteristics does Fuller consider essential (or nearly so)? Do you agree?

   Note that most of these issues will be explored in greater detail in later parts of this chapter.

3. With respect to the "limits" of adjudication, Professor Fuller mentions "polycentric" problems as one type of cases that are not well suited for adjudication in its traditional form. What is a "polycentric" problem? And how, according to Fuller, does it defy proper adjudication?

4. In a later book, Professor Fuller described the following "eight distinct routes to disaster" when attempting to "create and maintain a system of legal rules":

   > The first and most obvious lies in a failure to achieve rules at all, so that every issue must be decided on an ad hoc basis. The other routes are: (2) a failure to publicize, or at least to make available to the affected party, the rules he is expected to observe; (3) the abuse of retroactive legislation, which not only cannot itself guide action, but undercuts the integrity of rules prospective in effect, since it puts them under the threat of retrospective change; (4) a failure to make rules understandable; (5) the enactment of contradictory rules or (6) rules that require conduct beyond the powers of the affected party; (7) introducing such frequent changes in the rules that the subject cannot orient his action by them; and finally, (8) a failure of congruence between the rules as announced and their actual administration.

   Lon L. Fuller, The Morality of Law 38-39 (1964).

5. Professors Hart and Sacks, contemporaries of Professor Fuller, describe the proper exercise of the judicial decision-making process in terms of the process of "reasoned elaboration," which to them means "two principal things."

> It means, first of all, that the magistrate is obliged to resolve the issue before him on the assumption that the answer will be the same in all like cases. He is not to say to himself, "well, this morning it seems to me that a motorcycle is not a motor car [for the purpose of a speed statute]," assuming that another magistrate or even he himself will be free to think the opposite in another case. He is to decide the question, in other words, as a *question of law.*
>
> Secondly, the magistrate is obliged to relate his decision in some reasoned fashion to the speed statute out of which the question arises. He is not to think of himself as in the same position as a legislator taking part in the enactment of the statute in the first place. He is not to say simply, "*I* think that motorcycles should or should not be treated in the same way as ordinary automobiles for the purposes of regulating speed on public highways." He is obliged, instead, to respect the position of the legislature in the institutional system. He is to ask himself, "Ought this statute which the legislature has enacted to be read as including or not including a motorcycle?"

HENRY M. HART, JR. & ALBERT M. SACKS, THE LEGAL PROCESS: BASIC PROBLEMS IN THE MAKING AND APPLICATION OF LAW 143 (William N. Eskridge, Jr. & Philip P. Frickey eds., 1994).

C. THE ROLE OF FORMAL LOGIC

One of the most important components of the adjudicative process is logic, logic with respect to the way arguments and judicial decisions are constructed. Consider, in this regard, the following article.

Ruggero J. Aldisert, et al.

LOGIC FOR LAW STUDENTS: HOW TO THINK LIKE A LAWYER

69 U. Pitt. L. Rev. 1 (2007)

INTRODUCTION

Logic is the lifeblood of American law. In case after case, prosecutors, defense counsel, civil attorneys, and judges call upon the rules of logic to structure their arguments. Law professors, for their part, demand that students defend their comments with coherent, identifiable logic. By now we are all familiar with the great line spoken by Professor Kingsfield in *The Paper Chase*: "You come in here with a head full of mush and you leave thinking like a lawyer." What is thinking like a lawyer? It means employing logic to construct arguments.

Notwithstanding the emphasis on logical reasoning in the legal profession, our law schools do not give students an orientation in the principles of logic. Professor Jack L. Landau complained that "the idea of teaching traditional logic to law students does not seem to be very popular." Indeed, Professor Landau found that "not one current casebook on legal method, legal process, or the like contains a chapter on logic." In our view, this is tragic. The failure to ground legal education in principles of logic does violence to the essence of the law. Leaving students to distill the principles of logic on their own is like asking them to design a rocket without teaching them the rules of physics. Frustration reigns, and the resulting argument seems more mush-like than lawyerly. In these pages we make a small attempt to right the ship by offering a primer on the fundamentals of logical thinking.

Our goals are modest. At the risk of disappointing philosophers and mathematicians, we will not probe the depths of formal logic. Neither will we undertake to develop an abstract theory of legal thinking. This Article, rather, attempts something new: we endeavor to explain, in broad strokes, the core principles of logic and how they apply in the law school classroom. Our modest claim is that a person familiar with the basics of logical thinking is more likely to argue effectively than one who is not. We believe that students who master the logical tenets laid out in the following pages will be better lawyers and will feel more comfortable when they find themselves caught in the spotlight of a law professor on a Socratic binge.

Sifting through the dense jargon of logicians, we have identified a handful of ideas that are particularly relevant to the world of legal thinking. First, all prospective lawyers should make themselves intimately familiar with the fundamentals of deductive reasoning. Deductive reasoning, as Aristotle taught long ago, is based on the act of proving a conclusion by means of two other propositions. Perhaps 90 percent of legal issues can be resolved by deduction, so the importance of understanding this type of reasoning cannot be overstated. Second, students should acquaint themselves with the principles of inductive generalizations. Inductive generalizations, used correctly, can help students resuscitate causes that seem hopeless. Third, reasoning by analogy—another form of inductive reasoning—is a powerful tool in a lawyer's arsenal. Analogies help lawyers and judges solve legal problems not controlled by precedent and help law students deflect the nasty hypotheticals that are the darlings of professors. Finally, we comment briefly on the limitations of logic.

I. IT'S ELEMENTARY: DEDUCTIVE REASONING & THE LAW

A. The Syllogism

Logic anchors the law. The law's insistence on sound, explicit reasoning keeps lawyers and judges from making arguments based on untethered, unprincipled, and undisciplined hunches. Traditionally, logicians separate the wider universe of logical reasoning into two general categories: inductive and deductive. As we will see, both branches of logic play important roles in our legal system. We begin with deductive reasoning because it is the driving force behind most judicial opinions. Defined broadly, deduction is reasoning in which a conclusion is *compelled* by known facts. For example, if we know that Earth is bigger than Mars, and that Jupiter is bigger than Earth, then we also know that Jupiter *must* be bigger than Mars. Or, imagine that you know your dog becomes deathly ill every time he eats chocolate. Using deduction we know that if Spike wolfs down a Snickers bar, a trip to the vet will be necessary. From these examples, we can get an idea of the basic structure of deductive arguments: If A and B are true, then C must be true.

The specific form of deductive reasoning that you will find lurking below the surface of most judicial opinions and briefs is the "syllogism" — a label logicians attach to any argument in which a conclusion is inferred from two premises. For example:

> All men are mortal.
> Socrates is a man.
> Therefore, Socrates is mortal.

According to the traditional jargon, the syllogism's three parts are called the major premise, the minor premise, and the conclusion. The major premise states a broad and generally applicable truth: "All men are mortal." The minor premise states a specific and usually more narrowly applicable fact: "Socrates is a man." The conclusion then draws upon these premises and offers a new insight that is known to be true based on the premises: "Socrates is a mortal."

Gottfried Leibnitz expressed the significance of the syllogism three hundred years ago, calling its invention "one of the most beautiful, and also one of the most important, made by the human mind." For all its power, the basic principle of the syllogism is surprisingly straightforward: What is true of the universal is true of the particular. If we know that *all* cars have wheels, and that a Toyota is a car, then a Toyota must have wheels. The axiom may be stated this way: If we know that every member of a class has a certain characteristic, and that certain individuals are members of that class, then those individuals must have that characteristic.

It is no exaggeration to say that the syllogism lies at the heart of legal writing. Consider these examples taken from watershed Supreme Court opinions:

Marbury v. Madison
The Judicial Department's province and duty is to say what the law is.
The Supreme Court is the Judicial Department.
Therefore, the province and duty of the Supreme Court is to say what the law is.
. . . .

Brown v. Board of Education
Unequal educational facilities are not permitted under the Constitution.
A separate educational facility for black children is inherently unequal.
Therefore, a separate educational facility for black children is not permitted under the Constitution.
. . . .

We urge all law students to get in the habit of thinking in syllogisms. When briefing a case as you prepare a class assignment, the skeleton of the deductive syllogism should always poke through in your description of the case's rationale. Young attorneys should probably tattoo this on the back of their hands — or at least post it above their keyboards: Whenever possible, make the arguments in your briefs and memos in the form of syllogisms. A clear, well-constructed syllogism ensures each conclusion is well-supported with evidence and gives a judge recognizable guideposts to follow as he sherpas the law along his desired footpath.

But how, you might ask, does a new lawyer learn to construct valid syllogisms? Some people come to this ability instinctively. Just as some musicians naturally possess perfect pitch, some thinkers have logical instincts. Luckily for the rest of us, the skill can be learned through patience and practice. We start with the basics. To shape a legal issue in the form of a syllogism, begin by stating the general rule of law or widely-known legal rule that governs your case as your major premise. Then, in your next statement, the minor premise, describe the key facts of the legal problem at hand. Finally, draw your conclusion by examining how the major premise about the law applies to the minor premise about the facts. Like this:

> **Major Premise:** Cruel and unusual punishment by a state violates the Eighth Amendment.
> **Minor Premise:** Executing a minor is cruel and unusual punishment by a state.
> **Conclusion:** Executing a minor is forbidden by the Eighth Amendment.[22]

Although this might look simple, constructing logically-sound syllogisms requires a lot of grunt work. You must thoroughly research the law's nooks and crannies before you can confidently state the major premise. And you must become sufficiently knowledgeable about your case to reduce key facts to a brief yet accurate synopsis.

If you find yourself having trouble organizing a brief or memo, try shoehorning your argument into this generic model, which is based on the argument made by prosecutors in nearly every criminal case:

> Major premise: [**Doing something**] [violates the law.]
> Minor premise: *[The defendant]* [**did something.**]
> Conclusion: *[The defendant]* [violated the law.]

The prosecution's model can serve as a useful template for most legal problems. Using it will help you reduce your arguments to their most essential parts.

In addition to providing a useful template, the above example reflects the fact that the three parts of a syllogism — the two premises and the conclusion — are themselves built from three units. Logicians call these units "terms." Two terms appear in each statement: the "major term" in the major premise and conclusion, the "minor term" in the minor premise and conclusion, and the "middle term" in the major and minor premises but not in the conclusion. Notice that the middle term covers a broad range of facts, and that if the conclusion is to be valid, the minor term must be a fact that is included within the middle term. Although the

---

22. *See* Roper v. Simmons, 543 U.S. 551 (2003).

jargon can get confusing, the basic idea isn't hard to grasp: Each statement in a syllogism must relate to the other two.

B. Finding Syllogisms in Legal Writing

But wait! — you might be thinking — this syllogism business is too simple; opinions and memos are never so straightforward. Well, yes and no. The syllogism is simple, and indeed it does undergird most legal arguments, but sometimes you have to dig a bit below the surface to excavate syllogisms. The fact that syllogisms aren't immediately evident doesn't mean that the writing is sloppy, or that it doesn't use syllogisms. But it does mean that you'll have to work a bit harder as a reader. One logician notes that "an argument's basic structure may be obscured by an excess of verbiage, but an argument's structure may also be obscured for us because it is too sparse and has missing components. Such arguments may appear sounder than they are because we are unaware of important assumptions made by them."

Consider this one-sentence argument penned by Justice Blackmun in his *Roe v. Wade* opinion:

> This right of privacy, whether it be founded in the Fourteenth Amendment's concept of personal liberty and restrictions upon state action, as we feel it is, or, as the District Court determined, in the Ninth Amendment's reservation of rights to the people, is broad enough to encompass a woman's decision whether or not to terminate her pregnancy.[24]

Implicit within Justice Blackmun's statement is the following syllogism:

> **Major Premise:** The right of privacy is guaranteed by the Fourteenth or Ninth Amendment.
> **Minor Premise:** A woman's decision to terminate her pregnancy is protected by the right of privacy.
> **Conclusion:** Therefore, a woman's decision whether to terminate her pregnancy is protected by the Fourteenth or Ninth Amendment.

The ideas are floating around in Justice Blackmun's sentence, but it requires some work on the reader's part to parse them into two premises and a conclusion.

Sometimes it's more than a matter of rearranging sentences and rephrasing statements to match up with the syllogistic form. Sometimes a legal writer doesn't mention all parts of the syllogism, leaving you to read between the lines. Logicians are certainly aware that an argument can be founded on a syllogism although not all parts of the syllogism are expressed. They even have a name for such an argument: an enthymeme. Often, enthymemes are used for efficiency's sake. If a premise or conclusion is obvious, then the writer can save her precious words to make less obvious points. Even a kindergarten teacher might find the full expression of a syllogism to be unnecessary. The teacher could say, "Good girls get stars on their

---

24. 410 U.S. 113, 153 (1973).

foreheads; Lisa is a good girl; Lisa gets a star on her forehead." But she's more likely to say, "Lisa gets a star on her forehead because she is a good girl." In logic-speak, the teacher would be omitting the major premise because it is generally understood that good girls get stars on their foreheads.

. . . .

In addition to not handing the reader syllogisms on a platter, legal writers also have the tendency to pile one syllogism on top of another. Not surprisingly, logicians have a term for this, too, but for once it is a term that makes sense and is easy to remember. A series of syllogisms in which the conclusion of one syllogism supplies a premise of the next syllogism is known as a polysyllogism. Typically, polysyllogisms are used because more than one logical step is needed to reach the desired conclusion. Be on the lookout for something like this as you pick apart a complex legal opinion:

> All men are mortal.
> Socrates is a man.
> Therefore Socrates is mortal.

> All mortals can die.
> Socrates is mortal.
> Therefore Socrates can die.

> People who can die are not gods.
> Socrates can die.
> Therefore Socrates is not a god.

You have been warned. Watch for enthymemes and polysyllogisms in every opinion or legal memo or brief that you read, and be aware of them in your own writing. Your arguments will be improved.

C. Watch Out!: Flawed Syllogisms

A syllogism is a powerful tool because of its rigid inflexibility. If the premises of a syllogism are properly constructed, the conclusion *must* follow. But beware of bogus arguments masquerading as syllogisms. For example, consider the following:

> Some men are tall.
> Socrates is a man.
> Therefore Socrates is tall.

It looks something like a syllogism, but you have no doubt spotted the flaw: knowing that *some* men are tall isn't enough for you to conclude that a particular man is tall. He might fall into the group of other men about whom we know nothing, and who might be tall, but who also might be short. This type of non-syllogism got past the U.S. Supreme Court in the *Dred Scott* case, in which the Court held that people of African descent, whether or not they were slaves, could never be citizens of the United States. One dissenting opinion noted that the Court's ruling relied on a bad syllogism, simplified here:

> **Major Premise:** At the time of the adoption of the Constitution, *some* states considered members of the black race to be inferior and incapable of citizenship and of suing in federal court.
> **Minor Premise:** Dred Scott's ancestors at the time of the Constitution were members of the black race.
> **Conclusion:** Therefore, Dred Scott's ancestors were considered to be inferior and incapable of citizenship and of suing in federal court.

Mistakes of this sort remain extremely common in legal writing. Certain buzzwords, however, can help distinguish valid syllogisms from fallacious ones. Alarm bells should sound immediately if you spot terms in the major premise like "some," "certain," "a," "one," "this," "that," "sometimes," "many," "occasionally," "once," or "somewhere." Remember at all costs that the principle behind the syllogism is that what's true of the universal is true of the specific. In deductive reasoning, you reason from the general to the particular. Accordingly, if you're unsure about the nature of the general, you can't draw proper conclusions about the particular.

Logical errors, unfortunately, are often tough to catch. Here is a different one:

> **Major Premise:** All superheroes have special powers.
> **Minor Premise:** Superman has special powers.
> **Conclusion:** Superman is a superhero.

Unless you're an avid comic book reader, it might take a moment to spot the misstep. Knowing that every superhero has special powers doesn't allow you to conclude that everyone with special powers is a superhero. Recall again the golden rule of the syllogism: You can only draw a conclusion about the particular (Superman, in this case) after you demonstrate that it's part of the universal class. Thus, a correct syllogism would look like this:

> **Major Premise:** All superheroes have special powers. {General statement about a class}
> **Minor Premise:** Superman is a superhero. {Statement that an individual belongs to the class}
> **Conclusion:** Superman has special powers. {Conclusion that the individual has properties in common to other members of the class}

Remember this: Just because two things share a common property does not mean that they also share a second property....

. . . .

Certain logical errors crop up again and again, and so you should take particular care to avoid them. Don't cite inappropriate secondary authorities or cases from outside jurisdictions; logicians consider that an appeal to inappropriate authority. Don't rely on attacks on your opponent's character. Don't rely on appeals to emotion. Don't rely on fast talking or personal charm to carry the day. A cool head coupled with rigorous legal research, rather than rhetorical tricks, will turn a case in your favor.

It is critical to read every legal document you come across with care. Bad reasoning can seem persuasive at first glance. Logical fallacies are especially hard to spot in briefs, memos, and court opinions because of the dense writing and complex fact patterns. Yet the effort is worthwhile. The ability to detect and avoid logical missteps will improve your writing immensely and develop your ability to "think like a lawyer" — the skill that professors and partners so admire.

II. INDUCTIVE REASONING: GENERALIZATIONS

Deductive reasoning and its adherence to the "Socrates is Mortal" type of syllogism is the spine that holds our legal system together. Justice Cardozo estimated that at least nine-tenths of appellate cases "could not, with the semblance of reason, be decided in any way but one" because "the law and its applications alike are plain," or "the rule of law is certain, and the application alone is doubtful." . . . In the language of logic, this means that practicing lawyers spend most of their time worrying about the minor premises of syllogisms (i.e., can the facts of the case be fit into the territory governed by a particular rule?).

In law school, however, you will be asked to concentrate on the ten percent (or less) of cases that can't be resolved so easily. In the classroom, knotty and unsettled questions of law predominate. Where an issue of law is unsettled, and there is no binding precedent to supply a major premise for your syllogism, deductive logic is of no use to you. By focusing on such cases, your professors will drag you kicking and screaming into the land of induction, the second category of logic.

Inductive generalization is a form of logic in which big, general principles are divined from observing the outcomes of small events. In this form of inductive logic, you reason from multiple particulars to the general. To see how this works, suppose that you are asked to determine whether all men are mortal — the premise of the first syllogism we discussed. If nobody hands you the simple statement "All men are mortal," and you lack a way of deciding it, you have to turn to inductive reasoning. You might use what you know about particular men and their mortality as follows:

> Plato was a man, and Plato was mortal.
> Julius Caesar was a man, and Julius Caesar was mortal.
> George Washington was a man, and George Washington was mortal.
> John Marshall was a man, and John Marshall was mortal.
> Ronald Reagan was a man, and Ronald Reagan was mortal.
> Therefore, all men are mortal.

The principle underlying this way of thinking is that the world is sufficiently regular to permit the discovery of general rules. If what happened yesterday is likely to happen again today, we may use past experience to guide our future conduct. The contrast with deductive reasoning is stark. Whereas syllogisms are mechanical and exact — if the premises are true and properly assembled, the conclusion *must* be true — inductive logic is not so absolute. It does not produce conclusions *guaranteed* to be correct, no matter how many examples scholars assemble. Thousands of great men may live and die each year, but we will never know with absolute certainty whether every man is mortal. Thus, inductive reasoning is a logic of probabilities and generalities, not certainties. It yields workable rules, but not proven truths.

The absence of complete certainty, however, does not dilute the importance of induction in the law. As we stated at the outset, we look to inductive reasoning when our legal research fails to turn up a hefty, hearty precedent that controls the case. When there is no clear statute — no governing authority — to provide the major premise necessary for a syllogism, the law student must build the major premise himself. . . .

. . . .

[But in constructing inductive generalizations,] you must be careful to assemble a sufficient number of examples before shaping a far-reaching rule, or you will be guilty of the fallacy of "hasty generalization." In logic-speak, this fallacy occurs when you construct a general rule from an inadequate number of particulars. It is the bugaboo of inductive reasoning and often surfaces in casebooks and classroom discussions, as well as on TV talk-shows and newspaper editorials. Think about your overeager classmates who rely on nothing more than their personal life experiences to justify outlandish policy proposals. They're often guilty of creating bogus general rules from exceptional circumstances. Judges, lawyers, and law students all must be careful not to anoint isolated instances with the chrism of generality.

The difficulty comes in knowing how many instances are sufficient to make a generalization. Three? Ten? Forty thousand? This is where the art comes in. As a rule of thumb, the more examples you find, the stronger your argument becomes. . . .

. . . [Moreover,] the strength of an inductive argument rests not only on the number of examples you turn up to support your generalization, but also on the representativeness of the sample size. Keep this in mind when your opponent makes an argument based solely on the use of statistics, as is the case in many antitrust, securities, and discrimination claims.

. . . .

III. ANALOGY

Anyone who has struggled through a first-year torts course knows that hypothetical questions play a central role in the law school classroom. Professors invent elaborate factual scenarios and ask students to distill the correct result from a handful of cases read the night before. Then they change the situation slightly; does the answer change? Now alter a different parameter; same result, or a different one? The imaginative fact patterns do not end with law school; judges, too, rely on outlandish hypotheticals to test the validity of a lawyer's argument. Yet, notwithstanding the importance of hypothetical questions in legal thinking, the ability to manage them remains poorly taught and rarely practiced. We believe that the careful use of analogy — a form of inductive reasoning — can get you past a nasty hypothetical. Analogy can help a budding lawyer advance untested legal arguments in the classroom and the courtroom. We stress that mastering the principles of analogy is not just another garden-variety lawyer's skill. Rather, it is one of the most crucial aspects of the study and practice of law.

Unlike most concepts employed by logicians, the use of "analogy" is not confined to the realms of higher mathematics and philosophy. Most law students, and even most laypersons, are familiar with formal analogies of the "Sun is to Day and Moon is to ____?" variety. The use of informal, off-the-cuff analogies guides most of our own everyday decision-making. I own a Honda Civic that doesn't overheat, so I conclude that my friend's Honda Civic will never overheat. My eyes don't water when I cut an onion; I conclude that my brother's eyes won't water either. This type of reasoning has a simple structure: (1) *A* has characteristic *Y*; (2) *B* has characteristic *Y*; (3) *A* also has characteristic *Z*; (4) Because *A* and *B* both have *Y*, we conclude that *B* also shares characteristic *Z*. At base, analogy is a process of drawing similarities between things that appear different.

In the world of the law, analogies serve a very specific purpose. Attorneys use them to compare new legal issues to firmly established precedents. Typically, this means that a current case is compared to an older one, and the outcome of the new case is predicted on the basis of the other's outcome. Edward Levi, the foremost American authority on the role of analogy in the law, described analogical reasoning as a three step process: (1) establish similarities between two cases, (2) announce the rule of law embedded in the first case, and (3) apply the rule of law to the second case. This form of reasoning is different from deductive logic or inductive generalization. Recall that deduction requires us to reason from universal principles to smaller, specific truths. The process of generalization asks us to craft larger rules from a number of specific examples. Analogy, in contrast, makes one-to-one comparisons that require no generalizations or reliance on universal rules. In the language of logicians, analogy is a process of reasoning from the particular to the particular.

An example might help to clarify the distinction. Imagine you are asked to defend a client who received a citation for driving a scooter without a helmet. After scouring Westlaw, you find there's no controlling statute. There are, however, two precedents that could influence the result. One opinion holds that motorcyclists must wear helmets; the other case says that a helmet is not required to operate a bicycle. Does either control the issue in your case? Without a clear universal rule or past cases on point, deductive logic and inductive generalizations are of little help. Instead, you must rely on the power of analogy to convince a judge that helmet laws don't apply. To defend your client, you must suggest that driving a scooter is similar to riding a "fast bicycle." You might argue that small scooters can't go faster than well-oiled road bikes. Thus, a scooter presents no more danger to its operator or other drivers than a bicycle. You could also argue that scooters, like bikes, can't be driven on highways. The process of drawing these comparisons and explaining why they are important is the heart of reasoning by analogy. The idea is to find enough similarities between the new case and old precedent to convince a judge that the outcomes must be the same.

A proper analogy should identify the respects in which the compared cases, or fact scenarios, resemble one another and the respects in which they differ. What matters is *relevancy* — whether the compared traits resemble, or differ from, one another in relevant respects. A single apt comparison can be worth more than a host of not-quite-right comparisons. . . .

. . . .

IV. LOGICAL LIMITS: WHEN THERE IS MORE TO THE STORY

We hope we have convinced you that logic is the lifeblood of the law, and that understanding basic logical forms will assist you both in law school and in your practice as a lawyer. We would be remiss, however, if we were to send you out into the world without acknowledging that there is more to the law than assembling logical expressions.

Consider the following:

> All federal judges are body builders.
> Judge Aldisert is a federal judge.
> Therefore, Judge Aldisert is a body builder.

What's wrong with this statement? It's a rock-solid syllogism, adhering to the blueprint of logical validity expressed by the "Socrates" syllogism. Just the same, Judge Aldisert does not spend much time pumping iron. You see the problem, of course: the major premise is false. Not all federal judges are body builders. In fact, we doubt any of them are. The point is an obvious but important one: make sure your premises are true. If you use an untrue premise as a lawyer, it's an invitation to the other side to pillory you. If you do so as a judge, you may fashion a dangerous precedent. Consider the infamous *Dred Scott* case. The crucial syllogism used by the majority was as follows:

> **Major Premise:** At the time of the adoption of the Constitution, *all* states considered members of the black race to be inferior and incapable of citizenship and of suing in federal court.
> **Minor Premise:** Dred Scott's ancestors at the time of the Constitution were members of the black race.
> **Conclusion:** Therefore, Dred Scott's ancestors were considered to be inferior and incapable of citizenship and of suing in federal court.

As discussed in Part I, the dissenting opinion pointed out that only *some* state legislatures labeled blacks inferior at the time of the adoption of the Constitution. Other states — namely New Hampshire, Massachusetts, New York, New Jersey and North Carolina — maintained that all free-born inhabitants, even though descended from African slaves, possessed the right of franchise of electors on equal terms with other citizens. Once the "all" in the majority's major premise is replaced with "some," the syllogism fails to hold water.

Separately, logic is not the whole game. Even if your premises are true and your logical statements constructed properly, it is crucial to recognize that judges are motivated by more than the mandates of logic. As Judge Aldisert has said, "we judges come to our robes bearing the stigmata of our respective experiences." Judges have notions of how things should be — of what is wrong and what is right — and often strive to do justice as much as to fulfill the mandates of precedent. They have biases, too. In reading cases, writing briefs, and arguing before a court, you will be more effective if you flesh out the logical bones of your arguments and attempt to appeal to the judge in other ways as well.

But always bear in mind: *An argument that is correctly reasoned may be wrong, but an argument that is incorrectly reasoned can never be right.* You may find the discipline of parsing legalese into logical forms to be time-consuming and arduous at first, but as you become more comfortable with logic's framework, you will find that the exercise helps you more efficiently peel a case back to its essence. A solid footing in logic will help you feel more secure when you find yourself in a complex doctrinal thicket. And while the fundamentals of logic laid out in this article will not give you a magic carpet on which you can float above the legal briar patch, we believe they will give you a machete that will help you start hacking your way through the tangle.

Notes and Questions

1. Antonin Scalia & Bryan Garner, Making Your Case: The Art of Persuading Judges 41-43 (2008) ("Think Syllogistically")*:

> Leaving aside emotional appeal, persuasion is possible only because all human beings are born with a capacity for logical thought. It is something we all have in common. The most rigorous form of logic, and hence the most persuasive, is the syllogism. If you have never studied logic, you may be surprised to learn — like the man who was astounded to discover that he had been speaking prose all his life — that you have been using syllogistic reasoning all along. Argument naturally falls into this mode, whether or not you set out to make it do so. But the clearer the syllogistic progression, the better.
>
> Legal arguments can be expressed syllogistically in two ways. Some are positive syllogisms:

> | | |
> |---|---|
> | Major premise: | All S is P. |
> | Minor premise: | This case is S. |
> | Conclusion: | This case is P. |

> Others are negative:

> | | |
> |---|---|
> | Major premise: | Only S is P. |
> | Minor premise: | This case is not S. |
> | Conclusion: | This case is not P. |

> If the major premise (the controlling rule) and the minor premise (the facts invoking the rule) are true (you must establish that they're true), the conclusion follows inevitably.
>
> Legal argument generally has three sources of major premises: a text (constitution, statute, regulation, ordinance, or contract), precedent (caselaw, etc.), and policy (i.e., consequences of the decision). Often the major premise is self-evident and acknowledged by both sides.
>
> The minor premise, meanwhile, is derived from the facts of the case. There is much to be said for the proposition that "legal reasoning revolves mainly around the establishment of the minor premise."

So if you're arguing from precedent, your argument might go:

Major premise:	Our cases establish that a prisoner has a claim for harm caused by the state's deliberate indifference to serious medical needs.
Minor premise:	Guards at the Anderson Unit ignored the plaintiff's complaints of acute abdominal pain for 48 hours, whereupon his appendix burst.
Conclusion:	The plaintiff prisoner has a claim.

Or if you're arguing text:

Major premise:	Under the Indian Commerce Clause of the U.S. Constitution, states cannot tax Indian tribes for activities on reservations without the express authorization of Congress.
Minor premise:	Without congressional authorization, South Dakota has imposed its motor-fuel tax on tribes that sell fuel on reservations.
Conclusion:	South Dakota's tax is unconstitutional.

Or if you're arguing policy:

Major premise:	Only an interpretation that benefits the handicapped serves the policy objectives of the statute.
Minor premise:	The defendant's interpretation of the statute requires each wheelchair-bound employee to buy additional equipment at a cost of $1,800.
Conclusion:	The defendant's interpretation does not serve the policy objectives of the statute.

Figuring out the contents of a legal syllogism is a matter of finding a rule that works together with the facts of the case — really, a rule that is invoked by those facts. Typically, adversaries will be angling for different rules by emphasizing different facts. The victor will be the one who convinces decision-makers that his or her syllogism is closer to the case's center of gravity. What is this legal problem *mostly* about? Your task as an advocate is to answer that question convincingly.

2. A recent and explicit use of logic in a judicial decision occurred in *Henderson v. Shinseki*, 131 S. Ct. 1197 (2011), wherein the Court stated as follows:

> Contending that the 120-day filing deadline was meant to be jurisdictional, the Government maintains that *Bowles* is controlling. The Government reads *Bowles* to mean that all statutory deadlines for taking appeals in civil cases are jurisdictional. Since §7266(a) establishes a statutory deadline for taking an appeal in a civil case, the Government reasons, that deadline is jurisdictional.
>
> We reject the major premise of this syllogism. *Bowles* did not hold categorically that every deadline for seeking judicial review in civil litigation is jurisdictional.

Henderson, 131 S. Ct. at 1203.

Another example can be found in the opening paragraph of Justice Scalia's dissent in *United States v. Resendiz-Ponce*, 549 U.S. 102 (2007):

It is well established that an indictment must allege all the elements of the charged crime. As the Court acknowledges, it is likewise well established that "attempt" contains two substantive elements: the *intent* to commit the underlying crime, and the undertaking of *some action* toward the commission of that crime. It should follow, then, that when the Government indicts for attempt to commit a crime, it must allege both that the defendant had the intent to commit the crime, *and* that he took some action toward its commission. Any rule to the contrary would be an exception to the standard practice.

Id. at 11 (Scalia, J., dissenting) (citations omitted).

From these excerpts, can you reconstruct the "argument" in question in the form of a syllogism?

3. "There is, however, a more fundamental flaw in respondent's syllogism: the incorrect assumption that the rule of *Erie R. Co.* v. *Tompkins* constitutes the appropriate test of the validity and therefore the applicability of a Federal Rule of Civil Procedure." *Hanna v. Plumer*, 380 U.S. 460, 470 (1965).

4. For more on the use of logic in legal argument, see James A. Gardner, Legal Argument: The Structure and Language of Effective Advocacy (2d ed. 2007); Douglas Lind, Logic and Legal Reasoning (2001); and Anthony Weston, A Rulebook for Arguments (4th ed. 2009). For a recent article on this topic, see Cory S. Clements, Comment, *Perception and Persuasion in Legal Argumentation: Using Informal Fallacies and Cognitive Biases to Win the War of Words*, 2013 B.Y.U. L. Rev. 319.

D. THE PARTS OF A JUDICIAL DECISION

Though the various parts of a typical judicial decision are fairly well-known by most lawyers and law students, a brief summary is helpful if for no other reason than to ensure a consistency of terminology.

The typical judicial decision begins with the title or name of the case, which usually (though not always) consists of the names of at least one plaintiff and one defendant. After the name, there is often some sort of citation, typically to the court's own internal case number and the date of decision. If the decision is formally published, the citation will include a reference to the volume and page of the reporter in which the decision appears. If not obvious from the nature of the reporter, some indication will also be given of the issuing court. (Of course, in its original form as issued by the deciding court, the decision generally will begin with a caption, which includes the name of the court; the names of the parties (or other title for the case); the court's own internal case number; and a name for the decision issued, such as "Opinion.")

Following the name and citation of the case, there is often some introductory information that is inserted either by the court itself or by the publisher of the case. This introductory information might consist of a very brief summary of the case and its disposition (often called a syllabus), and/or headnotes describing certain key points of law discussed therein. The names of the attorneys of record and of the judges (or Justices) who decided the case are often included as well. The key thing to note about all of this introductory information is that it generally does not provide any *authoritative* guidance as to the decision actually reached by the court — i.e., in most jurisdictions it is not considered binding law. This is true even of that material prepared by the court itself. Thus, the syllabus typically should be regarded as no more than a non-binding synopsis, and the headnotes as research aids.

Next comes the body of the decision itself, usually (at least if lengthy and explanatory) called the court's *opinion*. The opinion typically consists of several components. Aside from the possibility of some form of brief introduction, judicial opinions usually consist of 1) a statement of the relevant *facts* and *procedural history* of the case, 2) a statement or discussion of the *relevant law*, and 3) the court's analysis, or the *application* of that law to those facts with respect to each issue. *See* BLACK'S LAW DICTIONARY 1125 (8th ed. 2004) (defining an "opinion" as a "court's written statement explaining its decision in a given case, usu. including the statement of facts, points of law, rationale, and dicta"). In a very general sense, that portion of the opinion in which the court applies relevant law to the facts and explains its rationale may be considered to be the court's *holding* in the case. (A more detailed description of the meaning of the term "holding," particularly in contrast to "dicta," can be found in part F *infra*.)

Finally, the court typically concludes with a recitation of its *judgment*. At the trial court level, the judgment may be thought of simply in terms of who won and what they got. Thus, a judgment in favor of a plaintiff might consist of an award of monetary damages or some form of equitable relief, like an injunction prohibiting the defendant from doing something. In the criminal context, a judgment in favor of the government typically consists of some adjudication or plea of guilt and the sentence thereafter imposed. If the defense prevails, the judgment might consist of a dismissal or an adjudication in favor of the defendant (in which situation the plaintiff would take nothing), or in the criminal context, an acquittal. At the appellate level, by contrast, the court's judgment typically consists only of an *affirmance* or a *reversal* of the judgment of the court below. Notice that this means that it is the lower court's *judgment* (not its holding or anything else) that is appealed. Notice also that a judgment may be affirmed for reasons independent of those that led to the lower court's judgment. *See, e.g., Chevron U.S.A. Inc. v. Natural Resources Defense Council, Inc.*, 467 U.S. 837, 842 (1984) ("Respondents do not defend the legal reasoning of the Court of Appeals. Nevertheless, since this Court reviews judgments, not opinions, we must determine whether the Court of Appeals' legal error resulted in an erroneous judgment on the validity of the regulations."). For these reasons, it is important to maintain a distinction between judgments and other, related concepts (such as holdings).

Notes and Questions

1. Again, most published judicial decisions consist of the following parts:
   a) the title of the case;
   b) the citation of the case;
   c) a syllabus and/or headnotes;
   d) the opinion of the court, which includes
      i) a statement of relevant facts and procedural history,
      ii) a statement of the applicable law, and
      iii) the court's analysis (i.e., the application of the law to the facts); and
   e) the judgment.

   As you read cases in this (or any) course or in practice, identifying these different parts will help you better understand those cases.

2. For a longer version of the foregoing that many have found helpful, see Orin S. Kerr, *How to Read a Legal Opinion: A Guide for New Law Students*, 11 GREEN BAG 2D 51 (2007).

3. Opinion writing is itself an art. For more on this topic, see RUGGERO J. ALDISERT, OPINION WRITING (2d ed. 2009).

1. Syllabus and Headnotes

Some might wonder why the syllabus and headnotes, even when prepared by the court itself, generally are not considered authoritative. Consider this question in light of the following article.

Gil Grantmore

THE HEADNOTE

5 Greenbag 2d 157 (2002)

Which Supreme Court opinion does the Court itself cite most often? *Marbury v. Madison,* you might suspect. But no; since 1945, the Court has cited *Marbury v. Madison* only 172 times. Another case has been cited more than twenty times as often. But it is a case that appears in no casebook, and that probably no living lawyer has ever read. Although the citation escapes notice — it truly comes in under the proverbial radar screen — it accompanies the release of every Supreme Court opinion, like a ritualistic incantation.

If I have sufficiently raised your curiosity, I will take the liberty of presenting a specimen of this citation in the only habitat in which it is ever found. As the reader may easily confirm, the first footnote in every Supreme Court case reads as follows:

> The syllabus constitutes no part of the opinion of the Court but has been prepared by the Reporter of Decisions for the convenience of the reader. See *United States* v. *Detroit Timber & Lumber Co.*, 200 U.S. 321, 337.

The effect, no doubt, is to signal to lawyers and judges that they should not cite or rely on the syllabus. Every experienced lawyer or judge with whom I have spoken has confirmed this understanding.

But in fact, *Detroit Timber* did not say the syllabus was irrelevant; instead, the Court paid careful attention to the headnote it was discussing. If the Court is meaning to advise that we ignore the syllabus, that advice is not grounded in the precedent that is cited. Moreover, we must recall, if this is the Court's advice, it is only unofficial advice: the footnote appears in every slip opinion (and correspondingly in the Supreme Court Reporter), but it does not appear in the official United States Reports. Thus, the final official version of the syllabus does not carry this caveat. Surely, there is a negative implication that can be drawn from this conscious omission.

I will argue that we should seize upon this negative implication and encourage reliance upon the syllabus, rather than on the Court's increasingly long-winded, turgid opinions. Ideally, anything not found in the syllabus should be presumptively classified as dictum. Lest this be thought an impossibly radical proposal, let me point out that it has long been the law in Ohio.

. . . .

I begin with a short discussion of *Detroit Timber* — which for all of its many years of service on behalf of the Court, deserves at least the dignity of a careful reading. It seems clear that *Detroit Timber* at least allowed the syllabus to have persuasive authority. I will then turn to the argument in favor of reversing the current priority between syllabus and opinion.

First, the *Detroit Timber* decision. The case arose in an earlier era, when the federal government was anxious to encourage development of the public domain. In 1878, Congress passed a statute allowing the equivalent of homesteading on land that was not suitable for farming or ranching, but only for logging or stone quarrying. The statute allowed individuals to file claims for up to 160 acres of land, provided that they intended to use the land themselves rather than buying on speculation or under contract for sale to a third-party. (The statute provided an automatic penalty if the claimant misrepresented his intentions: "he shall forfeit the money which he may have paid for said lands and all right and title to the same; and any grant or conveyance which he may have made, except in the hands of bona fide purchasers, shall be null and void.") The next step in the procedure was for the claimant to advertise his filing. If no adverse claim was filed within sixty days and the individual paid the statutory price for the land, then upon his transmitting the papers to the General Land Office "a patent shall issue thereon."

In *Detroit Timber*, a lumber mill had loaned money to a number of individuals (mostly employees) to pay the purchase fee and had helped them file the papers. It promptly entered into logging contracts with them. The company was then sold. The purchaser, Detroit Timber, had no actual knowledge of the fraudulent scheme. Although it would have found warning signs if it had carefully inspected the other company's records, the Supreme Court concluded that it was nevertheless a bona fide purchaser. To say that the buyer should have made "a searching inquiry" into the validity of the claim, the Court opined, "would shake the foundations of commercial business." For "no one is bound to assume that the party with whom he deals is a wrong doer."

After the purchase of the other company, Detroit Timber obtained deeds to twenty-seven tracts "in order to be relieved from the necessity of keeping accounts with respect to the different tracts." Since it already owned the logging rights, which were the only value of the land, the deeds from the patentees had only a nominal cost. The government's argument was that Detroit Timber's interest stemmed from the logging leases, not the later formal purchase of the land. It invoked the rule that a company acquiring an interest in the land before the patent was issued could not qualify as a b.f.p. The Court held, however, that once the patent was issued, it "related back" to the original filing of the claim, retroactively providing b.f.p. status to the timber lessee.

And now, finally, we come around to the famous, not-to-be-relied-upon syllabus. In an effort to fend off this "related back" argument, the government relied on *Hawley v. Diller*, or more specifically, on the syllabus in that case. The Court's brief discussion of this issue — the discussion that truly launched a thousand footnotes — is brief enough to quote in full:

> Counsel also say that the question is settled by the decision in *Hawley v. Diller*, *supra*, relying upon the second paragraph in the headnotes:
> "An entryman under this act acquires only an equity, and a purchaser from him cannot be regarded as a bona fide purchaser within the meaning of the act of Congress unless he become such after the government, by issuing a patent, has parted with the legal title."
> There are two or three answers to this contention. In the first place, the headnote is not the work of the court, nor does it state its decision — though a different rule, it is true, is prescribed in some states. It is simply the work of the reporter, [who] gives his understanding of the decision, and is prepared for the convenience of the profession in the examination of the records. In the second place, if the patent referred to in that headnote is a patent issued upon a wrongful entry, no such fact appeared in the case, because no patent was issued upon the entry charged to have been wrongful, but after that entry had been cancelled, a patent was issued to Diller on a new entry. If it refers to some other patent than one issued upon wrongful entry, it has no pertinency, for the doctrine of relation never carries a patent back to the date of any other entry other than that upon which it is issued. And finally, the headnote is a misinterpretation of the scope of the decision.
> That concludes the Court's discussion of the issue.

Detroit Timber clearly does not stand for the proposition that the headnote is irrelevant or inappropriate for citation. On the contrary, after explaining the genesis of the headnote, the Court goes on very carefully to consider its substance. True, the headnote did not carry the imprimatur of the Court. But it nevertheless seems to have been considered at least respectable persuasive authority. The common view today that the syllabus is valueless cannot be supported by *Detroit Timber*.

Interestingly, the syllabus seems to have had less standing at the time of *Detroit Timber* than it does today. Various versions of *Hawley* have different headnotes. In the U.S. Reports, the second headnote is as quoted by the Court. The headnote in the Lawyer's Edition begins with a list of issues in the case, and then, as the first numbered headnote, provides a differently phrased statement of the rule, but to the same effect. The same variant language appears in the Supreme Court Reporter. The unofficial reports do not reproduce the Reporter's syllabus; perhaps it was not available until after they themselves were published, given the usual efficiency of government printing offices. Thus, in contrast to the present, the Reporter's syllabus does not seem to have been considered official enough to warrant reproduction; it was merely a summary by one of several reporting services and was probably not available to many lawyers.

Today, the syllabus is issued as part of the slip opinion. Moreover, it is not purely a product of the Reporter's office. As Justice Ginsburg explains, "the justice who wrote the opinion may edit the syllabus and sometimes rewrite passages, as I more than occasionally do, mindful that busy lawyers and judges may not read more." Thus, the syllabus of *Detroit Timber* days is not the syllabus of today — today's is more widely available and more reliable. The argument for giving the syllabus at least persuasive effect — which is not foreclosed by *Detroit Timber* anyway — is even stronger today.

At the very least, then, it should be appropriate to cite the syllabus in briefs and opinions. After all, the Court cites the views of professors about its work product — surely, academics are no more reliable a source of interpretation than the person the Justices themselves have assigned the task of writing the syllabus. But a legitimate, if admittedly adventuresome, argument can be made for the Ohio rule, under which it is the syllabus rather than the opinion that has full precedential force.

First, it is an increasingly onerous burden to decode the Court's opinions. Their length appears to increase exponentially, as does the number of footnotes. It is no secret among lawyers, judges, and professors, however, that intellectual substance has failed to keep pace with the verbiage. What Holmes could say in a paragraph, today's judicial midgets — by which I mean to refer to the mini-judicial law clerks who do so much of the drafting rather than to disparage the intellectual stature of their employers — can only accomplish in eleven pages and a hundred footnotes. Enough is enough. Everything that really needs to be said can be said in a page or so, as Holmes would have done. We do not have Holmes with us today, but we do have the syllabus, and in our more bureaucratic days, the syllabus will have to do.

Second — the end all and be all of so many of today's scholars — there is the matter of original intent. When the Constitution was written, the judicial power was meant to embody the concept of precedent. But the Framers did not expect to see official publications of all rulings. It was the "entry on the official court record" which gave the decision precedential authority, and the decision retained its authority even when established "only by memory or by a lawyer's unpublished memorandum." The larger principle is that it is the court's judgment, not its opinion, which constitutes the true precedent — explanations from the bench (common in English practice), written opinions, lawyer's memoranda, or whatever, have value only as evidence of the Court's reasoning. In other words, the opinions are more like legislative history than statutes — the official constitutionally sanctioned action is the judgment, the opinion is merely explanatory of the reasons for the official act.

As evidence goes, one might think the formal opinions are reliable evidence of why the Justices voted to affirm or reverse. But this is surely a fiction. We have all heard that law clerks play a major role in drafting opinions, and whether or not this is true in general or in any given cases, the other Justices must sometimes find the nuances of the opinions as opaque as do the rest of us — possibly more opaque, since many important opinions come down only at the end of the Term, and the Justices have little time to review them carefully. The crux of the reasoning is displayed in the syllabus. We can safely assume that the other Justices agreed to at least that much; to think that they also agreed to the minutiae of these gargantuan opinions is absurd. Thus, the syllabus is really better evidence of the Justices' collective reasoning than the so-called "opinion of the Court." Since, as a matter of original intent, what has precedential value is the judgment, we should place the heaviest weight on the most reliable explanation of why the judgment was entered.

If the Ohio rule, in which the syllabus is truly "the law," seems to be too radical, we might consider the West Virginia approach as a compromise. The syllabus is a constitutional obligation of West Virginia courts. Normally, the West Virginia syllabus sets down the important points of law, leaving the factual issues to the body of the opinion. But opinions can also serve as sources of law in West Virginia. Thus, we could establish rough parity between opinion and syllabus, as an alternative to either the *Detroit Timber* or the Ohio regimes.

The syllabus itself, of course, is not always easy to understand. But it is short and accessible. The media rely on the syllabus when explaining the Court's decision. Making the syllabus a binding source of precedent would help narrow the gap between constitutional law as it is understood by citizens and as it is known by lawyers. This would seem to be a good idea. It is, after all, the People's Constitution. Or so the Constitution's own headnote — the Preamble — tells us.

Notes and Questions

1. The purported author of the above article, "Gil Grantmore," is fictional. The article was actually written by Professor Daniel A. Farber. "Gil Grantmore" appears to have been derived from Grant Gilmore, a former professor at Yale Law School (among others).

2. *Burbank v. Ernst*, 232 U.S. 162, 165 (1914) (Holmes, J.):

> Reliance . . . is placed upon the headnote of the decision . . . But the headnote is given no special force by statute or rule of court, as in some states. It inaccurately represents the reasoning of the judgment. In [a state court reporter] it is said to have been made by the court. However that may be, we look to the opinion for the original and authentic statement of the grounds of decision.

3. Syllabi, though intended to be sort of a summary of the court's opinion, are not necessarily short. For example, in recent years, Supreme Court syllabi frequently have been pages in length. Why is that?

4. As stated in the above article, the syllabi in a few states are authoritative — i.e., they are considered as having some binding precedential force.

E. THE VARIOUS TYPES OF OPINIONS

The previous discussion of judicial decisions presumed that all members of the court in question agreed with essentially every aspect of the opinion (or at least did not disagree to an extent warranting action). This of course will always be true with respect to a single-judge court. But when such agreement occurs on a multi-judge court, we refer to the decision as a *unanimous* decision.

Regrettably, unanimity is not always possible in judicial decision-making (at least not in the United States). This leads to a variety of different opinions, some of which constitute binding precedent and some not.

In order to create binding precedent, it is now accepted that a majority of the members of the court deciding the case must agree both as to the outcome (or judgment) and as to the reasoning behind the judgment (or holding). Thus, for example, on a three-judge panel (such as is typically used in the United States Court of Appeals), if two of the three judges can agree as to the judgment and the holding, the opinion thereby produced will be known as a *majority* opinion, and constitute binding precedent. *See* Black's Law Dictionary 1266 (10th ed. 2014) (defining a "majority opinion" as an "opinion joined in or by more than half the judges considering a given case"). In fact, a majority opinion is the *only* type of opinion that *is* binding precedent. Regardless of who wrote or delivered the majority opinion, that opinion generally is referred to as the opinion of the court, because it *is* the opinion of the court, or at least a majority of the members thereof. The same rule applies with respect to larger courts, such as the Supreme Court of the United States, currently a nine-judge court. So long as at least five of the nine Justices agree as to both the judgment and the holding, that opinion becomes the opinion of the Court. Of course, this includes unanimous decisions, but it also includes decisions in which only eight agree, or even five — so long as there is at least a majority.

All other types of opinions do not constitute binding precedent, and thus are not "law" in a strict sense. Nonetheless, many of these opinions have *persuasive* force, and sometimes carry the day in some future case. Accordingly, it is important to understand the names and nature of these other types of opinions.

American multi-judge courts typically consist of an odd number of members. This is quite intentional, as an odd number of judges is more likely to produce a majority decision. But what happens if, say, seven Justices on the Supreme Court deciding a particular case vote to affirm the judgment of the court of appeals, but only four can agree on the reasoning behind the affirmance (with the other three voting to affirm on some other basis). In that situation, one might say that the Court is split 4-3-2, with four voting to affirm for reason X, 3 voting to affirm for reason Y, and two voting to reverse the judgment of the court below. Notice that in this situation, there is a majority as to the judgment (affirm), but no majority opinion. So what do we call the opinion that received four votes? Such an opinion is referred to as a *plurality* opinion, as it lies in the majority as to the judgment, and it received more votes than any other opinion on that side of the ledger, yet it failed to capture at least five votes. *See* BLACK'S LAW DICTIONARY 1266 (defining a "plurality opinion" as an "opinion lacking enough judges' votes to constitute a majority, but receiving more votes than any other opinion"). Of course, other combinations are possible. For example, sometimes the Court is split 3-2-4; in that situation also, the opinion that received three votes would be the plurality opinion (assuming the three agree as to the same judgment as the two), despite the fact that it failed to receive more votes than the opinion that disagreed as to the judgment. So long as an opinion receives more votes than any other in the majority as to the judgment, that opinion will be the plurality opinion.

But what happens if a court is even more fractured? For example, what if the court of appeals is split 1-1-1, with two judges voting to affirm, but on different bases? Or what if the Supreme Court were to be split 4-4-1, or 3-3-3? In those situations, there is no majority opinion, nor is there even a plurality opinion. So how does a court decide which opinion is delivered first, and what do we call such an opinion? It appears that the answer to the first question is seniority — i.e., among the opinions in the majority as to the judgment, the opinion of the chief judge or Justice (or, lacking that, of the most senior member of that court) will be delivered first. That opinion will then become known as the lead opinion, though nothing more can really be said about it. Because it received no more votes than any other opinion, it is, in a sense, no more "important" than any other opinion.

This still leaves at least two other types of opinions: the concurrence, and the dissent. A *concurring* opinion is an opinion that is in the majority as to the judgment, but does not receive enough votes as to its reasoning to become a majority or plurality opinion and is not selected to be the lead opinion. *See* BLACK'S LAW DICTIONARY 352 (defining a "concurrence" as a "vote cast by a judge in favor of the judgment reached, often on grounds differing from those expressed in the opinion or opinions explaining the judgment," and a "concurring opinion" is a "separate written opinion explaining such a vote"). Often, the author of the concurring opinion will agree in whole or in part with the primary opinion, and issue the concurrence simply to add an additional line of reasoning or to offer another perspective on the views expressed in some other opinion. This might be described as a "regular" (or general) concurrence. But occasionally, the concurring judge will agree only with judgment reached by the majority of the court, and disagree completely with the reasoning of the others. In this situation, the concurrence is a concurrence in the judgment only. Sometimes (though less frequently today), a concurrence in the judgment is called a *special concurrence. See, e.g., Hopwood v. Texas,* 78 F.3d 932, 968 (5th Cir. 1996) (Wiener, J., specially concurring) ("I concur in the judgment of the panel opinion but, as to its conclusion on the issue of strict scrutiny and its gloss on the order of remand, I disagree for the reasons I have stated and therefore concur specially."). Of course, combinations of the two are also possible — i.e., a judge might concur in part (as to some issue or issues) but concur only in the judgment as to one or more others.

Finally, a *dissenting* opinion is an opinion issued by one or more judges who disagree with the judgment of the majority. *See* BLACK'S LAW DICTIONARY 1265 (defining a "dissenting opinion" as an "opinion by one or more judges who disagree with the decision reached by the majority"). Frequently, the dissenting judge or judges will disagree with the majority's view as to the relevant law and/or facts, though occasionally the dissent will agree as to the relevant law and facts, but simply disagree with the majority's analysis. Notice that the dissent becomes the dissent simply by virtue of being in the minority as to the judgment reached by the court, and not because of the number of votes such an opinion might receive. Thus (for example), if the Supreme Court were to be split 3-2-4, with five Justices voting to reverse (and four voting to affirm), despite the fact that the majority could not agree as to their reasoning (thus resulting in a three-vote plurality opinion and a two-vote concurrence), the four Justices voting to affirm would still find themselves in dissent, despite the fact that their opinion received more votes than any other. Moreover, keep in mind that here also, other combinations are possible. Indeed, depending upon the number and nature of the issues before the court, it has become fairly common for judges or Justices to concur in part and dissent in part.

Notes and Questions

1. *What happens when a court is equally divided?* The number of Justices currently on the Supreme Court is fixed by statute. *See* 28 U.S.C. § 1 (2012) ("The Supreme Court of the United States shall consist of a Chief Justice of the United States and eight associate justices, any six of whom shall constitute a quorum."). The same is true of the number of judges (three) that comprise a panel on the court of appeals. *See* 28 U.S.C. § 46 (2012). As stated above, American courts tend to have an odd number of judges (or Justices) for a reason, as an odd number will produce a majority decision at least as to the judgment of the court.

   But what happens if (say) one member of the Supreme Court becomes unavailable, for whatever reason, and the Court splits 4-4? According to the Court in *Neil v. Biggers,* 409 U.S. 188, 191-92 (1972), a judgment entered by an equally divided court results in the affirmation of the judgment below, and is not entitled to any binding precedential weight. As the Court explained in *Hertz v. Woodman*, 218 U.S. 205, 212-13 (1910):

> When this court in the exercise of its appellate powers is called upon to decide whether that which has been done in the lower court shall be reversed or affirmed, it is obvious that that which has been done must stand unless reversed by the affirmative action of a majority. It has therefore been the invariable practice to affirm, without opinion, any judgment or decree which is not decided to be erroneous by a majority of the court sitting in the cause.

For a more recent example of such a case, see *Costco Wholesale Corp. v. Omega, S.A.*, 131 S. Ct. 565 (2010).

There have been calls recently for temporarily adding judges or Justices to courts to avoid even-number splits. Assuming such a practice would be constitutionally (and perhaps even statutorily) permissible, would it be desirable? Why or why not?

2. *Opinion authorship and delivery.* The common practice today is for courts to name the particular judge or Justice who "delivered" the opinion of the court. Many lawyers presume that the jurist who delivered the opinion also was the author of that opinion, and that presumption probably holds true in most instances, though undoubtedly that jurist received considerable input from those other members of the court who joined in that opinion. It can get complicated, though, when more than one Justice delivers the opinion for the Court. *See, e.g., Planned Parenthood of Southeastern Pa. v. Casey*, 505 U.S. 833, 843 (opinion of the Court delivered jointly by Justices O'Connor, Kennedy, and Souter).

3. *Per curiam opinions.* Occasionally a court, for one reason or another, will decide that it would rather not identify the particular judge or Justice who delivered the opinion of the court, and instead will choose to take on something of a "united front." Such an opinion is typically identified as a *per curiam* opinion, "per curiam" literally meaning "by the court." *See* Black's Law Dictionary 1266 (10th ed. 2014) (defining a "per curiam opinion" as an "opinion handed down by an appellate court without identifying the individual judge who wrote the opinion"). A prominent, recent example of a per curiam opinion was the opinion issued by the Supreme Court in *Bush v. Gore*, 531 U.S. 98 (2000).

Per curiam opinions are more common than many realize. For example, according to the Supreme Court's website, of the 92 opinions issued during the October 2009 Term, 19 — more than 20% — were per curiam opinions. *See* http://www.supremecourt.gov/opinions/slipopinions/aspx.

Some lawyers believe that per curiam opinions are necessarily unanimous opinions, but that is not always true. For example, the last case decided during the October 2009 Term, *Sears v. Upton*, 130 S. Ct. 3259 (2010), though per curiam, did not involve the participation of Chief Justice Roberts and Justice Alito (*see id.* at 3267), and included a dissenting opinion by Justice Scalia, who was joined by Justice Thomas (*see id.* at 3267). And in *New York Times Co.*

v. United States, 403 U.S. 713 (1971), the Court's three-paragraph per curiam opinion was followed by six concurrences and three dissents.

Why do you think that courts issue per curiam opinions? What are the circumstances that might prompt a court to consider this option? Or should courts never issue per curiam opinions, on the ground that they are per se inappropriate? According to James Markham, Note, *Against Individually Signed Judicial Opinions,* 56 DUKE L.J. 923 (2006):

> Nothing in the Constitution or any other source of American law mandates the current practice of identifying the author of each opinion published in a given case, including majority opinions, concurrences, and dissents. The system could have evolved in other ways, and even today the [Supreme] Court occasionally departs from its standard operating procedure in somewhat haphazard fashion. Having a Justice's name attached to an opinion brings a measure of accountability and control to an otherwise secretive institution, but this accountability carries with it a cost in the Court's ability to appear independent and above the political fray, and detracts from the notion of the Court as something greater than the nine individuals who comprise it.

Id. at 926.

For more on per curiam opinions, see Laura Krugman Ray, *The Road to* Bush v. Gore: *The History of the Supreme Court's Use of the Per Curiam Opinion,* 79 NEBR. L. REV. 517 (2000); Ira P. Robbins, *Hiding Behind the Cloak of Invisibility: The Supreme Court and Per Curiam Opinions,* 86 TULANE L. REV. 1197 (2012); and Stephen L. Wasby, *The Per Curiam Opinion: Its Nature and Functions,* 76 JUDICATURE 29 (1992).

4. Sometimes the proliferation of opinions can get a little out of hand. For example, in *Bush v. Vera,* 517 U.S. 952, 990 (1996), Justice O'Connor filed an opinion concurring in the opinion she delivered on behalf of the Court. And in *Bazemore v. Friday,* 478 U.S. 385 (1986), the Court's brief per curiam opinion was followed by an opinion by Justice Brennan, concurring in part, that was "joined by all other Members of the Court" (*id.* at 388); a concurring opinion by Justice White that was joined by four other Justices (*id.* at 407); and an opinion dissenting in part, also delivered by Justice Brennan (*id.* at 409).

5. *Patching together different parts of a decision.* Most of the time, the different types of opinions described above will arrive neatly packaged and clearly identified; the opinion of the court will come first, followed by one or more wholly separable concurrences or dissents. Regrettably, it is becoming increasingly popular (at least on the Supreme Court) for the various Justices to join in only parts or subparts of various opinions, resulting in a hodgepodge of alliances and a patchwork-style opinion of the Court. (Several examples of such opinions can be found in this book.) In such situations, one must be careful to determine whether the relevant portion of any opinion represents the opinion of the Court or simply the opinion of some lesser number of Justices. The

headings currently provided in the United States Reporter help to some extent, though the prudent lawyer will "do the math" for herself.

6. *The* Marks *rule.* In *Marks v. United States,* 430 U.S. 188 (1977), the Court stated: "When a fragmented Court decides a case and no single rationale explaining the result enjoys the assent of five Justices, the holding of the Court may be viewed as that position taken by those Members who concurred in the judgments on the narrowest grounds." *Id.* at 193 (internal quotation marks omitted). This means that it might be possible to have a majority *holding* despite the lack of a majority *opinion.*

   For a more recent application and discussion of the *Marks* rule, see the various opinions in *United States v. Santos,* 553 U.S. 507 (2008).

   For more on the *Marks* rule, see Justin Marceau, *Plurality Decisions: Upward-Flowing Precedent and Acoustic Separation,* 45 CONN. L. REV. 933 (2013), and Mark Alan Thurmon, Note, *When the Court Divides: Reconsidering the Precedential Value of Supreme Court Plurality Decisions,* 42 DUKE L.J. 419 (1992).

7. *The different forms of appellate judgments.* Though appellate courts frequently use a variety of terms to describe their judgments, in the vast majority of cases, there are really only two options: affirm, or reverse. Of course, when there are multiple claims or issues, it might well be possible to affirm the lower court's judgment in part and reverse it in part, but this does not detract from the general principle that there are, in the main, only two options. The reason this is true goes back to the distinction between a holding and a judgment. If an appellate court agrees with the result reached by the lower court, it will affirm, regardless of whether it agrees with the reasoning of the lower court.

   The only other option relates to the concept of *vacatur.* In some situations, and usually for reasons unrelated to substantive correctness, an appellate court will vacate a lower court decision (i.e., erase it as a matter of precedent) without formally reversing it. (Vacatur is discussed in more detail in part I.2.)

   Unless the case originates in the court at issue, the appellate court will virtually always *remand* the case to the court below. This is true regardless of whether it affirms or reverses the lower court's judgment. The reason is that remand is typically (though not always) a housekeeping matter, for it is the trial court that ultimately will have to carry out the appellate court's judgment and (if reversed) conduct further proceedings consistent with its mandate. For symposia on the topic of remands, see 44 ARIZ. ST. L.J. 1017-1108 (2012), and 36 ARIZ. ST. L.J. 493-660 (2004).

8. Is our practice of opinion delivery inevitable? Probably not. According to Arthur J. Jacobson:

   > We can date the origins of the Supreme Court's opinion-delivery practices to the accession of John Marshall as Chief Justice in 1801. Before Marshall, a majority of decisions (71%) were announced in a single, short opinion issued in civilian

style, unsigned and unaccompanied by separate opinions. Alexander Dallas does report, however, that the opinion was "By the Court" (per curiam), in contrast with civilian reports, which need not make that announcement. Most of the rest (24%) were announced English-style, in seriatim opinions prepared by each Justice and read from the bench. . . . [There were] at least three occasions on which Dallas identified the opinion not as being given by the Court itself, but rather as having been delivered by the Chief Justice. It is this last method that Marshall pursued with crusading vigor.

For Marshall believed that it was only by presenting a united front that the Court could enhance its power vis-à-vis the legislature and the executive, as well as its prestige in the eyes of the public. . . . Marshall thus persuaded his colleagues not to write separately.

. . . .

Marshall's associates could not wholly be weaned from the practice of delivering opinions seriatim — they continued occasionally into the Taney era. But by 1808, the practice had begun to die. The practice of delivering per curiam opinions in the style of the pre-Marshall Court lasted somewhat longer. By the period 1814 to 1817, however, the Court was reporting only 4% of its opinions per curiam, and for the balance of the century, until its revival in the 1880s, the per curiam opinion all but disappeared.

The American practice of opinion delivery had its origin, then, in the political and institutional ambitions of a particular Chief Justice sitting at the head of a particular court facing a unique constellation of forces. Even so, Marshall's achievement of massing the Court while fixing responsibility for the opinion of the Court upon a single Justice, together with [Justice] Johnson's achievement of legitimating dissent from the mass, became the norm throughout the United States, in both state and intermediate federal appellate courts. Hence, the specific practice of the Supreme Court of the United States must have appealed to needs felt generally in the American judiciary.

Publishing Dissent, 62 Wash. & Lee L. Rev. 1607, 1621-22, 1626-27 (2005) (footnotes omitted).

9. Some of the Supreme Court's most famous opinions were individually signed by the Justices involved. *See, e.g., Brown v. Bd. of Educ.*, 347 U.S. 483 (1954). And as stated above, some opinions were delivered jointly by more than one Justice. *See, e.g., Planned Parenthood of Se. Pa. v. Casey*, 505 U.S. 833 (1992) (joint opinion). What is the significance of these practices — i.e., why do the Justices sometimes do this? For more on the latter practice, see Laura Krugman Ray, *Circumstance and Strategy: Jointly Authored Supreme Court Opinions*, 12 Nev. L.J. 727 (2012).

10. Regarding the concurrence, one legal scholar has written:

The modern judicial concurrence is a curious hybrid. A direct descendent of the *seriatim* opinion, it is now suspect because, unlike its ancestor, it lacks direct decisional force. Yet the concurrence may have a substantial effect on the outcome of a case. Such an opinion may prevent the court from reaching a majority opinion or, less dramatically, transform a unanimous holding into a fragmented majority. The concurrence as a practical matter may have a greater effect on subsequent cases than on the majority opinion it accompanies, especially if the concurrence is one proposing an independent legal basis for the majority's result. Further, such an opinion may offer the clearest possible expression of an individual justice's views, unhampered by the accommodation of a colleague's position.

Laura Krugman Ray, *The Justices Write Separately: Uses of the Concurrence by the Rehnquist Court*, 23 U.C. Davis L. Rev. 777, 780 (1990). *See also* Charles C. Turner et al., *Beginning to Write Separately: The Origins and Development of Concurring Judicial Opinions*, 35 J. Sup. Ct. Hist. 93 (2010).

11. Fred M. Vinson, *Work of the Federal Courts*, 69 S. Ct. v (1949):

> I should like to turn for a moment to the subject of dissents. . . .
>
> . . . .
>
> [T]he very nature of the Supreme Court's jurisdiction is such that the easy cases, the clear and indisputable cases, very seldom come before the Court. Our discretionary certiorari jurisdiction encompasses, for the most part, only the borderline cases — those in which there is conflict among lower courts or widespread uncertainty regarding problems of national importance. . . . Considering, therefore, the importance and difficulty of the cases which the Court must decide, it is not strange that there is some of the same disagreement on the Court as exists among others of the bench and bar concerning the questions decided.
>
> But I would not be understood as decrying the Supreme Court's dissenting opinions or minimizing their value. While it is true that division on the Court tends to break down what Chief Justice Stone has called "a much cherished illusion of certainty in the law and of infallibility of judges," my brother Douglas has pointed out, in a speech before the Section of Judicial Administration of the American Bar Association, that certainty and unanimity in the law are possible only under a fascist or communist system, where, indeed, they are indispensable. Democracy, in other words, must contemplate some division of opinion among judges, as among lawyers and other human beings, for unvarying unanimity can result only from some power that directs the judges to decide cases one way rather than another.
>
> The dissenting opinion itself is of value in many different respects. For example, an opinion circulated to the Court as a dissent sometimes has so much in logic, reason, and authority to support it that it becomes the opinion of the Court. I must confess that the writer of the original Court opinion usually fails to see the error of his ways and turns his opinion into a dissent, so that the sum total of opinions is not reduced. But my point remains: A dissenting opinion may have immediate effect in the decision of cases.
>
> In the second place, the dissent gives assurance to counsel and to the public that the decision was reached only after much discussion, thought, and research — that it received full and complete consideration before being handed down.
>
> In the third place, a dissent may have far-reaching influence in bringing to public attention the ramifications of the Court's opinion and by sounding a warning note against further extension of legal doctrine, or the dissenter's conviction that existing doctrine has been unduly limited.
>
> And, finally, to quote Chief Justice Hughes, "A dissent in a court of last resort is an appeal to the brooding spirit of the law, to the intelligence of a future day,

when a later decision may possibly correct the error into which the dissenting judge believes the court to have been betrayed."

I do not mean by what I have said that unanimity is not desirable or that the Court does not seek long and earnestly to find it in every case. I believe, however, as Chief Justice Hughes also pointed out, that it is more important that the independence of the judges should be "maintained and recognized than that unanimity should be secured through its sacrifice."

Id. at ix-xi.

12. How long should one persist in one's dissent? For a recent take on this subject, see Jon G. Heintz, Note, *Sustained Dissent and the Extended Deliberative Process*, 88 NOTRE DAME L. REV. 1939 (2013). For more on dissent, see Peter Bozzo et al., *Many Voices, One Court: The Origin and Role of Dissent in the Supreme Court*, 36 J. S. CT. HIST. 193 (2011); William A. Fletcher, *Dissent*, 39 GOLDEN GATE U. L. REV. 291 (2009); M. Todd Henderson, *From Seriatim to Consensus and Back Again: A Theory of Dissent*, 2007 S. CT. REV. 283; and Kevin M. Stack, Note, *The Practice of Dissent in the Supreme Court*, 105 YALE L.J. 2235 (1996). *See generally* RONALD K.L. COLLINS & DAVID SKOVER, ON DISSENT — ITS MEANING IN AMERICA (2013) and CASS SUNSTEIN, WHY SOCIETIES NEED DISSENT (2003).

13. For a recent treatment of plurality opinions, see James F. Spriggs II & David R. Stras, *Explaining Plurality Decisions*, 99 GEO. L.J. 515 (2011).

14. Sometimes agreement as to the result — i.e., the decision whether to affirm or reverse the judgment of a lower court — can mask differences as to the reasoning behind a court's decision. For example, in *Eastern Enterprises v. Apfel*, 524 U.S. 498 (1998), only four Justices concluded that the law in question (the Coal Industries Retiree Health Benefit Act of 1992) violated the Takings Clause of the United States Constitution, and only one Justice concluded that the act violated the Due Process Clause — and yet, a majority (five Justices) held that the act was unconstitutional. For a recent discussion of this and other "voting paradoxes," see David S. Cohen, *The Precedent-Based Voting Paradox*, 90 B.U. L. REV. 183 (2010).

15. For a recent article questioning the theory behind judicial reliance on majority opinions (and particularly bare majorities), see Jeremy Waldron, *Five to Four: Why Do Bare Majorities Rule on Courts?*, 123 YALE L.J. 1692 (2014). For more on these topics generally, see Ruth Bader Ginsburg, *Remarks on Writing Separately*, 65 WASH. L. REV. 133 (1990).

16. To what extent do judges (as opposed to law clerks) write their own opinions? For a recent study, see Jeffrey S. Rosenthal & Albert H. Yoon, *Judicial Ghostwriting: Authorship on the Supreme Court*, 96 CORNELL L. REV. 1307 (2011).

SIDEBAR: THE PRACTICE IN FOREIGN JUDICIAL SYSTEMS

How does the American practice of publishing separate concurrences and dissents differ from the practice employed in Great Britain and in civil law jurisdictions? Again, according to Professor Jacobson:

The American practice of publishing separate opinions differs not only from civilian practice but also from the practice of the common law jurisdiction from which all others issue. For English appellate judges do not denominate any of their "judgments" (English for "opinions") dissents or concurrences. A judge may in fact be dissenting from his panel's disposition, but the reports never say so. Similarly, a judge may in fact be concurring — he may agree with the disposition but disagree with the reasoning of a majority of the panel — but the reports never say that he's concurring. You have to read through all the judgments in order to discover that any one of them is a concurrence. Indeed, there could not as a logical matter be dissents or concurrences in the English system, because no appellate panel ever adopts a single judgment as the judgment of the court; that is American, not English, practice. The expectation in England was that each judge on an appellate panel would compose (or deliver orally from the bench) his own judgment.

American practice is thus at a curious fulcrum between civilian and English practice. The civilian appellate panel issues only one opinion, and it is the opinion of the court. Every opinion is per curiam, "by the court." The public record does not reveal dissenting or concurring opinions. No judge signs the opinion of the court. It is an institutional, not personal, opinion. The English appellate panel issues no judgment of the court. Rather, each judge on the panel (until recently) issues his own judgment. Every judgment is personal; none is institutional. Reading through the judgments permits one to say which judges agree with the court's disposition and share the reasons for it (one of these judgments could have been selected as the judgment of the court if that were the practice), which judges agree with the disposition but do not share the reasons (concur), and which judges disagree with the disposition (dissent). But no judgment comes with a label affixed to it, "opinion of the court," none with the label "concurrence," and none with "dissent."

The American practice differs from both of these, and shares an affinity with both. Unlike English practice, American practice requires, when possible, an opinion of the court. But unlike civilian practice, an individual judge (joined by others) signs it. Unlike civilian practice, the opinion of the court is not necessarily the only opinion: There may be concurrences and dissents. Unlike English practice, however, there need not be multiple opinions; it is not the expectation that every judge will write (or, in the English case, possibly speak). Thus, like the English practice and unlike the civilian, there is authorship of opinions, and like the civilian practice and unlike the English, there is an opinion of the court. It is only in this special place, where there is authorship of opinions together with an opinion of the court, that dissent and concurrence are possible.

62 Wash. & Lee L. Rev. at 1609-10 (footnotes omitted).

There are other differences between common-law and civil-law decisions (such as those issued by courts in France). According to Mitchel Lasser, French decisions

> are famously short: those of the Cour de cassation (the French supreme court in private and criminal law matters), for example, tend to run to less than a single typed page. The decisions also lack any serious description of the facts, almost never refer to past judicial decisions, and contain absolutely nothing that could be described as serious interpretive or policy analysis.

MITCHEL DE S. –O. –L'E. LASSER, JUDICIAL DELIBERATIONS: A COMPARATIVE ANALYSIS OF JUDICIAL TRANSPARENCY AND LEGITIMACY 30-31 (2004). According to Professor Lasser, though, this "official" portrait of French (and Continental) decision-making can be a little misleading to Americans, in that there is much more happening behind the scenes that renders the American and French processes more similar in fact than many might imagine. *See id.* at 38-60 (discussing the "unofficial" portrait).

F. HOLDING AND DICTA

The foregoing discussion of "binding precedent" spoke of the "holding" of a court. But how does one determine a court's holding? Does it include everything that a court says in the course of deciding a case, or is it something less? And how does one determine that portion of an opinion that is holding and that portion that is not?

Michael C. Dorf

DICTA AND ARTICLE III

142 U. Pa. L. Rev. 1997 (1994)

I. IMPRECISION IN THE USE OF THE TERM DICTA

A. The Problem

The term dicta typically refers to statements in a judicial opinion that are not necessary to support the decision reached by the court.[10] A dictum is usually contrasted with a holding, a term used to refer to a rule or principle that decides the case.

---

10. *See, e.g.*, Humphrey's Executor v. United States, 295 U.S. 602, 627 (1935) (noting that "general expressions" should not be controlling in subsequent suits).

It is commonplace that holdings carry greater precedential weight than dicta, "which may be followed if sufficiently persuasive but which are not controlling."[12] Chief Justice Marshall's exegesis in *Cohens v. Virginia*[13] of the principle that a court may give less precedential weight to its earlier dicta than to its holdings remains the standard:

> It is a maxim, not to be disregarded, that general expressions, in every opinion, are to be taken in connection with the case in which those expressions are used. If they go beyond the case, they may be respected, but ought not to control the judgment in a subsequent suit, when the very point is presented for decision. The reason of this maxim is obvious. The question actually before the court is investigated with care, and considered in its full extent. Other principles which may serve to illustrate it, are considered in their relation to the case decided, but their possible bearing on all other cases is seldom completely investigated.[14]

Chief Justice Marshall provides an instrumental justification for the maxim that dicta need not be followed. Dicta are less carefully considered than holdings, and, therefore, less likely to be accurate statements of the law. Thus, according to Marshall, accuracy is the primary virtue that the holding/dictum distinction serves.

Courts sometimes rely upon a second justification for discounting dicta that involves not accuracy but legitimacy. According to this view, dicta have no precedential effect because courts have legitimate authority only to decide cases, not to make law in the abstract.[15] This latter function is seen as the proper province of the political branches.

. . . .

Neither the accuracy-based justification nor the legitimacy-based justification for giving less weight to dicta than to holdings is unassailable. . . .

. . . .

. . . Nevertheless, both the adversary system and the premise that courts have less authority to prescribe general-purpose rules than do legislatures are so firmly rooted in American legal practice as to rank as axiomatic. . . .

If we accept that judicial accuracy and legitimacy will be advanced by discounting dicta more readily than holdings, we are left with a critical definitional question: How do we distinguish between dicta and holdings?

At first blush, this question appears easy to answer. A dictum is a statement which is not "necessary" to the decision in the precedent case. Or, as Chief Justice Marshall put it in *Cohens*, dicta are statements that "go beyond the case." The very issue in many disputed cases, however, is precisely how far the earlier case went. What consequences follow from it? The *Cohens* definition of dicta is unilluminating

---

12. *Humphrey's Executor*, 295 U.S. at 627; *see also* Kastigar v. United States, 406 U.S. 441, 454-55 (1972) (stating that broad language of dicta "cannot be considered binding authority").
13. 19 U.S. (6 Wheat.) 264 (1821).
14. *Id.* at 399-400.
15. *Cf.* James B. Beam Distilling Co. v. Georgia, 111 S. Ct. 2439, 2451 (1991) (Scalia, J., concurring in the judgment) (recognizing "that judges in a real sense 'make' law," but arguing that they may only do so in the context of resolving a factual dispute).

unless we have some independent method for gauging the scope of earlier holdings. But no universal agreement exists as to how to measure the scope of judicial holdings. Consequently, neither is there agreement as to how to distinguish between holdings and dicta.

Judges often appear to take for granted that discerning the difference between holding and dictum is a routine, noncontroversial matter. Yet an examination of the kinds of statements that courts label dicta reveals gross inconsistencies. . . . [W]e would find a consensus for the judgment that everything that is not holding is dictum and everything that is not dictum is holding, but little in the way of a substantive definition of either term.

The failure to define the terms holding and dictum with any precision has serious consequences. It enables courts to avoid the normal requirements of stare decisis. In order to overrule an earlier decision, it is not enough that a court have a present disposition to resolve the question differently. Something more is required. . . . This constraint will routinely operate on the judge, unless she can find some way to render the earlier decision irrelevant. One way to do this is to label the controlling principle from the earlier case dictum. Since dicta need not be followed, the controlling legal question becomes one of first impression, and the judge is free to rule as she likes. Because the term dictum has no fixed meaning, the ploy often goes unnoticed.

Of course, no legal category can be defined with complete precision. Thus, the fact that some statements could reasonably be characterized as either holding or dictum presents no special problem. One could find such borderline examples for any legal distinction. The holding/dictum distinction suffers from a much more fundamental difficulty than peripheral ambiguity, however. As currently understood, the distinction is almost entirely malleable. Consequently, attachment of the label dicta to past statements has been used as a means of avoiding the consequences of all kinds of legal pronouncements.

In order to discern legitimate from illegitimate uses of the holding/dictum distinction, it may be helpful to develop a typology of dicta. I turn now to that task.

B. Legitimate Dicta

To understand how the holding/dictum distinction has been used, we might ask a seemingly naive question: Given the limits that the case-or-controversy requirement places on a federal court's ability to make law in the abstract, why would a federal court ever make statements in dicta? After all, considerations of judicial restraint counsel that a federal court should not announce a rule broader than necessary to decide the case before it.[35] Such a narrow rule necessarily constitutes only holding, leaving no room for dicta. Moreover, as a rule or explanation, it would satisfy the reason-giving requirement implicit in Article III's invocation of the "judicial Power."

---

35. *See, e.g.*, Whitehouse v. Illinois Cent. R.R., 349 U.S. 366, 372-73 (1955) (claiming that judges must confine themselves to "deciding only what is necessary to the disposition of the immediate case").

Some departures from this minimalist principle constitute deliberate throw-aways — that is, statements a judge makes knowing them to have no direct prece-dential weight, but which she nevertheless hopes will be influential. Such conscious asides[36] are the paradigmatic instances of dicta.

Although in some sense a deliberate aside violates the rule against advisory opinions, not all asides are unjustifiable. . . .

Asides — justifiable or not — comprise one category of statements commonly labeled dicta. A second category is somewhat more amorphous. It consists of those elaborations of legal principles broader than the narrowest proposition that can decide the case. In other words, sometimes a court will depart from the minimalist principle not merely to clarify a tangential point, but because it wishes to decide the case on broad grounds. . . .

. . . .

. . . [N]ote the critical difference between this category of dictum and the first category, the aside. An aside is considered dictum because it forms no essential part of either the decision reached in the case or the rationale for the decision. Even if we assume that the court takes the opposite position on the issue addressed in the aside, neither the governing standard of law announced nor the outcome in the specific case will be changed.

. . . By contrast, one may classify a statement as overly broad (and therefore dictum) without reference to the opinion in which it appears, but merely by consid-ering the facts and outcome of the case in which it appears. Treating the question whether a statement is dictum as a feature of the opinion in which it appears will result in a broader view of holdings than will treating that question as a feature of the facts and outcome of the case in which it appears.

Notes and Questions

1. It is difficult to overstate the importance of the issue here: if a statement in an opinion is part of a court's holding, it is generally considered binding law, whereas if it is merely dicta, it is not. Thus, the distinction between holding and dicta can be a powerful tool in case law argument. Yet, as Professor Dorf indicates, though there is general agreement as to the *effect* of a determination as to holding or dicta, courts and commentators have struggled to come up with a coherent means of making this determination in the first instance. This has allowed courts and commentators (and lawyers) to argue about the scope of earlier court holdings. This also means that an argument based on an op-ponent's reliance upon dicta probably should also include an explanation as to why the passage in question is, indeed, dicta.

---

36. Those who believe that the category dicta includes more than just asides sometimes call asides obiter dicta. *See, e.g.,* KARL LLEWELLYN, THE CASE LAW SYSTEM IN AMERICA § 10, at 14 (Paul Gewirtz ed. & Michael Ansaldi trans., 1989).

2. In a thoughtful, even more recent article, Michael Abramowicz and Maxwell Stearns propose the following "definition" of a holding:

> A holding consists of those propositions along the chosen decisional path or paths of reasoning that (1) are actually decided, (2) are based upon the facts of the case, and (3) lead to the judgment. If not a holding, a proposition stated in a case counts as dicta.
>
> Each of the three numbered prongs is premised upon the power of the deciding jurist or court to select among one or more potential decisional paths in resolving a case. The first prong thus requires that for a proposition to be credited as a holding, it must be actually decided along the chosen decisional path or paths. The second proposition then limits the permissible range of articulated propositions that can be credited as holding by insisting that they be grounded in the facts of the case. And the third proposition, by linking the ultimate disposition to the selected decisional path, both constrains and broadens judicial discretion. While this prong ensures that holdings are limited to issues that lead to judgment, it also recognizes that particular findings might move us away from the judgment as the means of traveling along a path that eventually gets to that judgment. By analogy, a trip from a southern to a northern destination will sometimes require turns south, east, or west, depending upon the configuration of, and the relationships among, the various roads along the chosen route. So it is with legal reasoning. Thus, our definition allows a judge to draw one or more conceptual lines (or paths) from case facts to judgment, and to credit all issues resolved along the chosen path or paths to produce holdings. At the same time, it discounts as dicta issues on paths that do not originate in the facts in the case or that lead nowhere.

Michael Abramowicz & Maxwell Stearns, *Defining Dicta,* 57 STAN. L. REV. 953, 1065-66 (2005).

The Abramowicz and Stearns formulation ultimately might prove definitive (or as definitive as can be hoped); as of this writing, it is too soon to assess its influence. But it certainly seems to be a reasonable approach, does it not? Or can you think of improvements?

3. Does everything a court says in the course of an opinion, then, constitute holding? And must a proposition be expressly stated in order to be part of the holding? No and no.

> "Actually decided" does not mean "expressly stated." The "actually decided" requirement is broader in the sense that it includes implicit holdings that a court never quite explicitly announces. But it is narrower in that it excludes some statements that figure in the reasoning of the case, but that a fair construction of the opinion would not find to lie on the path from case facts to case disposition.

Id. at 1070. Recall also Gil Grantmore's observation (*supra* at D.1) that historically, it was the "court's judgment, not its opinion," that constituted the "true" precedent.

4. *What about alternative holdings?* What if a court provides two (or more) independent justifications for its decisions? Do each of these differing lines of reasoning constitute holding? Professors Abramowicz and Stearns say yes. *See id.* at 1042.

The Supreme Court appears to be in accord. As the Court stated in *Railroad Cos. v. Schutte*, 103 U.S. 118 (1880):

> It cannot be said that a case is not authority on one point because, although that point was properly presented and decided in the regular course of the consideration of the cause, something else was found in the end which disposed of the whole matter. Here the precise question was properly presented, fully argued, and elaborately considered in the opinion. The decision on this question was as much a part of the judgment of the court as was that on any other of the several matters on which the case as a whole depended.

See also Woods v. Interstate Realty Co., 337 U.S. 535, 537 (1949) ("[W]here a decision rests on two or more grounds, none can be relegated to the category of *obiter dictum*.")

5. As Professor Dorf suggests, part of what drives the holding/dicta distinction involves conceptions of the proper role of courts vis-à-vis legislatures. On this subject, Professors Abramowicz and Stearns write:

> Some might argue that courts have no less a role in setting out legal policy than legislatures, and therefore that there are no inherent limits on judicial lawmaking powers linked to the obligation to resolve particular cases. We respectfully disagree. Courts inevitably make positive law, but that is not inconsistent with observing that individual judges are subject to important normative constraints in undertaking that task. A central feature of the judicial system is that judges are randomly selected to hear cases and to resolve the issues presented by those cases. And because cases arise from circumstances beyond the control of the individual judge, any judge's ability to determine which issues to resolve is inherently limited. Proper definitions of holding and dicta can preserve this feature while still allowing judges control over case reasoning on issues fairly presented. To the extent that judges may resolve issues independent of the random generation of cases in need of resolution and of the factual bases of those cases, a central aspect of judicial legitimacy — and thus of judicial restraint — is undermined.

57 STAN. L. REV. at 1019 (footnotes omitted). But if this is true, then why do courts sometimes include dicta in their opinions? And is such inclusion sometimes "legitimate," as Professor Dorf suggests?

6. *What about decisional methodology?* Consider also the following passage:

> [A] judge's selection of a particular interpretive methodology will not necessarily credit that methodological choice as a holding. For example, imagine a Supreme Court statutory interpretation case in which the language of the statute points in one direction, while the legislative history points in the opposite direction. If a majority of five looked to legislative history in construing the statute, while the remaining four justices in dissent eschewed reliance on legislative history, does this establish a precedent that judges must consider legislative history? We do not think so. We do think, however, that the case does at least imply that

> where text and legislative history point in opposite directions, a court is permitted to consider both sources and sometimes may choose the interpretation suggested by the legislative history over that set out in the text.

Id. at 1071 (footnote omitted). Professors Abramowicz and Stearns further note that "[a]n important implication of this analysis is that a definition offered by a court to distinguish holding from dicta might itself be dicta." *Id.* n.370.

It is difficult to disagree with the notion that merely labeling some statement in an opinion as "holding" or "dicta" does not necessarily make it so. But what of the idea that a court's *decisional methodology* (as contrasted with the more specific doctrinal analysis used to decide the case) cannot constitute holding? This, it turns out, is a somewhat complicated (though as we will see when we consider theories of statutory interpretation, important) question as to which there is currently some disagreement. Consider, in contrast to Abramowicz and Stearns, the thoughts of Justice Scalia on this subject:

> [W]hen the Supreme Court of the federal system, or of one of the state systems, decides a case, not merely the *outcome* of that decision, but the *mode of analysis* that it applies will thereafter be followed by the lower courts within that system, and even by that supreme court itself.

Antonin Scalia, *The Rule of Law as a Law of Rules,* 56 U. CHI. L. REV. 1175, 1177 (1989). *See also Lampf, Pleva, Lipkind, Prupis, & Petigrow v. Gilbertson,* 501 U.S. 350, 364 (Scalia, J., concurring in part and concurring in the judgment) ("Although I accept the *stare decisis* effect of decisions we have made with respect to the statutes of limitations applicable to particular federal causes of action, I continue to disagree with the methodology the Court has very recently adopted for purposes of making those decisions."). At least one legal scholar agrees. *See* Jordan Wilder Connors, *Note, Treating Like Subdecisions Alike: The Scope of Stare Decisis as Applied to Judicial Methodologies,* 108 COLUM. L. REV. 681 (2008) (similarly arguing that stare decisis should attach to a court's decision-making methodology). *See also infra* at chapter 3, part D.2 (discussing this issue with respect to statutory interpretation).

7. *What about factual findings?* Should factual, as well as legal, findings count as holding? For one view, see Allison Orr Larsen, *Factual Precedents,* 162 U. PA. L. REV. 59, 62 (2013) (discussing the "tendency of lower courts to over-rely on Supreme Court opinions and to apply generalized statements of fact from old cases to new ones" and arguing that such fact-finding should be given no precedential value).

8. In *Bush v. Gore,* 531 U.S. 98 (2000), the Court stated (at 109): "Our consideration is limited to the present circumstances . . . ." May a court limit the effect of its holding in this manner — i.e., simply by adding some limiting language? At the other end of the spectrum, in *Ashcroft v. Iqbal,* 556 U.S. 662, 684 (2009), the Court stated: "Our decision in *Twombly* expounded the pleading standard for 'all civil actions,' and it applies to antitrust and discrimination suits alike." But may a court expand the scope of its holding simply by so stating? On the

other hand, if the Court's holding in *Twombly* does apply to all civil actions, is there any need for the Court to remind us of this fact?

9. A later court interpreting precedent seems obligated to do its best to faithfully interpret the scope of the earlier holding. But what the earlier holding means is, as some have said, the joint product of both courts, and it is possible that the later court might interpret the earlier court's holding in a manner in which the earlier court might disagree (had it known). Nonetheless, to a considerable extent, the later court gets the final word. This is true even when the later court limits the scope of an earlier holding to such an extent that the earlier holding is all but eliminated (at least until resurrected by an even later court). For more on this topic, see Jeff Todd, *Undead Precedent: The Curse of a Holding "Limited to Its Facts,"* 40 Tex. Tech L. Rev 67 (2007).

10. "The concurrence implies that *Sibbach* has slipped into desuetude, apparently for lack of sufficient citations. We are unaware of any rule to the effect that a holding of ours expires if the case setting it forth is not periodically revalidated." *Shady Grove Orthopedic Assoc. v. Allstate Ins. Co.*, 130 S. Ct. 1431, 1446 n.12 (2010) (opinion by Scalia, J.) (citation omitted).

11. "[W]e think it generally undesirable, where holdings of the Court are not at issue, to dissect the sentences of the United States Reports as though they were the United States Code." *St. Mary's Honor Ctr. v. Hicks*, 509 U.S. 502, 515 (1993).

12. "Dictum settles nothing, even in the court that utters it." *Jama v. Immigration and Customs Enforcement*, 543 U.S. 335, 352 n.12 (2005). *See also Kokkonen v. Guardian Life Ins. Co.*, 511 U.S. 375, 379 (1994) ("It is to the holdings of our cases, rather than their dicta, that we must attend . . . ."). Even so, dicta is often included in opinions for a reason, and later courts have the liberty of using dicta from earlier cases in fashioning holdings in later cases. Care accordingly should be used when working with dicta to ensure that the pendulum does not swing too far either way; though it might not be binding, it will not necessarily be disregarded in future decisions. *See, e.g.,* Judith M. Stinson, *Why Dicta Becomes Holding and Why It Matters*, 76 Brooklyn L. Rev. 219 (2010).

13. Pierre N. Leval, *Judging Under the Constitution: Dicta About Dicta*, 81 N.Y.U. L. Rev. 1249, 1282 (2006):

> To professors I would say: You have a responsibility to make sure that your students understand and are alert to the distinction between holding and dictum — and its importance. It is not something to be discussed only in a brief, first-year intro-to-law lecture. Students who graduate without a grasp of it are not well trained for the profession.
>
> To students and practitioners I would say that, in arguing to courts, you will need to be keenly aware what is holding and what is dictum. It is often the best way

to undermine unfavorable language in a prior opinion. By the same token, it can alert you that your argument is built on a house of cards.

To myself and other judges I would say three things: First, dictum can serve useful purposes. We have no need to purge dictum from our opinions and we shouldn't be embarrassed by its presence. We must only remember that it is not law. To avoid trespassing beyond the territory confided to us by the Constitution, to avoid creating law in circumstances likely to produce bad law, and to avoid creating confusion, we should not disguise dictum, but should forthrightly label it as what it is. Second, rather than reciting rules of law, which are not in dispute in the case, we should focus sharply on exactly what is in dispute and set forth rules in our opinions only as rulings on the disputed questions. Third, before relying on a formulation of law in a prior opinion, we must determine whether it was holding or dictum. We must make that inquiry even when the prior court was the Supreme Court. If a rule was declared only in dictum, the question remains undecided, and we have a constitutional duty to make our own determination of the answer. Unless we do, we have not done our job.

14. *See generally* Kent Greenawalt, *Reflections on Holding and Dictum*, 39 J. LEGAL EDUC. 431 (1989).

15. Not everyone agrees that the holding-dicta distinction matters (or matters much). For example, one recent study revealed that "lower courts made meaningful use of the holding-dicta distinction in fewer than 1 in every 3000 cases." David Klein & Neal Devins, *Dicta, Schmicta: Theory Versus Practice in Lower Court Decision Making*, 54 WM. & MARY L. REV. 2021, 2026 (2013).

SIDEBAR: A FURTHER WORD ON CASE LAW INTERPRETATION

In a recent article, Adam N. Steinman argued that when seeking to understand a judicial decision (and in particular, a decision by the Supreme Court), we should consider those "values that are traditionally employed when interpreting a case: (1) consistency with prior Supreme Court cases; (2) consistency with the governing textual sources; and (3) coherence with other parts of the opinion and relevancy given the case's factual and procedural posture." Adam N. Steinman, *The Irrepressible Myth of* Celotex: *Reconsidering Summary Judgment Burdens Twenty Years after the Trilogy*, 63 WASH. & LEE L. REV. 81, 122 (2006). According to Professor Steinman, these "simple values" are "consistent with basic principles of interpretation" and therefore "should not be controversial." *Id.* at 107.

It is true, is it not, that consistency with prior cases, consistency with governing textual sources, and internal coherence are important interpretive values? Can you think of any other important interpretive values?

But even if you agree with Professor Steinman's list, can you think of any problems with that list as presented? Consider the following critique:

> I agree that consistency with prior cases, consistency with governing textual sources, and internal coherence are important interpretive values. Nonetheless, there are aspects of Steinman's interpretive values with which I respectfully disagree. For one thing, I disagree with their order.[27] In fact, I would like to *reverse* the order. (Actually, if it was up to me, I would make the second value, "consistency with the governing textual sources," the first value, for I cannot see how the Court, in the course of one of its decisions, can change the meaning of a Federal Rule of Civil Procedure.[28] I understand, though, that once the Court interprets a governing textual source, it is that interpretation that controls, regardless of how difficult it might be for others to square that interpretation with the text so interpreted.[29]) Certainly, a case's "internal coherence with other parts of the majority opinion and with the case's factual and procedural posture" (the third value) is a more important interpretive value than is consistency with prior cases (the first value), for the Court may overrule itself,[31] and need not even say that it is doing so.[32]

Bradley Scott Shannon, *Responding to Summary Judgment*, 91 MARQ. L. REV. 815, 81920 (2008).

---

27. It might be more accurate to say that I disagree with the order in which they are presented, for, to be fair, I cannot find any express indication that they have been presented in any particular order. Of course, if they have not been presented in any particular order, that also might be a basis for criticism, unless one believes that each of these values should be given equal weight.

28. *See, e.g.,* Leatherman v. Tarrant County Narcotics Intelligence and Coordination Unit, 507 U.S. 163, 168 (1993) ("Perhaps if Rules 8 and 9 were rewritten today, claims against municipalities under § 1983 might be subjected to the added specificity requirement of Rule 9(b). But that is a result which must be obtained by the process of amending the Federal Rules, and not by judicial interpretation."). *Cf.* Am. Trucking Ass'ns v. Smith, 496 U.S. 167, 201 (Scalia, J., concurring in the judgment) (concluding that because "the Constitution does not change from year to year," "it does not conform to our decisions, but our decisions are supposed to conform to it").

29. *See, e.g.,* Allan Ides, *Judicial Supremacy and the Law of the Constitution*, 47 U.C.L.A. L. REV. 491, 500 (1999) ("[T]he judiciary possesses a recognized authority to interpret laws, and the product of those interpretations is law . . . even if the interpretation is somehow deemed incorrect . . . ."). *But see* Gary Lawson, *The Constitutional Case Against Precedent*, 17 HARV. J.L. & PUB. POL'Y 23 (1994) (arguing that, at least in constitutional cases, the practice of following precedent is unconstitutional, at least where the decision in question is inconsistent with the constitutional text being interpreted).

31. *See, e.g.,* Payne v. Tennessee, 501 U.S. 808, 828 (1991) (observing that "the Court has during the past 20 Terms overruled in whole or in part 33 of its previous constitutional decisions").

32. *See, e.g.,* Hudgens v. NLRB, 424 U.S. 507, 518 (1976) (recognizing the implicit overruling of *Amalgamated Food Employees Union v. Logan Valley Plaza*, 391 U.S. 308 (1968), by *Lloyd Corp. v. Tanner*, 407 U.S. 551 (1972)). *See also* Shalala v. Illinois Council on Long Term Care, Inc., 529 U.S. 1, 18 (2000) ("This Court does not *normally* overturn, or so dramatically limit, earlier authority *sub silentio*.") (emphasis supplied).

SIDEBAR: A WORD ABOUT CASE LAW TERMINOLOGY

Many courts today (particularly multi-judge courts) refer to themselves as "we," rather than "the Court." Does this distinction matter? If so, which is more appropriate? Why? Does the answer lie (at least in part) in the notion that a court is an institution, and exists irrespective of whoever might sit on the bench at any particular time? Does it matter that it is in reality people (judges) who actually decide cases, and not some faceless, incorporeal institution?

On this subject, Hugh Baxter has written:

> I recognize that any references to "the Court" as actor, or even "a majority of the Court" as actor, will strike some readers as bizarre personifications. The Supreme Court, after all, is an institution that operates through the (largely) independent judgment of its personnel, and the institution's personnel changes over time. I retain the conventional usage for two reasons. First, the idea of "the Court" structures the discourse that bears the Supreme Court's name: the various writings the Justices issue in the course of rendering decision either are written "for the Court," or if not, are correspondingly limited in their power. This basic institutional fact affects both the way in which the Justices operate and the legal effect of their writings. Second, in some instances a majority of Justices may agree even on the particulars of a possible legal change, and in that event, to the extent they cooperate effectively, they can act for the Court in selecting and deciding law-changing cases. The idea of "the Court" may be a legal construction, produced and maintained by the very legal communications it structures, but nonetheless — or rather, for that very reason — legal theory cannot simply "unmask" it as mere fiction. Fiction it may be, with respect to some other discourse, but it is hardly a fiction without legal significance or effect.

Hugh Baxter, *Managing Legal Change: The Transformation of Establishment Clause Law*, 46 UCLA L. REV. 343, 347-48 n.14 (1998).

Many lawyers and even judges, when seeking to denigrate some particular binding decision, refer to the decision as that of the "majority," rather than "the Court." Is that appropriate, or are those lawyers and judges simply acknowledging what is true — that a decision of a court is no more than whatever a simple majority of its members could agree upon?

Finally, in many of the cases included in this book, the court speaks of other cases "holding" this or that. But do cases themselves ever "hold" anything? Or is it the Court that decided the case the thing that (or "person" who) held?

G. THE BINDING EFFECT OF PRIOR DECISIONS IN RELATED PROCEEDINGS

There are several ways in which a judicial decision or ruling in a case can have a significant (and perhaps even determinative) impact on 1) a later proceeding in the same case, or 2) a subsequent (and sometimes even unrelated) case.

One way in which a prior decision or ruling can impact a later case is through the doctrine of preclusion. The doctrine of preclusion is typically divided into two types: claim preclusion, and issue preclusion. Claim preclusion (or "res judicata") may be roughly defined as "[a]n affirmative defense barring the same parties from litigating a second lawsuit on the same claim, or any other claim arising from the same transaction or series of transactions and that could have been — but was not — raised in the first suit." BLACK'S LAW DICTIONARY 1504 (10th ed. 2014). Issue preclusion (or "collateral estoppel") is "[t]he binding effect of a judgment as to matters actually litigated and determined in one action on later controversies between the parties involving a different claim from that on which the original judgment was based," or "[a] doctrine barring a party from relitigating an issue determined against that party in an earlier action, even if the second action differs significantly from the first one." *Id.* at 318. Claim and issue preclusion are somewhat complicated subjects, and are usually covered in a course on civil procedure.

But there are other ways in which a decision can impact a later proceeding in the same case or a related case. Perhaps the most common is the doctrine of law of the case. That doctrine is the subject of this section.

Finally, as you are probably already aware, a prior decision can impact a later case through the doctrine of precedent, or stare decisis. Various aspects of the doctrine of stare decisis (which literally means "to stand by decisions") are discussed in part H *infra*.

All of these various doctrines carry a common theme. As recently summarized by one legal scholar:

> Stare decisis is the judicial policy in favor of adhering to past precedent. Law of the case is the principle followed by . . . courts of refusing to alter a previous . . . determination made in the same case . . . . Res judicata is the policy that a final judgment rendered by a court with competent jurisdiction is conclusive on the questions involved between the parties and their privies. All three doctrines thus require, or at least strongly encourage, courts to adhere to previous decisions with which they may disagree.

Amanda Frost, *The Limits of Advocacy*, 59 DUKE L.J. 447, 474-75 n.103 (2009). *See also* ROBERT C. CASAD & KEVIN M. CLERMONT, RES JUDICATA: A HANDBOOK ON ITS THEORY, DOCTRINE, AND PRACTICE ch. 2 ("Related Doctrines") (2001).

1. Law of the Case

The "law of the case" doctrine reflects the general tendency of courts to adhere to prior rulings in the same case. This doctrine is the subject of the next case.

Christianson v. Colt Industries Operating Corp.

486 U.S. 800 (1988)

JUSTICE BRENNAN delivered the opinion of the Court.

This case requires that we decide a peculiar jurisdictional battle between the Court of Appeals for the Federal Circuit and the Court of Appeals for the Seventh Circuit. Each court has adamantly disavowed jurisdiction over this case. Each has transferred the case to the other. And each insists that the other's jurisdictional decision is "clearly wrong." The parties therefore have been forced to shuttle their appeals back and forth between Chicago and the District of Columbia in search of a hospitable forum, ultimately to have the merits decided, after two years, by a Court of Appeals that still insists it lacks jurisdiction to do so.

I

Respondent Colt Industries Operating Corp. is the leading manufacturer, seller, and marketer of M16 rifles and their parts and accessories. . . .

Petitioner Christianson is a former Colt employee . . . . Upon leaving respondent's employ in 1975, Christianson established petitioner International Trade Services, Inc. (ITS), and began selling M16 parts to various customers domestically and abroad. Petitioners' business depended on information that Colt considers proprietary . . .

[Petitioners commenced an action against Respondent in United States District Court. In their complaint, Petitioners alleged antitrust and tortious interference with business relationship claims that, in turn, were based (at least in part) on the alleged invalidity of Respondent's M16 patents.]

. . . .

The District Court awarded petitioners summary judgment as to liability on both the antitrust and the tortious-interference claims . . . . In the process, the District Court invalidated nine of Colt's patents, declared all trade secrets relating to the M16 unenforceable, enjoined Colt from enforcing "any form of trade secret right in any technical information relating to the M16," and ordered Colt to disgorge to petitioners all such information.

Respondent appealed to the Court of Appeals for the Federal Circuit, which, after full briefing and argument, concluded that it lacked jurisdiction and issued an unpublished order transferring the appeal to the Court of Appeals for the Seventh Circuit. See 28 U. S. C. § 1631. The Seventh Circuit, however, raising the jurisdictional issue *sua sponte,* concluded that the Federal Circuit was "clearly wrong" and transferred the case back. The Federal Circuit, for its part, adhered to its prior jurisdictional ruling, concluding that the Seventh Circuit exhibited "a monumental misunderstanding of the patent jurisdiction granted this court," and was "clearly wrong." Nevertheless, the Federal Circuit proceeded to address the merits in the "interest of justice," and reversed the District Court. We granted certiorari, and now vacate the judgment of the Federal Circuit.

II

As relevant here, 28 U. S. C. § 1295(a)(1) grants the Court of Appeals for the Federal Circuit exclusive jurisdiction over "an appeal from a final decision of a district court of the United States if the jurisdiction of that court was based, in whole or in part, on 28 U. S. C. § 1338." Section 1338(a), in turn, provides in relevant part that "the district court shall have original jurisdiction of any civil action arising under any Act of Congress relating to patents." Thus, the jurisdictional issue before us turns on whether this is a case "arising under" a federal patent statute, for if it is then the jurisdiction of the District Court was based at least "in part" on § 1338.

A

[The Court concludes that, under the well-pleaded complaint rule, Petitioners' action did not arise under § 1338, and therefore that the Court of Appeals for the Federal Circuit lacked appellate jurisdiction.]

. . . .

III

Colt offers three arguments for finding jurisdiction in the Federal Circuit, notwithstanding the well-pleaded complaint rule. . . . We find none of them persuasive.

. . . .

C

Colt's final argument is that the Federal Circuit was obliged not to revisit the Seventh Circuit's thorough analysis of the jurisdictional issue, but merely to adopt it as the law of the case. "As most commonly defined, the doctrine of the law of the case posits that when a court decides upon a rule of law, that decision should continue to govern the same issues in subsequent stages in the same case." *Arizona v. California,* 460 U. S. 605, 618 (1983) (dictum). This rule of practice promotes the finality and efficiency of the judicial process by "protecting against the agitation of settled issues." 1B J. Moore, J. Lucas, & T. Currier, Moore's Federal Practice ¶0.404[1], p. 188 (1984) (hereinafter Moore's). Colt is correct that the doctrine applies as much to the decisions of a coordinate court in the same case as to a court's own decisions. Federal courts routinely apply law-of-the-case principles to transfer decisions of coordinate courts. Indeed, the policies supporting the doctrine apply with even greater force to transfer decisions than to decisions of substantive law; transferee courts that feel entirely free to revisit transfer decisions of a coordinate court threaten to send litigants into a vicious circle of litigation.[5]

---

5. There is no reason to apply law-of-the-case principles less rigorously to transfer decisions that implicate the transferee's jurisdiction. Perpetual litigation of any issue — jurisdictional or nonjurisdictional — delays, and therefore threatens to deny, justice.

Colt's conclusion that jurisdiction therefore lay in the Federal Circuit is flawed, however, for three reasons. First, the Federal Circuit, in transferring the case to the Seventh Circuit, was the first to decide the jurisdictional issue. That the Federal Circuit did not explicate its rationale is irrelevant, for the law of the case turns on whether a court preciously "decided upon a rule of law" — which the Federal Circuit necessarily did — not on whether, or how well, it explained the decision. Thus, the law of the case was that the Seventh Circuit had jurisdiction, and it was the Seventh Circuit, not the Federal Circuit, that departed from the law of the case. Second, the law-of-the-case doctrine "merely expresses the practice of courts generally to refuse to reopen what has been decided, not a limit to their power." *Messenger v. Anderson,* 225 U. S. 436, 444 (1912) (Holmes, J.) (citations omitted). A court has the power to re-visit prior decisions of its own or of a coordinate court in any circumstance, although as a rule courts should be loath to do so in the absence of extraordinary circum-stances such as where the initial decision was "clearly erroneous and would work a manifest injustice." *Arizona v. California, supra,* at 618, n. 8 (citation omitted). Thus, even if the Seventh Circuit's decision was law of the case, the Federal Circuit did not exceed its power in revisiting the jurisdictional issue, and once it concluded that the prior decision was "clearly wrong" it was obliged to decline jurisdiction. Most impor-tantly, law of the case cannot bind this Court in reviewing decisions below. A petition for writ of certiorari can expose the entire case to review. *Panama R. Co. v. Napier Shipping Co.,* 166 U. S. 280, 283-84 (1897). Just as a district court's adherence to law of the case cannot insulate an issue from appellate review, a court of appeals' adherence to the law of the case cannot insulate an issue from this Court's review. *See Messenger, supra,* at 444.

IV

Our agreement with the Federal Circuit's conclusion that it lacked jurisdiction, com-pels us to disapprove of its decision to reach the merits anyway "in the interest of justice." "Courts created by statute can have no jurisdiction but such as the statute confers." The statute confers on the Federal Circuit authority to make a single deci-sion upon concluding that it lacks jurisdiction — whether to dismiss the case or, "in the interest of justice," to transfer it to a court of appeals that has jurisdiction. 28 U. S. C. § 1631.

The age-old rule that a court may not in any case, even in the interest of justice, extend its jurisdiction where none exists has always worked injustice in particular cases. Parties often spend years litigating claims only to learn that their efforts and expense were wasted in a court that lacked jurisdiction. Even more exasperating for the litigants (and wasteful for all concerned) is a situation where, as here, the liti-gants are bandied back and forth helplessly between two courts, each of which insists the other has jurisdiction. Such situations inhere in the very nature of jurisdictional lines, for as our cases aptly illustrate, few jurisdictional lines can be so finely drawn as to leave no room for disagreement on close cases.

That does not mean, however, that every borderline case must inevitably culmi-nate in a perpetual game of jurisdictional ping-pong until this Court intervenes to resolve the underlying jurisdictional dispute, or (more likely) until one of the parties surrenders to futility. Such a state of affairs would undermine public confidence in our judiciary, squander private and public resources, and commit far too much of this Court's calendar to the resolution of fact-specific jurisdictional disputes that lack national importance. "Surely a seemly system of judicial remedies regarding controverted transfer provisions of the United States Code should encourage, not discourage, quick settlement of questions of transfer." The courts of appeals should achieve this end by adhering strictly to principles of law of the case. Situations might arise, of course, in which the transferee court considers the transfer "clearly erroneous." *Arizona v. California,* 460 U. S., at 618, n. 8. But as "the doctrine of the law of the case is a heavy deterrent to vacillation on arguable issues," 1B Moore's ¶0.404[1], at 124, such reversals should necessarily be exceptional; courts will rarely transfer cases over which they have clear jurisdiction, and close questions, by definition, never have clearly correct answers. Under law-of-the-case principles, if the transferee court can find the transfer decision plausible, its jurisdictional inquiry is at an end. While adherence to the law of the case will not shield an incorrect jurisdictional decision should this Court choose to grant review, it will obviate the necessity for us to resolve every marginal jurisdictional dispute.

We vacate the judgment of the Court of Appeals for the Federal Circuit and remand with instructions to transfer the case to the Court of Appeals for the Seventh Circuit.

Notes and Questions

---

1. Can you summarize the law of the case doctrine as articulated by the Court in *Christianson?* And why did the Court reject Colt's argument that the Seventh Circuit's decision on the jurisdictional issue should be regarded as the law of the case here?

2. As indicated in *Christianson,* federal courts tend not to revisit prior decisions in the same case absent extraordinary circumstances. As stated in one early and influential decision, the law of the case

   > must be followed in all subsequent proceedings in the same case in the trial court or on a later appeal in the appellate court, unless the evidence on a subsequent trial was substantially different, controlling authority has since made a contrary decision of the law applicable to such issues, or the decision was clearly erroneous and would work a manifest injustice.

   White v. Murtha, 377 F.2d 428, 431-32 (5th Cir. 1967). Similar versions of this passage have been repeated often by other federal courts.

   Additional factors would seem to influence the reconsideration calculus as well. For example, the nature or import of the ruling in question would seem to play a role, with reconsideration less likely for more trivial matters. The stage in the proceedings also might be a factor, with courts more willing to reconsider rulings earlier rather than later. Can you think of any other potentially relevant factors?

3. What is the rationale behind the basic law of the case rule? As summarized by one leading treatise:

> A trial court could not operate if it were to yield to every request to reconsider each of the multitude of rulings that may be made between filing and final judgment. All too often, requests would be made for no purpose but delay and harassment. Other requests, made in subjective good faith, would reflect only the loser's misplaced attachment to a properly rejected argument. Even the sincere desire to urge again a strong position that perhaps deserves to prevail could generate more work than our courts can or should handle. A presumption against reconsideration makes sense.

18B CHARLES ALAN WRIGHT ET AL., FEDERAL PRACTICE AND PROCEDURE § 4478.1, at 692 (2d ed. 2002). On the other hand,

> a trial court could not operate justly if it lacked power to reconsider its own rulings as an action progresses toward judgment. Far too many things can go wrong, particularly with rulings made while the facts are still undeveloped or with decisions made under the pressures of time and docket.

Id. As a result, though reconsideration certainly is disfavored, "every order short of a final decree is subject to reopening at the discretion of the district judge." *Moses H. Cone Memorial Hosp. v. Mercury Constr. Corp.*, 460 U.S. 1, 12 (1983).

4. Many state courts expressly provide, by rule, for the reconsideration of prior rulings. Federal courts, on the other hand, have no such formal procedure. The closest analog appears to be Federal Rule of Civil Procedure 54(b), which currently provides in pertinent part:

> [A]ny order or other decision, however designated, that adjudicates fewer than all the claims or the rights and liabilities of fewer than all the parties [generally] does not end the action as to any of the claims or parties and may be revised at any time before the entry of judgment adjudicating all the claims and all the parties' rights and liabilities.

Should the federal rules be amended to include a more definite reconsideration procedure along these lines? Or is there some wisdom (intentional or not) in the federal courts' approach?

5. The law of the case doctrine actually encompasses a number of different procedural contexts. Most commonly, the doctrine is used to refer to the tendency of a single court (whether a trial or appellate court) to adhere to its own earlier rulings in the same case. But law of the case principles also lie at the core of "the duty of a trial court to adhere to the mandate of an appellate court" and (as in *Christianson*) "the comity concerns that take special hold when coordinate

courts come to consider a single case at different times." 18B CHARLES ALAN WRIGHT ET AL., FEDERAL PRACTICE AND PROCEDURE § 4478, at 637 (2d ed. 2002).

6. *The Mandate Rule.* As stated above, the law of the case doctrine is not limited to rulings within the same court. It also encompasses what is known as the mandate rule. As one treatise explains:

> Law-of-the-case terminology is often employed to express the principle that an inferior tribunal is bound to honor the mandate of a superior court within a single judicial system. There is nothing surprising about the basic principle, which inheres in the nature of judicial hierarchy and is confirmed by statute. Appellate courts, indeed, ordinarily do not enter the final judgment; that task is accomplished on remand to the district court.

18B CHARLES ALAN WRIGHT ET AL., FEDERAL PRACTICE AND PROCEDURE § 4478.3, at 733-34 (2d ed. 2002) (footnotes omitted). Thus, as stated by the Supreme Court in *Sibbald v. United States,* 37 U.S. (12 Pet.) 488 (1838):

> When the supreme court have executed their power, in a cause before them, and their final decree or judgment requires some further act to be done, it cannot issue an execution, but shall send a special mandate to the court below to award it. Whatever was before the court, and is disposed of, is considered as finally settled. The inferior court is bound by the decree as the law of the case; and must carry it into execution, according to the mandate. They cannot vary it, or examine it for any other purpose than execution; nor give any other or further relief; nor review it upon any matter decided on appeal, for error apparent; nor intermeddle with it, further than to settle so much as has been remanded. . . .
>
> If the special mandate . . . is not obeyed or executed, then the general power given to "all the courts of the United States to issue any writs which are necessary for the exercise of their respective jurisdictions, and agreeable to the principles and usages of law," . . . fairly arises, and a *mandamus,* or other appropriate writ will go.

Id. at 492 (citation omitted). *Accord Briggs v. Pennsylvania R. Co.,* 334 U.S. 304, 306 (1948). Other cases along this line include *In re Sanford Fork & Tool Co.,* 160 U.S. 247, 255-56 (1895), and *Quern v. Jordan,* 440 U.S. 332, 347 n.18 (1979).

7. *Coordinate Courts.* As we saw in *Christianson:*

> Law-of-the-case doctrine is not limited to proceedings within a single court or the duty of an inferior court to honor the mandate of a superior court in the same judicial system. The self-same case may move from one court to another by such means as transfer within a single system, realignment of appeals structures, removal, reference of specific questions by such means as abstention or certification, or remand after removal. The same dispute may instead be framed in formally separate actions, either simultaneously or sequentially, in circumstances that do not support claim preclusion or issue preclusion. For the most part, later courts tend to adhere to earlier rulings by other courts for the same reasons that inform general law-of-the-case practices. In some settings, indeed, there is at least a hint

of special deference that arises from comity, the desire to avoid strategic changes of court to reargue lost positions, and the need to avoid protracted jurisdictional disputes.

18B Charles Alan Wright et al., Federal Practice and Procedure § 4478.4, at 770 (2d ed. 2002).

For more on the law of the case doctrine, see 18 James Wm. Moore's Federal Practice §§ 134.20-.24 (3d ed. 2008).

8. *Case law exercise.* Fully understanding a judicial opinion involves much more than most non-lawyers (or even law students) realize. Consider, for example, the following concepts that were raised in *Christianson*:
    a) the use of the term "dictum" (in the *Arizona v. Colorado* parenthetical);
    b) citations to earlier Supreme Court cases (presumably for some specific purpose);
    c) citations to a legal treatise (*Moore's Federal Practice*) (presumably for some similar (or not) purpose);
    d) the role of judicial reason-giving (with respect to the Federal Circuit's jurisdiction ruling); and
    e) the special mention of a particular jurist (Holmes).

One might well wonder what "dictum" means; why courts cite to earlier court decisions (or to anything, for that matter); etc. One of these issues has already been discussed; many others will be. The broader point, though, is that a student of the law should seek out the meaning of unfamiliar terms and try to determine why courts do what they do (at which point one may intelligently criticize those practices and possibly formulate an even better way).

Try undertaking this exercise with respect to another judicial opinion (whether in this book or (even better) with respect to a case that has not been edited). You might be amazed how many legal concepts unrelated to the underlying decision are implicated therein.

2. Rehearing and Rehearing en Banc

"Rehearing" and "rehearing en banc" are special applications of the law of the case doctrine that are primarily applicable to appellate, as opposed to trial, courts. Consider the explanations of these doctrines as given in the following case.

Easley v. Reuss
532 F.3d 592 (7th Cir. 2008)

Per Curiam.

. . . .

In her petition for rehearing with suggestion for rehearing en banc, Ms. Easley requests that this court revisit its prior decision. We decline to do so, but we take this opportunity to explain our denial of further review in order to provide litigants with some guidance concerning the proper contents of petitions for rehearing and for rehearing en banc.

Appellate Rule 40 governs petitions for panel rehearing. It provides, in pertinent part, that "the petition must state with particularity each point of law or fact that the petitioner believes the court *has overlooked or misapprehended* and must argue in support of the petition." As suggested by the rule, petitions for panel rehearing should alert the panel to specific factual or legal matters that the party raised, but that the panel may have failed to address or may have misunderstood. It goes without saying that the panel cannot have "overlooked or misapprehended" an issue that was not presented to it. Panel rehearing is not a vehicle for presenting new arguments, and, absent extraordinary circumstances, we shall not entertain arguments raised for the first time in a petition for rehearing.

Petitions for rehearing en banc are governed by Appellate Rule 35. According to the Rule, if en banc rehearing is requested, the petition *must* begin with a statement that either:

> (A) the panel decision conflicts with a decision of the United States Supreme Court or of the court to which the petition is addressed (with citation to the conflicting case or cases) and consideration by the full court is therefore necessary to secure and maintain uniformity of the court's decisions; or
>
> (B) the proceeding involves one or more questions of exceptional importance, each of which must be concisely stated; for example, a petition may assert that a proceeding presents a question of exceptional importance if it involves an issue on which the panel decision conflicts with the authoritative decisions of other United States Courts of Appeals that have addressed the issue.

Again, as set forth in the language of the rule, en banc rehearing has a different focus than panel rehearing. Panel rehearings are designed as a mechanism for the panel to correct its own errors in the reading of the factual record or the law, rehearings en banc are designed to address issues that affect the integrity of the circuit's case law (intra-circuit conflicts) and the development of the law (questions of exceptional importance). Given the "heavy burden" that en banc rehearings impose on an "already overburdened court," such proceedings are reserved for the truly exceptional cases. Indeed, in the last calendar year, out of the thousands of cases resolved by this court, only one en banc opinion has been issued.

With these standards in mind, we turn to Ms. Easley's petition for rehearing, with suggestion for rehearing en banc. Ms. Easley's petition does not begin with the statement set forth in Appellate Rule 35 and required for all en banc petitions. By contrast, her statement in support of rehearing en banc appears to be aimed at satisfying the grounds set forth in Rule 40 for panel rehearing; she states: "This Court failed to address the state-created danger exception."[1] We, therefore, interpret Ms. Easley's petition as requesting panel rehearing.

. . . .

---

1. We previously have warned parties that make no effort to "fit their petitions within the criteria for en banc review" that sanctions may be imposed. However, because Ms. Easley also requests panel rehearing, and because her statement purports to satisfy the standards for panel rehearing, we do not believe sanctions are appropriate in this case.

There is good reason why this court did not address the "state-created danger exception" in its order disposing of Ms. Easley's appeal: Ms. Easley did not argue in her briefs before this court that the "state-created danger exception" applied. Indeed, prior to the submission of her petition for rehearing, the words "state-created danger" do not appear anywhere in Ms. Easley's filings with this court. . . . Similarly, the district court was not presented with any argument that the state-created danger doctrine applied, nor did Ms. Easley supply that court with any authority that may have alerted it to the fact that she was raising the issue. In short, Ms. Easley seeks to raise an issue in her petition for rehearing that was not presented to the district court and was neither briefed nor argued to this court prior to the rehearing petition. The time for presenting new, substantive arguments to this court has passed: "Having tried and appealed its case on one theory, an unsuccessful party may not then use a petition for rehearing as a device to test a new theory." *United States v. Sutherland*, 428 F.2d 1152, 1158 (5th Cir. 1970).

Petitions for rehearing and petitions for rehearing en banc are mechanisms governed by rule and designed to ensure the integrity of individual panel decisions and the consistent and thoughtful development of the law. The criteria for both petitions are explicit, and, in submitting petitions, we expect counsel to ensure that their petitions meet those criteria. Ms. Easley's petition does not satisfy the requirements for panel or en banc rehearing. Therefore, . . . we deny the petition for rehearing.

Notes and Questions

---

1. According to the *Easley* court, what is the distinction between rehearing and rehearing en banc? When does each apply?

2. For more on motions for rehearing and rehearing en banc, see 16AA Wright & Miller § 3981.1 (4th ed. 2008), and Stephen L. Wasby, *Why Sit En Banc?*, 63 HASTINGS L.J. 747 (2012).

SIDEBAR: THE DOCTRINE OF JUDICIAL ESTOPPEL

Another doctrine, somewhat related to the law of the case doctrine, is that of judicial estoppel. The leading case on judicial estoppel is *New Hampshire v. Maine*, 532 U.S. 742 (2001). As the Supreme Court explained in that case:

"Where a party assumes a certain position in a legal proceeding, and succeeds in maintaining that position, he may not thereafter, simply because his interests have changed, assume a contrary position, especially if it be to the prejudice of the party who has acquiesced in the position formerly taken by him." *Davis v. Wakelee,* 156 U. S. 680, 689 (1895). This rule, known as judicial estoppel, "generally prevents a party from prevailing in one phase of a case on an argument and then relying on a contradictory argument to prevail in another phase." *Pegram v. Herdrich,* 530 U. S. 211, 227 n.8 (2000).

Although we have not had occasion to discuss the doctrine elaborately, other courts have uniformly recognized that its purpose is "to protect the integrity of the judicial process" by "prohibiting parties from deliberately changing positions according to the exigencies of the moment." Because the rule is intended to prevent "improper use of judicial machinery," judicial estoppel "is an equitable doctrine invoked by a court at its discretion."

Courts have observed that "the circumstances under which judicial estoppel may appropriately be invoked are probably not reducible to any general formulation of principle." Nevertheless, several factors typically inform the decision whether to apply the doctrine in a particular case: First, a party's later position must be "clearly inconsistent" with its earlier position. Second, courts regularly inquire whether the party has succeeded in persuading a court to accept that party's earlier position, so that judicial acceptance of an inconsistent position in a later proceeding would create "the perception that either the first or the second court was misled." Absent success in a prior proceeding, a party's later inconsistent position introduces no "risk of inconsistent court determinations," and thus poses little threat to judicial integrity. A third consideration is whether the party seeking to assert an inconsistent position would derive an unfair advantage or impose an unfair detriment on the opposing party if not estopped.

In enumerating these factors, we do not establish inflexible prerequisites or an exhaustive formula for determining the applicability of judicial estoppel. Additional considerations may inform the doctrine's application in specific factual contexts.

For more on the doctrine of judicial estoppel, see 18 James Wm. Moore, Moore's Federal Practice §§ 134.30-.34 (3d ed. 2008).

SIDEBAR: THE ROOKER-FELDMAN DOCTRINE

Also somewhat related to the law of the case doctrine is the *Rooker-Feldman* doctrine. The doctrine takes its name from two Supreme Court cases, *Rooker v. Fidelity Trust Co.,* 263 U.S. 413 (1923), and *District of Columbia Court of Appeals v. Feldman,* 460 U.S. 462 (1983). As explained by the Court in *Exxon Mobil Corp. v. Saudi Basic Industries Corp.,* 544 U.S. 280 (2005):

> *Rooker* was a suit commenced in Federal District Court to have a judgment of a state court, adverse to the federal court plaintiffs, "declared null and void." In *Feldman,* parties unsuccessful in the District of Columbia Court of Appeals (the District's highest court) commenced a federal-court action against the very

> court that had rejected their applications. Holding the federal suits impermis-
> sible, we emphasized that appellate jurisdiction to reverse or modify a state-court
> judgment is lodged, initially by §25 of the Judiciary Act of 1789, and now by 28
> U. S. C. §1257, exclusively in this Court. Federal district courts, we noted, are
> empowered to exercise original, not appellate, jurisdiction. Plaintiffs in *Rooker*
> and *Feldman* had litigated and lost in state court. Their federal complaints, we
> observed, essentially invited federal courts of first instance to review and reverse
> unfavorable state-court judgments. We declared such suits out of bounds, *i.e.*,
> properly dismissed for want of subject-matter jurisdiction.

Id. at 283-84. In *Exxon Mobil*, the Court held that this doctrine

> is confined to cases of the kind from which the doctrine acquired its name: cases
> brought by state-court losers complaining of injuries caused by state-court judg-
> ments rendered before the district court proceedings commenced and inviting
> district court review and rejection of those judgments. *Rooker-Feldman* does
> not otherwise override or supplant preclusion doctrine or augment the circum-
> scribed doctrines that allow federal courts to stay or dismiss proceedings in def-
> erence to state-court actions.

Id. at 284.

For a more recent case on the *Rooker-Feldman* doctrine, see *Lance v. Dennis*,
546 U.S. 459 (2006).

H. THE CONCEPT OF PRECEDENT AND THE DOCTRINE OF STARE DECISIS

"Stare decisis," which literally means "to stand by things decided," is better known
in law as "[t]he doctrine of precedent, under which a court must follow earlier
judicial decisions when the same points arise again in litigation." BLACK'S LAW
DICTIONARY 1626 (10th ed. 2014). As one legal scholar explains: "Stare decisis is
an integral, accepted principle of American and common-law jurisprudence. The
idea that courts should follow past decisions, whether of the same or a higher court,
was accepted before this nation was born[2] and continues to be generally accepted
today." C. Steven Bradford, *Following Dead Precedent: The Supreme Court's Ill-
Advised Rejection of Anticipatory Overruling*, 59 FORDHAM L. REV. 39, 39 (1990).

As the passage above suggests, the doctrine of stare decisis as applied today is
usually thought of as having two components: one vertical, and one horizontal. *See*
BLACK'S LAW DICTIONARY 1626 (10th ed. 2014). *Vertical stare decisis* usually refers
to the generally accepted obligation of inferior courts in the same judicial system to

---

2. Blackstone wrote: "The doctrine of the law then is this: that precedents and rules must be followed,
unless flatly absurd or unjust; for though their reason be not obvious at first view, yet we owe such
a deference to former times as not to suppose that they acted wholly without consideration." 1 W.
Blackstone, Commentaries *70.

follow the holdings of superior courts, though it is actually somewhat broader than that. *Horizontal stare decisis* (or "true" stare decisis), by contrast, refers to the somewhat looser (though also generally accepted) obligation of a court to follow its own earlier holdings in later cases. Each of these concepts is discussed in turn below.

1. Vertical Stare Decisis Generally

Evan H. Caminker

WHY MUST INFERIOR COURTS OBEY SUPERIOR COURT PRECEDENTS?

46 Stan. L. Rev. 817 (1994)

I. THE DOCTRINE OF HIERARCHICAL PRECEDENT

A. The Duty to Obey Courts with Revisory Jurisdiction

Article III of the United States Constitution established the Supreme Court and also gave Congress the power to establish lower federal courts. Over the last two centuries, Congress has expanded the federal judiciary to include the Supreme Court, thirteen courts of appeals, and ninety-one district courts, the last staffed by more than 600 judges. These courts are arranged in three tiers that define the pattern of appellate review: District courts exercise original jurisdiction; courts of appeals engage in initial appellate review granted to losing litigants as a matter of right; and the Supreme Court engages in final but discretionary appellate review.

Generally, geographic boundaries determine the path of appellate review from one tier to the next. Litigants choose the district courts in which they file (or remove) their cases, though statutory and constitutional limitations on personal jurisdiction and venue constrain their choices. The court of appeals with jurisdiction over the geographic region including the litigants' chosen district court hears their appeal. A litigant who loses at the appellate level may seek the discretionary review of the Supreme Court, which supervises all inferior federal courts.[25]

---

25. However, exceptions to this general pattern exist. First, in some cases subject matter, not geography, determines the path of review: Cases concerning certain specific subjects are reviewable in the Court of Appeals for the Federal Circuit regardless of their district courts of origin. Second, a few cases skip the middle appellate tier. Special 3-judge district courts hear some cases, such as challenges to congressional apportionment. Appeals are made directly to the Supreme Court. Third, in exceptional circumstances the Supreme Court grants certiorari to review the decisions of district courts without awaiting the available appellate court review. Finally, some cases skip both the bottom and middle tiers because the Supreme Court exercises original jurisdiction.

Finally, the Article III judiciary forms part of a larger regime that includes the fifty state and various federal territorial judicial systems. If issues of federal law are presented, the United States Supreme Court may review the decisions of the highest court in each state or territory. In this sense, the Supreme Court sits atop more than fifty separate non-Article III judicial pyramids.

The duty to obey hierarchical precedent tracks the path of review followed by a particular case as it moves up the three federal judicial tiers: A court must follow the precedents established by the court(s) directly above it. District courts must follow both Supreme Court decisions and those issued by whichever court of appeals has revisory jurisdiction over its decisions, and courts of appeals must heed Supreme Court decisions.[28] However, a court can ignore precedents established by other courts so long as they lack revisory jurisdiction over it. Thus, a circuit court of appeals is not bound by decisions of coordinate circuit courts of appeals, and a district court judge may ignore the decisions of "foreign" courts of appeals as well as other district court judges, even within the same district.[31]

The doctrine also applies to state and territorial courts. These courts are bound by precedent set by the United States Supreme Court, which has the authority to review their federal law decisions. But the state and territorial authority judges are not bound by precedents established by courts that do not have the authority to review those judges' decisions, since, as in the Article III regime, authority to establish precedent follows the path of appellate review. Thus a state court need not follow the holdings of any inferior federal court, including the court of appeals in whose geographical region the state court sits.

In some specific circumstances, federal courts defer to legal interpretations by nonjudicial government actors or by state courts. These occasions do not, however, create exceptions to the doctrine of hierarchical precedent. Rather, within the Article III hierarchy, the inferior courts simply follow superior court precedents with respect to such interpretations.

Notes and Questions

1. The foregoing description of vertical stare decisis is so well established that most take it for granted. It is therefore not too surprising that Professor Caminker

---

28. The Tax Court most starkly illustrates the duty's path-dependent nature. Tax Court decisions are reviewable by Article III courts of appeals; which court will review a decision depends on factors such as where the disputed tax return was filed. When the Tax Court can identify in advance the court of appeals with revisory jurisdiction over a particular case, the Tax Court adheres to that court's precedents. Hence the Tax Court may decide similar cases differently because they are appealable to different federal circuits.

31. Present practice suggests a possible exception to path-dependent review. Numerous 3-judge district courts follow their local court of appeals' precedents even though only the Supreme Court may review their decisions.

ultimately concludes that "the doctrine of hierarchical precedent is sensible and, in the main, persuasively justified." *Id.* at 873. But as Professor Caminker demonstrates, the reasoning behind this conclusion is not as clear as one might suspect:

> No single rationale explains prevailing doctrine in its entirety; a persuasive account must combine various rationales for different levels of the judiciary. Obedience to Supreme Court precedents can be persuasively justified and obedience to circuit court precedents somewhat more tentatively so; but the arguments for obedience rely on value judgments that can reasonably be contested.

Id.

2. Comparing civil law views of "precedent" (such as dominate the courts of continental Europe), Professor Caminker writes:

> The fact that higher court precedents do not formally bind inferior courts in the hierarchical judicial systems of many civil law nations poses a challenge to those who presume that only the doctrine of hierarchical precedent staves off "chaos" in the United States courts. A central premise in civil law systems is that "judicial decisions are not a source of law. It would violate the rules against judicial lawmaking if decisions of courts were to be binding on subsequent courts." Hence, "no court is bound by the decision of any other court in a civil law jurisdiction. In theory, at least, even though the highest court has already spoken on the question and indicated a clear view of its proper resolution, the lowest court in the jurisdiction can decide differently." This system demonstrates that neither a formal nor rigid rule of adherence to precedent inheres in the notion of judicial hierarchy. Thus we must take care not to confuse the familiar with the necessary: The common law system's axiom that lower courts must obey superior court precedent needs justification.

Id. at 826. But Professor Caminker continues:

> Of course, [such a] system's courts would not always treat every legal issue of a case with plenary and de novo consideration. There are several reasons why a court, even when not obligated to do so, would likely adhere to its own precedents and those of reviewing — and perhaps even nonreviewing — courts. First, a deciding court might be persuaded by the prior court's reasoning. Second, adherence to precedent might be motivated by the personal or professional interests of the judge, such as avoiding the stigma associated with reversal. Third, a court might follow precedent simply to avoid "reinventing the wheel" by engaging in start-to-finish legal analysis, thus allowing a judge both to avoid becoming mired in unfamiliar legal thickets, and to concentrate her energies on interesting issues in which she wishes to develop expertise. Indeed, frequent adherence to precedent is a prerequisite to effective adjudication: Courts simply do not have the time to fully address each legal issue raised by every case.
>
> Clearly, removing the duty to obey hierarchical precedent would not stop its general practice. Indeed, given their incentives to obey, lower courts most likely would exercise their autonomy to eschew precedent only when they firmly believed that a higher court erred with respect to an important legal issue — in other words, in precisely those cases when autonomy seems most desirable.

Id. at 826-28.

3. As suggested above, vertical stare decisis is largely dependent upon the nature of the hierarchical structure. In the federal system, though, there are times when that nature is not entirely clear. Notice also that the structure of the federal courts is largely the product of congressional legislation. For a discussion of these and related issues, see Jeffrey C. Dobbins, *Structure and Precedent*, 108 Mich. L. Rev. 1453 (2010).

4. "Several state constitutions explicitly mandate obedience to hierarchical precedent within the state judicial system." Caminker, 46 Stan. L. Rev. at 838 n.87 (citing Georgia, Rhode Island, and South Carolina as examples). "However, I am unaware of any state constitutional provision binding state courts to United States Supreme Court decisions." *Id.*

5. State courts, of course, need not follow the same precedential rules as the federal courts. For example, "[t]he decisions of Florida's [five] district courts of appeal represent the law of Florida unless and until they are overruled by the Supreme Court of Florida." Michael Cavendish, *Diagonal Authority*, 8 Fla. Coastal L. Rev. 133, 133 (2006). Thus, "an un-contradicted district court of appeal decision binds the decisions of every state trial court in Florida," despite the fact that "[d]istrict court of appeal decisions do not bind sister district courts of appeal," *id.* at 141. Some states, though, do adhere to a model more analogous to that used in the federal courts.

6. Notice that "[t]he duty to follow the binding decisions of a higher authority does not depend on the correctness of those decisions." 18 James Wm. Moore, Moore's Federal Practice § 134.02[2], at 134-26 to -26.1 (3d ed. 2008). *Accord Hutto v. Davis*, 454 U.S. 370, 374-75 (1982) ("[U]nless we wish anarchy to prevail within the federal judicial system, a precedent of this Court must be followed by the lower federal courts no matter how misguided the judges of those courts may think it to be."). *See also Brown v. Allen*, 344 U.S. 443, 540 (1953) (Jackson, J., concurring) ("There is no doubt that if there were a super-Supreme Court, a substantial proportion of our reversals of state courts would also be reversed. We are not final because we are infallible, but we are infallible only because we are final.").

7. *The precedential effect of federal intermediate appellate court decisions.* In the federal system, the rule as to the precedential effect of decisions of the court of appeals is well known and well established. As stated by then-Circuit Judge Ruth Bader Ginsburg:

> The federal courts spread across the country owe respect to each other's efforts and should strive to avoid conflicts, but each has an obligation to engage independently in reasoned analysis. Binding precedent for all is set only by the Supreme Court, and for the district courts within a circuit, only by the court of appeals for that circuit.

In re Korean Air Lines Disaster of Sept. 1, 1983, 829 F.2d 1171, 1176 (D.C. Cir. 1987), *aff'd sub nom. Chan v. Korean Air Lines, Ltd.*, 490 U.S. 122 (1989). Thus, though all lower federal courts are bound by Supreme Court decisions, federal district courts generally are considered bound only by the court of appeals for the circuit in which the district court sits. But does this make sense? Should a district court instead be bound by *any* court of appeals decision? After all, is there not just one United States Court of Appeals?

2. State Law in Federal Courts

As the above discussion indicates, a general hierarchical adherence to precedent is well established, at least with respect to the law of each system. Thus, Supreme Court decisions as to issues of federal law are binding on the lower federal courts, and the same is generally true of state highest court decisions as to the law of that state. But in the United States, because we have federal and state systems of government and the courts of each system often have concurrent subject-matter jurisdiction (i.e., many courts can decide both federal and state claims), federal courts are sometimes called upon to decide issues of state law, and vice versa. In such "interjurisdictional" cases, what law is binding on the decisional court?

Commissioner of Internal Revenue v. Estate of Bosch
387 U.S. 456 (1967)

MR. JUSTICE CLARK delivered the opinion of the Court.

These two federal estate tax cases present a common issue for our determination: Whether a federal court or agency in a federal estate tax controversy is conclusively bound by a state trial court adjudication of property rights or characterization of property interests when the United States is not made a party to such proceeding.

. . . We hold that where the federal estate tax liability turns upon the character of a property interest held and transferred by the decedent under state law, federal authorities are not bound by the determination made of such property interests by a state trial court.

. . . .

. . . We cannot say that the authors of [the relevant federal estate tax provision with respect to marital deductions] intended that the decrees of state trial courts were to be conclusive and binding on the computation of the federal estate tax as levied by the Congress. If the Congress had intended state trial court determinations to have that effect on the federal actions, it certainly would have said so — which it did not do. . . . This also is in keeping with the long-established policy of the Congress, as expressed in the Rules of Decision Act. There it is provided that in the absence of federal requirements such as the Constitution or Acts of Congress, the "laws of the several states shall be regarded as rules of decision in civil actions in the courts of the United States, in cases where they apply." This Court has held that judicial decisions are "laws of the state" within the section. *Erie R. Co. v. Tompkins.* Moreover, even in diversity cases this Court has further held that while the decrees of "lower state courts" should be "attributed some weight the decision is not controlling" where the highest court of the State has not spoken on the point. And in *West v. A. T. & T. Co.*, 311 U. S. 223 (1940), this Court further held that "an intermediate appellate state court is a datum for ascertaining state law which is not to be disregarded by a federal court *unless it is convinced by other persuasive data that the highest court of the state would decide otherwise.*" At 237. (Emphasis supplied.) Thus, under some conditions, federal authority may not be bound even by an intermediate state appellate court ruling. It follows here then, that when the application of a federal statute is involved, the decision of a state trial court as to an underlying issue of state law should *a fortiori* not be controlling. This is but an application of the rule of *Erie,* where state law as announced by the highest court of the State is to be followed. This is not a diversity case but the same principle may be applied for the same reasons, *viz.,* the underlying substantive rule involved is based on state law and the State's highest court is the best authority on its own law. If there be no decision by that court then federal authorities must apply what they find to be the state law after giving "proper regard" to relevant rulings of other courts of the State. In this respect, it may be said to be, in effect, sitting as a state court. *Bernhardt v. Polygraphic Co.,* 350 U. S. 198 (1956).

Notes and Questions

---

1. Following *Estate of Bosch,* what sort of state case law is binding on the federal courts? Does it make sense that a federal court may sometimes disregard state appellate court decisions even when a similarly situated state trial court could not?

2. *The effect of a prior federal court ruling on state law.* It appears to be established that "a [federal] circuit court panel may not disregard or overrule a decision of an earlier panel on a matter of state law, unless there has been an intervening contrary decision of the state's highest court or the intervening enactment of a controlling statute." 18 James Wm. Moore, Moore's Federal Practice § 134.02[1][c], at 134-16 (3d ed. 2008). This is a corollary of the more general proposition that lower federal courts are bound by higher federal court determinations of state law. But does this practice make sense, given that federal court decisions with respect to state law generally are not binding on state courts?

3. Federal Law in State Courts

Donald H. Zeigler

GAZING INTO THE CRYSTAL BALL: REFLECTIONS ON THE STANDARDS STATE JUDGES SHOULD USE TO ASCERTAIN FEDERAL LAW

40 Wm. & Mary L. Rev. 1143 (1999)

Federal and state courts routinely interpret and apply each other's law. Federal courts must apply state law under the Rules of Decision Act as construed in *Erie Railroad Co. v. Tompkins* and its progeny. State courts must apply federal law under the Supremacy Clause. Federal courts use a single approach for ascertaining state law in cases in which it applies: they decide issues of state law the way they think the state supreme court would decide them.[4] State courts, by contrast, do not use a uniform approach for ascertaining federal law. Instead, they use a wide variety of approaches.

Virtually all state courts agree that they are bound by U.S. Supreme Court decisions interpreting federal law. When the Supreme Court has not spoken, however, there is little agreement on how to proceed. State courts vary greatly in the weight they give to lower federal court decisions: some consider themselves bound by such decisions; others ignore them entirely. Most state courts take a position somewhere between these two extremes. State courts generally give only brief, conclusory reasons for the approaches they follow. Courts deciding that they are not bound by lower federal court decisions almost never go on to articulate or explain the standards they use to ascertain federal law. . . .

. . . .

. . . . The few courts that explain why Supreme Court decisions are binding on state courts point to the Supremacy Clause and to the Supreme Court's power to review federal issues in state court decisions. . . .

State courts holding themselves bound by lower federal court interpretations of federal statutes may do so by analogy to the traditional federal court practice of following state court interpretations of state statutes. In 1825, the Supreme Court noted that there is a "principle, supposed to be universally recognized, that the judicial department of every government, where such department exists, is the appropriate organ for construing the legislative acts of that government."[150] . . . In

---

4. *See* Commissioner v. Estate of Bosch, 387 U.S. 456, 465 (1967) (noting that federal courts are bound by the decisions of a state's highest court in determining questions of state law and must ascertain what the state law should be after giving "proper regard" to lower state court holdings).
150. Elmendorf v. Taylor, 23 U.S. (10 Wheat.) 152, 159 (1825).

holding themselves bound by lower federal court constructions of federal statutes, state judges may simply be following the converse of this long-established practice in the federal courts. . . .

Courts that give reasons why they should not be bound by lower federal court decisions make both structural and practical arguments. These courts base the structural argument on the institutional framework chosen by the Founding Fathers: Lower federal and state courts exist side-by-side; both sets of courts can decide federal questions. Although both are subject to Supreme Court review, they do not sit in review of each other. Consequently, state courts are not bound by lower federal court decisions on issues of federal law. Some courts suggest that state courts have an independent responsibility to interpret federal law. . . .

Courts base the practical argument on the fact that the lower federal courts often disagree on the meaning of federal law. Obviously, a state court cannot follow two conflicting opinions. Some state courts give a similar reason in explaining why they do not grant their own circuit particular deference when other circuits disagree. No federal decision is definitive, and their own circuit may be wrong.

State courts give several reasons for following lower federal decisions, whether they consider themselves technically bound or not. They wish to avoid forum shopping between state and federal courts and to maintain good relations with the federal courts. They also seek to reduce confusion in the administration of justice, guarantee judicial certainty, and help insure the uniformity of federal law.

Notes and Questions

1. The adherence to Supreme Court precedent as to issues of federal law by state courts seems established. But what are the arguments in favor of adherence also to federal court of appeals precedent? What are the arguments against? Which is the better view? How does your state resolve this issue?

2. Professor Zeigler proposes "that the state courts adopt a uniform approach for ascertaining federal law," and that "[t]he approach should be the same that the Supreme Court mandated for the federal courts in the analogous situation when federal courts must ascertain state law" — namely, that "[t]he state courts should decide questions of federal law the way that they believe the Supreme Court would decide them." *Id.* at 1144-45. What do you think of this approach? Can you think of a better approach? Notice that Professor Zeigler's approach potentially suffers from the same problem as that articulated by the Supreme Court in *Estate of Bosch* with respect to state law in federal courts: courts of different judicial systems sitting in the same state might reach conflicting conclusions regarding the nature of the applicable law.

3. Notice that "[t]he issue of what standards states should use to ascertain federal law is probably itself a federal question." *Id.* at 1183 n.201. Thus (according to Professor Zeigler): "Congress or the Supreme Court probably could require state courts to use particular standards for ascertaining federal law." *Id.* at 1145 n.7. But to date, "[n]either institution has shown any inclination to do so." *Id.*

4. Though it appears that the Supreme Court of the United States has not yet directly addressed the issue of whether lower federal court decisions are binding on state courts as to questions of federal law, some of the Justices have weighed in on this question. For example, in *Lockhart v. Fretwell,* 506 U.S. 364 (1993), Justice Thomas offered the following:

    > The Supremacy Clause demands that state law yield to federal law, but neither federal supremacy nor any other principle of federal law requires that a state court's interpretation of federal law give way to a (lower) federal court's interpretation. In our federal system, a state trial court's interpretation of federal law is no less authoritative than that of the federal court of appeals in whose circuit the trial court is located. An Arkansas trial court is bound by this Court's (and by the Arkansas Supreme Court's and Arkansas Court of Appeals') interpretation of federal law, but if it follows the Eighth Circuit's interpretation of federal law, it does so only because it chooses to and not because it must.

    Id. at 375-76 (Thomas, J., concurring). Similarly, Justice Rehnquist once stated: "Although [a] state court would not be compelled to follow [a] federal [lower court] holding, the opinion might, of course, be viewed as highly persuasive." *Steffel v. Thompson,* 415 U.S. 452, 482 n.3 (1974).

5. *What about the application of the law of another state in a state court?* It has been held, as one might expect, that "[t]he courts of one state do not owe obedience to the courts of another state, except when following the law of another state under its choice-of-law rules." 18 JAMES WM. MOORE, MOORE'S FED. PRACTICE § 134.02[4][b], at 134-26.3 (3d ed. 2008). Thus (for example), a Washington court would only have to follow a decision of the Supreme Court of Oregon when deciding an issue of Oregon law. The same rule would seem to apply with respect to the use of foreign court decisions in American courts. Of course, all such decisions could serve as sources of persuasive authority to the extent otherwise considered appropriate.

4. Deference to Other Federal Courts as to the Law of a State Within Its Jurisdiction

As discussed previously, lower federal courts must follow higher federal court decisions, even as to state law. But to what extent, if any, must a federal court follow (or defer to) the decisions of any *other* federal courts with respect to issues of state law? Consider the following case.

Salve Regina College v. Russell

499 U.S. 225 (1991)

JUSTICE BLACKMUN delivered the opinion of the Court.

The concept of a federal general common law, lurking (to use Justice Holmes' phrase) as a "brooding omnipresence in the sky," was questioned for some time before being firmly rejected in *Erie R. Co. v. Tompkins,* 304 U. S. 64 (1938). *Erie* mandates that a federal court sitting in diversity apply the substantive law of the forum State, absent a federal statutory or constitutional directive to the contrary. See also 28 U. S. C. § 1652 ("The laws of the several states, except where the Constitution or treaties of the United States or Acts of Congress otherwise require or provide, shall be regarded as rules of decision in civil actions in the courts of the United States, in cases where they apply"). In decisions after *Erie,* this Court made clear that state law is to be determined in the same manner as a federal court resolves an evolving issue of federal law: "with the aid of such light as is afforded by the materials for decision at hand, and in accordance with the applicable principles for determining state law."

In this case, we must decide specifically whether a federal court of appeals may review a district court's determination of state law under a standard less probing than that applied to a determination of federal law.

I

The issue presented arises out of a contract dispute between a college and one of its students. . . .

. . . .

Soon after leaving Salve Regina College, respondent filed this civil action in the United States District Court for the District of Rhode Island. She asserted, among others, [a claim based on] nonperformance by the college of its implied agreement to educate respondent. Subject-matter jurisdiction in the District Court was based on diversity of citizenship. The parties agree that the law of Rhode Island applies to all substantive aspects of the action.

At the close of plaintiff-respondent's case in chief, [the college moved for a directed verdict]. . . . The court, however, denied the college's motion, . . . reasoning that "a legitimate factual issue" remained concerning whether "there was substantial performance by the plaintiff in her overall contractual relationship at Salve Regina."

At the close of all the evidence, the college renewed its motion for a directed verdict. It argued that under Rhode Island law the strict commercial doctrine of substantial performance did not apply in the general academic context. Therefore, according to petitioner, because respondent admitted she had not fulfilled the terms of the contract, the college was entitled to judgment as a matter of law.

The District Court denied petitioner's motion. Acknowledging that the Supreme Court of Rhode Island, to that point, had limited the application of the substantial-performance doctrine to construction contracts, the District Court nonetheless concluded, as a matter of law, that the Supreme Court of Rhode Island would apply that doctrine to the facts of respondent's case. The Federal District Judge based this conclusion, in part, on his observation that "I was a state trial judge for 18 and ½ years, and I have a feel for what the Rhode Island Supreme Court will do or won't do." Accordingly, the District Court submitted the breach-of-contract claim to the jury. . . .

The jury returned a verdict for respondent, and determined that the damages were $30,513.40. Judgment was entered. Both respondent and petitioner appealed.

The United States Court of Appeals for the First Circuit affirmed. . . . Rejecting petitioner's argument that, under Rhode Island law, the doctrine of substantial performance does not apply in the college-student context, the court stated:

> "In this case of first impression, the district court held that the Rhode Island Supreme Court would apply the substantial performance standard to the contract in question. In view of the customary appellate deference accorded to interpretations of state law made by federal judges of that state, we hold that the district court's determination that the Rhode Island Supreme Court would apply standard contract principles is not reversible error."

Petitioner college sought a writ of certiorari from this Court. It alleged that the Court of Appeals erred in deferring to the District Court's determination of state law. A majority of the Courts of Appeals, although varying in their phraseology, embrace a rule of deference similar to that articulated by the Court of Appeals in this case. Two Courts of Appeals, however, have broken ranks recently with their sister Circuits. They have concluded that a district-court determination of state law is subject to plenary review by the appellate court. We granted certiorari to resolve the conflict.

II

We conclude that a court of appeals should review *de novo* a district court's determination of state law. As a general matter, of course, the courts of appeals are vested with plenary appellate authority over final decisions of district courts. See 28 U. S. C. § 1291. The obligation of responsible appellate jurisdiction implies the requisite authority to review independently a lower court's determinations.

Independent appellate review of legal issues best serves the dual goals of doctrinal coherence and economy of judicial administration. District judges preside alone over fast-paced trials: Of necessity they devote much of their energy and resources to hearing witnesses and reviewing evidence. Similarly, the logistical burdens of trial advocacy limit the extent to which trial counsel is able to supplement the district judge's legal research with memoranda and briefs. Thus, trial judges often must resolve complicated legal questions without benefit of "extended reflection or extensive information."

Courts of appeals, on the other hand, are structurally suited to the collaborative juridical process that promotes decisional accuracy. With the record having been constructed below and settled for purposes of the appeal, appellate judges are able to devote their primary attention to legal issues. As questions of law become the focus of appellate review, it can be expected that the parties' briefs will be refined to bring to bear on the legal issues more information and more comprehensive analysis than was provided for the district judge. Perhaps most important, courts of appeals employ multi-judge panels that permit reflective dialogue and collective judgment. Over 30 years ago, Justice Frankfurter accurately observed:

> "Without adequate study there cannot be adequate reflection; without adequate reflection there cannot be adequate discussion; without adequate discussion there cannot be that fruitful interchange of minds which is indispensable to thoughtful, unhurried decision and its formulation in learned and impressive opinions." *Dick v. New York Life Ins. Co.*, 359 U. S. 437, 458-59 (1959) (dissenting opinion).

Independent appellate review necessarily entails a careful consideration of the district court's legal analysis, and an efficient and sensitive appellate court at least will naturally consider this analysis in undertaking its review. Petitioner readily acknowledges the importance of a district court's reasoning to the appellate court's review. Any expertise possessed by the district court will inform the structure and content of its conclusions of law and thereby become evident to the reviewing court. If the court of appeals finds that the district court's analytical sophistication and research have exhausted the state-law inquiry, little more need be said in the appellate opinion. Independent review, however, does not admit of unreflective reliance on a lower court's inarticulable intuitions. Thus, an appropriately respectful application of *de novo* review should encourage a district court to explicate with care the basis for its legal conclusions. See Fed. Rule Civ. Proc. 52(a) (requiring the district court to "state separately its conclusions of law").

Those circumstances in which Congress or this Court has articulated a standard of deference for appellate review of district-court determinations reflect an accommodation of the respective institutional advantages of trial and appellate courts. In deference to the unchallenged superiority of the district court's factfinding ability, Rule 52(a) commands that a trial court's findings of fact "shall not be set aside unless clearly erroneous, and due regard shall be given to the opportunity of the trial court to judge of the credibility of the witnesses." In addition, it is "especially common" for issues involving supervision of litigation to be reviewed for abuse of discretion. Finally, we have held that deferential review of mixed questions of law and fact is warranted when it appears that the district court is "better positioned" than the appellate court to decide the issue in question or that probing appellate scrutiny will not contribute to the clarity of legal doctrine.

Nothing about the exercise of diversity jurisdiction alters these functional components of decision-making or otherwise warrants departure from a rule of independent appellate review. Actually, appellate deference to the district court's determination of state law is inconsistent with the principles underlying this Court's decision in *Erie*. The twin aims of the *Erie* doctrine — "discouragement of forum-shopping and avoidance of inequitable administration of the laws" — are components of the goal of doctrinal coherence advanced by independent appellate review. As respondent has conceded, deferential appellate review invites divergent development of state law among the federal trial courts even within a single State. Moreover, by denying a litigant access to meaningful review of state-law claims, appellate courts that defer to the district courts' state-law determinations create a dual system of enforcement of state-created rights, in which the substantive rule applied to a dispute may depend on the choice of forum. Neither of these results, unavoidable in the absence of independent appellate review, can be reconciled with the command of *Erie*.

Although some might say that this Court has not spoken with a uniformly clear voice on the issue of deference to a district judge's determination of state law, a careful consideration of our cases makes apparent the duty of appellate courts to provide meaningful review of such a determination. In a series of cases decided soon after *Erie*, the Court noted that the appellate courts had applied general federal law instead of the law of the respective States, and remanded to the Courts of Appeals for consideration of the applicable principles of state law. It is true that in *Bernhardt v. Polygraphic Co. of America*, 350 U. S. 198 (1956), this Court remanded the case to the District Court for application of state law. The Court noted, however, that the law of the State was firmly settled, and emphasized: "Were the question in doubt or deserving further canvass, we would of course remand the case to the Court of Appeals to pass on this question of state law."

III

In urging this Court to adopt the deferential standard embraced by the majority of the Courts of Appeals, respondent offers two arguments. First, respondent suggests that the appellate courts professing adherence to the rule of deference actually are reviewing *de novo* the district-court determinations of state law. Second, respondent presses the familiar contention that district judges are better arbiters of unsettled state law because they have exposure to the judicial system of the State in which they sit. We reject each of these arguments.

A

Respondent primarily contends that the Courts of Appeals that claim to accord special consideration to the District Court's state-law expertise actually undertake plenary review of a determination of state law. According to respondent, this is simply *de novo* review "clothed in 'deferential' robes." In support of this contention, respondent refers to several decisions in which the appellate court has announced that it is bound to review deferentially a district court's determination of state law, yet nonetheless has found that determination to constitute reversible error. Respondent also relies on cases in which the Courts of Appeals, while articulating a rule of deference, acknowledge their obligation to scrutinize closely the District Court's legal conclusions.

We decline the invitation to assume that courts of appeals craft their opinions disingenuously. The fact that an appellate court overturns an erroneous determination of state law in no way indicates that the appellate court is not applying the rule of deference articulated in the opinion. The cases cited by respondent confirm this. . . .

Nor does it suffice to recognize that little substantive difference may separate the form of deference articulated and applied by the several Courts of Appeals and the independent appellate review urged by petitioner. Respondent argues that the subtle differences between these standards are insufficient to warrant intrusion into the manner in which appellate courts review state-law determinations. A variation of this argument forms the framework upon which the dissent in *McLinn* rests. See 739

F. 2d, at 1404 ("By giving 'substantial deference,' or 'great weight,' to the decisions of the district courts, appellate courts do not suspend their own thought processes").

As a practical matter, respondent and the dissent in *McLinn* frequently may be correct. We do not doubt that in many cases the application of a rule of deference in lieu of independent review will not affect the outcome of an appeal. In many diversity cases the controlling issues of state law will have been squarely resolved by the state courts, and a district court's adherence to the settled rule will be indisputably correct. In a case where the controlling question of state law remains unsettled, it is not unreasonable to assume that the considered judgment of the court of appeals frequently will coincide with the reasoned determination of the district court. Where the state-law determinations of the two courts diverge, the choice between these standards of review is of no significance if the appellate court concludes that the district court was clearly wrong.[4]

Thus, the mandate of independent review will alter the appellate outcome only in those few cases where the appellate court would resolve an unsettled issue of state law differently from the district court's resolution, but cannot conclude that the district court's determination constitutes clear error. These few instances, however, make firm our conviction that the difference between a rule of deference and the duty to exercise independent review is "much more than a mere matter of degree." When *de novo* review is compelled, no form of appellate deference is acceptable.

B

Respondent and her *amicus* also argue that *de novo* review is inappropriate because, as a general matter, a district judge is better positioned to determine an issue of state law than are the judges on the court of appeals. This superior capacity derives, it is said, from the regularity with which a district judge tries a diversity case governed by the law of the forum State, and from the extensive experience that the district judge generally has had as practitioner or judge in the forum State.

We are unpersuaded. As an initial matter, this argument seems to us to be founded fatally on overbroad generalizations. Moreover, and more important, the proposition that a district judge is better able to "intuit" the answer to an unsettled question of state law is foreclosed by our holding in *Erie*. The very essence of the *Erie* doctrine is that the bases of state law are presumed to be communicable by the parties to a federal judge no less than to a state judge. Almost 35 years ago, Professor Kurland stated: "Certainly, if the law is not a brooding omnipresence in the sky over the United States, neither is it a brooding omnipresence in the sky of Vermont, or New York or California." Similarly, the bases of state law are as equally communicable

---

4. Of course, a question of state law usually can be resolved definitively if the litigation is instituted in state court and is not finally removed to federal court, or if a certification procedure is available and is successfully utilized. Rhode Island provides a certification procedure.

See, however, *Lehman Brothers v. Schein*, 416 U. S. 386, 390-91 (1974) ("We do not suggest that where there is doubt as to local law and where the certification procedure is available, resort to it is obligatory. It does, of course, in the long run save time, energy, and resources and helps build a cooperative judicial federalism. Its use in a given case rests in the sound discretion of the federal court.").

to the appellate judges as they are to the district judge. To the extent that the available state law on a controlling issue is so unsettled as to admit of no reasoned divination, we can see no sense in which a district judge's prior exposure or nonexposure to the state judiciary can be said to facilitate the rule of reason.[5]

IV

The obligation of responsible appellate review and the principles of a cooperative judicial federalism underlying *Erie* require that courts of appeals review the state-law determinations of district courts *de novo*. The Court of Appeals in this case therefore erred in deferring to the local expertise of the District Court.

The judgment of the Court of Appeals is reversed, and the case is remanded for further proceedings consistent with this opinion.

It is so ordered.

CHIEF JUSTICE REHNQUIST, with whom JUSTICE WHITE and JUSTICE STEVENS join, dissenting.

I do not believe we need to delve into such abstractions as "deferential" review, on the one hand, as opposed to what the Court's opinion calls, at various places, "plenary," "independent," and "*de novo*" review, on the other, in order to decide this case. The critical language used by the Court of Appeals, and quoted in this Court's opinion, is this:

> "In view of the customary appellate deference accorded to interpretations of state law made by federal judges of that state, we hold that the district court's determination that the Rhode Island Supreme Court would apply standard contract principles is not reversible error."

In order to determine the Court of Appeals' views as to "customary appellate deference," it seems only fair to refer to the page in [one of the cases] to which the court cites. There we find this language:

> "In a diversity case such as this one, involving a technical subject matter primarily of state concern, we are 'reluctant to interfere with a reasonable construction of state law

---

5. "As a general proposition, a federal court judge who sits in a particular state, especially one who has practiced before its courts, may be better able to resolve complex questions as to the law of that state than is a federal judge who has no such personal acquaintance with the law of the state. For this reason, federal appellate courts frequently have voiced reluctance to substitute their own view of the state law for that of the district judge. As a matter of judicial administration, this seems defensible. But there is some tendency to go beyond that proposition and to say that if the trial court has reached a permissible conclusion under state law, the appellate court cannot reverse even if it thinks the state law to be otherwise, thereby treating the question of state law much as if it were a question of fact. The determination of state law, however, is a legal question, and although the considered decision of a district judge experienced in the law of a state naturally commands the respect of an appellate court, a party is entitled to meaningful review of that decision just as he is of any other legal question in the case, and just as he would have been if the case had been tried in a state court." 19 C. Wright, A. Miller, & E. Cooper, Federal Practice and Procedure § 4507, pp. 106-110 (1982).

made by a district judge, sitting in the state, who is familiar with that state's law and practices.'"

The court does not say that it *always* defers to a district court's conclusions of law. Rather, it states that it is reluctant to substitute its own view of state law for that of a judge "who is familiar with that state's law and practices." In this case, the court concluded that the opinion of a District Judge with 18 ½ years of experience as a trial judge was entitled to some appellate deference.

This seems to me a rather sensible observation. A district court's insights are particularly valuable to an appellate court in a case such as this where the state law is unsettled. In such cases, the courts' task is to try to *predict* how the highest court of that State would decide the question. A judge attempting to predict how a state court would rule must use not only his legal reasoning skills, but also his experiences and perceptions of judicial behavior in that State. It therefore makes perfect sense for an appellate court judge with no local experience to accord special weight to a local judge's assessment of state court trends.

If we must choose among Justice Holmes' aphorisms to help decide this case, I would opt for his observation that "the life of the law has not been logic: it has been experience." O. Holmes, The Common Law 1 (1881). And it does no harm to recall that the Members of this Court have no monopoly on experience; judges of the courts of appeals and of the district courts surely possess it just as we do. That the experience of appellate judges should lead them to rely, in appropriate situations, on the experience of district judges who have practiced law in the State in which they sit before taking the bench seems quite natural.

For this very reason, this Court has traditionally given special consideration or "weight" to the district judge's perspective on local law. See *Bernhardt v. Polygraphic Co. of America,* 350 U. S. 198, 204 (1956) ("Since the federal judge making those findings is from the Vermont bar, we give special weight to his statement of what the Vermont law is"); *United States v. Hohri,* 482 U. S. 64, 74 n. 6 (1987) ("Local federal district judges are likely to be familiar with the applicable state law. Indeed, a district judge's determination of a state-law question usually is reviewed with great deference"); *Bishop v. Wood,* 426 U. S. 341, 346, and n. 10 (1976) ("This Court has accepted the interpretation of state law in which the District Court and the Court of Appeals have concurred even if an examination of the state-law issue without such guidance might have justified a different conclusion").

But the Court today decides that this intuitively sensible deference is available only to this Court, and not to the courts of appeals. It then proceeds to instruct the courts of appeals and the district courts on their respective functions in the federal judicial system, and how they should go about exercising them. Questions of law are questions of law, they are told, whether they be of state law or federal law, and must all be processed through an identical decisional mold.

I believe this analysis unduly compartmentalizes things which have up to now been left to common sense and good judgment. Federal courts of appeals perform a different role when they decide questions of state law than they do when they decide questions of federal law. In the former case, these courts are not sources of law but only reflections of the jurisprudence of the courts of a State. While in deciding novel federal questions, courts of appeals are likely to ponder the policy implications as well as the decisional law, only the latter need be considered in deciding questions of state law. To my mind, therefore, it not only violates no positive law but also is a sensible allocation of resources to recognize these differences by deferring to the views of the district court where such deference is felt warranted.

I think we run a serious risk that our reach will exceed our grasp when we attempt to impose a rigid logical framework on the courts of appeals in place of a less precise but tolerably well-functioning approach adopted by those courts. I agree with the Court that a court of appeals should not "abdicate" its obligation to decide questions of state law presented in a diversity case. But by according weight to the conclusion of a particular district judge on the basis of his experience and special knowledge of state law, an appellate court does not "suspend its own thought processes." I think the Court of Appeals did no more than that here, and I therefore dissent from the reversal of its judgment.

Notes and Questions

1. What, if anything, marks the distinction between the Court's opinion and its adoption of an "independent appellate review" and that of the dissent? Consider in this context the Court's approval of an "appropriately respectful application of *de novo* review." What is that?

2. Since its decision in *Salve Regina*, the Court has been somewhat inconsistent in its own deference to lower federal courts on issues of federal law. Perhaps the most recent word can be found in *Town of Castle Rock v. Gonzales*, 545 U.S. 748 (2005), wherein the Court opined:

   > We have said that a "presumption of deference is given the views of a federal court as to the law of a State within its jurisdiction." That presumption can be overcome, however, and we think deference inappropriate here. The Tenth Circuit's opinion, which reversed the Colorado District Judge, did not draw upon a deep well of state-specific expertise, but consisted primarily of quoting language from the restraining order, the statutory text, and a state-legislative-hearing transcript. These texts, moreover, say nothing distinctive to Colorado, but use mandatory language that (as we shall discuss) appears in many state and federal statutes. As for case law: The only state-law cases about restraining orders that the Court of Appeals relied upon were decisions of Federal District Courts in Ohio and Pennsylvania and state courts in New Jersey, Oregon, and Tennessee. Moreover, if we were simply to accept the Court of Appeals' conclusion, we would necessarily have to decide conclusively a federal constitutional question .... We proceed, then, to our own analysis of whether Colorado law gave respondent a right to enforcement of the restraining order.

   Id. at 757-58. The Court's opinion was not unanimous on this point, though.

The majority's decision to plunge ahead with its own analysis of Colorado law imprudently departs from this Court's longstanding policy of paying "deference to the views of a federal court as to the law of a State within its jurisdiction." This policy is not only efficient, but it reflects "our belief that district courts and courts of appeals are better schooled in and more able to interpret the laws of their respective States." Accordingly, we have declined to show deference only in rare cases in which the court of appeals' resolution of state law was "clearly wrong" or otherwise seriously deficient.

Id. at 775 (Stevens, J., dissenting). Nonetheless, it appears that both the *Castle Rock* majority and dissent agreed that a presumption of deference is appropriate in at least some cases. Why, though, should the Supreme Court be allowed to defer, but the court of appeals not?

3. It seems reasonable to conclude, does it not, that federal judges likely have some superior understanding of the law of the state where they reside? After all, federal judges tend to be experienced lawyers, and with that experience often comes a deep understanding of local law. On the other hand, is there any reason to think that a judge sitting on the Court of Appeals for the Ninth Circuit in California would have any particular expertise with respect to Idaho state law simply because Idaho also lies in the Ninth Circuit? Or that nine Supreme Court Justices would not be better at discerning state law than a three-judge court of appeals panel (or a single-judge district court)? Is there ever an occasion for deferring to a lower court as to questions of law, questions that are usually reviewed de novo?

4. For a good summary of some of the issues in this area, see Aaron S. Bayer, *Home Circuit Rule*, Nat'l L.J. 12 (April 27, 2009). *See also* Jonathan Remy Nash, *Resuscitating Deference to Lower Federal Court Judges' Interpretations of State Law*, 77 S. Cal. L. Rev. 975 (2004).

Factors Etc., Inc. v. Pro Arts, Inc.

652 F.2d 278 (2d Cir. 1981)

Newman, Circuit Judge:

The merits of this appeal concern the interesting state law question whether [Elvis Presley] has a protected interest in publicizing his name and likeness after his death, or, as the matter has been put, is there a descendible right of publicity? Despite the fascination of this question, what divides the members of this panel and forms the basis for the majority's disposition of this appeal is the more esoteric question, apparently of first impression, concerning the deference a federal court exercising diversity jurisdiction should give to a ruling by a court of appeals deciding the law of a state within its circuit. Believing that conclusive deference should be given, except in certain situations not applicable here, we reverse the judgment of this case.

. . . .

The District Court, exercising its diversity jurisdiction, 28 U.S.C. § 1332 (1976), was obliged to apply the substantive law of the state to which the forum state, New York, would have turned had the suit been filed in state court. *Klaxon Co. v. Stentor Electric Manufacturing Co.*, 313 U.S. 487 (1941). . . .

. . . .

All members of the panel agree that we should turn to Tennessee law to determine what rights the Boxcar-Factors contract conveyed to Factors. We find, as the Sixth Circuit concluded in [*Memphis Development Foundation v. Factors Etc., Inc.*, 616 F.2d 956 (6th Cir.), *cert. denied*, 449 U.S. 953 (1980)], that Tennessee statutory and decisional law affords no answer to the question. We are thus brought to the issue that divides the panel: whether deference should be accorded to the decision in *Memphis Development.*

Somewhat to our surprise, there has been hardly a mention in the appellate reports of the appropriate deference a court of appeals should give to a decision made by the court of appeals in another circuit on the law of a state within that other circuit. It has frequently been observed that a court of appeals should give considerable weight to state law rulings made by district judges, within the circuit, who possess familiarity with the law of the state in which their district is located. The Supreme Court has expressed similar views concerning state law interpretations by a panel of circuit judges whose circuit includes the relevant state. *MacGregor v. State Mutual Life Assurance Co.*, 315 U.S. 280 (1942). But no case appears to have turned on whether one court of appeals should defer to another circuit as to the law of a state within that circuit.

In deciding *Memphis Development*, the Sixth Circuit was expounding Tennessee's version of the common law. It makes no difference that the Court was unable to find any Tennessee decisional law to guide its resolution of the issue before it, leaving it, as Judge Merritt candidly acknowledged, with "no way to assess" the predisposition of the Tennessee courts. The Sixth Circuit may have lacked any sure basis for predicting what the Tennessee courts would do and therefore felt obliged to make its decision "in the light of practical and policy considerations, the treatment of other similar rights in our legal system, the relative weight of the conflicting interests of the parties, and certain moral presuppositions concerning death, privacy, inheritability and economic opportunity." But this recourse to such general considerations did not alter the function that the Sixth Circuit was performing. In adjudicating a state-created right in the exercise of its diversity jurisdiction the Court was "for that purpose, in effect, only another court of the State." *Guaranty Trust Co. v. York*, 326 U.S. 99, 108 (1945). It had no power "to declare substantive rules of common law," *Erie Railroad Co. v. Tompkins*, 304 U.S. 64, 78 (1938); it could only declare the law of Tennessee. . . .

Of course reasonable minds may differ as to the preferable course that the common law of Tennessee ought to follow on the merits of Factors' claim. The writer would probably uphold a descendible right of publicity, were he serving on the Tennessee Supreme Court, and perhaps if he served on the Sixth Circuit when *Memphis Development* was decided. But the issue for this Court is not which view of the merits is wiser policy; it is whether, and under what circumstances, a ruling by a court of appeals, interpreting the common law of a state within its circuit, should be regarded as authoritative by the other federal courts of the nation. The answer is illuminated by consideration of the functioning of diversity jurisdiction.

One distinct shortcoming of diversity jurisdiction is the interruption of the orderly development and authoritative exposition of state law occasioned by sporadic federal court adjudications. Except in those few jurisdictions permitting a federal court to certify an unsettled question of state law to the state's highest court, a federal court's decision on state law cannot be corrected, for the benefit of the litigants in the particular case, by the state's authoritative tribunal. As long as diversity jurisdiction exists, this price must be paid. However, the opportunities for federal court departure from the normal paths of state law development should be held to a minimum, for the benefit of both the orderly development of state law and fairness to those subject to state law requirements. Both values are served by recognizing, within the federal system, the authoritativeness of decisions on the law of a particular state rendered by the court of appeals for the circuit in which the state is located. Orderly development is enhanced because the state legislature will know that the decision of the pertinent court of appeals will determine legal rights, unless superseded by a later state supreme court decision. This knowledge will focus state legislative efforts on the appropriateness of a statutory change. Fairness to the public is promoted by making clear that there is a single, authoritative answer to the particular state law issue, instead of leaving the matter subject to the varying interpretations of the courts of appeals for the several circuits.[6] If this Court were to disregard the Sixth Circuit's view and declare that Tennessee law recognizes a descendible right of publicity, what standard of conduct should guide Tennessee residents endeavoring to determine whether their publicity rights are to be valued only for a lifetime or beyond? Of course, lawyers frequently have to advise clients concerning unsettled issues of law, but the exercise of diversity jurisdiction should not add to their uncertainty. Diversity jurisdiction, especially in its post-*Erie* incarnation, should not create needless diversity in the exposition of state substantive law. . . .

We need not and do not conclude that the state law holdings of the pertinent court of appeals is automatically binding upon the federal courts of all the other circuits. The ultimate source for state law adjudication in diversity cases is the law as

---

6. Even if uniformity is achieved throughout the federal courts, the possibility remains that the courts of various states, obliged to consider Tennessee law because of their conflicts rules, might reach different predictions of Tennessee law. We think it more likely that state courts would share our interest in uniformity and accept a ruling by a pertinent federal court of appeals, subject to the same qualifications we adopt for ourselves. If in some instances a state court did not do so, that might lessen but would not eliminate the appropriateness of promoting uniform exercise of diversity jurisdiction within the federal court system. And the uniformity achieved for the period after the date of the decision of the pertinent federal court of appeals is not less worthy of achievement simply because prior to that decision other federal courts or courts of other states may have made different predictions about the course of Tennessee law. The possibility of these unavoidable departures from uniformity, just like decisions of federal or other state courts rendered before an authoritative ruling by the pertinent state's highest court, is an insufficient reason to create a needless departure from uniformity during what may be an extended period beginning after a decision by the pertinent federal court of appeals and ending, if at all, only in the event of a contrary decision by the pertinent state's highest court or legislature.

established by the constitution, statutes, or authoritative court decisions of the state. A federal court in another circuit would be obliged to disregard a state law holding by the pertinent court of appeals if persuaded that the holding had been superseded by a later pronouncement from state legislative or judicial sources, or that prior state court decisions had been inadvertently overlooked by the pertinent court of appeals. Neither circumstance exists in this case. Where, as here, the pertinent court of appeals has essayed its own prediction of the course of state law on a question of first impression within that state, the federal courts of other circuits should defer to that holding, perhaps always, and at least in all situations except the rare instance when it can be said with conviction that the pertinent court of appeals has disregarded clear signals emanating from the state's highest court pointing toward a different rule. However our sense of the common law might lead us to resolve the merits of this case were we judges of the Tennessee Supreme Court, as "outsiders" with respect to Tennessee law, we should defer to the views of the Sixth Circuit unless we can point to a clear basis in Tennessee law for predicting that the Tennessee courts, when confronted with a case such as this, would conclude that the Sixth Circuit's prediction was incorrect.[7] Since we are unable to find any such indication in Tennessee law, we accept *Memphis Development* as controlling authority and conclude that after Presley's death, Boxcar had no right of publicity in Presley's name and likeness to convey to Factors.

For these reasons the judgment of the District Court is reversed.

MANSFIELD, Circuit Judge (dissenting):

I respectfully dissent. I agree with the majority that . . . New York conflict of laws analysis would call for the application of Tennessee law to determine if Elvis Presley's right of publicity survived his death. However, with the utmost of respect for our distinguished and able colleagues on the Sixth Circuit, I see no warrant, if we disagree on the merits, for blindly following its decision in *Memphis Development* any more than we would defer to the decision of any other circuit court with which we might, as has occurred on numerous occasions, disagree or conflict. The reasoning of *Memphis Development* is not in any way derived from the local law of Tennessee. Its result is inconsistent with that of nearly every other case which has considered the issue, including the Sixth Circuit's own prior ruling on the preliminary injunction issued by the district court in *Memphis Development* and our opinion in *Factors I*. It is also contrary to all current views of scholarly commentators on the subject.

The majority starts with the proposition that deference is owed to the "interpretations" by a federal court of the law of a state within its jurisdiction, a principle with which I find no need to disagree. However, it then states that the "issue for the Court is whether, and under what circumstances, a ruling by a court of appeals, interpreting

---

7. As it happens, the author of *Memphis Development* is a distinguished member of the Tennessee bar, whose sense of what may be expected of the Tennessee Supreme Court surely surpasses our own. But since Judge Merritt's opinion so emphatically disclaims any basis for predicting how Tennessee will resolve the issue on the merits, we prefer to determine the authoritativeness of *Memphis Development* with regard to the territorial scope of the Sixth Circuit, rather than the heritage of the opinion's author.

the common law of a state within its circuit, should be recognized as authoritative by the other federal courts of the nation." With this statement of the issue I must disagree. Here there was *no interpretation of any* Tennessee law by the Sixth Circuit, only a declaration of what that court thought would be a preferable general common law rule for that state. The issue before us, therefore, is whether a federal court of appeals, called upon to anticipate what general common law rule with respect to a legal question might be appropriate for a state having no law whatsoever on the subject, must adhere to the diversity decision of a sister federal court of appeals within whose boundaries the state is located. Resolution of this issue requires us to look into the reasoning behind the policy of deference which the majority would apply and decide whether it is to be applied mechanically on a geographical basis or is instead subject to any limitations.

The weight given by higher federal courts to state law rulings made by federal judges sitting in that state results from the supposed greater familiarity that such a judge will have with the local law and the methods and tendencies of the state courts. . . .

To [some] extent a federal court of appeals might conceivably be considered to have more familiarity with the law of a state within its boundaries than would another federal court of appeals. Even this premise is open to serious question, however, for a number of reasons. Unlike a state court or a federal district court within a single state, the court of appeals of a circuit in which several states are located, which disposes of diversity appeals as only a small percentage of its business, is not likely to gain any special familiarity with the law of one of the states within its boundaries. The Sixth Circuit, for instance, physically encompasses seven different states. . . .

These facts weaken and, indeed, may even destroy the assumption that the able Sixth Circuit has some special knowledge or expertise in Tennessee law to which deference must be paid. In this case, for instance, it would be more logical to assume that, if familiarity with a particular state's law is to be the standard for deference, the United States district judge for the Western District of Tennessee, Judge Harry W. Wellford, who in a well reasoned opinion held Elvis Presley's property right in his name and image for commercial purposes to be descendible, had superior expertise with respect to Tennessee law. On the issue before us *MacGregor*, cited by the majority, is of no assistance for the reason that there the circuit court merely affirmed the "interpretation placed upon purely local law by a Michigan federal judge of long experience." Here, in contrast, the Sixth Circuit did not affirm Judge Wellford's decision, but reversed it.

Moreover, it is perfectly clear that the Sixth Circuit's decision in fact in no way depended on existent local law or methods. The opinion makes no effort, as is sometimes done, to determine what other states the Tennessee courts tend to look to, much less to be guided by analogous principles of Tennessee law. . . . We, however much "outsiders," are as fully qualified effectively to "declare" Tennessee law in such fashion as our sister circuit.

If under these circumstances we were able to bow to the Sixth Circuit's declaration of Tennessee law, it would have to be for reasons other than those underlying the usual deference given to federal judges who are experienced in the local law and practice of states located within their boundaries. The majority seeks to find such a basis in the overall "functioning of diversity jurisdiction." First it argues that recognizing the authoritativeness of the Sixth Circuit's ruling would enhance the "orderly development of state law." But our refusal to be bound by the Sixth Circuit here would not affect the development of Tennessee law at all. It is conceded as a matter of settled law that any Tennessee court decision or state legislation would wipe out the future significance of both *Memphis Development* and our decision. Moreover, the notion that consistency among the circuits will better "focus state legislative efforts on the appropriateness of a statutory change" is speculative at best and perhaps ill founded. If Tennessee constituents were laboring under conflicting federal court declarations of rights and duties, the legislature would be more likely to act sooner than if all decisions were consistent.

Second, while noting that lawyers must frequently advise clients concerning unsettled issues of law, the majority argues that failure to follow *Memphis Development* would promote uncertainty and "create needless diversity in the exposition of state substantive law." This ignores the fact that our development and formation of lasting rules of common law depends heavily on healthy differences of opinion. Soundness must not be sacrificed on the altar of consistency. If two members of this panel would "probably uphold a descendible right of publicity, were they sitting on the Tennessee Supreme Court," and the third would certainly do so, I think we should so hold rather than retreat behind unsupportable deferential niceties.

Even the consistency achieved under the majority's rule is fortuitous and arbitrary. Had the *Memphis Development* case arisen, for example, in the Ninth Circuit and had that circuit, without reference to Tennessee law or practice, declared that Tennessee law should not allow descendibility, would we be required to follow that version unless we could prove it wrong on some local basis overlooked by the Ninth Circuit? Apparently the majority, which would "determine the authoritativeness of *Memphis Development* with regard to the territorial scope of the Sixth Circuit," would agree that such a Ninth Circuit decision would be entitled to no more weight than the usual persuasive authority of a sister circuit with which, for good reason, we might disagree. The only difference here, where the Sixth Circuit eschewed any Tennessee law basis for its declaration, is that its physical geography includes that state. In my view the lack of logic behind the majority's geographical reasoning is further demonstrated by the fact that if we had stated our holding in *Factors I* to be a declaration of our view of Tennessee law, which we would certainly have done if the parties had not at that time agreed that New York law governed, the Sixth or any other circuit would have been free to take a contrary view and thus create the very inconsistency which the majority seeks to avoid.

In the unusual situation here, where an initial court of appeals diversity declaration is in no way derived from the law or practice of the state and interprets no existing state law, we should feel free to reach a different result if sound reasons recommend it, regardless of the unpersuasive views of a sister circuit from which the initial declaration emanated. Where, as here, the Sixth Circuit itself had no Tennessee law basis for its choice and we are persuaded that other reasons dictate a contrary decision (or prediction), there is no logical justification for a rule that would permit us to depart from the Sixth Circuit's views only upon a showing of "a clear *basis in Tennessee law* for predicting that the Sixth Circuit's prediction was incorrect."

Turning to the merits, sound principles commend a different result from that reached in *Memphis Development* on the issue of whether Elvis Presley's right of publicity survived his death. . . .

. . . .

For the reasons outlined I believe that Factors did have a valid and enforceable property right in the commercialization of Presley's persona and would therefore affirm the judgment of the district court granting it relief.

Notes and Questions

---

1. Which opinion do you find more persuasive — the majority, or the dissent? Why? Incidentally, in 1984, Tennessee amended its code to provide for a descendible right of publicity. *See* TENN. CODE ANN. §§ 47-25-1103 to -1104 (2010). Does this change your answer to the preceding questions? And do you believe the majority's view survives *Salve Regina* and its progeny? Why or why not?

2. How much weight, if any, should federal courts give to "foreign" state courts as to the law of another state? For example, should a federal court defer in any way to a decision by the Supreme Court of Georgia as to an issue of Florida law?

3. How much weight, if any, should state courts give to federal court rulings as to the law of that state? For example, should a Florida state court defer in any way to a decision by the United States Court of Appeals for the Eleventh Circuit (which encompasses Florida) as to an issue of Florida law? How about a decision by the United States Court of Appeals for the Ninth Circuit?

5. Certification to Another Court

The Court in *Salve Regina* mentioned the possibility of a federal court "certifying" questions of state law to a state court. What does "certify" mean? How does it work? Consider the following articles.

Jonathan Remy Nash

THE UNEASY CASE FOR TRANSJURISDICTIONAL ADJUDICATION

94 Va. L. Rev. 1869 (2008)

INTRODUCTION

Federal courts often are called upon to decide cases that include matters of state law, while state courts often are called upon to decide cases that raise matters of both federal and state law. The vast bulk of these cases are decided within the court system in which the cases originate, without the benefit of input from the other court system. In these cases of "intersystemic adjudication," the court system that decides the case will try to resolve "foreign" legal questions in the way that the other court system would by considering rulings from the other court system that have addressed the issue in question. Thus, under intersystemic adjudication, a court in one system undertakes to interpret issues arising under the laws of another system.

Recent commentary by academics and judges, however, suggests that the best way to resolve these cases is to have each court system definitively resolve those issues that arise under that court system's "native" law. These commentators advocate expanded use of what I shall call "transjurisdictional adjudication"—that is, the use of procedural devices that allow a court in one system to answer questions of law arising under that system's law in cases that are pending before courts in another system. Transjurisdictional adjudication and intersystemic adjudication constitute different approaches to "intersystemic judicial governance," that is, judicial adjudication of issues arising under more than one system of laws. In contrast to intersystemic adjudication, under transjurisdictional adjudication, a court in one system faced with a question arising under a second system's laws seeks an interpretation of that question from a court in the second system rather than conducting the interpretation itself.

. . . .

I. RESOLVING ISSUES ARISING UNDER ANOTHER SYSTEM'S LAW

State courts are often called upon to decide matters of federal law,[6] and federal courts are often called upon to decide matters of state law.[7] Both state and federal courts also may be called upon to decide cases in which state law causes of action implicate issues of, or are intertwined with, federal law,[8] or federal law causes of action that implicate issues of state law.[9]

When these situations arise, there are a few procedural devices that afford substantial opportunities for transjurisdictional dialogue and adjudication: certiorari review, abstention, and certification. By discretionary grant of certiorari, the

---

6. While settings in which courts of one state endeavor to discern the law of a sister state raise questions analogous to those I address here, they lie beyond the scope of this Article.

7. First, federal diversity jurisdiction authorizes—indeed, demands—that federal courts hear some cases in which issues of state law alone arise. Second, federal courts often hear state law causes of action that are supplemental to causes of action that arise under federal law. Third, it is possible that federal and state law are intertwined: state law might incorporate or implicate federal law, or federal law might incorporate or implicate state law.

8. For example, states often interpret state constitutional provisions to incorporate the legal standards of their federal analogs.

9. For example, the Supreme Court has held that the question of whether the Takings Clause applies to a property interest is not resolved by reference to the Takings Clause, but rather by reference to some independent source of law, such as state law.

Supreme Court has the power to review state courts' determinations of federal law. In order for the Court to review the case, the losing party must petition for a writ of certiorari, and then the Court must accept that petition and determine the scope of review. The state court has no discretion to request Supreme Court review, nor to deny review if the Court chooses to review the case. Further, remedies are available to the Court to address a state court's failure to abide by the Court's mandate. In a case in which some issues arise under state law and others under federal law, the Supreme Court will consider only those issues that arise under federal law (or, to the extent that the grant of certiorari is narrower, some subset thereof). Thus, the federal judicial system adjudicates the issues of federal law, while determinations of state law are left as the state courts resolved them.

There are also two other transjurisdictional procedural devices, abstention and certification, which offer federal courts the opportunity to obtain direct feedback from the state court system as to the appropriate resolution of state law issues. Under abstention, the federal court abstains from proceeding with the case in federal court to allow a pending state court case to resolve the state law issues in the federal court case, or to allow the parties to file such an action in state court. If the parties seek an *England* reservation and ask the federal court to retain jurisdiction over any remaining federal issues (and probably even if they object to the state court's attempt to resolve federal issues), the state court's jurisdiction will be limited to resolving the state law issues. The most commonly used form of abstention, *Pullman* abstention, is available only in cases where resolution of the state law questions might relieve the court of the need to confront unclear issues of federal constitutional law. While there are other forms of abstention that can apply in pure diversity cases, these abstention devices are quite limited in scope.

Certification is a procedural device that achieves the same result as abstention.[19] It is available in cases in which *Pullman* abstention can be invoked, as well as in pure diversity cases. Certification is also more streamlined than *Pullman* abstention, as the question of state law proceeds directly to the state's high court.

. . . .

Certiorari review, abstention, and certification thus each provide opportunities for transjurisdictional adjudication.[26] These devices are limited, however, in terms

---

19. In one way, the result achieved under certification is even greater: under certification it is guaranteed that the state high court will resolve the state law issue definitively (assuming that court agrees to answer the certified questions). By contrast, because state high courts generally retain the discretion to deny review of lower state court rulings, a state high court might never hear the case under abstention, with the lower state courts effectively providing the resolution.

26. These devices are among the few situations in which direct federal-state transjurisdictional dialogue and interaction are possible. One also might add federal court habeas review of state criminal convictions under 28 U.S.C. § 2254 to this mix. Habeas cases, however, are in the nature of collateral review, meaning that the federal court entry occurs only after the state court has rendered a final judgment. Thus, although they entail some measure of direct dialogue, that dialogue is decidedly one-sided.

Removal of cases to federal court is more complicated. Removal of federal question cases allows federal courts to resolve issues arising under federal law. The removal will generally apply to the entire case, however, so that state courts will lose the ability to resolve issues of state law to the extent that the case raises such issues.

of both scope and current use. Typically, then, state courts must resolve federal law issues without help from the federal judiciary,[27] and federal courts must resolve state law issues on their own.[28]

Jonathan Remy Nash

EXAMINING THE POWER OF FEDERAL COURTS TO CERTIFY QUESTIONS OF STATE LAW

88 Cornell L. Rev. 1672 (2003)

A federal court is frequently called upon to determine matters of state law. In such situations, the federal court must divine how the state's high court would decide the state law question at issue. On their own, federal courts can at best make only educated guesses as to how a state high court would decide an issue of state law. Thus, federal courts have often ruled on issues of state law only to be "corrected" subsequently by state high courts.

Most state high courts now offer federal courts faced with questions of state law, as well as similarly situated state courts, the opportunity to "certify" those questions to the state high courts. The state high court returns to the certifying court answers to the certified questions. With the issues of state law resolved, the certifying federal court presumably is then able to render judgment in the case in accordance with properly interpreted state law.

Certification advances the interests of the states and their courts, as well as the interests of the federal courts. States are assured that state law will be applied uniformly and in accordance with the interpretations given by each state's high court. State courts enjoy the benefit of having the final say on matters of state law. Federal courts are able to avoid the awkward, tenuous, and difficult chore of attempting to determine how a state high court would rule on a matter of state law. Indeed, from the viewpoint of federalism, certification's salutary effects are clear. For this reason, certification has become increasingly popular since its inception half a century ago.[8]

. . . .

27. State courts are bound by Supreme Court precedent on federal law and also by any decisions on federal law by a higher-ranked state court whose decisions would ordinarily be binding upon the state court. The state court also might look to lower federal courts' interpretations of [federal] law and interpretations of courts of other states, both of which might be persuasive.

28. The Court's decision in *Erie Railroad Co. v. Tompkins* does, however, mandate that federal courts decide state law issues in accordance with the laws of the state, as set out by the state legislature and judicial system.

8. Florida enacted the first statute that contemplated certification of questions to its supreme court in 1945. The device was not used, however, until 1960. Today, most states, as well as the District of Columbia and Puerto Rico, provide (whether through statute or court rule) authority for certification to their highest courts of questions of state law by federal courts.

Certification is designed to mitigate the problem of state courts' inability to decide definitively issues of state law arising in cases heard in federal court. The federal system at times calls upon state courts to hear cases that raise issues of federal law, and upon federal courts to hear cases that raise issues of state law. To the extent that state courts are called upon to determine matters of federal law, the United States Supreme Court has the power to hear appeals from such determinations, thereby affording it the opportunity to rectify erroneous interpretations and to ensure uniform application of federal law. The Court thus has the prerogative to be the final arbiter of disputes arising under federal law.

State high courts do not enjoy the same prerogative with respect to state law. Under *Erie Railroad Co. v. Tompkins,* federal courts faced with questions of state law are obligated to apply state law in the way, at best it can determine, that the state high court would. Accordingly, it is often said a state's highest court is the definitive authority of the law of that state, much as the United States Supreme Court is the definitive authority of federal law. This statement, however, may be somewhat misleading because, unlike the United States Supreme Court, state high courts often do not enjoy the right to rule definitively in all cases involving state law. Indeed, in most federal court cases involving issues of state law, no state court has any opportunity to rule upon the state law questions at issue.

Certification provides some remedy to state high courts in that it gives them the opportunity to provide definitive interpretations on matters of state law in federal court cases. It is the most common method affording states such an opportunity. Under certification procedure, a federal court "certifies" to a state's high court a question or questions of state law with which it is faced and upon which it would like the state court to rule.[19] The state court then responds to the question if it wishes.

. . . .

C. OVERVIEW OF THE CERTIFICATION PROCEDURE

Certification involves one court system enlisting the aid of a second court system to resolve a case, while affording the second court system the opportunity to announce a rule of law. The jurisprudence of certification reflects this judicial interdependence.

Assuming certification is an available option,[74] one or more of the parties to the federal case may request that the federal court invoke certification, or the federal

19. State laws vary as to which federal courts are authorized to certify questions to the state high court. In addition, some states permit courts of other states to certify questions of state law to the state high court.

74. As a threshold matter, certification of a question of state law will be an available option to a federal court only if the state whose law is at issue offers a certification procedure for the federal court to exercise. A federal court will not ask a state high court to respond to any questions of state law if there is no procedure under state law that authorizes certification. A more difficult question is whether federal courts might have the *power* to certify questions in the absence of a state certification procedure.

court may choose that option *sua sponte.* Either way, the federal court has final discretion over whether or not to employ certification. It is the federal court, not the parties, that invokes the procedure by promulgating and sending to the state high court a certificate that sets forth the questions of state law for which answers are sought. The certifying court normally includes a statement of the necessary background facts to provide context for the certified questions.

A state high court has discretion to accept or reject the certifying court's question. Assuming it chooses to accept the certification, the state high court proceeds in accordance with any governing statutes or rules. State courts considering certified questions do not engage in fact finding. Certification applies only to questions of law; thus, state courts have treated the collection by the certifying federal court of all necessary ancillary factual findings as a prerequisite to proper certification.

The state high court's involvement ends when it returns answers to the question or questions certified to the certifying court. Federal courts were initially uncertain as to whether a state court's response to a certified question bound the certifying court with respect to the question certified. . . . Although statements to the contrary have not disappeared entirely, modern federal courts generally agree that they are bound to follow state court responses to certified questions. The federal courts predominately base this view on the belief that *Erie* and its progeny require them to follow the answers rendered by state high courts in response to certified questions. However, a few opinions reach the same result via an alternative reasoning: these courts hold that state high court opinions are to be followed under the "law of the case" doctrine.

D. COSTS AND BENEFITS OF CERTIFICATION

Certification is generally viewed as furthering the interests of judicial federalism. Moreover, many commentators laud the procedure for imposing fewer costs on litigants than alternative systems with similar goals, such as abstention. While this may be true, certification costs, both temporal and monetary, are not insignificant. Indeed, a minority of commentators suggest that the procedure's costs outweigh its benefits. . . .

One benefit of certification is that it furthers the interests associated with judicial federalism. First, the procedure offers benefits to states in general, and to state judicial systems in particular. The prerogative of a state government to establish and define its own state law is enhanced by such a procedure, and it gives the state judiciary the opportunity to rule on important issues of state law in cases in which it might not otherwise have had the chance. Second, certification offers a federalism benefit to federal courts. Insofar as it allows a state court to determine pertinent issues of state law, certification spares a federal court the difficult chore of determining state law. Moreover, certification offers three benefits that abstention does not. First, it guarantees that the state's highest court — the only court capable of rendering a "definitive" statement of state law under *Erie* and its progeny — will decide the state law question where the state court accepts the certified question. Second, certification avoids procedural complications that might hinder the state court system's resolution of the state law question were abstention employed.

Third, certification offers a federalism benefit to litigants in the form of "fairness." Specifically, it provides federal court litigants the benefit of a resolution of their case based upon definitive state law, as determined by the state high court.

Although it does provide federalism benefits, certification does not uniformly advance the interests of judicial federalism. First, to the extent that one believes that diversity jurisdiction intentionally allows certain cases to be heard in a federal forum in order to avoid the possibility or appearance of bias that likely would be found in a state forum, certification hinders federalism because it may undermine that design by rechanneling cases to the state courts. As the Court explained in *Meredith,* the federal courts should not lightly shirk their responsibility to fulfill their "duty, if their jurisdiction is properly invoked, to decide questions of state law whenever necessary to the rendition of a judgment."

Second, Geri Yanover argues that federal courts' attempts to predict state law has a salutary impact on the subsequent development of state law. Third, James Rehnquist broadly criticizes the abstention doctrine on the ground that the Constitution remains neutral as to whether a federal or state forum is preferable in any particular case. As such, he argues that there is no federal interest in abstaining from hearing a pending case unless a case that raises identical issues was already filed in state court. Fourth, Judge Bruce Selya argues that certification's "fairness" benefit is generally overvalued and somewhat ephemeral. He notes that a litigant who loses a case by virtue of a federal court's ruling on state law, which ultimately is revealed to be flawed in a subsequent decision of the relevant state high court, "is no more greatly disadvantaged than a litigant who loses in a lower state court and is thereafter denied discretionary review, only to have the state's high court decide the issue favorably in some other case at a later date." Judge Selya further notes that, "more generally, litigants do not have an entitlement to something identifiable in the abstract as a 'right' answer."

Notwithstanding the above listed criticisms, the majority of commentators agree that certification furthers several highly valued federalism interests, and poll results show that this is also the view of a majority of federal and state judges. By contrast, the value of certification from the perspective of judicial economy and cost to litigants, both temporal and monetary, is subject to greater disagreement. As a threshold matter, it seems indisputable that, given a choice between abstention and certification, the latter procedure imposes less cost than does the former. . . .

Despite general recognition that the delay inherent in certification is less than the delay inherent in *Pullman* abstention, some commentators assert that the delay under certification is generally underestimated or undervalued by courts and in fact argues for more judicious use of the procedure. Generally, however, this is the minority view. Overall, the legal community views certification favorably; in particular the reaction of members of the federal and state judiciaries is overwhelmingly positive.

. . . However, it should be noted that the federalism benefits which certification offers mirror the reasons for eliminating or at least restricting the federal diversity jurisdiction. If one accepts the advisability of retaining the federal diversity jurisdiction, then the federalism benefit it provides must outweigh the benefits of restricting.

Notes and Questions

1. As the above articles indicate, certification, for a number of reasons, has become quite popular as a means by which a federal court may obtain "definitive" rulings by state high courts as to the meaning of state law. *See* Nash at 1682 ("Today, certification is the primary method by which federal courts faced with undecided questions of state law are able to enlist the aid of state courts to resolve those questions."). Nonetheless: "Neither the Supreme Court nor any other federal court has addressed in any detail either the federal jurisdictional basis for certification or the propriety, in light of the constitutional and statutory grants of diversity jurisdiction, of certification in pure diversity cases where no questions of federal law can be found." *Id.* at 1690. As Professor Nash also points out, "[t]ransjurisdictional adjudication is not the panacea that the commentators sometimes paint it to be." *Id.* at 1737.

2. Others have expressed mixed feelings about certification as well. For example, Justin Long explains:

> Previous scholarship on certified questions has generally focused on weighing its advantages and drawbacks, overwhelmingly from a federal perspective and mostly favorable to the practice. For example, one commonly cited advantage of certification is that it offers less delay and expense than federal court abstention, for both the parties and the courts. Because certification permits the litigants to short-circuit the ordinary state-court hierarchy by going directly to the state high court, it can save years of time and thousands of dollars in attorneys' fees. Certification, contrasted with abstention, also reduces the financial burden for the state courts, because only one court, the state's highest, would have to consider the issue. Despite the lower cost, certification promotes the same policies underlying abstention while still protecting federal-court jurisdiction over state law claims. . . . If a federal forum for diversity actions is a sound policy choice because of the potential for bias against out-of-state litigants in state courts, then certification is superior to abstention for protecting the federal interest at stake. Another common argument for certification avoids the risk that the federal court might get the law "wrong," by deciding the law in a way differently from how its authoritative interpreter would. Regardless of any other effects, at least the party that was denied its state law victory is harmed by a judgment that later proves contrary to the state high court's final holding. Furthermore, federal judges have expressed "embarrassment" when their predictions of unsettled state law turn out to be mistaken. Without certification or abstention, there is no avenue for state high court review of a potentially erroneous federal decision based on state law. Also, commentators have noted that certification avoids the risk of a federal court's possibly mistaken view of state law influencing the development of that law by opining before the state high court has had a chance to address the question. This influence might be seen as overbearing, given that state courts have a clear entitlement to shape the contours of their own law in their own fashion.
>
> Furthermore, variations between state and federal interpretations of state law open opportunities for forum shopping, the original flaw in state and federal

concurrent jurisdiction that *Erie* meant to discourage. Plaintiffs can choose where to file, and defendants can choose whether to remove, based on strategic considerations of how the lower state and federal courts have treated the open question of state law in the case. Certification's advocates contend that the procedure short-circuits this invidious forum shopping by allowing the state high court to declare the content of state law no matter in which forum the lawsuit started.

Justin R. Long, *Against Certification*, 78 GEO. WASH. R. REV. 114, 117-19 (2009). But in response to these arguments, Professor Long counters:

The initial argument that certification reduces courts' and litigants' expense seems not to affect the balance of respect between state and federal courts. This is because certification is more costly (to litigants and the courts) than a direct federal resolution of the state law matter, but is less costly than abstention. If certification's advocates are correct in arguing that federal courts show respect to states by asking state high courts to resolve state law issues, certification is a cheaper method of expressing respect than abstention. On the other hand, if . . . federal courts best express respect for states by resolving state law issues themselves, then both certification and abstention generally undermine those goals. The matter of expense does little to answer the ultimate question of state-federal comity.

In contrast, the argument that certification saves federal courts from reaching conclusions of state law that later fail upon state high-court consideration does affect the federal courts' purported expressions of comity. Federal courts' "wrong" interpretation of state law undeniably works to the detriment of one of the parties. An answer to a certified question would clearly solve that problem. But federal litigants are no more harmed by a view of state law that later turns out to be different than are litigants in the lower state courts confronted with the same circumstances. And state high courts are not generally in the business of error correction, any more than is the U.S. Supreme Court. The notion that a state high court should be more solicitous of the state-law rights of federal litigants than it would be of state litigants need only to be stated to reveal its federal-favoring slant. In fact, there is less reason for a state high court to accept a certified question in these circumstances than there is reason for the high court to accept review of state lower-court decisions to correct error. If the federal appellate court is mistaken about state law, its decision is precedential only over federal courts, and only to the extent federal law requires. In contrast, a state intermediate appellate court's application of the law to particular facts, even if rejected in subsequent litigation, can still be a precedential statement of state law (as to lower state courts and, to some extent, to federal courts) until the high court speaks.

Furthermore, the argument that certification is laudable for saving federal appellate courts from the "embarrassment" of getting state law "wrong" also fails. . . . If federal circuit courts and state high courts are "two households, both alike in dignity"—i.e., if the two institutions are equal in status as to state law interpretation—then the state court's later rejection of a doctrine announced in the federal forum is, indeed, a bit of an affront. Polite peers do not publicly display the unbalanced power one has over the other. If, in contrast, the federal courts sitting in diversity really did think of themselves as "inferior" courts for the sake of state law development, with the state high court as their supervising authority, there would be no more "embarrassment" about having a federal opinion overruled when the same issue percolated up to the state court in later litigation than there is now when the U.S. Supreme Court rejects a lower court interpretation of unsettled federal law.

Nor does a decision not to certify logically subvert the state courts' ability to craft their own law through overbearing federal influence. Although state courts often do rely on persuasive federal precedent in construing and constructing their own law, they have also proven an intermittent willingness to break from federal decisions they disfavor. To the extent state courts are cowed by federal decisions into reaching a state law result they otherwise would not, certification does offer a chance to write on a clean slate before the federal courts can influence the outcome. The argument's presumption of state court pliability, however, hardly expresses the sort of respect for state courts' control over state law that certification purportedly conveys. Indeed, some state high courts might prefer to have a federal court's ruminations on a matter before deciding it, much as high courts often prefer to let an issue percolate before reviewing it.

A final common argument for certification — avoidance of forum-shopping opportunities — also falters upon closer examination. First, and most plainly, the mere existence of diversity jurisdiction in the federal courts necessarily means at least some opportunity for forum shopping (to take advantage of federal jury-selection rules, or federal judges' perceived quality or independence, or federal docket speeds, etc.). In fact, Congress *intended* a difference between state and federal court resolution of claims in diversity, so as to protect out-of-state litigants from state-court bias. In addition, the opportunity for inconsistency exists only until the state high court decides the relevant question, because federal courts decline to decide their jurisdiction over state-law questions only where the state law is unclear. Furthermore, state high courts seem to accept certified questions more easily than they accept petitions for appeal from the lower state courts, which (paradoxically) suggests that litigants presenting open and important questions of state law who want the state high court to resolve their claim might be better off filing first in federal court, at least if federal courts are strongly inclined to certify questions of that sort. In any event, litigants who want a federal jury over a state law jury, or vice versa, will be unaffected by whether the ultimate legal questions are certified or not. Finally, even if certification does lead to an incremental decrease in undesirable forum shopping, state high courts do not (and should not) always value the uniformity of state law across state and federal courts over other concerns, such as concentrating on the best resolution to their own cases.

Id. at 120-24. Professor Long concludes that certification should only be used "where quirks of jurisdiction make impossible (or very unlikely) state-forum litigation over certain state law areas." *Id.* at 167.

Admittedly, the variations between state and federal court interpretations of the same questions of law can result in costs, including lack of uniformity, reduced judicial accountability, and slower development of finality in the law. While these costs are real, they do not outweigh the advantages of interactive federalism. . . .

First, in the absence of certification, different courts can reach different conclusions about the meaning of a particular law. If competing interpretations of the same issue prevail in the different fora, then litigants obtain a forum-shopping opportunity. However, the increase in potential forum shopping appears merely marginal. Even within a single system, like a single state's judiciary, lower courts might reach competing interpretations of a state-law question that had not yet been definitively resolved by the state high court. Of course, if the relevant question *has* been definitively resolved, then there would be no opportunity for forum shopping in either the lower state or federal courts; they simply apply the announced law. Courts also exhibit tolerance for forum shopping in other contexts. Plaintiffs often retain some discretion to frame a claim as either federal or state, thereby permitting them to pick their forum. Furthermore, defendants satisfying federal jurisdictional limits can choose to remove a case to federal court or not, according to their tactical judgment. The prevalence and acceptance of forum shopping by these means suggests that even relatively weak norms (like the norm that a plaintiff is "master" of the complaint) can overcome the intuition against permitting strategic choice of courts.

In addition, . . . [a]fter the federal court reaches a holding on state law, the losing party has no opportunity to appeal to a court with final authority over that state-law issue. This means that the fear of reversal that normally provides an incentive for lower court judges to attend carefully to state high court holdings does not apply. Like the forum-shopping objection, this objection seems to be founded on a very weak norm: the principle that litigants should have access to a final determination of the law in their cases from the highest court with relevant authority. Litigants in federal court, presenting federal questions, are denied the opportunity for a final and definitive declaration of the law from its final arbiter every time the U.S. Supreme Court denies certiorari. Similarly, in states with discretionary high-court review, litigants in the lower state courts are often denied the opportunity to get a definitive declaration of the law. If a federal court consistently applies a state-law interpretation inconsistent with prior holdings of the state high court, then other litigants will ordinarily bring actions in state court and the state high court will eventually have an opportunity to clarify its precedents.

Id. at 150-51.

3. According to a recent study, only North Carolina and Missouri lack a certification procedure. *See* Eric Eisenberg, Note, *A Divine Comity: Certification (At Last) in North Carolina*, 58 DUKE L.J. 69, 71 n.13 (2008).

4. Many state certification procedures are based on the Uniform Certification of Questions of Law Act, 12 U.L.A. 67 (1996).

5. Though certification is usually utilized by the district courts and the courts of appeals, it is sometimes utilized by the Supreme Court as well. For a recent example of certification by the Supreme Court, see *United States v. Juvenile Male*, 131 S. Ct. 2860 (2011) (certifying a question of Montana law to the Montana Supreme Court).

6. At least one federal court of appeals has held that "a court of appeals panel decision on a question of state law . . . prevents a subsequent panel from certifying that question to the state supreme court, because the only purpose of certifying the question to the state court would be to revisit the prior panel's decision, which is generally forbidden." 18 JAMES WM. MOORE, MOORE'S FEDERAL PRACTICE § 134.02[1][c], at 13421 (3d ed. 2008). Does this practice make sense? Why or why not?

7. *Certifying questions of federal law.* The Supreme Court of the United States is authorized to accept certified questions of *federal* law from the United States Court of Appeals pursuant to 28 U.S.C. § 1254(2) (2006). *See also* S. Ct. R. 19 (describing the procedure relating to such certification). Yet despite statutory authorization, the Supreme Court seems to disfavor the certification of federal questions. "Indeed, between 1946 and 2006 the Court accepted only four certifications." EUGENE GRESSMAN ET AL., SUPREME COURT PRACTICE 596 (9th ed. 2007). The Court's current attitude appears to be summarized by the following passage from *Wisniewski v. United States*, 353 U.S. 901 (1957), a per curiam decision dismissing a certificate from the United States Court of Appeals for the Eighth Circuit:

   > It is also the task of a Court of Appeals to decide all properly presented cases coming before it, except in the rare instances, as for example the pendency of another case before this Court raising the same issue, when certification may be advisable in the proper administration and expedition of judicial business.

   Id. at 902.

   There are some indications that the Court's attitude with respect to certification might be beginning to thaw, though. In *United States v. Seale*, 130 S. Ct. 12 (2009), Justice Stevens, joined by Justice Scalia, issued a statement regarding the dismissal of the certified question in that case. At the conclusion of the statement, Justice Stevens wrote:

   > The certification process has all but disappeared in recent decades. The Court has accepted only a handful of certified cases since the 1940s and none since 1981; it is a newsworthy event these days when a lower court even tries for certification. Section 1254(2) and this Court's Rule 19 remain part of our law because the certification process serves a valuable, if limited, function. We ought to avail ourselves of it in an appropriate case.

   Id. at 13.

   For a recent article advocating an increased use of certification to the Supreme Court of the United States, see Amanda L. Tyler, *Setting the Supreme Court's Agenda: Is There a Place for Certification?*, 78 GEO. WASH. L. REV. 1310 (2010).

8. In contrast to the ability of federal courts to certify questions of state law to state courts, state courts do not have the ability to certify questions of federal law to any federal court. One reason might be the belief that such a procedure would result in an advisory opinion by the federal court in contravention of Article III of the United States Constitution. *See* Bruce M. Selya, *Certified Madness: Ask a Silly Question . . .* , 29 SUFFOLK U. L REV. 677, 685-86 (1995). Another possible justification relates to the ability of the United States Supreme Court to accept review of issues of state law in cases on appeal from state courts. *See* 28 U.S.C. § 1257 (2006).

9. One legal scholar has proposed that questions of *statutory* ambiguity be certified to Congress. *See* Amanda Frost, *Certifying Questions to Congress*, 101 Nw. U. L. REV. 1 (2007).

6. Horizontal Stare Decisis

In the federal court system (as well as most state systems), not only do higher court decisions bind lower courts; they also bind the decisional court itself, though to a lesser extent. In this section, we will look first at how federal courts (primarily the Supreme Court) apply horizontal stare decisis in practice. Then we will look at the theoretical side of this fascinating issue.

a. Stare Decisis in Practice

Though the Supreme Court invokes stare decisis frequently, the doctrine is perhaps best summarized by a trio of cases decided over two decades ago: *Patterson v. McLean Credit Union*, 491 U.S. 164 (1989); *Payne v. Tennessee*, 501 U.S. 808 (1991); and *Planned Parenthood v. Casey*, 505 U.S. 833 (1992).

Patterson v. McLean Credit Union
491 U.S. 164 (1989)

JUSTICE KENNEDY delivered the opinion of the Court.

. . . .

We granted certiorari to decide whether petitioner's claim of racial harassment in her employment is actionable under [42 U.S.C.] § 1981, and whether the jury instruction given by the District Court on petitioner's § 1981 promotion claim was error. After oral argument on these issues, we requested the parties to brief and argue an additional question:

> "Whether or not the interpretation of 42 U. S. C. § 1981 adopted by this Court in *Runyon v. McCrary*, 427 U. S. 160 (1976), should be reconsidered."

We now decline to overrule our decision in *Runyon*. . . .

II

In *Runyon*, the Court considered whether § 1981 prohibits private schools from excluding children who are qualified for admission, solely on the basis of race. We held that § 1981 did prohibit such conduct, noting that it was already well established in prior decisions that § 1981 "prohibits racial discrimination in the making and enforcement of private contracts." The arguments about whether *Runyon* was decided correctly in light of the language and history of the statute were examined and discussed with great care in our decision. It was recognized at the time that a strong case could be made for the view that the statute does not reach private conduct, but that view did not prevail. Some Members of this Court believe that *Runyon* was decided incorrectly, and others consider it correct on its own footing, but the question before us is whether it ought now to be overturned. We conclude after reargument that *Runyon* should not be overruled, and we now affirm that § 1981 prohibits racial discrimination in the making and enforcement of private contracts.

The Court has said often and with great emphasis that "the doctrine of *stare decisis* is of fundamental importance to the rule of law." Although we have cautioned that "*stare decisis* is a principle of policy and not a mechanical formula of adherence to the latest decision," it is indisputable that *stare decisis* is a basic self-governing principle within the Judicial Branch, which is entrusted with the sensitive and difficult task of fashioning and preserving a jurisprudential system that is not based upon "an arbitrary discretion." The Federalist, No. 78, p. 490 (H. Lodge ed. 1888) (A. Hamilton). See also *Vasquez v. Hillery,* 474 U. S. 254, 265 (1986) *(stare decisis* ensures that "the law will not merely change erratically" and "permits society to presume that bedrock principles are founded in the law rather than in the proclivities of individuals").

Our precedents are not sacrosanct, for we have overruled prior decisions where the necessity and propriety of doing so has been established. Nonetheless, we have held that "any departure from the doctrine of *stare decisis* demands special justification." We have said also that the burden borne by the party advocating the abandonment of an established precedent is greater where the Court is asked to overrule a point of statutory construction. Considerations of *stare decisis* have special force in the area of statutory interpretation, for here, unlike in the context of constitutional interpretation, the legislative power is implicated, and Congress remains free to alter what we have done.

We conclude, upon direct consideration of the issue, that no special justification has been shown for overruling *Runyon.* In cases where statutory precedents have been overruled, the primary reason for the Court's shift in position has been the intervening development of the law, through either the growth of judicial doctrine or further action taken by Congress. Where such changes have removed or weakened the conceptual underpinnings from the prior decision, see, *e. g., Rodriguez de Quijas v. Shearson/American Express, Inc.,* 490 U. S. 477, 480-81 (1989), or where the later law has rendered the decision irreconcilable with competing legal doctrines or policies, the Court has not hesitated to overrule an earlier decision. Our decision in *Runyon* has not been undermined by subsequent changes or development in the law.

Another traditional justification for overruling a prior case is that a precedent may be a positive detriment to coherence and consistency in the law, either because of inherent confusion created by an unworkable decision or because the decision poses a direct obstacle to the realization of important objectives embodied in other laws, see, *e. g., Rodriguez de Quijas, supra,* at 484. In this regard, we do not find *Runyon* to be unworkable or confusing. Respondent and various *amici* have urged that *Runyon's* interpretation of § 1981, as applied to contracts of employment, frustrates the objectives of Title VII. The argument is that a substantial overlap in coverage between the two statutes, given the considerable differences in their remedial schemes, undermines Congress' detailed efforts in Title VII to resolve disputes about racial discrimination in private employment through conciliation rather than litigation as an initial matter. After examining the point with care, however, we believe that a sound construction of the language of § 1981 yields an interpretation which does not frustrate the congressional objectives in Title VII to any significant degree.

Finally, it has sometimes been said that a precedent becomes more vulnerable as it becomes outdated and after being "'tested by experience, has been found to be inconsistent with the sense of justice or with the social welfare.'" Whatever the effect of this consideration may be in statutory cases, it offers no support for overruling *Runyon*. In recent decades, state and federal legislation has been enacted to prohibit private racial discrimination in many aspects of our society. Whether *Runyon*'s interpretation of § 1981 as prohibiting racial discrimination in the making and enforcement of private contracts is right or wrong as an original matter, it is certain that it is not inconsistent with the prevailing sense of justice in this country. To the contrary, *Runyon* is entirely consistent with our society's deep commitment to the eradication of discrimination based on a person's race or the color of his or her skin.[1]

We decline to overrule *Runyon* and acknowledge that its holding remains the governing law in this area.

Payne v. Tennessee
501 U.S. 808 (1991)

CHIEF JUSTICE REHNQUIST delivered the opinion of the Court.

In this case we reconsider our holdings in *Booth v. Maryland,* 482 U.S. 496 (1987), and *South Carolina v. Gathers,* 490 U.S. 805 (1989), that the Eighth Amendment bars the admission of victim impact evidence during the penalty phase of a capital trial.

. . . .

We . . . hold that if the State chooses to permit the admission of victim impact evidence and prosecutorial argument on that subject, the Eighth Amendment erects no *per se* bar. A State may legitimately conclude that evidence about the victim and about the impact of the murder on the victim's family is relevant to the jury's decision

---

1. JUSTICE BRENNAN chides us for ignoring what he considers "two very obvious reasons" for adhering to *Runyon*. First, he argues at length that *Runyon* was correct as an initial matter. As we have said, however, it is unnecessary for us to address this issue because we agree that, whether or not *Runyon* was correct as an initial matter, there is no special justification for departing here from the rule of *stare decisis*.

JUSTICE BRENNAN objects also to the fact that our *stare decisis* analysis places no reliance on the fact that Congress itself has not overturned the interpretation of § 1981 contained in *Runyon*, and in effect has ratified our decision in that case. This is no oversight on our part. As we affirm today, considerations of *stare decisis* have added force in statutory cases because Congress may alter what we have done by amending the statute. In constitutional cases, by contrast, Congress lacks this option, and an incorrect or outdated precedent may be overturned only by our own reconsideration or by constitutional amendment. It does not follow, however, that Congress' failure to overturn a statutory precedent is reason for this Court to adhere to it. It is "impossible to assert with any degree of assurance that congressional failure to act represents" affirmative congressional approval of the Court's statutory interpretation. *Johnson v. Transportation Agency, Santa Clara County,* 480 U.S. 616, 671-72 (1987) (Scalia, J., dissenting). Congress may legislate, moreover, only through the passage of a bill which is approved by both Houses and signed by the President. See U.S. Const., Art. I, § 7, cl. 2. Congressional inaction cannot amend a duly enacted statute. We think also that the materials relied upon by JUSTICE BRENNAN as "more positive signs of Congress' views," which are the *failure* of an amendment to a *different statute* offered *before* our decision in *Runyon*, and the passage of an attorney's fee statute having nothing to do with our holding in *Runyon*, demonstrate well the danger of placing undue reliance on the concept of congressional "ratification."

as to whether or not the death penalty should be imposed. There is no reason to treat such evidence differently than other relevant evidence is treated.

Payne and his *amicus* argue that despite these numerous infirmities in the rule created by *Booth* and *Gathers,* we should adhere to the doctrine of *stare decisis* and stop short of overruling those cases. *Stare decisis* is the preferred course because it promotes the evenhanded, predictable, and consistent development of legal principles, fosters reliance on judicial decisions, and contributes to the actual and perceived integrity of the judicial process. See *Vasquez v. Hillery,* 474 U.S. 254, 265-266 (1986). Adhering to precedent "is usually the wise policy, because in most matters it is more important that the applicable rule of law be settled than it be settled right." *Burnet v. Coronado Oil & Gas Co.,* 285 U.S. 393, 406 (1932) (Brandeis, J., dissenting). Nevertheless, when governing decisions are unworkable or are badly reasoned, "this Court has never felt constrained to follow precedent." *Smith v. Allwright,* 321 U.S. 649, 665 (1944). *Stare decisis* is not an inexorable command; rather, it "is a principle of policy and not a mechanical formula of adherence to the latest decision." *Helvering v. Hallock,* 309 U.S. 106, 119 (1940). This is particularly true in constitutional cases, because in such cases "correction through legislative action is practically impossible." *Burnet,* 285 U.S., at 407 (Brandeis, J., dissenting). Considerations in favor of *stare decisis* are at their acme in cases involving property and contract rights, where reliance interests are involved; the opposite is true in cases such as the present one involving procedural and evidentiary rules.

Applying these general principles, the Court has during the past 20 Terms overruled in whole or in part 33 of its previous constitutional decisions. *Booth* and *Gathers* were decided by the narrowest of margins, over spirited dissents challenging the basic underpinnings of those decisions. They have been questioned by Members of the Court in later decisions, and have defied consistent application by the lower courts. Reconsidering these decisions now, we conclude, for the reasons heretofore stated, that they were wrongly decided and should be, and now are, overruled. We accordingly affirm the judgment of the Supreme Court of Tennessee.

JUSTICE SCALIA, with whom JUSTICE O'CONNOR and JUSTICE KENNEDY join as to Part II, concurring.

. . . .

II

The response to JUSTICE MARSHALL's strenuous defense of the virtues of *stare decisis* can be found in the writings of JUSTICE MARSHALL himself. That doctrine, he has reminded us, "is not 'an imprisonment of reason.'" If there was ever a case that defied reason, it was *Booth,* imposing a constitutional rule that had absolutely no basis in constitutional text, in historical practice, or in logic. JUSTICE MARSHALL has also explained that "'the jurist concerned with public confidence in, and acceptance of the judicial system might well consider that, however admirable its resolute adherence to the law as it was, a decision contrary to the public sense of justice as it is, operates, so far as it is known, to diminish respect for the courts and for law itself.'" *Booth*'s stunning *ipse dixit,* that a crime's unanticipated consequences must be deemed "irrelevant" to the sentence, conflicts with a public sense of justice keen enough that it has found voice in a nationwide "victims' rights" movement.

Today, however, JUSTICE MARSHALL demands of us some "special justification" — beyond the mere conviction that the rule of *Booth* significantly harms our criminal justice system and is egregiously wrong — before we can be absolved of exercising "power, not reason." I do not think that is fair. In fact, quite to the contrary, what would enshrine power as the governing principle of this Court is the notion that an important constitutional decision with plainly inadequate rational support *must* be left in place for the sole reason that it once attracted five votes.

It seems to me difficult for those who were in the majority in *Booth* to hold themselves forth as ardent apostles of *stare decisis.* That doctrine, to the extent it rests upon anything more than administrative convenience, is merely the application to judicial precedents of a more general principle that the settled practices and expectations of a democratic society should generally not be disturbed by the courts. It is hard to have a genuine regard for *stare decisis* without honoring the more general principle as well. A decision of this Court which, while not overruling a prior holding, nonetheless announces a novel rule, contrary to long and unchallenged practice, and pronounces it to be the Law of the Land — such a decision, no less than an explicit overruling, should be approached with great caution. It was, I suggest, *Booth,* and not today's decision, that compromised the fundamental values underlying the doctrine of *stare decisis.*

JUSTICE MARSHALL, with whom JUSTICE BLACKMUN joins, dissenting.

Power, not reason, is the new currency of this Court's decisionmaking. Four Terms ago, a five-Justice majority of this Court held that "victim impact" evidence of the type at issue in this case could not constitutionally be introduced during the penalty phase of a capital trial. By another 5-4 vote, a majority of this Court rebuffed an attack upon this ruling just two Terms ago. Nevertheless, having expressly invited respondent to renew the attack, today's majority overrules *Booth* and *Gardner* and credits the dissenting views expressed in those cases. Neither the law nor the facts supporting *Booth* and *Gathers* underwent any change in the last four years. Only the personnel of this Court did.

In dispatching *Booth* and *Gathers* to their graves, today's majority ominously suggests that an even more extensive upheaval of this Court's precedents may be in store. Renouncing this Court's historical commitment to a conception of "the judiciary as a source of impersonal and reasoned judgments," the majority declares itself free to discard any principle of constitutional liberty which was recognized or reaffirmed over the dissenting votes of four Justices and with which five or more Justices *now* disagree. The implications of this radical new exception to the doctrine of *stare decisis* are staggering. The majority today sends a clear signal that scores of established constitutional liberties are now ripe for reconsideration, thereby inviting the very type of open defiance of our precedents that the majority rewards in this case. Because I believe that this Court owes more to its constitutional precedents in general and to *Booth* and *Gathers* in particular, I dissent.

. . . .

II

The overruling of one of this Court's precedents ought to be a matter of great moment and consequence. Although the doctrine of *stare decisis* is not an "inexorable command," this Court has repeatedly stressed that fidelity to precedent is fundamental to "a society governed by the rule of law." *Akron v. Akron Center for Reproductive Health, Inc.,* 462 U.S. 416, 420 (1983).

Consequently, this Court has never departed from precedent without "special justification." Such justifications include the advent of "subsequent changes or developments in the law" that undermine a decision's rationale; the need "to bring a decision into agreement with experience and with facts newly ascertained"; and a showing that a particular precedent has become a "detriment to coherence and consistency in the law."

The majority cannot seriously claim that *any* of these traditional bases for overruling a precedent applies to *Booth* or *Gathers.* The majority does not suggest that the legal rationale of these decisions has been undercut by changes or developments in doctrine during the last two years. Nor does the majority claim that experience over that period of time has discredited the principle that "any decision to impose the death sentence be, and appear to be, based on reason rather than caprice or emotion," the larger postulate of political morality on which *Booth* and *Gathers* rest.

The majority does assert that *Booth* and *Gathers* "have defied consistent application by the lower courts," but the evidence that the majority proffers is so feeble that the majority cannot sincerely expect anyone to believe this claim. . . .

It takes little real detective work to discern just what *has* changed since this Court decided *Booth* and *Gathers*: this Court's own personnel. Indeed, the majority candidly explains why this particular contingency, which until now has been almost universally understood *not* to be sufficient to warrant overruling a precedent, *is* sufficient to justify overruling *Booth* and *Gathers*. . . .

This truncation of the Court's duty to stand by its own precedents is astonishing. By limiting full protection of the doctrine of *stare decisis* to "cases involving property and contract rights," the majority sends a clear signal that essentially *all* decisions implementing the personal liberties protected by the Bill of Rights and the Fourteenth Amendment are open to reexamination. Taking into account the majority's additional criterion for overruling — that a case either was decided or affirmed by a 5-4 margin "over spirited dissent" — the continued vitality of literally scores of decisions must be understood to depend on nothing more than the proclivities of the individuals who *now* comprise a majority of this Court.

In my view, this impoverished conception of *stare decisis* cannot possibly be reconciled with the values that inform the proper judicial function. Contrary to what the majority suggests, *stare decisis* is important not merely because individuals rely on precedent to structure their commercial activity but because fidelity to precedent is part and parcel of a conception of "the judiciary as a source of impersonal and reasoned judgments." Indeed, this function of *stare decisis* is in many respects even *more* critical in adjudication involving constitutional liberties than in adjudication involving commercial entitlements. Because enforcement of the Bill of Rights and the Fourteenth Amendment frequently requires this Court to rein in the forces of democratic politics, this Court can legitimately lay claim to compliance with its directives only if the public understands the Court to be implementing "principles founded in the law rather than in the proclivities of individuals."[3] . . .

Carried to its logical conclusion, the majority's debilitated conception of *stare decisis* would destroy the Court's very capacity to resolve authoritatively the abiding conflicts between those with power and those without. If this Court shows so little respect for its own precedents, it can hardly expect them to be treated more respectfully by the state actors whom these decisions are supposed to bind. By signaling its willingness to give fresh consideration to any constitutional liberty recognized by a 5-4 vote "over spirited dissent," the majority invites state actors to renew the very policies deemed unconstitutional in the hope that this Court may now reverse course, even if it has only recently reaffirmed the constitutional liberty in question.

. . . .

III

Today's decision charts an unmistakable course. If the majority's radical reconstruction of the rules for overturning this Court's decisions is to be taken at face value — and the majority offers us no reason why it should not — then the overruling of *Booth* and *Gathers* is but a preview of an even broader and more far-reaching assault upon this Court's precedents. Cast aside today are those condemned to face society's ultimate penalty. Tomorrow's victims may be minorities, women, or the indigent. Inevitably, this campaign to resurrect yesterday's "spirited dissents" will squander the authority and the legitimacy of this Court as a protector of the powerless.

I dissent.

Planned Parenthood of Southeastern Pa. v. Casey
505 U.S. 833 (1992)

JUSTICE O'CONNOR, JUSTICE KENNEDY, and JUSTICE SOUTER announced the judgment of the Court and delivered the opinion of the Court with respect to Parts I, II, III, V-A, V-C, and VI, an opinion with respect to Part V-E, in which JUSTICE STEVENS joins, and an opinion with respect to Parts IV, V-B, and V-D.

---

3. It does not answer this concern to suggest that Justices owe fidelity to the text of the Constitution rather than to the case law of this Court interpreting the Constitution. The text of the Constitution is rarely so plain as to be self-executing; invariably, this Court must develop mediating principles and doctrines in order to bring the text of constitutional provisions to bear on particular facts. Thus, to rebut the charge of personal lawmaking, Justices who would discard the mediating principles embodied in precedent must do more than state that they are following the "text" of the Constitution; they must explain why they are entitled to substitute *their* mediating principles for those that are already settled in the law. And such an explanation will be sufficient to legitimize the departure from precedent only if it measures up to the extraordinary standard necessary to justify overruling one of this Court's precedents.

I

Liberty finds no refuge in a jurisprudence of doubt. Yet 19 years after our holding that the Constitution protects a woman's right to terminate her pregnancy in its early stages, *Roe v. Wade*, 410 U. S. 113 (1973), that definition of liberty is still questioned. Joining the respondents as *amicus curiae,* the United States, as it has done in five other cases in the last decade, again asks us to overrule *Roe.*

. . . .

III

A

The obligation to follow precedent begins with necessity, and a contrary necessity marks its outer limit. With Cardozo, we recognize that no judicial system could do society's work if it eyed each issue afresh in every case that raised it. See B. Cardozo, The Nature of the Judicial Process 149 (1921). Indeed, the very concept of the rule of law underlying our own Constitution requires such continuity over time that a respect for precedent is, by definition, indispensable. At the other extreme, a different necessity would make itself felt if a prior judicial ruling should come to be seen so clearly as error that its enforcement was for that very reason doomed.

Even when the decision to overrule a prior case is not, as in the rare, latter instance, virtually foreordained, it is common wisdom that the rule of *stare decisis* is not an "inexorable command," and certainly it is not such in every constitutional case, see *Burnet v. Coronado Oil & Gas Co.,* 285 U. S. 393, 405-411 (1932) (Brandeis, J., dissenting). Rather, when this Court reexamines a prior holding, its judgment is customarily informed by a series of prudential and pragmatic considerations designed to test the consistency of overruling a prior decision with the ideal of the rule of law, and to gauge the respective costs of reaffirming and overruling a prior case. Thus, for example, we may ask whether the rule has proven to be intolerable simply in defying practical workability; whether the rule is subject to a kind of reliance that would lend a special hardship to the consequences of overruling and add inequity to the cost of repudiation; whether related principles of law have so far developed as to have left the old rule no more than a remnant of abandoned doctrine; or whether facts have so changed, or come to be seen so differently, as to have robbed the old rule of significant application or justification.

So in this case we may enquire whether *Roe*'s central rule has been found unworkable; whether the rule's limitation on state power could be removed without serious inequity to those who have relied upon it or significant damage to the stability of the society governed by it; whether the law's growth in the intervening years has left *Roe*'s central rule a doctrinal anachronism discounted by society; and whether *Roe*'s premises of fact have so far changed in the ensuing two decades as to render its central holding somehow irrelevant or unjustifiable in dealing with the issue it addressed.

1

Although *Roe* has engendered opposition, it has in no sense proven "unworkable," representing as it does a simple limitation beyond which a state law is unenforceable. While *Roe* has, of course, required judicial assessment of state laws affecting the exercise of the choice guaranteed against government infringement, and although the need for such review will remain as a consequence of today's decision, the required determinations fall within judicial competence.

2

The inquiry into reliance counts the cost of a rule's repudiation as it would fall on those who have relied reasonably on the rule's continued application. Since the classic case for weighing reliance heavily in favor of following the earlier rule occurs in the commercial context, see *Payne v. Tennessee, supra,* at 828, where advance planning of great precision is most obviously a necessity, it is no cause for surprise that some would find no reliance worthy of consideration in support of *Roe.*

While neither respondents nor their *amici* in so many words deny that the abortion right invites some reliance prior to its actual exercise, one can readily imagine an argument stressing the dissimilarity of this case to one involving property or contract. Abortion is customarily chosen as an unplanned response to the consequence of unplanned activity or to the failure of conventional birth control, and except on the assumption that no intercourse would have occurred but for *Roe*'s holding, such behavior may appear to justify no reliance claim. Even if reliance could be claimed on that unrealistic assumption, the argument might run, any reliance interest would be *de minimis.* This argument would be premised on the hypothesis that reproductive planning could take virtually immediate account of any sudden restoration of state authority to ban abortions.

To eliminate the issue of reliance that easily, however, one would need to limit cognizable reliance to specific instances of sexual activity. But to do this would be simply to refuse to face the fact that for two decades of economic and social developments, people have organized intimate relationships and made choices that define their views of themselves and their places in society, in reliance on the availability of abortion in the event that contraception should fail. The ability of women to participate equally in the economic and social life of the Nation has been facilitated by their ability to control their reproductive lives. The Constitution serves human values, and while the effect of reliance on *Roe* cannot be exactly measured, neither can the certain cost of overruling *Roe* for people who have ordered their thinking and living around that case be dismissed.

3

No evolution of legal principle has left *Roe*'s doctrinal footings weaker than they were in 1973. No development of constitutional law since the case was decided has implicitly or explicitly left *Roe* behind as a mere survivor of obsolete constitutional thinking.

. . . .

4

We have seen how time has overtaken some of *Roe*'s factual assumptions: advances in maternal health care allow for abortions safe to the mother later in pregnancy than was true in 1973, and advances in neonatal care have advanced viability to a point somewhat earlier. But these facts go only to the scheme of time limits on the realization of competing interests, and the divergences from the factual premises of 1973 have no bearing on the validity of *Roe*'s central holding, that viability marks the earliest point at which the State's interest in fetal life is constitutionally adequate to justify a legislative ban on nontherapeutic abortions. The soundness or unsoundness of that constitutional judgment in no sense turns on whether viability occurs at approximately 28 weeks, as was usual at the time of *Roe,* at 23 to 24 weeks, as it sometimes does today, or at some moment even slightly earlier in pregnancy, as it may if fetal respiratory capacity can somehow be enhanced in the future. Whenever it may occur, the attainment of viability may continue to serve as the critical fact, just as it has done since *Roe* was decided; which is to say that no change in *Roe*'s factual underpinning has left its central holding obsolete, and none supports an argument for overruling it.

5

The sum of the precedential enquiry to this point shows *Roe*'s underpinnings unweakened in any way affecting its central holding. While it has engendered disapproval, it has not been unworkable. An entire generation has come of age free to assume *Roe*'s concept of liberty in defining the capacity of women to act in society, and to make reproductive decisions; no erosion of principle going to liberty or personal autonomy has left *Roe*'s central holding a doctrinal remnant; *Roe* portends no developments at odds with other precedent for the analysis of personal liberty; and no changes of fact have rendered viability more or less appropriate as the point at which the balance of interests tips. Within the bounds of normal *stare decisis* analysis, then, and subject to the considerations on which it customarily turns, the stronger argument is for affirming *Roe*'s central holding, with whatever degree of personal reluctance any of us may have, not for overruling it.

    . . . .

CHIEF JUSTICE REHNQUIST, with whom JUSTICE WHITE, JUSTICE SCALIA, and JUSTICE THOMAS join, concurring in the judgment in part and dissenting in part.

The joint opinion, following its newly minted variation on *stare decisis,* retains the outer shell of *Roe,* but beats a wholesale retreat from the substance of that case. We believe that *Roe* was wrongly decided, and that it can and should be overruled consistently with our traditional approach to *stare decisis* in constitutional cases. . . .

    . . . .

II

The joint opinion of JUSTICES O'CONNOR, KENNEDY, and SOUTER cannot bring itself to say that *Roe* was correct as an original matter, but the authors are of the view that "the immediate question is not the soundness of *Roe*'s resolution of the issue, but the precedential force that must be accorded to its holding." Instead of claiming that *Roe* was correct as a matter of original constitutional interpretation, the opinion there-fore contains an elaborate discussion of *stare decisis*. This discussion of the principle of *stare decisis* appears to be almost entirely dicta, because the joint opinion does not apply that principle in dealing with *Roe*. *Roe* decided that a woman had a fun-damental right to an abortion. The joint opinion rejects that view. *Roe* decided that abortion regulations were to be subjected to "strict scrutiny" and could be justified only in the light of "compelling state interests." The joint opinion rejects that view. *Roe* analyzed abortion regulation under a rigid trimester framework, a framework which has guided this Court's decisionmaking for 19 years. The joint opinion rejects that framework.

Stare decisis is defined in Black's Law Dictionary as meaning "to abide by, or adhere to, decided cases." Whatever the "central holding" of *Roe* that is left after the joint opinion finishes dissecting it is surely not the result of that principle. While purporting to adhere to precedent, the joint opinion instead revises it. *Roe* continues to exist, but only in the way a storefront on a western movie set exists: a mere facade to give the illusion of reality.

In our view, authentic principles of *stare decisis* do not require that any portion of the reasoning in *Roe* be kept intact. "*Stare decisis* is not a universal, inexorable com-mand," especially in cases involving the interpretation of the Federal Constitution. Erroneous decisions in such constitutional cases are uniquely durable, because cor-rection through legislative action, save for constitutional amendment, is impossible. It is therefore our duty to reconsider constitutional interpretations that "depart from a proper understanding" of the Constitution. Our constitutional watch does not cease merely because we have spoken before on an issue; when it becomes clear that a prior constitutional interpretation is unsound we are obliged to reexamine the question.

The joint opinion discusses several *stare decisis* factors which, it asserts, point toward retaining a portion of *Roe*. Two of these factors are that the main "factual underpinning" of *Roe* has remained the same, and that its doctrinal foundation is no weaker now than it was in 1973. Of course, what might be called the basic facts which gave rise to *Roe* have remained the same — women become pregnant, there is a point somewhere, depending on medical technology, where a fetus becomes viable, and women give birth to children. But this is only to say that the same facts which gave rise to *Roe* will continue to give rise to similar cases. It is not a reason, in and of itself, why those cases must be decided in the same incorrect manner as was the first case to deal with the question. And surely there is no requirement, in considering whether to depart from *stare decisis* in a constitutional case, that a decision be more wrong now than it was at the time it was rendered. If that were true, the most outlandish constitutional decision could survive forever, based simply on the fact that it was no more outlandish later than it was when originally rendered.

Nor does the joint opinion faithfully follow this alleged requirement. The opin-ion frankly concludes that *Roe* and its progeny were wrong in failing to recognize that the State's interests in maternal health and in the protection of unborn human life exist throughout pregnancy. But there is no indication that these components of *Roe* are any more incorrect at this juncture than they were at its inception.

The joint opinion also points to the reliance interests involved in this context in its effort to explain why precedent must be followed for precedent's sake. Certainly it is true that where reliance is truly at issue, as in the case of judicial decisions that have formed the basis for private decisions, "considerations in favor of *stare decisis* are at their acme." But as the joint opinion apparently agrees, any traditional notion of reliance is not applicable here. The Court today cuts back on the protection afforded by *Roe,* and no one claims that this action defeats any reliance interest in the disavowed trimester framework. Similarly, reliance interests would not be diminished were the Court to go further and acknowledge the full error of *Roe,* as "reproductive planning could take virtually immediate account of" this action.

The joint opinion thus turns to what can only be described as an unconventional — and unconvincing — notion of reliance, a view based on the surmise that the availability of abortion since *Roe* has led to "two decades of economic and social developments" that would be undercut if the error of *Roe* were recognized. The joint opinion's assertion of this fact is undeveloped and totally conclusory. In fact, one cannot be sure to what economic and social developments the opinion is referring. Surely it is dubious to suggest that women have reached their "places in society" in reliance upon *Roe,* rather than as a result of their determination to obtain higher education and compete with men in the job market, and of society's increasing recognition of their ability to fill positions that were previously thought to be reserved only for men.

In the end, having failed to put forth any evidence to prove any true reliance, the joint opinion's argument is based solely on generalized assertions about the national psyche, on a belief that the people of this country have grown accustomed to the *Roe* decision over the last 19 years and have "ordered their thinking and living around" it. As an initial matter, one might inquire how the joint opinion can view the "central holding" of *Roe* so deeply rooted in our constitutional culture, when it so casually uproots and disposes of that same decision's trimester framework. Furthermore, at various points in the past, the same could have been said about this Court's erroneous decision[] that the Constitution allowed "separate but equal" treatment of minorities, see *Plessy v. Ferguson,* 163 U. S. 537 (1896) .... The "separate but equal" doctrine lasted 58 years after *Plessy* .... However, the simple fact that a generation or more had grown used to these major decisions did not prevent the Court from correcting its errors in those cases, nor should it prevent us from correctly interpreting the Constitution here. See *Brown v. Board of Education,* 347 U. S. 483 (1954) (rejecting the "separate but equal" doctrine).

Apparently realizing that conventional *stare decisis* principles do not support its position, the joint opinion advances a belief that retaining a portion of *Roe* is necessary to protect the "legitimacy" of this Court. Because the Court must take care to render decisions "grounded truly in principle," and not simply as political and social compromises, the joint opinion properly declares it to be this Court's duty to ignore the public criticism and protest that may arise as a result of a decision. Few would quarrel with this statement, although it may be doubted that Members of this Court, holding their tenure as they do during constitutional "good behavior," are at all likely to be intimidated by such public protests.

But the joint opinion goes on to state that when the Court "resolves the sort of intensely divisive controversy reflected in *Roe* and those rare, comparable cases," its decision is exempt from reconsideration under established principles of *stare decisis* in constitutional cases. This is so, the joint opinion contends, because in those "intensely divisive" cases the Court has "called the contending sides of a national controversy to end their national division by accepting a common mandate rooted in the Constitution," and must therefore take special care not to be perceived as "surrendering to political pressure" and continued opposition. This is a truly novel principle, one which is contrary to both the Court's historical practice and to the Court's traditional willingness to tolerate criticism of its opinions. Under this principle, when the Court has ruled on a divisive issue, it is apparently prevented from overruling that decision for the sole reason that it was incorrect, *unless opposition to the original decision has died away.*

The first difficulty with this principle lies in its assumption that cases that are "intensely divisive" can be readily distinguished from those that are not. The question of whether a particular issue is "intensely divisive" enough to qualify for special protection is entirely subjective and dependent on the individual assumptions of the Members of this Court. In addition, because the Court's duty is to ignore public opinion and criticism on issues that come before it, its Members are in perhaps the worst position to judge whether a decision divides the Nation deeply enough to justify such uncommon protection. Although many of the Court's decisions divide the populace to a large degree, we have not previously on that account shied away from applying normal rules of *stare decisis* when urged to reconsider earlier decisions. Over the past 21 years, for example, the Court has overruled in whole or in part 34 of its previous Constitutional decisions.

. . . .

There is also a suggestion in the joint opinion that the propriety of overruling a "divisive" decision depends in part on whether "most people" would now agree that it should be overruled. Either the demise of opposition or its progression to substantial popular agreement apparently is required to allow the Court to reconsider a divisive decision. How such agreement would be ascertained, short of a public opinion poll, the joint opinion does not say. But surely even the suggestion is totally at war with the idea of "legitimacy" in whose name it is invoked. The Judicial Branch derives its legitimacy, not from following public opinion, but from deciding by its best lights whether legislative enactments of the popular branches of Government comport with the Constitution. The doctrine of *stare decisis* is an adjunct of this duty, and should be no more subject to the vagaries of public opinion than is the basic judicial task.

. . . .

The sum of the joint opinion's labors in the name of *stare decisis* and "legitimacy" is this: *Roe v. Wade* stands as a sort of judicial Potemkin Village, which may be pointed out to passers-by as a monument to the importance of adhering to precedent. But behind the facade, an entirely new method of analysis, without any roots in constitutional law, is imported to decide the constitutionality of state laws regulating abortion. Neither *stare decisis* nor "legitimacy" are truly served by such an effort.

. . . .

JUSTICE SCALIA, with whom THE CHIEF JUSTICE, JUSTICE WHITE, and JUSTICE THOMAS join, concurring in the judgment in part and dissenting in part.

. . . .

The Court's reliance upon *stare decisis* can best be described as contrived. It insists upon the necessity of adhering not to all of *Roe,* but only to what it calls the "central holding." It seems to me that *stare decisis* ought to be applied even to the doctrine of *stare decisis,* and I confess never to have heard of this new, keep-what-you-want-and-throw-away-the-rest version.

Notes and Questions

---

1. *Patterson* resulted in three different opinions; *Payne,* in five; and *Casey,* in five. If the doctrine of stare decisis is that well established, why would this occur? Or is this an indication that the nature of the doctrine is more uncertain (or the force of the doctrine is weaker) than advertised?

2. In *Patterson,* the Court declined to overrule its earlier decision in *Runyon.* If *Runyon* had not been decided, would *Patterson* have come out the same way? If not, why should it matter that *Runyon* had already been decided?

3. Notice, in *Patterson,* the emphasis on the margin of the vote and of the date (or age) of the overruled decision. Notice also the importance of the dissenting opinion in the earlier, precedent-setting decision, even if it initially failed to carry the day.

4. Justice Marshall, in his dissent in *Payne,* went so far as to include a 17-case "endangered precedents" list. *See* 501 U.S. at 852 n.2. According to one subsequent study,

    > in the six year period after *Payne* at least four of the seventeen, or 23.5%, of the precedents identified by Justice Marshall have been overturned in part. Moreover, four other cases have been distinguished or limited in subsequent rulings by the Court, a sign that their precedential force is weakening. If the explicit overrulings are combined with the cases that have been distinguished, nearly fifty percent (47.0%) of the cases on the "endangered precedents" list have been either overruled in part or seriously weakened through the incremental process of distinguishing precedent.

    Christopher P. Banks, *Reversals of Precedent and Judicial Policy-Making: How Judicial Conceptions of Stare Decisis in the U.S. Supreme Court Influence Social Change,* 32 AKRON L. REV. 233, 247 (1999).

5. Would Justice Marshall be making so strong an appeal to stare decisis if he agreed with the underlying holding of the *Payne* Court? Would those Justices in the majority be more concerned about overruling *Booth* and *Gathers* if they did not agree with that holding? In other words, is stare decisis simply something to be invoked when one disagrees with the overruling of precedent? Or

does the doctrine have independent force — i.e., can it ever compel one to adhere to a precedent with which one disagrees? If so, is there any evidence of that here? In *Patterson*? In *Casey*?

6. What is the "rule" for adhering to precedent articulated by the Court in *Casey*? As we will see, this "test" has been quite influential. Are you persuaded that Justices O'Connor, Kennedy, and Souter properly applied that test in *Casey*?

7. Is Justice Scalia correct that stare decisis ought to be applied to the doctrine of stare decisis? (Recall the earlier discussion *supra* at 79-80 regarding decisional methodology vis-à-vis the concept of holding.) If so, did the Court follow that doctrine in its formulation of the doctrine in *Casey*? In other words, is the "rule" articulated in *Casey* the same as that articulated in *Patterson* and *Payne*? If not, then was the Court justified in altering the doctrine of stare decisis?

8. *Lawrence v. Texas*, 539 U.S. 558, 586-92 (2003) (Scalia, J., dissenting):

> "*Liberty finds no refuge in a jurisprudence of doubt.*" *Planned Parenthood of Southeastern Pa. v. Casey,* 505 U. S. 833, 844 (1992). That was the Court's sententious response, barely more than a decade ago, to those seeking to overrule *Roe v. Wade,* 410 U.S. 113 (1973). The Court's response today, to those who have engaged in a 17-year crusade to overrule *Bowers v. Hardwick,* 478 U. S. 186 (1986) [in which the Court permitted states to criminalize sodomy], is very different. The need for stability and certainty presents no barrier.
>
> . . . .
>
> I begin with the Court's surprising readiness to reconsider a decision rendered a mere 17 years ago in *Bowers.* I do not myself believe in rigid adherence to *stare decisis* in constitutional cases; but I do believe that we should be consistent rather than manipulative in invoking the doctrine. Today's opinions in support of reversal do not bother to distinguish — or indeed, even bother to mention — the paean to *stare decisis* coauthored by three Members of today's majority in *Casey.* There, when *stare decisis* meant preservation of judicially invented abortion rights, the widespread criticism of *Roe* was strong reason to *reaffirm* it:
>
>> "Where, in the performance of its judicial duties, the Court decides a case in such a way as to resolve the sort of intensely divisive controversy reflected in *Roe,* its decision has a dimension that the resolution of a normal case does not carry. To overrule under fire in the absence of the most compelling reason would subvert the Court's legitimacy beyond any serious question." 505 U. S., at 866-867.
>
> Today, however, the widespread opposition to *Bowers,* a decision resolving an issue as "intensely divisive" as the issue in *Roe,* is offered as a reason in favor of *overruling* it. Gone, too, is an "enquiry" (of the sort conducted in *Casey*) into whether the decision sought to be overruled has "proven 'unworkable.'"
>
> Today's approach to *stare decisis* invites us to overrule an erroneously decided precedent (including an "intensely divisive" decision) *if* (1) its foundations have been "eroded" by subsequent decisions; (2) it has been subject to "substantial and continuing" criticism; and (3) it has not induced "individual or societal reliance"

that counsels against overturning. The problem is that *Roe* itself — which today's majority surely has no disposition to overrule — satisfies these conditions to at least the same degree as *Bowers*.

. . . .

To tell the truth, it does not surprise me, and should surprise no one, that the Court has chosen today to revise the standards of *stare decisis* set forth in *Casey.* It has thereby exposed *Casey's* extraordinary deference to precedent for the result-oriented expedient that it is.

Is this a fair criticism of *Casey* and *Lawrence*? Why or why not?

9. *Does the force of stare decisis vary depending upon the nature of the issue?* In both *Patterson* and *Payne*, the Court suggested that the force of stare decisis should depend on the nature of the application. As Rafael Gely summarizes more generally:

> A three-tiered hierarchy of *stare decisis* has developed over the years. Statutory *stare decisis*, which refers to the role of precedent in interpreting statutes, involves a heightened adherence to precedent. Courts should, under this version of *stare decisis*, overrule statutory precedent only under the most compelling of circumstances. *Stare decisis* is, on the other hand, weakly applied in the context of constitutional precedent. The Supreme Court, for instance, has consistently followed the proposition that precedents should carry less weight in constitutional cases than in cases involving statutory interpretation. Application of *stare decisis* in the common law area is somewhere in between the constitutional and statutory cases. Therefore, common law precedents enjoy a presumption of correctness stronger than that applied to constitutional cases, but not as constraining as that enjoyed by statutory precedents.
>
> . . . .
>
> Various reasons have been advanced for the development of the three-tiered approach to *stare decisis.* Viewing common law precedent as the base form of *stare decisis,* the question then becomes: why should we raise or lower the base presumption in the case of statutory and constitutional precedent, respectively?
>
> The strong presumption applied to statutory precedent is based on the proposition that legislative silence amounts to legislative approval and that judicial interpretation of a statute over time becomes part of the statute itself. As such, any further judicial reinterpretation of the statute amounts to a statutory amendment, and thus, a usurpation of the legislature's power. . . .
>
> The conditions that support the heightened presumption in the statutory context are weakened in the context of constitutional case law. Constitutional precedent, therefore, is subject to a weak presumption of correctness. That is, in the constitutional context, *stare decisis* is at it[s] weakest. Unlike in the statutory context, the judiciary, not the legislature, is the ultimate arbiter of the Constitution. Since there is no other direct means by which to correct wrongly decided cases, and in order to allow for the adoption of necessary changes in the law, the "judiciary must not be constrained by precedent." Otherwise, "incorrect doctrine could never be changed." Similar to the legislative acquiescence argument, the argument in favor of a weak version of *stare decisis* in constitutional cases is motivated by the relationship between the judiciary and the legislature. Unlike the legislative acquiescence argument, it is the legislature's inability to readily amend a constitution,

instead of its silence, that requires the judiciary to adopt a different form of the use of precedent.

Rafael Gely, *Of Sinking and Escalating: A (Somewhat) New Look at Stare Decisis,* 60 U. PITT. L. REV. 89, 108-10 (1998). Do you find this explanation convincing? Consider, for example, *John R. Sand & Gravel Co. v. United States,* 552 U.S. 130 (2008), in which Justice Stevens, in dissent, stated:

> [T]he logic of the "special force" of *stare decisis* in the statutory context is that "Congress remains free to alter what we have done," *Patterson,* 491 U. S., at 172-173. But the amendment of an obscure statutory provision is not a high priority for a busy Congress, and we should remain mindful that enactment of legislation is by no means a cost-free enterprise.

Id. at 143 n.5 (Stevens, J., dissenting).

10. "It is revolting to have no better reason for a rule of law than that so it was laid down in the time of Henry IV. It is still more revolting if the grounds upon which it was laid down have vanished long since, and the rule simply persists from blind imitation of the past." Oliver Wendell Holmes, *The Path of the Law,* 10 HARV. L. REV. 457, 469 (1897).

11. **"A basic change in the law upon a ground no firmer than a change in our membership invites the popular misconception that this institution is little different from the two political branches of the Government. No misconception could do more lasting injury to this Court and to the system of law which it is our abiding mission to serve."** *Mitchell v. W. T. Grant Co.,* 416 U.S. 600, 636 (1974) (Stewart, J., dissenting).

12. "The policies underlying the doctrine [of stare decisis] — stability and predictability — are at their strongest when the Court is asked to change its mind, though nothing else of significance has changed." *John R. Sand & Gravel Co. v. United States,* 552 U.S. 130, 144 (2008) (Ginsburg, J., dissenting).

13. *Has the Supreme Court's standard changed?* More recently, in *Montejo v. Louisiana,* 129 S. Ct. 2079 (2009), the Supreme Court considered "the scope and continued viability of the rule announced by this Court in *Michigan* v. *Jackson,* 475 U. S. 625 (1986), forbidding police to initiate interrogation of a criminal defendant once he has requested counsel at an arraignment or similar proceeding." *Id.* at 2082. Regarding the precedential effect of *Jackson,* the Court (through Justice Scalia) stated:

> We do not think that *stare decisis* requires us to expand significantly the holding of a prior decision — fundamentally revising its theoretical basis in the process — in order to cure its practical deficiencies. To the contrary, the fact that a decision has proved "unworkable" is a traditional ground for overruling it. *Payne v. Tennessee,* 501 U. S. 808, 827 (1991). . . .

> Beyond workability, the relevant factors in deciding whether to adhere to the principle of *stare decisis* include the antiquity of the precedent, the reliance interests at stake, and of course whether the decision was well reasoned.

Id. at 2080-81. Is the *Montejo* Court's "test" for deciding whether to overrule one of its precedents the same as that used in its earlier decisions? If not, what has changed? And do you agree with this list of factors? In particular, to what extent, if any, should "workability" be a factor? If, for example, the Court "correctly" interprets some constitutional provision, why should it matter whether that interpretation is "workable"?

14. *What really matters?* Also in *Montejo*, Justice Alito, in a concurring opinion joined by Justice Kennedy, stated:

> Earlier this Term, in *Arizona* v. *Gant*, 129 S. Ct. 1710, 1713 (2009), the Court overruled *New York* v. *Belton*, 453 U. S. 454 (1981), even though that case had been on the books for 28 years, had not been undermined by subsequent decisions, had been recently reaffirmed and extended, had proven to be eminently workable (indeed, had adopted for precisely that reason), and had engendered substantial law enforcement reliance. The Court took this step even though we were not asked to overrule *Belton* and this new rule is almost certain to lead to a host of problems.
>
> Justice Scalia, who cast the deciding vote to overrule *Belton*, dismissed *stare decisis* concerns with the following observation: "It seems to me ample reason that the precedent was badly reasoned and produces erroneous results." This narrow view of *stare decisis* provides the only principle on which the decision in *Gant* can be justified.
>
> In light of *Gant*, the discussion of *stare decisis* in today's dissent is surprising. The dissent in the case at hand criticizes the Court for "acting on its own" in reconsidering *Michigan* v. *Jackson*, 475 U. S. 625 (1986). But the same was true in *Gant*, and in this case, the Court gave the parties and interested *amici* the opportunity to submit supplemental briefs on the issue, a step not taken in *Gant*.
>
> The dissent faults the Court for "casting aside the reliance interests of law enforcement," but in *Gant*, there were real and important law enforcement interests at stake. Even the Court conceded that the *Belton* rule had "been widely taught in police academies and that law enforcement officers had relied on the rule in conducting vehicle searches during the past 28 years." And whatever else might be said about *Belton*, it surely provided a bright-line rule.
>
> . . . .
>
> The dissent, finally, invokes *Jackson's* antiquity, stating that "the 23-year existence of a simple bright-line rule" should weigh in favor of its retention. But in *Gant*, the Court had no compunction about casting aside a 28-year-old bright-line rule. I can only assume that the dissent thinks that our constitutional precedents are like certain wines, which are most treasured when they are neither too young nor too old, and that *Jackson*, at 23, is in its prime, whereas *Belton*, at 28, had turned brownish and vinegary.
>
> I agree with the dissent that *stare decisis* should promote "'the evenhanded development of legal principles'" (quoting *Payne* v. *Tennessee*, 501 U. S. 808, 827-828 (1991)). The treatment of *stare decisis* in *Gant* fully supports the decision in the present case.

129 S. Ct. at 2092-94 (Alito, J., concurring). If Justice Alito's assessment of the Court's current view of stare decisis is correct, what, if anything, is left of this doctrine?

15. Randy Kozel argues that the primary consideration in deciding whether to overrule precedent is reliance interests, which should be "weighed against the value of reaching the correct result on the merits to determine whether *stare decisis* trumps in a given case." Randy J. Kozel, Stare Decisis *as Judicial Doctrine*, 67 WASH. & LEE L. REV. 411, 415 (2010). Is that the best approach? Or is the overruling of precedent ever so surprising as to disrupt reasonable expectations as to the state of the law? For example, does the fact that a case reaches the Supreme Court itself mean that any firm reliance on current law is probably misplaced?

    In a more recent article, Professor Kozel argues that the decision whether to overrule erroneous precedent should be "less about whether past reliance should be protected and more about how departures from precedent are likely to prove disruptive going forward." Randy J. Kozel, *Precedent and Reliance*, 62 EMORY L.J. 1459, 1461 (2013). Accordingly, "[d]eferring to a precedent whose overruling would have dramatic effects on settled expectations becomes a mechanism for controlling the degree of disruption that is injected into the legal system through the process of adjudicative change." *Id. See also* Hillel Y. Levin, *A Reliance Approach to Precedent*, 47 GA. L. REV. 1035 (2013).

16. "Just as the law of precedent gives earlier judges a check on the power of those who come behind it, the doctrine sometimes allows later judges to minimize the precedential effect of earlier decisions, providing a counter balancing check on their predecessors." Randy Beck, *Transtemporal Separation of Powers in the Law of Precedent*, 87 NOTRE DAME L. REV. 1405 (2012).

17. "The forty-nine states in the United States, other than Louisiana" also "follow a version of the doctrine of stare decisis that is similar to the English respect for precedent and its consideration of precedent as a source of law." Mary G. Algero, *The Sources of Law and the Value of Precedent: A Comparative and Empirical Study of a Civil Law State in a Common Law Nation*, 65 LA. L. REV. 775, 785 (2005).

18. For a more recent discussion of the doctrine of stare decisis (in the context of a fairly high-profile case), see *Citizens United v. Federal Election Comm'n*, 130 S. Ct. 876, 920-25 (2010) (Roberts, C.J., concurring). Another such discussion can be found in *Alleyne v. United States*, 133 S. Ct. 2151 (2013). *Alleyne* was particularly interesting in that the Court therein overruled *Harris v. United States*, 536 U.S. 545 (2002), with almost no discussion of stare decisis. More extended discussions of that doctrine, though, can be found in the concurring opinion of Justice Sotomayor, *see id.* at 2164, and the dissenting opinion of Justice Alito, *see id.* at 2167. Recalling his earlier opinions on this subject,

Justice Alito argued that "the Court ought to be consistent in its willingness to reconsider precedent," and if precedent "can be cast aside simply because a majority of this Court now disagrees with them, that same approach may properly be followed in future cases." *Id.* at 2172. Justice Alito concluded: "The Court's decision creates a precedent about precedent that may have greater precedential effect than the dubious decisions on which it relies." *Id.* at 2173.

SIDEBAR: ENGLISH AND CIVIL LAW VIEWS OF PRECEDENT

Formally speaking, the concept of precedent is predominantly a common law concept, though common law countries tend to vary somewhat in its application. Until relatively recently, for example, the English view of precedent had been fairly rigid, in that its courts considered themselves unable to deviate from prior decisions. *See, e.g., Helvering v. Hallock*, 309 U.S. 106, 121 (1940) ("This Court, unlike the House of Lords, has from the beginning rejected a doctrine of disability at self-correction.") (footnote omitted). That changed to a large extent in 1966 upon the issuance of the following "practice statement," found at [1966] 3 All E.R. 77 (H.L.):

> Before judgments were given in the House of Lords on July 26, 1966, LORD GARDINER, L.C., made the following statement on behalf of himself and the Lords of Appeal in Ordinary:
>
> Their lordships regard the use of precedent (1) as an indispensable foundation upon which to decide what is the law and its application to individual cases. It provides at least some degree of certainty upon which individuals can rely in the conduct of their affairs, as well as a basis for orderly development of legal rules.
>
> Their lordships nevertheless recognise that too rigid adherence to precedent may lead to injustice in a particular case and also unduly restrict the proper development of the law. They therefore to modify their present practice and, while treating former decisions of this House as normally binding, to depart from a previous decision when it appears right to do so.
>
> In this connexion they will bear in mind the danger of disturbing retrospectively the basis on which contracts, settlements of property and fiscal arrangements have been entered into and also the especial need for certainty as to the criminal law.
>
> This announcement is not intended to affect the use of precedent elsewhere than in this House.

The new United Kingdom Supreme Court appears to be adhering to this position. For example, in *Austin v. Southwark LBC*, (2011) AC 355, Lord Hope opined:

> The Supreme Court has not thought it necessary to reissue the Practice State-
> ment as a fresh statement of practice in the court's own name. This is because
> it has as much effect in this court as it did before the Appellate Committee in
> the House of Lords. It was part of the established jurisprudence relating to the
> conduct of appeals in the House of Lords which was transferred to this court by
> section 40 of the Constitutional Reform Act of 2005. So the question which we
> must consider is not whether the court has power to depart from the previous
> decisions of the House of Lords which have been referred to, but whether in the
> circumstances of this case it would be right for it to do so.

Id. ¶ 25, at 369-70.

And what about civil law systems? The general rule is that "civil law regimes
go further than declining to impose an obligation of precedent, and instead formally eschew precedent." Michael Abramowicz & Maxwell Stearns, *Defining Dicta*, 57 STAN. L. REV. 953, 996 n.120 (2005). But: "While civil law regimes formally
reject precedent, legal scholars have observed that, over time, such systems nonetheless begin to resemble common law systems in their effective, if not formal,
reliance upon precedent." *Id.*

b. Horizontal Stare Decisis in the United States Court of Appeals

Relatively speaking, stare decisis is easy to apply in the Supreme Court by virtue
of the fact that the Supreme Court is a "unitary" (single) court. Being a unitary
court, the Supreme Court need follow (or not) only its own prior decisions, and
not those of any other court. But what about the United States Court of Appeals,
which is, in a sense, a single court — after all, there is only one United States Court
of Appeals — but which has been divided into 13 circuits, each of which usually
decides cases in three-judge panels consisting of ever-changing groups of judges?
Consider this question in the context of the following case.

In re Korean Air Lines Disaster of September 1, 1983

829 F.2d 1171 (D.C. Cir. 1987)

RUTH BADER GINSBURG, Circuit Judge:

This case arises out of an air disaster and raises turbulent federal questions. On
September 1, 1983, Korean Air Lines (KAL) Flight 007, a commercial craft departing
from Kennedy Airport in New York and bound for Seoul, South Korea, was destroyed
over the Sea of Japan by Soviet Union military aircraft. Wrongful death actions were
filed against KAL in several federal district courts; the Judicial Panel on Multidistrict
Litigation transferred these actions to the District Court for the District of Columbia
for pretrial proceedings pursuant to 28 U.S.C. § 1407 . . . .

The nub of the controversy relates to the per passenger damage limitation of the Warsaw Convention, raised to $75,000 by an accord among airlines known as the Montreal Agreement. By motion for partial summary judgment, plaintiffs sought a declaration "that KAL is liable without any fault for compensatory damages without any limitation of $75,000." Plaintiffs grounded this motion on the inadequate type size of the liability limitation notice printed on KAL passenger tickets. The notice appeared in 8 point type; the Montreal Agreement specifies 10 point type. Denying plaintiffs' motion, the district court, on July 25, 1985, held that KAL could avail itself of the $75,000 per passenger limitation. In so ruling, the district court considered and rejected contrary Second Circuit precedent. [The district court later clarified that its order applied even as to actions originally commenced within the Second Circuit.]
. . . .

. . . We now affirm the district court's dispositions. On the Warsaw Convention/Montreal Agreement $75,000 per passenger damage limitation issue, we adopt as our opinion the comprehensive July 25, 1985 decision of the district court, reported at 664 F. Supp. 1463. We set out below our reasons for concluding that the district court properly adhered to its own interpretation of the Warsaw Convention/Montreal Agreement in all actions, including those transferred from district courts within the Second Circuit.

The Supreme Court, in *Van Dusen v. Barrack*, 376 U.S. 612 (1964), addressed and resolved this question: when a defendant in a diversity action moves for a venue transfer under 28 U.S.C. § 1404(a), which state's law applies post-transfer? The state law that would have applied in the transferor court adheres to the case, the Supreme Court held; in the Court's words, "with respect to state law," the venue change will accomplish "but a change of courtrooms."[4]

The *Van Dusen* interpretation of 28 U.S.C. § 1404(a), as the latter applies in diversity actions, rests on principles advanced in *Erie R.R. v. Tompkins*, 304 U.S. 64 (1938), and cases in the *Erie* line. Justice Goldberg explained for the Court in *Van Dusen*:

> Our interpretation of § 1404(a) is supported by the policy underlying *Erie*. We should ensure that the "accident" of federal diversity jurisdiction does not enable a party to utilize a transfer to achieve a result in federal court which could not have been achieved in the courts of the State where the action was filed. What *Erie* and the cases following it have sought was an identity or uniformity between federal and state courts; and the fact that in most instances this could be achieved by directing federal courts to apply the laws of the States "in which they sit" should not obscure that, in applying the same reasoning to § 1404(a), the critical identity to be maintained is between the federal district court which decides the case and the courts of the State in which the action was filed.

Defendants in *Van Dusen* sought to transfer the case from the Eastern District of Pennsylvania to the District of Massachusetts. (Massachusetts, but not Pennsylvania,

---

4. The *Van Dusen* Court expressly did not decide whether the law of the state in which the transferor court sits would apply if plaintiff rather than defendant sought the transfer, or if a state court in the transferor court's state would dismiss the case on forum non conveniens grounds. Wright, Miller & Cooper indicate that several courts have applied the law of the transferor court even when plaintiff, rather than defendant, moves for a transfer. A strong argument, however, favors application of the law of the transferee state in such instances.

limited the damages plaintiffs could recover.) Were the transfer to be made, the Supreme Court ruled, though all further proceedings would take place in the Massachusetts district court, Pennsylvania law, not Massachusetts law, would furnish the governing state prescriptions.

The question before us is whether the *Van Dusen* rule — that the law applicable in the transferor forum attends the transfer — should apply to transferred federal claims. It is a question meriting attention from Higher Authority. Congress, it appears, has not focused on the issue, nor has the Supreme Court addressed it. The Judicial Panel on Multidistrict Litigation assumed, on at least one occasion, that the *Van Dusen* rule would apply to transferred federal claims, but the Panel, from what we can glean, has given the matter only fleeting consideration. Recognizing that the question is perplexing, particularly in the context of 28 U.S.C. § 1407, a statute authorizing transfers only for pretrial purposes, we are persuaded by thoughtful commentary that "the transferee court should be free to decide a federal claim in the manner it views as correct without deferring to the interpretation of the transferor circuit." Marcus, *Conflict Among Circuits and Transfers Within the Federal Judicial System,* 93 YALE L.J. 677, 721 (1984); *see also* Steinman, *Law of the Case: A Judicial Puzzle in Consolidated and Transferred Cases and in Multidistrict Litigation,* 135 U. PA. L. REV. 595, 662-706 (1987).

As the district court stressed in response to our remand, the *Erie* policies served by the *Van Dusen* decision do not figure in the calculus when the law to be applied is federal, not state. Given the reality of conflict among the circuits on the proper interpretation of federal law, however, why deny to a plaintiff with a federal claim the "venue privilege" a diversity claimant enjoys? Plaintiffs in the *Van Dusen* situation could effectively pick Pennsylvania rather than Massachusetts law and retain the benefit of that choice after transfer. Why deny a similar right of selection and retention to plaintiffs who would fare better under the Second Circuit's interpretation of federal law than under the D.C. Circuit's interpretation?

The point has been cogently made that venue provisions are designed with geographical convenience in mind, and not to "guarantee that the plaintiff will be able to select the law that will govern the case." In diversity cases, however, federal courts are governed by *Klaxon* and therefore may not compose federal choice-of-law principles; instead, they must look to state prescriptions in determining which state's law applies. With "no federal choice-of-law principles that favor the application of the law of one state over the law of another," the diversity plaintiff's opening move or "venue privilege" ordinarily fills the gap — it "prevails by default." For the adjudication of federal claims, on the other hand, "the federal courts comprise a single system in which each tribunal endeavors to apply a single body of law"; there is no compelling reason to allow plaintiff to capture the most favorable interpretation of that law simply and solely by virtue of his or her right to choose the place to open the fray.

As summarized in the commentary we find persuasive:

> The *Van Dusen* Court stressed the venue privilege because under *Klaxon* there is no federal principle by which to select the state law that should govern diversity cases. Where federal claims are transferred, however, the principle that the transferee federal court is competent to decide federal issues correctly indicates that the transferee's interpretation should apply.

For federal courts, the most significant choice-of-law difference between issues of state law and issues of federal law is that they lack competence to develop rules of decision for the former and are presumptively competent to decide the latter. The federal courts have not only the power but the duty to decide issues of federal law correctly. There is no room in the federal system of review for rote acceptance of the decision of a court outside the chain of direct review. If a federal court simply accepts the interpretation of another circuit without independently addressing the merits, it is not doing its job.

Marcus, *supra*, 93 YALE L.J. at 679, 702.

Application of *Van Dusen* in the matter before us, we emphasize, would not produce uniformity. There would be one interpretation of federal law for the cases initially filed in districts within the Second Circuit, and an opposing interpretation for cases filed elsewhere. Applying divergent interpretations of the governing federal law to plaintiffs, depending solely upon where they initially filed suit, would surely reduce the efficiencies achievable through consolidated preparatory proceedings. Indeed, because there is ultimately a single proper interpretation of federal law, the attempt to ascertain and apply diverse circuit interpretation simultaneously is inherently self-contradictory. Our system contemplates differences between different states' laws; thus a multidistrict judge asked to apply divergent state positions on a point of law would face a coherent, if sometimes difficult, task. But it is logically inconsistent to require one judge to apply simultaneously different and conflicting interpretations of what is supposed to be a unitary federal law.

The district judge in the instant case observed that:

> If more than one interpretation of federal law exists, the Supreme Court of the United States can finally determine the issue and restore uniformity in the federal system. The uniformity achieved in this way is an "informed uniformity" unlike the "blind uniformity" which would result from one court applying the interpretation of another by rote.

We agree. The federal courts spread across the country owe respect to each other's efforts and should strive to avoid conflicts, but each has an obligation to engage independently in reasoned analysis. Binding precedent for all is set only by the Supreme Court, and for the district courts within a circuit, only by the court of appeals for that circuit.

We return, finally, to the most anomalous feature of this case. As earlier observed, we deal here not with an "all-purpose" transfer under 28 U.S.C. § 1404(a), but with a transfer under 28 U.S.C. § 1407 "for coordinated or consolidated pretrial proceedings." We have held, in accord with the district court, that the law of a transferor forum on a federal question — here, the law of the Second Circuit — merits close consideration, but does not have stare decisis effect in a transferee forum situated in another circuit. Should the several cases consolidated for pretrial preparation in the instant proceeding eventually return to transferor courts outside this circuit, would our district court's Warsaw Convention/Montreal Agreement ruling, which we have affirmed, have binding force? We believe it should, as "law of the case," for if it did not, transfers under 28 U.S.C. § 1407 could be counterproductive, *i.e.*, capable of generating rather than reducing the duplication and protraction Congress sought to check. On this issue in the case at hand, however, our circuit is not positioned to speak the last word.

We affirm the order of the district court that KAL is entitled to avail itself of the limitation on damages provided by the Warsaw Convention and raised to $75,000 by the Montreal Agreement; and we note again that the proper interpretation of the Convention and Agreement, as well as the scope of the transferee court's interpretive authority in a case such as this one, are matters in need of definitive resolution for our national court system.

Affirmed.

Notes and Questions

---

1. In *In re Korean Air Lines Disaster*, both the court and the concurrence (an opinion by Judge Douglas Ginsburg that is also well worth reading) agreed as to the existence of what the latter referred to as the "norm of independent judgment"—i.e., the ability of each federal circuit to resolve issues of federal law for itself. *Accord Air Line Pilots Ass'n, Int'l v. O'Neill*, 499 U.S. 65, 80 n.10 (1991) ("[A] Seventh Circuit case would not have controlled the outcome of this dispute, which arose in the Fifth Circuit."). Apparently because this rule is so well-known, though, neither of the aforementioned courts cited any authority in support of this proposition. So what is the source of this rule? Such a rule is difficult to discern from the text of the act that created the United States Court of Appeals, the Circuit Courts of Appeals Act of 1891, ch. 517, 26 Stat. 826 (also known as the Evarts Act). Moreover, there is some thought that "Congress may never have intended that the concept of law of the circuit develop," Richard L. Marcus, *Conflicts Among Circuits and Transfers Within the Federal Judicial System*, 93 YALE L.J. 677, 686 (1984), and some earlier courts held to the contrary, *see id.* at 703. Consider, for example, the following passage from *Shreve v. Cheesman*, 69 F. 785 (8th Cir. 1895):

> It is a principle of general jurisprudence that courts of concurrent or co-ordinate jurisdiction will follow the deliberate decisions of each other, in order to prevent unseemly conflicts, and to preserve uniformity of decision and harmony of action. This principle is nowhere more firmly established or more implicitly followed than in the circuit courts of the United States. A deliberate decision of a question of law by one of these courts is generally treated as a controlling precedent in every federal circuit court in the Union, until it is reversed or modified by an appellate court. . . . Nor has it been thought less vital to a wise administration of justice in the federal courts that the various judges who sit in the same court should not attempt to overrule the decisions of each other, especially upon questions involving rules of property or practice, except for the most cogent reasons.

Id. at 790-91.

Nonetheless, apparently due to some combination of the structure of appellate review established by the Evarts Act and a (somehow) related duty to consider questions of federal law independently (*see* Marcus, *supra*, at 686,

702-03), along with some apparent reliance on similar state court models (*see* Note, *Securing Uniformity in National Law: A Proposal for National Stare Decisis in the Courts of Appeals,* 87 YALE L.J. 1219, 1224-36 (1978)), "the independence of the circuits was quickly established" (Marcus, *supra,* at 703), and does not appear to have been seriously challenged since. *See, e.g.,* 18 JAMES WM. MOORE, MOORE'S FEDERAL PRACTICE § 134.02[1][c], at 134-23 (3d ed. 2008) ("The decisions of the court of appeals for one circuit are not binding upon the courts of appeal for other circuits. . . . However, the courts should consider the decisions of another circuit, if persuasive, in the interest of maintaining a reasonable uniformity of federal law.") But as the above-referenced Note indicates, numerous proposals for national unification have surfaced. For more on this subject, see Walter V. Schaefer, *Reducing Circuit Conflicts,* 69 A.B.A. J. 452 (April 1983).

Does the current rule of intercircuit independence (and therefore potential conflict) make sense? What are the advantages and disadvantages of such a system, as compared with a system where a decision of one appellate panel would be considered "binding" on the entire nation? Would the later application of such a precedent be any more "rote" than the application of an earlier precedent from the same circuit, or the Supreme Court? And what of the idea, expressed by the court in this case, of what is "supposed to be a unitary federal law"? Note (as the concurrence pointed out) that, at the time of this court's decision, "only the Second Circuit had spoken on the pertinent question." Note also the statement by the *In re Korean Air Lines Disaster* court that "there is ultimately a single proper interpretation of federal law." Note finally that not all states with intermediate appellate courts follow the federal model, and that some (such as California) follow the rule that a decision of such a court is binding on the entire state.

2. The *In re Korean Air Lines Disaster* court, toward the end of its opinion, spoke of the "law of the case" effect of its determination to apply its own law. What is that effect? Does it make sense to reject a strict application of another circuit's law as a matter of precedent, yet expect that circuit to strictly apply the District of Columbia circuit's law as a matter of law of the case?

3. If the District of Columbia Circuit in this case had followed Second Circuit law, could not review have been sought by the defendants in the Supreme Court? In other words, does the real issue here relate to whether one circuit should be bound by another with which it disagrees? Along this line, could not a later circuit, even though in some sense "bound" by an earlier circuit, overrule the first circuit, just as one circuit can overrule itself?

4. If the Supreme Court did not have to deal with circuit splits, it could focus more on error correction. Would that be preferable?

5. "The published decision of a [three-judge] panel of a court of appeals is a decision of the court and carries the weight of stare decisis." 18 JAMES WM. MOORE,

MOORE'S FEDERAL PRACTICE § 134.02[1][c], at 134-16 (3d ed. 2008). Thus, it has generally been established that "[o]ne panel of a circuit court cannot overrule another panel, unless a contrary decision of the United States Supreme Court or the enactment of a controlling [federal] statute intervenes . . . ." *Id.* at 134-16 to -18. Nonetheless, it has also been established that "a circuit court panel's decision may be overruled by the court sitting en banc." *Id.* at 134-20. *Accord* Amy E. Sloan, *The Dog That Didn't Bark: Stealth Procedures and the Erosion of Stare Decisis in the Federal Courts of Appeals*, 78 FORDHAM L. REV. 713, 718-19 (2009).

6. The concurring opinion in *In re Korean Air Lines Disaster* by Judge Douglas Ginsburg was joined by Judge Stephen F. Williams. Does this mean that the concurrence also has binding precedential effect, at least within the District of Columbia Circuit?

7. For a more recent take on intercircuit stare decisis, see Martha Dragich, *Uniformity, Inferiority, and the Law of the Circuit Doctrine*, 56 LOYOLA L. REV. 535 (2010).

c. *Horizontal Stare Decisis in the District Courts*

In contrast to the rule applicable in the Supreme Court and the various circuit courts of appeals, "[a] decision of a federal district court judge is not binding precedent in either a different judicial district, the same judicial district, or even upon the same judge in a different case." 18 JAMES WM. MOORE, MOORE'S FEDERAL PRACTICE § 134.02[1][d], at 134-24.1 (3d ed. 2008). But why should district court decisions not be binding on the other district courts, whether in the same district or elsewhere? According to one leading treatise: "The non-precedential status of district-court decisions is based not on a disrespect for district judges, but on the sheer unmanageability of a system in which the authority to lay down legal rules would be dispersed across a multitude of independent courts." *Id.* Do you find this reasoning persuasive, particularly in the age of computers?

Some courts have further suggested that district court decisions are not binding because those courts generally consist of trial, rather than appellate, courts, and thus have no general power of review over any lower courts and (thus) have little need to establish precedent for those courts. Yet, it has frequently been held that "district court decisions, in the absence of other authority, have stare decisis effect on bankruptcy courts in that district." *Id.*

For an argument in favor of district court stare decisis, see Joseph W. Mead, *Stare Decisis in the Inferior Courts of the United States*, 12 NEV. L.J. 787 (2012).

"Of course," even if not binding, "a decision by a federal district judge may be cited to any court for its persuasive effect." 18 JAMES WM. MOORE, MOORE'S FEDERAL PRACTICE § 134.02[1][d], at 134-24.1 to -24.2 (3d ed. 2008).

d. Stare Decisis in Theory

Henry M. Hart, Jr. & Albert M. Sacks

NOTE ON THE REASONS SUPPORTING A GENERAL PRACTICE OF ADHERENCE TO PRIOR HOLDINGS

**The Legal Process: Basic Problems in the Making and Application of Law
(William N. Eskridge, Jr. & Philip P. Frickey eds., 1994)**

A. *A TENTATIVE FORMULATION OF THE BASES OF THE DOCTRINE OF STARE DECISIS*

Consider the adequacy of the following formulation of the considerations which may be thought to support a general practice of adherence to prior holdings:

1. In Furtherance of Private Ordering —

(a) The desirability of enabling people to plan their affairs at the stage of primary private activity with the maximum attainable confidence that if they comply with the law as it has theretofore been announced, or can fairly be expected to be announced thereafter, they will not become entangled in litigation.

(b) The desirability of providing private counsel so far as possible with stable bases of reasoning. Think about this factor, in particular, from the point of view of efficient social engineering. The potential contribution of the legal profession in the avoidance of social friction is very large, is it not? A lawyer must have tools with which to work if he is to make this contribution.

(c) The desirability of encouraging the remedial processes of private settlement by minimizing the incentives of the parties to try to secure from a different judge a different decision than has been given by the same or other judges in the past.

2. In Furtherance of Fair and Efficient Adjudication —

(a) The desirability, from the point of view of the litigants, of expediting litigation and minimizing its costs by sparing them the necessity of relitigating every relevant proposition in every case.

(b) The need, from the point of view of the judicial system, of facilitating the dispatch of business — indeed, the sheer impossibility of reexamining *de novo* every relevant proposition in every case.

(c) The need of discouraging a rush of litigation whenever there is a change of personnel on the bench.

(d) The desirability, from the point of view of fairness to the litigants, of securing a reasonable uniformity of decision throughout the judicial system, both at any given time and from one time to another.

(e) The desirability of promoting genuine impersonality of decision by minimizing the elements of personal discretion, and of facilitating the operation of the check of professional criticism.

(f) The propriety of according respect to the conclusions of predecessor judges.

(g) The injustice of disappointing expectations fairly generated at the stage of primary private activity.

3. In Furtherance of Public Confidence in the Judiciary —

(a) The desirability of maximizing the acceptability of decisions, and the importance to this end of popular and professional confidence in (1) the impersonality of decisions and (2) their reasoned foundation, as manifested both by the respect accorded to them by successor judges and by their staying power.

(b) The necessity, considering the amorphous nature of the limits upon judicial power and the usual absence of an effective political check at the ballot box, that judges be subject to the discipline and the restraint of an obligation to build upon the prior law in a fashion which can withstand the test of professional criticism.

Is it sound to conclude that these factors warrant at least a presumption in favor of refusal to reexamine past holdings, which should yield only to a strong showing of probable error? Compare the practice of some courts of requiring counsel to ask and receive permission to argue that a prior decision should be overruled before listening to such an argument.

To what extent do these same factors counsel a policy of *stare dictis* as well as of *stare decisis*?

Notes and Questions

---

1. The justification for stare decisis offered by Professors Hart and Sacks has been very influential. Do you agree with it? Why or why not?

Frederick Schauer

PRECEDENT

39 Stan. L. Rev. 571 (1987)

What does it mean for a past event to be *precedent* for a current decision? And how does something we do *today* establish a precedent for the future? Can decisions really be controlled by the past and responsible to the future, or are appeals to precedent just so much window dressing, masking what is in reality a decision made for today only?[1] And even if precedent *can* constrain decisionmakers, why should a procedure for decisionmaking impose such a constraint? Why should the best decision for now be distorted or thwarted by obeisance to a dead past, or by obligation to an uncertain and dimly perceived future? Equally important is the question of weight. When precedent matters, just *how much* should it matter? If we are to be shackled to the past and beholden to the future, just how tight are those bonds, and what should it take to loose them?

An appeal to precedent is a form of argument, and a form of justification,[2] that is often as persuasive as it is pervasive. The bare skeleton of an appeal to precedent is easily stated: The previous treatment of occurrence *X* in manner *Y* constitutes, *solely because of its historical pedigree*, a reason for treating *X* in manner *Y* if and when *X* again occurs.

Appeals to precedent do not reside exclusively in courts of law. Forms of argument that may be concentrated in the legal system are rarely isolated there, and the argument from precedent is a prime example of the nonexclusivity of what used to be called "legal reasoning." Think of the child who insists that he should not have to wear short pants to school because his older brother was allowed to wear long pants when *he* was seven. Or think of the bureaucrat who responds to the supplicant for special consideration by saying that "we've never done it that way before." In countless instances, out of law as well as in, the fact that something was done before provides, by itself, a reason for doing it that way again.

Reliance on precedent is part of life in general. The law's lack of an exclusive claim on precedential reasoning suggests that we should dig beneath the use of precedent in this or even any legal system. I would thus like to look at precedent, at least initially, without the baggage of particular legal doctrines and without the encumbrances of a theory of law or judicial decision. By removing these potentially distorting constraints, we may see things that have previously been blocked from view. And having abstracted the analysis by looking at precedent outside of the law,

---

1. Recall Justice Roberts' fear that Supreme Court decisions might come to be treated like "a restricted railroad ticket, good for this day and train only." Smith v. Allwright, 321 U.S. 649, 669 (1943) (Roberts, J., dissenting).

2. There is no difference between the logical structure of an *argument* and that of a *justification*, but the different terms suggest separate events within a larger rhetorical setting. Arguments are made prior to a decision, and thus are made *to* a decisionmaker. Justifications, on the other hand, are provided after a decision is made or an action is taken, and are given *by* the decisionmaker.

we may then be able to glimpse a different picture of the use of precedent *in* law, and of what it means to "do law," to operate in a specifically legal form.

I. THE FORWARD-LOOKING ASPECT OF PRECEDENT

An argument from precedent seems at first to look backward. The traditional perspective on precedent, both inside and outside of law, has therefore focused on the use of yesterday's precedents in today's decisions.[4] But in an equally if not more important way, an argument from precedent looks forward as well, asking us to view today's decision as a precedent for tomorrow's decisionmakers. Today is not only yesterday's tomorrow; it is also tomorrow's yesterday. A system of precedent therefore involves the special responsibility accompanying the power to commit the future before we get there.

Thinking about the effect of today's decision upon tomorrow encourages us to separate the precedential effect of a decision from the canonical language, or authoritative characterization, that may accompany that decision. Looking at precedent only as a backward-looking constraint may produce a distorted preoccupation with the canonical statements of previous decisionmakers. The precedents of the past, especially judicial precedents, come neatly packaged, with selected facts and authoritative language. Dealing with the use of past precedents thus requires dealing with the presence of the previous decisionmaker's *words*.[5] These words may themselves have authoritative force, what Ronald Dworkin calls the "enactment force of precedent," and thus we often find it difficult to disentangle the effect of a past *decision* from the effect caused by its accompanying words. More pervasively, even a previous decisionmaker's noncanonical descriptions channel the way in which the present views those past decisions. So long as the words of the past tell

---

4. A noteworthy exception is MacCormick, *Formal Justice and the Form of Legal Argument*, 6 Etudes de Logique Juridique 103 (1976). Considering the future implications of today's decisions is central to the notion of adjudication according to principle. But principles, in and out of law, are expressed in words, and the existing discussion of principles involves the problem of imagining what future cases might later come within the domain now described by a particular set of words. That, as I will discuss presently, is distinct from the question of what later decisions might be taken to follow from the first decision. Implicit in what I say, therefore, is a distinction between what is said and what is done. Much of the discussion of principled decisionmaking focuses on being constrained tomorrow by what we *say* today. That is important, but it is not the same as being constrained by what we *do* today. Moreover, the focus of the "neutral principles" literature is on the commitments necessarily, or at least ideally, made by a single decisionmaker. That differs from the effect of a particular decision on some *other* decisionmaker possibly not sharing the same views.

More significantly, a careful study of precedent must confront the extent to which sticky and substantially nonnormative social or linguistic characterizations may impede the ability of a formulator of a principle to draw certain intrinsically sound distinctions or to employ certain intrinsically justifiable groupings. This problem, separate from the problem of decision according to principle, is central to understanding the concept of precedent.

5. This relationship among facts, facts as found by the court, decision of the court, and announced reasoning of the court is at the heart of the English debate about *ratio decidendi*. . . .

us how to view the deeds of the past, it remains difficult to isolate how much of the effect of a past decision is attributable to what a past court has *done* rather than to what it has *said*.

Nonjudicial precedents of the past also arrive at the present carrying with them their original characterizations. Suppose a child allowed to stay up past her bedtime in order to watch a television show her parents thought particularly educational. Two weeks later, the child again wants to stay up late to watch a television show. The child will probably argue, "Two weeks ago you said I could stay up late to watch an educational show. Well, this show is educational too, so you have to let me stay up late tonight." That argument moves discussion away from the decision to allow the child to watch a particular show to what the parents *said* in making the decision. And then the argument resembles one over application of a specifically formulated rule such as a statute. If the parents had set out a rule, in advance, that bedtime was 8 p.m. except when an educational show was on later than 8 p.m., the discussion would differ little from that in which a precedent is accompanied by simultaneous explanatory language. This is precisely because such language will be treated later like a specifically formulated rule.

. . . .

At the moment when we consider the wisdom of some currently contemplated decision, however, the characterization of that decision is comparatively open. There is no authoritative characterization apart from what we choose to create. In making a decision, we must acknowledge its many possible subsequent characterizations, and thus the many directions in which it might be extended. Yet despite this seeming indeterminacy of the future precedential effect of today's decision pervades legal and nonlegal argument. . . .

Thus, only the precedents of the past, and not forward-looking precedents, stand before us clothed with generations of characterizations and recharacterizations. When we look at today as a precedent for the future, we remove the distraction of the canonical effect of simultaneous explanatory language, and we can better understand how being constrained by precedent often involves something different from being constrained by specially formulated normative language.

II. ISOLATING THE ARGUMENT FROM PRECEDENT

We can use the past for many purposes, but not every use of the past involves reliance on precedent. Initially, we must differentiate an argument from precedent from an argument from experience. The first time a child sees a red coil on top of a stove he may touch it, but when he sees the red coil again he knows its dangers and keeps his fingers safely clear. When a physician sees a certain array of symptoms that in the past have indicated typhoid, she will probably diagnose typhoid when those symptoms again appear. And many judges would describe the process of sentencing as based substantially on this type of experiential reasoning.

In each of these cases, a present array of facts similar to some previous array leads a decisionmaker to draw on experience in reaching a conclusion. But despite the superficial similarity of these cases to the use of precedent, the reasoning process here is different. When reasoning from experience, the facts and conclusions of the past have no significance apart from what they teach us about the present. The probability that the present will be like the past both determines and exhausts the value of the previous experience. If we believe that the current case ought to be decided differently, no purely precedential residuum remains in the calculus. Moreover, if we now believe that the previous decision was incorrect, we will completely reject the value of the experience. But if we are truly arguing from precedent, then the fact that something was decided before gives it present value despite our current belief that the previous decision was erroneous.

An argument from experience need not be based on the experience of the present decisionmaker. Unwilling or unable to do as much thinking, looking, or testing as a previous decisionmaker, the current decisionmaker may choose to conserve present decisional resources by relying on the prior decisionmaker's experience: "If Cardozo decided this way, who am I to disagree?" Although people may describe this form of reasoning as "precedent," it is significantly different from a narrower, more central notion of precedent as a norm limiting the decisionmaker's flexibility. When the choice whether to rely on a prior decisionmaker is entirely in the hands of the present decisionmaker, the prior decision does not *constrain* the present decision, and the present decisionmaker violates no norm by disregarding it. I want to view precedent as a *rule* of precedent, and not as a nonrule-governed choice by a decisionmaker in an individual case to rely on the prior decisions of others.

If precedent is seen as a rule directing a decisionmaker to take prior decisions into account, then it follows that a pure argument from precedent, unlike an argument from experience, depends only on the *results* of those decisions, and not on the validity of the reasons supporting those results. That two plus two today equals four is true, but it does not become more true because two plus two equaled yesterday. When the strength of a current conclusion totally stands or falls on arguments for or against that conclusion, there is no appeal to precedent, even if the same conclusion has been reached in the past. If precedent matters, a prior decision now believed erroneous still affects the current decision simply because it is prior. Only if a rule makes relevant the result of a previous decision regardless of a decisionmaker's current belief about the correctness of that decision do we have the kind of argument from precedent routinely made in law and elsewhere.

In referring to past and present decisionmakers, I presuppose that, as institutions, the past and present decisionmakers are identical or of equal status. If a pure argument from precedent is valid, the earlier decision has a status that must be respected by a later decisionmaker, and that status is imposed by the rule of precedent independent of other status differentials. Lower courts, for example, are expected to respect the decisions of higher courts. But the hierarchical ordering of decisionmakers implicates considerations different from those involved when a decisionmaker is constrained by *its* previous actions as opposed to the orders of its superiors in the hierarchy.[11]

---

11. Note that while contemporary usage has collapsed much of the difference between precedent and *stare decisis*, it should be clear that I am talking about the latter in its strict sense.

A naked argument from precedent thus urges that a decisionmaker give weight to a particular result regardless of whether that decisionmaker believes it to be correct and regardless of whether that decisionmaker believes it valuable in any way to rely on that previous result. Shorn of any embellishments, the reasons for respecting an argument from precedent may seem far from obvious. But before turning to that issue, we must first deal with the logically prior questions of whether precedent *can* matter, and if so, how.

III. CAN PRECEDENT CONSTRAIN?

A. Rules of Relevance

Reasoning from precedent, whether looking back to the past or ahead to the future, presupposes an ability to identify the relevant precedent. Why does a currently contemplated decision sometimes have a precedent and sometimes not? Such a distinction can exist only if there is some way of identifying a precedent — some way of determining whether a past event is sufficiently similar to the present facts to justify assimilation of the two events. And when we think about the precedential effect in the future of the action we take today, we presuppose that some future events will be descriptively assimilated to today's.

No two events are exactly alike. For a decision to be precedent for another decision does not require that the facts of the earlier and the later cases be absolutely identical. Were that required, nothing would be a precedent for anything else. We must therefore leave the realm of absolute identity. Once we do so, however, it is clear that the relevance of an earlier precedent depends upon how we characterize the facts arising in the earlier case. It is a commonplace that these characterizations are inevitably theory-laden. In order to assess what is a precedent for what, we must engage in some determination of the relevant similarities between the two events. In turn, we must extract this determination from some other organizing standard specifying which similarities are important and which we can safely ignore.

A parent's decision to let a daughter wear high-heeled shoes at the age of thirteen is scarcely precedent when a son then asks to be permitted to wear high-heeled shoes at that age. But a parent's decision to let that daughter stay up until ten o'clock will be relied upon justifiably by the son when he reaches the same age. A judgment finding tort liability based on the ownership of a black dog is precedent for a judgment regarding the owner of a brown dog, but not for a judgment regarding the owner of a black car. This is so only because a principle, or standard, makes dogness relevant in a way that blackness is not. Consider who among Alan Alda, Menachem Begin, and Dave Righetti is most similar to Sandy Koufax. One is the same age, another has the same religion, and a third is employed in the same occupation. The same point about the role of theory in assessing similarity undergirds Holmes' facetious description of the "Vermont justice of the peace before whom a suit was brought by one farmer against another for breaking a churn. The justice took time to consider, and then said that he had looked through the statutes and could find nothing about churns, and gave judgment for the defendant."[14]

It should be clear, therefore, that only the intervention of organizing theory, in the form of *rules of relevance*, allows us to distinguish the precedential from the irrelevant. Precedent depends upon such rules. And these rules themselves are contingent upon both time and culture. . . .

With rule-dependency and context-dependency in mind, let us return to the forward-looking aspect of precedent. What is it to hope or fear that a decision will establish a precedent for some other decision in the future? Why do some people fear that allowing restrictions on Nazis because they are Nazis will establish a precedent for some other decision in the future? Why do some people fear that allowing restrictions on Nazis because they are Nazis will establish a precedent for restrictions on socialists because they are socialists, even though the distinction between a Nazi and a socialist is obvious, accessible, and easily justified? To worry about a precedential effect in the future, or to worry that a specific future event will be analogized to today's case, presupposes some rule of relevance. Rarely does someone at the time of the first decision think that almost the exact same facts will arise again. Rather, the thought is that this decision will establish a precedent for some different array of facts, one that contains some points of identity with the array of facts currently presented. Imagine a faculty meeting considering a request from a student for an excused absence from an examination in order to attend the funeral of a sister. Invariably someone will object that this case will establish a precedent allowing students to be excused from examinations to attend the funerals of grandparents, aunts, uncles, cousins, nieces, nephews, close friends, and pets. Implicit in this objection is a rule of relevance that treats death as a relevant similarity, "caring" as a relevant similarity, and any distinction between siblings and other meaningful relationships as irrelevant. In some form or another, this type of rule of relevance inheres in any assertion of similarity.

A rule of relevance may also be explained as a choice among alternative characterizations. To use the same example, the student's sister is simultaneously a woman, a sibling, a relative, a blood relative, and one with whom the student has a "meaningful relationship." How the relationship is characterized will determine whether later cases will be classed as similar. Thus, one who worries about establishing a precedent, or for that matter one who wants to establish a precedent, has in mind a characterization that the future will give to today's action, some category within which tomorrow's decisionmaker will place today's facts. The issue is one of *assimilation*, how we will group the facts and events of our world. The power of precedent depends upon some assimilation between the event at hand and some other event. This grouping may come from a simple characterization that includes both events, such as the phrase "censorship" to include restrictions on the speech of both Nazis and socialists. Or the assimilation of the two events may come from a more complex rule of relevance, such as the rule that enables people to group government assistance to New York City, Lockheed, Chrysler, and farmers while distinguishing all of these cases from loans to students and veterans. In this case there is still some "heading" under which some but not all instances are likely to be

---

14. Holmes, *The Path of the Law*, 10 HARV. L. REV. 457, 474-75 (1897).

grouped. Regardless of simplicity or complexity, some groupings of the two events under one heading remains necessary for the operation of a system of precedent. The task of a theory of precedent is to explain, in a world in which a single event may fit into many different categories, how and why some assimilations are plausible and others are not.

B. Categories of Decisions and Categories of the World

Identifying the central place of a rule of relevance is only the first step. We must still locate the source of the rules enabling us to call something similar to something else. Only by looking to the source can we determine if that source constrains, or if a decisionmaker may classify the black dogs as easily with the black cars as with the dogs of other colors.

1. The Articulated Characterization.

In seeking to locate the sources of characterization, we can take a large first step by noting the important distinction between decisions containing and those not containing canonical language. At times a decision will be accompanied by an articulated and authoritative characterization of the decision and its underlying facts. This *articulated characterization*, not unlike an articulated and specifically formulated rule, constrains the use of subsequent and inconsistent characterizations. Suppose the faculty grants the request of the student who wishes to attend the funeral of his sister. Suppose further that the grant of the request is accompanied by a written explanation specifying that the excuse was given so that the student could attend the funeral of a member of his immediate family. This characterization of a sister as a member of an immediate family will in subsequent cases constrain (although by no means absolutely) those who desire to characterize this precedent more broadly, such as by characterizing a sister as a relative, or as a close companion. A similar constraint would operate if the faculty that granted the first excuse attempted to narrow the precedent by denying an excuse in a subsequent case involving a father, mother, or brother.[19]

---

19. The two situations are not exactly equivalent, and a sort of "ratchet effect" seems to characterize the way in which constraints operate more in one direction than in another. Expansion seems more defensible than contraction, and it is important to think about why expansion of a given decision seems to flow more easily than contraction. A starting point may be the observation that we do not lead our lives under the *expressio unius* maxim. Except where something special about the context demands it, it is not a rule of discourse that what we say is all we have to say. But it *is* a rule of discourse that one does not willy-nilly go back on what one has already said. In some contexts, however, including most legislation and *perhaps* including case law, it is our understanding that what is said simultaneously says something and marks the outer limits of a domain. Thus the *expressio unius* maxim presupposes the existence of two groups — the group actually specified and the larger group, which could have been specified but what not. The question is one of deciding, given the absence of specification, what this larger group is. And this, in turn, will be largely a function of whether that larger group *could have* been specified. If there is no reason to suppose that it could not have been, then we are likely to take extension to that larger group in a later case as being as inconsistent with the first case as would be outright contradiction.

In classical legal theory, articulated characterizations are often considered mere dicta, but I do not want anything to turn on the questionable distinction between holding and dictum. Whether the characterizing language is treated as holding or dictum, that language cannot absolutely prevent a subsequent interpreter from recharacterizing the first case. But the interpreter must at least confront an argumentative burden not present without an articulated characterization. Thus the articulated characterization acts like a specifically formulated rule. Rules can be broken, but to justify breaking a rule is more difficult than to take the same course of conduct in pursuit of or in the absence of a rule. Where there is an articulated characterization, therefore, the question whether precedent can constrain may collapse into the question whether rules can constrain. The issue is then the extent to which authoritative language can control, channel, or constrain decisionmakers purporting to interpret that language. This issue has been rehearsed for decades, but it is different from the question whether a decision *qua* decision can also exert meaningful pressure on subsequent decisionmakers.

The special problem of precedent thus appears most clearly when we remove the obscuring smokescreen of an articulated characterization. No decision in the real world is completely devoid of characterizations. Even a mere statement of facts is undoubtedly a characterization. Nevertheless, it is heuristically useful to imagine an event and a decision, without an authoritative statement of what the event is an example of. In this case, it appears possible for a subsequent decisionmaker to adopt any rule of relevance at all — or at least so many alternative rules of relevance that precedent appears to impose no constraint. Precedent's forward-looking aspect reveals this open-ended quality, for the forward-looking use of precedent is somewhat closer to the notion of a collection of facts without an authoritative characterization. Prior to a decision, no single authoritative characterization presents itself in the way that it does with a decision already made. Instead, one concerned about what the future might do with today's decision worries that this decision might be taken by the future to constitute a component of any number of categories extending this decision in different directions. When one fears that restricting Nazis may establish a precedent for content-based restrictions on other speakers, the fear is fueled precisely by the absence, at the time the fear is expressed, of any authoritative characterization separating Nazis from socialists. When faculty members fear the precedential effect of allowing some excuses from examinations, the fears are expressed in ways not present when specifically formulated *rules* are proposed, exactly because the absence of either rules or a canonical statement of the action in this case leaves open a wide choice of possible characterizations for the future to place on this decision. In any situation that lacks an articulated characterization, the central problem of precedent remains: Are there constraints on the assessment of similarity when few events are intrinsically similar to others? When there is no authoritative rule of relevance for a particular situation, is it not then illusory to think of the precedent as in any way constraining?

2. The Roots of Characterization.

We can now rephrase the problem. For any given decision, are there restraints on the possible categories of assimilation connecting the facts now before us with the facts before a future decisionmaker? Or is the choice of category completely up to the future decisionmaker, who can choose the category that *a posteriori* justifies the decision made on nonprecedential grounds? The problem is to determine what constrains a decisionmaker's control over the categories of assimilation.

. . . .

. . . The notion of precedent largely depends upon the way in which the categories of the world are frequently larger or more powerful in channeling thought than the categories or comparisons that might be crafted to particular normative purposes. The categories of our existence, the categories that group beanbag chairs and metal desks together as "furniture" and motorcycles and trucks together as "vehicles," transcend specific normative ends. These conceptual categories intrude into diverse places and presumptively create assimilative groupings even where that assimilation may frustrate institutional or individual goals. The grouping of trucks and motorcycles as vehicles is a rule of language, not solely within the control of the regulations of the park department. We must distinguish the rule of language from the rule about the kinds of things we want in the park. If we collapse this distinction, we ignore what is most important — the way in which larger categories and rules of language that generate certain groupings significantly constrain the substantive rules in particular regulatory contexts.

IV. THE PRICE OF PRECEDENT

I have argued to this point only that precedent *can* matter, that we may coherently talk about one decision as constraining precedent for another. Sometimes an articulated characterization or an articulated rule of relevance may constrain significantly the range of a category of assimilation. And even without an articulated characterization, the characterizations implicit in our organization of the world, although themselves mutable, still channel the determination of relevant similarities within a decisionmaking institution and narrow the range of possible later analogies. That a system of precedent *can* be constraining says nothing, however, about either the desirability or the degree of those constraints.

In order to examine the justifications for a system of precedent, it is useful to begin by spending some time examining the consequences of adopting such a system. The most obvious consequence, of course, is that a decisionmaker constrained by precedent will sometimes feel compelled to make a decision contrary to the one she would have made had there been no precedent to be followed. Although this obvious consequence is no less important for its obviousness, and although I will discuss issues relating to this consequence in the following section, I want to concentrate now on the forward-looking aspect of precedent, and consider how this angle on precedent reveals consequences not quite so obvious.

A rule of precedent tells a current decisionmaker to follow the decision in a previous similar case. Using the language I have been employing here, we can say that a current decisionmaker is told to follow the decision of a previous case involving assimilable, if somewhat different, facts. But of course the current decisionmaker of today is the previous decisionmaker of tomorrow. Although it may seem counterintuitive, this fact causes the current decisionmaker to be constrained by precedent even if there has been no prior decision.

Even without an existing precedent, the conscientious decisionmaker must recognize that future conscientious decisionmakers will treat her decision as precedent, a realization that will constrain the range of possible decisions about the case at hand. If the future must treat what we do now as presumptively binding, then our current decision must judge not only what is best for now, but also how the current decision will affect the decision of other and future assimilable cases. Thus, the current decisionmaker must also take into account what would be best for some different but assimilable events yet to occur. The decisionmaker must then decide on the basis of what is best for *all* of the cases falling within the appropriate category of assimilation. In making this calculation, the decisionmaker will discount the future for the possibility that the future decisionmaker will disregard or distinguish today's decision. This discount cannot be complete, however, unless there is some reason to believe that future decisionmakers will feel no pull of precedent. But where future decisionmakers *can* be expected to feel the pull of precedent, today's conscientious decisionmakers are obliged to decide not only today's case, but tomorrow's as well. If the best solution to today's case is identical to the best solution for tomorrow's different but assimilable facts, then there is no problem. But if what is best for today's situation might not be best for a different (but likely to be assimilated) situation, then the need to consider the future as well as the present will result in at least some immediately suboptimal decisions.

    . . . .

Accepting the constraints of precedent thus entails taking into account an array of instances broader than the one immediately before the decisionmaker. And this in turn means that although in no case can we make a decision that is better than optimal for that case taken in isolation, in some cases we will make decisions that are worse than optimal for that case taken in isolation. It thus becomes plain that adopting a strategy of reliance on precedent is inherently risk averse, in the sense of giving up the possibility of the optimal result in every case in exchange for diminishing the possibility of bad results in some number of cases.

Thus, if the faculty in the case of the student wishing to attend the funeral of a sibling believes that future decisionmakers will assimilate siblings with all other relatives, and if it also believes that in some significant number of nonsibling relative cases it would be wrong to grant the excuse, then the faculty may plausibly deny the request in the present case even though it believes that it would be right to grant the excuse in this case if the case were taken in isolation. When we look at things this way, we see the price of precedent plainly presented. To the extent that a conscientious decisionmaker takes into account the fact that this distinction will, within a regime of precedent, substantially control future decisions with respect to similar but assimilable situations, then the conscientious current decisionmaker must partially make those future decisions as well. When this happens, there will be at least some cases in which the best decision within a regime of precedent is nevertheless a suboptimal decision for the case at hand, with each such case being a concrete example of the costs of a system in which precedent matters.

V. THE QUESTION OF WEIGHT

It should be apparent that the extent to which precedent constrains will vary with the size of the assimilating category. In other words, if the conclusions of one case apply to a sweepingly broad set of analogies (and encourage decisionmakers to make such analogies), then the constraints of precedent are likely to be substantial. Not only will a broad set of subsequent decisionmakers feel the impact of the original decision, but the original decisionmaker will feel a greater obligation in making a decision with such broad application. The bigger the group of cases the original decisionmaker is effectively deciding, the more constraining will be the mandate to treat all of those cases alike. Conversely, if the categories of assimilation are comparatively small, the decisionmaker need consider only a few cases beyond the instant case, and the constraints of precedent will be comparatively inconsequential.

Thus, the extent to which precedent constrains will vary not only with a decisionmaking institution's dependence on categories of assimilation external to its environment, but also on the *size* of those categories. To some extent the question of the size of the institution's categories of assimilation will be a function of the size of the particular categories existing in the larger world. But the strength of the constraints on precedent will also depend on just how much variation a particular decisionmaker is encouraged or allowed to acknowledge.

With respect to many decisions, a theoretically justifiable distinction between two events may be drawn if the full richness of individual variation is allowed to be a relevant factor. Distinguishing, for purposes of eligibility for a tax deduction, a failing steel industry from a prospering robotics industry is hardly unjustifiable. So too might we distinguish in the examination excuse example the good student from the marginal one. Of course, such distinctions are not necessarily wise or just. My point is only that distinctions like these cannot be considered arbitrary. The central question, then, is how many nonarbitrary variations between events will a given decisionmaker be allowed to pursue. If every nonarbitrary variation is open for consideration, then precedent poses only an illusory constraint. But if, instead, decisionmakers must look to that truncation of real world richness that comes from thinking about the world at large and rough groupings, then the constraints of precedent will be substantial.

    . . . .

Precedent [is not just presumptively binding]. The constraints of precedent attach in those instances in which some set of events now before us is deemed to be relevantly similar to some set of events of the past. The condition creating the presumption is similarity. But any overriding condition can always be expressed in terms of the absence of similarity. We never decide not to follow a precedent just because we do not feel like following it, but because something about the instant case is different from the precedent case. And if this is so, then burden-creating conditions and the burden-satisfying conditions are measured along the same plane — similarity and difference. It is as if the special burden of justification present in the case of racial classifications were capable of being overridden by showing that in this case the racial classification was not that bad, or was not really a racial classification. These are permissible arguments, but they are not arguments for overriding. They are arguments showing that the reasons for requiring an especially strong justification simply do not apply here.

In some sense, then, the question of weight is a red herring, for a precedent is always followed or distinguished. We never face a situation where a precedent presumptively ought to be followed, but some special overriding condition in this case leads us not to follow it. Rather, we say that this case is simply different — that there is actually no relevant precedent to follow or disregard. When the present situation presents factors that ought to control the disposition, we can and will translate those factors into a distinction between this case and the precedent case. Thus, the set of cases in which a precedent is applicable but overridden appears to be an empty one.

We must still address the question of how specifically we will describe the precedents of the past and the events of the present. Although it will always be *possible* to distinguish a precedent, this becomes comparatively harder if we describe and use the precedents of the past in general terms. If subsequent decisionmakers describe and carry on the relevant precedent as a case involving a "car," then an attempt to distinguish an instant case because it involves a red car will be unpersuasive, precisely because the breadth of the description in the first case substantially limits possible distinguishing factors in subsequent cases.

Thus, the question of strength once again dissolves into the question of size. Because we can always characterize any overriding event as a difference, it makes no sense to draw a distinction between whether a precedent is applicable and whether a precedent controls. Both inapplicability and noncontrollingness express themselves in terms of distinctions between the instant case and some putative precedent case. At the level at which we create the practices of precedent, the strength of the norms of precedent will be reflected in the generality of the categories in which decisions are made. A precedential category of "vehicles" will have greater force than smaller categories of "cars," "trucks," and "motorcycles," which in turn will have greater power over the future than categories of "Buicks" or "Toyotas." No precedential rule can begin to capture this question of size. We cannot say that the appropriate categories of distinction are just this big, or just this small. Instead, the rules of precedent are likely to resemble rules of language — a series of practices not substantially reducible to specifics. A system in which precedent operates as a comparatively strong constraint will be one in which decisionmakers ignore fine but justifiable differences in the pursuit of large similarities. At first glance, a precedent-governed system described this way, as one in which relevant differences are suppressed, seems no more justifiable than one characterized as treating prior decisions as important merely because they are prior. So why would any society want such a system?

VI. THE VIRTUES OF PRECEDENTIAL CONSTRAINT

I have looked at how precedent can constrain, at the strength of its constraints, and at the costs of such constraints in imposing a strategy of suboptimization. What remains is what to some might be the biggest question: Why should a decision-making mechanism incorporate substantial precedential constraints within it? Why should a decision in Case 1 constrain a decisionmaker in Case 2 and itself be constrained by the knowledge of this secondary impact?

A. The Argument from Fairness

Among the most common justifications for treating precedents as relevant is the argument from fairness, sometimes couched as an argument from justice. The argument is most commonly expressed in terms of the simple structure, "Treat like cases alike." To fail to treat similar cases similarly, it is argued, is arbitrary, and consequently unjust or unfair. We achieve fairness by decisionmaking rules designed to achieve consistency across a range of decisions. Where the consistency is among individuals at the same time, we express this decisional rule as "equality." Where the consistency among decisions takes place over time, we call our decisional rule "precedent." Equality and precedent are thus, respectively, the spatial and temporal branches of the same larger normative principle of consistency.

The idea of fairness as consistency forms the bedrock of a great deal of thinking about morality. Whether expressed as Kantian universalizability, as the decisions that people would make if cloaked in a Rawlsian veil of ignorance about their own circumstances, or simply as The Golden Rule, the principle emerges that decisions that are not consistent are, for that reason, unfair, unjust, or simply wrong.

How can we apply this broad principle of fairness more specifically as a potential justification for adopting a decision procedure in which precedent matters? Initially, the principle that like cases should be decided alike would seem to make an unassailable argument for precedent. But the difficulty of denying that like cases should be decided alike is precisely the problem. The statement is so broad as to be almost meaningless. The hard question is what we mean by "alike."

Recall the discussion of the potential *size* of categories of assimilation. From the perspective of the size of the categories involved, the question is not whether like cases should be decided alike, for at that level of abstraction the norm would engender unanimous agreement. Rather, the question is whether the categories of likeness should be large or small. If the categories of likeness, of assimilation, are so small as to enable a decisionmaker to take into account virtually every variation between separate events, then like cases are indeed being decided alike, yet the norm of precedent scarcely constrains. But if relatively large categories act to group many slightly different particular cases under general headings of likeness, then the stricture of deciding like cases alike makes reliance on precedent a substantial constraint.

The issue is thus not the sterile question of treating like cases alike. It is instead the more difficult question of whether we should base our decisionmaking norm on relatively large categories of likeness, or by contrast leave a decisionmaker more or less at liberty to consider any possible way in which this particular array of facts might be unique. The purely formal constraint of treating like cases alike does not speak to this question. Yet the first of these alternatives describes a system of precedent; the second describes a system in which the constraint of precedent is for all practical purposes absent.

Alone, therefore, the argument from fairness, the prescription to treat like cases alike, does not help us choose between a decisional system with a strong precedential constraint and one with virtually no precedential constraint. If we are to find arguments directly addressing the question of precedent, we must look for substantive reasons to choose the larger rather than smaller categories of decision.

B. The Argument from Predictability

The most commonly offered of the substantive reasons for choosing strong over weak precedential constraint is the principle of predictability. When a decisionmaker must decide this case in the same way as the last, parties will be better able to anticipate the future. The ability to predict what a decisionmaker will do helps us plan our lives, have some degree of repose, and avoid the paralysis of foreseeing only the unknown.

As a value, predictability is neither transcendent nor free from conflict with other values. Yet predictability plainly is, *ceteris paribus*, desirable. We attain predictability, however, only by diminishing our ability to adapt to a changing future. In the language of precedent, following a precedent at a particular time may produce a decision other than the decision deemed optimal on the facts of the particular instance. Where this divergence is absent, the effect of precedent is minimal. But if following precedent will produce a result different from that which would be produced without the constraint of the rule of precedent, then we have identified a case in which precedent matters. And thus we can rephrase the question: To what extent is a decisionmaking environment willing to tolerate suboptimal results in order that people may plan their lives according to decision previously made?

When we reformulate the question in this way, it becomes clear that the force of the argument from predictability, even if persuasive in the abstract, will vary with numerous factors whose weight cannot be generalized across all decisional environments. For example, how often will the use of large generalizations prevent making decisions on the basis of unique facts that would be dispositive in a particular case? To answer this question requires delving into a panoply of factors relating to the kinds of decisions that are to be made in a given decisionmaking environment. These factors may include the size of the relevant categories, the likelihood of significant factual variation, and many others that vary from environment to environment. I thus merely note, without intending to resolve, that one important issue is the expected *frequency* of suboptimal results.

The *consequences* of such a suboptimal decision provide a closely related concern, one touched on earlier. Once we realize that maintaining a serious regime of precedential constraint entails some number of suboptimal decisions, we see that we can express the price we pay for predictability in terms of some number of decisions in which the predicted result, and therefore the actual result if precedent is followed, is not in fact the best result. But the relationship of these costs to the possible benefits of predictability will vary across different kinds of decisions.

When Justice Brandeis noted that "in most matters it is more important that the applicable rule of law be settled than that it is settled right,"[55] he was reminding us of one side of the question. The other side, of course, is that sometimes it is more important that things be settled correctly than that they be settled for the sake of settlement. To take an extreme example, making all capital punishment decisions under a strict precedential rule would satisfy desires for predictability but would also entail putting to death some people who would live if their individual cases were scrutinized carefully. And, at the other extreme, many decisions involving the formalities of contracts or real estate transactions are decisions in which sacrificing optimality for predictability would involve negative consequences that are far from catastrophic.

Finally, it is worthwhile adding to the equation some variability in the value of predictability. Much of what we value about predictability is psychological. I feel better knowing that the letter carrier will come at the same time every day, that faculty meetings will not be scheduled on short notice, and that April brings the opening of the baseball season. Predictability thus often has value even when we cannot quantify it.

Thus, the value of predictability is really a question of balancing expected gain against expected loss. We ask how important predictability is for those affected by the decisions, and we then ask whether that amount of predictability is worth the price of the frequency of suboptimal results multiplied by the costs of those sub-optimal results. But there is no best answer to this calculation, for the answer will vary with the kinds of decisions that given decisionmakers are expected to make.

C. The Arguments from Strengthened Decisionmaking

1. Decisionmaking Efficiency.

When a precedent has no decisional significance as a precedent, the conscientious decisionmaker must look at each case in its own fullness. But when a rule external to the decisionmaker compels reliance on the decisions of others, it frees the decisionmaker from these responsibilities. Although a decisionmaker in a precedential system may in every case consider whether to disregard these constraints, this does not deny that a decisionmaker may choose to follow precedent, nor that a decisionmaker who chooses to rely on precedent is in most cases operating within the norms of the system. Thus, a decisionmaker choosing to rely on precedent may justifiably "relax," in the sense of engaging in less scrutiny of the case, where the decisionmaker chooses to rely on a precedent. And where a *rule* of precedent urges a decisionmaker to relax in this sense, the net product will be a substantial reduction in decisionmaking effort.

---

55. Burnet v. Coronado Oil & Gas Co., 285 U.S. 393, 406 (1932) (Brandeis, J., dissenting); *see also* Sheddon v. Goodrich, 8 Ves. 481, 497, 32 Eng. Rep. 441, 447 (1803) ("better that the law should be certain than that every judge should speculate upon improvements").

In this respect, efficiency may justify a rule of precedent. This argument properly relies on the fact that a regime of precedent allows less reconsideration of questions already considered than a system containing no rule of precedent. If we wish to conserve the decisional resources of the decisionmakers, therefore, we have an independent argument for a system of precedent.

There is something curious, however, about the argument from decisional efficiency. Suppose we have a string of three decisionmakers making three assimilable decisions. Under a regime of precedent, the second decisionmaker must defer to the first, but her deference is based on nothing about either the first or second decisionmakers, because it is also the case that the third decisionmaker must defer to the second. If we consider such a system efficient or otherwise desirable, we must either perceive some actual similarity between the decisionmakers or believe that there is some reason to impose a presumed similarity when none in fact exists. When there is actual similarity, a system of precedent enables a decisionmaker to rely on the similar decisionmaker's conclusion about a similar case. Having found the facts in the instant case similar to some decision in the past, the instant decisionmaker need go no further, because the system of precedent assumes that the same result would have been reached even if the instant decisionmaker started all over again.

2. Strengthening the Decisionmaking Institution.

But now let us abandon the assumption of similarity among decisionmakers. If we retain the assumption of assimilability of events, more than mere decisional efficiency must be at work. The system of precedent must operate to dampen the variability that would otherwise result from dissimilar decisionmakers. Why should we encourage this process? One possibility is that it might be thought important to create the aura of similarity among decisionmakers even where none may exist. Using a system of precedent to standardize decisions subordinates dissimilarity among decisionmakers, both in appearance and in practice.

Even more substantially, this subordination of decisional and decisionmaker variance is likely in practice to increase the power of the decisionmaking institution. If internal consistency strengthens external credibility, then minimizing internal inconsistency by standardizing decisions within a decisionmaking environment may generally strengthen that decisionmaking environment as an institution.

The considerations surrounding the argument from decisionmaking efficiency rest upon a broad notion about the value of stability in decisionmaking distinct from anything about the actual decisions made. It is also apparent that any attempt to stabilize decisionmaking in an unstable world is likely to produce some suboptimal results. The argument from enhanced decisionmaking, then, suggests that the efficiency advantages may justify putting on blinders to the full richness of human experience. This is by no means an implausible argument, but its strength will depend upon many of the same factors discussed in the context of the argument from predictability. Likewise, whether this strength is sufficient to outweigh its costs will vary with those same factors. Once it becomes clear that no argument from invariable principle supports either the argument from predictability or the argument from enhanced decisionmaking, the evaluation of these alternatives turns into a weighing of costs and benefits that varies with different decisionmaking settings. Further elaboration must be relegated to discussions of the goals to be served and the characteristics of decisionmaking in various decisionmaking settings.

D. Precedent and Stability

Although the various arguments for incorporating a rule of precedent into a particular decisional environment each retains its own irreducible core of justification, in some sense these arguments coalesce. Arguments premised on the values of reliance, predictability, and decisional efficiency all share a focus on stability for stability's sake. The extent to which stability will be promoted is largely a function of the size of the groupings employed within a decisional domain. We must ask whether, at the extremes, large numbers of differences between instances will be suppressed, thus generating comparatively few large categories, or whether all variation will be taken into account, thus generating many smaller categories. Naturally there will be gradations between these extremes. But by viewing the issue this way, we see that the various abstract and formal justifications for precedent all rest on conclusions about what ranges of events we wish to treat in like manner.

At times these size-determining factors may be based on substantive value choices. We may broadly draw the category of "person" in many contexts precisely because we believe it substantively evil to distinguish among people on the basis of race, gender, national origin, or even height. At other times the size of the categories will be controlled by the size of the categories at large in the world. Our language and its accompanying conceptual apparatus often inhibit attempts by decisionmakers to draw fine distinctions among the particulars that inhabit the larger categories of our existence. No amount of stress on particularization, for example, could completely prevent categories like "people," "dwellings," or "vehicles" from hindering a decisionmaker's efforts to see differences among people, dwellings, or vehicles. Finally, and perhaps most importantly, the size of the categories of assimilation may be a function of what we expect to accomplish in a decisionmaking setting. This is particularly germane here, for it links the principle of stability, hovering around all of the separate justifications for precedent, to the particular system actually generated.

Some decisionmaking environments emphasize today the richness and uniqueness of immediate experience. In those environments we seek the freedom to explore every possible argument or fact that might bear on making the best decision for *this* case, for it is precisely the *thisness* of the case that is most vital. At its extreme, such a system might, and arguably should, deny the relevance of precedent entirely. The virtues of stability would bow to the desire "to get it just right," and in such a framework a past decision would have little if any precedential force. More realistically, perhaps, such a system might still acknowledge precedent, but in small units. For if we see precedents as small units, full of rarely duplicated particulars, we are likely to find few cases in which the current small unit is like some small unit of the past.

By contrast, other decisional environments focus on yesterday and tomorrow, emphasizing the recurrent rather than the unique elements of the human condition. Here precedent has its greatest role to play, generating a format for decision-making that channels decisions toward consideration of a comparatively limited number of factors likely to be repeated over time. In the context of this essay, this would translate into the use of larger categories of assimilation, gathering many conceivably distinguishable particulars within the embrace of the larger categories.

Without a universal answer to the question of whether stability is a good thing, we cannot decide whether decision according to precedent is a good thing. Stability may be unimpeachable in the abstract, but in reality stability comes only by giving up some of our flexibility to explore fully the deepest corners of the events now before us. Whether this price is worth paying will vary with the purposes to be served within a decisional domain, and we get no closer to knowing those purposes by understanding the relationship between stability and categorical size. Still, focusing on this relationship is valuable, because it enables us to see more clearly just how stability is achieved and just what kind of price we must pay to obtain it.

Notes and Questions

1. See if you can summarize the major points made by Professor Schauer regarding precedent.

2. Professor Schauer has written on many of the topics in this book, and some of his other articles (all excellent) are excerpted later in this chapter. For a more complete account of his thoughts on these subjects, see FREDERICK SCHAUER, THINKING LIKE A LAWYER: A NEW INTRODUCTION TO LEGAL REASONING (2009).

3. Michael Abramowicz & Maxwell Stearns, *Defining Dicta*, 57 STAN. L. REV. 953, 1000-01 n.134 (2005):

> It is possible, for example, that a prior decision explored the legal issue in a sufficiently persuasive manner that a later judge, who initially would have resolved the issue differently, changes positions. Should this occur, the second judge is not basing the resolution on the fact of the precedent, however, but rather on the persuasiveness of the earlier reasoning. A judge is invariably free to do this, just as a judge may find a treatise, law review article, op-ed, or speech by a law professor persuasive on a relevant point of law.

4. Many, many books and articles have been written about precedent. For a recent empirical study of Supreme Court precedent (that also includes a nice bibliography on this subject), see Ryan C. Black & James F. Spriggs II, *Citation and Depreciation of U.S. Supreme Court Precedent*, 10 J. EMPIR. LEGAL STUDIES 325 (2013).

Gary Lawson

MOSTLY UNCONSTITUTIONAL: THE CASE AGAINST PRECEDENT REVISITED

5 Ave Maria L. Rev. 1 (2007)

In the American legal system, it is commonplace for actors to give varying degrees of legal weight to the decisions of prior actors. The generic name for this pervasive and familiar practice is the doctrine of *precedent*. Although all legal actors must consider the extent to which they ought to follow the prior decisions of others, the concept of precedent is associated most closely with the decision-making processes of judges. A court facing a legal problem must consider the weight, if any, that it will give to, inter alia, (1) prior executive or legislative decisions,[3] (2) decisions by courts situated above the deciding court in the judicial hierarchy (vertical precedent), (3) decisions by courts situated at the same level as the deciding court in the judicial hierarchy (horizontal precedent), and (4) decisions by courts or legal actors from foreign legal systems. The consensus view in the modern American legal culture is that some form of precedent is "part of our understanding of what law is."

In this short Article, I want to (re)examine one specific but important aspect of the doctrine of precedent: the weight that the Constitution requires or permits the United States Supreme Court to give prior United States Supreme Court decisions in constitutional cases. . . .[8] Conventional wisdom, in keeping with the view that precedent is an essential part of our understanding of law itself, holds that the Court is permitted, though not necessarily obliged, to give considerable, though not necessarily conclusive, weight to its prior decisions. The standard formulation is that the Court should not reject prior decisions, even when a current majority believes them on balance to be mistaken, without some "special justification" beyond the mere belief of error.[10]

Nearly fifteen years ago, I suggested that the Court, if it wants to conform to the Constitution, should *never* choose precedent over direct examination

---

3. The practice of giving weight to executive or legislative actors often goes under the heading of "deference," but it is actually a form of precedent that is conceptually indistinguishable from deference to prior judicial actors. Judicial deference to executive and legislative precedent is commonplace in many contexts. . . .

8. At all times in this Article, when I discuss what courts are obliged or permitted to do, I mean obliged or permitted *by the Constitution*. I *do not* mean to prescribe, as a matter of political morality, how public officials — whose action determine who gets shot by soldiers, federal marshals, or police — should do their jobs. One of my principal academic bugaboos is the persistent conflation of questions of legal *interpretation* with questions of political *morality*. It is one thing to establish the meaning of the Constitution. It is quite another thing to say that the meaning of the Constitution should, as a normative matter, guide conduct. All manner of mischief comes from confusing the two distinct enterprises. So that there is no mistake: my argument is designed *only* to establish what the Constitution says, not the extent (if any) to which anyone should care what the Constitution says.

10. *See* Dickerson v. United States, 530 U.S. 428, 443 (2000) (summarizing the conventional view).

of constitutional meaning.[11] After considering the issue further, and digesting a decade and a half of criticism of my argument by the legal academy, I want to change my conclusion (with apologies to Ford Prefect) from "never" to "mostly never." It turns out to be a bit of an overstatement to claim that the Supreme Court should *never* rely on past decisions in preference to direct, unmediated examination of the Constitution. But only a bit.

. . . .

I. REVISITING THE CASE AGAINST PRECEDENT

The federal Constitution grants to the federal courts one and only one power: "the judicial Power of the United States."[15] Federal courts have the capacity to receive power to appoint inferior officers if Congress chooses to grant it, and the chief justice personally has the power and duty to preside over presidential impeachment trials in the Senate, but the only power actually granted to the federal courts as an institution is the judicial power. It is remarkably difficult to give a full account of the original meaning of the phrase "the judicial Power," but fortunately the dispute focuses on the periphery, rather than the core. The central feature of the judicial power is clearly the power to decide cases according to governing law; the question that divides scholars is what ancillary powers go along with the basic power to decide cases.

In order to decide cases in accordance with governing law, one must know what law governs. That inquiry requires interpretation of the relevant sources of law — which is why the power of law interpretation is a necessary concomitant of the judicial power, just as it is a necessary concomitant of the legislative and executive powers — and also determination of which law governs in the case of conflict. In any given case, many different legal norms from many different sources — including constitutions, statutes, treaties, regulations, court decisions, traditional practices, and theories of justice — might potentially bear on the outcome. Depending on the legal system in place, any or all of these norms might legitimately claim the status of "law," and if they point in different directions, a court employing "the judicial Power" must determine which sources take priority. . . .

The federal Constitution contains only one express conflict-of-laws provision, but it is a doozy. The Supremacy Clause declares:

> This Constitution, and the Laws of the United States which shall be made in Pursuance thereof; and all Treaties made, or which shall be made, under the Authority of the United States, shall be the supreme Law of the Land; and the Judges in every State shall be bound thereby, any Thing in the Constitution or Laws of any State to the Contrary notwithstanding.

This clause is a specific directive to prefer three named federal legal sources over any other legal sources, including state law sources, in the event of a conflict. The

---

11. Gary Lawson, *The Constitutional Case Against Precedent*, 17 Harv. J.L. & Pub. Pol'y 23 (1994).
15. U.S. Const. art. III, § 1.

clause singles out state court judges for emphasis, but the basic conflict rule expressed in the first part of the clause is not limited to state court judges. By its terms, the Supremacy Clause speaks to *all* legal actors — federal and non-federal, judicial and non-judicial — and asserts the superiority of the Constitution, statutes, and treaties over competing sources of law. The Supremacy Clause conspicuously does not include "decisions by the United States Supreme Court" when naming the sources of law at the top of the legal food chain.

So, right away the Constitution itself establishes a prima facie case against the use of precedent: if a prior judicial decision conflicts with the Constitution, a statute, or a treaty, the prior decision must give way. If even a state constitution cannot prevail over the federal Constitution, it is hard to see how the views of three to five (depending on the size of the Supreme Court) lawyers or hacks (depending on the composition of the Supreme Court) can do so.

There is more. Within the set of legal trumps spelled out by the Supremacy Clause, there is an internal hierarchy. While the Supremacy Clause seems to place the Constitution, federal statutes, and treaties on the same legal plane, one can infer with a reasonable degree of confidence[23] that the Constitution is the ace of trumps and prevails in conflicts with statutes and treaties.[24] . . .

. . . .

Now suppose that a prior judicial decision speaks squarely to the resolution of a dispute brought before a court. Let us assume that prior judicial decisions count as law of some sort, even though they do not have the specifically designated legal status of the Constitution, federal statutes, and treaties. That status as law creates a prima facie obligation on the part of the court to apply the decision. But as soon as the other side interposes the Constitution, the court is now faced with two competing sources of law. If the Constitution says, "A," and the prior judicial decision says, "B," the Constitution must prevail. If a statute, which the Constitution specifically declares to be "Law," cannot defeat the Constitution, it is hard to see how a judicial decision could have a more exalted legal status.

. . . .

The question is whether anything can overcome that prima facie case.

II. WHY PRECEDENT?

The key to understanding the possible responses to this prima facie case against precedent is to recognize and keep clear . . . three distinct grounds on which one might give weight to the decision of a prior legal actor. I have elsewhere labeled those grounds *legal*, *epistemological*, and *economic*. The labels are not necessarily the most descriptive that one might imagine, but I will stick with them for now.

---

23. One can fairly ask whether a reasonable degree of confidence is enough. And one can fairly — and indeed must — answer: enough for what? The standard of proof that any proposition must meet depends to some extent on the purpose for which the proposition is advanced.

24. There is also a very good case that, contrary to current doctrine that applies a "last in time" rule, statutes must prevail over treaties in cases of conflict, but that is another topic. . . .

Legal deference involves giving weight to another actor's decision because some controlling legal authority requires it. Consider, for example, the role of jury verdicts in federal court. The Constitution contains provisions that specifically require subsequent decision makers to give a certain measure of respect to jury verdicts. . . .

. . . .

Epistemological deference, by contrast, results when one treats prior decisions as good evidence of the right answer. If one starts with the idea of independently determining the right answer to a question, it is possible that, along the way, one might run across someone who has already thought about the question carefully, was in a good position to get the right answer, and has relevant indicia of reliability. The fact that this other actor has reached a particular conclusion might well constitute good evidence, and perhaps even the best available evidence, of the right answer. Giving weight to that prior answer would simply be common sense, even in the absence of any legal command to do so. Unlike legal deference, epistemological deference focuses on case-specific reasons for thinking that a particular actor is a good source of guidance, though one can imagine general rules that might flow from these case-specific judgments.

Economic deference results from a cost-benefit analysis that suggests that giving weight to a prior decision is so much easier and cheaper (however "cheaper" is defined) than reconsidering the matter from scratch that deference to the prior decision is appropriate. This model of precedent recognizes that prior decisions may or may not be very good evidence of the right answer, but holds that figuring out either the right answer or whether the prior decision is good evidence of the right answer may be too expensive to be worthwhile. Such judgments can get very complicated; the "costs" of not having the right answer vary greatly with the context, as do the costs determining right answers, the costs of determining the costs of right answers, and the comparative costs of figuring out the right answer and figuring out the answer that is supposedly prescribed by precedent. Defenses of precedent that rely on the good consequences supposedly produced by the practice, such as predictability, stability, and objectivity, are forms of arguments for economic deference: they argue, in essence, that wrong answers are better than right answers when the social costs (however those are measured) of wrong answers are lower.

The practice of precedent could, in principle, be justified by any or all of these grounds. The precise shape of the doctrine obviously depends on the grounds by which it is justified.

III. DOES THE CONSTITUTION COMMAND RELIANCE ON PRECEDENT?

Jury verdicts must operate as precedent (of varying weight depending on the context) because the Constitution says that they must. If the Constitution similarly directs courts to give weight to prior judicial decisions, that would be the end of the matter.

With one modest but important exception (involving the finality of judgments) that does not bear on the limited topic of Supreme Court adherence to Supreme Court precedent,[37] the Constitution has no express clauses assigning weight to judicial decisions comparable to the provisions concerning juries. . . . The idea has occasionally been floated that the "judicial Power" includes a general obligation to prefer judicial decisions to the Constitution in at least some cases, but there is not much to support the claim.

The judicial power is the power to decide cases according to governing law. In the course of that task, courts must determine which law governs, which includes making conflict-of-laws judgments when multiple sources of law are brought into play. But, textually and structurally, even if judicial decisions count as law in some contexts (as they surely do in common law adjudication), one would need something as explicit as the jury clauses, or as structurally clear as the principle of finality of judgments, to permit any other consideration to leapfrog the Constitution in the conflict-of-laws hierarchy. The bare grant of the "judicial Power," with its accompanying inference of the power of judicial review, no more requires courts to prefer their prior legal conclusions to the Constitution than the grant of the "executive Power," with its accompanying inference of the power of executive review, requires the President to prefer his or her prior legal conclusions to the Constitution. And if one wishes to resort to history, the doctrine of precedent was certainly familiar in the Founding era, but not so well established and developed to be a part of the "judicial Power" in the super-strong sense that would be necessary to give judicial decisions preference over the Constitution. In sum, there is little to be said for a general constitutional *obligation* to follow precedent, and little is in fact said about it.

IV. DOES THE CONSTITUTION PERMIT RELIANCE ON PRECEDENT?

Very few people seriously maintain that courts are constitutionally *required* to follow precedent. The standard account of precedent holds that it is a *policy* rather than a legal command (though that position has implications that many of its adherents have not yet recognized). Accordingly, my earlier argument in *The Constitutional Case Against Precedent* did not contend merely that the Constitution does not *require* courts to follow precedent, but contended that the Constitution affirmatively *forbids* reliance on precedent in constitutional cases — where "reliance on precedent" is understood as treating precedent as something that can, in principle, change the outcome that would be reached by unmediated interpretation of the Constitution. That argument requires some modest revisions, which I provide here.

---

37. In order for the "judicial Power" vested in the federal courts to be an actual power, it must have the capacity to bind other actors, including executive actors who are charged with enforcement of judgments. As a result, judicial decisions have a constitutionally-based precedential effect of sorts *as judgments in specific cases.* . . .

A. The Case Against Permissive Legal Deference

The prima facie case against *requiring* adherence to precedent also functions as a prima facie case against *permitting* adherence to precedent. Courts have an obligation to decide cases in accordance with governing law. Once it is acknowledged that the Constitution is supreme law, and thus is *always* the governing law when it applies, a court would fail to exercise the "judicial Power" properly if it decided a case accordance with some other source of law that conflicted with the Constitution. For the same reasons that Article III does not *require* courts to follow precedent (and Article II does not *require* Presidents to follow precedent), Article III does not *authorize* courts to follow precedent (and Article II does not *authorize* Presidents to follow precedent). The conflict-of-laws rule stated in the Supremacy Clause and implicit in the entire constitutional structure is *incorporated* into Article III's grant of the "judicial Power" and is not *altered* or *superseded* by that grant. The power to apply governing law ordinarily also carries with it the power to determine which law governs, but not when the Constitution has already made that decision.

Frederick Schauer has responded that my argument depends upon the Constitution containing its own rules of interpretation, which he considers a logical impossibility. If the "meaning" of the Constitution is in fact what judges say it is, or what most actors in the legal system think it is, then there is a very good case that the "meaning" of Article III (or some other aspect of the Constitution) is that precedent may, on some nontrivial set of occasions, rule the day. Indeed, if practice determines constitutional meaning, my argument is obviously frivolous.

Schauer is partly right, but not in a way that saves precedent. One does, of course, need to bring extraconstitutional interpretative norms to bear in reading the Constitution, just as one must bring extra-Schauerian norms to bear in reading Schauer. But those extraconstitutional (and extra-Schauerian) norms are objectively discoverable, and they do not involve the *ipse dixit* of judges, lawyers, or any other concrete historical individuals. The Constitution means what a hypothetical reasonable observer at the time of its ratification, in possession of all relevant information, would have understood it to mean. This conclusion about constitutional meaning flows from reflection on background principles of human communication, the kind of document that one is interpreting (an instruction manual for a particular governmental structure), the character of jointly authored products, and the specific instructions for interpretation contained in the document (which one can readily understand through the application of the extraconstitutional norms that I have just described). When the Constitution is interpreted the same way that any normal person would interpret an eighteenth-century manual for constructing a compost heap, it follows that Article III does not authorize courts to prefer precedent, or anything else, to the Constitution in cases of conflict.

. . . .

B. The Case Against Permissive Economic Deference

At the risk of grossly over-generalizing about a voluminous body of scholarship, I suspect that most advocates of precedent ground their position not in some construction of Article III, but in the *practical* consequences that result from reliance on precedent. After all, if one is not arguing that the Constitution *requires* adherence to precedent as a legal rule, but merely that the Constitution *permits* adherence to precedent as a legal policy, it is natural to look at the justifications for that policy.

Fifteen years ago, I brushed aside those kinds of arguments as unworthy of serious consideration in a study of original meaning:

> The class of pro-precedent arguments that does not deserve careful attention involves the claim that following precedent serves important prudential interests, such as stability, predictability, judicial economy, fairness, and legitimacy. Even if the practice of following precedent in fact promotes these interests, that would at most establish that a well-crafted constitution would permit, or require, courts to follow precedent. I have no strong view, and do not mean to imply one here, on how a well-crafted constitution should handle precedent. My present concern is with the actual Constitution, however well- or ill-crafted it may be, and arguments from prudence go nowhere unless they are tied to the interpretation of some provision of the constitutional text.

I would say essentially the same thing today. There may very well be plenty of statutes and executive actions that are flatly inconsistent with the Constitution but which are normatively superior to the Constitution. Their normative superiority does not make them constitutional. Similarly, the practice of following precedent may well be, in many circumstances, a nice idea. But the Constitution does not contain a "Nice Idea" clause.

In the end, my disagreement with "pragmatists" who defend precedent on consequentialist grounds most likely results from the fact that we are asking different questions. I am asking what the Constitution means. They are (I believe) asking how courts should decide cases. Those two sets of questions are only contingently related and require application of very different disciplines. Questions about the Constitution's meaning are the province of legal interpretation. Questions about how courts should decide cases are the province of moral and political theory. It is entirely possible that modern American legal actors should, as a matter of political morality, make decisions without reference to a meaning of the Constitution. As an empirical matter, that is essentially what happens most of the time. If that is what pragmatic arguments for the precedent are saying, I have no comment on them (other than the perhaps tendentious suggestion that legal scholars, even very smart legal scholars, are unlikely to have much of anything useful to say about political morality).

. . . .

C. The Case Against — Well, Mostly Against — Epistemological Deference

In everyday life, we frequently rely on the views of others. Sometimes, we do so for reasons of convenience (economic deference). Other times, we do so because we recognize, or at least believe, that others know more than we do. When physicists tell me that gravity is not a force exerted by one object upon another, but rather is the result of the warping of the space-time continuum by mass, I take their word for it. I assume that they could prove their claim if I spent enough years learning the mathematics necessary to understand their arguments, and it is very hard for me to see how it would be in their interests to deceive me. I am willing to accept their prior decisions on the question of the nature of gravity as precedent. May courts, consistently with the Constitution, similarly rely on prior decisions when there is good reason to view those prior decisions as reliable?

The answer is that of course they may. The primary obligation of a court exercising the judicial power is to decide cases in accordance with governing law. That task requires discerning the content of the governing law. When the law in question is the Constitution, the proper way to discern its meaning is to ask how the relevant provisions, in context, would have been understood by a hypothetical reasonable observer at the time of their ratification. If someone else has already made that inquiry, and this someone else likely knows more about the subject than the judge in question, and there is good reason to think that this someone else applied the correct methodology honestly, and there is no good reason to think that this someone else would have cause to skew the result, then it makes perfectly good sense to defer to this someone else. If that is all that precedent involved, there would be a perfectly sensible constitutional case for it: judges have the obligation to get the right answer, and if the best evidence of the right answer is what someone else has already come up with, then go with it.

Precedent of this sort, however, is highly dependent on a wide range of conditions that frequently are not satisfied. For starters, it requires that the previous decision maker be better situated to get the right answer than the present decision maker. If the previous decision make was none too bright, an obligation to get the right answer would counsel strongly against giving that person's conclusions much, if any, weight. In addition, even the smartest person may not be a reliable guide if he or she is using the wrong method. Brilliant people asking the wrong questions are unlikely to get the right answers. Thus, for example, even though Justice Stephen Breyer is one of the smartest people ever to walk the planet, it would be foolhardy to rely on prior conclusions that he has reached about constitutional meaning because he is not actually looking for *original* constitutional meaning. Finally, even very smart people applying a correct method may be unreliable if they have motives to reach a particular result, and if there is reason to suspect that they have, consciously or not, yielded to those motives. In order to justify giving weight to a prior decision, many indicia of reliability have to align.

The chances of such an alignment in the modern world roughly approximate the chances of my beloved Seattle Mariners, Seattle Seahawks, and (at least as of 2006) Seattle Supersonics all winning a world championship in the same season. Even if one goes back to earlier times . . . there was never a golden age in which courts faithfully sought the original meaning of the Constitution through dispassionate application of a sound methodology. . . .

It is possible, however, that there are specific instances in which prior judicial actors carefully and honestly applied sound methodologies, and if one can pinpoint those instances, the conclusions reached in those cases would be entitled to some weight in the search for the right constitutional answers. If precedent is being used for epistemological reasons as good evidence of the right answer, and if all of the conditions for believing specific precedents to qualify as such evidence are met, the Constitution permits its use. This is a very thin doctrine of precedent, but it is a doctrine of precedent nonetheless, and I hereby endorse it.

. . . .

In the end, it is not strictly impossible to construct a narrowly tailored argument for affording weight to some especially reliable precedents in constitutional cases, but it is very, very difficult. Certainly there is no constitutional warrant for the broad-based deference currently afforded to past decisions by the Supreme Court. The Constitution does not allow itself to be overridden quite so easily. Thus, the constitutional case against precedent is not absolute. But it is mostly absolute.

Notes and Questions

1. What do you think of Professor Lawson's argument? What is his argument? Do you agree?

2. Most judges and legal scholars probably do not agree with Professor Lawson's position. But does Professor Lawson's view nonetheless comport with how the Supreme Court today in fact applies the doctrine of stare decisis?

3. Note Professor Lawson's observation regarding methodology. Is he not correct that someone (say, a judge or Justice) who utilizes a flawed analytical methodology is unlikely to reach a "correct" decision? And if so, would this be a relevant line of inquiry to pursue with respect to a judicial nominee in a Senate confirmation hearing? Perhaps the most relevant line of inquiry?

Michael Stokes Paulsen

DOES THE SUPREME COURT'S CURRENT DOCTRINE OF STARE DECISIS REQUIRE ADHERENCE TO THE SUPREME COURT'S CURRENT DOCTRINE OF STARE DECISIS?

86 N.C. L. Rev. 1165 (2008)

INTRODUCTION

What if one were to examine — as if without irony — the stare decisis effect that the Supreme Court should accord to its own current doctrine of stare decisis, under a fair application of the Court's current doctrine of stare decisis, in a case where the result turned on whether the doctrine of stare decisis should be adhered to as a matter of stare decisis or not? Would the Court find itself "tested by following" its own "promise of constancy, once given"?[1] Would the Court (or its doctrine) pass its own test? Or would the Court be forced to conclude that the doctrine of stare decisis does not meet the Court's own set of qualifications for when past decisions ought to be followed? And, if so, what follows from *that* conclusion?

In this short Article, I propose to examine, as if it could be taken seriously, the Supreme Court's current stated doctrine of stare decisis, as most comprehensively formulated and defended in *Planned Parenthood of Southeastern Pennsylvania v. Casey* and as exercised (or deviated from) in several prominent constitutional decisions of the Court in the fifteen years since *Casey* was decided. I propose to do so not from the standpoint of first premises, but from the more limited perspective of the Court's own doctrine of stare decisis. My analysis and critique here is thus an "internal" one — does the doctrine satisfy its own standards and purported justification? — rather than the "external" one of consistency with first principles of the Constitution. My conclusion, as one might guess from the framing of the question, is that the Court's doctrine about precedent fails its own test(s) of when precedents should be adhered to. Indeed, the doctrine fails *all* of the doctrine's own tests: It is embarrassingly unworkable. It certainly has not spawned reasonable reliance on the doctrine and practice of stare decisis continuing to remain stable; to the contrary, the Court's subsequent decisions have cast doubt on the content of the doctrine and seemingly left its stare decisis analysis as a remnant of abandoned doctrine. Changed factual circumstances cast some mild doubt on the validity of the doctrine, but the doctrine of stare decisis was never really much about facts in the first place. Finally, the Court's announced doctrine of stare decisis probably does not much contribute to, and in fact may well detract from, public perceptions of "judicial integrity," at least if one assumes a reasonably informed, intelligent, and not-hopelessly-naive public. In short, the doctrine serves poorly, if at all, the supposed rule-of-law values of promoting efficiency and stability, protecting reasonable reliance, and enhancing judicial credibility — the values asserted to justify the doctrine. The end result of this inquiry is that the current doctrine of stare decisis does not require adherence to the current doctrine of stare decisis. The doctrine may be repudiated, consistently with the doctrine.

I do not here address at any length for it appears to be no part of the Court's current doctrine of stare decisis — whether the current doctrine of stare decisis is *right* or *wrong*, on interpretive criteria apart from considerations of stare decisis. The whole point of the doctrine, after all, is to address when the Court should adhere to its prior decisions "whether or not mistaken" according to other possible criteria for constitutional adjudication. It is therefore immaterial, under the doctrine of stare decisis, for purposes of considering the stare decisis weight to be accorded the doctrine of stare decisis, whether the doctrine is sound.

---

1. Planned Parenthood of Se. Pa. v. Casey, 505 U.S. 833, 868 (1992).

All of this of course creates something of a quandary: If the doctrine of stare decisis suggests that the doctrine of stare decisis may (and perhaps should) be overruled or modified, precisely what should replace it? If the current doctrine of stare decisis is incoherent, what criteria should one apply to create a doctrine replacing or modifying it?

. . . .

I. THE CURRENT DOCTRINE OF STARE DECISIS

Planned Parenthood of Southeastern Pennsylvania v. Casey, decided in 1992, is, somewhat surprisingly, the Supreme Court's first systemic attempt to set forth a general theory of the role of precedent and "stare decisis" in constitutional adjudication. The Court had, of course, discussed the idea of stare decisis, and had invoked precedent, many, many times before. But one searches the first 500 volumes of the *U.S. Reports* in vain for a full-blown *theory* or *doctrine* of precedent. Think about it: after over 200 years in operation, *Casey*, in 1992, is the Court's first grand theology of precedent!

But *Casey*, barely fifteen years old as of this writing, is already not quite the Court's last word on the subject. Recent cases subsequent to *Casey* have treated the doctrine, too, embracing *Casey*'s treatment or distinguishing it in some manner, persuasive or not. If one is attempting to describe the "current doctrine of stare decisis," *Casey* is a good starting point and a proper prime focus of the inquiry, but it has to be taken in light of the glosses, modifications, and applications of subsequent decisions.

A. Three Preliminaries

Before digging into *Casey*'s explication of the factors comprising the doctrine, it may be useful to clear the doctrine of potentially confusing underbrush. I therefore begin with three straightforward, preliminary observations about the doctrine.

First, the doctrine of stare decisis is not constitutionally required, in any sense, and has never been so understood. Nothing in Article III of the Constitution (or in any other provision of the Constitution) mandates a practice of adherence to precedent; nothing in Article III specifies any rule or set of criteria for when a court should, must, or may follow a prior decision.

Nor does anything in Article III (or in any other provision of the Constitution) grant a *power* to the judiciary to prescribe binding rules that require future members of the judiciary to follow precedents. Indeed, to infer such a power would almost certainly be inconsistent with the probable claimed source of such power: If "the judicial Power" entails a power of courts to vest their decisions with prospective, quasi-legislative binding force — that is, if the judicial power of case-decision entails a power to prescribe binding rules of law — it is hard to see how the exercise of such power legitimately could be binding on future possessors of that same judicial power, who presumably have the same power to vest their decisions with authority. If courts legitimately can make constitutional law with their decisions, subsequent courts may repeal such enactments. If courts' interpretations of law purport merely to describe what has always been, is now, and ever shall be the objectively correct interpretation of the Constitution (or other law), it still would not imply that precisely the same interpretive power is thereby taken away from subsequent courts that might disagree with the supposedly objectively correct prior interpretation.[9]

And, to repeat, the Court has never so asserted. Rather, as the Court has said countless times, the doctrine of stare decisis is one of policy and practice only, not a strict rule of law or an inherent prescriptive power of the judiciary to bind present or future courts with its past decisions. To be sure, the Court could (one supposes) change its mind about this, too. But it would be quite hard to reconcile such an action with the enhanced notion of stare decisis thereby created; the act of creation would contradict the creation—an irony to which I return at the close of this Article. For now, it is sufficient to note that the judicial doctrine of stare decisis does not regard the judicial doctrine of stare decisis as being of constitutional dimension. To newly invent such a status would be, well, unprecedented.[11]

A second preliminary point can be stated more briefly: Stare decisis has never been thought absolute in American jurisprudence. It is a policy consideration, not an "inexorable command." The force of precedent is not strict. Thus, the doctrine of stare decisis is not constitutionally required and, even as a doctrine of mere policy, has never been regarded as absolute.

. . . . Courts overrule cases. Indeed, *Casey* itself overruled two of them.

The third preliminary point is slightly more difficult—defining exactly what is *meant* by the term stare decisis. We know it is a rule of practice and policy, not commanded by the Constitution or the product of a constitutionally delegated power. And we know it is not, and never has been, an absolute policy or practice. What, then, defines the essence of the doctrine? What *is* the non-absolute policy or practice to which the doctrine refers?

The short answer is that the doctrine of stare decisis is the judicial policy of (sometimes) adhering to a prior decision *irrespective of the prior decision's legal correctness* according to other interpretive criteria. As *Casey* put it fairly bluntly, it is the practice of adhering to a prior decision "whether or not mistaken." What defines the doctrine of stare decisis as a judicial practice—what gives the doctrine any punch at all—is adherence to what a court, by hypothesis, otherwise would regard as an erroneous exposition of the law. This distinguishes the doctrine of stare decisis from the milder doctrine of precedent as serving the more modest role of providing relevant interpretive information (the informed, considered views of

---

9. Similarly, one Congress cannot constitutionally purport to bar a subsequent Congress from repealing its legislative enactments, or otherwise limit a future Congress's ability to do so (except in the limited sense that there may be certain actions that, once taken, cannot be undone by a simple legislative repeal). The short point: Neither Congress nor the courts may make a rock so big that subsequent possessors of the same legislative or judicial power cannot move it.

11. For similar reasons, of course, my argument cannot depend on what the judiciary has said about the doctrine of stare decisis. I merely note that the judiciary's own articulation of the doctrine agrees with the position I have set forth.

prior, presumably competent interpreters) or serving as a starting point or baseline against which a departure ought to be justified or explained. The Supreme Court's current doctrine of stare decisis contemplates something more than mere *consideration* of prior cases' reasoning and conclusions; it is a doctrine about the judicial policy or practice of adhering, sometimes, to a decision the court would otherwise feel fully justified in concluding legally wrong.

The trick, then, for the Court in *Casey*, was to explain when and why precedent should be followed, and when and why it need not, apart from consideration of the precedent's correctness:

> When this Court reexamines a prior holding, its judgment is customarily informed by a series of prudential and pragmatic considerations designed to test the consistency of overruling a prior decision with the ideal of the rule of law, and to gauge the respective costs of reaffirming and overruling a prior case.

Both sides of the equation were involved in the *Casey* decision, which ended up reaffirming *Roe v. Wade* largely on the theory that stare decisis required such action yet overruled two of its decisions applying *Roe* on the theory that stare decisis permitted overruling those cases.

To the "prudential and pragmatic" end of informing the Court's judgment about which way to go in a particular instance, *Casey* identified a cluster of factors, interrelated and overlapping in some respects, relevant to the decision whether or not to overrule a prior decision. There are four primary, identified factors, plus an additional set of prudential, policy, and (seemingly) political judgments to lay on top of the more-legal factors. None is treated as dispositive; none is identified as essential; the relative weight of each is unclear. In short, current doctrine consists of a classic multifactor balancing test of incommensurable considerations. Let us consider each element in turn.

B. The Current Doctrine: When Should Wrong Precedent Be Followed (and When May It Be Overruled)?

1. Workability

First, *Casey* says, courts must consider the "workability" of a precedent decision or line of decisions. . . . *Casey* then summarized "workability," perhaps a bit cryptically, as a question of whether "the required determinations fall within judicial competence."

. . . .

. . . [T]he inquiry into workability appears to ask whether the rule of a precedent decision, besides being wrong, has tended to generate inconsistent applications, fostered unclarity and uncertainty, or proven difficult to manage in any kind of principled way — and on such account should be regarded as intolerable. "Workability" is not a hard-and-fast standard.

Moreover, that standard does not always even come into play in the first place. As noted above — and as illustrated by abundant examples in judicial practice before and since *Casey* — a finding of unworkability is not necessary for the Court to overrule a prior case. It is possible for a prior holding to be perfectly workable, but yet, in the Court's judgment, simply wrong. . . .

. . . .

"Workability" thus remains *a factor*. But it is hard to say much more beyond that. It is a factor of unclear weight and unclear application. It is perhaps fair to say, generally, that the more standardless, variable, and difficult-to-apply the holding of a particular case; the less it tends to yield predictable, principled results; the more unworkable that rule is; the greater the justification for discarding it. But a decision need not be unworkable to be overruled, and an unworkable decision need not be overruled.

2. Reliance

Casey's second factor in weighing the relative costs of reaffirming or overruling is whether a prior decision's rule "is subject to a kind of reliance that would lend a special hardship to the consequences of overruling and add inequity to the cost of repudiation." As to "special hardship," the Court invoked the "cost of a rule's repudiation as it would fall on those who have relied reasonably on the rule's continued application."

. . . .

The notion has a powerful intuitive appeal. It also has considerable legitimacy. But again, protecting legitimate, reasonable reliance interests is not an absolute rule. More fundamentally, it is not all that clear how reasonable it really is to rely on "reliance." . . . The simple fact is that legal rules change all the time. Legislatures are constantly creating new legal rules. These often frustrate well-informed prior expectations, causing folks to lose money they had invested or forcing them to invest some they had not planned on investing. This is what governments do: they upset prior expectations. Yet, no one thinks that this somehow gives those aggrieved by the new rule some vested legal right in the continuation of the prior legal regime. . . . The Court has held (rightly) that there is no constitutional legal right to have one's reasonable reliance interests prevail over a prospective change in the applicable legal rule.

What is true for legislative lawmaking is also true for judicial decisionmaking. Given that the courts have said, too many times to count, that the idea of stare decisis is not, and never has been, one of absolute adherence to a prior decision, and given the innumerable times that the Supreme Court has reconsidered and overruled its prior constitutional interpretations, there is not much more reason to expect that any given judicial interpretation will not change than there is to expect that a legislature will not enact a new statute.

. . . .

To some extent, this observation anticipates my critique, in the next Part, of the doctrine of stare decisis as applied to the doctrine of stare decisis. But one might as well begin unraveling a circular argument at any point on the circle: *reliance*, as that factor is employed in stare decisis, is little different from the argument one might employ with respect to an undesired legislative change in the law, and no more worthy of protection. Anything else — "stare decisis reliance" — is pure bootstrap, created by the existence of a doctrine of stare decisis in the first place.

What's more, it is hopelessly unclear how big a bootstrap it is. Under the current doctrine of stare decisis, it is uncertain precisely *what* should count as reasonable reliance and *how much* it should count, as weighed against correction of an erroneous rule of law embodied in a precedent. . . .

. . . .

It thus seems that the "reliance" thread of current doctrine can be summarized, not unfairly, as follows: Current doctrine treats reliance interests, of different kinds, as counseling, sometimes, to some extent, in favor of adhering to a decision otherwise thought to be wrong on independent interpretive criteria. Like workability, reliance is a *factor*, but one of uncertain content and uncertain weight. It perhaps can be said of the reliance factor, charitably, that the more that a legal rule has remained clear, stable, reasonably determinate, and certain in its application, and essentially uncontested over a sustained period of time, the more it will tend to have produced reasonable reliance; the more that such reasonable reliance has (then) tended to induce past, sunk action on the part of individuals, or institutions, that would require an enormous expenditure of resources, impose costs, or cause serious social or other dislocation in order to reverse or undo, the stronger the argument for protection of reliance interests.

But through all this, the *Plessy* problem remains and looms large. *Plessy* was as wrong as wrong precedent can be. Yet, the summary of reliance in the preceding paragraph *does* offer a pretty good argument for protecting the vested social, cultural, and even commercial reliance interests in maintaining segregation. . . . If "reliance" and stability interests ever should counsel against overruling a precedent, under the reasoning of *Casey*, *Plessy* would have been such a case. But that cannot possibly be right, can it?

The doctrinal escape hatch from this doctrinal problem — simply treating reliance considerations as a factor, not as dispositive — creates another problem. Under current doctrine, the need to correct error sometimes trumps reliance interests. But sometimes it does not. And there appears no clear rule or standard to identify when a case is of one type rather than another. That is the state of current reliance doctrine.

3. *Remnant of Abandoned Doctrine*

Casey's third identified factor is whether a precedent decision's premises, analysis, or holding have been significantly (or significantly *enough*) undermined by a subsequent case or by subsequent cases that the precedent has become a "doctrinal anachronism discounted by society," a "remnant of abandoned doctrine" that has been "left behind as a mere survivor of obsolete constitutional thinking."

Stripped of its wordiness, the "left behind" factor looks to *changed law* (as opposed to *changed facts*, the next factor I will discuss). If a case is a remnant, it may more readily be discarded. . . .

This, of course, raises an interesting (and inconvenient) question: How did precedents get out of whack with each other in the first place? How does something *get to be* a remnant of abandoned doctrine? How did there come to be subsequent decisions that undermined the first precedent? Did those cases fail to adhere to stare decisis?

The reality of the phenomenon is familiar to all lawyers and students of the law, who are trained from Day Two of law school to recognize how the second case in the book has departed, subtly or abruptly, from the first case in the book. Day Three is all about reconciling (or not) the first case and the second case, or choosing which one to apply, now that a third, unanticipated case comes along. This is the glorified, pseudo-mysterious "common law" method, so painfully memorable to all.

How does the doctrine of stare decisis permit this? The only logical answer is that, to whatever extent Case Two is in tension with Case One, it was to precisely that extent a departure from the idea of stare decisis. Occasionally, the departure or tension is acknowledged; sometimes it is disguised, which creates efficiency/workability problems.

Now we're on Day Three of the course. The third case has come along. When should Case One be thought a remnant? How great a degree of undermining needs to have been accomplished by Case Two in order to conclude that Case One has been left behind? Current stare decisis doctrine supplies no answer. There is no clear standard other than the Case Three court's evaluation of the state of law created by the precedents in tension with one another. It seems more accurate to say that the remnant-of-abandoned-doctrine argument merely posits that it is better to overrule a case in two (or more) steps than in one. But the remnant factor does not *require* that there always be this intermediate step, and there appears no logical reason why there should have to be one.

. . . .

. . . [H]owever, sometimes the Court says just the opposite — sometimes even in the same case. No, the Court says, we will not take the second step of the two-step and overrule, because Case Two — the undermining case — was itself an improper departure from precedent; *that* case is the one that needs to go.

. . . .

. . . [In summary,] a precedent that has been seriously undermined by subsequent precedents may more readily be overruled, but sometimes the reverse will hold true, and the Court may choose to reaffirm the earlier precedent and undermine the underminers. What becomes a remnant — what is left behind — is a function of the Court's subsequent decisions, not governed by any clear rules of stare decisis.

4. Changed Facts

Casey's stare decisis formula next asks "whether facts have so changed, or come to be seen so differently, as to have robbed the old rule of significant application or justification." The way this is expressed is slightly strange: facts have either changed "or come to be seen differently." Thus, even if facts have not *actually* changed, they might now be *viewed* differently. These real or perceived changes in social facts are then relevant where they have robbed the old rule of "application" *or* "justification."

But if changes in factual circumstances mean precedent no longer *applies* to very many real-world situations — its relevance has been overtaken by historical changes — that scarcely seems a reason to change the governing legal interpretation and abandon the precedent. Presumably, the precedent might still be right; it simply does not matter much any more.

The second part of *Casey*'s changed facts formulation is that factual changes (or changed perceptions) may deprive a rule of its *justification*. Again, as formulated, it is hard to see, in the abstract, what the Court might mean. The Court's subsequent discussion makes reasonably clear that this formulation is all about *Brown v. Board of Education*. It is an effort to supply a justification for *Brown*'s overruling of *Plessy* that might distinguish *that* overruling from others that might be urged upon the Court. . . . The Court in *Casey* seems to have been saying that *Plessy* was wrong when decided but that the *Brown* Court's overruling of it was not based on *Plessy*'s wrongness but on changed facts only.

. . . But th[is] factor, as used in *Casey* to explain the propriety of the Court's repudiation of *Plessy* . . . entails a subtle and disturbing implication — almost impossible to reconcile with the other factors comprising the Court's stare decisis doctrine — *that the meaning of the Constitution properly depends on how society views social facts at different times.*

. . . .

There is, I think, a great danger in this. If what makes it proper to *change* a legal interpretation is current social understandings of facts, then it is hard to argue that it was improper to *have made* a legal interpretation based on *then-current* social understandings of facts. The changed facts argument as explicated in *Casey* permits one to conclude that an awful case was not in fact awful when decided; it simply would be awful to adhere to it now. The Court did not actually make a grievous mistake back then; but it is right to change the rule for modern times. . . .

. . . .

Surely, this is a proposition worth examining long and questioning hard. . . .

I pose this very issue as a discussion question for that day of the basic Constitutional Law course: "Should the Constitution be interpreted in accordance with prevailing social understandings of the time?" My hope is that *Plessy* produces more than a few emphatic "no" answers. (It does.) But it is amazing, and disturbing, how many "yes" answers I receive. Some students evidently are not made uncomfortable by the proposition that *Plessy* was right in its day. I have had students argue seriously that *Brown* was right for its time and *Plessy* was right for *its* time; the meaning of the Constitution changes with the times and with folks' understanding of the proper result dictated by social facts.

. . . .

. . . If the changed facts notion is understood as an inquiry that permits overruling cases whenever social understandings, mores, and values have changed substantially, it has truly sweeping jurisprudential implications. "Changed facts," so understood, would be the stare decisis factor that swallowed stare decisis: courts should decide cases as current values dictate, and legitimately may overrule anything in their way. . . .

. . . [But this factor] might be understood to stand for something somewhat narrower: Where the Court had *justified its decision* at the time, at least in substantial part, by making factual statements or proceeding from factual premises that we would now conclude were simply wrong as a matter of fact, the inclusion of such factual misstatements within the stated rationale of decision gives a subsequent court special justification for overruling the precedent — that is, a justification for overruling beyond the fact of legal error. . . .

. . . .

A final possibility, narrower yet, seems the best way to understand this factor, though it is harder to square with the Court's discussion: changes in facts, in the times, or in social conditions, may *reveal*, or help to make clear, that a prior decision *always was* wrong as a matter of law; the Court was simply *blinded by* social context, social facts, or the latest trendy science or social science at the time of the error. . . .

. . . .

. . . In the end, the factor of changed facts is unclear on a number of scores. It can be understood to mean three entirely different things: one of which the Court seems to have said, but the logic of which is more extreme than the Court possibly could have intended; a second of which makes changed facts merely a pretense to be seized upon; and third of which seems to imply that focusing on different understandings of social facts is precisely the wrong thing upon which to base a decision and is evidence of a prior case's defects. It is also unclear exactly what *types* of changed facts are sufficient and *how much* social facts need to have changed in order to counsel more in favor of overruling. . . . And finally, the relationship of this factor to others, and its relative weight, is not at all clear. It is unclear whether a change in facts is necessary in order to overrule a precedent, or whether it is ever sufficient on its own to justify overruling.

5. *Judicial Integrity*

The final factor in *Casey*'s stare decisis analysis is a wide-ranging one that occupies several pages and consumes a great deal of the *Casey* Court's rhetorical attention. It goes by various names, but might usefully, if imprecisely, be termed "judicial integrity." . . .

. . . Shorn of the Court's overwrought formulations, the "judicial integrity" factor asks an understandable question: whether, even if a precedent is thought erroneous, it would seem arbitrary, capricious, or fickle for the Court to be changing its mind too often or too readily (especially if its decisions change along with personnel changes) or to be changing its interpretation in response to public, or political, or even scholarly criticism or pressure. . . .

The difficulty lies in transforming this intuition into a principled rule, susceptible of consistent application. . . .

It is even harder to find principled application. . . .

. . . [I]t stands as a fair description of "judicial integrity" that the impact of overruling-versus-adhering-to a case on public perceptions of judicial integrity will sometimes cut one way and sometimes cut the other way, with no clear, principled standard to control the decision.

So that is the state of current stare decisis doctrine: The factors are (1) workability, (2) reliance, (3) remnant of abandoned doctrine, (4) changed facts, and (5) judicial integrity. Each of the factors contains internal contradictions. Each admits of conflicting applications, and there are examples of such conflicts in each category. Each factor suffers from certain major analytic defects and unclarity. The relationship of each factor to the others, and their relative weight, is not defined. No factor is necessarily necessary. No factor is sufficient.

II. APPLYING THE DOCTRINE OF STARE DECISIS TO THE DOCTRINE OF STARE DECISIS

How does the current doctrine of stare decisis fare under these five criteria? Should the current doctrine of stare decisis be adhered to because it well serves the policies of workability-efficiency, protection of reliance interests, stability and predictability, and protection of judicial integrity? Or, perhaps, have changed facts, or changed law, undermined the doctrine in ways that might counsel in favor of it being overruled?

If one were to apply *Casey*'s criteria fairly, to the question of *whether the current decisional law of precedent should be followed*, it is hard to avoid the conclusion that the current doctrine of stare decisis does not require adherence to the current doctrine of stare decisis. Ironically, the doctrine, to the extent it can be thought to yield any clear direction, counsels in favor of overruling the doctrine. Nothing in any of the criteria set forth in *Casey* and subsequent cases — *none* of the factors of workability, reliance, changed law/remnant, changed facts, or judicial integrity — points in the direction of standing by what the Court has decided about when precedent should be followed. To the contrary, the current doctrine of stare decisis, applied to the current doctrine of stare decisis, tends to suggest that the doctrine undermines nearly all of the policies that the doctrine is supposed to serve. Current stare decisis doctrine therefore properly may, and even should, be abandoned, consistent with the evaluative criteria established by current stare decisis doctrine. To put it bluntly: The doctrine of stare decisis, as presently formulated, constitutes its own circular firing squad.

. . . .

A. Workability

Consider first "workability," and its companion value, the promotion of judicial efficiency: Does the current doctrine and practice of stare decisis supply a workable, coherent, readily administrable set of clear principles that promotes clarity, efficiency and predictability in adjudication, and that economizes on judicial work? Plainly not. As demonstrated above, the current doctrine of stare decisis supplies no clear standards. It is a laundry list mish-mash of factors, each of which has serious problems of unclarity and imprecision of application. The relative weight of each factor is also unclear — it is unspecified — as is the relationship of each to the others.

. . . .

B. Reliance

If reliance is the residue of predictability and stability, and if one of the objects of the doctrine of stare decisis is to protect reasonable, vested reliance interests, current doctrine must be judged a failure on this score as well. Surely, no reasonable person familiar with the Court's doctrine and practice of precedent would rely on current stare decisis doctrine remaining stable. No reasonable person would rely on the doctrine being applied in a consistent and predictable fashion. And no reasonable person would rely on the Court's adhering, in any given instance, to a decision it has concluded is wrong, simply for reasons of stare decisis. The Court's reliance on reliance has been unreliable. The Court finds protection-worthy reliance interests in all kinds of different things, when it suits its purposes (such as social reliance in a rule remaining the same because people desire it or are accustomed to it), but sometimes will simply rush on past such considerations or dismiss them as incidental.

. . . .

C. Remnant of Abandoned Doctrine

Has the doctrine of stare decisis remained stable and consistent over time, or has it been undermined by subsequent cases? . . .

. . . .

. . . [I]t is fair to observe that, though the Court's actions have not been perfectly consistent (again, undermining workability and reliance), the doctrinal evolution of the Court's decisions has left *Casey*'s discussion of stare decisis very much left behind. In practice, the doctrine is abandoned whenever the Court wishes to abandon it. The doctrine of stare decisis, as discussed in *Casey*, would thus seem to suggest that the doctrine of stare decisis has itself become, or is rapidly becoming, a remnant of abandoned doctrine. If subsequent decisions are fully as authoritative as to the meaning and content of current stare decisis doctrine (and how could they not be, consistent with such doctrine?), then there obviously has been a lot of undermining of the doctrine of stare decisis going on. . . .

D. Changed Facts

Have social or political facts changed, or come to be seen so differently, as to undermine the justification for continued adherence to the current doctrine of stare decisis? This is genuinely hard to evaluate, in part because of the difficulties presented by the "changed facts" factor itself. . . .

. . . .

. . . [But] the "changed facts" factor likewise could come to be seen as support-ing the overruling of current stare decisis doctrine.

E. Judicial Integrity

Finally, there is the grab-bag of considerations concerning public perceptions of judicial integrity. Does the furtherance of notions of (or public perceptions of) ju-dicial integrity require adherence to the current doctrine of stare decisis? *Casey* seems to require us to ask whether the current doctrine and practice of stare decisis is one on which the Court has "staked its authority" or "legitimacy" such that de-parture from it would undermine the people's belief in themselves and in the Court.

Surely any such assertion should be met with considerable skepticism, if not outright laughter. . . .

Moreover, more sensible notions of "judicial integrity" would seem to require acknowledgment that stare decisis is a doctrine of convenience, endlessly pliable, followed only when desired, and almost always invoked as a makeweight. . . .

. . . .

To review and recapitulate: the Court's current doctrine of stare decisis is unworkable, unsusceptible to principled application, inconsistent, unpredictable, and so unreliable as not to justify reliance upon it. The stated doctrine, as for-mulated in *Casey*, has been so greatly undermined by subsequent decisions and applications of the doctrine of stare decisis as to render the doctrine of stare decisis itself a remnant of abandoned doctrine. The doctrine does not further perceptions of judicial integrity, but probably undermines them. . . .

III. IF THE CURRENT DOCTRINE OF STARE DECISIS PERMITS ABANDONING OR MODIFYING THE CURRENT DOCTRINE OF STARE DECISIS, WHAT SHOULD REPLACE IT?

What should one do with a doctrine that is such a failure on its own terms? Given the irony that the current doctrine of stare decisis emphatically does not require adherence to the current doctrine of stare decisis, but suggests that it may and should be modified or replaced, what should replace it?

One bright idea might be to move in the direction of much stricter adher-ence to precedent — something closer to absolute stare decisis. The double para-dox with such a view is that, in the first place, such a move would be, well, *unpre-cedented* — unsupported by anything the Court has ever said about the authority of precedent. In the second place (and relatedly), there is the paradox that such a new, improved, better, stronger, faster stare decisis would be inconsistent with the act of adopting such a new rule. Given current doctrine, and long unsteady practice, for the judiciary to create a far stricter rule of stare decisis would be an act of activism overruling or drastically overhauling much prior law. This would be contrary to the far stricter rule of stare decisis being proposed.

No. The only direction in which the doctrine could be changed and not self-destruct, is in the direction of even looser "stare decisis." To be sure, it is hard to imagine a doctrine of stare decisis much looser than the current doctrine is, in practice, but at least this result could be made more honest. This would require disapproval of the tone, and some of the substance, of *Casey*'s discussion. It would require acknowledging that the decision to adhere to precedent or depart from it is really just a product of ad hoc, case-by-case decisionmaking. (The only problem is that the label "stare decisis" does not seem particularly apt for such a refashioned doctrine of precedent.)

All of this points in the direction of what I think is the proper approach. The doctrine of stare decisis may, and should be replaced by a much simpler, cleaner theory of the proper role of precedent in constitutional adjudication. The primary inquiry, in any situation, is whether a prior decision (or line of decisions) is *right* or *wrong*, on independent interpretive criteria one thinks are correct on grounds other than precedent. In conducting such an inquiry, precedent can serve an important "information function" of furnishing what one would hope would be useful, thoughtful arguments of prior interpreters concerning the proper understanding and application of a particular constitutional provision. This can promote efficiency: a subsequent interpreter need not re-invent the interpretive wheel for every issue. He or she may read prior opinions, with care but independent judgment, and use good prior reasoning as an efficient shortcut to correct conclusions today. This can also multiply competence: a subsequent interpreter may stand on the shoulders of others; moreover, a less competent or less confident interpreter may follow in others' footsteps, unless and until fully persuaded that the path is legally wrong. But where an interpreter is fully persuaded, after full and careful consideration of all relevant information, including the decisions of those who have gone before, that the standing interpretation is simply wrong, the interpreter should (indeed, I have argued elsewhere, *he must*) follow what he is persuaded is the correct interpretation of the Constitution, not what he has concluded is the incorrect interpretation of judges who have gone before him. This strikes me as a much more *modest*, sensible, coherent doctrine of precedent — one that does not make grandiose claims or require a grand theory that cannot be satisfied. It also appears to have been the original understanding of precedent, to boot.

Notes and Questions

---

1. Like the Lawson article, most judges and legal scholars probably do not agree with this article and its take on stare decisis. Nonetheless, Professor Paulsen's views, like Professor Lawson's, are thought-provoking. To what extent, if any, is Professor Paulsen's view of stare decisis consistent with Professor Lawson's? The Supreme Court's actual practice with respect to stare decisis?

2. *May stare decisis be overruled by court decision?* In the preceding article, Professor Paulsen argues that the Supreme Court should "overrule" its own doctrine of stare decisis. But could the Court really do so, logically speaking? For example, if the Court were to purport to eliminate the doctrine of stare decisis completely in the course of deciding some case, how would such a "holding" be enforced, given that there is no longer a doctrine of stare decisis? And this leads to a related question: How was the doctrine created in the first place? Must it have been announced in the course of deciding a case, or is it simply the product of a long-standing judicial practice of adhering to prior holdings in similar cases?

3. *May Congress abrogate stare decisis by statute?* What if Congress disagreed with a prior decision of the Supreme Court, and wanted the Court to revisit the issue underlying that decision without being burdened by that precedent. May Congress abrogate stare decisis by statute, either in general or with respect to particular subjects or cases? For a provocative argument in the affirmative, see Michael Stokes Paulsen, *Abrogating Stare Decisis by Statute: May Congress Remove the Precedential Effect of* Roe *and* Casey?, 109 YALE L.J. 1535 (2000). But for a counterargument, see Richard H. Fallon, Jr., *Stare Decisis and the Constitution: An Essay on Constitutional Methodology,* 76 N.Y.U. L. REV. 570 (2001).

4. *May stare decisis be abrogated by court rule?* Alternatively, may the federal courts abrogate stare decisis pursuant either to their statutory or their inherent rulemaking power? For an argument that they may not, see Bradley Scott Shannon, *May Stare Decisis Be Abrogated by Rule?,* 67 OHIO ST. L.J. 645 (2006).

5. For an argument that stare decisis already matters little in the Supreme Court, see Frederick Schauer, *Has Precedent Ever Really Mattered in the Supreme Court?,* 24 GA. ST. U. L. REV. 381 (2007).

6. For more on precedent generally, see MICHAEL J. GERHARDT, THE POWER OF PRECEDENT (2008), and Jeremy Waldron, *Stare Decisis and the Rule of Law: A Layered Approach,* 111 MICH. L. REV. 1 (2012).

7. Avoiding Precedent

What happens when an inferior court is bound by a decision of a superior (or otherwise binding) court with which it disagrees? Or if a precedent-setting court disagrees with its own earlier decision?

Disregarding seemingly illegitimate means of avoiding precedent (such as ignoring it or mischaracterizing it), an inferior court has little choice but to *follow* superior court precedent unless the lower court fairly may *distinguish* it. In other words, the lower court must find some legally significant difference between its case and the precedent-setting case that permits the later court to avoid the earlier decision. As Professor Schauer points out, precisely when a difference becomes legally sufficient is difficult to define, but its importance in litigation is difficult to overstate.

A court (such as the Supreme Court) that is bound only by its own earlier decisions may distinguish precedent as well, or (as we have also seen) it may *overrule* its earlier decision. Of course, if a party's ultimate goal is to convince a higher court to overrule precedent, counsel generally must "preserve" that argument at all levels of the judicial hierarchy (i.e., make the argument with the understanding that those courts below the precedent-setting court are powerless to address that argument).

8. Overruling by Implication

What happens when two (or more) decisions from the same court seem to conflict? Though this might seem like a theoretical impossibility, it does occur in practice on occasion. The general rule is that the later-decided case controls, though as with statutes, courts will work hard to interpret prior precedents in a way that avoids any conflicts. This general rule certainly holds when the earlier decision is expressly overruled, and would seem to hold true as well when the earlier decision is overruled by implication — i.e., in those situations where the court, for whatever reasons, fails to expressly overrule the earlier decision, but where the earlier is clearly contrary to the latter. *See, e.g., Asher v. Texas,* 128 U.S. 129, 131-32 (1888) ("Even if it were true that the decision referred to was not in harmony with some of the previous decisions, we had supposed that a later decision in conflict with prior ones had the effect to overrule them, whether mentioned and commented on or not"); 18 James Wm. Moore, Moore's Federal Practice § 134.05[6], at 134-46 (3d ed. 2008) ("Although a lower court is bound by a prior decision of a higher court until that decision is overruled, there are circumstances in which a prior decision will be overruled implicitly rather than explicitly. A lower court is not bound to follow a decision that has been implicitly overruled.").

Therefore, it should be apparent that no special language is necessary to overrule a prior decision; the simple existence of some later, irreconcilably inconsistent holding by the same court is sufficient.[17] Indeed, it does not seem particularly important whether the later court intended to overrule its prior holding or whether it was even aware that it was doing so. Thus, at the Supreme Court level, precedent — to the extent it exists — may be either followed, distinguished, or overruled. There are no other choices. Though it might be possible for a Court to be ignorant of or even to consciously disregard relevant precedent, the resulting holding, unless distinguishable, must be seen as overruling the earlier precedent. If that result was unintended or mistaken, it may of course be corrected in the future, in that the implicit overruling may itself be overruled. But until that time, the later decision must control — the two conflicting precedents cannot co-exist.

Some have criticized the practice of overruling by implication, and certainly, express overruling has some advantages. For one thing, express overruling more clearly

---

17. Conversely, the mere inclusion of language in a Court's opinion that "Case A is hereby overruled," if not supported by a holding to that effect, would not, in fact, result in the overruling of Case A.

informs the consumers of judicial decisions that a prior precedent is no longer good law. Express overruling also might cause the issuing court to more carefully consider whether overruling is truly appropriate (or to at least articulate those considerations expressly). Indeed, it might well be that reasons supporting express overruling outweigh those favoring overruling by implication.

But, while there might be *normative* concerns with overruling by implication, there do not appear to be any *legal* impediments to the use of this practice—i.e., there does not seem to be anything unconstitutional about it, and neither Congress nor the Court has repudiated this practice. Moreover, a consistent practice of express overruling, even if preferable, is not as easy as it might sound. For one thing, a serious commitment to express overruling would require a search of the relevant reporters for any and all precedents contrary to any aspect of the holding of each later case. Such a search, particularly considering the number of cases the Court might decide in any given year, seems impracticable. And even when express overruling is utilized, a somewhat related problem arises. Specifically, when the Court announces that one of its prior precedents has been overruled, it is probably the rare case in which *every* aspect of that prior holding is no longer good law. More typically, a later Court will only be overruling *certain* aspects of a prior holding—crucial aspects, to be sure, but less than all. Thus, though the Court typically announces overrulings without qualification, ideally it should be stating that it is overruling only those aspects of its prior holdings implicated by the current holding. Though this too has been done on occasion (at least to some extent), it is probably asking too much to expect courts to perform this exercise in every situation in which it arises. Overruling by implication avoids both of these problems (albeit by placing the burden of ascertaining the precise scope of a court's precedents on future courts and litigants). Thus, not only is overruling by implication permissible and done in fact, it also might be practically necessary, at least to some extent.

Bradley Scott Shannon, *Overruling by Implication*, 33 SEATTLE U. L. REV. 151, 153-57 (2009).

A recent example of this doctrine might be found in *John R. Sand & Gravel Co. v. United States,* 552 U.S. 130 (2008), wherein Justice Stevens, in dissent, stated:

> The majority points out quite rightly that the doctrine of *stare decisis* has "special force" in statutory cases. See *Patterson v. McLean Credit Union,* 491 U. S. 164, 172-173 (1989). But the doctrine should not prevent us from acknowledging when we have already overruled a prior case, even if we failed to say so explicitly at the time. In *Rasul v. Bush,* 542 U. S. 466 (2004), for example, we explained that in *Braden v. 30th Judicial Circuit Court of Ky.,* 410 U. S. 484 (1973), we had overruled so much of *Ahrens v. Clark,* 335 U. S. 188 (1948), as found that the habeas petitioners' presence within the territorial reach of the district court was a jurisdictional prerequisite. *Braden* held, contrary to *Ahrens,* that a prisoner's presence within the district court's territorial reach was *not* an "inflexible jurisdictional rule," 410 U. S., at 500. *Braden* nowhere stated that it was overruling *Ahrens,* although Justice Rehnquist began his dissent by noting: "Today the Court overrules *Ahrens v. Clark.*" 410 U. S., at 502. Thirty years later we acknowledged in *Rasul* what was by then clear: *Ahrens* was no longer good law. 542 U. S., at 478-479, and n. 9.

Id. at 143 n.5 (Stevens, J., dissenting).

This general rule regarding overruling by implication was modified to some extent, though, in *Rodriguez de Quijas v. Shearson/American Express, Inc.,* 490 U.S.

477 (1989). In *Rodriguez,* the Court was called upon to decide "whether a pre-dispute agreement to arbitrate claims under the Securities Act of 1933 is unenforceable" (*id.* at 478), an issue that in turn depended on the continued vitality of the Court's contrary holding in *Wilko v. Swan,* 346 U.S. 427 (1953). The court of appeals declined to follow that precedent, holding that "subsequent [Supreme Court] decisions have reduced *Wilko* to 'obsolescence.'" *Rodriguez,* 490 U.S. at 479. Though the Supreme Court affirmed the court of appeals' judgment (*see id.* at 486), the Court added:

> We do not suggest that the Court of Appeals on its own authority should have taken the step of renouncing *Wilko.* If a precedent of this Court has direct application in a case, yet appears to rest on reasons rejected in some other line of decisions, the Court of Appeals should follow the case which directly controls, leaving to this Court the prerogative of overruling its own decisions.

Id. at 484. Nonetheless, the Court then continued: "We now conclude that *Wilko* was incorrectly decided and is inconsistent with the prevailing uniform construction of other federal statutes governing arbitration agreements in the setting of business transactions." *Id.*

Though four Justices dissented from the Court's decision (*see id.* at 486 (Stevens, J., dissenting)), they also agreed with the Court's view regarding the court of appeals' treatment of *Wilko:*

> The Court of Appeals refused to follow *Wilko,* a controlling precedent of this Court. As the majority correctly acknowledges, the Court of Appeals therefore engaged in an indefensible brand of judicial activism. We, of course, are not subject to the same restraint when asked to upset one of our own precedents.

Id.

The *Rodriguez* Court's "requirement" that lower federal courts follow that precedent that "directly" controls, despite contrary indications in other, later cases, might seem reasonable at first blush. Certainly, one can understand a desire on the part of the Supreme Court to control the interpretation of its precedents. But does this "requirement" truly make sense? With regard to this question, C. Steven Bradford has argued:

> A lower court clearly violates its duty of allegiance to the Supreme Court when, simply because the lower court feels the earlier Supreme Court decision was analytically wrong, it rejects a precedent that the Supreme Court has not questioned. If a lower court has any duty to obey the Supreme Court, a blatant rejection of unquestioned Supreme Court doctrine violates that duty.
>
> The duty of the lower court is less clear when the Supreme Court has questioned its own precedent. In such cases, there is more than one Supreme Court decision to which the lower court owes obedience. The older, doubtful precedent requires the lower court to rule one way, but a newer case or series of Supreme Court cases argues for the opposite decision. To which line of decisions does the lower court owe obedience? If the later Supreme Court decision expressly overrules the earlier case, unquestionably the lower court should follow the latest pronouncement. Rejection of the precedent that the Supreme Court has itself overruled is not infidelity to the higher court. If this is

true, should not the lower court also follow the later case where the rejection is implicit rather than explicit? If the goal is allegiance to the Supreme Court, it is sophistry to require the lower court to follow doctrine that the Court has rejected, simply because the Supreme Court has not ruled on the particular issue confronting the lower court. How is fealty served when the lower court is clearly convinced that its ruling is contrary to the choice the Supreme Court itself would make? To disregard the current doctrine and apply the discredited case is the greater violation of the duty of loyalty.

C. Steven Bradford, *Following Dead Precedent: The Supreme Court's Ill-Advised Rejection of Anticipatory Overruling,* 59 FORDHAM L. REV. 39, 83 (1990).

Other legal scholars also have been critical of *Rodriguez de Quijas,* including Barry Friedman, *The Wages of Stealth Overruling (With Particular Attention to Miranda v. Arizona),* 99 GEO. L.J. 1 (2010), and (again) Bradley Scott Shannon, *Overruling by Implication,* 33 SEATTLE U. L. REV. 151 (2009). According to Professor Shannon, the Court's statement in that case regarding overruling by implication a) was dicta, b) has itself been overruled by implication, in that the Court continues to utilize this device, and c) does not survive the Court's own test regarding the adherence to precedent, and therefore should (and perhaps even must) be ignored by lower courts. *See id.* at 169-89.

PRACTICE PROBLEM :
OVERRULED BY IMPLICATION

8 U.S.C. § 1326 (2012) ("Reentry of removed aliens"), subsection (a) ("In general"), provides:

> Subject to subsection (b) of this section, any alien who —
> (1) has been denied admission, excluded, deported, or removed or has departed the United States while an order of exclusion, deportation, or removal is outstanding, and thereafter
> (2) enters, attempts to enter, or is at any time found in, the United States, unless
>> (A) prior to his reembarkation at a place outside the United States or his application for admission from foreign contiguous territory, the Attorney General has expressly consented to such alien's reapplying for admission; or
>> (B) with respect to an alien previously denied admission and removed, unless such alien shall establish that he was not required to obtain such advance consent under this chapter or any prior Act, shall be fined under title 18, or imprisoned not more than 2 years, or both.

Subsection (b) ("Criminal penalties for reentry of certain removed aliens"), further provides:

> Notwithstanding subsection (a) of this section, in the case of any alien described in such subsection —

. . . .

        (2) whose removal was subsequent to a conviction for commission of an aggravated felony, such alien shall be fined under such title, imprisoned not more than 20 years, or both . . . .

In *In re Winship*, 397 U.S. 358 (1970), the Supreme Court held that, in the jury trial context, the government must prove each element of a crime beyond a reasonable doubt to that jury.

In *Almendarez-Torres v. United States*, 523 U.S. 224 (1998), the Court held (by a margin of 5-4) that § 1326(b)(2), when applicable, does not constitute an additional element of this crime, but rather represents a mere "sentencing factor" (and therefore may be found by a judge, and by a preponderance of the evidence).

Finally, in *Jones v. United States*, 526 U.S. 227 (1999), the Court held, with respect to a different federal criminal statute, that "any factor . . . that increases the maximum penalty for a crime must be charged in the indictment, submitted to a jury, and proven beyond a reasonable doubt." The basic rule in *Jones* has been repeated by the Court several times since in a variety of contexts (though not with respect to 8 U.S.C. § 1326).

Assume that the government today would like to charge a defendant with violating § 1326(a), but further wants the defendant sentenced pursuant to § 1326(b)(2). Must the prior commission of an aggravated felony be charged and proved to a jury beyond a reasonable doubt (i.e., does the enhancement described in subsection (b)(2) constitute an "element" of this crime)? Please explain why or why not.

9. The Adoption of Precedent by Newly Created Courts

From time to time, Congress creates new judicial circuits. (Indeed, proposals to break up the Ninth Circuit into two or more circuits have been debated for decades.) Should the law of the prior circuit "bind" the newly created circuit of which it formerly was a part?

Bonner v. City of Prichard

661 F.2d 1206 (11th Cir. 1981)

GODBOLD, Chief Judge:

This is the first case to be heard by the United States Court of Appeals for the Eleventh Circuit, established October 1, 1981 pursuant to the Fifth Circuit Court of Appeals Reorganization Act of 1980, P.L. 96-452, 94 Stat. 1995, and this opinion is the first to be published by the Eleventh Circuit. Under P.L. 96-452 the United States Court of Appeals for the Fifth Circuit was divided into two circuits, the Eleventh and the "new Fifth." This court, by informal agreement of its judges prior to October 1,

1981, confirmed by formal vote on October 2, 1981, has taken this case en banc to consider what case law will serve as the established precedent of the Eleventh Circuit at the time it comes into existence. We hold that the decisions of the United States Court of Appeals for the Fifth Circuit (the "former Fifth" or the "old Fifth"), as that court existed on September 30, 1981, handed down by that court prior to the close of business on that date, shall be binding as precedent in the Eleventh Circuit, for this court, the district courts, and the bankruptcy courts in the circuit.

Section 9 of the Act provides for the handling of cases that prior to October 1, 1981 had been filed with the former Fifth Circuit. Subparagraphs (1) and (2) thereof provide:

> 1) If the matter has been submitted for decision, further proceedings in respect of the matter shall be had in the same manner and with the same effect as if this Act had not been enacted.
>
> (2) If the matter has not been submitted for decision, the appeal or proceeding, together with the original papers, printed records, and record entries duly certified, shall, by appropriate orders be transferred to the court to which it would have gone had this Act been in full force and effect at the time such appeal was taken or other proceeding commenced, and further proceedings in respect of the case shall be had in the same manner and with the same effect as if the appeal or other proceeding had been filed in such court.

In the former Fifth Circuit a case filed prior to October 1, 1981 was "submitted for decision" to that court within the meaning of § 9 of the Act on the date it was heard by an oral argument panel of that court or fully decided by a three judge screening panel without oral argument. Thus a case designated before October 1, 1981 for assignment to an oral argument calendar and scheduled for hearing after October 1, 1981 would not be "submitted for decision" to the old Fifth Circuit but, in due course, would be submitted to the Eleventh or the new Fifth. During the routine screening of this case in September 1981 the initiating judge assigned the case for oral argument. Since the case was not decided by a screening panel, and there were no oral argument panels sitting before October 1 to which it could be submitted, it was not (and could not be) "submitted for decision" before October 1. The appeal arose in the geographical confines of the Eleventh Circuit, so that, under § 9(2) of the Act, it became an Eleventh Circuit case to be submitted to and decided by that court, and it has been properly voted for hearing en banc by the members of that court.

. . . .

II. The Choice of Governing Law

Under the established federal legal system the decisions of one circuit are not binding on other circuits. . . . The various circuits differ somewhat in the extent to which they treat their own decisions as binding on themselves. Some appear at times to treat their own decisions as merely persuasive; others by rule or practice permit one panel to overrule another after prior notice to all judges of what is proposed, followed by no objection. The old Fifth followed the absolute rule that a prior decision of the circuit (panel or en banc) could not be overruled by a panel but only by the court sitting en banc. The Eleventh Circuit decides in this case that it chooses, and will follow, this rule.

The act of dividing the old Fifth Circuit into two circuits did not address the issue of what body of law would be adopted or otherwise would become the body of law of either of the two circuits for cases "submitted for decision" on and after October 1, 1981. To decide this case, and later Eleventh Circuit cases, we must decide whether this court shall adopt some established body of law as its body of precedent, and if so, effective as of its coming into existence, what established body of law will be chosen. For several reasons we choose the decisions of the United States Court of Appeals for the Fifth Circuit, as that court existed on September 30, 1981, handed down by that court prior to close of business on that date.[5] We consider that body of law worthy for governance of legal affairs within the jurisdiction of this new circuit.

Stability and predictability are essential factors in the proper operation of the rule of law. In *Moragne v. States Marine Lines, Inc.*, 398 U.S. 375 (1970), the Supreme Court states the reasons for following past decisions:

> Among these are the desirability that the law furnish a clear guide for the conduct of individuals, to enable them to plan their affairs with assurance against untoward surprise; the importance of furthering fair and expeditious adjudication by eliminating the need to relitigate every relevant proposition in every case; and the necessity of maintaining public faith in the judiciary as a source of impersonal and reasoned judgments.

Id. at 403. Our choice is strongly influenced by these considerations.

Adoption of the former Fifth Circuit precedents will maintain and promote stability and predictability in the states of Alabama, Georgia and Florida, which comprise the geographical territory of the Eleventh Circuit. Since 1866 these three states have been part of the former Fifth Circuit, which in addition has included Texas, Louisiana, Mississippi and the Canal Zone. During this extensive span of time the decisions of the Fifth Circuit have been precedents applied in the states that now constitute the Eleventh Circuit. District courts and bankruptcy courts in these states have rendered the initial decisions in many of the cases decided by the former Fifth Circuit. Judges presently on this court, who among them have 265 years of federal judicial service in the Fifth Circuit, have been instrumental in establishing its law. Lawyers from Alabama, Georgia and Florida, through the litigation of thousands of cases, have made significant contributions to the development of this jurisprudence. Bench and bar are schooled in it. Citizens of these states and their legal advisers have relied upon it and structured their legal relationships with one another and conducted their affairs in accordance with it. By adopting the former Fifth Circuit precedent we maintain the stability and predictability previously enjoyed. The decisions of the former Fifth Circuit, adopted as precedent by the Eleventh Circuit, will, of course,

---

5. We reserve for future consideration the effect on Eleventh Circuit law of other categories of decisions by the old Fifth Circuit — for example, decisions handed down by the old Fifth after September 30, 1981 in cases submitted to that court for decision before October 1; possible future en banc decisions by the *old* Fifth changing what appeared to have been its rule as of September 30, 1981.

be subject to the power of the Eleventh Circuit sitting en banc to overrule any such decision.

The Eighth Circuit was split in 1929 into the Eighth and Tenth. Two subsequent decisions by district courts in the new Tenth accepted the law of the Eighth as binding. In *Thompson v. St. Louis-San Francisco Ry. Co.*, 5 F.Supp. 785 at 789 (N.D.Okl. 1934), the court observed:

> The Tenth Circuit Court of Appeals, which is controlling of this court, has not passed upon the question, and since there is a difference in the holdings of two Circuit Courts of Appeals, the question is properly for the United States Supreme Court, rather than for this court's determination. However, it is not difficult to decide that the ruling of the Eighth Circuit Court of Appeals is controlling of the decision in question now before the court. This court was formerly a part of the Eighth Judicial Circuit, having become disengaged therefrom upon the creation of the Tenth Judicial Circuit. The decisions of the Eighth Judicial Circuit are binding upon this court in the absence of decisions of the Tenth Circuit. The Eighth Circuit Court of Appeals' decision was rendered by two of the present judges of the Tenth Circuit Court of Appeals, and in my opinion the decision is controlling of this court. The same conclusion was reached in *In re Meyers*, 1 F.Supp. 673, 674 (W.D.Okl.), *rev'd on other grounds sub nom. Barbee v. Spurrier Lumber Co.*, 64 F.2d 5 (10th Cir. 1933).

We find no convincing reason for taking any course other than for this court sitting en banc to adopt as precedent for the Eleventh Circuit the body of law of the old Fifth. We are not willing to reach the same result by an informal and unrevealed consensus among individual judges. This would be inconsistent with the methodology of orderly administration of justice. It would not give fair notice to litigants, district courts, bankruptcy courts, and government agencies of what to expect. An informal consensus not given the imprimatur of judicial decision could be upset by changes in the composition of the court.

Nor is our rule-making power an appropriate vehicle for establishing a body of precedent. Court rules generally address court procedures and court conduct of business. Congress has authorized the courts to "prescribe rules for the conduct of their business." 28 U.S.C.A. § 2071. Rule 47 of the Federal Rules of Appellate Procedure, adopted under that authority, authorizes the judges of the circuit to make rules of practice not inconsistent with FRAP, and in cases not provided for by FRAP authorizes the court of appeals "to regulate their practice in any manner not inconsistent with these rules." Neither the statute nor FRAP addresses the establishment of substantive law by court rule. The judges of this court, when judges of the former Fifth Circuit, maintained a distinct separation between their administrative and their judicial functions. The substantive law of the circuit was established by the exercise of judicial authority and procedural rules by administrative action. We consider it inappropriate to decide what this circuit's substantive law will be by any means other than judicial decision.

Theoretically, this court could decide to proceed with its duties without any precedent, deciding each legal principle anew, and relying upon decisions of the former Fifth Circuit and other circuits and district courts as only persuasive authority and not binding. This court, the trial courts, the bar and the public are entitled to a better result than to be cast adrift among the differing precedents of other jurisdictions, required to examine afresh every legal principle that eventually arises in the Eleventh Circuit. This approach would be inconsistent with the virtually wholesale adoption in this country of English common law. The Eleventh Circuit sitting en banc will be an available forum for pursuit of a better rule and for our rejection of any old Fifth Circuit precedents that we consider should be no longer followed. This means for correcting error, searching for a better rule, and reexamining past analyses will be the same in this court as in the old Fifth and all other circuits. Superimposing an additional level of inquiry by having every panel examine every issue as a new issue is, under the circumstances, both unnecessary and undesirable. We tend to think of *stare decisis* as only "it is decided." The full phrase is *stare decisis et non quieta movere* — "to adhere to precedents and *not to unsettle things which are established*." The prospect of decades of writing on a clean slate in pursuit of the possibility that in some case or cases we might find a rule we like better (or even conclude that an old Fifth Circuit decision is wrong) is at best unappealing, at worst catastrophic.

Failing to select a body of precedent would severely impede the operation of the court. Each panel decision on a principle not previously considered would create a new precedent and in turn an available argument that, pursuant to FRAP Rule 35, a rehearing en banc should be granted on the ground that because the case establishes a new precedent it "involves a question of exceptional importance." Every significant new principle — indeed every new principle, significant or not — would be a candidate for en banc consideration. This translates into a burden that this court could not discharge without seriously damaging its effectiveness, and it would mean years of waiting to determine the law of the circuit. We choose instead to begin on a stable, fixed, and identifiable base while maintaining the capacity for change.

Notes and Questions

1. A result very similar to *Bonner* was reached by the Federal Circuit in *South Corp. v. United States,* 690 F.2d 1368 (Fed. Cir. 1982), wherein the court adopted as precedent the holdings of its predecessor courts, the United States Court of Claims and the United States Court of Customs and Patent Appeals.

2. Not every court has taken the same approach as the *Bonner* court, though (certain language in *Bonner* to the contrary notwithstanding). For example, in *Estate of McMorris v. Commissioner of Internal Revenue,* 243 F.3d 1254 (10th Cir. 2001), the United States Court of Appeals for the Tenth Circuit (which was created out of the Eighth Circuit) finally decided (several decades after its creation) whether it was bound by a prior Eighth Circuit decision. Concluding it was not, the court opined:

   > This is an issue of first impression in our circuit, notwithstanding the Commissioner's assertion to the contrary. Specifically, he observes that the Eighth Circuit resolved this issue in his favor in *Jacobs v. Commissioner,* 34 F.2d 233 (8th Cir.

1929), shortly after Congress divided the former Eighth Circuit into the new Tenth and Eighth Circuits. He argues that "under the statute that created the Tenth Circuit, *Jacobs* is a decision that created law in the Eighth Circuit and, thus, should be treated as binding precedent here." There are two fundamental problems with the Commissioner's argument.

First, unlike the Eleventh Circuit, which chose to adopt all decisions issued by the former Fifth Circuit before its October 1, 1981, split as binding precedent, *see Bonner v. City of Prichard,* 661 F.2d 1206, 1209 (11th Cir. 1981) (en banc), we have never held that the decisions of our predecessor circuit are controlling in this court.[7] Second, even assuming we are bound by the decisions of the former Eighth Circuit, *Jacobs* does not fall within that category of cases. As the Commissioner concedes, the Eighth Circuit decided *Jacobs* almost four months *after* the Act creating our circuit took effect. Moreover, we are not persuaded by the Commissioner's argument that section 5(1) of that Act obligates us to treat the Eighth Circuit's post-split decision in *Jacobs* as a decision of the former Eighth Circuit simply because that case was argued and submitted prior to the effective date of the Act. 45 Stat. at 1348.

Notably, the Act creating the Eleventh Circuit contains nearly identical language, yet that circuit has never adopted the per se rule urged by the Commissioner in this case. The Eleventh Circuit has instead held that where an appeal was submitted before the split but decided by the Fifth Circuit thereafter, the decision has precedential effect only if the appeal arose in the geographical confines of the Eleventh Circuit. *See Stein v. Reynolds Sec., Inc.,* 667 F.2d 33, 34 (11th Cir. 1982). But as the estate points out in this case, *Jacobs* arose in Missouri, which always has been in the Eighth Circuit. The Commissioner offers no reason why an Eighth Circuit case decided after the split and arising outside the geographical confines of our circuit should be binding on this court, and we decline to announce such a rule here.

McMorris, 243 F.3d at 1258-59.

3. As mentioned in the introduction to this section, there has long been talk of splitting the Ninth Circuit into one (or more) circuits. For example, on January 3, 2013, a bill was introduced in the House of Representatives (titled the Ninth Circuit Court of Appeals Judgeship and Reorganization Act of 2013) which proposes to create a new Twelfth Circuit, composed of Alaska, Arizona, Idaho, Montana, Nevada, Oregon, and Washington. If a new Twelfth Circuit is formed, should it start with then-existing Ninth Circuit precedent? Why or why not?

---

7. Following the split, two district courts in our circuit concluded they were bound by the decisions of the former Eighth Circuit. *See Thompson v. St. Louis-San Francisco Ry. Co.,* 5 F. Supp. 785, 789 (N.D. Okla. 1934); *In re Meyers,* 1 F. Supp. 673, 674 (W.D. Okla. 1932), *rev'd on other grounds sub nom., Barbee v. Spurrier Lumber Co.,* 64 F.2d 5 (10th Cir. 1933). We seemed to reach a similar conclusion in *Boynton v. Moffat Tunnel Improvement Dist.,* 57 F.2d 772, 781 (10th Cir. 1932), where we discussed a former Eighth Circuit case in support of our holding and stated that "the decisions cited from the Supreme Court of the United States, from the Eighth Circuit Court of Appeals, and from this court, are binding upon us." However, we also relied on similar decisions by the Supreme Court and our own circuit and could have reached the same holding without reference to the Eighth Circuit case.

4. Though the "holding" by the court in *Bonner* might seem desirable, may a circuit truly adopt the entire law of another circuit in a wholesale fashion, as was purportedly done in that case? Why or why not?

5. Note the *Bonner* court's statement that it could only adopt the law of another circuit by judicial decision, and not by court rule. Why?

6. Read again the *Bonner* court's quote from the Supreme Court's decision in *Moragne*. Where do you think the *Moragne* Court got these "reasons for following past decisions"?

I. OTHER ASPECTS OF THE DOCTRINE OF STARE DECISIS

1. The Significance (or Insignificance) of Denials of Further Review

> The Supreme Court has always been reticent about the process by which it decides whether to grant the petition for certiorari. The rules say nothing about the process and only rarely does an opinion of the Court say anything. No statute governs it; the process seems to have evolved silently, a matter of custom and internally developed practice.

Peter Linzer, *The Meaning of Certiorari Denials*, 79 COLUM. L. REV. 1227, 1248-49 (1979). But though the *process* by which the Court grants or denies certiorari might be somewhat mysterious, what about the *precedential effect* of that decision?

Obviously, a *grant* of certiorari might well affect the precedential effect of the decision being reviewed, as the judgment below generally will either be affirmed or reversed. But what about the *denial* of further review?

In *Singleton v. Commissioner,* 439 U.S. 940, 942-46 (1978), Justice Stevens, respecting the denial of the petition for writ of certiorari in that case, opined:

> What is the significance of this Court's denial of certiorari? That question is asked again and again; it is a question that is likely to arise whenever a dissenting opinion argues that certiorari should have been granted. Almost 30 years ago Mr. Justice Frankfurter provided us with an answer to that question that should be read again and again.
>
> > "The Court now declines to review the decision of the Maryland Court of Appeals. The sole significance of such denial of a petition for writ of certiorari need not be elucidated to those versed in the Court's procedures. It simply means that fewer than four members of the Court deemed it desirable to review a decision of the lower court as a matter 'of sound judicial discretion.' A variety of considerations underlie denials of the writ, and as to the same petition different reasons may lead different Justices to the same result. This is especially true of petitions for review on writ of certiorari to a State court. Narrowly technical reasons may lead

to denials. Review may be sought too late; the judgment of the lower court may not be final; it may not be the judgment of the State court of last resort; the decision may be supportable as a matter of State law, not subject to review by this Court, even though the State court also passed on issues of federal law. A decision may satisfy all these technical requirements and yet may commend itself for review to fewer than four members of the Court. Pertinent considerations of judicial policy here come into play. A case may raise an important question but the record may be cloudy. It may be desirable to have different aspects of an issue further illuminated by the lower courts. Wise adjudication has its own time for ripening.

Since there are these conflicting and, to the uninformed, even confusing reasons for denying petitions for certiorari, it has been suggested from time to time that the Court indicate its reasons for denial. Practical considerations preclude. In order that the Court may be enabled to discharge its indispensable duties, Congress has placed the control of the Court's business, in effect, within the Court's discretion. During the last three terms the Court disposed of 260, 217, 224 cases, respectively, on their merits. For the same three terms the Court denied, respectively, 1,260, 1,105, 1,189 petitions calling for discretionary review. If the Court is to do its work it would not be feasible to give reasons, however brief, for refusing to take these cases. The time that would be required is prohibitive, apart from the fact as already indicated that different reasons not infrequently move different members of the Court in concluding that a particular case at a particular time makes review undesirable. It becomes relevant here to note that failure to record a dissent from a denial of a petition for writ of certiorari in nowise implies that only the member of the Court who notes his dissent thought the petition should be granted.

Inasmuch, therefore, as all that a denial of a petition for a writ of certiorari means is that fewer than four members of the Court thought it should be granted, this Court has rigorously insisted that such a denial carries with it no implication whatever regarding the Court's views on the merits of a case which it has declined to review. The Court has said this again and again; again and again the admonition has to be repeated." Opinion respecting the denial of the petition for writ of certiorari in *Maryland v. Baltimore Radio Show,* 338 U. S. 917-919.

When those words were written, Mr. Justice Frankfurter and his colleagues were too busy to spend their scarce time writing dissents from denials of certiorari. Such opinions were almost nonexistent. It was then obvious that if there was no need to explain the Court's action in denying the writ, there was even less reason for individual expressions of opinion about why certiorari should have been granted in particular cases. Times have changed. Although the workload of the Court has dramatically increased since Mr. Justice Frankfurter's day,[2] most present Members of the Court frequently file written dissents from certiorari denials. It is appropriate to ask whether the new practice serves any important goals or contributes to the strength of the institution.

---

2. By way of comparison to the figures cited by Mr. Justice Frankfurter, the Court during the three most recent Terms reviewed and decided 362, 483, and 323 cases respectively. And during each of these Terms, the Court denied certiorari in well over 3,000 cases.

One characteristic of all opinions dissenting from the denial of certiorari is manifest. They are totally unnecessary. They are examples of the purest form of dicta, since they have even less legal significance than the orders of the entire Court which, as Mr. Justice Frankfurter reiterated again and again, have no precedential significance at all.

Another attribute of these opinions is that they are potentially misleading. Since the Court provides no explanation of the reasons for denying certiorari, the dissenter's arguments in favor of a grant are not answered and therefore typically appear to be more persuasive than most other opinions. Moreover, since they often omit any reference to valid reasons for denying certiorari, they tend to imply that the Court has been unfaithful to its responsibilities or has implicitly reached a decision on the merits when, in fact, there is no basis for such an inference.

In this case, for example, the dissenting opinion suggests that the Court may have refused to grant certiorari because the case is "devoid of glamour and emotion." I am puzzled by this suggestion because I have never witnessed any indication that any of my colleagues has ever considered "glamour and emotion" as a relevant consideration in the exercise of his discretion or in his analysis of the law. With respect to the Court's action in this case, the absence of any conflict among the Circuits is plainly a sufficient reason for denying certiorari. Moreover, in allocating the Court's scarce resources, I consider it entirely appropriate to disfavor complicated cases which turn largely on unique facts. A series of decisions by the courts of appeals may well provide more meaningful guidance to the bar than an isolated or premature opinion of this Court. As Mr. Justice Frankfurter reminded us, "wise adjudication has its own time for ripening."

Admittedly these dissenting opinions may have some beneficial effects. Occasionally a written statement of reasons for granting certiorari is more persuasive than the Justice's oral contribution to the Conference. For that reason the written document sometimes persuades other Justices to change their votes and a petition is granted that would otherwise have been denied. That effect, however, merely justifies the writing and circulating of these memoranda within the Court; it does not explain why a dissent which has not accomplished its primary mission should be published.

It can be argued that publishing these dissents enhances the public's understanding of the work of the Court. But because they are so seldom answered, these opinions may also give rise to misunderstanding or incorrect impressions about how the Court actually works. Moreover, the selected bits of information which they reveal tend to compromise the otherwise secret deliberations in our Conferences. There are those who believe that these Conferences should be conducted entirely in public or, at the very least, that the votes on all Conference matters should be publicly recorded. The traditional view, which I happen to share, is that confidentiality makes a valuable contribution to the full and frank exchange of views during the decisional process; such confidentiality is especially valuable in the exercise of the kind of discretion that must be employed in processing the thousands of certiorari petitions that are reviewed each year. In my judgment, the importance of preserving the tradition of confidentiality outweighs the minimal educational value of these opinions.

In all events, these are the reasons why I have thus far resisted the temptation to publish opinions dissenting from denials of certiorari.

Notes and Questions

1. The "orthodox" view regarding the meaning of denials of petitions for writs of certiorari expressed above apparently stems from Justice Holmes' opinion in *United States v. Carver*, 260 U.S. 482 (1923), where, speaking for a unanimous Court, he plainly wrote: "The denial of a writ of certiorari imports no expression of opinion upon the merits of the case, as the bar has been told many times." *Id*. at 490.

2. *Singleton* dates from 1978. By contrast, the Supreme Court now denies about three times the number of petitions for a writ of certiorari. Does this fact reinforce the validity of the orthodox view?

3. If the orthodox view is correct, then why the need to dissent from denials of certiorari? As Professor Linzer again writes:

   > If a denial of certiorari were a purely discretionary act, largely or totally unconcerned with the merits of the particular case, it would be anomalous for Justices to note their dissents. The act of dissenting seems to imply that the majority, at least in part, considered the merits when it denied certiorari. In fact, the number of dissents has increased sharply in the last generation . . . . While many of the dissents do not expressly discuss the merits, some do, and many of the rest permit the reader to make at least a fair guess at the dissenter's substantive view of the decision below.

   79 COLUM. L. REV. at 1255.

4. Similarly, in *Brown v. Allen*, 344 U.S. 443 (1953), Justice Jackson wrote:

   > Perhaps the profession could accept denials as meaningless before the custom was introduced of noting dissents from them. Lawyers and lower judges will not readily believe that Justices of this Court are taking the trouble to signal a meaningless division of opinion about a meaningless act. It is just one of the facts of life that today every lower court does attach importance to denials and to presence or absence of dissents from denials, as judicial opinions and lawyers' arguments show.

   Id. at 543.

5. Is there any relevance (and significance) to the fact that of the cases accepted for review by the Supreme Court, the vast majority result in a reversal of the judgment below?

6. Though it might be true that the only thing those outside of the Supreme Court know about the denial of a petition for a writ of certiorari is that the petition

failed to receive at least four votes, the better question, of course, is why. Though those reasons might vary depending upon the case and the particular Justice in question, presumably there was *some* reason or reasons why the petition failed. What might those reasons be? Though that question also might be difficult to answer with certainty, it seems that one could fairly speculate that the possible reasons might include one or more of the following:

a) a belief that no material error was committed below (perhaps coupled with a belief that the reasons why are clear);

b) poor lawyering on the part of counsel for the petitioner (i.e., the argument for further review was not adequately made;

c) a fear that one or more of the attorneys in the case will not do an adequate job of advocacy were the petition to be granted (perhaps because one or more of those attorneys is not part of the Supreme Court bar's "inner circle");

d) the underlying issue is considered unimportant and/or is unlikely to arise again;

e) the Court's docket for the Term in question is considered full;

f) a perception that the case contains substantial factual and/or procedural problems that might lead to a poor decision on the merits;

g) inadequate consideration by lower courts (e.g., the absence of a circuit split);

h) those favoring a reversal of the underlying judgment are in the minority (i.e., they might have the votes necessary for granting the petition, but not for a majority opinion);

i) "cert. pool" incompetence (i.e., those law clerks responsible for reviewing such petitions failed to recognize a certiorari-worthy case); and

j) an unwillingness to attempt to answer a difficult or politically charged question.

Can you think of any other reasons why a petition might fail to receive the requisite number of votes?

7. What about dissents from the denial of a petition for a writ of certiorari? As has already been suggested, one reason a Justice (or Justices) might pen such a dissent is to express their views as to the merits. Are there any other, possible reasons for such dissents? Once again, it is difficult for those outside the Court to know why such opinions are filed, but it seems reasonable that the possible reasons might include one or more of the following:

a) an attempt to persuade others on the Court to reconsider their positions (i.e., they are written not so much as a dissent but rather as a last-ditch effort to sway colleagues);

b) a scolding (which, it is hoped, might be a different result in a similar, future case);

c) a signal to parties with similar issues to persist in their efforts to seek Supreme Court review;

d) to enhance the public's understanding of the work of the Court.

Can you think of any other, possible reasons?

8. In *Parker v. Ellis,* 362 U.S. 574, 576 (1960), the Supreme Court stated: "It is precisely because a denial of a petition for certiorari without more has no significance as a ruling that an explicit statement of the reason for a denial means what it says." *But see id.* at 588 (Warren, C.J., dissenting).

9. The practical effect of a denial of further review is to affirm the judgment of the lower court. Nonetheless: "There is a critical difference between a judgment of affirmance and an order denying a petition for a writ of certiorari. The former determines the rights of the parties; the latter expresses no opinion on the merits of the case." *Schiro v. Indiana,* 493 U.S. 910, 910-11 (1989) (opinion of Stevens, J., respecting the denial of the petition for writ of certiorari).

10. ASSOCIATION OF LEGAL WRITING DIRECTORS & DARBY DICKERSON, ALWD CITATION MANUAL: A PROFESSIONAL SYSTEM OF CITATION (4th ed. 2010) 99, sidebar 12.6 ("Information About Denials of Certiorari") states in part:

> A writ of certiorari is a device used by courts of last resort, such as the United States Supreme Court, that have discretion to select the cases they want to hear. If the party who lost in the court below seeks review in a court that has discretion to hear the appeal, that party files a "Petition for Writ of Certiorari." If the court grants the petition, it will hear the appeal. If the court denies the petition, it will not hear the appeal.
>
> Precedential Value
>
> Denials of certiorari — abbreviated "*cert. denied*" in citations — carry no precedential value and do not indicate that the higher court agreed with the lower court's decision. Accordingly, denials of certiorari typically should not be included as subsequent history. However, because denials inform readers that the lower court's decision has become final, the information should be included if the cited lower court decision is two years old or less. Two years was selected because that is the time within which most cases are resolved on appeal.
>
> "Particularly Important"
>
> The denial also should be included if the case is particularly important to the discussion in your paper. A denial of certiorari is important if the case is the focus of the discussion. It also is important when the higher court issues an opinion explaining why a petition for certiorari was denied or when a judge issues a dissenting opinion concerning the denial of certiorari.

The *ALWD Citation Manual* fails to explain, though, why a denial of a petition for a writ of certiorari becomes important simply because the underlying case is important to one's argument or when the denial is accompanied by an opinion. *Accord* THE BLUEBOOK: A UNIFORM SYSTEM OF CITATION 101 (19th ed. 2010) (similarly requiring the citation of denials of certiorari "or denials of similar discretionary appeals" when the denial is "particularly relevant," though without explaining why or how to determine when a denial is particularly relevant).

11. Increasingly (it appears), various Supreme Court Justices are issuing opinions in cases in which review is denied, though not with respect to the denial per se, but rather as to other issues relating to the underlying case. For a recent article on this phenomenon, see Tony Mauro, *Typically Quiet, Justices Open Up About Denials; Seven nondecision opinions issued this term-so far*, NAT'L L.J. 1 (Nov. 25, 2013).

12. Just as a denial of further review generally is regarded as having no precedential significance, a grant of further review generally has precedential significance only to the extent of those particular issues actually considered and decided. *See, e.g., United States v. Verdugo-Urquidez*, 494 U.S. 259, 272 (1990) ("The Court often grants certiorari to decide particular legal issues while assuming without deciding the validity of antecedent propositions, and such assumptions — even on jurisdictional issues — are not binding in future cases that directly raise the questions.").

2. Vacatur

With respect to judicial decisions, to "vacate" means "[t]o nullify or cancel; make void; invalidate." BLACK'S LAW DICTIONARY 1782 (10th ed. 2014). Obviously, when a lower court judgment is reversed, the underlying decision of that lower court is effectively (and appropriately) nullified. But to what extent, if any, is vacatur appropriate in the absence of a reversal of the underlying judgment? Consider this question in the context of the next case.

United States Bancorp Mortgage Co. v. Bonner Mall Partnership

513 U.S. 18 (1994)

JUSTICE SCALIA delivered the opinion of the Court.

In 1984 and 1985, Northtown Investments built the Bonner Mall in Bonner County, Idaho, with financing from a bank in that State. In 1986, respondent Bonner Mall Partnership (Bonner) acquired the mall, while petitioner U. S. Bancorp Mortgage Co. (Bancorp) acquired the loan and mortgage from the Idaho bank. In 1990, Bonner defaulted on its real estate taxes and Bancorp scheduled a foreclosure sale.

The day before the sale, Bonner filed a petition under Chapter 11 of the Bankruptcy Code, 11 U. S. C. § 1101 *et seq.*, in the United States Bankruptcy Court for the District of Idaho. It filed a reorganization plan that depended on the "new value exception" to the absolute priority rule. Bancorp moved to suspend the automatic stay of its foreclosure imposed by 11 U. S. C. § 362(a), arguing that Bonner's plan was unconfirmable as a matter of law for a number of reasons, including unavailability of the new value exception. The Bankruptcy Court eventually granted the motion, concluding that the new value exception had not survived enactment of the Bankruptcy Code. The court stayed its order pending an appeal by Bonner. The United States District Court for the District of Idaho reversed; Bancorp took an appeal in turn, but the Court of Appeals for the Ninth Circuit affirmed.

Bancorp then petitioned for a writ of certiorari. After we granted the petition and received briefing on the merits, Bancorp and Bonner stipulated to a consensual plan of reorganization, which received the approval of the Bankruptcy Court. The parties agreed that confirmation of the plan constituted a settlement that mooted the case. Bancorp, however, also requested that we exercise our power under 28 U. S. C. § 2106 to vacate the judgment of the Court of Appeals. Bonner opposed the motion. We set the vacatur question for briefing and argument.

Respondent questions our power to entertain petitioner's motion to vacate, suggesting that the limitation on the judicial power conferred by Article III "may, at least in some cases, *prohibit* an act of vacatur when no live dispute exists due to a settlement that has rendered a case moot."

The statute that supplies the power of vacatur provides:

> "The Supreme Court or any other court of appellate jurisdiction may affirm, modify, vacate, set aside or reverse any judgment, decree, or order of a court lawfully brought before it for review, and may remand the cause and direct the entry of such appropriate judgment, decree, or order, or require such further proceedings to be had as may be just under the circumstances."

Of course no statute could authorize a federal court to decide the merits of a legal question not posed in an Article III case or controversy. For that purpose, a case must exist at all the stages of appellate review. But reason and authority refute the quite different notion that a federal appellate court may not take any action with regard to a piece of litigation once it has been determined that the requirements of Article III no longer are (or indeed never were) met. That proposition is contradicted whenever an appellate court holds that a district court lacked Article III jurisdiction in the first instance, vacates the decision, and remands with directions to dismiss. In cases that become moot while awaiting review, respondent's logic would hold the Court powerless to award costs or even to enter an order of dismissal.

Article III does not prescribe such paralysis. "If a judgment has become moot while awaiting review, this Court may not consider its merits, but may make such disposition of the whole case as justice may require." As with other matters of judicial administration and practice "reasonably ancillary to the primary, dispute deciding function" of the federal courts, Congress may authorize us to enter orders necessary and appropriate to the final disposition of a suit that is before us for review.

The leading case on vacatur is *United States v. Munsingwear, Inc.*, 340 U. S. 36 (1950), in which the United States sought injunctive and monetary relief for violation of a price control regulation. The damages claim was held in abeyance pending a decision of the injunction. The District Court held that the respondent's prices complied with the regulations and dismissed the complaint. While the United States' appeal was pending, the commodity at issue was decontrolled; at the respondent's request, the case was dismissed as moot, a disposition in which the United States acquiesced. The respondent then obtained dismissal of the damages action on the ground of res judicata, and we took the case to review that ruling. The United States protested the unfairness of according preclusive effect to a decision that it had tried to appeal but could not. We saw no such unfairness, reasoning that the United States should have asked the Court of Appeals to vacate the District Court's decision before the appeal was dismissed. We stated that "the established practice of the Court in dealing with a civil case from a court in the federal system which has become moot while on its way here or pending our decision on the merits is to reverse or vacate the judgment below and remand with a direction to dismiss." We explained that vacatur "clears the path for future relitigation of the issues between the parties and eliminates a judgment, review of which was prevented through happenstance." Finding that the United States had "slept on its rights," we affirmed.

The parties in the present case agree that vacatur must be decreed for those judgments whose review is, in the words of *Munsingwear*, "prevented through happenstance" — that is to say, where a controversy presented for review has "become moot due to circumstances unattributable to any of the parties." They also agree that vacatur must be granted where mootness results from the unilateral action of the party who prevailed in the lower court. The contested question is whether courts should vacate where mootness results from a settlement. The centerpiece of petitioner's argument is that the *Munsingwear* procedure has already been held to apply in such cases. *Munsingwear*'s description of the "established practice" (the argument runs) drew no distinctions between categories of moot cases; opinions in later cases granting vacatur have reiterated the breadth of the rule, and at least some of those cases specifically involved mootness by reason of settlement.

But *Munsingwear,* and the post-*Munsingwear* practice, cannot bear the weight of the present case. To begin with, the portion of Justice Douglas' opinion in *Munsingwear* describing the "established practice" for vacatur was dictum; all that was needful for the decision was (at most) the proposition that vacatur should have been sought, not that it necessarily would have been granted. Moreover, as *Munsingwear* itself acknowledged, the "established practice" (in addition to being unconsidered) was not entirely uniform, at least three cases having been dismissed for mootness without vacatur within the four Terms preceding *Munsingwear*. Nor had the *post-Munsingwear* practice been as uniform as petitioner claims. Of course all of those decisions, both granting vacatur and denying it, were *per curiam,* with . . . [a] single exception . . . in which we declined to vacate. This seems to us a prime occasion for invoking our customary refusal to be bound by dicta and our customary skepticism towards *per curiam* dispositions that lack the reasoned consideration of a full opinion. Today we examine vacatur once more in the light shed by adversary presentation.

The principles that have always been implicit in our treatment of moot cases counsel against extending *Munsingwear* to settlement. From the beginning we have disposed of moot cases in the manner " 'most consonant to justice' in view of the nature and character of the conditions which have caused the case to become moot." The principle condition to which we have looked is whether the party seeking relief from the judgment below caused the mootness by voluntary action.

The reference to "happenstance" in *Munsingwear* must be understood as an allusion to this equitable tradition of vacatur. A party who seeks review of the merits of an adverse ruling, but is frustrated by the vagaries of circumstance, ought not in fairness be forced to acquiesce in the judgment. The same is true when mootness results from unilateral action of the party who prevailed below. Where mootness results from settlement, however, the losing party has voluntarily forfeited his legal remedy by the ordinary processes of appeal or certiorari, thereby surrendering his claim to the equitable remedy of vacatur. The judgment is not unreviewable, but simply unreviewed by his own choice. The denial of vacatur is merely one application of the principle that "a suitor's conduct in relation to the matter at hand may disentitle him to the relief he seeks."

In these respects the case stands no differently than it would if jurisdiction were lacking because the losing party failed to appeal at all. In *Karcher v. May,* 484 U. S. 72 (1987), two state legislators, acting in their capacities as presiding officers of the legislature, appealed from a federal judgment that invalidated a state statute on constitutional grounds. After the jurisdictional statement was filed the legislators lost their posts, and their successors in office withdrew the appeal. Holding that we lacked jurisdiction for want of a proper appellant, we dismissed. The legislators then argued that the judgments should be vacated under *Munsingwear.* But we denied the request, noting that "this controversy did not become moot due to circumstances unattributable to any of the parties. The controversy ended when the losing party — the State Legislature — declined to pursue its appeal. Accordingly, the *Munsingwear* procedure is inapplicable to this case." So too here.

It is true, of course, that respondent agreed to the settlement that caused the mootness. Petitioner argues that vacatur is therefore fair to respondent, and seeks to distinguish our prior cases on that ground. But that misconceives the emphasis on fault in our decisions. That the parties are jointly responsible for settling may in some sense put them on even footing, but petitioner's case needs more than that. Respondent won below. It is petitioner's burden, as the party seeking relief from the status quo of the appellate judgment, to demonstrate not merely equivalent responsibility for the mootness, but equitable entitlement to the extraordinary remedy of vacatur. Petitioner's voluntary forfeiture of review constitutes a failure of equity that makes the burden decisive, whatever respondent's share in the mooting of the case might have been.

As always when federal courts contemplate equitable relief, our holding must also take account of the public interest. "Judicial precedents are presumptively correct and valuable to the legal community as a whole. They are not merely the property of private litigants and should stand unless a court concludes that the public interest would be served by a vacatur." Congress has prescribed a primary route, by appeal as of right and certiorari, through which parties may seek relief from the legal consequences of judicial judgments. To allow a party who steps off the statutory path to employ the secondary remedy of vacatur as a refined form of collateral attack on the judgment would — quite apart from any considerations of fairness to the parties — disturb the orderly operation of the federal judicial system. *Munsingwear* establishes that the public interest is best served by granting relief when the demands of "orderly procedure" cannot be honored; we think conversely that the public interest requires those demands to be honored when they can.

Petitioner advances two arguments meant to justify vacatur on systemic grounds. The first is that appellate judgments in cases that we have consented to review by writ of certiorari are reversed more often than they are affirmed, are therefore suspect, and should be vacated as a sort of prophylactic against legal error. It seems to us inappropriate, however, to vacate mooted cases, in which we have no constitutional power to decide the merits, on the basis of assumptions about the merits. Second, petitioner suggests that "vacating a moot decision, and thereby leaving an issue temporarily unresolved in a Circuit, can facilitate the ultimate resolution of the issue by encouraging its continued examination and debate." We have found, however, that debate *among* the courts of appeal sufficiently illuminates the questions that come before us for review. The value of additional intra circuit debate seems to us far outweighed by the benefits that flow to litigants and the public from the resolution of legal questions.

A final policy question urged by petitioner is the facilitation of settlement, with the resulting economies for the federal courts. But while the availability of vacatur may facilitate settlement after the judgment under review has been rendered and certiorari granted (or appeal filed), it may *deter* settlement at an earlier stage. *Some* litigants, at least, may think it worthwhile to roll the dice rather than settle in the district court, or in the court of appeals, if, but only if, an unfavorable outcome can be washed away by a settlement related vacatur. And the judicial economies achieved by settlement at the district court level are ordinarily much more extensive than those achieved by settlement on appeal. We find it quite impossible to assess the effect of our holding, either way, upon the frequency or systemic value of settlement.

Although the case before us involves only a motion to vacate, by reason of settlement, the judgment of a court of appeals (with, of course, the consequential vacation of the underlying judgment of the district court), it is appropriate to discuss the relevance of our holding to motions at the court of appeals level for vacatur of district court judgments. Some opinions have suggested that vacatur motions at that level should be more freely granted, since district court judgments are subject to review as of right. Obviously, this factor does not affect the primary basis for our denying vacatur. Whether the appellate court's seizure of the case is the consequence of an appellant's right or of a petitioner's good luck has no bearing upon the lack of equity of a litigant who had voluntarily abandoned review. If the point of the proposed distinction is that district court judgments, being subject to review as of right, are more likely to be overturned and hence presumptively less valid: We again assert the inappropriateness of disposing of cases, whose merits are beyond judicial power to consider, on the basis of judicial estimates regarding their merits. Moreover, as petitioner's own argument described two paragraphs above points out, the reversal rate for cases in which this Court grants certiorari (a precondition for our vacatur) is over 50% — more than double the reversal rate for appeals to the courts of appeal.

We hold that mootness by reason of settlement does not justify vacatur of a judgment under review. This is not to say that vacatur can never be granted when mootness is produced in that fashion. As we have described, the determination is an equitable one, and exceptional circumstances may conceivably counsel in favor of such a course. It should be clear from our discussion, however, that those exceptional circumstances do not include the mere fact that the settlement agreement provides for vacatur — which neither diminishes the voluntariness of the abandonment of review nor alters any of the policy considerations we have discussed. Of course even in the absence of, or before considering the existence of, extraordinary circumstances, a court of appeals presented with a request for vacatur of a district court judgment may remand the case with instructions that the district court consider the request, which it may do pursuant to Federal Rule of Civil Procedure 60(b).

Petitioner's motion to vacate the judgment of the Court of Appeals for the Ninth Circuit is denied. The case is dismissed as moot.

Notes and Questions

1. Is vacatur ever appropriate? Take, for example, the *Munsingwear* situation described in *United States Bancorp*. Despite the fact that the loser in that case could not have appealed, due to no fault of its own, there remained a valid federal lower court decision, and presumably that court did the best that it could. Should that be a sufficient reason for according that decision whatever precedential effect it otherwise might be entitled? Or consider the problem from the perspective of statutory construction. Do you believe that when Congress enacted 28 U.S.C. § 2106, it intended to approve of the sort of practice urged in *United States Bancorp* (assuming it had the constitutional power to enact a statute of this nature in the first instance)? And even if it did, what sort of "exceptional circumstances" should it take to permit the vacatur of a decision following a settlement?

2. Assume that one party agrees to settle a case while it is on appeal on the condition (inter alia) that the other party join in (or at least not oppose) the first party's motion to vacate the decision below. In that situation, who would argue in opposition to vacatur? And if such a vacatur were granted by the court of appeals, who would appeal that decision to the Supreme Court?

3. "Of necessity our decision vacating the judgment of the Court of Appeals deprives that court's opinion of precedential effect, leaving this Court's opinion and judgment as the sole law of the case." *O'Connor v. Donaldson*, 422 U.S. 563, 578 n.12 (1975).

4. Many have been critical of discretionary vacatur. For example, Daniel Purcell identifies at least three problems with this practice.

   > First, vacatur casts doubt on the legitimacy of the judicial system, because it allows wealthy parties to purchase the law, and fortuitously-placed parties — usually plaintiffs — to sell the law, when the law is really not theirs to buy or sell. Second, vacatur stunts the growth of the law's organic progress by removing links from the chain of legal precedent. Third, vacatur can be seen as a judicially-created remedy that should only be granted where a legal right has been violated.

Daniel Purcell, *The Public Right to Precedent: A Theory and Rejection of Vacatur*, 85 CAL. L. REV. 867, 906 (1997). *See also* Jill E. Fisch, *Rewriting History: The Propriety of Eradicating Prior Decisional Law Through Settlement and Vacatur*, 76 CORNELL L. REV. 589 (1991) (reaching a similar conclusion).

5. Even when appellate courts decide cases, they frequently vacate, rather than reverse, lower court judgments. (We have already seen some examples in this book; *see, e.g., Christianson v. Colt Industries Operating Corp., supra.*) Why? Consider the following excerpt from Charles A. Sullivan, *On Vacation*, 43 HOUS. L. REV. 1143 (2006):

> The broader problem . . . is whether the . . . distinction between the status of reversed and vacated opinions exists, and, if it does, whether there is any principled reason for that distinction. Indeed, it is not clear why any opinion survives the extinction of the judgment it supports (whether that extinction is by vacatur or reversal), but, if some opinions do survive, it seems strange that the distinction is drawn between judgments which are vacated and those that are reversed.
>
> To this point, I have written as if the operative act of the higher court is dealing with the opinion of the inferior court. That is, of course, not true or, at least historically, was not.[34] The higher court deals with judgments, not opinions, and it is the judgment of the inferior court that is affirmed, reversed, or vacated. From a historical perspective, opinions were a kind of by-product of a court's central function, which was deciding cases. Indeed, in England, due to the erratic nature of the reporting system, the absence of a clear hierarchy of courts, and the practice of each jurist issuing his own views, opinions were seen not as the law per se but rather merely as "evidence" of the law. A subsequent court, in such a system, was never bound to follow the prior precedent since it might well have been misreported or simply have misunderstood the law. In the United States, due in large part to the development of the single opinion speaking for the Supreme Court as a whole and the relatively early emergence of effective reporting and search systems, opinions increasingly came to be viewed as not merely evidence of the law but as being the law. Within any jurisdiction, then, the rule of law requires a lower court to follow the higher court's pronouncements—although the rigors of such a system are admittedly mitigated by the distinction between holding and dictum and the ability of a court to "distinguish" the binding precedent. It is not surprising, therefore, that it is increasingly common in this country to treat opinions as the operative act of the court. While judgments continue to concern the parties (both in resolving the immediate dispute and affecting future suits under doctrines of preclusion), the rest of us worry not about the judgment but about the law made in the opinion.
>
>   . . . .
>
> With respect to this core function of dealing with judgments, an appellate court has very limited options. Whether the result is indicated by substantive

---

34. Edward A. Hartnett, *A Matter of Judgment, Not a Matter of Opinion*, 74 N.Y.U. L. REV. 123, 126 (1999) ("The operative legal act performed by a court is the entry of judgment; an opinion is simply an explanation of reasons for that judgment.").

or procedural law, the reviewing court has only five options: dismiss the appeal, which effectively affirms the judgment below; explicitly affirm that judgment; modify the judgment; reverse that judgment; or vacate it.[62] In choosing among these alternatives, the court must consider the immediate effects on the parties and the possible preclusive effects of the ultimate judgment rendered. And, of course, it must consider the precedential effects of its action. An affirmance will have significant effects on all three axes; but the decision to affirm itself normally justifies the immediate and preclusive effects, and precedential effects can be negated, as by issuing a not-for-publication opinion, or minimized, as by a summary affirmance.

Matters become more interesting with the choice between vacating and reversing. Both methods nullify the judgment below, which raises the question as to why there are two methods of negation. There does not seem to be a definitive answer. In some cases, vacation is used to indicate less disapproval or finality of the subject judgment. This seems to be the purpose of vacating the judgment issued by a panel when a circuit takes up the question en banc: while there may be reason to suspect that the panel's decision will ultimately be overturned on the rehearing, the panel's opinion is not disapproved because the full court has not yet reheard the case.[66] Similarly, the Supreme Court may vacate a decision not because it necessarily disapproves of the judgment below but to offer the court below the opportunity to reconsider the matter in light of some recent development, typically an intervening decision of the Court itself.

Beyond situations where the act of vacation seems designed mainly to permit the court to punt on the ultimate validity of the judgment, the choice between vacation and reversal is often not clear. . . .

Id. at 1149-57.

6. For a more recent application of vacatur, see *Camreta v. Greene*, 131 S. Ct. 2020 (2011).

3. The "Unpublished" Decision Problem

Appellate courts in recent years have grappled with the treatment of decisions that are "unpublished" in the sense that they are given this designation pursuant to some local court rule and (as a result) do not appear in "official" case reporters. May those courts further prohibit the citation of such decisions or deprive them of precedential effect? Consider these questions in the context of the next two cases.

---

62. *See* 28 U.S.C. § 2106 (2000) ("The Supreme Court or any other court of appellate jurisdiction may affirm, modify, vacate, set aside or reverse any judgment, decree, or order of a court lawfully brought before it for review.").

66. Vacating the panel's judgment will also revive the district court judgment, at least for the moment. This has the potential for preclusion because an unreviewed judgment is generally preclusive.

Anastasoff v. United States

223 F.3d 898, vacated as moot on reh'g en banc,

235 F.3d 1054 (8th Cir. 2000)

RICHARD S. ARNOLD, Circuit Judge.

Faye Anastasoff seeks a refund of overpaid federal income tax. On April 13, 1996, Ms. Anastasoff mailed her refund claim to the Internal Revenue Service for taxes paid on April 15, 1993. The Service denied her claim under 26 U.S.C. § 6511(b), which limits refunds to taxes paid in the three years prior to the filing of a claim. Although her claim was mailed within this period, it was received and filed on April 16, 1996, three years and one day after she overpaid her taxes, one day late. In many cases, "the Mailbox Rule," 26 U.S.C. § 7502, saves claims like Ms. Anastasoff's that would have been timely if received when mailed; they are deemed received when postmarked. But § 7502 applies only to claims that are untimely, and the parties agree that under § 6511(a), which measures the timeliness of the refund claim itself, her claim was received on time. The issue then is whether § 7502 can be applied, for the purposes of § 6511(b)'s three-year refund limitation, to a claim that was timely under § 6511(a). The District Court held that § 7502 could not apply to any part of a timely claim, and granted judgment for the Service. On appeal, Ms. Anastasoff argues that § 7502 should apply whenever necessary to fulfill its remedial purpose, i.e., to save taxpayers from the vagaries of the postal system, even when only part of the claim is untimely. We affirm the judgment of the District Court.

I.

We rejected precisely the same legal argument in *Christie v. United States*, No. 91-2375MN (8th Cir. Mar. 20, 1992) (per curiam) (unpublished). In *Christie*, as here, we considered a refund claim mailed just prior to § 6511(b)'s three-year bar and received just after. Like Ms. Anastasoff, the *Christie* taxpayers argued that § 7502 should operate regardless of the claim's timeliness under § 6511(a) to save their claim under § 6511(b). We [rejected that argument]. . . . Ms. Anastasoff does not attempt to distinguish *Christie*.

Although it is our only case directly in point, Ms. Anastasoff contends that we are not bound by *Christie* because it is an unpublished decision and thus not a precedent under 8th Circuit Rule 28A(i). We disagree. We hold that the portion of Rule 28A(i) that declares that unpublished opinions are not precedent is unconstitutional under Article III, because it purports to confer on the federal courts a power that goes beyond the "judicial."

The Rule provides:

> Unpublished opinions are not precedent and parties generally should not cite them. When relevant to establishing the doctrines of res judicata, collateral estoppel, or the law of the case, however, the parties may cite any unpublished opinion. Parties may also cite an unpublished opinion of this court if the opinion has persuasive value on a material issue and no published opinion of this or another court would serve as well.

Inherent in every judicial decision is a declaration and interpretation of a general principle or rule of law. *Marbury v. Madison,* 5 U.S. 137, 1 Cranch 137, 177-78 (1803). This declaration of law is authoritative to the extent necessary for the decision, and must be applied in subsequent cases to similarly situated parties. *James B. Beam Distilling Co. v. Georgia,* 501 U.S. 529, 544 (1991); *Cohens v. Virginia,* 6 Wheat. 264, 399 (1821). These principles, which form the doctrine of precedent, were well established and well regarded at the time this nation was founded. The Framers of the Constitution considered these principles to derive from the nature of the judicial power, and intended that they would limit the judicial power delegated to the courts by Article III of the Constitution. Accordingly, we conclude that 8th Circuit Rule 28A(i), insofar as it would allow us to avoid the precedential effect of our prior decisions, purports to expand the judicial power beyond the bounds of Article III, and is therefore unconstitutional. That rule does not, therefore, free us from our duty to follow this Court's decision in *Christie.*

II.

The doctrine of precedent was well established by the time the Framers gathered in Philadelphia. See, *e.g.,* 1 Sir William W. Blackstone, *Commentaries on the Laws of England* *69 (1765) ("it is an established rule to abide by former precedents"). To the jurists of the late eighteenth century (and thus by and large to the Framers), the doctrine seemed not just well established but an immemorial custom, the way judging had always been carried out, part of the course of the law. In addition, the Framers had inherited a very favorable view of precedent from the seventeenth century, especially through the writings and reports of Sir Edward Coke; the assertions of authority of precedent had been effective in past struggles of the English people against royal usurpations, and for the rule of law against the arbitrary power of government. In sum, the doctrine of precedent was not merely well established; it was the historic method of judicial decision-making, and well regarded as a bulwark of judicial independence in past struggles for liberty.

Modern legal scholars tend to justify the authority of precedents on equitable or prudential grounds.[7] By contrast, on the eighteenth-century view (most influentially expounded by Blackstone), the judge's duty to follow precedent derives from the nature of the judicial power itself. As Blackstone defined it, each exercise of the "judicial power" requires judges "to determine the law" arising upon the facts of the case. "To determine the law" meant not only choosing the appropriate legal principle but also expounding and interpreting it, so that "the law in that case, being solemnly declared and determined, what before was uncertain, and perhaps indifferent, is now

---

7. See, e.g., Frederick Schauer, Precedent, 39 Stan.L.Rev. 571, 595-602 (1987) (noting that the authority of precedent is commonly supported by arguments: (1) from fundamental fairness, i.e., that like cases should be treated alike; (2) from the need for predictability; and (3) as an aid to judicial decision-making, to prevent unnecessary reconsideration of established matters).

become a permanent rule."[9] In determining the law in one case, judges bind those in subsequent cases because, although the judicial power requires judges "to determine law" in each case, a judge is "sworn to determine, not according to his own judgements, but according to the known laws. Judges are not delegated to pronounce a new law, but to maintain and expound the old." The judicial power to determine law is a power only to determine what the law is, not to invent it. Because precedents are the "best and most authoritative" guide of what the law is, the judicial power is limited by them. . . .

In addition to keeping the law stable, this doctrine is also essential, according to Blackstone, for the separation of legislative and judicial power. In his discussion of the separation of governmental powers, Blackstone identifies this limit on the "judicial power," i.e., that judges must observe established laws, as that which separates it from the "legislative" power and in which "consists one main preservative of public liberty." If judges had the legislative power to "depart from" established legal principles, "the subject would be in the hands of arbitrary judges, whose decisions would be then regulated only by their own opinions."

The Framers accepted this understanding of judicial power (sometimes referred to as the declaratory theory of adjudication) and the doctrine of precedent implicit in it. Hamilton, like Blackstone, recognized that a court "pronounces the law" arising upon the facts of each case. . . . Like Blackstone, he thought that "the courts must declare the sense of the law," and that this fact means courts must exercise "judgment" about what the law is rather than "will" about what it should be. *The Federalist No. 78*, at 507-08. Like Blackstone, he recognized that this limit on judicial decision-making is a crucial sign of the separation of the legislative and judicial power. Hamilton concludes that "to avoid an arbitrary discretion in the courts, it is indispensable that they should be bound down by strict rules and precedents, which serve to define and point out their duty in every particular case that comes before them."

The Framers thought that, under the Constitution, judicial decisions would become binding precedents in subsequent cases. Hamilton anticipated that the record of federal precedents "must unavoidably swell to a very considerable bulk." But precedents were not to be recorded for their own sake. He expected judges to give them "long and laborious study" and to have a "competent knowledge of them." Likewise, Madison recognized "the obligation arising from judicial expositions of the law on succeeding judges." Madison expected that the accumulation of precedents would be beneficial: "among other difficulties, the exposition of the Constitution is frequently a copious source, and must continue so until its meaning on all great points shall have been settled by precedents." Although they drew different conclusions from the facts, the Anti-Federalists also assumed that federal judicial decisions would become authorities in subsequent cases. Finally, early Americans demonstrated the authority which they assigned to judicial decisions by rapidly establishing a reliable system of American reporters in the years following the ratification of the Constitution.

---

9. This need not be done by way of a reported opinion. The record of the judicial proceedings and decision alone is sufficient evidence of the legal principles necessary to support the decision to provide "light or assistance" when "any critical question arises."

We do not mean to suggest that the Framers expected or intended the publication (in the sense of being printed in a book) of all opinions. For the Framers, limited publication of judicial decisions was the rule, and they never drew that practice into question. Before the ratification of the Constitution, there was almost no private reporting and no official reporting at all in the American states. As we have seen, however, the Framers did not regard this absence of a reporting system as an impediment to the precedential authority of a judicial decision. Although they lamented the problems associated with the lack of a reporting system and worked to assure more systematic reporting, judges and lawyers of the day recognized the authority of unpublished decisions even when they were established only by memory or by a lawyer's unpublished memorandum.[14]

To summarize, in the late eighteenth century, the doctrine of precedent was well-established in legal practice (despite the absence of a reporting system), regarded as an immemorial custom, and valued for its role in past struggles for liberty. The duty of courts to follow their prior decisions was understood to derive from the nature of the judicial power itself and to separate it from a dangerous union with the legislative power. The statements of the Framers indicate an understanding and acceptance of these principles. We conclude therefore that, as the Framers intended, the doctrine of precedent limits the "judicial power" delegated to the courts in Article III. No less an authority than Justice (Professor) Joseph Story is in accord. See his *Commentaries on the Constitution of the United States* §§ 377-78 (1833):

> The case is not alone considered as decided and settled; but the principles of the decision are held, as precedents and authority, to bind future cases of the same nature. This is the constant practice under our whole system of jurisprudence. Our ancestors brought it with them, when they first emigrated to this country; and it is, and always has been considered, as the great security of our rights, our liberties, and our property. It is on this accord, that our law is justly deemed certain and founded in permanent principles, and not dependent upon the caprice or will of judges. A more alarming doctrine could not be promulgated by any American court, than that it was at liberty to disregard all former rules and decisions, and to decide for itself, without reference to the settled course of antecedent principles.
>
> This known course of proceeding, this settled habit of thinking, this conclusive effect of judicial adjudications, was in the full view of the framers of the constitution. It was required, and enforced in every state in the Union; and a departure from it would have been justly deemed an approach to tyranny and arbitrary power, to the exercise of mere discretion, and to the abandonment of all the just checks upon judicial authority.

III.

Before concluding, we wish to indicate what this case is not about. It is not about whether opinions should be published, whether that means printed in a book or

---

14. In this, they were following the common-law view, which considered entry on the official court record sufficient to give a decision precedential authority whether or not the decision was subsequently reported. This remained true even after reporting became more systematic.

available in some other accessible form to the public in general. Courts may decide, for one reason or another, that some of their cases are not important enough to take up pages in a printed report. Such decisions may be eminently practical and defensible, but in our view they have nothing to do with the authoritative effect of any court decision. The question presented here is not whether opinions ought to be published, but whether they ought to have precedential effect, whether published or not. We point out, in addition, that "unpublished" in this context has never meant "secret." So far as we are aware, every opinion and every order of any court in this country, at least of any appellate court, is available to the public. You may have to walk into a clerk's office and pay a per-page fee, but you can get the opinion if you want it. Indeed, most appellate courts now make their opinions, whether labeled "published" or not, available to anyone on line. This is true of our Court.

Another point about the practicalities of the matter needs to be made. It is often said among judges that the volume of appeals is so high that it is simply unrealistic to ascribe precedential value to every decision. We do not have time to do a decent enough job, the argument runs, when put in plain language, to justify treating every opinion as a precedent. If this is true, the judicial system is indeed in serious trouble, but the remedy is not to create an underground body of law good for one place and time only. The remedy, instead, is to create enough judgeships to handle the volume, or, if that is not practical, for each judge to take enough time to do a competent job with each case. If this means that backlogs will grow, the price must still be paid. At bottom, rules like our Rule 28A(i) assert that courts have the following power: to choose for themselves, from among all the cases they decide, those that they will follow in the future, and those that they need not. Indeed, some forms of the non-publication rule even forbid citation. Those courts are saying to the bar: "We may have decided this question the opposite way yesterday, but this does not bind us today, and, what's more, you cannot even tell us what we did yesterday." As we have tried to explain in this opinion, such a statement exceeds the judicial power, which is based on reason, not fiat.

Finally, lest we be misunderstood, we stress that we are not here creating some rigid doctrine of eternal adherence to precedents. Cases can be overruled. Sometimes they should be. On our Court, this function can be performed by the en banc Court, but not by a single panel. If the reasoning of a case is exposed as faulty, or if other exigent circumstances justify it, precedents can be changed. When this occurs, however, there is a burden of justification. The precedent from which we are departing should be stated, and our reasons for rejecting it should be made convincingly clear. In this way, the law grows and changes, but it does so incrementally, in response to the dictates of reason, and not because judges have simply changed their minds.

IV.

For these reasons, we must reject Ms. Anastasoff's argument that, under 8th Cir. R. 28A(i), we may ignore our prior decision in *Christie*. Federal courts, in adopting rules, are not free to extend the judicial power of the United States described in Article III of the Constitution. The judicial power of the United States is limited by the doctrine of precedent. Rule 28A(i) allows courts to ignore this limit. If we mark an opinion as unpublished, Rule 28A(i) provides that it is not precedent. Though prior decisions may be well-considered and directly on point, Rule 28A(i) allows us to depart from the law set out in such prior decisions without any reason to differentiate the cases. This discretion is completely inconsistent with the doctrine of precedent; even in constitutional cases, courts have always required a departure from precedent to be supported by some "special justification." Rule 28A(i) expands the judicial power beyond the limits set by Article III by allowing us complete discretion to determine which judicial decisions will bind us and which will not. Insofar as it limits the precedential effect of our prior decisions, the Rule is therefore unconstitutional.

Ms. Anastasoff's interpretation of § 7502 was directly addressed and rejected in *Christie*.[15] Eighth Cir.R. 28A(i) does not free us from our obligation to follow that decision. Accordingly, we affirm the judgment of the District Court.

HEANEY, Circuit Judge, concurring.

I agree fully with Judge Arnold's opinion. He has done the public, the court, and the bar a great service by writing so fully and cogently on the precedential effect of unpublished opinions. I write separately only to state that in my view, this is a case which should be heard en banc in order to reconsider our holding in *Christie*, and thus resolve an important issue.

Hart v. Massanari

266 F.3d 1155 (9th Cir. 2001)

KOZINSKI, Circuit Judge.

Appellant's opening brief cites *Rice v. Chater*, No. 95-35604, 1996 WL 583605 (9th Cir. Oct. 9, 1996). *Rice* is an unpublished disposition, not reported in the Federal Reporter except as a one-line entry in a long table of cases. *See* Decisions Without Published Opinions, 98 F.3d 1345, 1346 tbl. (9th Cir. 1996). The full text of the disposition can be obtained from our clerk's office, and is available on Westlaw® and LEXIS®. However, it is marked with the following notice: "This disposition is not appropriate for publication and may not be cited to or by the courts of this circuit except as provided by 9th Cir. R. 36-3." Our local rules are to the same effect: "Unpublished dispositions and orders of this Court are not binding precedent and generally may not be cited to or by the courts of this circuit." 9th Cir. R. 36-3.

We ordered counsel to show cause as to why he should not be disciplined for violating Ninth Circuit Rule 36-3. Counsel responds by arguing that Rule 36-3 may be unconstitutional. He relies on the Eighth Circuit's opinion in *Anastasoff v. United States*, 223 F.3d 898, *vacated as moot on reh'g en banc*, 235 F.3d 1054 (8th Cir. 2000).

---

15. On July 28, 2000, the Second Circuit decided *Weisbart v. United States Dep't of Treasury*, 2000 WL 1041231 (2d Cir. July 28, 2000). *Weisbart* appears to conflict with *Christie*. We express no view on whether we would follow *Weisbart* if it were not for the conclusive effect of *Christie*.

Anastasoff, while vacated, continues to have persuasive force. *See, e.g., Williams v. Dallas Area Rapid Transit,* 256 F.3d 260 (5th Cir. 2001) (Smith, J., dissenting from denial of reh'g en banc). It may seduce members of our bar into violating our Rule 36-3 under the mistaken impression that it is unconstitutional. We write to lay these speculations to rest.

I

A.

Anastasoff held that Eight Circuit Rule 28A(i), which provides that unpublished dispositions are not precedential — and hence not binding on future panels of that court — violates Article III of the Constitution. According to *Anastasoff,* exercise of the "judicial Power" precludes federal courts from making rulings that are not binding in future cases. Or, to put it differently, federal judges are not merely required to follow the law, they are also required to *make* law in every case. To do otherwise, *Anastasoff* argues, would invite judicial tyranny by freeing courts from the doctrine of precedent: "'A more alarming doctrine could not be promulgated by any American court, than that it was at liberty to disregard all former rules and decisions, and to decide for itself, without reference to the settled course of antecedent principles.'"[3]

We believe that *Anastasoff* overstates the case. Rules that empower courts of appeals to issue nonprecedential decisions do not cut those courts free from all legal rules and precedents; if they did, we might find cause for alarm. But such rules have a much more limited effect: They allow panels of the courts of appeals to determine whether future panels, as well as judges of the inferior courts of the circuit, will be bound by particular rulings. This is hardly the same as turning our back on all precedents, or on the concept of precedent altogether. Rather, it is an effort to deal with precedent in the context of a modern legal system, which has evolved considerably since the early days of common law, and even since the time the Constitution was adopted.

The only constitutional provision on which *Anastasoff* relies is that portion of Article III that vests the "judicial Power" of the United States in the federal courts. U.S. Const. art. III, § 1, cl. 1. *Anastasoff may* be the first case in the history of the Republic to hold that the phrase "judicial Power" encompasses a specific command that limits the power of the federal courts. There are, of course, other provisions of Article III that have received judicial enforcement, such as the requirement that the courts rule only in "Cases" or "Controversies," and that the pay of federal judges not be diminished during their good behavior. The judicial power clause, by contrast, has

---

3. In the passage cited by *Anastasoff,* Justice Story argued only that the judicial decisions of the Supreme Court were "conclusive and binding," and that inferior courts were not free to disregard the "decisions of the highest tribunal." He said nothing to suggest that the principle of binding authority constrained the "judicial Power," as *Anastasoff* does; rather, he recognized that the decisions of the Supreme Court were binding upon the states because they were the "supreme law of the land."

never been thought to encompass a constitutional limitation on how courts conduct their business.

There are many practices that are common or even universal in the federal courts. Some are set by statute, such as the courts' basic organization. Others are the result of tradition, some dating from the days of the common law, others of more recent origin. Among them are the practices of issuing written opinions that speak for the court rather than for individual judges, adherence to the adversarial (rather than inquisitorial) model of developing cases, limits on the exercise of equitable relief, hearing appeals with panels of three or more judges and countless others that are so much a part of the way we do business that few would think to question them. While well established, it is unclear that any of these practices have a constitutional foundation; indeed, Hart (no relation so far as we know), in his famous Dialogue, concluded that Congress could abolish the inferior federal courts altogether. *See* Henry M. Hart, Jr., *The Power of Congress to Limit the Jurisdiction of Federal Courts: An Exercise in Dialectic,* 66 Harv. L. Rev. 1362, 1363-64 (1953). While the greater power does not always include the lesser; the Dialogue does suggest that much of what the federal courts do could be modified or eliminated without offending the Constitution.

Anastasoff focused on one aspect of the way federal courts do business — the way they issue opinions — and held that they are subject to a constitutional limitation derived from the Framers' conception of what it means to exercise the judicial power. Given that no other aspect of the way courts exercise their power has ever been held subject to this limitation, we question whether the "judicial Power" clause contains any limitation at all, separate from the specific limitations of Article III and other parts of the Constitution. The more plausible view is that when the federal courts rule on cases or controversies assigned to them by Congress, comply with due process, accord trial by jury where commanded by the Seventh Amendment and generally comply with the specific constitutional commands applicable to judicial proceedings, they have ipso facto exercised the judicial power of the United States. In other words, the term "judicial Power" in Article III is more likely descriptive than prescriptive.

. . . .

. . . [I]n order to follow the path forged by *Anastasoff,* we would have to be convinced that the practice in question was one the Framers considered so integral and well-understood that they did not have to bother stating it, even though they spelled out many other limitations in considerable detail. Specifically, to adopt *Anastasoff*'s position, we would have to be satisfied that the Framers had a very rigid conception of precedent, namely that all judicial decisions necessarily served as binding authority on later courts.

This is, in fact, a much more rigid view of precedent than we hold today. As we explain below, most decisions of the federal courts are not viewed as binding precedent. No trial court decisions are; almost four-fifths of the merits decisions of courts of appeals are not.[7] To be sure, *Anastasoff* challenges the latter practice. We find it

---

7. Rules limiting the precedential effect of unpublished decisions exist in every federal circuit and all but four states (Connecticut, Delaware, New York and North Dakota). The near-universal adoption of the practice illustrates not only that the practice is consistent with the prevailing conception of the judicial power, but also that it reflects sound judicial policy.

significant, however, that the practice has been in place for a long time, yet no case prior to *Anastasoff* has challenged its constitutional legitimacy. The overwhelming consensus in the legal community has been that having appellate courts issue nonprecedential decisions is not inconsistent with the exercise of the judicial power.

To accept *Anastasoff*'s argument, we would have to conclude that the generation of the Framers had a much stronger view of precedent than we do. In fact, as we explain below, our concept of precedent today is far stricter than that which prevailed at the time of the Framing. The Constitution does not contain an express prohibition against issuing nonprecedential opinions because the Framers would have seen nothing wrong with the practice.

B.

. . . .

A survey of the legal landscape as it might have been viewed by the generation of the Framers casts serious doubt on the proposition — so readily accepted by *Anastasoff* — that the Framers viewed precedent in the rigid form that we view it today. Indeed, it is unclear that the Framers would have considered our view of precedent desirable. The common law, at its core, was a reflection of custom, and custom had a built-in flexibility that allowed it to change with circumstance. . . . It is entirely possible that lawyers of the eighteenth century, had they been confronted with the regime of rigid precedent that is in common use today, would have reacted with alarm.

The modern concept of binding precedent — where a single opinion sets the course on a particular point of law and must be followed by courts at the same level and lower within a pyramidal judicial hierarchy — came about only gradually over the nineteenth and early twentieth centuries. Lawyers began to believe that judges made, not found, the law. This coincided with monumental improvements in the collection and reporting of case authorities. As the concept of law changed and a more comprehensive reporting system began to take hold, it became possible for judicial decisions to serve as binding authority.

Early American reporters resembled their English ancestors — disorganized and meager — but the character of the reporting process began to change, after the Constitution was adopted, with the emergence of official reporters in the late eighteenth century and early nineteenth century. And, later in the nineteenth century, the West Company began to publish standardized case reporters, which were both accurate and comprehensive, making "it possible to publish in written form all of the decisions of courts." Case reports grew thicker, and the weight of precedent began to increase — weight, that is, in terms of volume.

The more cases were reported, the harder became the task of searching for relevant decisions. . . .

II

Federal courts today do follow some common law traditions. When ruling on a novel issue of law, they will generally consider how other courts have ruled on the same issue. This consideration will not be limited to courts at the same or higher level, or even to courts within the same system of sovereignty. Federal courts of appeals will cite decisions of district courts, even those in other circuits; the Supreme Court may cite the decisions of the inferior courts. It is not unusual to cite the decision of courts in foreign jurisdictions, so long as they speak to a matter relevant to the issue before us. The process even extends to non-case authorities, such as treatises and law review articles.

Citing a precedent is, of course, not the same as following it; "respectfully disagree" within five words of "learned colleagues" is almost a cliché. After carefully considering and digesting the views of other courts and commentators — often giving conflicting guidance on a novel legal issue — courts will then proceed to follow one line of authority or another, or sometimes strike out in a completely different direction. While we would consider it bad form to ignore contrary authority by failing even to acknowledge its existence, it is well understood that — in the absence of binding precedent — courts may forge a different path than suggested by prior authorities that have considered the issue. So long as the earlier authority is acknowledged and considered, courts are deemed to have complied with their common law responsibilities.

But precedent also serves a very different function in the federal courts today, one related to the horizontal and vertical organization of those courts. *See* John Harrison, *The Power of Congress Over The Rules of Precedent*, 50 Duke L.J. 503 (2000). A district judge may not respectfully (or disrespectfully) disagree with his learned colleagues on his own court of appeals who have ruled on a controlling legal issue, or with Supreme Court Justices writing for a majority of the Court. Binding authority within this regime cannot be considered and cast aside; it is not merely evidence of what the law is. Rather, caselaw on point *is* the law. If a court must decide an issue governed by a prior opinion that constitutes binding authority, the later court is bound to reach the same result, even if it considers the rule unwise or incorrect. Binding authority must be followed unless and until overruled by a body competent to do so.

In determining whether it is bound by an earlier decision, a court considers not merely the "reason and spirit of cases" but also "the letter of particular precedents." This includes not only the rule announced, but also the facts giving rise to the dispute, other rules considered and rejected and the views expressed in response to any dissent or concurrence. Thus, when crafting binding authority, the precise language employed is often crucial to the contours and scope of the rule announced.[26]

Obviously, binding authority is very powerful medicine. A decision of the Supreme Court will control that corner of the law unless and until the Supreme Court itself overrules or modifies it. Judges of the inferior courts may voice their criticisms, but follow it they must. The same is true as to circuit authority, although it usually covers a much smaller geographic area.[27] Circuit law, a concept wholly unknown at

---

26. This is consistent with the practice in our court — and all other collegial courts of which we are aware — in which the judges who join an opinion authored by another judge make substantive suggestions, often conditioning their votes on reaching agreement on mutually acceptable language.

the time of the Framing, binds all courts within a particular circuit, including the court of appeals itself. Thus, the first panel to consider an issue sets the law not only for all inferior courts in the circuit, but also future panels of the court of appeals.

Once a panel resolves an issue in a precedential opinion, the matter is deemed resolved, unless overruled by the court itself sitting en banc, or by the Supreme Court.[28] As *Anastasoff* itself states, a later three-judge panel considering a case that is controlled by the rule announced in an earlier panel's opinion has no choice but to apply the earlier-adopted rule; it may not any more disregard the earlier panel's opinion than it may disregard a ruling of the Supreme Court. Designating an opinion as binding circuit authority is a weighty decision that cannot be taken lightly, because its effects are not easily reversed. Whether done by the Supreme Court or the court of appeals through its "unwieldy" and time-consuming en banc procedures, overruling such authority requires a substantial amount of courts' time and attention — two commodities already in very short supply.

Controlling authority has much in common with persuasive authority. Using the techniques developed at common law, a court confronted with apparently controlling authority must parse the precedent in light of the facts presented and the rule announced. Insofar as there may be factual differences between the current case and the earlier one, the court must determine whether those differences are material to the application of the rule or allow the precedent to be distinguished on a principled basis. Courts occasionally must reconcile seemingly inconsistent precedents and determine whether the current case is closer to one or the other of the earlier opinions.

But there are also very important differences between controlling and persuasive authority. As noted, one of these is that, if a controlling precedent is determined to be on point, it must be followed. Another important distinction concerns the scope of controlling authority. Thus, an opinion of our court is binding within our circuit, not elsewhere in the country. The courts of appeals, and even the lower courts of other circuits, may decline to follow the rule we announce — and often do. This ability to develop different interpretations of the law among the circuits is considered a strength of our system. It allows experimentation with different approaches to the same legal problem, so that when the Supreme Court eventually reviews the issue it has the benefit of "percolation" within the lower courts. Indeed, the Supreme Court sometimes chooses not to grant certiorari on an issue, even though it might deserve definitive resolution, so it will have the benefit of a variety of views from the inferior courts before it chooses an approach to a legal problem.

The various rules pertaining to the development and application of binding authority do not reflect the developments of the English common law. They reflect, rather, the organization and structure of the federal courts and certain policy judgments about the effective administration of justice. Circuit boundaries are set by statute and can be changed by statute. When that happens, and a new circuit is created,

---

27. The exception is the Federal Circuit, which has a geographic area precisely the same as the Supreme Court, but much narrower subject-matter jurisdiction.

28. Or, unless Congress changes the law.

it starts without any circuit law and must make an affirmative decision whether to create its circuit law from scratch or to adopt the law of another circuit — generally the circuit from which it was carved — as its own. The decision whether to adopt wholesale the circuit law of another court is a matter of judicial policy, not a constitutional command.

How binding authority is overruled is another question that was resolved by trial and error with due regard to principles of sound judicial administration. Early in the last century, when the courts of appeals first grew beyond three judges, the question arose whether the courts could sit en banc to rehear cases already decided by a three judge panel. The lower courts disagreed, but in *Textile Mills Securities Corporation v. Commissioner,* the Supreme Court sustained the authority of the courts of appeals to sit en banc. En banc rehearing would give all active judges an opportunity to hear a case "where there is a difference in view among the judges upon a question of fundamental importance, and especially in a case where two of the three judges sitting in a case may have a view contrary to that of the other judges of the court." Congress codified the *Textile Mills* decision just five years later in 28 U.S.C. § 46(c), leaving the courts of appeals "free to devise their own administrative machinery to provide the means whereby a majority may order such a hearing."

That the binding authority principle applies only to appellate decisions, and not to trial court decisions, is yet another policy choice. There is nothing inevitable about this; the rule could just as easily operate so that the first district judge to decide an issue within a district, or even within a circuit, would bind all similarly situated district judges, but it does not. The very existence of the binding authority principle is not inevitable. The federal courts could operate, though much less efficiently, if judges of inferior courts had discretion to consider the opinions of higher courts, but "respectfully disagree" with them for good and sufficient reasons.[30]

III

While we agree with *Anastasoff* that the principle of precedent was well established in the common law courts by the time Article III of the Constitution was written, we do not agree that it was known and applied in the strict sense in which we apply binding authority today. It may be true, as *Anastasoff* notes, that "judges and lawyers of the day recognized the authority of unpublished decisions even when they were established only by memory or by a lawyer's unpublished memorandum," but precedents brought to the attention of the court in that fashion obviously could not serve as the

---

30. Some state court systems apply the binding authority principle differently than do the federal courts. In California, for example, an opinion by one of the courts of appeal is binding on all trial courts in the state, not merely those in the same district. However, court of appeal panels are not bound by the opinions of other panels, even those within the same district.

California's management of precedent differs from that of the federal courts in another important respect: The California Supreme Court may "depublish" a court of appeal opinion — i.e., strip a published decision of its precedential effect. California's depublication practice shows that it is possible to adopt more aggressive methods of managing precedent than those used by the federal courts.

kind of rigid constraint that binding authority provides today. Unlike our practice today, a single case was not sufficient to establish a particular rule of law, and case reporters often filtered out cases that they considered wrong, or inconsistent with their view of how the law *should* develop. The concept of binding case precedent, though it was known at common law, was used exceedingly sparingly. For the most part, common law courts felt free to depart from precedent where they considered the earlier-adopted rule to be no longer workable or appropriate.

Case precedent at common law thus resembled much more what we call persuasive authority than the binding authority which is the backbone of much of the federal judicial system today. The concept of binding precedent could only develop once two conditions were met: The development of a hierarchical system of appellate courts with clear lines of authority, and a case reporting system that enabled later courts to know precisely what was said in earlier opinions. As we have seen, these developments did not come about — either here or in England — until the nineteenth century, long after Article III of the Constitution was written.

While many consider the principle of binding authority indispensable — perhaps even inevitable — it is important to note that it is not an unalloyed good. While bringing to the law important values such as predictability and consistency, it also (for the very same reason) deprives the law of flexibility and adaptability. *See Planned Parenthood v. Casey*, 505 U.S. 833, 868 (1992) ("The promise of constancy, once given, binds its maker for as long as the power to stand by the decision survives and the understanding of the issue has not changed so fundamentally as to render the commitment obsolete.")[31] A district court bound by circuit authority, for example, has no choice but to follow it, even if convinced that such authority was wrongly decided. Appellate courts often tolerate errors in their caselaw because the rigors of the en banc process make it impossible to correct all errors.

A system of strict binding precedent also suffers from the defect that it gives undue weight to the first case to raise a particular issue. This is especially true in the circuit courts, where the first panel to consider an issue and publish a precedential opinion occupies the field, whether or not the lawyers have done an adequate job of developing and arguing the issue.

The question raised by *Anastasoff* is whether one particular aspect of the binding authority principle — the decision of which rulings of an appellate court are binding — is a matter of judicial policy or constitutional imperative. We believe *Anastasoff* erred in holding that, as a constitutional matter, courts of appeals may not decide which of their opinions will be deemed binding on themselves and the courts below them. For the reasons explained, the principle of strict binding authority is itself not constitutional, but rather a matter of judicial policy. Were it otherwise, it would cast doubt on the federal court practice of limiting the binding effect of

---

31. It also forces judges in certain instances to act in ways they may consider to be contrary to the Constitution. Some have argued that the duty of judges to follow the Constitution stands on a higher footing than the rule requiring adherence to precedent, and judges should not follow precedent when they believe that to do so would violate the Constitution. *See* Gary Lawson, *The Constitutional Case Against Precedent*, 17 Harv. J.L. & Pub. Pol'y 23, 27-28 (1994).

appellate decisions to the courts of a particular circuit. Circuit boundaries — and the very system of circuit courts — are a matter of judicial administration, not constitutional law. If, as *Anastasoff* suggests, the Constitution dictates that every "declaration of law must be applied in subsequent cases to similarly situated parties," then the Second Circuit would have no authority to disagree with a ruling of the Eighth Circuit that is directly on point, and the first circuit to rule on a legal issue would then bind not only itself and the courts within its own circuit, but all inferior or federal courts.

Another consequence of *Anastasoff*'s reasoning would be to cast doubt on the authority of courts of appeals to adopt a body of circuit law on a wholesale basis, as did the Eleventh Circuit in *Bonner,* and the Federal Circuit in *South Corp.* Circuits could, of course, adopt individual cases from other circuits as binding in a case raising a particular legal issue. But adopting a whole body of law, encompassing countless rules on matters wholly unrelated to the issues raised in a particular case, is a very different matter. If binding authority were a constitutional imperative, it could only be created through individual case adjudication, not by a decision unconstrained by the facts before the court or its prior caselaw.

Nor is it clear, under the reasoning of *Anastasoff,* how courts could limit the binding effect of their rulings to appellate decisions. Under *Anastasoff*'s reasoning, district court opinions should bind district courts, at least in the same district, or even nationwide. After all, the Constitution vests the same "judicial Power" in all federal courts, so *Anastasoff*'s conclusion that judicial decisions must have precedential effect would apply equally to the thousands of unpublished decisions of the district courts.

No doubt the most serious implication of *Anastasoff*'s constitutional rule is that it would preclude appellate courts from developing a coherent and internally consistent body of caselaw to serve as binding authority for themselves and the courts below them. Writing an opinion is not simply a matter of laying out the facts and announcing a rule of decision. Precedential opinions are meant to govern not merely the cases for which they are written, but future cases as well.

In writing an opinion, the court must be careful to recite all facts that are relevant to its ruling, while omitting facts that it considers irrelevant. Omitting relevant facts will make the ruling unintelligible to those not already familiar with the case; including inconsequential facts can provide a spurious basis for distinguishing the case in the future. The rule of decision cannot simply be announced, it must be selected after due consideration of the relevant legal and policy considerations. Where more than one rule could be followed — which is often the case — the court must explain why it is selecting one and rejecting the others. Moreover, the rule must be phrased with precision and with due regard to how it will be applied in future cases. A judge drafting a precedential opinion must not only consider the facts of the immediate case, but must also envision the countless permutations of facts that might arise in the universe of future cases. Modern opinions generally call for the most precise drafting and re-drafting to ensure that the rule announced sweeps neither too broadly nor too narrowly, and that it does not collide with other binding precedent that bears on the issue. Writing a precedential opinion, thus, involves much more than deciding who wins and who loses in a particular case. It is a solemn judicial act that sets the course of the law for hundreds or thousands of litigants and potential litigants. When properly done, it is an exacting and extremely time-consuming task.

It goes without saying that few, if any, appellate courts have the resources to write precedential opinions in every case that comes before them. The Supreme Court certainly does not. Rather, it uses its discretionary review authority to limit its merits docket to a handful of opinions per justice, from the approximately 9000 cases that seek review every Term.[34] While federal courts of appeals generally lack discretionary review authority, they use their authority to decide cases by unpublished — and nonprecedential — dispositions to achieve the same end: They select a manageable number of cases in which to publish precedential opinions, and leave the rest to be decided by unpublished dispositions or judgment orders. In our circuit, published dispositions make up approximately 16 percent of decided cases; in other circuits, the percentage ranges from 10 to 44, the national average being 20 percent.

That a case is decided without a precedential opinion does not mean it is not fully considered, or that the disposition does not reflect a reasoned analysis of the issues presented.[35] What it does mean is that the disposition is not written in a way that will be fully intelligible to those unfamiliar with the case, and the rule of law is not announced in a way that makes it suitable for governing future cases. . . . An unpublished disposition is, more or less, a letter from the court to parties familiar with the facts, announcing the result and the essential rationale of the court's decision. Deciding a large portion of our cases in this fashion frees us to spend the requisite time drafting precedential opinions in the remaining cases.

Should courts allow parties to cite to these dispositions, however, much of the time gained would likely vanish. Without comprehensive factual accounts and precisely crafted holdings to guide them, zealous counsel would be tempted to seize upon superficial similarities between their client's cases and unpublished dispositions. Faced with the prospect of parties citing these dispositions as precedent, conscientious judges would have to pay much closer attention to the way they word their unpublished rulings. Language adequate to inform the parties how their case has been decided might well be inadequate if applied to future cases arising from different facts. And, although three judges might agree on the outcome of the case before them, they might not agree on the precise reasoning or the rule to be applied to future cases. Unpublished concurrences and dissents would become much more common, as individual judges would feel obligated to clarify their differences with the majority, even when those differences had no bearing on the case before them. In short, judges would have to start treating unpublished dispositions — those they write, those written by other judges on their panels, and those written by judges on other panels — as mini-opinions. This new responsibility would cut severely into the time judges need

---

34. The United States Supreme Court decided seventy-seven cases in October Term 1999, which represents less than nine opinions per justice. By comparison, in 1999, each active judge in our court heard an average of 450 cases and had writing responsibility for an average of twenty opinions and 130 unpublished dispositions.

35. Sufficient restrictions on judicial decisionmaking exist to allay fears of irresponsible and unaccountable practices such as "burying" inconvenient decisions through nonpublication.

to fulfill their paramount duties: producing well-reasoned published opinions and keeping the law of the circuit consistent through the en banc process. The quality of published opinions would sink as judges were forced to devote less and less time to each opinion.[37]

Increasing the number of opinions by a factor of five, as *Anastasoff* suggests, doesn't seem to us a sensible idea, even if we had the resources to do so. Adding endlessly to the body of precedent — especially binding precedent — can lead to confusion and unnecessary conflict. Judges have a responsibility to keep the body of law "cohesive and understandable, and not muddy the water with a needless torrent of published opinions." Cases decided by nonprecedential disposition generally involve facts that are materially indistinguishable from those of prior published opinions. Writing a second, third or tenth opinion in the same area of the law, based on materially indistinguishable facts will, at best, clutter up the law books and databases with redundant and thus unhelpful authority. Yet once they are designated as precedent, they will have to be read and analyzed by lawyers researching the issue, materially increasing the costs to the client for absolutely no legitimate reason. Worse still, publishing redundant opinions will multiply significantly the number of inadvertent and unnecessary conflicts, because different opinion writers may use slightly different language to express the same idea. As lawyers well know, even small differences in language can have significantly different implications when read in light of future fact patterns, so differences in phrasing that seem trivial when written can later take on a substantive significance.

The risk that this may happen vastly increases if judges are required to write many more precedential opinions than they do now, leaving much less time to devote to each. Because conflicts — even inadvertent ones — can only be resolved by the exceedingly time-consuming and inefficient process of en banc review, an increase in intracircuit conflicts would leave much less time for us to devote to normal panel opinions. Maintaining a coherent, consistent and intelligible body of caselaw is not served by writing more opinions; it is served by taking the time to make the precedential opinions we do write as lucid and consistent as humanly possible.[39]

---

37. Recent figures tell a striking story. In 1999, our court decided some 4500 cases on the merits, about 700 by opinion and 3800 by unpublished disposition. Each active judge heard an average of 450 cases as part of a three judge panel and had writing responsibility in a third of those cases. That works out to an average of 150 dispositions — 20 opinions and 130 unpublished dispositions — per judge. In addition, each judge had to review, comment on, and eventually join or dissent from 40 opinions and 260 unpublished dispositions circulated by other judges with whom he sat.

39. *Anastasoff* suggests that the appointment of more judges would enable courts to write binding opinions in every case. We take no position as to whether there should be more federal judges, being a policy question for Congress to decide. We note, however, that Congress would have to increase the number of judges by something like a factor of five to allocate to each judge a manageable number of opinions each year. But adding more judges, and more binding precedents, creates its own set of problems by significantly increasing the possibility of conflict within the same circuit as each judge will have an increased body of binding caselaw to consider and reconcile.

That problem, in turn, could be ameliorated by increasing the number of circuits, but that would increase the number of inter-circuit conflicts, moving the problem up the chain of command to the Supreme Court, which likewise does not have the capacity to significantly increase the number of opinions it issues each year. In the end, we do not believe that more law makes for better law.

IV

Unlike the *Anastasoff* court, we are unable to find within Article III of the Constitution a requirement that all case dispositions and orders issued by appellate courts be binding authority. On the contrary, we believe that an inherent aspect of our function as Article III judges is managing precedent to develop a coherent body of circuit law to govern litigation in our court and the other courts of this circuit. We agree with *Anastasoff* that we — and all courts — must follow the law. But we do not think that this means we must also make binding law every time we issue a merits decision. The common law has long recognized that certain types of cases do not deserve to be authorities, and that one important aspect of the judicial function is separating the cases that should be precedent from those that should not. Without clearer guidance than that offered in *Anastasoff*, we see no constitutional basis for abdicating this important aspect of our judicial responsibility.

Contrary to counsel's contention, then, we conclude that Rule 36-3 is constitutional. We also find that counsel violated the rule. Nevertheless, we are aware that *Anastasoff* may have cast doubt on our rule's constitutional validity. Our rules are obviously not meant to punish attorneys who, in good faith, seek to test a rule's constitutionality. We therefore conclude that the violation was not willful and exercise our discretion not to impose sanctions.

The order to show case is DISCHARGED.

Notes and Questions

---

1. Which decision do you find more *persuasive* — *Anastasoff*, or *Hart*? Why? What reasons does each court give? What, if anything, is wrong with those arguments? For example, in *Hart*, the court presented a parade of horribles should the *Anastasoff* court's reasoning be adopted: court of appeals precedent might bind all circuits, new circuits might not be able to adopt wholesale a prior circuit's law, and district court decisions might have precedential effect. But in light of the discussion of those topics earlier in this chapter, is it so clear that any of these effects should be considered inappropriate, or even problematic?

2. The above cases involved local circuit "unpublished" decision rules. Since those cases were decided, the Supreme Court promulgated Federal Rule of Appellate Procedure 32.1 ("Citing Judicial Dispositions"), which provides as follows:

> (a) Citation Permitted. A court may not prohibit or restrict the citation of federal judicial opinions, orders, judgments, or other written dispositions that have been:
>> (i) designated as "unpublished," "not for publication," "nonprecedential," "not precedent," or the like; and
>> (ii) issued on or after January 1, 2007.

(b) Copies Required. If a party cites a federal judicial opinion, order, judgment, or written disposition that is not available in a publicly accessible electronic database, the party must file and serve a copy of that opinion, order, judgment, or disposition with the brief or other paper in which it is cited.

But as the advisory committee that drafted this rule indicates, the scope of Rule 32.1 is limited.

> It does not require any court to issue an unpublished opinion or forbid any court from doing so. It does not dictate the circumstances under which a court may choose to designate an opinion as "unpublished" or specify the procedure that a court must follow in making that determination. It says nothing about what effect a court must give to one of its unpublished opinions or to the unpublished opinions of another court. In particular, it takes no position on whether refusing to treat an unpublished opinion of a federal court as binding precedent is constitutional. Rule 32.1 addresses only the *citation* of federal judicial dispositions that have been *designated* as "unpublished" or "nonprecedential" — whether or not those dispositions have been published in some way or are precedential in some sense.

Fed. R. App. P. 32.1 advisory committee's note. And today, every circuit in fact has a local rule depriving its "unpublished" decisions of binding precedential effect. For example, Ninth Circuit Rule 36-3(a) provides: "**Not Precedent.** Unpublished dispositions and orders of this Court are not precedent, except when relevant under the doctrine of law of the case or rules of claim preclusion or issue preclusion."

3. For a variety of reasons, including volume and inherent lack of binding precedential force, only a small fraction of district court decisions are officially published, usually in the *Federal Supplement* (or, now, the *Federal Supplement 2d*).

   For the year ended September 30, 2011, the United States Court of Appeals (excluding the Federal Circuit) published only 15% of its opinions or orders filed in cases terminated on the merits. *See* Judicial Business of the United States Court, 2011 Annual Report of the Director, Table S-3, *available at* www.uscourts.gov/uscourts/statistics/JudicialBusiness/2011/JudicialBusiness2011.pdf. (Incidentally, all such opinions and orders were delivered in writing, rather than orally. *See id.*) Published opinions can be found in the *Federal Reporter*, and certain officially "unpublished" opinions can be found (ironically enough) in a publication known as the *Federal Appendix*.

   By contrast, virtually all of the Supreme Court's merits decisions are published in the *United States* and other reporters.

4. As you are probably aware, "unpublished" does not mean unavailable. Under the E-Government Act of 2002, Pub. L. No. 107-347, § 205(a), 116 Stat. 2899, 2913 (2002), each circuit is required to maintain a website of all written opinions, including "unpublished" opinions. Also, many such opinions are available on Westlaw and Lexis. And of course, most case files are publicly accessible,

meaning if one were aware of a particular opinion, one could physically go to the appropriate federal courthouse and find it.

5. As the advisory committee's note to Fed. R. App. P. 32.1 suggests, the authorities are divided as to whether local court rules that purport to deprive "unpublished" decisions of precedential value are constitutional, and the Supreme Court has yet to weigh in on this question. But for a non-constitutional argument that such rules are contrary to the Rules Enabling Act and are otherwise beyond the rulemaking power of the federal courts, see Bradley Scott Shannon, *May Stare Decisis Be Abrogated by Rule?*, 67 Ohio St. L.J. 645 (2006).

6. Even assuming that courts *may* issue "unpublished" decisions, there is still the normative questions of whether they *should*. It turns out that the answer to this question to a large extent tracks the reasons for and against stare decisis generally. For example, among the advantages of issuing unpublished decisions might be a time savings for the parties and for the court (in that they would not have to research the existence of precedent) and an ability to decide the case in a manner unconstrained by precedent. But some believe that the ability to issue unpublished decisions actually leads to lower quality decisions; enables courts to "hide" difficult or unpopular cases; and leads to inconsistent decisions in similar cases. Can you think of any other pros and cons that might be associated with this practice?

7. Can you think of a better solution to the "problems" that have led courts to issue "unpublished" opinions? For example, should Congress increase the number of federal judges? Or should courts simply refrain from issuing opinions in certain cases, and instead opt for summary affirmances or reversals?

8. Recall that the court of appeals' decision in *Anastasoff* was vacated by the court sitting en banc on the ground that the case was settled by the parties while awaiting further review. *See* 235 F.3d at 1056. In light of the Supreme Court's decision in *United States Bancorp* (*see supra* at 218), should this have occurred?

SIDEBAR: CITATION PRACTICE IN ENGLAND

In England, citation practice is governed by Practice Direction: Citation of Authorities (2012). Of particular interest is paragraph [10], which provides in part: "An unreported case should not usually be cited unless it contains a relevant statement of legal principle not found in reported authority."

J. PERSUASIVE AUTHORITY

Antonin Scalia & Bryan A. Garner

MASTER THE RELATIVE WEIGHT OF PRECEDENTS*

Making Your Case: The Art of Persuading Judges (2008)

From a juridical point of view, case authorities are of two sorts: those that are governing (either directly or by implication) and those that are persuasive.

Governing authorities are more significant and should occupy more of your attention. At the appellate level, at least, the decisions most important to your case will be those rendered by the very court before which you are appearing. (That is obviously true at the court of last resort, and in intermediate appellate courts it is often the rule that one panel cannot overrule another.) The next most important body of governing decisions (the most important at the trial-court level) is that of the court immediately superior to the court before which you are appearing. It is no use arguing at length in a trial court that your point is sustained by a proper reading of a supreme-court opinion, if the intermediate appellate court to which an appeal would be taken has already rejected that reading. Of course, when the intermediate appellate court has not spoken on the point, supreme-court opinions will be the most important.

One caveat: even when the governing authority is flatly against you, if you think it is wrong you should say so, lest on appeal you be held to have waived the point. If, for example, you are appearing before a district court bound by a prior court-of-appeals precedent, it is of little use to argue at length that this precedent misstates the law. Still, you should place on the record your view that it does so. And you should do the same in the intermediate appellate court so that there will be no doubt of your entitlement to raise that issue in the highest court of that jurisdiction.

Among the precedents that are nongoverning, there is a hierarchy of persuasiveness that far too many advocates ignore. The most persuasive nongoverning case authorities are the dicta of governing courts (quote them, but be sure to identify them as dicta) and the holdings of governing courts in analogous cases. Next are the holdings of courts of appeals coordinate to the court of appeals whose law governs your case; next, the holdings of trial courts coordinate to your court; finally (and rarely worth pursuing), the holdings of courts inferior to your court and courts of other jurisdictions.

. . . .

If you're arguing to an appellate court, decisions of lower courts will almost never be persuasive as authority unless (1) they are numerous and virtually unanimous, or (2) the cited case was written by a judge renowned enough to be named in parentheses after the citation (e.g., Learned Hand, J.). Lengthy discussion of conflicting lower-court decisions is largely a waste of time. . . .

Another consideration for citations is freshness. In some rare situations, the older citation will be the better one. A constitutional-law opinion by Joseph Story on circuit, for example, might be more persuasive than a more recent opinion by a federal court of appeals. But at least where opinions of governing courts are concerned, the more recent the citation the better. The judge wants to know whether the judgment you seek will be affirmed by the current court, not whether it would have been affirmed 30 years ago.

When you rely on nothing but persuasive authority, it is more important than ever to say why the rule you're promoting makes policy sense.

Notes and Questions

1. There are a host of non-binding ("persuasive") authorities available, including the following:
   a) dicta from binding cases;
   b) "unpublished" decisions from otherwise binding courts;
   c) non-binding case law (i.e., case law from lower courts or courts from other jurisdictions);
   d) *Restatements*;
   e) model and uniform acts;
   f) treatises and other books (legal encyclopedias, dictionaries, etc.);
   g) articles (particularly law review-type articles);
   h) legislative history (with respect to a relevant statute); and
   i) virtually anything else that is found to be persuasive.

2. When dealing with non-binding case law, there are some things to consider in gauging its usefulness — i.e., there are a number of factors that tend to make some authorities better (more persuasive) than others. These factors include the following:
   a) the margin of the decision (unanimity is best);
   b) the author of the decision (decisions by renowned and well-respected jurists carry more weight);
   c) the age of the decision (all else being equal, newer is better);
   d) whether the decision is "venerable" (e.g., *Marbury v. Madison*; note that this is an exception to (c) above);
   e) the prestige or influence of the issuing court;
   f) the strength and persuasiveness of the reasoning used;
   g) the number of similar decisions supporting your position (as opposed to the contrary position) (i.e., the "weight of authority");
   h) whether the decision represents the "modern trend" or the "better view"; and
   i) the relative position of the court (decisions from appellate courts of last resort are best).

   Can you think of any other, possibly relevant factors?

3. A study was recently conducted to determine which state courts are considered to be the most "influential" in terms of citations of decisions by other state courts. *See* Jake Dear & Edward W. Jessen, *"Followed Rates" and Leading State Cases, 1940-2005,* 41 U.C. DAVIS L. REV. 683 (2007). In terms of the number of state high court decisions that have been followed at least once by an out-of-state court between the years 1940 and 2005, California (not surprisingly) ranked first, followed by Washington, Colorado, Iowa, and Minnesota. *See id.* at 694.

4. Judges (and Justices) frequently deny the importance of legal scholarship to judicial decision making. In reality, though, legal scholarship appears to play a role, at least in the Supreme Court. *See* Lee Petherbridge & David L. Schwartz, *An Empirical Assessment of the Supreme Court's Use of Legal Scholarship,* 106 Nw. U. L. REV. 995 (2012). Among the authors' conclusions:

   1. Over the last sixty-one years, the Supreme Court has used legal scholarship in 32.21% of its decisions.
   2. The Supreme Court, on average, uses more than one work of legal scholarship per decision.
   3. The overall trend during the last sixty-one years has been an increase in the use of legal scholarship by the Supreme Court.

   Id. at 998. Moreover: "We find evidence that the Court disproportionately uses scholarship when cases are either more important or more difficult to decide as defined by several criteria." *Id.* at 998-99.

5. For a recent article discussing various issues associated with the use of Wikipedia as a persuasive authority, see Jason C. Miller & Hannah B. Murray, *Wikipedia in Court: When and How Citing Wikipedia and Other Consensus Websites Is Appropriate,* 84 ST. JOHN'S L. REV. 633 (2010). For works on the citation of nonlegal materials generally, see John J. Hasko, *Persuasion in the Court: Non-legal Materials in U.S. Supreme Court Opinions,* 94:3 LAW LIBR. J. 427 (2002-27), and Bezalel Stern, *Nonlegal Citations and the Failure of Law: A Case Study of the Supreme Court 2010-11 Term,* 35 WHITTIER L. REV. 75 (2103).

Frederick Schauer

AUTHORITY AND AUTHORITIES

94 Va. L. Rev. 1931 (2008)

A curious feature of the current controversy over the citation of foreign law is that it appears to be a debate about *citation*. And what makes that so curious is that engaging in a debate about citation, or even seeming to *care* about citation, stands in such marked contrast to the current legal *zeitgeist*. Legal sophisticates these days worry little about the ins and outs of citation, tending instead to cast their lot with the legal realists in believing that the citation of legal authorities in briefs, arguments, and opinions is scarcely more than a decoration. Citation may be professionally obligatory, the sophisticates grudgingly acknowledge, but it persists largely as an ornament fastened to reasons whose acceptance rarely depends on the assistance or weight of the cited authorities. So although learning the rules and practices of legal citation is necessary for speaking and writing the language of law, it is a mistake to think that the cited authorities have very much to do with the substance of legal argument or the determination of legal outcomes.

With this dismissive attitude towards legal citation so prevalent, the focus of the debate on the citation of foreign (or, sometimes, international) law seems almost quaint. Interestingly, however, the debate over the propriety of citing to non-American legal authority arises at the same time as the permissibility of other forms of citation has been at the vortex of a number of equally heated controversies. One such controversy erupted a few years ago with the Eighth Circuit's panel decision in *Anastasoff v. United States*, a case in which the court initially held unconstitutional a prohibition on the citation to (and precedential effect of) unpublished opinions on the grounds that the prohibition went beyond the court's judicial powers under Article III. Something of a firestorm ensued, one focused significantly on whether it was desirable or permissible to prohibit advocates in their briefs from citing to a particular kind of authority. What eventually followed was the new Federal Rule of Appellate Rule 32.1, prohibiting the circuits from adopting no-citation rules while allowing them to continue to adopt, if they wished, their own no-precedential-effect rules and practices. The new rule not only marked the denouement of the *Anastasoff* controversy in the Eighth Circuit, but also reflects a larger array of concerns that have arisen in all the federal circuits, and indeed in the state appellate courts as well. In the wake of growing concerns about how to manage a burgeoning caseload with little increase in the number of judges, these courts have wrestled with the desirability or permissibility, even if not the constitutionality, of various "no citation" rules, presumably to the sneers or yawns of the cogniscenti, especially those with realist sympathies. And when the Department of History at Middlebury College prohibited students from citing to Wikipedia in their term papers, legal observers debated the relevance of Middlebury's decision to the question of permissible and impermissible citations to Wikipedia and other allegedly unreliable sources in academic legal work.

Although the renewed attention to the citation of authorities initially seems anachronistic or otherwise odd, on further reflection it may not be so surprising after all. The issue in these controversies, after all, is not one of citation. It is one of authority, and law is, at bottom, an authoritative practice, a practice in which there is far more reliance than in, say, mathematics or the natural sciences on the source rather than the content (or even the correctness) of ideas, arguments, and conclusions. And as long as this is so, then something as seemingly trivial as citation practice turns out to be the surface manifestation of a deeply important facet of the nature of law itself. It is not without interest and importance that lawyers and judges refer to things they cite as *authorities* and that a brief is sometimes called a "memorandum of points and authorities." These usages and many like them reinforce the point that citation practice is intimately connected with the authoritative core of the idea of law. Rather than being little more than the characteristic form of legal jargon, the law's practice of using and announcing its authorities — its citation practice — is part and parcel of law's character. The various contemporary controversies about citation practice turn out, therefore, to be controversies about authority, and as a result they are controversies about the nature of law itself.

I. AUTHORITY 101

It may be useful to begin by reprising the conventional wisdom about the very idea of authority. According to this conventional wisdom, the characteristic feature of authority is its *content-independence*. The force of an authoritative directive comes not from its content, but from its source. And this is in contrast to our normal decisionmaking and reasoning processes. Typically, the reason for an action, a decision, or a belief is one that is grounded in the content of the reason. I eat spinach because it is good for me, and it actually being good for me is a necessary condition for it being a good reason. Similarly, when Judge Cardozo in *MacPherson v. Buick Motor Co.* held that privity was not a requirement for manufacturer liability to consumers, that conclusion was a product of his belief that it was the most fair, efficient, or otherwise desirable approach. Had he not believed that to be true, he would not have reached the conclusion he did, just as I would not eat spinach if I did not believe it was good for me. So let us call this kind of reason a *substantive reason*. Someone considering what to do, what to decide, or what to believe will take a reason as a good substantive reason only if she believes in what the reason actually *says* and believes that what the reason says is true.

Content-independent reasons, however, are different. They are reasons to act, decide, or believe that are based not on the substantive content of a reason, but instead on its source. What matters is not what the reason says but where it comes from. So when an exasperated parent yells, "Because I said so!" to a child, the parent typically has tried to explain to the child *why* she should do her homework or *why* he should clean up his room. When these content-based or substantive reasons have been unavailing, however, the exasperated parent resorts to the because-I-said-so argument precisely to make clear that the child should do as told regardless of whether the child agrees with those substantive reasons. And in much the same fashion, a judge in a New York lower court subsequent to *MacPherson* then has an obligation to reach the same conclusion as Judge Cardozo even if she does not believe that doing away with the privity requirement in such cases is a good idea. Her obligation arises simply from the fact that Judge Cardozo in *MacPherson* said so.

Like parents and judges of higher courts, those who are *in* authority typically rely, or at least can rely, on their role or position to provide reasons for their subjects to follow their rules, commands, orders, or instructions. Sergeants and teachers, among others, will often try to induce their subordinates or students to understand and agree with the substantive reasons for doing this or that, but the essence of authority exists not because of substantive agreement on the part of the subject, but apart from it. Maybe the sergeant would like me to understand *why* I should have a

sharp crease in my uniform pants, and surely the teacher would like me to understand *why* I must memorize and recite a Shakespeare sonnet. But in both cases, and
countless others, the authorities want it understood that I am expected to do what I
am told just because of who told me to do it, even if I do not accept the underlying
substantive reasons for so doing. Following H.L.A. Hart, we think of authority as
content-independent precisely because it is the source and not the content of the
directive that produces the reasons for following it. And so, when a rule is authoritative, its subjects are expected to obey regardless of their own evaluation of the
rule or the outcome it has indicated on a particular occasion.

It is highly controversial whether authority in this precise sense is a good idea
and, if so, in what context. A longstanding body of thinking argues that it is irrational for an autonomous agent to do something she would not otherwise have done
on the balance of substantive reasons just because a so-called authority says so. If
Barbara has decided after careful thought to spend her life as a lawyer rather than
a physician, why should she follow a different course just because her father has
said so? When Sam has concluded that he would like to smoke marijuana because
he believes it makes him feel good and has few side effects, is it rational for him to
put aside his own best judgment in favor of that of police officers and politicians?
When the sign says, "Don't Walk" but there is no car in sight, does it make sense
for me to stand obediently at the curb? And when a judge has determined what she
believes would be the best outcome in the case before her, can it be rational for her
to make a contrary ruling solely because a bare majority of judges on a higher court
has come to a different conclusion in a similar case? Authority may be ubiquitous
in our lives, but for generations its basic soundness has been an object of persistent
challenge. Yet although authority has long been criticized, it has for just as long been
defended. Socrates refused to escape from Athens on the eve of being put to death
precisely because he accepted the authority of the state that had unjustly, even in
his own mind, condemned him. President Dwight Eisenhower sent federal troops
to Little Rock, Arkansas in 1957 to enforce a Supreme Court decision — *Brown v.
Board of Education* — with whose outcome he disagreed, and he did so because
he accepted the authority of the Supreme Court, just as he expected the state of
Arkansas to accept the authority of the federal government. Questioning the idea
of authority may have a long history, but there is an equally long history of people accepting and endorsing it and consequently seeking to explain why it is often
appropriate for even a rational agent to defer to the views of others, even when she
disagrees with the judgments to which she is deferring.

For my purposes here, the ultimate rationality (or not) of authority from the
perspective of the subject is not the issue, because there can be little doubt that
authority exists, apart from the question of its desirability. We understand what
authority is, and we can identify instances of its effect, even as we disagree about its
normative desirability and the extent of its empirical prevalence in real-world decisionmaking. And thus we understand that authority provides reasons for action by
virtue of its status and not by virtue of the intrinsic or content-based soundness of
the actions that the authority is urging.

It is logically possible for those in authority — authorities — to prescribe only
those actions that their subjects would have selected on the balance of substantive

reasons even without the authoritative directive, but such a possibility is too fantastic to be taken seriously. As a practical matter, the universe of actual authoritative directives will encompass at least some decisionmaking occasions in which a subject who accepts an authority will have an authority-based and content-independent reason for doing something other than what the subject would otherwise have thought it correct to do. And also as a practical matter, these authoritative directives will sometimes be dispositive, thus requiring a subject actually to do or decide something other than what she would have done or decided in the absence of the authoritative directive. So although a source can be the repository of wisdom, experience, or information, when a source is authoritative it provides a potentially determinative reason for a decision other than the decision that the subject might have made after taking into account all of the knowledge, wisdom, and information she can obtain from herself or others. There is a key difference between *learning* how to do something from a book and taking something in that same book as correct just because it is in the book, and it is precisely this distinction that is captured by the concept of authority and by differentiation between substantive and content-independent reasons.

II. IS "PERSUASIVE AUTHORITY" AN OXYMORON?

With the basic concept of authority as necessary background, we can turn to the legal authorities that pervade and shape the formal discourse of the law. These authorities are not all of one type, however, and *mandatory* (or *binding*) authorities are commonly distinguished from *persuasive* authorities. Mandatory authorities, according to the standard account drummed into the minds of lawyers from their first year of law school on, are ones that bind a court to follow them, as in the case of the obligation of a lower court in New York to follow Judge Cardozo's decision in *MacPherson* solely because lower courts are bound to obey the decisions of higher courts in the same jurisdiction. And this binding obligation to follow the decision of a higher court (or an earlier decision of the same court, when a strong norm of stare decisis exists) is in contrast, so it is said, with a court's discretion to choose whether to follow a persuasive authority, such as a decision of a court in another jurisdiction or a so-called *secondary* authority like a treatise or law review article. A court may choose to follow such a decision or to rely on the conclusions of a secondary authority, but, unlike a court that is under an obligation to follow the decision of a higher court in the same jurisdiction, here a court is conventionally understood to be following only those decisions or conclusions whose reasoning the court finds persuasive. And thus proponents of the use of foreign law, for example, often argue that those who oppose its use seem to be making much ado about very little, because there is certainly no binding obligation for *any* court to follow a decision from another jurisdiction, whether domestic or foreign.

Yet perhaps this response is a bit too quick, and perhaps the fundamental distinction between binding and persuasive authority is deeply misguided. For once we understand that genuine authority is content-independent, we are in a position to see that persuasion and acceptance (whether voluntary or not) of authority are fundamentally opposed notions. To be *persuaded* that global warming is a real problem is to accept that there are sound substantive reasons supporting these conclusions and thus to have no need for authoritative pronouncements in reaching those conclusions. When a scientist reaches the conclusion that global warming is a problem, she does not do so because seven Nobel Prize winners have said it is so but because her own scientific knowledge or investigation justifies that conclusion. But when *I* conclude that global warming is a problem, I reach that conclusion not because I genuinely know that it is correct, for I have no authority-independent way of knowing. Rather, my conclusion is based on the fact that it is consistent with what various scientists whose authority I recognize and accept have said.[32] Thus, it is not that I am persuaded that global warming is a problem. Rather, I am persuaded that people whose judgment I trust are persuaded that global warming is a problem. At times we may have both substantive and content-independent reasons for believing the same thing, but it remains crucial to recognize that the two are fundamentally different.

The distinction is the same in law. It is one thing to conclude that the best theory of freedom of speech permits speakers to advocate racial hatred. It is quite another to say that advocating racial hatred is constitutionally protected in the United States because the Supreme Court said so (more or less) in *Brandenburg v. Ohio*. Here the contrast is the same as between the scientists and me with respect to global warming. A decision driven by the intrinsic or substantive reasons for a conclusion is very different from one based solely on authority, plain and simple. Those who accept scientific authority (which scientists rarely but not never do) will accept that global warming is a problem even if their own authority-independent reasoning leads to a different conclusion. Likewise, a lower court judge who accepts the authority of precedent (from a higher court) and a Supreme Court Justice who accepts the authority of previous Supreme Court decisions (according to the principle of stare decisis) are expected to conclude that advocacy of racial hatred is constitutionally protected even if they believe that such a conclusion is legally erroneous.[36]

But now we can see just how curious the ubiquitous references to persuasive authority turn out to be. It is true that standard texts on legal research, legal

---

32. It is characteristic of law and many other domains of authority that the system often tells the subjects who (or what) the authorities are, and thus the subject is not required (or entitled) to decide whether a given authority is entitled to source-based and content-independent deference. But in other contexts, including those in which the subject must decide whether to defer to an authority or must decide which of multiple authorities is entitled to deference, there arises the interesting question of how much knowledge the subject needs in order to defer to someone with greater knowledge.

36. The question of stare decisis has been much in the news and in Supreme Court opinions recently, as the Court and various commentators debate not only the question whether the Supreme Court is obligated to take its previous decision as authoritative but also whether the Court is in fact doing so. Although in this Article I do not directly engage the questions whether the Supreme Court should or does follow its own previous decisions even when it thinks them mistaken, the debate about stare decisis underscores the importance of understanding the concept of authority which undergirds these debates.

method, and legal writing almost invariably distinguish between binding — or mandatory — and persuasive authority. But if an agent is genuinely persuaded of some conclusion because she has come to accept the substantive reasons offered for that conclusion by someone else, then authority has nothing to do with it. Conversely, if authority is genuinely at work, then the agent who accepts the authoritativeness of a directive need not be persuaded by the substantive reasons that might support the same conclusion. As with the parent saying, "Because I said so," authority is in an important way the fallback position when substantive persuasion is ineffective. And thus being persuaded is fundamentally different from doing, believing, or deciding something because of the prescriptions or conclusions of an authority. But if this is so, then the very idea of a persuasive authority is self-contradictory, for persuasion and authority are inherently opposed notions. A judge who is genuinely persuaded by an opinion from another jurisdiction is not taking the other jurisdiction's conclusion as authoritative. Rather, she is *learning* from it, and in this sense she is treating it no differently in her own decisionmaking processes than she would treat a persuasive argument that she has heard from her brother-in-law or in the hardware store. Conversely, the judge who decides to treat a decision from another jurisdiction as worthy of following because of its source and not its content is treating it as authoritative and need not be persuaded by the substantive reasons that might have persuaded the court that reached that decision. Thus, the fundamental contrast between persuasion and authority renders the term "persuasive authority" self-contradictory. The use of a source can be one or the other — it can be persuasive or it can be authoritative — but it cannot be both at the same time.

Although courts often cite legal sources because they are genuinely and substantively persuaded, many — perhaps even most — judicial uses of so-called persuasive authority seem to stem from authority rather than persuasion. In *Thompson v. Oklahoma*, one of the earlier juvenile death penalty cases, for example, the plurality opinion of Justice Stevens reinforced its judgment by the fact that the Court's outcome was "consistent with the views that have been expressed by *respected* professional organizations, by other nations that share our Anglo-American heritage, and by the *leading* members of the Western European community." Similarly, in *Roper v. Simmons*, Justice Kennedy's opinion for the Court referred to the fact that there was "'virtual unanimity'" among other nations on the question of the death penalty for juveniles and explained that the Court's conclusion was consistent with the "overwhelming weight of international opinion." This is not the language of persuasion; it is the language of authority. It is the very actions of other nations, and not their justifications for those actions, that add weight to the Court's conclusion;[42] and the fact that the actual reasoning of these other courts and nations is not described at all in the opinion adds credence to this interpretation. It is simply the conclusion that other nations have reached that is supposed to make a difference.

---

42. I do not make the claim that such sources are typically outcome-determinative. Rather, the claim is that their authority as authority is used to strengthen a conclusion reached on other grounds or as one factor among several, which in combination produce the following court's conclusion.

Taking so-called persuasive authority as authoritative rather than persuasive is by no means peculiar to the issue of foreign law. In referring to the law of other jurisdictions, American courts persistently refer to the "weight of judicial opinion," the "consensus of the courts," the "consensus of judicial opinion," what the "majority" of courts in other jurisdictions have done, or what "most courts have held." Courts do not always use the language of authority, to be sure, and on occasion talk of having been "persuaded by the reasoning" of a court in another jurisdiction. But such uses seem considerably less frequent. As should be apparent, the task of determining the exact percentage of optional sources cited because of their authoritativeness versus those cited because of their persuasiveness is too daunting even to comprehend. But it seems apparent even without a systematic empirical examination that, with respect to a vast number of uses of so-called persuasive authority, persuasion seems to have very little to do with it. It is not that courts follow these optional sources because they are persuasive; rather, courts follow them because of their very existence.

Widespread judicial practice, therefore, appears to support the conclusion that persuasion is rarely part of the equation when persuasive authorities are being used. Yet although at first glance the idea of persuasive authority seems to be as empirically inaccurate as it is conceptually oxymoronic, the matter may not be quite so simple. Because the concept of *persuasive* authority is traditionally offered in opposition to the concept of *mandatory* authority, the distinction between the two hinges on whether the decisionmaker has a choice to use the authority. And here the contributions of Ronald Dworkin can be instructive. When Dworkin distinguishes rules from principles, he relies in part on the fact that the judge *must* apply a rule that applies to the facts at hand but has a choice about whether to apply a principle. Both rules and principles have *scopes* — they apply by their own terms to some but not all acts and events. But under Dworkin's distinction, the defining characteristic of a rule is that it must be applied whenever its triggering acts or events occur, while principles are never mandatory in this sense, even if it appears on their face that they apply to the matter at hand.

The value of Dworkin's analysis for our purposes here has little to do with any alleged distinction between rules and principles. Rather, Dworkin helps us grasp a valuable distinction between seemingly applicable authorities that must be applied and other seemingly applicable authorities whose application is optional and not obligatory. Transposing Dworkin's distinction between mandatory rules and less mandatory principles to the question of authority encourages us to distinguish mandatory from *optional* authorities. And "optional," rather than "persuasive," seems a word much better suited to capturing the distinction we are after between that which must be used and that which may be ignored. A judge in the Southern District of New York is *required* to follow Second Circuit and Supreme Court decisions but is not required to follow or even notice the conclusions of the Eastern District of New York, the New York Court of Appeals, the Third Circuit, *Wigmore on Evidence*, the *Harvard Law Review*, the High Court of Australia, the Constitutional Court of South Africa, or the European Court of Human Rights. Yet, although the Southern District judge may ignore all of the items on this list of optional authorities without fear of sanction, she is *permitted* by the applicable professional norms to use them, in a way that she is not permitted, for fear of criticism and professional embarrassment if nothing else, to provide citations to astrology, private conversations with her brother, articles in the *National Enquirer*, and (slightly more controversially) the Bible.

This much may appear banal, but a much more difficult and important question remains. If a court is not required to cite or use secondary authority, or authority from another jurisdiction — if the use of optional authorities is nonmandatory but nevertheless permissible — then on what basis does a judge select an optional authority? And is there anything at all authoritative about an optional authority whose use is solely at the discretion of the judge? The decisionmaker may select the optional authority because she is persuaded by the substantive reasons the authority offers in support of its conclusion, but we understand then that the authority is not being used *as* an authority. As such, little would differentiate the genuinely persuasive opinion of a court located in a different jurisdiction from the genuinely persuasive opinion of the judge's father-in-law. Moreover, when a judge is actually persuaded by the decision of another jurisdiction, whether foreign or domestic, we would expect the judge to explain both the reasoning of that other jurisdiction as well as the reasons why she found it persuasive. Good manners and perhaps the desire to give research direction to others will typically counsel the judge to acknowledge the source of what she has now taken on as *her* ideas and conclusions. The citation to the decision of another jurisdiction in these circumstances will accordingly not be a citation to authority as we now understand the idea of authority but will instead be the judicial equivalent of an academic paper that gives credit to the origins of the author's own thinking.

If an optional source of guidance is selected because of the substantive, first-order soundness of the source's reasoning, then the source, even if by tradition and convention we label it as an "authority," is not being used as an authority. But although that conclusion makes the idea of a persuasive authority once again appear self-contradictory, there remains still another possibility. At times, optional authorities are selected *as authorities* because the selector trusts the authority as an authority even if the selector does not agree with the conclusions or, more likely, believes herself unreliable in reaching some conclusion. So although a Tenth Circuit judge is under no obligation in a securities regulation case to rely on conclusions reached by the Second Circuit or found in the pages of the Loss and Seligman treatise on securities regulation, the judge might believe her own judgments about securities matters sufficiently unreliable that she would prefer to rely on a court or commentator she believes to be more expert. This could even be true if she perceives herself as having little ability to evaluate the soundness of the authority's conclusions and, indeed, even if she suspects that the authority's conclusions are erroneous. The Tenth Circuit judge who looks to the Second Circuit for guidance in securities cases is like a trial court relying on expert testimony or any other novice relying on expertise. And in such cases the decisionmaker is not so much persuaded by the expert's reasons and arguments as by (the decisionmaker's inexpert evaluation of) the expert's expertise, an expertise that operates in a genuinely authoritative manner.

Insofar as this picture of expertise-influenced selection of optional authorities is accurate, then an optional authority is genuinely authoritative when the selector of the authority is not (necessarily) persuaded by what some nonmandatory source says, but is (inexpertly) persuaded that the optional source is more likely reliable than the selector herself. So although a judge of the Southern District of New York is required to follow Second Circuit rulings he thinks wrong even if he thinks that the judges of the Second Circuit are morons, there are other circumstances in which a judge defers to an authority not because he is persuaded by the authority's conclusions or reasons but by the fact that the authority is an authority. In such circumstances, relying on the authority is genuinely optional and not mandatory, but it is nevertheless true that the reliance or obedience that ensues is one that is content-independent and, as such, an example of authentic authority.

Although optional authorities are often used in just this genuinely authoritative fashion, they are also employed frequently in a manner that hovers between the authoritative and the substantive. When a lawyer in a brief, a judge in an opinion, or a scholar in a law review article makes reference to an authority, it is often done to provide alleged "support" for some proposition. But the idea of "support" here is an odd one. The cited authority is often not one that supports the proposition in question any more than some other authority might negate it. And this makes the use of an authority as "support" a peculiar sense of authority, because the set of authorities does not necessarily point in one direction rather than another. Nevertheless, the conventions of legal citation do not appear to require only strong (authoritative) support. Rather, the conventions seem to require that a proposition be supported by a reference to some court (or other source) that has previously reached that conclusion, even if other courts or sources have reached a different and mutually exclusive conclusion, and even if there are more of the latter than the former. Thus, to support a legal proposition with a citation is often only to do no more than say that at least one person or court has said the same thing on some previous occasion.

When this kind of support appears in a law review article, it serves little purpose other than to acknowledge the provenance of an idea, and thus to think of the authority as supporting a conclusion is rather tenuous. But perhaps such support has greater import when it appears in a brief or judicial opinion. The requirement of at least some modicum of support reflects not only law's intrinsically authoritative nature but also law's inherent conservatism (in the non-political sense of that word). That is, a legal argument is often understood to be a better legal argument just because someone has made it before, and a legal conclusion is typically taken to be a better one if another court either reached it or credited it on an earlier occasion. The reference to a source in this context rarely refers to one that is more persuasive or authoritative than one that could be marshaled for an opposing proposition, but instead appears to be the legal equivalent of the line commonly used by the humorist Dave Barry — "I am not making this up."

So what does it mean for the author of a brief, a judicial opinion, or a law review article to say "I am not making this up"? One possibility is that there are not that many legal propositions whose affirmation and denial are both supportable. Were that the case, then the fact that a proposition was not novel would provide some genuine, even if minimal, decision-guiding force. But if, on the other hand, Karl Llewellyn's famous "thrust and parry" is representative of the legal domain generally, then it will typically be the case that there is some citation to a case, rule, or principle available to support virtually any legal proposition. And if that is so, then the requirement of "some" support will not be very much of a constraint. Judges frequently use the expression, "It won't write," to refer to situations in which there is *no* support or *no* argument for the result they would antecedently prefer to reach, but in a dense legal system it is arguable that this predicament will be rare indeed. To the extent that this conclusion is true, and thus to the extent that there are few judicial opinions or law review articles that will not write, a requirement of some support will be of little consequence.

But although the requirement of support may not be very constraining, it is worth noting that this variety of citation is a species, albeit a weak one, of genuine authority. The author of a brief or opinion who uses support to deny genuine novelty is asking the reader to take the supported proposition as being at least slightly more plausible because it has been said before than had it not been. And this is being done, typically, on the basis of the source's existence and not the substantive reasoning contained in it. One could well ask why the legal system is so concerned about the existence of one supporting "authority" even when the weight of authority might go in the other direction, but that is for another time. The point here is only that even this weaker and arguably more common form of citation to authority is a variant on genuine authority and consistent with the authoritative character of law itself.

III. MUST REAL AUTHORITY BE "BINDING"?

What emerges from the foregoing discussion is the conclusion that authority can be at the same time both optional and genuinely authoritative when it is selected for reasons other than its intrinsic persuasiveness. And thus we see the very misleading nature of the phrase "persuasive authority." But there is still more work to do, because we must now attend to the widespread view that a mandatory authority is *binding*. This view, however, may also be mistaken, for it may be possible for an authority to be both mandatory and non-binding, depending on what it is we mean by "binding."

It is commonplace in the foreign law debate for commentators, especially those sympathetic to the use of foreign or international law by American courts, to distinguish between "binding" (or, sometimes, "controlling") and "persuasive" (what we are now calling "optional") authority. They insist that the use of foreign law by American courts need not be perceived as threatening because its use would fall within the latter and not the former category. In other words, it is said, foreign law need not be considered binding or controlling in order for it to be valuable and citable. This conclusion may well be sound, but it is nevertheless important to clear up the widespread confusion arising from a failure to specify carefully what is meant by "binding." For when we typically think of some norm or constraint as binding, we think of it as inescapable, as leaving no choice, and, most importantly, as being absolute or non-overridable. When an authority is binding, therefore, the standard account is that the authority, especially if a precedent, must be followed or distinguished. A binding authority is one that, under this account, is determinative within its scope.

There is no reason, however, why an authoritative prescription need be understood as absolute or determinative. Just as rights, rules, and obligations can serve as reasons for action or decision even if they can be overridden at times by stronger rights, rules, and obligations, sources can also function as authorities without necessarily prevailing over all other sources, or even all other reasons for a decision. What there is a reason to do is different from what should be done, all things considered, just as what there is a right to do is different from what the right-holder actually gets to do, all things considered. Thus, my right to freedom of speech does not evaporate even when I am permissibly restricted from speaking because of a compelling state interest. And so too, my obligation to keep my luncheon appointments and to teach my classes at the designated times does not disappear even when it is overridden by, say, my obligation to attend to ailing relatives.

With this account of what are sometimes called "prima facie" rights and obligations in hand, we can see with little difficulty how authorities can be authoritative without being conclusively authoritative. The existence of an authoritative reason is not inconsistent with there being other outweighing authoritative reasons or outweighing reasons of other kinds. When a court rules that even the crisp rules of an applicable statute must yield at times to the demands of justice, it is saying that an undeniably applicable statute is to be understood as prima facie but not absolutely outcome producing. In this sense, it is certainly true that most authorities are not binding or controlling in an absolute way. And the suggestion that treating some source as authoritative requires that the prescriptions emanating from that source must be followed, come what may, is simply not part of the concept of authority at all.

Yet although neither mandatory nor optional authorities need be absolute in order to retain their authoritative status, it is important to recall from the conclusion in the previous section that even optional authorities can be genuinely authoritative. And this explains why those who object to the use of foreign law really do have, from their perspective, something to worry about. Neither the optional nor the non-conclusive aspect of using foreign law prevents it from being taken seriously as an authority, which is exactly what the objectors are concerned about. Similarly, when courts issue no-precedential-effect rules for a class of cases, their concern is not a worry that what the court has quickly and casually said in some earlier opinion will be totally controlling in a subsequent case. Rather, the worry is that what a court may have said entirely for the benefit of the parties and without careful (or any) consideration of the implications for other cases will even be used as a reason in subsequent cases.[74] The court simply wants to deny the

---

74. There is an interesting analytic point here. A court that makes a rule in Case 1 is, by virtue of the necessarily generalizing feature of all rules, making a rule that will presumptively apply in Case 2, Case 3, [etc.]. So when a court considers in Case 1 whether some rule will generate the correct result in Case 1 will also generate the correct result in, say, Case 2, Case 3, and Case 4, it is open to the possibility that it might be required to reach the wrong all-things-considered result in Case 1, the case before it, in order to avoid providing reasons for future incorrect results in Cases 2, 3, and 4. If a court wishes to avoid incorrect results in the cases before it, therefore, one way of doing so is to try to ensure that those results do not become reasons in other and future cases.

authority,[75] even if not the absolute authority, of its own casual, rushed, or simply overly party-focused statements.

Similarly, when the Middlebury College Department of History prohibited its students from citing to Wikipedia, it was not (only) worried that Middlebury students would take whatever is in Wikipedia as absolute and unchallenged gospel. That is a risk, but we would hope that for Middlebury students it is a remote one. What is less remote, however, is the possibility that Middlebury students will consider Wikipedia entries to be authoritative — to be serious sources of information — and this, even without the absolutism, is what the faculty presumably wishes to guard against. Indeed, Middlebury's prohibition on Wikipedia is similar to the strong warnings against citing *Corpus Juris Secondum* or *American Jurisprudence* that are, among other things, a staple of legal writing instruction for first-year law students.

Thus, there is a shared worry of Justice Scalia and others with respect to foreign law, of the Middlebury History Department with respect to Wikipedia, of overworked appellate courts that dash off brief opinions for the benefit of the parties, of a legal system that frowns on citation to legal encyclopedias, and indeed of a Supreme Court that warns about the uniqueness of *Bush v. Gore*, that will not treat its denials of certiorari as authoritative, and that in *every* one of its decisions warns against taking the syllabus as authority. And this is the worry that to recognize something as authority, even optional and non-conclusive authority, is to take it seriously as a source and thus to treat its guidance and information as worthy of respect. That a legal system premised to its core on the very notion of authority would worry about what it is treating as authoritative should come as little surprise.

IV. HOW DO AUTHORITIES BECOME AUTHORITATIVE?

Although I have drawn a seemingly sharp distinction between mandatory and optional authorities, the reality is more complex, and it is a reality that likely further fuels the worries of Justice Scalia, the Middlebury history department, the circuit judges guarding the purity of no-citation rules, and many others. For in reality, the status of a source as an authority is the product of an informal, evolving, and scalar process by which some sources become progressively more and more authoritative as they are increasingly used and accepted. It was formerly the practice in English courts, for example, to treat as impermissible the citation in an argument or judicial

---

75. The *Anastasoff* issue seems to involve the distinct questions of precedent-stripping and citation-prohibiting. Implicit in my argument here, however, is that the two may be more closely related than either the *Anastasoff* court or most of the commentators have appreciated. Citation is not just a pathway to precedent; it is the language the law uses to embody its precedential character. To prohibit the citation of decisions that may have precedential effect is to endorse the existence of secret law, the unacceptability of which explains the impetus for the new Rule 32.1 of the Federal Rules of Appellate Procedure. But a precedent-stripping rule without a no-citation rule may be toothless, because even formally nonprecedential but still citable decisions may exert constraining and path-dependency-creating effects on future decisions.

opinion to a secondary source written by a still-living author. If the author of a treatise or (rarely) an article were dead, then citation was permissible, but not otherwise. The reasons for this practice remain somewhat obscure, but that is not important here. What is important is the fact that the prohibition gradually withered, a withering that commenced more or less when the House of Lords in 1945 cited to a work by the then-living Arthur Goodhart. Once the first citation to a living secondary author appeared, subsequent courts became slightly less hesitant to do the same thing, and over time the practice became somewhat more acceptable.

There is nothing unusual about this example. Although H.L.A. Hart made famous the idea of a *rule of recognition*, it is rare that formal rules determine what is to be recognized as law or as a legitimate citation in a legal brief, argument, or opinion. Rather, as Brian Simpson has insightfully described, the recognition and non-recognition of law and legal sources is better understood as a *practice* in the Wittgensteinian sense: a practice in which lawyers, judges, commentators, and other legal actors gradually and in diffuse fashion determine what will count as law. Justice Scalia, the Middlebury history department, and the guardians of no-citation rules thus have some genuine basis for worrying that legitimizing the use of this or that source will set in motion a considerably more expansive process. Indeed, a legal citation has an important double aspect. A citation to a particular source is not only a statement by the citer that this is a good source but also a statement that sources *of this type* are legitimate. Citation practice is a practice, and thus an institution, and consequently every citation to a particular source legitimizes the institution of using sources of that type.

What is especially intriguing is the transformation of authoritativeness. How does it come to be that optional or even prohibited authorities over time turn into mandatory ones? Although the Tenth Circuit would be doing nothing wrong by failing to cite to the Second Circuit in a securities case, the failure to cite to the most prominent court on securities matters would likely raise some eyebrows. And the higher the eyebrows are raised, the more that what is in some sense optional is in another sense mandatory. For example, it is virtually impossible to argue or decide an evidence case in the Massachusetts Supreme Judicial Court without making reference to Liacos's *Handbook of Massachusetts Evidence* or its successor. Likewise, it was formerly difficult to argue a Charter of Rights and Freedoms case in the Supreme Court of Canada without nodding to American Supreme Court decisions. Jurisdictional boundaries are generally reliable markers of which authorities are optional and which are mandatory, but just as there are questionable within-jurisdiction authorities, so too can there be non-questionable out-of-jurisdiction authorities. And it is likely that a further fear of Justice Scalia and others about the citation of foreign and international law is that at some point these out-of-jurisdiction sources will become not only legitimate sources but also mandatory ones.

Thus, for Justice Scalia (and others) with reference to foreign and international law, for legal writing instructors counseling first-year law students about which authorities are permissible citations and which are not, and for appellate courts wrestling with no-citation rules, the question is nothing less than what to count as law. When Justice Breyer, in *Parents Involved in Community Schools v. Seattle School*

District No. 1, provides two pages of sources, mostly historical and administrative, and mostly not to be found in the briefs or the record below, his citation practice not only speaks volumes about what for him counts as law and what it is for him to *do* law, but also, and perhaps more importantly, his citations serve an authoritative (although less so because he was in dissent) function in telling lawyers and judges what they can *use* to make legal arguments and thus in telling lawyers and judges what law is. For Justice Scalia, Judge Posner, and others, the debate about foreign law is not a debate about citation. Instead, it is a debate about the rule of recognition or the *grundnorm*, to use Kelsen's term for a similar but not identical idea. What Justice Scalia fears is precisely that the political and legal decisions of another nation, the world community, or the creators of international law will have actual influence and effect — as authority in the strong sense — on American law. What Justice Scalia and Judge Posner fear may to some of us appear to be more opportunity than threat, but it seems a mistake to believe that from their lights they have nothing to worry about.

V. CONCLUSION: THE BOUNDARIES OF LAW

A large part of my goal here is to connect the seemingly trivial idea of citation to far less trivial questions about authority, a connection which then leads to rather more profound questions about what is a source of law and what is law itself. If law is an authoritative practice, then a great deal turns on what the authorities are. Why the Supreme Court and the Congress of the United States but not the President and Fellows of Harvard College or the editorial board of the *New York Times*? Why the Federal Trade Commission but not the board of directors of Wal-Mart? Why Loss and Seligman but not Marx and Engels? Why the *Harvard Law Review* but not the *Village Voice*? Why the writings of Thomas Jefferson but not of Jefferson Davis?

It is interesting that none of the rhetorical questions in the previous paragraph are strictly rhetorical. At least in American courts, citation practice is now undergoing rapid change, and we have seen a great increase not only in citations to non-American sources, but also to sources that not so many years ago would have been sneeringly dismissed as "non-legal." This change in citation practice reflects something deeper: a change in what counts as a *legal* argument. And what counts as a legal argument — as opposed to a moral, religious, economic, or political one — is the principal component in determining just what law is. To be clear, the claim I make here is not that citation practice or the selection of legal authorities is a marker or indicator of what law is. This is not (only) a "miner's canary" claim. Rather, the claim is that what counts as a good legal authority is the determinant and not just the indicator of what law is. Both the language and the decisionmaking modalities of law place weight on the preexisting. Citation is thus law's way of justifying its conclusions in law's characteristically incremental and partially backward-looking way. It may turn out, therefore, that far greater attention to disputes about citation and the nature of permissible legal authorities will yield greater insight not only into how law operates, but also into just what law is.

Chad Flanders

TOWARD A THEORY OF PERSUASIVE AUTHORITY

62 Okla. L. Rev. 55 (2009)

I. THE CONVENTIONAL PICTURE OF PERSUASIVE AUTHORITY

A. Binding Authority: Precedent and Stare Decisis

It will be best to introduce the conventional wisdom on the subject of persuasive authority by rehearsing what I hope are some familiar facts about authority that is "binding." Begin with the idea that decisions of a higher court in the United States constitutional system are binding on lower courts. Call this, following custom, "precedent." According to this familiar notion, lower courts *must* follow the decisions of a higher court on an identical matter. Of course, it will often be difficult to discern when the higher court has ruled on an identical matter: problems regarding distinguishing holding and dicta emerge here, but the basic principle is clear. At the very least, a lower court that does not follow the decision of a higher court on a similar matter will virtually guarantee that its decision will be overturned on appeal, should there be an appeal. But that is only to state the issue as a merely predictive (i.e., descriptive) matter. This would surely understate the normative force that precedent is supposed to have in our system: a lower court that does not follow the higher court's binding precedent has done something *wrong* as a legal matter. It has not discharged its role properly as a lower court. Thus, it is not simply that the court has done something which will, as a predictive matter, lead to the overturning of its judgment. A judgment which does not follow the higher court precedent is simply incorrect, even if it is not the subject of an appeal. By stressing this normative aspect, I mean to show how the higher court has authority over the lower court, and that this authority is not merely a matter of power, or at least it is not considered to be merely a matter of power. It is a matter of following the law, or of·"legality," and legality is a normative principle.

Closely related to this—at least in the conventional picture—is the idea of stare decisis. On this picture, at least on a first approximation, a single court is bound by the past decisions on relevantly similar matters of the same court. So where the picture of precedent is one in which higher constrains lower, the picture of stare decisis is one of the past constraining the present. For the Supreme Court, there is no higher authority, so all that binds it is its past decisions. The idea is that the past court stands in the same relation to the present court as a higher court stands to a lower court.

This is not quite right, though, because a court can change its mind. The dead hand of the court's own past is not totally binding in the same way that the command of a higher court is binding on a lower court. The question of when and why it can change is a vexed and mysterious one . . . . In the case of stare decisis, we seem not to be dealing with metaphors of the inexorable command of a superior, but with a metaphor of weight: the past decisions of the same court on similar matters should be given great weight, so that strong reasons need to be brought to bear to depart from that decision. The somewhat shaky nature of the force of past decisions can be seen by the need to shore up the doctrine of stare decisis with considerations such as the desire for stability or uniformity across time. Such considerations do not, and should not, apply in cases of applying precedent: the decision of the higher court may be cumbersome and awkward (not to mention false) and create confusion and uncertainty, but these factors do not give the lower court license to depart from the decision of a higher court.

We can say this, for now, knowing that we will return to this issue later: at least for the run of the mill case, the past decision of the same court will be binding on it *in much the same way* that the decision of a higher court would be. That is, it will function as if it were an inexorable command, simply to be followed and not revisited — not examined on the basis of its merits, but simply taken as given and as already decided. Even in the more complicated case, the past decision exerts some weight, so that reasons will have to be brought to bear to show why departure from the past case is warranted. In short, stare decisis has a dual aspect: a court's own past decision (1) can be treated as absolutely binding and perhaps simply cited without comment, or else (2) it can be treated as having a great weight.

But although stare decisis does have this dual aspect, at least one of those aspects shows it to be very clearly in the same category of "bindingness" as precedent is. And the second aspect, too, shows the strength of a past decision, even if that strength is not total, so that it simply forecloses any further discussion. There is at least some extra hurdle to overcome if the court determines that the past decision should be departed from; it cannot simply be noted and then departed from, it must receive an acknowledgment and rebuttal, showing why the decision no longer has any force. To fail to do so would also be a legal error: to fail to address a relevant and similar decision made earlier by the same court would render the decision at the very least defective and possibly mistaken — an inferior opinion, from the legal point of view.[24]

B. Persuasive Authority

By contrast, persuasive authority has neither of these elements; persuasive authority does not "bind" nor does a court *need* to reckon with it because of the gravitational pull it exerts or the weight that it has. Persuasive authority, to start, has no independent binding force; no court is bound to follow the dictates of an authority

---

24. It is not automatically a legal error because it could be assumed that the court has overruled the prior precedent *sub silentio*.

that is merely persuasive. Nor does persuasive authority, unlike decisions that have been made by the same court earlier, have weight that needs to be acknowledged and addressed just because of the type of decision it is.[27] A court need not mention any contrary persuasive authority unless it wants to; whereas a court would be mistaken, perhaps even mistaken as a matter of law, if a previous decision is contrary to the present one.[28] And this gives us at least the beginnings of what I want to claim is the first accepted truth about persuasive authority: persuasive authority is any authority which is not binding on courts. . . .

Here we are in a better position to see what this means because binding can mean being authoritative, as with precedent, or it can mean being required to give it consideration, as with stare decisis. . . . [W]e can say that cases that have a mandatory or binding authority are authoritative just by virtue of what they are, rather than what they say. A court must follow a decision relevant and on point by a higher court, and a court must at least consider and weigh — if only ultimately to reject — a past decision it has made. Precedent and stare decisis bind a court by virtue of pedigree, not solely by virtue of the merits of the cases decided. Persuasive authority does not bind in this way, and this gives us its first definition: authority that does not bind intrinsically.

Now, we will shortly get to what remains of persuasive authority's "authority" when it is defined by not being binding: this may seem to indicate it is not an authority at all, if it is only authoritative by virtue of what it says rather than what it is. But I want for the moment simply to focus on the negative aspect of persuasive authority — defining it by what it is not — and to provide some paradigmatic examples of authorities that are only persuasive.

In principle, subject to the constraints of being "authoritative" (whatever this turns out to mean), the set of persuasive authorities could be nearly limitless. The class of authorities that are binding is very small relative to the number of things that are non-binding. And what types of sources could be persuasive to a given judge is an open question.

But in practice, things turn out to be different. Not anything and everything is cited as persuasive authority. To orient ourselves, we can make a preliminary list of sources that are cited that are nonetheless non-binding on courts. I offer this list in a rough order to indicate what I believe to be, as an empirical matter, the frequency of use of these sources. I will try to suggest later . . . that there is more than simply an empirical grounding for this "ordering" of sources, and that it may also reflect a hierarchy of sorts among persuasive authorities. The important thing about this list, for the moment, is just that it contains those things which are not binding on courts, but to which courts, in the course of their reasoning, sometimes refer.

---

27. In fact, persuasive authorities need not be decisions from another *court* at all.
28. Hence the rule in many jurisdictions that parties have to present authorities from the court that are directly contrary to their position.

1. Other courts outside of the court's own jurisdiction, whether other circuit courts or other state courts (majority and concurring opinion).[33]

2. The laws of other states or of the federal government and agency regulations.

3. Legislative history or debates, especially if the question is one of statutory interpretation.[34]

4. Restatements of the law, such as the Restatement of Torts or Contracts.

5. Treatises, such as Laurence Tribe's *American Constitutional Law*.

6. Law review articles, notes, and comments.

7. Other academic sources, such as book-length treatments of an issue (e.g., John Rawls's *Theory of Justice*) or empirical or economic studies of a certain matter.

8. General interest sources (books, periodicals, and possibly literary sources).

9. General news sources (newspapers and magazines).

10. Internet sources, including blogs.

11. Moral principles themselves, such as the golden rule or the idea of equality.

12. Discouraged, but in principle possible sources: memorandum opinions and judgments, the Bible, the *National Enquirer*, the judge's father-in-law.[41]

All of these are sources that courts might cite, but are not binding on the courts. Citations to other courts are not binding because they are from places other than the court's own jurisdiction.[42] The binding authority these decisions may have in their own jurisdiction (their own state or own circuit or own nation) does not extend to any other jurisdiction. Therefore, although they are binding authorities in one aspect, they are not binding authorities when a court from outside their jurisdiction cites them. The lack of bindingness of sources 4-12 is even more obvious. A restatement of the law is composed by people, some of whom may be judges,

---

33. In their recent book, Justice Scalia and Bryan Garner suggest that dicta from the same court should have a higher place than this in a ranking of *persuasive* authority. ANTONIN SCALIA & BRYAN GARNER, MAKING YOUR CASE: THE ART OF PERSUADING JUDGES 53 (2008). I disagree. Dicta is too close to binding authority — and may actually be binding authority, given the slippery distinction between dicta and holding. . . . A harder example is a decision by the same court on an analogous matter. Is this to be considered along the lines of a holding, or as only persuasive? . . . But for the time being, I can bracket such cases, as I am only interested in a hierarchy of what is conventionally agreed to be persuasive authority.

34. There may be disagreement on this point. For some, legislative history may not be persuasive, but something more than this: it may be authoritative on matters of interpretation.

41. The last three are suggested by Schauer in *Authority and Authorities*. I deliberately leave off this list foreign courts. This is an obviously controversial example, which some *might* put under "forbidden authorities," but which others might put very high on the list.

42. There is, of course, the exception of when a higher court cites a lower court as persuasive authority. These are in the same jurisdiction, but the lower court does not bind the higher court.

but the restatement itself does not establish or promulgate a rule over anyone. Nor does a treatise, however eminent the author. And articles, novels, or blogs have no power to bind.

Given our first statement about persuasive authority, we know what unites these sources, at least partly, is what they are not: all of them share the feature of not being binding on the courts who cite them. No court is required to obey or even to confront Rawls's *Theory of Justice*, or even an article written on a case in the same jurisdiction that is well-written, insightful, and on-point. But we can also say something positive about them according to the conventional understanding of persuasive authority. Even though these sources do not have any power over courts by virtue of what they are (a source that is intrinsically authoritative), they still can have a power by virtue of what they *say*, if they say it persuasively.

In other words, if one of these sources makes an argument that a judge or court finds convincing, then to that extent, the source has some authority over the judge — whether that authority means that the judge should follow it because the reasoning is compelling, or merely that the judge has to take it into account. The important thing about the source's authority is that it is not a matter of will or fiat, it is a matter of persuasiveness, or even of reasonableness. In Habermas's winning phrase, the force of persuasive authority is the unforced force of the better argument. Habermas's formulation is particularly apt because it manages to capture the somewhat paradoxical idea that an authority could be authoritative merely be virtue of its persuasiveness — that there is something about a good argument that exerts control over us, even a control that is analogous (but perhaps only analogous) to the command of a superior officer.

Is it puzzling to speak of persuasive *authority*? Why not simply persuasive *sources*? Indeed, one might argue that the only persuasive authorities are the decisions of other courts because they at least have some authority over something — as opposed to the author of *A Theory of Justice*. But even that is a bit of a stretch: one jurisdiction has no authority over another, so its decision has no more power to bind than the words of John Rawls. So do we have persuasive authorities or persuasive sources, because persuasion and authority are opposed notions? . . . There is a perfectly familiar way that we might feel ourselves compelled by a particularly good argument or way of phrasing something. It can feel — and this may only be a feeling — that we are somehow, if only subtly, coerced into accepting the argument. It can have the feeling of being subject to an imperative. We might feel that we are, in a sense, commanded by reason, and have no choice but to submit to it. So to this extent it is not too far off to say that persuasive reasons can be authoritative, if only in a metaphorical and not a literal sense.

But we should be careful to cabin the authority that persuasive authorities possess. Suppose that a judge or a court finds a decision of another court outside of its jurisdiction extremely persuasive, so much so that he finds that he must follow its logic in the case before him. Is that decision binding? However binding it is on the conscience of the judge, it cannot be binding as a matter of law. Such are the limits of persuasive authority. It can have all the logical, moral, and even emotional power you like, but it can never rise to the level of having any legal force. It can only have any legal force once it is adopted into a decision by the court. Prior to its adoption, it is only as strong or as weak as its ability to persuade a court or a judge. Note that this means that even if the judge thinks that the argument is so powerful as to be unassailable, the judge makes no *legal* error if he disregards the argument in writing his own opinion. The judge can be faulted for bad (or unpersuasive) reasoning, but not for making a legal mistake.[53]

So we are left with two basic conventional points about persuasive authority. First, it is not binding. It does not have the power to be authoritative over other courts such that courts must follow it or must give it weight in their deliberations, no matter what the non-binding decision says. Second, the authority it holds flows from the persuasive content of the authority. A book or article or judicial opinion only compels by what it says, not by what it is. To have any legal force, a persuasive authority must be adopted into a legal decision — and it does so only by persuading a judge or a court. I take these two points to be fairly straightforward, and nearly universally accepted in law review articles and books on legal writing and research. I now want to try to introduce some nuances into them and to slowly encourage you, if not to reject them, at least to hold them somewhat qualifiedly and not uncritically.

II. RANKING PERSUASIVE AUTHORITIES

In the previous section, I made a list — admittedly provisional and incomplete — about various persuasive sources that courts have and could refer to: other court decisions, law reviews, treatises, blog postings, etc. The list was placed in a rough ordering of frequency of use, based on no more advanced empirical evidence than my own rough sense of citation counts.[55] All else being equal, courts are more likely to cite other courts than law review articles. What I want to point out is that there is no reason given on the conventional picture I sketched in the previous part why some sources should be cited more often than other sources. On the conventional picture, as I shall put it, the sources of persuasive authority are

---

53. Frederick Schauer makes the interesting suggestion that sometimes a certain circuit will be regarded as more authoritative on a certain issue (his example is the Second Circuit on securities regulation). Relying on the expertise of the court, he intimates, is treating that source as a genuinely non-persuasive authority — that is, using it as a source without regard to the content of its reasoning. First off, this does not distinguish court opinions from other persuasive sources courts may use in an "authoritative" way (a court may defer to an economist, say, without truly comprehending her methods). Second, it is not clear that the trust in the case is wholly divorced from the content of the reasoning. A court may hearken to the Second Circuit, but it will not follow it simply because it is the Second Circuit. In a similar way, a court may pay special attention to a decision by Richard Posner, but it will not defer to him *independently* of what he says. It just means that the court has previously found Posner a good judge to turn to when facing a difficult problem. I do not think it is the best analysis of these cases that the court will be persuaded by the "fact that the authority is an authority." Rather, the "authority" will be initially consulted because it/he/she is an authority; the decision to follow that authority, however, will be based on that authority's reasons.

55. Perhaps not coincidentally, this ranking of sources roughly mirrors the ranking found in *The Bluebook*.

undifferentiated: there is no reason why one kind of source should necessarily be cited more often than any other kind of source. Law review comments could have been cited more often than other court opinions, but they are not. This is just how it happens to be. There is no intrinsic reason why court opinions should be considered more "persuasive" than other sources.

This conclusion of course has to follow if the only reason why persuasive authorities have authority is because of their persuasiveness, rather than their pedigree. There does not seem to be any reason to assume that court opinions will always be more persuasive than other sources. A law review article might explain an issue and make an argument better than a Supreme Court opinion, especially one done under time pressure. And indeed, there is no general reason, at least in the conventional story, why a dissent in a court opinion from another jurisdiction might not have greater persuasive authority than a majority or concurring opinion. Also, an empirical study by a sociologist might provide more insight than legislative history could. A book by Richard Posner could be more persuasive than an opinion by Judge Richard Posner. And so on and so forth.

The undifferentiated nature of the list — the fact that persuasive authority is any source that is persuasive — does not give us any reason to make a hierarchy of sources in any normative sense, but only in the sense that, as a matter of fact, some sources get cited more often than others. Indeed, as a matter of principle, the list should be somewhat fluid. In some cases, it will be better to cite an empirical study; in other cases, it will be better to cite a court opinion. It will all depend on the context, and we should not expect one type of source to be, as a general matter, more persuasive. Thus, in the conventional picture, the repeated citation to other courts is a little anomalous. Why should courts have a special priority, if not in any evaluative sense, but on the basis of the numbers? Why legal authorities and not "the latest book from Habermas"?

But this may be too quick. Perhaps, contrary to the conventional picture strictly construed but still in the spirit of that picture, we can point to some general features of some types of sources that show why they tend to be more persuasive, or at least seem to be so. We can start near the bottom of the list, just to get an initial idea of how this could be so. Books on philosophy for instance, will less likely persuade, or be found to persuade, because they often will not directly address the issue that the court faces; or if it does address the issue, it will not approach it in exactly the same way. A general treatise on justice, for instance, like Rawls's *Theory of Justice*, will not always have much to say about whether one reading of a state regulation will be more correct than another interpretation. The considerations adduced by Rawls will simply be too abstract, and will not admit of any ready translation into the deciphering of the meaning of a state regulation. Rawls may at best simply be irrelevant. This is not to say that in some context Rawls will not be illuminating: for instance, there is a fair case to be made that Rawls is very useful in understanding the Equal Protection Clause. But in the ordinary, banal statutory interpretation case, Rawls might not be of much use.

Now let us return to the top of the list, and examine the opinions of courts from other jurisdictions. There are a number of things we can say about why court opinions will likely be found to be more relevant and useful, and hence more persuasive, than other sources such as a novel or a treatise. For starters, we might imagine that courts will routinely face the same type of problems. Whereas Rawls might only speak of justice in the abstract, courts repeatedly face questions concerning individual liability or questions of contract interpretation. Although one case from one court will probably never be exactly the same as a case from another, there will be certain situations that repeatedly arise and which parties will litigate in similar ways. So if one court is looking to find what another source will say in a similar situation, he may find it more likely that another *court*, as opposed to another book or article, will have faced that situation. To be sure, what another court says about what to do in that situation might not be very enlightening. But it will be more likely that what the court says could be relevant, and this relevancy would explain, at least partly, why courts cite other courts so much: they give insight on situations faced by courts on a regular basis.

More than this, we can say that courts will face like issues with the same sort of tools that another court has at its disposal. A court facing an issue, unlike an article or a book, will have to consider things such as canons of statutory construction, or questions of whether and when summary judgment is appropriate. Such terms are foreign to — taking my favored example — Rawls's *Theory of Justice*. So a court looking to see whether summary judgment would be appropriate will not find much help in looking to works in philosophy or sociology. Those sources will not confront the issue with the same techniques, nor, to put it perhaps a better way, will they work under the same constraints. That means that the decisions of other courts will be speaking the same language as the court which seeks to learn from and be persuaded by it.

Of course, these last two points may not sufficiently narrow our inquiry to the decisions of other courts. Law review articles, and especially notes and comments, may simply be a legal analysis of a case. A law review article will also be dealing with a situation that many courts will face — indeed, it could be precisely because the issue is a common one that the law review article is seeking to explain it. And the law review article could also try to deal with a case using legal tools and terminology. This point is well taken, and serves to show again the truth in the idea that the realm of persuasive authority is a relatively fluid one: what kind of source is persuasive in one instance will not always be persuasive in another instance. A court opinion, for the reasons stated above, will sometimes be helpful to another court, but a law review article could be helpful for precisely the same reasons.

Still, we should remind ourselves that here we are only looking at why citations to court opinions will likely be more frequent in the aggregate. We are not looking to show that courts will always prefer courts to other sources. And surely it pays to point out that there are many more court opinions than law review articles. As a result, it is more likely that a court will find a closer analogy to its own case in another court's decision rather than a law review article, especially if the situation at issue is not all that common. So, if only by virtue of the fact that there are more court opinions than law review articles that deal solely with cases, there will be a greater reliance — in the aggregate — on opinions of other courts. Note, too, that the law review article is parasitic on the court opinion: the author of the article is seeking to explicate a case, not merely a hypothetical.

But we can say more than this about court opinions and why other courts rely on them. Courts have to go through a process that law review authors do not encounter. Courts are presented with arguments from two competing sides (in most cases) and must weigh those arguments. Moreover, courts have to make a decision and that decision will actually have consequences in the real world. So courts are concerned with the practical effects of their decisions, in a way that law review articles generally need not be. In this way, being an authority actually matters, even if that authority is not over another court that may cite its opinion as a persuasive authority. A court will have to anticipate (and eventually deal with) the practical consequences of the decisions it makes. Finally, a judge writing an opinion may have to persuade a majority of his or her colleagues to agree with her. This will entail modifying the judge's position to anticipate objections, or perhaps even moderating the decision in order to forge a winning coalition. An opinion that wins over one judge on a three-judge panel may be less persuasive than an opinion that garners unanimity.

Again, we can minimize the actual difference these variances may make. Law review articles usually go through a process of review and revision and must (if they are any good) anticipate objections to their position. The process of having to defend an article may, in some instances, mimic the effect of the adversarial process and the obligation to win a majority for one's opinion. Also, a conscientious scholar will be interested not merely in the abstract theoretical virtues of her legal positions but in their practical consequences and their workability. Both of these things are true, and they show again how, in various contingent circumstances, a well written law review article will be more persuasive than a court opinion. But again we are only dealing now in *tendencies*. And given legal procedures and constraints, the tendency may be that a court's decision will be more persuasive to another court than a law review article more times than not. A judge may have to actually win votes for his or her position; a law review author need only convince a journal to publish her piece.

Further, note how this last tendency speaks not only to the fact that court decisions will be more relevant than law review articles or treatises most of the time, but that they actually may be *better* because they are the outcome of a process with constraints — hearing both sides of an argument and having to render a decision that can accommodate those arguments (or at least address them). This is not a claim that judges will be smarter than the average academic. Rather, it is a claim that there are structural features of court systems that will make their decisions possibly more compelling, simply as a matter of presentation and argument, to other courts. By this time, I should not need to emphasize again that I am talking about tendencies, not in absolutes. The hypothesis I am now offering is that courts are more likely to be considered "persuasive" both because they are more likely to be relevant, but also because they are more likely to be well-reasoned or better argued or simply in a generic sense more "persuasive" given the constraints of the legal way of doing things.

I said earlier that on the conventional way of looking at persuasive authority, the category of persuasive authority is undifferentiated. By that I meant that there was no pure ranking of the sources of persuasive authority, so that some authorities were automatically more persuasive than others. Indeed, this would be contrary to the animating idea of the conventional picture, which is that sources only have their authority to the extent that they are persuasive. And the "undifferentiated" thesis is that we cannot say, a priori, that some sources will be more persuasive than others. In some contexts, a novel or a philosophy book will be more relevant and useful, and hence, more persuasive than the decision of another court. Nothing I have said in this section has yet shown this to be false.

But the picture is, nonetheless, more complicated than this, because we can point to tendencies that explain why citation to other courts will be more frequent than citations to other authorities. We can say, as a general matter, that the decisions of other courts will be more relevant to courts because courts are routinely faced with similar situations and will have to resolve controversies using similar sorts of tools. And we can even hazard that courts have various checks and constraints that make their decision making better, and hence, more helpful to other courts. Again, these are generalizations. But they are generalizations that make the conventional picture more sophisticated, while still staying within the conventional picture. Nothing in what was said above requires that due to these features courts must defer to courts outside of their jurisdiction, or even that they have to refer to them at all. Importantly, I have not said in this section that some sources will be more persuasive than others because of their pedigree. I have only pointed to factors that show why courts might in more cases than not be more persuasive; I have not said that courts will be more persuasive *merely* because they are courts. A badly reasoned court decision will be less persuasive than a good law review article, even though it is the product of a court that has had arguments presented to it in an adversarial fashion and will have to produce an opinion that will win the votes of a majority of judges.[68] This is how the conventional picture says it should be. I want to suggest next that there are reasons for going beyond the conventional picture.

III. THE INTRINSIC PERSUASIVENESS OF SOME PERSUASIVE AUTHORITIES: FROM PERSUASIVE AUTHORITY TO SUPER PERSUASIVE AUTHORITY

In the previous Part, I tried as best I could to stay within the conventional picture regarding persuasive authority, but at the same time attempted to give that picture much more nuance. That nuance included showing how some authorities, namely courts, could be seen as *generally* more persuasive than other authorities. But is this all we can say about the authority of courts that are outside of the jurisdiction of the deciding court? . . .

I do not think . . . that this is all we can say about why courts cite other courts with a greater frequency than they do other persuasive sources. And to get to this

---

68. Indeed, there will even be distinctions between various courts being used as persuasive authorities. A recent court decision may be thought more persuasive than an older one. A court decision made by a higher level court may be thought to be more persuasive than the opinion of a lower level court (if only because the higher court has the benefit of the lower court's decision). Unanimous opinions will be more persuasive than majority opinions, etc.

conclusion, we have to depart from the traditional picture, which sees the authority of other courts as only persuasive authorities — that is, authoritative only insofar as they actually *persuade* the deciding court with their reasoning. In this section, I will suggest that other courts can have an authority just by virtue of being a *court* that decides, and not necessarily only because a judicial decision's reasoning is particularly persuasive. We might consider these to be "super-persuasive" authorities . . . . These authorities would have an additional weight, beyond their persuasiveness . . . . We might wonder: how could there be such sources? But they exist, and I will argue that they are a familiar part of the legal landscape.

Of course, super persuasive authorities would still ultimately be *optional* authorities — to use Frederick Schauer's helpful term — because they are not binding in the sense that courts must follow them or risk being in legal error. I will not be arguing that these super persuasive authorities *must* be cited by other courts. But I will suggest that some persuasive authorities do have an authority ordinarily thought to be held only by mandatory authorities. Courts who looked to other courts as being "super persuasive" not only borrow reasons from the other courts, but also look[ed] to that court's status *as a court* as a factor influencing their decision making. In this respect, I hope to show that the power of courts as persuasive authorities sometimes more closely approximates the pull that the past decisions of the same court can have, or even a higher court: they are authorities by virtue of what they are, and not (only) by virtue of what they say.

. . . In general, [courts] cite other courts because they are trying to make their decisions consistent with the decisions of those other courts. Why this is thought to be necessary in any given case will differ. But we can say, as a general matter, that sometimes courts will want to harmonize their decisions in other courts either because (1) there is some right answer for courts facing the question, and disagreement between courts implies that at least one court is wrong; (2) there is some independent good achieved by uniformity with other courts, such as stability or predictability across jurisdictional lines; or (3) because not to reach the same result as another court would be to fail to treat "like cases alike" on some relevantly similar factual situation, thus violating the legal principle of fairness.

. . . When does the court of another jurisdiction have authority just by virtue of being another court? I isolate three instances: First, when circuit courts cite other circuit courts, not merely for their informational or persuasive value, but because they seek to avoid a circuit split; second, when state courts aim to harmonize their interpretation of state "uniform" acts with other states based on the fact that those other states have adopted the same uniform act; and third, in common law jurisdictions, when states seek to harmonize their doctrines with the judicially crafted doctrines of other states. . . .

. . . .

D. Why Uniformity?

This pull towards conformity, present to a greater or lesser extent in all three examples cited above, should not strike us as a foreign or mysterious value in law — far from it. In addition to the above instances, uniformity is at the core of the doctrine of stare decisis. Stare decisis seeks uniformity across time and recognizes that there is a good to stability and uniformity in the same court. It is good that legal expectations be settled, and it is a legal imperative that like cases be treated alike, perhaps even at the risk of a substantive injustice. A court that simply disregarded its past decisions would disturb legitimately formed expectations, and it would also introduce unfairness, showing its rules to be arbitrary and ad hoc. Uniformity acts as a meta-constraint on a deciding court, but it is a constraint informed by substantive values that are uniquely legal. A court may, and should, decide each case on the merits. But it also must look at its own past and make sure that it is deciding each case in conformity with its own past. There is no mystery here in the bare legal value of uniformity, or as we might also put it, of consistency.

If stare decisis involves a uniformity across time, then the citation of other courts as authorities involves a uniformity across space with other courts. In the same way that a court looks to its own past decisions to try to bring its present self into conformity with its past self, courts may look to other courts to make their decisions congruent with one another. To be sure, courts do not have to cite other courts, or bring their caselaw into conformity with the law of other circuits, or of other states. But neither is stare decisis an "inexorable command": an old decision can be overturned if it is no longer applicable, if circumstances have changed, or if few people rely on the decision any longer. All of these are relevant considerations. But they do not stop stare decisis from dictating that the past decision of a court is something that the court should consider and assign weight. In a like manner, some court decisions may not always be very persuasive. The decisions of even a majority of courts can be wrong, and not useful, and should be departed from. Nonetheless, the decisions of other courts may deserve recognition and even consideration if the cases are very closely related or on point, and there are strong reasons for uniformity or consistency in that area of law.

Indeed, the more courts that have decided a matter in a certain way, the greater weight those decisions may be said to have, and not necessarily because consensus is a measure of truth. The reason decisions from other jurisdictions might deserve recognition is the same as the reason that the past decisions of the same court deserve recognition: to achieve uniformity to avoid the appearance of a checkerboard of legal principles across jurisdictions. The same values of settling expectations and of treating like cases alike are as much at play between courts as they are within the same courts. As one court put it, courts have an obligation to "promote predictability and stability through satisfaction of mutual expectations." There is no a priori reason why this interest in predictability and stability should stop at jurisdictional borders.

The only difference (and it is a major one) is that it may be harder to see cases as "similar" across jurisdictions, and so it may be harder to see uniformity across jurisdictions as a good to be achieved, because it is simply not a good to be had. There may be different laws, even different legal traditions, across jurisdictions. And this will prevent exactly similar cases from springing up across jurisdictions. It will tend to diminish the possibility that there was any uniformity of expectations to be preserved across the jurisdictions in the first place. Even among states in the United States, there will be a diversity of laws and legal cultures, and a court's duty should be to attend to the distinctiveness of its own jurisdiction. Moreover, uniformity is not a good above all else. The point that some make in objecting to the citation of foreign authorities has special weight when it is made in this spirit, emphasizing differences and distinctiveness, and opposing an unthinking uniformity achieved by following other courts.

However strong this point, and it is strong, it does not prevent us entirely from seeing the past decisions of the same court and relevant decisions of other courts as, at times, merely a matter of degree, and not a[n] absolute difference in kind. A past decision of the same court may be so poorly reasoned or so out of date that the past decision is like one of another country, not having any real pull on the court. It may not even deserve consideration in the court's decision; it may even be ignored. But at the other extreme, it may be that there is no compelling reason not to treat a case from another jurisdiction exactly like the case before the court. To do so would be morally arbitrary. In both cases, the "pull" that stare decisis or a particular persuasive authority can exert on the court is not irresistible: persuasive authorities can be disagreed with or distinguished, past decisions of the same court can be overruled. But in both cases, the pull exists not only towards the intrinsic persuasiveness of an authority but also toward uniformity in the law, and the good that uniformity brings and embodies (such as stability, reliability, and fairness). If this is right, then it shows how consensus among courts of different jurisdictions might be a good thing, and specifically a good thing legally — that is, realizes a good internal to law.

Notes and Questions

---

1. What is an "authority" in the legal sense? What do we mean by "persuasive" authority? How does an authority come to be considered persuasive? Are there any limits as to the nature of those authorities that may be cited to a court? Or is the use of the word "authority" itself a limiting factor?

2. Professor Flanders further posits that there might be a fourth category of "super persuasive" authority: the use of decisions of foreign courts by federal and state American courts, at least in those situations where international uniformity might be valued. *See id.* at 76, 86-88. Do you agree?

K. THE USE OF FOREIGN LAW

As the foregoing sections suggest, the use of foreign and international law by American courts has become both more common and increasingly subject to criticism in recent years. To a large extent, the following case to some extent brought this debate to the fore.

Roper v. Simmons

543 U.S. 551 (2005)

JUSTICE KENNEDY delivered the opinion of the Court.

This case requires us to address, for the second time in a decade and a half, whether it is permissible under the Eighth and Fourteenth Amendments to the Constitution of the United States to execute a juvenile offender who was older than 15 but younger than 18 when he committed a capital crime. In *Stanford* v. *Kentucky*, 492 U. S. 361 (1989), a divided Court rejected the proposition that the Constitution bars capital punishment for juvenile offenders in this age group. We reconsider the question.

. . . .

IV

Our determination that the death penalty is disproportionate punishment for offenders under 18 finds confirmation in the stark reality that the United States is the only country in the world that continues to give official sanction to the juvenile death penalty. This reality does not become controlling, for the task of interpreting the Eighth Amendment remains our responsibility. Yet at least from the time of the Court's decision in *Trop* [*v. Dulles*, 356 U.S. 86 (1958)], the Court has referred to the laws of other countries and to international authorities as instructive for its interpretation of the Eighth Amendment's prohibition of "cruel and unusual punishments."

As respondent and a number of *amici* emphasize, Article 37 of the United Nations Convention on the Rights of the Child, which every country in the world has ratified save for the United States and Somalia, contains an express prohibition on capital punishment for crimes committed by juveniles under 18. No ratifying country has entered a reservation to the provision prohibiting the execution of juvenile offenders. Parallel prohibitions are contained in other significant international covenants.

Respondent and his *amici* have submitted, and petitioner does not contest, that only seven countries other than the United States have executed juvenile offenders since 1990: Iran, Pakistan, Saudi Arabia, Yemen, Nigeria, the Democratic Republic of Congo, and China. Since then each of these countries has either abolished capital punishment for juveniles or made public disavowal of the practice. In sum, it is fair to say that the United States now stands alone in a world that has turned its face against the juvenile death penalty.

Though the international covenants prohibiting the juvenile death penalty are of more recent date, it is instructive to note that the United Kingdom abolished the juvenile death penalty before these covenants came into being. The United Kingdom's experience bears particular relevance here in light of the historic ties between our countries and in light of the Eighth Amendment's own origins. The Amendment was modeled on a parallel provision in the English Declaration of Rights of 1689, which provided: "Excessive Bail ought not to be required nor excessive Fines imposed; nor cruel and unusual Punishments inflicted." As of now, the United Kingdom has abolished the death penalty in its entirety; but, decades before it took this step, it recognized the disproportionate nature of the juvenile death penalty; and it abolished that penalty as a separate matter. . . . In the 56 years that have passed since the United Kingdom abolished the juvenile death penalty, the weight of authority against it there, and in the international community, has become well established.

It is proper that we acknowledge the overwhelming weight of international opinion against the juvenile death penalty, resting in large part on the understanding that the instability and emotional imbalance of young people may often be a factor in the crime. The opinion of the world community, while not controlling our outcome, does provide respected and significant confirmation for our own conclusions.

Over time, from one generation to the next, the Constitution has come to earn the high respect and even, as Madison dared to hope, the veneration of the American people. The document sets forth, and rests upon, innovative principles original to the American experience, such as federalism; a proven balance in political mechanisms through separation of powers; specific guarantees for the accused in criminal cases; and broad provisions to secure individual freedom and preserve human dignity. These doctrines and guarantees are central to the American experience and remain essential to our present-day self-definition and national identity. Not the least of the reasons we honor the Constitution, then, is because we know it to be our own. It does not lessen our fidelity to the Constitution or our pride in its origins to acknowledge that the express affirmation of certain fundamental rights by other nations and peoples simply underscores the centrality of those same rights within our own heritage of freedom.

The Eighth and Fourteenth Amendments forbid imposition of the death penalty on offenders who were under the age of 18 when their crimes were committed. The judgment of the Missouri Supreme Court setting aside the sentence of death imposed upon Christopher Simmons is affirmed.

JUSTICE SCALIA, with whom THE CHIEF JUSTICE and JUSTICE THOMAS join, dissenting.

. . . .

III

Though the views of our own citizens are essentially irrelevant to the Court's decision today, the views of other countries and the so-called international community take center stage.

The Court begins by noting that "Article 37 of the United Nations Convention on the Rights of the Child, which every country in the world has ratified *save for the United States* and Somalia, contains an express prohibition on capital punishment for crimes committed by juveniles under 18." The Court also discusses the International Covenant on Civil and Political Rights (ICCPR), which the Senate ratified only subject to a reservation that reads:

"The United States reserves the right, subject to its Constitutional constraints, to impose capital punishment on any person (other than a pregnant woman) duly convicted under existing or future laws permitting the imposition of capital punishment, including such punishment for crimes committed by persons below eighteen years of age."

Unless the Court had added to its arsenal the power to join and ratify treaties on behalf of the United States, I cannot see how this evidence favors, rather than refutes, its position. That the Senate and the President — those actors our Constitution empowers to enter into treaties, see Art. II, § 2 — have declined to join and ratify treaties prohibiting execution of under-18 offenders can only suggest that *our country* has either not reached a national consensus on the question, or has reached a consensus contrary to what the Court announces. That the reservation to the ICCPR was made in 1992 does not suggest otherwise, since the reservation still remains in place today. It is also worth noting that, in addition to barring the execution of under-18 offenders, the United Nations Convention on the Rights of the Child prohibits punishing them with life in prison without the possibility of release. If we are truly going to get in line with the international community, then the Court's reassurance that the death penalty is really not needed, since "the punishment of life imprisonment without the possibility of parole is itself a severe sanction," gives little comfort.

It is interesting that whereas the Court is not content to accept what the States of our Federal Union *say*, but insists on inquiring into what they *do* (specifically, whether they in fact *apply* the juvenile death penalty that their laws allow), the Court is quite willing to believe that every foreign nation — of whatever tyrannical political makeup and with however subservient or incompetent a court system — in fact *adheres* to a rule of no death penalty for offenders under 18. Nor does the Court inquire into how many of the countries that have the death penalty, but have forsworn (on paper at least) imposing that penalty on offenders under 18, have what no State of this country can constitutionally have: a *mandatory* death penalty for certain crimes, with no possibility of mitigation by the sentencing authority, for youth or any other reason. I suspect it is most of them. To forbid the death penalty for juveniles under such a system may be a good idea, but it says nothing about our system, in which the sentencing authority, typically a jury, always can, and almost always does, withhold the death penalty from an under-18 offender except, after considering all the circumstances, in the rare cases where it is warranted. The foreign authorities, in other words, do not even speak to the issue before us here.

More fundamentally, however, the basic premise of the Court's argument — that American law should conform to the laws of the rest of the world — ought to be rejected out of hand. In fact the Court itself does not believe it. In many significant respects the laws of most other countries differ from our law — including not only such explicit provisions of our Constitution as the right to jury trial and grand jury indictment, but even many interpretations of the Constitution prescribed by this Court itself. The Court-pronounced exclusionary rule, for example, is distinctively American. . . . Since then a categorical exclusionary rule has been "universally rejected" by other countries, including those with rules prohibiting illegal searches and police misconduct, despite the fact that none of these countries "appears to have any alternative form of discipline for police that is effective in preventing search violations." . . .

The Court has been oblivious to the views of other countries when deciding how to interpret our Constitution's requirement that "Congress shall make no law respecting the establishment of religion." Amdt. 1. Most other countries — including those committed to religious neutrality — do not insist on the degree of separation between church and state that this Court requires. . . .

And let us not forget the Court's abortion jurisprudence, which makes us one of only six countries that allow abortion on demand until the point of viability. Though the Government and *amici* in cases following *Roe* v. *Wade* urged the Court to follow the international community's lead, these arguments fell on deaf ears.

The Court's special reliance on the laws of the United Kingdom is perhaps the most indefensible part of its opinion. It is of course true that we share a common history with the United Kingdom, and that we often consult English sources when asked to discern the meaning of a constitutional text written against the backdrop of 18th-century English law and legal thought. If we applied that approach today, our task would be an easy one. As we explained in *Harmelin* v. *Michigan*, the "Cruell and Unusuall Punishments" provision of the English Declaration of Rights was originally meant to describe those punishments "'out of the Judges' Power'" — that is, those punishments that were not authorized by common law or statute, but that were nonetheless administered by the Crown or the Crown's judges. Under that reasoning, the death penalty for under-18 offenders would easily survive this challenge. The Court has, however — I think wrongly — long rejected a purely originalist approach to our Eighth Amendment, and that is certainly not the approach the Court takes today. Instead, the Court undertakes the majestic task of determining (and thereby prescribing) *our* Nation's *current* standards of decency. It is beyond comprehension why we should look, for that purpose, to a country that has developed, in the centuries since the Revolutionary War — and with increasing speed since the United Kingdom's recent submission to the jurisprudence of European courts dominated by continental jurists — a legal, political, and social culture quite different from our own. If we took the Court's directive seriously, we would also consider relaxing our double jeopardy prohibition, since the British Law Commission recently published a report that would significantly extend the rights of the prosecution to appeal cases where an acquittal was the result of a judge's ruling that was legally incorrect. We would also curtail our right to jury trial in criminal cases since, despite the jury system's deep roots in our shared common law, England now permits all but the most serious offenders to be tried by magistrates without a jury.

The Court should either profess its willingness to reconsider all these matters in light of the views of foreigners, or else it should cease putting forth foreigners' views as part of the *reasoned basis* of its decisions. To invoke alien law when it agrees with one's own thinking, and ignore it otherwise, is not reasoned decisionmaking, but sophistry.

The Court responds that "it does not lessen our fidelity to the Constitution or our pride in its origins to acknowledge that the express affirmation of certain fundamental rights by other nations and peoples simply underscores the centrality of those same rights within our own heritage of freedom." To begin with, I do not believe that approval by "other nations or peoples" should buttress our commitment to American principles any more than (what should logically follow) disapproval by "other nations and peoples" should weaken that commitment. More importantly, however, the Court's statement flatly misdescribes what is going on here. Foreign sources are cited today, *not* to underscore our "fidelity" to the Constitution, our "pride in its origins," and "our own American heritage." To the contrary, they are cited *to set aside* the centuries-old American practice — a practice still engaged in by a large majority of the relevant States — of letting a jury of 12 citizens decide whether, in the particular case, youth should be the basis for withholding the death penalty. What these foreign sources "affirm," rather than repudiate, is the Justices' own notion of how the world ought to be, and their diktat that it shall be so henceforth in America. The Court's parting attempt to downplay the significance of its extensive discussion of foreign law is unconvincing. "Acknowledgment" of foreign approval has no place in the legal opinion of this Court *unless it is part of the basis for the Court's judgment* — which is surely what it parades as today.

Notes and Questions

1. With respect to the use of foreign law, which opinion do you find more persuasive — the Court's, or the dissent? Why?

2. For a more recent Supreme Court case involving the use of foreign law, see *Graham v. Florida*, 130 S. Ct. 2011 (2010) (holding the Eighth Amendment similarly prohibits a sentence of life in prison without the possibility of parole for a juvenile convicted of a non-homicide offense). Interestingly, though, in *Miller v. Alabama*, 132 S. Ct. 2455 (2012), in which the Court held that the Eighth Amendment prohibits a sentence of life in prison without the possibility of parole for homicide offenses, the Court made no mention of foreign law.

Stephen Yeazell

WHEN AND HOW U.S. COURTS SHOULD CITE FOREIGN LAW

26 Const. Comment. 59 (2009)

There *is* a debate about U.S. courts citing foreign legal sources. A very small part of this debate is entirely legitimate — and I'll return to that. But first, let's be clear that there are many circumstances — accounting for the overwhelming majority of citations to foreign law — when a judge, sworn to uphold the Constitution, would be in dereliction of duty if he or she did *not* cite foreign legal sources.

Start with the easiest cases. In recent decades the Supreme Court, often in opinions written by Justices associated with a conservative wing of the Court, has vindicated parties' contractual power to manipulate the procedural rules under which their cases are decided. One such manipulation — found in large numbers of international contracts — is a choice of law clause, in which the parties stipulate that the law of Britain, or Mexico, or Italy will apply to any disputes arising under the agreement. U.S. courts regularly hear and decide such cases — applying the law of the nation designated in the clause. As you read these words, there are half a dozen U.S. courts that are assiduously citing foreign law, at the command of the U.S. Supreme Court or of similar mandates from their state supreme courts. They are doing so because the litigants have a choice of law clause and governing U.S. law says to respect that choice, and to respect it, the courts have to cite and discuss foreign law. That's not always easy or well done, a point to which I'll return, but it is a duty of a court under existing U.S. law.

A closely related second category comprises those cases where there's no choice of law clause but an ancient if sometimes indeterminate body of law (called "conflict of laws") dictates that the correct law to apply is foreign. So if on a trip to Austria to attend some opera, [Justice Ruth Bader Ginsburg] were injured in an auto accident involving her fellow Justice and opera buff, Antonin Scalia, and if, back in Washington, D.C., she brought suit against Justice Scalia to recover for her injuries, it's likely that a court would conclude that Austrian tort law applied to the case. And again, the U.S. court would be duty bound to cite and discuss Austrian statutes, treatises, and the like. Such a practice would be entirely uncontroversial; there is even a Federal Rule of Civil Procedure laying out the path by which litigants raise such issues of foreign law.[11]

A third kind of case — still in the uncontroversial category — arises when either a treaty or a statute explicitly refers to foreign law. One such statute — the Alien Tort Act — famously but mysteriously gives federal courts jurisdiction "of any civil action by an alien, for a tort only, committed in violation of the law of nations." Interpreting this statute has been difficult for the courts, but almost everyone who has looked at it has thought that to apply the statute a U.S. judge *has to* decide what acts do in fact violate "the law of nations." That phrase has been taken to refer not to the law of a single nation, but to the consensus reached by every (or almost every) nation even in the absence of a treaty. . . .

So far there's virtually no debate about the propriety of a federal or state judge citing foreign law; that law indisputably governs the case at hand, and courts all over the United States recognize their duty to find out what it is and apply it. The state of that law may be unclear, but judges are obliged to try to discern it just as they would a similarly relevant part of domestic law.

Let's get closer to the area where there's a legitimate disagreement. Even that disagreement is considerably narrower than one might gather from the comments. When should a U.S. court cite or look at foreign law in interpreting a U.S. statute or the Constitution? . . .

As even the deepest skeptics about citation of foreign law recognize, the U.S. Constitution is *full* of references to foreign law, so full that one cannot make

---

11. FED. R. CIV. P. 44.

sense out of many of its provisions without foreign law. As Justice Scalia has pith-ily acknowledged, "The reality is that I use foreign law more than anyone on the Court. But it's all old English law." Though no one debates this proposition, we've become so used to one brand of "foreign" law that we think it's domestic: it's so common that we call it "common law." Consider just Article I, section 9, which in the course of a few sentences defines Congressional power over "habeas corpus," "bills of attainder," and "letters of marque and reprisal." These references, all of which would have been well understood at the time of the ratification and which would continue to be so understood today, all refer to *foreign* law. Not only these but many of the provisions of the Bill of Rights, with its references to unreason-able searches, the right to jury trial at common law, and more — all assume a deep background in foreign law. The law in question, of course, is that of Great Britain, with which the United States had fought a long war to gain their independence. But when the new nation wanted to establish its government, it often did so by describ-ing familiar laws and practices that the Founders wished either to preserve (like right of trial by jury) or to reject (like bills of attainder).

Both sorts of law were indisputably foreign, but a U.S. court faced with a bill of attainder claim (a bill heavily taxing bonuses paid to executives at TARP-aided firms was recently attacked on the floor of Congress as a bill of attainder) would be bound by duty to examine the British practice of such bills. True, a House of Lords decision from the eighteenth century would not be dispositive, but it would surely be entirely appropriate, even though "no president accountable to the peo-ple" appointed the law lords. . . .

So what *are* the controversial cases? Even here, there may be less than meets the eye. Suppose a court confronts a case in which the question is the scope of the Commerce Clause or whether a statute falls within the ambit of the Necessary & Proper Clause of Article I. If the justices wrote an opinion resting on German precedents interpreting analogous provisions in the German Grundgesetz, people might rightly think they had taken leave of their senses. Surely the only relevant body of understandings are — depending on one's taste in constitutional interpreta-tion — the text of the Constitution, the Framers' writings and similar contemporary debate, the two hundred years of precedents from U.S. courts, and perhaps changes in popular understandings of the Constitution. But even this proposition might be subject to exceptions. The post-war Japanese constitution was famously modeled on that of the United States — even in places, some have argued, where it didn't fit the Japanese situation very well. Suppose the question was a case of first impres-sion for a U.S. court but that — one thinks this unlikely but surely possible — the Japanese Supreme Court had heard and decided a very closely analogous question. Yes, it's true that no U.S. President appointed the Japanese judges and no U.S. Senate confirmed them. And no one thinks the decision of the Japanese court would be dispositive. But would it really be irresponsible for a U.S. judge, seeking to under-stand the meaning of the U.S. Constitution, to seek counsel from a court interpret-ing the same clause in a sister democracy? I think not, though I also think that any such citation would have to be deeply contextualized — a point discussed below.

Now to the very small area of legitimate debate. Before exploring that small area, recall how many citations of foreign law are quite unremarkable; that is important to bear in mind, if only so we can discuss the debatable ones. In some recent cases, one or another justice, interpreting a provision of the Bill of Rights has cited to foreign practices. Which nations still execute minors?[29] . . . Some have condemned these practices as illegitimate; I take Chief Justice Roberts to be saying something like this. Certainly Justice Scalia has: "More fundamentally, however, the basic premise of the Court's argument — that American *law* should conform to the *laws* of the rest of the world — ought to be rejected out of hand."[30]

Maybe the Chief Justice and Justice Scalia are right, but a lot depends on exactly what they mean. The "unusual" part of "cruel and unusual" has an inescapably empirical content. Something is unusual if it doesn't happen very much; if it happens a lot, it's usual. What's the universe of reference in which a court has to decide whether a punishment is "unusual"? It might be the United States and only the United States; and it wouldn't be illogical so to conclude. But the appropriate constitutional reference might be broader. Suppose a state were to establish a particular form of juvenile rehabilitation that was pioneering in the United States, because the state in question had adapted its model from that used in several European countries. Let's further imagine that someone might think the punishment was cruel — perhaps because it involved a mild form of behavior modification. Would a U.S. judge — would Chief Justice Roberts or Justice Scalia — feel bound to strike down the new punishment because it was heretofore unknown in the United States? Or would they feel that they could appropriately cite to practices and law in the various nations that had pioneered this new treatment modality? I don't know the answer to that question. What I do know is that the U.S. legal system regularly encounters cases in which a conscientious judge, never suspected of "internationalist" leanings, would be obliged to look to the content of foreign law and in some cases to treat it as controlling. That's because U.S. law is simply chock full of reference and allusions to foreign law, some of it very old, some of it quite recent.

Often hidden in the sometimes fiery but often unilluminating dialogue about foreign law is a difficult problem — a problem that sounds less in national sovereignty and American values than in judicial craft. Often the problem with foreign law is not enough rather than too much. Justice Scalia has captured this problem with a recycled quip about the Court "looking over the heads of the crowd to pick out its friends." Justice Scalia has a point, though the point has an implication he might not favor — that the solution to "the foreign law problem" will sometimes be not less but more such citations.

. . . .

[Consider] the part of the majority opinion in *Roper v. Simmons* in which Justice Kennedy reviews the status of juvenile executions. I use *Roper* as an example because I am sympathetic with the Court's outcome; for me, only its methodology

---

29. That was the issue at stake in *Roper v. Simmons*, in which Justice Scalia dissented in part on the majority's reliance on foreign practices. Roper v. Simmons, 543 U.S. 551, 622-28 (2005) (Scalia, J., dissenting).

30. *Id.* at 624.

is at stake. In *Roper*, Justice Kennedy's opinion for the Court devotes five paragraphs to a treatment of foreign systems' stances on the question at hand. Foreign law is relevant to the disproportionality branch of the Eighth Amendment analysis on which the case turns: "Our determination that the death penalty is disproportionate punishment for offenders under 18 finds confirmation in the stark reality that the United States is the only country in the world that continues to give official sanction to the juvenile death penalty". The opinion for the majority demonstrates this contention by noting that all but two U.N. members states have ratified Article 37 of the United Nations Convention on the Rights of the Child; that of the seven countries other than the U.S. who actually executed juveniles since 1990, each had either abolished or abjured the practice; and that the United Kingdom, on whose declaration of rights the Eighth Amendment was based, had abolished juvenile execution decades before it abolished the death penalty altogether.

This is not enough of a good thing. Let us sidestep the question of whether one should ever look to international law or practice for the content of a U.S. constitutional norm.[39] *If* one is going to appeal to foreign law, the appeal has to be effective. Effective use of foreign law requires that it be treated as respectfully as state law — surveyed carefully and contextually rather than mentioned in passing references. Justice Kennedy doesn't think he can mention in passing that many states have abolished capital punishment for juveniles; instead he devotes most of the opinion to this proposition, and for good measure attaches an appendix with charts showing in several different ways the changing fortunes of juvenile execution.

Not so for the foreign references. As a result, the discussion of foreign law is weaker than that of domestic law. As Justice Scalia has suggested in another context, one should subtract from the denominator in the UN Convention those nations that have abolished capital punishment for *all* cases; it's politically costless for such a nation to ratify Article 37, forbidding juvenile executions, because the polity in question has already decided not to execute anyone. Justice Scalia is likely also correct in noting that a fuller consideration of this matter would note that some nations maintain a *mandatory* death penalty for some crimes; and that one might examine more closely the actual practices of some nations that claim to have abolished the death penalty for juveniles. None of these points is in principle unanswerable. Moreover, none of them arises because the law involved is foreign: the objections are those involving analysis and craft, not any special feature of foreign law. But their answers call for deeper, more nuanced exploration of foreign law when a court thinks it relevant — as the majority does in *Roper* — to the content of such multi-national norms as capital punishment.

International law, if it is to be used, should be used well — not as an ornament or afterthought. . . . [I]f one wants to make claims about international consensus, that requires more and better exploration. In that exploration context matters. . . .

. . . .

[T]he point is simple: "good" citation of foreign law will have the same characteristics as good citation of domestic law; they will be complete, careful, and

---

39. Some might argue that no foreign source should ever be cited except when required.

contextualized. Hit-and-run citations are bad whether they use foreign or domestic sources. Thus stated, the point becomes commonplace. But given the occasionally hysterical rhetoric surrounding discussion of foreign law, lowering the volume of the discussion to the commonplace may be a useful contribution.

Notes and Questions

1. Note, as Professor Yeazell points out, the many legitimate uses of foreign and international law. What are those uses?

2. Professor Yeazell mentions Federal Rule of Civil Procedure 44.1. Rule 44.1 provides:

> A party who intends to raise an issue about a foreign country's law must give notice by a pleading or other writing. In determining foreign law, the court may consider any relevant material or source, including testimony, whether or not submitted by a party or admissible under the Federal Rules of Evidence. The court's determination must be treated as a ruling on a question of law.

Of course, in addition to explaining its relevance, the prudent lawyer will also ensure that the court has an accurate translation of the law in question (if in another language).

3. Oklahoma State Question 755, also known as the "Save Our State" Amendment, reads as follows:

> This measure amends the State Constitution. It changes a section that deals with the courts of this state. It would amend Article 7, Section 1. It makes courts rely on federal and state law when deciding cases. It forbids courts from considering or using international law. It forbids courts from considering or using Sharia Law.
>
> International law is also known as the law of nations. It deals with the conduct of international organizations and independent nations, such as countries, states and tribes. It deals with their relationship with each other. It also deals with some of their relationships with persons.
>
> The law of nations is formed by the general assent of civilized nations. Sources of international law also include international agreements, as well as treaties.
>
> Sharia Law is Islamic law. It is based on two principal sources, the Koran and the teachings of Mohammed.

Oklahoma State Question 755 was passed by the citizens of Oklahoma on November 2, 2010; in fact, it received more than 70% of the vote. Do you see any problems with this measure? A federal district court permanently enjoined the certification of this measure, thus preventing it from ever taking effect. *See Awad v. Ziriax*, 966 F. Supp. 2d 1198 (W.D. Okla. 2013).

4. For more on the use of foreign law by American courts, see Stephen G. Ca-labresi, *"A Shining City on a Hill": American Exceptionalism and the Supreme Court's Practice of Relying on Foreign Law*, 86 B.U. L. REV. 1335 (2006); Vicki C. Jackson, *Constitutional Comparisons: Convergence, Resistance, Engagement*, 119 HARV. L REV. 109 (2005); John O. McGinnis, *Foreign to Our Constitution*, 100 NW. U. L. REV. 303 (2006); and Eugene Volokh, *Foreign Law in American Courts*, 66 OKLA. L. REV. 219 (2014).

L. WHAT IS A "HEARING"?

Many legal proceedings require or permit a "hearing" on the matter at issue prior to a ruling by the relevant adjudicatory body. But beyond basic constitutional due process guarantees — i.e., reasonable notice and an opportunity to be heard — what does such a "hearing" require? Professor Fuller speaks of the need for an opportunity to present proofs and reasoned arguments to the adjudicator. But does a "hearing" necessarily include a right to present one's arguments orally, whether in-person or by some electronic means?

Perez-Llamas v. Utah Court of Appeals

2005 UT 18, 110 P.3d 706 (2005)

PER CURIAM:

Luis Perez-Llamas was stopped by a highway patrol officer and arrested when marijuana was discovered in a shrink-wrapped tire in the van in which he was traveling. Perez-Llamas unsuccessfully moved to suppress the evidence and then entered a conditional guilty plea to possession with intent to distribute a controlled substance, a second degree felony. The district court imposed the sentence applicable to the level of conviction but suspended that sentence in favor of a 364-day jail term. On the same date Perez-Llamas was sentenced, he filed an application for a certificate of probable cause, which the district court denied. Perez-Llamas then filed an application on appeal with the court of appeals. The State filed a response within five days, and the court of appeals issued an order denying the application seven days later. The court of appeals held Perez-Llamas had failed to meet the substantive criteria for obtaining the certificate. Perez-Llamas then filed the instant petition for extraordinary relief.

In his petition before this court, Perez-Llamas does not seek review on the merits. Rather, he requests an order directing the court of appeals to provide him with a hearing pursuant to rule 27(e) of the Rules of Criminal Procedure. We conclude the court of appeals in fact provided Perez-Llamas with a hearing within the context of rule 27 and the Appellate Rules. Accordingly, we deny the petition for extraordinary relief.

ANALYSIS

. . . .

Rule 27(a)(2) provides: "A sentence of fine, imprisonment, or probation shall be stayed if an appeal is taken and a certificate of probable cause is issued." Subpart (b) of rule 27 sets forth procedures and standards expressly directed to the trial court. In particular, that subpart requires a finding by "clear and convincing evidence that the defendant is not likely to flee during pendency of the appeal and that the defendant will not pose a danger to the safety of any other person or the community." Subpart (c) provides for appeal in the event the trial court denies the initial application for a certificate. Subpart (d) delineates various procedural and substantive requirements for an application for a certificate. Subpart (d)(3) appears to be expressly limited to materials required in support of an application on appeal, whereas subpart (d)(2) appears to set forth requirements for any application for a certificate, whether filed with the trial court or the appellate court. Subpart (d)(2) additionally requires a convicted defendant to demonstrate that the issues on appeal "raise a substantial question of law or fact reasonably likely to result in a reversal, an order for a new trial or sentence that does not include a term of incarceration." Subpart (e) initially draws a distinction between applications to the trial court and the appellate court by dictating which officer of the State must be served with a copy of the application and supporting materials. It is apparent that this distinction was drawn for the limited purpose of assuring proper service on the State. The remaining balance of subpart (e) appears to address all applications for a certificate. It provides in relevant part:

> An opposing memorandum may be filed by the appropriate State officer within 10 days after receipt of the application. A hearing on the application shall be held within 10 days after the appropriate court receives the opposing memorandum, or if no opposing memorandum is filed, within 15 days after the application is filed with the court.

Utah R. Crim. P. 27(e).

Rule 27 provides what is essentially an expedited procedure for determining a convicted defendant's eligibility for release on bail pending resolution of the appeal. Plainly, the short time frame contemplated for adjudication of an application, both before the trial court and on appeal, is significant. If a convicted defendant is otherwise eligible for release pending appeal, the rule contemplates a speedy resolution of the application to avoid protracted incarceration prior to that release.

Perez-Llamas asserts rule 27(e) requires the appellate court to provide an "oral" hearing, either in the form of argument on the legal merits of the petition or in the form of a full evidentiary review. While rule 27(e) does require a "hearing," its evident focus is on the materials that are to be submitted in connection with an application or the appeal of a denial of an application and on the timing of the adjudication of the application. Apart from the requirement that a hearing be afforded within the designated time frame, the rule offers no independent definition or description of what constitutes a hearing. Accordingly, we find it useful to address Perez-Llamas' contention by looking to the context in which the procedure prescribed by rule 27(e) would have its effect in both the trial court and the appellate court.

Trial courts are primarily responsible for collecting evidence and adjudicating matters in the first instance. With respect to legal arguments, such as those presented on motions to dismiss or summary judgment, trial courts often will receive pleadings and conduct oral hearings to assist in the adjudication of those motions. With respect to matters requiring a judge to resolve conflicting factual disputes, an evidentiary hearing may be held. In the trial court, rulings on an oral or evidentiary hearing are often rendered within a short time after the hearing. Indeed, the trial court may announce its ruling from the bench, with findings of fact and conclusions of law issued shortly thereafter.

The trial process is also structured in a manner that allows each aspect of the process to inform subsequent aspects. In criminal cases, the judge who presided over the trial or plea that resolved the case ordinarily will be the same judge who conducts a sentencing hearing and imposes sentence. Similarly, the same sentencing judge ordinarily will entertain any application for a certificate of probable cause. While adjudication of the application may involve factors not examined in the trial or sentencing process, those earlier processes can provide important background and context for determining whether a convicted defendant is a flight risk or a danger to the public, and whether a convicted defendant's appeal is reasonably likely to result in a reversal or other significant alteration to his conviction or sentence. To the extent there are additional disputed facts relevant to disposition of the application, or the trial judge needs to collect information not readily available in the written application and response, an oral hearing or evidentiary hearing may be necessary to properly resolve the application.

By contrast, appellate courts do not conduct evidentiary hearings in the ordinary course, as their review typically focuses upon the legal correctness of a lower tribunal's decision. In the unusual circumstances where an appellate court does directly collect and analyze testimony and evidence, it will appoint a special master for that purpose.

Oral argument is the typical method by which information is presented in person to the judges of an appellate court. However, oral argument is conducted for the limited purpose of obtaining information that is *supplemental* to the written briefs. At the appellate level, the parties are expected to make their full case in the written pleadings and the reception of supplemental information at oral argument is not always necessary. Indeed, it may only delay resolution of a matter that is less complex or more time- sensitive than a plenary appeal of a judgment below. In short, oral argument is a tool for assisting the appellate court in its decision making process, not an independent due process right vested in the parties.

The Appellate Rules recognize this fact by placing the decision to hold oral argument within the discretion of the appellate court. For instance, rule 23 of the Rules of Appellate Procedure governs with respect to motions not amounting to a request to dismiss a case or to rule on the merits. Rule 23 does not require oral argument, and such argument is held only when the appellate court deems it appropriate. As for plenary treatment of a case on the merits, rule 29 of the Appellate Rules provides that the appellate court in its discretion may choose not to hold oral argument if the appeal is deemed frivolous, the issue on appeal has already been decided, or "the facts and legal arguments are adequately presented in the briefs and record and the decisional process would not be significantly aided by oral argument." Moreover, rule 2 of the Appellate Rules allows the appellate court to suspend all provisions of the Appellate Rules except those that impose jurisdictional limits on the appellate court's authority to entertain an appeal or a petition.

Given this context, we do not believe that the reference to a "hearing" in rule 27(e) requires both the trial court and the appellate court to follow precisely the same procedures in adjudicating an application for a certificate of probable cause. Nor do we believe "hearing" has a fixed meaning as a recitation of a list of prescribed judicial procedures to be followed. Rather, "hearing" refers to the adjudication process itself, and is peculiar to the context in which it is applied. For example, notice and the opportunity to be "heard" are frequently recited as the essential elements of due process. Yet, this does not always mean a party's voice must be orally transmitted to the ear of a judge. Rather a party must simply be afforded a meaningful opportunity to submit relevant information and persuasive legal reasoning to the court.

Before the trial court, an oral hearing on the legal merits of the application, or even an evidentiary hearing, may be the ordinary and appropriate course for an application for a certificate of probable cause. Moreover, where the trial court setting is more adapted to rendering decisions quickly, it would be reasonable to anticipate a hearing and a ruling on an application for a certificate of probable cause within the time frame contemplated by the rule.

In the appellate court, an oral hearing is not necessary or required to address the denial of an application for a certificate of probable cause. The appellate court may look to relevant provisions of the Appellate Rules for guidance. As noted above, the criteria set forth by rule 29 of the Appellate Rules provide relevant guidelines to the circumstances when oral argument is appropriate as a general matter. Rule 2 also may be relevant in cases where the appellate court deems it necessary to suspend other rules.

In this case, there is no allegation that Perez-Llamas was deprived of the opportunity to present appropriate argument and affidavit in written form to the court of appeals. Moreover, he has not articulated how the presentation of additional information at oral argument would have generated a different outcome. The court of appeals reviewed the substantive criteria set forth by rule 27 in a timely manner and denied the application. We conclude that Perez-Llamas has not shown any violation of the provisions of rule 27 of the Rules of Criminal Procedure. Accordingly, the petition for extraordinary relief is denied.

Notes and Questions

---

1. Not surprisingly, the Supreme Court of the United States also has weighed in on the issue of the necessity of oral argument, at least as it relates to the right to due process. In *FCC v. WJR, The Goodwill Station, Inc.,* 337 U.S. 265 (1949), the Court considered the question as follows:

Most broadly stated, the important question presented by this case is the extent to which due process of law, as guaranteed by the Fifth Amendment, requires federal administrative tribunals to accord the right of oral argument to one claiming to be adversely affected by their action, more particularly upon questions of law. . . . [A]s we understand the Court of Appeals' decision, it has ruled that Fifth Amendment procedural due process requires an opportunity for oral argument to be given "on every question of law raised before a judicial or quasi-judicial tribunal, including questions raised by demurrer or as if on demurrer, except such questions of law as may be involved in interlocutory orders such as orders for the stay of proceedings *pendente lite,* for temporary injunctions and the like," and on this basis has remanded this cause to the Federal Communications Commission for oral argument.

. . . .

Taken at its literal and explicit import, the Court's broad constitutional ruling cannot be sustained. So taken, it would require oral argument upon every question of law, apart from the excluded interlocutory matters, arising in administrative proceedings of every sort. This would be regardless of whether the legal question were substantial or insubstantial; of the substantive nature of the asserted right or interest involved; of whether Congress had provided a procedure, relating to the particular interest, requiring oral argument or allowing it to be dispensed with; and regardless of the fact that full opportunity for judicial review may be available.

We do not stop to consider the effects of such a ruling, if accepted, upon the work of the vast and varied administrative as well as judicial tribunals of the federal system and the equally numerous and diversified interests affected by their functioning; or indeed upon the many and different types of administrative and judicial procedures which Congress has provided for dealing adjudicatively with such interests. It is enough to say that due process of law, as conceived by the Fifth Amendment, has never been cast in so rigid and all-inclusive confinement.

On the contrary, due process of law has never been a term of fixed and invariable content. This is as true with reference to oral argument as with respect to other elements of procedural due process. For this Court has held in some situations that such argument is essential to a fair hearing, in others that argument submitted in writing is sufficient.

The decisions cited are sufficient to show that the broad generalization made by the Court of Appeals is not the law. Rather it is in conflict with this Court's rulings, in effect, that the right of oral argument as a matter of procedural due process varies from case to case in accordance with differing circumstances, as do other procedural regulations. Certainly the Constitution does not require oral argument in all cases where only insubstantial or frivolous questions of law, or indeed even substantial ones, are raised. Equally certainly it has left wide discretion to Congress in creating the procedures to be followed in both administrative and judicial proceedings, as well as in their conjunction.

Without in any sense discounting the value of oral argument wherever it may be appropriate or, by virtue of the particular circumstances, constitutionally required, we cannot accept the broad formula upon which the Court of Appeals rested its ruling. To do so would do violence not only to our own former decisions but also, we think, to the constitutional power of Congress to devise differing administrative and legal procedures appropriate for the disposition of issues affecting interests widely varying in kind.[10]

It follows also that we should not undertake in this case to generalize more broadly than the particular circumstances require upon when and under what circumstances procedural due process may require oral argument. That is not a matter, under our decisions, for broadside generalization and indiscriminate application. It is rather one for case-to-case determination, through which alone account may be taken of differences in the particular interest affected, circumstances involved, and procedures prescribed by Congress for dealing with them. Only thus may the judgment of Congress, expressed pursuant to its power under the Constitution to devise both judicial and administrative procedures, be taken into account. Any other approach would be, in these respects, highly abstract, indeed largely in a vacuum.

Respondent does not contend that it was denied any opportunity to present for the Commission's consideration any matter of fact or law in connection with its application or that the Commission has not given all matters submitted by it due and full consideration. We cannot say, in view of the statute and of the subject matter involved, that the Commission abused its discretion in hearing respondent's application on the written submission.[18]

2. Federal Rule of Civil Procedure 78(b) provides: "By rule or order, the court may provide for submitting and determining motions on briefs, without oral hearings." Similarly, Federal Rule of Appellate Procedure 34(a) provides:

(1) *Party's Statement.* Any party may file, or a court may require by local rule, a statement explaining why oral argument should, or need not, be permitted.

(2) *Standards.* Oral argument must be allowed in every case unless a panel of three judges who have examined the briefs and record unanimously agrees that oral argument is unnecessary for any of the following reasons:

(A) the appeal is frivolous;

(B) the dispositive issue or issues have been authoritatively decided; or

(C) the facts and legal arguments are adequately presented in the briefs and record, and the decisional process would not be significantly aided by oral argument.

---

10. For example, what may be appropriate or constitutionally required by way of procedure, including opportunity for oral argument, in protection of an alien's claims of right to enter the country, may be very different from what is required to determine an alleged citizen's right of entry or reentry; a claimed right of naturalization; a claim of just compensation for land condemned; or the right to defend against an indictment for crime.

18. Federal Rule 78, the terms of which were noted by the dissent in the Court of Appeals, provides in part, as to United States District Courts: "To expedite its business, the court may make provision by rule or order for the submission and determination of motions without oral hearing upon brief written statements of reasons in support and opposition." Similar notice may be taken of Rule 7(2) of this Court which, governing not only motion practice in appellate cases but motions for leave to initiate original proceedings, provides in part: "Oral argument will not be heard on any motion unless the court specially assigns it therefor."

See also FED. R. APP. P. 34(f) ("The parties may agree to submit a case for decision on the briefs, but the court may direct that the case be argued.").

Finally, Supreme Court Rule 28 provides:

> 1. Oral argument should emphasize and clarify the written arguments in the briefs on the merits. Counsel should assume that all Justices have read the briefs before oral argument. Oral argument read from a prepared text is not favored.
>
> 2. The petitioner or appellant shall open and may conclude the argument. A cross-writ of certiorari or cross-appeal will be argued with the initial writ of certiorari or appeal as one case in the time allowed for that one case, and the Court will advise the parties who shall open and close.
>
> 3. Unless the Court directs otherwise, each side is allowed one-half hour for argument. Counsel is not required to use all the allotted time. Any request for additional time to argue shall be presented by motion under Rule 21 in time to be considered at a scheduled Conference prior to the date of oral argument and no later than 7 days after the respondent's or appellee's brief on the merits is filed, and shall set out specifically and concisely why the case cannot be presented within the half-hour limitation. Additional time is rarely accorded.
>
> 4. Only one attorney will be heard for each side, except by leave of the Court on motion filed in time to be considered at a scheduled Conference prior to the date of oral argument and no later than 7 days after the respondent's or appellee's brief on the merits is filed. Any request for divided argument shall be presented by motion under Rule 21 and shall set out specifically and concisely why more than one attorney should be allowed to argue. Divided argument is not favored.
>
> 5. Regardless of the number of counsel participating in oral argument, counsel making the opening argument shall present the case fairly and completely and not reserve points of substance for rebuttal.
>
> 6. Oral argument will not be allowed on behalf of any party for whom a brief has not been filed.
>
> 7. By leave of the Court, and subject to paragraph 4 of this Rule, counsel for an *amicus curiae* whose brief has been filed as provided in Rule 37 may argue orally on the side of a party, with the consent of that party. In the absence of consent, counsel for an *amicus curiae* may seek leave of the Court to argue orally by a motion setting out specifically and concisely why oral argument would provide assistance to the Court not otherwise available. Such a motion will be granted only in the most extraordinary circumstances.

3. For more on the meaning of the term "hearing" in varying contexts, see *United States v. Florida East Coast Railway,* 410 U.S. 224 (1973).

1. The Purpose and Value of Oral Argument

As the *Perez-Llamas* court indicated, a judicial hearing usually may properly be conducted either with or without oral argument. If true, then it seems as though the better question might be whether oral argument might be valuable in any particular case, and if so, why, and to what extent? Consider, in this vein, the following excerpt.

Antonin Scalia & Bryan A. Garner

APPRECIATE THE IMPORTANCE OF ORAL ARGUMENT, AND KNOW YOUR OBJECTIVES*

Making Your Case: The Art of Persuading Judges (2008)

Many lawyers view oral argument as just a formality, especially in courts that make a practice of reading the briefs in advance. Sure, it gives counsel a chance to show off before the client. But as far as affecting the outcome is concerned, what can 20 minutes or half an hour of oral argument add to what the judge has already learned from reading a few hundred pages of briefs, underlining significant passages and annotating the margins?

This skepticism has proved false in every study of judicial behavior we know. Does oral argument change a well-prepared judge's mind? Rarely. What often happens, though, is that the judge is undecided at the time of oral argument (the case is a close one), and oral argument makes the difference. It makes the difference because it provides information and perspective that the briefs don't and can't contain.

A brief is logical and sequential. If it contains five points, they will often be addressed in some logical order, not necessarily in the order of their importance. The amount of space devoted to each point, moreover, has more to do with its complexity than its strength. Someone who has read your brief, therefore — and especially someone who has read it some days ago — may have a distorted impression of your case. The reader may think that point #1, which it takes a third of your brief to explain, is the most significant aspect of your argument, whereas in fact point #3, which covers half as many pages, is really your trump card. Oral argument can put things in perspective: "Your Honors, we have four points to our brief, all of which we think merit your attention. But the heart of our argument is point #3, on issue preclusion, and I'll turn to that now."

Oral argument also provides information that the brief can't contain. Most obviously, it gives the appellee an opportunity to reply to responses and new points contained in the appellant's reply brief. At least as important, it provides both sides the opportunity to answer questions that have arisen in the judges' minds. The most obvious of these should have been anticipated and answered in the briefing, but repetition of the answers to a persistent doubter can be helpful. And the judges are bound to have in mind questions unanticipated by the briefs — either because the answer is too obvious or because the question is too subtle. Oral argument is the time to lay these judicial doubts to rest. And finally, the quality of oral argument can convey to the court that the brief already submitted is the product of a highly capable and trustworthy attorney, intimately familiar with the facts and the law of the case.

In descending order of importance, your objectives in oral argument are these:

---

* © Antonin Scalia and Bryan A. Garner. Reproduced from their book *Making Your Case: The Art of Persuading Judges* (Thomson Reuters. 2008).

1. To answer any questions and satisfy any doubts that have arisen in the judges' minds.

2. If you're counsel for the appellee, to answer new and telling points raised in the appellant's reply brief. Oral argument is your only chance.

3. To call to the judges' minds and reinforce the substantive points made in your brief.

4. To demonstrate to the court, by the substance and manner of your presentation, that you are trustworthy, open, and forthright.

5. To demonstrate to the court, by the substance and manner of your presentation, that you have thought long and hard about this case and are familiar with all its details.

6. To demonstrate to the court, mostly by the manner of your presentation, that you are likeable and not mean-spirited.

Notes and Comments

---

1. Is not oral argument more appropriate for some matters and less appropriate for others? What are the factors that a court might use to fairly make this determination?

    In addition to the "objectives" listed by Scalia and Garner, some of the advantages or benefits of oral argument include the following:
    a) it allows the parties to raise and discuss new or additional facts or intervening changes in the law;
    b) it can facilitate the explanation of complex matters;
    c) it seems to make the process more "public" (i.e., more transparent);
    d) in some sense, it gives the parties their "day in court";
    e) it might provide a greater sense that the court considered the parties' arguments;
    f) it can accelerate a decision, in that it forces the court to prepare for the hearing and also creates the possibility of a ruling "from the bench";
    g) it provides a vehicle for the judges on a multi-judge court to communicate with one another; and
    h) it can improve understanding for judges who tend to be more "audio" learners.

    On the other hand, there are several disadvantages of oral argument, including:

    a) it tends to be regarded as unnecessary in most cases;
    b) it is expensive and time-consuming;
    c) it can create less incentive for parties to write good briefs;

d) it tends not to be done well (and therefore tends to be of limited assistance); and

e) it provides no occasion for passion (at least in contract to a closing argument at trial).

Can you think of any other arguments, pro or con, for having oral argument?

2. Much has been written on oral argument. For a Supreme Court perspective, see DAVID C. FREDRICK, THE ART OF ORAL ADVOCACY (2003), and EUGENE GRESSMAN ET AL., SUPREME COURT PRACTICE 748-52 (9th ed. 2007) ("Importance of Oral Argument"). For an exhaustive (though somewhat dated) treatment, see ROBERT L. STERN, APPELLATE PRACTICE IN THE UNITED STATES 358-442 (1981). For a criticism, see Robert J. Martineau, *The Value of Appellate Oral Argument: A Challenge to the Conventional Wisdom*, 72 IOWA L. REV. 1 (1986), and for a response to Professor Martineau, see Myron H. Bright, *The Spoken Word: In Defense of Oral Argument*, 72 IOWA L. REV. 35 (1986). For more recent takes (that also consider the value of oral argument at the trial court level), see Mark R. Kravitz, *Written and Oral Persuasion in the United States Courts: A District Judge's Perspective on Their History, Function, and Future*, 10 J. APP. PRAC. & PROCESS 247 (2009), and Mark Spottswood, *Live Hearings and Paper Trials*, 38 FL. ST. U. L. REV. 827 (2011).

3. "[T]he great Chief Justice John Marshall often allowed oral argument in a single case to proceed for days. He and his colleagues spent five days, for instance, hearing argument in the landmark case of *Gibbons v. Ogden*." Joseph T. Thai & Andrew M. Coats, *The Case for Oral Argument in the Supreme Court of Oklahoma*, 62 OKLA. L. REV. 695, 699 (2008) (footnote omitted).

4. The use of oral argument in the United States Court of Appeals seems to be declining. For example, for the year ending September 30, 2011, 75% of the appeals before the United States Court of Appeals (excluding the Federal Circuit) were terminated on the merits on the briefs, meaning only 25% were terminated after oral argument. *See* Judicial Business of the United States Court, 2011 Annual Report of the Director, Table S-1, *available at* www.uscourts.gov/uscourts/statistics/JudicialBusiness/2011/JudicialBusiness2011.pdf. For a recent article on this topic, see David R. Cleveland & Steven Wisotsky, *The Decline of Oral Argument in the Federal Courts of Appeals: A Modest Proposal for Reform*, 13 J. APP. PRAC. & PROCESS 119 (2012).

5. ALI/UNIDROIT Principles of Transnational Civil Procedure (2004), Principle 19 ("Oral and Written Presentations") provides in part: "Pleadings, formal requests (motions), and legal argument ordinarily should be presented initially in writing, but the parties should have the right to present oral argument on important substantive and procedural issues." *Id.* Principle 19.1.

6. Though common-law countries generally appear to be embracing more of a written style of advocacy, the oral tradition remains much more entrenched

outside of the United States. For a study of this phenomenon, see Suzanne Ehrenberg, *Embracing the Writing-Centered Legal Process*, 89 IOWA L. REV. 1159 (2004). *See also* ROBERT J. MARTINEAU, APPELLATE JUSTICE IN ENGLAND AND THE UNITED STATES: A COMPARATIVE ANALYSIS (1990).

M. THE NEED TO PROVIDE REASONS FOR THE DECISION

Though Professor Fuller did not regard adjudicatory reason-giving as indispensable, he did believe that it generally promoted the fairness and effectiveness of the proceedings. Do you agree? Consider this question as you read the following cases.

In re Shell Oil Co.

966 F.2d 1130 (7th Cir. 1992)

EASTERBROOK, Circuit Judge.

On March 3 the district judge remanded the case to state court. The order reads, in full: "IT IS HEREBY ORDERED that Plaintiff's Motion for Remand is hereby granted." The court did not provide a reason.

Whether we have the authority to issue the writ of mandamus [Defendant] Shell seeks depends on the unstated reason for the remand. . . .

. . . Here, . . . we have no idea why the district judge remanded the case. "Appellate judges are no better than average mind readers, which creates difficulties in reviewing unexplained acts." . . .

The Rules of Civil Procedure require district judges to state reasons when issuing injunctions or deciding cases after trial (or in mid-trial). They do not call for reasons when a judge dismisses a claim before trial or grants summary judgment. Frustration at our inability to provide intelligent review on the (rare) occasions when district judges disposed of cases on the merits without explanation led us to adopt Circuit Rule 50, which provides: "Whenever a district court dismisses a claim or counterclaim or grants summary judgment, the district judges shall give his or her reasons for the dismissal of the claim or counterclaim or the granting of summary judgment, either orally on the record or by written statement." Rule 50 was designed to close the gaps in the Rules of Civil Procedure, so that every dispositive order would be explained — for the benefit of the parties (who should not have to wonder why a judge acted) as well as this court.

. . . [T]his case show[s] that our drafting was not sufficiently comprehensive. . . . Just which remands are reviewable depends on the reasons the district court provides, as [our prior cases] show. Unless the district courts explain their orders, we cannot carry out our own duties. Neither the parties nor a reviewing court should be compelled to guess at the reasons for a decision — especially not when the reason determines whether we are entitled to be a "reviewing court" in the first place!

Pending a revision of Circuit Rule 50, district courts should accommodate both the litigants and this tribunal by stating reasons for their remand orders. Reasons need not be elaborate; often a sentence will do. When as in this case the unstated reason is important to our jurisdiction, we shall issue a limited writ directing the district court to provide the essential information.

Taylor v. McKeithen

407 U.S. 191 (1972)

PER CURIAM.

The 1970 self-reapportionment of the Louisiana Legislature was challenged in this lawsuit on the dual grounds that it offended both the one-man, one-vote principle and the prohibition against voting arrangements designed to dilute the voting strength of racial minorities. After the United States Attorney General interposed an objection to the election law change under § 5 of the Voting Rights Act of 1965, the District Court appointed a Special Master to prepare a court-imposed plan. The Master was verbally instructed to hold hearings and to devise a proposal to maintain the integrity of political subdivisions and to observe natural or historical boundaries "as nearly as possible." He was also instructed that "no consideration whatsoever was to be given to the location of the residence of either incumbents in office or of announced or prospective candidates."

The Special Master held four days of hearings, during which over 100 persons were heard. Proposed plans were received by him. No one was denied a hearing. He then submitted his recommendations to the District Court and after a hearing it was adopted by the court.

. . . .

Despite the District Court's findings, however, the Court of Appeals reversed without opinion and adopted the Attorney General's alternative division of New Orleans. The petitioners are the original plaintiffs and they now seek review of this summary reversal.

. . . .

Because this record does not fully inform us of the precise nature of the litigation and because we have not had the benefit of the insight of the Court of Appeals, we grant the petition for writ of certiorari, vacate the judgment below, and remand the case to the Court of Appeals for proceedings in conformity with this opinion.[4]

MR. JUSTICE BLACKMUN concurs in the Court's judgment.

---

4. We, of course, agree that the courts of appeals should have wide latitude in their decisions of whether or how to write opinions. That is especially true with respect to summary affirmances. But here the lower court summarily reversed without any opinion on a point that had been considered at length by the District Judge. Under the special circumstances of this case, we are loath to impute to the Court of Appeals reasoning that would raise a substantial federal question when it is plausible that its actual ground of decision was of more limited importance.

Mr. Justice Rehnquist, with whom The Chief Justice and Mr. Justice Powell join, dissenting.

The short recitation of specific facts in the Court's opinion makes clear that the issues in this case, as viewed by both petitioners and respondents, are well developed in the record. The federal questions adverted to by the Court in its opinion are undoubtedly important ones. They are either presented by the proceedings below on this record, or they are not; this Court, in exercising its certiorari jurisdiction, may wish to consider such problems as are presented in this case at this time, or it may not. While an opinion from the Court of Appeals fully explaining the reason for its reversal of the District Court would undoubtedly be of assistance to our exercise of certiorari jurisdiction here, it is by no means essential. I do not believe that the Court's vacation of the judgment below with a virtually express directive to the Court of Appeals that it write an opinion is an appropriate exercise of this Court's authority.

The courts of appeals are statutory courts, having the power to prescribe rules for the conduct of their own business so long as those rules are consistent with applicable law and rules of practice and procedure prescribed by this Court. No existing statute or rule of procedure prohibits the Fifth Circuit from issuing a short opinion and order, as it has done here, or from deciding cases without any opinion at all. The courts of appeals, and particularly the Fifth Circuit, which has experienced the heaviest caseload of all the circuits, need the maximum possible latitude to deal with the "flood tide" of appeals that the "ever growing explosive increase" of federal judicial business has produced.

If there are important federal questions presented in this record, this Court should address itself to them. Instead of doing that, it calls upon the Fifth Circuit to write an *amicus curiae* opinion to aid us. I think decisions as to whether opinions should accompany judgments of the court of appeals, and the desirable length and content of those opinions are matters best left to the judges of the court of appeals. I therefore dissent from the order of vacation and remand.

Notes and Questions

1. In *Shell Oil*, was there really no way for the court of appeals to determine the reason for the district court's remand order short of sending the case back to the district court for a more detailed explanation? For the Supreme Court to assess the propriety of the reversal by the court of appeals in *Taylor*? Are there not certain presumptions an appellate court can make, depending upon the record? And to the extent any appellate review is de novo, why does it matter how the lower court reached its decision?

2. On remand, the court of appeals in *Taylor* responded with a lengthy opinion explaining its earlier judgment. *See* 499 F.2d 893 (5th Cir. 1974). There was no further review by the Supreme Court.

Frederick Schauer

GIVING REASONS

47 Stan. L. Rev. 633 (1995)

Sometimes people who make decisions give reasons to support and explain them. And sometimes they do not. The conventional picture of legal decisionmaking, with the appellate opinion as its archetype and "reasoned elaboration" as its credo,[1] is one in which giving reasons is both the norm and the ideal. Results unaccompanied by reasons are typically castigated as deficient on precisely those grounds. In law, and often elsewhere, giving reasons is seen as a necessary condition of rationality. To characterize a conclusion as an *ipse dixit* — a bare assertion unsupported by reasons — is no compliment.

The conventional picture, however, may be mistaken. Like voters who simply say aye or nay, like publishers and journal editors who turn down submissions without explanation, like employers and admissions officers who send rejection letters that announce outcomes without providing justifications, like homeowners who rarely explain to painters and carpenters whose proposals they have rejected why someone else was chosen, and like referees in sporting events who make calls that are ordinarily unsupported by explanations, many decisionmaking environments eschew the very feature that the conventional picture of legal decisionmaking takes as an essential component of rationality. Even within the law itself, decisionmaking devoid of reason-giving is more prevalent than might at first be apparent. When juries deliver verdicts, when the Supreme Court denies certiorari, when state supreme courts refuse review, when federal courts of appeals dispose of cases from the bench or without opinion, when trial judges rule on objections and frequently when they rule on motions, when lawyers exercise peremptory challenges and sometimes when judges dismiss jurors for cause, when housing and zoning authorities refuse to grant variances from their regulations, and sometimes when judges impose sentences, the conclusion stands alone, unsupported by reasons, justifications, or explanations.

Are all of these examples instances of irrationality? Some may be explained by the efficiencies of saving time, but is that the only justification for failing to give reasons? Do the examples suggest that there may be fewer grounds for treating reason-giving as a necessary condition of rationality than many scholars have supposed? Perhaps at times it is better not to give reasons than to give them. If so, when might that be? The practice of giving reasons in law has rarely been analyzed, perhaps because we assume the practice is central to what makes the legal enterprise distinctive, and is indeed virtually definitional of rationality. Yet once we see that the practice of giving reasons is not omnipresent, we are better situated to try to

---

1. The phrase "reasoned elaboration" originated in HENRY M. HART, JR. & ALBERT M. SACKS, THE LEGAL PROCESS: BASIC PROBLEMS IN THE MAKING AND APPLICATION OF LAW 143-52 (William N. Eskridge, Jr. & Philip P. Frickey eds., 1994).

understand what is gained — and at what price — when a decisionmaking environment requires giving reasons.

My aim is to explore the logic and morality of giving reasons — the practice of engaging in the linguistic act of providing a reason to justify what we do or what we decide. By "logic" I mean the structural relationship between a reason and what it is a reason for; and by "morality" I mean the question of what commitments, if any, attach to giving a reason, announcing it publicly, and writing it down in canonical form. If offering a reason consists of taking a decision to its next level of generality, as I will argue it ordinarily does, then is the offeror committed to the reason, and thereby to the other decisions that lie within its scope, or only to the actual decision itself? If only to the actual decision, then what role does the reason play? And if to the reason as well as to the result, then might there be stronger arguments against giving reasons than traditionally recognized?

This inquiry into the practice of giving reasons is part of the larger topic of the role of generality in law. Consider *rules*, *principles*, *standards*, *canons*, *maxims*, and, of course, *laws*. The institution we call "law" is soaked with generality, for one of its central features is the use of norms reaching beyond particular events and individual disputes. Indeed, it is more than mere coincidence that the very name for the enterprise — law — is the same one that scientists use to designate exceptionless empirical generalizations.

Although many of the devices of generality are familiar, reason-giving is both the most common and the least analyzed. When lawyers argue and when judges write opinions, they seek to *justify* their conclusions, and they do so by offering *reasons*. The reasons they provide, however, are broader than the outcomes they are reasons for. Indeed, if a reason were no more general than the outcome it purports to justify, it would scarcely count as a reason. The act of *giving* a reason, therefore, is an exercise in generalization. The lawyer or judge who gives a reason steps behind and beyond the case at hand to something more encompassing. By learning more about reasons, we may learn more about the place of generality in law, and indeed about the relationship of generality to rationality.

I

I start with a crucial preliminary. When referring to "reasons," I mean less by that word than is customary in the literature of law, moral philosophy, and normative theory. I certainly mean nothing so grand as Reason itself, the capacity of thought and rationality. But even when we get less grandiose than Reason, and think only of "reasons," the common uses still carry too much freight. Although philosophers debate whether reasons are the causes of the actions they are reasons for, whether they are internal or external, and whether they are propositions or beliefs or facts, they often use the word "reason" in such a way as to suggest that "good reason" is redundant and "bad reason" oxymoronic. To *have* a reason for a decision is to have a good reason, and what some might think a bad reason is simply no reason at all.

Here, by contrast, it is important that there be the possibility of bad reasons, or at least a thin sense of how *giving* a reason might differ from *having* a reason.

For my purposes, therefore, "reason" labels what follows the word "because" in, "We reach this result because" or, "I find for the plaintiff because" or, "You should come to this conclusion because." Under this definition, a judge who says she has decided for the plaintiff because it is raining in Calcutta offers a reason — "because it is raining in Calcutta" — even though the reason, unconnected to any sound basis for decision, is a bad one indeed. But although it is a bad reason, it still exhibits the feature of legal practice that I seek to analyze — the explicit act of offering a justification or explanation for the result reached.

This definition of "reason" may be jarring, yet it appears unavoidable. For when we look for alternative terms, we discover that words like "justification" and "explanation" contain the same linguistic ambiguities as does "reason." A *justification* may be what *does* justify a decision, such that something offered as a justification will not actually *be* a justification if it proves faulty. Alternatively, a justification may be the act of offering something in the *form* of a justification, such that what is offered remains a justification even if a bad one. Similarly, the *explanation* of some phenomenon may be that which in fact explains what happened, or it may be the verbal act of attempting to explain something without regard to the soundness of the explanation. My definition of "reason" tracks the latter of each of these pairs, for my focus is the statement rather than soundness of what is stated. It follows that I am concerned not with *having* a reason, but instead with *giving* a reason, and with what follows from the very act of giving one, whether it is a good reason or not.

II

It will be useful in further setting the stage to note the variety of legal modes in which reason-giving is absent. The voice is not one of persuasion or argument, but one of authority, of command. Statutes say, "Do it!"; they do not say, "Do it because." The bare assertion characteristic of statutes suggests a relationship between the authority implicit in a statute and the nonuse of reasons in statutes. Only rarely do statutes offer reasons to justify their prescriptions, and then usually out of concern about potential interpretive problems in difficult cases. Typically, drafters of statutes, like sergeants and parents, simply do not see the need to give reasons, and often see a strong need not to: The act of giving a reason is the antithesis of authority. When the voice of authority fails, the voice of reason emerges. Or vice versa. But whatever the hierarchy between reason and authority, reasons are what we typically give to support what we conclude precisely when the mere fact we have concluded is not enough. And reasons are what we typically avoid when the assertion of authority is thought independently important.

A second category of reason-avoidance in the law occurs when legal decisionmakers facing specific controversies simply announce results without giving reasons to support them. When juries deliver verdicts, when the Supreme Court denies certiorari, and when trial judges rule on objections, for example, the decisionmakers speak with a declarative rather than an imperative voice. Yet here as well, each outcome is unaccompanied by an articulate explanation of why the decisionmaker reached the announced conclusion. Reasons do play a role in producing such decisions — jurors give reasons to each other when they deliberate, Supreme Court justices have reasons for denying certiorari, and trial judges have reasons for overruling objections — but the form in which the conclusions are announced cuts off access to those reasons, suggesting that the reasons are none of the reader's (or hearer's) business.

A third category, a mixed case, is the class of decisions announced in the form of an authoritative restatement of (some of) the facts, yet still without a statement of the reasons supporting the outcome. The "no-action" letters or advisory opinions of some administrative agencies, for example, commonly repeat some of the facts presented by the requester of the opinion, but the restatement of facts is followed only by a bald pronouncement of intended inaction. Trial judges sometimes employ this approach, coupling a narrative of their conclusions of fact with a quite uninformative list of their conclusions of law, and jury verdicts may take this form when juries are required to answer special questions in conjunction with their general verdicts.

In contrast to these reason-barren decisionmaking modes stands the practice of giving reasons. Commonly associated with appellate argument and appellate opinions, the practice of explicitly providing reasons to support conclusions is also found in presidential veto messages, commission and committee reports, numerous trial court opinions at preliminary or final stages, some arbitration opinions, and the explanatory opinions or private letter rulings of agencies such as the Internal Revenue Service. At times the practice of giving reasons is explicitly mandated, as with the requirement in the Administrative Procedure Act that decisions "shall include a statement of findings and conclusions, and the reasons or basis therefor, on all the material issues of fact, law, or discretion presented on the record." And, of course, a host of less formal deliberative settings exist in which we expect conclusions to be explicitly supported by a statement of reasons underlying those conclusions. Thus in many contexts, yet tantalizingly not in many others, a decisionmaker is expected to provide, ordinarily in writing, a statement of the reasons supporting her conclusion. It is now time to examine the structure and status of those reasons, for such an understanding will enable us to see when it is important that reasons be given, and when it is equally important that they not be.

III

Consider the logical structure of a reason. I intend to argue that reasons are typically propositions of greater generality than the conclusions they are reasons for, so we must start by looking at the idea of generality itself. Initially, the dimension of generality is a measure of the size of the field of extension of some term or principle. When we say that one term is more general than another, we usually mean that the former includes all of the latter, and more. The class of mammals is more general than the class of dogs, and the class of dogs more general than the class of Dalmatians. The class of law students is less general than the class of university students, which is in turn less general than the class of students.

So too with rules or principles. "Write thank-you notes" is less general than "Show appreciation for social kindnesses," and "Do unto others as you would have them do unto you" is the most general of all. In law, "Intentional misrepresentation by fiduciaries is unlawful" is more general than "The directors of Delaware corporations shall not deceive the shareholders," which is more general than "It is unlawful for the directors of the Delaware Widget Corporation to include false or misleading representations in proxy statements."

. . . .

The extreme of nongenerality is "specificity" or "particularity." "Susan's two-year-old Dalmatian is named Ralph." "Mary should write a thank-you note to John for having her to dinner on March 23, 1991." "Jane acted unlawfully in signing, as a member of the Board of Directors of Delaware Widget Corporation, the April 28, 1987, proxy statement containing false statements about the profitability of Delaware Widget's plant in Dover, Delaware." And although a statement can be more particular (less general) than another without being this specific, generality and particularity mark opposite directions on the same scale.

With the distinction between the general and the particular in hand, consider a typical case of reason-giving. To give a reason for attending a dinner party despite illness, I might first give a characterization — a statement of some facts about the situation. I say that although I have a cold, I had promised to attend the dinner party and knew that the host had relied on my acceptance of the invitation. And then I include that characterization within a more general principle, saying perhaps that it is rude and therefore unacceptable to break social promises except in dire emergencies. Similarly, consider a housing authority's decision to deny a building permit. The housing authority, asked to give a reason for its decision, first provides a characterization but not limited to this case: "The plans indicate that the house will be three stories high [the characterization], and we do not permit buildings taller than two stories [the general principle]." So too in law. When a court gives a reason, it typically either calls forth a preexisting rule that encompasses this case (as well as others), as when a court says that a complaint will not be accepted because it (and many others) is barred by a six-year statute of limitations, or, if candidly acknowledging that it is making new law, it announces a new rule that includes cases other than the one at hand. When then-Judge Cardozo concluded in *MacPherson v. Buick Motor Co.* that Buick was liable to Mr. MacPherson despite a lack of contractual privity, Cardozo gave as a reason the new rule that in *all* such cases, lack of privity would not bar recovery, and gave as a reason for that rule the even more general proposition that liability should be placed on those with the power to locate and correct defects. When the California Supreme Court in *Knight v. Kaiser Co.* refused to allow the plaintiff to claim that the sand pile under which her son died was an "attractive nuisance," it supported its conclusion by explaining why sand piles — *all* sand piles, and not just the sand pile under which the plaintiff's son was asphyxiated — were not to be considered attractive nuisances. When the United States Supreme Court decided *Ernst & Ernst v. Hochfelder*, it justified its refusal to allow the plaintiff to recover for securities fraud under rule 10b-5 by explaining why *no* defendant without the state of mind known as scienter could be held liable, the consequences being that *this* defendant without scienter could not be held liable.

The feature of giving reasons that I wish to highlight is now clear. The key point, indeed the linchpin for the entire analysis, is that, ordinarily, *to provide a reason for a decision is to include that decision within a principle of greater generality than the decision itself.*[21] When we provide a reason for a particular decision, we typically provide a rule, principle, standard, norm, or maxim broader than the decision itself, and this is so even if the form of articulation is not exactly what we normally think of as a principle. "I criticize Mary because she did not write a thank-you note" presupposes (or conversationally implies) that there is a principle pursuant to which people in Mary's situation should write thank-you notes, and that Mary's behavior, falling within the scope of the principle, is open to criticism for not comporting with the principle. "The members of the Board of Directors of Delaware Widget Corporation are liable to the stockholders because they signed a proxy statement containing misleading facts about the company's facilities" similarly calls forth (or creates) as its justification a rule more general than one pertaining only to the behavior of *these* directors with respect to *this* proxy statement containing *these* facts about *this* plant. To provide a reason in a particular case is thus to transcend the very particularity of that case.

The same structure also operates when we justify a rule or principle itself. Just as providing a reason for an outcome ordinarily takes the outcome to a greater level of generality, so too does providing a reason for a reason, or a reason for a rule or principle. When the Supreme Court in *New York Times Co. v. Sullivan* established the so-called "actual malice" rule, it gave as its reason the proposition that *anything* resembling a seditious libel action — not just those civil defamation actions to which the actual malice rule applied — violated the First Amendment. The scope of instances encompassed by the reason — all state actions carrying the same risks to freedom of speech and press as a seditious libel prosecution — is broader than the scope of instances encompassed by the actual malice rule that the reason was provided to support. To justify a principle is to put the class of instances encompassed by it within a wider class of instances encompassed by a more general principle, and thus to maintain that the narrower principle is sound because it is subsumed under the stipulated-to-be-sound broader principle.

A parallel relationship therefore exists at numerous levels of argument, and the process of providing a reason is ordinarily nothing more than (but nothing less

---

21. I say "ordinarily" because some reasons might seem less general than the decisions that they support. An answer to why it is true that every American car has an engine could be that Fords have engines, Chevrolets have engines, Cadillacs have engines, and so on. Sometimes when a decisionmaker announces an analogy as a reason for some result, it is unclear that the analogy is more general than the result. And when we narrow a principle because it encompasses an intuitively unacceptable result . . . , the reason for narrowing the principle is less general than the result the principle supports. Although it might be argued that all of these instances are just different versions of giving reasons more general than their results (narrowing a previous principle still yields a reason more general than the particular result, for example), I will not pursue this possibility, for nothing in my analysis turns on whether *all* reasons are more general than the results they support. It is sufficient for my purposes that many are, and my interest here is the class of generalizations offered as reasons for decisions, without regard to whether this class exhausts the class of all reasons.

than) the process of locating a result within a greater degree of generality. Reasons, therefore, are commonly results, rules, principles, maxims, standards, or norms taken to the next level of generality. But regardless of the level of generality, and whether we are seeking to justify a result or a rule, the central point is that to say "*x* because *y*" is not only to say *x*, but to say *y* as well.[24] When put this way the claim seems trivially tautological, but its consequences are both interesting and problematic.

IV

The notion of greater generality thus locates the logical relationship between a reason and what it is a reason for. To explore the implications of this relationship, I begin with some simple conversational examples to introduce the central issue of *commitment*, and to put on the table the question whether various conversational and social practices establish fixed points from which it may be unreasonable to expect legal practice, situated at least partially within social practice, to depart.

You ask why I am carrying an umbrella, and I respond that the weather forecast predicted rain. Although the response is not explicitly prescriptive, it embraces the mandate, "Carry an umbrella when rain is forecast," which is more general than the fact that I am carrying this umbrella on this day in response to a more general forecast. In everyday social practice, to provide a reason for an act is paradigmatically to provide, if only implicitly, a general prescription — a rule, standard, or guideline — encompassing that act.

Although it requires contextual implications to move from reason ("because the weather forecast predicted rain") to norm ("Carry an umbrella when the weather forecast predicts rain"), the move involves few contestable conversational rules. If "because the weather forecast predicted rain" does not implicitly embrace "Carry an umbrella when the weather forecast predicts rain," then there is no point in giving the reason at all.[25] So although the move from the reason to the norm presupposes compliance with the sincerity conditions of discourse, that is, that one

---

24. An important question, though not mine here, is whether saying *x*, without more, commits the speaker to at least some *y* of a degree of generality larger than *x* alone. The issue is important to the possibility that naked results might have precedential effect. If conventions of categorization place a particular in a larger category even when there is no explicit statement to that effect, then (and only then) can a particular establish a rule capable of being followed in the future.

25. Nothing here addresses the weight of the reason. If you ask why I am carrying an umbrella, and I say that I am carrying an umbrella because the weather forecast calls for rain, and you then observe that the weather forecast called for rain yesterday but that I was not carrying an umbrella yesterday, a perfectly legitimate response on my part is that although yesterday's weather forecast gave me a reason to carry an umbrella yesterday, the fact that I had to carry two armloads of books to my office yesterday gave me a stronger reason not to carry an umbrella. What I have a reason to do is not necessarily what I should do, all things considered. My claim is that there is a commitment to the reason, not a commitment to its conclusiveness, although a strong version of Legal Realism might question whether and when this distinction (and its kin — burdens of proof, standards of review, and levels of scrutiny) makes a decisional difference.

ordinarily means what one says, my point is basically a logical one. If in saying, "*x* because *y*," one is not (at least at that moment, and under those conditions) affirming *y*, then one is either being dishonest or self-contradictory. So if I decline a dinner invitation *because of* illness, I have, to say the least, a heavy burden of explanation if the host sees me at a restaurant with friends on that very day, even though no explanation would be called for had I not claimed illness.

This is familiar ground, for it undergirds what (among other things) goes on in the standard law school socratic dialogue when a student, asked to give a reason for an assertion, is bombarded with an array of carefully crafted hypotheticals designed to test the student's commitment to the reason she has just offered.[27] Implicit in the process is the notion that one offers a reason for a result (or a rule) is, at least at that time, committed to the reason as well as to the less general result. And equally implicit is the corollary that to be committed to a reason is to be committed to the results encompassed by that reason. Because reasons are typically more general than the results they are reasons for, to offer a reason is to offer a statement encompassing at least one result other than the one that prompted giving the reason in the first place. The minimal sincerity conditions of ordinary conversational practice thus indicate that the giver of a reason is, at least at the moment of giving the reason, committed to no less than one result other than the result that prompted giving the reason.

But now things get troubling. We have been assuming simultaneity, such that if I say, "*x* because *y*," then I am committed, because of obligations of sincerity and noncontradiction, to *y*, at least at that time and under what I take to be the same conditions leading me to conclude *x*. But let us eliminate the condition of simultaneity and consider the possibility of cross-temporal commitment to reasons as well as results. Does giving a reason *now* commit the giver of the reason *later*? Consider first a silly hypothetical case. A friend and I are talking about food.[30] The talk turns to lobster, and I say I adore it. She asks why. I say I adore lobster because I like the red color, find the taste and texture of shellfish very appealing, and enjoy the very process of cracking the shells and working to remove the flesh inside.

Two weeks later, I am at her house for dinner. She serves crab legs. But because I was bitten by a crab at the ocean as a child, I have grown up with a great distaste for crab, even though it is the only shellfish I dislike. Consequently, I cannot and do not eat the crab legs.

Now, is my host justifiably *more* aggrieved when I refuse to eat the crab legs under these circumstances than if I had previously said nothing? Am I now obliged, if I do not eat the crab legs, to offer not only an explanation, but an *apology*?

---

27. One perfectly legitimate response to such questioning tends to be neither encouraged nor accepted: "Professor X, the rule I offered would generate a bad result for the hypothetical you just posed, but of course you know as well as I do that the generation of one or even several bad results by faithful application of a rule is no argument against a rule, since all rules are overinclusive or underinclusive vis-à-vis some ideal conception of the right result. So I will stick with the rule I offered, even in the face of the bad result you suggested, because I believe that this rule will generate, in application, fewer bad results than any other rule we can imagine."

30. This part is neither hypothetical nor silly.

Intuitively, I think the answer to these questions is yes, precisely because the crab legs fall within the literal scope of the reason I had given previously. Just by giving the reason, I induced reliance on the part of another, and inducing reasonable reliance places obligations on the one who does so. The reason accordingly resembles a promise, and having given this reason I am no less committed to the particulars lying within its scope than I would be to the particulars lying within the scope of something like, "I will eat shellfish." The commitment creates a prima facie obligation to act in conformity with it, and requires me to offer something — at least an apology — when I am unwilling or unable to keep it.[31]

This example tests the extent to which general assertions (of which reasons are a species, at least in this context) carry the same kinds of promissory commitments vis-à-vis future actions or decisions as do locutions more explicitly seen as promises. One possibility, of course, is that they do not. Perhaps the word "promise," or a close equivalent varying with conversational context, is a necessary condition for commitment in the future to what we say now. Perhaps someone relies at her peril on an assertion not explicitly flagged as a promise. If so, anyone relying on what I say, absent my use of words like "promise," does so at her own risk, and I have no reason to feel committed to complying with my past assertions.

Yet this seems wrong. Even when we do not use words like "promise," and we ordinarily do not, we expect that others will rely in the future on what we say today, at least absent intervening distinctions obvious to both of us. If it sounds right that the dinner host has reason to feel slightly more aggrieved by my refusal to eat crab than she would have been had I not given a reason for liking lobster that linguistically encompasses crab, then it appears that even in ordinary conversation we make prima facie commitments to future decisions when we give reasons more general than the particular decisions or statements that they are given as reasons for.

V

Now consider the same question — whether there exists at least a prima facie commitment to future decisions lying within the scope of a general reason — in the context of legal decisionmaking. We start with an actual case. In *New York v. United States*, the Supreme Court held[33] that federal legislation exceeds the bounds of congressional power under Article I, or violates the Tenth Amendment, or both, when it commands a state legislature to legislate in a particular way. The case involved the Low-Level Radioactive Waste Policy Act. One portion of the Act — the "take title" provision — required states to either regulate low-level radioactive waste in a certain way or take title to the waste and provide for its lawful disposal. In explaining

---

31. I accept that the *degree* of commitment may vary, such that the reason "because there is no shellfish I do not like" may, because of listener expectations, create a stronger commitment than "because lobster meat is sweet."

33. Of course my summary of what the Court "held," what materials I use to reach that conclusion, and just what it is for a court to "hold" something, are exactly the points at issue.

why this provision violated the Constitution, Justice O'Connor's majority opinion stated that "the Federal Government may not compel the States to enact or administer a federal regulatory program."

New York v. United States is both a bad and a good example for the point I wish to pursue. It is bad because it is a constitutional case from the Supreme Court of the United States, and is thus part of the decisionmaking milieu in which the indeterminacy claims of Legal Realism are at their acme. Given the operation of the selection effect,[37] the open-endedness of textual norms, and the extant array of Supreme Court opinions (to say nothing of other legitimate sources), the likelihood of serious formal legal constraint in most Supreme Court decisions is small, and such cases thus provide a poor vehicle for pursuing a series of arguments about the possibility of constraint. Accordingly, I use this case as a metaphor for the possibility of constraint, and the sources thereof, rather than as a claim about constraint in these circumstances.

I pick *New York v. United States* as my metaphor, however, because it contains two desirable features. First, it includes the above-quoted sentence, a crisp example of a reason broader than the result in the case, and one plainly embracing a range of statutes other than the one before the Court. Second, the Court was quite clear that this reason was conclusive. It was not a factor to be balanced, nor something that would decide the case if all other things were equal (which they never are). Indeed, the Court made it clear that this principle could not be overridden even in cases of compelling interest. Based upon what the Court said, this case was decided the way it was *because* of the Court's statement that any act of Congress infringing on this principle was *eo ipso* unconstitutional.

Now suppose a different statute comes before the same decisionmakers in 1995. Upon looking at this statute, enacted under different conditions, the reaction of the justices who made up the 1992 majority is (1) that the statute is an act of Congress compelling the states to enact a federal regulatory program, and thus within the literal reach of the reason offered previously; and (2) that had the justices contemplated the possible existence of such an act in 1992, they never would have said what they said in 1992. The question is then on the table: Are 1992's decisionmakers committed in 1995 to the result indicated by the reasons *they* gave in 1992, even though when faced with 1995's situation they realize that what they said in 1992 was not what they should have said?[42] The question in the legal case is the same as in the crab case: Are reasons actually given to be considered commitments, of the same genus as contracts and promises, or are they simply noncommiting

---

37. That is, the proposition that cases that reach trial and appellate courts are not "a random sample of the mass of underlying cases," and its various effects on studies of the legal system.

42. The possibility of drawing a distinction now (in 1995) is a red herring. If the previously articulated principle did not draw the distinction, then drawing the distinction now, even if plausible, is inconsistent with the previously articulated principle. "All *a* except *y*" is inconsistent with and not mere supplementation of "all *a*" . . . .

statements subject to unimpeded defeat in the event of changed or newly discovered circumstances?[43]

One quaint response could be that the Court's statement in *New York v. United States* was merely *dicta* and not the *holding* of the Court. As a result, according to the traditional dicta/holding distinction, the Court in 1995 would not be bound by its 1992 statement. But this will not do. First, the 1992 statement is not dicta in the sense that it is an aside unnecessary to the result. The statement is the very proposition that generates the result, or so the Court said. Without this proposition, there is, we can assume, no reason for the result. And because this reason directly supports the Court's result, it does not become dicta just because the Court could have given a narrower reason. Under that logic all reasons would be dicta, since all reasons can always be narrowed to the point at which their degree of generality is no greater than the outcome they support. If a reason that can be narrower is for that reason dicta, then anything other than the announcement of an outcome is dicta. Once we recognize that reasons are usually, as here, results taken to a greater level of generality, then an argument from the dicta/holding distinction for the non-committing character of dicta collapses into an argument against the committing character of reasons. The argument from dicta, therefore, does not add a new argument, but only restates the argument against the claim that reasons, when given, create commitments. The argument from dicta may be relevant to thinking about the future effect of a statement *not* standing in some sort of "vertical" justificatory relationship to the immediate result,[46] but it does not help in thinking about the relation of reasons to commitments.

If a reason is the result itself at a greater level of generality, then a legal reason has the same logical structure as the reason in the crab case. And as in the crab case, such a reason appears to be a prima facie commitment to other outcomes falling within its scope. While any conclusion about the conditions of commitment is an empirical assessment of social practice, this assessment nevertheless appears sound. First, if the commitment-creating intuition in the crab case correctly reflects background social practice, then such social practice is likely to substantially influence legal practices existing against that background. This is not to say that legal practice might not diverge from social practice. It is to say, however,

---

43. My reference to "unimpeded defeat" should be read in conjunction with both note 25 *supra* and my repeated references to commitment as prima facie. When there is a subsequent commitment to reasons, the weight of the commitment will produce some outcomes different from the ones that would have been produced without the commitment. This is because the weight of the commitment increases the weight of the countervailing factor necessary to override the commitment. The existence of a commitment will thus, over time, produce an array of results in which the existence of the commitment turned out to be dispositive, even though it is not necessarily dispositive in every case. A noncommitting reason, by contrast, carries no independent decisional force in future cases, and stands as no barrier to a court reaching the result it would have reached even in the absence of any previous action.

46. Even this is not so clear. What is the point of making a statement, even if orthogonal to the result to which it is connected, unless the maker of the statement is at least slightly committed to, and therefore constrained by, that statement in the future?

that the existence of a background social practice suggests, in the absence of more explicit counterconventions, that legal practices are best understood in ways consistent with, rather than contradictory to, the background social practice. Insofar as there is a background social practice pursuant to which we are prima facie expected to mean tomorrow what we say today, legal practice is more plausibly understood as consistent rather than inconsistent with that practice.

The conclusion that, in law, giving reasons commits the giver is also supported by the fact that quotations directly justifying a result have considerable purchase in legal argument. Direct quotes from previous cases do not always control; lawyers argue that such quotes are taken out of context and they strain to distinguish the cases in which the quotes first appeared. Still, the deployment of a direct quote to support the argued result at least appears to shift the burden of persuasion by imposing a burden of denial on the lawyer seeking to resist the effect of the quote. If this hypothesis is correct, it would further support the conclusion that the legal practice of commitment, exemplified in the notion that the 1995 Court would be more constrained as a consequence of the 1992 statement than it would have been had the 1992 statement not existed, is broadly consistent with the social practice of commitment we saw in the crab example.

To repeat, the argument for commitment *in the law* is stronger if the argument for commitment as a social practice — the crab case — is sound. If a social practice exists pursuant to which reasons given in ordinary discourse constrain and commit future action, it establishes a baseline of minimal commitment below which it would be difficult for the legal system (or any other social subsystem) to go. Just as legal language has only a limited ability to depart from ordinary language, even while legal usage may diverge from ordinary usage, legal commitment practice cannot completely depart from social commitment practice.

The phenomenon, however, is not symmetrical. If an antecedent social practice of commitment exists, it may contaminate legal practice, making it difficult for the legal system to choose a model of noncommitment even if it wanted to. But if there is no social practice of commitment, if my inference from the crab case is as wrong as the case is silly, institutions might still create their own practices of commitment. Still, it is less likely that there is a legal practice of commitment to reasons if the social practice of commitment does not exist.

The argument for the nonexistence of commitment to reasons in legal practice likely stems from a common law tradition of particularity. Law is not about generality, the tradition holds, but about particular situations and decisions in cases that the infinite variety of human experience ensures will never repeat themselves. So although the reason given by a court reflects a decisionmaker's thinking at the time of her decision, and perhaps also demonstrates respect for the subject of the decision, it should not, so the argument goes, be considered a commitment. Because the concrete dominates the abstract, and the particular dominates the general, the argument continues, the same justices who gave reasons in 1992 may say in 1995 that the issue looks different upon seeing different facts and a different situation. Moreover, abstract reasoning is necessarily deficient, and rules are incomplete until applied, so any abstract conclusion must be considered genuinely tentative and defeasible until actual cases provide the privileged knowledge that only the concrete can give us.

But if this argument against a commitment model of reasons is sound, then surely the practice of *giving* reasons has developed far beyond what the use of those reasons could justify. For example, if reasons were not commitments of at least some weight, then it would make sense to write opinions as if they were no-action letters, with detailed statements of fact followed by naked statements of result. But because judicial opinions are much more than that, and because the reasons they provide serve as more than biographical guides to the feelings of those who write them, much suggests that the existing practices of opinion-writing and reason-giving are not those that would have been expected to flow from a thoroughgoing commitment to particularity. Instead, the actual practice of writing and using opinions seems more consistent with a contract/commitment model of the force of legal reasons.

VI

Description is not justification. But if giving reasons is centrally explained by a reason's generality and the reason giver's commitment to that generality, then giving a reason is like setting forth a rule. Justifying reason-giving will thus track justifying rule-based decisionmaking and, conversely, justifying the avoidance of reason-giving will parallel justifying highly particularistic decisionmaking. In other words, justifying the practice of giving reasons and treating those reasons as commitments will implicate familiar questions about the advantages and disadvantages of rules. Because I and others have said much about these questions in other contexts, I will only focus on a few of the most relevant dimensions.

If a decisionmaker is prima facie committed in the future to the reasons she gives for a conclusion now, and if those reasons are typically more general than the conclusion they support, then she commits herself to deciding some number of cases whose full factual detail she cannot possibly now comprehend. One consequence of a commitment model, therefore, is the treatment of consistency for consistency's sake as an independent value, although it is debatable when and whether we should do so. Moreover, a decisionmaker committed to her present reasons commits her future self to treating the very pastness of the past as a reason for decision in accordance with that past, and it is equally debatable when and whether we should do that. Apart from this familiar terrain in the literature on precedent, however, there is another way current knowledge of future commitment constrains what we do in the present. Think of a judge who reaches a conclusion but then, after struggling with the opinion, says, "It won't write." Just what does that mean, and what assumptions does it reflect?

One possibility is that a judge who says that an outcome "won't write" is simply rejecting a creation model of judicial power. Such a judge refuses to reach any result unauthorized by an identifiable preexisting legal rule encompassing some plausible presentation of the facts in the present case. In other words, the judge decides (by "hunch," by "gestalt," by "situation sense," or by some other nonformulaic method) that a case ought to be decided in a particular way. She then tries to find a preexisting legal rule that encompasses most of what seems relevant in the case and that produces the desired result. If such a rule exists, all well and good. If it does not, however, then a judge who believes that her role prohibits her from creating new law will not reach this result. "It won't write."

But suppose the judge has a sufficiently post-Realist understanding of her role such that she recognizes that she is "permitted" to reach a result for which she cannot find a preexisting rule, so long as she can write a reason for it. But we have seen that a reason is, itself, a type of rule. As a result, a judge required to give a reason is a judge required either to call forth a preexisting rule or to create a new one. We can understand why a judge who believed she should not create rules would say, "It won't write," when there is no preexisting rule, but why would a judge who did not think that judicial rule-creation was uncommon or undesirable ever say such a thing?

Perhaps the very fact of writing (or writing publicly, although the two are hardly the same) serves as a constraint. Perhaps there are things we can think but cannot write down. But why would a judge believe an outcome to be correct when it could not be explained by a reason? Perhaps the result itself is indefensible, but that begs the question, for then we can ask what makes a result indefensible. One possibility is that there is a reason for the result, albeit a legally, socially, or morally impermissible one. The judge might believe, for example, that the plaintiff should win because the plaintiff is white. This is a reason, but its social and moral unacceptability operates as a constraint.[59] So perhaps to say that an outcome "won't write" is to say that it is justifiable only by illegitimate reasons.

Judges and other decisionmakers rarely think their *own* outcomes illegitimate, however, so it is unlikely that the perception that there are things we can think but not write down only concerns morally and socially impermissible reasons. So if neither a prohibition on rule-creation nor outcome-impermissibility explains, "It won't write," then the only remaining explanation is one premised on the equation of rationality with some minimum quantum of generality. The idea of an outcome that is not patently illegitimate, but still incapable of being justified in writing, appears based on a decisionmaking norm about the size of the field within which decisions should be made. Perhaps some decisions are simply too narrow to be rational. Perhaps some norms require a decisionmaker to include a decision within a type, field, or class at least somewhat bigger than the particular case. In other words, perhaps the constraint of unwritability (and therefore of reason-giving) is based on the idea that generality is a necessary condition of rationality.

I am not sure, however, that this is so. More importantly, I am not sure that the legal system operates as if this were so. If the legal system operated on the assumption that giving reasons served an important decision-disciplining function, it would be less tolerant of reason-avoiding (or reason-hiding) in jury verdicts, sentencing, certiorari denials, no-action letters, exclusion of jurors, rulings on objections, and summary affirmances. In short, these situations suggest that the legal system functions as if openly placing a result within a larger category is not a

---

59. If the reason were morally unacceptable but, at the same time, socially acceptable, then a judge who believed it would not hesitate to write it down.

necessary condition of rationality. Yet the legal system does appear to suppose that it *is* sometimes desirable for legal decisionmakers to be committed to, and therefore constrained by, a range of results larger than the case at hand. This might, as noted above, stem from a preference for stability, but it might also be a corrective against the potential for the bias built into excess particularity. Although there is no basis for presuming that particular decisions are necessarily a function of decisionmaker partiality, it might be supposed that particular decisions *are* often, empirically, the result of decisionmaker partiality, and that an artificial constraint of giving reasons, and therefore of generality, is designed to counteract this tendency.

If we think that giving reasons ensures generality, and generality is a way to improve the quality of decisions, then there is a plausible argument that subsequent decisionmakers, even within the same decisionmaking institution, should not be committed to and constrained by the reasons offered by their predecessors. If those predecessors were compelled to offer reasons and to be committed to the results encompassed by those reasons because it would make *their* decisions better, then their commitment need not carry over to subsequent decisionmakers. Other arguments for commitment, however, especially arguments for cross-temporal stability, and for intrainstitutional stability in the face of changing personnel, might militate in favor of a broader conception of commitment. Here the arguments closely track the argument supporting a strong regime of precedential constraint. Rather than rehearse those arguments, I merely note that the arguments in favor of precedent or stare decisis as a strong constraint often require decisionmakers at a later time to subjugate, in the service of stability for stability's sake, their own best judgment to the erroneous (as they see it) judgment of earlier decisionmakers.[66] Similarly, arguments against strong precedential constraint, which stress case-by-case optimization and question why the value of stability should compel decisionmakers to repeat the mistakes of the past, also apply to the question why decisionmakers should subjugate their own best judgment to general statements made in the past, and thus also to the question why decisionmakers should be required to give reasons, a practice likely to have that effect.

VII

Precedential constraint permits courts to influence outcomes in future cases that they may now only dimly perceive. Reason-giving has the same potential. If the reasons provided by courts constrain future decisions, then giving reasons can be opposed as undesirably encouraging courts to influence decisions arising in contexts at which they can only guess. Consider, in this regard, the aversion to advisory opinions. Although some state courts issue advisory opinions, and although courts in other countries sometimes issue advisory opinions or evaluate the constitutionality of proposed legislation without the encumbrance of the "case or controversy"

---

66. When the later decisionmaker agrees with the earlier decision, the constraint of precedent is redundant, as is the constraint of commitment to reasons under those circumstances.

requirement, federal courts in the United States are different. Here the advisory opinion is anathema, and for numerous well-massaged reasons American federal courts will not decide cases removed from the context of a real controversy between real parties.

The aversion to advisory opinions, however, stands in tension with the commitment model of legal reasons. If a court is constrained by the reasons it gives in addition to the result it reaches, and if reasons are results taken to a greater level of generality and so include a wider class of acts, then under a commitment model a court giving reasons *is* deciding a class of cases not now before the court, and a class of cases for which the supposed crucible of experience is missing. Thus every time a court gives a reason it is, in effect, giving an advisory opinion.

If legal practice thus tolerates a wide range of decisions based on speculative imaginings about possible cases within the extension of a reason, then requiring a concrete case seems peculiar. For example, suppose the reason given to support the result in one actual case encompasses a thousand potential cases. Since giving the reason represents some commitment to a decision when one of those thousand cases actually arises, the case or controversy requirement dictates that only one out of 1001 cases be real before a court offers its judgment on the other thousand. Why is it so important, then, that there be even one real case, given that the decision also decides a thousand cases that have yet to occur?

This question is not rhetorical. There may be good grounds for wanting one real case before effectively deciding a thousand other ones. It might be desirable to cabin the courts, for example, and the aversion to advisory opinions is a strategic way of preventing overreaching. But my concern here involves the interplay between the particular and the general, and with the claim that seeing *a* particular is an important part of making general decisions. Now it is true that seeing one particular may, at times, help a decisionmaker imagine other cases. But just as human weakness and partiality might prevent us from imagining what others would imagine, so too might real cases distort by "hogging the stage," occupying so much of the foreground of our phenomenology that they narrow rather than broaden the imagination, and dominate a form of decisionmaking that seeks desirable outcomes for many possible cases whose own details can only be the product of guesswork. Although there may be good reasons to worry about the distorting effects of uninformed speculation, there may be equally good reasons to worry about the distorting effects of decisionmaking overinformed by the grip of a particular instance. Perhaps this is what people mean by "result-oriented," a curious phrase that few outside the legal culture take as the pejorative it is within the culture. But to the extent that it remains a pejorative, it is because real cases produce reasons whose array of results is, on balance, more detrimental than the good produced by the right result in the original case, such that it would have been better to reach the wrong result in the original case.

From this perspective, one possible approach to reason-giving is to give better reasons, ones that will not produce a hundred wrong results in exchange for one right one. Another is to reject the commitment model of giving reasons, but this is difficult given the commitment model of social practice. A third approach is not to give reasons at all. If reasons are what cause the right outcome in this case to generate wrong outcomes in others, then weakening the reason-giving requirement can produce the right outcome now without negative side effects. In effect, lowering the cost of reaching the right result may make it easier to reach the right result more often.

The argument against giving reasons thus tracks the argument against advisory opinions, and the legal culture's attraction to reasons and aversion to advisory opinions is inconsistent in that both involve deciding hypothetical cases possibly arising under facts we can only dimly perceive now. We might even say that the legal culture is wrong to think itself averse to advisory opinions, because advisory opinions are given all the time. On the other hand, the legal system may be right to think that rendering advisory opinions is bad idea. If so, then giving reasons may be a worse idea than many people suspect.

VIII

The thesis I advance, therefore, is that giving reasons *is* committing, although not inviolably so. Having given a reason, the reason-giver has, by virtue of an existing social practice, committed herself to deciding those cases within the scope of the reason in accordance with the reason. Insofar as the word "commitment" might be too strong to capture the defeasible commitments to which I refer, it could be said simply that the very act of giving a reason provides an independent ground (i.e., a "reason" for action, in a different sense of "reason") for following that reason in future cases. These grounds compete with other bases in decisionmaking, especially the desire to decide *this* case in the right way, but the grounds emanating from the practice of giving reasons still reduce the reason-giver's freedom of decision in future cases.

As a device of institutional design, reason-giving can thus be seen as contingent rather than necessary, a style of decisionmaking with disadvantages of excess commitment that might at times outweigh its advantages. But there are advantages to giving reasons, the most obvious being the very commitment that is at times a disadvantage. Although decisionmakers are typically loath to commit themselves out of reluctance to constrain their own future decisions,[72] others might nevertheless want to compel decisionmakers to commit themselves. When the forces of institutional design require decisionmakers to give reasons, it may be that these forces have more cause to want commitment than do the decisionmakers themselves. Decisionmakers usually desire flexibility and the freedom to try to reach the optimal outcome in each case. But from an institutional perspective, the virtues of decisionmaker flexibility and case-by-case optimization are sometimes best

---

72. The dynamics of reliance complicate the statement in the text. Insofar as a decisionmaker's commitment induces reliance on the part of those likely affected by future decisions, decisionmakers may voluntarily commit themselves in order to encourage such reliance. In some contexts, decisionmakers may encourage reliance because relying parties may value reliance sufficiently to "pay" for it, as in contracts, by making commitments in return.

tempered by an appreciation of the values of reliance and stability for stability's sake.[73] When designers of institutions (including the democratic process itself) believe it would be beneficial for decisionmakers to commit themselves, and when the designers believe the decisionmakers are likely to undercommit, then imposing a requirement of reason-giving on the decisionmakers — that they state in advance how they are likely to decide cases other than the one before them and that in the future they treat their prior statements as constraining — is a valuable way of achieving the proper level of commitment.

Distinct from the question of commitment, however, is the decision-disciplining function of giving reasons. Again, decisionmakers themselves are unlikely to fully apprehend and appreciate this function, for most decisionmakers underestimate the need for external quality control of their own decisions. But when institutional designers have grounds for believing that decisions will systemically be the product of bias, self-interest, insufficient reflection, or simply excess haste, requiring decisionmakers to give reasons may counteract some of these tendencies. Under some circumstances, the very time required to give reasons may reduce excess haste and thus produce better decisions. A reason-giving mandate will also drive out illegitimate reasons when they are the only plausible explanation for particular outcomes.

Additionally, giving reasons may be a sign of respect. As noted at the outset, announcing an outcome without giving a reason is consistent with the exercise of authority, for such an announcement effectively indicates that neither discussion nor objection will be tolerated. When the source of a decision rather than the reason behind it compels obedience, there is less warrant for explaining the basis for the decision to those who are subject to it. But when decisionmakers expect voluntary compliance, or when they expect respect for decisions because the decisions are right rather than because they emanate from an authoritative source, then giving reasons becomes a way to bring the subject of the decision into the enterprise. Even if compliance is not the issue, giving reasons is still a way of showing respect for the subject, and a way of opening a conversation rather than forestalling one.

That giving reasons is a way of opening a conversation may in fact be an independent basis for a reason-giving requirement. In some contexts, discussion and conversation are to be avoided, even apart from the question of authority. Discussion takes time and may, on occasion, heighten rather than dampen disagreement. Yet discussion can be the vehicle by which the subject of the decision feels more a part of the decision, producing the possibility of compromise and the respect for a final decision that comes from inclusion.

---

73. The value of reliance, however, is best evaluated against a baseline of antecedent understandings by the relier. Whether reliance is a good thing may thus depend on what will be believed by a subject with less reliable means of determining what a decisionmaker is likely to do in the future. If we are concerned with maximizing enforcement, for example, it may be beneficial to keep risk-averse enforcement subjects in a state of some uncertainty about likely enforcement action. When this is so, discouraging decisionmakers from giving reasons may help produce an optimal compliance level.

Yet as I have stressed throughout, the advantages of giving reasons come at a price. Not only does giving reasons take time and sometimes open up conversations best kept closed, it also commits the decisionmaker in ways that are rarely recognized. Specifically, giving reasons requires decisionmakers to decide cases they can scarcely imagine arising under conditions about which they can only guess, in a future they can only imperfectly predict. Moreover, the commitment that comes from giving reasons is a commitment of categorization and a commitment of generalization. To give a reason is both to create a category larger than the decision at hand and to generalize. Reason-giving is therefore in tension with and potentially a check on maximal contextualization, on case-by-case determination, and on recognition of the power of the particular. Conversely, reason-giving is the kin of abstraction, of rule-based decisionmaking, and of decontextualization. As soon as giving a reason puts this case into a larger category including other cases, the pull away from the particular and toward the general has begun. In many decisionmaking environments, the pull away from the particular and away from context is precisely what is desired by institutional designers. When that is the case, a requirement that decisionmakers give reasons can be one — although by no means the only — instrument of achieving that goal. But when particularization and contextualization are desired, and categorization and abstraction are resisted, then requiring decisionmakers to give reasons for their decisions impedes the aims of particularization and contextualization. This says little about whether and when giving reasons, all things considered, should be required. It does say, however, that when context, case-by-case decisionmaking, and flexibility are thought important, the benefits of requiring decisionmakers to give reasons do not come without a price.

Notes and Questions

---

1. According to Professor Schauer, what are the benefits of reason-giving? What are the costs?

2. As the above authorities suggest, many lawyers and judges regard it as important — if not essential — for courts to provide reasons in support of their judgments. And indeed, there are several reasons why a court might want to provide such reasons. One was provided by the court of appeals in *In re Shell Oil*: to allow that court to determine whether it had jurisdiction of the appeal. According to James Hardisty of the University of Washington School of Law, the possible reasons for providing reasons might include the following:
   a) to give parties an idea of basis for decision;
   b) to give the feeling that decision is just;
   c) to assist appellate courts in review;
   d) to provide guidance (and possibly even precedent) for private parties in the future;

e) to (possibly) cause better results, in that the articulation of reasons might help lead to a better decision;
f) to cause the parties to accept the decision more readily (they receive more information, they get the impression the court considered the arguments and gave thought to the issues, etc.);
g) to increase acceptance of the decision by other judges;
h) to create the impression of objectivity;
i) to help harmonize this and other, related areas of the law;
j) to create a restraint on arbitrary and capricious decisionmaking;
k) to provide more guidance to legislators, if considering acting; and
l) to prevent commentators from becoming law makers (such as occurs in civil systems).

Courts generally are not required to provide reasons for their decisions, though; it is a matter of discretion. So why might a court decline to provide such reasons? Among the possible reasons are:

a) to increase efficiency; giving reasons takes considerable time;
b) to avoid provoking arguments;
c) to indicate some uncertainty as to the relevant rule or even the result (i.e., sometimes the most rhetorically powerful argument is that which is unarticulated, and seemingly self-evident);
d) to eliminate (or diminish) the precedential effect of the decision; and
e) to allow a judge to arrive at and express a correct/wise/just/good judgment which the judge perceives by intuition but is not able to give the reasons why.

Can you think of any other arguments, pro or con? *See also* Chad M. Oldfather, *Writing, Cognition, and the Nature of the Judicial Function*, 96 Geo. L.J. 1283, 1317 (2008):

> Prior scholarship has identified three primary functions served by judicial opinions. The first is to discipline judges in the decision making process. The key idea here is that the act of writing helps to ensure that judges properly reason through the issues put before them. The second is to facilitate the system of precedent. Opinions memorialize judicial decisions so they can function as authoritative statements of law governing the resolution of future cases. The third is to legitimize those decisions. Roughly stated, opinions provide the parties and the public with assurance that a given decision is not arbitrary, but rather is the product of the reasoned application of appropriate legal standards.

3. "We have repeatedly emphasized the importance of a statement of the grounds of decision, both as to facts and law, as an aid to litigants and to this Court." *Pub. Serv. Comm'n of Wis. v. Wis. Tel. Co.,* 289 U.S. 67, 69 (1933).

4. "It is wrong and highly abusive for a judge to exercise his power without the normal procedures and trappings of the adversary system — a motion, an opportunity for the other side to respond, a statement of reasons for the decision, reliance on legal authority." *In re Complaint of Judicial Misconduct,* 425 F.3d 1179, 1185 (9th Cir. 2005) (Kozinski, J., dissenting).

5. As the *In re Shell Oil* court indicated, under the Federal Rules of Civil Procedure, there are few times in which federal district courts are required to issue written opinions. *See* FED. R. CIV. P. 52. Nonetheless, Federal Rule of Civil Procedure 56(a), which relates to summary judgment, was recently amended to provide: "The court should state on the record the reasons for granting or denying the motion." Why was this language added? Note that a statement of reasons in this context still is not required; it is only encouraged. Why?

6. ALI/UNIDROIT Principles of Transnational Civil Procedure (2004), Principle 23 ("Decision and Reasoned Explanation") provides in part: "The judgment should be accompanied by a reasoned explanation of the essential factual, legal, and evidentiary basis of the decision." Principle 23.2.

7. In *Harrington v. Richter*, 131 S. Ct. 770 (2011), the Supreme Court held that 28 U.S.C. § 2254(d), which relates to federal habeas corpus with respect to state convictions, "does not require a state court to give reasons before its decision can be deemed to have been 'adjudicated on the merits.'" *Id.* at 785.

8. For more on this topic, see HENRY M. HART, JR. & ALBERT M. SACKS, THE LEGAL PROCESS: BASIC PROBLEMS IN THE MAKING AND APPLICATION OF LAW 383-403 (William N. Eskridge, Jr. & Philip P. Frickey eds., 1994); Mathilde Cohen, *Sincerity and Reason Giving: When May Legal Decisionmakers Lie?*, 59 DEPAUL L. REV. 1091 (2010); Donald J. Kochan, *The "Reason-Giving Lawyer: An Ethical, Practical, and Pedagogical Perspective*, 26 GEO. J. OF LEGAL ETHICS 261 (2013); and Martin Shapiro, *The Giving Reasons Requirement*, 1992 U. CHI. LEGAL FORUM 179.

N. THE PROPRIETY OF SUA SPONTE DECISIONS

To what extent should a court be permitted to make decisions sua sponte — i.e., on its own motion? Professor Fuller, as you might recall, seemed to frown on this practice (at least with respect to the practice of deciding cases on grounds not argued by the parties). Consider this question in the context of the following cases.

Day v. McDonough
547 U.S. 198 (2006)

JUSTICE GINSBURG delivered the opinion of the Court.

This case concerns the authority of a U. S. District Court, on its own initiative, to dismiss as untimely a state prisoner's petition for a writ of habeas corpus. The Antiterrorism and Effective Death Penalty Act of 1996 (AEDPA) sets a one-year limitation period for filing such petitions, running from "the date on which the judgment became final by the conclusion of direct review or the expiration of the time for seeking such review." The one-year clock is stopped, however, during the time the petitioner's "properly filed" application for state postconviction relief "is pending." Under Eleventh Circuit precedent, that tolling period does not include the 90 days in which a petitioner might have sought certiorari review in this Court challenging state-court denial of postconviction relief.

In the case before us, the State's answer to the federal habeas petition "agreed the petition was timely" because it was "filed after 352 days of untolled time." Inspecting the pleadings and attachments, a Federal Magistrate Judge determined that the State had miscalculated the tolling time. Under Circuit precedent, the untolled time was 388 days, rendering the petition untimely by some three weeks. After affording the petitioner an opportunity to show cause why the petition should not be dismissed for failure to meet the statutory deadline, and finding petitioner's responses inadequate, the Magistrate Judge recommended dismissal of the petition. The District Court adopted the Magistrate Judge's recommendation, and the Court of Appeals affirmed, concluding that "a concession of timeliness by the state that is patently erroneous does not compromise the authority of a district court *sua sponte* to dismiss a habeas petition as untimely, under AEDPA."

The question presented is whether a federal court lacks authority, on its own initiative, to dismiss a habeas petition as untimely, once the State has answered the petition without contesting its timeliness. Ordinarily in civil litigation, a statutory time limitation is forfeited if not raised in a defendant's answer or in an amendment thereto. Fed. Rules Civ. Proc. 8(c), 12(b), and 15(a). And we would count it an abuse of discretion to override a State's deliberate waiver of a limitations defense. In this case, however, the federal court confronted no intelligent waiver on the State's part, only an evident miscalculation of the elapsed time under a statute designed to impose a tight time constraint on federal habeas petitioners. In the circumstances here presented, we hold, the federal court had discretion to correct the State's error and, accordingly, to dismiss the petition as untimely under AEDPA's one-year limitation.

. . . .

II

A statute of limitations defense, the State acknowledges, is not "jurisdictional," hence courts are under no *obligation* to raise the time bar *sua sponte*. In this respect, the limitations defense resembles other threshold barriers — exhaustion of state remedies, procedural default, nonretroactivity — courts have typed "nonjurisdictional," although recognizing that those defenses "implicate values beyond the concerns of the parties."

On the exhaustion of state remedies doctrine, requiring state prisoners, before invoking federal habeas jurisdiction, to pursue remedies available in state court, *Granberry v. Greer*, 481 U. S. 129 (1987), is the pathmarking case. We held in *Granberry* that federal appellate courts have discretion to consider the issue of exhaustion despite the State's failure to interpose the defense at the district-court level.

Id. at 133.[4] Later, in *Caspari v. Bohlen,* 510 U. S. 383, 389 (1994), we similarly held that "a federal court may, but need not, decline to apply the nonretroactivity rule announced in *Teague v. Lane,* 489 U. S. 288, 310 (1989) (plurality opinion), if the State does not argue it."

While the issue remains open in this Court, see *Trest v. Cain,* 522 U. S. 87, 90 (1997),[5] the Courts of Appeals have unanimously held that, in appropriate circumstances, courts, on their own initiative, may raise a petitioner's procedural default, *i. e.,* a petitioner's failure properly to present an alleged constitutional error in state court, and the consequent adequacy and independence of state-law grounds for the state-court judgment.

Petitioner Day relies heavily on Rule 4 of the Rules Governing Section 2254 Cases in the United States District Courts (Habeas Rules), *i. e.,* the procedural Rules governing federal habeas petitions from state prisoners, in urging, that AEDPA's limitation may be raised by a federal court *sua sponte* only at the preanswer, initial screening stage. Habeas Rule 4 provides that district courts "must promptly examine" state prisoner petitions and must dismiss the petition "if it plainly appears that the petitioner is not entitled to relief." Once an answer has been ordered and filed, Day maintains, the court loses authority to rule the petition untimely *sua sponte.*[6] At that point, according to Day, the Federal Rules of Civil Procedure hold sway. Under the Civil Procedure Rules, a defendant forfeits a statute of limitations defense, see Fed. Rule Civ. Proc. 8(c), not asserted in its answer, see Rule 12(b), or an amendment thereto, see Rule 15(a).

The State, on the other hand, points out that the statute of limitations is akin to other affirmative defenses to habeas petitions, notably exhaustion of state remedies, procedural default, and nonretroactivity. Indeed, the statute of limitations is explicitly aligned with those other defenses under the current version of Habeas Rule 5(b), which provides that the State's answer to a habeas petition "must state whether any claim in the petition is barred by a failure to exhaust state remedies, a procedural bar, non- retroactivity, or a statute of limitations." The considerations of comity, finality, and the expeditious handling of habeas proceedings that motivated AEDPA, the State maintains, counsel against an excessively rigid or formal approach to the affirmative defenses now listed in Habeas Rule 5. Citing *Granberry* as the instructive case, the State urges express recognition of an "intermediate approach." In lieu of an inflexible rule requiring dismissal whenever AEDPA's one-year clock has run, or, at the opposite extreme, a rule treating the State's failure initially to plead the one-year bar as an

---

4. In AEDPA, enacted nearly a decade after *Granberry,* Congress expressly provided that "a State shall not be deemed to have waived the exhaustion requirement or be estopped from reliance upon the requirement unless the State, through counsel, expressly waives the requirement."

5. *Trest* held that a Court of Appeals was not obliged to raise procedural default on its own initiative, but declined to decide whether courts have discretion to do so.

6. Were we to accept Day's position, courts would never (or, at least, hardly ever) be positioned to raise AEDPA's time bar *sua sponte.* As this Court recognized in *Pliler v. Ford,* 542 U. S. 225, 232 (2004), information essential to the time calculation is often absent — as it was in this case — until the State has filed, along with its answer, copies of documents from the state-court proceedings.

absolute waiver, the State reads the statutes, Rules, and decisions in point to permit the "exercise of discretion in each case to decide whether the administration of justice is better served by dismissing the case on statute of limitations grounds or by reaching the merits of the petition." Employing that "intermediate approach" in this particular case, the State argues, the petition should not be deemed timely simply because a government attorney calculated the days in between petitions incorrectly.

We agree, noting particularly that the Magistrate Judge, instead of acting *sua sponte*, might have informed the State of its obvious computational error and entertained an amendment to the State's answer. Recognizing that an amendment to the State's answer might have obviated this controversy,[9] we see no dispositive difference between that route, and the one taken here.

In sum, we hold that district courts are permitted, but not obliged, to consider, *sua sponte*, the timeliness of a state prisoner's habeas petition. We so hold, noting that it would make scant sense to distinguish in this regard AEDPA's time bar from other threshold constraints on federal habeas petitioners. We stress that a district court is not required to double-check the State's math. If, as this Court has held, "district judges have no obligation to act as counsel or paralegal to *pro se* litigants," then, by the same token, they surely have no obligation to assist attorneys representing the State. Nevertheless, if a judge does detect a clear computational error, no Rule, statute, or constitutional provision commands the judge to suppress that knowledge. Cf. Fed. Rule Civ. Proc. 60(a) (clerical errors in the record "arising from oversight or omission may be corrected by the court at any time of its own initiative or on the motion of any party").

Of course, before acting on its own initiative, a court must accord the parties fair notice and an opportunity to present their positions. Further, the court must assure itself that the petitioner is not significantly prejudiced by the delayed focus on the limitation issue, and "determine whether the interests of justice would be better served" by addressing the merits or by dismissing the petition as time barred.[11] Here, the Magistrate Judge gave Day due notice and a fair opportunity to show why the limitation period should not yield dismissal of the petition. The notice issued some nine months after the State answered the petition. No court proceedings or action occurred in the interim, and nothing in the record suggests that the State "strategically" withheld the defense or chose to relinquish it. From all that appears in the record, there was merely an inadvertent error, a miscalculation that was plain under Circuit precedent, and no abuse of discretion in following this Court's lead in *Granberry* and *Caspari*.

For the reasons stated, the judgment of the Court of Appeals is
Affirmed.

Justice Scalia, with whom Justice Thomas and Justice Breyer join, dissenting.

---

9. The Court is unanimous on this point.
11. A district court's discretion is confined within these limits. As earlier noted, should a State intelligently choose to waive a statute of limitations defense, a district court would not be at liberty to disregard that choice.

The Court today disregards the Federal Rules of Civil Procedure (Civil Rules) in habeas corpus cases, chiefly because it believes that this departure will make no difference. Even if that were true, which it is not, I could not join this novel presumption *against* applying the Civil Rules.

The Civil Rules "govern the procedure in the United States district courts in all suits of a civil nature." Rule 1. This includes "proceedings for habeas corpus," but only "to the extent that the practice in such proceedings is not set forth in statutes of the United States or the [Habeas Rules]." Thus, "the Federal Rules of Civil Procedure apply in the context of habeas suits to the extent that they are not inconsistent with the Habeas Corpus Rules" and do not contradict or undermine the provisions of the habeas corpus statute.

As the Court notes, the Civil Rules adopt the traditional forfeiture rule for unpleaded limitations defenses. The Court does not identify any "inconsistency" between this forfeiture rule and the statute, Rules, or historical practice of habeas proceedings — because there is none. Forfeiture of the limitations defense is demonstrably not inconsistent with traditional habeas practice, because, as the Court acknowledges, habeas practice included no statute of limitations until 1996. Forfeiture is perfectly consistent with Habeas Rule 5(b), which now provides that the State's "answer *must* state whether any claim in the petition is barred by statute of limitations." And forfeiture is also consistent with (and indeed, arguably suggested by) Habeas Rule 4, because Rule 4 provides for *sua sponte* screening and dismissal of habeas petitions on, *prior* to the filing of the State's responsive pleading.[1]

Most importantly, applying the forfeiture rule to the limitations period of 28 U. S. C. § 2244(d) does not contradict or undermine any provision of the habeas statute. Quite the contrary, on its most natural reading, the statute calls for the forfeiture rule. AEDPA expressly enacted, without further qualification, "a 1-year *period of limitation*" for habeas applications by persons in custody pursuant to the judgments of state courts. We have repeatedly stated that the enactment of time-limitation periods such as that in § 2244(d), without further elaboration, produces defenses that are nonjurisdictional and thus subject to waiver and forfeiture. Absent some affirmative incompatibility with habeas practice, there is no reason why a habeas limitation period should be any different. By imposing an unqualified "period of limitation" against the background understanding that a defense of "limitations" must be raised in the answer, the statute implies that the usual forfeiture rule is applicable.

Instead of identifying an inconsistency between habeas corpus practice and the usual civil forfeiture rule, the Court urges that "it would make scant sense to distinguish in this regard AEDPA's time bar from other threshold constraints on federal habeas petitioners" that may be raised *sua sponte* — namely, exhaustion of state remedies, procedural default, nonretroactivity, and (prior to AEDPA) abuse of the

---

1. The Court observes that "were we to accept Day's position, courts would never (or, at least, hardly ever) be positioned to raise AEDPA's time bar *sua sponte*," because "information essential to the time calculation is often absent" at the Rule 4 prescreening stage. But to be distressed at this phenomenon is to beg the question — that is, to assume that courts *ought* to "be positioned to raise AEDPA's time bar *sua sponte*." That is precisely the question before us.

writ. But unlike AEDPA's statute of limitations, these defenses were all created by the habeas courts themselves, in the exercise of their traditional equitable discretion, because they were seen as necessary to protect the interests of comity and finality that federal collateral review of state criminal proceedings necessarily implicates. Unlike these other defenses, no time limitation — not even equitable laches — was imposed to vindicate comity and finality. AEDPA's 1-year limitations period is entirely a recent creature of statute. If comity and finality did not compel any time limitation at all, it follows *a fortiori* that they do not compel making a legislatively created, forfeitable time limitation *nonforfeitable.*

In what appears to be the chief ground of its decision, the Court also observes that "the Magistrate Judge, instead of acting *sua sponte,* might have informed the State of its obvious computation error and entertained an amendment to the State's answer" under Civil Rule 15(a). Although "an amendment to the State's answer might have obviated this controversy," the Court concedes, "we see no dispositive difference between that route, and the one taken here." But this consideration cuts in the opposite direction. If there truly were no "dispositive difference" between following and disregarding the rules that Congress has enacted, the natural conclusion would be that there is no compelling reason to *disregard* the Civil Rules.[2] Legislatively enacted rules are surely entitled to more respect than this apparent presumption that, when nothing substantial hangs on the point, they do *not* apply as written. And, unlike the novel regime that the Court adopts today, which will apparently require the development of new rules from scratch, there already exists a well-developed body of law to govern the district courts' exercise of discretion under Rule 15(a). Ockham is offended by today's decision, even if no one else is.

But, in fact, there are at least two notable differences between the Civil Rules and the *sua sponte* regime of such cases of *Granberry* and *Caspari*— *both* of which involve sufficiently significant departures from ordinary civil practice as to require clear authorization from the statute, the Rules, or historical habeas practice. First, the *Granberry* regime allows the forfeited procedural defense to be raised for the first time on appeal, either by the State or by the appellate court *sua sponte.* Ordinary civil practice does not allow a forfeited affirmative defense whose underlying facts were not developed below to be raised for the first time on appeal. The ability to raise even constitutional errors in criminal trials for the first time on appeal is narrowly circumscribed. Comity and finality justified this departure from ordinary practice for historically rooted equitable defenses such as exhaustion. But limitations was not such a defense.

---

2. I agree with the Court that today's decision will have little impact on the outcome of district court proceedings. In particular, I agree that "if a district judge does detect a clear computation error, no Rule, statute, or constitutional provision commands the judge to suppress that knowledge." Rather, a judge may call the timeliness issue to the State's attention and invite a motion to amend the pleadings under Civil Rule I5(a), under which "leave shall be freely given when justice so requires." In fact, in providing for leave whenever "justice so requires," the Civil Rules fully accommodate the comity and finality interests that the Court thinks require a departure from the Civil Rules. Requiring the State to take the affirmative step of amending its own pleading at least observes the formalities of our adversary system, which is a nontrivial value in itself.

Also, *Granberry* and the like raise the possibility that the courts can impose a procedural defense over the State's affirmative decision to waive that defense. The Court takes care to point out that this is not such a case, but it invites such cases in the future. After all, the principal justification for allowing such defenses to be raised *sua sponte* is that they "'implicate values beyond the concerns of the parties,'" including "'judicial efficiency and conservation of judicial resources'" and "the expeditious handling of habeas proceedings." There are many reasons why the State may wish to disregard the statute of limitations, including the simple belief that it would be unfair to impose the limitations defense on a particular defendant. On the Court's reasoning, a district court would not abuse its discretion in overriding the State's conscious waiver of the defense in order to protect such "'values beyond the concerns of the parties.'"[3]

Under the Civil Rules, by contrast, amending a party's pleading over his objection would constitute a clear abuse of the trial court's discretion.

In sum, applying the ordinary rule of forfeiture to the AEDPA statute of limitations creates no inconsistency with the Habeas Rules. On the contrary, it is the Court's unwarranted expansion of the timeliness rule enacted by Congress that is inconsistent with the statute, the Habeas Rules, the Civil Rules, and traditional practice. I would hold that the ordinary forfeiture rule, as codified in the Civil Rules, applies to the limitations period of § 2244(d). I respectfully dissent.

Notes and Questions

---

1. Which opinion do you find more persuasive — the majority, or the dissent? Why? Notice, inter alia, the Court's observation that there was no "intelligent" waiver of the defense at issue by the State. What is that? Since when have we required that parties act "intelligently"? Cannot defenses be waived unintelligently as well as intelligently?

---

3. In order to avoid this seemingly unavoidable conclusion, the Court asserts, without relevant citation or reasoning, that "should a State intelligently choose to waive a statute of limitations defense, a district court would not be at liberty to disregard that choice." This assertion is contrary to our statement in *Granberry* — a case which, on the Court's view, it makes "scant sense to distinguish" — that an appellate court may dismiss an unexhausted petition *sua sponte* in "cases in which the State fails, *whether inadvertently or otherwise,* to raise an arguably meritorious nonexhaustion defense." To support its assertion, the Court cites nothing but its own earlier statement: "Ordinarily in civil litigation; a statutory time limitation is forfeited if not raised in a defendant's answer or in an amendment thereto. And we would count it an abuse of discretion to override the State's deliberate waiver of a limitations defense." But as the statement itself shows, the "ordinary" inability to override the State's "intelligent" waiver is coupled with an "ordinary" automatic forfeit of the defense if it is not timely raised. The Court does not say why it makes sense, for the statute of limitations of § 2244(d)(1)(A), to reject (as it does) the first part of the ordinary practice (automatic forfeiture), while embracing the second (inability to override intelligent waiver). The *reason* for rejecting the first part surely applies just as well to the second: Section 2244(d)(1)(A) supposedly "'implicates value beyond the concerns of the parties,'" including "'judicial efficiency,'" "'conservation of judicial resources,'" and "expeditious handling of habeas proceedings."

2. Just prior to the Supreme Court's decision in *Day*, the United States Court of Appeals for the Third Circuit, in *United States v. Bendolph*, 409 F.3d 155 (3d Cir. 2005) (en banc), similarly held

> that, upon finding a potential AEDPA [(Antiterrorism and Effective Death Penalty Act)] statute of limitations problem in a habeas case arising under 28 U.S.C. §§ 2254 or 2255, a court may act *sua sponte* at any point in the proceedings, regardless of the government's position, provided the court (i) gives notice of the issue [to the petitioner] and an opportunity to respond; and (ii) if the case has passed the [pleadings] stage, also analyzes the prejudice [associated with a dismissal].

Bendolph, 409 F.3d at 169. But a substantial minority, led by Judge Nygaard, dissented from that portion of the court's holding that authorized a district court to raise such a defense on its own motion after the government had failed to raise that defense in its answer to the petition. *Id.* at 170 (Nygaard, J., concurring in part and dissenting in part). According to Judge Nygaard:

> [G]enerally it is not appropriate for a court to *sua sponte* raise non-jurisdictional defenses not raised by the parties. This rule exists because ours is an adversarial system, which relies on advocacy by trained counsel. *Cf. United States v. Burke*, 504 U.S. 229, 246 (1992) (Scalia, J., concurring) ("The rule that points of law not argued will not be considered is more than just a prudential rule of convenience; its observance, at least in the vast majority of cases, distinguishes our adversary system of justice from the inquisitorial one.") In an adversarial system, it is not for the courts to bring to light the best arguments for either side; that responsibility is left to the parties themselves. *McNeil v. Wisconsin*, 501 U.S. 171, 181 n. 2 (1991) ("What makes a system adversarial rather than inquisitorial is the presence of a judge who does not (as an inquisitor does) conduct the factual and legal investigation himself, but instead decides on the basis of facts and arguments pro and con *adduced by the parties*."). As the Supreme Court has explained, "the determination of what may be useful to the defense can properly and effectively be made only by an advocate." *Dennis v. United States*, 384 U.S. 855, 875 (1966).
>
> 　　We should decline to raise non-jurisdictional defenses for another reason as well: fairness to the other party. Typically, it is not fair for courts to act as surrogate counsel for one side but not the other. *See United States v. Pryce*, 938 F.2d 1343, 1352 (D.C. Cir. 1991) (Silberman, J., dissenting in part) ("We thus ordinarily have no right to consider issues not raised by a party in either briefing or argument because of the unfairness of such a practice to the other party.").
>
> 　　Of course I acknowledge that there are exceptions to this rule of restraint. . . . However, when a court examines a habeas petition for facial deficiencies pursuant to Rule 4, and finding none orders the government to answer, only to have the government fail to raise timeliness as a defense, each of those values become substantially less significant. . . .
>
> 　　. . . The very purpose of affirmative defenses, such as the statute of limitations, is to conserve judicial resources by requiring the parties to raise them *early* in the proceedings. Rescuing the government from its folly or inadvertence by permitting a district court to raise the statute of limitations after the parties have begun to address the merits of the petition subverts that purpose, and may even have the opposite effect. If the statute of limitations is raised late in the proceedings, the parties must then brief yet an additional issue, which consumes the resources

of all involved. I recognize that by permitting a district court to dismiss a habeas petition as untimely, some resources may be saved. But the same can be said for dismissing any lawsuit at any point. Yet it is not the general practice of this Court to raise the statute of limitations or other affirmative defenses either in civil or criminal cases in order to conserve judicial resources. Courts exist to resolve disputes. The resources of the courts should be used to that end. . . .

. . . .

"In our adversary system, it is enough for judges to judge." *Dennis,* 384 U.S. at 875. Advocacy is best left to the parties. Thus, as a general rule, courts should not raise non-jurisdictional defenses on behalf of parties who did not raise the defenses themselves. The Supreme Court has permitted departures from that general rule only when values beyond the interests of the parties are implicated. No such values are sufficiently implicated by a *sua sponte* dismissal for lack of timeliness where, as here, the government has failed to raise the statute of limitations in its answer.

. . . .

Even if a *sua sponte* dismissal of the petitions in this case would serve values beyond the interests of the parties, I would still dissent because of the damage dismissal would work upon two countervailing values the majority fails to consider: the related notions of waiver and fundamental fairness.

The majority's decision renders the concept of waiver a nullity. . . .

As for the issue of fairness, *Pliler v. Ford,* 542 U.S. 225 (2004), is instructive. In *Pliler,* the Supreme Court reversed a decision by the Ninth Circuit, which required district courts to give *pro se* habeas petitioners a warning that if they dismiss their petitions in order to first exhaust state remedies, AEDPA's statute of limitations might bar them from refiling a future petition in federal court. According to the Ninth Circuit, the failure to provide the *pro se* habeas petitioner in that case with such a warning deprived him of the opportunity to make a "meaningful" choice concerning his petition. The Supreme Court disagreed. It held that district courts need not warn *pro se* litigants that AEDPA's statute of limitations might preclude them from filing any future petitions if they withdraw a timely petition. According to the Court, explaining habeas procedure and calculating the statute of limitations are tasks normally reserved for trained counsel, and "requiring district courts to advise a *pro se* litigant in such a manner would undermine the district judges' role as impartial decisionmakers."

While one might argue that it is the *pro se* habeas petitioners — who are without the assistance of trained counsel — who need to be warned by district courts of AEDPA's labyrinthine pitfalls most of all, the Court's decision in *Pliler* is clear: district courts may not act as *de facto* counsel in habeas proceedings. Fairness dictates that we apply this rule equally to both sides, but the majority does not. The majority permits a district court to act as *de facto* counsel for the government, working together toward the common goal of dismissal of the petition. That is unfair. A habeas petitioner gets no help from the courts, and the government needs none either. If, as Justice Thomas explained in *Pliler,* calculating the statute of limitations is a job ordinarily reserved for trained counsel, then that job should be left in the able hands of the government's attorneys. Any other rule contravenes the fundamental notion that "the judiciary is on *no* side. We judges must be strictly neutral with respect to all cases that come before us." *Pryce,* 938 F.2d at 1352 (Silberman, J., dissenting in part).

> The Court today permits and perpetuates a double standard. It also sends a disturbing message: We will aid the government in a habeas proceeding, but not the petitioner. The mistakes of the government may be excused or ignored, but any error by the petitioner is fatal — perhaps figuratively, but too often literally. The favored-party status the majority affords to the government in habeas cases undermines both the appearance and fact of judicial neutrality, and I will have no part in it.

Bendolph, 409 F.3d at 172-76 (Nygaard, J., concurring in part and dissenting in part).

3. Despite the fact that the American legal system is generally considered to be an adversarial system, is a court limited to the arguments raised by the parties? Apparently not. *See, e.g., Kamen v. Kemper Financial Services, Inc.,* 500 U.S. 90, 99 (1991) ("When an issue or claim is properly before the court, the court is not limited to the particular legal theories advanced by the parties, but rather retains the independent power to identify and apply the proper construction of governing law."). *See also Davis v. United States,* 512 U.S. 452 (1994), in which Justice Scalia opined:

> I agree with the Court that it is *proper,* given the Government's failure to raise the point, to render judgment without taking account of § 3501. But the refusal to consider arguments not raised is a sound prudential practice, rather than a statutory or constitutional mandate, and there are times when prudence dictates the contrary.

Id. at 464 (Scalia, J., concurring). Assuming these sentiments are true, though, this does not dispose of the more difficult question of determining when a court *should* engage in sua sponte decisionmaking.

4. In his dissent, Justice Scalia discussed *Granberry v. Greer,* 481 U.S. 129 (1987), and the problems caused by arguments raised for the first time on appeal. In what way, if any, is that problem related to the sua sponte problem? (Raising arguments for the first time on appeal is discussed in greater detail in part O *infra.*)

Greenlaw v. United States
554 U.S. 237 (2008)

JUSTICE GINSBURG delivered the opinion of the Court.

This case concerns the role of courts in our adversarial system. The specific question presented: May a United States Court of Appeals, acting on its own initiative, order an increase in a defendant's sentence? Petitioner Michael J. Greenlaw was convicted of various offenses relating to drugs and firearms, and was sentenced to imprisonment for 442 months. He appealed urging, *inter alia,* that his sentence was unreasonably long. After rejecting all of Greenlaw's arguments, the Court of Appeals determined, without Government invitation, that the applicable law plainly required a prison sentence 15 years longer than the term the trial court had imposed. Accordingly, the appeals court instructed the trial court to increase Greenlaw's sentence to 622 months. We hold that, absent a Government appeal or cross-appeal, the sentence Greenlaw received should not have been increased. We therefore vacate the Court of Appeals' judgment.

    . . . .

II

In our adversary system, in both civil and criminal cases, in the first instance and on appeal, we follow the principle of party presentation. That is, we rely on the parties to frame the issues for decision and assign to courts the role of neutral arbiter of matters the parties present. To the extent courts have approved departures from the party presentation principle in criminal cases, the justification has usually been to protect a *pro se* litigant's rights. See *Castro* v. *United States*, 540 U. S. 375, 381-383 (2003). But as a general rule, "our adversary system is designed around the premise that the parties know what is best for them, and are responsible for advancing the facts and arguments entitling them to relief." *Id.*, at 386 (SCALIA, J., concurring in part and concurring in judgment).[3] As cogently explained:

> "Courts do not, or should not, sally forth each day looking for wrongs to right. We wait for cases to come to us, and when they do we normally decide only questions presented by the parties. Counsel almost always know a great deal more about their cases than we do, and this must be particularly true of counsel for the United States, the richest, most powerful, and best represented litigant to appear before us." *United States* v. *Samuels*, 808 F. 2d 1298, 1301 (CA8 1987) (R. Arnold, J., concurring in denial of reh'g en banc).

The cross-appeal rule, pivotal in this case, is both informed by, and illustrative of, the party presentation principle. Under that unwritten but longstanding rule, an appellate court may not alter a judgment to benefit a nonappealing party. This Court, from its earliest years, has recognized that it takes a cross-appeal to justify a remedy in favor of an appellee. We have called the rule "inveterate and certain."

Courts of Appeals have disagreed, however, on the proper characterization of the cross-appeal rule: Is it "jurisdictional," and therefore exceptionless, or a "rule of practice," and thus potentially subject to judicially created exceptions? Our own opinions contain statements supporting both characterizations.

In *El Paso Natural Gas Co.* v. *Neztsosie*, 526 U. S. 473, 480 (1999), we declined to decide "the theoretical status" of the cross-appeal rule. It sufficed to point out that the rule was "firmly entrenched" and served to advance "institutional interests in fair notice and repose." "Indeed," we noted, "in more than two centuries of repeatedly

---

3. Cf. Kaplan, Civil Procedure — Reflections on the Comparison of Systems, 9 Buffalo L. Rev. 409, 431-432 (1960) (U. S. system "exploits the free-wheeling energies of counsel and places them in adversary confrontation before a detached judge"; "German system puts its trust in a judge of paternalistic bent acting in cooperation with counsel of somewhat muted adversary zeal").

endorsing the cross-appeal requirement, not a single one of our holdings has ever recognized an exception to the rule." Following the approach taken in *Neztsosie*, we again need not type the rule "jurisdictional" in order to decide this case.

   . . . .

III

A

In ordering the District Court to add 15 years to Greenlaw's sentence, despite the absence of a cross-appeal by the Government, the Court of Appeals identified Federal Rule of Criminal Procedure 52(b) as the source of its authority. Rule 52(b) reads: "A plain error that affects substantial rights may be considered even though it was not brought to the court's attention." Nothing in the text or history of Rule 52(b) suggests that the rulemakers, in codifying the plain-error doctrine, meant to override the cross-appear requirement.

   Nor do our opinions support a plain-error exception to the cross-appeal rule. This Court has indeed noticed, and ordered correction of, plain errors not raised by defendants, but we have done so only to benefit a defendant who had himself petitioned the Court for review on other grounds. In no case have we applied plain-error doctrine to the detriment of a petitioning party. Rather, in every case in which correction of a plain error would result in modification of a judgment to the advantage of a party who did not seek this Court's review, we have invoked the cross-appeal rule to bar the correction.

   . . . .

B

Amicus supporting the Eighth Circuit's judgment links the argument based on Rule 52(b) to a similar argument based on 28 U. S. C. §2106. Section 2106 states that federal appellate courts "may affirm, modify, vacate, set aside or reverse any judgment lawfully brought before it for review." For substantially the same reasons that Rule 52(b) does not override the cross-appeal requirement, §2106 does not do so either. Section 2106 is not limited to plain errors, much less to sentencing errors in criminal cases — it applies to all cases, civil and criminal, and to all errors. Were the construction *amicus* offers correct, §2106 would displace the cross-appeal rule cross-the-board. The authority described in §2106, we have observed, "must be exercised consistent with the requirements of the Federal Rules of Civil Procedure as interpreted by this Court." No different conclusion is warranted with respect to the "inveterate and certain" cross-appeal rule.

   . . . .

D

In increasing Greenlaw's sentence by 15 years on its own initiative, the Eighth Circuit did not advert to the procedural rules setting deadlines for launching appeals and cross-appeals. Unyielding in character, these rules may be seen as auxiliary to the cross-appeal rule and the party presentation principle served by that rule. Federal

Rule of Appellate Procedure 3(a)(1) provides that "an appeal permitted by law may be taken *only by filing a notice of appeal* within the prescribed time." Complementing Rule 3(a)(1), Rule 4(b)(B)(ii) instructs that, when the Government has the right to cross-appeal in a criminal case, its notice "*must be filed* within 30 days after the filing of a notice of appeal by any defendant." The filing time for a notice of appeal or cross-appeal, Rule 4(b)(4) states, may be extended "for a period not to exceed 30 days." Rule 26(b) bars any extension beyond that time.

The firm deadlines set by the Appellate Rules advance the interests of the parties and the legal system in fair notice and finality. Thus a defendant who appeals but faces no cross-appeal can proceed anticipating that the appellate court will not enlarge his sentence. And if the Government files a cross-appeal, the defendant will have fair warning, well in advance of briefing and argument, that pursuit of his appeal exposes him to the risk of a higher sentence. Given early warning, he can tailor his arguments to take account of that risk. Or he can seek the Government's agreement to voluntary dismissal of the competing appeals before positions become hardened during the hours invested in preparing the case for appellate court consideration.

The strict time limits on notices of appeal and cross-appeal would be undermined, in both civil and criminal cases, if an appeals court could modify a judgment in favor of a party who filed no notice of appeal. In a criminal prosecution, moreover, the defendant would appeal at his peril, with nothing to alert him that, on his own appeal, his sentence would be increased until the appeals court so decreed. In this very case, Greenlaw might have made different strategic decisions had he known soon after filing his notice of appeal that he risked a 15-year increase in an already lengthy sentence.

E

. . . .

. . . Greenlaw was unsuccessful on all his appellate issues. There was no occasion for the Court of Appeals to vacate his sentence and no warrant, in the absence of a cross-appeal, to order the addition of 15 years to his sentence.[9]

For the reasons stated, the judgment of the United States Court of Appeals for the Eighth Circuit is vacated, and the case is remanded for further proceedings consistent with this opinion.

---

9. For all its spirited argument, the dissent recognizes the narrow gap between its core position and the Court's. The cross-appeal rule, rooted in the principle of party presentation, the dissent concedes, should hold sway in the "vast majority of cases." Does this case qualify as the "rare" exception to the "strong rule of practice" the dissent advocates? Greenlaw was sentenced to imprisonment for 442 months. The Government might have chosen to insist on 180 months more, but it elected not to do so. Was the error so "grossly prejudicial," so harmful to our system of justice, as to warrant *sua sponte* correction? By what standard is the Court of Appeals to make such an assessment? Without venturing to answer these questions, the dissent would simply "entrust the decision to initiate error correction to the sound discretion of the courts of appeals." The "strong rule" thus may be broken whenever the particular three judges composing the appellate panel see the sentence as a "wrong to right." The better answer, consistent with our jurisprudence, as reinforced by Congress, entrusts "the decision whether to initiate error correction" in this matter to top counsel for the United States.

JUSTICE BREYER, concurring in the judgment.

I agree with JUSTICE ALITO that the cross-appeal requirement is simply a rule of practice for appellate courts, rather than a limitation on their power, and I therefore join Parts I-III of his opinion. Moreover, as a general matter, I would leave application of the rule to the courts of appeals, with our power to review their discretion "seldom to be called into action." But since this case is now before us, I would consider whether the Court of Appeals here acted properly. Primarily for the reasons stated by the majority in footnote 9 of its opinion, I believe that the court abused its discretion in *sua sponte* increasing the petitioner's sentence. Our precedent precludes the creation of an exception to the cross-appeal requirement based solely on the obviousness of a lower court's error. And I cannot see how the interests of justice are significantly disserved by permitting petitioner's release from prison at roughly age 62, after almost 37 years behind bars, as opposed to age 77.

JUSTICE ALITO, with whom JUSTICE STEVENS joins, and with whom JUSTICE BREYER joins as to Parts I, II, and III, dissenting.

I respectfully dissent because I view the cross-appeal requirement as a rule of appellate practice. It is akin to the rule that courts invoke when they decline to consider arguments that the parties have not raised. Both rules rest on premises about the efficient use of judicial resources and the proper role of the tribunal in an adversary system. Both are sound and should generally be followed. But just as the courts have made them, the courts may make exceptions to them, and I do not understand why a reviewing court should enjoy less discretion to correct an error *sua sponte* than it enjoys to raise and address an argument *sua sponte*. Absent congressional direction to the contrary, and subject to our limited oversight as a supervisory court, we should entrust the decision to initiate error correction to the sound discretion of the courts of appeals.

. . . .

II

Since a cross-appeal has no effect on the appellate court's subject-matter jurisdiction, the cross-appeal requirement is best characterized as a rule of practice. It is a rule created by the courts to serve interests that are important to the Judiciary. The Court identifies two of these interests: notice to litigants and finality. One might add that the cross-appeal requirement serves a third interest: the appellate court's interest in being adequately briefed on the issues that it decides. Although these are substantial interests in the abstract, I question how well an inflexible cross-appeal requirement serves them.

Notice. With respect to notice, the benefits of an unyielding cross-appeal requirement are insubstantial. When the Government files a notice of cross-appeal, the defendant is alerted to the possibility that his or her sentence may be increased as a result of the appellate decision. But if the cross-appeal rule is, as I would hold, a strong rule of practice that should be followed in all but exceptional instances, the Government's failure to file a notice of cross-appeal would mean in the vast majority of cases that the defendant thereafter ran little risk of an increased sentence. And the rare cases where that possibility arose would generally involve errors so plain that no conceivable response by the defendant could alter the result. It is not unreasonable to consider an appealing party to be on notice as to such serious errors of law in his favor. And while there may be rare cases in which the existence of such a legal error would come as a complete surprise to the defendant or in which argument from the parties would be of assistance to the court, the solution to such a problem is not to eliminate the courts of appeals' authority to correct egregious errors. Rather, the appropriate response is for the court of appeals to request supplemental briefing or — if it deems that insufficient — simply to refuse to exercise its authority. In short, the Court's holding does not increase the substance of the notice that a defendant receives; it merely accelerates that notice by at most a few weeks in a very small number of cases.

The Court contends that "given early warning, the defendant can tailor his arguments to take account of the risk of a higher sentence or he can seek the Government's agreement to voluntary dismissal of the competing appeals." But the Court does not explain how a notice of cross-appeal, a boilerplate document, helps the defendant "tailor his arguments." Whether the cross-appeal rule is ironclad, as the Court believes, or simply a strong rule of practice, a defendant who wishes to appeal his or her sentence is always free to seek the Government's commitment not to cross-appeal or to terminate a cross-appeal that the Government has already taken.

Finality. An inflexible cross-appeal rule also does little to further the interest of the parties and the Judiciary in the finality of decisions. An appellate court's decision to grant a nonappealing party additional relief does not interrupt a long, undisturbed slumber. The error's repose begins no earlier than the deadline for filing a cross-appeal, and it ends as soon as the reviewing court issues its opinion — and often much sooner. Here, for example, the slumber was broken when the Government identified the error in its brief as appellee.

Orderly Briefing. I do not doubt that adversarial briefing improves the quality of appellate decisionmaking, but it hardly follows that appellate courts should be denied the authority to correct errors that seriously prejudice nonappealing parties. Under my interpretation of the cross-appeal rule, a court of appeals would not be obligated to address errors that are prejudicial to a nonappealing party; a court of appeals would merely have the authority to do so in appropriate cases. If a court of appeals noticed such an error and concluded that it was appropriate to address the issue, the court could, if it wished, order additional briefing. If, on the other hand, the court concluded that the issue was not adequately addressed by the briefs filed by the parties in the ordinary course and that additional briefing would interfere with the efficient administration of the court's work, the court would not be required to decide the issue. Therefore, I do not see how the courts of appeals' interest in orderly briefing is furthered by denying those courts the discretionary authority to address important issues that they find it appropriate to decide.

Indeed, the inflexible cross-appeal rule that the Court adopts may disserve the interest in judicial efficiency in some cases. For example, correcting an error that prejudiced a nonappealing defendant on direct review might obviate the need for a collateral attack. Because the reviewing court is in the best position to decide whether a departure from the cross-appeal rule would be efficient, rigid enforcement of that rule is more likely to waste judicial resources than to conserve them.

In sum, the Court exaggerates the interests served by the cross-appeal requirement. At the same time, it overlooks an important interest that the rule disserves: the interest of the Judiciary and the public in correcting grossly prejudicial errors of law that undermine confidence in our legal system. We have repeatedly stressed the importance of that interest, and it has justified departures from our traditional adversary framework in other contexts. The Court mentions one of those contexts, but there are others that deserve mention.

The most well-known is plain-error review. Federal Rule of Criminal Procedure 52(b) authorizes reviewing courts to correct "a plain error that affects substantial rights even though it was not brought to the court's attention." Although I agree with the Court that this Rule does not independently justify the Eighth Circuit's decision, I believe that the Rule's underlying policy sheds some light on the issue before us. We have explained that courts may rely on Rule 52(b) to correct only those plain errors that "seriously affect the fairness, integrity or public reputation of judicial proceedings." We have thus recognized that preservation of the "fairness, integrity or public reputation of judicial proceedings" may sometimes justify a departure from the traditional adversarial framework of issue presentation.

Perhaps the closest analogue to the cross-appeal requirement is the rule of appellate practice that restrains reviewing courts from addressing arguments that the parties have not made. Courts typically invoke this rule to avoid resolving a case based on an unaired argument, even if the argument could change the outcome. But courts also recognize that the rule is not inflexible, and sometimes they depart from it.

A reviewing court will generally address an argument *sua sponte* only to correct the most patent and serious errors. Because the prejudicial effect of the error and the impact of error correction on judicial resources are matters best determined by the reviewing court, the court's decision to go beyond the arguments made by the parties is committed to its sound discretion.

This authority provides a good model for our decision in this case. The Court has not persuaded me that the interests at stake when a reviewing court awards a nonappealing party additional relief are qualitatively different from the interests at stake when a reviewing court raises an issue *sua sponte*. Authority on the latter point recognizes that the interest of the public and the Judiciary in correcting grossly prejudicial errors of law may sometimes outweigh other interests normally furthered by fidelity to our adversarial tradition. I would recognize the same possibility here. And just as reviewing courts enjoy discretion to decide for themselves when to raise and decide arguments *sua sponte*, I would grant them substantial latitude to decide when to enlarge an appellee's judgment in the absence of a cross-appeal.[1]

---

1. The Court argues that petitioner's original sentence was neither so fundamentally unfair nor so harmful to our system of justice as to warrant *sua sponte* correction by the Court of Appeals. But these considerations, which may well support a conclusion that the Court of Appeals should not have exercised its authority in this case, surely do not justify the Court's broad rule that *sua sponte* error correction on behalf of the Government is inappropriate in all cases.

III

The approach I advocate is not out of step with our precedent. The Court has never decided whether the cross-appeal requirement is "subject to exceptions or an unqualified limit on the power of appellate courts." That question was reserved in *Neztsosie*, even as the Court recognized that lower courts had reached different conclusions. I would simply confirm what our precedent had assumed: that there are exceptional circumstances when it is appropriate for a reviewing court to correct an error for the benefit of a party that has not cross-appealed the decision below.

. . . .

Even today, the Court refuses to decide whether the cross-appeal requirement admits of exceptions in appropriate cases. While calling the rule "inveterate and certain," the Court allows that "there might be circumstances in which it would be proper for an appellate court to initiate plain-error review." . . .

. . . .

IV

For the reasons given above, I would hold that the courts of appeals enjoy the discretion to correct error *sua sponte* for the benefit of nonappealing parties. The Court errs in vacating the judgment of the Eighth Circuit, and I respectfully dissent.[3]

Notes and Questions

---

1. Which opinion do you find the more persuasive, the majority, or the dissent? Why?

2. Is *Greenlaw* fairly distinguishable from *Day*? If so, on what basis?

3. What do you think of Justice Alito's question as to "why a reviewing court should enjoy less discretion to correct an error *sua sponte* than it enjoys to raise and address an argument *sua sponte*"? Is he correct? Sometimes correct?

---

3. Neither the parties nor our *amicus* have addressed whether, under the assumption that the Court of Appeals enjoys discretion to initiate error correction for the benefit of a nonappealing party, the Eighth Circuit abused that discretion in this case. As framed by petitioner, the question presented asked only whether the cross-appeal requirement is subject to exceptions. Because the parties have not addressed the factbound subsidiary question, I would affirm without reaching it.

Wood v. Milyard
132 S. Ct. 1826 (2012)

JUSTICE GINSBURG delivered the opinion of the Court.

This case concerns the authority of a federal court to raise, on its own motion, a statute of limitations defense to a habeas corpus petition. After state prisoner Patrick Wood filed a federal habeas petition, the State twice informed the U. S. District Court that it "would not challenge, but is not conceding, the timeliness of Wood's habeas petition." Thereafter, the District Court rejected Wood's claims on the merits. On appeal, the Tenth Circuit directed the parties to brief the question whether Wood's federal petition was timely. Post-briefing, the Court of Appeals affirmed the denial of Wood's petition, but solely on the ground that it was untimely.

Our precedent establishes that a court may consider a statute of limitations or other threshold bar the State failed to raise in answering a habeas petition. *Granberry* v. *Greer*, 481 U. S. 129, 134 (1987) (exhaustion defense); *Day* v. *McDonough*, 547 U. S. 198, 202 (2006) (statute of limitations defense). Does court discretion to take up timeliness hold when a State is aware of a limitations defense, and intelligently chooses not to rely on it in the court of first instance? The answer *Day* instructs is "no": A court is not at liberty, we have cautioned, to bypass, override, or excuse a State's deliberate waiver of a limitations defense. *Id.*, at 202, 210, n. 11. The Tenth Circuit, we accordingly hold, abused its discretion by resurrecting the limitations issue instead of reviewing the District Court's disposition on the merits of Wood's claims.

I

. . . .

Wood filed a federal habeas petition in 2008, which the District Court initially dismissed as untimely. On reconsideration, the District Court vacated the dismissal and instructed the State to file a preanswer response "limited to addressing the affirmative defenses of timeliness and/or exhaustion of state court remedies." On timeliness, the State responded in its preanswer response: "Respondents will not challenge, but are not conceding, the timeliness of Wood's federal habeas petition." Consistently, in its full answer to Wood's federal petition, the State repeated: "Respondents are not challenging, but do not concede, the timeliness of the petition."

Disposing of Wood's petition, the District Court dismissed certain claims for failure to exhaust state remedies, and denied on the merits Wood's two remaining claims — one alleging a double jeopardy violation and one challenging the validity of Wood's waiver of his Sixth Amendment right to a jury trial. On appeal, the Tenth Circuit ordered the parties to brief, along with the merits of Wood's double jeopardy and Sixth Amendment claims, "the timeliness of Wood's application for federal habeas relief." After briefing, the Court of Appeals affirmed the denial of Wood's petition without addressing the merits; instead, the Tenth Circuit held the petition time barred. In so ruling, the Court of Appeals concluded it had authority to raise timeliness on its own motion. It further ruled that the State had not taken that issue off the table by declining to interpose a statute of limitations defense in the District Court.

We granted review to resolve two issues: first, whether a court of appeals has the authority to address the timeliness of a habeas petition on the court's own initiative;[2] second, assuming a court of appeals has such authority, whether the State's representations to the District Court in this case nonetheless precluded the Tenth Circuit from considering the timeliness of Wood's petition.

II

. . . .

B

"Ordinarily in civil litigation, a statutory time limitation is forfeited if not raised in a defendant's answer or in an amendment thereto." *Day*, 547 U. S., at 202 (citing Fed. Rules Civ. Proc. 8(c), 12(b), and 15(a)). See also Habeas Corpus Rule 5(b) (requiring the State to plead a statute of limitations defense in its answer).[4] An affirmative defense, once forfeited, is "excluded from the case," and, as a rule, cannot be asserted on appeal.

In *Granberry* v. *Greer*, we recognized a modest exception to the rule that a federal court will not consider a forfeited affirmative defense. The District Court in *Granberry* denied a federal habeas petition on the merits. On appeal, the State argued for the first time that the petition should be dismissed because the petitioner had failed to exhaust relief available in state court. See Habeas Corpus Rule 5(b) (listing "failure to exhaust state remedies" as a threshold bar to federal habeas relief). Despite the State's failure to raise the nonexhaustion argument in the District Court, the Seventh Circuit accepted the argument and ruled for the State on that ground. We granted certiorari to decide whether a court of appeals has discretion to address a nonexhaustion defense that the State failed to raise in the district court.

Although "expressing our reluctance to adopt rules that allow a party to withhold raising a defense until after the 'main event' is over," we nonetheless concluded that the bar to court of appeals' consideration of a forfeited habeas defense is not absolute. The exhaustion doctrine, we noted, is founded on concerns broader than those of the parties; in particular, the doctrine fosters respectful, harmonious relations between the state and federal judiciaries. With that comity interest in mind, we held that federal appellate courts have discretion, in "exceptional cases," to consider a nonexhaustion argument "inadvertently" overlooked by the State in the District Court.[5]

---

2. The Tenth Circuit's conclusion that it had authority to raise an AEDPA statute of limitations defense *sua sponte* conflicts with the view of the Eighth Circuit. Compare 403 Fed. Appx. 335, 337 n. 2 (CA10 2010) (case below), with *Sasser* v. *Norris*, 553 F. 3d 1121, 1128 (CA8 2009) ("The discretion to consider the statute of limitations defense *sua sponte* does not extend to the appellate level.").

4. We note here the distinction between defenses that are "waived" and those that are "forfeited." A waived claim or defense is one that a party has knowingly and intelligently relinquished; a forfeited plea is one that a party has merely failed to preserve. That distinction is key to our decision in Wood's case.

5. Although our decision in *Granberry* did not expressly distinguish between forfeited and waived defenses, we made clear in *Day* that a federal court has the authority to resurrect only forfeited defenses.

In *Day*, we affirmed a federal district court's authority to consider a forfeited habeas defense when extraordinary circumstances so warrant. There, the State miscalculated a time span, specifically, the number of days running between the finality of Day's state-court conviction and the filing of his federal habeas petition. As a result, the State erroneously informed the District Court that Day's petition was timely. A Magistrate Judge caught the State's computation error and recommended that the petition be dismissed as untimely, notwithstanding the State's timeliness concession. The District Court adopted the recommendation, and the Court of Appeals upheld the trial court's *sua sponte* dismissal of the petition as untimely.

Concluding that it would make "scant sense" to treat AEDPA's statute of limitations differently from other threshold constraints on federal habeas petitioners, we held "that district courts are permitted, but not obliged, to consider, *sua sponte*, the timeliness of a state prisoner's habeas petition." Affording federal courts leeway to consider a forfeited timeliness defense was appropriate, we again reasoned, because AEDPA's statute of limitations, like the exhaustion doctrine, "implicates values beyond the concerns of the parties."

We clarified, however, that a federal court does not have *carte blanche* to depart from the principle of party presentation basic to our adversary system. See *Greenlaw v. United States*, 554 U. S. 237, 243-244 (2008). Only where the State does not "strategically withhold the limitations defense or choose to relinquish it," and where the petitioner is accorded a fair opportunity to present his position, may a district court consider the defense on its own initiative and "determine whether the interests of justice would be better served by addressing the merits or by dismissing the petition as time barred." It would be "an abuse of discretion," we observed, for a court "to override a State's deliberate waiver of a limitations defense." In Day's case itself, we emphasized, the State's concession of timeliness resulted from "inadvertent error," not from any deliberate decision to proceed straightaway to the merits.

Consistent with *Granberry* and *Day*, we decline to adopt an absolute rule barring a court of appeals from raising, on its own motion, a forfeited timeliness defense. The institutional interests served by AEDPA's statute of limitations are also present when a habeas case moves to the court of appeals, a point *Granberry* recognized with respect to a nonexhaustion defense. We accordingly hold, in response to the first question presented, that courts of appeals, like district courts, have the authority — though not the obligation — to raise a forfeited timeliness defense on their own initiative.

C

We turn now to the second, case-specific, inquiry. Although a court of appeals has discretion to address, *sua sponte*, the timeliness of a habeas petition, appellate courts should reserve that authority for use in exceptional cases. For good reason, appellate courts ordinarily abstain from entertaining issues that have not been raised and preserved in the court of first instance. That restraint is all the more appropriate when the appellate court itself spots an issue the parties did not air below, and therefore would not have anticipated in developing their arguments on appeal.

Due regard for the trial court's processes and time investment is also a consideration appellate courts should not overlook. It typically takes a district court more time to decide a habeas case on the merits, than it does to resolve a petition on threshold procedural grounds. When a court of appeals raises a procedural impediment to dis-position on the merits, and disposes of the case on that ground, the district court's labor is discounted and the appellate court acts not as a court of review but as one of first view.

In light of the foregoing discussion of the relevant considerations, we hold that the Tenth Circuit abused its discretion when it dismissed Wood's petition as untimely. In the District Court, the State was well aware of the statute of limitations defense available to it and of the arguments that could be made in support of the defense. Yet the State twice informed the District Court that it "will not challenge, but is not conceding" the timeliness of Wood's petition. Essentially, the District Court asked the State: Will you oppose the petition on statute of limitations grounds? The State answered: Such a challenge would be supportable, but we won't make the challenge here.

"Waiver is the 'intentional relinquishment or abandonment of a known right.'" The State's conduct in this case fits that description. Its decision not to contest the timeliness of Wood's petition did not stem from an "inadvertent error," as did the State's concession in *Day*. Rather, the State, after expressing its clear and accurate understanding of the timeliness issue, deliberately steered the District Court away from the question and towards the merits of Wood's petition. In short, the State knew it had an "arguable" statute of limitations defense, yet it chose, in no uncertain terms, to refrain from interposing a timeliness "challenge" to Wood's petition. The District Court therefore reached and decided the merits of the petition. The Tenth Circuit should have done so as well.

For the reasons state, the judgment of the Court of Appeals for the Tenth Circuit is reversed, and the case is remanded for further proceedings consistent with this opinion.

JUSTICE THOMAS, with whom JUSTICE SCALIA joins, concurring in the judgment.

In *Day*, the Court held that a federal district court may raise *sua sponte* a for-feited statute of limitations defense to a habeas corpus petition. Relying on *Day* and *Granberry*, the Court now holds that a court of appeals may do the same. Because I continue to think that *Day* was wrongly decided and that *Granberry* is inapposite, I cannot join the Court's opinion.

As the dissent in *Day* explained, the Federal Rules of Civil Procedure apply in ha-beas corpus cases to the extent that they are consistent with the Habeas Corpus Rules, the habeas corpus statute, and the historical practice of habeas proceedings. As rel-evant here, the Rules of Civil Procedure provide that a defendant forfeits his statute of limitations defense if he fails to raise it in his answer or in an amendment thereto. That forfeiture rule is fully consistent with habeas corpus procedure. As an initial matter, the rule comports with the Habeas Rules' instruction that a State "must" plead any limitations defense in its answer. Moreover, the rule does not conflict with the habeas statute, which imposes a 1-year period of limitations without any indica-tion that the typical forfeiture rules do not apply. Finally, the rule does not interfere with historical practice. Prior to the enactment of a habeas statute of limitations in the Antiterrorism and Effective Death Penalty Act of 1996 (AEDPA), habeas practice included no limitations period at all, much less one immune to forfeiture.

As the dissent in *Day* further explained, AEDPA's statute of limitations is distinguishable from the equitable defenses that we have traditionally permitted federal habeas corpus courts to raise *sua sponte*. Those judicially created defenses were rooted in concerns of comity and finality that arise when federal courts collaterally review state criminal convictions. But those same concerns did not lead this Court to recognize any equitable time bar against habeas petitions. Thus, nothing in this Court's pre-existing doctrine of equitable defenses supported the *Day* Court's "decision to beef up the presumptively forfeitable 'limitations period' of §2244(d) by making it the subject of *sua sponte* dismissal."

For these reasons, I believe that the *Day* Court was wrong to hold that district courts may raise *sua sponte* forfeited statute of limitations defenses in habeas cases. I therefore would not extend *Day*'s reasoning to proceedings in the courts of appeals. Appellate courts, moreover, are particularly ill suited to consider issues forfeited below. Unlike district courts, courts of appeals cannot permit a State to amend its answer to add a defense, nor can they develop the facts that are often necessary to resolve questions of timeliness.

In light of these considerations, I cannot join the Court's holding that a court of appeals has discretion to consider *sua sponte* a forfeited limitations defense. Nor can I join the Court's separate holding that the Court of Appeals abused its discretion by raising a defense that had been deliberately waived by the State. As the dissent in *Day* noted, there is no principled reason to distinguish between forfeited and waived limitations defenses when determining whether courts may raise such defenses *sua sponte*. Therefore, I concur only in the judgment.

Notes and Questions

---

1. Which opinion do you find more persuasive — the majority, or the concurrence? Why? If the concurrence agrees that the court of appeals' judgment should be reversed, what are its concerns? And what of the Court's purported distinction between forfeited and waived defenses? Do you find that distinction convincing? In this context?

2. Is *Wood* fairly distinguishable from *Greenlaw*? From *Day*? If so, on what basis? Notice, *inter alia*, that *Wood* and *Greenlaw* involved sua sponte decisionmaking by the court of appeals, whereas in *Day* it occurred in the district court. Does that make a difference? If so, how much? And why? Can you formulate a "rule" regarding sua sponte decisionmaking in federal court that encompasses all three cases?

3. In *Wood*, the Court purported to "hold" that courts of appeals have discretion to raise the timeliness of a habeas petition sua sponte. But did it? Notice that the Court reversed the court of appeals' judgment in this case.

4. In *Carducci v. Regan,* 714 F.2d 171, 177 (D.C. Cir. 1983), the court (through then-Circuit Judge Scalia) opined:

> The premise of our adversarial system is that appellate courts do not sit as self-directed boards of legal inquiry and research, but essentially as arbiters of legal questions presented and argued by the parties before them. Thus, Rule 28(a)(4) of the Federal Rules of Appellate Procedure requires that the appellant's brief contain "the contentions of the appellant with respect to the issues presented, and the reasons therefor, with citations to the authorities, statutes and parts of the record relied upon." Failure to enforce this requirement will ultimately deprive us in substantial measure of that assistance of counsel which the system assumes — a deficiency that we can perhaps supply by other means, but not without altering the character of our institution. Of course not all legal arguments bearing upon the issue in question will always be identified by counsel, and we are not precluded from supplementing the contentions of counsel through our own deliberation and research. But where counsel has made no attempt to address the issue, we will not remedy the defect, especially where, as here, "important questions of far-reaching significance" are involved. We therefore decline to entertain appellant's asserted but unanalyzed constitutional claim.

5. "I believe that the adversary process functions most effectively when we rely on the initiative of lawyers, rather than the activism of judges, to fashion the questions for review." *New Jersey v. T. L. O.,* 468 U.S. 1214, 1216 (1984) (Stevens, J., joined by Brennan and Marshall, JJ., dissenting from sua sponte reargument and addition of a question not raised by the parties).

6. Some of the most famous cases in the history of the Supreme Court were decided on the basis of arguments that were not raised by the parties. *See* Amanda Frost, *The Limits of Advocacy,* 59 DUKE L.J. 447, 467-69 (2009) (citing, *inter alia, Erie R.R. v. Tompkins,* 304 U.S. 64 (1938)).

7. As Professor Frost argues in the preceding article, sua sponte decisionmaking seems to be grounded in part on the notion that courts have something of an obligation to get the law "right," even if that means bypassing the arguments of the parties. *See also* Sarah M. R. Cravens, *Involved Appellate Judging,* 88 MARQ. L. REV. 251 (2004). But for a somewhat contrary view, *see* Gary Lawson, *Stipulating the Law,* 109 MICH. L. REV. 1191 (2011).

8. Why does a court seemingly have an *obligation* to raise some matters sua sponte (such as subject-matter jurisdiction) but not all matters? Is a court *prohibited* from raising some matters sua sponte?

9. ALI/UNIDROIT Principles of Transnational Civil Procedure (2004), Principle 10 ("Party Initiative and Scope of Proceedings") provides: "The proceeding should be initiated through the claim or claims of the plaintiff, not by the court acting on its own motion." Principle 10.1. *See also* Principle 10.3 ("The scope of the proceedings is determined by the claims and defenses of the parties in the pleadings, including amendments."). Comment P-10A continues: "All modern legal systems recognize the principle of party initiative concerning the scope and particulars of the dispute. It is within the framework of party initiative that the court carries out its responsibility for just adjudication."

10. Federal Rule of Civil Procedure 56 was recently amended to include what has now become Rule 56(f) ("Judgment Independent of the Motion"), which provides: "After giving notice and a reasonable time to respond, the court may: (1) grant summary judgment for a nonmovant; (2) grant the motion on grounds not raised by a party; or (3) consider summary judgment on its own after identifying for the parties material facts that may not be genuinely in dispute." Do you think that this is a good rule? A bad rule? A necessary rule?

11. Sua sponte decisionmaking is not limited to questions of law, as courts sometimes engage in their own factual determinations as well. For more on this topic as it arises in the Supreme Court, see Allison Larsen, *Confronting Supreme Court Fact Finding*, 98 VA. L. REV. 1255 (2012).

12. On this topic generally, *see* Bradley Scott Shannon, *Some Concerns About Sua Sponte*, 73 OHIO ST. L.J. FURTHERMORE 27 (2012).

SIDEBAR: AMICUS CURIAE PRACTICE

The consideration of amicus curiae ("friend of the court") briefs (and therefore arguments) by United States courts is a growing trend that raises many of the same issues as does sua sponte judicial decisionmaking. As Professor Frost explains:

> The widespread participation of amicus curiae at all stages of litigation is also in tension with the party presentation principle. Although many amicus briefs simply underscore the petitioners' and respondents' arguments, some stake out new territory, and no rule forbids them from doing so. To the contrary, the rules of procedure governing amicus filings in the U.S. Supreme Court state that amicus briefs should discuss aspects of the case given short shrift or entirely overlooked by the parties, and discourage amicus briefs that simply reiterate the litigants' arguments.
>
> . . . .
>
> Most remarkable in light of the party presentation norm, the Supreme Court occasionally appoints amicus curiae to argue a position that *no* party supports, even when those issues are not jurisdictional.

Amanda Frost, *The Limits of Advocacy*, 59 DUKE L.J. 447, 465-66 (2009) (footnotes omitted).

Amicus curiae practice in the Supreme Court is governed by S. Ct. R. 37. What are the possible pros and cons associated with this practice? Should it be allowed? Limited in any way?

ALI/UNIDROIT Principles of Transnational Civil Procedure (2004), Principle 13 ("*Amicus Curiae* Submissions") provides:

> Written submissions concerning important legal issues in the proceeding and matters of background information may be received from third parties with the consent of the court, upon consultation with the parties. The court may invite such a submission. The parties must have the opportunity to submit written comment addressed to the matters contained in such a submission before it is considered by the court.

> For recent surveys of Supreme Court amicus practice (which appears to be growing), see Anthony J. Franze & R. Reeves Anderson, *The Supreme Court's reliance on amicus curiae in the 2011-12 term*, Nat'l L.J. 18 (2012), and Mark Walsh, *Frequent Filers: It was another big term for amicus briefs at the high court*, ABA J. 16 (Sept. 2013). For a critical view of amicus practice, see John Harrington, Note, *Amici Curiae in the Federal Courts of Appeals: How Friendly Are They?*, 55 Case W. Res. L. Rev. 667 (2005). For a perspective on amicus practice in civil law countries, see Steven Kochevar, Comment, *Amici Curiae in Civil Law Jurisdictions*, 122 Yale L.J. 1653 (2013). *See also generally* Joseph D. Kearney & Thomas W. Merrill, *The Influence of Amicus Curiae Briefs on the Supreme Court*, 148 U. Pa. L. Rev. 743 (2000); Samuel Krislov, *The Amicus Curiae Brief: From Friendship to Advocacy*, 72 Yale L.J. 694 (1963); and Linda Sandstrom Simard, *An Empirical Study of Amici Curiae in Federal Courts: A Fine Balance of Access, Efficiency, and Adversarialism*, 27 Rev. Lit. 669 (2008).

O. DECIDING ISSUES FOR THE FIRST TIME ON APPEAL

Should an appellate court decide a case without the benefit of trial court consideration? Or should the appellate court await trial court consideration, and limit its role to that of review? Consider these questions in the context of the following case.

Weisgram v. Marley Co.
528 U.S. 440 (2000)

Justice Ginsburg delivered the opinion of the Court.

This case concerns the respective authority of federal trial and appellate courts to decide whether, as a matter of law, judgment should be entered in favor of a verdict loser. The pattern we confront is this. Plaintiff in a product liability action gains a jury verdict. Defendant urges, unsuccessfully before the federal district court but successfully on appeal, that expert testimony plaintiff introduced was unreliable, and therefore inadmissible, under the analysis required by *Daubert v. Merrell Dow Pharmaceuticals, Inc.,* 509 U. S. 579 (1993). Shorn of the erroneously admitted expert testimony, the record evidence is insufficient to justify a plaintiff's verdict. May the court of appeals then instruct the entry of judgment as a matter of law for defendant, or must that tribunal remand the case, leaving to the district court's discretion the choice between final judgment for defendant or a new trial of plaintiff's case?

Our decision is guided by Federal Rule of Civil Procedure 50, which governs the entry of judgment as a matter of law, and by the Court's pathmarking opinion in *Neely v. Martin K. Eby Constr. Co.,* 386 U. S. 317 (1967). As *Neely* teaches, courts of appeals should "be constantly alert" to "the trial judge's first-hand knowledge of witnesses, testimony, and issues"; in other words, appellate courts should give due consideration to the first-instance decisionmaker's 'feel' for the overall case." But the court of appeals has authority to render the final decision. If, in the particular case, the appellate tribunal determines that the district court is better positioned to decide whether a new trial, rather than judgment for defendant, should be ordered, the court of appeals should return the case to the trial court for such an assessment. But if, as in the instant case, the court of appeals concludes that further proceedings are unwarranted because the loser on appeal has had a full and fair opportunity to present the case, including arguments for a new trial, the appellate court may appropriately instruct the district court to enter judgment against the jury-verdict winner. Appellate authority to make this determination is no less when the evidence is rendered insufficient by the removal of erroneously admitted testimony than it is when the evidence, without any deletion, is insufficient.

I

Firefighters arrived at the home of Bonnie Weisgram on December 30, 1993, to discover flames around the front entrance. Upon entering the home, they found Weisgram in an upstairs bathroom, dead of carbon monoxide poisoning. Her son, petitioner Chad Weisgram, individually and on behalf of Bonnie Weisgram's heirs, brought a diversity action in the United States District Court for the District of North Dakota seeking wrongful death damages. He alleged that a defect in an electric baseboard heater, manufactured by defendant (now respondent) Marley Company and located inside the door to Bonnie Weisgram's home, caused both the fire and his mother's death.

At trial, Weisgram introduced the testimony of three witnesses, proffered as experts, in an endeavor to prove the alleged defect in the heater and its causal connection to the fire. The District Court overruled defendant Marley's objections, lodged both before and during trial, that this testimony was unreliable and therefore inadmissible under Federal Rule of Evidence 702 as elucidated by *Daubert.* At the close of Weisgram's evidence, and again at the close of all the evidence, Marley unsuccessfully moved under Federal Rule of Civil Procedure 50(a) for judgment as a matter of law on the ground that plaintiffs had failed to meet their burden of proof on the issues of defect and causation. The jury returned a verdict for Weisgram. Marley again requested judgment as a matter of law, and additionally requested, in the alternative, a new trial, pursuant to Rules 50 and 59; among arguments in support of its post-trial motions, Marley reasserted that the expert testimony essential to prove Weisgram's case was unreliable and therefore inadmissible. The District Court denied the motions and entered judgment for Weisgram. Marley appealed.

The Court of Appeals for the Eighth Circuit held that Marley's motion for judgment as a matter of law should have been granted. Writing for the panel majority, Chief Judge Bowman first examined the testimony of Weisgram's expert witnesses, the sole evidence supporting plaintiffs' product defect charge. Concluding that the testimony was speculative and not shown to be scientifically sound, the majority held the expert evidence incompetent to prove Weisgram's case. The court then considered the remaining evidence in the light most favorable to Weisgram, found it insufficient to support the jury verdict, and directed judgment as a matter of law for Marley. In a footnote, the majority "rejected any contention that it was required to remand for a new trial." It recognized its discretion to do so under Rule 50(d), but stated: "We can discern no reason to give the plaintiffs a second chance to make out a case of strict liability. This is not a close case. The plaintiffs had a fair opportunity to prove their claim and they failed to do so." The dissenting judge disagreed on both points, concluding that the expert evidence was properly admitted and that the appropriate remedy for improper admission of expert testimony is the award of a new trial, not judgment as a matter of law.

Courts of Appeals have divided on the question whether Federal Rule of Civil Procedure 50 permits an appellate court to direct the entry of judgment as a matter of law when it determines that evidence was erroneously admitted at trial and that the remaining, properly admitted evidence is insufficient to constitute a submissible case.[2] We granted certiorari to resolve the conflict and we now affirm the Eighth Circuit's judgment.

II

Federal Rule of Civil Procedure 50 . . . governs motions for judgment as a matter of law in jury trials. It allows the trial court to remove cases or issues from the jury's consideration "when the facts are sufficiently clear that the law requires a particular result." Subdivision (d) controls when, as here, the verdict loser appeals from the trial court's denial of a motion for judgment as a matter of law:

> "The party who prevailed on that motion may, as appellee, assert grounds entitling the party to a new trial in the event the appellate court concludes that the trial court erred in denying the motion for judgment. If the appellate court reverses the judgment, nothing in this rule precludes it from determining that the appellee is entitled to a new trial, or from directing the trial court to determine whether a new trial shall be granted."

---

2. The Tenth Circuit has held it inappropriate for an appellate court to direct the entry of judgment as a matter of law based on the trial court's erroneous admission of evidence, because to do so would be unfair to a party who relied on the trial court's evidentiary rulings.

Under this Rule, Weisgram urges, when a court of appeals determines that a jury verdict cannot be sustained due to an error in the admission of evidence, the appellate court may not order the entry of judgment for the verdict loser, but must instead remand the case to the trial court for a new trial determination. Nothing in Rule 50 expressly addresses this question.

In a series of pre-1967 decisions, this Court refrained from deciding the question, while emphasizing the importance of giving the party deprived of a verdict the opportunity to invoke the discretion of the trial judge to grant a new trial. Then, in *Neely*, the Court reviewed its prior jurisprudence and ruled definitively that if a motion for judgment as a matter of law is erroneously denied by the district court, the appellate court does have the power to order the entry of judgment for the moving party.

Neely first addressed the compatibility of appellate direction of judgment as a matter of law (then styled "judgment *n.o.v.*") with the Seventh Amendment's jury trial guarantee. . . . The Court next turned to "the statutory grant of appellate jurisdiction to the courts of appeals in 28 U. S. C. § 2106,"[6] which it found "certainly broad enough to include the power to direct entry of judgment *n.o.v.* on appeal." The remainder of the *Neely* opinion effectively complements Rules 50(c) and 50(d), providing guidance on the appropriate exercise of the appellate court's discretion when it reverses the trial court's denial of a defendant's Rule 50(b) motion for judgment as a matter of law.

Neely represents no volte-face in the Court's understanding of the respective competences of trial and appellate forums. Immediately after declaring that appellate courts have the power to order the entry of judgment for a verdict loser, the Court cautioned:

> "Part of the Court's concern has been to protect the rights of the party whose jury verdict has been set aside on appeal and who may have valid grounds for a new trial, some or all of which should be passed upon by the district court, rather than the court of appeals, because of the trial judge's first-hand knowledge of witnesses, testimony, and issues — because of his 'feel' for the overall case. These are very valid concerns to which the court of appeals should be constantly alert."[7]

Nevertheless, the Court in *Neely* continued, due consideration of the rights of the verdict winner and the closeness of the trial court to the case "does not justify an

---

6. Section 2106 reads:

"The Supreme Court or any other court of appellate jurisdiction may affirm, modify, vacate, set aside or reverse any judgment, decree, or order of a court lawfully brought before it for review, and may remand the cause and direct the entry of such appropriate judgment, decree, or order, or require such further proceedings to be had as may be just under the circumstances."

7. *Iacurci v. Lummus Co.,* 387 U. S. 86 (1967) *(per curiam),* decided shortly after *Neely,* is illustrative. There, the Court reversed the appellate court's direction of the entry of judgment as a matter of law for the defendant and instructed the appeals court to remand the case to the trial court for a new trial determination; the Court pointed to the jury's failure to respond to four out of five special interrogatories, which left issues of negligence unresolved, and concluded that in the particular circumstances, the trial judge "was in the best position to pass upon the question of a new trial in light of the evidence, his charge to the jury, and the jury's verdict and interrogatory answers." 387 U. S., at 88.

ironclad rule that the court of appeals should never order dismissal or judgment for the defendant when the plaintiffs verdict has been set aside on appeal." "Such a rule," the Court concluded, "would not serve the purpose of Rule 50 to speed litigation and to avoid unnecessary retrials." *Neely* ultimately clarified that if a court of appeals determines that the district court erroneously denied a motion for judgment as a matter of law, the appellate court may (1) order a new trial at the verdict winner's request or on its own motion, (2) remand the case for the trial court to decide whether a new trial or entry of judgment for the defendant is warranted, or (3) direct the entry of judgment as a matter of law for the defendant.

III

The parties before us — and Court of Appeals opinions — diverge regarding *Neely*'s scope. Weisgram, in line with some appellate decisions, posits a distinction between cases in which judgment as a matter of law is requested based on plaintiff's failure to produce enough evidence to warrant a jury verdict, as in *Neely*, and cases in which the proof introduced becomes insufficient because the court of appeals determines that certain evidence should not have been admitted, as in the instant case. Insufficiency caused by deletion of evidence, Weisgram contends, requires an "automatic remand" to the district court for consideration whether a new trial is warranted.[9]

Weisgram relies on cases holding that, in fairness to a verdict winner who may have relied on erroneously admitted evidence, courts confronting questions of judgment as a matter of law should rule on the record as it went to the jury, without excising evidence inadmissible under Federal Rule of Evidence 702. These decisions are of questionable consistency with Rule 50(a)(1), which states that in ruling on a motion for judgment as a matter of law, the court is to inquire whether there is any "legally sufficient evidentiary basis for a reasonable jury to find for the opponent of

---

9. Weisgram misreads the Court's decision in *Montgomery Ward & Co. v. Duncan*, 311 U. S. 243 (1940), to support his position. The Court in *Montgomery Ward* directed that a trial judge who grants the verdict loser's motion for judgment *n.o.v.* should also rule conditionally on that party's alternative motion for a new trial. The conditional ruling would be reviewed by the court of appeals only if it reversed the entry of judgment *n.o.v.* Proceeding in this manner would avoid protracting the proceedings by obviating the need for multiple appeals. Rule 50 was amended in 1963 to codify *Montgomery Ward*'s instruction. See Fed. Rule Civ. Proc. 50(c)(1). In the course of its elaboration, the *Montgomery Ward* Court observed that a "motion for judgment cannot be granted unless, as a matter of law, the opponent of the movant failed to make a case." In contrast, the Court stated, a new trial motion may invoke the court's discretion, bottomed on such standard new trial grounds as "the verdict is against the weight of the evidence," or "the damages are excessive," or substantial errors were made "in admission or rejection of evidence."

Many rulings of evidence, of course, do not bear dispositively on the adequacy of the proof to support a verdict. For example, the evidence erroneously admitted or excluded may strengthen or weaken one side's case without being conclusive as to the litigation's outcome. Or, the evidence may abundantly support a jury's verdict, but one or another item may have been unduly prejudicial to the verdict loser and excludable on that account. Such run-of-the-mine, ordinarily nondispositive, evidentiary rulings, we take it, were the sort contemplated in *Montgomery Ward*.

the motion." Inadmissible evidence contributes nothing to a "legally sufficient evidentiary basis."

As *Neely* recognized, appellate rulings on post-trial pleas for judgment as a matter of law call for the exercise of "informed discretion," and fairness to the parties is surely key to the exercise of that discretion. But fairness concerns should loom as large when the verdict winner, in the appellate court's judgment, failed to present sufficient evidence as when the appellate court declares inadmissible record evidence essential to the verdict winner's case. In both situations, the party whose verdict is set aside on appeal will have had notice, before the close of the evidence, of the alleged deficiency. On appeal, both will have the opportunity to argue in support of the jury's verdict or, alternatively, for a new trial. And if judgment is instructed for the verdict loser, both will have a further chance to urge a new trial in a rehearing petition.[11]

Since *Daubert*, moreover, parties relying on expert evidence have had notice of the exacting standards of reliability such evidence must meet. It is implausible to suggest, post-*Daubert*, that parties will initially present less than their best expert evidence in the expectation of a second chance should their first try fail. We therefore find unconvincing Weisgram's fears that allowing courts of appeals to direct the entry of judgment for defendants will punish plaintiffs who could have shored up their cases by other means had they known their expert testimony would be found inadmissible. In this case, for example, although Weisgram was on notice every step of the way that Marley was challenging his experts, he made no attempt to add or substitute other evidence.

After holding Weisgram's expert testimony inadmissible, the Court of Appeals evaluated the evidence presented at trial, viewing it in the light most favorable to Weisgram, and found the properly admitted evidence insufficient to support the verdict. Weisgram offered no specific grounds for a new trial to the Eighth Circuit.[13] Even in the petition for rehearing, Weisgram argued only that the appellate court had misapplied state law, did not have the authority to direct judgment, and had failed to give adequate deference to the trial court's evidentiary rulings. The Eighth Circuit concluded that this was "not a close case." In these circumstances, the Eighth Circuit did not abuse its discretion by directing entry of judgment for Marley, instead of returning the case to the District Court for further proceedings.

---

11. We recognize that it is awkward for an appellee, who is wholeheartedly urging the correctness of the verdict, to point out, in the alternative, grounds for a new trial. A petition for rehearing in the court of appeals, however, involves no conflicting tugs. We are not persuaded by Weisgram's objection that the 14 days allowed for the filing of a petition for rehearing is insufficient time to formulate compelling grounds for a new trial. This time period is longer than the ten days allowed a verdict winner to move for a new trial after a trial court grants judgment as a matter of law. Nor do we foreclose the possibility that a court of appeals might properly deny a petition for rehearing because it pressed an argument that plainly could have been formulated in a party's brief.

13. Cf. *Neely* [at 327] (observing that it would not be clear that litigation should be terminated for evidentiary insufficiency when, for example, the trial court excluded evidence that would have strengthened the verdict winner's case or "itself caused the insufficiency by erroneously imposing too high a burden of proof").

Neely recognized that there are myriad situations in which the determination whether a new trial is best made by the trial judge. *Neely* held, however, that there are also cases in which a court of appeals may appropriately instruct the district court to enter judgment as a matter of law against the jury-verdict winner. We adhere to *Neely's* holding and rationale, and today hold that the authority of courts of appeals to direct the entry of judgment as a matter of law extends to cases in which, on excision of testimony erroneously admitted, there remains insufficient evidence to support the jury's verdict.

For the reasons stated, the judgment of the Court of Appeals for the Eighth Circuit is

Affirmed.

Notes and Questions

1. The Court's decision in *Weisgram* was unanimous.

2. What are the benefits of having the court of appeals simply decide the case, as was done in *Weisgram*? What are the problems associated with this practice, as opposed to remanding the case to the district court for further consideration consistent with the court of appeals' decision? Which do you think is, on balance, the better practice? Or does it depend on the circumstances?

3. Federal Rule of Civil Procedure 50 was amended following *Weisgram*, and now conforms to it. Specifically, Rule 50(e) now provides in pertinent part: "If the appellate court reverses the judgment, it may order a new trial, direct the trial court to determine whether a new trial should be granted, or direct the entry of judgment." Was this a wise change? Why or why not?

4. Did the court of appeals in *Weisgram* enter judgment in favor of the appellant sua sponte, or at the urging of that party? Or is the answer unclear?

5. With respect to 28 U.S.C. § 2106 (quoted in the Court's footnote 6), does the power to "affirm, modify, vacate, set aside or reverse any judgment" truly include the power to decide issues for the first time on appeal?

6. For a more recent example of a case in which the Supreme Court finally decided a case on appeal rather than allowing further consideration on remand, see *Republic of the Philippines v. Pimentel*, 128 S. Ct. 2180 (2008).

7. *Singleton v. Wulff*, 428 U.S. 106 (1976), involved a challenge to the constitutionality of a state statute. Though the district court dismissed the action for lack of standing, the court of appeals not only reversed the judgment of dismissal, but

then proceeded to determine that the statute in question was unconstitutional. *See id.* at 111-12. In reversing the court of appeals, the Supreme Court stated:

> It is a general rule, of course, that a federal appellate court does not consider an issue not passed upon below. In *Hormel v. Helvering,* 312 U. S. 552, 556 (1941), the Court explained that this is "essential in order that parties may have the opportunity to offer all the evidence they believe relevant to the issues and in order that litigants may not be surprised on appeal by final decision there of issues upon which they have had no opportunity to introduce evidence." We have no idea what evidence, if any, petitioner would, or could, offer in defense of this statute, but this is only because petitioner has had no opportunity to proffer such evidence. Moreover, even assuming that there is no such evidence, petitioner should have the opportunity to present whatever legal arguments he may have in defense of the statute. We think he was justified in not presenting those arguments to the Court of Appeals, and in assuming, rather, that he would be allowed to answer the complaint, should the Court of Appeals reinstate it.
>
> The matter of what questions may be taken up and resolved for the first time on appeal is one left primarily to the discretion of the courts of appeals, to be exercised on the facts of individual cases. We announce no general rule. Certainly there are circumstances in which a federal appellate court is justified in resolving an issue not passed on below, as where the proper resolution is beyond any doubt, or where "injustice might otherwise result." Suffice it so say that this is not such a case. The issue resolved by the Court of Appeals has never been passed upon in any decision of this Court. This being so, injustice was more likely to be caused than avoided by deciding the issue without petitioner's having had an opportunity to be heard.

Id. at 120-21. Does the *Singleton* Court in fact articulate any sort of general rule regarding when an appellate court may properly consider arguments not considered below? Does the "rule" the Court does articulate seem workable? Note, in this regard, the Court's statement that the examples of exceptions to the general rule mentioned in its opinion "are not intended to be exclusive." *Id.* at 121 n.8.

8. In *United States v. Locke,* 471 U.S. 84, 92 n.9 (1985), the Court more recently noted:

> When the nonconstitutional questions have not been passed on by the lower court, we may vacate the decision below and remand with instructions that those questions be decided, or we may choose to decide those questions ourselves without the benefit of lower court analysis. The choice between these options depends on the extent to which lower court factfinding and analysis of the nonconstitutional questions will be necessary or useful to our disposition of those questions.

9. *The appellee exception.* Though it has generally been held that an appellant may not raise arguments that were not "passed upon" by the court below, an *appellee* may support the judgment below with reasons other than those relied upon by the deciding court, so long as those reasons appear in the record (i.e., were presented to the court below). As stated by the Court in *United States v. American Ry. Exp. Co.*, 265 U.S. 425, 435 (1923):

> It is true that a party who does not appeal from a final decree of the trial court cannot be heard in opposition thereto when the case is brought here by appeal of the adverse party. In other words, the appellee may not attack the decree with a view either to enlarging his own rights thereunder or of lessening the rights of his adversary, a matter dealt with below. But it is likewise settled that the appellee may, without taking a cross-appeal, urge in support of a decree any matter appearing in the record, although his argument may involve an attack upon the reasoning of the lower court or an insistence upon a matter overlooked or ignored by it.

Accord Chevron U.S.A. Inc. v. Natural Resources Defense Council, Inc., 467 U.S. 837, 842 n.7 ("Respondents rely on the arguments rejected by the Court of Appeals in support of the judgment, and may rely on any ground that finds support in the record."). This rule was recently reaffirmed in *Greenlaw v. United States*, 128 S. Ct. 2559, 2567 n.5 (2008).

Of course, if the issue was not *raised* below, the usual rule applies. As the Supreme Court stated in *14 Penn Plaza LLC v. Pyett*, 556 U.S. 247 (2009):

> Without cross-petitioning for certiorari, a prevailing party may, of course, defend its judgment on any ground properly raised below whether or not that ground was relied upon, rejected, or even considered by the District Court or the Court of Appeals. But this Court will affirm on grounds that have not been raised below only in exceptional cases. This is not an exceptional case. As a result, we find that respondents' alternative arguments for affirmance have been forfeited. We will not resurrect them on respondents' behalf.

556 U.S. at 273 (quotation marks omitted).

10. As mentioned by the *Penn Plaza* Court in the previous note, appellate courts will sometimes consider issues or arguments that were not raised in the trial court, though only in "exceptional cases." The problem, of course, is knowing when a case is "exceptional." As explained by Robert J. Martineau, *Considering New Issues on Appeal: The General Rule and the Gorilla Rule*, 40 VANDERBILT L. REV. 1023 (1987):

> One aspect of the appellate process that most bedevils judges and lawyers occurs when a party attempts to raise an issue in the appellate court that it did not present to the trial court. This question creates problems for the following reasons: (1) the general rule against considering new issues on appeal; (2) the perception that it is unfair to the appellant if the new issue is not considered, yet it is unfair to the appellee if the new issue is considered; and (3) the failure or inability of appellate courts to articulate any principled basis for determining when and under what circumstances a new issue will be considered. As a result, it is almost impossible to predict in a particular case whether or not the appellate court will consider a new issue raised by the appellant. This uncertainty reduces the value of being the successful party in the trial court and adds to the already overwhelming caseload of American appellate courts by encouraging appeals. Further, in many appeals,

which would have been taken in any event, it can add two issues: whether or not to consider the new issue, as well as the merits of the issue itself.

    . . . .

The rationale [behind the general rule] is that if the party who objects to the trial court's action is forced to state its objection and to offer an alternative, the adversary or the trial court or both can decide whether to agree with the objecting party, offer a third alternative, or set out in the record the factual or legal basis for the trial court's action. If the adversary or the court accepts the objecting party's proposal, there is no error insofar as that party is concerned and thus no basis for appeal. If the adversary or the trial court follows a course of action that differs both from the action originally objected to and the objecting party's alternative proposal, the objecting party may be satisfied and once again not pursue an appeal. If the trial court proceeds as originally planned notwithstanding the objection, both the adversary and the trial court can ensure that the record supports the factual and legal basis for the action, thus making it easier for the adversary to defend the action on appeal and less likely that the appellate court will find the trial court's action reversible error.

The validity of this approach should be examined from the viewpoints of the private and public interests involved in the court proceeding. The private interests are those of the litigants in the particular case. From the perspective of the party who is affected adversely by the trial court action, common sense dictates that the party should be compelled to "speak up now or forever hold your peace" if the party realizes or should realize at the time the action is taken that the effect will be adverse to its interests. In various legal contexts, this principle is characterized as waiver, clean hands, and invited error. At the heart of these doctrines is the essential point that a person should not benefit from his own inaction or, stated obversely, a person has an obligation to assert his rights at the first opportunity or within a specified time. The various rules of procedure that require a matter to be raised in a particular document, by a particular time, or in a particular way, with the failure to do so resulting in a forfeiture of the right or claim are merely expressions of the same principle. Implicit in the general rule against considering new issues on appeal is the recognition that courts must come to a conclusion if they are to perform their function of resolving disputes; but to reach conclusions, courts must enforce rules of procedure. It is not unreasonable to expect that persons who avail themselves of a forum should follow that forum's rules of procedure, and not be heard to complain about an adverse effect from their failure to do so.

From the viewpoint of the adversary whose interests are advanced by the trial court's action, requiring the objecting party to speak up at the time the action occurs is not only highly desirable but a matter of simple fairness. If the adverse party is aware of the objection the party can . . . urge that the action not be taken, an alternative can be adopted, or make as complete record as possible to support the action. If no objection is made, the adverse party may think that the other party agrees with the action or for tactical reasons decides not to raise an objection. In either case the adverse party may fail to develop a record that would support the action taken or forgo taking some step that would avoid the alleged error. The failure to object is particularly important with regard to the development of the record. The party seeking to have the trial court act is unlikely to attempt to put the basis for the request in the record when there is no objection from the other party. That is just "gilding the lily" insofar as the trial court proceedings are concerned.

Competent trial counsel always are conscious of the hazards of trying to prove that which does not have to be proven and of appearing to waste the court's time in doing so.

The public interests to consider include those of the trial and appellate courts and other present and future litigants who look to the courts to resolve disputes. It is difficult to see any positive effect on the trial court other than the time saved initially when no objection is made. Three results can flow from considering a new issue on appeal. First, the appellate court will consider the new issue to be reversible error requiring either the entry of a new judgment or, more likely, further proceedings in the trial court. Second, the appellate court will not find reversible error, in which case the trial court's original judgment will stand (unless some other reversible error is found). Third, the appellate court will find reversible error not only on the new issue but on some other properly preserved issue that requires further proceedings in the trial court. From the viewpoint of the trial court, the effect of considering the new issue may be neutral at best, requiring no additional time on its part. At worst the new issue may require substantial additional proceedings in the trial court and possibly a new trial, which is the most likely result of reversible error. Furthermore, the appellate court is unlikely to consider the new issue unless the court perceives some likelihood that reversible error exists.

Invariably, there is a negative effect on the appellate court when new issues are raised on appeal. Each time an appellant asks the appellate court to consider an issue not raised in the trial court, the appellate court must devote time to deciding whether to consider the issue and, if it decides to do so, must then spend additional time examining its merits. Inevitably, the more an appellate court is willing to consider new issues, the more likely it is that additional appeals will be taken. A losing party who will not appeal if the party knows that the appellate court will not consider new issues may do so if it thinks that the appellate court may consider the issue. The same principle applies in a case in which other issues are properly preserved on appeal. The losing party may decide to raise an issue overlooked in the trial court just in case the other issues are found to be without merit. The work of the appellate court is increased in either instance.

Litigants in other present and future cases necessarily are affected whenever an appellate court devotes time to a new issue or a trial court is compelled to spend time on a case that has been reversed and remanded by the appellate court as a result of considering the new issue. Any additional time spent on one case necessarily delays the consideration of cases involving other litigants. The only advantage to other litigants occurs if they also seek to raise a new issue in the appellate court.

. . . .

If the courts attempted to develop objective criteria for determining when an exception should be recognized and simply deferred on the application of the criteria, inconsistency in the recognition of exceptions to the general rule would not be a matter of great concern. The cases indicate, however, that very few courts have attempted to develop objective criteria. In the overwhelming majority of cases the court merely decides whether or not to recognize an exception, giving no rationale for its action. If the court refuses to consider the new issue it merely recites the general rule. If the court does consider the new issue, it simply states the exception to the rule (with or without citing authority for allowing the exception). The question is resolved in conclusory terms with little or no analysis to support whatever decision is made. As a result, the dominant characteristic of the application of the general rule and its exceptions is inconsistency.

. . . .

If courts are free to disregard the general rule whenever they wish to do so, in effect there is no general rule. The current situation is destructive of the adversary system, causes substantial harm to the interests that the general rule is designed to protect, and is an open invitation to the appellate judges to "do justice" on ad hoc rather than principles bases.

11. Should an appellate court focus on reaching the correct result, or simply in correcting lower court error? Does the answer depend on the circumstances? Does the answer depend upon what we mean by "correct result"? Is it possible to achieve both?

12. Why might an appellate court want to decide an issue that was not raised or decided below? Some of the reasons were suggested by the *Weisgram* Court; certainly a decision by an appellate court (as opposed to a remand and possible second appeal) is quicker, and to the extent the issue is predominantly legal, an appellant court would seem to be every bit as competent (assuming the corresponding factual record has been adequately developed). Moreover, there might be some situations in which consideration for the first time on appeal might simply be more fair, or more just. Can you think of any other reasons?

On the other hand, there certainly seem to be some reasons why this practice should be exceptional. Among the possible reasons why appellate courts should not decide issues that were not raised below are the following:

a) the necessary factual record might not be developed (coupled with the notion that appellate courts tend to be ill-suited for further factual development);

b) the appellate court is likely to be much less familiar with the case, and thus is more likely to make a less-informed decision or to require additional time in which to gain familiarity;

c) further appellate review of such decisions is much less likely (i.e., appellate review of district court decisions is generally of right, whereas Supreme Court review is generally discretionary, not to mention rare);

d) a sound resolution of the issue at the trial court level might obviate the need for appellate review;

e) the appellate court is deprived of the benefit of the trial court's decision (and, typically, its reasoning therefor);

f) because this practice is largely left to the discretion of the appellate court, it is difficult for the parties to predict whether and to what extent it might be allowed;

g) it adds to the burden of the appellate courts; and

h) it to some extent ignores the fact that the case will eventually be remanded to the trial court in any event.

Can you think of any other, contrary arguments?

13. One of the most difficult aspects of the waiver rule arises when the law has changed in some manner while a case in on appeal. On the one hand, the general rule is that arguments not raised in the trial court will not be considered on appeal. On the other hand, a change in the law is not the sort of argument that one should be expected to have made — i.e., how can one make an argument relating to law that is not yet law? Yet, it is almost certain that some litigant *did* make such an argument — after all, how could the law have changed otherwise (assuming the change was not made sua sponte). So why not everyone else? For a more extended discussion of this dilemma, see Mark I. Levy, *Changes in Law*, Nat'l L.J. at 13 (Dec. 3, 2007).

14. "[T]his is a court of final review and not first view . . . ." *Adarand Constructors, Inc. v. Mineta*, 534 U.S. 103, 110 (2001) (internal quotation marks omitted).

15. For a recent take on this topic, see Joan Steinman, *Appellate Courts as First Responders: The Constitutionality and Propriety of Appellate Courts' Resolving Issues in the First Instance*, 87 Notre Dame L. Rev. 1521 (2012).

16. Concerns with respect to sua sponte decisionmaking, amicus briefs, deciding (or even considering) issues for the first time on appeal, and even the distinction between holding and dicta (among other issues) all share a common thread. What is that thread?

P. THE RETROACTIVE AND PROSPECTIVE APPLICATION OF DECISIONS

1. The Problem

What happens when the law (case law, statutory law, etc.) changes in some respect following the occurrence of some significant act or event? Consider the following timeline:

act or ⟶ case ⟶ trial ⟶ direct
event   commenced   (judgment)   appeal(s)

If the law changes at some point along the timeline — i.e., after the underlying act or event giving rise to litigation occurs, but before all direct appeals have been exhausted — which law applies, the old law or the new law? Here, we will consider what happens when there is a change in case law. In Chapter 3, we will consider what happens when there is a change in statutory law.

"Historically, rules of law announced in judicial decisions were applied retroactively — that is, to conduct or events that had occurred prior to the dates of those decisions." Bradley Scott Shannon, *The Retroactive and Prospective Application of Judicial Decisions*, 26 HARV. J.L. & PUB. POL'Y 811, 812 (2003). This was true with respect to the law-changing decision itself as well as to other cases not yet final (i.e., cases that were still on appeal or could be appealed). (Of course, judicial decisions also were generally applied to cases that arose after the law-changing decision. *See* Thomas S. Currier, *Time and Change in Judge-Made Law: Prospective Overruling*, 51 VA. L. REV. 201, 205 (1965) ("It is the common-law tradition that judicial precedents normally have retroactive as well as prospective effect.").) Thus, as late as 1958, Professors Hart and Sacks were able to conclude: "Contrary to what has sometimes been supposed, the Supreme Court of the United States seems never to have sanctioned the practice of prospective overruling in the judicial elaboration of federal law." HENRY M. HART, JR. & ALBERT M. SACKS, THE LEGAL PROCESS: BASIC PROBLEMS IN THE MAKING AND APPLICATION OF LAW 608-09 (William N. Eskridge, Jr. & Philip P. Frickey eds., 1994). As you might recall, Professor Fuller (a contemporary of Professors Hart and Sacks) seemed to agree from a more theoretical perspective. *See supra* at 38-39.

At the same time, though, there had been rumblings to the effect that decisions ought not apply retroactively when the legal rule announced seems "new" in some significant way. *See, e.g., Great N. Ry. Co. v. Sunburst Oil & Ref. Co.*, 287 U.S. 358, 363-66 (1932) (Cardozo, J.); *Griffin v. Illinois*, 351 U.S. 12, 25-26 (1956) (Frankfurter, J., concurring in the judgment). By the mid-1960s, the Supreme Court began to experiment with this device. The jurisprudential roller coaster that ensued would last almost thirty years, and in the area of habeas corpus the final chapter perhaps has yet to be written.

2. Basic Concepts

Henry M. Hart, Jr. & Albert M. Sacks

A FURTHER NOTE ON THE CONFLICT OF LAWS IN TIME

**The Legal Process: Basic Problems in the Making and Application of Law
(William N. Eskridge, Jr. & Philip P. Frickey eds., 1994)**

To what extent is it, or should it be, an aim of a legal system to see that people are able to tell at the stage of primary private activity just what the legal consequences of their actions will be? To what extent should the legal system set itself the task of fulfilling expectations generated at this stage of activity? What kinds of outstanding official determinations ought to be indubitably good, come wind come weather, for the indefinite future?

The problems which these questions suggest pervade the whole legal order. But they are especially acute in the regime of self-applying regulation. For this method of legal control invariably requires people to act first and have their actions judged afterward.

One of the uncertainties to which all kinds of primary activity are subject is the uncertainty about where, if at all, litigation challenging primary action will be brought.

In the United States, litigation may occur in any one of [fifty] states, not to mention foreign countries, and in either a state or federal court. To assure that the place of litigation does not materially affect the primary law by which the relations of the parties are determined is one of the main functions of the body of law conventionally known as the conflict of laws. What is meant is the conflict of territorial laws, or of the laws of different governments.

A distinct body of laws concerns itself with what may be called the conflict of laws in time. Here the governmental unit whose laws are to be deemed authoritative is assumed to be known. But the substantive content of its laws is constantly changing. New judicial decisions are announced; new statutes enacted; new administrative regulations, orders and interpretations issued. Again and again, in many varied types of situations, the [question] presents itself: Should this matter be settled in accordance with the law as it was or appeared to be at one or another past point of time or in accordance with the law as it appears to be now?

Obviously, people who live in a society with inescapably changing laws must inescapably accept many of the changes. A man may buy a house, for example, with certain expectations about his powers and duties as an owner and about the powers and duties of others with respect to him. But no one is likely to suggest that he ought thereby to acquire a complete immunity from duly enacted statutes or evolving judicial doctrines which disappoint these expectations. No one would suppose, for example, that he could justly complain about later increases in the tax rate. To some extent the Constitution *does* give protection to expectations based upon executed contracts, viewed in the light of the law in force at the time of execution. But, as we shall see, the protection has had to be sharply limited. The law cannot stand still; and some at least of the public purposes which it exists to serve must imperatively be served.

a. A Brief Note on Terminology

The following cases use a variety of terms that can be confusing unless one has some understanding of the concepts to which they relate.

"Retroactivity" (or "retrospectivity") refers to a rule of law that is applied both in the law-announcing case and in other, similar cases not yet final.

"Modified" (or "selective") "prospectivity" means that the rule of law is applied in the law-announcing case (as well as to cases arising after that case), but not in other cases involving facts occurring prior to the law-announcing decision.

Finally, "pure prospectivity" refers to a rule of law that is announced in some case, but applied only to cases involving facts occurring after the law-changing decision (somewhat similar to the manner in which most statutes operate).

3. The Modern Cases

Linkletter v. Walker

381 U.S. 618 (1965)

MR. JUSTICE CLARK delivered the opinion of the Court.

In *Mapp* v. *Ohio*, 367 U. S. 643 (1961), we held that the exclusion of evidence seized in violation of the search and seizure provisions of the Fourth Amendment was required of the States by the Due Process Clause of the Fourteenth Amendment. In so doing we overruled *Wolf* v. *People of State of Colorado*, 338 U. S. 25 (1949), to the extent that it failed to apply the exclusionary rule to the States.[1] This case presents the question whether this requirement operates retrospectively upon cases finally decided in the period prior to *Mapp*. The Court of Appeals for the Fifth Circuit held that it did not, and we granted certiorari in order to settle what has become a most troublesome question in the administration of justice.[2] We agree with the Court of Appeals.

. . . .

. . . Petitioner has two points: (1) that the Court of Appeals erred in holding that *Mapp* was not retrospective; and (2) that even though *Mapp* be held not to operate retrospectively, the search in his case was subsequent to that in *Mapp*, and while his final conviction was long prior to our disposition of it, his case should nevertheless be governed by *Mapp*.

Initially we must consider the term "retrospective" for the purposes of our opinion. A ruling which is purely prospective does not apply even to the parties before the court.[3] However, we are not here concerned with pure prospectivity since we applied the rule announced in *Mapp* to reverse Miss Mapp's conviction. That decision also has been applied to cases still pending on direct review at the time it was rendered. Therefore, in this case, we are concerned only with whether the exclusionary

---

1. Although *Mapp* may not be considered to be an overruling decision in the sense that it did not disturb the earlier holding of *Wolf* that the search and seizure provisions of the Fourth Amendment are applicable to the States, its effect was to change existing law with regard to enforcement of the right.

2. A split of authority has developed in the various courts of appeals concerning the retrospectivity of *Mapp*.

About the only point upon which there was agreement . . . was that our opinion in *Mapp* did not foreclose the question.

The state courts which have considered the question have almost unanimously decided against application to cases finalized prior to *Mapp*.

Commentators have also split over the question of absolute retroactivity.

3. It has been suggested that this Court is prevented by Article III from adopting the technique of purely prospective overruling. Note, 71 Yale L.J. 907, 933 (1962). However, no doubt was expressed of our power under Article III in *England* v. *Louisiana State Board of Medical Examiners*, 375 U. S. 411 (1964). See also *Griffin* v. *People of State of Illinois*, 351 U. S. 12, 20 (1956) (concurring opinion of Frankfurter, J.).

principle enunciated in *Mapp* applies to state court convictions which had become final[5] before rendition of our opinion.

I.

While to some it may seem "academic" it might be helpful to others for us to briefly outline the history and theory of the problem presented.

At common law there was no authority for the proposition that judicial decisions made law only for the future.[6] Blackstone stated the rule that the duty of the court was not to "pronounce a new law, but to maintain and expound the old one." 1 Blackstone, Commentaries 69 (15th ed. 1809). This Court followed that rule in *Norton* v. *Shelby County*, 118 U. S. 425, 442 (1886), holding that unconstitutional action "confers no rights; it imposes no duties; it affords no protection; it creates no office; it is, in legal contemplation, as inoperative as though it had never been passed." The judge rather than being the creator of the law was but its discoverer. Gray, Nature and Sources of the Law 222 (1st ed. 1909). In the case of the overruled decision, *Wolf*, here, it was thought to be only a failure at true discovery and was consequently never the law; while the overruling one, *Mapp*, was not "new law but an application of what is, and theretofore had been, the true law."

On the other hand, Austin maintained that judges do in fact do something more than discover law; they make it interstitially by filling in with judicial interpretation the vague, indefinite, or generic statutory or common-law terms that alone are but the empty crevices of the law. Implicit in such an approach is the admission when a case is overruled that the earlier decision was wrongly decided. However, rather than being erased by the later overruling decision it is considered as an existing juridical fact until overruled, and intermediate cases finally decided under it are not to be disturbed.

The Blackstonian view ruled English jurisprudence and cast its shadow over our own as evidenced by *Norton*. However, some legal philosophers continued to insist that such a rule was out of tune with actuality largely because judicial repeal oftime did "work hardship to those who had trusted to its existence." Cardozo, Address to the N.Y. Bar Assn., 55 Rep. N.Y. State Bar Assn. 263, 296-97 (1932). The Austinian view gained some acceptance over a hundred years ago when it was decided that although legislative divorces were illegal and void, those previously granted were immunized by a prospective application of the rule of the case. And as early as 1863 this Court drew on the same concept in *Gelpcke* v. *City of Dubuque*, 1 Wall. 175 (1863). The Supreme Court of Iowa had repeatedly held that the Iowa Legislature had the power to authorize municipalities to issue bonds to aid in the construction of railroads.

---

5. By final we mean where the judgment of conviction was rendered, the availability of appeal exhausted, and the time for petition for certiorari had elapsed before our decision in *Mapp* v. *Ohio*.

6. "I know of no authority in this court to say that, in general, state decisions shall make law only for the future. Judicial decisions have had retrospective operation for near a thousand years." *Kuhn* v. *Fairmont Coal Co.*, 215 U. S. 349, 372 (1910) (dissenting opinion of Holmes, J.).

After the City of Dubuque had issued such bonds, the Iowa Supreme Court reversed itself and held that the legislature lacked such power. In *Gelpcke,* which arose after the overruling decision, this Court held that the bonds issued under the apparent authority granted by the legislature were collectible. "However we may regard the late overruling case in Iowa as affecting the future, it can have no effect upon the past." The theory was, as Mr. Justice Holmes stated in *Kuhn,* "that a change of judicial decision after a contract has been made on the faith of an earlier one the other way is a change of the law." And in 1932 Mr. Justice Cardozo in *Great Northern Ry. Co.* v. *Sunburst Oil & Refining Co.,* 287 U. S. 358, applied the Austinian approach in denying a federal constitutional due process attack on the prospective application of a decision of the Montana Supreme Court. He said that a State "may make a choice for itself between the principle of forward operation and that of relation backward." Mr. Justice Cardozo based the rule on the avoidance of "injustice or hardship" citing a long list of state and federal cases supporting the principle that the courts had the power to say that decisions though later overruled "are law none the less for intermediate transactions." Eight years later Chief Justice Hughes in *Chicot County Drainage Dist.* v. *Baxter State Bank,* 308 U. S. 371 (1940), in discussing the problem made it clear that the broad statements of *Norton* "must be taken with qualifications." He reasoned that the actual existence of the law prior to the determination of unconstitutionality "is an operative fact and may have consequences which cannot justly be ignored. The past cannot always be erased by a new judicial declaration." He laid down the rule that the "effect of the subsequent ruling as to invalidity may have to be considered in various aspects."

One form of limited retroaction which differs somewhat from the type discussed above is that which was established in *United States* v. *Schooner Peggy,* 1 Cranch 103 (1801). There, a schooner had been seized under an order of the President which commanded that any armed French vessel found on the high seas be captured. An order of condemnation was entered on September 23, 1800. However, while the case was pending before this Court the United States signed an agreement with France providing that any property captured and not "definitively condemned" should be restored. Chief Justice Marshall said:

> "It is in the general true that the province of an appellate court is only to enquire whether a judgment when rendered was erroneous or not. But if subsequent to the judgment and before the decision of the appellate court, a law intervenes and positively changes the rule which governs, the law must be obeyed, or its obligation denied and where individual rights are sacrificed for national purposes the court must decide according to existing laws, and if it be necessary to set aside the judgment which cannot be affirmed but in violation of law, the judgment must be set aside."

This same approach was subsequently applied in instances where a statutory change intervened, *Carpenter* v. *Wabash R. Co.,* 309 U. S. 23 (1940); where a constitutional amendment was adopted, *United States* v. *Chambers,* 291 U. S. 217 (1934); and where judicial decision altered or overruled earlier case law, *Vandenbark* v. *Owens-Illinois Glass Co.,* 311 U. S. 538 (1941).

Under our cases it appears (1) that a change in law will be given effect while a case is on direct review, and (2) that the effect of the subsequent ruling of invalidity on prior final judgments when collaterally attacked is subject to no set "principle of absolute retroactive invalidity" but depends upon a consideration of "particular relations and particular conduct of rights claimed to have become vested, of status, of prior determinations deemed to have finality"; and "of public policy in the light of the nature both of the statute and of its previous application."

. . . .

. . . Thus, the accepted rule today is that in appropriate cases the Court may in the interest of justice make the rule prospective. . . .

While the cases discussed above deal with the invalidity of statutes or the effect of a decision overturning long-established common-law rules there seems to be no impediment — constitutional or philosophical — to the use of the same rule in the constitutional area where the exigencies of the situation require such an application. It is true that heretofore, without discussion, we have applied new constitutional rules to cases finalized before the promulgation of the rule. Petitioner contends that our method of resolving those prior cases demonstrates that an absolute rule of retroaction prevails in the area of constitutional adjudication. However, we believe that the Constitution neither prohibits nor requires retrospective effect. As Justice Cardozo said [in *Sunburst*], "We think the Federal Constitution has no voice upon the subject."

Once the premise is accepted that we are neither required to apply, nor prohibited from applying, a decision retroactively, we must then weigh the merits and demerits in each case by looking to the prior history of the rule in question, its purpose and effect, and whether retrospective operation will further or retard its operation. . . .

. . . .

III.

We believe that the existence of the *Wolf* doctrine prior to *Mapp* is "an operative fact and may have consequences which cannot justly be ignored. The past cannot always be erased by a new judicial declaration." The thousands of cases that were finally decided on *Wolf* cannot be obliterated. The "particular conduct, private and official," must be considered. Here "prior determinations deemed to have finality and acted upon accordingly" have "become vested." And finally, "public policy in the light of the nature both of the *Wolf* doctrine and of its previous application" must be given its proper weight. In short, we must look to the purpose of the *Mapp* rule; the reliance placed upon the *Wolf* doctrine; and the effect on the administration of justice of a retrospective application of *Mapp*.

. . . *Mapp* had as its prime purpose the enforcement of the Fourth Amendment through the inclusion of the exclusionary rule within its rights. . . . We cannot say that this purpose would be advanced by making the rule retrospective. The misconduct of the police prior to *Mapp* has already occurred and will not be corrected by releasing the prisoners involved. Nor would it add harmony to the delicate state-federal relationship of which we have spoken as part and parcel of the purpose of *Mapp*. Finally, the ruptured privacy of the victims' homes and effects cannot be restored. Reparation comes too late.

It is true that both the accused and the States relied upon *Wolf*. . . . Final judgments of conviction were entered prior to *Mapp*. Again and again this Court refused to reconsider *Wolf* and gave its implicit approval to hundreds of cases in their application of the rule. In rejecting the *Wolf* doctrine as to the exclusionary rule the purpose was to deter the lawless action of the police and to effectively enforce the Fourth Amendment. That purpose will not at this late date be served by the wholesale release of the guilty victims.

Finally, there are interests in the administration of justice and the integrity of the judicial process to consider. To make the rule of *Mapp* retrospective would tax the administration of justice to the utmost. Hearings would have to be held on the excludability of evidence long since destroyed, misplaced or deteriorated. If it is excluded, the witnesses available at the time of the original trial will not be available or if located their memory will be dimmed. To thus legitimate such an extraordinary procedural weapon that has no bearing on guilt would seriously disrupt the administration of justice.

. . . .

Nor can we accept the contention of petitioner that the *Mapp* rule should date from the day of the seizure there, rather than that of the judgment of this Court. The date of the seizure in *Mapp* has no legal significance. It was the judgment of this Court that changed the rule and the date of that opinion is the crucial date. In the light of the cases of this Court this is the better cutoff time. See *United States* v. *Schooner Peggy, supra.*

All that we decide today is that though the error complained of might be fundamental it is not of the nature requiring us to overturn all final convictions based upon it. After full consideration of all the factors we are not able to say that the *Mapp* rule requires retrospective application.

Affirmed.

MR. JUSTICE BLACK, with whom MR. JUSTICE DOUGLAS joins, dissenting.

. . . Despite the Court's resounding promises throughout the *Mapp* opinion that convictions based on such "unconstitutional evidence" would "'find no sanction in the judgments of the courts,'" Linkletter, convicted in the state court by use of "unconstitutional evidence," is today denied relief by the judgment of this Court because his conviction became "final" before *Mapp* was decided. Linkletter must stay in jail; Miss Mapp, whose offense was committed before Linkletter's, is free. This different treatment of Miss Mapp and Linkletter points up at once the arbitrary and discriminatory nature of the judicial contrivance utilized here to reap the promise of *Mapp* by keeping all people in jail who are unfortunate enough to have had their unconstitutional convictions affirmed before June 19, 1961.

. . . The Court offers no defense based on any known principle of justice for discriminating among defendants who were similarly convicted by use of evidence unconstitutionally seized. . . .

. . . .

Interesting as the question may be abstractly, this case should not be decided on the basis of arguments about whether judges "make" law or "discover" it when performing their duty of interpreting the Constitution. . . .

. . . .

. . . Even using the Court's own balancing process, however, I think those now in prison under convictions resting on the use of unconstitutionally seized evidence should have their convictions set aside and be granted new trials conducted in conformity with the Constitution.

. . . .

The plain facts here are that the Court's opinion cuts off many defendants who are now in jail from any hope of relief from unconstitutional convictions. The opinion today also beats a timid retreat from the wholesome and refreshing principles announced in *Noia*. No State should be considered to have a vested interest in keeping prisoners in jail who were convicted because of lawless conduct by the State's officials. Careful analysis of the Court's opinion shows that it rests on the premise that a State's assumed interest in sustaining convictions obtained under the old, repudiated rule outweighs the interests both of that State and of the individuals convicted in having wrongful convictions set aside. It certainly offends my sense of justice to say that a State holding in jail people who were convicted by unconstitutional methods has a vested interest in keeping them there that outweighs the right of persons adjudged guilty of crime to challenge their unconstitutional convictions at any time. No words can obscure the simple fact that the promises of *Mapp* and *Noia* are to a great extent broken by the decision here. I would reverse.

Notes and Questions

1. The development of modern Supreme Court prospectivity doctrine (at least with respect to federal law) generally is thought to begin with *Linkletter*. *See, e.g.,* John Bernard Corr, *Retroactivity: A Study in Supreme Court Doctrine "As Applied,"* 61 N.C. L. Rev. 745, 746 (1983).

2. Why, as late as 1965 (the year *Linkletter* was decided), was retroactivity considered "a most troublesome question in the administration of justice?" Why was this question not definitively settled decades, if not centuries, earlier?

3. Note that *Linkletter* was a habeas corpus case, meaning Linkletter, a convicted criminal, was attempting to attack his conviction collaterally. To what extent did this fact weigh in the Court's reasoning? As compared with civil and criminal cases on direct review, is not habeas corpus the most sympathetic application of prospectivity? On the other hand, why should Linkletter be denied the benefit of the *Mapp* rule (presuming there are no statutory prohibitions to the contrary), so long as his habeas corpus petition is timely? (Note that the constitutional provision at issue had not changed for more than 100 years.) Is the real problem here the notion that such petition could be brought long after the underlying conviction became final? If so, would not the better solution be a shorter statute of limitations for habeas corpus petitions? Or would

that solution cause problems of its own? Alternatively, does the problem lie in *Mapp* itself, and the Court's (apparent) failure to consider the consequences of its decision in that case?

4. Does it necessarily follow that a rejection of a Blackstonian "declaratory" theory of the law requires (or even permits) a rejection of retroactivity in the case law context?

5. The *Linkletter* Court's holding notwithstanding, do there appear to be any constitutional impediments to prospectivity in this context? Consider, e.g., the following argument:

> "One of the great inherent restraints upon this Court's departure from the field of interpretation to enter that of lawmaking has been the fact that its judgments could not be limited to prospective application. This Court and in fact all departments of the Government have always heretofore realized that prospective lawmaking is the function of Congress rather than of the courts. We continue to think that this function should be exercised only by Congress under our constitutional system."

   Linkletter, 381 U.S. at 627 n.12 (quoting *James v. United States,* 366 U.S. 213, 225 (1961) (Black, J., dissenting)). Does this argument have any merit? And even if not, might there exist other, non-constitutional reasons for rejecting prospectivity? If so, what might those reasons be?

6. In *Johnson v. New Jersey,* 384 U.S. 719 (1966), the Supreme Court held that the three-part test articulated in *Linkletter* with respect to criminal cases on collateral review applied as well to criminal cases on direct review. *See also Stovall v. Denno,* 388 U.S. 293, 300-01 (1967) (reaffirming the notion that "no distinction is justified between convictions now final . . . and convictions at various stages of trial and direct review," as "[w]e regard the factors of reliance and burden on administration of justice as entitled to such overriding significance as to make that distinction unsupportable"). How can this result be squared with the *Linkletter* Court's purported distinction between cases on direct, as opposed to collateral, review?

7. In *Stovall,* the Court also stated:

> We recognize that [the defendants in the precedent-setting decision] are, therefore, the only victims of pretrial confrontations in the absence of their counsel to have the benefit of the rules established in their cases. That they must be given that benefit is, however, an unavoidable consequence of the necessity that constitutional adjudications not stand as mere dictum. Sound policies of decision-making, rooted in the command of Article III of the Constitution that we resolve issues solely in concrete cases or controversies, and in the possible effect upon the incentive of counsel to advance contentions requiring a change in the law, militate against denying [these defendants] the benefit of today's decisions. Inequity arguably results from according the benefit of a new rule to the parties in the case in which it is announced but not to other litigants similarly situated in the trial or

appellate process who have raised the same issue. But we regard the fact the parties involved are chance beneficiaries as an insignificant cost for adherence to sound principles of decision-making.

388 U.S. at 301. This language seems to suggest that "pure" prospectivity — i.e., the announcement of a new rule of law that is only to be applied in future cases — is unconstitutional. Do you agree? And do you also agree that a rule of law included in a court's opinion but not applied to the parties before that court is dictum? If so, does this mean that all opinions containing dicta are unconstitutional? Consider the fact that even pure prospectivity results in a case being decided on some basis (albeit not in accordance with the "new" rule). Or is something else at work here? Finally, do you agree that "modified" (or "selective") prospectivity — i.e., deciding the case before the court based on a new rule of law, but refusing to apply that rule to cases that predate the precedent-setting case, such as was done in *Stovall* — and the inequity it causes, embodies "sound principles of decision-making?" Or does there exist another alternative for courts desiring legal change in a manner that minimizes the disruptions caused thereby?

Chevron Oil Co. v. Huson
404 U.S. 97 (1971)

MR. JUSTICE STEWART delivered the opinion of the Court.

The respondent, Gaines Ted Huson, suffered a back injury while working on an artificial island drilling rig owned and operated by the petitioner, Chevron Oil Co., and located on the Outer Continental Shelf off the Gulf coast of Louisiana. The injury occurred in December 1965. Allegedly, it was not until many months later that the injury was discovered to be a serious one. In January 1968 the respondent brought suit for damages against the petitioner in federal district court. The respondent's delay in suing the petitioner ultimately brought his case to this Court.

The issue presented is whether the respondent's action is time barred and, more particularly, whether state or federal law determines the timeliness of the action. That issue must be resolved under the Outer Continental Shelf Lands Act, 43 U. S. C. § 1331 *et seq.,* which governs injuries occurring on fixed structures on the Outer Continental Shelf. When this lawsuit was initiated, there was a line of federal court decisions interpreting the Lands Act to make general admiralty law, including the equitable doctrine of laches, applicable to personal injury suits such as the respondent's. The petitioner did not question the timeliness of the action as a matter of laches. While pretrial discovery proceedings were still under way, however, this Court announced its decision in *Rodrigue v. Aetna Casualty & Surety Co.,* 395 U. S. 352. That decision entirely changed the complexion of this case. For it established that the Lands Act does *not* make admiralty law applicable to actions such as this one. Relying on *Rodrigue,* the District Court held that Louisiana's one-year limitation on personal injury actions, rather than the admiralty doctrine of laches, must govern this case. It concluded, therefore, that the respondent's action was time barred and granted summary judgment for the petitioner.

On appeal, the respondent argued that *Rodrigue* should not be applied retroactively to bar actions filed before the date of its announcement. But the Court of Appeals declined to reach that question. Instead, it held that the interpretation of the Lands Act in *Rodrigue* does not compel application of the state statute of limitations or prevent application of the admiralty doctrine of laches. It concluded that the doctrine of laches should have been applied by the District Court and, therefore, reversed that court's judgment and remanded the case for trial. We granted certiorari to consider the Court of Appeals' construction of the Lands Act and of *Rodrigue*. We hold that the Lands Act, as interpreted in *Rodrigue*, requires that the state statute of limitations be applied to personal injury actions. We affirm the judgment of the Court of Appeals, however, on the ground that *Rodrigue* should not be invoked to require application of the Louisiana time limitation retroactively to this case.

. . . .

II

Although we hold that Louisiana's one-year statute of limitations must be applied under the Lands Act as interpreted in *Rodrigue,* we do not blind ourselves to the fact that this is, in relevant respect, a pre-*Rodrigue* case. The respondent's injury occurred more than three years before the announcement of our decision in *Rodrigue.* He instituted the present lawsuit more than one year before *Rodrigue.* Yet, if the Louisiana statute of limitations controls in this case, his action was time barred more than two years before *Rodrigue.* In these circumstances, we must consider the respondent's argument that the state statute of limitations should be given nonretroactive application under *Rodrigue.*

In recent years, the nonretroactive application of judicial decisions has been most conspicuously considered in the area of the criminal process. But the problem is by no means limited to that area. The earliest instances of nonretroactivity in the decisions of this Court — more than a century ago — came in cases of nonconstitutional, noncriminal state law. It was in a noncriminal case that we first held that a state court may apply its decisions prospectively. And, in the last few decades, we have recognized the doctrine of nonretroactivity outside the criminal area many times, in both constitutional and nonconstitutional cases.

In our cases dealing with the nonretroactivity question, we have generally considered three separate factors. First, the decision to be applied nonretroactively must establish a new principle of law, either by overruling clear past precedent on which litigants may have relied, or by deciding an issue of first impression whose resolution was not clearly foreshadowed. Second, it has been stressed that "we must weigh the merits and demerits in each case by looking to the prior history of the rule in question, its purpose and effect, and whether retrospective operation will further or retard its operation." *Linkletter v. Walker, supra,* at 629. Finally, we have weighed the inequity imposed by retroactive application, for "where a decision of this Court could produce substantial inequitable results if applied retroactively, there is ample basis in our cases for avoiding the 'injustice or hardship' by a holding of nonretroactivity."

Upon consideration of each of these factors, we conclude that the Louisiana one-year statute of limitations should not be applied retroactively in the present case. *Rodrigue* was not only a case of first impression in this Court under the Lands Act, but it also effectively overruled a long line of decisions by the Court of Appeals for the Fifth Circuit holding that admiralty law, including the doctrine of laches, applies through the Lands Act. When the respondent was injured, for the next two years until he instituted his lawsuit, and for the ensuing year of pretrial proceedings, these Court of Appeals decisions represented the law governing his case. It cannot be assumed that he did or could foresee that this consistent interpretation of the Lands Act would be overturned. The most he could do was to rely on the law as it then was. "We should not indulge in the fiction that the law now announced has always been the law and, therefore, that those who did not avail themselves of it waived their rights." *Griffin v. Illinois,* 351 U. S. 12, 26 (Frankfurter, J., concurring in the judgment).

To hold that the respondent's lawsuit is retroactively time barred would be anomalous indeed. A primary purpose underlying the absorption of state law as federal law in the Lands Act was to aid injured employees by affording them comprehensive and familiar remedies. Yet retroactive application of the Louisiana statute of limitations to this case would deprive the respondent of any remedy whatsoever on the basis of superseding legal doctrine that was quite unforeseeable. To abruptly terminate this lawsuit that has proceeded through lengthy and, no doubt, costly discovery stages for a year would surely be inimical to the beneficial purpose of the Congress.

It would also produce the most "substantial inequitable results" to hold that the respondent "slept on his rights" a time when he could not have known the time limitation that the law imposed upon him. In *Cipriano v. City of Houma,* we invoked the doctrine of nonretroactive application to protect property interests of "cities, bondholders, and others connected with municipal utilities"; and, in *Allen v. State Board of Elections,* we invoked the doctrine to protect elections held under possibly discriminatory voting laws. Certainly, the respondent's potential redress for his allegedly serious injury—an injury that may significantly undercut his future earning power—is entitled to similar protection. . . . [N]onretroactive application here simply preserves his right to a day in court.[10]

Both a devotion to the underlying purpose of the Land Act's absorption of state law and a weighing of the equities requires nonretroactive application of the state statute of limitations here. Accordingly, although holding that the opinion of the Court of Appeals reflects a misapprehension of *Rodrigue,* we affirm its judgment remanding this case to the trial court.

---

10. We do not hold here that *Rodrigue,* in its entirety, must be applied nonretroactively. Rather, we hold only that state statutes of limitations, applicable under *Rodrigue's* interpretation of the Lands Act, should not be applied retroactively. Retroactive application of all state substantive remedies under *Rodrigue* would not work a comparable hardship or be so inconsistent with the purpose of the Lands Act. (*Rodrigue*). Accordingly, the law governing the retroactive application of judicial decisions (rather than of statutes) was implicated.

Notes and Questions

1. *Chevron Oil* at least purported to provide the retroactivity/prospectivity standard applicable in cases on direct review, and that standard was, in fact, applied in a number of later cases. Nonetheless, some tension remained between that standard and the Court's holding in *Schooner Peggy*. See, e.g., *Saint Francis College v. Al-Khazraji*, 481 U.S. 604, 608 (1987) (recognizing that "[t]he usual rule is that federal cases should be decided in accordance with the law existing at the time of decision," yet upholding the application of *Chevron Oil* to avoid an intervening shortening of the applicable statute of limitations). Can *Chevron Oil* be reconciled with *Schooner Peggy*? In this regard, note that the *Chevron Oil* Court failed to even mention *Schooner Peggy*.

2. Note also that although *Chevron Oil* in some sense involved the interpretation of a federal statute, the pivotal issue involved the retroactive effect of a judicial decision (*Rodrigue*). Accordingly, the law governing the retroactive application of judicial decisions (rather than of statutes) was implicated.

3. What is the relevance of the fact that Huson's injury and the commencement of his action occurred prior to the Court's decision in *Rodrigue*? Admittedly, Huson would not have been aware of *Rodrigue;* but are not courts generally in the business of applying the law to events that occurred in the past? For example, is it not clear that if *Rodrigue* had not yet been decided, the *Chevron Oil* Court would have reached the same interpretation of the Lands Act? So why should the result be different here? On the other hand, if the *Chevron Oil* Court had been confronted with this issue pre-*Rodrigue,* was some form of prospectivity its only option? Do courts have any ability to decide cases according to "prior" law, and yet express their dissatisfaction with that law? If so, then is the real problem here the fact that the *Chevron Oil* Court was more or less "stuck" with its earlier decision in *Rodrigue?* Might one then wonder whether the *Rodrigue* Court fully considered the implications of its decisions, the "usual" rule of retroactive application in later cases notwithstanding?

4. The first part of the "nonretroactivity" standard articulated by the Court concerned whether the prior decision at issue involved a "new" principle of law. What does "new" mean in this context? How does one determine whether a principle is of sufficient "newness" so as to demand prospective application? Does this standard seem likely to produce clear and easily derived answers?

5. The third part of the Court's "nonretroactivity" standard concerns a balancing of the equities were the prior decision to be applied retroactively. How does one go about making that determination? For example, in *Chevron Oil,* Huson certainly knew when he was injured, and there is no indication in the Court's opinion that the seriousness of his injury did not manifest itself within a year of

the date of that injury. Under these circumstances, how is it inequitable to bar his action in this case? Consider the fact that similarly situated persons subject to the Louisiana one-year statute of limitations would be barred. Is that not the point of a statute of limitations defense? And what is the relevance of the fact that Huson might not have been aware that he was subject to a one-year statute of limitations? Does the success of such a defense ever rise or fall on such a basis? Under what circumstances should a court ever concern itself with what a party might have perceived the law to be? Do you see any problems with such an approach?

6. Read again the Court's footnote 10. Does it make sense to apply one part of *Rodrigue* prospectively, but not all?

Griffith v. Kentucky
479 U.S. 314 (1987)

JUSTICE BLACKMUN delivered the opinion of the Court.

These cases, one state and one federal, concern the retrospective application of *Batson* v. *Kentucky*, 476 U. S. 79 (1986).

In *Batson*, this Court ruled that a defendant in a state criminal trial could establish a prima facie case of racial discrimination violative of the Fourteenth Amendment, based on the prosecution's use of peremptory challenges to strike members of the defendant's race from the jury venire, and that, once the defendant had made the prima facie showing, the burden shifted to the prosecution to come forward with a neutral explanation for those challenges. In the present cases we consider whether that ruling is applicable to litigation pending on direct state or federal review or not yet final when *Batson* was decided. We answer that question in the affirmative.

. . . .

II

Twenty-one years ago, this Court adopted a three-pronged analysis for claims of retroactivity of new constitutional rules of criminal procedure. In *Linkletter*, the Court held that *Mapp* v. *Ohio*, which extended the Fourth Amendment exclusionary rule to the States, would not be applied retroactively to a state conviction that had become final before *Mapp* was decided. The Court explained that "the Constitution neither prohibits nor requires retrospective effect" of a new constitutional rule, and that a determination of retroactivity must depend on "weighing the merits and demerits in each case." The Court's decision not to apply *Mapp* retroactively was based on "the purpose of the *Mapp* rule; the reliance placed upon the previous doctrine; and the effect on the administration of justice of a retrospective application of *Mapp*."

Shortly after the decision in *Linkletter*, the Court held that the three-pronged analysis applied both to convictions that were final and to convictions pending on direct review. In [*Stovall*], the Court concluded that, for purposes of applying the three factors of the analysis, "no distinction is justified between convictions now final and convictions at various stages of trial and direct review." Thus, a number of new rules of criminal procedure were held not to apply retroactively either to final cases or to cases pending on direct review.

In *United States* v. *Johnson*, 457 U. S. 537 (1982), however, the Court shifted course. In that case, we reviewed at some length the history of the Court's decisions in the area of retroactivity and concluded, in the words of Justice Harlan: " 'Retroactivity' must be rethought." Specifically, we concluded that the retroactivity analysis for convictions that have become final must be different from the analysis for convictions that are not final at the time the new decision is issued.[8] We observed that, in a number of separate opinions since *Linkletter*, various Members of the Court "have asserted that, at a minimum, all defendants whose cases were still pending on direct appeal at the time of the law-changing decision should be entitled to invoke the new rule." The rationale for distinguishing between cases that have become final and those that have not, and for applying new rules retroactively to cases in the latter category, was explained at length by Justice Harlan in *Desist* and *Mackey*. In *United States* v. *Johnson*, we embraced to a significant extent the comprehensive analysis presented by Justice Harlan in those opinions.

In Justice Harlan's view, and now in ours, failure to apply a newly declared constitutional rule to criminal cases pending on direct review violates basic norms of constitutional adjudication. First, it is a settled principle that this Court adjudicates only "cases" and "controversies." Unlike a legislature, we do not promulgate new rules of constitutional criminal procedure on a broad basis. Rather, the nature of judicial review requires that we adjudicate specific cases, and each case usually becomes the vehicle for announcement of a new rule. But after we have decided a new rule in the case selected, the integrity of judicial review requires that we apply that rule to all similar cases pending on direct review. Justice Harlan observed:

> "If we do not resolve all cases before us on direct review in light of our best understanding of governing constitutional principles, it is difficult to see why we should so adjudicate any case at all. In truth, the Court's assertion of power to disregard current law in adjudicating cases before us that have not already run the full course of appellate review, is quite simply an assertion that our constitutional function is not one of adjudication but in effect of legislation."

As a practical matter, of course, we cannot hear each case pending on direct review and apply the new rule. But we fulfill our judicial responsibility by instructing the lower courts to apply the new rule retroactively to cases not yet final. Thus, it is the nature of judicial review that precludes us from "simply fishing one case from the stream of appellate review, using it as a vehicle for pronouncing new constitutional standards, and then permitting a stream of similar cases subsequently to flow by unaffected by that new rule."

---

8. We noted in *Johnson* that our review did not address the area of civil retroactivity. That area continues to be governed by the standard announced in *Chevron Oil Co.* v. *Huson*, 404 U. S. 97, 106-107 (1970).

Second, selective application of new rules violates the principle of treating simi-larly situated defendants the same. As we pointed out in *United States* v. *Johnson*, the problem with not applying new rules to cases pending on direct review is "the *actual inequity* that results when the Court chooses which of many similarly situated defendants should be the chance beneficiary" of a new rule. Although the Court had tolerated this inequity for a time by not applying new rules retroactively to cases on direct review, we noted: "The time for toleration has come to an end."

. . . .

III

. . . .

We therefore hold that a new rule for the conduct of criminal prosecutions is to be applied retroactively to all cases, state or federal, pending on direct review or not yet final, with no exception for cases in which the new rule constitutes a "clear break" with the past. . . .

It is so ordered.

JUSTICE WHITE, with whom THE CHIEF JUSTICE and JUSTICE O'CONNOR join, dissenting.

Last Term this Court decided that the rule announced in *Batson* v. *Kentucky* should not apply on collateral review of convictions that became final before the de-cision in *Batson* was announced. *Allen* v. *Hardy*, 478 U. S. 255 (1986). In reaching this judgment, the Court weighed the three [*Stovall*] factors . . . . No Justice suggested that this test is unworkable. The question, then, is why the Court feels constrained to fashion a different rule for cases on direct review. . . .

. . . .

. . . I would adhere to the approach set out in *Stovall* and recognize no distinction for retroactivity purposes between cases on direct and collateral review.

Notes and Questions

---

1. Note the significance of *Griffith*: the Supreme Court abandoned the modified prospectivity approach utilized in *Linkletter* and instead adopted a strict rule of retroactivity, at least with respect to criminal cases on direct review. Why did the Court so decide to "change course"? What are the arguments in favor of this "new" approach? What are the arguments against? In particular, why should "civil retroactivity" be treated differently?

2. *Teague v. Lane and the Standard Applicable to Habeas Corpus Cases.* Shortly after deciding *Griffith*, the Supreme Court, in *Teague v. Lane*, 489 U.S. 288 (1989), was asked to consider whether the Sixth Amendment's fair cross sec-tion requirement applies to a petit jury. (Previously, in *Taylor v. Louisiana*, 419

U.S. 522 (1975), the Court held that the Sixth Amendment requires that the jury *venire* be drawn from a fair cross section of the community.) But the Court never resolved that question. Instead, a plurality of the Court, in an opinion authored by Justice O'Connor, concluded that "a decision extending the fair cross section requirement to the petit jury would not be applied retroactively to cases on collateral review." *Id.* at 316 (plurality opinion).

The plurality began by observing:

> In the past, the Court has, without discussion, often applied a new constitutional rule of criminal procedure to the defendant in the case announcing the new rule, and has confronted the question of retroactivity later when a different defendant sought the benefit of that rule. In several cases, however, the Court has addressed the retroactivity question in the very case announcing the new rule. These two lines of cases do not have a unifying theme, and we think it is time to clarify how the question of retroactivity should be resolved for cases on collateral review.
>
> . . . .
>
> In our view, the question whether a decision announcing a new rule should be given prospective or retroactive effect should be faced at the time of that decision. Retroactivity is properly treated as a threshold question, for, once a new rule is applied to the defendant in the case announcing the rule, evenhanded justice requires that it be applied retroactively to all who are similarly situated. Thus, before deciding whether the fair cross section requirement should be extended to the petit jury, we should ask whether such a rule would be applied retroactively to the case at issue.

Id. at 299-301 (plurality opinion) (citations and quotation marks omitted).

Though the plurality then acknowledged that "[t]his retroactivity determination would normally entail application of the *Linkletter* standard," it further decided "that our approach to retroactivity for cases on collateral review requires modification." *Id.* at 301. During the course of an extended discussion on the nature and function of collateral review, the plurality adopted Justice Harlan's suggestion "that it is 'sounder, in adjudicating habeas petitions, generally to apply the law prevailing at the time a conviction became final.'" *Id.* at 306 (quoting *Mackey v. United States*, 401 U.S. 667, 689 (1971) (Harlan, J., concurring in part and dissenting in part)). The application of the law prevailing at the time of conviction, according to the plurality, means that "new" rules of law — that is, rules of law arising only after the time of conviction — should not be given retroactive effect. *Id.* at 306-07. As for what it means for a rule to be considered "new," the plurality explained:

> It is admittedly often difficult to determine when a case announces a new rule, and we do not attempt to define the spectrum of what may or may not constitute a new rule for retroactivity purposes. In general, however, a case announces a new rule when it breaks new ground or imposes a new obligation on the States or the Federal Government. To put it differently, a case announces a new rule if the result was not *dictated* by precedent existing at the time the defendant's conviction became final.

Id. at 306.

The plurality then concluded that the application of the fair cross section requirement to the petit jury, if adopted, would be such a rule. *See id.*

The plurality then turned to Justice Harlan's exceptions to the non-retroactive application of "new" rules:

> Justice Harlan identified only two exceptions to his general rule of nonretroactivity for cases on collateral review. First, a new rule should be applied retroactively if it places "certain kinds of primary, private individual conduct beyond the power of the criminal law-making authority to proscribe." Second, a new rule should be applied retroactively if it requires the observance of "those procedures that . . . are implicit in the concept of ordered liberty."

Id. at 307 (internal quotations marks and citations omitted) (quoting *Mackey*, 401 U.S. at 692-93 (Harlan, J., concurring in part and dissenting in part)). The plurality then modified the second exception to require that "the procedure at issue must implicate the fundamental fairness of the trial" and that the procedure be "central to an accurate determination of innocence or guilt." *Id.* at 312-13. "Unless they fall within an exception to the general rule, new constitutional rules of criminal procedure will not be applicable to those cases which have become final before the new rules are announced." *Id.* at 310. But applying this new standard to Teague, the plurality concluded that the new rule at issue did not meet either exception. *See id.* at 311-16.

Finally, the plurality added:

> Were we to recognize the new rule urged by petitioner in this case, we would have to give petitioner the benefit of that new rule even though it would not be applied retroactively to others similarly situated. In the words of Justice Brennan, such an inequitable result would be "an unavoidable consequence of the necessity that constitutional adjudications not stand as mere dictum." . . .
>
> If there were no other way to avoid rendering advisory opinions, we might well agree that the inequitable treatment described above is "an insignificant cost of adherence to sound principles of decision-making." But there is a more principled way of dealing with the problem. We can simply refuse to announce a new rule in a given case unless the rule would be applied retroactively to the defendant in the case and to all others similarly situated.

Id. at 316 (citations omitted) (quoting *Stovall v. Denno*, 388 U.S. 293, 301 (1967)).

The chief criticism of the plurality opinion came in the form of a dissenting opinion authored by Justice Brennan and joined by Justice Marshall. In particular, Justice Brennan criticized the triggering definition of a "new" rule of law — that the rule was not dictated by precedent existing at the time the defendant's conviction became final — as "extremely broad." *Id.* at 333 (Brennan, J., dissenting).

> Few decisions on appeal or collateral review are "*dictated*" by what came before. Most such cases involve a question of law that is at least debatable, permitting a rational judge to resolve the case in more than one way. Virtually no case that prompts a dissent on the relevant legal point, for example, could be said to be "*dictated*" by prior decisions.

Teague, 489 U.S. at 333 (Brennan, J., dissenting). "By the plurality's test, therefore, a great many cases could only be heard on habeas if the rule urged by the petitioner fell within one of the two exceptions the plurality has sketched. Those exceptions, however, are narrow." *Id.* at 333-34.

Though the pivotal portions of Justice O'Connor's opinion failed to garner more than four votes, the retroactivity analysis employed by the *Teague* plurality was endorsed by a majority of the Court later that same year in *Penry v. Lynaugh,* 492 U.S. 302 (1989).

Today, parties litigating in this area also must consider the Antiterrorism and Effective Death Penalty Act of 1996 (commonly referred to as the AEDPA), particularly that portion codified at 28 U.S.C. §§ 2254, 2255 (2012). For a recent case interpreting the AEDPA and how it relates to *Teague,* see *Greene v. Fisher,* 132 S. Ct. 38, 44-45 (2011). For a recent application of *Teague,* see *Chaidez v. United States,* 133 S. Ct. 1103 (2013), in which the Supreme Court held that *Padilla v. Kentucky,* 559 U.S. 356 (2010) (holding that the Sixth Amendment requires an attorney for a criminal defendant to provide advice about the risk of deportation relating to a guilty plea) was a "new rule" and therefore did not apply retroactively to cases that were final on direct review. *See also* Laurie L. Levenson, *Retroactivity of cases on criminal defendants' rights: Of the past term's decisions, it's clear that one is not retroactive, another will allow for collateral attach of convictions,* NAT'L L.J. 26 (Aug. 13, 2012).

3. In *Danforth v. Minnesota,* 552 U.S. 264 (2008), the Supreme Court held that state courts are not prohibited by *Teague* from giving even broader effect to new rules of criminal procedure than might be required by federal courts. *Danforth* includes a fine historical discussion of much of the law in this area.

4. American Trucking, Beam, *and the beginning of the demise of* Chevron Oil. In *American Trucking Ass'ns, Inc. v. Smith,* 496 U.S. 167 (1990), and in *James B. Beam Distilling Co. v. Georgia,* 501 U.S. 529 (1991), the Supreme Court considered whether its reasoning in *Griffith* should apply as well to the more typical (i.e., non-habeas corpus) civil context. Unfortunately, neither case (both of which are well worth reading) resulted in a clear majority opinion. But the Court finally clarified its view on this issue in the next case.

Harper v. Virginia Department of Taxation
509 U.S. 86 (1993)

JUSTICE THOMAS delivered the opinion of the Court.

In *Davis v. Michigan Dept. of Treasury,* 489 U. S. 803 (1989), we held that a State violates the constitutional doctrine of intergovernmental tax immunity when it taxes retirement benefits paid by the Federal Government but exempts from taxation all retirement benefits paid by the State or its political subdivisions. Relying on the retroactivity analysis of *Chevron Oil Co. v. Huson,* 404 U. S. 97 (1971), the Supreme

Court of Virginia twice refused to apply *Davis* to taxes imposed before *Davis* was decided. In accord with *Griffith* v. *Kentucky*, 479 U. S. 314 (1987), and *James B. Beam Distilling Co.* v. *Georgia*, 501 U. S. 529 (1991), we hold that this Court's application of a rule of federal law to the parties before the Court requires every court to give retroactive effect to that decision. We therefore reverse.

I

. . . .

Petitioners, 421 federal civil service and military retirees, sought a refund of [Virginia state] taxes "erroneously or improperly assessed" in violation of *Davis*' nondiscrimination principle. The trial court denied relief. Applying the factors set forth in *Chevron Oil Co.* v. *Huson*, the court reasoned that "*Davis* decided an issue of first impression whose resolution was not clearly foreshadowed," that "prospective application of *Davis* will not retard its operation," and that "retroactive application would result in inequity, injustice and hardship."

The Supreme Court of Virginia affirmed. It too concluded, after consulting *Chevron* and the plurality opinion in *American Trucking Assns., Inc.* v. *Smith*, 496 U. S. 167 (1990), that "the *Davis* decision is not to be applied retroactively." . . .

Even as the Virginia courts were denying relief to petitioners, we were confronting a similar retroactivity problem in *James B. Beam Distilling Co.* v. *Georgia*. At issue was *Bacchus Imports, Ltd.* v. *Dias*, 468 U. S. 263 (1984), which prohibited States from imposing higher excise taxes on imported alcoholic beverages than on local products. The Supreme Court of Georgia had used the analysis described in *Chevron* to deny retroactive effect to a decision of this Court. Six Members of this Court disagreed, concluding instead that *Bacchus* must be applied retroactively to claims arising from facts predating that decision. After deciding *Beam*, we vacated the judgment in Harper and remanded for further consideration.

On remand, the Supreme Court of Virginia again denied tax relief. It reasoned that because Michigan did not contest the *Davis* plaintiffs' entitlement to a refund, this Court "made no ruling" regarding the retroactive application of its rule "to the litigants in that case." Concluding that *Beam* did not foreclose application of *Chevron*'s retroactivity analysis because "the retroactivity issue was not decided in *Davis*," the court "reaffirmed its prior decision in all respects."

When we decided *Davis*, 23 States gave preferential tax treatment to benefits received by employees of state and local governments relative to the tax treatment of benefits received by federal employees. Like the Supreme Court of Virginia, several other state courts have refused to accord full retroactive effect to *Davis* as a controlling statement of federal law. Two of the courts refusing to apply *Davis* retroactively have done so after this Court remanded for reconsideration in light of *Beam*. By contrast, the Supreme Court of Arkansas has concluded as a matter of federal law that *Davis* applies retroactively.

After the Supreme Court of Virginia reaffirmed its original decision, we granted certiorari a second time. We now reverse.

II

Both the common law and our own decisions have "recognized a general rule of retrospective effect for the constitutional decisions of this Court." Nothing in the Constitution alters the fundamental rule of "retrospective operation" that has governed "judicial decisions for near a thousand years." *Kuhn* v. *Fairmont Coal Co.,* 215 U. S. 349 (1910) (Holmes, J., dissenting). In *Linkletter,* however, we developed a doctrine under which we could deny retroactive effect to a newly announced rule of criminal law. Under *Linkletter,* a decision to confine a new rule to prospective application rested on the purpose of the new rule, the reliance placed upon the previous view of the law, and "the effect on the administration of justice of a retrospective application" of a new rule. In the civil context, we similarly permitted the denial of retroactive effect to "a new principle of law" if such a limitation would avoid "injustice or hardship" without unduly undermining the "purpose and effect" of the new rule.[9]

We subsequently overruled *Linkletter* in *Griffith* v. *Kentucky,* 479 U. S. 314 (1987), and eliminated limits on retroactivity in the criminal context by holding that all "newly declared rules" must be applied retroactively to all "criminal cases pending on direct review." This holding rested on two "basic norms of constitutional adjudication." First, we reasoned that "the nature of judicial review" strips us of the quintessentially "legislative" prerogative to make rules of law retroactive or prospective as we see fit. Second, we concluded that "selective application of new rules violates the principle of treating similarly situated parties the same."

Dicta in *Griffith,* however, stated that "civil retroactivity continued to be governed by the standard announced in *Chevron Oil.*" We divided over the meaning of this dicta in *American Trucking.* The four Justices in the plurality used "the *Chevron Oil* test" to consider whether to confine "the application of *American Trucking Assns., Inc.* v. *Scheiner,* 483 U. S. 266 (1987), to taxation of highway use prior to June 23, 1987, the date we decided *Scheiner.*" Four other Justices rejected the plurality's "anomalous approach" to retroactivity and declined to hold that "the law applicable to a particular case is the law which the parties believe in good faith to be applicable to the case." Finally, despite concurring in the judgment, Justice Scalia "shared" the dissent's "perception that prospective decisionmaking is incompatible with the judicial role."

Griffith and *American Trucking* thus left unresolved the precise extent to which the presumptively retroactive effect of this Court's decisions may be altered in civil cases. But we have since adopted a rule requiring the retroactive application of a civil decision such as *Davis.* Although *Beam* did not produce a unified opinion for the Court, a majority of Justices agreed that a rule of federal law, once announced and applied to the parties to the controversy, must be given full retroactive effect by all courts adjudicating federal law. . . .

---

9. We need not debate whether *Chevron Oil* represents a true "choice-of-law principle" or merely "a remedial principle for the exercise of equitable discretion by federal courts." Regardless of how *Chevron Oil* is characterized, our decision today makes it clear that "the *Chevron Oil* test cannot determine the choice of law by relying on the equities of the particular case" and that the federal law applicable to a particular case does not turn on "whether litigants actually relied on an old rule or how they would suffer from retroactive application" of a new one.

Beam controls this case, and we accordingly adopt a rule that fairly reflects the position of a majority of Justices in *Beam*: When this Court applies a rule of federal law to the parties before it, that rule is the controlling interpretation of federal law and must be given full retroactive effect in all cases still open on direct review and as to all events, regardless of whether such events predate or postdate our announcement of the rule. This rule extends *Griffith*'s ban against "selective application of new rules." Mindful of the basic norms of constitutional adjudication that animated our view of retroactivity in the criminal context, we now prohibit the erection of selective temporal barriers to the application of federal law in noncriminal cases. In both civil and criminal cases, we can scarcely permit "the substantive law to shift and spring" according to "the particular equities of individual parties' claims" of actual reliance on an old rule and of harm from a retroactive application of the new rule. Our approach to retroactivity heeds the admonition that "the Court has no more constitutional authority in civil cases than in criminal cases to disregard current law or to treat similarly situated litigants differently."

The Supreme Court of Virginia "applied the three-pronged *Chevron Oil* test in deciding the retroactivity issue" presented by this litigation. When this Court does not "reserve the question whether its holding should be applied to the parties before it," however, an opinion announcing a rule of federal law "is properly understood to have followed the normal rule of retroactive application" and must be "read to hold that its rule should apply retroactively to the litigants then before the Court." Furthermore, the legal imperative "to apply a rule of federal law retroactively after the case announcing the rule has already done so" must "prevail over any claim based on a *Chevron Oil* analysis."

. . . .

III

. . . .

We [also] reject the Department's defense of the decision below [based on state law]. The Supremacy Clause does not allow federal retroactivity doctrine to be supplanted by the invocation of a contrary approach to retroactivity under state law. Whatever freedom state courts may enjoy to limit the retroactive operation of their own interpretations of state law, see *Great Northern R. Co.* v. *Sunburst Oil & Refining Co.*, 287 U. S. 358 (1932), cannot extend to their interpretations of federal law.

. . . .

Because we have decided that *Davis* applies retroactively to the tax years at issue in petitioners' refund action, we reverse the judgment below. We do not enter judgment for petitioners, however, because federal law does not necessarily entitle them to a refund. Rather, the Constitution requires Virginia "to provide relief consistent with federal due process principles." Under the Due Process Clause, "a State found to have imposed an impermissibly discriminatory tax retains flexibility in responding to this determination." If Virginia "offers a meaningful opportunity for taxpayers to withhold contested tax assessments and to challenge their validity in a predeprivation hearing," the "availability of a predeprivation hearing constitutes a procedural safeguard sufficient by itself to satisfy the Due Process Clause." On the other hand, if no such predeprivation remedy exists, "the Due Process Clause of the Fourteenth Amendment obligates the State to provide meaningful backward-looking relief to rectify any unconstitutional deprivation." In providing such relief, a State may either award full refunds to those burdened by an unlawful tax or issue some other order that "creates in hindsight a nondiscriminatory scheme."

. . . Because this issue has not been properly presented, we leave to Virginia courts this question of state law and the performance of other tasks pertaining to the crafting of any appropriate remedy. Virginia "is free to choose which form of relief it will provide, so long as that relief satisfies the minimum federal requirements we have outlined." State law may provide relief beyond the demands of federal due process, but under no circumstances may it confine petitioners to a lesser remedy.

IV

We reverse the judgment of the Supreme Court of Virginia, and we remand the case for further proceedings not inconsistent with this opinion.

So ordered.

JUSTICE SCALIA, concurring.

I am surprised to see an appeal to *stare decisis* in today's dissent. In *Teague* v. *Lane*, Justice O'Connor wrote for a plurality that openly rejected settled precedent controlling the scope of retroactivity on collateral review. "This retroactivity determination," the opinion said, "would normally entail application of the *Linkletter* standard, but we believe that our approach to retroactivity for cases on collateral review requires modification." The dissent in Teague was a sort of anticipatory echo of today's dissent, criticizing the plurality for displaying "infidelity to the doctrine of *stare decisis*[]." . . .

I joined the plurality opinion in *Teague*. Not only did I believe the rule it announced was correct, but I also believed that abandonment of our prior collateral-review retroactivity rule was fully in accord with the doctrine of *stare decisis*, which as applied by our Court has never been inflexible. The *Teague* plurality opinion set forth good reasons for abandoning *Linkletter*—reasons justifying a similar abandonment of *Chevron Oil.* It noted, for example, that *Linkletter* had not led to consistent results; but neither has *Chevron Oil.* Proof that what it means is in the eye of the beholder is provided quite nicely by the separate opinions filed today: Of the four Justices who would still apply *Chevron Oil,* two find *Davis* retroactive, two find it not retroactive. Second, the *Teague* plurality opinion noted that *Linkletter* had been criticized by commentators, but the commentary cited in the opinion criticized not just *Linkletter,* but the Court's retroactivity jurisprudence in general, of which it considered *Chevron Oil* an integral part, see Beytagh, Ten Years of Non-Retroactivity: A Critique and a Proposal, 61 Va. L. Rev. 1557 (1975). Other commentary, of course, has also regarded the issue of retroactivity as a general problem of jurisprudence. See, *e.g.,* Fallon & Meltzer, New Law, Non-Retroactivity, and Constitutional Remedies, 104 Harv. L. Rev.

1731 (1991); Mishkin, Forward: The High Court, The Great Writ, and the Due Process of Time and Law, 79 Harv. L Rev 56 (1965).

Finally, the plurality opinion in *Teague* justified the departure from *Linkletter* by implicitly relying on the well-settled proposition that *stare decisis* has less force where intervening decisions "have removed or weakened the conceptual underpinnings from the prior decision." *Patterson* v. *McLean Credit Union*, 491 U. S. 164, 173 (1989). Justice O'Connor endorsed the reasoning expressed by Justice Harlan . . . , and noted that the Court had already adopted the first part of Justice Harlan's retroactivity views in *Griffith*. Again, this argument equally — indeed, even more forcefully — supports reconsideration of *Chevron Oil*. *Griffith* returned this Court, in criminal cases, to the traditional view (which I shall discuss at greater length below) that prospective decisionmaking "violates basic norms of constitutional adjudication." One of the conceptual underpinnings of *Chevron Oil* was that retroactivity presents a *similar* problem in both civil and criminal contexts. Thus, after *Griffith*, *Chevron Oil* can be adhered to *only by rejecting the reasoning of Chevron Oil* — that is, only by asserting that the issue of retroactivity is *different* in the civil and criminal settings. That is a particularly difficult proof to make, inasmuch as Griffith rested on "basic norms of constitutional adjudication" and "the nature of judicial review."[1]

What most provokes comment in the dissent, however, is not its insistence that today a rigid doctrine of *stare decisis* forbids tinkering with retroactivity, which four Terms ago did not; but rather the irony of its invoking *stare decisis* in defense of prospective decisionmaking *at all*. Prospective decisionmaking is the hand-maid of judicial activism, and the born enemy of *stare decisis*. It was formulated in the heyday of legal realism and promoted as a "technique of judicial lawmaking" in general, and

---

1. The dissent attempts to distinguish between retroactivity in civil and criminal settings on three grounds, none of which has ever been adopted by this Court. The dissent's first argument begins with the observation that "nonretroactivity in criminal cases historically has favored the government's reliance interests over the rights of criminal defendants." But while it is true that prospectivity was usually employed in the past (during the brief period when it was used in criminal cases) to favor the government, there is no basis for the implicit suggestion that it would usually favor the government in the future. That phenomenon was a consequence, not of the nature of the doctrine, but of the historical "accident" that during the period prospectivity was in fashion legal rules favoring the government were more frequently overturned. But more fundamentally, to base a rule of full retroactivity in the criminal-law area upon what the dissent calls "the generalized policy of favoring individual rights over government prerogative" makes no more sense than to adopt, because of the same "generalized policy," a similarly gross rule that no decision favoring criminal defendants can ever be overruled. The law is more discerning than that. The dissent's next argument is based on the dubious empirical assumption that civil litigants, but not criminal defendants, will often receive some benefit from a prospective decision. That assumption does not even hold even in this case: Prospective invalidation of Virginia's taxing scheme would afford petitioners the enormous future "benefit" of knowing that others in the State are being taxed more. But empirical problems aside, the dissent does not explain why, if a receipt-of-some-benefit principle is important, we should use such an inaccurate proxy as the civil/criminal distinction, or how this newly discovered principle overcomes the "basic norms of constitutional adjudication" on which *Griffith* rested. Finally, the dissent's "equal treatment" argument ably distinguishes between cases in which a prospectivity claim is properly raised, and those in which it is not. But that does nothing to distinguish between civil and criminal cases; obviously, a party may procedurally default on a claim in either context.

more specifically as a means of making it easier to overrule prior precedent. Thus, the dissent is saying, in effect, that *stare decisis* demands the preservation of methods of destroying *stare decisis* recently invented in violation of *stare decisis*.

Contrary to the dissent's assertion that *Chevron Oil* articulated "our traditional retroactivity analysis," the jurisprudence it reflects "came into being," as Justice Harlan observed, less than 30 years ago with *Linkletter*. It is so un-ancient that one of the current members of this Court was sitting when it was invented. The true *traditional* view is that prospective decisionmaking is quite incompatible with the judicial power, and that courts have no authority to engage in the practice. *Linkletter* itself recognized that "at common law there was no authority for the proposition that judicial decisions made law only for the future." And before *Linkletter,* the academic proponents of prospective judicial decisionmaking acknowledged that their proposal contradicted traditional practice. Indeed, the roots of the contrary tradition are so deep that Justice Holmes was prepared to hazard the guess that "judicial decisions have had retrospective operation for near a thousand years." *Kuhn* v. *Fairmont Coal Co.*, 215 U. S. 349, 372 (1910) (dissenting opinion).

JUSTICE O'CONNOR asserts that "when the Court changes its mind, the law changes with it." That concept is quite foreign to the American legal and constitutional tradition. It would have struck John Marshall as an extraordinary assertion of raw power. The conception of the judicial role that he possessed, and that was shared by succeeding generations of American judges until very recent times, took it to be "the province and duty of the judicial department to say what the law *is*," *Marbury* v. *Madison*, 1 Cranch 137, 177 (1803) (emphasis added) — not what the law *shall be*. That original and enduring American perception of the judicial role sprang not from the philosophy of Nietzsche but from the jurisprudence of Blackstone, which viewed retroactivity as an inherent characteristic of the judicial power, a power "not delegated to pronounce a new law, but to maintain and expound the old one." 1 W. Blackstone, Commentaries 69 (1765). Even when a "former determination is most evidently contrary to reason or contrary to the divine law," a judge overruling that decision would "not pretend to make a new law, but to vindicate the old one from misrepresentation. For if it be found that the former decision is manifestly absurd or unjust, it is declared, not that such a sentence was *bad law*, but that it was *not* law." Fully retroactive decisionmaking was considered a principal distinction between the judicial and the legislative power: "It is said that that which distinguishes a judicial from a legislative act is, that the one is a determination of what the existing law is in relation to some existing thing already done or happened, while the other is a predetermination of what the law shall be for the regulation of all future cases." The critics of the traditional rule of full retroactivity were well aware that it was grounded in what one of them contemptuously called "another fiction known as the Separation of powers."

Prospective decisionmaking was known to foe and friend alike as a practical tool of judicial activism, born out of disregard for *stare decisis*. In the eyes of its enemies, the doctrine "smacked of the legislative process," "encroached on the prerogatives of the legislative department of government," removed "one of the great inherent restraints upon this Court's departing from the field of interpretation to enter that of lawmaking," caused the Court's behavior to become "assimilated to that of a legislature," and tended "to cut the courts loose from the force of precedent, allowing them to restructure artificially those expectations legitimately created by extant law and thereby mitigate the practical force of *stare decisis*." All this was not denied by the doctrine's friends, who also viewed it as a device to "augment the power of the courts to contribute to the growth of the law in keeping with the demands of society," as "a deliberate and conscious technique of judicial lawmaking," [and] as a means of "facilitating more effective and defensible judicial lawmaking."

Justice Harlan described this Court's embrace of the prospectivity principle as "the product of the Court's disquietude with the impacts of its fast-moving pace of constitutional innovation." The Court itself, however, glowingly described the doctrine as the cause rather than the effect of innovation, extolling it as a "technique" providing the "impetus for the implementation of long overdue reforms." Whether cause or effect, there is no doubt that the era which gave birth to the prospectivity principle was marked by a newfound disregard for *stare decisis*. As one commentator calculated, "by 1959, the number of instances in which the Court had reversals involving constitutional issues had grown to sixty; in the two decades which followed, the Court overruled constitutional cases on no less than forty-seven occasions." It was an era when this Court cast overboard numerous settled decisions, and indeed even whole areas of law, with an unceremonious "heave-ho." See, *e.g., Mapp* v. *Ohio*, 367 U. S. 643 (1961) (overruling *Wolf* v. *Colorado*, 338 U. S. 25 (1949)); *Gideon* v. *Wainwright*, 372 U. S. 335 (1963) (overruling *Betts* v. *Brady*, 316 U. S. 455 (1942)); *Miranda* v. *Arizona*, 384 U. S. 436 (1966) (overruling *Crooker* v. *California*, 357 U. S. 433 (1958)). To argue now that one of the jurisprudential tools of judicial activism from that period should be extended on the grounds of *stare decisis* can only be described as paradoxical.[2]

In sum, I join the opinion of the Court because the doctrine of prospective decisionmaking is not in fact protected by our flexible rule of *stare decisis*; and because no friend of *stare decisis* would want it to be.

JUSTICE KENNEDY, with whom JUSTICE WHITE joins, concurring in part and concurring in the judgment.

I remain of the view that it is sometimes appropriate in the civil context to give only prospective application to a judicial decision. "Prospective overruling allows courts to respect the principle of *stare decisis* even when they are impelled to change

---

2. Contrary to the suggestion in the dissent, I am not arguing that we should "cast overboard our *entire* retroactivity doctrine with an unceremonious heave-ho." There is no need. We cast over the first half six Terms ago in *Griffith*, and deep-sixed most of the rest two Terms ago in *Beam* — in neither case unceremoniously (in marked contrast to some of the overrulings cited in the text). What little, if any, remains is teetering at the end of the plank and needs no more than a gentle nudge. But if the entire doctrine had been given a quick and unceremonious end, there could be no complaint on the grounds of *stare decisis*; as it was born, so should it die. I do not know the basis for the dissent's contention that I find the jurisprudence of the era that produced the doctrine of prospectivity "distasteful." Much of it is quite appetizing. It is only the cavalier treatment of *stare decisis* and the invention of prospectivity that I have criticized here.

the law in light of new understanding." When a court promulgates a new rule of law, prospective application functions "to avoid injustice or hardship to civil litigants who have justifiably relied on prior law." And in my view retroactivity in civil cases continues to be governed by the standard announced in *Chevron Oil*. Thus, for the reasons explained by Justice O'Connor, I cannot agree with the Court's broad dicta that appears to embrace in the civil context the retroactivity principles adopted for criminal cases in *Griffith*. As Justice O'Connor has demonstrated elsewhere, the differences between the civil and criminal contexts counsel strongly against adoption of *Griffith* for civil cases. I also cannot accept the Court's conclusion, which is based on Justice Souter's opinion in *Beam*, that a decision of this Court must be applied in a retroactive manner simply because the rule of law there announced happened to be applied to the parties then before the Court. For these reasons, I do not join Part II of the Court's opinion.

I nonetheless agree with the Court that *Davis* must be given retroactive effect. The first condition for prospective application of any decision is that it must announce a new rule of law. The decision must "overrule clear past precedent on which litigants may have relied" or "decide an issue of first impression whose resolution was not clearly foreshadowed." Because *Davis* did neither, it did not announce new law and therefore must be applied in a retroactive manner.

. . . .

Because I do not believe that *Davis* announced a new principle of law, I have no occasion to consider Justice O'Connor's argument that equitable considerations may inform the formulation of remedies when a new rule is announced. In any event, I do not read Part III of the Court's opinion as saying anything inconsistent with what Justice O'Connor proposes.

On this understanding, I join Parts I and III of the Court's opinion and concur in its judgment.

JUSTICE O'CONNOR, with whom THE CHIEF JUSTICE joins, dissenting.

Today the Court applies a new rule of retroactivity to impose crushing and unnecessary liability on the States, precisely at a time when they can least afford it. Were the Court's decision the product of statutory or constitutional command, I would have no choice but to join it. But nothing in the Constitution or statute requires us to adopt the retroactivity rule the majority now applies. In fact, longstanding precedent requires the opposite result. Because I see no reason to abandon our traditional retroactivity analysis as articulated in *Chevron Oil*, and because I believe the Supreme Court of Virginia correctly applied *Chevron Oil* in this case, I would affirm the judgment below.

I

This Court's retroactivity jurisprudence has become somewhat chaotic in recent years. Three Terms ago, the case of *American Trucking* produced three opinions, none of which garnered a majority. One Term later, *Beam* yielded five opinions; there, no single writing carried more than three votes. As a result, the Court today finds itself confronted with such disarray that, rather than relying on precedent, it must resort to vote-counting: Examining the various opinions in *Beam*, it discerns six votes for a single proposition that, in its view, controls this case.

If we had given appropriate weight to the principle of *stare decisis* in the first place, our retroactivity jurisprudence never would have become so hopelessly muddled. After all, it was not that long ago that the law of retroactivity for civil cases was considered well settled. . . . In *American Trucking*, however, a number of Justices expressed a contrary view, and the jurisprudential equivalent of entropy took over. Whatever the merits of any retroactivity test, it cannot be denied that resolution of the case before us would be simplified greatly had we not disregarded so needlessly our obligation to follow precedent in the first place.

I fear that the Court today, rather than rectifying that confusion, reinforces it still more. In the usual case, of course, retroactivity is not an issue; the courts simply apply their best understanding of current law in resolving each case that comes before them. But where the law changes in some respect, the courts sometimes may elect not to apply the new law; instead, they apply the law that governed when the events giving rise to the suit took place, especially where the change in law is abrupt and the parties may have relied on the prior law. This can be done in one of two ways. First, a court may choose to make the decision purely prospective, refusing to apply it not only to the parties before the court but also to *any* case where the relevant facts predate the decision. Second, a court may apply the rule to some but not all cases where the operative events occurred before the court's decision, depending on the equities. The first option is called "pure prospectivity" and the second "selective prospectivity."

As the majority notes, six Justices in *Beam* expressed their disagreement with selective prospectivity. Thus, even though there was no majority opinion in that case, one can derive from that case the proposition the Court announces today: Once "this Court applies a rule of federal law to the parties before it, that rule must be given full retroactive effect in all cases still open on direct review." But no decision of this Court forecloses the possibility of pure prospectivity — refusal to apply a new rule in the very case in which it is announced and every case thereafter. . . .

Rather than limiting its pronouncement to the question of selective prospectivity, the Court intimates that pure prospectivity may be prohibited as well. The intimation is incorrect. As I have explained before and will touch upon only briefly here:

> "When the Court changes its mind, the law changes with it. If a Court decides, in the context of a civil case or controversy, to change the law, it must make a determination whether the new law or the old is to apply to conduct occurring before the law-changing decision." . . .

Nor can the Court's suggestion be squared with our cases, which repeatedly have announced rules of purely prospective effect.

In any event, the question of pure prospectivity is not implicated here. The majority first holds that once a rule *has been* applied retroactively, the rule must be applied retroactively to all cases thereafter. Then it holds that *Davis* in fact retroactively applied the rule it announced. Under the majority's approach, that should end the matter: Because the Court applied the rule retroactively in *Davis*, it must do so here as well. Accordingly, there is no reason for the Court's careless dictum regarding pure prospectivity, much less dictum that is contrary to clear precedent.

Plainly enough, Justice Scalia would cast overboard our entire retroactivity doctrine with precisely the "unceremonious 'heave-ho'" he decries in his concurrence. Behind the undisguised hostility to an era whose jurisprudence he finds distasteful, Justice Scalia raises but two substantive arguments, both of which were raised in *Beam*, and neither of which has been adopted by a majority of this Court. Justice White appropriately responded to those arguments then, and there is no reason to repeat the responses now. As Justice Frankfurter explained more than 35 years ago:

> "We should not indulge in the fiction that the law now announced has always been the law. It is much more conducive to law's self-respect to recognize candidly the considerations that give prospective content to a new pronouncement of law." *Griffin* v. *Illinois*, 351 U. S. 12, 26 (1956) (opinion concurring in judgment).

II

I dissented in *James B. Beam* because I believed that the absolute prohibition on selective prospectivity was not only contrary to precedent, but also so rigid that it produced unconscionable results. I would have adhered to the traditional equitable balancing test of *Chevron Oil* as the appropriate method of deciding the retroactivity question in individual cases. But even if one believes the prohibition on selective prospectivity desirable, it seems to me that the Court today takes that judgment to an illogical — and inequitable — extreme. It is one thing to say that, where we have considered prospectivity in a prior case and rejected it, we must reject it in every case thereafter. But it is quite another to hold that, because we did *not* consider the possibility of prospectivity in a prior case and instead applied a rule retroactively through inadvertence, we are foreclosed from considering the issue forever thereafter. Such a rule is both contrary to established precedent and at odds with any notion of fairness or sound decisional practice. Yet that is precisely the rule the Court appears to adopt today.

A

Under the Court's new approach, we have neither authority nor discretion to consider the merits of applying *Davis* retroactively. Instead, we must inquire whether any of our previous decisions happened to have applied the *Davis* rule retroactively to the parties before the Court. Deciding whether we in fact have applied *Davis* retroactively turns out to be a rather difficult matter. Parsing the language of the *Davis* opinion, the Court encounters a single sentence it declares determinative: "The State having conceded that a refund is appropriate in these circumstances, to the extent appellant has paid taxes pursuant to this invalid tax scheme, he is entitled to a refund."

One might very well debate the meaning of the single sentence on which everyone relies. But the debate is as meaningless as it is indeterminate. In *Brecht* v. *Abrahamson*, 507 U. S. 619 (1993), we reaffirmed our longstanding rule that, if a decision does not "squarely address an issue," this Court remains "free to address it on the merits" at a later date. . . . . Regardless of how one reads the solitary sentence upon which the Court relies, surely it does not "squarely address" the question of retroactivity; it does not even mention retroactivity. At best, by addressing the question of remedies, the sentence implicitly "assumes" the rule in *Davis* to be retroactive. Our decision in *Brecht*, however, makes it quite clear that unexamined assumptions do not bind this Court.

The Court offers no justification for disregarding the settled rule we so recently applied in *Brecht*. Nor do I believe it could, for the rule is not a procedural nicety. On the contrary, it is critical to the soundness of our decisional processes. It should go without saying that any decision of this Court has wide-ranging applications; nearly every opinion we issue has effects far beyond the particular case in which it issues. The rule we applied in *Brecht*, which limits the stare decisis effect of our decisions to questions actually considered and passed on, ensures that this Court does not decide important questions by accident or inadvertence. By adopting a contrary rule in the area of retroactivity, the Court now permanently binds itself to its every unexamined assumption or inattention. Any rule that creates a grave risk that we might resolve important issues of national concern sub silentio, without thought or consideration, cannot be a wise one.

.   .   .   .

The Court's decision today cannot be justified by comparisons to our decision in *Griffith*, which abandoned selective retroactivity in the criminal context. As I explained in *American Trucking*, there are significant differences between criminal and civil cases that weigh against such an extension. First, nonretroactivity in criminal cases historically has favored the government's reliance interests over the rights of criminal defendants. As a result, the generalized policy of favoring individual rights over governmental prerogative can justify the elimination of prospectivity in the criminal arena. The same rationale cannot apply in civil cases, as nonretroactivity in the civil context does not necessarily favor plaintiffs or defendants; "nor is there any policy reason for protecting one class of litigants over another." More important, even a party to civil litigation who is "deprived of the full retroactive benefit of a new decision may receive some relief." Here, for example, petitioners received the benefit of prospective invalidation of Virginia's taxing scheme. From this moment forward, they will be treated on an equal basis with all other retirees, the very treatment our intergovernmental immunity cases require. The criminal defendant, in contrast, is usually interested only in one remedy — reversal of his conviction. *That* remedy can be obtained only if the rule is applied retroactively.

Nor can the Court's rejection of selective retroactivity in the civil context be defended on equal treatment grounds. It may well be that there is little difference between the criminal defendant in whose case a decision is announced and the defendant who seeks certiorari on the same question two days later. But in this case there is a tremendous difference between the defendant in whose case the *Davis* rule was announced and the defendant who appears before us today: The latter litigated and preserved the retroactivity question while the former did not. The Michigan Department of Taxation did not even brief the question of retroactivity in *Davis*. Respondent, in contrast, actually prevailed on the question in the court below.

.   .   .   .

III

Even if the Court is correct that *Davis* must be applied retroactively in this case, there is the separate question of the *remedy* that must be given. The questions of retroactivity and remedy are analytically distinct. As Justice Souter explained in *Beam*, retroactivity is a matter of choice of law "since the question is whether the court should apply the old rule or the new one." When the retroactivity of a decision of this Court is in issue, the choice-of-law issue is a federal question.

The question of remedy, however, is quite different. The issue is not whether to apply new law or old law, but what relief should be afforded once the prevailing party has been determined under applicable law. The question of remedies is in the first instance a question of state law. In fact, the only federal question regarding remedies is whether the relief afforded is sufficient to comply with the requirement of due process.

. . . .

In my view, if the Court is going to restrict authority to temper hardship by holding our decisions nonretroactive through the *Chevron Oil* factors, it must afford courts the ability to avoid injustice by taking equity into account when formulating the remedy for violations of novel constitutional rules. Surely the Constitution permits this Court to refuse plaintiffs full backwards-looking relief under *Chevron Oil*; we repeatedly have done so in the past. I therefore see no reason why it would not similarly permit state courts reasonably to consider the equities in the exercise of their sound remedial discretion.

Notes and Questions

---

1. What do you think of the rule articulated in *Harper*? Does it make sense to apply the same rule in both criminal and civil cases on direct review? On the other hand, does Justice O'Connor raise any legitimate concerns? If so, how should those concerns be addressed?

2. On this subject, Professors Hart and Sacks write:

   > Acceptance of the possibility of overruling prior decisions with no more than prospective effect relieves a court of one of the major practical restraints upon free changes of law. It thus forces attention upon the question of what, if any, considerations other than that of protection of reasonable reliance underlie the policy of *stare decisis*. And it heightens the importance of the problem of determining the appropriate limits upon the exercise of judicial discretion in saying what the law should be. Do we have a working theory of the judicial function which would be adequate to prevent judges from assuming political functions and to avoid a disintegrating chaos of doctrine if the propriety of prospective overruling were universally accepted?

> HENRY M. HART, JR. & ALBERT M. SACKS, THE LEGAL PROCESS: BASIC PROBLEMS IN THE MAKING AND APPLICATION OF LAW 606 (William N. Eskridge, Jr. & Philip P. Frickey eds., 1994).

3. Though the Supreme Court now seems to have rejected prospectivity, at least as a general matter, you should be aware that many state courts, which tended to follow the Supreme Court's lead with respect to prospectivity, still adhere to various forms of that doctrine.

4. Notice the discussion of stare decisis with respect to the Court's retroactivity analysis. Should that analysis be considered part of the Court's holding, or is it mere decisional methodology? In other words, aside from the issue of whether *Chevron Oil* should be "overruled," is there not the antecedent question of whether a court's retroactivity analysis is deserving of stare decisis? But assuming the answer to this antecedent question is yes, was the *Harper* Court justified in overruling *Chevron Oil*?

4. Possible Constitutional Limitations on the Retroactive Application of Decisions

Though retroactivity has long been the norm with respect to judicial decisions, can retroactivity nonetheless run afoul of constitutional considerations? Consider this question in the context of the next case.

Rogers v. Tennessee
532 U.S. 451 (2001)

JUSTICE O'CONNOR delivered the opinion of the Court.

This case concerns the constitutionality of the retroactive application of a judicial decision abolishing the common law "year and a day rule." At common law, the year and a day rule provided that no defendant could be convicted of murder unless his victim had died by the defendant's act within a year and a day of the act. See, *e.g., Louisville, E. & St. L. R. Co. v. Clarke,* 152 U.S. 230, 239 (1894); 4 W. Blackstone, Commentaries on the Laws of England 197-98 (1769). The Supreme Court of Tennessee abolished the rule as it had existed at common law in Tennessee and applied its decision to petitioner to uphold his conviction. The question before us is whether, in doing so, the court denied petitioner due process of law in violation of the Fourteenth Amendment.

. . . .

II

Although petitioner's claim is one of due process, the Constitution's *Ex Post Facto* Clause figures prominently in his argument. The Clause provides simply that "no

State shall pass any ex post facto Law." Art. I, § 10, cl. 1. The most well-known and oft-repeated explanation of the scope of the Clause's protection was given by Justice Chase, who long ago identified, in dictum, four types of laws to which the Clause extends:

> "1st. Every law that makes an action done before the passing of the law, and which was innocent when done, criminal; and punishes such action. 2d. Every law that aggravates a crime, or makes it greater than it was, when committed. 3d. Every law that changes the punishment, and inflicts a greater punishment, than the law annexed to the crime, when committed. 4th. Every law that alters the legal rules of evidence, and receives less, or different, testimony, than the law required at the time of the commission of the offense, in order to convict the offender." *Calder v. Bull,* 3 Dall. 386 (1798) *(seriatim* opinion of Chase, J.).

As the text of the Clause makes clear, it "is a limitation upon the powers of the Legislature, and does not of its own force apply to the Judicial Branch of government." *Marks v. United States,* 430 U.S. 188, 191 (1977).

We have observed, however, that limitations on *ex post facto* judicial decision-making are inherent in the notion of due process. In *Bouie v. City of Columbia,* we considered the South Carolina Supreme Court's retroactive application of its construction of the State's criminal trespass statute to the petitioners in that case. The statute prohibited "entry upon the lands of another . . . after notice from the owner or tenant prohibiting such entry . . . ." 378 U.S., at 349, n. 1. The South Carolina court construed the statute to extend to patrons of a drug store who had received no notice prohibiting their entry into the store, but had refused to leave the store when asked. Prior to the court's decision, South Carolina cases construing the statute had uniformly held that conviction under the statute required proof of notice before entry. None of those cases, moreover, had given the "slightest indication that that requirement could be satisfied by proof of the different act of remaining on the land after being told to leave."

We held that the South Carolina court's retroactive application of its construction to the store patrons violated due process. Reviewing decisions in which we had held criminal statutes "void for vagueness" under the Due Process Clause, we noted that this Court has often recognized the "basic principle that a criminal statute must give fair warning of the conduct that it makes a crime." Deprivation of the right to fair warning, we continued, can result both from vague statutory language and from an unforeseeable and retroactive judicial expansion of statutory language that appears narrow and precise on its face. For that reason, we concluded that "if a judicial construction of a criminal statute is 'unexpected and indefensible by reference to the law which had been expressed prior to the conduct in issue,' the construction must not be given retroactive effect." We found that the South Carolina court's construction of the statute violated this principle because it was so clearly at odds with the statute's plain language and had no support in prior South Carolina decisions.

Relying largely upon *Bouie,* petitioner argues that the Tennessee court erred in rejecting his claim that the retroactive application of its decision to his case violates due process. Petitioner contends that the *Ex Post Facto* Clause would prohibit the retroactive application of a decision abolishing the year and a day rule if accomplished by the Tennessee Legislature. He claims that the purposes behind the Clause are so fundamental that due process should prevent the Supreme Court of Tennessee from accomplishing the same result by judicial decree. In support of this claim, petitioner takes *Bouie* to stand for the proposition that "in evaluating whether the retroactive application of a judicial decree violates Due Process, a critical question is whether the Constitution would prohibit the same result attained by the exercise of the state's legislative power."

To the extent petitioner argues that the Due Process Clause incorporates the specific prohibitions of the *Ex Post Facto* Clause as identified in *Calder,* petitioner misreads *Bouie*. To be sure, our opinion in *Bouie* does contain some expansive language that is suggestive of the broad interpretation for which petitioner argues. Most prominent is our statement that "if a state legislature is barred by the *Ex Post Facto* Clause from passing . . . a law, it must follow that a State Supreme Court is barred by the Due Process Clause from achieving precisely the same result by judicial construction." 378 U.S., at 353-354; see also *id.,* at 353 ("An unforeseeable, judicial enlargement of a criminal statute, applied retroactively, operates precisely like an *ex post facto* law"); *id.,* at 362 ("The Due Process Clause compels the same result" as would the constitutional proscription against *ex post facto* laws "where the State has sought to achieve precisely the same impermissible effect by judicial construction of the statute"). This language, however, was dicta. Our decision in *Bouie* was rooted firmly in well established notions of *due process*. Its rationale rested on core due process concepts of notice, foreseeability, and, in particular, the right to fair warning as those concepts bear on the constitutionality of attaching criminal penalties to what previously had been innocent conduct. And we couched it holding squarely in terms of that established due process right, and not in terms of the *ex post facto* related dicta to which petitioner points. *Id.,* at 355 (concluding that "the South Carolina Code did not give the petitioners fair warning, at the time of their conduct . . . , that the act for which they now stand convicted was rendered criminal by the statute"). Contrary to petitioner's suggestion, nowhere in the opinion did we go so far as to incorporate jot-for-jot the specific categories of *Calder* into due process limitations on the retroactive application of judicial decisions.

Nor have any of our subsequent decisions addressing *Bouie*-type claims interpreted *Bouie* as extending so far. Those decisions instead have uniformly viewed *Bouie* restricted to its traditional due process roots. In doing so, they have applied *Bouie*'s check on retroactive judicial decisionmaking not by reference to the *ex post facto* categories set out in *Calder,* but, rather, in accordance with the more basic and general principle of fair warning that *Bouie* so clearly articulated.

Petitioner observes that the Due Process and *Ex Post Facto* Clauses safeguard common interests — in particular, the interests in fundamental fairness (through notice and fair warning) and the prevention of arbitrary and vindictive use of the laws. While this is undoubtedly correct, petitioner is mistaken to suggest that these considerations compel extending the strictures of the *Ex Post Facto* Clause to the context of common law judging. The *Ex Post Facto* Clause, by its own terms, does not apply to courts. Extending the Clause to courts through the rubric of due process thus would circumvent the clear constitutional text. It also would evince too little regard for the important institutional and contextual differences between legislating, on the one hand, and common law decisionmaking, on the other.

Petitioner contends that state courts acting in their common law capacity act much like legislatures in the exercise of their lawmaking function, and indeed may in some cases even be subject to the same kinds of political influences and pressures that justify *ex post facto* limitations upon legislatures. A court's "opportunity for discrimination," however, "is more limited than a legislature's, in that it can only act in construing existing law in actual litigation." *James v. United States,* 366 U.S. 213, 247 n. 3 (1961) (Harlan, J., concurring in part and dissenting in part). Moreover, "given the divergent pulls of flexibility and precedent in our case law system," *ibid.,* incorporation of the *Calder* categories into due process limitations on judicial decisionmaking would place an unworkable and unacceptable restraint on normal judicial processes and would be incompatible with the resolution of uncertainty that marks any evolving legal system.

That is particularly so where, as here, the allegedly impermissible judicial application of a rule of law involves not the interpretation of a statute but an act of common law judging. In the context of common law doctrines (such as the year and a day rule), there often arises a need to clarify or even to reevaluate prior opinions as new circumstances and fact patterns present themselves. Such judicial acts, whether they be characterized as "making" or "finding" the law, are a necessary part of the judicial business in States in which the criminal law retains some of its common law elements. Strict application of *ex post facto* principles in that context would unduly impair the incremental and reasoned development of precedent that is the foundation of the common law system. The common law, in short, presupposes a measure of evolution that is incompatible with stringent application of *ex post facto* principles. It was on account of concerns such as these that *Bouie* restricted due process limitations on the retroactive application of judicial interpretations of criminal statutes to those that are "unexpected and indefensible by reference to the law which had been expressed prior to the conduct in issue."

We believe this limitation adequately serves the common law context as well. It accords common law courts the substantial leeway they must enjoy as they engage in the daily task of formulating and passing upon criminal defenses and interpreting such doctrines as causation and intent, reevaluating and refining them as may be necessary to bring the common law into conformity with logic and common sense. It also adequately respects the due process concern with fundamental fairness and protects against vindictive or arbitrary judicial lawmaking by safeguarding defendants against unjustified and unpredictable breaks with prior law. Accordingly, we conclude that a judicial alteration of a common law doctrine of criminal law violates the principle of fair warning, and hence must not be given retroactive effect, only where it is "unexpected and indefensible by reference to the law which had been expressed prior to the conduct in issue."

JUSTICE SCALIA makes much of the fact that, at the time of the framing of the Constitution, it was widely accepted that courts could not "change" the law, and that (according to JUSTICE SCALIA) there is no doubt that the *Ex Post Facto* Clause would have prohibited a legislative decision identical to the Tennessee court's decision here. This latter argument seeks at bottom merely to reopen what has long been settled by the constitutional text and our own decisions: that the *Ex Post Facto* Clause does not apply to judicial decisionmaking. The former argument is beside the point. Common law courts at the time of the framing undoubtedly believed that they were finding rather than making law. But, however one characterizes their actions, the fact of the matter is that common law courts then, as now, were deciding cases, and in doing so were fashioning and refining the law as it existed in light of reason and experience. Due process clearly did not prohibit this process of judicial evolution at the time of the framing, and it does not do so today.

III

Turning to the particular facts of the instant case, the Tennessee court's abolition of the year and a day rule was not unexpected and indefensible. The year and a day rule is widely viewed as an outdated relic of the common law. Petitioner does not even so much as hint that good reasons exist for retaining the rule, and so we need not delve too deeply into the rule and its history here. Suffice it to say that the rule is generally believed to date back to the 13th century, when it served as a statute of limitations governing the time in which an individual might initiate a private action for murder known as an "appeal of death"; that by the 18th century the rule had been extended to the law governing public prosecutions for murder; that the primary and most frequently cited justification for the rule is that 13th century medical science was incapable of establishing causation beyond a reasonable doubt when a great deal of time had elapsed between the injury to the victim and his death; and that, as practically every court recently to have considered the rule has noted, advances in medical and related science have so undermined the usefulness of the rule as to render it without question obsolete.

For this reason, the year and a day rule has been legislatively or judicially abolished in the vast majority of jurisdictions recently to have addressed the issue. Citing *Bouie,* petitioner contends that the judicial abolition of the rule in other jurisdictions is irrelevant to whether he had fair warning that the rule in Tennessee might similarly be abolished and, hence, to whether the Tennessee court's decision was unexpected and indefensible as applied to him. In discussing the apparent meaning of the South Carolina statute in *Bouie,* we noted that "it would be a rare situation in which the meaning of a statute of another State sufficed to afford a person 'fair warning' that his own State's statute meant something quite different from what its words said." This case, however, involves not the precise meaning of the words of a particular statute, but rather the continuing viability of a common law rule. Common law courts frequently look to the decisions of other jurisdictions in determining whether to alter or modify a common law rule in light of changed circumstances, increased knowledge, and general logic and experience. Due process, of course, does not require a person to apprise himself of the common law of all 50 States in order to guarantee that his actions will not subject him to punishment in light of a developing trend in the law that has not yet made its way to his State. At the same time, however, the fact that a vast number of jurisdictions have abolished a rule that has so clearly outlived its purpose is surely relevant to whether the abolition of the rule in a particular case can be said to be unexpected and indefensible by reference to the law as it then existed.

Finally, and perhaps most importantly, at the time of petitioner's crime the year and a day rule had only the most tenuous foothold as part of the criminal law of the State of Tennessee. The rule did not exist as part of Tennessee's statutory criminal code. And while the Supreme Court of Tennessee concluded that the rule persisted at common law, it also pointedly observed that the rule had never once served as a ground of decision in any prosecution for murder in the State. Indeed, in all the reported Tennessee cases, the rule has been mentioned only three times, and each time in dicta.

. . . .

These cases hardly suggest that the Tennessee court's decision was "unexpected and indefensible" such that it offended the due process principle of fair warning articulated in *Bouie* and its progeny. This is so despite the fact that, as JUSTICE SCALIA correctly points out, the court viewed the year and a day rule as a "substantive principle" of the common law of Tennessee. As such, however, it was a principle in name only, having never once been enforced in the State. The Supreme Court of Tennessee also emphasized this fact in its opinion, and rightly so, for it is surely relevant to whether the court's abolition of the rule in petitioner's case violated due process limitations on retroactive judicial decisionmaking. And while we readily agree with JUSTICE SCALIA that fundamental due process prohibits the punishment of conduct that cannot fairly be said to have been criminal at the time the conduct occurred, nothing suggests that this is what took place here.

There is, in short, nothing to indicate that the Tennessee court's abolition of the rule in petitioner's case represented an exercise of the sort of unfair and arbitrary action against which the Due Process Clause aims to protect. Far from a marked and unpredictable departure from prior precedent, the court's decision was a routine exercise of common law decisionmaking in which the court brought the law into conformity with reason and common sense. It did so by laying to rest an archaic and outdated rule that had never been relied upon as a ground of decision in any reported Tennessee case.

The judgment of the Supreme Court of Tennessee is accordingly affirmed.

It is so ordered.

JUSTICE SCALIA, with whom JUSTICE STEVENS and JUSTICE THOMAS join, and with whom JUSTICE BREYER joins as to Part II, dissenting.

The Court today approves the conviction of a man for a murder that was not murder (but only manslaughter) when the offense was committed. It thus violates a principle — encapsulated in the maxim *nulla poena sine lege* — which "dates from the ancient Greeks" and has been described as one of the most "widely held value-judgments in the entire history of human thought." J. Hall, General Principles of Criminal Law 59 (2d ed. 1960). Today's opinion produces, moreover, a curious constitution that only a judge could love. One in which (by virtue of the *Ex Post Facto* Clause) the elected representatives of all the people cannot retroactively make murder what was not murder when the act was committed; but in which unelected judges can do precisely that. One in which the predictability of parliamentary lawmaking cannot validate the retroactive creation of crimes, but the predictability of judicial lawmaking can do so. I do not believe this is the system that the Framers envisioned — or, for that matter, that any reasonable person would imagine.

I

A

To begin with, let us be clear that the law here was altered after the fact. Petitioner, whatever else he was guilty of, was innocent of murder under the law as it stood at the time of the stabbing, because the victim did not die until after a year and a day had passed. The requisite condition subsequent of the murder victim's death within a year and a day is no different from the requisite condition subsequent of the rape victim's raising a "hue and cry" which we held could not retroactively be eliminated in *Carmell v. Texas,* 529 U.S. 513 (2000). Here, as there, it operates to bar conviction. Indeed, if the present condition differs at all from the one involved in *Carmell* it is the fact that it does not merely pertain to the "quantum of evidence" necessary to corroborate a charge, but is an actual *element* of the crime — a "substantive principle of law," the failure to establish which "entirely precludes a murder prosecution." Though the Court spends some time questioning whether the year-and-a-day rule was ever truly established in Tennessee, the Supreme Court of Tennessee said it was, and this reasonable reading of state law by the State's highest court is binding upon us.

Petitioner's claim is that his conviction violated the Due Process Clause of the Fourteenth Amendment, insofar as that Clause contains the principle applied against the legislature by the *Ex Post Facto* Clause of Article I. We first discussed the relationship between these two Clauses in *Bouie v. City of Columbia,* 378 U.S. 347 (1964). There, we considered Justice Chase to have spoken for the Court in *Calder v. Bull,* 3 Dall. 386, 390 (1798), when he defined an *ex post facto* law as, *inter alia,* one that "aggravates a crime, or makes it greater than it was, when committed." We concluded that, "if a state legislature is barred by the *Ex Post Facto* Clause from passing such a law, it must follow that a State Supreme Court is barred by the Due Process Clause from achieving precisely the same result by judicial construction." The Court seeks to avoid the obvious import of this language by characterizing it as mere dicta. The *ratio decidendi* of *Bouie* was that the principle applied to the legislature through the *Ex Post Facto* Clause was contained in the Due Process Clause insofar as judicial action is concerned. I cannot understand why the Court derives such comfort from the fact that later opinions applying *Bouie* have referred to the Due Process Clause rather than the *Ex Post Facto* Clause; that is entirely in accord with the rationale of the case, which I follow and which the Court discards.

The Court attempts to cabin *Bouie* by reading it to prohibit only "unexpected and indefensible" judicial law revision, and to permit retroactive judicial changes so long as the defendant has had "fair warning" that the changes might occur. This reading seems plausible because *Bouie* does indeed use those quoted terms; but they have been wrenched entirely out of context. The "fair warning" to which *Bouie* and subsequent cases referred was not "fair warning that the law might be changed," but fair warning *of what constituted the crime at the time of the offense.* And *Bouie* did not express disapproval of "unexpected and indefensible changes in the law" (and thus implicitly approve "expected or defensible changes"). It expressed disapproval of "*judicial construction* of a criminal statute" that is "unexpected and indefensible *by reference to the law which had been expressed prior to the conduct in issue.*" It thus implicitly approved only a judicial construction that was an expected or defensible application of prior cases interpreting the statute. Extending this principle from statutory crimes to common-law crimes would result in the approval of retroactive holdings that accord with prior cases expounding the common law, and the disapproval of retroactive holdings that clearly depart from prior cases expounding the common law. According to *Bouie,* not just "unexpected and indefensible" retroactive changes in the common law of crimes are bad, but *all* retroactive changes.

Bouie rested squarely upon the fundamental principle that "the required criminal law must have existed when the conduct at issue occurred" (*Nulla poena sine lege.*) Proceeding from that principle, *Bouie* said that "a State Supreme Court is barred by the Due Process Clause from achieving precisely the same result prohibited by the *Ex Post Facto* Clause by judicial construction." There is no doubt that "fair warning" of the legislature's intent to change the law does not insulate retroactive *legislative* criminalization. Such a statute violates the *Ex Post Facto* Clause, no matter that, at the time the offense was committed, the bill enacting the change was pending and assured of passage — or indeed, had already been passed but not yet signed by the President whose administration had proposed it. It follows from the analysis of *Bouie* that "fair warning" of impending change cannot insulate retroactive *judicial* criminalization either.

Nor is there any reason in the nature of things why it should. According to the Court, the exception is necessary because prohibiting retroactive judicial criminalization would "place an unworkable and unacceptable restraint on normal judicial processes," would be "incompatible with the resolution of uncertainty that marks any evolving legal system," and would "unduly impair the incremental and reasoned development of precedent that is the foundation of the common law system." That assessment ignores the crucial difference between simply applying a law to a new set of circumstances and changing the law that has previously been applied to the very circumstances before the court. Many criminal cases present some factual nuance that arguably distinguishes them from cases that have come before; a court applying the penal statute to the new fact pattern does not purport to *change* the law. That, however, is not the action before us here, but rather, a square, head-on *overruling* of prior law — or, more accurately, something even more extreme than that: a judicial opinion acknowledging that under prior law, for reasons that used to be valid, the accused could not be convicted, but decreeing that, because of changed circumstances, "we hereby abolish the common law rule," and upholding the conviction by applying the new rule to conduct that occurred before the change in law was announced. Even in civil cases, and even in modern times, such retroactive revision of a concededly valid legal rule is extremely rare. With regard to criminal cases, I have no hesitation in affirming that it was unheard of at the time the original Due Process Clause was adopted. As I discuss in detail in the following section, proceeding in that fashion would have been regarded as contrary to the judicial traditions embraced within the concept of due process of law.

B

The Court's opinion considers the judgment at issue here "a routine exercise of common law decisionmaking," whereby the Tennessee court "brought the law into conformity with reason and common sense," by "laying to rest an archaic and outdated rule." This is an accurate enough description of what modern "common law decision-making" consists of — but it is not an accurate description of the theoretical model of common-law decisionmaking accepted by those who adopted the Due Process Clause. At the time of the framing, common-law jurists believed (in the words of Sir Francis Bacon) that the judge's "office is *jus dicere,* and not *jus dare;* to interpret law, and not to make law, or give law." Bacon, Essays, Civil and Moral, in 3 Harvard Classics 130 (C. Eliot ed. 1909) (1625). Or as described by Blackstone, whose Commentaries were widely read and "accepted by the framing generation as the most satisfactory exposition of the common law of England," see *Schick v. United States,* 195 U.S. 65, 69 (1904), "judicial decisions are the principal and most authoritative *evidence,* that can be given, of the existence of such a custom as shall form a part of the common law," 1 W. Blackstone, Commentaries *69.

Blackstone acknowledged that the courts' exposition of what the law was could change. *Stare decisis,* he said, "admits of exception, where the former determination is most evidently contrary to reason. . . ." But "in such cases the subsequent judges do not pretend to make a new law, but to vindicate the old one from misrepresentation." To fit within this category of bad law, a law must be "manifestly absurd or unjust." It would not suffice, he said, that "the particular reason for the law can at this distance of time not be precisely assigned." "For though its reason be not obvious at first view, yet we owe such a deference to former times as not to suppose they acted wholly without consideration."[1] By way of example, Blackstone pointed to the seemingly unreasonable rule that one cannot inherit the estate of one's half brother. Though he accepted that the feudal reason behind the law was no longer obvious, he wrote "yet it is not *in a common law judge's power* to alter it."[2] Moreover, "the unreasonableness of a custom in modern circumstances will not affect its validity if the Court is satisfied of a reasonable origin." Allen 140-41. "A custom once reasonable and tolerable, if after it becomes grievous, and not answerable to the reason, whereupon it was grounded, yet is to be . . . taken away by act of parliament." 2 E. Coke, Institutes of the Laws of England * 664; see also *id.,* at *97 ("No law, or custome of England can be taken

---

1. Inquiring into a law's original reasonableness was perhaps tantamount to questioning whether it existed at all. "In holding the origin to have been unreasonable, the Court nearly always doubts or denies the actual origin and continuance of the custom *in fact.*" C. Allen, Law in the Making 140 (3d ed. 1939).

2. The near-dispositive strength Blackstone accorded *stare decisis* was not some mere personal predilection. Chancellor Kent was of the same view: "If a decision has been made upon solemn argument and mature deliberation, the presumption is in favor of its correctness; and the community have *a right* to regard it as a just declaration or exposition of the law, and to regulate their actions and contracts by it." 1 J. Kent, Commentaries *475-*476. See also Hamilton's statement in The Federalist: "To avoid an arbitrary discretion in the courts, it is indispensable that they should be bound down by strict rules and precedents which serve to define and point out their duty in every particular case that comes before them." The Federalist No. 78, p. 471 (C. Rossiter ed. 1961).

away, abrogated, or adnulled, but by authority of parliament"); Of Oaths before an Ecclesiastical Judge Ex Officio, 12 Co. Rep. *26, *29 (1655) ("The law and custom of England is the inheritance of the subject, which he cannot be deprived of without his assent in Parliament").

There are, of course, stray statements and doctrines found in the historical record that — read out of context — could be thought to support the modern-day proposition that the common law was always meant to evolve. Take, for instance, Lord Coke's statement in the Institutes that "the reason of the law ceasing, the law itself ceases." This maxim is often cited by modern devotees of a turbulently changing common law — often in its Latin form *(cessante ratione legis, cessat ipse lex)* to create the impression of great venerability. In its original context, however, it had nothing to do with the power of common-law courts to change the law. At the point at which it appears in the Institutes, Coke was discussing the exception granted abbots and mayors from the obligation of military service to the King which attached to land ownership. Such service would be impracticable for a man of the cloth or a mayor. But, said Coke, "if they convey over the lands to any naturall man and his heires," the immunity "by the conveyance over ceaseth." In other words, the service which attached to the land would apply to any subsequent owner not cloaked in a similar immunity. It was in describing this change that Coke employed the Latin maxim *cessante ratione legis, cessat ipse lex.* It had to do, not with a changing of the common-law rule, but with a change of circumstances that rendered the common-law rule no longer applicable to the case.

The same is true of the similar quotation from Coke: "*Ratio legis est anima legis, et mutata legis ratione, mutatur et lex*" — reason is the soul of the law; the reason of the law being changed, the law is also changed. This is taken from Coke's report of *Milborn's Case,* 7 Co. Rep. 6b, 7a (1587), a suit involving a town's responsibility for a murder committed within its precincts. The common-law rule had been that a town could be amerced for failure to apprehend a murderer who committed his crime on its streets during the day, but not a murderer who struck after nightfall, when its citizens were presumably asleep. Parliament, however, enacted a statute requiring towns to close their gates at night, and the court reasoned that thereafter a town that left its gates open could be amerced for the nocturnal homicide as well, since the town's violation of the Act was negligence that facilitated the escape. This perhaps partakes more of a new right of action implied from legislation than of any common-law rule. But to the extent it involved the common law, it assuredly did not *change* the prior rule: A town not in violation of the statute would continue to be immune. *Milborn's Case* simply held that the rule would not be extended to towns that wrongfully failed to close their gates — which involves no overruling, but nothing more than normal, case-by-case common-law adjudication.

It is true that framing-era judges in this country considered themselves authorized to reject English common-law precedent they found "barbarous" and "ignorant." That, however, was not an assertion of *judges'* power to *change* the common law. For, as Blackstone wrote, the common law was a law for England, and did not automatically transfer to the American Colonies; rather, it had to be adopted. See 1 Blackstone *107,*108 (observing that "the common law of England, as such, has no allowance or authority" in "our American plantations"). In short, the colonial courts felt themselves perfectly free to pick and choose which parts of the English common law they would adopt.[3] As stated by [N. Chipman, A Dissertation on the Act Adopting the Common and Statute Laws of England, in Reports and Dissertations 128 (1793)]: "If no reason can be assigned, in support of rules, or precedents, *not already adopted in practice,* to adopt such rules, is certainly contrary to the principles of our government." This discretion not to adopt would not presuppose, or even support, the power of colonial courts subsequently to change the accumulated colonial common law. The absence of belief in *that* power is demonstrated by the following passage from 1 Horwitz 5: "Massachusetts Chief Justice Hutchison could declare in 1767 that 'laws should be established, else Judges and Juries must go according to their Reason, that is, their Will.' It was also imperative 'that *the Judge* should never be the *Legislator*: Because, then, the Will of the Judge would be the Law: and this tends to a State of Slavery.'" Or, as Judge Swift put it, courts "ought never to be allowed to depart from the well known boundaries of express law, into the wide fields of discretion."

Nor is the framing era's acceptance of common-law crimes support for the proposition that the Framers accepted an evolving common law. The acknowledgment of a new crime, not thitherto rejected by judicial decision, was not a *changing* of the common law, but an *application* of it. At the time of the framing, common-law crimes were considered unobjectionable, for "'a law founded on the law of nature may be retrospective, because it always existed.'" Of course, the notion of a common-law crime is utterly anathema today, which leads one to wonder why that is so. The obvious answer is that we now agree with the perceptive chief justice of Connecticut, who wrote in 1796 that common-law crimes "partake of the odious nature of an ex post facto law." But, as Horwitz makes clear, a widespread sharing of Swift's "preoccupation with the unfairness of administering a system of judge-made criminal law was a distinctly *post-revolutionary* phenomenon, reflecting a profound change in sensibility. For the inarticulate premise that lay behind Swift's warnings against the danger of judicial discretion was *a growing perception that judges no longer merely discovered law; they also made it.*" In other words, the connection between *ex post facto* lawmaking and common-law judging would not have become widely apparent *until* common-law judging *became* lawmaking, not (as it had been) law declaring. This did not happen until the 19th century, *after* the framing.

What happened in the present case, then, is precisely what Blackstone said — and the Framers believed — would not suffice. The Tennessee Supreme Court made no pretense that the year-and-a-day rule was "bad" law from the outset; rather, it asserted, the need for the rule, as a means of assuring causality of the death, had disappeared with time. Blackstone — and the Framers who were formed by Blackstone — would clearly have regarded that *change* in law as a matter for the legislature, beyond the *power* of the court. It may well be that some common-law decisions of the era in

---

3. In fact, however, "most of the basic departures from English common law were accomplished not by judicial decision but by local statute, so that by the time of the American Revolution one hears less and less about the unsuitability of common law principles to the American environment." 1 M. Horwitz, Transformation of American Law 1780-1860, p. 5 (1977).

fact changed the law while purporting not to. But that is beside the point. What is important here is that it was an undoubted point of principle, at the time the Due Process Clause was adopted, that courts could not "change" the law. That explains why the Constitution restricted only the legislature from enacting *ex post facto* laws. Under accepted norms of judicial process, an *ex post facto* law (in the sense of a judicial holding, not that a prior decision was erroneous, but that the prior valid law is hereby retroactively *changed)* was simply not an option for the courts. This attitude subsisted, I may note, well beyond the founding era, and beyond the time when due process guarantees were extended against the States by the Fourteenth Amendment. In an 1886 admiralty case, for example, this Court said the following: "The rights of persons in this particular under the maritime law of this country are not different from those under the common law, and as it is the duty of courts to declare the law, not to make it, we cannot change this rule." *The Harrisburg,* 119 U.S. 199, 213-214 (1886).

It is not a matter, therefore, of "extending the *Ex Post Facto* Clause to courts through the rubric of due process," and thereby "circumventing the clear constitutional text." It is simply a matter of determining what due judicial process consists of — and it does not consist of retroactive creation of crimes. The *Ex Post Facto* Clause is relevant only because it demonstrates beyond doubt that, however much the acknowledged and accepted role of common-law courts could evolve (as it has) in other respects, retroactive revision of the criminal law was regarded as so fundamentally unfair that an alteration of the judicial role which permits *that* will be a denial of due process. Madison wrote that "*ex-post-facto* laws . . . are contrary to the first principles of the social compact, and to every principle of social legislation." The Federalist No. 44, p. 282 (C. Rossiter ed. 1961). I find it impossible to believe, as the Court does, that this strong sentiment attached only to retroactive laws passed by the legislature, and would not apply equally (or indeed with even greater force) to a court's production of the same result through disregard of the traditional limits upon judicial power. Insofar as the "first principles of the social compact" are concerned, what possible difference does it make that "a court's opportunity for discrimination" by retroactively changing a law "is more limited than a legislature's, in that it can only act in construing existing law in actual legislation"? The injustice to the individuals affected is no less.

II

Even if I agreed with the Court that the Due Process Clause is violated only when there is lack of "fair warning" of the impending retroactive change, I would not find such fair warning here. It is not clear to me, in fact, what the Court believes the fair warning consisted of. Was it the mere fact that "the year and a day rule is widely viewed as an outdated relic of the common law"? So are many elements of common-law crimes, such as "breaking the close" as an element of burglary, or "asportation" as an element of larceny. See W. LaFave & A. Scott, Criminal Law 631-633, 708-710 (1972). Are all of these "outdated relics" subject to retroactive judicial rescission? Or perhaps the fair warning consisted of the fact that "the year and a day rule has been legislatively or judicially abolished in the vast majority of jurisdictions recently to have addressed the issue." But why not count in petitioner's favor (as giving him no reason to expect a change in law) those even more numerous jurisdictions that have chosen *not* "recently to have addressed the issue"? And why not also count in petitioner's favor (rather than *against* him) those jurisdictions that have abolished the rule *legislatively,* and those jurisdictions that have abolished it through *prospective* rather than *retroactive* judicial rulings? That is to say, even if it was predictable that the rule would be changed, it was *not* predictable that it would be changed *retroactively,* rather than in the *prospective* manner to which legislatures are restricted by the *Ex Post Facto* Clause, or in the *prospective* manner that most other courts have employed.

In any event, as the Court itself acknowledges, "due process . . . does not require a person to apprise himself of the common law of all 50 States in order to guarantee that his actions will not subject him to punishment in light of a developing trend in the law that has not yet made its way to his State." The Court tries to counter this self-evident point with the statement that "at the same time, however, the fact that a vast number of jurisdictions have abolished a rule that has so clearly outlived its purpose is surely relevant to whether the abolition of the rule in a particular case can be said to be unexpected and indefensible by reference to the law as it then existed." This retort rests upon the fallacy that I discussed earlier: that "expected or defensible" "abolition" of prior law was approved by *Bouie.* It was not — and according such conclusive effect to the "defensibility" (by which I presume the Court means the "reasonableness") of the change in law will validate the retroactive creation of many new crimes.

Finally, the Court seeks to establish fair warning by discussing at great length how unclear it was that the year-and-a-day rule was ever the law in Tennessee. As I have already observed, the Supreme Court of Tennessee is the authoritative expositor of Tennessee law, and has said categorically that the year-and-a-day rule was the law. Does this Court mean to establish the principle that fair warning of impending change exists — or perhaps fair warning can be dispensed with — when the prior law is not crystal clear? Yet another boon for retroactively created crimes.

I reiterate that the only "fair warning" discussed in our precedents, and the only "fair warning" relevant to the issue before us here, is fair warning *of what the law is.* That warning, unlike the new one that today's opinion invents, goes well beyond merely "safeguarding defendants against *unjustified* and *unpredictable* breaks with prior law." It safeguards them against *changes in the law after the fact.* But even accepting the Court's novel substitute, the opinion's conclusion that this watered-down standard has been met seems to me to proceed on the principle that a large number of almost-valid arguments makes a solid case. As far as I can tell, petitioner has nothing that could fairly be called a "warning" that the Supreme Court of Tennessee would retroactively eliminate one of the elements of the crime of murder.

To decide this case, we need only conclude that due process prevents a court from (1) acknowledging the validity, when they were rendered, of prior decisions establishing a particular element of a crime; (2) changing the prior law so as to eliminate that element; and (3) applying that change to conduct that occurred under the prior regime. A court would remain free to apply common-law criminal rules to new fact patterns so long as that application is consistent with a fair reading of prior cases. It would remain free to conclude that a prior decision or series of decisions establishing a particular element of a crime was in error, or to apply that conclusion retroactively (so long as the "fair notice" requirement of *Bouie* is satisfied). It would even remain free, insofar as the *ex post facto* element of the Due Process Clause is concerned, to "reevaluate and refine" the elements of common-law crimes to its heart's content, so long as it does so prospectively. (The majority of the state courts that have abolished the year-and-a-day rule have done so in this fashion.) And, of course (as Blackstone and the Framers envisioned), legislatures would be free to eliminate outmoded elements of common-law crimes for the future *by law*. But what a court cannot do, consistent with due process, is what the Tennessee Supreme Court did here: avowedly *change* (to the defendant's disadvantage) the criminal law governing past acts.

For these reasons, I would reverse the judgment of the Supreme Court of Tennessee.

Notes and Questions

---

1. Because the "retroactive" application of judicial decisions is (essentially) the norm, there appear to be very few constitutional limits to this practice. Nonetheless, the *Rogers* Court does acknowledge one, based on due process: judicial interpretations of statutes or changes to the common law that are "unexpected and indefensible by reference to the law which had been expressed prior to the conduct in issue." But how is this standard to be applied? What is a state (or federal) court to do when the change it is trying to make falls into this category? Is it forever prohibited from changing that area of the law? And what about Justice Scalia's approach? In light of the Court's jurisprudence in this area, is prospectivity a realistic option?

2. For arguments that due process considerations should apply with respect to applications of stare decisis—i.e., the idea that nonparties also should be bound by prior judicial decisions in which they did not participate—see Amy Coney Barrett, *Stare Decisis and Due Process*, 74 U. Colo. L. Rev. 1011 (2003), and Max Minzner, *Saving Stare Decisis: Preclusion, Precedent, and Procedural Due Process*, 2010 BYU L. Rev. 597.

Q. LEGISLATIVE VERSUS JUDICIAL RESOLUTION

Sometimes a court will decline to decide an issue in deference to possible future resolution by the legislature. But to not decide is to decide. Thus, when a court states that an issue is more appropriately decided by the legislature, it is actually making at least two decisions: that decision (i.e., the legislature-versus-court decision), and (perhaps by implication) the decision as to the underlying dispute, which presumably will be "decided" by default.

Regarding this issue, Professors Hart and Sacks rather pointedly state:

> For the Supreme Court to put as crucial for decision the question, "Is it wiser and more appropriate for the law with respect to this matter to be developed legislatively or judicially?" is to pose an issue which the Court does not have jurisdiction to determine. It is for the Congress to determine whether federal law should or should not be developed legislatively. The Court has no writ to control the judgment of the Congress on this matter. And it ought not to have. For the determination whether legislatively developed law in the form of an enactment is to be preferred to judicially developed law in the form of reasoned ground for decision is inherently and inescapably discretionary. Upon such a question the Anglo-American legal tradition yields no principles of decision which are susceptible of reasoned elaboration and of even-handed and impartial application now in one field of law and then in another. The determination, therefore, is one which ought to be made by a political arm of the government. By the same token, it is one which ought not to be made by the judicial arm.
>
> What the Justices are *not* empowered to do should be contrasted with what they *are* empowered to do — and obliged, by the deepest presuppositions of the legal order, to do faithfully and as wisely as may be. They are *not* commissioned to decide whether the method of legislative growth of the law is to be preferred to the method of judicial growth. They *are* commissioned to "administer justice."[5] Does it not follow, then, that any discussion in a judicial opinion of the legislature as a preferable forum is both irrelevant and eyewash *unless it can be shown to have a rational bearing upon the question of what constitutes a just decision of the case before the court*?

HENRY M. HART, JR. & ALBERT M. SACKS, THE LEGAL PROCESS: BASIC PROBLEMS IN THE MAKING AND APPLICATION OF LAW 517 (William N. Eskridge, Jr. & Philip P. Frickey eds., 1994).

Notes and Questions

1. The above discussion provides a few of the reasons why courts should decide cases rather than defer to the legislature. Note that a judicial resolution also might assist a legislature should the latter decide to become involved, and (if

---

5. The full text of 28 U.S.C. § 453 (1948), which prescribes the form of oath for federal judges, is as follows (emphasis added):

> Each justice or judge of the United States shall take the following oath or affirmation before performing the duties of his office: "I, do solemnly swear (or affirm) that I *will administer justice without respect to persons, and do equal right to the poor and to the rich,* and that I will faithfully and impartially discharge and perform all the duties incumbent upon me as according to the best of my abilities and understanding, agreeably to the Constitution and laws of the United States. So help me God."

the issue is time-sensitive) might be the only means of achieving a just resolution. Are there any other, possible reasons?

On the other hand, might there nonetheless be valid (even if not conclusive) reasons why a court might defer? For example, might deference sometimes be the more politically expedient course? Are there some problems that are not well suited for judicial resolution? (Recall, for example, Professor Fuller's discussion of "polycentric" problems.) Might a court's limited time sometimes be better spent on other matters? Can you think of any other reasons to the contrary?

SIDEBAR: LEGISLATIVE VERSUS ADJUDICATIVE FACTS AND RELATIVE INSTITUTIONAL COMPETENCE

Part of what is lurking behind the judicial-versus-legislative resolution debate might be the differences between what are known as "adjudicative" facts as opposed to "legislative" facts. As summarized by Brianne J. Gorod, *The Adversarial Myth: Appellate Court Extra-Record Factfinding*, 61 Duke L.J. 101 (2011):

> In the vast majority of cases, courts apply settled principles of law to disputed facts; the main work of the court is to resolve the parties' disputes about what happened to whom and when. How the court resolves those disputes will determine how the rule of law should be applied, but it will have no effect on the rule of law itself. These facts related to the particular parties before the court — so-called "adjudicative facts" — are what courts and commentators most often have in mind when they refer to the "facts of the case."[123]
>
> But there is another kind of fact that is no less important (and, in fact, arguably more important) to the courts' resolution of legal disputes. Unlike "adjudicative" facts that deal with the particular, so-called "legislative" facts deal with the general, providing descriptive (and sometimes predictive) information about the larger world. Not to be confused with facts found by a legislature, they are often called "legislative" facts because they are general and used in the course of developing legal rules. These legislative facts can take various forms; they might help the court understand the history of a given practice, identify current realities, or make predictions about the effects of different legal rules that the Court might adopt. While there will be many cases in which legislative facts will play no role at all, when they do play a role, they are often critical.

---

123. In perhaps the most famous scene in the classic film *The Paper Chase*, the movie's protagonist is asked to "recite the facts of Hawkins versus McGee." The facts he was expected to recite were these "adjudicative facts," background facts about what happened to the plaintiff that brought him into court — namely, that his hand had been injured, the doctor made it worse when he operated, and the plaintiff now sought compensation for his "hairy hand." *See* The Paper Chase (Thompson Films 1973); *see also* Hawkins v. McGee, 146 A. 641 (N.J. 1929).

. . . .

> Despite the significant distinction between adjudicative and legislative facts, there is no established manner for courts to find legislative facts. . . .
>
> . . . .
>
> In fact, the primary federal rule that governs courts' finding of facts not presented by the parties explicitly excludes from its ambit the finding of legislative facts. Federal Rule of Evidence 201 provides that courts, "whether requested or not," can take "judicial notice" of a fact "not subject to reasonable dispute in that it is either (1) generally known within the territorial jurisdiction of the trial court or (2) capable of accurate and ready determination by resort to sources whose accuracy cannot reasonably be questioned." But the rule explicitly provides that "this rule governs only judicial notice of adjudicative facts." Thus, the rule's requirement that a party, "upon timely request," be given "an opportunity to be heard as to the propriety of taking judicial notice and the tenor of the matter noticed" does not apply to legislative facts.

Id. at 131-32, 134-36 (some footnotes omitted).

For more on "legislative fact" fact finding by the Supreme Court, see Allison Orr Larsen, *Confronting Supreme Court Fact Finding*, 98 VA. L. REV. 1255 (2012).

Generally speaking, between Congress and the federal judiciary, which institution do you believe is more competent at finding adjudicative facts? Legislative facts? *Cf. Turner Broadcasting System, Inc. v. FCC*, 520 U.S. 180, 195 (1997) ("We owe Congress' findings deference in part because the institution is far better equipped to amass and evaluate the vast amounts of data bearing upon legislative questions.") (citations and internal quotation marks omitted).

Recall also Professor Fuller's discussion of polycentric problems and how such problems are "unsuited to solution by adjudication" (*supra* at 40-43). Are such problems more amenable to legislative, or perhaps administrative, solution?

R. JUDICIAL IMPARTIALITY

Professor Fuller stresses the need for impartiality on the part of the arbiter. How does this play out in practice?

Cheney v. United States District Court for the District of Columbia, No. 03-475
Memorandum of Justice Scalia
541 U.S. 913 (2004)

I have before me a motion to recuse in these cases consolidated below. The motion is filed on behalf of respondent Sierra Club. The other private respondent, Judicial

Watch, Inc., does not join the motion and has publicly stated that it "does not believe the presently-known facts about the hunting trip satisfy the legal standards requiring recusal." (The District Court, a nominal party in this mandamus action, has of course made no appearance.) Since the cases have been consolidated, however, recusal in the one would entail recusal in the other.

I

The decision whether a judge's impartiality can "'reasonably be questioned'" is to be made in light of the facts as they existed, and not as they were surmised or reported. The facts here were as follows:

For five years or so, I have been going to Louisiana during the Court's long December-January recess, to the duck-hunting camp of a friend whom I met through two hunting companions from Baton Rouge, one a dentist and the other a worker in the field of handicapped rehabilitation. The last three years, I have been accompanied on this trip by a son-in-law who lives near me. Our friend and host, Wallace Carline, has never, as far as I know, had business before this Court. He is not, as some reports have described him, an "energy industry executive" in the sense that summons up boardrooms of ExxonMobil or Con Edison. He runs his own company that provides services and equipment rental to oil rigs in the Gulf of Mexico.

During my December 2002 visit, I learned that Mr. Carline was an admirer of Vice President Cheney. Knowing that the Vice President, with whom I am well acquainted (from our years serving together in the Ford administration), is an enthusiastic duck hunter, I asked whether Mr. Carline would like to invite him to our next year's hunt. The answer was yes; I conveyed the invitation (with my own warm recommendation) in the spring of 2003 and received an acceptance (subject, of course, to any superseding demands on the Vice President's time) in the summer. The Vice President said that if he did go, I would be welcome to fly down to Louisiana with him. (Because of national security requirements, of course, he must fly in a Government plane.) That invitation was later extended — if space was available — to my son-in-law and to a son who was joining the hunt for the first time; they accepted. The trip was set long before the Court granted certiorari in the present case, and indeed before the petition for certiorari had even been filed.

We departed from Andrews Air Force Base at about 10 a.m. on Monday, January 5, flying in a Gulfstream jet owned by the Government. We landed in Patterson, Louisiana, and went by car to a dock where Mr. Carline met us, to take us on the 20-minute boat trip to his hunting camp. We arrived at about 2 p.m., the 5 of us joining about 8 other hunters, making about 13 hunters in all; also present during our time there were about 3 members of Mr. Carline's staff, and, of course, the Vice President's staff and security detail. It was not an intimate setting. The group hunted that afternoon and Tuesday and Wednesday mornings; it fished (in two boats) Tuesday afternoon. All meals were in common. Sleeping was in rooms of two or three, except for the Vice President, who had his own quarters. Hunting was in two- or three-man blinds. As it turned out, I never hunted in the same blind with the Vice President. Nor was I alone with him at any time during the trip, except, perhaps, for instances so brief and unintentional that I would not recall them — walking to or from a boat, perhaps, or going to or from dinner. Of course we said not a word about the present case. The Vice President left the camp Wednesday afternoon, about two days after our arrival. I stayed on to hunt (with my son and son-in-law) until late Friday morning, when the three of us returned to Washington on a commercial flight from New Orleans.

II

Let me respond, at the outset, to Sierra Club's suggestion that I should "resolve any doubts in favor of recusal." That might be sound advice if I were sitting on the Court of Appeals. There, my place would be taken by another judge, and the case would proceed normally. On the Supreme Court, however, the consequence is different: The Court proceeds with eight Justices, raising the possibility that, by reason of a tie vote, it will find itself unable to resolve the significant legal issue presented by this case. Thus, as Justices stated in their 1993 Statement of Recusal Policy: "We do not think it would serve the public interest to go beyond the requirements of the statute, and to recuse ourselves, out of an excess of caution, whenever a relative is a partner in the firm before us or acted as a lawyer at an earlier stage. Even one unnecessary recusal impairs the functioning of the Court." Moreover, granting the motion is (insofar as the outcome of the particular case is concerned) effectively the same as casting a vote against the petitioner. The petitioner needs five votes to overturn the judgment below, and it makes no difference whether the needed fifth vote is missing because it has been cast for the other side, or because it has not been cast at all.

Even so, recusal is the course I must take — and will take — when, on the basis of established principles and practices, I have said or done something which requires that course. I have recused for such a reason this very Term. See *Elk Grove Unified School Dist.* v. *Newdow*, 540 U.S. 945 (cert. granted, Oct. 14, 2003). I believe, however, that established principles and practices do not require (and thus do not permit) recusal in the present case.

A

My recusal is required if, by reason of the actions described above, my "impartiality might reasonably be questioned." 28 U.S.C. § 455(a). Why would that result follow from my being in a sizable group of persons, in a hunting camp with the Vice President, where I never hunted with him in the same blind or had other opportunity for private conversation? The only possibility is that it would suggest I am a friend of his. But while friendship is a ground for recusal of a Justice where the personal fortune or the personal freedom of the friend is at issue, it has traditionally *not* been a ground for recusal where *official action* is at issue, no matter how important the official action was to the ambitions or the reputation of the Government officer.

A rule that required Members of this Court to remove themselves from cases in which the official actions of friends were at issue would be utterly disabling. Many Justices have reached this Court precisely because they were friends of the incumbent President or other senior officials — and from the earliest days down to modern times

Justices have had close personal relationships with the President and other officers of the Executive. John Quincy Adams hosted dinner parties featuring such luminaries as Chief Justice Marshall, Justices Johnson, Story, and Todd, Attorney General Wirt, and Daniel Webster. Justice Harlan and his wife often "'stopped in'" at the White House to see the Hayes family and pass a Sunday evening in a small group, visiting and singing hymns. Justice Stone tossed around a medicine ball with members of the Hoover administration mornings outside the White House. Justice Douglas was a regular at President Franklin Roosevelt's poker parties; Chief Justice Vinson played poker with President Truman. A no-friends rule would have disqualified much of the Court in *Youngstown Sheet & Tube Co.* v. *Sawyer*, 343 U.S. 579 (1952), the case that challenged President Truman's seizure of the steel mills. Most of the Justices knew Truman well, and four had been appointed by him. A no-friends rule would surely have required Justice Holmes's recusal in *Northern Securities Co.* v. *United States*, 193 U.S. 197 (1904).

It is said, however, that this case is different because the federal officer (Vice President Cheney) is actually a *named party*. That is by no means a rarity. At the beginning of the current Term, there were before the Court (excluding habeas actions) no fewer than 83 cases in which high-level federal Executive officers were named in their official capacity — more than 1 in every 10 federal civil cases then pending. That an officer is named has traditionally made no difference to the proposition that friendship is not considered to affect impartiality in official-action suits. Regardless of whom they name, such suits, when the officer is the plaintiff, seek relief not for him personally but for the Government; and, when the officer is the defendant, seek relief not against him personally, but against the Government. That is why federal law provides for *automatic substitution* of the new officer when the originally named officer has been replaced. The caption of Sierra Club's complaint in this action designates as a defendant "Vice President Cheney, *in his official capacity* as Vice President of the United States and Chairman of the National Energy Policy Development Group." . . . Sierra Club has *relied* upon the fact that this is an official-action rather than a personal suit as a basis for denying the petition. . . .

Richard Cheney's name appears in this suit only because he was the head of a Government committee that allegedly did not comply with the Federal Advisory Committee Act, and because he may, by reason of his office, have custody of some or all of the Government documents that the plaintiffs seek. If some other person were to become head of that committee or to obtain custody of those documents, the plaintiffs would name that person and Cheney would be dismissed. Unlike the defendant in *United States* v. *Nixon*, or *Clinton* v. *Jones*, Cheney is represented here, not by his personal attorney, but by the United States Department of Justice in the person of the Solicitor General. And the courts at all levels have referred to his arguments as (what they are) the arguments of "the government."

The recusal motion, however, asserts the following:

> "Critical to the issue of Justice Scalia's recusal is understanding that this is not a run-of-the-mill legal dispute about an administrative decision. Because his own conduct is central to this case, the Vice President's 'reputation and his integrity are on the line.' (Chicago Tribune.)"

I think not. Certainly as far as the legal issues immediately presented to me are concerned, this *is* "a run-of-the-mill legal dispute about an administrative decision." I am asked to determine what powers the District Court possessed under FACA, and whether the Court of Appeals should have asserted mandamus or appellate jurisdiction over the District Court. Nothing this Court says on those subjects will have any bearing upon the reputation and integrity of Richard Cheney. Moreover, even if this Court affirms the decision below and allows discovery to proceed in the District Court, the issue that would ultimately present itself *still* would have no bearing upon the reputation and integrity of Richard Cheney. That issue would be, quite simply, whether some private individuals were *de facto* members of the National Energy Policy Development Group (NEPDG). It matters not whether they were caused to be so by Cheney or someone else, or whether Cheney was even aware of their *de facto* status; if they *were de facto* members, then (according to D.C. Circuit law) the records and minutes of NEPDG would be made public.

The recusal motion asserts, however, that Richard Cheney's " 'reputation and his integrity are on the line' " because

> "respondents have alleged, *inter alia*, that the Vice President, as the head of the Task Force and its sub-groups, was responsible for the involvement of energy industry executives in the operations of the Task Force, as a result of which the Task Force and its sub-groups became subject to FACA."

As far as Sierra Club's *complaint* is concerned, it simply is not true that Vice President Cheney is singled out as having caused the involvement of energy executives. But even if the allegation had been made, it would be irrelevant to the case. FACA assertedly requires disclosure if there were private members of the task force, *no matter who* they were — "energy industry executives" or Ralph Nader; and *no matter who* was responsible for their membership — the Vice President or no one in particular. I do not see how the Vice President's " 'reputation and integrity are on the line' " any more than the agency head's reputation and integrity are on the line in virtually all official-action suits, which accuse his agency of acting (to quote the Administrative Procedure Act) "arbitrarily, capriciously, with an abuse of discretion, or otherwise not in accordance with law." Beyond the always-present accusation, there is nothing illegal or immoral about making "energy industry executives" members of a task force on energy; some people probably think it would be a good idea. If, in doing so, or in allowing it to happen, the Vice President went beyond his assigned powers, that is no worse than what every agency head has done when his action is judicially set aside.

To be sure, there could be political consequences from disclosure of the fact (if it be so) that the Vice President favored business interests, and especially a sector of business with which he was formerly connected. But political consequences are not my concern, and the possibility of them does not convert an official suit into a private one. That possibility exists to a greater or lesser degree in virtually all suits involving agency action. To expect judges to take account of political consequences — and to assess the high or low degree of them — is to ask judges to do precisely what they should not do. It seems to me quite wrong (and quite impossible) to make recusal depend upon what degree of political damage a particular case can be expected to inflict.

In sum, I see nothing about this case which takes it out of the category of normal official-action litigation, where my friendship, or the appearance of my friendship, with one of the named officers does not require recusal.

B

The recusal motion claims that "the fact that Justice Scalia and his daughter were the Vice President's guest on Air Force Two on the flight down to Louisiana" means that I "accepted a sizable gift from a party in a pending case," a gift "measured in the thousands of dollars."

Let me speak first to the value, though that is not the principal point. Our flight down cost the Government nothing, since space-available was the condition of our invitation. And, though our flight down on the Vice President's plane was indeed free, since we were not returning with him we purchased (because they were least expensive) round-trip tickets that cost precisely what we would have paid if we had gone both down and back on commercial flights. In other words, none of us saved a cent by flying on the Vice President's plane. . . .

The principal point, however, is that social courtesies, provided at Government expense by officials whose only business before the Court is business in their official capacity, have not hitherto been thought prohibited. Members of Congress and others are frequently invited to accompany Executive Branch officials on Government planes, where space is available. That this is not the sort of gift thought likely to affect a judge's impartiality is suggested by the fact that the Ethics in Government Act of 1978, which requires annual reporting of transportation provided or reimbursed, excludes annual reporting of transportation provided by the United States. I daresay that, at a hypothetical charity auction, much more would be bid for dinner for two at the White House than for a one-way flight to Louisiana on the Vice President's jet. Justices accept the former with regularity. While this matter was pending, Justices and their spouses were invited (*all* of them, I believe) to a December 11, 2003, Christmas reception at the residence of the Vice President — which included an opportunity for a photograph with the Vice President and Mrs. Cheney. Several of the Justices attended, and in doing so were fully in accord with the proprieties.

III

When I learned that Sierra Club had filed a recusal motion in this case, I assumed that the motion would be replete with citations of legal authority, and would provide some instances of cases in which, because of activity similar to what occurred here, Justices have recused themselves or at least have been asked to do so. In fact, however, the motion cites only two Supreme Court cases assertedly relevant to the issue here discussed, and nine Court of Appeals cases. Not a single one of these even involves an official action suit. And the motion gives not a single instance in which, under even remotely similar circumstances, a Justice has recused or been asked to recuse. Instead, the argument section of the motion consists almost entirely of references to, and quotations from, newspaper editorials.

The core of Sierra Club's argument is as follows:

"Sierra Club makes this motion because damage to the integrity of the system is being done right now. As of today, 8 of the 10 newspapers with the largest circulation in the United States, 14 of the largest 20, and 20 of the largest 30 have called on Justice Scalia to step aside. Of equal import, there is no counterbalance or controversy: not a single newspaper has argued against recusal. Because the American public, as reflected in the nation's newspaper editorials, has unanimously concluded that there is an appearance of favoritism, any objective observer would be compelled to conclude that Justice Scalia's impartiality has been questioned. These facts more than satisfy Section 455(a), which mandates recusal merely when a Justice's impartiality 'might reasonably be questioned.'"

The implications of this argument are staggering. I must recuse because a significant portion of the press, which is deemed to be the American public, demands it.

The motion attaches as exhibits the press editorials on which it relies. Many of them do not even have the facts right. . . .

. . . With regard to the *law*, the vast majority of the editorials display no recognition of the central proposition that a federal officer is not ordinarily regarded to be a personal party in interest in an official-action suit. And those that do display such recognition facilely assume, contrary to all precedent, that in such suits mere political damage (which they characterize as a destruction of Cheney's reputation and integrity) is ground for recusal. Such a blast of largely inaccurate and uninformed opinion cannot determine the recusal question. It is well established that the recusal inquiry must be "made from the perspective of a *reasonable* observer who is *informed of all the surrounding facts and circumstances*."

IV

While Sierra Club was apparently unable to summon forth a single example of a Justice's recusal (or even motion for a Justice's recusal) under circumstances similar to those here, I have been able to accomplish the seemingly more difficult task of finding a couple of examples establishing the negative: that recusal or motion for recusal did *not* occur under circumstances similar to those here.

[Justice Scalia provided examples involving personal relationships between Justice White and Robert Kennedy and between Justice Jackson and Franklin Roosevelt.]

V

Since I do not believe my impartiality can reasonably be questioned, I do not think it would be proper for me to recuse. That alone is conclusive; but another consideration moves me in the same direction: Recusal would in my judgment harm the Court. If I were to withdraw from this case, it would be because some of the press has argued that the Vice President would suffer political damage *if* he should lose this appeal, and *if*, on remand, discovery should establish that energy industry representatives were *de facto* members of NEPDG — and because some of the press has elevated that possible political damage to the status of an impending stain on the reputation and integrity of the Vice President. But since political damage often comes from the Government's losing official-action suits; and since political damage can readily be characterized as a stain on reputation and integrity; recusing in the face of such charges would give elements of the press a veto over participation of any Justices who had social contacts with, or were even known to be friends of, a named official. That is intolerable.

My recusal would also encourage so-called investigative journalists to suggest improprieties, and demand recusals, for other inappropriate (and increasingly silly) reasons. The Los Angeles Times has already suggested that it was improper for me to sit on a case argued by a law school dean whose school I had visited several weeks before — visited not at his invitation, but at his predecessor's. The same paper has asserted that it was improper for me to speak at a dinner honoring Cardinal Bevilacqua given by the Urban Family Council of Philadelphia because (according to the Times's false report) that organization was engaged in litigation seeking to prevent same-sex civil unions, and I had before me a case presenting the question (whether same-sex civil unions were lawful? — no) whether homosexual sodomy could constitutionally be *criminalized*. While the political branches can perhaps survive the constant baseless allegations of impropriety that have become the staple of Washington reportage, this Court cannot. The people must have confidence in the integrity of the Justices, and that cannot exist in a system that assumes them to be corruptible by the slightest friendship or favor, and in an atmosphere where the press will be eager to find foot-faults.

As I noted at the outset, one of the private respondents in this case has not called for my recusal, and had expressed confidence that I will rule impartially, as indeed I will. Counsel for the other private respondent seek to impose, it seems to me, a standard regarding friendship, the appearance of friendship, and the acceptance of social favors, that is more stringent than what they themselves observe. Two days before the brief in opposition to the petition in this case was filed, lead counsel for Sierra Club, a friend, wrote me a warm note inviting me to come to Stanford Law School to speak to one of his classes. (Judges teaching classes at law schools normally have their transportation and expenses paid.) I saw nothing amiss in that friendly letter and invitation. I surely would have thought otherwise if I had applied the standards urged in the present motion.

There are, I am sure, those who believe that my friendship with persons in the current administration might cause me to favor the Government in cases brought against it. That is not the issue here. Nor is the issue whether personal friendship with the Vice President might cause me to favor the Government in cases in which *he* is named. None of those suspicions regarding my impartiality (erroneous suspicions, I hasten to protest) bears upon recusal here. The question, simply put, is whether someone who thought I could decide this case impartially despite my friendship with the Vice President would reasonably believe that I *cannot* decide it impartially because I went hunting with that friend and accepted an invitation to fly there with him on a Government plane. If it is reasonable to think that a Supreme Court Justice can be bought so cheap, the Nation is in deeper trouble than I had imagined.

As the newspaper editorials appended to the motion make clear, I have received a good deal of embarrassing criticism and adverse publicity in connection with the matters at issue here — even to the point of becoming (as the motion cruelly but accurately states) "fodder for late-night comedians." If I could have done so in good conscience, I would have been pleased to demonstrate my integrity, and immediately silence the criticism, by getting off the case. Since I believe there is no basis for recusal, I cannot. The motion is

Denied.

Notes and Questions

---

1. 28 U.S.C. § 455 (2006) ("Disqualification of justice, judge, or magistrate judge"), the statute referred to in the above opinion, provides in part:

    (a) Any justice, judge, or magistrate judge of the United States shall disqualify himself in any proceeding in which his impartiality might reasonably be questioned.

    (b) He shall also disqualify himself in the following circumstances:

    (1) Where he has a personal bias or prejudice concerning a party, or personal knowledge of disputed evidentiary facts concerning the proceeding;

    (2) Where in private practice he served as a lawyer in the matter in controversy, or a lawyer with whom he previously practiced law served during such association as a lawyer concerning the matter, or the judge or such lawyer has been a material witness concerning it;

    (3) Where he has served in governmental employment and in such capacity participated as counsel, adviser or material witness concerning the proceeding or expressed an opinion concerning the merits of the particular case in controversy;

    (4) He knows that he, individually or as a fiduciary, or his spouse or minor child residing in his household, has a financial interest in the subject matter in controversy or in a party to the proceeding, or any other interest that could be substantially affected by the outcome of the proceeding;

    (5) He or his spouse, or a person within the third degree of relationship to either of them, or the spouse of such a person:

    (i) Is a party to the proceeding, or an officer, director, or trustee of a party;

    (ii) Is acting as a lawyer in the proceeding;

    (iii) Is known by the judge to have an interest that could be substantially affected by the outcome of the proceeding;

    (iv) Is to the judge's knowledge likely to be a material witness in the proceeding.

    . . . .

    (e) No justice, judge, or magistrate judge shall accept from the parties to the proceeding a waiver of any ground for disqualification enumerated in subjection (b). Where the ground for disqualification arises only under subsection (a), waiver may be accepted provided it is preceded by a full disclosure on the record of the basis for disqualification.

In light of this statute, do you believe that Justice Scalia made the correct decision in this case? Why or why not? And what is a party to do if it disagrees with a Justice's analysis under this statute?

2. Can you think of any ways in which 28 U.S.C. § 455 might be improved?

3. In *Cheney*, the Supreme Court ultimately held in favor of the Vice-President. *See* 542 U.S. 367 (2004). Though Justice Scalia sided with Cheney, the decision was not close.

4. Many were critical of Justice Scalia's opinion in *Cheney*, including Monroe H. Freedman, *Duck-Blind Justice: Justice Scalia's Memorandum in the* Cheney *Case*, 18 GEO. J. LEGAL ETHICS 229 (2004); David Feldman, Note, *Duck Hunting, Deliberating, and Disqualification:* Cheney v. U.S. District Court *and the Flaws of 28 U.S.C. § 455(A)*, 15 B.U. PUB. INT. L.J. 319 (2006); and Timothy J. Goodson, Comment, *Duck, Duck, Goose: Hunting for Better Recusal Practices in the United States Supreme Court in Light of* Cheney v. United States District Court, 84 N.C. L. REV. 181 (2005).

5. Justice Scalia's son, Eugene, is a partner in the Washington, D.C., office of the Gibson, Dunn & Crutcher law firm. Gibson, Dunn regularly represents clients before the Supreme Court. Justice Scalia recently refused to recuse himself in a case involving Wal-Mart, a Gibson, Dunn client, on the ground that Eugene opted to exclude from his partner compensation any money attributed to the firm's Supreme Court litigation. According to a March 30, 2011 *American Bar Association Journal* article, the pay cut satisfies current Supreme Court recusal guidelines. Do you agree?

6. Seeking the disqualification of a judge can place a party (and counsel) in a difficult position, particularly when such a request is denied. For more on this rather touchy subject, see Michael Downey, *The Delicate Balance of Booting Judges: Clients deserve impartiality, but alleging that a judge can't do the job fairly is a risky undertaking*, NAT'L L.J. (online) (Nov. 4, 2013).

7. There are various non-statutory codes of judicial conduct that might have some relevance to a disqualification or recusal-type situation, the most prominent perhaps being that promulgated by the American Bar Association. *See* AMERICAN BAR ASSOCIATION, MODEL CODE OF JUDICIAL CONDUCT (2010). *See also* CODE OF CONDUCT FOR UNITED STATES JUDGES, *available at* http://www.uscourts.gov/RulesAndPolicies/CodesOfConduct/ CodeConductUnitedStatesJudges.aspx. Many states also have their own codes of judicial conduct.

Caperton v. A.T. Massey Coal Co., Inc.

129 S. Ct. 2252 (2009)

JUSTICE KENNEDY delivered the opinion for the Court.

In this case the Supreme Court of Appeals of West Virginia reversed a trial court judgment, which had entered a jury verdict of $50 million. Five justices heard the case, and the vote to reverse was 3 to 2. The question presented is whether the Due Process Clause of the Fourteenth Amendment was violated when one of the justices in the majority denied a recusal motion. The basis for the motion was that the justice had received campaign contributions in an extraordinary amount from, and through the efforts of, the board chairman and principal officer of the corporation found liable for the damages.

Under our precedents there are objective standards that require recusal when "the probability of actual bias on the part of the judge or decisionmaker is too high to be constitutionally tolerable." *Withrow* v. *Larkin*, 421 U. S. 35, 47 (1975). Applying those precedents, we find that, in all the circumstances of this case, due process requires recusal.

I

In August 2002 a West Virginia jury returned a verdict that found [Massey] liable for fraudulent misrepresentation, concealment, and tortious interference with existing contractual relations. The jury awarded [Caperton] the sum of $50 million in compensatory and punitive damages.

In June 2004 the state trial court denied Massey's post-trial motions challenging the verdict and the damages award, finding that Massey "intentionally acted in utter disregard of Caperton's rights and ultimately destroyed Caperton's businesses because, after conducting cost-benefit analyses, Massey concluded it was in its financial interest to do so." In March 2005 the trial court denied Massey's motion for judgment as a matter of law.

Don Blankenship is Massey's chairman, chief executive officer, and president. After the verdict but before the appeal, West Virginia held its 2004 judicial elections. Knowing the Supreme Court of Appeals would consider the appeal in the case, Blankenship decided to support an attorney who sought to replace Justice McGraw. Justice McGraw was a candidate for reelection to that court. The attorney who sought to replace him was Brent Benjamin.

In addition to contributing the $1,000 statutory maximum to Benjamin's campaign committee, Blankenship donated almost $2.5 million to "And For The Sake Of The Kids," a political organization formed under 26 U. S. C. §527. The §527 organization opposed McGraw and supported Benjamin. Blankenship's donations accounted for more than two-thirds of the total funds it raised. This was not all. Blankenship spent, in addition, just over $500,000 on independent expenditures — for direct mailings and letters soliciting donations as well as television and newspaper advertisements — "to support Brent Benjamin."

To provide some perspective, Blankenship's $3 million in contributions were more than the total amount spent by all other Benjamin supporters and three times the amount spent by Benjamin's own committee. Caperton contends that Blankenship spent $1 million more than the total amount spent by the campaign committees of both candidates combined.

Benjamin won. He received 382,036 votes (53.3%), and McGraw received 334,301 votes (46.7%).

In October 2005, before Massey filed its petition for appeal in West Virginia's highest court, Caperton moved to disqualify now-Justice Benjamin under the Due Process Clause and the West Virginia Code of Judicial Conduct, based on the conflict caused by Blankenship's campaign involvement. Justice Benjamin denied the motion in April 2006. He indicated that he "carefully considered the bases and accompanying exhibits proffered by the movants." But he found "no objective information to show that this Justice has a bias for or against any litigant, that this Justice has prejudged the matters which comprise this litigation, or that this Justice will be anything but fair and impartial." In December 2006 Massey filed its petition for appeal to challenge the adverse jury verdict. The West Virginia Supreme Court of Appeals granted review.

In November 2007 that court reversed the $50 million verdict against Massey. The majority opinion, authored by then-Chief Justice Davis and joined by Justices Benjamin and Maynard, found that "Massey's conduct warranted the type of judgment rendered in this case." It reversed, nevertheless, based on two independent grounds — first, that a forum-selection clause contained in a contract to which Massey was not a party barred the suit in West Virginia, and, second, that res judicata barred the suit due to an out-of-state judgment to which Massey was not a party. Justice Starcher dissented, stating that the "majority's opinion is morally and legally wrong." Justice Albright also dissented, accusing the majority of "misapplying the law and introducing sweeping 'new law' into our jurisprudence that may well come back to haunt us."

Caperton sought rehearing, and the parties moved for disqualification of three of the five justices who decided the appeal. Photos had surfaced of Justice Maynard vacationing with Blankenship in the French Riviera while the case was pending. Justice Maynard granted Caperton's recusal motion. On the other side Justice Starcher granted Massey's recusal motion, apparently based on his public criticism of Blankenship's role in the 2004 elections. In his recusal memorandum Justice Starcher urged Justice Benjamin to recuse himself as well. He noted that "Blankenship's bestowal of his personal wealth, political tactics, and 'friendship' have created a cancer in the affairs of this Court." Justice Benjamin declined Justice Starcher's suggestion and denied Caperton's recusal motion.

The court granted rehearing. Justice Benjamin, now in the capacity of acting chief justice, selected Judges Cookman and Fox to replace the recused justices. Caperton moved a third time for disqualification, arguing that Justice Benjamin had failed to apply the correct standard under West Virginia law — i.e., whether "a reasonable and prudent person, knowing these objective facts, would harbor doubts about Justice Benjamin's ability to be fair and impartial." Caperton also included the results of a public opinion poll, which indicated that over 67% of West Virginians doubted Justice

Benjamin would be fair and impartial. Justice Benjamin again refused to withdraw, noting that the "push poll" was "neither credible nor sufficiently reliable to serve as the basis for an elected judge's disqualification."

In April 2008 a divided court again reversed the jury verdict, and again it was a 3-to-2 decision. Justice Davis filed a modified version of his prior opinion, repeating the two earlier holdings. She was joined by Justice Benjamin and Judge Fox. Justice Albright, joined by Judge Cookman, dissented: "Not only is the majority opinion unsupported by the facts and existing case law, but it is also fundamentally unfair. Sadly, justice was neither honored nor served by the majority." The dissent also noted "genuine due process implications arising under federal law" with respect to Justice Benjamin's failure to recuse himself.

Four months later — a month after the petition for writ of certiorari was filed in this Court — Justice Benjamin filed a concurring opinion. He defended the merits of the majority opinion as well as his decision not to recuse. He rejected Caperton's challenge to his participation in the case under both the Due Process Clause and West Virginia law. Justice Benjamin reiterated that he had no " 'direct, personal, substantial, pecuniary interest' in this case." Adopting "a standard merely of 'appearances,' " he concluded, "seems little more than invitation to subject West Virginia's justice system to the vagaries of the day — a framework in which predictability and stability yield to supposition, innuendo, half-truths, and partisan manipulations."

We granted certiorari.

II

It is axiomatic that "a fair trial in a fair tribunal is a basic requirement of due process." As the Court has recognized, however, "most matters relating to judicial disqualification do not rise to a constitutional level." The early and leading case on the subject is *Tumey* v. *Ohio*, 273 U. S. 510 (1927). There, the Court stated that "matters of kinship, personal bias, state policy, remoteness of interest, would seem generally to be matters merely of legislative discretion."

The *Tumey* Court concluded that the Due Process Clause incorporated the common-law rule that a judge must recuse himself when he has a "direct, personal, substantial, pecuniary interest" in a case. This rule reflects the maxim that "no man is allowed to be a judge in his own cause; because his interest would certainly bias his judgment, and, not improbably, corrupt his integrity." The Federalist No. 10, p. 59 (J. Cooke ed. 1961) (J. Madison). Under this rule, "disqualification for bias or prejudice was not permitted"; those matters were left to statutes and judicial codes. Personal bias or prejudice "alone would not be sufficient basis for imposing a constitutional requirement under the Due Process Clause."

As new problems have emerged that were not discussed at common law, however, the Court has identified additional instances which, as an objective matter, require recusal. These are circumstances "in which experience teaches that the probability of actual bias on the part of the judge or decisionmaker is too high to be constitutionally tolerable." *Withrow*, 421 U. S., at 47. To place the present case in proper context, two instances where the Court has required recusal merit further discussion.

A

The first involved the emergence of local tribunals where a judge had a financial interest in the outcome of a case, although the interest was less than what would have been considered personal or direct at common law.

This was the problem addressed in *Tumey*. There, the mayor of a village had the authority to sit as a judge (with no jury) to try those accused of violating a state law prohibiting the possession of alcoholic beverages. Inherent in this structure were two potential conflicts. First, the mayor received a salary supplement for performing judicial duties, and the funds for that compensation derived from the fines assessed in a case. No fines were assessed upon acquittal. The mayor-judge thus received a salary supplement only if he convicted the defendant. Second, sums from the criminal fines were deposited to the village's general treasury fund for village improvements and repairs.

The Court held that the Due Process Clause required disqualification "both because of the mayor-judge's direct pecuniary interest in the outcome, and because of his official motive to convict and to graduate the fine to help the financial needs of the village." It so held despite observing that "there are doubtless mayors who would not allow such a consideration as $12 costs in each case to affect their judgment in it." The Court articulated the controlling principle:

> "Every procedure which would offer a possible temptation to the average man as a judge
> to forget the burden of proof required to convict the defendant, or which might lead him
> not to hold the balance nice, clear and true between the State and the accused, denies the
> latter due process of law."

The Court was thus concerned with more than the traditional common-law prohibition on direct pecuniary interest. It was also concerned with a more general concept of interests that tempt adjudicators to disregard neutrality.

. . . .

B

The second instance requiring recusal that was not discussed at common law emerged in the criminal contempt context, where a judge had no pecuniary interest in the case but was challenged because of a conflict arising from his participation in an earlier proceeding. This Court characterized that first proceeding (perhaps pejoratively) as a " 'one-man grand jury.' " [*In re Murchison*, 349 U. S. 133, 133 (1955).]

. . . .

Following *Murchison* the Court held in *Mayberry* v. *Pennsylvania*, 400 U. S. 455, 466 (1971), "that by reason of the Due Process Clause of the Fourteenth Amendment a defendant in criminal contempt proceedings should be given a public trial before a judge other than the one reviled by the contemnor." The Court reiterated that this rule rest on the relationship between the judge and the defendant: "A judge, vilified as was this Pennsylvania judge, necessarily becomes embroiled in a running, bitter controversy. No one so cruelly slandered is likely to maintain that calm detachment necessary for fair adjudication."

Again, the Court considered the specific circumstances presented by the case. It noted that "not every attack on a judge disqualifies him from sitting." . . . The inquiry is an objective one. The Court asks not whether the judge is actually, subjectively biased, but whether the average judge in his position is "likely" to be neutral, or whether there is an unconstitutional "potential for bias."

III

Based on the principles described in these cases we turn to the issue before us. This problem arises in the context of judicial elections, a framework not presented in the precedents we have reviewed and discussed.

Caperton contends that Blankenship's pivotal role in getting Justice Benjamin elected created a constitutionally intolerable probability of actual bias. Though not a bribe or criminal influence, Justice Benjamin would nevertheless feel a debt of gratitude to Blankenship for his extraordinary efforts to get him elected. That temptation, Caperton claims, is as strong and inherent in human nature as was the conflict the Court confronted in *Tumey* . . . when a mayor-judge (or the city) benefited financially from a defendant's conviction, as well as the conflict identified in *Murchison* and *Marberry* when a judge was the object of a defendant's contempt.

Justice Benjamin was careful to address the recusal motions and explain his reasons why, on his view of the controlling standard, disqualification was not in order. In four separate opinions issued during the course of the appeal, he explained why no actual bias had been established. He found no basis for recusal because Caperton failed to provide "objective evidence" or "objective information," but merely "subjective belief" of bias. Nor could anyone "point to any actual conduct or activity on his part which could be termed "improper." In other words, based on the facts presented by Caperton, Justice Benjamin conducted a probing search into his actual motives and inclinations; and he found none to be improper. We do not question his subjective findings of impartiality and propriety. Nor do we determine whether there was actual bias.

Following accepted principles of our legal tradition respecting the proper performance of judicial functions, judges often inquire into their subjective motives and purposes in the ordinary course of deciding a case. This does not mean the inquiry is a simple one. "The work of deciding cases goes on every day in hundreds of courts throughout the land. Any judge, one might suppose, would find it easy to describe the process which he had followed a thousand times and more. Nothing could be farther from the truth." B. Cardozo, The Nature of the Judicial Process 9 (1921).

The judge inquires into reasons that seem to be leading to a particular result. Precedent and *stare decisis* and the text and purpose of the law and the Constitution; logic and scholarship and experience and common sense; and fairness and disinterest and neutrality are among the factors at work. To bring coherence to the process, and to seek respect for the resulting judgment, judges often explain the reasons for their conclusions and rulings. There are instances when the introspection that often attends this process may reveal that what the judge assumed to be a proper, controlling factor is not the real one at work. If the judge discovers that some personal bias or improper consideration seems to be the actuating cause of the decision or to be an influence so difficult to dispel that there is a real possibility of undermining neutrality, the judge may think it necessary to consider withdrawing from the case.

The difficulties of inquiring into actual bias, and the fact that the inquiry is often a private one, simply underscore the need for objective rules. Otherwise there may be no adequate protection against a judge who simply misreads or misapprehends the real motives at work in deciding the case. The judge's own inquiry into actual bias, then, is not one that the law can easily superintend or review, though actual bias, if disclosed, no doubt would be grounds for appropriate relief. In lieu of exclusive reliance on that personal inquiry, or on appellate review of the judge's determination respecting actual bias, the Due Process Clause has been implemented by objective standards that do not require proof of actual bias. In defining these standards the Court has asked whether, "under a realistic appraisal of psychological tendencies and human weakness," the interest "poses such a risk of actual bias or prejudgment that the practice must be forbidden if the guarantee of due process is to be adequately implemented." *Withrow*, 421 U. S., at 47.

We turn to the influence at issue in this case. Not every campaign contribution by a litigant or attorney creates a probability of bias that requires a judge's recusal, but this is an exceptional case. We conclude that there is a serious risk of actual bias — based on objective and reasonable perceptions — when a person with a personal stake in a particular case had a significant and disproportionate influence in placing the judge on the case by raising funds or directing the judge's election campaign when the case was pending or imminent. The inquiry centers on the contribution's relative size in comparison to the total amount of money contributed to the campaign, the total amount spent in the election, and the apparent effect such contribution had on the outcome of the election.

Applying this principle, we conclude that Blankenship's campaign efforts had a significant and disproportionate influence in placing Justice Benjamin on the case. Blankenship contributed some $3 million to unseat the incumbent and replace him with Benjamin. His contributions eclipsed the total amount spent by all other Benjamin supporters and exceeded by 300% the amount spent by Benjamin's campaign committee. Caperton claims Blankenship spent $1 million more than the total amount spent by the campaign committees of both candidates combined.

Massey responds that Blankenship's support, while significant, did not cause Benjamin's victory. In the end the people of West Virginia elected him, and they did so based on many reasons other than Blankenship's efforts. Massey points out that every major state newspaper, but one, endorsed Benjamin. It also contends that then-Justice McGraw cost himself the election by giving a speech during the campaign, a speech the opposition seized upon for its own advantage.

Justice Benjamin raised similar arguments. . . .

Whether Blankenship's campaign contributions were a necessary and sufficient cause of Benjamin's victory is not the proper inquiry. Much like determining whether a judge is actually biased, proving what ultimately drives the electorate to choose a particular candidate is a difficult endeavor, not likely to lend itself to a certain conclusion. This is particularly true where, as here, there is no procedure for judicial factfinding and the sole trier of fact is the one accused of bias. Due process requires an objective inquiry into whether the contributor's influence on the election under all the circumstances "would offer a possible temptation to the average judge to lead him not to hold the balance nice, clear and true." In an election decided by fewer than

50,000 votes, Blankenship's campaign contributions — in comparison to the total amount contributed to the campaign, as well as the total amount spent in the election — had a significant and disproportionate influence on the electoral outcome. And the risk that Blankenship's influence engendered actual bias is sufficiently substantial that it "must be forbidden if the guarantee of due process is to be adequately implemented."

The temporal relationship between the campaign contributions, the justice's election, and the pendency of the case is also critical. . . . Just as no man is allowed to be a judge in his own cause, similar fears of bias can arise when — without the consent of the other parties — a man chooses the judge in his own cause. And applying this principle to the judicial election process, there was here a serious, objective risk of actual bias that required Justice Benjamin's recusal.

Justice Benjamin did undertake an extensive search for actual bias. But, as we have indicated, that is just one step in the judicial process; objective standards may also require recusal whether or not actual bias exists or can be proved. . . . The failure to consider objective standards requiring recusal is not consistent with the imperatives of due process. We find that Blankenship's significant and disproportionate influence — coupled with the temporal relationship between the election and the pending case — " " "offer a possible temptation to the average judge to lead him not to hold the balance nice, clear and true." " " On these extreme facts the probability of actual bias rises to an unconstitutional level.

IV

Our decision today addresses an extraordinary situation where the Constitution requires recusal. Massey and its *amici* predict that various adverse consequences will follow from recognizing a constitutional violation here — ranging from a flood of recusal motions to unnecessary interference with judicial elections. We disagree. The facts now before us are extreme by any measure. The parties point to no other instance involving judicial campaign contributions that presents a potential for bias comparable to the circumstances in this case.

. . . .

One must also take into account the judicial reforms the States have implemented to eliminate even the appearance of partiality. Almost every State — West Virginia included — has adopted the American Bar Association's objective standard: "A judge shall avoid impropriety and the appearance of impropriety." . . .

. . . .

"The Due Process Clause demarks only the outer boundaries of judicial disqualifications. Congress and the states, of course, remain free to impose more rigorous standards for judicial disqualification than those we find mandated here today." Because the codes of judicial conduct provide more protection than due process requires, most disputes over disqualification will be resolved without resort to the Constitution. Application of the constitutional standard implicated in this case will thus be confined to rare instances.

The judgment of the Supreme Court of Appeals of West Virginia is reversed, and the case is remanded for further proceedings not inconsistent with this opinion.

CHIEF JUSTICE ROBERTS, with whom JUSTICE SCALIA, JUSTICE THOMAS, and JUSTICE ALITO join, dissenting.

I, of course, share the majority's sincere concerns about the need to maintain a fair, independent, and impartial judiciary — and one that appears to be such. But I fear that the Court's decision will undermine rather than promote these values.

Until today, we have recognized exactly two situations in which the Federal Due Process Clause requires disqualification of a judge: when the judge has a financial interest in the outcome of the case, and when the judge is trying a defendant for certain criminal contempts. Vaguer notions of bias or the appearance of bias were never a basis for disqualification, either at common law or under our constitutional precedents. Those issues were instead addressed by legislation or court rules.

Today, however, the Court enlists the Due Process Clause to overturn a judge's failure to recuse because of a "probability of bias." Unlike the established grounds for disqualification, a "probability of bias" cannot be defined in any limited way. The Court's new "rule" provides no guidance to judges and litigants about when recusal will be constitutionally required. This will inevitably lead to an increase in allegations that judges are biased, however groundless those charges may be. The end result will do far more to erode public confidence in judicial impartiality than an isolated failure to recuse in a particular case.

I

There is a "presumption of honesty and integrity in those serving as adjudicators." All judges take an oath to uphold the Constitution and apply the law impartially, and we trust that they will live up to this promise. We have thus identified only *two* situations in which the Due Process Clause requires disqualification of a judge: when the judge has a financial interest in the outcome of the case, and when the judge is presiding over certain types of criminal contempt proceedings.

. . . .

Our decisions in this area have also emphasized when the Due Process Clause does *not* require recusal:

> "All questions of judicial qualification may not involve constitutional validity. Thus matters of kinship, personal bias, state policy, remoteness of interest, would seem generally to be matters of legislative discretion."

Subject to the two well-established exceptions described above, questions of judicial recusal are regulated by "common law, statute, or the professional standards of the bench and bar."

In any given case, there are a number of factors that could give rise to a "probability" or "appearance" of bias: friendship with a party or lawyer, prior employment experience, membership in clubs or associations, prior speeches and writings, religious affiliation, and countless other considerations. We have never held that the Due

Process Clause requires recusal for any of these reasons, even though they could be viewed as presenting a "probability of bias." Many state *statutes* require recusal based on a probability or appearance of bias, but "that alone would not be sufficient basis for imposing a *constitutional* requirement under the Due Process Clause." States are, of course, free to adopt broader recusal rules than the Constitution requires — and every State has — but these developments are not continuously incorporated into the Due Process Clause.

II

In departing from this clear line between when recusal is constitutionally required and when it is not, the majority repeatedly emphasizes the need for an "objective" standard. The majority's analysis is "objective" in that it does not inquire into Justice Benjamin's motives or decisionmaking process. But the standard the majority articulates — "probability of bias" — fails to provide clear, workable guidance for future cases. At the most basic level, it is unclear whether the new probability of bias standard is somehow limited to financial support in judicial elections, or applies to judicial recusal questions more generally.

But there are other fundamental questions as well. With a little help from the majority, courts will now have to determine:

[the principal dissent raised 40 hypothetical questions]

These are only a few uncertainties that quickly come to mind. Judges and litigants will surely encounter others when they are forced to, or wish to, apply the majority's decision in different circumstances. Today's opinion requires state and federal judges simultaneously to act as political scientists (why did candidate X win the election?), economists (was the financial support disproportionate?), and psychologists (is there likely to be a debt of gratitude?).

The Court's inability to formulate a "judicially discernible and manageable standard" strongly counsels against the recognition of a novel constitutional right. The need to consider these and countless other questions helps explain why the common law and this Court's constitutional jurisprudence have never required disqualification on such vague grounds as "probability" or "appearance" of bias.

III

A

To its credit, the Court seems to recognize that the inherently boundless nature of its new rule poses a problem. But the majority's only answer is that the present case is an "extreme" one, so there is no need to worry about other cases. The Court repeats this point over and over.

But this is just so much whistling past the graveyard. Claims that have little chance of success are nonetheless frequently filed. The success rate for certiorari petitions before this Court is approximately 1.1%, and yet the previous Term some 8,241 were filed. Every one of the "*Caperton* motions" or appeals or §1983 actions will claim that the judge is biased, or probably biased, bringing the judge and the judicial system into disrepute. And all future litigants will assert that their case is *really* the most extreme thus far.

Extreme cases often test the bounds of established legal principles. There is a cost to yielding to the desire to correct the extreme case, rather than adhering to the legal principle. That cost is demonstrated so often that it is captured in a legal aphorism: "Hard cases make bad law."

. . . .

B

And why is the Court so convinced that this is an extreme case? It is true that Don Blankenship spent a large amount of money in connection with this election. But this point cannot be emphasized strongly enough: Other than a $1,000 direct contribution from Blankenship, *Justice Benjamin and his campaign had no control over how this money was spent.* . . .

Moreover, Blankenship's independent expenditures do not appear "grossly disproportionate" compared to other such expenditures in this very election. . . .

It is also far from clear that Blankenship's expenditures affected the outcome of the election. . . .

It is an old cliché, but sometimes the cure is worse than the disease. I am sure there are cases where a "probability of bias" should lead the prudent judge to step aside, but the judge fails to do so. Maybe this is one of them. But I believe that opening the door to recusal claims under the Due Process Clause, for an amorphous "probability of bias," will itself bring our judicial system into undeserved disrepute, and diminish the confidence of the American people in the fairness and integrity of their courts. I hope I am wrong.

I respectfully dissent.

JUSTICE SCALIA, dissenting.

The principal purpose of this Court's exercise of its certiorari jurisdiction is to clarify the law. As THE CHIEF JUSTICE's dissent makes painfully clear, the principal consequence of today's decision is to create vast uncertainty with respect to a point of law that can be raised in all litigated cases in (at least) those 39 states that elect their judges. This course was urged upon us on grounds that would preserve the public's confidence in the judicial system.

The decision will have the opposite effect. What above all else is eroding public confidence in the Nation's judicial system is the perception that litigation is just a game, that the party with the most resourceful lawyer can play it to win, that our seemingly interminable legal proceedings are wonderfully self-perpetuating but incapable of delivering real-world justice. The Court's opinion will reinforce that perception, adding to the vast arsenal of lawyerly gambits what will come to be known as the *Caperton* claim. The facts relevant to adjudicating it will have to be litigated — and likewise the law governing it, which will be indeterminate for years to come, if not forever. Many billable hours will be spent in poring through volumes of campaign finance reports, and many more in contesting nonrecusal decisions through every available means.

A Talmudic maxim instructs with respect to Scripture: "Turn it over, and turn it over, for all is therein." Divinely inspired text may contain the answers to all earthly questions, but the Due Process Clause most assuredly does not. The Court today continues its quixotic quest to right all wrongs and repair all imperfections through the Constitution. Alas, the quest cannot succeed — which is why some wrongs and imperfections have been called nonjusticiable. In the best of all possible worlds, should judges sometimes recuse even where the clear commands of our prior due process law do not require it? Undoubtedly. The relevant question, however, is whether we do more good than harm by seeking to correct this imperfection through expansion of our constitutional mandate in a manner ungoverned by any discernible rule. The answer is obvious.

Notes and Questions

---

1. On remand, after appointing a replacement for Justice Benjamin, the Supreme Court of Appeals of West Virginia once again reversed the lower court's judgment in favor of A.T. Massey. *See* 690 S.E. 2d 322 (2009).

2. What do you think of the Court's due process standard — that recusal is required when "the probability of actual bias on the part of the judge or decision maker is too high to be constitutionally tolerable"? Is this a standard that can be easily and fairly (and predictably) applied in future cases?

3. If Justice Benjamin would have been a federal judge or justice, would his recusal have been required under 28 U.S.C. § 455 (2006)?

4. Recall Professor Fuller's discussion of impartiality as an essential component of a properly functioning adjudicative process. Does this mean that there are situations in which a judge might have to recuse himself or herself irrespective of the Constitution or any statute?

5. If *Caperton* really was an "extreme" case (as all of the Justices seem to believe), then why did the Supreme Court of the United States accept review? Should it have? In this vein, consider Justice Scalia's proposition that "[t]he principal purpose of this Court's exercise of its certiorari jurisdiction is to clarify the law."

   And what of the dissent's concern that this case would lead to the filing of "*Caperton* motions" in numerous other cases? Though it is probably too soon to appraise the full effect of *Caperton*, Westlaw and Lexis searches conducted in 2014 each revealed more than 300 case citations.

6. Justice Scalia, in his dissent, stated that 39 states elect their judges. Should judges be elected? Is that part of the problem? Consider, for example, Justice

O'Connor's concerns with respect to judicial elections as expressed in *Republican Party v. White*, 536 U.S. 765 (2002):

> I join the opinion of the Court but write separately to express my concerns about judicial elections generally. . . . I am concerned that, even aside from what candidates might say while campaigning, the very practice of electing judges undermines th[e state's] interest [in an impartial judiciary].
>
> We of course want judges to be impartial, in the sense of being free from any personal stake in the outcome of the cases to which they are assigned. But if judges are subject to regular elections they are likely to feel that they have at least some personal stake in the outcome of every publicized case. Elected judges cannot help being aware that if the public is not satisfied with the outcome of a particular case, it could hurt their reelection prospects. Even if judges were able to suppress their awareness of the potential electoral consequences of their decisions and refrain from acting on it, the public's confidence in the judiciary could be undermined simply by the possibility that judges would be unable to do so.
>
> Moreover, contested elections generally entail campaigning. And campaigning for a judicial post today can require substantial funds. Unless the pool of judicial candidates is limited to those wealthy enough to independently fund their campaigns, a limitation unrelated to judicial skill, the cost of campaigning requires judicial candidates to engage in fundraising. Yet relying on campaign donations may leave judges feeling indebted to certain parties or interest groups. Even if judges were able to refrain from favoring donors, the mere possibility that judges' decisions may be motivated by the desire to repay campaign contributors is likely to undermine the public's confidence in the judiciary.
>
> Despite these significant problems, 39 States currently employ some form of judicial elections for their appellate courts, general jurisdiction trial courts, or both. Judicial elections were not always so prevalent. The first 29 States of the Union adopted methods for selecting judges that did not involve popular elections. As the Court explains, however, beginning with Georgia in 1812, States began adopting systems for judicial elections. From the 1830's until the 1850's, as part of the Jacksonian movement toward greater popular control of public office, this trend accelerated. By the beginning of the 20th century, however, elected judiciaries increasingly came to be viewed as incompetent and corrupt, and criticism of partisan judicial elections mounted. . . .
>
> In response to such concerns, some States adopted a modified system of judicial selection that became known as the Missouri Plan (because Missouri was the first State to adopt it for most of its judicial posts). Under the Missouri Plan, judges are appointed by a high elected official, generally from a list of nominees put together by a nonpartisan nominating commission, and then subsequently stand for unopposed retention elections in which voters are asked whether the judges should be recalled. If a judge is recalled, the vacancy is filled through a new nomination and appointment. This system obviously reduces threats to judicial impartiality, even if it does not eliminate all popular pressure on judges. The Missouri Plan is currently used to fill at least some judicial offices in 15 States.
>
> Thirty-one States, however, still use popular elections to select some or all of their appellate and/or general jurisdiction trial court judges, who thereafter run for reelection periodically. Of these, slightly more than half use nonpartisan elections, and the rest use partisan elections. Most of the States that do not have any

form of judicial elections choose judges through executive nomination and legislative confirmation.

Minnesota has chosen to select its judges through contested popular elections instead of through an appointment system or a combined appointment and retention election system along the lines of the Missouri Plan. In doing so the State has voluntarily taken on the risks to judicial bias described above. As a result, the State's claim that it needs to significantly restrict judges' speech in order to protect judicial impartiality is particularly troubling. If the State has a problem with judicial impartiality, it is largely one the State brought upon itself by continuing the practice of popularly electing judges.

Id. at 788-92 (O'Connor, J., concurring). On the other hand, does the federal system, in which judges are nominated by the President and appointed with the advice and consent of the Senate, carry with it its own, equally serious problems with respect to bias?

7. After leaving the bench, Justice O'Connor has become very active in the judicial appointment area. *See, e.g.,* "The O'Connor Judicial Selection Plan," *available at* http://iaals.du.edu/initiatives/quality-judges-initiative/recommended-models/the-oconnor-judicial-selection-plan-how-it-works-why-it-matters. For more on the current state of state judicial reform, see Aaron S. Bayer, *Judicial Section Reform: All Over the Map*, Nat'l L.J. 10 (June 3, 2013).

8. ALI/UNIDROIT Principles of Transnational Civil Procedure (2004), Principle 1 ("Independence, Impartiality, and Qualifications of the Court and Its Judges") provides in part:

1.1 The court and the judges should have judicial independence to decide the dispute according to the facts and the law, including freedom from improper internal and external influence.

1.2 Judges should have reasonable tenure in office. Nonprofessional members of the court should be designated by a procedure assuring their independence from the parties, the dispute, and other persons interested in the resolution.

1.3 The court should be impartial. A judge or other person having decisional authority must not participate if there is reasonable ground to doubt such person's impartiality. There should be a fair and effective procedure for addressing contentions of judicial bias.

Similarly, Rule 10 ("Impartiality of the Court") provides in part:

10.1 A judge or other person having decisional authority must not participate if there are reasonable grounds to doubt such person's impartiality.

10.2 A party must have the right to make reasonable challenge of the impartiality of a judge, referee, or other person having decisional authority. A challenge must be made promptly after the party has knowledge of the basis for challenge.

10.3 A challenge of a judge must be heard and determined either by a judge other than the one so challenged or, if by the challenged judge, under procedure affording immediate appellate review or reconsideration by another judge.

9. For an argument that legislative control of Supreme Court recusal practices is itself unconstitutional, see Louis J. Virelli III, *The (Un)Constitutionality of Supreme Court Recusal Standards*, 2011 Wis. L. Rev. 1181.

10. For a recent article on some of the problems caused by recusals on the Supreme Court, see Tony Mauro, *Justices Kagan, Alito Recusals Adding Up in New Court Term*, Nat'l L.J. 17 (Oct. 21, 2013). For more on recusal generally, see *James Sample et al., Fair Courts: Setting Recusal Standards* (Brennan Center for Justice 2008); James Sample, *Supreme Court Recusal: From* Marbury *to the Modern Day*, 26 Geo. J. Legal Ethics 95 (2013); Symposium, *The State of Recusal: Judicial Disqualification, Due Process, and the Public's Post-*Caperton *Perception of the Integrity of the Judicial System*, 58 Drake L. Rev. 657-818 (2010); and Kristen L. Henke, Comment, *If It's Not Broke, Don't Fix It: Ignoring Criticisms of Supreme Court Recusals*, 57 St. Louis U. L.J. 521 (2013).

11. A bill was recently introduced in Congress (the "Supreme Court Ethics Act of 2013") that would require the Supreme Court to promulgate a code of ethics for the Justices of the Supreme Court. Assuming such an act would be constitutional, would it be a good idea? Why or why not?

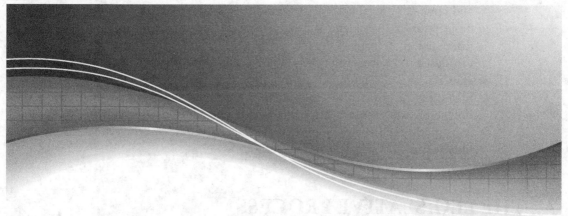

CHAPTER 3

The Legislative Branch:
The Enactment and
Interpretation of Statutes

It is difficult to overstate the importance of statutory law in modern legal practice. As one leading treatise in this area states:

> There has been an enormous increase in the use of statute law. The importance of ready access to its provisions, for lawyers and laymen alike, has also increased. The need for change, particularly in the social and economic fields, has been too rapid for the slower processes of the judicial system. Growth in the law today comes primarily from the legislature and not from the courts. No longer is the common law the starting point of most inquiries. Litigation frequently begins and ends with the statute, and when judicial action is called for, the statute is often the key to the decision.

1A NORMAN J. SINGER, STATUTES AND STATUTORY CONSTRUCTION § 28:1, at 637 (6th ed. 2002).

Statutory law is also important because of its relative supremacy. Indeed, as discussed in the Introduction, aside from the Constitution, federal statutes take priority over all other forms of law. *See* U.S. CONST. art. VI.

The purpose of this chapter, accordingly, is to provide an introduction as to how statutes (particularly federal statutes) are created and how they are interpreted and applied by legal actors (particularly by courts). The chapter will begin with a description of the federal legislative process and the codification of statutes. The discussion then turns to the interpretation of statutes and the various theories and tools used by courts (and others) to ascertain statutory meaning. The chapter concludes with a discussion of various issues relating to the application of statutes, including the issue of whether statutes apply retroactively or only prospectively; how to resolve statutory conflicts; the fate of statutes declared unconstitutional by courts; and the issue of whether Congress, by statute, may overturn federal court judgments.

A. THE LEGISLATIVE PROCESS

In order to understand statutes, it is important to understand the process by which they are made. This is true for several reasons.

For one thing, understanding the legislative process is helpful when performing statutory law research. Not only will such an understanding help you find relevant statutes, it will also help you trace the statute back to the act, and then the bill, that led to the statute. This, in turn, will help you locate materials generated in connection with that process, such as congressional committee reports, materials that can assist in ascertaining the meaning of a statute. And if a statute has been amended, understanding the legislative process will help you locate the original text of the statute and how it has changed over time.

Understanding the legislative process also helps us understand how statutes ought to be interpreted. We will explore theories of statutory interpretation later in this chapter. What you should realize now, though, is that any successful theory of statutory interpretation generally should comport with the way statutes are actually enacted. Any theory that fails to account for this reality seems destined to fail, in that it is not likely to consistently produce accurate results. *See, e.g.*, Jarrod Shobe, *Intertemporal Statutory Interpretation and the Evolution of Legislative Drafting*, 114 COLUM. L. REV. 807, 811 (2014) ("Scholars must first understand the institutional realities of how Congress works before they can create fully developed theories of statutory interpretation and fully informed prescriptive recommendations for how courts and Congress could and should interact."). In addition, viewing the entire act from which a particular code section was taken can shed new light as to the meaning of that provision that cannot be derived simply from looking at that section in isolation.

The following summary, prepared by the former Parliamentarian of the United States House of Representatives, is intended to provide a brief overview of how this process works at the federal level. You should be aware, though, that the actual process is much more complicated, and varies widely depending upon the particular legislation under consideration.

John V. Sullivan, Parliamentarian
United States House of Representatives

HOW OUR LAWS ARE MADE

July 24, 2007

I. INTRODUCTION

This brochure is intended to provide a basic outline of the numerous steps of our federal lawmaking process from the source of an idea for a legislative proposal through its publication as a statute. The legislative process is a matter about which every person should be well informed in order to understand and appreciate the work of Congress.

It is hoped that this guide will enable readers to gain a greater understanding of the federal legislative process and its role as one of the foundations of our representative system. One of the most practical safeguards of the American democratic way of life is this legislative process with its emphasis on the protection of the minority, allowing ample opportunity for all sides to be heard and make their views known. The fact that a proposal cannot become a law without consideration and approval by both Houses of Congress is an outstanding virtue of our bicameral legislative system. The open and full discussion provided under the Constitution often results in the notable improvement of a bill by amendment before it becomes law or in the eventual defeat of an inadvisable proposal.

As the majority of laws originate in the House of Representatives, this discussion will focus principally on the procedure in that body.

II. THE CONGRESS

Article I, Section 1, of the United States Constitution, provides that:

> All legislative Powers herein granted shall be vested in a Congress of the United States, which shall consist of a Senate and House of Representatives.

The Senate is composed of 100 Members — two from each state, regardless of population or area — elected by the people in accordance with the 17th Amendment to the Constitution. The 17th Amendment changed the former constitutional method under which Senators were chosen by the respective state legislatures. A Senator must be at least 30 years of age, have been a citizen of the United States for nine years, and, when elected, be an inhabitant of the state for which the Senator is chosen. The term of office is six years and one-third of the total membership of the Senate is elected every second year. The terms of both Senators from a particular state are arranged so that they do not terminate at the same time. Of the two Senators from a state serving at the same time the one who was elected first — or if both were elected at the same time, the one elected for a full term — is referred to as the "senior" Senator from that State. The other is referred to as the "junior" Senator. If a Senator dies or resigns during the term, the governor of the state must call a special election unless the state legislature has authorized the governor to appoint a successor until the next election, at which time a successor is elected for the balance of the term. Most of the state legislatures have granted their governors the power of appointment.

Each Senator has one vote.

As constituted in the 110th Congress, the House of Representatives is composed of 435 Members elected every two years from among the 50 states, apportioned to their total populations. The permanent number of 435 was established by federal law following the Thirteenth Decennial Census in 1910, in accordance with Article I, Section 2, of the Constitution. . . .

. . . .

A Representative must be at least 25 years of age, have been a citizen of the United States for seven years, and, when elected, be an inhabitant of the state in which the Representative is chosen. Unlike the Senate where a successor may be appointed by a governor when a vacancy occurs during a term, if a Representative dies or resigns during the term, the executive authority of the state must call a special election pursuant to state law for the choosing of a successor to serve for the unexpired portion of the term.

Each Representative has one vote.

In addition to the Representatives from each of the States, a Resident Commissioner from the Commonwealth of Puerto Rico and Delegates from the District of Columbia, American Samoa, Guam, and the Virgin Islands are elected pursuant to federal law. The Resident Commissioner, elected for a four-year term, and the Delegates, elected for two-year terms, have most of the prerogatives of Representatives including the right to vote in committees to which they are elected. . . . However, the Resident Commissioner and the Delegates do not have the right to vote on matters before the House.

Under the provisions of Section 2 of the 20th Amendment to the Constitution, Congress must assemble at least once every year, at noon on the third day of January, unless by law they appoint a different day.

A Congress lasts for two years, commencing in January of the year following the biennial election of Members. A Congress is divided into two regular sessions.

The Constitution authorizes each House to determine the rules of its proceedings. Pursuant to that authority, the House of Representatives adopts its rules on the opening day of each Congress, ordinarily on the opening day of the first session. The Senate considers itself a continuing body and operates under continuous standing rules that it amends from time to time.

Unlike some other parliamentary bodies, both the Senate and the House of Representatives have equal legislative functions and powers with certain exceptions. For example, the Constitution provides that only the House of Representatives may originate revenue bills. By tradition, the House also originates appropriations bills. As both bodies have equal legislative powers, the designation of one as the "upper" House and the other as the "lower" House is not appropriate.

The chief function of Congress is the making of laws. In addition, the Senate has the function of advising and consenting to treaties and to certain nominations by the President. Under the 25th Amendment to the Constitution, a vote in each House is required to confirm the President's nomination for Vice-President when there is a vacancy in that office. In the matter of impeachments, the House of Representatives presents the charges — a function similar to that of a grand jury — and the Senate sits as a court to try the impeachment. No impeached person may be removed without a two-thirds vote of those Senators voting, a quorum being present. The Congress under the Constitution and by statute also plays a role in presidential elections. Both Houses meet in joint session on the sixth day of January, following a presidential election, unless by law they appoint a different day, to count the electoral votes. If no candidate receives a majority of the total electoral votes, the House of Representatives, each state delegation having one vote, chooses the President from among the three candidates having the largest number of electoral votes. The Senate, each Senator having one vote, chooses the Vice President from the two candidates having the largest number of votes for that office.

III. SOURCES OF LEGISLATION

Sources of ideas for legislation are unlimited and proposed drafts of bills originate in many diverse quarters. Primary among these is the idea and draft conceived by a Member. This may emanate from the election campaign during which the Member had promised, if elected, to introduce legislation on a particular subject. The Member may have also become aware after taking office of the need for amendment to or repeal of an existing law or the enactment of a statute in an entirely new field.

In addition, the Member's constituents, either as individuals or through citizen groups, may avail themselves of the right to petition and transmit their proposals to the Member. The right to petition is guaranteed by the First Amendment to the Constitution. Similarly, state legislatures may "memorialize" Congress to enact specified federal laws by passing resolutions to be transmitted to the House and Senate as memorials. If favorably impressed by the idea, a Member may introduce the proposal in the form in which it has been submitted or may redraft it. In any event, a Member may consult with the Legislative Counsel of the House or the Senate to frame the ideas in suitable legislative language and form.

In modern times, the "executive communication" has become a prolific source of legislative proposals. The communication is usually in the form of a message or letter from a member of the President's Cabinet, the head of an independent agency, or the President himself, transmitting a draft of a proposed bill to the Speaker of the House of Representatives and the President of the Senate. Despite the structure of separation of powers, Article II, Section 3, of the Constitution imposes an obligation on the President to report to Congress from time to time on the "State of the Union" and to recommend for consideration such measures as the President considers necessary and expedient. Many of these executive communications follow on the President's message to Congress on the state of the Union. The communication is then referred to the standing committee or committees having jurisdiction of the subject matter of the proposal. The chairman or the ranking minority member of the relevant committee often introduces the bill, either in the form in which it was received or with desired changes. This practice is usually followed even when the majority of the House and the President are not of the same political party, although there is no constitutional or statutory requirement that a bill be introduced to effectuate the recommendations.

The most important of the regular executive communications is the annual message from the President transmitting the proposed budget to Congress. The President's budget proposal, together with testimony by officials of the various branches of the government before the Appropriations Committees of the House and Senate, is the basis of the several appropriation bills that are drafted by the Committee on Appropriations of the House and Senate.

The drafting of statutes is an art that requires great skill, knowledge, and experience. In some instances, a draft is the result of a study covering a period of a year or more by a commission or committee designated by the President or a member of the Cabinet. The Administrative Procedure Act and the Uniform Code of Military Justice are two examples of enactments resulting from such studies. In addition, congressional committees sometimes draft bills after studies and hearings covering periods of a year or more.

IV. FORMS OF CONGRESSIONAL ACTION

The work of Congress is initiated by the introduction of a proposal in one of four forms: the bill, the joint resolution, the concurrent resolution, and the simple resolution. The most customary form used in both Houses is the bill. During the 109th Congress (2005-2006), 10,558 bills and 143 joint resolutions were introduced in both Houses. Of the total number introduced, 6,436 bills and 102 joint resolutions originated in the House of Representatives.

For the purpose of simplicity, this discussion will be confined generally to the procedure on a measure of the House of Representatives, with brief comment on each of the forms.

Bills

A bill is the form used for most legislation, whether permanent or temporary, general or specific, public or private.

The form of a House bill is as follows:

A BILL
For the establishment, etc. [as the title may be]
Be it enacted by the Senate and House of Representatives of the United States of America in Congress assembled, That, etc.

The enacting clause was prescribed by law in 1871 and is identical in all bills, whether they originate in the House of Representatives or in the Senate.

Bills may originate in either the House of Representatives or the Senate with one notable exception. Article I, Section 7, of the Constitution provides that all bills for raising revenue shall originate in the House of Representatives but that the Senate may propose or concur with amendments. By tradition, general appropriation bills also originate in the House of Representatives.

There are two types of bills — public and private. A public bill is one that affects the public generally. A bill that affects a specified individual or a private entity rather than the population at large is called a private bill. A typical private bill is used for relief in matters such as immigration and naturalization and claims against the United States.

A bill originating in the House of Representatives is designated by the letters "H.R." followed by a number that it retains throughout all of its parliamentary stages. The letters signify "House of Representatives" and not, as is sometimes incorrectly assumed, "House resolution". A Senate bill is designated by the letter "S." followed by its number. The term "companion bill" is used to describe a bill introduced in one House of Congress that is similar or identical to a bill introduced in the other House of Congress.

A bill that has been agreed to in identical form in both bodies becomes the law of the land only after —

(1) Presidential approval; or

(2) failure by the President to return it with objections to the House in which it originated within 10 days (Sundays excepted) while Congress is in session; or

(3) the overriding of a presidential veto by a two-thirds vote in each House.

Such a bill does not become law without the President's signature if Congress by their final adjournment prevent its return with objections. This is known as a "pocket veto". For a discussion of presidential action on legislation, see Part XVIII.

Joint Resolutions

Joint resolutions may originate either in the House of Representatives or in the Senate — not, as is sometimes incorrectly assumed, jointly in both Houses. There is little practical difference between a bill and a joint resolution and the two forms are often used interchangeably. One difference in form is that a joint resolution may include a preamble preceding the resolving clause. Statutes that have been initiated as bills have later been amended by a joint resolution and vice versa. Both are subject to the same procedure except for a joint resolution proposing an amendment to the Constitution. When a joint resolution amending the Constitution is approved by two-thirds of both Houses, it is not presented to the President for approval. Rather, such a joint resolution is sent directly to the Archivist of the United States for submission to the several states where ratification by the legislatures of three-fourths of the states within the period of time prescribed in the joint resolution is necessary for the amendment to become part of the Constitution.

. . . .

A joint resolution originating in the House of Representatives is designated "H.J. Res." followed by its individual number which it retains throughout all its parliamentary stages. One originating in the Senate is designated "S.J. Res." followed by its number.

Joint resolutions, with the exception of proposed amendments to the Constitution, become law in the same manner as bills.

Concurrent Resolutions

A matter affecting the operations of both Houses is usually initiated by a concurrent resolution. In modern practice, and as determined by the Supreme Court in *INS v. Chadha*, 462 U.S. 919 (1983), concurrent and simple resolutions normally are not legislative in character since not "presented" to the President for approval, but are merely used for expressing facts, principles, opinions, and purposes of the two Houses. A concurrent resolution is not equivalent to a bill and its use is narrowly limited within these bounds. The term "concurrent", like "joint", does not signify simultaneous introduction and consideration in both Houses.

A concurrent resolution originating in the House of Representatives is designated "H. Con. Res." followed by its individual number, while a Senate concurrent resolution is designated "S. Con. Res." together with its number. . . .

Simple Resolutions

A matter concerning the rules, operation, or the opinion of either House alone is initiated by a simple resolution. A resolution affecting the House of Representatives is designated "H. Res." followed by its number, while a Senate resolution is designated "S. Res." together with its number. Simple resolutions are considered only by the body in which they are introduced. . . .

V. INTRODUCTION AND REFERRAL TO COMMITTEE

Any Member, Delegate or the Resident Commissioner from Puerto Rico in the House of Representatives may introduce a bill at any time while the House is in session by simply placing it in the "hopper", a wooden box provided for that purpose located on the side of the rostrum in the House Chamber. Permission is not required to introduce the measure. The Member introducing the bill is known as the primary sponsor. Except in the case of private bills, an unlimited number of Members may cosponsor a bill. . . .

In the Senate, a Senator usually introduces a bill or resolution by presenting it to one of the clerks at the Presiding Officer's desk, without commenting on it from the floor of the Senate. However, a Senator may use a more formal procedure by rising and introducing the bill or resolution from the floor. A Senator usually makes a statement about the measure when introducing it on the floor. . . .

In the House of Representatives, it is no longer the custom to read bills — even by title — at the time of introduction. The title is entered in the Journal and placed in the Congressional Record, thus preserving the purpose of the custom. The bill is assigned its legislative number by the Clerk. The bill is then referred as required by the rules of the House to the appropriate committee or committees by the Speaker, the Member elected by the Members to be the Presiding Officer of the House, with the assistance of the Parliamentarian. . . .

. . . .

Perhaps the most important phase of the legislative process is the action by committees. The committees provide the most intensive consideration to a proposed measure as well as the forum where the public is given their opportunity to be heard. A tremendous volume of work, often overlooked by the public, is done by the Members in this phase. There are, at present, 20 standing committees in the House and 16 in the Senate as well as several select committees. In addition, there are four standing joint committees of the two Houses, with oversight responsibilities but no legislative jurisdiction. The House may also create select committees or task forces to study specific issues and report on them to the House. A task force may be established formally through a resolution passed by the House or informally through organization of interested Members by the House leadership.

. . . .

Each committee is provided with a professional staff to assist it in the innumerable administrative details involved in the consideration of bills and its oversight responsibilities. . . .

VI. CONSIDERATION BY COMMITTEE

One of the first actions taken by a committee is to seek the input of the relevant departments and agencies about a bill. Frequently, the bill is also submitted to the General Accountability Office with a request for an official report of views on the necessity or desirability of enacting the bill into law. Normally, ample time is given for the submission of the reports and they are accorded serious consideration. However, these reports are not binding on the committee in determining whether or not to act favorably on the bill. Reports of the departments and agencies in the executive branch are submitted first to the Office of Management and Budget to determine whether they are consistent with the program of the President. Many committees adopt rules requiring referral of measures to the appropriate subcommittee unless the full committee votes to retain the measure at the full committee.

Committee Meetings

Standing committees are required to have regular meeting days at least once a month. The chairman of the committee may also call and convene additional meetings. . . .

A subpoena may be authorized and issued at a meeting by a vote of a committee or subcommittee with a majority of members present. The power to authorize and issue subpoenas also may be delegated to the chairman of the committee. A subpoena may require both testimonial and documentary evidence to be furnished to the committee. A subpoena is signed by the chairman of the committee or by a member designated by the committee.

All meetings for the transaction of business of standing committees or subcommittees, except the Committee on Standards of Official Conduct, must be open to the public, except when the committee or subcommittee, in open session with a majority present, determines by record vote that all or part of the remainder of the meeting on that day shall be closed to the public. Members of the committee may authorize congressional staff and departmental representatives to be present at any meeting that has been closed to the public. Open committee meetings may be covered by the media. Permission to cover hearings and meetings is granted under detailed conditions as provided in the rules of the House.

. . . .

Public Hearings

If the bill is of sufficient importance, the committee may set a date for public hearings. The chairman of each committee, except for the Committee on Rules, is required to make public announcement of the date, place, and subject matter of any hearing at least one week before the commencement of that hearing, unless the committee chairman with the concurrence of the ranking minority member or the committee by majority vote determines that there is good cause to begin the hearing at an earlier date. . . .

Each hearing by a committee or subcommittee, except the Committee on Standards of Official Conduct, is required to be open to the public except when the committee or subcommittee, in open session and with a majority present, determines by record vote that all or part of the remainder of the hearing on that day shall be closed to the public because disclosure of testimony, evidence, or other matters to be considered would endanger national security, would compromise sensitive law enforcement information, or would violate a law or rule of the House. . . .

. . . .

Markup

After hearings are completed, the subcommittee usually will consider the bill in a session that is popularly known as the "markup" session. The views of both sides are studied in detail and at the conclusion of deliberation a vote is taken to determine the action of the subcommittee. It may decide to report the bill favorably to the full committee, with or without amendment, or unfavorably, or without recommendation. The subcommittee may also suggest that the committee "table" it or postpone action indefinitely. Each member of the subcommittee, regardless of party affiliation, has one vote. Proxy voting is no longer permitted in House committees.

Final Committee Action

At full committee meetings, reports on bills may be made by subcommittees. Bills are read for amendment in committees by section and members may offer germane amendments. Committee amendments are only proposals to change the bill as introduced and are subject to acceptance or rejection by the House itself. A vote of committee members is taken to determine whether the full committee will report the bill favorably, adversely, or without recommendation. . . .

. . . .

VII. REPORTED BILLS

If the committee votes to report the bill to the House, the committee staff writes a committee report. The report describes the purpose and scope of the bill and the reasons for its recommended approval. Generally, a section-by-section analysis sets forth precisely what each section is intended to accomplish. All changes in existing law must be indicated in the report and the text of laws being repealed must be set out. This requirement is known as the "Ramseyer" rule. A similar rule in the Senate is known as the "Cordon" rule. Committee amendments also must be set out at the beginning of the report and explanations of them are included. Executive communications regarding the bill may be referenced in the report.

. . . .

Committee reports are perhaps the most valuable single element of the legislative history of a law. They are used by the courts, executive departments, and the public as a source of information regarding the purpose and meaning of the law.

Contents of Reports

The report of a committee on a measure must include: (1) the committee's oversight findings and recommendations; (2) a statement required by the Congressional Budget Act of 1974, if the measure is a bill or joint resolution providing new budget authority (other than continuing appropriations) or an increase or decrease in revenues or tax expenditures; (3) a cost estimate and comparison prepared by the Director of the Congressional Budget Office; and (4) a statement of general performance goals and objectives, including outcome-related goals and objectives, for which the measure authorizes funding. . . .

. . . .

In addition, each report of a committee on a public bill or public joint resolution must contain a statement citing the specific powers granted to Congress in the Constitution to enact the law proposed by the bill or joint resolution. . . .

. . . .

VIII. LEGISLATIVE OVERSIGHT BY STANDING COMMITTEES

Each standing committee, other than the Committee on Appropriations, is required to review and study, on a continuing basis, the application, administration, execution, and effectiveness of the laws dealing with the subject matter over which the committee has jurisdiction and the organization and operation of federal agencies and entities having responsibility for the administration and evaluation of those laws.

The purpose of the review and study is to determine whether laws and the programs created by Congress are being implemented and carried out in accordance with the intent of Congress and whether those programs should be continued, curtailed, or eliminated. In addition, each committee having oversight responsibility is required to review and study any conditions or circumstances that may indicate the necessity or desirability of enacting new or additional legislation within the jurisdiction of that committee, and must undertake, on a continuing basis, future research and forecasting on matters within the jurisdiction of that committee. Each standing committee also has the function of reviewing and studying, on a continuing basis, the impact or probable impact of tax policies on subjects within its jurisdiction.

. . . .

XIII. ENGROSSMENT AND MESSAGE TO SENATE

The preparation of a copy of the bill in the form in which it has passed the House can be a detailed and complicated process because of the large number and complexity of amendments to some bills adopted by the House. Frequently, these amendments are offered during a spirited debate with little or no prior formal preparation. The amendment may be for the purpose of inserting new language, substituting different words for those set out in the bill, or deleting portions of the bill. In some cases, amendments offered from the floor are written in longhand. Each amendment must be inserted in precisely the proper place in the bill, with the spelling and punctuation exactly as it was adopted by the House. It is extremely important that the Senate receive a copy of the bill in the precise form in which it has passed the House. The preparation of such a copy is the function of the Enrolling Clerk.

In the House, the Enrolling Clerk is under the Clerk of the House. In the Senate, the Enrolling Clerk is under the Secretary of the Senate. The Enrolling Clerk receives all the papers relating to the bill, including the official Clerk's copy of the bill as reported by the standing committee and each amendment adopted by the House. From this material, the Enrolling Clerk prepares the engrossed copy of the bill as passed, containing all the amendments agreed to by the House. At this point, the measure ceases technically to be called a bill and is termed "An Act" signifying that it is the act of one body of the Congress, although it is still popularly referred to as a bill. The engrossed bill is printed on blue paper and is signed by the Clerk of the House. Bills may also originate in the Senate with certain exceptions. For a discussion of bills originating in the Senate, see Part XVI.

XIV. SENATE ACTION

The Parliamentarian, in the name of the Vice President, as the President of the Senate, refers the engrossed bill to the appropriate standing committee of the Senate in conformity with the rules of the Senate. . . .

Committee Consideration

Senate committees give the bill the same detailed consideration as it received in the House and may report it with or without amendment. . . .

. . . .

After final action on the amendments the bill is ready for engrossment and the third reading, which is by title only. The Presiding Officer then puts the question on the passage and a voice vote is usually taken although a yea-and-nay vote is in order if demanded by one-fifth of the Senators present. A simple majority is necessary for passage. . . .

The original engrossed House bill, together with the engrossed Senate amendments, if any, or the original engrossed Senate bill, as the case may be, is then returned to the House with a message stating the action taken by the Senate. Where the Senate has adopted amendments, the message requests that the House concur in them.

. . . .

XV. FINAL ACTION ON AMENDED BILL

On their return to the House, the official papers relating to the amended measure are placed on the Speaker's table to await House action on the Senate amendments. . . . If the amendments are of a minor or noncontroversial nature, any Member, usually the chairman of a committee that reported the bill, may, at the direction of the committee, ask unanimous consent to take the bill with the amendments from the Speaker's table and agree to the Senate amendments. At that point, the Clerk reads the title of the bill and the Senate amendments. If there are no objections, the amendments are then declared to be agreed to, and the bill is ready to be enrolled for presentation to the President. . . .

Request for a Conference

The mere fact that each House may have separately passed its own bill on a subject is not sufficient to make either bill eligible for conference. One House must first take the additional step of amending and then passing the bill of the other House to form the basis for a conference. . . . In the case of a Senate bill with House amendments, the House may insist on the House amendments and request a conference. . . .

If the Senate agrees to the request for a conference, a similar committee is appointed by unanimous consent by the Presiding Officer of the Senate. . . .

. . . .

Custody of Papers

. . . .

A bill cannot become a law of the land until it has been approved in identical form by both Houses of Congress. When the bill has finally been approved by both Houses, all the original papers are transmitted to the Enrolling Clerk of the body in which the bill originated.

XVI. BILL ORIGINATING IN SENATE

The preceding discussion has described the legislative process for bills originating in the House. When a bill originates in the Senate, this process is reversed. . . .

XVII. ENROLLMENT

When the bill has been agreed to in identical form by both bodies — either: (1) without amendment by the second House to consider it; (2) by the first House's concurrence in the second House's amendments; or (3) by agreement in both bodies to the conference report — a copy of the bill is enrolled for presentation to the President.

The preparation of the enrolled bill is a painstaking and important task because it must reflect precisely the effect of all amendments, either by way of deletion, substitution, or addition, agreed to by both bodies. . . .

. . . .

XVIII. PRESIDENTIAL ACTION

Article I, Section 7, of the Constitution provides in part that —

> Every Bill which shall have passed the House of Representatives and the Senate, shall, before it becomes a Law, be presented to the President of the United States.

In actual practice, the Clerk, or the Secretary of the Senate when the bill originated in that body, delivers the original enrolled bill to a clerk at the White House and obtains a receipt. The fact of the delivery is then reported to the House by the Clerk. Delivery to a White House clerk has customarily been regarded as presentation to the President and as commencing the constitutional period for presidential action.

Copies of the enrolled bill usually are transmitted by the White House to the various departments interested in the subject matter so that they may advise the President on the issues surrounding the bill.

If the President approves the bill, he signs it and usually writes the word "approved" and the date. However, the Constitution requires only that the President sign it.

The bill may become law without the President's signature by virtue of the constitutional provision that if the President does not return a bill with objections within 10 days (excluding Sundays) after it has been presented to the President, it becomes law as if the President had signed it. However, if Congress by their adjournment prevent its return, it does not become law. This is known as a "pocket veto"; that is, the bill does not become law even though the President has not sent his objections to the Congress. The Congress has interpreted the President's ability to pocket veto a bill to be limited to adjournment "sine die" of a Congress and not to interim adjournments or first session adjournments where the originating House of Congress through its agents is able to receive a veto message for subsequent reconsideration by that same Congress when it reconvenes. The extent of pocket veto authority has not been definitively decided by the courts.

Notice of the signing of a bill by the President is sent by message to the House in which it originated and that House informs the other, although this action is not necessary for the act to be valid. The action is also noted in the Congressional Record.

A bill becomes law on the date of approval or passage over the President's veto, unless it expressly provides a different effective date.

Veto Message

By the terms of the Constitution, if the President does not approve the bill "he shall return it, with his Objections to that House in which it shall have originated, who shall enter the Objections at large on their Journal, and proceed to reconsider it". A bill returned with the President's objections need not be voted on at once when laid before the House since the vetoed bill can be postponed, referred to committee, or tabled before the question on passage is pending. A vetoed bill is always privileged until directly voted upon, and a motion to take it from the table or from committee is in order at any time.

The question of override is put by the Speaker as follows: "Will the House, on reconsideration, pass the bill, the objections of the President to the contrary notwithstanding?" Under the Constitution, a vote by the yeas and nays is required to pass a bill over the President's veto. The Clerk activates the electronic system and calls the roll with those in favor of passing the bill answering "Aye", and those opposed "No". If fewer than two-thirds of the Members present vote in the affirmative, a quorum being present, the bill is rejected, and a message is sent to the Senate advising that body of the House action. However, if two-thirds vote in the affirmative, the bill is sent with the President's objections to the Senate, unless that body has acted first, together with a message advising it of the action in the House.

If the Senate joins the House and votes two-thirds in the affirmative to pass the bill, the measure becomes the law of the land notwithstanding the objections of the President, and it is ready for publication as a binding statute.

Line Item Veto

From 1997 until it was declared unconstitutional in 1998, the Line Item Veto Act provided the President authority to cancel certain individual items contained in a bill or joint resolution that he had signed into law. The law allowed the President to cancel only three types of fiscal items: a dollar amount of discretionary budget authority, an item of new direct spending, and a tax change benefitting a class of 100 or fewer. While the Act has not been repealed, the Supreme Court in *Clinton* v. *City of New York*, 524 U.S. 417 (1998), struck down the Line Item Veto Act as unconstitutional.

XIX. PUBLICATION

One of the important steps in the enactment of a valid law is the requirement that it shall be made known to the people who are to be bound by it. There would be no justice if the state were to hold its people responsible for their conduct before it made known to them the unlawfulness of such behavior. In practice, our laws are published immediately upon their enactment so that the public will be aware of them.

If the President approves a bill, or allows it to become law without signing it, the original enrolled bill is sent from the White House to the Archivist of the United States for publication. If a bill is passed by both Houses over the objections of the President, the body that last overrides the veto transmits it. It is then assigned a public law number, and paginated for the Statutes at Large volume covering that session of Congress. The public and private law numbers run in sequence starting anew at the beginning of each Congress and are prefixed for ready identification by the number of the Congress. For example, the first public law of the 110th Congress is designated Public Law 110-1 and the first private law of the 110th Congress is designated Private Law 110-1.

Slip Laws

The first official publication of the statute is in the form generally known as the "slip law". In this form, each law is published separately as an unbound pamphlet. The heading indicates the public or private law number, the date of approval, and the bill number. The heading of a slip law for a public law also indicates the United States Statutes at Large citation. If the statute has been passed over the veto of the President, or has become law without the President's signature because he did not return it with objections, an appropriate statement is inserted instead of the usual notation of approval.

The Office of the Federal Register, National Archives and Records Administration prepares the slip laws and provides marginal editorial notes giving the citations to laws mentioned in the text and other explanatory details. The marginal notes also give the United States Code classifications, enabling the reader immediately to determine where the statute will appear in the Code. Each slip law also includes an informative guide to the legislative history of the law consisting of the committee report number, the name of the committee in each House, as well as the date of consideration and passage in each House, with a reference to the Congressional Record by volume, year, and date. A reference to presidential statements relating to the approval of a bill or the veto of a bill when the veto was overridden and the bill becomes law is included in the legislative history as a citation to the Weekly Compilation of Presidential Documents.

. . . Section 113 of title 1 of the United States Code provides that slip laws are competent evidence in all the federal and state courts, tribunals, and public offices.

Statutes at Large

The United States Statutes at Large, prepared by the Office of the Federal Register, National Archives and Records Administration, provide a permanent collection of the laws of each session of Congress in bound volumes. . . . Each volume contains a complete index and a table of contents. A legislative history appears at the end of each law. There are also extensive marginal notes referring to laws in earlier volumes and to earlier and later matters in the same volume.

Under the provisions of a statute originally enacted in 1895, these volumes are legal evidence of the laws contained in them and will be accepted as proof of those laws in any court in the United States.

The Statutes at Large are a chronological arrangement of the laws exactly as they have been enacted. The laws are not arranged according to subject matter and do not reflect the present status of an earlier law that has been amended.

United States Code

The United States Code contains a consolidation and codification of the general and permanent laws of the United States arranged according to subject matter under 50 title headings, largely in alphabetical order. It sets out the current status of the laws, as amended, without repeating all the language of the amendatory acts except where necessary. The Code is declared to be prima facie evidence of those laws. Its purpose is to present the laws in a concise and usable form without requiring recourse to the many volumes of the Statutes at Large containing the individual amendments.

The Code is prepared by the Law Revision Counsel of the House of Representatives. New editions are published every six years and cumulative supplements are published after the conclusion of each regular session of the Congress. The Code is also available in electronic format.

Twenty-four of the 50 titles have been revised and enacted into positive law, and one title has been eliminated by consolidation with another title. Titles that have been revised and enacted into positive law are legal evidence of the law and may be updated by direct amendment. Eventually all the titles will be revised and enacted into positive law.

Notes and Questions

1. For a graphical representation of the federal legislative process by artist Mike Wirth, see: http://www.mikewirthart.com/wp-content/uploads/2010/05/how-lawsmadeWIRTH2.jpg.

2. Of course, there are scores of books and other publications on the federal legislative process. But for a similar summary of this process, see Robert B. Dove, Parliamentarian, United States Senate, *Enactment of a Law* (updated February 1997). For an online summary of the federal legislative process, see United States House of Representatives, The Legislative Process, http://www.house.gov/content/learn/legislative_process/. For a more sophisticated (and perhaps more pragmatic) treatment, see WILLIAM N. ESKRIDGE, JR. ET AL., CASES AND MATERIALS ON STATUTORY INTERPRETATION 24-38 (2012), an excellent book on statutory interpretation generally.

3. Some might remember the Schoolhouse Rock! cartoon version of the federal legislative process, "I'm Just a Bill," which may be found at http://www.youtube.com/watch?v=tyeJ55o3El0.

4. For a recent and ambitious attempt to answer the question, "What role should the realities of the legislative drafting process play in the theories and doctrines of statutory interpretation and administrative law?," Abbe R. Gluck & Lisa Schultz Bressman, *Statutory Interpretation from the Inside—An Empirical Study of Congressional Drafting, Delegation, and the Canons: Part I*, 65 STAN. L. REV. 901, 905 (2013), see *id.* and Lisa Schultz Bressman & Abbe R. Gluck, *Statutory Interpretation from the Inside—An Empirical Study of Congressional Drafting, Delegation, and the Canons: Part II*, 66 STAN. L. REV. 725 (2014). For a recent and sophisticated chronicling of the evolution of the legislative drafting process in Congress (and how that understanding might impact statutory interpretation), see Jarrod Shobe, *Intertemporal Statutory Interpretation and the Evolution of Legislative Drafting*, 114 COLUM. L. REV. 807 (2014). Of course, the relationship between the courts and Congress is a two-way street, and Congress, no less than the courts, should always be looking for ways to improve the legislative drafting process as a normative matter and with an eye toward the way in which statutes are likely (and reasonably) to be interpreted by other political actors.

5. What happens when (or if) Congress fails to follow the constitutionally prescribed procedure for enacting statutes? For an argument that the federal legislative process should be subject to judicial review, see Ittai Bar-Simon-Tov, *The Puzzling Resistance to Judicial Review of the Legislative Process*, 91 B.U. L. REV. 1915 (2011). *See also* Hanah Metchis Volokh, *A Read-the-Bill Rule for Congress*, 76 MO. L. REV. 135 (2011).

6. The above summaries of course relate to the federal legislative process. But each state has its own, somewhat similar legislative process. Questions relating to state statutes should be answered in relation to the particular process of the enacting state.

B. STATUTES AS LAW

At the end of John V. Sullivan's summary of the federal legislative process, he spoke of portions of the United States Code as being only "prima facie evidence of those laws," whereas some titles have been "enacted into positive law" and are "legal evidence of the law." *See supra* at 443. What, exactly, do these phrases mean? The answers to these questions, which relate to the process of codification, are the topics of the following excerpt.

Mary Whisner

THE *UNITED STATES CODE*, PRIMA FACIE EVIDENCE, AND POSITIVE LAW

101 Law Libr. J. 545 (2009)

Pretty much every legal researcher in the United States has to deal with federal statutes. Even in what is mostly a state practice, federal issues arise. Just handling divorces? Think about possible social security benefits post-retirement and who will claim the kids as dependents on federal tax returns. Defending clients charged with state crimes? Remember the criminal procedure guarantees from the United States Constitution. Helping a client set up a business? Don't forget federal labor, trademark, tax, and environmental laws.

Most of us can find our way around the *United States Code, United States Code Annotated, United States Code Service,* and *United States Statutes at Large.* But I still had some questions about codification, so I went exploring, and in this article I will share with you what I learned.

THE BASIC SPIEL

First there are the basics that we often teach to students:

- When a law is enacted — passed by the House and the Senate and signed by the President — it is given a public law number reflecting when it was passed (which "Congress") and the order it came within that Congress. For example, Pub. L. No. 108-1 was the first law of the 108th Congress.[2]
- Laws are published in chronological order in United States Statutes at Large (Stat.).
- Because that chronological arrangement isn't efficient for researchers (imagine looking at every volume since 1935 to find all the amendments

---

2. An item beyond the basic spiel: this numbering system began with the 85th Congress, in 1957. *See* Charles S. Zinn, *Revision of the United States Code*, 51 Law Libr. J. 388, 389 (1958). Before then, the number of the Congress was not included.

to the Social Security Act!), the laws are sorted into subjects ("codified") in the *United States Code* (U.S.C.).

- The U.S.C. is divided into fifty titles with broad subjects — e.g., title 7, Agriculture; title 8, Aliens (i.e., immigration and naturalization); title 20, Education. You can't assume too much about the title groupings though. For instance, federal employment discrimination laws are in title 42, Public Welfare, and not title 20, Labor, as you might guess.

- Titles are divided into sections. If you look at the table of contents, you'll see that they're grouped into chapters and subchapters, but you don't cite those — just the title and the section.

- Small changes are made in codification to make cross-references work — for instance, changing a reference to a section within the act to a section in the Code.

- Private publishers put out annotated editions of the *United States Code* — *United States Code Annotated* (U.S.C.A.) and *United States Code Service* (U.S.C.S.) — that are even more useful for researchers. They include the text of the laws, with the same numbering system as U.S.C., and following each section of the code they also list relevant secondary sources and give brief summaries of cases.

- These sets are generally much more current than the U.S.C. — another big bonus for researchers. You update by checking pocket parts and supplements at the end of the sets. The versions on Westlaw or LexisNexis are even more up to date.

Sometimes a student asks, "If the U.S.C. is easier for researchers, why would we ever look at *Statutes at Large*?" I start with this answer: Sometimes you care about the whole act as Congress passed it, before it was split up and codified, and sometimes you want to see when a particular provision was added. Moreover, if there's any change in language between *Statutes at Large* and U.S.C., the language in *Statutes at Large* governs. The *United States Code* is only prima facie evidence of the law for much of the code. But some titles (marked with asterisks at the front of the bound volumes) have been enacted into positive law.

And that's where the questions can start us on our way out to sea. What is "positive law"? What difference does it really make in practice? How often does it come up that there's a typo or some other change in the *United States Code*? What other changes would there be, anyway? Why did Congress enact those titles as positive law? Is Congress going to enact any more?

After we look at sample pages from the official and annotated codes, someone often asks, "If U.S.C.A. and U.S.C.S. are so handy, why should we bother with U.S.C.?" Short answer: Because the *Bluebook* says you have to. A longer answer would add that it's often helpful to be able to see a chapter or subchapter printed on big pages without annotations to figure out how the sections fit together. Sometimes you want a copy of just the statute, without all the pages of annotations in between sections. And then one could add: "Well, because it's official, and if there's a typo in one of the others, the U.S.C. version would count." But then you'd only have somebody ask: "Come on, how often does that really happen?"

It is questions like these that I want to address here. We still won't have time to spell out all the details about positive law and codification in a short class, but we will know more ourselves and be better able to answer student questions.[6]

PRIMA FACIE EVIDENCE OF THE LAW

The *United States Code* self-referentially provides that it is "prima facie" evidence of the general and permanent laws in force at a given date — except that the titles that have been enacted as positive law are "legal evidence of the laws therein contained."[7] In contrast, the *Statutes at Large* are "legal evidence of laws."[8] The difference between prima facie and legal evidence is this:

If you go into court and cite a section of the *United States Code*, your adversary may bring in a dozen *Statutes at Large* to show that what is in the Code is not an accurate statement. As a result, he may prevail because the *Statutes at Large* are legal evidence of the law, whereas the *Code* is only prima facie evidence.[9]

And there are cases where that has happened. For example, the Treasury Department once relied on a provision in the *United States Code* that did not reflect an amendment, so the agency's regulation imposed a requirement on taxpayers that was not in the current statute. The I.R.S. tried to collect, based on the regulation, but the court went back to the *Statutes at Large* and held for the taxpayer.[10]

. . . .

WHY ONLY PRIMA FACIE EVIDENCE?

Why is the *United States Code* only prima facie evidence of the laws? The rule could certainly be otherwise. Congress could have said that the *United States Code* is the definitive statement of the law, without resort to *Statutes at Large*, as some states do for their codes. Why didn't it? The short answer is: because too many mistakes find their way into a project as big as a code of all the laws of the United States. The Senate insisted that the new code not be binding, just in case.

The first official codification of federal laws was the *Revised Statutes of the United States*. In 1873, the code was enacted as law (you'll find it in volume 18 of *Statutes at Large*), and it repealed all earlier statutes. But, alas, there were inaccuracies in the code — plenty of them. Sixty-nine errors were caught while the volume was still in production and were corrected in a statute that was published as an appendix. Over the next few years, people found 183 more errors (and one error in the correcting statute), leading to another statute with corrections.

---

6. Mike Lynch wrote an article that answers many questions about codification. Michael J. Lynch, *The U.S. Code, the Statutes at Large, and Some Peculiarities of Codification*, Legal Reference Services Q., no. 1, 1997, at 69.

7. 1 U.S.C. § 204(a) (2006).

8. *Id.* § 112.

9. Zinn, *supra* note 2, at 389-90.

10. Royer's, Inc. v. United States, 265 F.2d 615 (3d Cir. 1959).

The *Revised Statutes* were not kept up to date. Research became increasingly cumbersome . . . .

. . . .

[In 1926, Congress passed the first United States Code, but due to concerns regarding possible errors, the Senate] insisted that the code would be only prima facie evidence of the laws. And that is what was enacted — a code that purported to cover all the general and permanent laws then in effect, but allowed for the possibility of errors or omissions, to be resolved by resort to the *Statutes at Large.*

In retrospect, it appears that the Senate's caution was well placed. In 1928, the legislative reference service of the Library of Congress prepared a list of several hundred provisions of permanent law that had been left out of the *United States Code.*

Although accepting the Senate's requirement that the code be only prima facie evidence of law, Representative Roy G. Fitzgerald, the chairman of the House Committee on Revision of the Laws, hoped, that "either officially or unofficially, if time shows that this work can be relied upon, it will become more and more the exemplification of the law of the United States." Perhaps one day, Congress would be able to pass an act that "will cause the code officially to supersede and positively repeal all other legislation."

Fitzgerald said that he and his committee also had "other ambitions." They hoped to "present from time to time different titles of this code with real revisions, so that the obsolete matter may be cut out and the law may be stated tersely and clearly." He didn't serve long enough to see it happen, but eventually Congress did take up the project of revising and enacting individual titles.

TITLE BY TITLE ENACTMENT

Congress did not enact any titles as positive law for some time. But in the early years of the code, it did do some clean-up work. . . .

In 1941, several bills were introduced to codify title 1 and title 3, but it was not until July 30, 1947, that the first titles were enacted . . . .

Until 1974, codification fell under the jurisdiction of the House Judiciary Committee and "the committees with jurisdiction over the subject matter found in the titles." . . . The Office of Law Revision Counsel was created in 1974 as part of a reorganization of House governance and committees. This office has several responsibilities, including assigning places in the *United States Code* to new legislation and preparing titles for enactment as positive law.

When Congress amends a law in one of the titles it has not enacted as positive law, then it refers to the original law (for instance, the Truth in Lending Act). If it amends something in a title that is positive law (for instance, title 4), then it refers directly to the title and section being amended. . . .

When Congress enacts something new, without reference to an earlier statute, if it is general and permanent, the office assigns it to an appropriate place in the code.

Before beginning work on this piece, I had the impression that no new titles had been enacted for a long time, decades perhaps. But I was wrong. Granted, the pace of codification has been less than rocket-like, but there were two new titles in the 1990s and two in this decade. The office currently has several titles in the works. . . .

While I was surprised to see this work underway . . . what really startled me was the prospect of *new* titles. Yes, after being encompassed within 50 titles for its entire life, the *United States Code* is poised to move beyond — to 51, National and Commercial Space Programs; 52, Voting and Elections; 53, Small Business; 54, National Park System; and 55, Environment. . . .

CONCLUSION

The *United States Code* is a staple of legal research because — complex and confusing as it might be — it is much easier to use and deal with than the potentially dozens of volumes of *Statutes at Large* on a given topic. But legal researchers should be mindful that much of the *United States Code* is still only prima facie evidence of the laws, while the *Statutes at Large* are legal evidence of the laws. As more titles are enacted as positive law, the balance will shift, but it will be a very long time until the entire code is positive law.

Notes and Questions

---

1. As the Whisner article indicates, the positive law codification of the United States Code is carried out by the Office of the Law Revision Counsel of the United States House of Representatives. For more information about the work of the Office of the Law Revision Counsel, see http://uscode.house/gov.

2. As the Whisner article also indicates, the legal effect of the United States Code is governed by 1 U.S.C. § 204 (2012). As of 2013, the following titles have been enacted into positive law:

   1   General Provisions
   3   The President
   4   Flag and Seal, Seat of Government, and the States
   5   Government Organization and Employees
   9   Arbitration
   10 Armed Forces
   11 Bankruptcy
   13 Census
   14 Coast Guard

17   Copyrights
18   Crimes and Criminal Procedure
23   Highways
28   Judiciary and Judicial Procedure
31   Money and Finance
32   National Guard
34   Navy
35   Patents
36   Patriotic and National Observances, Ceremonies, and Organizations
37   Pay and Allowances of the Uniformed Services
38   Veterans' Benefits
39   Postal Service
40   Public Buildings, Property, and Works
41   Public Contracts
44   Public Printing and Documents
46   Shipping
49   Transportation
51   National and Commercial Space Programs

1 U.S.C. § 204 note (2012). Also, though title 26 is not positive law, the Internal Revenue Code (which is essentially the same) is. *See id.*

If a portion of the code has not been enacted as positive law, the ultimate authority remains the Statutes at Large. As 1 U.S.C. § 112 (2012) provides (in pertinent part):

> The United States Statutes at Large shall be legal evidence of laws, concurrent resolutions, treaties, international agreements other than treaties, proclamations by the President, and proposed or ratified amendments to the Constitution of the United States therein contained, in all the courts of the United States, the several States, and the Territories and insular possessions of the United States.

3. In *United States Nat'l Bank v. Independent Ins. Agents*, 508 U.S. 439 (1993), the Supreme Court confirmed:

> Though the appearance of a provision in the current edition of the United States Code is "prima facie" evidence that the provision has the force of law, 1 U. S. C. § 204(a), it is the Statutes at Large that provides the "legal evidence of laws," § 112, and despite its omission from the Code [a statute] remains on the books if the Statutes at Large so dictates.

United States Nat'l Bank, 508 U.S. at 448.

4. Not every statute enacted by Congress finds its way into the text of the United States Code, sometimes making statutory research difficult. This is particularly true of statutes that are not (to use Whisner's words) "general and permanent." For more on this problem, see Will Tress, *Lost Laws: What We Can't Find in the United States Code*, 40 GOLDEN GATE U. L. REV. 129 (2010).

5. For more on the federal codification process generally, see Tobias A. Dorsey, *Some Reflections on Not Reading the Statutes*, 10 Green Bag 2d 283 (2007).

6. Though the United States Code is the "official" code, there are, of course, other, unofficial codes, the two most prominent being the United States Code Annotated (U.S.C.A.) and the United States Code Service (U.S.C.S.). Because both the U.S.C.A. and the U.S.C.S. are annotated (i.e., they contain a wealth of related material, such as case citations, beyond the text of the statute in question), they are in many ways superior vehicles for performing statutory research.

   The United States Code is also available in electronic format. Perhaps the best (as well as the most reliable) such sources are those provided by the Library of Congress ("Thomas," http://thomas.loc.gov/home/thomas.php) and the Legal Information Institute at the Cornell University Law School (http://www.law.cornell.edu/uscode/text).

7. All of the states also have statutory codes that are somewhat similar to the federal code. *See* National Survey of State Laws (Richard A. Leiter ed.) (6th ed. 2008).

SIDEBAR: CODES IN CIVIL LAW COUNTRIES

Most civil law countries (such as France and Germany) also have codes, though due to their coverage and preeminence, "codification" in that context takes on a somewhat different meaning. According to *Black's Law Dictionary*, a "civil code" is a "comprehensive and systematic legislative pronouncement of the whole private, noncommercial law in a legal system of the continental civil-law tradition." Black's Law Dictionary 299 (10th ed. 2014). As one legal scholar elaborates:

> "codification" is the process by which the top authority in a political unit puts into effect for the legal system of that political unit a single, newly conceived, legally binding "code." I define a "code" in turn as a body of rules that, while not necessarily comprehensive or perfectly clear and consistent, is intended to cover all or most aspects of a major area of law within the legal system, such as civil law, criminal law, or procedural law. "Codification" excludes a reissuance or recension of an existing code of laws currently in force, or a revision of such a code unless the revision radically changes either the structure or content of that code. A "codification" is also to be distinguished from an unofficial "compilation" that constitutes a collection of legal rules (perhaps with added commentary or structure) but that does not itself have the force of law.

John W. Head, *Codes, Cultures, Chaos, and Champions: Common Features of Legal Codification Experiences in China, Europe, and North America*, 13 Duke Comp. & Int'l L. 1, 5-6 (2003). In other words, in many civil law countries, codes, where applicable, are intended to comprise essentially the whole of the binding law in that area, thus leaving courts to apply those provisions in situations in which the intended result might not be obvious (though without themselves making law, at least not formally). This means, though, that many civil law code provisions are written in extraordinarily broad terms so as to encompass a broad array of unforeseeable circumstances.

PRACTICE PROBLEM: THE FEDERAL LEGISLATIVE PROCESS

As we saw in the Sullivan excerpt, the federal legislative process typically takes the following general course:

bill → act → statute(s) (code section(s))

In practice, though, most lawyers do not monitor the legislative process itself. Rather, most lawyers simply deal with enacted statutes. But they also know that the process that led to the enactment of the statute in question often includes important information and therefore can be worth researching. Accordingly, lawyers researching the legislative history of a statute tend to think of the legislative process in reverse:

statute → statutory history → public law (act) → legislative history materials (the original bill, committee reports, etc.)

Consider, for example, a statute with which you might already be familiar: 28 U.S.C. § 1391 (2012), the general federal district court civil venue statute. As the citation indicates, this statute can be found in title 28 of the United States Code at code section 1391. If you were to locate this statute in the United States Code, the first thing you would see, of course, is the current text of this code section. But just after the statutory text, you would find a wealth of additional information (divided into several categories, including "Source," "Historical and Revision Notes," "Amendments," and effective date information), information that provides (among other things) the *history* of this statute. This history usually will tell you when the statute was first enacted and each time the statute has been amended (in chronological order). For example, with respect to 28 U.S.C. § 1391, you would notice that this statute was last amended on December 7, 2011 by Public Law 112-63 at title II, section 202, and that this amendment may be found in volume 125 of Statutes at Large ("Stat.") starting at page 763.

The Statutes at Large reference provides additional information about this 2011 amendment to 28 U.S.C. § 1391. For example, the Statutes at Large states that this amendment was part of the Federal Courts Jurisdiction and Venue Clarification Act of 2011. It also tells you how this code section was changed — what was deleted and what was added. It provides an effective date. And it provides references (or citations) to legislative history, such as the original bill numbers, a house committee report, and those portions of the Congressional Record when the bill was considered.

Additional legislative history materials relating to this Act can be found in the "Legislative History" section of the United States Code Congressional and Administrative News ("U.S.C.C.A.N."). Looking up Public Law 112-63 in U.S.C.C.A.N. leads to House Report No. 112-10, which can be found starting at 576.

To make sure that you understand this process, try repeating it with respect to another federal statute of your choice (or as selected by your instructor).

SIDEBAR: TREATIES

Treaties, like court rules (such as the Federal Rules of Civil Procedure), are generally thought to operate at essentially the same level as statutes. For example, if a treaty to which the United States is a party conflicts with a United States statute, the more recent of the two generally will take priority. *See, e.g., United States v. Dion*, 476 U.S. 734, 738 (1986). By contrast, if a treaty to which the United States is a party conflicts with a provision of the United States Constitution, the Constitution generally will take priority (at least domestically), even if such a resolution places the United States in violation of international law outside of the United States. *See, e.g., Reid v. Covert*, 354 U.S. 1, 16-17 (1957).

Perhaps the most significant, recent case on the effect of treaties is *Medellin v. Texas*, 552 U.S. 491 (2008). In *Medellin*, the Supreme Court, through Chief Justice Roberts, stated:

> This Court has long recognized the distinction between treaties that automatically have effect as domestic law, and those that — while they constitute international law commitments — do not by themselves function as binding federal law. The distinction was well explained by Chief Justice Marshall's opinion in *Foster v. Neilson*, 2 Pet. 253, 315 (1829), which held that a treaty is "equivalent to an act of the legislature," and hence self-executing, when it "operates of itself without the aid of any legislative provision." When, in contrast, "treaty stipulations are not self-executing they can only be enforced pursuant to legislation to carry them into effect." *Whitney v. Robertson*, 124 U.S. 190, 194 (1888). In sum, while treaties "may comprise international commitments they are not domestic law unless Congress has either enacted implementing statutes or the treaty itself conveys an intention that it be 'self-executing' and is ratified on these terms."

Id. at 504-05. The Court continued:

The requirement that Congress, rather than the President, implement a non-self-executing treaty derives from the text of the Constitution, which divides the treaty-making power between the President and the Senate. The Constitution vests the President with the authority to "make" a treaty. Art. II, § 2. If the Executive determines that a treaty should have domestic effect of its own force, that determination may be implemented "in making" the treaty, by ensuring that it contains language plainly providing for domestic enforceability. If the treaty is to be self-executing in this respect, the Senate must consent to the treaty by the requisite two-thirds vote, *ibid.*, consistent with all other constitutional restraints.

Once a treaty is ratified without provisions clearly according it domestic effect, however, whether the treaty will ever have such effect is governed by the fundamental constitutional principle that " 'the power to make the necessary laws is in Congress; the power to execute in the President.' " *Hamdan v. Rumsfeld*, 548 U.S. 557, 591 (2006). As already noted, the terms of a non-self-executing treaty can become domestic law only in the same way as any other law — through passage of legislation by both Houses of Congress, combined with either the President's signature or a congressional override of a Presidential veto. See Art. I, § 7. Indeed, "the President's power to see that the laws are faithfully executed refutes the idea that he is to be a lawmaker." *Youngstown*, 343 U.S., at 587.

Id. at 526. The Court further observed that "[t]he interpretation of a treaty, like the interpretation of a statute, begins with its text. Because a treaty ratified by the United States is 'an agreement among sovereign powers,' we have also considered as 'aids to its interpretation' the negotiation and drafting history of the treaty as well as 'the postratification understanding' of signatory nations." *Id.* at 507.

For more on the legal effect of treaties, see Carlos Manual Vazquez, *Treaties As Law of the Land: The Supremacy Clause and the Judicial Enforcement of Treaties*, 122 HARV. L. REV. 599 (2008).

SIDEBAR: INITIATIVES AND REFERENDA

At the state level, statutes — and even constitutional provisions — sometimes may be enacted via processes other than the more usual legislative process, processes generally known as initiatives and referenda. According to the Initiative & Referendum Institute at the University of Southern California:

> **Ballot measures** or **ballot propositions** are proposals to enact new laws or constitutional amendments or repeal existing laws or constitutional amendments that are placed on the ballot for approval or rejection by the electorate. There are several different types of ballot measures.
>
> An ***initiative*** is a proposal of a new law or constitutional amendment that is placed on the ballot by petition, that is, by collecting signatures of a certain number of citizens. Twenty-four states have the initiative process. Of the 24 states, 18

allow initiatives to propose constitutional amendments and 21 states allow initiatives to propose statutes. In most cases, once a sufficient number of signatures has been collected, the proposal is placed on the ballot for a vote of the people ("direct initiative"). In some cases, the proposal first goes to the legislature, and if approved by the legislature, is not voted on by the people ("indirect initiative"). For constitutional amendments, 16 states allow direct initiatives and two allow indirect initiatives. For statutes, 11 states allow direct initiatives for statutes, seven allow indirect initiatives, and two states (Utah and Washington) allow both direct and indirect initiatives.

A *referendum* (sometimes "popular referendum") is a proposal to repeal a law that was previously enacted by the legislature, and that is placed on the ballot by citizen petition. A total of 24 states permit referendums, most of them states that also permit initiatives. Although the Progressives considered the referendum as important as the initiative, in practice, referendums are fairly rare, especially compared to initiatives.

A *legislative measure* or *legislative proposition* (or sometimes "referred" measure) is a proposal placed on the ballot by the legislature. All states permit legislative measures and all states except Delaware require constitutional amendments to be approved by the voters at large. In some states, legislatures place nonbinding advisory measures on the ballot. Legislative measures are much more common than initiatives and referendums, and are about twice as likely to be approved. Some states, such as Florida, also allow certain commissions to refer measures to the ballot.

There is no provision for any sort of ballot proposition at the national level in the United States. However, the initiative and referendum are available in thousands of counties, cities and towns across the country and are utilized far more frequently than their statewide counterpart.

INITIATIVE & REFERENDUM INSTITUTE AT THE UNIVERSITY OF SOUTHERN CALIFORNIA, *What Are Ballot Propositions, Initiatives, and Referendums?*, http://iandrinstitute.org/Quick%20Fact%20-%20What%20is%20I&R.htm. For a map showing the current availability of initiatives and referenda in the various states, *see id.* at http://iandrinstitute.org/statewide_i%26r.htm.

As the above excerpt indicates, the United States Constitution does not provide for the creation of federal law by initiative or referendum. As one legal scholar explains:

> The United States is one of the very few democracies that do not permit a national referendum. Leaders in several other nations have often put issues before the voters at large. President Corazon Aquino submitted the 1986 Philippine constitution to the people for ratification, and the constitution provides for both the initiative and referendum. Spanish citizens voted to remain in the North Atlantic Treaty Organization. The Irish and Italians have voted on the divorce issue. The Swiss vote with frequency on both major and mundane issues. Charles de Gaulle put before French voters the issue of whether France should give up Algeria and won their support for his policy. The British have voted in a national referendum on whether to remain in the European Common Market. Polish authorities recently placed two important economic issues on the national

ballot and suffered embarrassing defeats. And several nations have settled border or boundary disputes by putting these matters to the people.

Thomas E. Cronin, Direct Democracy 4 (1989).

For additional information on initiatives and referenda, see David B. Mableby, Direct Legislation (1984), and M. Dane Waters, Initiatives and Referendum Almanac (2003). State ballot measures generally may be tracked using Ballotpedia (http://ballotpedia.org/wiki/index.php/Main_Page). For a criticism of "direct democracy," see Erwin Chemerinsky, *Challenging Direct Democracy*, 2007 Mich. St. L. Rev. 293.

Of course, once enacted, legislation that is the product of state initiatives and referenda must be interpreted and applied just like any other statute, and similarly may be challenged for unconstitutionality. For example, in *Romer v. Evans*, 517 U.S. 620 (1996), the Supreme Court of the United States considered a challenge to "Amendment 2," an amendment to the Colorado Constitution adopted pursuant to a statewide referendum. "Amendment 2" provided (in pertinent part):

> Neither the State of Colorado, through any of its branches or departments, nor any of its agencies, political subdivisions, municipalities or school districts, shall enact, adopt or enforce any statute, regulation, ordinance or policy whereby homosexual, lesbian or bisexual orientation, conduct, practices or relationships shall constitute or otherwise be the basis of or entitle any person or class of persons to have or claim any minority status, quota preferences, protected status or claim of discrimination.

Romer, 517 U.S. at 624. In a 6-3 vote, the Court invalidated "Amendment 2" as violative of the federal Constitution's Equal Protection Clause. *See id.* at 623. For a more recent attack on a state ballot initiative (this one relating to California's Proposition 8, which amended the California Constitution to define marriage as a union between a man and a woman), see *Hollingsworth v. Perry*, 133 S. Ct. 2652 (2013).

In some states, the sponsorship and promotion of initiatives can become something of an industry, particularly following the success of California Proposition 13 in 1978. For example, in Washington, Tim Eyman became relatively well known for his sponsorship of a number of state initiatives during the late 1990s through the early part of this century. But not everyone was happy with his efforts. One such citizen, David Goldstein, proposed his own initiative, which became known as Initiative 831, and which read as follows:

> WHEREAS, Tim Eyman's ill-conceived anti-tax initiatives are an irresponsible means of legislating tax policy, an abuse of the initiative process, and an insult to our system of representative democracy; and
>
> WHEREAS, Tim Eyman is an admitted liar, who paid himself $45,000 from campaign funds, while publicly denying any personal gain from the state-wide initiatives he sponsored; and
>
> WHEREAS, Tim Eyman diverted $165,000 of campaign contributions to a for-profit corporation he controls, with the intention of paying himself an additional $157,000; and

> WHEREAS, Motivated by self-aggrandizement and personal gain, Tim Eyman has consistently misrepresented the initiatives he sponsored, and misappropriated funds donated to support them; and
>
> WHEREAS, Tim Eyman readily admits, in his own words, that "I just feel like an ass";
>
> NOW, THEREFORE, BE IT RESOLVED, That the citizens of the State of Washington do hereby proclaim that Tim Eyman is a Horse's Ass.
>
> BE IT FURTHER RESOLVED, That copies of this resolution be immediately transmitted to Tim Eyman, his wife, and his mother. So there.

Initiative 831 never made it to a ballot.

C. THE INTERPRETATION OF STATUTES

1. Basic Concepts

Of course, once statutes are enacted and codified, they must be read, interpreted, and applied, especially by lawyers and judges. How is this accomplished? That is the subject of this part.

Before beginning, it might be observed that the interpretation of statutes is but one type of textual interpretation, i.e., the interpretation of written communication. Even when confined to the law, you will find that there are all sorts of texts — constitutions, orders, contracts, letters, etc. — that are in need of interpretation, and to a large extent, similar interpretive problems and methods apply. But in some ways, statutory interpretation — because of the nature of statutes, how they are enacted, and their role in the hierarchy of legal authorities — is unique.

The following excerpt lays something of a foundation for the interpretation of statutes.

Reed Dickerson

"FOUR CONSTITUTIONAL ASSUMPTIONS"

The Interpretation and Application of Statutes (1975)

A. INTRODUCTION

The [proper interpretation and application of statutes] rests on several constitutional assumptions. However obvious they may seem, they need to be expressed and kept continuously in the foreground, because without necessarily intending to reject them courts often act as if they were false.

B. FIRST ASSUMPTION: LEGISLATIVE SUPREMACY

The first assumption is that the general powers of government are constitutionally allocated among the three central branches in such a way that, although it does not enjoy an exclusive power to make substantive law, the legislative branch exercises lawmaking power that takes precedence over the lawmaking powers respectively exercised by the executive and judicial branches.

The facts that this separation of powers is not absolute, and that the allocation is complicated rather than simple, in no wise detract from the simple assertion that, within the domains of lawmaking in which they are constitutionally permitted to operate and within the differing means by which they make their pronouncements, any conflict between the legislative will and the judicial will must be resolved in favor of the former. It is assumed, therefore, that within these boundaries the judicial branch must remain appropriately deferential to the properly promulgated views of the legislature. Although the courts, too, make general law, they do this in the absence or supplementation of statute. . . .

. . . .

C. SECOND ASSUMPTION: EXCLUSIVENESS OF STATUTORY VEHICLE

A second constitutional assumption is that the legislative will can be communicated as effective law only if the legislature promulgates its views in the way prescribed by the applicable constitution. The exclusive means by which a legislature may create new law is enacting a statute or its procedural equivalent. . . .

If this second assumption is correct, it means that not even the most reliable document of legislative history, such as a conference committee report, may have the force of law. Certainly, it may not be given weight equal to that of the statute to which it relates. If it has weight, it must be because it is part of proper legislative context (if it can meet the applicable standards), or because it is used for a purpose other than ascertaining the meaning of a statute.

D. THIRD ASSUMPTION: RELIANCE ON ACCEPTED MEANS OF COMMUNICATION

A third constitutional assumption is that, as a communication from the legislature to one or more legislative audiences, a statute is subject to the accepted standards of communication in effect in the given environment. This tacitly underlies the applicable constitution and is therefore part of it. Any other assumption would unjustifiably magnify the risk that legislative supremacy would in fact be subverted, because it is the very nature of language, which is founded on accepted usage, to comply with that usage most of the time.

Thus, a court seeking to discharge its constitutional duty of deference to the expressions of the legislative will made in the constitutionally prescribed way is obliged to ascertain the meaning of those expressions according to accepted standards of communication. . . .

. . . .

This premise should be kept constantly in mind, because courts have often felt free to recognize and resolve uncertainties of meaning contrary to the preponderance of factual probabilities or plausibilities of meaning. That they may have been motivated by what they have believed to be the public good is not, in the light of the constitutional separation of powers, adequate justification.

E. FOURTH ASSUMPTION: NECESSITY OF REASONABLE AVAILABILITY

A fourth constitutional assumption is that a legislature is required to make the laws that it enacts reasonably available to the persons who are affected by them. Although the United States Constitution and some state constitutions are silent on the subject, the notion of providing a reasonable opportunity to know what the law is inheres in the constitutional requirement that the legislature must communicate its commands and pronouncements by means of a specified kind of vehicle developed and launched in a specified way. It would make no sense to assume, on the one hand, that the Constitution is deeply concerned with the creation of such a vehicle and, on the other hand, that it is unconcerned with whether the vehicle reaches its intended destination.

. . . A constitutional opportunity for the persons affected to adjust to the new law necessarily implies a constitutional policy of providing a reasonable opportunity to know what the new law provides. The effectiveness of the law is thus conditioned, not on actual knowledge of the law, but on a reasonable opportunity to acquire that knowledge. Because this standard cannot be met unless the opportunity to know extends to all aspects of the legislature's communication, no material extrinsic to the statute can properly be treated as part of the total legislative communication unless it meets the minimum standards of availability to which the statute itself is constitutionally subject. This it can do only as part of proper legislative context; otherwise it runs afoul our second constitutional assumption, already discussed.

Notes and Questions

1. Try to restate each of Professor Dickerson's four constitutional assumptions into single sentences using your own words.

2. "There are two basic reasons why [problems of statutory interpretation arise]: the indefiniteness of language and the unforeseeable variety of problems." MICHAEL SINCLAIR, GUIDE TO STATUTORY INTERPRETATION 85 (2000).

3. *Statutory interpretation as textual interpretation.* As stated previously, statutory interpretation is but a specific example of the general problem of textual interpretation. One might consider whether and to what extent the principles of statutory interpretation should apply to the interpretation of other legal texts (constitutions, contracts, etc.), and vice versa. For more on this subject, see (e.g.) Kevin M. Stack, *The Divergence of Constitutional and Statutory Interpretation*, 75 U. COLO. L. REV. 1 (2004).

4. *Statutory interpretation versus statutory construction.* In the area of textual interpretation, some have attempted to distinguish the terms "interpretation" and "construction." Generally speaking, "interpretation" has been defined as the process of determining the meaning to be given to the words at issue, whereas "construction" involves the process of determining the legal consequences that follow from the words so interpreted. *See, e.g.,* Randy E. Barnett, *Interpretation and Construction*, 34 HARV. J.L. & PUB. POL'Y 65 (2011); Edwin W. Patterson, *The Interpretation and Construction of Contracts*, 64 COLUM. L. REV. 833 (1964); Lawrence B. Solum, *The Interpretation-Construction Distinction*, 27 CONST. COMMENT. 95 (2010). Others, though, have rejected the notion that there is any such distinction. *See, e.g.,* ANTONIN SCALIA & BRYAN A. GARNER, READING LAW: THE INTERPRETATION OF LEGAL TEXTS 13-15 (2012).

   For simplicity, this book will use the single phrase "statutory interpretation" to represent both concepts.

5. *Statutory ambiguity v. statutory vagueness.* When interpreting any legal text, two important problems relate to what might be referred to as *ambiguity* and *vagueness.* As Professor Barnett explains:

   > *Ambiguity* refers to words that have more than one sense or meaning. *Vagueness* refers to the penumbra or borderline of a word's meaning, where it may be unclear whether a certain object is included within it or not. . . . In other words, language is ambiguous when it has *more than one sense*; it is vague when its meaning admits of *borderline cases* that cannot definitively be ruled in or out of its meaning.
   >
   > When it comes to resolving ambiguity, the context of a statement usually reveals which sense is meant. . . .
   >
   > . . . .
   >
   > In contrast, with vague provisions, the terms themselves — even when interpreted contextually — simply do not contain the information necessary to decide matters of application.

   Barnett, *supra* note 4, at 65, 67-68.

   As you read cases involving issues of statutory interpretation, consider whether the interpretive problem is one of ambiguity or more one of vagueness.

2. Historical Development

Historically, the interpretation of statutes by courts has been a matter of common law development — i.e., the courts themselves have devised "rules" (and later, theories) for determining the meaning of the statute in question. Though courts have not been consistent in their use of any single rule or theory, some rules, as well as the cases with which they are associated, have had considerable staying power, in that they continue to be used by courts despite being decades, or even centuries, old. The cases that follow are cases of this type. They continue to exert influence on courts today.

a. Early Landmarks

Heydon's Case

76 Eng. Rep. 637 (Ex. 1584)

In an information upon an intrusion in the Exchequer (A), against Heydon, for intruding into certain lands, &c. in the county of Devon: upon the general issue, the jurors gave a special verdict to this effect.

First, they found that parcel of the lands in the information was ancient copyholds of the manor of Ottery, whereof the warden and canons regular of the late college of Ottery were seised in the right of the said college; and that the warden and canons of said college, 22 H. 7. at a court of the said manor, granted the same parcel by copy, to Ware the father and Ware the son, for their lives, at the will of the lord, according to the custom of the said manor; and that the rest of the land in the information was occupied by S. and G. at the will of the warden and canons of the said college for the time being, in the time of H. 8. And further that the said S. and G. so possessed, and the said Ware and Ware so seised as aforesaid, the said warden and canons by their deed indented, dated 12 January anno 30 H. 8. did lease the same to Heydon the defendant for eighty years, rendering certain rents severally for several parcels; and found that the said several rents in Heydon's lease reserved, were the ancient and accustomed rents of the several parcels of the lands, and found, that after the said lease they did surrender their college, and all the possessions thereof to King Hen. 8. And further found the statute of (b) 31 Hen. 8. and the branch of it, *scil.* by which it is enacted, "That if any abbot, &c. or other religious and ecclesiastical house or place, within one year next before the first day of this present Parliament, hath made, or hereafter shall make any lease or grant for life, or for a term of years, of any manors, messuages, lands, &c. and in the which any estate or interest for life, year or years, at the time of the making of such grant or lease, then had his being or continuance, or hereafter shall have his being or continuance, and not determined at the making of such lease, &c. Or if the usual and old rents and farms accustomed to be yielden and reserved by the space of twenty years next before the first day of this present Parliament, is not, or be not, or hereafter shall not be thereupon reserved or yielded, &c. that all and every such lease, &c. shall be utterly void." And further found, that the particular estates aforesaid were determined, and before the intrusion Heydon's lease began; and that Heydon entered, &c. And the great doubt which was often debated at the Bar and Bench, on this verdict, was, whether the copyhold estate of Ware and Ware for their lives, at the will of the Lords, according to the custom of the said manor, should, in judgment of law be called an estate and interest for lives, within the said general words and meaning of the said Act. And after all the Barons openly argued in Court in the same term, *scil.* Pasch. 26 Eliz. and it was unanimously resolved by Sir Roger Manwood, Chief Baron, and the other Barons of the Exchequer, that the said lease made to Heydon was void; for it was agreed by them, that the said copyhold estate was an estate for life, within the words and meaning of the said Act. And it was resolved by them, that for the sure and true (*a*) interpretation of all statutes in general (be they penal (B) or beneficial, restrictive or enlarging of the common law,) four things are to be discerned and considered: —

(*b*) 1st. What was the common law before the making of the Act.

(*c*) 2nd. What was the mischief and defect for which the common law did not provide.

3rd. What remedy the Parliament hath resolved and appointed to cure the disease of the commonwealth.

And, 4th. The true reason of the remedy; and then the office of all the Judges is always to make such (*d*) construction as shall suppress the mischief, and advance the remedy, and to suppress subtle inventions and evasions for continuance of the mischief, and *pro privato commodo*, and to add force and life to the cure and remedy, according to the true intent of the makers of the Act, *pro bono publico*. And it was said, that in this case the common law was, that religious and ecclesiastical persons might have made leases for as many years as they pleased, the mischief was that when they perceived their houses would be dissolved, they made long and unreasonable leases: now the stat of 31 H. 8. doth provide the remedy, (†) and principally for such religious and ecclesiastical houses which should be dissolved after the Act (as the said college in our case was) that all leases of any land, whereof any estate or interest for life or years was then in being, should be void; and their reason was, that it was not necessary for them to make a new lease so long as a former had continuance; and therefore the intent of the Act was to avoid doubling of estates, and to have but one single estate in being at a time: for doubling of estates implies in itself deceit, and private respect, to prevent the intention of the Parliament. And if the copyhold estate for two lives, and the lease for eighty years shall stand together, here will be doubling of estates *simul & semel*, which will be against the true meaning of Parliament.

Notes and Questions

1. Can you summarize the interpretive "rule" articulated by the court in *Heydon's Case*? What do you think of this rule as a theory of statutory interpretation?

2. It seems plausible that a court could determine the state of the common law prior to the statute, as well as the "remedy" created by the statute. But how is a court to determine "the mischief and defect for which the common law did not provide"? Or the "true reason for the remedy"?

3. The rule articulated in *Heydon's Case* has become known as the "mischief rule." Though *Heydon's Case* was an English case, the mischief rule eventually found its way into American jurisprudence. For example, in *Hamilton v. Rathbone*, 175 U.S. 414, 419 (1899), the Supreme Court stated:

> The general rule is perfectly well settled that, where a statute is of doubtful meaning and susceptible upon its face of two constructions, the court may look into prior and contemporaneous acts, the reasons which induced the act in question, the mischiefs intended to be remedied, the extraneous circumstances, and the purpose intended to be accomplished by it, to determine the proper construction.

Nonetheless, the *Hamilton* Court then continued:

> But where the act is clear upon its face, and when standing alone it is fairly susceptible of but one construction, that construction must be given to it. . . .
>
>   . . . .
>
>   . . . The whole doctrine applicable to the subject may be summed up in the single observation that prior acts may be resorted to, to *solve*, but not to *create* an ambiguity.

Id. at 419-21.

Church of the Holy Trinity v. United States
143 U.S. 457 (1892)

MR. JUSTICE BREWER delivered the opinion of the court.

Plaintiff in error is a corporation, duly organized and incorporated as a religious society under the laws of the State of New York. E. Walpole Warren was, prior to September, 1887, an alien residing in England. In that month the plaintiff in error made a contract with him, by which he was to remove to the city of New York and enter into its service as rector and pastor; and in pursuance of such contract, Warren did so remove and enter upon such service. It is claimed by the United States that this contract on the part of the plaintiff in error was forbidden by the act of February 26, 1885, 23 Stat. 332, c. 164, and an action was commenced to recover the penalty prescribed by that act. The Circuit Court held that the contract was within the prohibition of the statute, and rendered judgment accordingly, (36 Fed. Rep. 303;) and the single question presented for our determination is whether it erred in that conclusion.

The first section describes the act forbidden, and is in these words:

"*Be it enacted by the Senate and House of Representatives of the United States of America in Congress assembled*, That from and after the passage of this act it shall be unlawful for any person, company, partnership, or corporation, in any manner whatsoever, to prepay the transportation, or in any way assist or encourage the importation or migration of any alien or aliens, any foreigner or foreigners, into the United States, its Territories, or the District of Columbia, under contract or agreement, parol or special, express or implied, made previous to the importation or migration of such alien or aliens, foreigner or foreigners, to perform labor or service of any kind in the United States, its Territories, or the District of Columbia."

It must be conceded that the act of the corporation is within the letter of this section, for the relation of rector to his church is one of service, and implies labor on the one side with compensation on the other. Not only are the general words labor and service both used, but also, as it were to guard against any narrow interpretation and emphasize a breadth of meaning, to them is added "of any kind;" and, further, as noticed by the Circuit Judge in his opinion, the fifth section, which makes specific exceptions, among them professional actors, artists, lecturers, singers and domestic servants, strengthens the idea that every other kind of labor and service was intended to be reached by the first section. While there is great force to this reasoning, we cannot think Congress intended to denounce with penalties a transaction like that in the present case. It is a familiar rule, that a thing may be within the letter of the statute and yet not within the statute, because not within its spirit, nor within the intention of its makers. This has been often asserted, and the reports are full of cases illustrating its application. This is not the substitution of the will of the judge for that of the legislator, for frequently words of general meaning are used in a statute, words broad enough to include an act in question, and yet a consideration of the whole legislation, or of the circumstances surrounding its enactment, or of the absurd results which follow from giving such broad meaning to the words, makes it unreasonable to believe that the legislator intended to include the particular act. . . .

. . . In *United States v. Kirby*, 7 Wall. 482, 486, the defendants were indicted for the violation of an act of Congress, providing "that if any person shall knowingly and wilfully obstruct or retard the passage of the mail, or of any driver or carrier, or of any horse or carriage carrying the same, he shall, upon conviction, for every such offence pay a fine not exceeding one hundred dollars." The specific charge was that the defendants knowingly and wilfully retarded the passage of one Farris, a carrier of the mail, while engaged in the performance of his duty, and also in like manner retarded the steamboat General Buell, at that time engaged in carrying the mail. To this indictment the defendants pleaded specially that Farris had been indicted for murder by a court of competent authority in Kentucky; that a bench warrant had been issued and placed in the hands of the defendant Kirby, the sheriff of the county, commanding him to arrest Farris and bring him before the court to answer the indictment; and that in obedience to this warrant, he and the other defendants, as his posse, entered upon the steamboat General Buell and arrested Farris, and used only such force as was necessary to accomplish that arrest. The question as to the sufficiency of this plea was certified to this court, and it was held that the arrest of Farris upon the warrant from the state court was not an obstruction of the mail, or the retarding of the passage of a carrier of the mail, within the meaning of the act. In its opinion the court says: "All laws should receive a sensible construction. General terms should be so limited in their application as not to lead to injustice, oppression or an absurd consequence. It will always, therefore, be presumed that the legislature intended exceptions to its language which would avoid results of this character. The reason of the law in such cases should prevail over its letter. The common sense of man approves the judgment mentioned by Puffendorf, that the Bolognian law which enacted 'that whoever drew blood in the streets should be punished with the utmost severity,' did not extend to the surgeon who opened the vein of a person that fell down in the street in a fit. The same common sense accepts the ruling, cited by Plowden, that the statute of 1st Edward II., which enacts that a prisoner who breaks prison shall be guilty of felony, does not extend to a prisoner who breaks out when the prison is on fire, 'for he is not to be hanged because he would not stay to be burnt.' And we think that a like common sense will sanction the ruling we make, that the act of Congress which punishes the obstruction or retarding of the passage of the mail, or of its carrier, does not apply to a case of temporary detention of the mail caused by the arrest of the carrier upon an indictment for murder." . . .

Among other things which may be considered in determining the intent of the legislature is the title of the act. We do not mean that it may be used to add to or take from the body of the statute, but it may help to interpret the meaning. . . .

It will be seen that words as general as those used in the first section of this act were by that decision limited, and the intent of Congress with respect to that act was gathered partially, at least, from its title. Now, the title of this act is, "An act to prohibit the importation and migration of foreigners and aliens under contract or agreement to perform labor in the United States, its Territories and the District of Columbia." Obviously the thought expressed in this reaches only to the work of the manual laborer, as distinguished from that of the professional man. No one reading such a title would suppose that Congress had in its mind any purpose of staying the coming into this country of ministers of the gospel, or, indeed, of any class whose toil is that of the brain. The common understanding of the terms labor and laborers does not include preaching and preachers; and it is to be assumed that words and phrases are used in their ordinary meaning. So whatever of light is thrown upon the statute by the language of the title indicates an exclusion from its penal provisions of all contracts for the employment of ministers, rectors and pastors.

Again, another guide to the meaning of a statute is found in the evil which it is designed to remedy; and for this the court properly looks at contemporaneous events, the situation as it existed, and as it was pressed upon the attention of the legislative body. The situation which called for this statute was briefly but fully stated by Mr. Justice Brown when, as District Judge, he decided the case of *United States v. Craig*, 28 Fed. Rep. 795, 798: "The motives and history of the act are matters of common knowledge. It had become the practice for large capitalists in this country to contract with their agents abroad for the shipment of great numbers of an ignorant and servile class of foreign laborers, under contracts, by which the employer agreed, upon the one hand, to prepay their passage, while, upon the other hand, the laborers agreed to work after their arrival for a certain time at a low rate of wages. The effect of this was to break down the labor market, and to reduce other laborers engaged in like occupations to the level of the assisted immigrant. The evil finally became so flagrant that an appeal was made to Congress for relief by the passage of the act in question, the design of which was to raise the standard of foreign immigrants, and to discountenance the migration of those who had not sufficient means in their own hands, or those of their friends, to pay their passage."

It appears, also, from the petitions, and in the testimony presented before the committees of Congress, that it was this cheap unskilled labor which was making the trouble, and the influx of which Congress sought to prevent. It was never suggested that we had in this country a surplus of brain toilers, and, least of all, that the market for the services of Christian ministers was depressed by foreign competition. Those were matters to which the attention of Congress, or of the people, was not directed. So far, then, as the evil which was sought to be remedied interprets the statute, it also guides to an exclusion of this contract from the penalties of the act.

. . . .

But beyond all these matters no purpose of action against religion can be imputed to any legislation, state or national, because this is a religious people. This is historically true. From the discovery of this continent to the present hour, there is a single voice making this affirmation. . . .

. . . .

. . . In the face of all these [examples of this being a Judeo-Christian nation], shall it be believed that a Congress of the United States intended to make it a misdemeanor for a church of this country to contract for the services of a Christian minister residing in another nation?

Suppose in the Congress that passed this act some member had offered a bill which in terms declared that, if any Roman Catholic church in this country should contract with Cardinal Manning to come to this country and enter into its service as pastor or priest; or any Episcopal church should enter into a like contract with Canon Farrar; or any Baptist church should make similar arrangements with Rev. Mr. Spurgeon; or any Jewish synagogue with some eminent Rabbi, such contract should be adjudged unlawful and void, and the church making it be subject to prosecution and punishment, can it be believed that it would have received a minute of approving thought or a single vote? Yet it is contended that such was in effect the meaning of this statute. The construction invoked cannot be accepted as correct. It is a case where there was presented a definite evil, in view of which the legislature used general terms with the purpose of reaching all phases of that evil, and thereafter, unexpectedly, it is developed that the general language thus employed is broad enough to reach cases and acts which the whole history and life of the country affirm could not have been intentionally legislated against. It is the duty of the courts, under those circumstances, to say that, however broad the language of the statute may be, the act, although within the letter, is not within the intention of the legislature, and therefore cannot be within the statute.

The judgment will be reversed, and the case remanded for further proceedings in accordance with this opinion.

Notes and Questions

1. How would you summarize the interpretive rule used by the Court in *Holy Trinity*? What do you think of this rule? The rule articulated by the *Holy Trinity* Court led in part to a theory of statutory interpretation known as intentionalism.

2. Is there any serious question that the Congress that enacted the act at issue in *Holy Trinity* did not intend that act to apply to the hiring of an English pastor

by an American church? On the other hand, is it not equally clear that such hiring fits squarely within the terms of that act? And what of the fact that another section of the act specifically excluded certain types of workers, and yet made no mention of pastors; is this not evidence that Congress also could have excluded pastors (or otherwise could have limited the reach of this act), and yet, for whatever reason, decided not to? At what point should Congress be "punished" for its own poor drafting (if that is indeed what occurred here)? In other words, is the Court's decision truly better than a decision adverse to the church, followed by some form of statutory amendment?

3. What would possess the government to prosecute a church for this "offense"? What of the role of prosecutorial discretion? On the other hand, once the decision to prosecute was made and the penalty prescribed was imposed, was a favorable decision from the Supreme Court the church's only reasonable means of obtaining relief?

4. The penalty at issue consisted of a $1,000 fine. *See United States v. Church of the Holy Trinity*, 36 F. 303, 303 (C.C.S.D.N.Y. 1888). Was it possible that the Church of the Holy Trinity realized that bringing E. Walpole Warren to the United States might result in such a penalty, and simply decided to assume that risk? Is that ever a possibility in this context?

5. The *Holy Trinity* Court relied in part on its earlier decision in *United States v. Kirby*. But does *Kirby* necessarily support the *Holy Trinity* Court's decision? Or is *Kirby* somehow distinguishable?

6. The *Holy Trinity* Court also relied on the fact that the title to the act at issue referred only to "labor." But is it really "obvious" that this term refers "only to the work of the manual laborer, as distinguished from that of the professional man?" What authority does the Court cite in support of that interpretation? And though "cheap unskilled labor" indeed might have served as the impetus for this legislation, is it possible that an intrusion of foreign "brain toilers" might also have been viewed as a problem worthy of congressional action? In any event, should the title of the act be allowed to override the text of the act?

7. According to the Court, "it is to be assumed that words and phrases are used in their ordinary meaning." Why? In all contexts?

8. The Court also suggested that the "motives and history of the act are matters of common knowledge." But if that is true, then why did the Circuit Court reach a contrary result?

9. There are other interesting aspects of the *Holy Trinity* decision. For example, are we truly a "religious" (and specifically, a Judeo-Christian) people? (Consider this question in light of the current debate over the propriety of the Pledge of Allegiance.) And if not today, were we in 1885, when this act was enacted? Is

that not the relevant date for such an inquiry? Or is this inquiry even relevant? Would the *Holy Trinity* Court have found this act inapplicable to all "religious" organizations? Any "brain toiler" whatsoever?

10. The statute at issue in *Holy Trinity* was later amended in a manner more consistent with the Court's reading. Does this support or refute the propriety of the Court's holding in that case?

Caminetti v. United States
242 U.S. 470 (1917)

MR. JUSTICE DAY delivered the opinion of the Court.

These three cases were argued together, and may be disposed of in a single opinion. In each of the cases there was a conviction and sentence for violation of the so-called White Slave Traffic Act of June 24, 1910, 36 Stat. 825, the judgments were affirmed by the Circuit Courts of Appeals, and writs of certiorari bring the cases here.

In the Caminetti case, the petitioner was indicted in the United States District Court for the Northern District of California, upon the sixth day of May, 1913, for alleged violations of the act. The indictment was in four counts, the first of which charged him with transporting and causing to be transported and aiding and assisting in obtaining transportation for a certain woman from Sacramento, California, to Reno, Nevada, in interstate commerce for the purpose of debauchery, and for an immoral purpose, to wit, that the aforesaid woman should be and become his mistress and concubine. A verdict of not guilty was returned as to the other three counts of this indictment. As to the first count defendant was found guilty and sentenced to imprisonment for eighteen months and to pay a fine of $1,500.00. Upon writ of error to the United States Circuit Court of Appeals for the Ninth Circuit, that judgment was affirmed. 220 Fed. Rep. 545.

. . . .

It is contended that the act of Congress is intended to reach only "commercialized vice," or the traffic of women for gain, and that the conduct for which the several petitioners were indicted and convicted, however reprehensible in morals, is not within the purview of the statute when properly construed in the light of its history and the purposes intended to be accomplished by its enactment. In none of the cases was it charged or proved that the transportation was for gain or for the purpose of furnishing women for prostitution for hire, and it is insisted that, such being the case, the acts charged and proved, upon which conviction was had, do not come within the statute.

It is elementary that the meaning of a statute must, in the first instance, be sought in the language in which the act is framed, and if that is plain, and if the law is within the constitutional authority of the law-making body which passed it, the sole function of the courts is to enforce it according to its terms.

Where the language is plain and admits of no more than one meaning the duty of interpretation does not arise and the rules which are to aid doubtful meanings need no discussion. There is no ambiguity in the terms of this act. It is specifically made an offense to knowingly transport or cause to be transported, etc., in interstate commerce, any woman or girl for the purpose of prostitution or debauchery, or for "any other immoral purpose," or with the intent and purpose to induce any such woman or girl to become a prostitute or to give herself up to debauchery, or to engage in any other immoral practice.

Statutory words are uniformly presumed, unless the contrary appears, to be used in their ordinary and usual sense, and with the meaning commonly attributed to them. To cause a woman or girl to be transported for the purposes of debauchery, and for an immoral purpose, to wit, becoming a concubine or mistress, for which Caminetti . . . w[as] convicted . . . , would seem by the very statement of the facts to embrace transportation for purposes denounced by the act, and therefore fairly within its meaning.

While such immoral purpose would be more culpable in morals and attributed to baser motives if accompanied with the expectation of pecuniary gain, such considerations do not prevent the lesser offense against morals of furnishing transportation in order that a woman may be debauched, or become a mistress or a concubine from being the execution of purposes within the meaning of this law. To say the contrary would shock the common understanding of what constitutes an immoral purpose when those terms are applied, as here, to sexual relations.

In *United States v. Bitty*, 208 U.S. 393, it was held that the act of Congress against the importation of alien women and girls for the purpose of prostitution "and any other immoral purpose" included the importation of an alien woman to live in concubinage with the person importing her. . . .

. . . .

This definition of an immoral purpose was given prior to the enactment of the act now under consideration, and must be presumed to have been known to Congress when it enacted the law here involved. . . .

But it is contended that though the words are so plain that they cannot be misapprehended when given their usual and ordinary interpretation, and although the sections in which they appear do not in terms limit the offense defined and punished to acts of "commercialized vice," or the furnishing or procuring of transportation of women for debauchery, prostitution or immoral practices for hire, such limited purpose is to be attributed to Congress and engrafted upon the act in view of the language of § 8 and the report which accompanied the law upon its introduction into and subsequent passage by the House of Representatives.

In this connection, it may be observed that while the title of an act cannot overcome the meaning of plain and unambiguous words used in its body, the title of this act embraces the regulation of interstate commerce "by prohibiting the transportation therein for immoral purposes of women and girls, and for other purposes." It is true that § 8 of the act provides that it shall be known and referred to as the "White-slave traffic Act," and the report accompanying the introduction of the same into the House of Representatives set forth the fact that a material portion of the legislation suggested was to meet conditions which had arisen in the past few years, and that the legislation was needed to put a stop to a villainous interstate and international traffic in women and girls. Still, the name given to an act by way of designation or description, or the report which accompanies it, cannot change the plain import of its words.

If the words are plain, they give meaning to the act, and it is neither the duty nor the privilege of the courts to enter speculative fields in search of a different meaning.

Reports to Congress accompanying the introduction of proposed laws may aid the courts in reaching the true meaning of the legislature in cases of doubtful interpretation. But, as we have already said, and it has been so often affirmed as to become a recognized rule, when words are free from doubt they must be taken as the final expression of the legislative intent, and are not to be added to or subtracted from by considerations drawn from titles or designating names or reports accompanying their introduction, or from any extraneous sources. In other words, the language being plain, and not leading to absurd or wholly impracticable consequences, it is the sole evidence of the ultimate legislative intent.

The fact, if it be so, that the act as it is written opens the door to blackmailing operations upon a large scale, is no reason why the courts should refuse to enforce it according to its terms, if within the constitutional authority of Congress. Such considerations are more appropriately addressed to the legislative branch of the government, which alone had authority to enact and may if it sees fit amend the law.

. . . .

The judgment in each of the cases is
Affirmed.

MR. JUSTICE MCREYNOLDS took no part in the consideration or decision of these cases.

MR. JUSTICE MCKENNA, with whom concurred the CHIEF JUSTICE and MR. JUSTICE CLARKE, dissenting.

Undoubtedly in the investigation of the meaning of a statute we resort first to its words, and when clear they are decisive. The principle has attractive and seemingly disposing simplicity, but that it is not easy of application or, at least, encounters other principles, many cases demonstrate. The words of a statute may be uncertain in their signification or in their application. If the words be ambiguous, the problem they present is to be resolved by their definition; the subject-matter and the lexicons become our guides. But here, even, we are not exempt from putting ourselves in the place of the legislators. If the words be clear in meaning but the objects to which they are addressed be uncertain, the problem then is to determine the uncertainty. And for this a realization of conditions that provoked the statute must inform our judgment. Let us apply these observations to the present case.

The transportation which is made unlawful is of a woman or girl "to become a prostitute or to give herself up to debauchery, or to engage in any other immoral practice." Our present concern is with the words "any other immoral practice," which, it is asserted, have a special office. The words are clear enough as general descriptions; they fail in particular designation; they are class words, not specifications. Are they controlled by those which precede them? If not, they are broader in generalization and include those that precede them, making them unnecessary and confusing. To what conclusion would this lead us? "Immoral" is a very comprehensive word. It means a dereliction of morals. In such sense it covers every form of vice, every form of conduct that is contrary to good order. It will hardly be contended that in this sweeping sense it is used in the statute. But if not used in such sense, to what is it limited and by what limited? If it be admitted that it is limited at all, that ends the imperative effect assigned to it in the opinion of the court. But not insisting quite on that, we ask again, By what is it limited? By its context, necessarily, and the purpose of the statute.

For the context I must refer to the statute; of the purpose of the statute Congress itself has given us illumination. It devotes a section to the declaration that the "Act shall be known and referred to as the 'White-slave traffic Act.'" And its prominence gives it prevalence in the construction of the statute. It cannot be pushed aside or subordinated by indefinite words in other sentences, limited even there by the context. It is a peremptory rule of construction that all parts of a statute must be taken into account in ascertaining its meaning, and it cannot be said that § 8 has no object. But it gives more than a title; it makes distinctive the purpose of the statute. The designation "White-slave traffic" has the sufficiency of an axiom. If apprehended, there is no uncertainty as to the conduct it describes. It is commercialized vice, immoralities having a mercenary purpose, and this is confirmed by other circumstances.

The author of the bill was Mr. Mann, and in reporting it from the House Committee on Interstate and Foreign Commerce he declared for the Committee that it was not the purpose of the bill to interfere with or usurp in any way the police power of the States, and further that it was not the intention of the bill to regulate prostitution or the places where prostitution or immorality was practiced, which were said to be matters wholly within the power of the States and over which the federal government had no jurisdiction. And further explaining the bill, it was said that the sections of the act had been "so drawn that they are limited to cases in which there is the act of transportation in interstate commerce of women for purposes of prostitution." . . .
        . . . .

In other words, it is vice as a business at which the law is directed, using interstate commerce as a facility to procure or distribute its victims.

[An opinion of the Attorney General similarly concluded that this act was not concerned with the suppression or regulation of immorality in general.]

Of course, neither the declarations of the report of the Committee on Interstate Commerce of the House nor the opinion of the Attorney General are conclusive of the meaning of the law, but they are highly persuasive. The opinion was by one skilled in the rules and methods employed in the interpretation or construction of laws, and informed besides of the conditions to which the act was addressed. The report was by the committee charged with the duty of investigating the necessity for the act and to inform the House of the results of that investigation, both of evil and remedy. The report of the committee has, therefore, a higher quality than debates on the floor of the House. The representations of the latter may indeed be ascribed to the exaggerations of advocacy or opposition. The report of the committee is the execution of a duty and has the sanction of duty. There is a presumption, therefore, that the measure it recommends has the purpose it declares and will accomplish it as declared.

This being the purpose, the words of the statute should be construed to execute it, and they may be so construed even if their literal meaning be otherwise. [*Holy Trinity Church v. United States*] . . . .

It is hardly necessary to say that the application of the rule does not depend upon the objects of the legislation, to be applied or not applied as it may exclude or include good things or bad things. Its principle is the simple one that the words of a statute will be extended or restricted to execute its purpose.

Another pertinent illustration of the rule is *Reich v. Smythe*, 13 Wall. 162, in which the court declared that if at times it was its duty to regard the words of a statute, at times it was also its duty to disregard them, limit or extend them, in order to execute the purpose of the statute. And applying the principle, it decided that in a tariff act the provision that a duty should be imposed on horses, etc., and other *live animals* imported from foreign countries should not include canary birds, ignoring the classification of nature. And so again in *Silver v. Ladd*, 7 Wall. 219, where the benefit of the Oregon Donation Act was extended by making the words "single man" used in the statute mean an unmarried woman, disregarding a difference of genders clearly expressed in the law.

The rule that these cases illustrate is a valuable one and in varying degrees has daily practice. It not only rescues legislation from absurdity (so far the opinion of the court admits its application), but it often rescues it from invalidity, a useful result in our dual form of governments and conflicting jurisdictions. It is the dictate of common sense. Language, even when most masterfully used, may miss sufficiency and give room for dispute. Is it a wonder therefore, that when used in the haste of legislation, in view of conditions perhaps only partly seen or not seen at all, the consequences, it may be, beyond present foresight, it often becomes necessary to apply the rule? And it is a rule of prudence and highest sense. It rescues from crudities, excesses and deficiencies, making legislation adequate to its special purpose, rendering unnecessary repeated qualifications and leaving the simple and best exposition of a law the mischief it was intended to redress. Nor is this judicial legislation. It is seeking and enforcing the true sense of a law notwithstanding its imperfection or generality of expression.

There is much in the present case to tempt to a violation of the rule. Any measure that protects the purity of women from assault or enticement to degradation finds an instant advocate in our best emotions; but the judicial function cannot yield to emotion — it must, with poise of mind, consider and decide. It should not shut its eyes to the facts of the world and assume not to know what everybody else knows. And everybody knows that there is a difference between the occasional immoralities of men and women and that systematized and mercenary immorality epitomized in the statute's graphic phrase "White-slave traffic." And it was such immorality that was in the legislative mind and not the other. The other is occasional, not habitual — inconspicuous — does not offensively obtrude upon public notice. Interstate commerce is not its instrument as it is of the other, nor is prostitution its object or its end. It may, indeed, in instances, find a convenience in crossing state lines, but this is its accident, not its aid.

There is danger in extending a statute beyond its purpose, even if justified by a strict adherence to its words. The purpose is studied, all effects measured, not left at random — one evil practice prevented, opportunity given to another. The present case warns against ascribing such improvidence to the statute under review. Blackmailers of both sexes have arisen, using the terrors of the construction now sanctioned by this court as a help — indeed, the means — for their brigandage. The result is grave and should give us pause. It certainly will not be denied that legal authority justifies the rejection of a construction which leads to mischievous consequences, if the statute be susceptible of another construction.

United States v. Bitty, 208 U.S. 393, is not in opposition. The statute passed upon was a prohibition against the importation of alien women or girls, a statute, therefore, of broader purpose than the one under review. Besides, the statute finally passed upon was an amendment to a prior statute and the words construed were an addition to the prior statute and necessarily, therefore, had an added effect. The first statute prohibited the importation of any alien woman or girl into the United States "*for the purposes of prostitution*." The second statute repeated the words and added "*or for any other immoral purpose*" (italics mine). Necessarily there was an enlargement of purpose, and besides the act was directed against the importation of foreign corruption and was construed accordingly. The case, therefore, does not contradict the rule; it is an example of it.

For these reasons I dissent from the opinion and judgment of the court, expressing no opinion of the other propositions in the cases.

Notes and Questions

1. Which opinion do you find to be the better reasoned, the opinion of the Court (i.e., the opinion of the majority), or the dissent? Why? Upon what rule of interpretation does each primarily rely?

2. The Court states that "[w]here the language is plain and admits of no more than one meaning the duty of interpretation does not arise and the rules which are to aid doubtful meanings need no discussion." But is the meaning of a statute ever so plain? Even if so, was the statute at issue in *Caminetti*? And even if so, does such a meaning comport with the Court's interpretation?

3. Recalling the questions raised with respect to *Holy Trinity*, what would possess the government to prosecute someone like Caminetti for this offense? How likely is it that an offense of this nature is prosecuted uniformly across the country (or even within a particular district)? What about the blackmail argument? And how likely is it that a man would knowingly risk eighteen months imprisonment and a $1,500 fine (in 1913) to live with a woman out of wedlock in another state? Should the answers to these questions have any bearing on the interpretation of the act at issue?

4. Can *Caminetti* be squared with *Holy Trinity*? Notice that the *Caminetti* Court makes no express mention of *Holy Trinity* (though that earlier case unquestionably was brought to its attention; *see, e.g.*, 242 U.S. at 482).

5. In which case — *Holy Trinity* or *Caminetti* — is it more likely that Congress "intended" the result reached by the Court? To what extent is this a relevant inquiry, if at all?

6. What do you think of the Court's definition of "immoral purpose"? Must that phrase be interpreted (for purposes of this statute) as including the transporting of a woman to be one's mistress or concubine? If not, then how is one to reasonably choose among alternative possible definitions?

7. What do you think of the Court's invocation of *Bitty*? Is the Court's reasoning here persuasive? Or might the situation at issue in *Bitty* be distinguishable? Is it fair to presume (as the Court seemingly does) that the Congress that enacted the White Slave Traffic Act was aware of the meaning given by the Supreme Court in *Bitty* to the statute in that case?

8. Near the end of its opinion, the Court stated: "Reports to Congress accompanying the introduction of proposed laws may aid the courts in reaching the true meaning of the legislation in cases of doubtful interpretation." Why? The Court also spoke of an exception to its interpretive theory where the language of the statute "lead[s] to absurd or wholly impracticable consequences." Do you agree? What are the pros and cons of such an exception? Notice that the *Caminetti* Court did not invoke either of these devices. Should it have? Would either have made difference?

9. The current version of the statute at issue in *Caminetti*, 18 U.S.C. § 2421 (2006), now provides: "Whoever knowingly transports any individual in interstate or foreign commerce . . . with intent that such individual engage in prostitution, or in any sexual activity for which any person can be charged with a criminal offense, or attempts to do so, shall be fined under this title or imprisoned not more than 10 years, or both." If Caminetti were to be charged with this crime today, would he be guilty?

10. Though *Caminetti* is said to provide an example of the "plain meaning" rule, versions of this rule predate *Caminetti*. For example, in *Sturges v. Crowninshield*, 17 U.S. (4 Wheat.) 122 (1819), the Court (through Chief Justice Marshall) opined:

> [A]lthough the spirit of an instrument, especially of a constitution, is to be respected no less than its letter, yet the spirit is to be collected chiefly from its words. It would be dangerous in the extreme to infer from extrinsic circumstances, that a case for which the words of an instrument expressly provide, shall be exempted from its operation. Where words conflict with each other, where the different clauses of an instrument bear upon each other, and would be inconsistent unless the natural and common import of words be varied, construction becomes necessary, and a departure from the obvious meaning of words is justifiable. But if, in any case, the plain meaning of a provision, not contradicted by any other provision in the same instrument, is to be disregarded, because we believe the framers of that

instrument could not intend what they say, it must be one in which the absurdity and injustice of applying the provision to the case, would be so monstrous, that all mankind would, without hesitation, unite in rejecting the application.

Id. at 202-03.

11. Regardless of what you might think of the Court's articulation and application of the plain meaning rule, the Court is correct, is it not, that Congress alone may enact and amend statutes, and thus that courts cannot simply interpret statutes as they might like them to read?

12. Notice the dissent's comparison of committee reports with floor debates as possible sources of evidence of legislative intent, as well as its preference for the former.

13. "We do not inquire what the legislature meant; we ask only what the statute means." OLIVER WENDELL HOLMES, COLLECTED LEGAL PAPERS 207 (1920).

United States v. American Trucking Associations, Inc.

310 U.S. 534 (1940)

MR. JUSTICE REED delivered the opinion of the Court.

This appeal requires determination of the power of the Interstate Commerce Commission under the Motor Carrier Act, 1935, to establish reasonable requirements with respect to the qualifications and maximum hours of service of employees of motor carriers, other than employees whose duties affect safety of operation.

After detailed consideration, the Motor Carrier Act, 1935, was passed. It followed generally the suggestion of form made by the Federal Coordinator of Transportation. The difficulty and wide scope of the problems raised by the growth of the motor carrier industry were obvious. Congress sought to set out its purpose and the range of its action in a declaration of policy which covered the preservation and fostering of motor transportation in the public interest, tariffs, the coordination of motor carriage with other forms of transportation and cooperation with the several states in their efforts to systematize the industry.

While efficient and economical movement in interstate commerce is obviously a major objective of the Act, there are numerous provisions which make it clear that Congress intended to exercise its powers in the non-transportation phases of motor carrier activity. Safety of operation was constantly before the committees and Congress in their study of the situation.

The pertinent portions of the section of the Act immediately under discussion read as follows:

"SEC. 204 (a). It shall be the duty of the Commission—

"(1) To regulate common carriers by motor vehicle as provided in this part, and to that end the Commission may establish reasonable requirements with respect to continuous and adequate service, transportation of baggage and express, uniform systems of accounts, records, and reports, preservation of records, qualifications and maximum hours of service of employees, and safety of operation and equipment.

"(2) To regulate contract carriers by motor vehicle as provided in this part, and to that end the Commission may establish reasonable requirements with respect to uniform systems of accounts, records, and reports, preservation of records, qualifications and maximum hours of service of employees, and safety of operation and equipment.

"(3) To establish for private carriers of property by motor vehicle, if need therefor is found, reasonable requirements to promote safety of operation, and to that end prescribe qualifications and maximum hours of service of employees, and standards of equipment."

Shortly after the approval of the Act, the Commission on its own motion undertook to and did fix maximum hours of service for "employees whose functions in the operation of motor vehicles make such regulations desirable because of safety considerations." A few months after this determination, the Fair Labor Standards Act was enacted. Section 7 of this act limits the work-week at the normal rate of pay of all employees subject to its terms and § 18 makes the maximum hours of the Fair Labor Standards Act subject to further reduction by applicable federal or state law or municipal ordinances. There were certain employees excepted, however, from these regulations by § 13 (b). It reads as follows:

"Sec. 13 (b). The provisions of section 7 shall not apply with respect to (1) any employee with respect to whom the Interstate Commerce Commission has power to establish qualifications and maximum hours of service pursuant to the provisions of section 204 of the Motor Carrier Act, 1935."

This exception brought sharply into focus the coverage of employees by Motor Carrier Act, § 204 (a). Clerical, storage and other non-transportation workers are under this or the Fair Labor Standards Act, dependent upon the sweep of the word employee in this act. The Commission again examined the question of its jurisdiction and in Ex parte No. MC-28 again reached the conclusion that its power under "section 204 (a) (1) and (2) is limited to prescribing qualifications and maximum hours of service for those employees whose activities affect the safety of operation." It added: "The provisions of section 202 evince a clear intent of Congress to limit our jurisdiction to regulating the motor-carrier industry as a part of the transportation system of the nation. To extend that regulation to features which are not characteristic of transportation or inherent in that industry strikes us as an enlargement of our jurisdiction unwarranted by any express or implied provision in the act, which vests in us all the powers we have." The Wage and Hour Division of the Department of Labor arrived at the same result in an interpretation.

Shortly thereafter appellees, an association of truckmen and various common carriers by motor, filed a petition with the Commission in the present case seeking an exercise of the Commission's jurisdiction under § 204 (a) to fix reasonable requirements "with respect to qualifications and maximum hours of service of all employees of common and contract carriers, except employees whose duties are related to safety of operations; (3) to disregard its report and order in Ex parte MC-28." The Commission reaffirmed its position and denied the petition. The appellees petitioned a three-judge district court to compel the Commission to take jurisdiction and consider the establishment of qualifications and hours of service of all employees of common and contract carriers by motor vehicle. The Administrator of the Wage and Hour Division was permitted to intervene. The district court reversed the Commission, set aside its order and directed it to take jurisdiction of the appellees' petition. 31 F. Supp. 35. A direct appeal to this Court was granted.

In the broad domain of social legislation few problems are enmeshed with the difficulties that surround a determination of what qualifications an employee shall have and how long his hours of work may be. Upon the proper adjustment of these factors within an industry and in relation to competitive activities may well depend the economic success of the enterprises affected as well as the employment and efficiency of the workers. The Motor Carrier Act lays little emphasis upon the clause we are called upon now to construe, "qualifications and maximum hours of service of employees." None of the words are defined by the section, 203, devoted to the explanation of the meaning of the words used in the Act. They are a part of an elaborate enactment drawn and passed in an attempt to adjust a new and growing transportation service to the needs of the public. To find their content, they must be viewed in their setting.

In the interpretation of statutes, the function of the courts is easily stated. It is to construe the language so as to give effect to the intent of Congress. There is no invariable rule for the discovery of that intention. To take a few words from their context and with them thus isolated to attempt to determine their meaning, certainly would not contribute greatly to the discovery of the purpose of the draftsmen of a statute, particularly in a law drawn to meet many needs of a major occupation.

There is, of course, no more persuasive evidence of the purpose of a statute than the words by which the legislature undertook to give expression to its wishes. Often these words are sufficient in and of themselves to determine the purpose of the legislation. In such cases we have followed their plain meaning. When that meaning has led to absurd or futile results, however, this Court has looked beyond the words to the purpose of the act. Frequently, however, even when the plain meaning did not produce absurd results but merely an unreasonable one "plainly at variance with the policy of the legislation as a whole" this Court has followed that purpose, rather than the literal words. When aid to construction of the meaning of words, as used in the statute, is available, there certainly can be no "rule of law" which forbids its use, however clear the words may appear on "superficial examination." The interpretation of the meaning of statutes, as applied to justiciable controversies, is exclusively a judicial function. This duty requires one body of public servants, the judges, to construe the meaning of what another body, the legislators, has said. Obviously there is danger that the courts' conclusion as to legislative purpose will be unconsciously influenced by the judges' own views or by factors not considered by the enacting body. A lively appreciation of the danger is the best assurance of escape from its threat but hardly justifies an acceptance of a literal interpretation dogma which withholds from the courts available information for reaching a correct conclusion. Emphasis should be laid, too, upon the necessity for appraisal of the purposes as a whole of Congress in analyzing the meaning of clauses or sections of general acts. A few words of general connotation appearing in the text of statutes should not be given a wide meaning, contrary to a settled policy, "excepting as a different purpose is plainly shown."

The language here under consideration, if construed as appellees contend, gives to the Commission a power of regulation as to qualifications and hours of employees quite distinct from the settled practice of Congress. That policy has been consistent in legislating for such regulation of transportation employees in matters of movement and safety only. . . . In the face of this course of legislation, coupled with the supporting interpretation of the two administrative agencies concerned with its interpretation, . . . it cannot be said that the word "employee" as used in § 204 (a) is so clear as to the workmen it embraces that we would accept its broadest meaning. The word, of course, is not a word of art. It takes color from its surroundings and frequently is carefully defined by the statute where it appears.

We are especially hesitant to conclude that Congress intended to grant the Commission other than the customary power to secure safety in view of the absence in the legislative history of the Act of any discussion of the desirability of giving the Commission broad and unusual powers over all employees. . . .

The Commission and the Wage and Hour Division, as we have said, have both interpreted § 204 (a) as relating solely to safety of operation. In any case such interpretations are entitled to great weight. This is particularly true here where the interpretations involve "contemporaneous con[s]truction of a statute by the men charged with the responsibility of setting its machinery in motion, of making the parts work efficiently and smoothly while they are yet untried and new." Furthermore, the Commission's interpretation gains much persuasiveness from the fact that it was the Commission which suggested the provisions' enactment to Congress.

It is important to remember that the Commission has three times concluded that its authority was limited to securing safety of operation. . . . Under the circumstances it is unlikely that Congress would not have explicitly overruled the Commission's interpretation had it intended to exempt others than employees who affected safety from the Labor Standards Act.

It is contended by appellees that the difference in language between subsections (1) and (2) and subsection (3) is indicative of a congressional purpose to restrict the regulation of employees of private carriers to "safety of operation" while inserting broader authority in (1) and (2) for employees of common and contract carriers. Appellants answer that the difference in language is explained by the difference in the powers. As (1) and (2) give powers beyond safety for service, goods, accounts and records, language limiting those subsections to safety would be inapt.

Appellees call our attention to certain pending legislation as sustaining their view of the congressional purpose in enacting the Motor Carrier Act. We do not think it can be said that the action of the Senate and House of Representatives on this pending transportation legislation throws much light on the policy of Congress or the meaning attributed by that body to § 204 (a). Aside from the very pertinent fact that the legislation is still unadopted, the legislative history up to now points only to a hesitation to determine a controversy as to the meaning of the present Motor Carrier Act, pending a judicial determination.

One amendment made to the then pending Motor Carrier Act has relevance to our inquiry. . . . The words, "except the provisions of section 204 relative to qualifications and maximum hours of service of employees and safety of operation or standards of equipment," [as found in § 203 (b)], were added by amendment in the

House after the passage of S. 1629 in the Senate with the addition of the disputed clause to § 204 (a) (1) and (2). It is evident that the exempted vehicles and operators include common, contract and private carriers. It seems equally evident that where these vehicles or operators were common or contract carriers, it was not intended by Congress to give the Commission power to regulate the qualifications and hours of service of employees, other than those concerned with the safety of operations.

Our conclusion, in view of the circumstances set out in this opinion, is that the meaning of employees in § 204 (a) (1) and (2) is limited to those employees whose activities affect the safety of operation. The Commission has no jurisdiction to regulate the qualifications or hours of service of any others. The decree of the district court is accordingly reversed and it is directed to dismiss the complaint of the appellees.

Reversed.

The CHIEF JUSTICE, MR. JUSTICE MCREYNOLDS, MR. JUSTICE STONE, and MR. JUSTICE ROBERTS are of the opinion that the decree should be affirmed for the reasons stated in the opinion of the district court, 31 F. Supp. 35.

Notes and Questions

---

1. Can the reasoning of the Court in *American Trucking* be reconciled with that in *Caminetti*? If not, what was the interpretive rule articulated by the *American Trucking* Court?

2. In its statutory interpretation analysis, the Court began by speaking of the "intent of Congress," but then shifted to a discussion of the "purpose of the legislation." Are these two phrases one and the same, or do they refer to separate and distinct concepts?

3. How, if at all, does an "absurd" result differ from a result that is "plainly at variance with the policy of the legislation as a whole"? How is one to determine the latter?

4. Notice that the Court deferred to (or at least agreed with) the interpretation reached by administrative agency charged with its enforcement. Is it not likely, in such circumstances, that the agency's interpretation is correct?

5. The Court stated that in light of the agency's prior interpretation of the statute in question, "it is unlikely that Congress would not have explicitly overruled the [agency's] interpretation" had it intended a contrary result. Is this a valid presumption? To what extent should we expect Congress to be aware of prior agency interpretations? Or to expect Congress to include express statutory language when intending to overrule such interpretations?

6. The Court was correct, was it not, in rejecting the consideration of similar legislation pending (but not yet enacted)? The same also can be said, can it not, of the appropriateness of the Court's consideration of the history of the Act in question (i.e., how that Act was amended, as it worked its way through Congress), for whatever such an exercise might be worth? What is the difference between these two possible forms of "authority" as means of ascertaining legislative intent or the purpose of a statute?

7. The Court states that "[t]here is no invariable rule for the discovery of [the intent of Congress]." Assuming this is true, why not? Should there be such a rule, or would it necessarily be so complicated and include so many exceptions as to not be worthwhile?

8. *American Trucking* became known for the Court's use of statutory purpose as a means of interpreting statutes. Purposivism remained a powerful theory of statutory interpretation for several decades, leading to the following summarizing Note.

Henry M. Hart, Jr. & Albert M. Sacks

NOTE ON THE RUDIMENTS OF STATUTORY INTERPRETATION

**The Legal Process: Basic Problems in the Making and Application of Law
(William N. Eskridge, Jr. & Philip P. Frickey eds., 1994)**

Consider the adequacy of the following summation:

A. THE GENERAL NATURE OF THE TASK OF INTERPRETATION

The function of a court in interpreting a statute is to decide what meaning ought to be given to the directions of the statute in the respects relevant to the case before it.

Comment: Before deciding that this statement is so nearly indeterminate as to be meaningless, notice what it does *not* say. It does not say that the court's function is to ascertain the intention of the legislature with respect to the matter at issue.

B. THE MOOD IN WHICH THE TASK SHOULD BE DONE

1. Respect the position of the legislature as the chief policy-determining agency of the society, subject only to the limitations of the constitution under which it exercises its powers;

2. Respect the constitutional procedures for the enactment of bills;

3. Be mindful of the dependence of the legislature upon the good faith and good sense of the agencies of authoritative interpretation;

4. Be mindful of the nature of language and, in particular, of its special nature when used as a medium for giving authoritative general directions; and

5. Be mindful of the nature of law and of the fact that every statute is a part of the law and partakes of the qualities of law, and particularly of the quality of striving for even-handed justice.

C. A CONCISE STATEMENT OF THE TASK

In interpreting a statute a court should:

1. Decide what purpose ought to be attributed to the statute and to any subordinate provision of it which may be involved; and then

2. Interpret the words of the statute immediately in question so as to carry out the purpose as best it can, making sure, however, that it does not give the words either —

(a) a meaning they will not bear, or

(b) a meaning which would violate any established policy of clear statement.

D. THE DOUBLE ROLE OF THE WORDS AS GUIDES TO INTERPRETATION

The words of a statute, taken in their context, serve both as guides in the attribution of general purpose and as factors limiting the particular meanings that can properly be attributed.

When the words fit with all the relevant elements of their context to convey a single meaning, as applied to the matter in hand, the mind of the interpreter moves to a confident conclusion almost instantaneously; and this double aspect of the operation of the words will not be apparent. . . .

It is in such cases that courts sometimes say that "the need for interpretation does not arise." In a just analysis, however, interpretation seems always to be involved when meaning is communicated.

Interpretation requires a conscious effort when the words do not fit with their context to convey any single meaning. It is in such cases that the words will be seen to play a double part, first, as a factor together with relevant elements of the context in the formulation of hypotheses about possible purposes, and, second, as a separately limiting factor in checking the hypotheses.

E. THE MEANING THE WORDS WILL BEAR

The proposition that a court ought never to give the words of a statute a meaning they will not bear is a corollary of the propositions that courts are bound to respect the constitutional position of the legislature and the constitutional procedures for the enactment of legislation.

The words of the statute are what the legislature has enacted as law, and all that it has the power to enact. Unenacted intentions or wishes cannot be given effect as law.

In deciding whether words will bear a particular meaning, a court needs to be linguistically wise and not naive. It needs to understand, especially, that meaning depends upon context. But language is a social institution. Humpty Dumpty was wrong when he said that you can make words mean whatever you want them to mean.

The language belongs to the whole society and not to the legislature in office for the time being. Courts on occasion can correct mistakes, as by inserting or striking out a negative, when it is completely clear from the context that a mistake has been made. But they cannot permit the legislative process, and all the other processes which depend upon the integrity of language, to be subverted by the misuse of words.

Unabridged dictionaries are historical records (as reliable as the judgment and industry of the editors) of the meanings with which words have in fact been used by writers of good repute. They are often useful in answering hard questions of whether, in an appropriate context, a particular meaning is linguistically permissible.

So-called maxims of construction, such as *ejusdem generis*, *expressio unius est exclusio alterius*, *noscitur a sociis*, and *reddendo singula singulis*, are useful as reassurances about the meaning which particular configurations of words *may* have in an appropriate context. They should not be treated as rules about the meaning which the configurations invariably *must* have.

As these maxims suggest, the proposition that words must not be given a meaning they will not bear operates almost wholly to *prevent* rather than to *compel* expansion of the scope of statutes. The meaning of words can almost always be narrowed if the context seems to call for narrowing.

F. POLICIES OF CLEAR STATEMENT

In various types of situations wise policy counsels against giving words an unusual meaning even though it may be linguistically permissible.

Like the first requirement just considered that words must bear the meaning given them, these policies of clear statement may on occasion operate to defeat the actual, consciously held intention of particular legislators, or of the members of the legislature generally. Like that requirement, in other words, they constitute conditions on the effectual exercise of legislative power. But the requirement should be thought of as constitutionally imposed. The policies have been judicially developed to promote objectives of the legal system which transcend the wishes of any particular session of the legislature.

In general, the requisite clearness of statement of a statutory provision should be thought of as varying according to the position of those to whom it is primarily addressed. Correspondingly, the degree of clearness which particular words actually have should be judged in light of that position. This means that attention should be paid not only to the linguistic usages of the addressees as a class but to the extent to which the various elements of the context are known or available to them. *E.g.*, committee reports and legislative debates.

The need for clarity is at its greatest in words addressed to private persons. Words addressed primarily to judges, on the other hand, may fairly presuppose the powers of analysis and ratiocination which judges supposedly have. Words addressed to officials of other kinds may presuppose the characteristic capacity for understanding of those officials.

Two policies of clear statement call for particular mention.

The first of these, familiar and long-standing, requires that words which mark the boundary between criminal and non-criminal conduct should speak with more than ordinary clearness. This policy has special force when the conduct on the safe side of the line is not, in the general understanding of the community, morally blameworthy.

The second forbids a court to understand a legislature as directing a departure from a generally prevailing principle or policy of the law unless it does so clearly. This policy has special force when the departure is so great as to raise a serious question of constitutional power. This general policy lies behind the various presumptions referred to in discussing the attribution of purpose.

G. THE ATTRIBUTION OF PURPOSE

1. Enacted Statements of Purpose

A formally enacted statement of purpose in a statute should be accepted by the court if it appears to have been designed to serve as a guide to interpretation, is consistent with the words and context of the statute, and is relevant to the question of meaning at issue.

In all other situations, the purpose of a statute has in some degree to be inferred.

2. Inferring purpose: The Nature of the Problem

In drawing such inferences the court needs to be aware that the concept of purpose is not simple.

(a) Purposes may be shaped with differing degrees of definiteness.

The definiteness may be such that resolution of a doubt about purpose resolves, without more, a question of specific application.

Or a purpose may be deliberately formulated with great generality, openly contemplating the exercise of further judgment by the interpreter even after he has fully grasped the legislature's thought. *E.g.*, the direction to the Federal Trade Commission to prevent, in certain ways, "unfair methods of competition in commerce."

(b) Purposes, moreover, may exist in hierarchies or constellations. *E.g.* (to give a very simple illustration), to do *this* only so far as possible without doing *that*.

(c) One form of such a constellation or relationship is invariable in the law and of immense importance. The purpose of a statute must always be treated as including not only an immediate purpose or group of related purposes but a larger and subtler purpose as to how the particular statute is to be fitted into the legal system as a whole.

An isolated enactment, not part of a comprehensive code, always raises the question: What purpose is to be attributed to the statute with respect to the treatment of related matters falling outside the four corners of its immediate application? As contemplating judicial solution of such problems without any reference to the statute whatever? As precluding judicial change in previously announced law relating to them? Or as encouraging or directing judicial change in accordance with the underlying policy or principle of the statute?

A provision in a comprehensive code presents always a distinctive question of interpretive method. In interpreting such a provision, the court must necessarily be aware that the sole agency of growth of the law thereafter will have to be the legislature, if the provision is read as precluding exercise of creative activity on its part. It has to attribute a purpose to the statute in this regard.

3. Inferring Purpose: The Technique

In determining the more immediate purpose which ought to be attributed to a statute, and to any subordinate provision of it which may be involved, a court should try to put itself in imagination in the position of the legislature which enacted the statute.

The court, however, should not do this in the mood of a cynical political observer, taking account of all the short-run currents of political expedience that swirl around any legislative session.

It should assume, unless the contrary unmistakably appears, that the legislature was made up of reasonable persons pursuing reasonable purposes reasonably.

It should presume conclusively that these persons, whether or not entertaining concepts of reasonableness shared by the court, were trying responsibly and in good faith to discharge their constitutional powers and duties.

The court should then proceed to do, in substance, just what Lord Coke said it should do in *Heydon's Case*. The gist of this approach is to infer purpose by comparing the new law with the old. Why would reasonable men, confronted with the law as it was, have enacted this new law to replace it? Answering this question, as Lord Coke said, calls for a close look at the "mischief" thought to inhere in the old law and at "the true reason of the remedy" provided by the statute for it.

The most reliable guides to an answer will be found in the instances of unquestioned application of the statute. Even in the case of a new statute there almost invariably *are* such instances, in which, because of the perfect fit of words and context, the meaning seems unmistakable.

Once these points of reference are established, they throw a double light. The purposes necessarily implied in them illuminate facets of the general purpose. At the same time they provide a basis for reasoning by analogy to the disputed application in hand. *E.g.*, why would the legislature distinguish, for purposes of punishment, between an escaper serving only a single sentence and one serving the first of several? What is crucial here is the realization that law is being made, and that law is not supposed to be irrational.

4. Inferring Purpose: Aids from the Context

The whole context of a statute may be examined in aid of its interpretation, and should be whenever substantial doubt about its meaning exists in the interpreter's mind, or is suggested by him.

Not only the state of the law immediately before enactment but the course of its prior development is relevant.

The court may draw on general public knowledge of what was considered to be the mischief that needed remedying.

Formal public announcements of those concerned with the preparation or advocacy of the measure may be freely consulted. *E.g.*, messages of the chief executive, reports of commissions, and the like.

The internal legislative history of the measure (that is, its history from the filing of the bill to enactment) may be examined, if this was reduced to writing officially and contemporaneously. But in the use which is made of this material two closely related limitations should be scrupulously observed.

First. The history should be examined for the light it throws on *general purpose*. Evidence of specific intention with respect to particular applications is competent only to the extent that the particular applications illuminate the general purpose and are consistent with other evidence of it.

Second. Effect should not be given to evidence from the internal legislative history if the result would be to contradict a purpose otherwise indicated and to yield an interpretation disadvantageous to private persons who had no reasonable means of access to the history.

5. Inferring Purpose: Post-Enactment Aids

The judicial, administrative, and popular construction of a statute, subsequent to its enactment, are all relevant to attributing a purpose to it.

The court's own prior interpretation of a statute in related applications should be accepted, on the principle of *stare decisis*, unless they are manifestly out of accord with other indications of purpose. Once these applications are treated as fixed, they serve as points of reference for juristic thinking in the same fashion as verbally clear applications in the case of a new statute.

An administrative or popular construction is relevant for different reasons. Such a construction affords weighty evidence that the words *may* bear the meaning involved. In the absence of reasons of self-interest or the like for discounting the construction, it is persuasive evidence that the meaning is a natural one. Considerations of the stability of transactions and of existing understandings counsel in favor of its acceptance, if possible. In cases where the construction has been widely accepted and consistently adhered, it may be said to fix the meaning — to *be* the meaning which experience has demonstrated the words to bear.

6. Inferring Purpose: Presumptions

The court's last resort, when doubt about the immediate purpose of a statute remains, is resort to an appropriate presumption drawn from some general policy of law.

This is likely to be its only resort when the question concerns more nearly ultimate policy, or the mode of fitting the statute into the general fabric of the law.

Reflection about these presumptions is the most important task in the development of a workable and working theory of statutory interpretation.

H. INTERPRETING THE WORDS TO CARRY OUT THE PURPOSE

The degree of definiteness to be attributed to the legislative purpose in the enactment of the statute is decisive of the nature of the task of interpretation which remains after the purpose has been grasped.

The task, if it still involves significant choices, is essentially one of creative elaboration of the principles and policies initially formulated in the statute.

The main burden of the task should be carried by the institution (court or administrative agency) which has the first-line responsibility for applying the statute authoritatively.

This agency should give sympathetic attention to indications in the legislative history of the lines of contemplated growth, if the history is available. It should give weight to popular construction of self-operating elements of the statute, if that is uniform. Primarily, it should strive to develop a coherent and reasoned pattern of applications intelligibly related to the general purpose.

A uniform interpretation by an administrative agency charged with official responsibility of any kind under the statute should be given weight by a court.

An interpretation by an administrative agency charged with first-line responsibility for the authoritative application of the statute should be accepted by the court as conclusive, if it is consistent with the purpose properly to be attributed to the statute, and if it has been arrived at with regard to the factors which should be taken into account in elaborating it.

Notes and Questions

1. What do you think of the adequacy of the above "summation"?

2. In addition to the summation set forth above, Professors Hart and Sacks also set forth the following "conclusions" with respect to the process of statutory interpretation:

> *Avoid linguistic naivete.* Avoid, in particular, the one-word, one-meaning fallacy. Words may have many different meanings. There are more ideas in the world to be expressed than there are words in any language in which to express them.
>
> *Meaning depends upon context.* The way in which you tell which of various possible meanings of a word is the right one is by reference to the context. (To verify this, look at the way any unabridged dictionary is made up.)
>
> *An essential part of the context of every statute is its purpose.* Every statute must be conclusively presumed to be a purposive act. The idea of a statute without an intelligible purpose is foreign to the idea of law and inadmissible.
>
> *The meaning of a statute is never plain unless it fits with some intelligible purpose.* Any judicial opinion . . . , which finds a plain meaning in a statute without consideration of its purpose, condemns itself on its face. The opinion is linguistically, philosophically, legally, and generally ignorant. It is deserving of nothing but contempt. (There are lots of opinions of this kind being handed down every day by both English and American courts.)
>
> *The first task in the interpretation of any statute (or of any provision of a statute) is to determine what purpose ought to be attributed to it.* The principal problem in the development of a workable technique of interpretation is the formulation of accepted and acceptable criteria for the attribution of purpose.
>
> *Deciding what purpose ought to be attributed to a statute is often difficult. But at least three things about it are always easy.* (a) The statute ought always to be presumed to be the work of reasonable men pursuing reasonable purposes reasonably, unless the contrary is made unmistakably to appear. (b) The general words of a statute ought never to be read as directing an irrational pattern of particular applications. (c) What constitutes an irrational pattern of particular applications ought always to be judged in the light of the overriding and organizing purpose.

Id. at 1124-25.

b. The Modern Standard

American Trucking became known for the Court's use of statutory purpose as a means of interpreting statutes, and with the help of Professors Hart and Sacks, purposivism became a powerful theory of statutory interpretation. But by the 1980s, the Court started to move in a different direction, a direction that resulted in a new theory of statutory interpretation that remains the dominant (though by no means exclusive) theory today.

Griffin v. Oceanic Contractors, Inc.

458 U.S. 564 (1982)

JUSTICE REHNQUIST delivered the opinion of the Court.

This case concerns the application of 46 U. S. C. § 596, which requires certain masters and vessel owners to pay seamen promptly after their discharge and authorizes seamen to recover double wages for each day that payment is delayed without sufficient cause. The question is whether the district courts, in the exercise of discretion, may limit the period during which this wage penalty is assessed, or whether imposition of the penalty is mandatory for each day that payment is withheld in violation of the statute.

I

On February 18, 1976, petitioner signed an employment contract with respondent in New Orleans, agreeing to work as a senior pipeline welder on board vessels operated by respondent in the North Sea. The contract specified that petitioner's employment would extend "until December 15, 1976 or until Oceanic's 1976 pipeline committal in the North Sea is fulfilled, whichever shall occur first." The contract also provided that respondent would pay for transportation to and from the worksite, but that if petitioner quit the job prior to its termination date, or if his services were terminated for cause, he would be charged with the cost of transportation back to the United States. Respondent reserved the right to withhold $137.50 from each of petitioner's first four paychecks "as a cash deposit for the payment of your return transportation in the event you should become obligated for its payment." On March 6, 1976, petitioner flew from the United States to Antwerp, Belgium, where he reported to work at respondent's vessel, the "Lay Barge 27," berthed in the Antwerp harbor for repairs.

On April 1, 1976, petitioner suffered an injury while working on the deck of the vessel readying it for sea. Two days later he underwent emergency surgery in Antwerp. On April 5, petitioner was discharged from the hospital and went to respondent's Antwerp office, where he spoke with Jesse Williams, the welding superintendent, and provided a physician's statement that he was not fit for duty. Williams refused to acknowledge that petitioner's injury was work-related and denied that respondent was liable for medical and hospital expenses, maintenance, or unearned wages. Williams also refused to furnish transportation back to the United States, and continued to retain $412.50 in earned wages that had been deducted from petitioner's first three paychecks for that purpose. Petitioner returned to his home in Houston, Tex., the next day at his own expense. He was examined there by a physician who determined that he would be able to resume work on May 3, 1976. On May 5, petitioner began working as a welder for another company operating in the North Sea.

In 1978 he brought suit against respondent under the Jones Act, § 20, 38 Stat. 1185, as amended, 46 U. S. C. § 688, and under general maritime law, seeking damages for respondent's failure to pay maintenance, cure, unearned wages, repatriation expenses, and the value of certain personal effects lost on board respondent's vessel. Petitioner also sought penalty wages under Rev. Stat. § 4529, as amended, 46 U. S. C.

§ 596, for respondent's failure to pay over the $412.50 in earned wages allegedly due upon discharge. The District Court found for petitioner and awarded damages totaling $23,670.40.

Several findings made by that court are particularly relevant to this appeal. First, the court found that petitioner's injury was proximately caused by an unseaworthy condition of respondent's vessel. Second, the court found that petitioner was discharged from respondent's employ on the day of the injury, and that the termination of his employment was caused solely by that injury. Third, it found that respondent's failure to pay petitioner the $412.50 in earned wages was "without sufficient cause." Finally, the court found that petitioner had exercised due diligence in attempting to collect those wages.

In assessing penalty wages under 46 U. S. C. § 596, the court held that "the period during which the penalty runs is to be determined by the sound discretion of the district court and depends on the equities in the case." It determined that the appropriate period for imposition of the penalty was from the date of discharge, April 1, 1976, through the date of petitioner's reemployment, May 5, 1976, a period of 34 days. Applying the statute, it computed a penalty of $6,881.60. Petitioner appealed the award of damages as inadequate.

The Court of Appeals for the Fifth Circuit affirmed. 664 F. 2d 36 (1981). That court concluded, *inter alia*, that the District Court had not erred in limiting assessment of the penalty provided by 46 U. S. C. § 596 to the period beginning April 1 and ending May 5. The court recognized that the statute required payment of a penalty for each day during which wages were withheld until the date they were actually paid, which in this case did not occur until September 17, 1980, when respondent satisfied the judgment of the District Court. Nevertheless, the court believed itself bound by prior decisions within the Circuit, which left calculation of the penalty period to the sound discretion of the district courts. It concluded that the District Court in this case had not abused its discretion by assessing a penalty only for the period during which petitioner was unemployed.

We granted certiorari to resolve a conflict among the Circuits regarding the proper application of the wage penalty statute. We reverse the judgment of the Court of Appeals as to that issue.

II

A

The language of the statute first obligates the master or owner of any vessel making coasting or foreign voyages to pay every seaman the balance of his unpaid wages within specified periods after his discharge. It then provides:

> "Every master or owner who refuses or neglects to make payment in the manner hereinbefore mentioned without sufficient cause shall pay to the seaman a sum equal to two days' pay for each and every day during which payment is delayed beyond the respective periods . . . ."

The statute in straightforward terms provides for the payment of double wages, depending upon the satisfaction of two conditions. First, the master or owner must have refused or failed to pay the seaman his wages within the periods specified. Second, this failure or refusal must be "without sufficient cause." Once these conditions are satisfied, however, the unadorned language of the statute dictates that the master or owner "*shall pay* to the seaman" the sums specified "*for each and every day* during which payment is delayed." The words chosen by Congress, given their plain meaning, leave no room for the exercise of discretion either in deciding whether to exact payment or in choosing the period of days by which the payment is to be calculated. As this Court described the statute many years ago, it "affords a definite and reasonable procedure by which the seaman may establish his right to recover double pay where his wages are unreasonably withheld." Our task is to give effect to the will of Congress, and where its will has been expressed in reasonably plain terms, "that language must ordinarily be regarded as conclusive."

The District Court found that respondent had refused to pay petitioner the balance of his earned wages promptly after discharge, and that its refusal was "without sufficient cause." Respondent challenges neither of these findings. Although the two statutory conditions were satisfied, however, the District Court obviously did not assess double wages "for each and every day" during which payment was delayed, but instead limited the assessment to the period of petitioner's unemployment. Nothing in the language of the statute vests the courts with the discretion to set such a limitation.

B

Nevertheless, respondent urges that the legislative purpose of the statute is best served by construing it to permit some choice in determining the length of the penalty period. In respondent's view, the purpose of the statute is essentially remedial and compensatory, and thus it should not be interpreted literally to produce a monetary award that is so far in excess of any equitable remedy as to be punitive.

Respondent, however, is unable to support this view of legislative purpose by reference to the terms of the statute. "There is, of course, no more persuasive evidence of the purpose of a statute than the words by which the legislature undertook to give expression to its wishes." *United States* v. *American Trucking Assns., Inc.*, 310 U. S. 534, 543 (1940). See *Caminetti* v. *United States*, 242 U. S. 470, 490 (1917). Nevertheless, in rare cases the literal application of a statute will produce a result demonstrably at odds with the intentions of its drafters, and those intentions must be controlling. We have reserved "some 'scope for adopting a restricted rather than a literal or usual meaning of its words where acceptance of that meaning would thwart the obvious purpose of the statute.'" This, however, is not the exceptional case.

As the Court recognized [previously], the "evident purpose" of the statute is "to secure prompt payment of seamen's wages and thus to protect them from the harsh consequences of arbitrary and unscrupulous action of their employers, to which, as a class, they are peculiarly exposed." This was to be accomplished "by the imposition of a liability which is not exclusively compensatory, but designed to prevent, by its coercive effect, arbitrary refusals to pay wages, and to induce prompt payment when payment is possible." Thus, although the sure purpose of the statute is remedial, Congress has chosen to secure that purpose through the use of potentially punitive sanctions designed to deter negligent or arbitrary delays in payment.

The legislative history of the statute leaves little if any doubt that this understanding is correct. The law owes its origins to the Act of July 20, 1790, passed by the First Congress. Although the statute as originally enacted gave every seaman the right to collect the wages due under his contract "as soon as the voyage is ended," it did not provide for the recovery of additional sums to encourage compliance. Such a provision was added by the Shipping Commissioners Act of 1872, which provided for the payment of "a sum not exceeding the amount of two days' pay for each of the days, not exceeding ten days, during which payment is delayed." The Act of 1872 obviously established a ceiling of 10 days on the period during which the penalty could be assessed and, by use of the words "not exceeding," left the courts with discretion to choose an appropriate penalty within that period.

Congress amended the law again in 1898. As amended, it read in relevant part:

> "Every master or owner who refuses or neglects to make payment in manner hereinbefore mentioned without sufficient cause shall pay to the seaman a sum equal to one day's pay for each and every day during which payment is delayed beyond the respective periods."

The amending legislation thus effected two changes: first, it removed the discretion theretofore existing by which courts might award less than an amount calculated on the basis of each day during which payment was delayed, and, second, it removed the 10-day ceiling which theretofore limited the number of days upon which an award might be calculated. The accompanying Committee Reports identify the purpose of the legislation as "the amelioration of the condition of the American seaman," and characterize the amended wage penalty in particular as "designed to secure the promptest possible payment of wages." Nothing in the legislative history of the 1898 Act suggests that Congress intended to do anything other than what the Act's enacted language plainly demonstrates: to strengthen the deterrent effect of the statue by removing the courts' latitude in assessing the wage penalty.

The statute was amended for the last time in 1915 to increase further the severity of the penalty by doubling the wages due for each day during which payment of earned wages was delayed. There is no suggestion in the Committee Report or in the floor debates that, in so doing, Congress intended to reinvest the courts with the discretion it had removed in the Act of 1898. Resort to the legislative history, therefore, merely confirms that Congress intended the statute to mean exactly what its plain language says.

III

Respondent argues, however, that a literal construction of the statute in this case would produce an absurd and unjust result which Congress could not have intended. The District Court found that the daily wage to be used in computing the penalty was $101.20. If the statute is applied literally, petitioner would receive twice this amount for each day after his discharge until September 17, 1980, when respondent satisfied the District Court's judgment. Petitioner would receive over $300,000 simply because respondent improperly withheld $412.50 in wages. In respondent's view, Congress could not have intended seamen to receive windfalls of this nature without regard to the equities of the case.

It is true that interpretations of a statute which would produce absurd results are to be avoided if alternative interpretations consistent with the legislative purpose are available. See *United States* v. *American Trucking Assns., Inc.* In refusing to nullify statutes, however hard or unexpected the particular effect, this Court has said:

> "Laws enacted with good intention, when put to the test, frequently, and to the surprise of the law maker himself, turn out to be mischievous, absurd or otherwise objectionable. But in such case the remedy lies with the law making authority, and not with the courts."

It is highly probable that respondent is correct in its contention that a recovery in excess of $300,000 in this case greatly exceeds any actual injury suffered by petitioner as a result of respondent's delay in paying his wages. But this Court has previously recognized that awards made under this statute were not intended to be merely compensatory[.] . . .

It is in the nature of punitive remedies to authorize awards that may be out of proportion to actual injury; such remedies typically are established to deter particular conduct, and the legislature not infrequently finds that harsh consequences must be visited upon those whose conduct it would deter. It is probably true that Congress did not precisely envision the grossness of the difference in this case between the actual wages withheld and the amount of the award required by the statute. But it might equally well be said that Congress did not precisely envision the trebled amount of some damages awards in private antitrust actions, or that, because it enacted the Endangered Species Act, "the survival of a relatively small number of three-inch fish would require the permanent halting of a virtually completed dam for which Congress had expended more than $1 million." It is enough that Congress intended that the language it enacted would be applied as we have applied it. The remedy for any dissatisfaction with the results in particular cases lies with Congress and not with this Court. Congress may amend the statute; we may not.

. . . .

IV

The District Court found that respondent's refusal to pay petitioner earned wages following his discharge was without sufficient cause. It applied the wage penalty only for the period of nonpayment during which petitioner was unable to work. It made no finding, however, that respondent's continuing delay in payment beyond that period was for sufficient cause. Under the plain language of the statute, therefore, its decision to limit the penalty period was error. The judgment of the Court of Appeals affirming that decision accordingly is reversed, and the case is remanded for proceedings consistent with this opinion.

JUSTICE STEVENS, with whom JUSTICE BLACKMUN joins, dissenting.

In final analysis, any question of statutory construction requires the judge to decide how the legislature intended its enactment to apply to the case at hand. The language of the statute is usually sufficient to answer that question, but "the reports are full of cases" [(*Holy Trinity*)] in which the will of the legislature is not reflected in a literal reading of the words it has chosen. In my opinion this is such a case.

Qualifying language in 46 U. S. C. § 596 supports a much narrower construction than the Court adopts. For over 50 years after the statute's most recent amendment in 1915, federal judges consistently construed it to avoid the absurd result the Court sanctions today. Their reading of the statute was consistent with the specific purposes achieved by the amendments in 1898 and 1915, as well as with the meaning of the statute when an award for unearned wages was first authorized.

. . . .

. . . Whether those decisions were entirely consistent with the meaning a grammarian might have placed on the statute is less significant than the fact that they were entirely consistent with this Court's decisions and with one another, and the fact that their holdings must have come to the attention of Congress.

It was not until 1966 that a contrary reading of the statute was adopted . . . and another eight years before that case was followed in another Circuit. I cannot deny that there is wisdom in the rule of construction that mandates close adherence to literal statutory text, but it is also true that a consistent course of judicial construction can become as much a part of a statute as words inserted by the legislature itself. . . .

. . . .

The construction permitting the district court to exercise some discretion in tailoring the double-wage award to the particular equities of the case is just as consistent with the legislative history of § 596 as the Court's new literal approach to this statute. . . .

. . . .

The Court's construction of the amendment is, however, both drastic and dramatic. Instead of effecting a modest enlargement of the judge's discretion to do justice in these cases, the Court's construction effects a complete prohibition of judicial discretion. . . . Such a major change in both the potential amount of the statutory recovery and the character of the judge's authority would normally be explained in the committee reports or the debates if it had been intended.

. . . .

I respectfully dissent.

United States v. Ron Pair Enterprises, Inc.

489 U.S. 235 (1989)

JUSTICE BLACKMUN delivered the opinion of the Court.

In this case we must decide the narrow statutory issue whether § 506(b) of the Bankruptcy Code of 1978 entitles a creditor to receive postpetition interest on a nonconsensual oversecured claim allowed in a bankruptcy proceeding. We conclude that it does, and we therefore reverse the judgment of the Court of Appeals.

I

Respondent Ron Pair Enterprises, Inc., filed a petition for reorganization under Chapter 11 of the Bankruptcy Code on May 1, 1984, in the United States Bankruptcy

Court for the Eastern District of Michigan. The Government filed timely proof of a prepetition claim of $52,277.93, comprised of assessments for unpaid withholding and Social Security taxes, penalties, and prepetition interest. The claim was perfected through a tax lien on property owned by respondent. Respondent's First Amended Plan of Reorganization, filed October 1, 1985, provided for full payment of the prepetition claim, but did not provide for postpetition interest, since the property securing the claim had a value greater than the amount of the principal debt. At the Bankruptcy Court hearing, the parties stipulated that the claim was oversecured, but the court subsequently overruled the Government's objection. The Government appealed to the United States District Court for the Eastern District of Michigan. That court reversed the Bankruptcy Court's judgment, concluding that the plain language of § 506(b) entitled the Government to postpetition interest.

The United States Court of Appeals for the Sixth Circuit, in its turn, reversed the District Court. 828 F. 2d 367 (1987). While not directly ruling that the language of § 506(b) was ambiguous, the court reasoned that reference to pre-Code law was appropriate "in order to better understand the context in which the provision was drafted and therefore the language itself." The court went on to note that under pre-Code law the general rule was that postpetition interest on an oversecured prepetition claim was allowable only where the lien was consensual in nature. In light of this practice, and of the lack of any legislative history evincing an intent to change the standard, the court held that § 506(b) codified the pre-existing standard, and that postpetition interest was allowable only on consensual claims. Because this result was in direct conflict with the view of the Court of Appeals for the Fourth Circuit, and with the views of other courts, we granted certiorari to resolve the conflict.

II

Section 506, enacted as part of the extensive 1978 revision of the bankruptcy laws, governs the definition and treatment of secured claims, *i. e.*, claims by creditors against the estate that are secured by a lien on property in which the estate has an interest. Subsection (a) of § 506 provides that a claim is secured only to the extent of the value of the property on which the lien is fixed; the remainder of that claim is considered unsecured. Subsection (b) is concerned specifically with oversecured claims, that is, any claim that is for an amount less than the value of the property securing it. Thus, if a $50,000 claim were secured by a lien on property having a value of $75,000, the claim would be oversecured, provided the trustee's costs of preserving or disposing of the property were less than $25,000. Section 506(b) allows a holder of an oversecured claim to recover, in addition to the prepetition amount of the claim, "interest on such claim, and any reasonable fees, costs, or charges provided for under the agreement under which such claim arose."

The question before us today arises because there are two types of secured claims: (1) voluntary (or consensual) secured claims, each created by agreement between the debtor and the creditor and called a "security interest" by the Code, and (2) involuntary secured claims, such as a judicial or statutory lien, which are fixed by operation of law and do not require the consent of the debtor. The claim against respondent's estate was of this latter kind. Prior to the passage of the 1978 Code, some Courts of Appeals drew a distinction between the two types for purposes of determining post-petition interest. The question we must answer is whether the 1978 Code recognizes and enforces this distinction, or whether Congress intended that all oversecured claims be treated the same way for purposes of postpetition interest.

III

Initially, it is worth recalling that Congress worked on the formulation of the Code for nearly a decade. It was intended to modernize the bankruptcy laws, and as a result made significant changes in both the substantive and procedural laws of bankruptcy. In particular, Congress intended "significant changes from current law in the treatment of secured creditors and secured claims." In such a substantial overhaul of the system, it is not appropriate or realistic to expect Congress to have explained with particularity each step it took. Rather, as long as the statutory scheme is coherent and consistent, there generally is no need for a court to inquire beyond the plain language of the statute.

A

The task of resolving the dispute over the meaning of § 506(b) begins where all such inquiries must begin: with the language of the statute itself. In this case it is also where the inquiry should end, for where, as here, the statute's language is plain, "the sole function of the courts is to enforce it according to its terms." *Caminetti v. United States*, 242 U. S. 470, 485 (1917). The language before us expresses Congress' intent — that postpetition interest be available — with sufficient precision so that reference to legislative history and to pre-Code practice is hardly necessary.

The relevant phrase in § 506(b) is: "There shall be allowed to the holder of such claim, interest on such claim, and any reasonable fees, costs, or charges provided for under the agreement under which such claim arose." "Such claim" refers to an over-secured claim. The natural reading of the phrase entitles the holder of an oversecured claim to postpetition interest and, in addition, gives one having a secured claim created pursuant to an agreement the right to reasonable fees, costs, and charges provided for in that agreement. Recovery of postpetition interest is unqualified. Recovery of fees, costs, and charges, however, is allowed only if they are reasonable and provided for in the agreement under which the claim arose. Therefore, in the absence of an agreement, postpetition interest is the only added recovery available.

This reading is also mandated by the grammatical structure of the statute. The phrase "interest on such claim" is set aside by commas, and separated from the reference to fees, costs, and charges by the conjunctive words "and any." As a result, the phrase "interest on such claim" stands independent of the language that follows. "Interest on such claim" is not part of the list made up of "fees, costs, or charges," nor is it joined to the following clause so that the final "provided for under the agreement" modifies it as well. The language and punctuation Congress used cannot be read in any other way.[4] By the plain language of the statute, the two types of recovery are distinct.[5]

B

The plain meaning of legislation should be conclusive, except in "rare cases in which the literal application of a statute will produce a result demonstrably at odds with the intentions of its drafters." *Griffin v. Oceanic Contractors, Inc.*, 458 U. S. 564, 571 (1982). In such cases, the intention of the drafters, rather than the strict language, controls. *Ibid.* It is clear that allowing postpetition interest on nonconsensual over-secured liens does not contravene the intent of the framers of the Code. Allowing such interest does not conflict with any other section of the Code, or with any important state or federal interest; nor is a contrary view suggested by the legislative history. Respondent has not articulated, nor can we discern, any significant reason why Congress would have intended, or any policy reason would compel, that the two types of secured claims be treated differently in allowing postpetition interest.

C

Respondent urges that pre-Code practice drew a distinction between consensual and nonconsensual liens for the purpose of determining entitlement to postpetition interest, and that Congress' failure to repudiate that distinction requires us to enforce it. . . . We disagree.

. . . .

. . . Although the payment of postpetition interest is arguably somewhat in tension with the desirability of paying all creditors as uniformly as practicable, Congress expressly chose to create that alleged tension. There is no reason to suspect that Congress did not mean what the language of the statute says.

D

But even if we saw the need to turn to pre-Code practice in this case, it would be of little assistance. The practice of denying postpetition interest to holders of non-consensual liens, while allowing it to holders of consensual liens, was an exception

---

4. The Court of Appeals for the Fourth Circuit pointed out that, had Congress intended to limit post-petition interest to consensual liens, § 506(b) could have said: "there shall be allowed to the holder of such claim, as provided for under the agreement under which such claim arose, interest on such claim and any reasonable fees, costs or charges." A less clear way of stating this, closer to the actual language, would be: "there shall be allowed to the holder of such claim, interest on such claim and reasonable fees, costs, and charges provided for under the agreement under which such claim arose."

5. It seems to us that the interpretation adopted by the Court of Appeals in this case not only requires that the statutory language be read in an unnatural way, but that it is inconsistent with the remainder of § 506 and with terminology used throughout the Code. Adopting the Court of Appeals' view would mean that § 506(b) is operative only in regard to consensual liens, *i. e.*, that only a holder of an oversecured claim arising from an agreement is entitled to any added recovery. But the other portions of § 506 make no distinction between consensual and nonconsensual liens. Moreover, had Congress intended § 506(b) to apply only to consensual liens, it would have clarified its intent by using the specific phrase, "security interest," which the Code employs to refer to liens created by agreement.

to an exception, recognized by only a few courts and often dependent on particular circumstances. It was certainly not the type of "rule" that we assume Congress was aware of when enacting the Code; nor was it of such significance that Congress would have taken steps other than enacting statutory language to the contrary.

. . . .

The judgment of the Court of Appeals is reversed.

JUSTICE O'CONNOR, with whom JUSTICE BRENNAN, JUSTICE MARSHALL, and JUSTICE STEVENS join, dissenting.

The Court's decision is based on two distinct lines of argument. First, the Court concludes that the language of § 506(b) of the Bankruptcy Code is clear and unambiguous. Second, the Court takes a very narrow view of [prior precedent]. I disagree with both aspects of the Court's opinion, and with the conclusion to which they lead.

The relevant portion of § 506(b) provides that "there shall be allowed to the holder of an oversecured claim, interest on such claim, and any reasonable fees, costs, or charges provided for under the agreement under which such claim arose." The Court concludes that the only natural reading of § 506(b) is that recovery of postpetition interest is "unqualified." As Justice Frankfurter remarked some time ago, however: "The notion that because the words of a statute are plain, its meaning is also plain, is merely pernicious oversimplification."

Although "the use of the comma is exceedingly arbitrary and indefinite," the Court is able to read § 506(b) the way that it does only because of the comma following the phrase "interest on such claim." Without this "capricious" bit of punctuation, the relevant portion of § 506(b) would read as follows: "there shall be allowed to the holder of an oversecured claim, interest on such claim and any reasonable fees, costs, or charges provided for under the agreement under which such claim arose." The phrase "interest on such claims" would be qualified by the phrase "provided for under the agreement under which such claim arose," and nonconsensual liens would not accrue postpetition interest. This conclusion is not altered by the fact that the words "and any" follow the phrase "interest on such claim." Those words simply indicate that interest accrues only on the amount of the claim, and not on "fees, costs, or charges" that happen to be incurred by the creditor.

The Court's reliance on the comma is misplaced. "Punctuation is not decisive of the construction of a statute." Under this rule of construction, the Court has not hesitated in the past to change or ignore the punctuation in legislation in order to effectuate congressional intent.

Although punctuation is not controlling, it can provide useful confirmation of conclusions drawn from the words of a statute. The Court attempts to buttress its interpretation of § 506(b) by suggesting that any other reading would be inconsistent with the remaining portions of § 506, which "make no distinction between consensual and nonconsensual liens." But § 506(b), regardless of how it is read, does distinguish between types of liens. The phrase "provided for under the agreement under which such claim arose" certainly refers to consensual liens, and must qualify some preceding language. Even under the Court's interpretation, "reasonable fees, costs, or charges" can only be awarded if provided for in a consensual lien. Thus, limiting postpetition interest to consensual liens simply reinforces a distinction that already exists in § 506(b). For the same reason, I find unavailing the Court's assertion that Congress would have used the phrase "security interest" if it wanted to limit postpetition interest to consensual liens.

Even if I believed that the language of § 506(b) were clearer than it is, I would disagree with the Court's conclusion, for [prior precedent] counsels against inferring congressional intent to change pre-Code bankruptcy law. . . .

. . . .

For the reasons set forth above, I respectfully dissent.

Notes and Questions

1. The *Griffin* and *Ron Pair* decisions established (roughly, anyway) the standard currently applied by the Supreme Court (and presumably all other federal courts) with respect to the interpretation of federal statutes. What is that standard? What are its implications? Notice first that the standard now applied is not simply a recapitulation of the "plain meaning" rule, for it does speak of an exception. Still, is not the text of the statute preeminent, or at least the starting point of the analysis? On the other hand, note the possibility of showing that some text-based interpretation is demonstrably at odds with the intention of Congress. How should one go about doing that?

2. What do you think of the *Griffin/Ron Pair* standard? Can you think of any problems with this standard? Can you formulate a better standard for resolving questions of this nature? To a large extent, these cases ushered in a theory of statutory interpretation known as textualism, the theory that has become the dominant (though by no means exclusive) theory used in federal courts today. *See, e.g.,* William N. Eskridge, Jr., Book Review, *The New Textualism and Normative Canons*, 113 COLUM. L. REV. 531, 532 (2013) ("[V]irtually all theorists and judges are 'textualists,' in the sense that all consider the text the starting point for statutory interpretation and follow statutory plain meaning if the text is clear."); Jarrod Shobe, *Intertemporal Statutory Interpretation and the Evolution of Legislative Drafting*, 114 COLUM. L. REV. 807, 851 (2014) ("There has been a generally acknowledged trend toward textualist interpretation in the Supreme Court and other courts over the last fifty years.").

3. *Legislative history versus statutory history.* In *Griffin*, the Court refers to the "legislative history" of the statute at issue. Most of what the Court discusses, though, relates to what is often referred to as the *statutory* history of this provision — that is, the history of this statute in terms of how it read when initially enacted and how it has been amended since that time. Can you see how such an inquiry might be relevant to gaining an understanding of the statute as it currently stands? And does this strike you (generally, anyway) as a more

persuasive interpretive device than resort to more typical *legislative* history (committee reports and the like)?

4. *Unintended applications versus unintended results in particular cases.* The result suggested by the *Griffin* Court (an award of over $300,000 for the wrongful withholding of $412.50 in wages) is absurd, is it not? If not, what level of absurdity is required to overcome the presumption attached to a literal reading of a statute? On the other hand, to what extent should it even matter whether the result reached is absurd, if consistent with the literal language of the statute? Where does one draw the line between the quest for a reasonable interpretation of statutory language and the quest for an interpretation with which one personally might agree? Moreover, is it not possible that Congress sometimes makes mistakes, or simply engages in sloppy drafting? Are the Courts supposed to fix all such errors? If so, by what standard? And how great is the problem, really? As the *Griffin* Court observed, is not Congress able to amend a statute following the issuance of a Supreme Court interpretation with which it does not agree?

5. In *Griffin*, it seems that both the majority and the dissent were concerned with the proper role of discretion in the exercise of the judicial function. To what extent can the *Griffin/Ron Pair* standard be explained in those terms?

6. The dissent in *Griffin* observed that the statute at issue had been in force for more than 50 years before any federal appellate court arrived at the interpretation adopted by the majority. To what extent should this fact be relevant? For example, how likely is it that a court sitting in 1982 is going to be able to discern the meaning of a statute last amended in 1915 better than a court sitting at some earlier time? More generally, to what extent should a court defer to an earlier court as to questions of statutory interpretation? Or is a court (and particularly the Supreme Court) under a continuing obligation to interpret statutes correctly (at least in their view), meaning that there should be little if any obligation to adhere to prior precedent in this area?

7. The dissent in *Griffin* suggested that Congress must have been aware of prior federal court decisions in this area. But can we reasonably expect that Congress was aware of all prior federal court decisions? Prior Supreme Court decisions? Should Congress be so aware?

8. The dissent in *Griffin* also suggested that an interpretation such as that reached by the majority "would normally be explained in the committee reports or the debates if it had been intended." Do you think this is true (both here in particular or generally)? And do you think this would be a wise policy, if adopted? Do we really want a standard of interpretation where courts are essentially bound by whatever is included in a committee report?

9. Concerning *Ron Pair*, do you think it is more likely that Congress intended that oversecured creditors receive postpetition interest a) only if such interest

is provided for pursuant to some consensual security agreement, b) only as to consensual security arrangements (though regardless of whether such interest was provided for under the relevant agreement), or c) without regard to whether the arrangement was consensual? What would be the best way to draft a statute corresponding to each of these various options? And which option does § 506(b) most resemble? How does the answer to that question compare to your answer to the first question?

10. Note, in *Ron Pair*, the comparison with other, related provisions in the Bankruptcy Code. Does such a comparison strike you as persuasive? Is it not fair to presume that Congress probably used identical words and phrases similarly (unless expressly defined otherwise) within related portions of the United States Code, and, conversely, that the use of a different word or phrase likely signals a change in meaning?

11. An interesting application of the *Griffin/Ron Pair* standard can be found in *United States v. Locke*, 471 U.S. 84 (1985). At issue in *Locke* was 43 U.S.C. § 1744, which required holders of unpatented mining claims who wished to retain those claims to file certain paperwork "prior to December 31" of each year. Not surprisingly, the Court held that the phrase "prior to December 31" means on or before December 30. *See* 471 U.S. at 93-96. Remarkably, the Court was not unanimous on this issue. *See id.* at 120-25 (Stevens, J., joined by Brennan, J., dissenting). Is the *Locke* Court's reading of this statute absurd? Why or why not?

12. For more recent, "textbook" applications of the *Griffin/Ron Pair* standard, see *Schindler Elevator Corp. v. United States ex rel. Kirk*, 131 S. Ct. 1885 (2011) (interpreting the meaning of the term "report" for purposes of the False Claims Act), and *Dean v. United States*, 129 S. Ct. 1849 (2009) (interpreting the meaning of the term "discharged" for purposes of 18 U.S.C. § 924(c)(1)(A)).

c. A Case Study in Modern Statutory Interpretation

Smith v. United States
508 U.S. 223 (1993)

JUSTICE O'CONNOR delivered the opinion of the Court.

We decide today whether the exchange of a gun for narcotics constitutes "use" of a firearm "during and in relation to a drug trafficking crime" within the meaning of 18 U.S.C. § 924(c)(1). We hold that it does.

I

Petitioner John Angus Smith and his companion went from Tennessee to Florida to buy cocaine; they hoped to resell it at a profit. While in Florida, they met petitioner's acquaintance, Deborah Hoag. Hoag agreed to, and in fact did, purchase cocaine for petitioner. She then accompanied petitioner and his friend to her motel room, where they were joined by a drug dealer. While Hoag listened, petitioner and the dealer discussed petitioner's MAC-10 firearm, which had been modified to operate as an automatic. The MAC-10 apparently is a favorite among criminals. It is small and compact, lightweight, and can be equipped with a silencer. Most important of all, it can be devastating: A fully automatic MAC-10 can fire more than 1,000 rounds per minute. The dealer expressed his interest in becoming the owner of a MAC-10, and petitioner promised that he would discuss selling the gun if his arrangement with another potential buyer fell through.

Unfortunately for petitioner, Hoag had contacts not only with narcotics traffickers but also with law enforcement officials. In fact, she was a confidential informant. Consistent with her post, she informed the Broward County Sheriff's Office of petitioner's activities. The Sheriff's Office responded quickly, sending an undercover officer to Hoag's motel room. Several others were assigned to keep the motel room under surveillance. Upon arriving at Hoag's motel room, the undercover officer presented himself to petitioner as a pawnshop dealer. Petitioner, in turn, presented the officer with a proposition: He had an automatic MAC-10 and silencer with which he might be willing to part. Petitioner then pulled the MAC-10 out of a black canvas bag and showed it to the officer. The officer examined the gun and asked petitioner what he wanted for it. Rather than asking for money, however, petitioner asked for drugs. He was willing to trade his MAC-10, he said, for two ounces of cocaine. The officer told petitioner that he was just a pawnshop dealer and did not distribute narcotics. Nonetheless, he indicated that he wanted the MAC-10 and would try to get the cocaine. The officer then left, promising to return within an hour.

Rather than seeking out cocaine as he had promised, the officer returned to the Sheriff's Office to arrange for petitioner's arrest. But petitioner was not content to wait. The officers who were conducting surveillance saw him leave the motel room carrying a gun bag; he then climbed into his van and drove away. The officers reported petitioner's departure and began following him. When law enforcement authorities tried to stop petitioner, he led them on a high-speed chase. Petitioner eventually was apprehended.

Petitioner, it turns out, was well armed. A search of his van revealed the MAC-10 weapon, a silencer, ammunition, and a "fast-feed" mechanism. In addition, the police found a MAC-11 machine gun, a loaded .45 caliber pistol, and a .22 caliber pistol with a scope and a homemade silencer. Petitioner also had a loaded 9 millimeter handgun in his waistband.

A grand jury sitting in the District Court for the Southern District of Florida returned an indictment charging petitioner with, among other offenses, two drug trafficking crimes — conspiracy to possess cocaine with intent to distribute and attempt to possess cocaine with intent to distribute in violation of 21 U.S.C. §§ 841(a)(1), 846, and 18 U.S.C. § 2. Most important here, the indictment alleged that petitioner knowingly used the MAC-10 and its silencer during and in relation to a drug trafficking crime. Under 18 U.S.C. § 924(c)(1), a defendant who so uses a firearm must be sentenced to five years' incarceration. And where, as here, the firearm is a "machinegun" or is fitted with a silencer, the sentence is 30 years. The jury convicted petitioner on all counts.

On appeal, petitioner argued that § 924(c)(1)'s penalty for using a firearm during and in relation to a drug trafficking offense covers only situations in which the firearm is used as a weapon. According to petitioner, the provision does not extend to defendants who use a firearm solely as a medium of exchange or for barter. The Court of Appeals for the Eleventh Circuit disagreed. 957 F. 2d 835 (1992). The plain language of the statute, the court explained, imposes no requirement that the firearm be used as a weapon. Instead, any use of "the weapon to facilitate *in any manner* the commission of the offense" suffices.

Shortly before the Eleventh Circuit decided this case, the Court of Appeals for the District of Columbia Circuit arrived at the same conclusion. In *United States v. Phelps*, 877 F. 2d 28 (1989), however, the Court of Appeals for the Ninth Circuit held that trading a gun in a drug-related transaction could not constitute use of a firearm during and in relation to a drug trafficking offense within the meaning of § 924(c)(1). We granted certiorari to resolve the conflict among the Circuits. We now affirm.

II

Section 924(c)(1) requires the imposition of specified penalties if the defendant, "during and in relation to any crime of violence or drug trafficking crime, uses or carries a firearm." By its terms, the statute requires the prosecution to make two showings. First, the prosecution must demonstrate that the defendant "used or carried a firearm." Second, it must prove that the use or carrying was "during and in relation to" a "crime of violence or drug trafficking crime."

A

Petitioner argues that exchanging a firearm for drugs does not constitute "use" of the firearm within the meaning of the statute. He points out that nothing in the record indicates that he fired the MAC-10, threatened anyone with it, or employed it for self-protection. In essence, petitioner argues that he cannot be said to have "used" a firearm unless he used it as a weapon, since that is how firearms most often are used. Of course, § 924(c)(1) is not limited to those cases in which a gun is used; it applies with equal force whenever a gun is "carried." In this case, however, the indictment alleged only that petitioner "used" the MAC-10. Accordingly, we do not consider whether the evidence might support the conclusion that petitioner carried the MAC-10 within the meaning of § 924(c)(1). Instead we confine our discussion to what the parties view as the dispositive issue in this case: whether trading a firearm for drugs can constitute "use" of the firearm within the meaning of § 924(c)(1).

When a word is not defined by statute, we normally construe it in accord with its ordinary or natural meaning. Surely petitioner's treatment of his MAC-10 can be described as "use" within the everyday meaning of that term. Petitioner "used" his MAC-10 in an attempt to obtain drugs by offering to trade it for cocaine. Webster's defines "to use" as "to convert to one's service" or "to employ." Black's Law Dictionary contains a similar definition: "to make use of; to convert to one's service; to employ; to avail oneself of; to carry out a purpose or action by means of." Indeed, over 100 years ago we gave the word "use" the same gloss, indicating that it means "'to employ'" or "'to derive service from.'" Petitioner's handling of the MAC-10 in this case falls squarely within those definitions. By attempting to trade his MAC-10 for the drugs, he "used" or "employed" it as an item of barter to obtain cocaine; he "derived service" from it because it was going to bring him the very drugs he sought.

In petitioner's view, § 924(c)(1) should require proof not only that the defendant used the firearm, but also that he used it *as a weapon*. But the words "as a weapon" appear nowhere in the statute. Rather, § 924(c)(1)'s language sweeps broadly, punishing any "use" of a firearm, so long as the use is "during and in relation to" a drug trafficking offense. Had Congress intended the narrow construction petitioner urges, it could have so indicated. It did not, and we decline to introduce that additional requirement on our own.

Language, of course, cannot be interpreted apart from context. The meaning of a word that appears ambiguous if viewed in isolation may become clear when the word is analyzed in light of the terms that surround it. Recognizing this, petitioner and the dissent argue that the word "uses" has a somewhat reduced scope in § 924(c)(1) because it appears alongside the word "firearm." Specifically, they contend that the average person on the street would not think immediately of a guns-for-drugs trade as an example of "using a firearm." Rather, that phrase normally evokes an image of the most familiar use to which a firearm is put — use as a weapon. Petitioner and the dissent therefore argue that the statute excludes uses where the weapon is not fired or otherwise employed for its destructive capacity. Indeed, relying on that argument — and without citation to authority — the dissent announces its own, restrictive definition of "use." "To use an instrumentality," the dissent argues, "ordinarily means to use it for its intended purpose."

There is a significant flaw to this argument. It is one thing to say that the ordinary meaning of "uses a firearm" *includes* using a firearm as a weapon, since that is the intended purpose of a firearm and the example of "use" that most immediately comes to mind. But it is quite another to conclude that, as a result, the phrase also *excludes* any other use. Certainly that conclusion does not follow from the phrase "uses a firearm" itself. As the dictionary definitions and experience make clear, one can use a firearm in a number of ways. That one example of "use" is the first to come to mind when the phrase "uses a firearm" is uttered does not preclude us from recognizing that there are other "uses" that qualify as well. In this case, it is both reasonable and normal to say that petitioner "used" his MAC-10 in his drug trafficking offense by trading it for cocaine; the dissent does not contend otherwise.

The dissent's example of how one might "use" a cane suffers from a similar flaw. To be sure, "use" as an adornment in a hallway is not the first "use" of a cane that comes to mind. But certainly it does not follow that the *only* "use" to which a cane might be put is assisting one's grandfather in walking. Quite the opposite: The most infamous use of a cane in American history had nothing to do with walking at all, and the use of a cane as an instrument of punishment was once so common that "to cane" has become a verb meaning "to beat with a cane." In any event, the only question in this case is whether the phrase "uses a firearm" in § 924(c)(1) is most reasonably read as *excluding* the use of a firearm in a gun-for-drugs trade. The fact that the phrase clearly *includes* using a firearm to shoot someone, as the dissent contends, does not answer it.

The dissent relies on one authority, the United States Sentencing Commission, Guidelines Manual, as "reflecting" its interpretation of the phrase "uses a firearm."

But the Guidelines do not define "using a firearm" as using it for its intended purposes, which the dissent apparently assumes are limited to firing, brandishing, displaying, and possessing. In fact, if we entertain for the moment the dubious assumption that the Sentencing Guidelines are relevant in the present context, they support the opposite view. Section 2B3.1(b)(2), upon which the dissent relies, provides for increases in a defendant's offense level, and therefore his sentence, if the offense involved a firearm. The extent of the adjustment varies according to the nature of the gun's involvement. There is a seven-point upward adjustment if the firearm "was discharged"; a six-point enhancement if a gun was "otherwise *used*"; and a five-point adjustment if the firearm was brandished, displayed, or possessed. Unless the six-point enhancement for "other uses" is mere surplusage, there must be "uses" for a firearm *other than* its "intended purposes" of firing, brandishing, displaying, or possessing. The dissent points out that there may be *some* uses that are not firing or brandishing but constitute use as a weapon nonetheless. But nothing in [the Guidelines] suggests that the phrase "other uses" must be so limited. On the contrary, it is perfectly reasonable to construe [the Guidelines] as including uses, such as trading and bludgeoning, that do not constitute use for the firearm's "intended purpose."

It is true that the Guidelines commentary defines "otherwise used" as conduct that falls short of "discharging a firearm but is more than brandishing, displaying, or possessing it." That definition, however, simply reflects the peculiar hierarchy of culpability established in USSG § 2B3.1(b)(2). It clarifies that between the most culpable conduct of discharging the firearm and less culpable actions such as "brandishing, displaying, or possessing" lies a category of "other uses" for which the Guidelines impose intermediate punishment. It does not by its terms exclude from its scope trading, bludgeoning, or any other use beyond the firearm's "intended purpose."

We are not persuaded that our construction of the phrase "uses a firearm" will produce anomalous applications. As we already have noted, and will explain in greater detail later, § 924(c)(1) requires not only that the defendant "use" the firearm, but also that he use it "during and in relation to" the drug trafficking crime. As a result, the defendant who "uses" a firearm to scratch his head, or for some other innocuous purpose, would avoid punishment for that conduct altogether: Although scratching one's head with a gun might constitute "use," that action cannot support punishment under § 924(c)(1) unless it facilitates or furthers the drug crime; that the firearm served to relieve an itch is not enough. Such a defendant would escape the six-point enhancement provided in [the Guidelines] as well. As the Guidelines definition of "otherwise used" makes clear, the six-point enhancement does not apply unless the use is "more than" brandishing. While pistol-whipping a victim with a firearm might be "more than" brandishing, scratching one's head is not.

In any event, the "intended purpose" of a firearm is not that it be used in any offensive manner whatever, but rather that it be used in a particular fashion — by firing it. The dissent's contention therefore cannot be that the defendant must use the firearm "as a weapon," but rather that he must fire it or threaten to fire it, "as a gun." Under the dissent's approach, then, even the criminal who pistol-whips his victim has not used a firearm within the meaning of § 924(c)(1), for firearms are intended to be fired or brandished, not used a bludgeons. It appears that the dissent similarly would limit the scope of "other uses" covered by [the Guidelines]. The universal view of the courts of appeals, however, is directly to the contrary. No court of appeals ever has held that using a gun to pistol-whip a victim is anything but the "use" of a firearm . . . .

To the extent there is uncertainty about the scope of the phrase "uses a firearm" in § 924(c)(1), we believe the remainder of § 924 appropriately sets it to rest. Just as a single word cannot be read in isolation, nor can a single provision of a statute. . . . Here, Congress employed the words "use" and "firearm" together not only in § 924(c)(1), but also in § 924(d)(1), which deals with forfeiture of firearms. Under § 924(d)(1), any "firearm or ammunition intended to be used" in the various offenses listed in § 924(d)(3) is subject to seizure and forfeiture. Consistent with petitioner's interpretation, § 924(d)(3) lists offenses in which guns might be used as offensive weapons. But it also lists offenses in which the firearm is *not* used as a weapon but instead as an item of barter or commerce. For example, any gun intended to be "used" in an interstate "transfer, sale, trade, gift, transport, or delivery" of a firearm prohibited under § 922(a)(5) where there is a pattern of such activity, or in a federal offense involving "the exportation of firearms," is subject to forfeiture. In fact, none of the offenses listed in four of the six subsections of § 924(d)(3) involves the bellicose use of a firearm; each offense involves use as an item of commerce. Thus, it is clear from § 924(d)(3) that one who transports, exports, sells, or trades a firearm "uses" it within the meaning of § 924(d)(1) — even though those actions do not involve using the firearm as a weapon. Unless we are to hold that using a firearm has a different meaning in § 924(c)(1) than it does in § 924(d) — and clearly we should not — we must reject petitioner's narrow interpretation.

The evident care with which Congress chose the language of § 924(d)(1) reinforces our conclusion in this regard. Although § 924(d)(1) lists numerous firearm-related offenses that render guns subject to forfeiture, Congress did not lump all of those offenses together and require forfeiture solely of guns "used" in a prohibited activity. Instead, it carefully varied the statutory language in accordance with the guns' relation to the offense. For example, with respect to some crimes, the firearm is subject to forfeiture not only if it is "used," but also if it is "involved in" the offense. Examination of the offenses to which the "involved in" language applies reveals why Congress believed it necessary to include such an expansive term. One of the listed offenses, violation of § 922(a)(6), is the making of a false statement material to the lawfulness of a gun's transfer. Because making a material misstatement in order to acquire or sell a gun is not "use" of the gun even under the broadest definition of the word "use," Congress carefully expanded the statutory language. As a result, a gun with respect to which a material misstatement is made is subject to forfeiture because, even though the gun is not "used" in the offense, it is "involved in" it. Congress, however, did not so expand the language for offenses in which firearms were "intended to be used," even though the firearms in many of those offenses function as items of commerce rather than as weapons. Instead, Congress apparently was of the view that one could use a gun by trading it. In light of the common meaning of the word "use" and the structure and language of the statute, we are not in any position to disagree.

The dissent suggests that our interpretation produces a "strange dichotomy" between "using" a firearm and "carrying" one. We do not see why that is so. Just as a defendant may "use" a firearm within the meaning of § 924(c)(1) by trading it for drugs *or* using it to shoot someone, so too would a defendant "carry" the firearm by keeping it on his person whether he intends to exchange it for cocaine or fire it in self-defense. The dichotomy arises, if at all, only when one tries to extend the phrase "uses a firearm" to any use " 'for any purpose whatever.' " For our purposes, it is sufficient to recognize that, because § 924(d)(1) includes both using a firearm for *trade* and using a firearm as a *weapon* as "using a firearm," it is most reasonable to construe § 924(c)(1) as encompassing both of those "uses" as well.

Finally, it is argued that § 924(c)(1) originally dealt with use of a firearm during crimes of violence; the provision concerning use of a firearm during and in relation to drug trafficking offenses was added later. From this, the dissent infers that "use" *originally* was limited to use of a gun "as a weapon." That the statute in its current form employs the term "use" more broadly is unimportant, the dissent contends, because the addition of the words " 'drug trafficking crime' would have been a peculiar way to *expand* its meaning." Even if we assume that Congress had intended the term "use" to have a more limited scope when it passed the original version of § 924(c) in 1968, we believe it clear from the face of the statute that the Congress that amended § 924(c) in 1986 did not. Rather, the 1986 Congress employed the term "use" expansively, covering both use as a weapon, as the dissent admits, and use as an item of trade or barter, as an examination of § 924(d) demonstrates. Because the phrase "uses a firearm" is broad enough in ordinary usage to cover use of a firearm as an item of barter or commerce, Congress was free in 1986 so to employ it. The language and structure of § 924 indicate that Congress did just that. Accordingly, we conclude that using a firearm in a guns-for-drugs trade may constitute "using a firearm" within the meaning of § 924(c)(1).

B

Using a firearm, however, is not enough to subject the defendant to the punishment required by § 924(c)(1). Instead, the firearm must be used "during and in relation to" a "crime of violence or drug trafficking crime." Petitioner does not deny that the alleged use occurred "during" a drug trafficking crime. Nor could he. The indictment charged that petitioner and his companion conspired to possess cocaine with intent to distribute. There can be no doubt that the gun-for-drugs trade was proposed during and in furtherance of that interstate drug conspiracy. Nor can it be contended that the alleged use did not occur during the "attempt" to possess cocaine with which petitioner also was charged; the MAC-10 served as an inducement to convince the undercover officer to provide petitioner with the drugs that petitioner sought.

Petitioner, however, does dispute whether his use of the firearm was "in relation to" the drug trafficking offense. The phrase "in relation to" is expansive.... Nonetheless, the phrase does illuminate § 924(c)(1)'s boundaries. According to Webster's, "in relation to" means "with reference to" or "as regards." The phrase "in relation to" thus, at a minimum, clarifies that the firearm must have some purpose or effect with respect to the drug trafficking crime; its presence or involvement cannot be the result of accident or coincidence. As one court has observed, the "in relation to" language "allays explicitly the concern that a person could be" punished under § 924(c)(1) for committing a drug trafficking offense "while in possession of a firearm" even though the firearm's presence is coincidental or entirely "unrelated" to the crime. Instead, the gun at least must "facilitate, or have the potential of facilitating," the drug trafficking offense.

We need not determine the precise contours of the "in relation to" requirement here, however, as petitioner's use of his MAC-10 meets any reasonable construction of it. The MAC-10's presence in this case was not the product of happenstance. On the contrary, "far more than in the ordinary case" under § 924(c)(1), in which the gun merely facilitates the offense by providing a means of protection or intimidation, here "the gun was an integral part of the transaction." Without it, the deal would not have been possible. The undercover officer posing as a pawnshop dealer expressly told petitioner that he was not in the narcotics business and that he did not get involved with drugs. For a MAC-10, however, he was willing to see if he could track down some cocaine.

Relying on the decision of the Court of Appeals for the Ninth Circuit in *Phelps* and on the legislative record, petitioner insists that the relationship between the gun and the drug offense in this case is not the type of connection Congress contemplated when it drafted § 924(c)(1). With respect to that argument, we agree with the District of Columbia Circuit's observation:

> "It may well be that Congress, when it drafted the language of § 924(c), had in mind a more obvious use of guns in connection with a drug crime, but the language of the statute is not so limited; nor can we imagine any reason why Congress would not have wished its language to cover this situation. Whether guns are used as the medium of exchange for drugs sold illegally or as a means to protect the transaction or dealers, their introduction into the scene of drug transactions dramatically heightens the danger to society."

One need look no further than the pages of the Federal Reporter to verify the truth of that observation. In *Phelps*, the defendant arranged to trade his MAC-10 for chemicals necessary to make methamphetamine. The Ninth Circuit held that the gun was not used or carried "in relation to" the drug trafficking offense because it was used as an item of barter and not as a weapon. The defendant, however, did not believe his MAC-10's capabilities were so limited. When he was stopped for a traffic violation, "the MAC 10, suddenly transmogrified from an item of commerce into an offensive weapon, was still in the defendant's possession. He opened fire and shot a deputy sheriff."

C

Finally, the dissent and petitioner invoke the rule of lenity. The mere possibility of articulating a narrower construction, however, does not by itself make the rule of lenity applicable. Instead, that venerable rule is reserved for cases where, "after 'seizing every thing from which aid can be derived,'" the Court is "left with an ambiguous statute." This is not such a case. Not only does petitioner's use of his MAC-10 fall squarely within the common usage and dictionary definitions of the terms "uses a firearm," but Congress affirmatively demonstrated that it meant to include transactions like petitioner's as "using a firearm" by so employing those terms in § 924(d).

Imposing a more restrictive reading of the phrase "uses a firearm" does violence not only to the structure and language of the statute, but to its purpose as well. When Congress enacted the current version of § 924(c)(1), it was no doubt aware that drugs and guns are a dangerous combination. In 1989, 56 percent of all murders in New York City were drug related; during the same period, the figure for the Nation's Capital was as high as 80 percent. The fact that a gun is treated momentarily as an item of commerce does not render it inert or deprive it of destructive capacity. Rather, as experience demonstrates, it can be converted instantaneously from currency to cannon. We therefore see no reason why Congress would have intended courts and juries applying § 924(c)(1) to draw a fine metaphysical distinction between a gun's role in a drug offense as a weapon of violence and death in either capacity.

We have observed that the rule of lenity "cannot dictate an implausible interpretation of a statute, nor one at odds with the generally accepted contemporary meaning of a term." That observation controls this case. Both a firearm's use as a weapon and its use as an item of barter fall within the plain language of § 924(c)(1), so long as the use occurs during and in relation to a drug trafficking offense; both must constitute "uses" of a firearm for § 924(d)(1) to make any sense at all; and both create the very dangers and risks that Congress meant § 924(c)(1) to address. We therefore hold that a criminal who trades his firearm for drugs "uses" it during and in relation to a drug trafficking offense within the meaning of § 924(c)(1). Because the evidence in this case showed that petitioner "used" his MAC-10 machine gun and silencer in precisely such a manner, proposing to trade them for cocaine, petitioner properly was subjected to § 924(c)(1)'s 30-year mandatory minimum sentence. The judgment of the Court of Appeals, accordingly, is affirmed.

JUSTICE BLACKMUN, concurring.

I join the Court's opinion in full because I understand the discussion in Part II-B not to foreclose the possibility that the "in relation to" language of 18 U.S.C. § 924(c)(1) requires more than mere furtherance or facilitation of a crime of violence or drug-trafficking crime. I agree with the Court that because petitioner's use of his MAC-10 meets any reasonable construction of the phrase, it is unnecessary to determine in this case the precise contours of "in relation to" as it appears in § 924(c)(1).

JUSTICE SCALIA, with whom JUSTICE STEVENS and JUSTICE SOUTER join, dissenting.

Section 924(c)(1) mandates a sentence enhancement for any defendant who "during and in relation to any crime of violence or drug trafficking crime uses a firearm." The Court begins its analysis by focusing upon the word "use" in this passage, and explaining that the dictionary definitions of that word are very broad. It is, however, a "fundamental principle of statutory construction (and, indeed, of language itself) that the meaning of a word cannot be determined in isolation, but must be drawn from the context in which it is used." That is particularly true of a word as elastic as "use," whose meanings range all the way from "to partake of" (as in "he uses tobacco") to "to be wont or accustomed" (as in "he used to smoke tobacco").

In the search for statutory meaning, we give nontechnical words and phrases their ordinary meaning. To use an instrumentality ordinarily means to use it for its intended purpose. When someone asks, "Do you use a cane?," he is not inquiring whether you have your grandfather's silver-handled walking stick on display in the hall; he wants to know whether you *walk* with a cane. Similarly, to speak of "using a firearm" is to speak of using it for its distinctive purpose, *i.e.*, as a weapon. To be sure, "one can use a firearm in a number of ways," including as an article of exchange, just as one can "use" a cane as a hall decoration — but that is not the ordinary meaning of "using" the one or the other.[1] The Court does not appear to grasp the distinction between how a word *can* be used and how it *ordinarily is* used. It would, indeed, be "both reasonable and normal to say that petitioner 'used' his MAC-10 in his drug trafficking offense by trading it for cocaine." It would also be reasonable and normal to say that he "used" it to scratch his head. When one wishes to describe the action of employing the instrument of a firearm for such unusual purposes, "use" is assuredly a verb one could select. But that says nothing about whether the *ordinary* meaning of the phrase "uses a firearm" embraces such extraordinary employments. It is unquestionably *not* reasonable and normal, I think, to say simply "do not use firearms" when one means to prohibit selling or scratching with them.

The normal usage is reflected, for example, in the United States Sentencing Guidelines, which provide for enhanced sentences when firearms are "discharged," "brandished, displayed, or possessed," or "otherwise used." As to the latter term, the Guidelines say: "'Otherwise used' with reference to a dangerous weapon (including a firearm) means that the conduct did not amount to the discharge of a firearm but was more than brandishing, displaying, or possessing a firearm or other dangerous weapon." "Otherwise used" in this provision obviously means "otherwise used as a weapon."[2]

---

1. The Court asserts that the "significant flaw" in this argument is that "to say that the ordinary meaning of 'uses a firearm' *includes* using a firearm as a weapon" is quite different from saying that the ordinary meaning "also *excludes* any other use." The two are indeed different—but it is precisely the latter that I assert to be true: The ordinary meaning of "uses a firearm" does *not* include using it as an article of commerce. I think it perfectly obvious, for example, that the objective falsity requirement for a perjury conviction would not be satisfied if a witness answered "no" to a prosecutor's inquiry whether he had ever "used a firearm," even though he had once sold his grandfather's Enfield rifle to a collector.
2. The Court says that it is "not persuaded that its construction of the phrase 'uses a firearm' will produce anomalous applications." But as proof it points only to the fact that § 924(c)(1) fortuitously contains *other language*—the requirement that the use be "during and in relation to any crime of violence or drug trafficking crime"—that happens to prevent untoward results. That language does not, in fact, prevent all untoward results: Though it excludes an enhanced penalty for the burglar who scratches his head with the barrel of a gun, it requires one for the burglar who happens to use a gun handle, rather than a rock, to break the window affording him entrance—hardly a distinction that ought to make a sentencing difference if the gun has no other connection to the crime. But in any event, an excuse that turns upon the language of § 924(c)(1) is good only for that particular statute. The Court *cannot* avoid "anomalous applications" when it applies its anomalous meaning of "use a firearm" in other contexts—for example, the Guidelines provision just described in the text.

In a vain attempt to show the contrary, it asserts that the phrase "otherwise used" in the Guidelines means used for any other purpose at all (the Court's preferred meaning of "use a firearm"), *so long as it is more "culpable" than brandishing.* But whence does it derive that convenient limitation? It appears nowhere in the text—as well it should not, since the whole purpose of the Guidelines is to take out of the hands of individual judges determinations as to what is "more culpable" and "less culpable." The definition of "otherwise used" in the Guidelines merely says that it means "more than" brandishing and less than firing. The Court is confident that "scratching one's head" with a firearm is not "more than" brandishing it. I certainly agree—but only because the "more" use referred to is more use *as a weapon.* Reading the Guidelines as they are written (rather than importing the Court's *deus ex machina* of a culpability scale), and interpreting "use a firearm" in the strange fashion the Court does, produces a full seven-point upward sentence adjustment for firing a gun at a storekeeper during a robbery; a mere five-point adjustment for pointing a gun at the storekeeper (which falls within the Guidelines' definition of "brandishing"); but an intermediate *six*-point adjustment for using the gun to pry open the cash register or prop open the door. Quite obviously ridiculous. When the Guidelines speak of "otherwise using" a firearm, they mean, in accordance with normal usage, otherwise "using" it as a weapon—for example, placing the gun barrel in the mouth of the storekeeper to intimidate him.

Given our rule that ordinary meaning governs, and given the ordinary meaning of "uses a firearm," it seems to me inconsequential that "the words 'as a weapon' appear nowhere in the statute"; they are reasonably implicit. Petitioner is not, I think, seeking to introduce an "additional requirement" into the text, but is simply construing the text according to its normal import.

The Court seeks to avoid this conclusion by referring to the next subsection of the statute, § 924(d), which does not employ the phrase "uses a firearm," but provides for the confiscation of firearms that are "used in" referenced offenses which include the crimes of transferring, selling, or transporting firearms in interstate commerce. The Court concludes from this that *whenever* the term appears in this statute, "use" of a firearm must include nonweapon use. I do not agree. We are dealing here not with a technical word or an "artfully defined" legal term, but with common words that are, as I have suggested, inordinately sensitive to context. Just as adding the direct object "a firearm" to the verb "use" *narrows* the meaning of that verb (it can no longer mean "partake of"), so also adding the modifier "in the offense of transferring, selling, or transporting firearms" to the phrase "use a firearm" *expands* the meaning of that phrase (it then includes, as it previously would not, nonweapon use). But neither the narrowing nor the expansion should logically be thought to apply to *all* appearances of the affected word or phrase. Just as every appearance of the word "use" in the statute need not be given the narrow meaning that word acquires in the phrase "use a firearm," so also every appearance of the phrase "use a firearm" need not be given the expansive connotation that phrase acquires in the broader context "use a firearm in crimes such as unlawful sale of firearms." When, for example, the statute provides that its prohibition on certain transactions in firearms "shall not apply to the loan or rental of a firearm to any person for temporary use for lawful sporting purposes," I have no doubt that the "use" referred to is *only* use as a sporting *weapon*, and not the use of pawning the firearm to pay for a ski trip. Likewise when, in § 924(c)(1), the phrase "uses a firearm" is not employed in a context that necessarily envisions the unusual "use" of a firearm as a commodity, the normally understood meaning of the phrase should prevail.

Another consideration leads to the same conclusion: § 924(c)(1) provides increased penalties not only for one who "uses" a firearm during and in relation to any crime of violence or drug trafficking crime, but also for one who "carries" a firearm in those circumstances. The interpretation I would give the language produces an eminently reasonable dichotomy between "using a firearm" (as a weapon) and "carrying a firearm" (which in the context "uses or carries a firearm" means carrying it in such manner as to be ready for use as a weapon). The Court's interpretation, by contrast, produces a strange dichotomy between "using a firearm for any purpose whatever, including barter," and "carrying a firearm."[3]

---

3. The Court responds to this argument by abandoning all pretense of giving the phrase "uses a firearm" even a *permissible* meaning, much less its ordinary one. There is no problem, the Court says, because it is not contending that "uses a firearm" means "uses for *any* purpose," only that it means "uses as a weapon or for trade." Unfortunately, that is not one of the options that our mother tongue makes available. "Uses a firearm" can be given a broad meaning ("uses for any purpose") or its more ordinary narrow meaning ("uses as a weapon"); but it can not possibly mean "uses as a weapon or for trade."

Finally, although the present prosecution was brought under the portion of § 924(c)(1) pertaining to use of a firearm "during and in relation to any drug trafficking crime," I think it significant that that portion is affiliated with the preexisting provision pertaining to use of a firearm "during and in relation to any crime of violence," rather than with the firearm trafficking offenses defined in § 922 and referenced in § 924(d). The word "use" in the "crime of violence" context has the unmistakable import of use as a weapon, and that import carries over, in my view, to the subsequently added phrase "or drug trafficking crime." Surely the word "use" means the same thing as to both, and surely the 1986 addition of "drug trafficking crime" would have been a peculiar way to *expand* its meaning (beyond "use as a weapon") for crimes of violence.

Even if the reader does not consider the issue to be as clear as I do, he must at least acknowledge, I think, that it is eminently debatable — and that is enough, under the rule of lenity, to require finding for the petitioner here. "At the very least, it may be said that the issue is subject to some doubt. Under these circumstances, we adhere to the familiar rule that, 'where there is ambiguity in a criminal statute, doubts are resolved in favor of the defendant.'"[4]

For the foregoing reasons, I respectfully dissent.

Notes and Questions

---

1. Which opinion do you find to be the more persuasive, the Court's or the dissent's? Why?

2. Notice the various discussions of the meaning of statutory terms a) in isolation, b) in the context of the sentence in which the term appears, c) in the context of the statute at issue, and d) in the context of other, related statutes.

3. Notice the many authorities (including "nonlegal" authorities) relied upon in the various opinions in *Smith*, and the arguments constructed therefrom. Notice also the specific nonlegal authorities selected. Why did the various Justices choose the authorities that they did?

4. When attempting to discern the meaning of a word in a statute, should reference be made to a general dictionary (such as *Webster's*), or to a law dictionary (such as *Black's*)? Or does it depend upon the word and/or the context, or audience? And where does one turn to discern the meaning of a phrase?

---

4. The Court contends that giving the language its ordinary meaning would frustrate the purpose of the statute, since a gun "can be converted instantaneously from currency to cannon." Stretching language in order to write a more effective statute than Congress devised is not an exercise we should indulge in. But in any case, the ready ability to use a gun that is at hand as a weapon is perhaps one of the reasons the statute sanctions not only *using* a firearm, but *carrying* one. Here, however, the Government chose not to indict under that provision.

5. At one point in its opinion, the Court stated: "Had Congress intended the narrow construction petitioner urges, it could have so indicated." It is true, is it
not, that Congress probably could have been more precise in its wording of
this statute? But is it not also possible that Congress *did* intend the construction
urged by the petitioner, and believed that this statute would be so construed?
And is it not also true that Congress probably cannot foresee all of the possible,
future applications of its statutes? Assume, for example, that Congress did not
foresee trading a gun for drugs. Should a court in that situation try to interpret
the statute in the manner it believes the enacting Congress would have preferred, or as the statute is written?

6. Notice, finally, the Court's invocation of the supposed purpose of the statute at
issue (despite taking a largely textualist interpretive approach generally). How
did the Court ascertain that purpose?

7. Can you think of any legitimate reason why the government in *Smith* failed to
indict under the "carrying" portion of § 924(c)(1)? Is that not (as opposed to poor
drafting on the part of Congress) the greater problem here? And does not the inclusion of the phrase "or carrying" shed light on the meaning of the term "use"?

8. Notice Justice Scalia's distinction between how a word *can* be used and how it
ordinarily is used. (Note, in this regard, that the Court and the dissent appear
to be working from the same dictionary, yet arrive at different conclusions.)
Other factors aside, is not ordinary use more in accord with general principles
of textual (including statutory) interpretation?

9. What is the "rule of lenity"? And what, if anything, is left of the doctrine in light
of the result reached in this case?

Bailey v. United States
516 U.S. 137 (1995)

JUSTICE O'CONNOR delivered the opinion of the Court.

These consolidated petitions each challenge a conviction under 18 U. S. C.
§ 924(c)(1). In relevant part, that section imposes a 5-year minimum term of imprisonment upon a person who "during and in relation to any crime uses or carries a
firearm." We are asked to decide whether evidence of proximity and accessibility of a
firearm to drugs or drug proceeds is alone sufficient to support a conviction for "use"
of a firearm during and in relation to a drug trafficking offense under 18 U. S. C.
§ 924(c)(1).

I

In May 1989, petitioner Roland Bailey was stopped by police officers after they noticed that his car lacked a front license plate and an inspection sticker. When Bailey

failed to produce a driver's license, the officers ordered him out of the car. As he stepped out, the officers saw Bailey push something between the seat and the front console. A search of the passenger compartment revealed one round of ammunition and 27 plastic bags containing a total of 30 grams of cocaine. After arresting Bailey, the officers searched the trunk of his car where they found, among a number of items, a large amount of cash and a bag containing a loaded 9-mm. pistol.

Bailey was charged with several counts, including using and carrying a firearm in violation of 18 U. S. C. § 924(c)(1). A prosecution expert testified at trial that drug dealers frequently carry a firearm to protect their drugs and money as well as themselves. Bailey was convicted by the jury on all charges, and his sentence included a consecutive 60-month term of imprisonment on the § 924(c)(1) conviction.

The Court of Appeals for the District of Columbia Circuit rejected Bailey's claim that the evidence was insufficient to support his conviction under § 924(c)(1). The court held that Bailey could be convicted for "using" a firearm during and in relation to a drug trafficking crime if the jury could reasonably infer that the gun facilitated Bailey's commission of a drug offense. In Bailey's case, the court explained, the trier of fact could reasonably infer that Bailey had used the gun in the trunk to protect his drugs and drug proceeds and to facilitate sales. Judge Douglas H. Ginsburg, dissenting in part, argued that prior Circuit precedent required reversal of Bailey's conviction.

. . . .

II

Section 924(c)(1) requires the imposition of specified penalties if the defendant, "during and in relation to any crime of violence or drug trafficking crime, uses or carries a firearm." Petitioners argue that "use" signifies active employment of a firearm. The Government opposes that definition and defends the proximity and accessibility test adopted by the Court of Appeals. We agree with petitioners, and hold that § 924(c)(1) requires evidence sufficient to show an *active employment* of the firearm by the defendant, a use that makes the firearm an operative factor in relation to the predicate offense.

This action is not the first one in which the Court has grappled with the proper understanding of "use" in § 924(c)(1). In *Smith*, we faced the question whether the barter of a gun for drugs was a "use," and concluded that it was. As the debate in *Smith* illustrated, the word "use" poses some interpretational difficulties because of the different meanings attributable to it. Consider the paradoxical statement: "I *use* a gun to protect my house, but I've never had to *use* it." "Use" draws meaning from its context, and we will look not only to the word itself, but also to the statute and the sentencing scheme, to determine the meaning Congress intended.

We agree with the majority below that "use" must connote more than mere possession of a firearm by a person who commits a drug offense. Had Congress intended possession alone to trigger liability under § 924(c)(1), it easily could have so provided. This obvious conclusion is supported by the frequent use of the term "possess" in the gun-crime statutes to describe prohibited gun-related conduct.

Where the Court of Appeals erred was not in its conclusion that "use" means more than mere possession, but in its standard for evaluating whether the involvement of a firearm amounted to something more than mere possession. Its proximity and accessibility standard provides almost no limitation on the kind of possession that would be criminalized; in practice, nearly every possession of a firearm by a person engaged in drug trafficking would satisfy the standard, "thereby erasing the line that the statutes, and the courts, have tried to draw." *United States* v. *McFadden, supra,* at 469 (Breyer, C.J., dissenting). . . .

. . . .

We start, as we must, with the language of the statute. See *United States* v. *Ron Pair Enterprises, Inc.,* 489 U. S. 235, 241 (1989). The word "use" in the statute must be given its "ordinary or natural" meaning, a meaning variously defined as "to convert to one's service," "to employ," "to avail oneself of," and "to carry out a purpose or action by means of." These various definitions of "use" imply action and implementation.

We consider not only the bare meaning of the word but also its placement and purpose in the statutory scheme. "'The meaning of statutory language, plain or not, depends on context.'" Looking past the word "use" itself, we read § 924(c)(1) with the assumption that Congress intended each of its terms to have meaning. "Judges should hesitate to treat as surplusage statutory terms in any setting, and resistance should be heightened when the words describe an element of a criminal offense." Here, Congress has specified two types of conduct with a firearm: "uses" or "carries."

Under the Government's reading of § 924(c)(1), "use" includes even the action of a defendant who puts a gun into place to protect drugs or to embolden himself. This reading is of such breadth that no role remains for "carry." The Government admits that the meaning of "use" and "carry" converge under its interpretation, but maintains that this overlap is a product of the particular history of § 924(c)(1). Therefore, the Government argues, the canon of construction that instructs that "a legislature is presumed to have used no superfluous words," *Platt* v. *Union Pacific R. Co.,* 99 U. S. 48, 58 (1879), is inapplicable. We disagree. Nothing here indicates that Congress, when it provided these two terms, intended that they be understood to be redundant.

We assume that Congress used two terms because it intended each term to have a particular, nonsuperfluous meaning. While a broad reading of "use" undermines virtually any function for "carry," a more limited, active interpretation of "use" preserves a meaningful role for "carries" as an alternative basis for a charge. Under the interpretation we enunciate today, a firearm can be used without being carried, *e. g.,* when an offender has a gun on display during a transaction, or barters with a firearm without handling it; and a firearm can be carried without being used, *e. g.,* when an offender keeps a gun hidden in his clothing throughout a drug transaction.

. . . .

The amendment history of § 924(c)(1) casts further light on Congress' intended meaning. The original version, passed in 1968, read:

"(c) Whoever —

"(1) uses a firearm to commit any felony which may be prosecuted in a court of the United States, or

"(2) carries a firearm unlawfully during the commission of any felony which may be prosecuted in a court of the United States, "shall be sentenced to a term of imprisonment for not less than one year nor more than 10 years."

The phrase "uses a firearm to commit" indicates that Congress originally intended to reach the situation where the firearm was actively employed during commission of the crime. This original language would not have stretched so far as to cover a firearm that played no detectable role in the crime's commission. For example, a defendant who stored a gun in a nearby closet for retrieval in case the deal went sour would not have "used a firearm to commit" a crime. This version also shows that "use" and "carry" were employed with distinctly different meanings.

Congress' 1984 amendment to § 924(c) altered the scope of predicate offenses from "any felony" to "any crime of violence," removed the "unlawfully" requirement, merged the "uses" and "carries" prongs, substituted "during and in relation to" the predicate crimes for the earlier provisions linking the firearm to the predicate crimes, and raised the minimum sentence to five years. The Government argues that this amendment stripped "uses" and "carries" of the qualifications ("to commit" and "unlawfully during") that originally gave them distinct meanings, so that the terms should now be understood to overlap. Of course, in *Smith* we recognized that Congress' subsequent amendments to § 924(c) employed "use" expansively, to cover both use as a weapon and use as an item of barter. But there is no evidence to indicate that Congress intended to expand the meaning of "use" so far as to swallow up any significance for "carry." If Congress had intended to deprive "use" of its active connotations, it could have simply substituted a more appropriate term — "possession" — to cover the conduct it wished to reach.

The Government nonetheless argues that our observation in *Smith* that "§ 924(c)(1)'s language sweeps broadly" precludes limiting "use" to active employment. But our decision today is not inconsistent with *Smith*. Although there we declined to limit "use" to the meaning "use as a weapon," our interpretation of § 924(c)(1) nonetheless adhered to an active meaning of the term. In *Smith*, it was clear that the defendant had "used" the gun; the question was whether that particular use (bartering) came within the meaning of § 924(c)(1). *Smith* did not address the question we face today of what evidence is required to permit a jury to find that a firearm had been used at all.

To illustrate the activities that fall within the definition of "use" provided here, we briefly describe some of the activities that fall within "active employment" of a firearm, and those that do not.

The active-employment understanding of "use" certainly includes brandishing, displaying, bartering, striking with, and, most obviously, firing or attempting to fire a firearm. We note that this reading compels the conclusion that even an offender's reference to a firearm in his possession could satisfy § 924(c)(1). Thus, a reference to a firearm calculated to bring about a change in the circumstances of the predicate offense is a "use," just as the silent but obvious and forceful presence of a gun on a table can be a "use."

The example given above — "I *use* a gun to protect my house, but I've never had to *use* it" — shows that "use" takes on different meanings depending on context. In the first phrase of the example, "use" refers to an ongoing, inactive function fulfilled by a firearm. It is this sense of "use" that underlies the Government's contention that "placement for protection" — *i. e.*, placement of a firearm to provide a sense of security or to embolden — constitutes "use." It follows, according to this argument, that a gun placed in a closet is "used," because its mere presence emboldens or protects its owner. We disagree. Under this reading, mere possession of a firearm by a drug offender, at or near the site of a drug crime or its proceeds or paraphernalia, is a "use" by the offender, because its availability for intimidation, attack, or defense would always, presumably, embolden or comfort the offender. But the inert presence of a firearm, without more, is not enough to trigger § 924(c)(1). Perhaps the nonactive nature of this asserted "use" is clearer if a synonym is used: storage. A defendant cannot be charged under § 924(c)(1) merely for storing a weapon near drugs or drug proceeds. Storage of a firearm, without its more active employment, is not reasonably distinguishable from possession.

A possibly more difficult question arises where an offender conceals a gun nearby to be at the ready for an imminent confrontation. Some might argue that the offender has "actively employed" the gun by hiding it where he can grab and use it if necessary. In our view, "use" cannot extend to encompass this action. If the gun is not disclosed or mentioned by the offender, it is not actively employed, and it is not "used." To conclude otherwise would distort the language of the statute as well as create an impossible line-drawing problem. How "at the ready" was the firearm? Within arm's reach? In the room? In the house? How long before the confrontation did he place it there? Five minutes or 24 hours? Placement for later active use does not constitute "use." An alternative rationale for why "placement at the ready" is a "use" — that such placement is made with the intent to put the firearm to a future active use — also fails. As discussed above, § 924(d)(1) demonstrates that Congress knew how to draft a statute to reach a firearm that was "intended to be used." In § 924(c)(1), it chose not to include that term, but instead established the 5-year mandatory minimum only for those defendants who actually "use" the firearm.

While it is undeniable that the active-employment reading of "use" restricts the scope of § 924(c)(1), the Government often has other means available to charge offenders who mix guns and drugs. The "carry" prong of § 924(c)(1), for example, brings some offenders who would not satisfy the "use" prong within the reach of the statute. And Sentencing Guidelines § 2D1.1(b)(1) provides an enhancement for a person convicted of certain drug-trafficking offenses if a firearm was possessed during the offense. But the word "use" in § 924(c)(1) cannot support the extended applications that prosecutors have sometimes placed on it, in order to penalize drug-trafficking offenders for firearms possession.

The test set forth by the Court of Appeals renders "use" virtually synonymous with "possession" and makes any role for "carry" superfluous. The language of § 924(c)(1), supported by its history and context, compels the conclusion that Congress intended "use" in the active sense of "to avail oneself of." To sustain a conviction under the "use" prong of § 924(c)(1), the Government must show that the defendant actively employed the firearm during and in relation to the predicate crime.

III

Having determined that "use" denotes active employment, we must conclude that the evidence was insufficient to support . . . Bailey's . . . conviction for "use" under § 924(c)(1).

The police stopped Bailey for a traffic offense and arrested him after finding cocaine in the driver's compartment of his car. The police then found a firearm inside a bag in the locked car trunk. There was no evidence that Bailey actively employed the firearm in any way. . . . We reverse . . . .

Bailey . . . [was] charged under both the "use" and "carry" prongs of § 924(c)(1). Because the Court of Appeals did not consider liability under the "carry" prong of § 924(c)(1) . . . , we remand for consideration of that basis for upholding the conviction[].

Notes and Questions

---

1. Do you agree that *Bailey* was correctly decided, at least as to result? Why or why not?

2. The Court invokes a "canon of construction" to aid in its interpretation of the statute at issue. What is that canon?

3. In *Muscarello v. United States*, 524 U.S. 125 (1998), the Court held that, for the purpose of 18 U.S.C. § 924(c)(1), the phrase "carries a firearm" is not limited to the carrying of firearms on the person, but rather applies as well to a person who knowingly possesses and conveys firearms in a vehicle, including the locked glove compartment or trunk of a car, which the person accompanies. The Court's opinion generated a vigorous four-Justice dissent, led by Justice Ginsburg, in which she noted:

   > Popular films and television productions provide corroborative illustrations. In "The Magnificent Seven," for example, O'Reilly (played by Charles Bronson) says: "You think I am brave because I carry a gun; well, your fathers are much braver because they carry responsibility, for you, your brothers, your sisters, and your mothers." And in the television series "M*A*S*H," Hawkeye Pierce (played by Alan Alda) presciently proclaims: "I will not carry a gun. I'll carry your books, I'll carry a torch, I'll carry a tune, I'll carry on, carry over, carry forward, Cary Grant, cash and carry, carry me back to Old Virginia, I'll even 'hari-kari' if you show me how, but I will not carry a gun!"

   Id. at 144 n.6 (Ginsburg, J., dissenting).

Watson v. United States
522 U.S. 74 (2007)

JUSTICE SOUTER delivered the opinion of the Court.

The question is whether a person who trades his drugs for a gun "uses" a firearm "during and in relation to a drug trafficking crime" within the meaning of 18 U. S. C. § 924(c)(1)(A). We hold that he does not.

I

A

Section 924(c)(1)(A) sets a mandatory minimum sentence, depending on the facts, for a defendant who, "during and in relation to any crime of violence or drug trafficking crime, uses or carries a firearm." The statute leaves the term "uses" undefined, though we have spoken to it twice before.

Smith v. *United States*, 508 U. S. 223 (1993) raised the converse of today's question, and held that "a criminal who trades his firearm for drugs 'uses' it during and in relation to a drug trafficking offense within the meaning of § 924(c)(1)." We rested primarily on the "ordinary or natural meaning" of the verb in context, and understood its common range as going beyond employment as a weapon: "it is both reasonable and normal to say that petitioner 'used' his MAC-10 in his drug trafficking offense by trading it for cocaine."

Two years later, the issue in *Bailey* v. *United States*, 516 U. S. 137 (1995) was whether possessing a firearm kept near the scene of drug trafficking is "use" under § 924(c)(1). We looked again to "ordinary or natural" meaning, and decided that mere possession does not amount to "use": "§ 924(c)(1) requires evidence sufficient to show an *active employment* of the firearm by the defendant, a use that makes the firearm an operative factor in relation to the predicate offense."[3]

B

The third case on the reach of § 924(c)(1)(A) began to take shape when petitioner, Michael A. Watson, told a Government informant that he wanted to acquire a gun. On the matter of price, the informant quoted no dollar figure but suggested that Watson could pay in narcotics. Next, Watson met with the informant and an undercover law enforcement agent posing as a firearms dealer, to whom he gave 24 doses of oxycodone hydrochloride (commonly, OxyContin) for a .50 caliber semiautomatic pistol. When law enforcement officers arrested Watson, they found the pistol in his car, and a later search of his house turned up a cache of prescription medicines, guns, and ammunition. Watson said he got the pistol "to protect his other firearms and drugs."

A federal grand jury indicted him for distributing a Schedule II controlled substance and for "using" the pistol during and in relation to that crime, in violation of § 924(c)(1)(A). Watson pleaded guilty across the board, reserving the right to challenge the factual basis for a § 924(c)(1)(A) conviction and the added consecutive sentence of 60 months for using the gun. The Court of Appeals affirmed, 191 Fed. Appx. 326 (CA5 2006) (*per curiam*), on Circuit precedent foreclosing any argument that Watson had not "used" a firearm.

---

3. In 1998, Congress responded to *Bailey* by amending § 924(c)(1). The amendment broadened the provision to cover a defendant who "in furtherance of any crime of violence or drug trafficking crime, possesses a firearm." 18 U. S. C. § 924(c)(1)(A). The amendment did not touch the "use" prong of § 924(c)(1).

We granted certiorari to resolve a conflict among the Circuits on whether a person "uses" a firearm within the meaning of 18 U. S. C. § 924(c)(1)(A) when he trades narcotics to obtain a gun. We now reverse.

II

A

The Government's position that Watson "used" the pistol under § 924(c)(1)(A) by receiving it for narcotics lacks authority in either precedent or regular English. To begin with, neither *Smith* nor *Bailey* implicitly decides this case. While *Smith* held that firearms may be "used" in a barter transaction, even with no violent employment, the case addressed only the trader who swaps his gun for drugs, not the trading partner who ends up with the gun. *Bailey*, too, is unhelpful, with its rule that a gun must be made use of actively to satisfy § 924(c)(1)(A), as "an operative factor in relation to the predicate offense." The question here is whether it makes sense to say that Watson employed the gun at all; *Bailey* does not answer it.

With no statutory definition or definitive clue, the meaning of the verb "uses" has to turn on the language as we normally speak it; there is no other source of a reasonable inference about what Congress understood when writing or what its words will bring to the mind of a careful reader. So, in *Smith* we looked for "everyday meaning," revealed in phraseology that strikes the ear as "both reasonable and normal." This appeal to the ordinary leaves the Government without much of a case.

The Government may say that a person "uses" a firearm simply by receiving it in a barter transaction, but no one else would. A boy who trades an apple to get a granola bar is sensibly said to use the apple, but one would never guess which way this commerce actually flowed from hearing that the boy used the granola. Cf. *United States* v. *Stewart*, 246 F. 3d 728, 731 (CADC 2001) ("When a person pays a cashier a dollar for a cup of coffee in the courthouse cafeteria, the customer has not used the coffee. He has only used the dollar bill."). So, when Watson handed over the drugs for the pistol, the informant or the agent "used" the pistol to get the drugs, just as *Smith* held, but regular speech would not say that Watson himself used the pistol in the trade. . . .

B

The Government would trump ordinary English with two arguments. First, it relies on *Smith* for the pertinence of a neighboring provision, 18 U. S. C. § 924(d)(1), which authorizes seizure and forfeiture of firearms "intended to be used in" certain criminal offenses listed in § 924(d)(3). Some of those offenses involve receipt of a firearm, from which the Government infers that "use" under § 924(d) necessarily includes some receipt of a gun even in a barter transaction. *Smith* is cited for the proposition that the term must be given the same meaning in both subsections, and the Government urges us to import "use" as "receipt in barter" into § 924(c)(1)(A).

We agree with the Government that § 924(d) calls for attention; the reference to intended use in a receipt crime carries some suggestion that receipt can be "use" (more of a hint, say, than speaking of intended "use" in a crime defined as exchange).

But the suggestion is a tepid one and falls short of supporting what is really an attempt to draw a conclusion too specific from a premise too general.

The *Smith* majority rested principally on ordinary speech in reasoning that § 924(c)(1) extends beyond use as a weapon and includes use as an item of barter, and the *Smith* opinion looks to § 924(d) only for its light on that conclusion. It notes that the "intended to be used" clause of § 924(d)(1) refers to offenses where "the firearm is *not* used as a weapon but instead as an item of barter or commerce," with the implication that Congress intended "use" to reach commercial transactions, not just gun violence, in § 924(d) generally. It was this breadth of treatment that led the *Smith* majority to say that, "unless we are to hold that using a firearm has a different meaning in § 924(d) — and clearly we should not — we must reject petitioner's narrow interpretation."

The Government overreads *Smith*. While the neighboring provision indicates that a firearm is "used" nonoffensively, and supports the conclusion that a gun can be "used" in barter, beyond that point its illumination fails. This is so because the utility of § 924(d)(1) is limited by its generality and its passive voice; it tells us a gun can be "used" in a receipt crime, but not whether both parties to a transfer use the gun, or only one, or which one. The nearby subsection (c)(1)(A), however, requires just such a specific identification. It provides that a person who uses a gun in the circumstances described commits a crime, whose perpetrator must be clearly identifiable in advance.

The agnosticism on the part of § 924(d)(1) about who does the using is entirely consistent with common speech's understanding that the first possessor is the one who "uses" the gun in the trade, and there is thus no cause to admonish us to adhere to the paradigm of a statute "as a symmetrical and coherent regulatory scheme, in which the operative words have a consistent meaning throughout," or to invoke the "standard principle of statutory construction that identical words and phrases within the same statute should normally be given the same meaning." Subsections (d)(1) and (c)(1)(A) as we read them are not at odds over the verb "use"; the point is merely that in the two subsections the common verb speaks to different issues in different voices and at different levels of specificity. The provisions do distinct jobs, but we do not make them guilty of employing the common verb inconsistently.

C

The second effort to trump regular English is the claim that failing to treat receipt in trade as "use" would create unacceptable asymmetry with *Smith*. At bottom, this atextual policy critique says it would be strange to penalize one side of a gun-for-drugs exchange but not the other: "the danger to society is created not only by the person who brings the firearm to the drug transaction, but also by the drug dealer who takes the weapon in exchange for his drugs during the transaction."

The position assumes that *Smith* must be respected, and we join the Government at least on this starting point. A difference of opinion within the Court (as in *Smith*) does not keep the door open for another try at statutory construction, where *stare decisis* has "special force since the legislative power is implicated, and Congress remains free to alter what we have done." *Patterson* v. *McLean Credit Union*, 491 U. S. 164, 172-173 (1989). What is more, in 14 years Congress has taken no step to modify *Smith*'s holding, and this long congressional acquiescence "has enhanced even the usual precedential force" we accord to our interpretations of statutes.

The problem, then, is not with the sturdiness of *Smith* but with the limited malleability of the language *Smith* construed, and policy-driven symmetry cannot turn "receipt-in-trade" into "use." Whatever the tension between the prior result and the outcome here, law depends on respect for language and would be served better by statutory amendment (if Congress sees asymmetry) than by racking statutory language to cover a policy it fails to reach.

The argument is a peculiar one, in fact, given the Government's take on the current state of § 924(c)(1)(A). It was amended after *Bailey* and now prohibits not only using a firearm during and in relation to a drug trafficking crime, but also possessing one "in furtherance of" such a crime. The Government is confident that "a drug dealer who takes a firearm in exchange for his drugs generally will be subject to prosecution" under this new possession prong. This view may or may not prevail, and we do not speak to it today, but it does leave the appeal to symmetry underwhelming in a contest with the English language, on the Government's very terms.

Given ordinary meaning and the conventions of English, we hold that a person does not "use" a firearm under § 924(c)(1)(A) when he receives it in trade for drugs. The judgment of the Court of Appeals is reversed, and the case is remanded for further proceedings consistent with this opinion.

It is so ordered.

JUSTICE GINSBURG, concurring in the judgment.

It is better to receive than to give, the Court holds today, at least when the subject is guns. Distinguishing, as the Court does, between trading a gun for drugs and trading drugs for a gun, for purposes of the 18 U. S. C. § 924(c)(1) enhancement, makes scant sense to me. I join the Court's judgment, however, because I am persuaded that the Court took a wrong turn in *Smith* v. *United States*, 508 U. S. 223 (1993), when it held that trading a gun for drugs fits within § 924(c)(1)'s compass as "use" of a firearm "during and in relation to any drug trafficking crime." For reasons well stated by JUSTICE SCALIA in his dissenting opinion in *Smith*, I would read the word "use" in § 924(c)(1) to mean use as a weapon, not use in a bartering transaction. Accordingly, I would overrule *Smith*, and thereby render our precedent both coherent and consistent with normal usage. Cf. *Henslee* v. *Union Planters Nat. Bank & Trust Co.*, 335 U. S. 595, 600 (1949) (Frankfurter, J., dissenting) ("Wisdom too often never comes, and so one ought not to reject it merely because it comes late.").

Notes and Questions

1. Is *Watson* reconcilable with *Smith*? May one reasonably be said to "use" a gun by trading it for drugs, but not when trading drugs for a gun? To what extent does or should the answer depend on the fact that the statute in question was amended, post-*Smith*, so that this same sentencing enhancement also applies to a defendant who simply "possesses" a firearm "in furtherance" of a drug trafficking crime?

2. The *Watson* Court speaks repeatedly of ordinary meaning. But to whom? A reasonable member of Congress? Someone trained in the law, such as a lawyer or a judge? The typical "man (or woman) on the street"? The typical person charged with an offense of this nature?

3. Notice that the Court recognized the "'standard principle of statutory construction that identical words and phrases within the same statute should normally be given the same meaning,'" but did not find it applicable in this case.

4. With respect to footnote 3, how did the Court know that the 1998 amendment to 18 U.S.C. § 924(c)(1) was in response to *Bailey*? Assuming it was in response to *Bailey*, do you think that Congress was "saying" that *Bailey* was wrongly decided, or that there might have been an "unintended" gap in that statute as originally drafted? And how does the fact that this statute was amended impact the argument with respect to statutory stare decisis, if at all?

5. The Court asserts that *Smith* "must be respected" because "in 14 years Congress has taken no step to modify *Smith*'s holding." But may one read that much into congressional "acquiescence," or (more accurately) failure to act? Can one confidently say that Congress in fact approves of *Smith*? And even if one can, would it be because the Court correctly interpreted the text of the relevant statute, or because Congress simply liked the result, in sort of an "I wish we would have thought of that" fashion?

6. Notice that, following *Smith* (in which the Court found the statute applicable), Congress did nothing to contract the statute's scope, but that following *Bailey* (in which the Court found the statute inapplicable), Congress amended the statute to expand its scope. Assuming Congress's responses to these two cases were not coincidental, might this mean that a legislature, being an elected body, generally is more likely to expand criminal liability and enhance criminal punishments than do the opposite? If so, then does Congress's supposed reaction to any particular Supreme Court case tell one anything about the "correctness" of the Court's interpretation of some criminal law-related statute?

7. The court of appeals in *Watson* affirmed the judgment of the district court in an unpublished (and therefore nonprecedential), per curiam opinion. Is that at all troubling, particularly given the Supreme Court's subsequent reversal of the judgment?

3. Tools of Statutory Interpretation

In the previous Section, we saw some of the various techniques or "tools" of statutory interpretation that are used by courts today to help ascertain statutory meaning and scope. In this Section, we will now look at such tools more comprehensively.

a. *The Parts of a Statute*

Statutes, being the product of an act, generally constitute parts of a larger whole. An understanding of these various component parts and how they fit together is often helpful to gaining an understanding of the meaning of an act as codified. Similarly, statutes *themselves* can consist of parts that can serve as aids to interpretation. As one leading treatise summarizes:

> The text of a statute is an instrument of communication. Therefore, textual considerations are relevant for the purpose of resolving differences concerning the way an act should be interpreted and applied. How a statute is constructed has much to do with how it is construed. An understanding of the parts of an act, particularly from the standpoint of their relevance and significance for interpretation, is important both to the author or draftsman of a legislative measure and to those who are concerned with the operation of the statute.

1A NORMAN J. SINGER, STATUTES AND STATUTORY CONSTRUCTION § 20:1, at 118-19 (6th ed. 2002).

For example, we have already seen that the *title* of an act can provide some information regarding the meaning or purpose of an act. As Professor Singer states:

> Originally in England, bills were not given titles. Even when used, titles were not considered part of the act. Although a similar view was also followed in early American legislative history, the custom gradually developed to caption legislative acts to identify the subject matter. Eventually, the draftsmen of state constitutions inserted provisions requiring titles on all statutes. The federal Constitution does not impose any requirements concerning titles for acts of Congress.
>
> State constitutional provisions usually prescribe that the subject or object of an act be expressed in the title.

1A NORMAN J. SINGER, STATUTES AND STATUTORY CONSTRUCTION § 18:1, at 38-39 (6th ed. 2002).

The importance of the title in the interpretation of federal statutes is limited, though, particularly at the federal level. A fairly detailed discussion of the use of headings and titles in federal statutes can be found in *Brotherhood of Railroad Trainmen v. Baltimore & Ohio R.R.*, 331 U.S. 519 (1947), wherein the Court stated:

> That the heading of [the section of the act at issue] fails to refer to all the matters which the framers of that section wrote into the text is not an unusual fact. The heading is but a short-hand reference to the general subject-matter involved. . . . [H]eadings and titles are not meant to take the place of the detailed provisions of the text. Nor are they necessarily designed to be a reference guide or a synopsis. Where the text is complicated and prolific, headings and titles can do no more than indicate the provisions in a most general manner; to attempt to refer to each specific provision would often be ungainly as well as useless. As a result, matters in the text which deviate from those falling within the general pattern are frequently unreflected in the headings and titles. Factors of this type have led to the wise rule that the title of a statute and the heading of a section cannot limit

the plain meaning of the text. For interpretive purposes, they are of use only when they shed light on some ambiguous word or phrase. They are but tools available for the resolution of doubt. But they cannot undo or limit that which the text makes plain.

Id. at 528-29 (citations omitted). The above language was more recently reaffirmed in *Carter v. United States*, 530 U.S. 255, 267 (2000).

Another component of some statutes that can shed some light on statutory meaning is a statutory *statement of purpose*. For example, the statutorily defined purposes of the Endangered Species Act are codified at 16 U.S.C. § 1531(b) (2006), which provides:

> The purposes of this chapter are to provide a means whereby the ecosystems upon which endangered species and threatened species depend may be conserved, to provide a program for the conservation of such endangered species and threatened species, and to take such steps as may be appropriate to achieve the purposes of the treaties and conventions set forth in subsection (a) of this section.

But like titles, statements of purpose — which tend to be vague, ambitious, and somewhat hortatory — should not be given undue emphasis. As the Supreme Court has stated:

> "[N]o legislation pursues its purposes at all costs. Deciding what competing values will or will not be sacrificed to the achievement of a particular objective is the very essence of legislative choice — and it frustrates rather than effectuates legislative intent simplistically to assume that *whatever* furthers the statute's primary objective must be the law."

Rodriguez v. United States, 480 U.S. 522, 525-26 (1987). *See also* William N. Eskridge, Jr., Book Review, *The New Textualism and Normative Canons*, 113 Colum. L. Rev. 531, 560 (2013) ("Enacted statutory purposes are usually multiple (and potentially conflicting) and are set at a high level of generality, which makes them less than determinate aids for understanding how to apply statutory texts.").

Indeed, the National Conference of Commissioners on Uniform State Laws counsels against the inclusion of a purpose clause.

> A well drafted act requires no extraneous statement within itself of what it seeks to accomplish or the reasons prompting its enactment. Comments and annotations supply this detail to aid in its passage and interpretation. A purpose clause may create uncertainty by giving support to specious arguments that the substantive provisions of the act should be ignored because they are inconsistent with the purpose clause.

National Conference of Commissioners on Uniform State Laws, *Drafting Rules* 20 (2006).

b. *Statutory Definitions*

Determining the meaning of a statute usually requires a determination of the words and phrases comprising that statute. And determining the meaning of statutory terms is aided considerably by the inclusion of statutory definitions. As one leading treatise summarizes:

> The legislative process culminates in an official, authoritative expression of legal standards and directives. As a part of its legislative function a legislature may, besides enacting the original text of a law, also prescribe that words used elsewhere in the same statute or in other statutes are to carry specified meanings. Or it may, without reference to particular words, enact directives specifying how provisions in the same or other statutes are to be construed and applied. . . .
>
> . . . .
>
> Statutory definitions of words used elsewhere in the same statute furnish official and authoritative evidence of legislative intent and meaning, and are usually given controlling effect. Such internal legislative construction is of the highest value and prevails over executive or administrative construction and other extrinsic aids. A legislature is free to define terms for purpose of legislation, even though it does not follow a pharmacological or dictionary definition.
>
> Where a definition clause is clear it should ordinarily control the meaning of words used in the remainder of the act because of its authoritative nature. But the courts are not bound to follow a statutory definition where obvious incongruities in the statute would thereby be created, or where one of the major purposes of the legislation would be defeated or destroyed. . . .
>
> The problem of definition is not an easy one — for it never stops. Inevitably, the definition must itself be defined, and the definition of the definition, itself, will need interpretation.

1A Norman J. Singer, Statutes and Statutory Construction §§ 27:1-27:2 (6th ed. 2002).

Many, if not most, statutory definitions are specific to particular acts, and typically will be located fairly closely to the code sections to which they relate. But sometimes legislatures prescribe statutory definitions that are generally applicable to the entire code (unless another section prescribes otherwise). For example, at the federal level, the Dictionary Act, 1 U.S.C. §§ 1-6 (2012), sets forth definitions and rules of construction that are applicable to "any Act of Congress, unless the context indicates otherwise." 1 U.S.C. § 1 (2012). The Dictionary Act was recently cited by the Supreme Court in *Mohamad v. Palestinian Authority*, 132 S. Ct. 1702 (2012) (relying on the Act's definition of "person"). It might be observed that statutory definitions, whether specific or general, tend to be *stipulative* rather than *reportative* — i.e., they mean whatever the legislature wants them to mean, and might not exactly match common usage.

One of the more interesting — and more controversial — federal statutory definitions is found in the Defense of Marriage Act, which generally defines "marriage" as meaning "only a legal union between one man and one woman as husband and wife." 1 U.S.C. § 7 (2012). This definition was recently found unconstitutional by the Supreme Court in *United States v. Windsor*, 133 S. Ct. 2675 (2013). Also somewhat controversial is the Born-Alive Infants Protection Act of 2002, which generally defines "person" as including "every infant member of the species homo sapiens who is born alive at any stage of development." 1 U.S.C. § 8 (2012).

Curiously, 28 U.S.C. § 1369 (2006) defines the term "injury," *see* § 1369(c)(3), but does not otherwise use that term in that statute.

For more on statutory definitions, see Jeanne Frazier Price, *Wagging, Not Barking: Statutory Definitions*, 60 CLEVE. ST. L. REV. 999 (2013).

c. The Use of Dictionaries

In the absence of statutory definitions, courts charged with the interpretation and application of statutes must somehow discern the meaning of statutory terms through the use of other devices. One such device that has become quite prominent in recent years is the dictionary.

Nix v. Hedden

149 U.S. 304 (1893)

MR. JUSTICE GRAY, after stating the case, delivered the opinion of the court.

The single question in this case is whether tomatoes, considered as provisions, are to be classed as "vegetables" or as "fruit," within the meaning of the Tariff Act of 1883.

The only witness called at the trial testified that neither "vegetables" nor "fruit" had any special meaning in trade or commerce, different from that given in the dictionaries; and that they had the same meaning in trade to-day that they had in March, 1883.

The passages cited from the dictionaries define the word "fruit" as the seed of plants, or that part of plants which contains the seed, and especially the juicy, pulpy products of certain plants, covering and containing the seed. These definitions have no tendency to show that tomatoes are "fruit," as distinguished from "vegetables," in common speech, or within the meaning of the Tariff Act.

There being no evidence that the words "fruit" and "vegetables" have acquired any special meaning in trade or commerce, they must receive their ordinary meaning. Of that meaning the court is bound to take judicial notice, as it does in regard to all words in our own tongue; and upon such a question dictionaries are admitted, not as evidence, but only as aids to the memory and understanding of the court.

Botanically speaking, tomatoes are the fruit of a vine, just as are cucumbers, squashes, beans and peas. But in the common language of the people, whether sellers or consumers of provisions, all these are vegetables, which are grown in kitchen gardens, and which, whether eaten cooked or raw, are, like potatoes, carrots, parsnips, turnips, beets, cauliflower, cabbage, celery and lettuce, usually served at dinner in, with or after the soup, fish or meats which constitute the principal part of the repast, and not, like fruits generally, as dessert.

The attempt to class tomatoes with fruit is not unlike a recent attempt to class beans as seeds, of which Mr. Justice Bradley, speaking for this court, said: "We do not see why they should be classified as seeds, any more than walnuts should be so classified. Both are seeds in the language of botany or natural history, but not in commerce nor in common parlance. On the other hand, in speaking generally of provisions, beans may well be included under the term 'vegetables.' As an article of food on our tables, whether baked or boiled, or forming the basis of soup, they are used as a vegetable, as well when ripe as when green. This is the principal use to which they are put. Beyond the common knowledge which we have on this subject, very little evidence is necessary, or can be produced." *Robertson v. Salomon*, 130 U. S. 412, 414.

Judgment affirmed.

Notes and Questions

1. What do you think of the Court's holding in *Nix*? Its analysis? Do you agree?

2. We have already seen several cases in which the Supreme Court turned to dictionaries to assist in the interpretation of statues. Some of these uses were no doubt proper. But "[a]ll of us, including the Justices of the Supreme Court, have used dictionaries uncritically, without asking or understanding what purposes they are intended to serve." Ellen P. Aprill, *The Law of the Word: Dictionary Shopping in the Supreme Court*, 30 Ariz. St. L.J. 275, 277 (1998). This practice should be avoided. Thus, when using a dictionary as an aid to statutory interpretation, one should not simply search for and select the definition that leads to the particular result sought; rather, one should endeavor to select a dictionary most likely to contain an accurate definition, and be prepared to explain why the dictionary and the definition selected is superior to any others. As one legal scholar has stated: "There are a wide variety of dictionaries from which to choose, and all of them usually provide several entries for each word. The selection of a particular dictionary and a particular definition is not obvious and must be defended on some other grounds of suitability." Note, *Looking It Up: Dictionaries and Statutory Interpretation*, 107 Harv. L. Rev. 1437, 1445 (1994).

3. Regarding the use of dictionaries to ascertain the "linguistically correct meaning of particular words," Professors Hart and Sacks write:

> Judges answer many questions of the linguistically correct meaning of particular words out of their own experience and judgment. And counsel argue such questions on the basis of *their* experience and judgment. It is nice, however, when such questions can be answered by reference to impersonal authority. Such an authority is provided by reputable dictionaries.
>
> A dictionary, it is vital to observe, never says what meaning a word *must* bear in a particular context. Nor does it ever purport to say this. An unabridged dictionary is simply an historical record, not necessarily all-inclusive, of the meanings which words in fact *have* borne, in the judgment of the editors, in the writings of reputable authors. The editors make up this record by collecting examples of uses of the word to be defined, studying each use *in context*, and then forming a judgment about the meaning in that context. A good dictionary always gives examples of the use of the word *in context* in each of the meanings ascribed to it.

> The editors of dictionaries are never victims of the one-word, one-meaning fallacy.

HENRY M. HART, JR. & ALBERT M. SACKS, THE LEGAL PROCESS: BASIC PROBLEMS IN THE MAKING AND APPLICATION OF LAW 1190 (William N. Eskridge, Jr. & Philip P. Frickey eds., 1994). *Accord* Aprill, 30 ARIZ. ST. L.J. at 285 ("The role of context is crucial for modern lexicographers. Like many modern philosophers and psychologists of language, they do not view the meaning of a word as an absolute or existing in isolation.")

4. It is important to keep in mind that "[m]odern lexicographers see their task as describing how speakers of English use words. They do not seek or claim to prescribe how language should be used." Aprill, 30 ARIZ. ST. L.J. at 283. Modern dictionaries, in other words, tend to be more descriptive than prescriptive.

5. Dictionaries "are inevitably incomplete and subject to severe constraints on length." Aprill, 30 ARIZ. ST. L.J. at 285. Thus, "the meaning of a word as used in a particular statute will not necessarily be included among the listed definitions." *Id.* at 298. Unless the word in question is highly technical, though, this seems unlikely.

6. There is no doubt that the Supreme Court makes considerable use of dictionaries, and more use than it has in earlier times. *See* James J. Brudney & Lawrence Baum, *Oasis or Mirage: The Supreme Court's Thirst for Dictionaries in the Rehnquist and Roberts Eras*, 55 WM. & MARY L. REV. 483, 495-96 (2013). There is also no doubt that other courts will follow suit in the future.

7. *General dictionaries v. specialized dictionaries.* The general dictionary most frequently cited by the Supreme Court today is *Webster's Third New International Dictionary. See* Samuel A. Thumma & Jeffrey L. Kirchmeier, *The Lexicon Has Become a Fortress: The United States Supreme Court's Use of Dictionaries*, 47 BUFF. L. REV. 227, 263 (1999). General dictionaries, largely because of space limitations, tend to include only general definitions for common words. As a result, "general dictionaries exhibit serious deficiencies not only for technical legal terms, but also for the use of common words in a legal context." Aprill, 30 ARIZ. ST. L.J. at 303. For these reasons, the better answer sometimes lies in law dictionaries.

   The most frequently cited law dictionary by the Supreme Court is *Black's Law Dictionary. See* Thumma & Kirchmeier, *supra*, at 263. But there are others.

   For a more recent update of Thumma and Kirchmeier's work, see Jeffrey L. Kirchmeier & Samuel A. Thumma, *Scaling the Lexicon Fortress: The United States Supreme Court's Use of Dictionaries in the Twenty-First Century*, 94 MARQUETTE L. REV. 77 (2010), which includes appendices of words and phrases that have been defined by the Court in recent cases as well as the dictionaries used by the Court and various individual Justices. The authors also observe that "[a] majority of the Court has never explicitly offered any definitive guidance in selecting dictionary publishers or editions, specific definitions, how much weight to give to definitions, or whether to use a dictionary at all." *Id.* at 129.

8. *Variations among dictionaries.* "Dictionaries will differ in the definitions they include for a single word." Aprill, 30 ARIZ. ST. L.J. at 298. In light of this fact, what is a lawyer (or judge) likely to do if they are not satisfied by the definitions found in the first dictionary consulted?

9. *The ages of the dictionary.* One should also be sensitive to the date of the dictionary, particularly in relation to the date of the statute or other instrument being interpreted. For example, *Webster's Third New International Dictionary* was published in 1961 — more than 50 years ago. Though reprints of *Webster's Third* include an addendum of new words and meanings, those entries — even if consulted — date from the date of the reprint. Moreover: "Because of the inevitable time delay between collection of citations and publication of a dictionary, dictionaries must lag behind current use of the language. A dictionary with a 1996 publication date will not describe completely how language is being used in 1996." Aprill, 30 ARIZ. ST. L.J. at 287.

   At the other end of the spectrum, when interpreting the meaning of an old text, it seems to make sense to choose a dictionary contemporaneous with that text. *See* Aprill, 30 ARIZ. ST. L.J. at 288.

10. *Order of definitions.* When any given word has more than one meaning (which is often, if not usually, the case), what is the significance of the ordering (or numbering) of the various definitions provided? In order to know the answer, one must know how the particular dictionary in question was constructed. For example, *Webster's Third New International Dictionary*, Explanatory Notes 12.4 and 12.5 (at 17a), explains:

   > The system of separating by numbers and letters reflects something of the semantic relationship between various senses of a word. It is only a lexical convenience. It does not evaluate senses or establish an enduring hierarchy of importance among them. The best sense is the one that most aptly fits the context of an actual genuine utterance.
   >
   > The order of senses is historical: the one known to have been first used in English is entered first.

   An example of a case in which an understanding of the ordering of definitions might have made a difference can be found in *Smith v. United States*, 507 U.S. 197 (1993). In *Smith*, the issue was whether the Federal Tort Claims Act (FTCA) applied to tortious acts or omissions committed by persons acting on behalf of the United States in Antarctica. That issue, in turn, depended upon whether Antarctica should be considered a "foreign country," for if so, the FTCA was inapplicable. In the course of its opinion, the Court stated:

> Though the FTCA offers no definition of "country," the commonsense meaning of the term undermines petitioner's attempt to equate it with "sovereign state." The first dictionary definition of "country" is simply "a region or tract of land." Webster's New International Dictionary 609 (2d ed. 1945). To be sure, this is not the only possible interpretation of the term, and it is therefore appropriate to examine other parts of the statute before making a final determination. But the ordinary meaning of the language itself, we think, includes Antarctica, even though it has no recognized government.

Id. at 201. The Court ultimately concluded that claims arising in Antarctica, "a sovereignless region without civil tort law of its own," were beyond the scope of the FTCA. *Id.* at 198.

11. *Chisom v. Roemer*, 501 U.S. 380 (1991), involved the issue whether the term "representatives" as used in one portion of the Voting Rights Act included elected state judges. The Court concluded that it did. *See id.* at 404. Justice Scalia, joined by Chief Justice Rehnquist and Justice Kennedy, dissented. *See id.* Regarding the meaning of this term, Justice Scalia wrote:

> The Court, petitioners, and petitioners' *amici* have labored mightily to establish that there is *a* meaning of "representatives" that would include judges. But our job is not to scavenge the world of English usage to discover whether there is any possible meaning of "representatives" which suits our preconception that the statute includes judges; our job is to determine whether the *ordinary* meaning includes them, and if it does not, to ask whether there is any solid indication in the text or structure of the statute that something other than ordinary meaning is intended.
>
> There is little doubt that the ordinary meaning of "representatives" does not include judges, see Webster's Second New International Dictionary 2114 (1950). The Court's feeble argument to the contrary is that "representatives" means those who "are chosen by popular election." On that hypothesis, the fan-elected members of the baseball all-star teams are "representatives" — hardly a common, if even permissible, usage. Surely the word "representatives" connotes one who is not only *elected by* the people, but who also, at a minimum, *acts on behalf of* the people. Judges do that in a sense — but not in the ordinary sense. As the captions of the pleadings in some States still display, it is the prosecutor who represents "the People"; the judge represents the Law — which often requires him to rule against the People. It is precisely because we do not *ordinarily* conceive of judges as representatives that we held judges not within the Fourteenth Amendment's requirement of "one person, one vote." The point is not that a State could not make judges in some senses representative, or that all judges must be conceived of in the Article III mold, but rather, that giving "representatives" its ordinary meaning, the ordinary speaker in 1982 would not have applied the word to judges, see Holmes, The Theory of Legal Interpretation, 12 Harv. L. Rev. 417 (1899).

Id. at 410-11 (Scalia, J., dissenting). Justice Scalia is correct, is he not, that few ordinarily think of "representatives" as including judges, even elected judges? On the other hand, no one would confuse baseball players with state government officials, would they? More importantly, is there any reason to think that federal voting rights-type legislation would be drafted so as to apply to elected state legislators, but not elected state judges? Is resort to a dictionary an appropriate (or sufficient) means of resolving this dispute?

12. "[I]t is one of the surest indexes of a mature and developed jurisprudence not to make a fortress out of the dictionary . . . ." *Cabell v. Markham*, 148 F.2d 737, 739 (2d Cir.) (L. Hand, J.), *aff'd*, 326 U.S. 404 (1945).

13. For more on dictionaries, see Antonin Scalia & Bryan A. Garner, Reading Law: The Interpretation of Legal Texts 415-24 ("A Note on the Use of Dictionaries") (2012). *See also* Lawrence Solan, *When Judges Use the Dictionary*, 68 Am. Speech 50 (1993), and Phillip A. Rubin, Note, *War of the Words: How Courts Can Use Dictionaries Consistent with Textualist Principles*, 60 Duke L.J. 167 (2010).

14. For a recent Supreme Court battle concerning the use of dictionaries in statutory interpretation, see *Taniguchi v. Kan Pacific Saipan, Ltd.*, 132 S. Ct. 1997 (2012) (regarding the meaning of the term "interpreter" for purposes of 28 U.S.C. § 1920 and the awarding of costs to the prevailing party in a federal civil action). For another recent case involving the use of dictionaries in statutory interpretation, see *Bullock v. BankChampaign, N.A.*, 133 S. Ct. 1754 (2013) (interpreting the statutory term "defalcation").

PRACTICE PROBLEM: DICTIONARIES

Webster's Third New International Dictionary includes numerous definitions for the word "dog," including (in the order presented) "a carnivorous mammal (*Canis familiaris*)"; "a mean worthless fellow"; "any of various usu. simple mechanical devices for holding, gripping, or fastening something"; "ostentatious display"; and "something inferior of its kind." *Black's Law Dictionary* includes two definitions for the word "dog": "[s]omething undesirable, esp. a lawsuit," and a "stock or other investment that suffers public disdain and repeated price declines or poor performance."

Assume that a city has enacted a statute that reads, "No dogs in the park."

For the purpose of selecting the most appropriate meaning of the word "dog" as used in this statute, which dictionary would you choose? Why? Please explain.

And which definition (or definitions) in the dictionary you have selected supplies the most appropriate definition(s) for the word "dog" as used in this statute? Why? Please explain.

d. *The Use of Canons of Construction*

As we have seen, courts often rely on various maxims (or "canons") of construction to ascertain the "linguistically correct meaning of typical forms of word arrangements" such as are found in statutes. HENRY M. HART, JR. & ALBERT M. SACKS, THE LEGAL PROCESS: BASIC PROBLEMS IN THE MAKING AND APPLICATION OF LAW 1190 (William N. Eskridge, Jr. & Philip P. Frickey eds., 1994). But what, specifically, do we mean by canons of construction? As Professors Hart and Sacks explain:

> An act of Congress declares it to be a felony to "transport or cause to be transported in interstate commerce any woman or girl for the purpose of prostitution or debauchery, *or for any other immoral purpose.*" Suppose that the defendant transported a woman in interstate commerce for the purpose of assisting him to obtain money by false pretenses from an elderly and defenseless widow. Is the court forced to choose between convicting the defendant under the statute or holding this purpose not to be "immoral"? Will the word "immoral" bear the meaning of "sexually immoral, exclusive of other kinds of immorality"?
>
> A dictionary will scarcely answer this question, for dictionaries do not record the various meanings that historically have been attached to particular forms of word arrangements. But courts and lawyers have been concerned with such problems for centuries, and their conclusions about permissible meanings in many typical forms of word arrangements are embodied in many familiar "maxims of construction." In the case put, of course, the maxim *ejusdem generis* gives the simple answer. A general expression concluding a series of related particular expressions does not have to be taken with the generality it would have in another context. It may be limited to applications falling within the same kind or genus as the particular expressions.
>
> Maxims or canons of interpretation, such as *ejusdem generis*, are sometimes spoken of as "rules," as if they were of invariable application in the verbal situations which they describe. Students often become disillusioned with the maxims when they discover that they are not thus invariably applied. Commentators have often pointed out, with the joyous air of a debunker, that this cannot be so, since for every maxim of construction there is almost always an opposite. See, *e.g.*, Llewellyn, *Remarks on the Theory of Appellate Decision and the Rules or Canons About How Statutes Are to be Construed*, 3 Vand. L. Rev. 395, 401-08 (1950). A recent casebook says bluntly that canons of construction "are useful only as facades, which for an occasional judge may add lustre to an argument persuasive for other reasons."
>
> All this, it is ventured, involves a misunderstanding of the function of the canons, and at bottom of the problem of interpretation itself. Of course there are pairs of maxims susceptible of being invoked for opposite conclusions. Once it is understood that meaning depends upon context, and that contexts vary, how could it be otherwise? Maxims should not be treated, any more than a dictionary, as saying what meaning a word or group of words *must* have in a given context. They simply answer the question whether a particular meaning is linguistically permissible, if the context warrants it. Is this not a useful function?

Id. at 1190-91. But Professors Hart and Sacks close by asking: "Does the view of the maxims of construction here presented assign them too limited a function? May they also be used, sometimes, as indicating a presumptive, or linguistically more probable meaning?" *Id.* at 1192.

Though the use of canons of construction became somewhat less popular in the 1960s and 1970s, they have enjoyed something of a resurgence as courts have adopted a more textualist approach to statutory interpretation. What follows is one attempt to catalog most of the more commonly used canons.

William N. Eskridge, Jr. & Philip P. Frickey

FOREWORD: LAW AS EQUILIBRIUM

108 Harv. L. Rev. 26 (1994)

APPENDIX

THE REHNQUIST COURT'S CANONS OF STATUTORY CONSTRUCTION

This Appendix collects the canons of statutory construction that have been used or developed by the Rehnquist Court, from the 1986 through the 1993 Terms of the Court (inclusive). The Appendix divides the canons into three conventional categories: the textual canons setting forth conventions of grammar and syntax, linguistic inferences, and textual integrity; extrinsic source canons, which direct the interpreter to authoritative sources of meaning; and substantive policy canons which embody public policies drawn from the Constitution, federal statutes, or the common law.

TEXTUAL CANONS

- Plain meaning rule: follow the plain meaning of statutory text, except when text suggests an absurd result or a scrivener's error.

Linguistic Inferences

- *Expressio unius*: expression of one thing suggests the exclusion of others.
- *Noscitur a sociis*: interpret a general term to be similar to more specific terms in a series.
- *Ejusdem generis*: interpret a general term to reflect the class of objects reflected in more specific terms accompanying it.
- Follow ordinary usage of terms, unless Congress gives them a specified or technical meaning.
- Follow dictionary definitions of terms, unless Congress has provided a specific definition. Consider dictionaries of the era in which the statute was enacted. Do not consider "idiosyncratic" dictionary definitions.
- "May" is usually precatory, while "shall" is usually mandatory.
- "Or" means in the alternative.

Grammar and Syntax

- Punctuation rule: Congress is presumed to follow accepted punctuation standards, so that placements of commas and other punctuation are assumed to be meaningful.

. . . .

Textual Integrity

- Each statutory provision should be read by reference to the whole act. Statutory interpretation is a "holistic" endeavor.
- Avoid interpreting a provision in a way that would render other provisions of the Act superfluous or unnecessary.

. . . .

- Avoid interpreting a provision in a way that is inconsistent with the structure of the statute.

. . . .

- Interpret the same or similar terms in a statute the same way.
- Specific provisions targeting a particular issue apply instead of provisions more generally covering the issue.
- Provisos and statutory exceptions should be read narrowly.
- Do not create exceptions in addition to those specified by Congress.

EXTRINSIC SOURCE CANONS

Agency Interpretations

- Rule of deference to agency interpretations, unless contrary to plain meaning of statute or unreasonable.
- Rule of extreme deference when there is express delegation of lawmaking duties to agency.
- Presumption that agency interpretation of its own regulations is correct.

Continuity in Law

- Rule of continuity: assume that Congress does not create discontinuities in legal rights and obligations without some clear statement.
- Presumption that Congress uses same term consistently in different statutes.
- Super-strong presumption of correctness for statutory precedents.
- Presumption that international agreements do not displace federal law.
- Borrowed statute rule: when Congress borrows a statute, it adopts by implication interpretations placed on that statute, absent express statement to the contrary.

- Re-enactment rule: when Congress re-enacts a statute, it incorporates settled interpretations of the re-enacted statute. The rule is inapplicable when there is no settled standard Congress could have known.
- Acquiescence rule: consider unbroken line of lower court decisions interpreting statute, but do not give them weight.

Extrinsic Legislative Sources

- Interpret provision consistent with subsequent statutory amendments, but do not consider subsequent legislative discussions.
- Consider legislative history if the statute is ambiguous.
- Committee reports are authoritative legislative history, but cannot trump a textual plain meaning, and should not be relied on if they are "imprecise."
- Committee report language that cannot be tied to a specific statutory provision cannot be credited. House and Senate reports inconsistent with one another should be discounted.
- Presumption against interpretation considered and rejected by floor vote of a chamber of Congress or committee.
- Floor statements can be used to confirm apparent meaning.
- Contemporaneous and subsequent understandings of a statutory scheme (including understandings by President and Department of Justice) may sometimes be admissible.
- The "dog didn't bark" canon: presumption that prior legal rule should be retained if no one in legislative deliberations even mentioned the rule or discussed any changes to the rule.

SUBSTANTIVE POLICY CANONS

Constitution-Based Canons

- Avoid interpretations that would render a statute unconstitutional. Inapplicable if statute would survive constitutional attack, or if statutory text is clear.

1. Separation of Powers

- Super-strong rule against congressional interference with President's authority over foreign affairs and national security.
- Rule against congressional invasion of the President's core executive powers.
- Rule against review of President's core executive actions for "abuse of discretion."
- Rule against congressional curtailment of judiciary's "inherent powers" or its "equity" powers.

. . . .

- Presumption that Congress does not delegate authority without sufficient guidelines.
- Presumption against "implying" causes of action into federal statutes.
- Presumption that U.S. law conforms to U.S. international obligations.
- Rule against congressional abrogation of Indian treaty rights.
- Presumption favoring severability of unconstitutional provisions.

2. Federalism

- Super-strong rule against federal invasion of "core state functions."
- Super-strong rule against federal abrogation of states' Eleventh Amendment immunity from lawsuits in federal courts.
- Rule against inferring enforceable conditions on federal grants to the states.
- Rule against congressional expansion of federal court jurisdiction that would siphon cases away from state courts.
- Rule against reading a federal statute to authorize states to engage in activities that would violate the dormant commerce clause.
- Rule favoring concurrent state and federal court jurisdiction over federal claims.
- Rule against federal pre-emption of traditional state functions, or against federal disruption of area of traditional state regulation.

. . . .

- Presumption that states can tax activities within their borders, including Indian tribal activities, but also presumption that states cannot tax on Indian lands.
- Presumption against congressional derogation from state's land claims based upon its entry into Union on an "equal footing" with all other states.
- Presumption against federal habeas review of state criminal convictions supported by independent state ground.
- Presumption of finality of state convictions for purposes of habeas review.
- Principle that federal equitable remedies must consider interests of state and local authorities.
- Presumption that Congress borrows state statutes of limitations for federal statutory schemes, unless otherwise provided.

3. Due Process

- Rule of lenity: rule against applying punitive sanctions if there is ambiguity as to underlying criminal liability or criminal penalty.
- Rule of lenity applies to civil sanction that is punitive or when underlying liability is criminal.
- Rule against criminal penalties imposed without showing of specific intent.
- Rule against interpreting statutes to be retroactive, even if statute is curative or restorative.
- Rule against interpreting statutes to deny a right to a jury trial.
- Presumption in favor of judicial review, especially for constitutional questions, but not for agency decisions not to prosecute.

. . . .

- Presumption that judgments will not be binding upon persons not party to adjudication.
- Presumption against national service of process unless authorized by Congress.
- Presumption against foreclosure of private enforcement of important federal rights.

Statute-Based Canons

- *In pari materia*: similar statutes should be interpreted similarly, unless legislative history or purpose suggests material differences.
- Presumption against repeals by implication.
- Purpose rule: interpret ambiguous statutes so as best to carry out their statutory purposes.
- Narrow interpretation of statutory exemptions.
- Presumption against creating exemptions in a statute that has none.

. . . .

Common Law-Based Canons

- Presumption in favor of following common law usage where Congress has employed words or concepts with well settled common law traditions. Follow evolving common law unless inconsistent with statutory purposes.
- Rule against extraterritorial application of U.S. law, except for antitrust laws.
- Super-strong rule against waivers of United States sovereign immunity.

. . . .

- Rule presuming against attorney fee-shifting in federal courts and federal statutes, and narrow construction of fee-shifting statutes to exclude unmentioned costs.
- Presumption that jury finds facts, judge declares law.
- Rule presuming that law takes effect on date of enactment.

. . . .

- Presumption favoring enforcement of forum selection clauses.

Notes and Questions

---

1. For another excellent and fairly comprehensive list of canons of construction, see ANTONIN SCALIA & BRYAN A. GARNER, READING LAW: THE INTERPRETATION OF LEGAL TEXTS xi-xvi (2012). In *Reading Law*, Scalia and Garner also include a more controversial list of "Thirteen Falsities Exposed." *See id.* at xvii.

2. For a thorough critique of Scalia and Garner's canons of construction, see William N. Eskridge, Jr., Book Review, *The New Textualism and Normative Canons*, 113 COLUM. L. REV. 531 (2013).

3. Sometimes canons of construction are codified by legislatures. Indeed: "Each state, the District of Columbia, and the United States have a set of laws directing interpreters as to how the legislature wishes its statutes to be construed." Jacob Scott, *Codified Canons and the Common Law of Interpretation*, 98 GEO. L.J. 341, 350 (2010).

PRACTICE PROBLEM: CANONS OF CONSTRUCTION[1]

A federal criminal statute prohibits "willful interference with the delivery of mail." An arrest warrant is issued for an accused murderer who happens to be a postman. While delivering the mail, he is arrested by a county sheriff. A federal prosecutor indicts the sheriff for violating the mail statute by interfering with the postman. Should the prosecution succeed? Why or why not? Please explain.

e. Rules of Clear Statement

The above discussion of canons of construction arguably merges that concept with another, related concept that some find somewhat separable: *rules of clear statement*. See if you can understand the distinction from the following case.

---

1. This problem (which undoubtedly was derived from *United States v. Kirby*, 74 U.S. (7 Wall.) 482 (1868)) was taken from Bryan A. Garner, *Outtakes from a Treatise*, ABA J. 22 (Oct. 2012), and Bryan A. Garner, *A Text on Textualism, Part 2*, ABA J. 27 (Nov. 2012), which also provide other good examples of statutory interpretation problems.

Equal Employment Opportunity Commission v. Arabian American Oil Co.

499 U.S. 244 (1991)

CHIEF JUSTICE REHNQUIST delivered the opinion of the Court.

These cases present the issue whether Title VII applies extraterritorially to regulate the employment practices of United States employers who employ United States citizens abroad. The United States Court of Appeals for the Fifth Circuit held that it does not, and we agree with that conclusion.

Petitioner Boureslan is a naturalized United States citizen who was born in Lebanon. The respondents are two Delaware corporations, Arabian American Oil Company (Aramco), and its subsidiary, Aramco Service Company (ASC). Aramco's principal place of business is Dhahran, Saudi Arabia, and it is licensed to do business in Texas. ASC's principal place of business is Houston, Texas.

In 1979, Boureslan was hired by ASC as a cost engineer in Houston. A year later he was transferred, at his request, to work for Aramco in Saudi Arabia. Boureslan remained with Aramco in Saudi Arabia until he was discharged in 1984. After filing a charge of discrimination with the Equal Employment Opportunity Commission (EEOC or Commission), he instituted this suit in the United States District Court for the Southern District of Texas against Aramco and ASC. He sought relief under both state law and Title VII of the Civil Rights Act of 1964, 78 Stat. 253, as amended, 42 U. S. C. §§ 2000e-2000e-17, on the ground that he was harassed and ultimately discharged by respondents on account of his race, religion, and national origin.

Respondents filed a motion for summary judgment on the ground that the District Court lacked subject-matter jurisdiction over Boureslan's claim because the protections of Title VII do not extend to United States citizens employed abroad by American employers. The District Court agreed and dismissed Boureslan's Title VII claim; it also dismissed his state-law claims for lack of pendent jurisdiction and entered final judgment in favor of respondents. A panel for the Fifth Circuit affirmed. After vacating the panel's decision and rehearing the case en banc, the court affirmed the District Court's dismissal of Boureslan's complaint. Both Boureslan and the EEOC petitioned for certiorari. We granted both petitions for certiorari to resolve this important issue of statutory interpretation.

Both parties concede, as they must, that Congress has the authority to enforce its laws beyond the territorial boundaries of the United States. Whether Congress has in fact exercised that authority in these cases is a matter of statutory construction. It is our task to determine whether Congress intended the protections of Title VII to apply to United States citizens employed by American employers outside of the United States.

It is a longstanding principle of American law "that legislation of Congress, unless a contrary intent appears, is meant to apply only within the territorial jurisdiction of the United States." This "canon of construction is a valid approach whereby unexpressed congressional intent may be ascertained." It serves to protect against unintended clashes between our laws and those of other nations which could result in international discord.

In applying this rule of construction, we look to see whether "language in the relevant Act gives any indication of a congressional purpose to extend its coverage beyond places over which the United States has sovereignty or has some measure of legislative control." We assume that Congress legislates against the backdrop of the presumption against extraterritoriality. Therefore, unless there is "the affirmative intention of the Congress clearly expressed," we must presume it "is primarily concerned with domestic conditions."

Boureslan and the EEOC contend that the language of Title VII evinces a clearly expressed intent on behalf of Congress to legislate extraterritorially. They rely principally on two provisions of the statute. First, petitioners argue that the statute's definitions of the jurisdictional terms "employer" and "commerce" are sufficiently broad to include United States firms that employ American citizens overseas. Second, they maintain that the statute's "alien exemption" clause necessarily implies that Congress intended to protect American citizens from employment discrimination abroad. Petitioners also contend that we should defer to the EEOC's consistently held position that Title VII applies abroad. We conclude that petitioners' evidence, while not totally lacking in probative value, falls short of demonstrating the affirmative congressional intent required to extend the protections of Title VII beyond our territorial borders.

Title VII prohibits various discriminatory employment practices based on an individual's race, color, religion, sex, or national origin. An employer is subject to Title VII if it has employed 15 or more employees for a specified period and is "engaged in an industry affecting commerce." An industry affecting commerce is "any activity, business, or industry in commerce or in which a labor dispute would hinder or obstruct commerce or the free flow of commerce and includes any activity or industry 'affecting commerce' within the meaning of the Labor-Management Reporting and Disclosure Act of 1959." "Commerce," in turn, is defined as "trade, traffic, commerce, transportation, transmission, or communication among the several States; or between a State and any place outside thereof; or within the District of Columbia, or a possession of the United States; or between points in the same State but through a point outside thereof."

Petitioners argue that by its plain language, Title VII's "broad jurisdictional language" reveals Congress's intent to extend the statute's protections to employment discrimination anywhere in the world by a United States employer who affects trade "between a State and any place outside thereof." More precisely, they assert that since Title VII defines "States" to include States, the District of Columbia, and specified territories, the clause "between a State and any place outside thereof" must be referring to areas beyond the territorial limit of the United States.

Respondents offer several alternative explanations for the statute's expansive language. They contend that the "or between a State and any place outside thereof" clause "provides the jurisdictional nexus required to regulate commerce that is not wholly within a single state, presumably as it affects both interstate and foreign commerce" but not to "regulate conduct exclusively *within* a foreign country." They also argue that since the definitions of the terms "employer," "commerce," and "industry affecting commerce" make no mention of "commerce with foreign nations," Congress cannot be said to have intended that the statute apply overseas. In support of this argument, respondents point to Title II of the Civil Rights Act of 1964, governing public accommodation, which specifically defines commerce as it applies to foreign nations. Finally, respondents argue that while language present in the first bill considered by the House of Representatives contained the terms "foreign commerce" and "foreign nations," those terms were deleted by the Senate before the Civil Rights Act of 1964 was passed. They conclude that these deletions "are inconsistent with the notion of a clearly expressed congressional intent to apply Title VII extraterritorially."

We need not choose between these competing interpretations as we would be required to do in the absence of the presumption against extraterritorial application discussed above. Each is plausible, but no more persuasive than that. The language relied upon by petitioners — and it is they who must make the affirmative showing — is ambiguous, and does not speak directly to the question presented here. The intent of Congress as to the extraterritorial application of this statute must be deduced by inference from boilerplate language which can be found in any number of congressional Acts, none of which have ever been held to apply overseas.

Petitioners' reliance on Title VII's jurisdictional provisions also finds no support in our case law; we have repeatedly held that even statutes that contain broad language in their definitions of "commerce" that expressly refer to "*foreign* commerce" do not apply abroad....

....

... Many Acts of Congress are based on the authority of that body to regulate commerce among the several States, and the parts of these Acts setting forth the basis for legislative jurisdiction will obviously refer to such commerce in one way or another. If we were to permit possible, or even plausible, interpretations of language such as that involved here to override the presumption against territorial application, there would be little left of the presumption.

Petitioners argue that Title VII's "alien exemption provision" "clearly manifests an intention" by Congress to protect United States citizens with respect to their employment outside of the United States. The alien-exemption provision says that the statute "shall not apply to an employer with respect to the employment of aliens outside any State." Petitioners contend that from this language a negative inference should be drawn that Congress intended Title VII to cover United States *citizens* working abroad for United States employers....

....

If petitioners are correct that the alien-exemption clause means that the statute applies to employers overseas, we see no way of distinguishing in its application between United States employers and foreign employers. Thus, a French employer of a United States citizen in France would be subject to Title VII — a result at which even petitioners balk. The EEOC assures us that in its view the term "employer" means only "American employer," but there is no such distinction in this statute and no indication that the EEOC in the normal course of its administration had produced a reasoned basis for such a distinction. Without clearer evidence of congressional intent to do so than is contained in the alien-exemption clause, we are unwilling to ascribe to that body a policy which would raise difficult issues of international law by imposing this country's employment-discrimination regime upon foreign corporations operating in foreign commerce.

This conclusion is fortified by the other elements in the statute suggesting a purely domestic focus. . . .

Similarly, Congress failed to provide any mechanisms for overseas enforcement of Title VII. . . .

It is also reasonable to conclude that had Congress intended Title VII to apply overseas, it would have addressed the subject of conflicts with foreign laws and procedures. . . .

Finally, the EEOC, as one of the two federal agencies with primary responsibility for enforcing Title VII, argues that we should defer to its "consistent" construction of Title VII . . . "to apply to discrimination against American citizens outside the United States." . . .

    . . . .

    . . . [But w]e are of the view that, even when considered in combination with petitioners' other arguments, the EEOC's interpretation is insufficiently weighty to overcome the presumption against extraterritorial application.

Our conclusion today is buttressed by the fact that "when it desires to do so, Congress knows how to place the high seas within the jurisdictional reach of a statute." Congress' awareness of the need to make a clear statement that a statute applies overseas is amply demonstrated by the numerous occasions on which it has expressly legislated the extraterritorial application of a statute. . . .

Petitioners have failed to present sufficient affirmative evidence that Congress intended Title VII to apply abroad. Accordingly, the judgment of the Court of Appeals is

Affirmed.

Justice Scalia, concurring in part and concurring in the judgment.

I join the judgment of the Court and its opinion except that portion asserting that the views of the [EEOC] — not only with respect to the particular point at issue here but apparently as a general matter — are not entitled to the deference normally accorded administrative agencies under *Chevron U. S. A. Inc. v. Natural Resources Defense Council, Inc.*, 467 U. S. 837 (1984). . . .

    . . . .

I would resolve these cases by assuming, without deciding, that the EEOC was entitled to deference on the particular point in question. But deference is not abdication, and it requires us to accept only those agency interpretations that are reasonable in light of the principles of construction courts normally employ. Given the presumption against extraterritoriality that the Court accurately describes, and the requirement that the intent to overcome it be "clearly expressed," it is in my view not reasonable to give effect to mere implications from the statutory language as the EEOC has done.

On all other points, I join the opinion of the Court.

Justice Marshall, with whom Justice Blackmun and Justice Stevens join, dissenting.

Like any issue of statutory construction, the question whether Title VII protects United States citizens from discrimination by United States employers abroad turns solely on congressional intent. As the majority recognizes, our inquiry into congressional intent in this setting is informed by the traditional "canon of construction which teaches that legislation of Congress, unless a contrary intent appears, is meant to apply only within the territorial jurisdiction of the United States." *Foley Bros., Inc. v. Filardo*, 336 U. S. 281, 285 (1949). But contrary to what one would conclude from the majority's analysis, this canon is *not* a "clear statement" rule, the application of which relieves a court of the duty to give effect to all available indicia of the legislative will. Rather, as our case law applying the presumption against extraterritoriality well illustrates, a court may properly rely on this presumption only after exhausting all of the traditional tools "whereby unexpressed congressional intent may be ascertained." When these tools are brought to bear on the issue in this case, the conclusion is inescapable that Congress *did* intend Title VII to protect United States citizens from discrimination by United States employers operating overseas. Consequently, I dissent.

I

Because it supplies the driving force of the majority's analysis, I start with "the canon that legislation of Congress, unless a contrary intent appears, is meant to apply only within the territorial jurisdiction of the United States." The majority recasts this principle as "the need to make *a clear statement* that a statute applies overseas." So conceived, the presumption against extraterritoriality allows the majority to derive meaning from various instances of statutory silence — from Congress' failure, for instance, "to mention foreign nations or foreign proceedings," "to provide any mechanisms for overseas enforcement," or to "address the subject of conflicts with foreign laws and procedures." At other points, the majority relies on its reformulation of the presumption to avoid the "need to choose between competing interpretations" of affirmative statutory language that the majority concludes "does not speak *directly* to the question" of extraterritoriality. In my view, the majority grossly distorts the effect of this rule of construction upon conventional techniques of statutory interpretation.

. . . .

The range of factors that the Court considered in *Foley Brothers* demonstrates that the presumption against extraterritoriality is *not* a "clear statement" rule. Clear-statement rules operate less to reveal *actual* congressional intent than to shield important values from an *insufficiently strong* legislative intent to displace them. When they apply, such rules foreclose inquiry into extrinsic guides to interpretation and even compel courts to select less plausible candidates from within the range of permissible constructions. The Court's analysis in *Foley Brothers* was by no means so narrowly constrained. Indeed, the Court considered the entire range of conventional sources "whereby *unexpressed* congressional intent may be ascertained," including legislative history, statutory structure, and administrative interpretations. Subsequent applications of the presumption against extraterritoriality confirm that we have not imposed the drastic clear-statement burden upon Congress before giving effect to its intention that a particular enactment apply beyond the national boundaries.

. . . .

The majority also overstates the strength of the presumption by drawing on language from cases involving a wholly independent rule of construction: "that 'an act of congress ought never to be construed to violate the law of nations if any other possible construction remains.'" . . .

. . . Nothing nearly so dramatic is at stake when Congress merely seeks to regulate the conduct of United States nationals abroad.

Because petitioners advance a construction of Title VII that would extend its extraterritorial reach only to United States nationals, it is the weak presumption of *Foley Brothers*, not . . . [a] clear statement rule, that should govern our inquiry here. Under *Foley Brothers*, a court is not free to invoke the presumption against extraterritoriality until it has exhausted all available indicia of Congress' intent on this subject. Once these indicia are consulted and given effect in this case, I believe there can be no question that Congress intended Title VII to protect United States citizens from discrimination by United States employers abroad.

Notes and Questions

---

1. The dissent in *Arabian American Oil* speaks of the difference between "canons of construction" and "clear statement" rules. What is the difference? Why are these two devices given different treatments? *Cf.* HENRY M. HART, JR. & ALBERT M. SACKS, THE LEGAL PROCESS: BASIC PROBLEMS IN THE MAKING AND APPLICATION OF LAW 1209 (William N. Eskridge, Jr. & Philip P. Frickey eds., 1994) ("Judicial opinions on the interpretation of statutes are replete with references to presumptions, or suggestions of the existence of presumptions, amounting to what are here called policies of clear statement. In effect, these presumptions all say to the legislature, 'if you mean *this*, you must say so plainly.'").

2. Following the Court's decision in *Arabian American Oil*, Congress amended Title VII to extend its protections to United States citizens working overseas. *See* Civil Rights Act of 1991, § 109(a), 105 Stat. 1077, *codified at* 42 U.S.C. § 2000e(f) (2000) ("With respect to employment in a foreign country," the term "employee" "includes an individual who is a citizen of the United States."). Does this necessarily mean that the Court's decision in *Arabian American Oil* was incorrect?

3. The clear statement rule articulated in *Aramco* was essentially reaffirmed in *Morrison v. Nat'l Australia Bank Ltd.*, 561 U.S. 247 (2010).

4. The Supreme Court has identified a number of clear statement rules, though (regrettably) the Court does not always use consistent terminology to describe this concept. Another example can be found in *Gonzales v. Thaler*, 132 S. Ct. 641 (2012), in which the Court reaffirmed the "clear-statement principle" relating

to purportedly jurisdictional statutes. *See also FAA v. Cooper*, 132 S. Ct. 1441 (2012) ("We have said on many occasions that a waiver of sovereign immunity must be 'unequivocally expressed' in statutory text."); *Gregory v. Ashcroft*, 501 U.S. 452 (1991) ("In traditionally sensitive areas, such as legislation affecting the federal balance, the requirement of clear statement assures that the legislature has in fact faced, and intended to bring into issue, the critical matters involved in the judicial decision.").

5. For a critical view of constitutionally based clear statement rules, see John F. Manning, *Clear Statement Rules and the Constitution*, 110 COLUM. L. REV. 399 (2010). For a criticism of clear statement rules generally, see William N. Eskridge, Jr. & Phillip P. Frickey, *Quasi-Constitutional Law: Clear Statement Rules as Constitutional Lawmaking*, 45 VAND. L. REV. 593 (1995).

f. Statutory History

As you might recall, the earlier discussion of the amendment to 28 U.S.C. § 1391 brought about as a result of the Federal Courts Jurisdiction and Venue Clarification Act of 2011 (*see supra* at 452-53) contained a description of the history of that statute. In a strict sense, *statutory history* refers to the development of a statute over time — how the statute appeared as first enacted, and how the statute has been amended since. But this phrase can also have a broader meaning. As Professors Hart and Sacks explain:

> Is it a sound conclusion that the state of the prior law ought always to be taken into account in determining the purpose of a statute, and is always relevant, therefore, in every case of interpretation except one in which the purpose of the statute has already been authoritatively determined? How could it be otherwise? Can any purposive act be understood without regard to the circumstances which prompted the act?
>
> Orthodox legal doctrine answers the opening question in the last paragraph in the affirmative, although everyday practice is sometimes forgetful of the dictates of doctrine. To say that the prior law is to be taken into account, however, is only to indicate a direction of inquiry. Sometimes the mere comparison of the new statute with the preexisting law yields an irresistible inference as to what the purpose of the statute was. But often the comparison does no more than raise questions and indicate possibilities. What then are wanted are contemporaneous explanations to help in resolving doubts about possible purposes.
>
> Such explanations may be provided simply by common knowledge of the history of the times. Or they may be a matter of historical record in public documents other than those which relate to the progress of the bill from the time of its introduction into the legislature to its enactment. In either event, no Anglo-American court, it seems, would doubt the propriety of considering the explanations, at least in cases of acknowledged ambiguity in the statute.

HENRY M. HART, JR. & ALBERT M. SACKS, THE LEGAL PROCESS: BASIC PROBLEMS IN THE MAKING AND APPLICATION OF LAW 1211 (William N. Eskridge, Jr. & Philip P. Frickey eds., 1994).

Statutory history is a commonly used tool of statutory interpretation with a well-established pedigree. A study of the history of a statute will often yield seemingly accurate insights into statutory meaning.

g. The Use of Legislative History

A somewhat more controversial tool of statutory interpretation is *legislative history*. Though courts and legal scholars are somewhat divided over the legitimacy of the use of legislative history materials as an aid to the interpretation of statutes, the consensus seems to be that such materials have some place in that endeavor. Certainly, the Supreme Court's decisions in *Griffin* and *Ron Pair* so indicate.

The more difficult question relates to the precise contours of such use. Notice first that under the *Griffin/Ron Pair* scheme, legislative history plays a very limited role. This approach is consistent with that taken by Professors Hart and Sacks, who instruct:

> Consider the difference between going to the legislative history with a question about general purpose carefully formulated after analysis of the statute and the rest of its context, and plunging into the morass of successive versions of the bill, committee hearings, committee reports, floor debates, and conference reports with a blank mind waiting to be instructed, on the assumption that it is equally probable that the legislature did or did not "intend" a particular result and trying to find out which.

HENRY M. HART, JR. & ALBERT M. SACKS, THE LEGAL PROCESS: BASIC PROBLEMS IN THE MAKING AND APPLICATION OF LAW 1233 (William N. Eskridge, Jr. & Philip P. Frickey eds., 1994).

Second, as explained in more detail below, there seems to be a consensus that some types of legislative history are more legitimate than others.

Notes and Questions

---

1. When legislative history materials are used, it is important to have a sense of which types are generally considered to be more "important" (or authoritative, or relevant) than others. For example, one prominent legal scholar has suggested the following "hierarchy of legislative history sources," ranked from most authoritative to least authoritative:

   - committee reports
   - sponsor statements
   - rejected proposals
   - floor and hearing colloquy
   - views of nonlegislator drafters
   - legislative inaction
   - subsequent legislative history

William N. Eskridge, Jr., *The New Textualism*, 37 UCLA L. REV. 621, 636 (1990). Of course, the value of any particular item is going to depend to some extent on its specific contents and on the context in which it is being used.

2. Some — most notably, Justice Antonin Scalia — see little or no place for legislative history in statutory interpretation. For example, in *Blanchard v. Bergeron*, 489 U.S. 87 (1989), Justice Scalia criticized the Court's use of legislative history (in the form of certain committee reports that cited certain lower federal court decisions) as follows:

> Congress is elected to enact statutes rather than point to cases, and its Members have better uses for their time than poring over District Court opinions. That the Court should refer to the citation of three District Court cases in a document issued by a single committee of a single house as the action *of Congress* displays the level of unreality that our unrestrained use of legislative history has attained. I am confident that only a small proportion of the Members of Congress read either one of the Committee Reports in question, even if (as is not always the case) the Reports happened to have been published before the vote; that very few of those who did read them set off for the nearest law library to check out what was actually said in the four cases at issue (or in the more than 50 other cases by the House and Senate Reports); and that *no* Member of Congress came to the judgment that the District Court cases would trump [a court of appeals decision] because the latter was dictum. As anyone familiar with modern-day drafting of congressional committee reports is well aware, the references to the cases were inserted, at best by a committee staff member on his or her own initiative, and at worst by a committee staff member at the suggestion of a lawyer-lobbyist; and the purpose of those references was not primarily to inform the Members of Congress what the bill meant . . . , but rather to influence judicial construction. What a heady feeling it must be for a young staffer, to know that his or her citation of obscure district court cases can transform them into the law of the land, thereafter dutifully to be observed by the Supreme Court itself.
>
> I decline to participate in this process. It is neither compatible with our judicial responsibility of assuring reasoned, consistent, and effective application of the statutes of the United States, nor conducive to a genuine effectuation of congressional intent, to give legislative force to each snippet of analysis, and even every case citation, in committee reports that are increasingly unreliable evidence of what the voting Members of Congress actually had in mind.

Id. at 98-99 (Scalia, J., concurring in part and concurring in the judgment).

In *Wisconsin Public Intervenor v. Mortier*, 501 U.S. 597 (1991), Justice Scalia, after reviewing certain committee reports, further opined:

> Of course that does not necessarily say anything about what Congress as a whole thought. Assuming that all the members of the three Committees in question (as opposed to just the relevant Subcommittees) actually adverted to the interpretive point at issue here — which is probably an unrealistic assumption — and assuming further that they were in *unanimous* agreement on the point, they would still represent less than two-fifths of the Senate, and less than one-tenth of the House. It is most unlikely that many Members of either Chamber read the

pertinent portions of the Committee Reports before voting on the bill — assuming (we cannot be sure) that the Reports were available before the vote. Those pertinent portions, though they dominate our discussion today, constituted less than a quarter-page of the 82-page House Agriculture Committee Report, and less than a half-page each of the 74-page Senate Agriculture Committee Report, the 46-page Senate Commerce Committee Report, and the 73-page Senate Agriculture Committee Supplemental Report. Those Reports in turn were a miniscule portion of the total number of reports that the Members of Congress were receiving (and presumably even writing) during the period in question. In the Senate, at least, there was a vote on an amendment (the Commerce Committee proposal) that would have changed the result of the supposed interpretation. But the full Senate could have rejected that *either* because a majority of its Members disagreed with the Commerce Committee's proposed policy; *or* because they disagreed with the Commerce Committee's and the Agriculture Committee's interpretation (and thus thought the amendment superfluous); *or* because they were blissfully ignorant of the entire dispute and simply thought that the Commerce Committee, by asking for recommittal and proposing 15 amendments, was being a troublemaker; *or* because three different minorities (enough to make a majority) had each of these respective reasons. We have no way of knowing; indeed, we have no way of knowing that they had any *rational* motive at all.

All we know for sure is that the full Senate adopted the text that we have before us here, as did the full House, pursuant to the procedures prescribed by the Constitution; and that that text, having been transmitted to the President and approved by him, again pursuant to the procedures prescribed by the Constitution, became law. On the important question before us today, whether that law denies local communities throughout the Nation significant powers of self-protection, we should try to give the text its fair meaning, whatever various committees might have had to say — thereby affirming the proposition that we are a Government of laws, not of committee reports. That is, at least, the way I prefer to proceed.

If I believed, however, that the meaning of a statute is to be determined by committee reports, I would have to conclude that a meaning opposite to our judgment has been commanded three times over — not only by one committee in each House, but by *two* Committees in one of them. Today's decision reveals that, in their judicial application, Committee reports are a forensic rather than an interpretive device, to be invoked when they support the decision and ignored when they do not. To my mind that is infinitely better than honestly giving them dispositive effect. But it would be better still to stop confusing the Wisconsin Supreme Court, and not to use committee reports at all.

Id. at 620-21 (Scalia, J., concurring in the judgment).

And in *Conroy v. Aniskoff*, 507 U.S. 511 (1993), Justice Scalia, in a concurring opinion, stated:

The Court begins its analysis with the observation: "The statutory command in § 525 is unambiguous, unequivocal, and unlimited." In my view, discussion of that point is where the remainder of the analysis should have ended. Instead, however, the Court feels compelled to demonstrate that its holding is consonant with legislative history, including some dating back to 1917 — a *full quarter century* before the provision at issue was enacted. That is not merely a waste of research time and ink; it is a false and disruptive lesson in the law. It says to the bar that even an "unambiguous and unequivocal" statute can never be dispositive; that, presumably under penalty of malpractice liability, the oracles of legislative history, far into the dimmy past, must always be consulted. This undermines the clarity of law, and condemns litigants (who, unlike us, must pay for it out of their own pockets) to subsidizing historical research by lawyers.

The greatest defect of legislative history is its illegitimacy. We are governed by laws, not by the intentions of legislators. As the Court said in 1844: "The law as it passed is the will of the majority of both houses, *and the only mode in which that will is spoken is in the act itself.*" *Aldridge* v. *Williams*, 3 How. 9, 24 (emphasis added). But not the least of the defects of legislative history is its indeterminacy. If one were to search for an interpretive technique that, *on the whole*, was more likely to confuse than to clarify, one could hardly find a more promising candidate than legislative history. And the present case nicely proves that point.

Judge Harold Leventhal used to describe the use of legislative history as the equivalent of entering a crowded cocktail party and looking over the heads of the guests for one's friends. If I may pursue the metaphor: The legislative history of § 205 of the Soldiers' and Sailors' Civil Relief Act contains a variety of diverse personages, a selected few of whom — its "friends" — the Court has introduced to us in support of its result. But there are many other faces in the crowd, most of which, I think, are set against today's result.

. . . .

I confess that I have not personally investigated the entire legislative history — or even that portion of it which relates to the four statutes listed above. The excerpts I have examined and quoted were unearthed by a hapless law clerk to whom I assigned the task. The other Justices have, in the aggregate, many more law clerks than I, and it is quite possible that if they all were unleashed upon this enterprise they would discover, in the legislative materials dating back to 1917 *or earlier*, many faces friendly to the Court's holding. Whether they would or would not makes no difference to me — and evidently makes no difference to the Court, which gives lipservice to legislative history but does not trouble to set forth and discuss the foregoing material that others found so persuasive. In my view, that is as it should be, except for the lipservice. The language of the statute is entirely clear, and if that is not what Congress meant then Congress has made a mistake and Congress will have to correct it. We should not pretend to care about legislative intent (as opposed to the meaning of the law), lest we impose upon the practicing bar and their clients obligations that we do not ourselves take seriously.

Id. at 518-28 (Scalia, J., concurring in the judgment).

For more recent examples of Justice Scalia's (unchanged) views on the use of legislative history, see *Graham Co. Soil and Water Conservation Dist. v. United States*, 559 U.S. 280, 302 (2010) (Scalia, J., concurring in part and concurring in the judgment), and *Milavetz, Gallop & Milavetz, P.A. v. United States*, 559 U.S. 229, 253 (2010) (Scalia, J., concurring in part and concurring in the judgment).

3. Justice Scalia is not alone in his skepticism of legislative history. For example, in *Schwegmann Bros. v. Calvert Distillers Corp.*, 341 U.S. 384 (1951), Justice Robert Jackson opined:

I agree with the Court's judgment and with its opinion insofar as it rests upon the language of the Miller-Tydings Act. But it does not appear that there is either necessity or propriety in going back of it into legislative history.

Resort to legislative history is only justified where the face of the Act is inescapably ambiguous, and then I think we should not go beyond Committee reports, which presumably are well considered and carefully prepared. I cannot deny that I have sometimes offended against that rule. But to select casual statements from floor debates, not always distinguished for candor or accuracy, as a basis for making up our minds what law Congress intended to enact is to substitute ourselves for the Congress in one of its important functions. The Rules of the House and Senate, with the sanction of the Constitution, require three readings of an Act in each House before final enactment. That is intended, I take it, to make sure that each House knows what it is passing and passes what it wants, and that what is enacted was formally reduced to writing. It is the business of Congress to sum up its own debates in its legislation. Moreover, it is only the words of the bill that have presidential approval, where that approval is given. It is not to be supposed that, in signing a bill, the President endorses the whole Congressional Record. For us to undertake to reconstruct an enactment from legislative history is merely to involve the Court in political controversies which are quite proper in the enactment of a bill but should have no place in its interpretation.

Moreover, there are practical reasons why we should accept whenever possible the meaning which an enactment reveals on its face. Laws are intended for all of our people to live by; and the people go to law offices to learn what their rights under those laws are. Here is a controversy which affects every little merchant in many States. Aside from a few offices in the larger cities, the materials of legislative history are not available to the lawyer who can afford neither the cost of acquisition, the cost of housing, or the cost of repeatedly examining the whole congressional history. Moreover, if he could, he would not know any way of anticipating what would impress enough members of the Court to be controlling. To accept legislative debates to modify statutory provisions is to make the law inaccessible to a large part of the country.

By and large, I think our function was well stated by Mr. Justice Holmes: "We do not inquire what the legislature meant; we ask only what the statute means." Holmes, Collected Legal Papers, 207. And I can think of no better example of legislative history that is unedifying and unilluminating than that of the Act before us.

Id. at 395-97 (Jackson, J., concurring).

4. "One determines what Congress would have done by examining what it did." *Legal Services Corp. v. Velazquez*, 531 U.S. 533, 560 (2001) (Scalia, J., dissenting).

5. As indicated above—and as evidenced by the continued use of such materials—most of the Justices on the Supreme Court disagree with Justice Scalia and support the use of legislative history in statutory interpretation, at least to some extent. For one such defense, see Stephen Breyer, *On the Uses of Legislative History in Interpreting Statutes*, 65 S. Cal. L. Rev. 845 (1992).

6. *Is the tide turning?* In *Exxon Mobil Corp. v. Allapattah Services, Inc.*, 545 U.S. 546, 568-69 (2005), the Court stated:

> As we have repeatedly held, the authoritative statement is the statutory text, not the legislative history or any other extrinsic material. Extrinsic materials have a role in statutory interpretation only to the extent they shed a reliable light on the enacting Legislature's understanding of otherwise ambiguous terms. Not all extrinsic materials are reliable sources of insight into legislative understandings, however, and legislative history in particular is vulnerable to two serious criticisms. First, legislative history is itself often murky, ambiguous, and contradictory. Judicial investigation of legislative history has a tendency to become, to borrow Judge Leventhal's memorable phrase, an exercise in "'looking over a crowd and picking out your friends.'" Second, judicial reliance on legislative materials like committee reports, which are not themselves subject to the requirements of Article I, may give unrepresentative committee members — or, worse yet, unelected staffers and lobbyists — both the power and the incentive to attempt strategic manipulations of legislative history to secure results they were unable to achieve through the statutory text. We need not comment here on whether these problems are sufficiently prevalent to render legislative history inherently unreliable in all circumstances, a point on which Members of this Court have disagreed. It is clear, however, that in this instance both criticisms are right on the mark.

Whether *Exxon Mobil* marks a turning point in the Court's use of legislative history remains to be seen; certainly, it has not yet resulted in its demise. If nothing else, though, the criticisms made by Justice Scalia and others, as well as the various responses to those criticisms, seem to have resulted in a somewhat more limited and more discriminating use of such materials.

What do you think is the proper place for such materials?

7. For an argument that, in using legislative history, courts should consider how it is viewed by Congress itself — i.e., in relation to the Rules of the House and Senate — see Victoria Nourse, *A Decision Theory of Statutory Interpretation: Legislative History by the Rules*, 122 Yale L.J. 70 (2012).

8. *Federal Rules Advisory Committee Notes as "legislative history."* In *Tome v. United States*, 513 U.S. 150 (1995), which involved the proper interpretation of Federal Rule of Evidence 801(d)(1)(B), Justice Scalia opined:

> I concur in the judgment of the Court, and join its opinion except for Part II-B. That Part, which is devoted entirely to a discussion of the Advisory Committee's Notes pertinent to Rule 801(d)(1)(B), gives effect to those Notes not only because they are "a respected source of scholarly commentary," but also because they display the "purpose," or "intent," of the draftsmen.
>
> I have previously acquiesced in, and indeed myself engaged in, similar use of the Advisory Committee Notes. More mature consideration has persuaded me that is wrong. Having been prepared by a body of experts, the Notes are assuredly persuasive scholarly commentaries — ordinarily *the* most persuasive — concerning the meaning of the Rules. But they bear no special authoritativeness as the work of the draftsmen, any more than the views of Alexander Hamilton (a

draftsman) bear more authority than the views of Thomas Jefferson (not a drafts-man) with regard to the meaning of the Constitution. It is the words of the Rules that have been authoritatively adopted — by this Court, or by Congress if it makes a statutory change. In my view even the adopting Justices' thoughts, unpromulgated as Rules, have no authoritative (as opposed to persuasive) effect, any more than their thoughts regarding an opinion (reflected in exchanges of memoranda before the opinion issues) authoritatively demonstrate the meaning of that opinion. And the same for the thoughts of congressional draftsmen who prepare statutory amendments to the Rules. Like a judicial opinion and like a statute, the promulgated Rule says what it says, regardless of the intent of the drafters. The Notes are, to be sure, submitted to us and to the Members of Congress as the thoughts of the body initiating the recommendations; but there is no certainty that either we or they read those thoughts, nor is there any procedure by which we formally endorse or disclaim them. That being so, the Notes cannot, by some power inherent in the draftsmen, change the meaning that the Rules would otherwise bear.

Id. at 167-68 (Scalia, J., concurring in part and concurring in the judgment). Justice Scalia recently reaffirmed his position with respect to the use of advisory committee notes in *Krupski v. Costa Crociere S.p.A.*, 560 U.S. 538, 557 (2010) (Scalia, J., concurring in part and concurring in the judgment). *See also Wal-Mart Stores, Inc. v. Dukes*, 131 S. Ct. 2541, 2559 (2011) (Scalia, J.) ("Of course it is the Rule itself, not the Advisory Committee's description of it, that governs.").

What do you think of Justice Scalia's views on the use of federal rule advisory committee notes? Even if one were to agree with his view of the use of legislative history, does the same reasoning necessarily translate to this, the federal rulemaking, context?

9. There are other uses for legislative history besides statutory interpretation. For more on this topic, see Mary Whisner, *Other Uses of Legislative History*, 105 Law Libr. J. 243 (2013). This article also includes an appendix listing state statutes providing for the use of legislative history in state statutory interpretation.

SIDEBAR: THE ENGLISH PERSPECTIVE

For years, the British House of Lords refused to consider legislative history in its interpretation of acts of Parliament. But in 1983, the House of Lords relaxed its prohibition against the use of legislative history, and adopted a stance more consistent with that used by the United States Supreme Court. In *Pepper v. Hart*, [1993] A.C. 593 (H.L.), 1 All E.R. 42 [1993], Lord Browne-Wilkinson stated:

My Lords, I have come to the conclusion that, as a matter of law, there are sound reasons for making a limited modification to the existing rule (subject to strict safeguards) unless there are constitutional or practical reasons which outweigh them. In my judgment, subject to the questions of the privileges of the

> House of Commons, reference to Parliamentary material should be permitted
> as an aid to the construction of legislation which is ambiguous or obscure or the
> literal meaning of which leads to an absurdity. Even in such cases references in
> court to Parliamentary material should only be permitted where such material
> clearly discloses the mischief aimed at or the legislative intention lying behind
> the ambiguous or obscure words. In the case of statements made in Parliament,
> as at present advised I cannot foresee that any statement other than the statement
> of the Minister or other promoter of the Bill is likely to meet these criteria.

h. *Legislative Inaction*

One of the more difficult issues in statutory interpretation has been ascertaining
the proper role, if any, of what might be termed *legislative inaction*. In broad terms,
legislative inaction can encompass a variety of concepts. According to William N.
Eskridge, Jr., *Interpreting Legislative Inaction*, 87 MICH. L. REV. 67 (1988):

> Three related doctrines emerge from the Court's past treatment of legislation inaction
> issues: (1) the "acquiescence rule," positing that if Congress does not overturn a judicial
> or administrative interpretation it probably acquiesces in it; (2) the "reenactment rule,"
> which posits that a reenactment of the statute incorporates any settled interpretations
> of the statute by courts or agencies; and (3) the "rejected proposal rule," which posits
> that proposals rejected by Congress are an indication that the statute cannot be inter-
> preted to resemble the rejected proposals.

Id. at 69. But Professor Eskridge cautions: "These rules are not inevitably followed,
though. In some cases, the Court finds great meaning in 'positive inaction.' In
other cases the Court finds such an inquiry nothing more than 'the pursuit of a
mirage.'" *Id.*

i. The Rejected Proposal Rule

Of the three doctrines identified by Professor Eskridge, the "rejected proposal rule"
ranks the highest in his "hierarchy of legislative history sources" (*see supra* at 546-47).
But though courts have considered rejected proposals in statutory interpretation
on occasion, this concept also has been subjected to some criticism. This is particularly true when the rejected proposal was introduced subsequent to the statute
in question. For example, in *Pension Benefit Guaranty Corp. v. The LTV Corp.*, 496
U.S. 633 (1990), the Supreme Court opined:

> The Court of Appeals also relied on the legislative history of the 1987 amendments
> to ERISA effected by the Pension Protection Act. This history reveals that Congress in
> 1987 considered, but did not enact, a provision that expressly would have authorized
> the PBGC to prohibit follow-on plans. But subsequent legislative history is a "hazard-
> ous basis for inferring the intent of an earlier" Congress. It is a particularly dangerous
> ground on which to rest an interpretation of a prior statute when it concerns, as it does
> here, a proposal that does not become law. Congressional inaction lacks "persuasive
> significance" because "several equally tenable inferences" may be drawn from such in-
> action, "including the inference that the existing legislation already incorporated the

offered change." These admonitions are especially apt in the instant case because Congress was aware of the action taken by the PBGC with respect to LTV at the time it rejected the proposed amendment. Despite Congress' awareness of the PBGC's belief that the adoption of follow-on plans was a ground for restoration, Congress did not amend § 4047 to restrict the PBGC's discretion. The conclusion that Congress thought the PBGC was properly exercising its authority is at least as plausible as any other. Thus, the legislative history surrounding the 1987 amendments provides no more support than the 1974 legislative history for the Court of Appeals' holding that the PBGC's interpretation of § 4047 contravened clear congressional will.

Id. at 649-50. More emphatically, in *United States v. Estate of Romani*, 523 U.S. 517 (1998), Justice Scalia stated:

I join the opinion of the Court except that portion which takes seriously, and thus encourages in the future, an argument that should be laughed out of court. The Government contended that 31 U. S. C. § 3713(a) must have priority over the Federal Tax Lien Act of 1966, because in 1966 and again in 1970 Congress "failed to enact" a proposal put forward by the American Bar Association that would have subordinated § 3713(a) to the Tax Lien Act, citing hearings before the House Committee on Ways and Means, and a bill proposed in, but not passed by, the Senate. The Court responds that these rejected proposals "provide no support for the hypothesis that both Houses of Congress silently endorsed" the supremacy of § 3713 because those proposals contained other provisions as well, and might have been rejected because of those other provisions, or because Congress thought the existing law already made § 3713 supreme. This implies that, if the proposals had not contained those additional features, or if Members of Congress (or some part of them) had somehow made clear in the course of rejecting them that they wanted the existing supremacy of the Tax Lien Act to subsist, the rejection *would* "provide support" for the Government's case.

That is not so, for several reasons. First and most obviously, Congress cannot express its will by a *failure* to legislate. The act of refusing to enact a law (if that can be called an act) has utterly no legal effect, and thus has utterly no place in a serious discussion of the law. The Constitution sets forth the only manner in which the Members of Congress have the power to impose their will upon the country: by a bill that passes both Houses and is either signed by the President or repassed by a supermajority after his veto. Art. I, § 7. Everything else the Members of Congress do is either prelude or internal organization. Congress can no more express its will by not legislating than an individual Member can express his will by not voting.

Second, even if Congress *could* express its will by not legislating, the will of a later Congress that a law enacted by an earlier Congress should bear a particular meaning is of no effect whatever. The Constitution puts Congress in the business of writing new laws, not interpreting old ones. "Later enacted laws do not declare the meaning of earlier law." If the *enacted* intent of a later Congress cannot change the meaning of an earlier statute, then it should go without saying that the later *unenacted intent* cannot possibly do so. It should go without saying, and it should go without arguing as well.

I have in the past been critical of the Court's using the so-called legislative history of an enactment (hearings, committee reports, and floor debates) to determine its meaning. Today, however, the Court's fascination with the files of Congress (we must consult them, because they are there) is carried to a new silly extreme. Today's opinion ever-so-carefully analyzes, not legislative history, but the history of legislation-that-never-was. If we take this sort of material seriously, we require conscientious counsel to investigate (at clients' expense) not only the hearings, committee reports, and floor debates pertaining to the history of the law at issue (which is bad enough), but to find, and then investigate the hearings, committee reports, and floor debates pertaining to, later bills on the same subject that were never enacted. This is beyond all reason, and we should say so.

Id. at 535-37 (Scalia, J., concurring in part and concurring in the judgment).

ii. The Acquiescence Rule

The "acquiescence rule" — i.e., the failure of a legislature (such as Congress) to enact or amend a statute in response to some event (such as an interpretation of a statute by the Supreme Court) — also has sometimes been used by courts to divine legislative intent. But how accurate (and therefore legitimate) is the use of this device? Consider the following excerpt.

Henry M. Hart, Jr. & Albert M. Sacks

THE IMPLICATIONS OF THE FAILURE OF CONGRESS TO LEGISLATE

The Legal Process: Basic Problems in the Making and Application of Law (William N. Eskridge, Jr. & Philip P. Frickey eds., 1994)

A. THE COMPETENCE AND RELEVANCE OF LEGISLATIVE INACTION

Was Chief Justice Stone [in his dissenting opinion in *Girouard v. United States*, 328 U.S. 61, 70 (1946),] right in giving the weight he did to the failure of Congress to pass any of the various bills introduced for the purpose of overriding the earlier decisions? In countenancing the formulation . . . that, as a result, the interpretation announced in those decisions now had "congressional sanction and approval"?

The Chief Justice seems to be saying that Congress had somehow passed a law — a curious kind of negative law-against-overruling — taking away a power which the Court would otherwise have had to correct its earlier interpretation, if on later consideration it deemed it to be erroneous. But how could Congress do this without complying with the constitutional prerequisites for the enactment of bills?

Suppose, for example, that the President thought that the Court should retain its power of reconsideration — as very possibly in this matter President Roosevelt did. Can Congress circumvent the President's veto power?

Suppose that the two houses of Congress had passed a concurrent resolution, not presented to the President for approval, endorsing the [prior decisions] and purporting to forbid the Court to reconsider or overrule it. To what weight would such a resolution be entitled?

Note that a concurrent resolution would at least be a formal expression of the opinion of both branches of Congress, adopted in accordance with the constitutional grant of authority to each house to "determine the rules of its proceedings." Does either house have a rule which says that the rejection of a bill at any stage of its consideration shall be equivalent to enactment of a bill of opposite tenor? Would any such rule be constitutional? Wise, when a bill has not run the full gamut of legislative investigation and debate?

Apart from the question of the competence of legislative inaction as a guide to judicial decision, what of its relevance?

If a legislature were under a duty to consider every question of public policy which is mooted in a court or elsewhere and to declare itself one way or the other, inaction would obviously be significant. But is there such a duty? Would it be tolerable if there were?

If a legislature has discretion whether to legislate or not to legislate, how can significance rationally be attached to its decision not to do so? Compare the Supreme Court's own steady insistence that its discretionary denial of a petition for writ of certiorari imports no expression of opinion upon the merits whatsoever.

Consider the variety of reasons which legislators may have either for opposing a bill or simply withholding the votes necessary for its forward progress:

(1) Complete disinterest;

(2) Belief that other measures have a stronger claim on the limited time and energy of the body;

(3) Belief that the bill is sound in principle but politically inexpedient to be connected with;

(4) Unwillingness to have the bill's sponsors get credit for its enactment;

(5) Belief that the bill is sound in principle but defective in material particulars;

(6) Tentative approval, but belief that action should be withheld until the problem can be attacked on a broader front;

(7) Indecision, with or without one or another of the foregoing attitudes also;

(8) Belief that the matter should be left to be handled by the normal processes of judicial development of decisional law, including the overruling of outstanding decisions to the extent that the sound growth of the law requires;

(9) Positive approval of existing law as expressed in outstanding decisions of the Supreme Court;

(10) Ditto of the courts of appeals' decisions also;

(11) Ditto also of district court decisions;

(12) Ditto also of one or more varieties of outstanding administrative determinations;

(13) Etc., etc., etc., etc.

By what processes of rationalization can a court ever say, when a bill has failed of enactment, that a majority of the members held attitude (9), or (10), or (11), or (12), rather than one or more of the others, so that the failure was tantamount to "sanction and approval" of an outstanding decision, and a bar to its reconsideration and overruling?

Notice that attitudes (9) through (11) are actually extremely subtle ones. They presuppose approval of the naked rules of decisions, irrespective of the soundness of their reasoning. They presuppose disapproval of any subsequent departure from those rules, irrespective of the persuasiveness of the judicial considerations counseling such departure. [In some instances,] they presuppose a deliberate purpose to perpetuate irrational discrepancies in the law.

How ready should a court be to attribute such an attitude to a legislator, let alone to a majority of the legislators?

How likely is it, in actuality, that any legislator would have such an attitude? That he would ever pose the problem in this way to himself in the first place? That, if so, he would know enough about *stare decisis* and its limitations to be able to pose the problem accurately, and understand what he was deciding? Are not the attitudes, basically, attitudes about how judicial power should be exercised? Is *that* within the constitutional sphere of responsibility of Congress?

Try to express the doctrine in the form of a statute. Would you expect such a statute, if enacted, to be upheld?

Think about the potential sweep of a doctrine of legislative action by not acting. It can be extended, can it not, beyond the mere prohibition of overruling of an outstanding decision or line of decisions to an inhibition against any kind of creative development of the law by the courts at all? . . .

. . . .

Does legislative inaction ever prove anything except that the necessary majorities to enact a bill in the two houses were not summoned?

iii. The Reenactment Rule

The "reenactment rule" is well-described in *Lorillard v. Pons*, 434 U.S. 575 (1978), wherein the Court stated:

> Congress is presumed to be aware of an administrative or judicial interpretation of a statute and to adopt that interpretation when it reenacts a statute without change. So too, where, as here, Congress adopts a new law incorporating sections of a prior law, Congress normally can be presumed to have had knowledge of the interpretation given to the incorporated law, at least insofar as it affects the new statute.

Id. at 580-81. For a more recent application of this doctrine, see *Forest Grove Sch. Dist. v. T.A.*, 557 U.S. 230, 239-40 (2009) (quoting *Lorillard*). Indeed, if anything, the *Forest Grove* Court only strengthened this presumption. *See id.* at 240 ("Accordingly, absent a clear expression in the Amendments of Congress' intent to repeal some portion of that provision or to abrogate our [prior decisions], we will continue to read [the statute in question] to authorize the relief respondent seeks.") Still, a three-Justice dissent, led by Justice Souter, argued that "there is no authority for a heightened standard before Congress can alter a prior judicial interpretation of a statute." *Id.* at 250 (Souter, J., dissenting).

Does the presumption set forth in *Lorillard* seem valid? Even if so, how far should it be extended? Consider the following excerpt from Justice Scalia's concurring opinion in *Jerman v. Carlisle, McNellie, Rini, Kramer & Ulrich LPA*, 559 U.S. 573 (2010):

> I join the Court's opinion except for its reliance upon two legal fictions. A portion of the Court's reasoning consists of this: The language in the Fair Debt Collection Practices Act (FDCPA or Act) tracks language in the Truth in Lending Act (TILA); and in the nine years between the enactment of TILA and the enactment of the FDCPA, three Court of Appeals had "interpreted TILA's bona fide error defense as referring to clerical errors." Relying on our statement in *Bragdon* v. *Abbott*, 524 U. S. 624, 645 (1998), that Congress's repetition, in a new statute, of statutory language with a "settled" judicial interpretation indicates "the intent to incorporate its judicial interpretations as well," the Court concludes that these three Court of Appeals cases "support an inference that Congress understood the statutory formula it chose for the FDCPA consistent with the Federal Court of Appeals interpretations of TILA."
>
> Let me assume (though I do not believe it) that what counts is what Congress "intended," even if that intent finds no expression in the enacted text. When a large majority of the Circuits, over a lengthy period of time, have uniformly reached a certain conclusion as to the meaning of a particular statutory text, it may be reasonable to assume that Congress was aware of those holdings, took them to be correct, and intended the same meaning in adopting that text.[1] It seems to me unreasonable, however, to assume that, when Congress has a bill before it that contains language used in an earlier statute, it is aware of, and approves as correct, a mere three Court of Appeals decisions interpreting that earlier statute over the previous nine years. Can one really believe that a majority in both Houses of Congress knew of those three cases, and accepted them as correct (even when, as was the case here, some District Court opinions and a State Supreme Court opinion had concluded, to the contrary, that the defense covered legal errors)? This is a legal fiction, which has nothing to be said for it except that it can sometimes make our job easier. The Court acknowledges that "the interpretations of three Federal Courts of Appeals may not have 'settled' the meaning of TILA's bona fide error defense," but says "there is no reason to suppose that Congress disagreed with those interpretations." Perhaps not; but no reason to suppose that it knew of and agreed with them either — which is presumably the proposition for which the Court cites them.

Id. at 606-07 (Scalia, J., concurring in part and concurring in the judgment).

Based on these various opinions, can you formulate a rule describing the extent that legislative reenactments of prior statutory text should be presumed as including judicial interpretations of that text?

---

1. Of course where so many federal courts have read the language that way, the text was probably clear enough that resort to unexpressed congressional intent would be unnecessary. Or indeed it could be said that such uniform and longstanding judicial interpretation had established the public meaning of the text, whether the Members of Congress were aware of the cases or not. That would be the understanding of the text by reasonable people familiar with its legal context.

i. *Subsequent Legislative History*

At the bottom of Professor Eskridge's hierarchy of legislative history sources (just below legislative inaction) is *subsequent legislative history*. Though subsequent legislative history has been used by federal courts on occasion, its legitimacy is somewhat questionable. As a result, it tends to be given little weight. For example, in *Consumer Product Safety Commission v. GTE Sylvania, Inc.*, 447 U.S. 102 (1980), the Court stated: "In evaluating the weight to be attached to [post-enactment] statements, we begin with the oft-repeated warning that 'the views of a subsequent Congress form a hazardous basis for inferring the intent of an earlier one.'" *Id.* at 117 (quoting *United States v. Price*, 361 U.S. 304, 313 (1960)). The Court further explained:

> Such history does not bear strong indicia of reliability . . . because as time passes memories fade and a person's perception of his earlier intention may change. Thus, even when it would otherwise be useful, subsequent legislative history will rarely override a reasonable interpretation of a statute that can be gleaned from its language and legislative history prior to its enactment.

Id. at 118 n.13.

In *Sullivan v. Finkelstein*, 496 U.S. 617 (1990), Justice Scalia was even more emphatic:

> I join the opinion of the Court, except for footnote 8, which responds on the merits to "two arguments based on subsequent legislative history."
>
> The legislative history of a statute is the history of its consideration and enactment. "Subsequent legislative history" — which presumably means the *post*-enactment history of a statute's consideration and enactment — is a contradiction in terms. The phrase is used to smuggle into judicial consideration legislators' expressions *not* of what a bill currently under consideration means (which, the theory goes, reflects what their colleagues understood they were voting for), but of what a law *previously enacted* means.
>
> It seems to be a rule for the use of subsequent legislative history that the legislators or committees of legislators whose post-enactment views are consulted must belong to the institution that passed the statute. Never, for example, have I seen floor statements of Canadian MP's cited concerning the meaning of a United States statute; only statements by Members of Congress qualify. No more connection than that, however, is required. It is assuredly *not* the rule that the legislators or committee members in question must have considered, or at least voted upon, the particular statute in question — or even that they have been members of the particular Congress that enacted it. The subsequent legislative history rejected as inconclusive in today's footnote, for example, tells us (according to the Court's analysis) what committees of the 99th and 95th Congresses thought the 76th Congress intended.
>
> In my opinion, the views of a legislator concerning a statute already enacted are entitled to no more weight than the views of a judge concerning a statute not yet passed. In some situations, of course, the expression of a legislator relating to a previously enacted statute may bear upon the meaning of a provision in a bill under consideration — which provision, if passed, may in turn affect judicial interpretation of the previously enacted statute, since statutes *in pari materia* should be interpreted harmoniously. Such an expression would be useful, if at all, not because it was subsequent

legislative history of the earlier statute, but because it was plain old legislative history of the later one.

> Arguments based on subsequent legislative history, like arguments based on antecedent futurity, should not be taken seriously, not even in a footnote.

Id. at 631-32 (Scalia, J., concurring in part). Do you agree with Justice Scalia's skepticism regarding the use of subsequent legislative history? Or should such materials retain a place in statutory interpretation?

j. The Interpretation of Borrowed Statutes

Somewhat related to the doctrine associated with the congressional reenactment of statutes (though seemingly much more legitimate) is the doctrine relating to the "borrowing" of statutes from other jurisdictions, such as from one state to another or to or from the federal government. The interpretation of borrowed statutes was discussed in some detail by the Supreme Court in *Shannon v. United States*, 512 U.S. 573 (1994). In *Shannon*, the defendant (no known relation to the author of this book) argued that under the Insanity Defense Reform Act of 1984 (IDRA), the jury should have been instructed that a verdict of not guilty by reason of insanity (NGI) would result in his involuntary commitment. After concluding that the text of the Act itself failed to support the defendant's argument, the Court continued:

> Shannon asserts, however, that an express statutory directive is not necessary because, by modeling the IDRA on D. C. Code Ann. § 24-301 (1981), Congress impliedly adopted the District of Columbia Circuit's decision in *Lyles* and the practice endorsed by that decision of instructing the jury as to the consequences of an NGI verdict. For this argument he relies on *Capital Traction Co. v. Hof*, 174 U. S. 1, 36 (1899), in which we stated:
>
> > "By a familiar canon of interpretation, heretofore applied by this court whenever Congress has borrowed from the statutes of a State provisions which had received in that State a known and settled construction before their enactment by Congress, that construction must be deemed to have been adopted by Congress together with the text which it expounded, and the provisions must be construed as they were understood at the time in the State."
>
> See also *Carolene Products Co. v. United States*, 323 U. S. 18, 26 (1944) ("The general rule is that adoption of the wording of a statute from another legislative jurisdiction carries with it the previous judicial interpretations of the wording"); *Cathcart v. Robinson*, 5 Pet. 264, 280 (1831). The canon of interpretation upon which Shannon relies, however, is merely a "presumption of legislative intention" to be invoked only "under suitable conditions." We believe that the "conditions" are not "suitable" in this case. Indeed, although Congress may have had the District of Columbia Code in mind when it passed the IDRA, it did not, in the language of *Hof*, "borrow" the terms of the IDRA from the District of Columbia Code. Rather, Congress departed from the scheme embodied in D. C. Code Ann. § 24-301 in several significant ways.
>
> The IDRA, for example, requires a defendant at trial to prove insanity by clear and convincing evidence; the District of Columbia statute, by contrast, employs a preponderance standard. A commitment hearing must be held under the IDRA within 40 days of an NGI verdict; the period is 50 days under the District of Columbia scheme.

Under the IDRA, a defendant whose offense involved bodily injury to another or serious damage to another's property, or the substantial risk thereof, must demonstrate at the hearing by clear and convincing evidence that he is entitled to release; under the District of Columbia scheme, an acquittee, regardless of the character of his offense, need only meet the preponderance standard. The IDRA provides that an acquittee, once committed, may be released when he no longer presents a substantial risk of harm to others or to their property; an acquittee under the District of Columbia system may be released from commitment when he "will not in the reasonable future be dangerous to himself or others." Finally, in the IDRA, Congress rejected the broad test for insanity that had been utilized under the District of Columbia provision, and instead adopted a more restrictive formulation under which a person is deemed insane if he is unable "to appreciate the nature and quality or the wrongfulness of his acts." We believe that these significant differences between the IDRA and D. C. Code Ann. § 24-301 render the canon upon which Shannon relies inapplicable in this case.[8]

Notes and Questions

1. Following *Shannon*, under what circumstances *will* a court adopt the interpretations of other courts as to borrowed statutes?

2. Note that although the borrowing of statutes is not particularly common at the federal level, it is very common at the state level, particularly with respect to the adoption of uniform and model acts. Besides interpretations of such acts, any definitions and/or commentary included in the original uniform or model act, even if not formally adopted in a particular jurisdiction, can be helpful in understanding the meaning of the borrowed statute. Note also that the concept of "borrowed" statutes goes well beyond statutes derived from uniform or model acts. For example, sometimes merely similar (or partially similar) acts are used as the starting point for other, later statutes.

4. Special Problems in Statutory Interpretation

What happens when the interpretation of a statute through traditional means yields a fairly clear, yet seemingly anomalous, answer? This is, generally speaking,

---

8. In addition, we note that the canon upon which Shannon relies is a canon of *statutory construction*. It stems from the notion that a court, in interpreting "borrowed" statutory language, should apply the same construction to that language that was placed upon it by the courts in the jurisdiction from which it was borrowed. In this case, however, the court in the jurisdiction from which the statutory text was supposedly borrowed — that is, the *Lyles* court — did not purport to construe the language of the District of Columbia Code provision; rather, in holding that jurors should be informed of the consequences of an NGI verdict, the court appears to have relied on its supervisory power over the Federal District Courts in the District of Columbia. Thus, we conclude that the canon is also inapplicable in this case because there was no "known and settled construction" of the statute that Congress could have adopted by virtue of borrowing language from the District of Columbia statutory scheme.

the subject of this section. This section will first address the so-called "absurdity doctrine" and the related issue of what have been called "scrivener's errors." The last subsection will discuss some of the problems legislatures face in trying to anticipate all the various contexts in which a statute might be applied.

a. The Absurdity Doctrine and the Problem of Scrivener's Errors

In *Griffin* and *Ron Pair*, the Supreme Court suggested that it generally would not interpret a statute in a manner that would produce "absurd results." What does "absurd" mean in this context? How absurd must the result be? And what about simple typographical (or "scrivener's") errors? Presumably, the latter should be ignored — assuming they can be recognized. These are some of the problems raised in the following case and the notes that follow.

Green v. Bock Laundry Machine Co.

490 U.S. 504 (1989)

JUSTICE STEVENS delivered the opinion of the Court.

This case presents the question whether Rule 609(a)(1) of the Federal Rules of Evidence requires a judge to let a civil litigant impeach an adversary's credibility with evidence of the adversary's prior felony convictions. Because the Courts of Appeals have answered that question in different ways, we granted certiorari to resolve the conflict.

While in custody at a county prison, petitioner Paul Green obtained work-release employment at a car wash. On his sixth day at work, Green reached inside a large dryer to try to stop it. A heavy rotating drum caught and tore off his right arm. Green brought this product liability action against respondent Bock Laundry Co. (Bock), manufacturer of the machine. At trial Green testified that he had been instructed inadequately concerning the machine's operation and dangerous character. Bock impeached Green's testimony by eliciting admissions that he had been convicted of conspiracy to commit burglary and burglary, both felonies. The jury returned a verdict for Bock. On appeal Green argued that the District Court had erred by denying his pretrial motion to exclude the impeaching evidence. The Court of Appeals summarily affirmed the District Court's ruling.

. . . .

I

Federal Rule of Evidence 609(a) provides:

> "General Rule. For the purpose of attacking the credibility of a witness, evidence that the witness has been convicted of a crime shall be admitted if elicited from the witness or established by public record during cross-examination but only if the crime (1) was punishable by death or imprisonment in excess of one year under the law under which the witness was convicted, and the court determines that the probative value of

admitting this evidence outweighs its prejudicial effect to the defendant, or (2) involved dishonesty or false statement, regardless of the punishment."

By its terms the Rule requires a judge to allow impeachment of any witness with prior convictions for felonies not involving dishonesty "only if" the probativeness of the evidence is greater than its prejudice "to the defendant." It follows that impeaching evidence detrimental to the prosecution in a criminal case "shall be admitted" without any such balancing.

The Rule's plain language commands weighing of prejudice to a defendant in a civil trial as well as in a criminal trial. But that literal reading would compel an odd result in a case like this. Assuming that all impeaching evidence has at least minimal probative value, and given that the evidence of plaintiff Green's convictions had some prejudicial effect on his case — but surely none on defendant Bock's — balancing according to the strict language of Rule 609(a)(1) inevitably leads to the conclusion that the evidence was admissible. In fact, under this construction of the Rule, impeachment detrimental to a civil plaintiff always would have to be admitted.

No matter how plain the text of the Rule may be, we cannot accept an interpretation that would deny a civil plaintiff the same right to impeach an adversary's testimony that it grants to a civil defendant. The Sixth Amendment to the Constitution guarantees a criminal defendant certain fair trial rights not enjoyed by the prosecution, while the Fifth Amendment lets the accused choose not to testify at trial. In contrast, civil litigants in federal court share equally the protections of the Fifth Amendment's Due Process Clause. Given liberal federal discovery rules, the inapplicability of the Fifth Amendment's protection against self-incrimination, and the need to prove their case, civil litigants almost always must testify in depositions or at trial. Denomination as a civil defendant or plaintiff, moreover, is often happenstance based on which party filed first or the nature of the suit. Evidence that a litigant or his witness is a convicted felon tends to shift a jury's focus from the worthiness of the litigant's position to the moral worth of the litigant himself. It is unfathomable why a civil plaintiff — but not a civil defendant — should be subjected to this risk. Thus we agree with the Seventh Circuit that as far as civil trials are concerned, Rule 609(a)(1) "can't mean what it says."

Out of this agreement flow divergent courses, each turning on the meaning of "defendant." The word might be interpreted to encompass all witnesses, civil and criminal, parties or not. It might be read to connote any party offering a witness, in which event Rule 609(a)(1)'s balance would apply to civil, as well as criminal, cases. Finally, "defendant" may refer only to the defendant in a criminal case. These choices spawn a corollary question: must a judge allow prior felony impeachment of all civil witnesses, or is Rule 609(a)(1) inapplicable to civil cases, in which event Rule 403 would authorize a judge to balance in such cases? Because the plain text does not resolve these issues, we must examine the history leading to the enactment of Rule 609 as law.

II

. . . .

. . . [The Court concludes] that only the accused in a criminal case should be protected from unfair prejudice by the balance set out in Rule 609(a)(1).

III

That conclusion does not end our inquiry. We next must decide whether Rule 609(a)(1) governs all prior felonies impeachment, so that no discretion may be exercised to benefit civil parties, or whether Rule 609(a)(1)'s specific reference to the criminal defendant leaves Rule 403 balancing available in the civil context.

Several courts, often with scant analysis of the interrelationship between Rule 403 and Rule 609(a)(1), have turned to Rule 403 to weigh prejudice and probativeness of impeaching testimony in civil cases. . . . Prodigious scholarship highlighting the irrationality and unfairness of impeaching credibility with evidence of felonies unrelated to veracity indicates that judicial exercise of discretion is in order. If Congress intended otherwise, however, judges must adhere to its decision.

A general statutory rule usually does not govern unless there is no more specific rule. Rule 403, the more general provision, thus comes into play only if Rule 609, though specific regarding criminal defendants, does not pertain to civil witnesses. The legislative history evinces some confusion about Rule 403's applicability to a version of Rule 609 that included no balancing language. That confusion is not an obstacle because the structure of the Rules as enacted resolves the question.

Rule 609(a) states that impeaching convictions evidence "shall be admitted." With regard to subpart (2), which governs impeachment by *crimen falsi* convictions, it is widely agreed that this imperative, coupled with the absence of any balancing language, bars exercise of judicial discretion pursuant to Rule 403. Subpart (1), concerning felonies, is subject to the same mandatory language; accordingly, Rule 403 balancing should not pertain to this subsection either.

Any argument that Rule 403 overrides Rule 609 loses force when one considers that the Rule contains its own weighing language, not only in subsection (a)(1), but also in sections (b), pertaining to older convictions, and (d), to juvenile adjudications. These latter balances, like Rule 609 in general, apply to both civil and criminal witnesses. . . . The absence of balances within only two aspects of the Rule — *crimen falsi* convictions and felony convictions of witnesses other than those whose impeachment would prejudice a criminal defendant — must be given its proper effect. Thus Rule 609(a)(1)'s exclusion of civil witnesses from its weighing language is a specific command that impeachment of such witnesses be admitted, which overrides a judge's general discretionary authority under Rule 403. Courts relying on Rule 403 to balance probative value against prejudice to civil witnesses depart from the mandatory language of Rule 609.

In summary, we hold that Federal Rule of Evidence 609(a)(1) requires a judge to permit impeachment of a civil witness with evidence of prior felony convictions regardless of ensuant unfair prejudice to the witness or the party offering the testimony. Thus no error occurred when the jury in this product liability suit learned through impeaching cross-examination that plaintiff Green was a convicted felon. The judgment of the Court of Appeals is

Affirmed.

JUSTICE SCALIA, concurring in the judgment.

We are confronted here with a statute which, if interpreted literally, produces an absurd, and perhaps unconstitutional result. Our task is to give some alternative meaning to the word "defendant" in Federal Rule of Evidence 609(a)(1) that avoids this consequence; and then to determine whether Rule 609(a)(1) excludes the operation of Federal Rule of Evidence 403.

I think it entirely appropriate to consult all public materials, including the background of Rule 609(a)(1) and the legislative history of its adoption, to verify that what seems to us an unthinkable disposition (civil defendants but not civil plaintiffs receive the benefit of weighing prejudice) was indeed unthought of, and thus to justify a departure from the ordinary meaning of the word "defendant" in the Rule. For that purpose, however, it would suffice to observe that counsel have not provided, nor have we discovered, a shred of evidence that anyone has ever proposed or assumed such a bizarre disposition. The Court's opinion, however, goes well beyond this. Approximately four-fifths of its substantive analysis is devoted to examining the evolution of Federal Rule of Evidence 609, from the 1942 Model Code of Evidence, to the 1953 Uniform Rules of Evidence, to the 1965 *Luck* case and the 1970 statute overriding it, to the Subcommittee, Committee, and Conference Committee Reports, and to the so-called floor debates on Rule 609 — all with the evident purpose, not merely of confirming that the word "defendant" cannot have been meant literally, but of determining what, precisely, the Rule does mean.

I find no reason to believe that any more than a handful of the Members of Congress who enacted Rule 609 were aware of its interesting evolution from the 1942 Model Code; or that any more than a handful of them (if any) voted, with respect to their understanding of the word "defendant" and the relationship between Rule 609 and Rule 403, on the basis of the referenced statements in the Subcommittee, Committee, or Conference Committee Reports, or floor debates — statements so marginally relevant, to such minute details, in such relatively inconsequential legislation. The meaning of terms on the statute books ought to be determined, not on the basis of which meaning can be shown to have been understood by a larger handful of the Members of Congress; but rather on the basis of which meaning is (1) most in accord with context and ordinary usage, and thus most likely to have been understood by the *whole* Congress which voted on the words of the statute (not to mention the citizens subject to it), and (2) most compatible with the surrounding body of law into which the provision must be integrated — a compatibility which, by a benign fiction, we assume Congress always has in mind. I would not permit any of the historical and legislative material discussed by the Court, or all of it combined, to lead me to a result different from the one that these factors suggest.

I would analyze this case, in brief, as follows:

(1) The word "defendant" in Rule 609(a)(1) cannot rationally (or perhaps even constitutionally) mean to provide the benefit of prejudice-weighing to civil defendants and not civil plaintiffs. Since petitioner has not produced, and we have not ourselves discovered, even a snippet of support for this absurd result, we may confidently assume that the word was not used (as it normally would be) to refer to all defendants and only all defendants.

(2) The available alternatives are to interpret "defendant" to mean (a) "civil plaintiff, civil defendant, prosecutor, and criminal defendant," (b) "civil plaintiff and defendant and criminal defendant," or (c) "criminal defendant." Quite obviously, the last does the least violence to the text. It adds a qualification that the word "defendant" does not contain but, unlike the others, does not give the word a meaning ("plaintiff" or "prosecutor") it simply will not bear. The qualification it adds, moreover, is one that could understandably have been omitted by inadvertence — and sometimes is omitted in normal conversation ("I believe strongly in defendants' rights"). Finally, this last interpretation is consistent with the policy of the law in general and the Rules of Evidence in particular of providing special protection to defendants in criminal cases.*

(3) As well described by the Court, the "structure of the Rules" makes it clear that Rule 403 is not to be applied in addition to Rule 609(a)(1).

I am frankly not sure that, despite its lengthy discussion of ideological evolution and legislative history, the Court's reasons for both aspects of its decisions are much different from mine. I respectfully decline to join that discussion, however, because it is natural for the bar to believe that the juridical importance of such material matches its prominence in our opinions — thus producing a legal culture in which, when counsel arguing before us assert that "Congress has said" something, they now frequently mean, by "Congress," a committee report; and in which it was not beyond the pale for a recent brief to say the following: "Unfortunately, the legislative debates are not helpful. Thus, we turn to the other guidepost in this difficult area, statutory language."

For the reasons stated, I concur in the judgment of the Court.

JUSTICE BLACKMUN, with whom JUSTICE BRENNAN and JUSTICE MARSHALL join, dissenting.

Federal Rule of Evidence 609(a) has attracted much attention during its relatively short life. This is due in no small part to its poor and inartful drafting. As noted by the majority, the Rule's use of the word "defendant" creates inescapable ambiguity. The majority concludes that Rule 609(a)(1) cannot mean what it says on its face. I fully agree.

I fail to see, however, why we are required to solve this riddle of statutory interpretation by reading the inadvertent word "defendant" to mean "criminal defendant." I am persuaded that a better interpretation of the Rule would allow the trial court to consider the risk of prejudice faced by any party, not just a criminal defendant. Applying the balancing provisions of rule 609(a)(1) to all parties would have prevented the admission of unnecessary and inflammatory evidence in this case and would prevent other similar unjust results until Rule 609(a) is repaired, as it must be. The result the Court reaches today, in contrast, endorses "the irrationality and

---

* Acknowledging the statutory ambiguity, the dissent would read "defendant" to mean "any party" because, it says, this interpretation "extends the protection of judicial supervision to a larger class of litigants" than the interpretation the majority and I favor, which "takes protection *away* from litigants." But neither side in this dispute can lay claim to generosity without begging the policy question whether judicial supervision is better than the automatic power to impeach. We could as well say — and with much more support in both prior law, and this Court's own recommendation — that our reading "extends the protection of the right to impeach with prior felony convictions to a larger class of litigants" than the dissent's interpretation, which "takes protection *away* from litigants."

unfairness" of denying the trial court the ability to weigh the risk of prejudice to any party before admitting evidence of a prior felony for purposes of impeachment.

Notes and Questions

---

1. Do you agree that a literal reading of Rule 609 as it stood in *Green* produced a ridiculous result, and one that was not espoused by the drafters of that rule? Note in this regard that no opinion supported a literal reading of this rule.

2. Which do you think was more likely—that Rule 609 was poorly drafted, or that the drafters did not consider the various ways in which this rule might be applied? Does the answer to this question help a court to determine how the rule should be interpreted?

3. Federal Rule of Evidence 609(a) was amended following the Supreme Court's decision in *Green*. Rule 609(a) now reads:

   > For the purpose of attacking the character for truthfulness of a witness,
   > (1) evidence that a witness other than an accused has been convicted of a crime shall be admitted, subject to Rule 403, if the crime was punishable by death or imprisonment in excess of one year under the law under which the witness was convicted, and evidence that an accused has been convicted of such a crime shall be admitted if the court determines that the probative value of admitting this evidence outweighs its prejudicial effect to the accused; and
   > (2) evidence that any witness has been convicted of a crime shall be admitted regardless of the punishment, if it readily can be determined that establishing the elements of the crime required proof or admission of an act of dishonesty or false statement by the witness.

   (Incidentally, Federal Rule of Evidence 403 provides: "The court may exclude relevant evidence if its probative value is substantially outweighed by a danger of one or more of the following: unfair prejudice, confusing the issues, misleading the jury, undue delay, wasting time, or needlessly presenting cumulative evidence.") Does the fact that this rule was amended, and the way in which it was amended, support the Court's decision? Why or why not? Is that relevant to assessing the correctness of the Court's holding?

4. How does one know for sure that a particular interpretation is absurd? And even if one can know with reasonable certainty that Congress could not have intended some particular result, is it the court's job to fix that? For an argument that the absurdity doctrine is inconsistent with a textualist approach to statutory interpretation, see John F. Manning, *The Absurdity Doctrine*, 116 HARV. L. REV. 2387 (2003).

5. *Scrivener's errors contrasted.* Some believe that the absurdity doctrine may be contrasted with the concept of the scrivener's error. As Justice Antonin Scalia explains:

Congress can enact foolish statutes as well as wise ones, and it is not for the courts to decide which is which and rewrite the former. I acknowledge an interpretative doctrine of what the old writers call *lapsus linguae* (slip of the tongue), and what our modern cases call "scrivener's error," where on the very face of the statute it is clear to the reader that a mistake of expression (rather than of legislative wisdom) has been made. For example, a statute may say "defendant" when only "criminal defendant" (i.e., not "civil defendant") makes sense.[23] The objective import of such a statute is clear enough, and I think it not contrary to sound principles of interpretation, in such extreme cases, to give the totality of context precedence over a single word.[24] But to say that the legislature obviously misspoke is worlds away from saying that the legislature obviously overlegislated. *Church of the Holy Trinity* is cited to us whenever counsel wants us to ignore the narrow, deadening text of the statute, and pay attention to the life-giving legislative intent. It is nothing but an invitation to judicial lawmaking.

ANTONIN SCALIA, A MATTER OF INTERPRETATION 20-21 (1997). Obviously, Justice Scalia believes that *Church of the Holy Trinity* represents an example of the Court's invocation of the absurdity doctrine (of which he disapproves), whereas *Green* represents an example of a scrivener's error (of which he approves). Do you agree with this distinction? That *Green* was an example of the latter, rather than the former?

Even if one agrees that there should be a distinction in treatment between scrivener's errors, on the one hand, and what might be described as absurd results, on the other, the difficulty lies in categorizing a statute as an example of one and not the other. For instance, though Professor Manning also recognizes the legitimacy of scrivener's errors, he takes a rather narrow view of when they arise. *See* Manning, *The Absurdity Doctrine*, 116 HARV. L. REV. at 2459-60 n.265.

PRACTICE PROBLEM: SEXUAL BATTERY IN FLORIDA

In Florida, "statutory" sexual battery is generally defined as a "sexual battery" committed by a person 18 years of age or older on a person less than 12 years of age, regardless of the victim's "consent." FLA. CODE § 794.011(2)(a). A separate statute also proscribes "sexual activity" between a person 24 years of age or older and a person 16 or 17 years of age. FLA. CODE § 794.05. Why do you think that the Florida Legislature enacted the latter statute? Can you think of any reason why such a statute should apply to 16- or 17-year-old victims, and not victims between the ages of 12 and 15? Is such a scheme "absurd"?

---

23. *See* Green v. Bock Laundry Mach. Co., 490 U.S. 504 (1989).
24. *Id.* at 527 (Scalia, J., concurring).

b. Dealing with the Unanticipated: The Problem of New Applications of Old Statutes

What happens when courts are forced to deal with "a problem which Congress apparently did not explicitly consider" (*Richards v. United States*, 369 U.S. 1, 9 (1962))? Consider this question in the context of the following cases.

McBoyle v. United States

283 U.S. 25 (1931)

MR. JUSTICE HOLMES delivered the opinion of the Court.

The petitioner was convicted of transporting from Ottawa, Illinois, to Guymon, Oklahoma, an airplane that he knew to have been stolen, and was sentenced to serve three years' imprisonment and to pay a fine of $2,000. The judgment was affirmed by the Circuit Court of Appeals for the Tenth Circuit. A writ of certiorari was granted by this Court on the question whether the National Motor Vehicle Theft Act applies to aircraft. That Act provides: "Sec. 2. That when used in this Act: (a) The term 'motor vehicle' shall include an automobile, automobile truck, automobile wagon, motor cycle, or any other self-propelled vehicle not designed for running on rails . . . ."

Section 2 defines the motor vehicles of which the transportation in interstate commerce is punished in § 3. The question is the meaning of the word 'vehicle' in the phrase "any other self-propelled vehicle not designed for running on rails." No doubt etymologically it is possible to use the word to signify a conveyance working on land, water or air, and sometimes legislation extends the use in that direction, e. g., land and air, water being separately provided for, in the Tariff Act. But in everyday speech 'vehicle' calls up the picture of a thing moving on land. Thus in Rev. Stats. § 4, intended, the Government suggests, rather to enlarge than to restrict the definition, vehicle includes every contrivance capable of being used "as a means of transportation on land." And this is repeated, expressly excluding aircraft, in the Tariff Act. So here, the phrase under discussion calls up the popular picture. For after including automobile truck, automobile wagon and motor cycle, the words "any other self-propelled vehicle not designed for running on rails" still indicate that a vehicle in the popular sense, that is a vehicle running on land, is the theme. It is a vehicle that runs, not something, not commonly called a vehicle, that flies. Airplanes were well known in 1919, when this statute was passed; but it is admitted that they were not mentioned in the reports or in the debates in Congress. It is impossible to read words that so carefully enumerate the different forms of motor vehicles and have no reference to any kind of aircraft, as including airplanes under a term that usage more and more precisely confines to a different class. The counsel for the petitioner have shown that the phraseology of the statute as to motor vehicles follows that of earlier statutes of Connecticut, Delaware, Ohio, Michigan and Missouri, not to mention the late Regulations of Traffic for the District of Columbia, none of which can be supposed to leave the earth.

Although it is not likely that a criminal will carefully consider the text of the law before he murders or steals, it is reasonable that a fair warning should be given to the world in language that the common world will understand, of what the law intends to do if a certain line is passed. To make the warning fair, so far as possible the line should be clear. When a rule of conduct is laid down in words that evoke in the common mind only the picture of vehicles moving on land, the statute should not be extended to aircraft, simply because it may seem to us that a similar policy applies, or upon the speculation that, if the legislature had thought of it, very likely broader words would have been used.

Judgment reversed.

Notes and Questions

---

1. Do you agree with the Court's analysis? Why or why not?

2. Is there any other aspect of this case that might have contributed to the Court's conclusion?

3. 18 U.S.C. § 2312 (2012), the statute at issue in *McBoyle*, currently provides: "Whoever transports in interstate or foreign commerce a motor vehicle, vessel, or aircraft, knowing the same to have been stolen, shall be fined under this title or imprisoned not more than 10 years, or both." Does the addition of the "or aircraft" language either confirm or refute the holding reached in that case? And why the addition of the term "vessel"?

In re Blanchflower
834 A.2d 1010 (N.H. 2003)

NADEAU, J.

Robin Mayer, co-respondent in the divorce proceeding of petitioner, David G. Blanchflower, and the respondent, Sian E. Blanchflower, challenges an order of the [trial court] denying her motion to dismiss the petitioner's amended ground for divorce of adultery. We accepted this matter as an interlocutory appeal under Supreme Court Rule 8, and now reverse and remand.

The record supports the following facts. The petitioner filed for divorce from the respondent on grounds of irreconcilable differences. He subsequently moved to amend the petition to assert the fault ground of adultery under RSA 458:7, II. Specifically, the petitioner alleged that the respondent has been involved in a "continuing adulterous affair" with the co-respondent, a woman, resulting in the irremediable breakdown of the parties' marriage. The co-respondent sought to dismiss the amended petition, contending that a homosexual relationship between two people, one of whom is married, does not constitute adultery under RSA 458:7, II. The trial court disagreed, and the co-respondent brought this appeal.

Before addressing the merits, we note this appeal is not about the status of homosexual relationships in our society or the formal recognition of homosexual unions. The narrow question before us is whether a homosexual sexual relationship between a married person and another constitutes adultery within the meaning of RSA 458:7, II.

RSA 458:7 provides, in part: "A divorce from the bonds of matrimony shall be decreed in favor of the innocent party for any of the following causes: II. Adultery of either party." The statute does not define adultery. Accordingly, we must discern its meaning according to our rules of statutory construction.

"In matters of statutory interpretation, this court is the final arbiter of the intent of the legislature as expressed in the words of a statute considered as a whole." We first look to the language of the statute itself and, where terms are not defined therein, "we ascribe to them their plain and ordinary meanings."

The plain and ordinary meaning of adultery is "voluntary sexual intercourse between a married man and someone other than his wife or between a married woman and someone other than her husband." *Webster's Third New International Dictionary* 30 (unabridged ed. 1961). Although the definition does not specifically state that the "someone" with whom one commits adultery must be of the opposite gender, it does require sexual intercourse.

The plain and ordinary meaning of sexual intercourse is "sexual connection esp. between humans: COITUS, COPULATION." Coitus is defined to require "insertion of the penis in the vagina," which clearly can only take place between persons of the opposite gender.

We also note that "a law means what it meant to its framers and its mere repassage does not alter that meaning." The statutory compilation in which the provision now codified as RSA 458:7 first appeared is the Revised Statutes of 1842. No definition of adultery was contained in that statute. Our cases from that approximate time period, however, support the inference that adultery meant intercourse.

Cases from this period also indicate that adultery as a ground for divorce was equated with the crime of adultery and was alleged as such in libels for divorce. Although the criminal adultery statute in the 1842 compilation also did not define adultery, roughly contemporaneous case law is instructive. "Adultery is committed whenever there is an intercourse from which spurious issue may arise." As "spurious issue" can only arise from intercourse between a man and a woman, criminal adultery could only be committed with a person of the opposite gender.

We note that the current criminal adultery statute still requires sexual intercourse . . . . Based upon the foregoing, we conclude that adultery under RSA 458:7, II does not include homosexual relationships.

We reject the petitioner's argument that an interpretation of adultery that excludes homosexual conduct subjects homosexuals and heterosexuals to unequal treatment, "contrary to New Hampshire's public policy of equality and prohibition of discrimination based on sex and sexual orientation." Homosexuals and heterosexuals engaging in the same acts are treated the same because our interpretation of the term "adultery" excludes all non-coital sex acts, whether between persons of the same or opposite gender. The only distinction is that persons of the same gender cannot, by definition, engage in the one act that constitutes adultery under the statute.

The petitioner also argues that "public policy would be well served by applying the same law to a cheating spouse, whether the promiscuous spouse chooses a paramour of the same sex or the opposite sex." This argument is tied to the premise, as argued by the petitioner, that "the purpose underlying the adultery fault ground is based upon the fundamental concept of marital loyalty and public policy's disfavor of one spouse's violation of the marriage contract with another."

We have not, however, seen any such purpose expressed by the legislature. As noted above, the concept of adultery was premised upon a specific act. To include in that concept other acts of a sexual nature, whether between heterosexuals or homosexuals, would change beyond recognition this well-established ground for divorce and likely lead to countless new marital cases alleging adultery, for strategic purposes. In any event, "it is not the function of the judiciary to provide for present needs by an extension of past legislation." Similarly, "we will not undertake the extraordinary step of creating legislation where none exists. Rather, matters of public policy are reserved for the legislature."

The dissent defines adultery not as a specific act of intercourse, but as "extramarital intimate sexual activity with another." This standard would permit a hundred different judges and masters to decide just what individual acts are so sexually intimate as to meet the definition. The dilemma faced by Justice Stewart and his fellow justices applying their personal standards to the issue of pornography in movies demonstrates the value of a clear objective definition of adultery in marital cases. *See Jacobellis v. Ohio*, 378 U.S. 184 (1964).

We are also unpersuaded by the dissent's contention that "it is improbable that the legislature intended to require an innocent spouse in a divorce action to prove the specific intimate sexual acts in which the guilty spouse engaged." Citing [prior cases], the dissent notes that adultery usually has no eyewitnesses and therefore "ordinarily must be proved by circumstantial evidence." While this is true, it does not support the dissent's point. For over a hundred and fifty years judges, lawyers and clients have understood that adultery meant intercourse as we have defined it. It is an act determined not by the subjective test of an individual justice but by an objective determination based upon the facts. What must be proved to establish adultery and what evidence may be used to prove it are separate issues. Adultery cases have always required proof of the specific sexual act engaged in, namely, sexual intercourse. That circumstantial evidence may be used to establish the act does not negate or undermine the requirement of proof that the act actually occurred. . . .

Reversed and remanded.

DALIANIS and DUGGAN, JJ., concurred; BROCK, C.J., and BRODERICK, J., dissented.

BROCK, C.J., and BRODERICK, J., dissenting.

We agree with the majority that this appeal is "not about the status of homosexual relationships in our society or the formal recognition of homosexual unions." These issues are not remotely before us. We respectfully dissent because we believe that the majority's narrow construction of the word "adultery" contravenes the legislature's intended purpose in sanctioning fault-based divorce for the protection of the injured spouse.

To strictly adhere to the primary definition of adultery in the 1961 edition of *Webster's Third New International Dictionary* and a corollary definition of sexual intercourse, which on its face does not require coitus, is to avert one's eyes from the sexual realities of our world. While we recognize that "we first look to the plain and ordinary meaning of words to interpret our statutes, it is one of the surest indexes of a mature and developed jurisprudence not to make a fortress out of the dictionary; but to remember that statutes always have some purpose or object to accomplish."

New Hampshire permits both fault-based and no-fault divorces. No-fault divorces are governed by RSA 458:7-a, which permits divorce "irrespective of the fault of either party, on the ground of irreconcilable differences which have caused the irremediable breakdown of the marriage." RSA 458:7 governs fault-based divorce. Unlike no-fault divorces, a fault-based divorce presumes that there is an innocent and a guilty spouse, and permits divorce "in favor of the innocent party" for any of nine possible causes, including impotency, adultery, extreme cruelty, felony conviction for which a party has been imprisoned, habitual drunkenness, and abandonment. Under our fault-based law, the innocent spouse is entitled to a divorce because the guilty spouse has breached a marital covenant, such as the covenant to be sexually faithful.

The purpose of permitting fault-based divorces is to provide some measure of relief to an innocent spouse for the offending conduct of a guilty spouse. The law allows the court to consider fault in assessing the equitable division of the marital assets, and in so doing, as in the case of adultery, seeks to justly resolve the unseemly dissolution of a confidential and trusting relationship. We should therefore view the purpose and fabric of our divorce law in a meaningful context, as the legislature presumably intended, and not so narrow our focus as to undermine its public goals.

From the perspective of the injured spouse, the very party fault-based divorce law is designed to protect, "an extramarital relationship is just as devastating irrespective of the specific sexual act performed by the promiscuous spouse or the sex of the new paramour." Indeed, to some, a homosexual betrayal may be more devastating. Accordingly, consistent with the overall purpose of New Hampshire's fault-based divorce law, we would interpret the word "adultery" in RSA 458:7, II to mean a spouse's extramarital intimate sexual activity with another, regardless of the specific intimate sexual acts performed, the marital status, or the gender of the third party.

The majority intimates that to construe adultery to include homosexual conduct invades the exclusive province of the legislature to establish public policy. We recognize that questions of public policy are reserved for the legislature. Questions of statutory interpretation are our domain, however. We do not intend to add a new cause of action for divorce, which is a purely legislative responsibility.

Defining the word "adultery" to include intimate extramarital homosexual sexual activity by a spouse is consonant with the decisions of other [state] courts that have considered this issue. . . .

. . . .

The majority suggests that to define "adultery" so as to include intimate extramarital homosexual activity by a spouse is to propose a test so vague as to be unworkable. Apparently, a similar test has been adopted in the three jurisdictions previously cited and remains good law. Further, while such a definition is more inclusive than one reliant solely upon heterosexual sexual intercourse, we do not believe that "intimate extramarital sexual activity" either requires a more explicit description or would be subject to such a widely varying judicial view. As Justice Stewart stated with regard to defining the term "hard-core pornography,"

> I shall not today attempt further to define the kinds of material I understand to be embraced within that shorthand description; and perhaps I could never succeed in intelligibly doing so. But I know it when I see it.

Jacobellis v. Ohio, 378 U.S. 184, 197 (1964) (Stewart, J., concurring).

We believe that the majority's interpretation of the word "adultery" is overly narrow in scope. It is improbable that our legislature intended to require an innocent spouse in a divorce action to prove the specific intimate sexual acts in which the guilty spouse engaged. There are usually no eyewitnesses to adultery. It ordinarily must be proved by circumstantial evidence. Nor does it seem reasonable that the legislature intended to allow a guilty spouse to defend against an adultery charge by arguing that, while he or she engaged in intimate sexual activity with another, the relationship was not adulterous because it did not involve coitus. It is hard to comprehend how the legislature could have intended to exonerate a sexually unfaithful or even promiscuous spouse who engaged in all manner of sexual intimacy, with members of the opposite sex, except sexual intercourse, from a charge of adultery. Sexual infidelity should not be so narrowly proscribed.

It is much more likely that our legislature intended the innocent spouse to establish adultery through circumstantial evidence showing, by a preponderance of the evidence, that the guilty spouse had engaged in intimate sexual activity outside of the marriage, regardless of the specific sexual acts involved or the gender of the guilty spouse's lover. Under our fault-based divorce law, a relationship is adulterous because it occurs outside of marriage and involves intimate sexual activity, not because it involves only one particular sexual act. Accordingly, we respectfully dissent.

Notes and Questions

---

1. Which opinion do you find to be the more persuasive — the majority, or the dissent? Why? What interpretative approach or theory does each principally rely on?

2. It is almost certainly true, is it not, that the New Hampshire legislature, in 1842, did not intend to include a "homosexual sexual relationship" among the grounds for a fault-based divorce? On the other hand, is it not also true that such relationships existed at that time? In light of that fact, are there any reasons why that legislature might have nonetheless decided not to include such a ground?

3. It does not appear that the New Hampshire statute at issue in *Blanchflower*, RSA 458:7, II, has been amended subsequent to the court's decision in that case. If not, why not? Can any conclusions regarding the correctness of the court's decision be drawn from this fact?

4. Consider, again, the federal Defense of Marriage Act (*see supra* at 525). According to one legal scholar, this Act "had no immediate tangible effect because [it was] enacted before same-sex marriage was a reality" — i.e., "no such union had been recognized as a marriage anywhere in the United States." Note, *Litigating the Defense of Marriage Act: The Next Battleground for Same-Sex Marriage*, 117 HARV. L. REV. 2684, 2684, 2686 (2004). If that is true, then why the perceived need for the Act?

5. Can a statute ever be drafted to include all results a legislature might have intended? At the same time, is any situation conceivably covered by a statute ever completely unforeseeable?

   These sorts of issues seem to arise with surprising frequency. One particularly famous example can be found in *Riggs v. Palmer*, 22 N.E. 188, 115 N.Y. 506 (1889). *Riggs* involved a grandson who murdered his grandfather so that he might take under the latter's will. Though the statute in question was silent as to this issue, the Court of Appeals of New York held against the grandson. In so holding, the court stated:

   > It was the intention of the law-makers that the donees in a will should have the property given to them. But it never could have been their intention that a donee who murdered the testator to make the will operative should have any benefit under it. If such a case had been present to their minds, and it had been supposed necessary to make some provision of law to meet it, it cannot be doubted that they would have provided for it.

   Id. at 509. There was a vigorous dissent. Who was correct? Is there any way to achieve the result reached by the majority without interpreting the statute in a manner that was unsupported by the text?

D. THEORIES OF STATUTORY INTERPRETATION

As discussed previously, over the past century or so, three main theories of statutory interpretation have been dominant, at least in the United States: intentionalism, purposivism, and textualism. The following is a brief explanation of each of these theories and their historical development.

William N. Eskridge, Jr. & Philip P. Frickey

STATUTORY INTERPRETATION AS PRACTICAL REASONING

42 Stan. L. Rev. 321 (1990)

Traditional theories [of statutory interpretation] have always considered a variety of factors relevant for statutory interpretation. In the post-World War II era, however, legal scholars have preferred theories that offer a unitary foundation for statutory interpretation. Much of the theoretical debate has been over which of the competing foundations is the best one. The three main theories today emphasize (1) the actual or presumed intent of the legislature enacting the statute ("intentionalism"); (2) the actual or presumed purpose of the statute ("purposivism" or "modified intentionalism"); and (3) the literal commands of the statutory text ("textualism"). We call these theories "foundationalist," because each seeks an objective ground ("foundation") that will reliably guide the interpretation of all statutes in all situations.

Each of the three grand theories seeks to reconcile statutory interpretation by unelected judges with the assumptions of majoritarian political theory. Toward this end, each seeks an objective standard that will constrain the discretion of judicial interpreters. . . .

A. INTENTIONALISM

The most popular grand theory is probably intentionalism. Under this view, the Court acts as the enacting legislature's faithful servant, discovering and applying the legislature's original intent. Traditional treatises on statutory interpretation generally acknowledge the primacy of legislative intent, qualifying the canons of construction with the caveat, "unless the legislature otherwise intends." Although traditional intentionalism was subjected to withering attack in the 1930s and 1940s, recent scholarship has revived academic interest in the theory and posited some form of intentionalism as the anchor for a grand theory of interpretation.

Intentionalism makes a strong claim to be the only legitimate foundation for statutory interpretation in a representative democracy. If the legislature is the primary lawmaker and courts are its agents, then requiring the courts to follow the legislature's intentions disciplines judges by inhibiting judicial lawmaking, and in so doing seems to further democracy by affirming the will of elected representatives. Not surprisingly, then, a number of Supreme Court opinions state that original legislative intent is the touchstone for statutory interpretation.

. . . .

B. PURPOSIVISM

The legal realists — especially Max Radin — raised some of the objections to intentionalism noted above and proposed as an alternative theory a flexible "mischief" approach to statutory interpretation. Professors Henry Hart and Albert Sacks in the 1950s expanded the realists' approach into a "purposivist" theory of interpretation that seemed as faithful to the principle of legislative supremacy as intentionalism, but without the rigidity and definitional problems of intentionalism. According to the Hart and Sacks legal process materials, "every statute must be conclusively presumed to be a purposive act. The idea of a statute without an intelligible purpose is foreign to the idea of law and inadmissible." Because "every statute and every doctrine of unwritten law developed by the decisional process has some kind of purpose or objective," identifying that purpose and deducing the interpretation with which it is most consistent resolves interpretive ambiguities.

As an alternative to intentionalism, purposivism has been rather successful, and some commentators believe that it is now the "traditional" theory of statutory interpretation. . . .

C. TEXTUALISM

The legal realists and legal process thinkers discredited intentionalism as a grand strategy for statutory interpretation; in its place they suggested purposivism. That theory has in turn been extensively criticized, especially by scholars influenced by the law and economics movement. As argued above, the recent trend is to view the legislature as not necessarily purposive; "attributing" purposes to ad hoc statutory deals is nothing if not judicial lawmaking. Accordingly, several judges of the law and economics school have responded to the critique of purposivism by urging as a grand theory the return to some version of the old "plain meaning rule": The beginning, and usually the end, of statutory interpretation should be the apparent meaning of the statutory language.

The arguments for textualism are strong ones. As suggested above, textualism appeals to the rule-of-law value that citizens ought to be able to read the statute books and know their rights and duties. By emphasizing the statutory words chosen by the legislature, rather than (what seems to be) more abstract and judicially malleable interpretive sources, textualism also appeals to the values of legislative supremacy and judicial restraint.

There are at least two varieties of textualism. The stricter version posits the statutory text as (at least ordinarily) the sole legitimate interpretive source. A characteristically pithy Holmesianism says it well: "We do not inquire what the legislature meant; we ask only what the statute means." The second, and less ambitious, variety of textualism uses statutory language not in place of, but rather as the best guide to, legislative intent or purpose. "There is, of course, no more persuasive evidence of the purpose of a statute than the words by which the legislature undertook to give expression to its wishes."[73] Similarly, "when words are free from doubt they must be taken as the final expression of the legislative intent."[74]

Notes and Questions

---

1. Reconsider the Court's decisions in *Griffin* and *Ron Pair*. How would you characterize the Court's approach in those cases? Does each fit neatly into one of three "traditional" categories, or is either (or both) more of a hybrid?

---

73. United States v. American Trucking Ass'ns, 310 U.S. 534, 543 (1940), *followed and quoted in* Huffman v. Western Nuclear, Inc., 108 S. Ct. 2087, 2092 (1988).
74. Caminetti v. United States, 242 U.S. 470, 490 (1917).

2. For a video of a 2009 Federalist Society debate between United States Court of Appeals Judges (and former law professors) Frank Easterbrook and Guido Calabresi (and moderated by Professor John Manning) that demonstrates many of the differences between textualism and earlier approaches, see http://www.youtube.com/watch?v=ss2yAzXyUiI&feature=bf_prev&list=SP5C35B705C674BD9B.

1. Intentionalism vs. Textualism

Henry M. Hart, Jr. & Albert M. Sacks

WHY SHOULD WORD MEANINGS BE RESPECTED AT ALL?

**The Legal Process: Basic Problems in the Making and Application of Law
(William N. Eskridge, Jr. & Philip P. Frickey eds., 1994)**

It has thus far been assumed that the problem posed by the words of a statute is simply to determine whether they will bear an otherwise indicated meaning. But why is this inquiry important? Why should a court confine itself to meanings which the words of a statute will bear?

The principle of institutional settlement may be thought to yield a short answer. That principle, obviously, forbids a court to substitute its own ideas for what the legislature has duly enacted. What the legislature *has* thus enacted should not be frustrated or defeated. What it *has* thus enacted should be declared to be law, if at all, only upon the court's independent responsibility and not upon a pretense of legislative responsibility.

Suppose, however, that a court is trying in good faith to do what it thinks the legislature wanted or now wants. May it twist the words then, or disregard them altogether?

This question gains some point from the uncritical reading that is occasionally given to the conventional proposition that "the ultimate aim of rules of interpretation is to ascertain the intention of the legislature in the enactment of the statute." If "intention," thus taken as the ultimate touchstone, is understood as referring to a subjective state of mind, then the way is opened for the conclusion that it is a mere technicality to let the words stand in the way whenever other indications seem to point with assurance to what the legislature was really driving at.

The question gains special point because of the current practice in the federal courts . . . of free reference to evidences of purpose and meaning garnered from the internal legislative history of a statute. If these evidences point persuasively toward a particular conclusion about the intended effect of a statute, why be stuffy about the fact that the words do not seem to bear this meaning?

What weight should be given, in answering these questions, to the usual constitutional provisions with respect to the procedure for the enactment of bills?

Should these provisions be read as specifying the exclusive means by which the legislature may express its intention — as saying, in other words, that it may do so only by agreeing in a prescribed way that the particular collection of words embodied in a particular bill shall become law? If so, a court would be flouting the Constitution by treating anything else as law.

Or should a legislature be thought of as a kind of glorified board of directors whose unenacted intentions and wishes are entitled to respect also?

In what sense can a body of individuals such as a legislature be said to have formed an "intention" otherwise than by agreeing, in accordance with its rules, to take some kind of formal action? In the absence of such action, how can a court know what that "intention" is?

What meaning can be given not only to constitutional rules but to the legislature's own rules for the enactment of bills if an "intention" which has been neither formed nor expressed in accordance with the rules can be treated as law?

Suppose it were known, by some kind of Gallup poll, that a clear majority of each branch of a legislature approved a particular bill at the time of its introduction. Would it be possible to be sure that the respective majorities would still approve the bill after it had been through the testing procedure of committee hearing and floor debate in both houses? That the bill would even be able to make its way through that procedure in either house, to the point of final vote upon enactment?

Is legislative procedure a mere routine? Or does it have a function in the shaping of legislative intention which cannot be properly be ignored? If it does, then the particular collocation of words which was the product of that procedure cannot be ignored either.

Consider, more broadly, the role which language plays not only in the legislative process but in every other process for the settlement of problems of group concern. Can the integrity of any of these processes be maintained if the integrity of language, as a healthily functioning social institution, is not maintained also?

John F. Manning

TEXTUALISM AND LEGISLATIVE INTENT

91 Va. L. Rev. 419 (2005)

For much of our history, the Supreme Court has unflinchingly proclaimed that legislative "intent" is the touchstone of federal statutory interpretation.[1] The rationale is familiar: In a constitutional system predicated upon legislative supremacy (within constitutional boundaries), judges — as Congress's faithful agents — must try to ascertain as accurately as possible what Congress meant by the words it used.

---

1. See, e.g., United States v. Am. Trucking Ass'ns, 310 U.S. 534, 542 (1940) ("In the interpretation of statutes, the function of the courts is easily stated. It is to construe the language so as to give effect to the intent of Congress.").

On this premise, federal judges long assumed that when a statute was vague or ambiguous, interpreters should seek clarification, if possible, in the bill's internal legislative history. Thus, when a sponsor or committee expressed an understanding of the bill or the mischiefs at which it was aimed, federal courts often took that as probative evidence of the text's meaning. And because a legislature — like any other user of language — might speak imprecisely, or use language loosely or idiosyncratically, federal judges long assumed that a statute's semantic detail, however clear, must yield when it conflicts sharply with the apparent spirit or purpose that inspired its enactment.

For the latter half of the twentieth century, these principles — referred to herein as "classical intentionalism" — reflected the orthodoxy, at least among federal judges. Near the close of that century, however, a competing philosophy known as "textualism" emerged, producing a rather significant effect on both judicial behavior and academic writing. As discussed below, textualism does not admit of a simple definition, but in practice is associated with the basic proposition that judges must seek and abide by the public meaning of the enacted text, understood in context (as all texts must be). Hence, even in cases of ambiguity, many textualist judges typically refuse to treat legislative history as "authoritative" evidence of legislative intent. Given the undeniable complexity of the legislative process, interpreters simply cannot know if a requisite majority of enactors knew of or assented to the contents of any particular piece of legislative history. In addition, textualists choose the letter of the statutory text over its spirit; again, the intricacy and opacity of the legislative process make them reluctant to ascribe an apparent mismatch between text and purpose to a lapse in legislative expression rather than the ever-present possibility of an awkward legislative compromise.

The leading exponents of modern textualism — Justice Scalia on the U.S. Supreme Court and Judge Easterbrook on the U.S. Court of Appeals for the Seventh Circuit — often justify these deviations from class intentionalism with an alluring but ultimately inexact proposition: Building on the realist tradition, they emphasize that multi-member legislatures do not have an actual but unexpressed "intent" on any materially contested interpretive point; judges must therefore abandon any pretense of using such an intent as the aim of interpretation. Instead, courts should listen for "the ring the words of a statute would have had to a skilled user of words at the time, thinking about the same problem." Textualists thus aspire "to read the words of a statutory text as any ordinary Member of Congress would have read them, and apply the meaning so determined." Such an approach, they insist, does not replicate the fanciful pursuit of Congress's true intentions; rather, it more plausibly captures "a sort of 'objectified' intent — the intent that a reasonable person would gather from the text of the law, placed alongside the remainder of the *corpus juris*."

In a characteristically insightful article, Professor Caleb Nelson has suggested that the difference between new textualists and classical intentionalists may not be as cosmic as modern textualist rhetoric sometimes suggests.[12] Several considerations,

---

12. See Caleb Nelson, What Is Textualism?, 91 Va. L. Rev. 347 (2005).

he argues, demonstrate that the leading modern textualists do, in fact, care about Congress's actual rather than objectified intent. A few examples suffice to reveal the gist of his analysis: First, textualists reject internal legislative history precisely because they regard a sponsor's or committee's views as an unreliable proxy for the intentions of the body as a whole. Second, modern textualists sometime sacrifice clear semantic meaning in order to avoid scrivener's errors, a practice that makes sense only if one is seeking the true intention of the enacting body. Third, textualists sometimes even engage in the "imaginative reconstruction" of legislative intent — that is, in some contexts they eschew close textual exegesis and try instead to imagine how the legislature would have resolved a particular interpretive question under the circumstances at bar. Such considerations lead Professor Nelson to conclude that textualists talk a good game but in the end want to know the same thing as do intentionalists — what the legislature subjectively intended. They just have different presuppositions about how to read — or, perhaps more accurately, how to approximate — that intent.

So what does Professor Nelson see as the salient factor that distinguishes modern textualists from classical intentionalists? Simply put, he detects a heightened tendency among textualists to prefer rules over standards. For example, textualists are quick to enforce statutorily embedded rules against the claim that inevitable over- or under-inclusiveness warrants an (intent-based) exception. And they enthusiastically deploy canons of construction, with special emphasis on the more rule-like of the canons. Given his previous conclusion that textualists seek legislative intent, he chalks up their rule-like tendencies to an implicit judgment that rule-following will more likely approximate legislative intent. (That is, textualists appear to believe that deviating from a clear text in the name of intent will typically produce more misapproximations of legislative intent than will hewing to the text, and that a strong presumption against intent-based exceptions to rules will therefore prevent more errors than it leaves in place.) Similarly, their attraction to rule-based canons reflects an implicit belief that such canons accurately reflect congressional habits of mind; that their application will thus capture true congressional desires more often than case-by-case analysis of intent; and that consistent judicial deployment of such preference-estimating canons will become self-fulfilling as legislative drafters first become familiar with and then take account of predictable canons of construction.

This Essay will examine Professor Nelson's central contention that, contrary to some of their rhetoric, textual judges do care about legislative intent. If by that he means that textualists believe that the legislative majority as a whole possesses a background subjective intention about the words it adopts, I believe that his conclusion misses the fact that textualists, given their assumptions about the legislative process, necessarily believe that intent is a construct. To be sure, textualists have sought to devise a constructive intent that satisfies the minimum conditions for meaningfully tracing statutory meaning to the legislative process. That much is uncontroversial. In any system predicated on legislative supremacy, a faithful agent will of course seek the legislature's intended meaning in some sense, and modern textualists do situate themselves in that tradition. But to say that they simply practice intentionalism by other means is to understate the important link for textualists between recognizing the cumbersome, chaotic, path-dependent, and opaque character of the legislative process and their rejection (in what may perhaps be overstated rhetoric) of the classical intentionalists' understanding of legislative intent.

What characterizes classical intentionalism is its tendency to anthropomorphize the legislature. In important respects, intentionalists believe that a legislative command can and should be treated as one would treat the speech of an individual human actor. That is, they believe that a legislative majority can have coherent but unexpressed background intentions about its statutory utterances that can be used to clarify or even alter the significance that a reasonable person conversant with relevant social and linguistic conventions would otherwise attach to the chosen words in context. Textualists, by contrast, deny that Congress has a collective will apart from the outcomes of the complex legislative process that conditions its ability to translate raw policy impulses or intentions into finished legislation. For them, intended meaning never emerges unfiltered; it must survive a process that includes committee approval, logrolling, the need for floor time, threatened filibusters, conference committees, veto threats, and the like. For better or worse, only the statutory text navigates all those hurdles. Accordingly, whereas intentionalists believe that legislatures have coherent and identifiable but *unexpressed* policy intentions, textualists believe that the only meaningful collective legislative intentions are those reflected in the *public meanings* of the final statutory text.

. . . .

I. LEGISLATIVE SUPREMACY AND LEGISLATIVE INTENT

As a matter of political theory, any conceptions of judging rooted in the related premises of legislative supremacy and the faithful agent theory is, quite simply, unintelligible without an underlying conception of legislative intent. As Joseph Raz has explained "it makes no sense to give any person or body law-making power unless it is assumed that the law they make is the law they intended to make." . . .

Classical intentionalism of course starts with similar premises. But as traditionally practiced by the Supreme Court, it refines that basic idea in a crucial respect. Consistent with an important strain of modern language theory, classical intentionalists emphasize that meaning depends on what the speaker *actually* intends to convey. In that sense, classical intentionalists treat Congress much as they would treat an individual speaker: If an individual uses a term that has multiple potential meanings, the true meaning of that term as used on a particular occasion depends on the meaning intended by the speaker. So when the words of a statute leave a residue of ambiguity, intentionalists find it appropriate to examine the bill's internal legislative history for further evidence of what members of Congress "intended." More important, because people often speak loosely, listeners must adjust their understanding when circumstances suggest that an individual has poorly expressed his or her intentions. By the same token, intentionalists insist that judges enforce the spirit rather than the letter of the law when the enacted words fail to capture the legislature's apparent purposes, as revealed by the tenor of the legislation as a whole, the mischiefs giving rise to its enactment, the policy expressed in similar statutes, and whatever other circumstances may shed light on the policy of the enactment. Classical intentionalism thus presupposes that interpreters should try to ascertain how the legislative majority would have handled a problem that the fair import of the enacted text either does not resolve or resolves in a manner that does not adequately reflect the legislature's apparent aims.

Like classical intentionalists, textualists work within the faithful agent framework; they believe that in our system of government, federal judges have a duty to ascertain and implement as accurately as possible the instructions set down by Congress (within constitutional bounds). To this extent, Professor Nelson and I certainly agree. But textualists deny that a legislature has any shared intention that lies behind but differs from the reasonable import of the words adopted; that is, they think it impossible to tell how the body as a whole actually intended (or, more accurately, would have intended) to resolve a policy question not clearly or satisfactorily settled by the text. Building upon the realist tradition, textualists do not believe that the premises governing an individual's intended meaning translate well to a complex, multi-member legislative process. As one author has put it, Congress is a "they," not an "it," and legislative policies are reduced to law only through a cumbersome and highly intricate lawmaking process.

Invoking the economic and game-theoretic insights of public choice theory, textualists thus emphasize that laws frequently reflect whatever bargain competing interest groups could strike rather than the fully principled policy judgment of a single-minded majority. Moreover, a tortuous and largely opaque legislative process makes it difficult if not impossible for judges to retrace all the steps that contributed to the final wording of the enacted text. Bills "must run the gamut of the process," which involves "committees, fighting for time on the floor, compromise because other members want some unrelated objective, passage, exposure to veto, and so on." Legislative outcomes necessarily hinge on arbitrary (or at least nonsubstantive) factors such as the sequence in which alternatives are presented. And no issue is considered in isolation; indeed, legislators frequently choose their words strategically in order to elide disagreements and smooth a bill's passage. Strategic voting — including logrolling across different substantive areas — further complicates matters by introducing additional nonsubstantive and untraceable considerations into the shaping of a bill. Based on such factors, Judge Easterbrook thinks it is "impossible for a court — even one that knows each legislators' complete table of preferences — to say what the whole body would have done with a proposal it did not consider in fact." Hence, if a bill's final shape depends to a large extent on these varied procedural idiosyncrasies, textualists deem it fanciful to try to reconstruct the actual but unexpressed intent of the legislative majority on any seriously contested interpretive question.

. . . While the textualists' view of the legislative process requires them to reject the classical intentionalists' anthropomorphic treatment of the legislature, it by no means necessitates a wholesale rejection of any useful conception of legislative intent. To satisfy the requirements of legislative supremacy, one need not believe, as classical intentionalists do, that a multi-member legislature has a human-like capacity to form single-minded but unexpressed intentions about the words used in a

statute. Rather, as Professor Raz has explained, the demands of legislative supremacy require only that legislators intend to enact a law that will be decoded according to prevailing interpretive conventions. If so, then society can at least attribute
to each legislator the intention "to say what one would ordinarily be understood as
saying, given the circumstances in which one said it." Or as the leading philosophical textualist, Jeremy Waldron, has put it:

> A legislator who votes for (or against) a provision like "No vehicle shall be per-
> mitted to enter any state or municipal park" does so on the assumption that — to put it
> crudely — what the words mean to him is identical to what they will mean to those to
> whom they are addressed (in the event that the provision is passed). That such assump-
> tions pervade the legislative process shows how much law depends on language, on the
> shared conventions that constitute a language, and on the reciprocity of intentions that
> conventions comprise.

These premises closely reflect Justice Scalia's and Judge Easterbrook's commitment
to "objectified intent," a concept predicated on the notion that a judge should read
a statutory text just as any reasonable person conversant with applicable social conventions would read it. Ascribing that sort of objectified intent to legislators offers
an intelligible way for textualists to hold them accountable for whatever law they
have passed, whether or not they have *any* actual intent, singly or collectively, respecting its details.

In that sense, textualism might be understood as a judgment about the most
reliable (or perhaps the least unreliable) way of discerning legislative instructions.
If one cannot accurately ascertain what the body as a whole would have done with
matters unspecified or even misspecified by the text, then perhaps the best one
can do is to approximate the way a reasonable person in the legislator's position
would have read the words actually adopted. Certainly, the aspiration to decode
the legislature's instructions as accurately as possible gives textualists something in
common with classical intentionalists. To say that textualism is just intentionalism
by other means, however, threatens to obscure the central point that for textualists intent is a construct; it does not depend on the conclusion that a hypothetical legislative majority actually subscribed to the likely meaning that a reasonable
person, conversant with the relevant conventions, would attach to the enacted text.
Legislative intent, to the extent textualists invoke it, is a framework for analysis
designed to satisfy the minimum conditions for meaningful communication by a
multi-member body without actual intentions to judges, administrators, and the
public, who all form a community of shared conventions for decoding language in
context.

To underscore the constructive nature of objectified intent, it is helpful to note
that modern textualists are not literalists; they do not look exclusively for the "ordinary meaning" of words and phrases. Rather, they emphasize the relevant linguistic
community's (or sub-community's) shared understandings and practices. I have
explored the implications of this position more fully in previous writing. For now,
it suffices to note that textualists therefore want to know how "a *skilled*, objectively
reasonable user of words" would have understood the statutory text, an approach
that entails ascertaining the "assumptions shared by speakers and the intended

audience." Accordingly, where appropriate in context, textualists seek out technical meaning, including the specialized connotations and practices common to the specialized sub-community of lawyers.[53] Textualists assign common-law terms their full array of common-law connotations; they supplement otherwise unqualified texts with settled common-law practices, where such practices traditionally pertained to the subject matters covered within the statute; and they apply sufficiently well-settled canons of construction, including substantive canons such as the rule of lenity.

What textualists do not suggest is that distilling technical meaning from trade practice, the common law, technical norms of construction, and the like necessarily reflects the actual (*viz.* subjective) understanding of a multi-person legislative majority. Consider, for example, *Babbitt v. Sweet Home Chapter of Communities for a Greater Oregon*,[58] in which the Court construed a provision of the Endangered Species Act of 1973 ("ESA") making it unlawful to "*take* any endangered species within the United States or the territorial seas of the United States." At issue was whether a "taking" occurs when a defendant *indirectly* harms an endangered species by modifying its habitat. The Court deferred to the Secretary of the Interior's interpretation that habitat modification fell within the Act's reach, noting that the ESA broadly defined "take" to mean "harass, harm, pursue, hunt, shoot, wound, kill, trap, capture, or collect" — at least some of which surely encompass the indirect effects of habitat modification.

In dissent, Justice Scalia argued that "take" is "a term of art" in wildlife law and, as such, "describes a class of acts (not omissions) done directly and intentionally (not indirectly and by accident) to particular animals (not populations of animals)." Although acknowledging that the Act's definition section broadly defined "take," the dissent emphasized that nothing in the definition precluded the Court from reading the enumerated list of prohibited acts in light of the common law tradition

---

53. Professor Nelson provocatively suggests that if textualists merely read texts according to prevailing social and linguistic conventions, then they should in fact be purposivists, since purposivism had long represented the prevailing mode of statutory interpretation when textualism came onto the scene. See Caleb Nelson, A Response to Professor Manning, 91 Va. L. Rev. 451, 455-57 (2005). This contention, I believe, ultimately proves too much. As I have argued in detail in previous writing, modern textualism ultimately rests on several normative premises derived from the constitutional structure. Prominent among these structural norms is this: By adopting an effective supermajority requirement, the legislative process of bicameralism and presentment affords political minorities extraordinary authority to block legislation or to insist upon compromise as the price of assent. At least in the strong form that federal judges practiced prior to the advent of modern textualism, purposivism threatened the integrity of any resulting legislative compromise by enforcing the spirit over the letter of the law — that is, the statute's apparent background purpose rather than the precise details bargained for in the adopted text. If one accepts that analytical framework, textualists appropriately rejected purposivism on normative grounds, even if purposivism did constitute a previously established mode of interpretation. To suggest otherwise would be to say that textualists must treat as part of every specific compromise a convention that directs courts to ignore the precise terms of that compromise whenever there is good reason to do so. Only facetiously could one say that embracing such a convention satisfies the modern textualists' perceived constitutional duty to protect the specific compromises forged in the legislative process of bicameralism and presentment.
58. 515 U.S. 687 (1995).

equating a "taking" with direct rather than indirect acts.[62] Of interest here, he identified that tradition not only by locating the technical meaning of "take" in standard dictionaries, but also by examining sources as unobvious (to the ordinary reader) as a nineteenth-century Supreme Court decision, Blackstone's *Commentaries*, a statute implementing a migratory bird treaty, and a treaty governing polar bear conservation. His opinion appears to capture the technical meaning quite admirably, but it also highlights the fact that when textualists *impute* to legislators the understanding of a reasonable member of the relevant linguistic community (here, lawyers or wildlife aficionados), they do not purport to describe what legislators actually knew when they voted for a bill. In the unlikely event that any meaningful proportion of legislators had any actual intent about what "take" means, I doubt that many in fact knew of nor assented to the specialized legal meaning reflected in the sources cited by Justice Scalia.

So while textualists do care about "legislative intent" in the refined sense described by Professor Raz, to suggest that they are classical intentionalists by other means obscures the fact that textualists reject perhaps the most important premise of classical intentionalism: the idea that behind most legislation lies some sort of policy judgment that is meaningfully identifiable, shared by a legislative majority, and yet imprecisely expressed in the public meaning of the text that has made its way through Congress's many filters. Textualists focus on the *end product of the legislative process*, as reflected in the way a reasonable person conversant with applicable conventions would read the enacted words in context. Because of the fractured, tortuous, and often concealed nature of legislative bargaining, textualists believe that such a construct is the best that interpreters can do — that objectified intent provides the most, if not the only, plausible way for a faithful agent to show fidelity to his principal. In the end, this conviction maps importantly onto distinctions between rules and standards, but not in precisely the way Professor Nelson suggests. Because the modern textualists' approach to levels of statutory generality sharpens the distinct process assumptions that inform their approach, I turn now to a brief consideration of that question.

II. LEGISLATIVE BARGAINS AND LEVELS OF STATUTORY GENERALITY

A central precept of textualism is that interpreters must respect the level of generality at which the text expresses legislative policy judgments — that is, that judges should treat rules as rules and standards as standards. Specifically, although textualists find it appropriate in cases of ambiguity to consult a statute's apparent purpose or policy

---

62. Justice Scalia thus explained:

> The Act's definition of "take" does expand the word slightly (and not unusually), so as to make clear that it includes not just a completed taking, but the process of taking, and all of the acts that are customarily identified with or accompany that process ("to harass, harm, pursue, hunt, shoot, wound, kill, trap, capture, or collect"); and so as to include attempts.

(provided that it is derived from sources other than legislative history), they resist altering a statute's clear semantic import in order to make the text more congruent with its apparent background purpose. The underlying problem of fit reflected in such a choice of course has always troubled the law of statutory interpretation. No matter how precisely framed, laws will sometimes be over- or under-inclusive in relation to their apparent background aims. When a sufficiently dramatic mismatch between means and ends occurs (or, more accurately, appears to occur), classical intentionalists ascribe that divergence to legislative inadvertence. Classical intentionalists think it possible for judges to identify the collective policy judgment that the legislative majority *would have* arrived at had it framed the statute to avoid imprecision in the chosen words. Hence, they are willing to adjust the level of generality at which legislation speaks in order to make the textual expression of policy more congruent with what the majority would have wanted had it confronted the precise issue. Textualists, in contrast, chalk up statutory awkwardness to the (unknowable) exigencies of the legislative process with many and diverse veto points. They believe that smoothing over the rough edges in a statute threatens to upset whatever complicated bargaining led to its being cast in the terms that it was. Hence, for textualists, respecting the level of generality preserves the carefully designed process in which varied gatekeepers may block or slow legislation or exact a compromise as the price of assent.

West Virginia University Hospitals v. Casey[71] supplies perhaps the clearest example of this line of demarcation. Under 42 U.S.C. § 1988 (2000), prevailing plaintiffs in certain types of civil rights actions are entitled to recover "a reasonable attorney's fee." In *Casey*, the prevailing plaintiff sought to recover as part of its fees the fees of experts who were engaged to assist in preparing the lawsuit and to testify at trial. Under modern textualism, of course, one could not say that the matter begins and ends with the conclusion that an "expert fee" is literally not an "attorney's fee." At least one would need to consider whether the phrase "attorney's fee" is a term of the trade that includes more than a lawyer's billable hours. As used in the legal profession, that term might in fact encompass many items essential to a representation — such as paralegal services, secretarial services, messengers, photocopying, Westlaw charges, and so forth. Hence, the operative phrase has an underlying ambiguity that must be resolved by considering the phrase in context.

Justice Scalia's opinion for the Court in *Casey* found the semantic context decisive, crediting evidence of the way a reasonable person would have *used* the relevant language in context. His opinion emphasized the fact that countless other fee-shifting statutes — some enacted before and some after § 1988 — had explicitly provided for "attorney's fees" and "expert fees" as separate items of recovery. Under the maxim *expressio unius est exclusio alterius*, "it is generally presumed that Congress acts intentionally and purposely in the disparate inclusion or exclusion" of particular statutory language. Accordingly, the Court held that the relevant "statutory *usage* shows beyond question that attorney's fees and expert fees are distinct items of expense." Although acknowledging that the resulting emphasis on usage

---

71. 499 U.S. 83 (1991).

made the *policy* of § 1988 incongruent with that of similar fee-shifting statutes, the Court explained that interpreting a statute to promote policy coherence was a permissible judicial function where "a statutory term is ambiguous." Where consideration of the semantic context points clearly to a particular meaning, the Court stressed that "it is not our function to eliminate clearly expressed inconsistency of policy and to treat alike subjects that different Congresses have chosen to treat differently." In short, in ascribing meaning to the term "attorney's fee," Justice Scalia favored establishing congressional usage over arguments from congressional policy in determining which elements of statutory context to treat as determinative.

For the classical intentionalist, however, a clear pattern of usage would not end the matter; it would still remain necessary to measure the phrase "attorney's fee" against the policy impulses that apparently underlay the majority's enactment of the specific legislation. In his dissenting opinion in *Casey*, Justice Stevens thus criticized the Court for "putting on its thick grammarian's spectacles and ignoring the available evidence of congressional purpose and the teaching of prior cases." In particular, he reasoned that if a prevailing plaintiff could recover a reasonable "attorney's fee," it made no sense to deny the plaintiff similar recovery for an expert, whose services merely provided a lower cost substitute for attorney time. Moreover, because the Court had previously recognized that a prevailing plaintiff could recover paralegal fees and other costs of representation under § 1988, it would surely appear arbitrary not to allow the recovery of expert fees needed to make the legal representation effective. In addition, no one disputed that Congress enacted § 1988 to overturn the Court's decision in *Alyeska Pipeline Service Co. v. Wilderness Society*, which had rejected the federal courts' common law practice of shifting litigation costs in certain federal cases. Because the pre-*Alyeska* regime had shifted attorney's fees and expert fees, Justice Stevens thought it fair to infer that § 1988's purpose was to restore the status quo ante. Finally, although the dissent did not mention the point, because Congress had provided for the recovery of expert fees in virtually every other important fee-shifting statute, one might think it arbitrary to read into § 1988 an unexplained departure from an otherwise clear pattern of congressional policy preferences.

Simply put, textualists believe that the impulse to make the semantic details of a statute more coherent with its apparent animating policy — the impulse that underlies classic intentionalism — poses too great a risk to whatever legislative bargain or bargains were needed to ensure enactment.[84] Put differently, they believe that

---

84. Although somewhat tangential to the present comparison of modern textualism and classical intentionalism, it is worth noting that the textualists' preference for a statute's letter over its spirit does not hinge on the distinction between objective and subjective intent. Rather, the legislative process concerns that inform textualism cut more deeply. In this regard, it is helpful to contrast textualism with another post-realist response to classical intentionalism — the Legal Process school founded by Henry Hart and Albert Sacks at Harvard Law School. Much like modern textualists, Hart and Sacks subscribed to the faithful agent theory while simultaneously rejecting the idea that "the court's function is to ascertain the intention of the legislature with respect to the matter at issue." Also like modern textualists, Hart and Sacks proposed an objective rather than subjective standard for reading the work product of the legislature.

the reasonable reader standard supplies the best, and indeed the only meaningful, way to take seriously a legislative process that has many twists and turns; that gives the most intensely interested or even outlying legislative actors many opportunities to stop, slow, or reshape initiatives that have apparent majority support; and that emphasizes the legislative majority's need to compromise as a way to secure a bill's passage. The results of such a process are likely to look awkward for reasons that have nothing to do with failures of human foresight or lapses in drafting skill. Accordingly, for textualists, any attempt to overlay coherence on a statutory text that otherwise seems to have problems of fit unacceptably threatens to undermine the bargaining process that produced it.

Notes and Questions

1. Can you summarize the major differences between intentionalism and textualism, at least according to Professor Manning? What are those differences?

2. In *Lawson v. FMR LLC*, 134 S. Ct. 1158 (2014), Justice Scalia recently opined:

> I agree with the Court's conclusion that 18 U. S. C. § 1514A protects employees of private contractors from retaliation when they report covered forms of fraud. As the Court carefully demonstrates, that conclusion logically flows from §1514A's text and broader context. I therefore join the Court's opinion in principal part.
>
> I do not endorse, however, the Court's occasional excursions beyond the interpretative terra firma of text and context, into the swamps of legislative history. Reliance on legislative history rests upon several frail premises. First, and most important: That the statute means what Congress intended. It does not. Because we are a government of laws, not of men, and are governed by what Congress enacted rather than by what it intended, the sole object of the interpretative enterprise is to determine what a law *says*. Second: That there *was* a congressional "intent" apart from that reflected in the enacted text. On most issues of detail that come before this Court, I am confident that the majority of Senators and Representatives had no views whatever on how the issues should be resolved — indeed, were unaware of the issues entirely. Third: That the views expressed in a committee report or a floor statement represent those of all the Members of that House. Many of them almost certainly did not read the report or hear the statement, much less agree with it — not to mention the Members of the other House and the President who signed the bill.

Id. at 1176-77 (Scalia, J., concurring in principal part and concurring in the judgment). Do you agree? Agree in part? Did not those who approved of this law intend *something* of substance? If so, might it be worthwhile trying to determine what that intent might have been? Or does the problem lie more in the likely futility of any such endeavor?

3. For a more modern defense of intentionalism, see Michael Sinclair, A Guide to Statutory Interpretation 89-102 (2000).

2. Purposivism vs. Textualism

John F. Manning

WHAT DIVIDES TEXTUALISTS FROM PURPOSIVISTS?

106 Colum. L. Rev. 70 (2006)

INTRODUCTION

For a not inconsiderable part of our history, the Supreme Court held that the "letter" (text) of a statute must yield to its "spirit" (purpose) when the two conflicted.[1] Traditionally, the Court's "purposivism" rested on the following intuitions: In our constitutional system, federal courts act as faithful agents of Congress; accordingly, they must ascertain and enforce Congress's commands as accurately as possible. Statutes are active instruments of policy, enacted to serve some background purpose or goal. Ordinarily, a statutory text will adequately reflect its intended purpose. Sometimes, however, the text of a particular provision will seem incongruous with the statutory purpose reflected in various *contextual* cues — such as the overall tenor of the statute, patterns of policy judgments made in related legislation, the "evil" that inspired Congress to act, or express statements found in the legislative history. Since legislators act under the constraints of limited resources, bounded foresight, and inexact human language, unanticipated problems of fit have long been viewed as unavoidable. It is said that just as individuals sometimes inadvertently misstate their intended meaning, so too does Congress. Accordingly, the Court long assumed that when the clear import of a statute's text deviated sharply from its purpose, (1) Congress must have expressed its true intentions imprecisely, and (2) a judicial faithful agent could properly adjust the enacted text to capture what Congress would have intended had it expressly confronted the apparent mismatch between text and purpose.

Near the close of the twentieth century, however, the "new textualism" challenged the prevailing judicial orthodoxy by arguing that the Constitution, properly understood, requires judges to treat the clear import of an enacted text as conclusive, even when the text fits poorly with its apparent background purposes. The textualist critique — which took shape largely in judicial opinions written by Justice Scalia and Judge Easterbrook — initially stressed two related themes: First, textualists emphasized that the statutory text alone has survived the constitutionally

---

1. See, e.g., Church of the Holy Trinity v. United States, 143 U.S. 457, 459 (1892).

prescribed process of bicameralism and presentment. Accordingly, they argued that when a statute is clear in context, purposivist judges disrespect the legislative process by relying upon unenacted legislative intentions or purposes to alter the meaning of a duly enacted text.

Second, building upon the intent skepticism of the legal realists, the new textualists contended that the purposivist judge's aspiration to identify and rely upon the *actual* intent of any multimember lawmaking body is fanciful. In brief, textualists have contended that the final wording of a statute may reflect an otherwise unrecorded legislative compromise, one that may — or may not — capture a coherent set of purposes. A statute's precise phrasing depends, moreover, on often untraceable procedural considerations, such as the sequence of alternatives presented (agenda manipulation) or the effect of strategic voting (including logrolling). Given the opacity, complexity, and path dependency of this process, textualists believe that it is unrealistic for judges ever to predict with accuracy what Congress would have "intended" if it had expressly confronted a perceived mismatch between the statutory text and its apparent purpose. In place of traditional conceptions of "actual" legislative intent, modern textualists urge judges to focus on what they consider the more realistic — and objective — measure of how "a skilled, objectively-reasonable user of words" would have understood the statutory text in context.

Despite the significant differences thus championed by textualists, recent scholarship has sought to minimize the division between textualism and the (related) approaches that it has sought to displace: intentionalism and purposivism. Proceeding along that line, Professor Molot's thoughtful and reflective Article in this Issue argues that the line separating textualists and purposivists has grown fainter over time.[17] Modern textualists, he states, are sensitive to context as well as text. He also suggests that modern purposivists, with whom his allegiance more closely lies, feel the pinch of the statutory text more sharply than purposivists of the past. Based on these trends, he argues that we should conclude that text and purpose are both always relevant and that interpreters should proceed by calibrating how strong the respective textual and purposive cues appear in any particular interpretive case. In effect, Professor Molot proposes an approach more holistic than that of modern textualism — one that recalls Chief Justice Marshall's admonition that "where the mind labours to discover the design of the legislature, it seizes every thing from which aid can be derived."

Writing from a textualist perspective, I argue here that textualism and purposivism do in fact share more conceptual common ground than textualists (myself included) have sometimes emphasized. Nonetheless, salient differences remain in the two methods' philosophies and approaches that trace back to quite distinctive conceptions of the legislative process. In Part I, I survey the common ground. First, because modern textualists understand that the meaning of statutory language (like all language) depends wholly on context, their asserted distinction between enacted text and unenacted intentions or purposes is somewhat imprecise. In any case posing a meaningful interpretive question, the very process of ascertaining

---

17. Jonathan T. Molot, The Rise and Fall of Textualism, 106 Colum. L. Rev. 1 (2006).

textual meaning inescapably entails resorting to extrastatutory—and thus unen-acted—contextual cues. Indeed, when modern textualists find a statutory text to be ambiguous, they believe that statutory purpose—if derived from sources other than the legislative history—is itself a relevant ingredient of statutory context. Second, although textualists criticize purposivism as involving a fruitless search for subjective legislative intent, that characterization may reflect the fact that textual-ism originated in reaction to the Court's traditional (and perhaps anachronistic) understanding of purposivism. As Hart and Sacks took pains to demonstrate in their influential Legal Process materials, one can also plausibly cast purposivism as an objective framework that aspires to reconstruct the policy that a hypothetical "reasonable legislator" would have adopted in the context of the legislation, and not the search for a specific policy that Congress *actually* intended to adopt.

In Part II, I isolate what continues to distinguish textualism from purposivism and then offer a refinement of the legislative process justification for textualism. In particular, I first suggest that textualists and purposivists emphasize different ele-ments of context. Textualists give precedence to *semantic context*—evidence that goes to the way a reasonable person would use language under the circumstances. Purposivists give priority to *policy context*—evidence that suggests the way a rea-sonable person would address the mischief being remedied. To be sure, practitio-ners of each methodology will consider both forms of contextual evidence in cases of ambiguity. But textualists give determinative weight to clear semantic cues even then they conflict with evidence from the policy context. Purposivists allow suf-ficiently pressing policy cues to overcome such semantic evidence.

Part II next considers competing normative justifications for the two approaches, and ultimately offers a defense of the textualists' primary reliance on semantic context. I acknowledge that purposivist theory rests on the serious intu-ition that legislators enact statutes to achieve policy aims, and that legislators sim-ply do not focus on the semantic fine points of (what is often complex and lengthy) legislation. For purposivists, therefore, subordinating a statute's semantic detail to its background purpose respects legislative supremacy while also promoting the normatively attractive goals of policy coherence and adaptability.

Despite the obvious appeal of the foregoing attributes, I suggest that modern textualism offers a convincing rejoinder: Certainly, focusing on the way a reason-able user of language employs words reflects a meaningful theory of legislative supremacy; even if legislators do not collectively form any specific subjective inten-tion about the way they would apply a statute to any given fact situation, a court can at least ascribe to them the plausible intention to adopt what a reasonable person conversant with applicable social conventions would have understood them to be adopting. From this starting point, textualists contend that semantic detail offers a singularly effective medium for legislators to set the level of generality at which policy will be articulated—and thus to specify the limits of often messy legislative compromises. Because the lawmaking procedures prescribed by Article I, Section 7 of the Constitution and the congressionally prescribed rules of legislative proce-dure unmistakably afford political minorities extraordinary power to block legisla-tion or insist upon compromise as the price of assent, textualists believe that adjust-ing a statute's semantic detail unacceptably risks diluting that crucial procedural right. If judges transform awkward but precise semantic formulations into reasonably coherent policy outcomes, then the legislators who occupy Congress's many and diverse veto gates cannot rely upon statutory wording as a predictable means for setting the desirable limits on bills that they are willing to let through only upon acceptance of bargained-for conditions.

. . . .

I. TEXTUALISM AND LEGAL PROCESS PURPOSIVISM: COMMON GROUND

The distinction between textualism and purposivism is not, as is often assumed, cut-and-dried. Properly understood, textualism is not and could not be defined either by a strict preference for enacted text over unenacted context, or by a wholesale rejection of the utility of purpose. Because the meaning of language depends on the way a linguistic community uses words and phrases in context, textualists recognize that meaning can never be found exclusively within the enacted text. This feature of textualism, moreover, goes well beyond the often subconscious process of reading words in context in order to pinpoint the "ordinary" meaning of a word that may mean several things in common parlance. Rather, because legal communication often entails the use of specialized conventions, textualists routinely consult unenacted sources of context whose contents might be obscure to the ordinary reader without further inquiry. Moreover, because textualists understand that speakers use language purposively, they recognize that evidence of purpose (if derived from sources other than the legislative history) may also form an appropriate ingredient of the context used to define the text.

Conversely, certain features of purposivism reflect textualist practices and assumptions more deeply than textualists sometimes acknowledge. Although Professor Molot properly notes that this trend has perhaps become more pronounced in the judicial opinions of avowedly purposivist judges in recent years, many important conceptual similarities were already present in the (now canonical) mid-twentieth-century account of purposivism developed in the Legal Process materials of Professors Hart and Sacks. Although Legal Process purposivists believe that interpretation entails the attribution of purpose, they do not deny that semantic meaning of the text casts light — perhaps the most important light — on the purposes to be attributed. Nor do they deny that, in such a pursuit, the judge should carefully consult the technical conventions that distinctively pertain to legalese. Perhaps most important, much like modern textualists, Hart-and-Sacks-style purposivists recognize that a judge's task, properly conceived, is not to seek actual legislative intent; rather, their method of interpretation poses the objective question of how a hypothetical "reasonable legislator" (as opposed to a real one) would have resolved the problem addressed by the statute.

In considering the similarities discussed in this Part, the reader should keep in mind that, in contrast with Professor Molot, I believe that significant practical and theoretical differences continue to separate textualism from purposivism, however enlightened the two philosophies have become in relation to each other.

Accordingly, the objective here is to highlight the key similarities between the two in a way that will help to define more sharply (in Part II) the differences that remain.

A. Textualism and Extrastatutory Context (Including Purpose)

In contrast with their ancestors in the "plain meaning" school of the late nineteenth and early twentieth centuries, modern textualists do not believe that it is possible to infer meaning from "within the four corners" of a statute.[28] Rather, they assert that language is intelligible only by virtue of a community's shared conventions for understanding the words in context.[29] While rejecting the idea of subjective legislative intent, they contend that the effective communication of legislative commands is in fact possible because one can attribute to legislators the minimum intention "to say what one would be normally understood as saying, given the circumstances to which one said it." Textualists thus look for what they call "'objectified' intent — the intent that a reasonable person would gather from the text of the law, placed alongside the remainder of the corpus juris." Because one can make sense of others' communications only by placing them in their appropriate social and linguistic context, textualists further acknowledge that "in textual interpretation, context is everything."

The resulting recognition of the importance of context makes it more difficult for textualists to distinguish themselves from purposivists on the straightforward ground that textualism relies exclusively on the *enacted text* when that text is clear. To highlight this point, it is helpful to consider different ways in which context may be brought to bear. Because context of course is essential even to determine the way words are used in everyday parlance,[34] textualists (like everyone else) necessarily resort to context even in cases in which the meaning of the text appears intuitively obvious. In such cases, contextual understandings may be so routinely accepted that their application occurs at a subconscious level that may feel "automatic." For instance, even though social and linguistic context is essential to the conclusion that a "no dogs in the park" ordinance would not ordinarily apply to a domesticated pet pig, it is forgivably intuitive (if technically inaccurate) to state that applying that ordinance to a pig sacrifices the plain meaning of the enacted text. Barring the presence of some idiosyncratic term of art (a matter to be addressed shortly),

---

28. White v. United States, 191 U.S. 545, 551 (1903). Often, the formalist decisions of the late nineteenth and early twentieth centuries spoke as if the determination that a statute had a "plain meaning" foreclosed any necessity to consider context. See, e.g., Caminetti v. United States, 242 U.S. 470, 485 (1917) ("Where the language is plain and admits of no more than one meaning the duty of interpretation does not arise.").

29. Modern textualism thus resonates with [Ludwig] Wittgenstein's [philosophical] insights about language.

34. At a minimum, because commonly used words frequently have multiple meanings depending on the context of their use, interpreters must consult context to ascertain the relevant meaning. If someone declares, "I took the boat out on the bay," the word "bay" obviously refers to a body of water; but if the same person states, "I put the saddle on the bay," it is equally obvious that he or she means a horse.

nearly all users of English, including legislators, would reflexibly understand that the social meaning of "dog," however elastic, does not reach that far.

As I have discussed in detail in earlier writings, however, modern textualism necessarily — and quite properly — draws upon contextual cues far less obvious to the ordinary user of language. Because textualists want to know the way a reasonable user of language would understand a statutory phrase in the circumstances in which it is used, they must always ascertain the unstated "assumptions shared by the speakers and the intended audience." In particular, when operating within the realm of legal parlance (a relevant linguistic subcommunity), textualism's premise requires that interpreters consider specialized conventions and linguistic practices peculiar to the law.[40] A given statutory phrase may reflect the often elaborate (but textually unspecified) connotations of a technical term of art. Or by dint of some settled common law practice, unstated exceptions or qualifications may form part of the background against which lawyers understand the workings of a given category of statute.[42] Textualists also rely on off-the-rack canons of construction peculiar to the legal community, including some substantive (policy-oriented) canons that have come to be accepted as background assumptions by virtue of longstanding prescription. Such interpretive techniques inevitably require judges to go well beyond the four corners of the text to determine the often abstruse details of technical meaning.

Consider, for example, how far outside the text modern textualists may sometimes have to travel to decipher an obscure legal term of art. Thus, in *Moskal v. United States*,[45] the Court construed a statute that made it a crime to transport in interstate commerce "any falsely made, forged, altered, or counterfeited securities." At issue was whether an automobile title (concededly a "security") was "falsely made" because someone had filled in a fraudulent odometer reading. Invoking its understanding of "ordinary meaning," the Court held that such titles were " 'falsely made' in the sense that they were made to contain false, or incorrect, information." In a carefully researched dissent, Justice Scalia concluded that the term "falsely made" was a term of art that referred only to forgeries, not to authentic documents

---

40. Even within the realm of ordinary meaning, textualists must be sensitive to the fact that words sometimes have colloquial meanings that are widely understood but too obscure to have made their way into standard dictionaries. Context is essential to understanding such nuance. Consider the following examples. First, although an airplane may technically satisfy the dictionary definition of "vehicle," no English speaker would refer to a motorized airplane as a "motor vehicle." In common parlance, the latter term has come to mean a car, truck, or perhaps a motorcycle. Thus, in McBoyle v. United States, 283 U.S. 25, 26 (1931), the Court refused to apply the National Motor Vehicle Theft Act to the theft of an airplane. Writing for the Court, Justice Holmes started by observing that "no doubt etymologically it is possible to use the word 'vehicle' to signify a conveyance working on land, water or air." "But," he added, "in everyday speech 'vehicle' calls up the picture of a thing moving on land." Second, although water literally falls within the "mineral" kingdom (it is not an animal or vegetable), few would use the term "mineral rights" to describe the right to exploit water reserves, as opposed to coal, oil, gas, and shale. See Andrus v. Charleston Stone Prods. Co., 436 U.S. 604, 610-11 (1978).

42. So, for example, textualists read otherwise unqualified statutes of limitations in light of the settled judicial practice of equitable tolling. They also read criminal statutes in light of customary but textually unspecified state-of-mind requirements and defenses.

45. 498 U.S. 103 (1990).

containing false information. In doing so, he culled that unobvious meaning from (a) Blackstone's *Commentaries*; (b) numerous state forgery statutes that had used "falsely made" as a synonym for forgery; (c) the decisions of several federal courts (including dicta from the Supreme Court) and eight state courts; and (d) the "apparently unanimous" understanding of all the major criminal law treatises published prior to the relevant federal enactment. However convincingly this evidence demonstrates the background understanding of a term of legal art, the important point is that Justice Scalia's avowedly textualist analysis invoked authoritative evidence from outside the enacted text.

Decisions such as *Moskal* underscore the fact that the statutory meaning derived by textualists is a construct. Textualists do not (and, given their assumptions about actual legislative intent, could not) claim that a constitutionally sufficient majority of legislators *actually* subscribed to the meaning that a textualist judge would ascribe to a hypothetical reasonable legislator conversant with the applicable social and linguistic conventions. Even if Justice Scalia's dissent in *Moskal* accurately captures the technical meaning of "falsely made" (as I believe it does), his reasoning highlights the fact that textualists necessarily *impute* meaning to a statute. Even if a meaningful proportion of legislators formed an actual intent about the meaning of "falsely made," one cannot know whether a majority subscribed to (or even knew of) the specialized legal meaning found in the external sources cited by the dissent. This uncertainty does not, however, make the dissent's approach illegitimate; it merely underscores the fact Justice Scalia's "reasonable" legislator purports to capture the understanding of an idealized, rather than an actual, legislator.

There is an additional wrinkle: Because speakers use language purposively, textualists recognize that the relevant context for a statutory text includes the mischiefs the authors were addressing. Thus, when a statute is ambiguous,[50] textualists think it quite appropriate to resolve that ambiguity in light of the statute's apparent overall purpose. To be sure, textualists generally forgo reliance on legislative history as an authoritative source of such purpose, but that reaction goes to the reliability and legitimacy of a certain type of evidence of purpose rather than to the use of purpose as such.[52] In fact, in cases of ambiguity, textualists are sometimes willing to

---

50. As used here, the concept of ambiguity refers to circumstances in which the usage indicated by the semantic context does not speak decisively, but rather leaves more than one reasonable alternative understanding on the table.

52. In previous writing, I have argued that the textualists' rejection of legislative history is best explained by reference to the constitutional norm against legislative self-delegation. The constitutionally ordained legislative process of bicameralism and presentment is designed to check factional influence, promote caution and deliberation, and provoke public discussion. To prevent the circumvention of that process, the Court has consistently forbidden Congress to reserve delegated authority for its own components, agents, or members. In recent years, some textualists have justified their reluctance to credit internal legislative history on the ground that it effectively transfers authority from the body as a whole to the committees or sponsors who, under established judicial practice, are capable of producing particularly "authoritative" expressions of legislative intent. Whatever the proper rationale (if any) for the textualists' rejection of legislative history, the important point for present purposes is this: Rejecting legislative history merely eliminates one potential basis for inferring purpose. It does not require a categorical rejection of purpose as an organizing principle in statutory interpretation.

make rough estimates of purpose from sources such as the overall tenor or structure of the statute, its title, or public knowledge of the problems that inspired its enactment. This practice is significant for two reasons. First, it shows that modern textualists consider purpose to be part of the relevant interpretive landscape. Second, it reveals their concomitant belief that interpreters can (at least sometimes) draw a suitably objective inference of purpose — presumably one that a "reasonable user of words" would arrive at after reading the entire text in context. Accordingly, when semantic ambiguity creates the necessary leeway, textualists will try to construct a plausible hypothetical purpose (if possible) not because they believe that it "is what the lawmakers must have had in mind, but because it is the judiciary's role to make sense rather than nonsense out of the *corpus juris*."

B. Legal Process Purposivism and the Enacted Text

Contrary to popular perception, prevailing methods of purposivism rely on many of the methods that textualists hold dear. In determining what purpose to attribute to a statute, purposivists pay close attention to text, structure, sources of technical or specialized meaning, and maxims of construction (both semantic and substantive). In addition, the most influential version of purposivism also purports to filter those sources through an objective construct that does not seek actual legislative intent, but rather invokes an idealized, hypothetical legislator as the benchmark for understanding what legislation means. A brief consideration of these similarities will further illuminate the remaining differences (examined in Part II).

Although Professor Molot (quite perceptively, I believe) finds potent evidence of an increasingly text-based approach in the opinions of contemporary purposivists on the Supreme Court, I take as my main point of departure the work of Professors Hart and Sacks, whose celebrated Legal Process materials developed a highly influential rationalist approach to legal analysis in general and statutory interpretation in particular. I do so for several reasons. First, for many, their materials have come to represent the canonical statement of purposivism. Second, their work offers a rich account of the conceptual basis for purposivism. Third, they provide a particularly apt point of comparison with textualism because their purposivism eschews any inquiry into subjective legislative intent and instead proposes an objective criterion for reading legislative commands. Accordingly, while occasionally buttressing my analysis with judicial opinions (old and new), I use the Legal Process materials as an approximate proxy for the now generally dominant version of purposivism.[60]

While purposivism is characterized by the conviction that judges should interpret a statute in a way that carries out its reasonably apparent purpose and fulfills its background justification, purposivists start — and most of the time end — their inquiry with the semantic meaning of the text. For example, in the most important

---

60. In drawing examples from Supreme Court opinions, I rely on opinions written by Justices Stevens, Souter, and Breyer — the present Court's most enthusiastic proponents of the type of reasoning that underlies purposivism.

purposivist precedent of the twentieth century, *United States v. American Trucking Ass'ns*, the Court emphasized that "there is no more persuasive evidence of the purpose of a statute than the words by which the legislature undertook to give expression to its wishes," and that deciphering the conventional meaning of statutory language is frequently (though not always) "sufficient to determine the purpose of the legislation."[61] Or as Hart and Sacks themselves have stressed, "the words of a statute, taken in their context, serve both as guides in the attribution of general purpose and as factors limiting the particular meanings that can properly be attributed." Of course, as discussed below, purposivists are far less willing than textualists to adhere to the conventional social meaning of a given statutory provision when contrary indications of purpose cut strongly against such meaning. But that does not alter the fact that the first impulse of even the strongest purposivist is to try to read the statute in light of the accepted semantic import of the text.

It is also significant that purposivists take seriously the obligation to examine the semantic context carefully to ascertain colloquial or technical nuances in the usage of statutory language; they do not treat the text as a mere place holder for concocting plausible inferences about purpose. They realize that "words of art bring their art with them," and that any good interpreter must seek the often "recondite connotations" of the technical terms that Congress sometimes borrows from the legal, scientific, business, or other subcommunities. Again, much like modern textualists, purposivists accept "the recurrent possibilities of reading general language as subject to assumed but unexpressed qualifications in terms of customary defenses or other limiting policies of law." As compared with textualists, purposivists tend to worry more about the potential indeterminacy of the traditional canons of construction — including the risk (made famous by Karl Llewellyn) that two or more conflicting canons may apply to the same interpretive question. Nonetheless, they rely on those canons to help determine "whether a particular meaning is linguistically permissible, if the context warrants it." In other words, even if purposivists define the task of interpretation as that of attributing a sensible purpose to the legislature, they take seriously the entire range of semantic cues in doing so.

Perhaps most importantly, purposivism has not always sought its justification in the Court's traditional premise that following the spirit rather than the letter of the law will more likely capture the *subjective* intent of the legislature. Although this is not the occasion for a comprehensive account of their work, it is significant that Hart and Sacks urged interpreters to consider a broad variety of sources, such as the statutory language and structure, well-settled background legal assumptions, accepted maxims of interpretation, any relevant canons of clear statement, and the political context surrounding the enactment (including "general public knowledge" of "the mischief" that inspired the legislation and any "legislative history" suggesting the "*general purpose*" of the statute). None of this material, however, was to be considered with an eye toward ascertaining the subjective "intention of the

---

61. 310 U.S. 534, 543 (1940). Hart and Sacks aptly describe *American Trucking* as the "landmark case in the overthrow of the plain meaning rule."

legislature with respect to the matter in issue." Rather, in considering all of these matters, the judge was to presume "that the legislature was made up of reasonable persons pursuing reasonable purposes reasonably." Interpreters were to derive a constructive rather than subjective purpose by asking how a *reasonable person* familiar with the operative text, the background rules of interpretation, and the full context of the legislation would have resolved the interpretive problem at hand. Accordingly, the theory of Legal Process purposivism, much like that of modern textualism, treats the attribution of meaning as a construct.

II. TEXTUALISM, PURPOSIVISM, AND LEGISLATIVE SUPREMACY

Despite the apparent similarities described above, significant practical and theoretical differences persist between textualists and purposivists. Why? Each side gives priority to different elements of statutory context. Textualists give primacy to the *semantic* context — evidence about the way a reasonable person conversant with relevant social and linguistic practices would have used the words. Purposivists give precedence to *policy* context — evidence that goes to the way a reasonable person conversant with the circumstances underlying enactment would suppress the mischief and advance the remedy. This difference accounts for the distinct questions that each methodology poses for the hypothetical interpreter. As noted, textualists ask how "a skilled, objectively reasonable user of words" would have understood the text, in the circumstances in which it was uttered. Legal Process purposivists ask how "reasonable persons pursuing reasonable purposes reasonably" would have resolved the policy issue addressed by the words.

Ultimately, the justifications for their disparate preferences are rooted in competing understandings of the legislative process as it relates to the constitutional ideal of legislative supremacy. Purposivists in the Legal Process tradition think it unrealistic and arbitrary to suppose that Congress collectively knows or cares about the semantic detail of often complex statutes. For them, enforcing the overarching policy of a statute rather than the minutiae of its semantic detail better serves legislative supremacy while also promoting the independently valuable aims of policy coherence and adaptability of the law to unforeseen circumstances.

Textualists (again, myself included) believe that the purposivist approach disregards the central place of legislative compromise embedded in both the constitutional structure and the corresponding congressional rules of legislative procedure. Textualists contend that once one gives up the idea of ascertaining subjective legislative intent, as Legal Process purposivists do, legislative supremacy is most meaningfully served by attributing to legislators the understanding that a reasonable person conversant with applicable conventions would attach to the enacted text in context. From that starting point, textualists argue that purposivism cannot deal adequately with legislative compromise because semantic detail, in the end, is the only effective means that legislators possess to specify the limits of an agreed-upon legislative bargain. When interpreters disregard clear contextual clues about semantic detail, it becomes surpassingly difficult for legislative actors to agree reliably upon terms that give half a loaf.

This Part considers first the descriptive claim that textualists and purposivists divide over what forms of context merit priority in cases where semantic and policy cues point in different directions. It next considers the legislative process justifications that underpin both approaches.

A. Semantic Versus Policy Context

Starting from the sort of prima facie ambiguity that troubles interpreters, each side of the debate emphasizes different aspects of the context that lies beyond the face of any statute. Textualists start with contextual evidence that goes to customary usage and habits of speech; they believe that a statute may have a clear semantic meaning, even if that meaning is not plain to the ordinary reader without further examination. They try "to assemble the various pieces of linguistic data, dictionary definitions, and canons into the best (most coherent, most explanatory) account of the meaning of the statute." This inquiry, as I have noted, also includes consideration of specialized trade usage, substantive canons of clear statement (including the rule of lenity), and colloquial nuances that may be widely understood but that are unrecorded in standard dictionaries. When textualists state that background purpose is beside the point when the text of a statute is clear in context, that is shorthand for a technically more accurate, but less intuitively worded, observation: When contextual evidence of semantic usage points decisively in one direction, that evidence takes priority over contextual evidence that relates to questions of policy. The latter category includes matters such as public knowledge of the mischief the lawmakers sought to address; the way competing interpretations of a discrete statutory provision fit with the policy reflected in the statute's preamble, title, or overall structure; and the way alternative readings of the statute fit with the policy expressed in similar statutes. For purposivists, of course, the converse is true: Even when clear contextual evidence of semantic usage exists, priority is accorded to (sufficiently powerful) contextual evidence of the policy considerations that apparently justified the statute.

West Virginia University Hospitals, Inc. v. Casey boldly illustrates this line of division. . . .

. . . .

In short, textualists give precedence to contextual evidence concerning likely semantic usage while purposivists do the same with contextual cues that reflect policy considerations. Although it may be a mere matter of characterization rather than substance, reframing the textualists' position in this way casts textualists' burden of explanation differently. In cases such as *Casey*, they cannot simply rely on the straightforward notion that they prefer the clear terms of the duly enacted text, for that description begs the question of how best to attribute meaning to a text with a prima facie ambiguity. Instead, starting from the longstanding constitutional premise that federal judges must act as faithful agents of Congress, textualists must show why semantic rather than policy context constitutes a superior means of fulfilling the faithful agent's duty to respect legislative supremacy. It is to that question that I now turn.

B. Coherence, Compromise, and Legislative Supremacy

Both textualists and purposivists acknowledge that their approaches attribute meaning to a statute based on what purport to be objective criteria for ascertaining legislative instructions. Neither side seeks to justify its interpretive results as the reflection of some subjective congressional understanding. For textualists, the metric is the understanding of a hypothetical reasonable person conversant with applicable social and linguistic conventions. For purposivists in the Hart and Sacks tradition, the metric is the understanding of a hypothetical reasonable policymaker conversant with all of the circumstances surrounding the enactment. Even if the textualist approach more accurately reflects the semantic meaning of the enacted text, the question of which approach to prefer cannot be answered by reference to language theory. Since each approach rests on a construct that captures a plausible way to make sense of the instructions issued by the legislature, the choice between them must rest on political theory.

In particular, the choice will ultimately depend on which criterion more appropriately describes the duties of federal judges who, under the premises of our system of government, operate subject to the constraints of legislative supremacy (within constitutional boundaries). Purposivists argue that legislative supremacy is better served not by the judge who attends to every last clue about the social usage of the chosen words, but rather by someone who is sensitive to the policy concerns underlying the legislative choice — even when they contradict the apparent import of the text. Properly understood, textualism rests on the competing idea that the accepted semantic meaning of the enacted text represents a meaningful — indeed, superior — basis for implementing legislative supremacy. In particular, textualists believe that judicial adherence to semantic detail (when clear) is essential if one wishes legislators to be able to strike reliable bargains. In the end, I believe that the latter position is easier to square with important features of both constitutionally and congressionally prescribed rules of legislative procedure that demonstrably give political minorities the right to block legislation or to condition their assent upon compromise. To set the stage for that analysis, I first offer a sympathetic account of the legislative supremacy justification for purposivism.

1. Purposivists and Legislative Supremacy.

Purposivists have offered a highly thoughtful defense of the position that policy context assures greater fidelity to legislative supremacy in our constitutional system. Max Radin, a prominent legal realist who had a late-career conversion to purposivism, offered a particularly crisp defense of using policy rather than semantic context. Radin started from the premise that "the legislature that put the statute on the books had the constitutional right and power to set the statute's purpose as a desirable one for the community, and the court or administrator has the undoubted duty to obey it." Because the words in a statute have been selected "primarily to let us know the statutory purpose," they must be read with that function in mind:

> To say that the legislature is "presumed" to have selected its phraseology with meticulous care as to every word is in direct contradiction to known facts and injects an improper element into the relation of courts to the statutes. The legislature has no constitutional warrant to demand reverence for the words in which it frames its directives. If the purposes of the statute cannot be learned except by examining the precise words and by troubling our ingenuity to discover why this word was used rather than another of approximately similar effect, then this process of anxious cogitation must be employed. But it is rarely necessary.

In other words, in our constitutional system, courts have responsibility for seeing that a statute's apparent purposes are fulfilled. Their job is not simply to decode each semantic detail recorded in the enacted text. Rather, "if the purpose is clear, the implemental part of the statute should be subordinated to it."

Radin's premise that legislative supremacy does not lie in judicial adherence to semantic detail must be taken seriously. As discussed, the textualists' approach to constructing semantic meaning will sometimes produce results that cannot easily be ascribed to the actual understanding of the requisite legislative majority. To return to Justice Scalia's *Moskel* dissent, one cannot suppose that most (or even many) legislators bothered to ascertain that the statutory term in question ("falsely made") had a technical meaning ("forged") that could be discovered by excavating old state statutes, dusty criminal law treatises, and scattered federal and state case law. Nor can one assume that legislators peruse statutes (if at all) with a conscious awareness of technical grammatical rules such as the recently dispositive "'rule of the last antecedent,' according to which a limiting clause or phrase should ordinarily be read as modifying only the noun or phrase that it immediately follows." Nor can one maintain that all of the canons of construction readily invoked by textualists — such as the presumption against linguistic surplusage or the maxim disfavoring implied repeals — reflect legislators' actual knowledge of the contents of legislation.

Most textualists, of course, would have little difficulty accepting the foregoing conclusions, given their embrace of "objectified intent" and their concomitant rejection of the utility and relevance of subjective legislative intent. But by acknowledging the constructive nature of the meaning they attribute to statutes, textualists do leave themselves open to the basic question posed by Radin's analysis: Why should one presume that legislative supremacy entails pursuing semantic meaning to the far corners of hoary treatise, technical rule of grammar, or obscure canon of construction, rather than reading a statutory phrase in a way that will best serve the overall policy that the legislation evidently aimed to accomplish? Apart from the purposivists' guiding premise that legislators vote for policies rather than semantic details, their approach claims various normative benefits that stand independent of the legislative process justification. Reading a given phrase in light of the likely statutory purpose should make any given statute more internally coherent.

Focusing on policy rather than semantic context will also make any given statute more coherent with the policy aims of other statutes. And, of course, emphasizing the policy rather than the semantic context will also make any given statute more coherent with the policy aims of other statutes. And, of course, emphasizing the policy rather than the semantic context will enable judges and administrators to adapt a statute more readily to unforeseen circumstances over time. Quite plainly, therefore, textualists must provide affirmative reasons for their belief that giving priority to semantic rather than policy context better respects Congress's primacy in framing legislative policy.

2. *Semantic Import and Legislative Compromise.*

Properly understood, textualism rests upon three related premises. First, searching for semantic meaning represents a theoretically sound basis for attributing statutory outcomes to legislative choice, thereby satisfying the minimum requirement for legislative supremacy. Second, because the approach advanced by purposivists does not itself plausibly capture *actual* legislative preferences, purposivism has no superior claim to the attention of judges acting as faithful agents. Third, and most important, the legislative process prescribed by Article I, Section 7 of the Constitution and the rules of procedure prescribed by each House place an obvious emphasis on giving political minorities the power to block legislation or, of direct relevance here, to insist upon compromise as the price of assent. Giving precedence to semantic context (when clear) is necessary to enable legislators to set the level of generality at which they wish to express their policies. In turn, this ability alone permits them to strike compromises that go so far and no farther. Ultimately, then, the affirmative justification for textualism lies in the idea that semantic meaning is the currency of legislative compromise. . . .

. . . .

CONCLUSION

When modern textualism first emerged near the end of the past century, textualists tended to cast their approach as a challenge to the strong form of atextual, purposive interpretation that the Court had long practiced. Textualists argued that judges should read the words of a statute as a reasonable person familiar with applicable social and linguistic conventions would read them. Contrary to the tenets of purposivism, textualists further contended that when the text was clear in context, judges should not adjust it to make it more consistent with the apparent background purposes that could be gleaned from extrinsic circumstances. Textualists asserted that this approach was more faithful to the background constitutional notion of legislative supremacy because it favored the enacted text — the only thing that had cleared the constitutional process of bicameralism and presentment — over unenacted evidence of purpose. Moreover, whereas focusing on the text was said to represent an objective measure of statutory meaning, focusing on purpose unrealistically sought to discover the unknowable subjective intentions of a complex, path-dependent, and opaque multimember lawmaking body.

As the debate over interpretation has deepened, however, it has become increasingly clear that the straightforward account of what divides textualists from purposivists requires refinement. Textualists of course believe that language has meaning only in context. This recognition requires them routinely to consult extratextual sources. (Indeed, in cases of ambiguity, textualists are even willing to treat indicia of purpose as legitimate parts of the relevant context.) And the most sophisticated version of modern purposivism plausibly defends the search for purpose as the objective pursuit of how "reasonable persons pursuing reasonable purposes reasonably" would have resolved the issue before the court. Because these considerations are somewhat in tension with the traditional account of modern textualism, the standard justification for that approach is incomplete.

Properly understood, textualism means that in resolving ambiguity, interpreters should give precedence to semantic context (evidence about the way reasonable people use words) rather than policy context (evidence about the way reasonable people would solve problems). Purposivists claim that this approach is backwards. There is no reason, they assert, to believe that legislators vote on the basis of semantic minutiae. Rather, Congress passes laws for a reason, and the dictates of legislative supremacy obligate the interpreter to help the legislature realize the statute's overarching goals. Under that perfectly plausible conception of legislative supremacy, law is likely to be more coherent, better tailored to the problem at hand, and more adaptable to unforeseen circumstances.

In the end, I believe that textualism continues to represent a superior account of legislative supremacy, despite the need for a more nuanced form of justification. Surely, it is hard to deny that one plausible version of legislative supremacy ascribes to legislators an intention to adopt texts that will be interpreted according to the accepted social and linguistic conventions for reading language (in context). If so, then giving precedence to (clear) semantic detail fits more tightly with the framework of constitutional and congressional rules of procedure that lay heavy emphasis on the right to insist upon compromise. Article I, Section 7's requirements of bicameralism and presentment, and the congressional rules of procedure that flesh out that process, empower political minorities to block or slow legislation or, more important, to exact compromise as the price of their assent. By allowing legislators to set the level of generality at which they express their policies, semantic detail enables legislators with leverage in the process to express the limits that are necessary to secure their assent. Let me be clear: Not every turn of phrase is bargained for; many are surely the product of happenstance or insufficient foresight. But if legislators are to be able to record their compromises in a predictable and effective way, they must have the capacity to use words to do so. If the Court feels free to adjust the semantic meaning of statutes when the rules embedded in the text seem awkward in relation to the statute's apparent goals, then legislators cannot reliably use words to articulate the boundaries of the frequently awkward compromises that are necessary to secure a bill's enactment.

Notes and Questions

1. Can you summarize what Professor Manning sees as the major differences between purposivism and textualism? What are those differences?

2. For a more modern argument in favor of at least some consideration of purpose in statutory interpretation, see David M. Driesen, *Purposeless Construction*, 48 WAKE FOREST L. REV. 97 (2013). *See also* John F. Manning, *The New Purposivism*, 2011 S. CT. REV. 113.

3. For a more recent article that argues that textualism, among its other virtues, best promotes fair notice of the law, see Note, *Textualism as Fair Notice*, 123 HARV. L. REV. 542 (2009).

4. There are other theories or approaches to statutory interpretation besides intentionalism, purposivism, and textualism. *See, e.g.*, WILLIAM N. ESKRIDGE, JR., DYNAMIC STATUTORY INTERPRETATION (1994).

Hillel Y. Levin

THE FOOD STAYS IN THE KITCHEN: EVERYTHING I NEEDED TO KNOW ABOUT STATUTORY INTERPRETATION I LEARNED BY THE TIME I WAS NINE

12 Green Bag 2d 337 (2009)

On March 23, 1986, the following proclamation, henceforth known as Ordinance 7.3, was made by the Supreme Lawmaker, Mother:

> I am tired of finding popcorn kernels, pretzel crumbs, and pieces of cereal all over the family room. From now on, no food may be eaten outside the kitchen.

Thereupon, litigation arose.

FATHER, C.J., issued the following ruling on March 30, 1986:

Defendant Anne, age 14, was seen carrying a glass of water into the family room. She was charged with violating Ordinance 7.3 ("the Rule"). We hold that drinking water outside of the kitchen does not violate the Rule.

The Rule prohibits "food" from being eaten outside of the kitchen. This prohibition does not extend to water, which is a beverage rather than food. Our interpretation is confirmed by Webster's Dictionary, which defines food to mean, in relevant part, a "material consisting essentially of protein, carbohydrate, and fat used in the body of an organism to sustain growth, repair, and vital processes and to furnish energy" and "nutriment in solid form." Plainly, water, which contains no protein, carbohydrate, or fat, and which is not in solid form, is not a food.

Customary usage further substantiates our distinction between "food" and water. Ordinance 6.2, authored by the very same Supreme Lawmaker, declares: "after you get home from school, have some food and something to drink, and then do your homework." This demonstrates that the Supreme Lawmaker speaks of food and drink separately and is fully capable of identifying one or both as appropriate. After all, if "food," as used in the Family Code, included beverages, then the word "drink" in Ordinance 6.2 would be redundant and mere surplusage. Thus, had the Supreme Lawmaker wished to prohibit beverages from being taken out of the kitchen, she could have easily done so by declaring that "no food or drink is permitted outside the kitchen."

Our understanding of the word "food" to exclude water is further buttressed by the evident purpose of the Rule. The Supreme Lawmaker enacted the Rule as a response to the mess produced by solid foods. Water, even when spilled, does not produce a similar kind of mess.

Some may argue that the cup from which the Defendant was drinking water may, if left in the family room, itself be a mess. But we are not persuaded. The language of the Rule speaks to the Supreme Lawmaker's concern with small particles of food rather than to a more generalized concern with the containers in which food is held. A cup or other container bears a greater resemblance to other bric-a-brac, such as toys and backpacks, to which the Rule does not speak, than it does to the food spoken of in the Rule. Although we need not divine the Supreme Lawmaker's reasons for such a distinction, there are at least two plausible explanations. First, it could be that small particles of food left around the house are more problematic than the stray cup or bowl because they find their way into hard-to-reach places and may lead to rodent infestation. Second, it is possible that the Supreme Lawmaker was unconcerned with the containers being left in the family room because citizens of this jurisdiction have been meticulous about removing such containers.

BABYSITTER SUE, J., issued the following ruling on April 12, 1986:

Defendant Beatrice, age 12, is charged with violating Ordinance 7.3 by drinking a beverage, to wit: orange juice, in the family room.

The Defendant relies on our ruling of March 30, 1986, which "held that drinking water outside of the kitchen does not violate the Ordinance," and urges us to conclude that all beverages are permitted in the family room under Ordinance 7.3. While we believe this is a difficult case, we agree. As we have previously explained, the term "food" does not extend to beverages.

Our hesitation stems not from the literal meaning of the Ordinance, which strongly supports the Defendant's claim, but rather from an understanding of its purpose. As we have previously stated, and as evidenced by the language of the Ordinance itself, the Ordinance was enacted as a result of the Supreme Lawmaker's concern with mess. Unlike the case with water, if the Defendant were to spill orange juice on the couch or rug in the family room, the mess would be problematic — perhaps even more so than the mess produced by crumbs of food. It is thus difficult to infer why the Supreme Lawmaker would choose to prohibit solid foods outside of the kitchen but to permit orange juice.

Nevertheless, we are bound by the plain language of the Ordinance and by precedent. We are confident that if the Supreme Lawmaker disagrees with the outcome in this case, she can change or clarify the law accordingly.

GRANDMA, SENIOR J., issued the following ruling on May 3, 1986:

Defendant Charlie, age 10, is charged with violating Ordinance 7.3 by eating popcorn in the family room. The Defendant contends, and we agree, that the Ordinance does not apply in this case.

Ordinance 7.3 was enacted to prevent messes outside of the kitchen. This purpose is demonstrated by the language of the Ordinance itself, which refers to food being left "all over the family room" as the immediate cause of its adoption.

Such messes are produced only when one transfers food from a container to his or her mouth outside of the kitchen. During that process — what the Ordinance refers to as "eating" — crumbs and other food particles often fall out of the eater's hand and only the floor or sofa.

As the record shows, the Defendant placed all of the popcorn into his mouth prior to leaving the kitchen. He merely masticated and swallowed while in the family room. At no time was there any danger that a mess would be produced.

We are certain that there was no intent to prohibit merely the chewing or swallowing of food outside of the kitchen. After all, the Supreme Lawmaker has expressly permitted the chewing of gum in the family room. It would be senseless and absurd to treat gum differently from popcorn that has been ingested prior to leaving the kitchen.

If textual support is necessary to support this obvious and commonsensical interpretation, abundant support is available. First, the Ordinance prohibits food from being "eaten" outside of the kitchen. The term "eat" is defined to mean "to take in through the mouth as food: ingest, chew, and swallow in turn." The Defendant, having only chewed and swallowed, did not "eat." Further, the Ordinance prohibits the "eating" rather than the "bringing" of food outside of the kitchen; and indeed, food is often brought out of the kitchen and through the family room, as when school lunches are delivered to the front door for carpool pickup. There is no reason to treat food enclosed in a brown bag any differently from food enclosed within the Defendant's mouth.

Finally, if any doubt remains as to the meaning of this Ordinance as it pertains to the chewing and swallowing of food, we cannot punish the Defendant for acting reasonably and in good faith reliance upon the text of the Ordinance and our past pronouncements as to its meaning and intent.

UNCLE RICK, J., issued the following ruling on May 20, 1986:

Defendant Charlie, age 10, is charged with violating Ordinance 7.3 ("the Rule") by bringing a double thick mint chocolate chip milkshake into the family room.

Were I writing on a clean slate, I would surely conclude that the Defendant has violated the Rule. A double thick milkshake is "food" because it contains protein, carbohydrate, and/or fat. Further, the purpose of the Rule — to prevent messes — would be undermined by permitting a double thick milkshake to be brought into the family room. Indeed, it makes little sense to treat a milkshake differently from a pretzel or a scoop of ice cream.

However, I am not writing on a clean slate. Our precedents have now established that all beverages are permitted outside of the kitchen under the Rule. The Defendant relied on those precedents in good faith. Further, the Supreme Lawmaker has had ample opportunity to clarify or change the law to prohibit any or all beverages from being brought out of the kitchen, and she has elected not to exercise that authority. I can only conclude that she is satisfied with the status quo.

GRANDMA, SENIOR J., issued the following ruling on July 2, 1986:

Defendant Anne, age 14, is charged with violating Ordinance 7.3 by eating apple slices in the family room.

As we have repeatedly held, the Ordinance pertains only to messy foods. Moreover, the Ordinance explicitly refers to "popcorn kernels, pretzel crumbs, and pieces of cereal." Sliced apples, not being messy (and certainly being no worse than orange juice and milkshakes, which have been permitted by our prior decisions), and being wholly dissimilar from the crumbly foods listed in the Ordinance, do not come within the meaning of the Ordinance.

We also find it significant that the consumption of healthy foods such as sliced apples is a behavior that this jurisdiction supports and encourages. It would be odd to read the Ordinance in a way that would discourage such healthy behaviors by limiting them to the kitchen.

AUNT SARAH, J., issued the following ruling on August 12, 1986:

Defendant Beatrice, age 13, is charged with violating Ordinance 7.3 by eating pretzels, popcorn, cereal, and birthday cake in the family room. Under ordinary circumstances, the Defendant would clearly be subject to the Ordinance. However, the circumstances giving rise to the Defendant's action in this case are far from ordinary.

The Defendant celebrated her thirteenth birthday on August 10, 1986. For the celebration, she invited four of her closest friends to sleep over. During the evening, and as part of the festivities, the celebrants watched a movie in the family room. Chief Justice Father provided those present with drinks and snacks, including the aforesaid pretzels, popcorn, and cereal, for consumption during the movie-watching. Father admonished the Defendant to clean up after the movie, and there is no evidence in the record suggesting that the Defendant failed to do so.

We frankly concede that the Defendant's action[s] were violative of the plain meaning of the Ordinance. However, given the special and unique nature of the occasion, the fact that Father, a representative of the Supreme Lawmaker — as well as of this Court — implicitly approved of the Defendant's actions, and the apparent efforts of the Defendant in upholding the spirit of the Ordinance by cleaning up after her friends, we believe that the best course of action is to release the Defendant.

In light of the growing confusion in the interpretation of this ambiguous Ordinance, we urge the Supreme Lawmaker to exercise her authority to clarify and/or change the law if and as she deems it appropriate.

FATHER, C.J., issued the following ruling on September 17, 1986:

Defendant Derek, age 9, was charged with violating Ordinance 7.3 ("the Rule") by eating pretzels, potato chips, popcorn, a bagel with cream cheese, cottage cheese, and a chocolate bar in the family room.

The Defendant argues that our precedents have clearly established a pattern permitting food to be eaten in the family room so long as the eater cleans up any mess. He further maintains that it would be unjust for this Court to punish him after having permitted past actions such as drinking water, orange juice, and a milkshake, as well as swallowing popcorn, eating apple slices, and eating pretzels, popcorn, and cereal on a special occasion. The Defendant avers that there is no rational distinction between his sister's eating foods in the family room during a movie on a special occasion and his eating foods in the family room during a weekly television show.

We agree. The citizens of this jurisdiction look to the rulings of this Court, as well as to general practice, to understand their rights and obligations as citizens. In the many months since the Rule was originally announced, the cumulative rulings of this Court on the subject would signify to any citizen that, whatever the technical language of the Rule, the real Rule is that they must clean up after eating any food outside of the kitchen. To draw and enforce any other line now would be arbitrary and, as such, unjust.

On November 4, 1986, the following proclamation, henceforth known as The New Ordinance 7.3, was made by the Supreme Lawmaker, Mother:

> Over the past few months, I have found empty cups, orange juice stains, milkshake spills, slimy spots of unknown origin, all manner of crumbs, melted chocolate, and icing from cake in the family room. I thought I was clear the first time! And you've all had a chance to show me that you could use your common sense and clean up after yourselves. So now let me be clearer: No food, gum, or drink of any kind, on any occasion or in any form, is permitted in the family room. Ever. Seriously. I mean it.

Notes and Questions

---

1. The above piece is supposed to be sort of funny. But it also shows how "judges" can evade what might seem to some to be a fairly clear statutory meaning, and that is not funny at all. Of course, as this article also demonstrates, the "legislature" can always amend the statute in question to produce greater clarity. But this does not seem to be a very desirable solution, for in the interim, damage has been done. Is there anything else a "legislature" can do to avoid these sorts of problems? Or does the solution lie more in selecting judges who have a better understanding of their role and of statutory interpretation theory?

2. For an all-time classic treatment of various perspectives on statutory interpretation, see Lon L. Fuller, *The Case of the Speluncean Explorers*, 112 HARV. L. REV. 1851 (1999) (fiftieth anniversary symposium reproduction).

3. Numerous books and articles have been written on statutory interpretation, including KENT GREENAWALT, STATUTORY INTERPRETATION: 20 QUESTIONS

(1999), and Felix Frankfurter *Reflections on the Reading of Statutes*, 47 COLUM. L. REV. 527 (1947).

4. There also exist excellent summaries as to the current state of statutory interpretation, including George Costello, *Statutory Interpretation: General Principles and Recent Trends*, CRS REPORT FOR CONGRESS (updated March 30, 2006). For other, more exhaustive treatments, see ANTONIN SCALIA, A MATTER OF INTERPRETATION (1997); RONALD BENTON BROWN & SHARON JACOBS BROWN, STATUTORY INTERPRETATION: THE SEARCH FOR LEGISLATIVE INTENT (2002); FRANK B. CROSS, THE THEORY AND PRACTICE OF STATUTORY INTERPRETATION (1999); and PETER L. STRAUSS, LEGISLATION: UNDERSTANDING AND USING STATUTES (2006).

5. For an attempt to "standardize" statutory interpretation, see UNIFORM STATUTE AND RULE CONSTRUCTION ACT (1995), a work that is well worth reading. To date, though, the Uniform Act has been adopted only in New Mexico.

6. There have been other, recent calls for a more formal and systematic approach to statutory interpretation. Among them are Nicholas Quinn Rosenkranz, *Federal Rules of Statutory Interpretation*, 115 HARV. L. REV. 2085 (2002), and Gary E. O'Connor, *Restatement (First) of Statutory Interpretation*, 7 N.Y.U. J. LEGIS. & PUB. POL'Y 333 (2004). But such efforts have not yet come to fruition, perhaps due in part to some uncertainty regarding their propriety. As stated by Amanda Frost:

> Academics debate the degree to which Congress could enact legislation that purported to control the judiciary's interpretive methodology, especially its interpretation of legislative enactments. Some argue that Congress has significant leeway to tell the courts how to interpret its statutes, while others contend that the Constitution prohibits legislative interference in the judicial power.

Amanda Frost, *The Limits of Advocacy*, 59 DUKE L.J. 447, 477 (2009). There is, in other words, some debate as to whether any particular theory of statutory interpretation could be *imposed* upon the federal courts by some external source (e.g., Congress).

7. Somewhat related to the foregoing issue is the issue whether a court's *own* decisions regarding statutory interpretation methodology should constitute holding — i.e., be binding on the court in later cases. (This is a subset of the debate as to whether a court's decisional methodology constitutes holding, a topic discussed in Chapter 2; *see supra* at 79-80.) As we saw previously, the authorities are somewhat divided with respect to the binding effect of decisional methodology generally. With respect to statutory interpretations methodology in particular, at least as a practical matter, courts generally do not seem to regard decisions in this area as binding (or they are oblivious to the issue). For example, more than fifty years ago, Professors Hart and Sacks wrote the following "Note on What to Expect from a Theory of Statutory Interpretation":

To work effectively with statutes, just as with cases, it is necessary to have some kind of guiding notion, either articulate or inarticulate, about what you are doing and why. These materials proceed on the assumption that a working theory which is consciously developed and articulate is better than one which is taken for granted upon unexamined premises and hence inarticulate. They try to provide the wherewithal for the development of such a. But in embarking upon this enterprise it is important not to be misled about the nature of it.

Do not expect anybody's theory of statutory interpretation, whether it is your own or somebody else's, to be an accurate statement of what courts actually do with statutes. The hard truth of the matter is that American courts have no intelligible, generally accepted, and consistently applied theory of statutory interpretation.

When an effort is made to formulate a sound and workable theory, therefore, the most that can be hoped for is that it will have some foundation in experience and in the best practice of the wisest judges, and that it will be well calculated to serve the ultimate purposes of law.

HENRY M. HART, JR. & ALBERT M. SACKS, THE LEGAL PROCESS: BASIC PROBLEMS IN THE MAKING AND APPLICATION OF LAW 1169 (William N. Eskridge, Jr. & Philip P. Frickey eds., 1994). Similarly, Amanda Frost more recently wrote:

Of course, there is no single accepted method of interpretation. . . . When it comes to interpreting statutes, judges differ over whether to look to the intentions of the legislature and the broader purpose of the legislative enactment, or to limit their analysis to the statute's plain language. . . . Each judge has the authority to employ the interpretive approach she thinks best.

Amanda Frost, *The Limits of Advocacy*, 59 DUKE L.J. 447, 476-77 (2009).

Do you agree? Irrespective of whether you agree with the Supreme Court's current approach to statutory interpretation, do you believe that the Court today has "no intelligible, generally accepted, and consistently applied theory of statutory interpretation," binding or not? If not, should there be? And would it be wise for counsel today to omit an argument based on the text of the statute on this ground?

For more on these subjects, see Sydney Foster, *Should Courts Give Stare Decisis Effect to Statutory Interpretation Methodology?*, 96 GEO. L.J. 1863 (2008); Linda D. Jellum, *"Which Is To Be Master," the Judiciary or the Legislature? When Statutory Directives Violate Separation of Powers*, 56 UCLA L. REV. 837 (2009); and Jennifer M. Bandy, Note, *Interpretive Freedom: A Necessary Component of Article III Judging*, 61 DUKE L.J. 651 (2011). It might be observed that some *state* courts do consider statutory interpretation methodology, once declared and applied, to be binding. *See* Abbe R. Gluck, *Statutory Interpretation Methodology as "Law": Oregon's Path-Breaking Interpretive Framework and its Lessons for the Nation*, 47 WILLAMETTE L. REV. 539 (2011), and Abbe R. Gluck, *The States as Laboratories of Statutory Interpretation: Methodological Consensus and the New Modified Textualism*, 119 YALE L.J. 1750, 1846-61 (2010).

8. *Legislative Drafting Manuals.* Legislative drafting manuals also provide good summaries of statutory interpretation-related principles. Both the United

States Senate and United States House of Representatives have their own drafting manuals, as do a number of states. *See, e.g.*, OFFICE OF THE LEGISLATIVE COUNSEL, U.S. HOUSE OF REPRESENTATIVES, HOUSE LEGISLATIVE COUNSEL'S MANUAL ON DRAFTING STYLE (1995), *available at* http://www.house.gov/legcoun/pdf/draftstyle.pdf. For a recent article in this area, see B.J. Ard, Comment, *Interpreting by the Book: Legislative Drafting Manuals and Statutory Interpretation*, 120 YALE L.J. 185 (2010).

9. Another effort to improve legislative drafting was introduced by President Bill Clinton through his issuance of Executive Order 12988, 61 Fed. Reg. 4729 (Feb. 7, 1996), *reprinted in* 28 U.S.C. § 519 (2006). In that order, the President commanded

> each agency promulgating new regulations, reviewing existing regulations, developing legislative proposals concerning regulations, and developing new legislation shall adhere to the following requirements:
>
> (1) The agency's proposed legislation and regulations shall be reviewed by the agency to eliminate drafting errors and ambiguity;
>
> (2) The agency's proposed legislation and regulations shall be written to minimize litigation; and
>
> (3) The agency's proposed legislation and regulations shall provide a clear legal standard for affected conduct rather than a general standard, and shall promote simplification and burden reduction.

Id. at 4731. Moreover, in conducting such reviews,

> each agency formulating proposed legislation and regulations shall make every reasonable effort to ensure:
>
> (1) that the legislation, as appropriate
>
> (A) specifies whether all causes of action arising under the law are subject to statutes of limitation;
>
> (B) specifies in clear language the preemptive effect, if any, to be given the law;
>
> (C) specifies in clear language the effect on existing Federal law, if any, including all provisions repealed, circumscribed, displaced, impaired, or modified;
>
> (D) provides a clear legal standard for affected conduct;
>
> (E) specifies whether arbitration and other forms of private dispute resolution are appropriate under enforcement and relief provisions, subject to constitutional requirements;
>
> (F) specifies whether the provisions of the law are severable if one or more is found to be unconstitutional;
>
> (G) specifies in clear language the retroactive effect, if any, to be given to the law;
>
> (H) specifies in clear language the applicable burdens of proof;
>
> (I) specifies in clear language whether it grants private parties a right to sue and, if so, the relief available and the conditions and terms for authorized awards of attorney's fees, if any;

(J) specifies whether State courts have jurisdiction under the law and, if so, whether and under what conditions an action would be removable to Federal court;

(K) specifies whether administrative proceedings are to be required before parties may file suit in court and, if so, describes those proceedings and requires the exhaustion of administrative remedies;

(L) sets forth the standards governing the assertion of personal jurisdiction, if any;

(M) defines key statutory terms, either explicitly or by reference to other statutes that explicitly define those terms;

(N) specifies whether the legislation applies to the Federal Government or its agencies;

(O) specifies whether the legislation applies to States, territories, the District of Columbia, and the Commonwealths of Puerto Rico and the Northern Mariana Islands;

(P) specifies what remedies are available such as money damages, civil penalties, injunctive relief, and attorney's fees; and

(Q) addresses other important issues affecting clarity and general draftsmanship of legislation set forth by the Attorney General, with the concurrence of the Director of the Office of Management and Budget ("OMB") and after consultation with affected agencies, that are determined to be in accordance with the purposes of this order.

Id. at 4731-32. What do you think of the terms of this executive order? Is there anything you would add? Delete?

10. *Statutory Interpretation in the state courts.* States, of course, have to deal with their own issues of statutory interpretation (whether interpreting their own statutes or federal statutes). And federal courts sometimes have to interpret state statutes. For more on these subjects, see Abbe R. Gluck, *The States as Laboratories of Statutory Interpretation: Methodological Consensus and the New Modified Textualism*, 119 YALE L.J. 1750 (2010).

PRACTICE PROBLEM: NO DOGS IN THE PARK

Assume that a city (such as New York City) passed an ordinance (or statute) prohibiting dogs in a certain park (such as Central Park). In its entirety, the statute reads: "No dogs in the park."

A. What does this statute mean? What, exactly, does it prohibit? For example, what does (or can) the word "dog" mean? What is the most common (or ordinary) meaning of this word? What is the meaning of this word in this context? And what does it mean to be "in the park"? How do you know? Consider these questions as you determine whether the following things are prohibited by this statute:

1. a beagle
2. a wild dingo
3. someone's pet pig
4. a guide or police dog
5. a hotdog vendor (or specifically, his merchandise)
6. a statue of Balto, the famous Alaskan sled dog
7. a person dressed as Walt Disney's Pluto
8. a large balloon version of Charles Schulz's Snoopy leftover from Macy's Thanksgiving Day Parade
9. a chihuahua flying in an airplane several thousand feet above the park

B. What was the intent of the city in enacting this statute? What was the purpose (or purposes) of this statute? How do you know? Do the answers to these questions help you answer the above questions (or change any of your answers)? What additional information would you like to have in order to better answer these questions?

As silly as some of the above questions might seem, they collectively raise some important issues that are inherent in any question of statutory interpretation. In fact, this very hypothetical (or variants of it) has been used repeatedly by judges and scholars in this area to illustrate various points. Consider two such examples:

- *Martin v. Coventry Fire Dist.*, 981 F.2d 1358, 1361 (1st Cir. 1992) (Breyer, C.J.) ("The Secretary quite properly understands, however, that statutory language, like all language, derives its meaning from context. A sign that says 'no animals in the park' does not mean 'no picnic oysters,' nor does it mean 'no children,' nor is it 'ambiguous' in the respect.").

- Frank H. Easterbrook, *Statute's Domains*, 50 U. Chi. L. Rev. 533, 535-36 (1983):

Consider, for example, whether a statute providing for the leashing of "dogs" also requires the leashing of cats (because the statute really covers the category of "animals") or wolves (because the statute really covers the category of "canines") or lions ("dangerous animals"). Most people would say that the statute does not go beyond dogs, because after all the verbal torturing of the words has been completed it is still too plain for argument what the statute means. Perhaps it is a quibble, but in my terminology this becomes a decision that the statute "applies" only to dogs. For rules about the rest of the animal kingdom we must look elsewhere.

The distinction between application and interpretation is a line worth drawing—however difficult to maintain—because of the malleability of words. To find the leash statute limited to dogs after a bout of interpretation inevitably has the air of arbitrariness. Why *not* treat it as a statute about "animals" or "dangerous animals" or "canines"? . . . The philosophy of language, and most particularly the work of Ludwig Wittgenstein, has established that sets of words do not possess intrinsic meanings and cannot be given them; to make matters worse, speakers do not even have determinative intents about the meanings of their own words. Thus when a speaker says "dogs" we cannot be certain that he did not mean "dangerous animals" unless that question was present to his mind and the structure of the utterance indicates his resolution of the problem. When Congress enacts a $10,000 jurisdictional amount, we cannot be certain whether it means $10,000 in nominal dollars or real (inflation-adjusted) ones. When the Constitution says that the President must be thirty-five years old, we cannot be certain whether it means thirty-five as the number of revolutions of the world around the sun, as a percentage of average life expectancy (so that the Constitution now has age fifty as a minimum), or as a minimum number of years after puberty (so the minimum now is thirty or so). Each of these treatments has some rational set of reasons, goals, values, and the like to recommend it. If the meaning of language depends on a community of understanding among readers, none is "right." But unless the community of readers is to engage in ceaseless (and thus pointless) babble — and unless, moreover, the community is willing to entrust almost boundless discretion to judges as oracles of the community's standards — there is a need for some broader set of rules about when to engage in the open-ended process of construction.

In a world of language skepticism, every attempt to "construe" a statute is a transfer of a substantial measure of decision-making authority from the speaker to the interpreter.

For more on this topic, see John F. Manning, *Federalism and the Generality Problem in Constitutional Interpretation*, 122 HARV. L. REV. 2003, 2010-11 (2009) (an article that also includes (at 2011-15) a fine explanation of the historical shift in the Supreme Court from an essentially purposivist approach to statutory interpretation to a more textualist approach).

E. THE RETROACTIVE AND PROSPECTIVE APPLICATION OF STATUTES

Recall the problem presented in Chapter 2 regarding the retroactive and prospective application of judicial decisions (*see supra* at 354). As we now know, the general rule in federal courts today (at least with respect to cases on direct review) is that changes in case law generally apply both retroactively and prospectively — i.e., they apply to acts and events that arise both before and after the date of the "law-changing" decision in question.

But what about changes in statutory law? In the absence of express legislative direction one way or the other, do statutory changes apply only to acts and events that arise after the effective date of the statute, or also to acts and events that arise sooner? As with case law, the answer here has proved elusive, and has resulted in considerable upheaval over the past several decades. But here also, the law has finally arrived at some level of stability, though as with application of changes in case law on collateral review, the final chapter in the statutory area perhaps has yet to be written.

Bradley v. School Board

416 U.S. 696 (1974)

MR. JUSTICE BLACKMUN delivered the opinion of the Court.

In this protracted school desegregation litigation, the District Court awarded the plaintiff-petitioners expenses and attorneys' fees for services rendered from March 10, 1970, to January 29, 1971. 53 F. R. D. 28 (ED Va. 1971). The United States Court of Appeals for the Fourth Circuit, one judge dissenting, reversed. 472 F. 2d 318 (1972). We granted certiorari, 412 U. S. 937 (1973), to determine whether the allowance of attorneys' fees was proper. Pertinent to the resolution of the issue is the enactment in 1972 of § 718 of Title VII, the Emergency School Aid Act, 20 U. S. C. § 1617 (1970 ed., Supp. II), as part of the Education Amendments of 1972, Pub. L. 92-318, 86 Stat. 235, 369.

. . . .

II

. . . .

After initial submission of the case to the Court of Appeals, but prior to its decision, the Education Amendments of 1972, of which § 718 of Title VII of the Emergency School Aid Act is a part, became law. Section 718, 20 U. S. C. § 1617 (1970 ed., Supp. II), grants authority to a federal court to award a reasonable attorney's fee when appropriate in a school desegregation case.[12] The Court of Appeals, sitting en banc, then heard argument as to the applicability of § 718 to this and other litigation.[13] In the other cases it held that only legal services rendered after July 1, 1972, the effective date of § 718, see Pub. L. 92-318, § 2(c)(1), 86 Stat. 236, were compensable under that statute. *Thompson v. School Board of the City of Newport News*, 472 F. 2d 177 (CA4 1972). In the instant case the court held that, because there were no orders pending or appealable on either May 26, 1971, when the District Court made its fee award, or on July 1, 1972, when the statute became effective, § 718 did not sustain the allowance of counsel fees.

III

In *Northcross v. Board of Education of the Memphis City Schools*, 412 U. S. 427, 428 (1973), we held that under § 718 "the successful plaintiff 'should ordinarily recover

---

12. "§ 1617. Attorney fees.

"Upon the entry of a final order by a court of the United States against a local educational agency, a State (or any agency thereof), or the United States (or any agency thereof), for failure to comply with any provision of this chapter or for discrimination on the basis of race, color, or national origin in violation of title VI of the Civil Rights Act of 1964, or the fourteenth amendment to the Constitution of the United States as they pertain to elementary and secondary education, the court, in its discretion, upon a finding that the proceedings were necessary to bring about compliance, may allow the prevailing party, other than the United States, a reasonable attorney's fee as part of the costs."

13. The fee issue had been argued in the Court of Appeals on March 7, 1972. The Education Amendments of 1972 were approved by the President on June 23. The argument before the en banc court took place on October 2.

an attorney's fee unless special circumstances would render such an award unjust.'" We decide today a question left open in *Northcross*, namely, "whether § 718 authorizes an award of attorneys' fees insofar as those expenses were incurred prior to the date that that section came into effect." *Id.*, at 429 n. 2.

The District Court in this case awarded counsel fees for services rendered from March 10, 1970, when petitioners filed their motion for further relief, to January 29, 1971, when the court declined to implement the plan proposed by the petitioners. It made its award on May 26, 1971, after it had ordered into effect the noninterim desegregation plan which it had approved. The Board appealed from that award, and its appeal was pending when Congress enacted § 718. The question, properly viewed, then, is not simply one relating to the propriety of retroactive application of § 718 to services rendered prior to its enactment, but rather, one relating to the applicability of that section to a situation where the propriety of a fee award was pending resolution on appeal when the statute became law.

This Court in the past has recognized a distinction between the application of a change in the law that takes place while a case is on direct review, on the one hand, and its effect on a final judgment under collateral attack, on the other hand. *Linkletter v. Walker*, 381 U. S. 618, 627 (1965). We are concerned here only with direct review.

A

We anchor our holding in this case on the principle that a court is to apply the law in effect at the time it renders its decision, unless doing so would result in manifest injustice or there is statutory direction or legislative history to the contrary.

The origin and justification for this rule are found in the words of Mr. Chief Justice Marshall in *United States v. Schooner Peggy*, 1 Cranch 103 (1801):

> "It is in the general true that the province of an appellate court is only to enquire whether a judgment when rendered was erroneous or not. But if subsequent to the judgment and before the decision of the appellate court, a law intervenes and positively changes the rule which governs, the law must be obeyed, or its obligation denied. If the law be constitutional . . . I know of no court which can contest its obligation. It is true that in mere private cases between individuals, a court will and ought to struggle hard against a construction which will, by a retrospective operation, affect the rights of parties, but in great national concerns . . . the court must decide according to existing laws, and if it be necessary to set aside a judgment, rightful when rendered, but which cannot be affirmed but in violation of law, the judgment must be set aside." *Id.*, at 110.[16]

---

16. *Schooner Peggy* concerned a condemnation following the seizure of a French vessel by an American ship. The trial court found that the vessel was within French territorial waters at the time of seizure and, hence, was not a lawful prize. On appeal, the Circuit Court reversed, holding that the vessel in fact was on the high seas. A decree was entered accordingly. While the case was pending on appeal to this Court, a convention with France was entered into providing in part: "Property captured, and not yet *definitively* condemned, or which may be captured before the exchange of ratifications . . . shall be mutually restored." 1 Cranch, at 107. This Court reversed, holding that it must apply the terms of the convention despite the propriety of the Circuit Court's decision when it was rendered, and that the vessel was to be restored since, by virtue of the pending appeal, it had not been "*definitively* condemned," *id.*, at 108.

In the wake of *Schooner Peggy*, however, it remained unclear whether a change in the law occurring while a case was pending on appeal was to be given effect only where, by its terms, the law was to apply to pending cases, as was true of the convention under consideration in *Schooner Peggy*, or, conversely, whether such a change in the law must be given effect *unless* there was clear indication that it was *not* to apply in pending cases. For a very long time the Court's decisions did little to clarify this issue.

Ultimately, in *Thorpe v. Housing Authority of the City of Durham*, 393 U. S. 268 (1969), the broader reading of *Schooner Peggy* was adopted, and this Court ruled that "an appellate court must apply the law in effect at the time it renders its decision." *Id.*, at 281. In that case, after the plaintiff Housing Authority had secured a state court eviction order, and it had been affirmed by the Supreme Court of North Carolina, *Housing Authority of the City of Durham v. Thorpe*, 267 N. C. 431, 148 S. E. 2d 290 (1966), and this Court had granted certiorari, 385 U. S. 967 (1966), the Department of Housing and Urban Development ordered a new procedural prerequisite for an eviction. Following remand by this Court for such further proceedings as might be appropriate in light of the new directive, 386 U. S. 670 (1967), the state court adhered to its decision. 271 N. C. 468, 157 S. E. 2d 147 (1967). This Court again granted certiorari. 390 U. S. 942 (1968). Upon review, we held that, although the circular effecting the change did not indicate whether it was to be applied to pending cases or to events that had transpired prior to its issuance, it was, nonetheless, to be applied to anyone residing in the housing project on the date of its promulgation. The Court recited the language in *Schooner Peggy*, quoted above, and noted that that reasoning "had been applied where the change was constitutional, statutory, or judicial," 393 U. S., at 282 (footnotes omitted), and that it must apply "with equal force where the change is made by an administrative agency acting pursuant to legislative authorization." *Ibid. Thorpe* thus stands for the proposition that even where the intervening law does not explicitly recite that it is to be applied to pending cases, it is to be given recognition and effect.

Accordingly, we must reject the contention that a change in the law is to be given effect in a pending case only where that is the clear and stated intention of the legislature. While neither our decision in *Thorpe* nor our decision today purports to hold that courts must always thus apply new laws to pending cases in the absence of clear legislative direction to the contrary, we do note that insofar as the legislative history of § 718 is supportive of either position, it would seem to provide at least implicit support for the application of the statute to pending cases.[23]

---

23. The legislation that ultimately resulted in the passage of § 718 grew out of a bill that would have provided for the establishment of a $15 million federal fund from which successful litigants in school discrimination cases would be paid a reasonable fee "for services rendered, and costs incurred, *after the date of enactment of this Act.*" S. 683, § 11(a), 92d Cong., 1st Sess. (1971) (emphasis supplied). The bill was reported out of the Senate Committee on Labor and Public Welfare as S. 1557, with the relevant clause intact in § 11. See S. Rep. No. 92-61, pp. 55-56 (1971). The section, however, was stricken in the Senate, 117 Cong. Rec. 11338-11345 (1971), and the present language of § 718 took its place. *Id.*, at 11521-11529 and 11724-11726. The House, among other amendments, deleted all mention of counsel fees. In conference, the fee provision was restored. S. Rep. No. 92-798, p. 143 (1972).

Thus, while there is no explicit statement that § 718 may be applied to services rendered prior to enactment, we are reluctant specifically to read into the statute the very fee limitation that Congress eliminated.

B

The Court in *Thorpe*, however, observed that exceptions to the general rule that a court is to apply a law in effect at the time it renders its decision "had been made to prevent manifest injustice," citing *Greene v. United States*, 376 U. S. 149 (1964). Although the precise category of cases to which this exception applies has not been clearly delineated, the Court in *Schooner Peggy* suggested that such injustice could result "in mere private cases between individuals," and implored the courts to "struggle hard against a construction which will, by a retrospective operation, affect the rights of parties." 1 Cranch, at 110. We perceive no such threat of manifest injustice present in this case. We decline, accordingly, to categorize it as an exception to *Thorpe*'s general rule.

The concerns expressed by the Court in *Schooner Peggy* and in *Thorpe* relative to the possible working of an injustice center upon (a) the nature and identity of the parties, (b) the nature of their rights, and (c) the nature of the impact of the change in the law upon those rights.

In this case, the parties consist, on the one hand, of the School Board, a publicly funded governmental entity, and, on the other, a class of children whose constitutional right to a nondiscriminatory education has been advanced by this litigation. The District Court rather vividly described what it regarded as the disparity in the respective abilities of the parties adequately to present and protect their interests. Moreover, school desegregation litigation is of a kind different from "mere private cases between individuals." With the Board responsible for the education of the very students who brought suit against it to require that such education comport with constitutional standards, it is not appropriate to view the parties as engaged in a routine private lawsuit. In this litigation the plaintiffs may be recognized as having rendered substantial service both to the Board itself, by bringing it into compliance with its constitutional mandate, and to the community at large by securing for it the benefits assumed to flow from a nondiscriminatory educational system. *Brown v. Board of Education*, 347 U. S., at 494.

. . . .

Application of § 718 to such litigation would thus appear to have been anticipated by Mr. Chief Justice Marshall in *Schooner Peggy* when he noted that in "great national concerns . . . the court must decide according to existing laws." 1 Cranch, at 110. Indeed, the circumstances surrounding the passage of § 718, and the numerous expressions of congressional concern and intent with respect to the enactment of that statute, all proclaim its status as having to do with a "great national concern."

The second aspect of the Court's concern that injustice may arise from retrospective application of a change in law relates to the nature of the rights effected by the change. The Court has refused to apply an intervening change to a pending action where it has concluded that to do so would infringe upon or deprive a person of a right that had matured or become unconditional. See *Greene v. United States*, 376 U. S., at 160; *Claridge Apartments Co. v. Commissioner*, 323 U. S. 141, 164 (1944); *Union Pacific R. Co. v. Laramie Stock Yards Co.*, 231 U. S. 190, 199 (1913). We find here no such matured or unconditional right affected by the application of § 718. It cannot be claimed that the publicly elected School Board had such a right in the funds allocated to it by the taxpayers. These funds were essentially held in trust for the public, and at all times the Board was subject to such conditions or instructions on the use of the funds as the public wished to make through its duly elected representatives.

The third concern has to do with the nature of the impact of the change in law upon existing rights, or, to state it another way, stems from the possibility that new and unanticipated obligations may be imposed upon a party without notice or an opportunity to be heard. . . . Here no increased burden was imposed since § 718 did not alter the Board's constitutional responsibility for providing pupils with a nondiscriminatory education. Also, there was no change in the substantive obligation of the parties. From the outset, upon the filing of the original complaint in 1961, the Board engaged in a conscious course of conduct with the knowledge that, under different theories, discussed by the District Court and the Court of Appeals, the Board could have been required to pay attorneys' fees. Even assuming a degree of uncertainty in the law at that time regarding the Board's constitutional obligations, there is no indication that the obligation under § 718, if known, rather than simply the common-law availability of an award, would have caused the Board to order its conduct so as to render this litigation unnecessary and thereby preclude the incurring of such costs.

The availability of § 718 to sustain the award of fees against the Board therefore merely serves to create an additional basis or source for the Board's potential obligation to pay attorneys' fees. It does not impose an additional or unforeseeable obligation upon it.

Accordingly, upon considering the parties, the nature of the rights, and the impact of § 718 upon those rights, it cannot be said that the application of the statute to an award of fees for services rendered prior to its effective date, in an action pending on that date, would cause "manifest injustice," as that term is used in *Thorpe*, so as to compel an exception of the case from the rule of *Schooner Peggy*.

C

Finally, we disagree with the Court of Appeals' conclusion that § 718 by its very terms is inapplicable to the petitioners' request for fees "because there was no 'final order' pending unresolved on appeal," 472 F. 2d, at 331, when § 718 became effective, or on May 26, 1971, when the District Court made its award.

. . . .

We are in agreement, however, with the dissenting judge of the Court of Appeals when he observed, 472 F. 2d, at 337, that the award made by the District Court for services from March 10, 1970, to January 29, 1971, did not precisely fit § 718's requirement that the beneficiary of the fee order be "the prevailing party." In January 1971 the petitioners had not yet "prevailed" and realistically did not do so until April 5. Consequently, any fee award was not appropriately to be made until April 5. Thereafter, it may include services at least through that date. This, of course, will be attended to on remand.

Accordingly, we hold that § 718 is applicable to the present situation, and that in this case the District Court in its discretion may allow the petitioners reasonable attorneys' fees for services rendered from March 10, 1970, to or beyond April 5, 1971. The judgment of the Court of Appeals is vacated and the case is remanded for further proceedings consistent with this opinion.

Notes and Questions

1. What is the rule of retroactivity articulated in *Bradley*?

2. Does it seem fair to apply the statute at issue in *Bradley* to events that occurred prior to its enactment? Why or why not? Did the statute at issue, by its own terms, so provide?

3. The *Bradley* Court relied upon the Court's holding in *Schooner Peggy*, a case that involved the application of a treaty. Does *Schooner Peggy* seem apposite in the *Bradley* context?

4. The *Bradley* Court suggested that there might be an exception to the general rule in *Thorpe* where necessary to "prevent manifest injustice." When might this occur? Does the standard suggested by the Court seem workable? Predictable?

Bowen v. Georgetown University Hospital
488 U.S. 204 (1988)

JUSTICE KENNEDY delivered the opinion of the Court.

Under the Medicare program, health care providers are reimbursed by the Government for expenses incurred in providing medical services to Medicare beneficiaries. See Title XVIII of the Social Security Act, 79 Stat. 291, as amended, 42 U. S. C. § 1395 *et seq.* (the Medicare Act). Congress has authorized the Secretary of Health and Human Services to promulgate regulations setting limits on the levels of Medicare costs that will be reimbursed. The question presented here is whether the Secretary may exercise this rulemaking authority to promulgate cost limits that are retroactive.

. . . .

II

It is axiomatic that an administrative agency's power to promulgate legislative regulations is limited to the authority delegated by Congress. In determining the validity of the Secretary's retroactive cost-limit rule, the threshold question is whether the Medicare Act authorizes retroactive rulemaking.

Retroactivity is not favored in the law. Thus, congressional enactments and administrative rules will not be construed to have retroactive effect unless their language requires this result. By the same principle, a statutory grant of legislative rulemaking authority will not, as a general matter, be understood to encompass the power to promulgate retroactive rules unless that power is conveyed by Congress in express terms. Even where some substantial justification for retroactive rulemakings is presented, courts should be reluctant to find such authority absent an express statutory grant.

The Secretary contends that the Medicare Act provides the necessary authority to promulgate retroactive cost-limit rules in the unusual circumstances of this case. He rests on alternative grounds: first, the specific grant of authority to promulgate regulations to "provide for the making of suitable retroactive corrective adjustments," 42 U. S. C. § 1395x(v)(1)(A)(ii); and second, the general grant of authority to promulgate cost limit rules, §§ 1395x(1)(A), 1395hh, 1395ii. We consider these alternatives in turn.

A

. . . .

. . . [T]he retroactive rule cannot be upheld as an exercise of the Secretary's authority to make retroactive corrective adjustments.

B

The statutory provisions establishing the Secretary's general rulemaking power contain no express authorization of retroactive rulemaking. Any light that might be shed on this matter by suggestions of legislative intent also indicates that no such authority was contemplated. In the first place, where Congress intended to grant the Secretary the authority to act retroactively, it made that intent explicit. As discussed above, § 1395x(1)(A)(ii) directs the Secretary to establish procedures for making retroactive corrective adjustments; in view of this indication that Congress considered the need for retroactive agency action, the absence of any express authorization for retroactive cost-limit rules weighs heavily against the Secretary's position.

The legislative history of the cost-limit provision directly addresses the issue of retroactivity. In discussing the authority granted by § 223(b) of the 1972 amendments, the House and Senate Committee Reports expressed a desire to forbid retroactive cost-limit rules: "The proposed new authority to set limits on costs would be exercised on a prospective, rather than retrospective, basis so that the provider would know in advance the limits to Government recognition of incurred costs that are not reimbursable." H. R. Rep. No. 92-231, p. 83 (1971); see S. Rep. No. 92-1230, p. 188 (1972).

The Secretary's past administrative practice is consistent with this interpretation of the statute. The first regulations promulgated under § 223(b) provided that "these limits will be imposed prospectively." 20 CFR § 405.460(a) (1975). Although the language was dropped from subsection (a) of the regulation when it was revised in 1979, the revised regulation continued to refer to "the prospective periods to which limits are being applied," and it required that notice of future cost limits be published in the Federal Register "prior to the beginning of a cost period to which limits will be applied." 42 CFR §§ 405.460(b)(2), (3) (1980). Finally, when the regulations were amended again in 1982, the Secretary reinserted the requirement that the limits be applied with prospective effect, noting that the language had been "inadvertently omitted" in the previous amendment but that the reinsertion would "have no effect on the way we develop or apply the limits." 47 Fed. Reg. 43282, 23286 (1982); see 42 CFR § 405.460(a)(2) (1983).

Other examples of similar statements by the agency abound. . . .

The Secretary nonetheless suggests that, whatever the limits on his power to promulgate retroactive regulations in the normal course of events, judicial invalidation of a prospective rule is a unique occurrence that creates a heightened need, and thus a justification, for retroactive curative rulemaking. The Secretary warns that congressional intent and important administrative goals may be frustrated unless an invalidated rule can be cured of its defect and made applicable to past time periods. The argument is further advanced that the countervailing reliance interests are less compelling than in the usual case of retroactive rulemaking, because the original, invalidated rule provided at least some notice to the individuals and entities subject to its provisions.

Whatever weight the Secretary's contentions might have in other contexts, they need not be addressed here. The case before us is resolved by the particular statutory scheme in question. Our interpretation of the Medicare Act compels the conclusion that the Secretary has no authority to promulgate retroactive cost-limit rules.

The 1984 reinstatement of the 1981 cost-limit rule is invalid. The judgment of the Court of Appeals is

Affirmed.

Notes and Questions

---

1. What is the rule of retroactivity articulated in *Bowen*? Is that rule consistent with the rule articulated in *Bradley*? If not, which do you find the more reasonable?

2. Should the *Bowen* rule be considered a clear statement rule? *Cf. Gozlon-Peretz v. United States*, 498 U.S. 395, 404 (1991) ("[A]bsent a clear direction by Congress to the contrary, a law takes effect on the date of its enactment."). Or are the presumptions relating to retroactivity in some way unlike other rules relating to statutory interpretation?

Landgraf v. USI Film Products

511 U.S. 244 (1994)

JUSTICE STEVENS delivered the opinion of the Court.

The Civil Rights Act of 1991 (1991 Act or Act) creates a right to recover compensatory and punitive damages for certain violations of Title VII of the Civil Rights Act of 1964. See Rev. Stat. § 1977A(a), 42 U. S. C. § 1981a(a), as added by § 102 of the 1991 Act, Pub. L. 102-166, 105 Stat. 1071. The Act further provides that any party may demand a trial by jury if such damages are sought. We granted certiorari to decide whether these provisions apply to a Title VII case that was pending on appeal when the statute was enacted. We hold that they do not.

I

From September 4, 1984, through January 17, 1986, petitioner Barbara Landgraf was employed in the USI Film Products (USI) plant in Tyler, Texas. She worked the 11 p.m. to 7 a.m. shift operating a machine that produced plastic bags. A fellow employee named John Williams repeatedly harassed her with inappropriate remarks and physical contact. Petitioner's complaints to her immediate supervisor brought her no relief, but when she reported the incidents to the personnel manager, he conducted an investigation, reprimanded Williams, and transferred him to another department. Four days later petitioner quit her job.

. . . .

On July 21, 1989, petitioner commenced this action against USI, its corporate owner, and that company's successor-in-interest. After a bench trial, the District Court found that Williams had sexually harassed petitioner causing her to suffer mental anguish. However, the court concluded that she had not been constructively discharged. The court said:

> "Although the harassment was serious enough to establish that a hostile work environment existed for Landgraf, it was not so severe that a reasonable person would have felt compelled to resign. This is particularly true in light of the fact that at the time Landgraf resigned from her job, USI had taken steps to eliminate the hostile working environment arising from the sexual harassment. Landgraf voluntarily resigned from her employment with USI for reasons unrelated to the sexual harassment in question."

Because the court found that petitioner's employment was not terminated in violation of Title VII, she was not entitled to equitable relief, and because Title VII did not then authorize any other form of relief, the court dismissed her complaint.

On November 21, 1991, while petitioner's appeal was pending, the President signed into law the Civil Rights Act of 1991. The Court of Appeals rejected petitioner's argument that her case should be remanded for a jury trial on damages pursuant to the 1991 Act. Its decision not to remand rested on the premise that "a court must 'apply the law in effect at the time it renders its decision, unless doing so would result in manifest injustice or there is statutory direction or legislative history to the contrary.' *Bradley* v. *Richmond School Bd.*, 416 U. S. 696, 711 (1974)." Commenting first on the provision for a jury trial in § 102(c), the court stated that requiring the defendant "to retry this case because of a statutory change enacted after the trial was completed would be an injustice and a waste of judicial resources. We apply procedural rules to pending cases, but we do not invalidate procedures followed before the new rule was adopted." The court then characterized the provision for compensatory and punitive damages in § 102 as "a seachange in employer liability for Title VII violations" and concluded that it would be unjust to apply this kind of additional and unforeseeable obligation to conduct occurring before the effective date of the Act. Finding no clear error in the District Court's factual findings, the Court of Appeals affirmed the judgment for respondents.

We granted certiorari and set the case for argument with *Rivers* v. *Roadway Express, Inc.*, [511 U. S. 298 (1994)]. Our order limited argument to the question whether § 102 of the 1991 Act applies to cases pending when it became law.

Accordingly, for purposes of our decision, we assume that the District Court and the Court of Appeals properly applied the law in effect at the time of the discriminatory conduct and that the relevant findings of fact were correct. We therefore assume that petitioner was the victim of sexual harassment violative of Title VII, but that the law did not then authorize any recovery of damages even though she was injured. We also assume, *arguendo*, that if the same conduct were to occur today, petitioner would be entitled to a jury trial and that the jury might find that she was constructively discharged, or that her mental anguish or other injuries would support an award of damages against her former employer. Thus, the controlling question is whether the Court of Appeals should have applied the law in effect at the time the discriminatory conduct occurred, or at the time of its decision in July 1992.

II

. . . .

. . . Our first question . . . is whether the statutory text on which petitioner relies manifests an intent that the 1991 Act should be applied to cases that arose and went to trial before its enactment.

III

Petitioner's textual argument relies on three provisions of the 1991 Act: §§ 402(a), 402(b), and 109(c). Section 402(a), the only provision of the Act that speaks directly to the question before us, states:

> "Except as otherwise specifically provided, this Act and the amendments made by this Act shall take effect upon enactment."

That language does not, by itself, resolve the question before us. A statement that a statute will become effective on a certain date does not even arguably suggest that it has any application to conduct that occurred at an earlier date. . . .

. . . .

The relevant legislative history of the 1991 Act reinforces our conclusion that §§ 402(a), 109(c) and 402(b) cannot bear the weight petitioner places upon them. The 1991 bill as originally introduced in the House contained explicit retroactivity provisions similar to those found in the [vetoed] 1990 bill. However, the Senate substitute that was agreed upon omitted those explicit retroactivity provisions. The legislative history discloses some frankly partisan statements about the meaning of the final effective date language, but those statements cannot plausibly be read as reflecting any general agreement. The history reveals no evidence that Members believed that an agreement had been tacitly struck on the controversial retroactivity issue, and little to suggest that *Congress* understood or intended the interplay of §§ 402(a), 402(b) and 109(c) to have the decisive effect petitioner assigns them. Instead, the history of the 1991 Act conveys the impression that legislators agreed to disagree about whether and to what extent the Act would apply to preenactment conduct.

Although the passage of the 1990 bill may indicate that a majority of the 1991 Congress also favored retroactive application, even the will of the majority does not become law unless it follows the path charted in Article I, § 7, cl. 2 of the Constitution. See *INS* v. *Chadha*, 462 U. S. 919, 946-951 (1983). In the absence of the kind of unambiguous directive found in § 15 of the 1990 bill, we must look elsewhere for guidance on whether § 102 applies to this case.

IV

It is not uncommon to find "apparent tension" between different canons of statutory construction. As Professor Llewellyn famously illustrated, many of the traditional canons have equal opposites.[16] In order to resolve the question left open by the 1991 Act, federal courts have labored to reconcile two seemingly contradictory statements found in our decisions concerning the effect of intervening changes in the law. Each statement is framed as a generally applicable rule for interpreting statutes that do not specify their temporal reach. The first is the rule that "a court is to apply the law in effect at the time it renders its decision," *Bradley*, 416 U. S., at 711. The second is the axiom that "retroactivity is not favored in the law," and its interpretive corollary that "congressional enactments and administrative rules will not be construed to have retroactive effect unless their language requires this result." *Bowen*, 488 U. S., at 208.

We have previously noted the "apparent tension" between those expressions. We found it unnecessary in *Kaiser* [*Aluminum & Chemical Corp.* v. *Bonjorno*, 494 U. S. 827 (1990)] to resolve that seeming conflict "because under either view, where the congressional intent is clear, it governs," and the prejudgment interest statute at issue in that case evinced "clear congressional intent" that it was "not applicable to judgments entered before its effective date." In the case before us today, however, we have concluded that the Civil Rights Act of 1991 does not evince any clear expression of intent on § 102's application to cases arising before the Act's enactment. We must, therefore, focus on the apparent tension between the rules we have espoused for handling similar problems in the absence of an instruction from Congress.

We begin by noting that there is no tension between the *holdings* in *Bradley* and *Bowen*, both of which were unanimous decisions. Relying on another unanimous decision — *Thorpe* v. *Housing Authority of Durham*, 393 U. S. 268 (1969) — we held in *Bradley* that a statute authorizing the award of attorney's fees to successful civil rights plaintiffs applied in a case that was pending on appeal at the time the statute was enacted. *Bowen* held that the Department of Health and Human Services lacked statutory authority to promulgate a rule requiring private hospitals to refund

---

16. See Llewellyn, Remarks on the Theory of Appellate Decision and the Rules or Canons about How Statutes are to be Construed, 3 Vand. L. Rev. 395 (1950). Llewellyn's article identified the apparent conflict between the canon that

"a statute imposing a new penalty or forfeiture, or a new liability or disability, or creating a new right of action will not be construed as having retroactive effect" and the countervailing rule that

"remedial statutes are to be liberally construed and if a retroactive interpretation will promote the ends of justice, they should receive such construction."

Medicare payments for services rendered before promulgation of the rule. Our opinion in *Bowen* did not purport to overrule *Bradley* or to limit its reach. In this light, we turn to the "apparent tension" between the two canons mindful of another canon of unquestionable vitality, the "maxim not to be disregarded that general expressions, in every opinion, are to be taken in connection with the case in which those expressions are used." *Cohens* v. *Virginia*, 6 Wheat. 264, 399 (1821).

A

As Justice Scalia has demonstrated, the presumption against retroactive legislation is deeply rooted in our jurisprudence, and embodies a legal doctrine centuries older than our Republic.[17] Elementary considerations of fairness dictate that individuals should have an opportunity to know what the law is and to conform their conduct accordingly; settled expectations should not be lightly disrupted.[18] For that reason, the "principle that the legal effect of conduct should ordinarily be assessed under the law that existed when the conduct took place has timeless and universal appeal." *Kaiser*, 494 U. S., at 855 (Scalia, J., concurring). In a free, dynamic society, creativity in both commercial and artistic endeavors is fostered by a rule of law that gives people confidence about the legal consequences of their actions.

It is therefore not surprising that the antiretroactivity principle finds expression in several provisions of our Constitution. The *Ex Post Facto* Clause flatly prohibits retroactive application of penal legislation.[19] Article I, § 10, cl. 1 prohibits States from passing another type of retroactive legislation, laws "impairing the Obligation of Contracts." The Fifth Amendment's Takings Clause prevents the Legislature (and other government actors) from depriving private persons of vested property rights except for a "public use" and upon payment of "just compensation." The prohibitions on "Bills of Attainder" in Art. I, §§ 9-10, prohibit legislatures from singling out disfavored persons and meting out summary punishment for past conduct. The Due Process Clause also protects the interests in fair notice and repose that may be compromised by retroactive legislation; a justification sufficient to validate a statute's prospective application under the Clause may not suffice to warrant its retroactive application.

---

17. See *Kaiser Aluminum & Chemical Corp.* v. *Bonjorno*, 494 U. S. 827, 842-44 (1990) (Scalia, J., concurring). See also, *e.g.*, *Dash* v. *Van Kleeck*, 7 Johns. *477, *503 (N.Y. 1811) ("It is a principle of the *English* common law, as ancient as the law itself, that a statute, even of its omnipotent parliament, is not to have a retrospective effect") (Kent, C. J.); Smead, The Rule Against Retroactive Legislation: A Basic Principle of Jurisprudence, 20 Minn. L. Rev. 775 (1936).

18. See *General Motors Corp.* v. *Romein*, 503 U. S. 181, 191 (1992) ("Retroactive legislation presents problems of unfairness that are more serious than those posed by prospective legislation, because it can deprive citizens of legitimate expectations and upset settled transactions"); Munzer, A Theory of Retroactive Legislation, 61 Texas L. Rev. 425, 471 (1982) ("The rule of law is a defeasible entitlement of persons to have their behavior governed by rules publicly fixed in advance"). See also L. Fuller, The Morality of Law 51-62 (1964) (hereinafter Fuller).

19. Article I contains two *Ex Post Facto* Clauses, one directed to Congress (§ 9, cl. 3), the other to the States (§ 10, cl. 1). We have construed the Clauses as applicable only to penal legislation. See *Calder* v. *Bull*, 3 Dall. 386, 390-91 (1798) (opinion of Chase, J.).

These provisions demonstrate that retroactive statutes raise particular concerns. The Legislature's unmatched powers allow it to sweep away settled expectations suddenly and without individualized consideration. Its responsivity to political pressures poses a risk that it may be tempted to use retroactive legislation as a means of retribution against unpopular groups or individuals. As Justice Marshall observed in his opinion in *Weaver* v. *Graham*, 450 U. S. 24 (1981), the *Ex Post Facto* Clause not only ensures that individuals have "fair warning" about the effect of criminal statutes, but also "restricts government power by restraining arbitrary and potentially vindictive legislation." *Id.*, at 28-29 (citations omitted).[20]

The Constitution's restrictions, of course, are of limited scope. Absent a violation of one of those specific provisions, the potential unfairness of retroactive civil legislation is not a sufficient reason for a court to fail to give a statute its intended scope. Retroactivity provisions often serve entirely benign and legitimate purposes, whether to respond to emergencies, to correct mistakes, to prevent circumvention of a new statute in the interval immediately preceding its passage, or simply to give comprehensive effect to a new law Congress considers salutary. However, a requirement that Congress first make its intention clear helps ensure that Congress itself has determined that the benefits of retroactivity outweigh the potential for disruption or unfairness.

While statutory retroactivity has long been disfavored, deciding when a statute operates "retroactively" is not always a simple or mechanical task. Sitting on Circuit, Justice Story offered an influential definition in *Society for Propagation of the Gospel* v. *Wheeler*, 22 F. Cas. 756 (No. 13,156) (CCDNH 1814), a case construing a provision of the New Hampshire Constitution that broadly prohibits "retrospective" laws both criminal and civil. Justice Story first rejected the notion that the provision bars only explicitly retroactive legislation, *i.e.*, "statutes enacted to take effect from a time anterior to their passage." Such a construction, he concluded, would be "utterly subversive of all the objects" of the prohibition. Instead, the ban on retrospective legislation

---

20. See *Richmond* v. *J. A. Croson Co.*, 488 U. S. 469, 513-514 (1989) ("Legislatures are primarily policymaking bodies that promulgate rules to govern future conduct. The constitutional prohibitions against the enactment of *ex post facto* laws and bills of attainder reflect a valid concern about the use of the political process to punish or characterize past conduct of private citizens. It is the judicial system, rather than the legislative process, that is best equipped to identify past wrongdoers and to fashion remedies that will create the conditions that presumably would have existed had no wrong been committed") (Stevens, J., concurring in part and concurring in judgment); *James* v. *United States*, 366 U. S. 213, 247 n. 3 (1961) (retroactive punitive measures may reflect "a purpose not to prevent dangerous conduct generally but to impose by legislation a penalty against specific persons or classes of persons").

James Madison argued that retroactive legislation also offered special opportunities for the powerful to obtain special and improper legislative benefits. According to Madison, "bills of attainder, ex post facto laws, and laws impairing the obligation of contracts" were "contrary to the first principles of sound legislation," in part because such measures invited the "influential" to "speculate on public measures," to the detriment of the "more industrious and less informed part of the community." The Federalist No. 44, p. 301 (J. Cooke ed. 1961). See Hochman, The Supreme Court and the Constitutionality of Retroactive Legislation, 73 Harv. L. Rev. 692, 693 (1960) (a retroactive statute "may be passed with an exact knowledge of who will benefit from it").

embraced "all statutes, which, though operating only from their passage, affect vested rights and past transactions." "Upon principle," Justice Story elaborated,

> "every statute, which takes away or impairs vested rights acquired under existing laws, or creates a new obligation, imposes a new duty, or attaches a new disability, in respect to transactions or considerations already past, must be deemed retrospective."

Though the formulas have varied, similar functional conceptions of legislative "retroactivity" have found voice in this Court's decisions and elsewhere.

A statute does not operate "retrospectively" merely because it is applied in a case arising from conduct antedating the statute's enactment, or upsets expectations based in prior law.[24] Rather, the court must ask whether the new provision attaches new legal consequences to events completed before its enactment. The conclusion that a particular rule operates "retroactively" comes at the end of a process of judgment concerning the nature and extent of the change in the law and the degree of connection between the operation of the new rule and a relevant past event. Any test of retroactivity will leave room for disagreement in hard cases, and is unlikely to classify the enormous variety of legal changes with perfect philosophical clarity. However, retroactivity is a matter on which judges tend to have "sound instincts" and familiar considerations of fair notice, reasonable reliance, and settled expectations offer sound guidance.

Since the early days of this Court, we have declined to give retroactive effect to statutes burdening private rights unless Congress had made clear its intent. . . . The presumption against statutory retroactivity has consistently been explained by reference to the unfairness of imposing new burdens on persons after the fact. Indeed, at common law a contrary rule applied to statutes that merely *removed* a burden on private rights by repealing a penal provision (whether criminal or civil); such repeals were understood to preclude punishment for acts antedating the repeal.

The largest category of cases in which we have applied the presumption against statutory retroactivity has involved new provisions affecting contractual or property rights, matters in which predictability and stability are of prime importance. The presumption has not, however, been limited to such cases. . . .

Our statement in *Bowen* that "congressional enactments and administrative rules will not be construed to have retroactive effect unless their language requires this result" was in step with this long line of cases. *Bowen* itself was a paradigmatic case of retroactivity in which a federal agency sought to recoup, under cost limit regulations issued in 1984, funds that had been paid to hospitals for services rendered earlier; our search for clear congressional intent authorizing retroactivity was consistent with the approach taken in decisions spanning two centuries.

---

24. Even uncontroversially prospective statutes may unsettle expectations and impose burdens on past conduct: a new property tax or zoning regulation may upset the reasonable expectations that prompted those affected to acquire property; a new law banning gambling harms the person who had begun to construct a casino before the law's enactment or spent his life learning to count cards. See [L. Fuller, The Morality of Law 60 (1964)] ("If every time a man relied on existing law in arranging his affairs, he were made secure against any change in legal rules, the whole body of our law would be ossified forever."). Moreover, a statute "is not made retroactive merely because it draws upon antecedent facts for its operation."

The presumption against statutory retroactivity had special force in the era in which courts tended to view legislative interference with property and contract rights circumspectly. In this century, legislation has come to supply the dominant means of legal ordering, and circumspection has given way to greater deference to legislative judgments. But while the *constitutional* impediments to retroactive civil legislation are now modest, prospectivity remains the appropriate default rule. Because it accords with widely held intuitions about how statutes ordinarily operate, a presumption against retroactivity will generally coincide with legislative and public expectations. Requiring clear intent assures that Congress itself has affirmatively considered the potential unfairness of retroactive application and determined that it is an acceptable price to pay for the countervailing benefits. Such a requirement allocates to Congress responsibility for fundamental policy judgments concerning the proper temporal reach of statutes, and has the additional virtue of giving legislators a predictable background rule against which to legislate.

B

Although we have long embraced a presumption against statutory retroactivity, for just as long we have recognized that, in many situations, a court should "apply the law in effect at the time it renders its decision," *Bradley*, 416 U. S. at 711, even though that law was enacted after the events that gave rise to the suit. There is, of course, no conflict between that principle and a *presumption* against retroactivity when the statute in question is unambiguous. . . .

Even absent specific legislative authorization, application of new statutes passed after the events in suit is unquestionably proper in many situations. When the intervening statute authorizes or affects the propriety of prospective relief, application of the new provision is not retroactive. . . .

We have regularly applied intervening statutes concerning or ousting jurisdiction, whether or not jurisdiction lay when the underlying conduct occurred or when the suit was filed. . . . Application of a new jurisdictional rule usually "takes away no substantive right but simply changes the tribunal that is to hear the case." Present law normally governs in such situations because jurisdictional statutes "speak to the power of the court rather than to the rights or obligations of the parties."

Changes in procedural rules may often be applied in suits arising before their enactment without raising concerns about retroactivity. . . . Because rules of procedure regulate secondary rather than primary conduct, the fact that a new procedural rule was instituted after the conduct giving rise to the suit does not make application of the rule at trial retroactive.[29]

---

29. Of course, the mere fact that a new rule is procedural does not mean that it applies to every pending case. A new rule concerning the filing of complaints would not govern an action in which the complaint had already been properly filed under the old regime, and the promulgation of a new rule of evidence would not require an appellate remand for a new trial. Our orders approving amendments to federal procedural rules reflect the common-sense notion that the applicability of such provisions ordinarily depends on the posture of the particular case. Contrary to Justice Scalia's suggestion, we do not restrict the presumption against statutory retroactivity to cases involving "vested rights." (Neither is Justice Story's definition of retroactivity, quoted *supra*, so restricted.) Nor do we suggest that concerns about retroactivity have no application to procedural rules.

Petitioner relies principally upon *Bradley v. Richmond School Bd.*, 416 U. S. 696 (1974), and *Thorpe v. Housing Authority of Durham*, 393 U. S. 268 (1969), in support of her argument that our ordinary interpretive rules support application of § 102 to her case. In *Thorpe*, we held that an agency circular requiring a local housing authority to give notice of reasons and opportunity to respond before evicting a tenant was applicable to an eviction proceeding commenced before the regulation issued. *Thorpe* shares much with both the "procedural" and "prospective-relief" cases. Thus, we noted in *Thorpe* that new hearing procedures did not affect either party's obligations under the lease agreement between the housing authority and the petitioner and, because the tenant had "not yet vacated," we saw no significance in the fact that the housing authority had "decided to evict her before the circular was issued." The Court in *Thorpe* viewed the new eviction procedures as "essential to remove a serious impediment to the successful protection of constitutional rights."

Our holding in *Bradley* is similarly compatible with the line of decisions disfavoring "retroactive" application of statutes. In *Bradley*, the District Court had awarded attorney's fees and costs, upon general equitable principles, to parents who had prevailed in an action seeking to desegregate the public schools of Richmond, Virginia. While the case was pending before the Court of Appeals, Congress enacted § 718 of the Education Amendments of 1972, which authorized federal courts to award the prevailing parties in school desegregation cases a reasonable attorney's fee. The Court of Appeals held that the new fee provision did not authorize the award of fees for services rendered before the effective date of the amendments. This Court reversed. We concluded that the private parties could rely on § 718 to support their claim for attorney's fees, resting our decision "on the principle that a court is to apply the law in effect at the time it renders its decision, unless doing so would result in manifest injustice or there is statutory direction or legislative history to the contrary."

Although that language suggests a categorical presumption in favor of application of *all* new rules of law, we now make it clear that *Bradley* did not alter the well-settled presumption against application of the class of new statutes that would have genuinely "retroactive" effect. Like the new hearing requirement in *Thorpe*, the attorney's fee provision at issue in *Bradley* did not resemble the cases in which we have invoked the presumption against statutory retroactivity. Attorney's fee determinations, we have observed, are "collateral to the main cause of action" and "uniquely separable from the cause of action to be proved at trial." Moreover, even before the enactment of § 718, federal courts had authority (which the District Court in *Bradley* had exercised) to award fees based upon equitable principles. As our opinion in *Bradley* makes clear, it would be difficult to imagine a stronger equitable case for an attorney's fee award than a lawsuit in which the plaintiff parents would otherwise have to bear the costs of desegregating their children's public schools. In light of the prior availability of a fee award, and the likelihood that fees would be assessed under pre-existing theories, we concluded that the new fee statute simply "did not impose an additional or unforeseeable obligation" upon the school board.

In approving application of the new fee provision, *Bradley* did not take issue with the long line of decisions applying the presumption against retroactivity. Our opinion distinguished, but did not criticize, prior cases that had applied the anti-retroactivity canon. The authorities we relied upon in *Bradley* lend further support to the conclusion that we did not intend to displace the traditional presumption against applying statutes affecting substantive rights, liabilities, or duties to conduct arising before their enactment. *Bradley* relied on *Thorpe* and on other precedents that are consistent with a presumption against statutory retroactivity, including decisions involving explicitly retroactive statutes,[31] the retroactive application of intervening *judicial* decisions,[32] statutes altering jurisdiction, and repeal of a criminal statute. Moreover, in none of our decisions that have relied upon *Bradley* or *Thorpe* have we cast doubt on the traditional presumption against truly "retrospective" application of a statute.

When a case implicates a federal statute enacted after the events in suit, the court's first task is to determine whether Congress has expressly prescribed the statute's proper reach. If Congress has done so, of course, there is no need to resort to judicial default rules. When, however, the statute contains no such express command, the court must determine whether the new statute would have retroactive effect, *i.e.*, whether it would impair rights a party possessed when he acted, increase a party's liability for past conduct, or impose new duties with respect to transactions already completed. If the statute would operate retroactively, our traditional presumption teaches that it does not govern absent clear congressional intent favoring such a result.

V

We now ask whether, given the absence of guiding instructions from Congress, § 102 of the Civil Rights Act of 1991 is the type of provision that should govern cases arising before its enactment. As we observed *supra*, there is no special reason to think that all the diverse provisions of the Act must be treated uniformly for such purposes. To the contrary, we understand the instruction that the provisions are to "take effect upon enactment" to mean that courts should evaluate each provision of the Act in light of ordinary judicial principles concerning the application of new rules to pending cases and preenactment conduct.

Two provisions of § 102 may be readily classified according to these principles. The jury trial right set out in § 102(c)(1) is plainly a procedural change of the sort that would ordinarily govern in trials conducted after its effective date. If § 102 did no more than introduce a right to jury trial in Title VII cases, the provision would

---

31. In *Bradley*, we cited *Schooner Peggy* for the "current law" principle, but we recognized that the law at issue in *Schooner Peggy* had expressly called for retroactive application.

32. At the time *Bradley* was decided, it was by no means a truism to point out that rules announced in intervening judicial decisions should normally be applied to a case pending when the intervening decision came down. In 1974, our doctrine on judicial retroactivity involved a substantial measure of discretion, guided by equitable standards resembling the *Bradley* "manifest injustice" test itself. See *Chevron Oil Co.* v. *Huson*, 404 U. S. 97, 106-107 (1971); *Linkletter* v. *Walker*, 381 U. S. 618, 636 (1965). While it was accurate in 1974 to say that a new rule announced in a judicial decision was only *presumptively* applicable to pending cases, we have since established a firm rule of retroactivity. See *Harper* v. *Virginia Dept. of Taxation*, 509 U. S. 86 (1993); *Griffith* v. *Kentucky*, 479 U. S. 314 (1987).

presumably apply to cases tried after November 21, 1991, regardless of when the underlying conduct occurred. However, because § 102(c) makes a jury trial available only "if a complaining party seeks compensatory or punitive damages," the jury trial option must stand or fall with the attached damages provision.

Section 102(b)(1) is clearly on the other side of the line. That subsection authorizes punitive damages if the plaintiff shows that the defendant "engages in a discriminatory practice with malice or with reckless indifference to the federally protected rights of an aggrieved individual." The very labels given "punitive" or "exemplary" damages, as well as the rationales that support them, demonstrate that they share key characteristics of criminal sanctions. Retroactive imposition of punitive damages would raise a serious constitutional question. Before we entertained that question, we would have to be confronted with a statute that explicitly authorized punitive damages for preenactment conduct. The Civil Rights Act of 1991 contains no such explicit command.

The provisions of § 102(a)(1) authorizing the recovery of compensatory damages is not easily classified. It does not make unlawful conduct that was lawful when it occurred; as we have noted, *supra*, § 102 only reaches discriminatory conduct already prohibited by Title VII. Concerns about a lack of fair notice are further muted by the fact that such discrimination was in many cases (although not this one) already subject to monetary liability in the form of backpay. Nor could anyone seriously contend that the compensatory damages provisions smack of a "retributive" or other suspect legislative purpose. Section 102 reflects Congress' desire to afford victims of discrimination more complete redress for violations of rules established more than a generation ago in the Civil Rights Act of 1964. At least with respect to its compensatory damages provisions, then, § 102 is not in a category in which objections to retroactive application on grounds of fairness have their greatest force.

Nonetheless, the new compensatory damages provision would operate "retrospectively" if it were applied to conduct occurring before November 21, 1991. Unlike certain other forms of relief, compensatory damages are quintessentially backward-looking. Compensatory damages may be *intended* less to sanction wrongdoers than to make victims whole, but they do so by a mechanism that affects the liabilities of defendants. They do not "compensate" by distributing funds from the public coffers, but by requiring particular employers to pay for harms they caused. The introduction of a right to compensatory damages is also the type of legal change that would have an impact on private parties' planning. In this case, the event to which the new damages provision relates is the discriminatory conduct of respondents' agent John Williams; if applied here, that provision would attach an important new legal burden to that conduct. The new damages remedy in § 102, we conclude, is the kind of provision that does not apply to events antedating its enactment in the absence of clear congressional intent.

In cases like this one, in which prior law afforded no relief, § 102 can be seen as creating a new cause of action, and its impact on parties' rights is especially pronounced. Section 102 confers a new right to monetary relief on persons like petitioner who were victims of a hostile work environment but were not constructively discharged, and the novel prospect of damages liability for their employers. Because Title VII previously authorized recovery of backpay in some cases, and because compensatory damages under § 102(a) are in addition to any backpay recoverable, the new provision also resembles a statute increasing the amount of damages available under a preestablished cause of action. Even under that view, however, the provision would, if applied in cases arising before the Act's effective date, undoubtedly impose on employers found liable a "new disability" in respect to past events. The *extent* of a party's liability, in the civil context as well as the criminal, is an important legal consequence that cannot be ignored.[36] Neither in *Bradley* itself, nor in any case before or since in which Congress had not clearly spoken, have we read a statute substantially increasing the monetary liability of a private party to apply to conduct occurring before the statute's enactment.[37]

It will frequently be true, as petitioner and *amici* forcefully argue here, that retroactive application of a new statute would vindicate its purpose more fully. That consideration, however, is not sufficient to rebut the presumption against retroactivity. Statutes are seldom crafted to pursue a single goal, and compromises necessary to their enactment may require adopting means other than those that would most effectively pursue the main goal. A legislator who supported a prospective statute might reasonably oppose retroactive application of the same statute. Indeed, there is reason to believe that the omission of the 1990 version's express retroactivity provisions was a factor in the passage of the 1991 bill. Section 102 is plainly not the sort of provision that *must* be understood to operate retroactively because a contrary reading would render it ineffective.

The presumption against statutory retroactivity is founded upon sound considerations of general policy and practice, and accords with long held and widely shared expectations about the usual operation of legislation. We are satisfied that it applies to § 102. Because we have found no clear evidence of congressional intent that § 102 of the Civil Rights Act of 1991 should apply to cases arising before its enactment, we conclude that the judgment of the Court of Appeals must be affirmed.

It is so ordered.

JUSTICE SCALIA, with whom JUSTICE KENNEDY and JUSTICE THOMAS join, concurring in the judgment.

I

I of course agree with the Court that there exists a judicial presumption, of great antiquity, that a legislative enactment affecting substantive rights does not apply

---

36. The state courts have consistently held that statutes changing or abolishing limits on the amount of damages available in wrongful death actions should not, in the absence of clear legislative intent, apply to actions arising before their enactment.

37. We have sometimes said that new "remedial" statutes, like new "procedural" ones, should presumptively apply to pending cases. While that statement holds true for some kinds of remedies, we have not classified a statute introducing damages liability as the sort of "remedial" change that should presumptively apply in pending cases. "Retroactive modification" of damage remedies may "normally harbor much less potential for mischief than retroactive changes in the principles of liability," but that potential is nevertheless still significant.

retroactively absent *clear statement* to the contrary. *Kaiser Aluminum & Chemical Corp.* v. *Bonjourno*, 494 U. S. 827, 840 (1990) (Scalia, J., concurring). The Court, however, is willing to let that clear statement be supplied, not by the text of the law in question, but by individual legislators who participated in the enactment of the law, and even legislators in an earlier Congress which tried and failed to enact a similar law. For the Court not only combs the floor debate and committee reports of the statute at issue, but also reviews the procedural history of an earlier, unsuccessful, attempt by a *different* Congress to enact similar legislation.

This effectively converts the "clear statement" rule into a "discernible legislative intent" rule — and even that understates the difference. The Court's rejection of the floor statements of certain Senators because they are "frankly partisan" and "cannot plausibly be read as reflecting any general agreement" reads like any other exercise in the soft science of legislative historicizing,[1] undisciplined by any distinctive "clear statement" requirement. If it is a "clear statement" we are seeking, surely it is not enough to insist that the statement can "plausibly be read as reflecting general agreement"; the statement must *clearly* reflect general agreement. No legislative history can do that, of course, but only the text of the statute itself. That has been the meaning of the "clear statement" retroactivity rule from the earliest times. I do not deem that clear rule to be changed by the Court's dicta regarding legislative history in the present case.

The 1991 Act does not expressly state that it operates retroactively, but petitioner contends that its specification of prospective-only application for two sections, §§ 109(c) and 402(b), implies that its other provisions are retroactive. More precisely, petitioner argues that since § 402(a) states that "except as otherwise specifically provided, the 1991 Act shall take effect upon enactment"; and since §§ 109(c) and 402(b) specifically provide that those sections shall operate only prospectively; the term "shall take effect upon enactment" in § 402(a) must mean *retroactive* effect. The short response to this refined and subtle argument is that refinement and subtlety are no substitute for clear statement. "Shall take effect upon enactment" is presumed to mean "shall have prospective effect upon enactment," and that presumption is too strong to be overcome by any negative inference derived from §§ 109(c) and 402(b).

II

The Court's opinion begins with an evaluation of petitioner's argument that the text of the statute dictates its retroactive application. The Court's rejection of that argument cannot be as forceful as it ought, so long as it insists upon compromising the clarity of the ancient and constant assumption that legislation is prospective, by attributing a comparable pedigree to the nouveau *Bradley* presumption in favor of

---

1. In one respect, I must acknowledge, the Court's effort may be unique. There is novelty as well as irony in the Court's supporting the judgment that the floor statements on the 1991 Act are unreliable by citing Senator Danforth's floor statement on the 1991 Act to the effect that floor statements on the 1991 Act are unreliable.

applying the law in effect at the time of decision. As I have demonstrated elsewhere and need not repeat here, *Bradley* and *Thorpe* simply misread our precedents and invented an utterly new and erroneous rule. See generally *Bonjourno*, 494 U. S., at 840 (Scalia, J., concurring).

Besides embellishing the pedigree of the *Bradley-Thorpe* presumption, the Court goes out of its way to reaffirm the holdings of those cases. I see nothing to be gained by overruling them, but neither do I think the indefensible should needlessly be defended. And *Thorpe*, at least, is really indefensible. The regulation at issue there required that "before *instituting an eviction proceeding* local housing authorities should inform the tenant of the reasons for the eviction." The Court imposed that requirement on an eviction proceeding *instituted eighteen months before the regulation issued*. That application was plainly retroactive and was wrong. The result in *Bradley* presents a closer question; application of an attorney's fees provision to ongoing litigation is arguably not retroactive. If it *were* retroactive, however, it would surely not be saved (as the Court suggests) by the existence of another theory under which attorney's fees might have been discretionarily awarded.

III

My last, and most significant, disagreement with the Court's analysis of this case pertains to the meaning of retroactivity. The Court adopts as its own the definition crafted by Justice Story in a case involving a provision of the New Hampshire Constitution that prohibited "retrospective" laws: a law is retroactive only if it "takes away or impairs vested rights acquired under existing laws, or creates a new obligation, imposes a new duty, or attaches a new disability, in respect to transactions or considerations already past."

One might expect from this "vested rights" focus that the Court would hold all changes in rules of procedure (as opposed to matters of substance) to apply retroactively. And one would draw the same conclusion from the Court's formulation of the test as being "whether the new provision attaches new legal consequences to events completed before its enactment" — a test borrowed directly from our *ex post facto* Clause jurisprudence, where we have adopted a substantive-procedural line. In fact, however, the Court shrinks from faithfully applying the test that it has announced. It first seemingly defends the procedural-substantive distinction that a "vested rights" theory entails. But it soon acknowledges a broad and ill defined (indeed, utterly undefined) exception: "Our orders approving amendments to federal procedural rules reflect the common-sense notion that the applicability of such provisions ordinarily depends on the posture of the particular case." Under this exception, "a new rule concerning the filing of complaints would not govern an action in which the complaint had already been properly filed," and "the promulgation of a new jury trial rule would ordinarily not warrant retrial of cases that had previously been tried to a judge." It is hard to see how either of these refusals to allow retroactive application preserves any "vested right." " 'No one has a vested right in any given mode of procedure.' "

The seemingly random exceptions to the Court's "vested rights" (substance-*vs.*-procedure) criterion must be made, I suggest, because that criterion is fundamentally wrong. It may well be that the upsetting of "vested substantive rights" was the proper touchstone for interpretation of New Hampshire's constitutional prohibition, as it is for interpretation of the United States Constitution's *ex post facto* Clauses. But I doubt that it has anything to do with the more mundane question before us here: absent clear statement to the contrary, what is the presumed temporal application of a statute? For purposes of *that* question, a *procedural* change should no more be presumed retroactive than a *substantive* one. The critical issue, I think, is not whether the rule affects "vested rights," or governs substance or procedure, but rather what is the relevant activity that the rule regulates. Absent clear statement otherwise, only such relevant activity which occurs *after* the effective date of the statute is covered. Most statutes are meant to regulate primary conduct, and hence will not be applied in trials involving conduct that occurred before their effective date. But other statutes have a different purpose and therefore a different relevant retroactivity event. A new rule of evidence governing expert testimony, for example, is aimed at regulating the conduct of trial, and the event relevant to retroactivity of the rule is introduction of the testimony. Even though it is a procedural rule, it would unquestionably not be applied to *testimony already taken* — reversing a case on appeal, for example, because the new rule had not been applied at a trial which antedated the statute.

The inadequacy of the Court's "vested rights" approach becomes apparent when a change in one of the incidents of trial alters substantive entitlements. The opinion classifies attorney's fees provisions as procedural and permits "retroactive" application (in the sense of application to cases involving pre-enactment conduct). It seems to me, however, that holding a person liable for attorney's fees affects a "substantive right" no less than holding him liable for compensatory or punitive damages, which the Court treats as affecting a vested right. If attorney's fees can be awarded in a suit involving conduct that antedated the fee-authorizing statute, it is because the purpose of the fee award is not to affect that conduct, but to encourage suit for the vindication of certain rights — so that the retroactivity event is the filing of suit, whereafter encouragement is no longer needed. Or perhaps because the purpose of the fee award is to *facilitate* suit — so that the retroactivity event is the termination of suit, whereafter facilitation can no longer be achieved.

The "vested rights" test does not square with our consistent practice of giving immediate effect to statutes that alter a court's jurisdiction. The Court explains this aspect of our retroactivity jurisprudence by noting that "a new jurisdictional rule will often not involve 'retroactivity' in Justice Story's sense because it 'takes away no substantive right but simply changes the tribunal that is to hear the case.'" That may be true sometimes, but surely not always. A jurisdictional rule can deny a litigant a forum for his claim entirely, or may leave him with an alternate forum that will deny relief for some collateral reason (*e.g.*, a statute of limitations bar). Our jurisdiction cases are explained, I think, by the fact that the purpose of provisions conferring or eliminating jurisdiction is to permit or forbid the exercise of judicial power — so that the relevant event for retroactivity purposes is the moment at which that power is sought to be exercised. Thus, applying a jurisdiction-eliminating statute to undo past judicial action would be applying it retroactively; but applying it to prevent any judicial action after the statute takes effect is applying it prospectively.

Finally, statutes eliminating previously available forms of prospective relief provide another challenge to the Court's approach. Courts traditionally withhold requested injunctions that are not authorized by then-current law, even if they were authorized at the time suit commenced and at the time the primary conduct sought to be enjoined was first engaged in. The reason, which has nothing to do with whether it is possible to have a vested right to prospective relief, is that "obviously, this form of relief operates only *in futuro*." Since the purpose of prospective relief is to affect the future rather than remedy the past, the relevant time for judging its retroactivity is the very moment at which it is ordered.[3]

I do not maintain that it will always be easy to determine, from the statute's purpose, the relevant event for assessing its retroactivity. As I have suggested, for example, a statutory provision for attorney's fees presents a difficult case. Ordinarily, however, the answer is clear — as it is in both *Landgraf* and *Rivers*. Unlike the Court, I do not think that any of the provisions at issue is "not easily classified." They are all directed at the regulation of primary conduct, and the occurrence of the primary conduct is the relevant event.

JUSTICE BLACKMUN, dissenting.

Perhaps from an eagerness to resolve the "apparent tension" between *Bradley* and *Bowen*, the Court rejects the "most logical reading," and resorts to a presumption against retroactivity. This approach seems to me to pay insufficient fidelity to the settled principle that the "starting point for interpretation of a statute 'is the language of the statute itself,'" and extends the presumption against retroactive legislation beyond its historical reach and purpose.

A straightforward textual analysis of the Act indicates that § 102's provision of compensatory damages and its attendant right to a jury trial apply to cases pending on appeal on the date of enactment. This analysis begins with § 402(a) of the Act: "Except as otherwise specifically provided, this Act and the amendments made by this Act shall take effect upon enactment." Under the "settled rule that a statute must, if possible, be construed in such fashion that every word has operative effect," *United States* v. *Nordic Village, Inc.*, 503 U. S. 30, 36 (1992), § 402(a)'s qualifying clause, "except as otherwise specifically provided," cannot be dismissed as mere surplusage or an "insurance policy" against future judicial interpretation. Instead, it most logically refers to the Act's two sections "specifically providing" that the statute does not apply to cases pending on the date of enactment: (a) § 402(b), which provides, in effect, that the Act did not apply to the then pending case of *Wards Cove Packing Co.* v. *Atonio*, 490 U. S. 642 (1989), and (b) § 109(c), which states that the Act's protections of overseas employment "shall not apply with respect to conduct occurring before the date of the

---

3. A focus on the relevant retroactivity event also explains why the presumption against retroactivity is not violated by interpreting a statute to alter the future legal effect of past transactions — so-called secondary retroactivity, see *Bowen* v. *Georgetown Univ. Hospital*, 488 U. S. 204, 219-220 (1988) (Scalia, J., concurring) (citing McNulty, Corporations and the Intertemporal Conflict of Laws, 55 Calif. L. Rev. 12, 58-60 (1967)). A new ban on gambling applies to existing casinos and casinos under construction, even though it "attaches a new disability" to those past investments. The relevant retroactivity event is the primary activity of gambling, not the primary activity of constructing casinos.

enactment of this Act." Self-evidently, if the entire Act were inapplicable to pending cases, §§ 402(b) and 109(c) would be "entirely redundant." Thus, the clear implication is that, while § 402(b) and § 109(c) do not apply to pending cases, other provisions — including § 102 — do. "'Absent a clearly expressed legislative intention to the contrary, this language must be regarded as conclusive.'" The legislative history of the Act, featuring a welter of conflicting and "some frankly partisan" floor statements, but no committee report, evinces to such contrary legislative intent. Thus, I see no reason to dismiss as "unlikely" the most natural reading of the statute, in order to embrace some other reading that is also "possible."

Even if the language of the statute did not answer the retroactivity question, it would be appropriate under our precedents to apply § 102 to pending cases. The well-established presumption against retroactive legislation, which serves to protect settled expectations, is grounded in a respect for vested rights. This presumption need not be applied to remedial legislation, such as § 102, that does not proscribe any conduct that was previously legal.

At no time within the last generation has an employer had a vested right to engage in or to permit sexual harassment; "'there is no such thing as a vested right to do wrong.'" *Freeborn* v. *Smith*, 2 Wall 160, 175 (1865). See also 2 N. Singer, Sutherland on Statutory Construction § 41.04, p. 349 (4th ed. 1986) (procedural and remedial statutes that do not take away vested rights are presumed to apply to pending actions). Section 102 of the Act expands the remedies available for acts of intentional discrimination, but does not alter the scope of the employee's basic right to be free from discrimination or the employer's corresponding legal duty. There is nothing unjust about holding an employer responsible for injuries caused by conduct that has been illegal for almost 30 years.

Accordingly, I respectfully dissent.

Notes and Questions

---

1. What is the rule articulated by the Court in *Landgraf*? How does it differ from the rules in *Bradley* and *Bowen*? Are you persuaded by the Court's attempt to distinguish *Thorpe* and *Bradley*?

2. Notice the concurring opinion by Justice Scalia (which received three votes). (Notice also the reference to Justice Scalia's concurring opinion in *Kaiser Aluminum & Chemical Corp. v. Bonjourno*, 494 U.S. 827 (1990), which is well worth reading.) Do you find that opinion more or less persuasive than the Court's? Why?

3. Notice also that Justice Blackmun, who delivered the opinion of the Court in *Bradley*, was the lone dissenter in *Landgraf*.

4. *The effective date of a statute.* The act at issue in *Landgraf* contained an express effective date provision. Regrettably, many acts contain no such provision.

When an act contains no express effective date provision, the act (like the act in *Landgraf*) is deemed to become effective upon enactment — i.e., upon the completion of the constitutionally prescribed procedure for the making of this type of law. *See, e.g., Gozlon-Peretz v. United States,* 498 U.S. 395, 404 (1990) ("It is well established that, absent a clear direction by Congress to the contrary, a law takes effect on the date of its enactment.") Of course, when an act does contain an express effective date provision, that provision is controlling.

Notice, though, that an effective date provision is controlling only as far as it goes. In *Landgraf,* for example, the statute provided simply that the act "shall take effect upon enactment." The Court was correct, was it not, that such a provision "does not even arguably suggest that it has any application to conduct that occurred at an earlier date." On the other hand, what does "conduct" mean? Such a provision might well mean that a party who received a bench trial prior to the effective date of the act is not now entitled to a jury trial, even though the act now so provides. But what if a case to which the act applies has not yet gone to trial as of the effective date of the act? Can one say for certain that a party would then not be entitled to a jury trial, even though the events that gave rise to the case occurred at some earlier time? Notice that the *Landgraf* Court found that the provision at issue in that case "does not, by itself, resolve the question before us."

5. Notice carefully the Court's definition of retroactive legislation. What is that definition? Does a statute apply "retroactively" merely because it relates to or affects past conduct or events?

   Compare Justice Scalia's definition of retroactive legislation. What is that definition? How does it differ from the Court's? Which do you find the more sensible? More workable?

6. *The effect of a repeal.* 1 U.S.C. § 109 (2000) ("Repeal of statutes as affecting existing liabilities") provides:

   > The repeal of any statute shall not have the effect to release or extinguish any penalty, forfeiture, or liability incurred under such statute, unless the repealing Act shall so expressly provide, and such statute shall be treated as still remaining in force for the purpose of sustaining any proper action or prosecution for the enforcement of such penalty, forfeiture, or liability. The expiration of a temporary statute shall not have the effect to release or extinguish any penalty, forfeiture, or liability incurred under such statute, unless the temporary statute shall so expressly provide, and such statute shall be treated as still remaining in force for the purpose of sustaining any proper action or prosecution for the enforcement of such penalty, forfeiture, or liability.

7. Recall from Chapter 2 that, in contrast to the rule applied as to statutes, essentially the opposite rule applies with respect to the effect of a judicial decision, at least regarding the presumption as to retroactivity. (Review again note 32 of the *Landgraf* decision.) Does this disparity in treatment between changes in statutory law and case law make sense? Why or why not?

8. Along this same line, consider *Rivers v. Roadway Express, Inc.*, 511 U.S. 298 (1994), the companion case to *Landgraf*. In *Rivers*, the Court (again through Justice Stevens) stated:

> "The principle that statutes operate only prospectively, while judicial decisions operate retrospectively, is familiar to every law student," and this case illustrates the second half of that principle as well as the first. Even though applicable Sixth Circuit precedents were otherwise when this dispute arose, the District Court properly applied *Patterson* [(a case decided while this case was pending)] to this case. . . . The essence of judicial decisionmaking — applying general rules to particular situations — necessarily involves some peril to individual expectations because it is often difficult to predict the precise application of a general rule until it has been distilled in the crucible of litigation. See L. Fuller, Morality of Law 56 (1964) ("No system of law — whether it be judge-made or legislatively enacted — can be so perfectly drafted as to leave no room for dispute").
>
> *Patterson* did not overrule any prior decision of this Court; rather, it held and therefore established that the prior decisions of the Courts of Appeals which read § 1981 to cover discriminatory contract termination were *incorrect*. They were not wrong according to some abstract standard of interpretive validity, but by the rules that necessarily govern our hierarchical federal court system. It is this Court's responsibility to say what a statute means, and once the Court has spoken, it is the duty of other courts to respect that understanding of the governing rule of law. A judicial construction of a statute is an authoritative statement of what the statute meant before as well as after the decision of the case giving rise to that construction.[12] Thus, *Patterson* provides the authoritative interpretation of the phrase "make and enforce contracts" in the Civil Rights Act of 1866 before the 1991 amendment went into effect on November 21, 1991. That interpretation provides the baseline for our conclusion that the 1991 amendment would be "retroactive" if applied to cases arising before that date.
>
> Congress, of course, has the power to amend a statute that it believes we have misconstrued. It may even, within broad constitutional bounds, make such a change retroactive and thereby undo what it perceives to be the undesirable past consequences of a misinterpretation of its work product. No such change, however, has the force of law unless it is implemented through legislation. Even when Congress intends to supersede a rule of law embodied in one of our decisions with what it views as a better rule established in earlier decisions, its intent to reach conduct preceding the "corrective" amendment must clearly appear. We cannot say that such an intent clearly appears with respect to § 101. For this reason, and

---

12. When Congress enacts a new statute, it has the power to decide when the statute will become effective. The new statute may govern from the date of enactment, from a specified future date, or even from an expressly announced earlier date. But when this Court construes a statute, it is explaining its understanding of what the statute has meant continuously since the date when it became law. In statutory cases the Court has no authority to depart from the congressional command setting the effective date of a law that it has enacted. Thus, it is not accurate to say that the Court's decision in *Patterson* "changed" the law that previously prevailed in the Sixth Circuit when this case was filed. Rather, given the structure of our judicial system, the *Patterson* opinion finally decided what § 1981 had *always* meant and explained why the Courts of Appeals had misinterpreted the will of the enacting Congress.

because it creates liabilities that had no legal existence before the Act was passed, § 101 does not apply to preenactment conduct.

Id. at 311-13.

Do you agree that the principles governing the retroactive and prospective application of statutes and judicial decisions are familiar to every law student (or even every judge or law professor)? More importantly, notice the main point of this excerpt: that when a court authoritatively interprets a statute, that interpretation essentially dates from the effective date of that statute as it was part thereof.

9. Not long after *Landgraf*, the Supreme Court decided *Lindh v. Murphy*, 521 U.S. 320 (1997). In *Lindh*, the issue was "whether that [portion of the Antiterrorism and Effective Death Penalty Act of 1996] dealing with petitions for habeas corpus governs applications in noncapital cases that were already pending when the Act was passed." *Id.* at 322-23. The Court, in an opinion delivered by Justice Souter, held that it did not. *See id.* Chief Justice Rehnquist authored a vigorous four-Justice dissent. *See id.* at 337 (Rehnquist, C.J., dissenting).

10. In contrast to the law governing the retroactive and prospective effect of *statutes*, consider Federal Rule of Civil Procedure 86(a), which provides:

> These rules and any amendments take effect at the time specified by the Supreme Court, subject to 28 U.S.C. § 2074. They govern:
> > (1) proceedings in an action commenced after their effective date; and
> > (2) proceedings after that date in an action then pending unless:
> > > (A) the Supreme Court specifies otherwise; or
> > > (B) the court determines that applying them in a particular action would be infeasible or work an injustice.

Is it clear when the application of a new or amended rule to an action already pending would "be infeasible or work an injustice"? On the other hand, can you think of a better standard? For example, a rule that provided that rule changes would only be applied to future cases certainly would be clearer. But would it necessarily be fairer? Effectuate those changes as well?

Vartelas v. Holder
132 S. Ct. 1479 (2012)

JUSTICE GINSBURG delivered the opinion of the Court.

Panagis Vartelas, a native of Greece, became a lawful permanent resident of the United States in 1989. He pleaded guilty to a felony (conspiring to make a counterfeit security) in 1994, and served a prison sentence of four months for that offense. Vartelas traveled to Greece in 2003 to visit his parents. On his return to the United States a week later, he was treated as an inadmissible alien and placed in removal proceedings.

Under the law governing at the time of Vartelas' plea, an alien in his situation could travel abroad for brief periods without jeopardizing his resident alien status.

In 1996, Congress enacted the Illegal Immigration Reform and Immigrant Responsibility Act (IIRIRA), 110 Stat. 3009–546. That Act effectively precluded foreign travel by lawful permanent residents who had a conviction like Vartelas'. Under IIRIRA, such aliens, on return from a sojourn abroad, however brief, may be permanently removed from the United States. See 8 U. S. C. §1101(a)(13)(C)(v); §1182(a)(2).

This case presents a question of retroactivity not addressed by Congress: As to a lawful permanent resident convicted of a crime before the effective date of IIRIRA, which regime governs, the one in force at the time of the conviction, or IIRIRA? If the former, Vartelas' brief trip abroad would not disturb his lawful permanent resident status. If the latter, he may be denied reentry. We conclude that the relevant provision of IIRIRA, §1101(a)(13)(C)(v), attached a new disability (denial of reentry) in respect to past events (Vartelas' pre-IIRIRA offense, plea, and conviction). Guided by the deeply rooted presumption against retroactive legislation, we hold that §1101(a)(13)(C)(v) does not apply to Vartelas' conviction. The impact of Vartelas' brief travel abroad on his permanent resident status is therefore determined not by IIRIRA, but by the legal regime in force at the time of his conviction.

. . . .

II

As earlier explained, pre-IIRIRA, a resident alien who once committed a crime of moral turpitude could travel abroad for short durations without jeopardizing his status as a lawful permanent resident. Under IIRIRA, on return from foreign travel, such an alien is treated as a new arrival to our shores, and may be removed from the United States. Vartelas does not question Congress' authority to restrict reentry in this manner. Nor does he contend that Congress could not do so retroactively. Instead, he invokes the principle against retroactive legislation, under which courts read laws as prospective in application unless Congress has unambiguously instructed retroactivity. See *Landgraf* v. *USI Film Products*, 511 U. S. 244, 263 (1994).

The presumption against retroactive legislation, the Court recalled in *Landgraf*, "embodies a legal doctrine centuries older than our Republic." Several provisions of the Constitution, the Court noted, embrace the doctrine, among them, the *Ex Post Facto* Clause, the Contract Clause, and the Fifth Amendment's Due Process Clause. Numerous decisions of this Court repeat the classic formulation Justice Story penned for determining when retrospective application of a law would collide with the doctrine. It would do so, Story stated, when such application would "tak[e] away or impai[r] vested rights acquired under existing laws, or creat[e] a new obligation, impos[e] a new duty, or attac[h] a new disability, in respect to transactions or considerations already past."[4]

---

4. The dissent asserts that Justice Story's opinion "bear[s] no relation to the presumption against retroactivity." That is a bold statement in view of this Court's many references to Justice Story's formulation in cases involving the presumption that statutes operate only prospectively in the absence of a clear congressional statement to the contrary.

Vartelas urges that applying IIRIRA to him, rather than the law that existed at the time of his conviction, would attach a "new disability," effectively a ban on travel outside the United States, "in respect to [events] . . . already past," *i.e.*, his offense, guilty plea, conviction, and punishment, all occurring prior to the passage of IIRIRA. In evaluating Vartelas' argument, we note first a matter not disputed by the Government: Congress did not expressly prescribe the temporal reach of the IIRIRA provision in question, 8 U. S. C. §1101(a)(13). See *Landgraf*, 511 U. S., at 280 (Court asks first "whether Congress has expressly prescribed [new §1101(a)(13)'s] proper reach"). . . . Accordingly, we proceed to the dispositive question whether, as Vartelas maintains, application of IIRIRA's travel restraint to him "would have retroactive effect" Congress did not authorize. See *Landgraf*, 511 U. S., at 280.

Vartelas presents a firm case for application of the antiretroactivity principle. Neither his sentence, nor the immigration law in effect when he was convicted and sentenced, blocked him from occasional visits to his parents in Greece. Current §1101(a)(13)(C)(v), if applied to him, would thus attach "a new disability" to conduct over and done well before the provision's enactment.

. . . .

III

The Government, echoed in part by the dissent, argues that no retroactive effect is involved in this case, for the Legislature has not attached any disability to past conduct. Rather, it has made the relevant event the alien's post-IIRIRA act of returning to the United States. We find this argument disingenuous. Vartelas' return to the United States occasioned his treatment as a new entrant, but the reason for the "new disability" imposed on him was not his lawful foreign travel. It was, indeed, his conviction, pre-IIRIRA, of an offense qualifying as one of moral turpitude. That past misconduct, in other words, not present travel, is the wrongful activity Congress targeted in §1101(a)(13)(C)(v).

. . . .

Fernandez-Vargas v. *Gonzales*, 548 U. S. 30 (2006), featured by the Government and the dissent, is similarly inapposite. That case involved 8 U. S. C. §1231(a)(5), an IIRIRA addition, which provides that an alien who reenters the United States after having been removed can be removed again under the same removal order. We held that the provision could be applied to an alien who reentered illegally before IIRIRA's enactment. Explaining the Court's decision, we said: "[T]he conduct of remaining in the country . . . is the predicate action; the statute applies to stop an indefinitely continuing violation . . . . It is therefore the alien's choice to continue his illegal presence . . . after the effective date of the new la[w] that subjects him to the new . . . legal regime, not a past act that he is helpless to undo." Vartelas, we have several times stressed, engaged in no criminal activity after IIRIRA's passage. He simply took a brief trip to Greece, anticipating a return without incident as in past visits to his parents. No "indefinitely continuing" crime occurred; instead, Vartelas was apprehended because of a pre-IIRIRA crime he was "helpless to undo."

The Government further refers to lower court decisions in cases involving 18 U. S. C. §922(g), which prohibits the possession of firearms by convicted felons.

"[L]ongstanding prohibitions on the possession of firearms by felons," *District of Columbia* v. *Heller*, 554 U. S. 570, 626 (2008), however, target a present danger, *i.e.*, the danger posed by felons who bear arms.[7]

In sum, Vartelas' brief trip abroad post-IIRIRA involved no criminal infraction. IIRIRA disabled him from leaving the United States and returning as a lawful permanent resident. That new disability rested not on any continuing criminal activity, but on a single crime committed years before IIRIRA's enactment. The antiretroactivity principle instructs against application of the new proscription to render Vartelas a first-time arrival at the country's gateway.

. . . .

For the reasons stated, the judgment of the Court of Appeals for the Second Circuit is reversed, and the case is remanded for further proceedings consistent with this opinion.

It is so ordered.

JUSTICE SCALIA, with whom JUSTICE THOMAS and JUSTICE ALITO join, dissenting.

As part of the Illegal Immigration Reform and Immigrant Responsibility Act of 1996 (IIRIRA), Congress required that lawful permanent residents who have committed certain crimes seek formal "admission" when they return to the United States from abroad. 8 U. S. C. §1101(a)(13)(C)(v). This case presents a straightforward question of statutory interpretation: Does that statute apply to lawful permanent residents who, like Vartelas, committed one of the specified offenses before 1996, but traveled abroad after 1996? Under the proper approach to determining a statute's temporal application, the answer is yes.

I

The text of §1101(a)(13)(C)(v) does not contain a clear statement answering the question presented here. So the Court is correct that this case is governed by our

---

7. The dissent notes two statutes of the same genre: laws prohibiting persons convicted of a sex crime against a victim under 16 years of age from working in jobs involving frequent contact with minors, and laws prohibiting a person "who has been adjudicated as a mental defective or who has been committed to a mental institution" from possessing guns, 18 U. S. C. §922(g)(4). The dissent is correct that these statutes do not operate retroactively. Rather, they address dangers that arise postenactment: sex offenders with a history of child molestation working in close proximity to children, and mentally unstable persons purchasing guns. The act of flying to Greece, in contrast, does not render a lawful permanent resident like Vartelas hazardous. Nor is it plausible that Congress' solution to the problem of dangerous lawful permanent residents would be to pass a law that would deter such persons from ever leaving the United States.

As for student loans, it is unlikely that the provision noted by the dissent, 20 U. S. C. §1091(r), would raise retroactivity questions in the first place. The statute has a prospective thrust. It concerns "[s]uspension of eligibility" when a student receiving a college loan commits a drug crime. The suspension runs "from the date of th[e]conviction" for specified periods, *e.g.*, two years for a second offense of possession. Moreover, eligibility may be restored before the period of ineligibility ends if the student establishes, under prescribed criteria, his rehabilitation.

longstanding interpretive principle that, in the absence of a contrary indication, a statute will not be construed to have retroactive application. See, *e.g., Landgraf* v. *USI Film Products*, 511 U. S. 244, 280 (1994). The operative provision of this text — the provision that specifies the act that it prohibits or prescribes — says that lawful permanent residents convicted of offenses similar to Vartelas's must seek formal "admission" before they return to the United States from abroad. Since Vartelas returned to the United States after the statute's effective date, the application of that text to his reentry does not give the statute a retroactive effect.

In determining whether a statute applies retroactively, we should concern ourselves with the statute's actual operation on regulated parties, not with retroactivity as an abstract concept or as a substitute for fairness concerns. It is impossible to decide whether a statute's application is retrospective or prospective without first identifying a reference point — a moment in time to which the statute's effective date is either subsequent or antecedent. (Otherwise, the obvious question — retroactive in reference to what? — remains unanswered.) In my view, the identity of that reference point turns on the activity a statute is intended to regulate. For any given regulated party, the reference point (or "retroactivity event") is the moment at which the party does what the statute forbids or fails to do what it requires. With an identified reference point, the retroactivity analysis is simple. If a person has engaged in the primary regulated activity *before* the statute's effective date, then the statute's application *would* be retroactive. But if a person engages in the primary regulated activity *after* the statute's effective date, then the statute's application is prospective only. In the latter case, the interpretive presumption against retroactivity does not bar the statute's application.

Under that commonsense approach, this is a relatively easy case. Although the *class* of aliens affected by §1101(a)(13)(C)(v) is defined with respect to past crimes, the *regulated activity* is reentry into the United States. By its terms, the statute is all about controlling admission at the border. It specifies six criteria to identify lawful permanent residents who are subject to formal "admission" procedures, most of which relate to the circumstances of departure, the trip itself, or reentry. The titles of the statutory sections containing §1101(a)(13)(C)(v) confirm its focus on admission, rather than crime: The provision is located within Title III of IIRIRA ("Inspection, Apprehension, Detention, Adjudication, and Removal of Inadmissible and Deportable Aliens"), under Subtitle A ("Revision of Procedures for Removal of Aliens"), and §301 ("Treating Persons Present in the United States Without Authorization as Not Admitted"). 110 Stat. 3009–575. And the specific subsection of IIRIRA at issue (§301(a), entitled "'Admission' Defined") is an amendment to the definition of "entry" in the general "Definitions" section of the Immigration and Nationality Act (INA). The original provision told border officials how to regulate admission — not how to punish crime — and the amendment does as well.

Section 1101(a)(13)(C)(v) thus has no retroactive effect on Vartelas because the reference point here — Vartelas's readmission to the United States after a trip abroad — occurred years after the statute's effective date. Although Vartelas cannot change the fact of his prior conviction, he could have avoided *entirely* the consequences of §1101(a)(13)(C)(v) by simply remaining in the United States or, having left, remaining in Greece. That §1101(a)(13)(C)(v) had no effect on Vartelas until he performed a post-enactment activity is a clear indication that the statute's application is purely prospective. See *Fernandez-Vargas v. Gonzales*, 548 U. S. 30, 45, n. 11, 46 (2006) (no retroactive effect where the statute in question did "not operate on a completed preenactment act" and instead turned on "a failure to take timely action that would have avoided application of the new law altogether").

II

The Court avoids this conclusion by insisting that "[p]ast misconduct, . . . not present travel, is the wrongful activity Congress targeted" in §1101(a)(13)(C)(v). That assertion does not, however, have any basis in the statute's text or structure, and the Court does not pretend otherwise. Instead, the Court simply asserts that Vartelas's "lawful foreign travel" surely could not be the "reason for the 'new disability' imposed on him." But the reason for a prohibition has nothing to do with whether the prohibition is being applied to a past rather than a future act. It may be relevant to other legal inquiries — for example, to whether a legislative act violates one of the Ex Post Facto Clauses in Article I, see, *e.g., Smith v. Doe*, 538 U. S. 84, 92 (2003), or one of the Due Process Clauses in the Fifth and Fourteenth Amendments, see, *e.g., Williamson v. Lee Optical of Okla., Inc.*, 348 U. S. 483, 487 (1955), or the Takings Clause in the Fifth Amendment, see, *e.g., Kelo v. New London*, 545 U. S. 469, 477–483 (2005), or the Obligation of Contracts Clause in Article I, see, *e.g., United States Trust Co. of N. Y. v. New Jersey*, 431 U. S. 1, 29 (1977). But it has no direct bearing upon whether the statute is retroactive.[*]

The Court's failure to differentiate between the statutory-interpretation question (whether giving certain effect to a provision would make it retroactive and hence presumptively unintended) and the validity question (whether giving certain effect to a provision is unlawful) is on full display in its attempts to distinguish §1101(a)(13)(C)(v) from similar statutes. . . .

The Court's confident assertion that Congress surely would not have meant this statute to apply to Vartelas, whose foreign travel and subsequent return to the United States were innocent events, simply begs the question presented in this case. Ignorance, of course, is no excuse *(ignorantia legis neminem excusat)*; and his return was entirely lawful only if the statute before us did not render it unlawful. Since IIRIRA's effective date in 1996, lawful permanent residents who have committed crimes of moral turpitude are forbidden to leave the United States and return without formally seeking "admission." As a result, Vartelas's numerous trips abroad and "uneventful" reentries into the United States after the passage of IIRIRA were lawful only *if* §1101(a)(13)(C)(v) does not apply to him — which is, of course, precisely the matter in dispute here.

---

[*] I say no *direct* bearing because if the prospective application of a statute would raise constitutional doubts because of its effect on preenactment conduct, *that* would be a reason to presume a legislative intent not to apply it unless the conduct in question is post-enactment — that is, to consider it retroactive when the conduct in question is pre-enactment. See *Clark v. Martinez*, 543 U. S. 371, 380-381 (2005). That is not an issue here. If the statute had expressly made the new "admission" rule applicable to those aliens with prior convictions, its constitutionality would not be in doubt.

The Court's circular reasoning betrays its underlying concern: Because the Court believes that reentry after a brief trip abroad *should* be lawful, it will decline to apply a statute that clearly provides otherwise for certain criminal aliens. (The same instinct likely produced the Court's questionable statutory interpretation in *Rosenberg* v. *Fleuti*, 374 U. S. 449 (1963).) The Court's test for retroactivity — asking whether the statute creates a "new disability" in "respect to past events" — invites this focus on fairness. Understandably so, since it is derived from a Justice Story opinion interpreting a provision of the New Hampshire Constitution that *forbade* retroactive laws — a provision comparable to the Federal Constitution's *ex post facto* prohibition and bearing no relation to the presumption against retroactivity. What is unfair or irrational (and hence should be forbidden) has nothing to do with whether applying a statute to a particular act is prospective (and thus presumptively intended) or retroactive (and thus presumptively unintended). On the latter question, the "new disability in respect to past events" test provides no meaningful guidance.

I can imagine countless laws that, like §1101(a)(13)(C)(v), impose "new disabilities" related to "past events" and yet do not operate retroactively. For example, a statute making persons convicted of drug crimes ineligible for student loans. See, *e.g.*, 20 U. S. C. §1091(r)(1). Or laws prohibiting those convicted of sex crimes from working in certain jobs that involve repeated contact with minors. See, *e.g.*, Cal. Penal Code Ann. §290.95(c) (West Supp. 2012). Or laws prohibiting those previously committed for mental instability from purchasing guns. See, *e.g.*, 18 U. S. C. §922(g)(4). The Court concedes that it would not consider the last two laws inapplicable to pre-enactment convictions or commitments. The Court does not deny that these statutes impose a "new disability in respect to past events," but it distinguishes them based on the *reason* for their enactment: These statutes "address dangers that arise postenactment." So much for the new-disability-in-respect-to-past-events test; it has now become a new-disability-not-designed-to-guard-against-future-danger test. But why is guarding against future danger the *only* reason Congress may wish to regulate future action in light of past events? It obviously is not. So the Court must invent yet another doctrine to address my first example, the law making persons convicted of drug crimes ineligible for student loans. According to the Court, that statute differs from §1101(a)(13)(C)(v) because it "has a prospective thrust." I cannot imagine what that means, other than that the statute regulates post-enactment conduct. But, of course, so does §1101(a)(13)(C)(v). Rather than reconciling any of these distinctions with Justice Story's formulation of retroactivity, the Court leaves to lower courts the unenviable task of identifying new-disabilities-not-designed-to-guard-against-future-danger-and-also-lacking-a-prospective-thrust.

And anyway, is there any doubt that §1101(a)(13)(C)(v) is intended to guard against the "dangers that arise postenactment" from having aliens in our midst who have shown themselves to have proclivity for crime? Must that be rejected as its purpose simply because Congress has not sought to achieve it by all possible means — by ferreting out such dangerous aliens and going through the expensive and lengthy process of deporting them? At least some of the post-enactment danger can readily be eliminated by forcing lawful permanent residents who have committed certain crimes to undergo formal "admission" procedures at our borders. Indeed, by limiting criminal aliens' opportunities to travel and then return to the United States, §1101(a)(13)(C)(v) may encourage self-deportation. But all this is irrelevant. The positing of legislative "purpose" is always a slippery enterprise compared to the simple determination of whether a statute regulates a future event — and it is that, rather than the Court's pronouncement of some forward-looking *reason*, which governs whether a statute has retroactive effect.

Finally, I cannot avoid observing that even if the Court's concern about the fairness or rationality of applying §1101(a)(13)(C)(v) to Vartelas were relevant to the statutory interpretation question, that concern is greatly exaggerated. In disregard of a federal statute, convicted criminal Vartelas repeatedly traveled to and from Greece without ever seeking formal admission at this country's borders. When he was finally unlucky enough to be apprehended, and sought discretionary relief from removal under former §212(c) of the INA, 8 U. S. C. §1182(c) (1994 ed.), the Immigration Judge denying his application found that Vartelas had made frequent trips to Greece and had remained there for long periods of time, that he was "a serious tax evader," that he had offered testimony that was "close to incredible," and that he had not shown hardship to himself or his estranged wife and children should he be removed. In decrying the "harsh penalty" imposed by this statute on Vartelas, the Court ignores those inconvenient facts. But never mind. Under any sensible approach to the presumption against retroactivity, these factual subtleties should be irrelevant to the temporal application of §1101(a)(13)(C)(v).

This case raises a plain-vanilla question of statutory interpretation, not broader questions about frustrated expectations or fairness. Our approach to answering that question should be similarly straightforward: We should determine what relevant activity the statute regulates (here, reentry); absent a clear statement otherwise, only such relevant activity which occurs after the statute's effective date should be covered (here, post-1996 reentries). If, as so construed, the statute is unfair or irrational enough to violate the Constitution, that is another matter entirely, and one not presented here. Our interpretive presumption against retroactivity, however, is just that — a tool to ascertain what the statute means, not a license to rewrite the statute in a way the Court considers more desirable.

I respectfully dissent.

Notes and Questions

---

1. The Court and the dissent agree with respect to several relevant retroactivity propositions. What are those propositions? What is the proposition (or propositions) on which they disagree?

2. What is the Court's current test regarding the retroactive or prospective application of statutes? Is that test superior or inferior to the approach taken by the dissent? Why?

3. In *United States v. Sec. Indus. Bank*, 459 U.S. 70, 79 (1982), the Court stated: "The principle that statutes operate only prospectively, while judicial decisions operate retrospectively, is familiar to every law student." Is it? Is it familiar even to the members of the Supreme Court?

1. Possible Constitutional Limitations to the Retroactive Application of Statutes

Though statutes generally are construed as applying only prospectively (in the absence of express language to the contrary), it should be recognized that there are few constitutional provisions preventing Congress from enacting retroactive legislation. Thus, in many situations, the most significant impediments to retroactive legislation are simply matters of policy. For example, a statute making a certain type of expense deductible for federal income tax purposes that was enacted in September but made to apply retroactively to all such expenses incurred during that same calendar year would probably be more popular (i.e., more politically expedient) than a similar statute imposing a tax on a certain type of income previously exempt from taxation. But there might well be no constitutional impediment to enacting either statute. (A recent example of an arguably retroactive statute, at least in part, can be found in the Fraud Enforcement and Recovery Act of 2009, Public Law 111-21, 123 Stat. 1617, which provides that certain portions of that Act "shall take effect as if enacted on June 7, 2008, and apply to all claims under the False Claims Act that are pending on or after that date." 123 Stat. 1625.)

But as the Court's opinion in *Landgraf*, as well as the dissenting opinion in *Vartelas*, indicates, there are some constitutional impediments to certain types of retroactive legislation. Most prominently, Article I, § 10, cl. 1 provides that "[n]o state shall . . . pass any Bill of Attainder, ex post facto Law, or Law impairing the Obligation of Contracts." The next case discusses the contours of what is perhaps the most significant such impediment, the ex post facto clause.

Calder v. Bull
3 U.S. (3 Dall.) 386 (1798)

IN error from the State of Connecticut. The cause was argued at the last term (in the absence of the Chief Justice) and now the court delivered their opinions *seriatim*.

CHASE, Justice. — The decision of one question determines (in my opinion) the present dispute. I shall, therefore, state from the record no more of the case, than I think necessary for the consideration of that question only.

The legislature of Connecticut, on the 2d Thursday of May 1795, passed a resolution or law, which, for the reasons assigned, set aside a decree of the Court of Probate for Hartford, on the 21st of March 1793, which decree disapproved of the will of Normand Morrison (the grandson), made the 21st of August 1779, and refused to record the said will; and granted a new hearing by the said court of probate, with liberty of appeal therefrom, in six months. A new hearing was had, in virtue of this resolution or law, before the said court of probate, who, on the 27th of July 1795, approved the said will, and ordered it to be recorded. At August 1795, appeal was then had to the superior court at Hartford, who, at February term 1796, affirmed the decree of the court of probate. Appeal was had to the supreme court of errors of Connecticut, who, in June 1796, adjudged that there were no errors. More than eighteen months elapsed from the decree of the court of probate (on the 1st of March 1793), and thereby Caleb Bull and wife were barred of all right of appeal, by a statute of Connecticut. There was no law of that state whereby a new hearing or trial, before the said court of probate, might be obtained. Calder and wife claimed the premises in question, in right of the wife, as heiress of N. Morrison, physician; Bull and wife claimed under the will of N. Morrison, the grandson.

The counsel for the plaintiffs in error contend, that the said resolution or law of the legislature of Connecticut, granting a new hearing, in the above case, is an *ex post facto* law, prohibited by the constitution of the United States; that any law of the federal government, or of any of the state government, contrary to the constitution of the United States, is void; and that this court possesses the power to declare such law void.

It appears to me a self-evident proposition, that the several state legislatures retain all the powers of legislation, delegated to them by the state constitutions; which are not expressly taken away by the constitution of the United States. The establishing courts of justice, the appointment of judges, and the making of regulations for the administration of justice within each state, according to its laws, on all subjects not entrusted to the federal government, appears to me to be the peculiar and exclusive province and duty of the state legislatures. All the powers delegated by the people of the United States to the federal government are defined, and no *constructive* powers can be exercised by it, and all the powers that remain in the state governments are indefinite; except only in the constitution of Massachusetts.

The effect of a resolution or law of Connecticut, above stated, is to revise a decision of one of its inferior courts, called the court of probate for Hartford, and to direct a new hearing of the case by the same court of probate, that passed the decree against the will of Normand Morrison. By the existing law of Connecticut, a right to recover certain property had vested in Calder and wife (the appellants), in consequence of a decision of a court of justice, but in virtue of a subsequent resolution or law, and the new hearing thereof, and the decision in consequence, this right to recover certain property was divested, and the right to the property declared to be in Bull and wife, the appellees. The sole inquiry is, whether this resolution or law of Connecticut, having such operation, is an *ex post facto* law, within the prohibition of the federal constitution?

Whether the legislature of any of the states can revise and correct by law, a decision of any of its courts of justice, although not prohibited by the constitution of the state, is a question of very great importance, and not necessary now to be determined; because the resolution or law in question does not go so far. I cannot subscribe to the omnipotence of a state legislature, or that it is absolute and without control; although its authority should not be expressly restrained by the constitution, or fundamental law of the state. The people of the United States erected their constitutions or forms of government, to establish justice, to promote the general welfare, to secure the blessings of liberty, and to protect their persons and property from violence. The purposes for which men enter into society will determine the nature and terms of the social compact; and as they are the foundation of the legislative power, they will decide what are the proper objects of it. The nature, and ends of legislative power will limit the exercise of it. This fundamental principle flows from the very nature of our free republican governments, that no man should be compelled to do what the laws do not require; nor to refrain from acts which the laws permit. There are acts which the federal, or state legislature cannot do, without exceeding their authority. There are certain vital principles in our free republican governments, which will determine and overrule an apparent and flagrant abuse of legislative power; as to authorize manifest injustice by positive law; or to take away that security for personal liberty, or private property, for the protection whereof the government was established. An act of the legislature (for I cannot call it a law), contrary to the great first principles of the social compact, cannot be considered a rightful exercise of legislative authority. The obligation of a law, in governments established on express compact, and on republican principles, must be determined by the nature of the power on which it is founded.

A few instances will suffice to explain what I mean. A law that punished a citizen for an innocent action, or, in other words, for an act, which, when done, was in violation of no existing law; a law that destroys or impairs the lawful private contracts of citizens; a law that makes a man a judge in his own cause; or a law that takes property from A. and gives it to B.: it is against all reason and justice, for a people to entrust a legislature with such powers; and therefore, it cannot be presumed that they have done it. The genius, the nature and spirit of our state governments, amount to a prohibition of such acts of legislation; and the general principles of law and reason forbid them. The legislature may enjoin, permit, forbid and punish; they may declare new crimes; and establish rules of conduct for all its citizens in future cases; they may command what is right, and prohibit what is wrong; but they cannot change innocence into guilt; or punish innocence as a crime; or violate the right of an antecedent lawful private contract; or the right of private property. To maintain that our federal, or state legislature possesses such powers, if they had not been expressly restrained; would, in my opinion, be a political heresy, altogether inadmissible in our free republican governments.

All the restrictions contained in the constitution of the United States on the power of the state legislatures, were provided in favor of the authority of the federal government. The prohibition against their making any *ex post facto* laws was introduced for greater caution, and very probably arose from the knowledge, that the parliament of Great Britain claimed and exercised a power to pass such laws, under the denomination of bills of attainder, or bills of pains and penalties; the first inflicting capital, and the other less punishment. These acts were legislative judgments; and an exercise of judicial power. Sometimes, they respected the crime, by declaring acts to be treason, which were not treason, when committed; at other times, they violated the rules of evidence (to supply a deficiency of legal proof) by admitting one witness, when the existing law required two; by receiving evidence without oath; or the oath of the wife against the husband; or other testimony, which the courts of justice would not admit; at other times, they inflicted punishments, where the party was not, by law, liable to any punishment; and in other cases, they inflicted greater punishment, than the law annexed to the offence. The ground for the exercise of such legislative power was this, that the safety of the kingdom depended on the death, or other punishment, of the offender: as if traitors, when discovered, could be so formidable, or the government so insecure! With very few exceptions, the advocates of such laws were stimulated by ambition, or personal resentment and vindictive malice. To prevent such and similar acts of violence and injustice, I believe, the federal and state legislatures were prohibited from passing any bill of attainder, or any *ex post facto* law.

The constitution of the United States, article I., section 9, prohibits the legislature of the United States from passing any *ex post facto* law; and, in § 10, lays several restrictions on the authority of the legislatures of the several states; and, among them, "that no state shall pass any *ex post facto* law."

It may be remembered, that the legislatures of several of the states, to wit, Massachusetts, Pennsylvania, Delaware, Maryland, and North and South Carolina, are expressly prohibited, by their state constitutions, from passing any *ex post facto* law.

I shall endeavor to show what law is to be considered an *ex post facto* law, within the words and meaning of the prohibition in the federal constitution. The prohibition, "that no state shall pass any *ex post facto* law," necessarily requires some explanation; for, naked and without explanation, it is unintelligible, and means nothing. Literally, it is only, that a law shall not be passed concerning, and after the fact, or thing done, or action committed. I would ask, what fact; or what nature or kind; and by whom done? That Charles I., king of England, was beheaded; that Oliver Cromwell was protector of England; that Louis XVI., late king of France, was guillotined; are all facts that have happened; but it would be nonsense to suppose, that the states were prohibited from making any law, after either of these events, and with reference thereto. The prohibition, in the letter, is not to pass any law concerning, and after the fact; but the plain and obvious meaning and intention of the prohibition is this: that the legislatures of the several states, shall not pass laws, after a fact done by a subject or citizen, which shall have relation to such fact, and shall punish him for having done it. The prohibition, considered in this light, is an additional bulwark in favor of the personal security of the subject, to protect his person from punishment by legislative acts, having a retrospective operation. I do not think it was inserted, to secure the citizen in his private rights of either property or contracts. The prohibitions not to make anything but gold and silver coin in tender in payment of debts, and not to pass any law impairing the obligation of contracts, were inserted to secure private rights; but the restriction not to pass any *ex post facto* law, was to secure the person of the subject from injury or punishment, in consequence of such law. If the prohibition against making *ex post facto* laws was intended to secure personal rights from being affected or injured by such laws, and the prohibition is sufficiently extensive for that object, the other restraints I have enumerated, were unnecessary, and therefore, improper; for both of them are retrospective.

I will state what laws I consider *ex post facto* laws, within the words and the intent of the prohibition. 1st. Every law that makes an action done before the passing of the law, and which was innocent when done, criminal; and punishes such action. 2d. Every law that aggravates a crime, or makes it greater than it was, when committed. 3d. Every law that changes the punishment, and inflicts a greater punishment, than the law annexed to the crime, when committed. 4th. Every law that alters the legal rules of evidence, and receives less, or different testimony, than the law required at the time of the commission of the offence, in order to convict the offender. All these, and similar laws, are manifestly unjust and oppressive. In my opinion, the true distinction is between *ex post facto* laws, and retrospective laws. Every *ex post facto* law must necessarily be retrospective; but every retrospective law is not an *ex post facto* law: the former only are prohibited. Every law that takes away or impairs rights vested, agreeable to existing laws, is retrospective, and is generally unjust, and may be oppressive; and it is a good general rule, that a law should have no retrospect: but there are cases in which laws may justly, and for the benefit of the community, and also of individuals, relate to a time antecedent to their commencement; as statutes of oblivion or of pardon. They are certainly retrospective, and literally both concerning and after the facts committed. But I do not consider any law *ex post facto*, within the prohibition, that mollifies the rigor of the criminal law: but only those that create or aggravate the crime; or increase the punishment, or change the rules of evidence, for the purpose of conviction. Every law that is to have an operation before the making thereof, as to commence at an antecedent time; or to save time from the statute of limitations; or to excuse acts which were unlawful, and before committed, and the like, is retrospective. But such laws may be proper or necessary, as the case may be. There is a great and apparent difference between making an unlawful act lawful; and the making an innocent action criminal, and punishing it as a crime. The expressions "*ex post facto* laws," are technical, they had been in use long before the revolution, and had acquired an appropriate meaning, by legislators, lawyers and authors. The celebrated and judicious Sir William Blackstone, in his commentaries, considers an *ex post facto* law precisely in the same light as I have done. His opinion is confirmed by his successor, Mr. Wooddeson; and by the author of the *Federalist*, who I esteem superior to both, for his extensive and accurate knowledge of the true principles of government.

. . . .

I am of the opinion, that the fact, contemplated by the prohibition, and not to be affected by a subsequent law, was some fact to be done by a citizen or subject. . . .

In the present case, there is no fact done by Bull and wife, plaintiffs in error, that is in any manner affected by the law or resolution of Connecticut . . . . The decree of the court of probate of Hartford (on the 21st of March), in consequence of which Calder and wife claim a right to the property in question, was given before the said law or resolution, and in that sense, was affected and set aside by it; and in consequence of the law allowing a hearing and the decision in favor of the will, they have lost what they would have been entitled to, if the law or resolution, and the decision in consequence thereof, had not been made. The decree of the court of probate is the only fact, on which the law or resolution operates. In my judgment, the case of the plaintiffs in error, is not within the letter of the prohibition; and for the reasons assigned, I am clearly of the opinion, that it is not within the intention of the prohibition; and if within the intention, but out of the letter, I should not, therefore, consider myself justified to construe it within the prohibition, and therefore, that the whole was void.

It was argued by counsel for the plaintiffs in error, that the legislature of Connecticut had no constitutional power to make the resolution (or law) in question, granting a new hearing, &c. Without giving an opinion, at this time, whether this court has jurisdiction to decide that any law made by congress, contrary to the constitution of the United States, is void: I am fully satisfied, that this court has no jurisdiction to determine that any law of any state legislature, contrary to the constitution of such state, is void. Further, if this court had such jurisdiction, yet it does not appear to me, that the resolution (or law) in question, is contrary to the charter of Connecticut, or its constitution, which is said by counsel to be composed of its acts of assembly, and usages and customs. I should think, that the courts of Connecticut are the proper tribunals to decide, whether laws contrary to the constitution thereof, are void. In the present case, they have, both in the inferior and superior courts, determined that the resolution (or law) in question was not contrary to either their state, or the federal constitution.

. . . .

It was further urged, that if the provision does not extend to prohibit the making any law, after a fact, then all *choses in action*; all lands by devise; all personal property by bequest, or distribution; by *elegit*; by execution; by judgments, particularly on *torts*; will be unprotected from the legislative power of the states; rights vested may be divested at the will and pleasure of the state legislatures; and therefore, that the true construction and meaning of the prohibition is, that the states pass no law to deprive a citizen of any right vested in him by existing law.

It is not to be presumed, that the federal or state legislatures will pass laws to deprive citizens of rights vested in them by existing laws; unless for the benefit of the whole community; and on making full satisfaction. The restraint against making any *ex post facto* laws was not considered by the framers of the constitution, as extending to prohibit the depriving a citizen even of a vested right to property; or the provision "that private property should not be taken for public use, without just compensation," was unnecessary.

. . . .

Judgment affirmed.

Notes and Questions

---

1. Notice that in *Calder*, there was no opinion of the Court en banc; rather, the four justices who considered the case (Justices Chase, Paterson, Iredell, and Cushing) issued *seriatim* opinions, and no justice formally joined in the opinion of any other. All four justices voted to affirm the judgment of the lower court, though, and all seemed to agree with the reasoning set forth in Justice Chase's lead opinion.

2. The ex post facto clause is alive and well, as evidenced by the number of recent Supreme Court decisions discussing its reach. *See, e.g., Stogner v. California*, 539 U.S. 607 (2003); *Carmell v. Texas*, 529 U.S. 513 (2000).

3. Though there is little doubt that there are other constitutional limits to the retroactive application of statutes, the Supreme Court has had some difficulty deciding on the precise basis for such limits and the scope of their application. For example, in *Eastern Enterprises v. Apfel*, 524 U.S. 498 (1998), a plurality of the Court (in an opinion delivered by Justice O'Connor and joined by Chief Justice Rehnquist and Justices Scalia and Thomas) concluded that the statute in question, as applied in that case, effected an unconstitutional taking under the Fifth Amendment's Takings Clause. *See id.* at 503-38 (opinion by O'Connor, J.). In the course of so concluding, Justice O'Connor wrote:

> Retroactivity is generally disfavored in the law, *Bowen* v. *Georgetown Univ. Hospital*, 488 U. S. 204, 208 (1988), in accordance with "fundamental notions of justice" that have been recognized throughout history, *Kaiser Aluminum & Chemical Corp.* v. *Bonjorno*, 494 U. S. 827, 855 (1990) (SCALIA, J., concurring). See also, e. g., *Dash* v. *Van Kleeck*, 7 Johns. *477, *503 (NY 1811) ("It is a principle in the *English* common law, as ancient as the law itself, that a statute, even of its omnipotent parliament, is not to have a retrospective effect"); H. Broom, Legal Maxims 24 (8th ed. 1911) ("Retrospective laws are, as a rule, of questionable policy, and contrary to the general principle that legislation by which the conduct of mankind is to be regulated ought to deal with future acts, and ought not to change the character of past transactions carried on upon the faith of the then existing law"). In his Commentaries on the Constitution, Justice Story reasoned: "Retrospective laws are, indeed, generally unjust; and, as has been forcibly said, neither accord with sound legislation nor with the fundamental principles of the social compact." 2 J. Story, Commentaries on the Constitution § 1398 (5th ed. 1891). A similar principle abounds in the laws of other nations. "Retroactive legislation," we have explained, "presents problems of unfairness that are more serious than those posed by prospective legislation, because it can deprive citizens of legitimate expectations and upset settled transactions." *General Motors Corp.* v. *Romein*, 503 U. S. 181, 191 (1992).
>
> Our Constitution expresses concern with retroactive laws through several of its provisions, including the *Ex Post Facto* and Takings Clauses. *Landgraf, supra*, at 266. In *Calder* v. *Bull*, 3 Dall. 386 (1798), this Court held that the *Ex Post Facto* Clause is directed at the retroactivity of penal legislation, while suggesting that that Takings Clause provides a similar safeguard against retrospective legislation concerning property rights. *See id.*, at 394 (opinion of Chase, J.) ("The restraint against making any *ex post facto laws* was not considered, by the framers of the constitution, as extending to prohibit the depriving a citizen even of a *vested right to property;* or the provision, 'that *private* property should not be taken for public use, without just compensation,' was unnecessary").

Eastern Enterprises, 524 U.S. at 532-34.

Though Justice Kennedy agreed that the statute in question was unconstitutional, he "disagree[d] with the plurality's Takings Clause analysis," and instead concluded that the statute "must be invalidated as contrary to essential due process principles." *Id.* at 539 (Kennedy, J., concurring in the judgment and dissenting in part). Conversely, though Justice Breyer (joined by Justices Stevens, Souter, and Ginsburg) agreed that a due process (rather than a takings) analysis represented the proper line of inquiry (at least in this case), he concluded that the statute in question nonetheless was constitutional. *See id.* at 553-68 (Breyer, J., dissenting).

Perhaps the most interesting aspect of *Eastern Enterprises* was the concurrence by Justice Thomas.

> JUSTICE O'CONNOR's opinion correctly concludes that the Coal Act's imposition of retroactive liability on petitioner violates the Takings Clause. I write separately to emphasize that the *Ex Post Facto* Clause of the Constitution even more clearly reflects the principle that "retrospective laws are, indeed, generally unjust." Since *Calder* v. *Bull*, however, this Court has considered the *Ex Post Facto* Clause to apply only in the criminal context. I have never been convinced of the soundness of this limitation, which in *Calder* was principally justified because a contrary interpretation would render the Takings Clause unnecessary. In an appropriate case, therefore, I would be willing to reconsider *Calder* and its progeny to determine whether a retroactive civil law that passes muster under our current Takings Clause jurisprudence is nonetheless unconstitutional under the *Ex Post Facto* Clause.

Eastern Enterprises, 524 U.S. at 538-39 (Thomas, J., concurring).

4. There are several articles on the constitutional limits to statutory retroactivity, including Daniel E. Troy, *Toward a Definition and Critique of Retroactivity*, 51 ALA. L. REV. 1329 (2000).

F. STATUTORY AND OTHER CONFLICTS

Occasionally, two statutes will seem to conflict with one another. In that event, which should be applied? The general rule is that the later-enacted statute controls (the thought being that the later implicitly repealed the earlier), though courts will work hard to avoid any such conflicts where possible, as implied repeals are disfavored.

An example of these principles can be found in *Radzanower v. Touche Ross & Co.*, 426 U.S. 148 (1976), wherein the Court stated:

> It is a basic principle of statutory construction that a statute dealing with a narrow, precise, and specific subject is not submerged by a later enacted statute covering a more generalized spectrum. "Where there is no clear intention otherwise, a specific statute will not be controlled or nullified by a general one, regardless of the priority of enactment." "The reason and philosophy of the rule is, that when the mind of the legislator has been turned to the details of a subject, and he has acted upon it, a subsequent statute in general terms, or treating the subject in a general manner, and not expressly contradicting the original act, shall not be considered as intended to affect the more particular or positive previous provisions, unless it is absolutely necessary to give the latter act such a construction, in order that its words shall have any meaning at all." T. Sedgwick, The Interpretation and Construction of Statutory and Constitutional Law 98 (2d ed. 1874).

. . . .

The issue thus boils down to whether a "clear intention otherwise" can be discovered — whether, in short, it can be fairly concluded that the [later statute] operated as a *pro tanto* repeal of [the earlier statute]. "It is, of course, a cardinal principle of statutory construction that repeals by implication are not favored." There are, however,

> "two well-settled categories of repeals by implication — (1) where provisions in the two acts are in irreconcilable conflict, the later act to the extent of the conflict constitutes an implied repeal of the earlier one; and (2) if the later act covers the whole subject of the earlier one and is clearly intended as a substitute, it will operate similarly as a repeal of the earlier act. But, in either case, the intention of the legislature to repeal must be clear and manifest."

It is evident that the "two acts" in this case fall into neither of those categories.

The statutory provisions at issue here cannot be said to be in "irreconcilable conflict" in the sense that there is a positive repugnancy between them or that they cannot mutually coexist. It is not enough to show that the two statutes produce differing results when applied to the same factual situation, for that no more than states the problem. Rather, "when two statutes are capable of co-existence, it is the duty of the courts to regard each as effective." As the Court put the matter in discussing the interrelationship of the antitrust laws and the securities laws: "Repeal is to be regarded as implied only if necessary to make the later enacted law work, and even then only to the minimum extent necessary. This is the guiding principle to reconciliation of the two statutory schemes."

Id. at 153-55. These same sentiments were repeated by the Court more recently in *National Ass'n of Home Builders v. Defenders of Wildlife*, 127 S. Ct. 2518, 2532 (2007). Again, though, when Congress expressly repeals an earlier statute, the later statute will control.

What about conflicts between statutes and other types of laws? As stated in Chapter 1, in the event of irreconcilable conflict, the Constitution will take priority over a statute (hence the ability of courts to declare statutes unconstitutional), though a statute will take priority over virtually everything else (understanding that some other types of laws, such as treaties and court rules, generally are regarded as operating at essentially the same level). But here also, courts generally will work hard to avoid any such conflicts.

Consider, for example, *United States v. Locke*, 471 U.S. 84 (1985), which involved an appeal of a district court judgment in which the district court held a federal statute unconstitutional in the context of a civil action in which the United States was a party. As such, a direct appeal to the Supreme Court was permitted under 28 U.S.C. § 1252. Before dealing with the merits of that appeal, the Court stated:

> Appeal under 28 U. S. C. § 1252 brings before this Court not merely the constitutional question decided below, but the entire case. The entire case includes nonconstitutional questions actually decided by the lower court as well as nonconstitutional grounds presented to, but not passed on, by the lower court. These principles are important aids in the prudential exercise of our appellate jurisdiction, for when a case arrives here by appeal under 28 U. S. C. § 1252, this Court

will not pass on the constitutionality of an Act of Congress if a construction of the Act is fairly possible, or some other nonconstitutional ground fairly available, by which the constitutional question can be avoided.

Id. at 92. Among the cases cited by the Court in support of this proposition was Justice Brandeis's oft-cited concurrence in *Ashwander v. TVA*, 297 U.S. 288, 341 (1936). This canon of avoidance of constitutional questions had been repeated often and in many other contexts. For a more recent example, see *Clinton v. Jones*, 520 U.S. 681, 690 (1997).

Though the same concept is true to some extent as between statutes and cases (thus sometimes leading to the "canon" that statutes in derogation of the common law are to be narrowly construed), greater caution should be exercised in that area, the reason being that Congress often has as its goal the "repeal" of earlier case law to the contrary. Indeed, that is often the very purpose of the legislation at issue.

Notes and Questions

1. 28 U.S.C. § 2072(b) (2012), which is part of the Rules Enabling Act, provides (in part): "All laws in conflict with such rules shall be of no further force or effect after such rules have taken effect." As a result of this statute, a valid federal court rule (such as a federal rule of civil procedure) takes priority over an earlier, contrary federal statute.

   In 2007, when the Federal Rules of Civil Procedure were "restyled" — rewritten and, to some extent, reorganized — some were concerned that the resulting changes might conflict with certain, earlier statutes, even though no substantive change in the Rules was intended. Accordingly, Federal Rule of Civil Procedure 86(b) was also added, which provides: "If any provision in Rules 1-5.1, 6-73, or 77-86 conflicts with another law, priority in time for the purpose of 28 U.S.C. § 2072(b) is not affected by the amendments taking effect on December 1, 2007." Rule 86(b) itself took effect on December 1, 2007. But because Rule 86(b) was *itself* a part of one of the rules encompassed by that rule, and because Rule 86(b) obviously conflicts with § 2072(b), does this mean that Rule 86(b) has no effect?

G. THE FATE OF UNCONSTITUTIONAL STATUTES

As mentioned in the previous section, courts sometimes "declare" statutes unconstitutional. In that event, what happens to that statute? In other words, what is the effect, from a statutory perspective, of such a declaration? Consider the following case.

Ayotte v. Planned Parenthood

546 U.S. 320 (2006)

JUSTICE O'CONNOR delivered the opinion of the Court.

We do not revisit our abortion precedents today, but rather address a question of remedy: If enforcing a statute that regulates access to abortion would be unconstitutional in medical emergencies, what is the appropriate judicial response? We hold that invalidating the statute entirely is not always necessary or justified, for lower courts may be able to render narrower declaratory and injunctive relief.

I

A

In 2003, New Hampshire enacted the Parental Notification Prior to Abortion Act. The Act prohibits physicians from performing an abortion on a pregnant minor (or a woman for whom a guardian or conservator has been appointed) until 48 hours after written notice of the pending abortion is delivered to her parent or guardian. Notice may be delivered personally or by certified mail. Violations of the Act are subject to criminal and civil penalties.

The Act allows for three circumstances in which a physician may perform an abortion without notifying the minor's parent. First, notice is not required if "the attending abortion provider certifies in the pregnant minor's record that the abortion is necessary to prevent the minor's death and there is insufficient time to provide the required notice." Second, a person entitled to receive notice may certify that he or she has already been notified. Finally, a minor may petition a judge to authorize her physician to perform an abortion without parental notification. The judge must so authorize if he or she finds that the minor is mature and capable of giving informed consent, or that an abortion without notification is in the minor's best interests. These judicial bypass proceedings "shall be confidential and shall be given precedence over other pending matters so that the court may reach a decision promptly and without delay," and access to the courts "shall be afforded [to the] pregnant minor 24 hours a day, 7 days a week." The trial and appellate courts must each rule on bypass petitions within seven days.

The Act does not explicitly permit a physician to perform an abortion in a medical emergency without parental notification.

B

Respondents are Dr. Wayne Goldner, an obstetrician and gynecologist who has a private practice in Manchester, and three clinics that offer reproductive health services. All provide abortions for pregnant minors, and each anticipates having to provide emergency abortions for minors in the future. Before the Act took effect, respondents brought suit under 42 U. S. C. § 1983, alleging that the Act is unconstitutional because it fails "to allow a physician to provide a prompt abortion to a minor whose health would be endangered" by delays inherent in the Act. Respondents also challenged the adequacy of the Act's life exception and of the judicial bypass' confidentiality provision.

The District Court declared the Act unconstitutional, see 28 U. S. C. § 2201(a), and permanently enjoined its enforcement. It held, first, that the Act was invalid for failure "on its face [to] comply with the constitutional requirement that laws restricting a woman's access to abortion must provide a health exception." It also found that the Act's judicial bypass would not operate expeditiously enough in medical emergencies. In the alternative, the District Court held the Act's life exception unconstitutional because it requires physicians to certify with impossible precision that an abortion is "necessary" to avoid death, and fails to protect their good faith medical judgment.

The Court of Appeals for the First Circuit affirmed. Citing our decisions in *Stenberg v. Carhart*, 530 U. S. 914, 929-930 (2000), *Planned Parenthood of Southeastern Pa. v. Casey*, 505 U. S. 833, 879 (1992) (plurality opinion), and *Roe v. Wade*, 410 U. S. 113, 164-165 (1973), it observed: "Complementing the general undue burden standard for reviewing abortion regulations, the Supreme Court has also identified a specific and independent constitutional requirement that an abortion regulation must contain an exception for the preservation of the pregnant woman's health." It went on to conclude that the Act is unconstitutional because it does not contain an explicit health exception, and its judicial bypass, along with other provisions of state law, is not a substitute. The Court of Appeals further found the Act unconstitutional because, in its view, the life exception forces physicians to gamble with their patients' lives prohibiting them from performing an abortion without notification until they are certain that death is imminent, and is intolerably vague. Because the district and appellate courts permanently enjoined the Act's enforcement on the basis of the above infirmities, neither reached respondents' objection to the judicial bypass' confidentiality provision.

We granted certiorari to decide whether the courts below erred in invalidating the Act in its entirety because it lacks an exception for the preservation of pregnant minors' health. We now vacate and remand for the Court of Appeals to reconsider its choice of remedy.

II

As the case comes to us, three propositions — two legal and one factual — are established. First, States unquestionably have the right to require parental involvement when a minor considers terminating her pregnancy, because of their "strong and legitimate interest in the welfare of their young citizens, whose immaturity, inexperience, and lack of judgment may sometimes impair their ability to exercise their rights wisely." Accordingly, we have long upheld state parental involvement statutes like the Act before us, and we cast no doubt on those holdings today.

Second, New Hampshire does not dispute, and our precedents hold, that a State may not restrict access to abortions that are "'necessary, in appropriate medical judgment, for the preservation of the life or health of the mother.'"

Third, New Hampshire has not taken real issue with the factual basis of this litigation: In some very small percentage of cases, pregnant minors, like adult women, need immediate abortions to avert serious and often irreversible damage to their health.

New Hampshire has maintained that in most if not all cases, the Act's judicial bypass and the State's "competing harms" statutes should protect both physician and patient when a minor needs an immediate abortion. But the District Court and Court of Appeals found neither of these provisions to protect minors' health reliably in all emergencies. And New Hampshire has conceded that, under our cases, it would be unconstitutional to apply the Act in a manner that subjects minors to significant health risks.

III

We turn to the question of remedy: When a statute restricting access to abortion may be applied in a manner that harms women's health, what is the appropriate relief? Generally speaking, when confronting a constitutional flaw in a statute, we try to limit the solution to the problem. We prefer, for example, to enjoin only the unconstitutional applications of a statute while leaving other applications in force, or to sever its problematic portions while leaving the remainder intact.

Three interrelated principles inform our approach to remedies. First, we try not to nullify more of a legislature's work than is necessary, for we know that "a ruling of unconstitutionality frustrates the intent of the elected representatives of the people." It is axiomatic that a "statute may be invalid as applied to one state of facts and yet valid as applied to another." Accordingly, the "normal rule" is that "partial, rather than facial invalidation is the required course," such that a "statute may be declared invalid to the extent that it reaches too far, but otherwise left intact."

Second, mindful that our constitutional mandate and institutional competence are limited, we restrain ourselves from "rewriting state law to conform it to constitutional requirements" even as we strive to salvage it. Our ability to devise a judicial remedy that does not entail quintessentially legislative work often depends on how clearly we have already articulated the background constitutional rules at issue and how easily we can articulate the remedy. In *United States* v. *Grace*, for example, we crafted a narrow remedy much like the one we contemplate today, striking down a statute banning expressive displays only as it applied to public sidewalks near the Supreme Court but not as it applied to the Supreme Court Building itself. We later explained that the remedy in *Grace* was a "relatively simple matter" because we had previously distinguished between sidewalks and buildings in our First Amendment jurisprudence. But making distinctions in a murky constitutional context, or where line-drawing is inherently complex, may call for a "far more serious invasion of the legislative domain" than we ought to undertake.

Third, the touchstone for any decision about remedy is legislative intent, for a court cannot "use its remedial powers to circumvent the intent of the legislature." After finding an application or portion of a statute unconstitutional, we must next ask: Would the legislature have preferred what is left of its statute to no statute at all? All the while, we are wary of legislatures who would rely on our intervention, for "it would certainly be dangerous if the legislature could set a net large enough to catch all possible offenders, and leave it to the courts to step inside" to announce to whom the statute may be applied. "This would, to some extent, substitute the judicial for the legislative department of the government."

In this case, the courts below chose the most blunt remedy — permanently enjoining the enforcement of New Hampshire's parental notification law and thereby invalidating it entirely. That is understandable, for we, too, have previously invalidated an abortion statute in its entirety because of the same constitutional flaw. In *Stenberg,* we addressed a Nebraska law banning so-called "partial birth abortion" unless the procedure was necessary to save the pregnant woman's life. We held Nebraska's law unconstitutional because it lacked a health exception. But the parties in *Stenberg* did not ask for, and we did not contemplate, relief more finely drawn.

In the case that is before us, however, we agree with New Hampshire that the lower courts need not have invalidated the law wholesale. Respondents, too, recognize the possibility of a modest remedy: They pleaded for any relief "just and proper" and conceded at oral argument that carefully crafted injunctive relief may resolve this case. Only a few applications of New Hampshire's parental notification statute would present a constitutional problem. So long as they are faithful to legislative intent, then, in this case the lower courts can issue a declaratory judgment and an injunction prohibiting the statute's unconstitutional application.

There is some dispute as to whether New Hampshire's legislature intended the statute to be susceptible to such a remedy. New Hampshire notes that the Act contains a severability clause providing that "if any provision of this subdivision or the application thereof to any person or circumstance is held invalid, such invalidity shall not affect the provisions or applications of this subdivision which can be given effect without the invalid provisions or applications." Respondents, on the other hand, contend that New Hampshire legislators preferred no statute at all to a statute enjoined in the way we have described. Because this is an open question, we remand for the lower courts to determine legislative intent in the first instance.

Notes and Questions

---

1. A more recent take on the effect of statutory unconstitutionality (albeit in dissent) can be found in *National Federation of Indep. Business v. Sebelius,* 132 S. Ct. 2566 (2012) (the "Obamacare" case). In their joint dissent, Justices Scalia, Kennedy, Thomas, and Alito opined:

   > When an unconstitutional provision is but a part of a more comprehensive statute, the question arises as to the validity of the remaining provisions. The Court's authority to declare a statute partially unconstitutional has been well established since *Marbury* v. *Madison,* 1 Cranch 137 (1803) when the Court severed an unconstitutional provision from the Judiciary Act of 1789. And while the Court has sometimes applied "at least a modest presumption in favor of severability," C. Nelson, Statutory Interpretation 144 (2010), it has not always done so.

An automatic or too cursory severance of statutory provisions risks "rewriting a statute and giving it an effect altogether different from that sought by the measure viewed as a whole." The Judiciary, if it orders severance, then assumes the legislative function; for it imposes on the Nation, by the Court's decree, its own new statutory regime, consisting of policies, risks, and duties that Congress did not enact. That can be a more extreme exercise of the judicial power than striking the whole statute and allowing Congress to address the conditions that pertained when the statute was considered at the outset.

The Court has applied a two-part guide as the framework for severability analysis. The test has been deemed "well established." *Alaska Airlines, Inc.* v. *Brock*, 480 U. S. 678, 684 (1987). First, if the Court holds a statutory provision unconstitutional, it then determines whether the now truncated statute will operate in the manner Congress intended. If not, the remaining provisions must be invalidated. . . .

Second, even if the remaining provisions can operate as Congress designed them to operate, the Court must determine if Congress would have enacted them standing alone and without the unconstitutional portion. If Congress would not, those provisions, too, must be invalidated.

The two inquiries — whether the remaining provisions will operate as Congress designed them, and whether Congress would have enacted the remaining provisions standing alone — often are interrelated. In the ordinary course, if the remaining provisions cannot operate according to the congressional design (the first inquiry), it almost necessarily follows that Congress would not have enacted them (the second inquiry). This close interaction may explain why the Court has not always been precise in distinguishing between the two. There are, however, occasions in which the severability standard's first inquiry (statutory functionality) is not a proxy for the second inquiry (whether the Legislature intended the remaining provisions to stand alone).

Id. at 2668-69.

Is this analysis consistent with that in *Ayotte*? Regardless, how is a court to determine the "two inquiries" described in the Affordable Care Act case?

2. *Facial vs. as applied challenges to constitutionality.* Regarding the fate of unconstitutional statutes, consider also *Ada v. Guam Society of Obstetricians and Gynecologists*, 506 U.S. 1011 (1992) (Scalia, J., joined by Rehnquist, C.J., and White, J., dissenting from the denial of certiorari):

Statutes are ordinarily challenged, and their constitutionality evaluated, "as applied" — that is, the plaintiff contends that application of the statute in the particular context in which he has acted, or in which he proposes to act, would be unconstitutional. The practical effect of holding a statute unconstitutional "as applied" is to prevent its future application in a similar context, but not to render it utterly inoperative. To achieve the latter result, the plaintiff must succeed in challenging the statute "on its face." Our traditional rule has been, however, that a facial challenge must be rejected unless there exists *no set of circumstances* in which the statute can constitutionally be applied. "Courts are not," we have said, "roving commissions assigned to pass judgment on the validity of the Nation's laws." The only exception to this rule recognized in our jurisprudence is the facial challenge based upon First Amendment free-speech grounds. We have applied to statutes restricting speech a so-called "overbreadth" doctrine, rendering such a statute invalid in all its applications (*i.e.*, facially invalid) if it is invalid in any of them.

. . . .

Facial invalidation based on overbreadth [outside of the First Amendment area] impermissibly interferes with the state process of refining and limiting — through judicial decision or enforcement discretion — statutes that cannot be constitutionally applied in all cases covered by their language. And it prevents the State (or territory) from punishing people who violate a prohibition that is, in the context in which it is applied, entirely constitutional.

3. As you might have surmised, unconstitutional statutes are not removed from the code in which they are found. Indeed, often they are never repealed.

This can lead to a somewhat interesting problem: What happens when one court declares a statute unconstitutional, but then a later court overrules the earlier court's decision? Most courts and commentators have concluded that the statute is then "revived," though for a contrary viewpoint, see William Michael Treanor & Gene B. Sperling, *Prospective Overruling and the Revival of "Unconstitutional" Statutes*, 93 COLUM. L. REV. 1902 (1993).

4. In *Ayotte*, the New Hampshire act at issue contained an express severability clause that was to take effect should some portion of the act be held invalid. On the subject of "fallback" law generally, Michael Dorf explains:

To address the risk that a court will declare all or part of a law unconstitutional, legislatures sometimes include "fallback" provisions that take effect on condition of such total or partial invalidation. The attraction of fallback law is obvious. A fallback provision enables the legislature to avoid having to go back to the drawing board should a court find the law invalid. The fallback fills the legal vacuum that would otherwise exist during the time between the invalidating decision and the enactment, if any, of new, valid legislation. Fallback measures ensure that the same session of the legislature that produced the original law gets to say, in advance, what the law will be in the event that the original is subsequently invalidated.

However, fallback law also has disadvantages. Fallback provisions will not always cure the original provisions they back up, and even when they do, other constitutional and practical difficulties can arise. . . . Upon finding a law unconstitutional, a court must do its best to implement the remaining will of the very legislature that enacted the invalid law, and in crafting fallback law, a legislature must do its best to anticipate how the courts will respond. In an American system of separation of powers, each institution has at best a limited ability to predict or control how the other will respond to its work product.

. . . The most widely used kind of fallback provision is a severability clause, which provides that in the event that the original law is held partly invalid, a fallback of the original law minus the invalid provision or application will take effect.

Less commonly, fallback law takes the form of substitute provisions, rather than merely the truncated version of the original law that a severability clause produces. For example, section 274(f) of the Balanced Budget and Emergency Deficit Control Act of 1985 (also known as the Gramm-Rudman-Hollings Act) provided that in the event that certain features of the Act were held invalid, a collection of fallback provisions would go into effect. Having invalidated the triggering provisions, the Supreme Court in *Bowsher v. Synar* declared these fallback provisions effective.[4]

The distinction between severability and "substitutive" fallback law is not always sharp, and in some sense, every severability provision establishes a kind of substitutive fallback provision. The truncated law is not simply smaller; it is also different from the original law.

Michael C. Dorf, *Fallback Law*, 107 COLUM. L. REV. 303, 304-05 (2007).

5. Sometimes the act in question contains no express "fallback" provision. In that event, a court will still attempt to sever the invalid portion and preserve that which remains. According to Professor Dorf, one such example can be found in *United States v. Booker*, 543 U.S. 220 (2005), wherein the Supreme Court, after declaring portions of the Federal Sentencing Guidelines unconstitutional, proceeded (through a different majority of the Court) to cure the deficiency by making the Guidelines advisory, rather than mandatory. *See id.* at 244-68.

H. MAY CONGRESS RETROACTIVELY REOPEN FEDERAL COURT JUDGMENTS WITH WHICH IT DISAGREES?

It is often stated that if Congress disagrees with some interpretation of federal statutory law, it may enact contrary legislation. *See, e.g., Illinois Brick Co. v. Illinois*, 431 U.S. 720, 736 (1977) ("Congress is free to change this Court's interpretation of its legislation."). And Congress in fact does so with some frequency. In fact, one study conducted for the period 1967 to 1990 detected 187 such congressional overrides. *See* William N. Eskridge, *Overriding Supreme Court Statutory Interpretation Decisions*, 101 YALE L.J. 331 (1991). *See also* Matthew R. Christiansen & William N. Eskridge, Jr., *Congressional Overrides of Supreme Court Interpretation Decisions, 1967-2011*, 92 TEXAS L. REV. 1317 (2014) (refining and updating Professor Eskridge's 1991 congressional override study).

But may Congress, by statute, alter final federal court *judgments*? Consider the next case.

Plaut v. Spendthrift Farm, Inc.
514 U.S. 211 (1995)

JUSTICE SCALIA delivered the opinion of the Court.

The question presented in this case is whether § 27A(b) of the Securities Exchange Act of 1934, to the extent that it requires federal courts to reopen final judgments in

---

4. 478 U.S. 714, 734-36 (1986).

private civil actions under § 10(b) of the Act, contravenes the Constitution's separa-tion of powers or the Due Process Clause of the Fifth Amendment.

I

In 1987, petitioners brought a civil action against respondents in the United States District Court for the Eastern District of Kentucky. The complaint alleged that in 1983 and 1984 respondents had committed fraud and deceit in the sale of stock in violation of § 10(b) of the Securities Exchange Act of 1934 and Rule 10b-5 of the Securities and Exchange Commission. The case was mired in pretrial proceedings in the District Court until June 20, 1991, when we decided *Lampf, Pleva, Lipkind, Prupis & Petigrow v. Gilbertson*, 501 U. S. 350. *Lampf* held that "litigation instituted pursuant to § 10(b) and Rule 10b-5 must be commenced within one year after the discovery of the facts constituting the violation and within three years after such vio-lation." We applied that holding to the plaintiff-respondents in *Lampf* itself, found their suit untimely, and reinstated a summary judgment previously entered in favor of the defendant-petitioners. On the same day we decided *James B. Beam Distilling Co. v. Georgia*, 501 U. S. 529 (1991), in which a majority of the Court held, albeit in different opinions, that a new rule of federal law that is applied to the parties in the case announcing the rule must be applied as well to all cases pending on direct review. See *Harper v. Virginia Dept. of Taxation*, 509 U. S. 86, 92 (1993). The joint effect of *Lampf* and *Beam* was to mandate application of the 1-year/3-year limita-tions period to petitioners' suit. The District Court, finding that petitioners' claims were untimely under the *Lampf* rule, dismissed their action with prejudice on August 13, 1991. Petitioners filed no appeal; the judgment accordingly became final 30 days later. See 28 U. S. C. § 2107(a); *Griffith v. Kentucky*, 479 U. S. 314, 321, n. 6 (1987).

On December 19, 1991, the President signed the Federal Deposit Insurance Corporation Improvement Act of 1991, 105 Stat. 2236. Section 476 of the Act — a sec-tion that had nothing to do with FDIC improvements — became § 27A of the Securities Exchange Act of 1934, and was later codified as 15 U. S. C. § 78aa-1. It provides:

"(a) Effect on pending causes of action

"The limitation period for any private civil action implied under . . . § 10(b) of the Securities Exchange Act of 1934[] that was commenced on or before June 19, 1991, shall be the limitation period provided by the laws ap-plicable in the jurisdiction, including principles of retroactivity, as such laws existed on June 19, 1991.

"(b) Effect on dismissed causes of action

"Any private civil action implied under section [10(b)] . . . that was com-menced on or before June 19, 1991 —

"(1) which was dismissed as time barred subsequent to June 19, 1991, and

"(2) which would have been timely filed under the limitation period provided by the laws applicable in the jurisdiction, including principles of retroactivity, as such laws existed on June 19, 1991,

> "shall be reinstated on motion by the plaintiff not later than 60 days after December 19, 1991."

On February 11, 1992, petitioners returned to the District Court and filed a motion to reinstate the action previously dismissed with prejudice. The District Court found that the conditions set out in §§ 27A(b)(1) and (2) were met, so that petitioners' motion was required to be granted by the terms of the statute. It nonetheless denied the motion, agreeing with respondents that § 27A(b) is unconstitutional. The United States Court of Appeals for the Sixth Circuit affirmed. We granted certiorari.[1]

. . . .

III

Respondents submit that § 27A(b) violates both the separation of powers and the Due Process Clause of the Fifth Amendment. Because the latter submission, if correct, might dictate a similar result in a challenge to state legislation under the Fourteenth Amendment, the former is the narrower ground for adjudication of the constitutional question in this case, and we therefore consider it first. We conclude that in § 27A(b) Congress has exceeded its authority by requiring the federal courts to exercise "the judicial Power of the United States," U. S. Const., Art. III, § 1, in a manner repugnant to the text, structure, and traditions of Article III.

Our decisions to date have identified two types of legislation that require federal courts to exercise the judicial power in a manner that Article III forbids. The first appears in *United States* v. *Klein*, 13 Wall. 128 (1872), where we refused to give effect to a statute that was said "to prescribe rules of decision to the Judicial Department of the government in cases pending before it." Whatever the precise scope of *Klein*, however, later decisions have made clear that its prohibition does not take hold when Congress "amends applicable law." *Robertson* v. *Seattle Audubon Soc.*, 503 U. S. 429, 441 (1992). Section 27A(b) indisputably does set out substantive legal standards for the Judiciary to apply, and in that sense changes the law (even if solely retroactively). The second type of unconstitutional restriction upon the exercise of judicial power identified by past cases is exemplified by *Heyburn's Case*, 2 Dall. 409 (1792), which stands for the principle that Congress cannot vest review of the decisions of Article III courts in officials of the Executive Branch. Yet under any application of § 27A(b) only courts are involved; no officials of other departments sit in direct review of their decisions. Section 27A(b) therefore offends neither of these previously established prohibitions.

We think, however, that § 27A(b) offends a postulate of Article III just as deeply rooted in our law as those we have mentioned. Article III establishes a "judicial

---

1. Last Term this Court affirmed, by an equally divided vote, a judgment of the United States Court of Appeals for the Fifth Circuit that held § 27A constitutional. *Morgan Stanley & Co.* v. *Pacific Mut. Life Ins. Co.*, 511 U. S. 658 (1994) (*per curiam*). That ruling of course lacks precedential weight. *Trans World Airlines, Inc.* v. *Hardison*, 432 U. S. 63, 73 n. 8 (1977).

department" with the "province and duty to say what the law is" in particular cases and controversies. *Marbury* v. *Madison*, 1 Cranch 137, 177 (1803). The record of history shows that the Framers crafted this charter of the judicial department with an expressed understanding that it gives the Federal Judiciary the power, not merely to rule on cases, but to *decide* them, subject to review only by superior courts in the Article III hierarchy — with an understanding, in short, that "a judgment conclusively resolves the case" because "a 'judicial Power' is one to render dispositive judgments." Easterbrook, Presidential Review, 40 Case W. Res. L. Rev. 905, 926 (1990). By retroactively commanding the federal courts to reopen final judgments, Congress has violated this fundamental principle.

. . . .

B

Section 27A(b) effects a clear violation of the separation-of-powers principle we have just discussed. It is, of course, retroactive legislation, that is, legislation that prescribes what the law *was* at an earlier time, when the act whose effect is controlled by the legislation occurred — in this case, the filing of the initial Rule 10b-5 action in the District Court. When retroactive legislation requires its own application in a case already finally adjudicated, it does no more and no less than "reverse a determination once made, in a particular case." The Federalist No. 81, at 545. Our decisions stemming from *Heyburn's Case* — although their precise holdings are not strictly applicable here — have uniformly provided fair warning that such an act exceeds the powers of Congress. Today those clear statements must either be honored, or else proved false.

It is true, as petitioners contend, that Congress can always revise the judgments of Article III courts in one sense: When a new law makes clear that it is retroactive, an appellate court must apply that law in reviewing judgments still on appeal that were rendered before the law was enacted, and must alter the outcome accordingly. See *United States* v. *Schooner Peggy*, 1 Cranch 103 (1801); *Landgraf* v. *USI Film Products*, 511 U. S. 244, 273-280 (1994). Since that is so, petitioners argue, federal courts must apply the "new" law created by § 27A(b) in finally adjudicating cases as well; for the line that separates lower court judgments that are pending on appeal (or may still be appealed), from lower court judgments that are final, is determined by statute, see, *e.g.*, 28 U. S. C. § 2107(a) (30-day time limit for appeal to federal court of appeals), and so cannot possibly be a *constitutional* line. But a distinction between judgments from which all appeals have been forgone or completed, and judgments that remain on appeal (or subject to being appealed), is implicit in what Article III creates: not a batch of unconnected courts, but a judicial *department* composed of "inferior Courts" and "one supreme Court." Within that hierarchy, the decision of an inferior court is not (unless the time for appeal has expired) the final word of the department as a whole. It is the obligation of the last court in the hierarchy that rules on the case to give effect to Congress's latest enactment, even when that has the effect of overturning the judgment of an inferior court, since each court, at every level, must "decide according to existing laws." *Schooner Peggy, supra,* at 109. Having achieved finality, however, a judicial decision becomes the last word of the judicial department with regard to a particular case or controversy, and Congress may not declare by retroactive legislation that the law applicable *to that very case* was something other than what the courts said it was. Finality of a legal judgment is determined by statute, just as entitlement to a government benefit is a statutory creation; but that no more deprives the former of its constitutional significance for separation-of-powers analysis than it deprives the latter of its significance for due process purposes.

. . . .

We know of no previous instance in which Congress has enacted retroactive legislation requiring an Article III court to set aside a final judgment, and for good reason. The Constitution's separation of legislative and judicial powers denied it the authority to do so. Section 27A(b) is unconstitutional to the extent that it requires federal courts to reopen final judgments entered before its enactment. The judgment of the Court of Appeals is affirmed.

Notes and Questions

---

1. Make sure that you understand the distinction between the issue in *Landgraf* and the holding of the Court in *Plaut*. What is that distinction?

2. As stated above, Congress is permitted to "override" prior federal court statutory interpretation decisions, at least as a prospective matter, and in fact does so on occasion. Does this fact say anything about the propriety of the presumption that legislative inaction is somehow indicative of legislative approval? That courts should be more reluctant to overrule statutory interpretation decisions?

The Executive Branch: Presidential Signing Statements, Executive Orders, Regulations, and the Role of Agencies in the Interpretation of Statutes

In the federal system, the Executive Branch is headed by the President, though it includes many other persons, departments, and agencies. Though known more for its role in ensuring that federal law is faithfully executed, the Executive Branch, like the other branches, is responsible (or partially responsible) for the making of certain types of law. A complete exploration of this subject is a matter best reserved for a course devoted solely to Administrative Law. Nonetheless, this Chapter will focus on four of the most important aspects of this Executive Branch law-making power: the issuance of presidential signing statements and executive orders; the creation of regulations; and the role of agencies in the interpretation of statutes (particularly in relation to courts).

A. PRESIDENTIAL SIGNING STATEMENTS

In Chapter 3, we saw that the President plays a role in the federal legislative process. Typically, in order for a bill to become a law, the President must sign it within 10 days of presentation. Sometimes, though, in addition to signing the bill, the President will issue a "signing statement" in which the President gives his or her views regarding subjects relating to the new law. What is the role of such signing statements? To what extent are they even legitimate? These questions and more are discussed in the following excerpt.

T.J. Halstead

PRESIDENTIAL SIGNING STATEMENTS: CONSTITUTIONAL AND INSTITUTIONAL IMPLICATIONS

Congressional Research Service Report for Congress
Updated September 17, 2007

INTRODUCTION

Presidential signing statements are official pronouncements issued by the President contemporaneously to the signing of a bill into law that, in addition to commenting on the law generally, have been used to forward the President's interpretation of the statutory language; to assert constitutional objections to the provisions contained therein; and, concordantly, to announce that the provisions of the law will be administered in a manner that comports with the Administration's conception of the President's constitutional prerogatives. While the history of presidential issuance of signing statements dates to the early 19th century, the practice has become the source of significant controversy in the modern era as Presidents have increasingly employed the statements to assert constitutional objections to congressional enactments. The number and scope of such assertions in the George W. Bush Administration in particular has given rise to extensive debate over the issuance of signing statements, with the American Bar Association (ABA) recently publishing a report declaring that these instruments are "contrary to the rule of law and our constitutional separation of powers" when they "claim the authority or state the intention to disregard or decline to enforce all or part of a law or to interpret such a law in a manner inconsistent with the clear intent of Congress."[3]

However, in analyzing the constitutional basis for, and legal effect of, presidential signing statements, it becomes apparent that no constitutional or legal

---

3. American Bar Association, Report of the Task Force on Presidential Signing Statements and the Separation of Powers Doctrine at p. 5 (August 2006).

deficiencies adhere to the issuance of such statements in and of themselves. Rather, it appears that the appropriate focus of inquiry in this context is on the assertions of presidential authority contained therein, coupled with an examination of substantive executive action taken or forborne with regard to the provisions of law implicated in a presidential signing statement. Applying this analytical rubric to the current controversy, it seems evident that the issues involved center not on the simple issue of signing statements, but rather on the view of presidential authority that govern the substantive actions of the Administration in question. This report focuses on the use of signing statements by recent Administrations, with particular emphasis on the current Administration.

HISTORICAL USAGE AND CONSTITUTIONAL BASIS

There is no explicit constitutional provision authorizing the issuance of presidential signing statements. Article I of the Constitution provides only that the President "shall sign" a bill of which he approves, while in vetoing a measure the President is required to return the measure "with his Objections to that House in which it shall have originated." However, Presidents have issued such statements since the Monroe Administration, and there is little evident constitutional or legal support for the proposition that the President may be constrained from issuing a statement regarding a provision of law.

The first controversy arising in this context stemmed from a signing statement issued by Andrew Jackson in 1830 that raised objections to an appropriations bill that involved internal improvements. The bill specifically addressed road examinations and surveys. In his signing statement President Jackson declared that the road in question, which was to reach from Detroit to Chicago, should not extend beyond the territory of Michigan. A subsequently issued House report criticized Jackson's action, characterizing it as in effect constituting a line item veto. Likewise, a signing statement issued by President Tyler in 1842 expressing doubts about the constitutionality of a bill regarding the appointment of congressional districts was characterized by a select committee of the House as "a defacement of the public record and archives." Perhaps sensitized by this rebuke, Presidents Polk and Pierce apologized for the issuance of such statements, noting that such action departed from the traditional practice of notifying Congress of the approval of a bill via an oral message from the President's private secretary. This conception of a signing statement as an unusual instrument was again noted by President Grant in 1875, when he declared that his use of a signing statement was an "unusual method of conveying the notice of approval."

Signing statements remained comparatively rare through the end of the 19th century, but had become common instruments by 1950. President Truman, for instance, issued nearly 16 signing statements per year, on average, with the figure steadily increasing up to the modern day. Concurrent with the rise in the number of statements issued, the usage of signing statements to voice constitutional objections to acts of Congress has become increasingly prevalent over the past 60 years. This type of executive action began in earnest during the Reagan Administration, as one aspect of a comprehensive strategy employed by the Reagan Administration to aggressively assert the constitutional prerogatives of the presidency.

A. Signing Statements in the Reagan Administration.

President Reagan expanded the use and impact of the presidential signing statement, transforming it into a mechanism for the assertion of presidential authority and intent. President Reagan issued 250 signing statements, 86 of which (34%) objected to one or more of the statutory provisions signed into law. One key aspect of President Reagan's approach in this context centered on attempts to establish the signing statement as part of the legislative history of an enactment, and, concordantly, to persuade courts to take the statements into consideration in judicial rulings. This goal was illustrated in a memorandum drafted by Samuel A. Alito, Jr., then serving in the Office of Legal Counsel (OLC) of the Department of Justice, announcing a "primary objective" to "ensure that Presidential signing statements assume their rightful place in the interpretation of legislation." To this end, Attorney General Edwin Meese III entered into an agreement in 1986 with the West Publishing Company for signing statements to be included in the legislative histories contained in its U.S. Code Congressional and Administrative News publication.

This strategy met with a degree of success in two major Supreme Court cases that were decided during this time period. In *INS v. Chadha*, which struck down as unconstitutional the congressional practice of subjecting various executive branch actions to a legislative veto, the Court noted that "11 Presidents, from Mr. Wilson through Mr. Reagan, who have been presented with this issue have gone on record at some point to challenge congressional vetoes as unconstitutional." Likewise, in *Bowsher v. Synar*, which struck down provisions of the Gramm-Rudman Deficit Reduction Act on the basis that they impermissibly imbued a legislative branch officer with executive authority, the Court noted: "in his signing statement, the President expressed his view that the act was constitutionally defective because of the Comptroller General's ability to exercise supervisory authority over the President." While these citations by the Court lend credence to validity of signing statements as constitutional presidential instruments, it does not appear that the statements were in fact relied upon in any determinative degree by the Court. Indeed, as discussed in further detail below, the contents of signing statements do not seem to have factored prominently in judicial decisions.

. . . .

B. Signing Statements in the George H.W. Bush Administration.

The Administration of President George H.W. Bush (Bush I) continued to employ signing statements to further presidential prerogatives, issuing 228 signing statements, 107 of which (47%) raised constitutional or legal objections. In particular, the Bush I Administration was highly sensitive to perceived encroachments upon executive power by Congress, as illustrated by an OLC opinion drafted by Deputy Attorney General William P. Barr. In this memo, Barr identified ten categories of legislative action he considered constitutionally problematic and noted that the

Administration had objected to many of these perceived intrusions through the issuance of signing statements.

   . . . .

C. Signing Statements in the Clinton Administration.

While the policy aims of his Administration might have differed, President Clinton's conception of executive power revealed itself to be largely consonant with the philosophical underpinnings of the Reagan and Bush I Administrations. Accordingly, President Clinton also made active use of signing statements as a mechanism to assert presidential prerogatives. President Clinton issued 381 signing statements, 70 of which (18%) voiced concerns or objections.

   . . . .

D. Signing Statements in the George W. Bush Administration.

Like its predecessors, the Administration of George W. Bush (Bush II) has employed the signing statement to voice constitutional objections to, or concerns with, congressional enactments, or to enunciate the Administrations interpretation of an enactment it deems ambiguous. However, while the nature and scope of the objections raised by the Bush II Administration mirror those of prior Administrations, the sheer number of challenges contained in the signing statements issued by President Bush indicate that the current Administration is using this presidential instrument relative to all levels and elements of the executive branch and to aggressively assert presidential prerogatives in its relations with the Congress and the Judiciary. These factors, in turn, have generated a significant degree of controversy regarding the issuance of presidential signing statements.

At first glance, it does not appear that President Bush has departed significantly from prior practice in the signing statement context, having issued 152 signing statements as compared to 381 during the Clinton Administration. However, the qualitative difference in the Bush II approach becomes apparent when considering the number of individual challenges or objections to statutory provisions that are contained in these statements. Of President Bush's 152 signing statements, 118 (78%) contain some type of constitutional challenge or objection, as compared to 70 (18%) during the Clinton Administration. Even more significant, however, is the fact that these 118 signing statements are typified by multiple constitutional and statutory objections, containing challenges to more than 1,000 distinct provisions of law.

   . . . .

LEGAL AND CONSTITUTIONAL IMPLICATIONS OF SIGNING STATEMENTS

As has been illustrated, there is a long history of presidential issuance of signing statements, and these statements provide "one way in which a President may indicate his intent to refuse to enforce a provision of a congressionally enacted law that he believes to be unconstitutional." However, there is little evident support for the notion that objections or concerns raised in a signing statement may be given substantive legal effect. . . .

   . . . .

   This persistent practice on the part of presidents gives rise to the question of whether a President can refuse to comply with a law he believes to be unconstitutional. The Supreme Court has not directly addressed this issue, but a long line of precedent could be taken to indicate a consistent view on the part of the Court that the Take Care Clause[56] imposes a duty on the President to ensure that officials obey Congress's instructions, and, conversely, that the Clause does not imbue the President with the authority to dispense with congressional enactments. . . .

   Despite these declarations from the Court, the executive branch has consistently maintained that the President possesses authority to decline to enforce enactments he views as unconstitutional. . . .

   . . . .

SUBSTANTIALITY OF CONSTITUTIONAL OBJECTIONS

While presidential authority to refuse to enforce laws he considers unconstitutional is a matter of significant constitutional importance, the issue is ultimately of little concern with regard to the legality or effect of signing statements themselves. As the judicial maxims discussed above establish, there is little evident support for the notion that signing statements are instruments with legal force and effect in and of themselves. If an action taken by a President in fact contravenes legal or constitutional provisions, that illegality is not augmented or assuaged merely by the issuance of a signing statement. Commentators argue that this dynamic lends credence to the notion that signing statements have been employed by the Bush II Administration not to flatly reject congressional enactments, but, rather, are intended to sensitize other parties to the President's conception of executive authority. Moreover, the usage of signing statements as an instrument to expand executive authority generally, as opposed to a mechanism by which the President has claimed summary authority to dispense with the laws enacted by Congress, becomes more apparent when the merits of the objections that typify signing statements are examined. In particular, such analysis indicates that while there are instances in which signing statements are predicated on specific and supportable concerns, the majority of the objections raised for example in President Bush's signing statements are largely unsubstantive or are so general as to appear to be hortatory assertions of executive power.

   . . . .

---

56. The Take Care Clause states that the President "shall take Care that the Laws be faithfully executed." U.S. Const. Art. II, sec. 3, cl. 3.

INSTITUTIONAL IMPLICATIONS OF SIGNING STATEMENTS

The generalized nature of the constitutional objections and assertions of authority that pervade signing statements, coupled with the fact that such instruments do not have any legal force in and of themselves, lends support to the notion that the Bush II Administration is employing these instruments as a means by which it can make broad claims to extensive and exclusive authority. This approach necessarily raises questions regarding the impact of signing statements on the exercise of executive authority in relation to the traditional roles of Congress and the Judiciary.

Statutory Construction and the Courts.

With regard to the Judicial Branch, the primary consideration is whether the courts have in fact begun to give a degree of determinative weight to signing statements in a manner akin to traditional sources of legislative history. As noted above, one of the factors that appears to have motivated the increase in the issuance of signing statements beginning in the Reagan Administration was to encourage judicial reliance upon the viewpoints contained therein. After persuading West Publishing Company to include signing statements along with legislative histories contained in the *United States Code Congressional and Administrative News*, Attorney General Edwin Meese stated that this inclusion would facilitate the use of signing statements by courts "for future construction of what the statute actually means."

Despite these efforts, it does not appear that courts have incorporated signing statements in the manner hoped for by the Reagan Administration, presumably due to traditional practice as motivated by constitutional precepts. In particular, it could be argued that while there is little support for the notion that the Constitution somehow implicitly forbids the issuance of signing statements, the nature of the President's role in vetoing or approving legislation has nonetheless militated against courts granting interpretive weight to signing statements. Specifically, while the Constitution provides that the President is to note his objections upon the veto of a bill, there is no corresponding requirement that he announce his reasons for its approval. In turn, there is a constitutionally prescribed procedure by which Congress is to consider objections raised by a President in formulating a response to a veto, but not for congressional response to a signing statement. While this dichotomy does not require that courts disregard signing statements (as there is likewise no corresponding constitutional validation of committee reports, floor debates and other legislative history), it arguably lends weight to the notion that presidential signing statements should be discounted when they conflict with congressional explanations that have traditionally enjoyed judicial deference. In particular, a well established rule for resolving conflicts in legislative history establishes that when the two Houses have disagreed on the meaning of identical language in a bill that did not go to conference, the explanation that was before both Houses prevails in the event that the court turns to the legislative history. The rationale is that congressional intent should depend upon the actions of both Houses. Accordingly, given that Congress has no opportunity to act in response to interpretations set forth in signing statements, there is lessened support for the notion that courts should rely upon them to interpret the aim of a congressional enactment.

A related issue arising from this constitutional provision centers on the fact that the President may only approve or veto a bill in its entirety. The President does not possess inherent line-item veto authority, and it is well established that Congress cannot grant the President such authority by statute. Thus, it could be argued that if the courts were to give determinative weight to signing statements in negating statutory provisions a President would effectively possess power analogous to a line item veto. However, there is no indication that this has occurred, rendering this dynamic of greater interest in relation to the impact of signing statements on executive branch interaction with Congress.

Information contained in signing statements may be entitled to more significant judicial consideration if the President or his Administration worked closely with Congress in developing the legislation, and if the approved version incorporated the President's recommendations. This principle can be applied not only to bills introduced at the Administration's behest, but also to bills the final content of which resulted from compromise negotiations between the Administration and Congress. In such circumstances, of course, signing statements are used to explain rather than negate congressional action, and are most valuable as lending support to congressional explanations.

Although signing statements are not generally treated as a significant part of legislative history by the courts, they nonetheless affect interpretation by virtue of the effect of directives contained therein on actions taken by administering agencies. Courts grant a high degree of deference to interpretations of agencies charged with implementing statutes, premised on the notion that Congress has authorized the agency to "speak with the force of law" through a rulemaking or other formal process. Congress has not authorized the President to speak with the force of law through signing statements. So, although signing statements may influence or even control agency implementation of statutes, it is the implementation, and not the signing statement itself, that would be measured against the statute's requirements. At most, signing statements might be considered analogous to informal agency actions, entitled to respect only to the extent that they have the power to persuade.

Ultimately, it does not appear that the courts have relied on signing statements in any appreciably substantive fashion. As touched upon above, the references made to signing statements in the Supreme Court's decisions in *Bowsher v. Synar* and *INS v. Chadha* were perfunctory in nature. Furthermore, in *Hamdan v. Rumsfeld*, the Supreme Court made no reference whatsoever to the President's signing statement in rejecting the contention that the Detaining Treatment Act did not apply to pending habeas petitions of Guantanamo detainees.

Impact on Congress.

One of the main complaints lodged by the ABA Task Force in opposition to the issuance of presidential signing statements is based on the viewpoint that the objections and challenges raised therein improperly circumvent the veto process delineated in the Constitution. According to this argument, the President, by refusing to veto a bill that contains provisions he does not intend to enforce, expands the presidential role in lawmaking beyond the constitutional parameters of "recommending laws he thinks wise and vetoing laws he thinks bad," and deprives Congress of the opportunity override a presidential veto.

While this position has a degree of intuitive appeal in light of the maxims pronounced in cases such as *Youngstown*, it could misapprehend the nature of signing statements as presidential instruments as well as the actual substantive concerns that underlie their issuance. First, as the signing statements discussed above illustrate, it is exceedingly rare for a President to make a direct announcement that he will categorically refuse to enforce a provision he finds troublesome. Instead, the concerns voiced in the statements are generally vague, with regard both to the nature of the objection and what circumstances might give rise to an actual conflict. The ABA Task Force Report's concern on this point also seems to assume that the interpretation and application of congressional enactments is a black and white issue, when, in reality, inherent ambiguity in the text almost always allows for competing interpretations of what the provision at issue requires. Given this dynamic, it is not surprising that a President's interpretation of a law, as announced in a signing statement, would be informed by a broad conception of executive authority. More fundamentally, a signing statement does not have the effect of a veto. A bill that is vetoed does not become law unless reenacted by a supermajority vote of the Congress. Conversely, a bill that is signed by the President retains its legal effect and character, irrespective of any pronouncements made in a signing statement, and remains available for interpretation and application by the courts (if the provision is justiciable) and monitoring by Congress.

A closely related argument, also raised in the ABA Report, is that signing statements that raise objections to provisions of an enactment constitute the exercise of a line-item veto. In *Clinton v. New York*, the Supreme Court held that the Line Item Veto Act violated the constitutional requirement of bicameralism and presentment by authorizing the President to essentially create a law which had not been voted upon by either House or presented to the President for approval and signature. Accordingly, this argument posits that when the President issues a signing statement objecting to certain provisions of a bill or declaring that he will treat a provision as advisory so as to avoid a constitutional conflict, he is, in practical effect, exercising an unconstitutional line-item veto. The counterpoints to this argument are similar to those adhering to the premise that signing statements constitute an abuse of the veto process. While an actual refusal of a President to enforce a legal provision may be characterized as an "effective" line-item veto, the provision nonetheless retains its full legal character and will remain actionable, either in the judicial or congressional oversight contexts.

Ultimately, both of these objections, as with the general focus of concern on signing statements as presidential instruments, may obscure the substantive issue that has apparently motivated the increased use of the constitutional signing statement by President Bush: an expansive conception of presidential authority, coupled with a willingness to utilize fully mechanisms that will aid in furthering and buttressing that philosophy. Given the general and hortatory nature of the language that characterizes these signing statements, it seems apparent that President Bush is using that instrument as part of a comprehensive strategy to strengthen and expand executive authority generally, as opposed to a de facto line item veto. Indeed, while the breadth and number of provisions called into question by President Bush draw attention to the institution of the signing statement itself, Professors Curtis A. Bradley and Eric A. Posner have stated that "critics of the Bush administration's use of signing statements have not identified a single instance where the Bush Administration followed through on the language in the signing statement and refused to enforce the statute as written."

This declaration is arguably belied by a report from the Government Accountability Office (GAO) that identified six provisions of law that were addressed in various signing statements that it determined were not "executed as written" by the executive branch. . . .

While these examples may be cited in support of the proposition that presidential signing statements constitute the effective exercise of a line item veto, it should be noted that GAO stated in its report that "although we found the agencies did not execute the provisions as enacted, we cannot conclude that agency noncompliance was the result of the President's signing statements." This statement is significant, in that while it may of course be argued that these examples of noncompliance constitute prima facie evidence that signing statements are being given substantive legal effect under the current administration, the fact remains that the GAO report presents no particularized information, beyond their existence, that these departments and agencies were relying on the relevant presidential signing statements as a basis to support such noncompliance. Specifically, the GAO report does not identify any declarations or documents that indicate that presidential signing statements played a role in the actions taken by the aforementioned departments and agencies. Furthermore, it could be argued that the scope and nature of the noncompliance in the provisions identified by GAO militates against a summary conclusion that the pertinent signing statements motivated such noncompliance.

. . . .

[S]ome might argue that the Bush II Administration's practice of issuing signing statements is beneficial, in that the statements alert Congress to the universe of provisions that are held in disregard by the executive branch, in turn affording Congress the opportunity not only to engage in systematic monitoring and oversight to ensure that its enactments are complied with, but to assert its prerogatives to counteract the broad claims of authority that undergird the statements. In particular, while the focus on the institution of the presidential signing statement as a source of controversy may be misplaced, congressional interest in the protection of its own institutional prerogatives could ultimately motivate a reaction to the Bush II Administration's expansive view of presidential authority as expressed not only in signing statements, but in executive orders, OLC opinions, internal White House Memoranda, and refusals to accede to congressional and legislative branch agency requests for information. All of these tools have been used by President Bush to exert control over executive personnel in their administration of statutory obligations and interaction with Congress. Additionally, the broad and persistent nature of the claims of executive authority forwarded by President Bush appear designed to inure Congress, as well as others, to the belief that the President in fact possesses expansive and exclusive powers upon which the other branches may not intrude.

Three bills have been introduced in the 110th Congress with the aim of restraining the use of signing statements, but it does not appear that any of these proposals would appreciably alter or confine the current administration's approach. . . .

. . . .

While the broad and continuing assertions of authority made by President Bush in numerous signing statements have the potential to impact Congress at a practical and institutional level, both by discouraging federal officials from engaging in open interaction with congressional committees and staff and by arguably discounting the constitutional prerogatives enjoyed by Congress, the aforementioned legislative proposals may be seen as failing to address the purpose and impact of these instruments. By focusing its efforts on attempting to constrain the President from issuing signing statements that call the validity of its enactments into question, Congress could leave unaddressed any risks posed to its institutional power by the broad conception of presidential authority that arguably motivates their issuance. It does not seem likely that a reduction in the number of challenges raised in signing statements, whether caused by procedural limitations or political rebuke, will necessarily result in any change in a President's conception and assertion of executive authority. Accordingly, a more effective congressional response might be to focus on any substantive actions taken by the Bush II Administration that are arguably designed to embed that conception of presidential power in the constitutional framework.

CONCLUSION

Presidential signing statements have a long historical pedigree and there is no discernible constitutional or legal impediment to their issuance. While such statements have become increasingly common since the Reagan Administration and have increasingly been utilized by Presidents to raise constitutional or interpretive objections to congressional enactments, that increased usage does not render them unconstitutional. While the broad assertions of executive authority contained in these statements carry significant implications, both practical and constitutional, for the traditional relationship between the executive branch and Congress, they do not have legal force or effect, and have not been utilized to effect the formal nullification of laws. Instead, it appears that recent administrations, as made apparent by the voluminous challenges lodged by President George W. Bush, have employed these instruments in an attempt to leverage power and control away from Congress by establishing these broad assertions of authority as a constitutional norm. It can be argued that the appropriate focus of congressional concern should center not on the issuance of signing statements themselves, but on the broad assertions of presidential authority forwarded by Presidents and the substantive actions taken to establish that authority. Accordingly, a robust oversight regime focusing on substantive execution action, as opposed to the vague and generalized assertions of authority typical of signing statements, might allow Congress in turn to more effectively assert its constitutional prerogatives and ensure compliance with its enactments.

Notes and Questions

1. Can you summarize what might be considered an appropriate role for presidential signing statements in statutory interpretation?

2. As the CRS Report indicates, the Constitution says very little about presidential signing statements. What the Constitution does say is this:

> Every bill which shall have passed the House of Representatives and the Senate, shall, before it become a Law, be presented to the President of the United States; If he approve he shall sign it, but if not he shall return it, with his Objections to that House in which it shall have originated, who shall . . . proceed to reconsider it. If after such Reconsideration two thirds of that House shall agree to pass the Bill, it shall be sent, together with the Objections, to the other House, by which it shall likewise be reconsidered, and if approved by two thirds of that House, it shall become a Law. . . . If any Bill shall not be returned by the President within ten Days (Sundays excepted) after it shall have been presented to him, the Same shall be a Law, in like Manner as if he had signed it, unless the Congress by their Adjournment prevents its Return, in which Case it shall not be a Law.

U.S. Const. Art. I, § 7, cl. 2. Article II, section 3 further provides that the President "shall . . . recommend to [Congress's] Consideration such Measures as he shall judge necessary and expedient," and that the President "shall take Care that the Laws be faithfully executed." Do any of these provisions shed any further light on these issues?

3. As the CRS Report also indicates, during the Bush II Administration, the American Bar Association took a particular interest in presidential signing statements. *See* AMERICAN BAR ASSOCIATION, TASK FORCE ON PRESIDENTIAL SIGNING STATEMENTS AND THE SEPARATION OF POWERS DOCTRINE, REPORT WITH RECOMMENDATIONS (2006). The "Recommendation" of the Task Force reads as follows:

> RESOLVED, That the American Bar Association opposes, as contrary to the rule of law and our constitutional system of separation of powers, the issuance of presidential signing statements that claim the authority or state the intention to disregard or decline to enforce all or part of a law the President has signed, or to interpret such a law in a manner inconsistent with the clear intent of Congress;
> FURTHER RESOLVED, That the American Bar Association urges the President, if he believes that any provision of a bill pending before Congress would be

unconstitutional if enacted, to communicate such concerns to Congress prior to passage;

FURTHER RESOLVED, That the American Bar Association urges the President to confine any signing statements to his views regarding the meaning, purpose and significance of bills presented by Congress, and if he believes that all or part of a bill is unconstitutional, to veto the bill in accordance with Article I, § 7 of the Constitution of the United States, which directs him to approve or disapprove each bill in its entirety;

FURTHER RESOLVED, That the American Bar Association urges Congress to enact legislation requiring the President promptly to submit to Congress an official copy of all signing statements he issues, and in any instance in which he claims the authority, or states the intention, to disregard or decline to enforce all or part of a law he has signed, or to interpret such a law in a manner inconsistent with the clear intent of Congress, to submit to Congress a report setting forth in full the reasons and legal basis for the statement; and further requiring that all such submissions be available in a publicly accessible database; and

FURTHER RESOLVED, That the American Bar Association urges Congress to enact legislation enabling the President, Congress, or other entities or individuals, to seek judicial review, to the extent constitutionally permissible, in any instance in which the President claims the authority, or states the intention, to disregard or decline to enforce all or part of a law he has signed, or interprets such a law in a manner inconsistent with the clear intent of Congress, and urges Congress and the President to support a judicial resolution of the President's claim or interpretation.

The Report that accompanied this Recommendation can be found at http://www.abanet.org/op/signingstatements/aba_final_signing_statements_recommendation-report_7-24-06.pdf.

4. According to one source, through the end of 2013, President Barack Obama has issued only 25 signing statements. *See* http://www.coherentbabble.com/listBHOall.htm.

5. On March 9, 2009, President Obama issued the following "Memorandum for the Heads of Executive Departments and Agencies on Presidential Signing Statements," published at 74 Fed. Reg. 10669:

For nearly two centuries, Presidents have issued statements addressing constitutional or other legal questions upon signing bills into law (signing statements). Particularly since omnibus bills have become prevalent, signing statements have often been used to ensure that the constitutionality of discrete statutory provisions do not require a veto of the entire bill.

In recent years, there has been considerable public discussion and criticism of the use of signing statements to raise constitutional objections to statutory provisions. There is no doubt that the practice of issuing such statements can be abused. Constitutional signing statements should not be used to suggest that the President will disregard statutory requirements on the basis of policy disagreements. At the same time, such signing statements serve a legitimate function in our system, at least when based on well-founded constitutional objections. In appropriately limited circumstances, they represent an exercise of the President's constitutional obligation to take care that the laws be faithfully executed, and they promote a healthy dialogue between the executive branch and the Congress.

With these considerations in mind and based upon advice of the Department of Justice, I will issue signing statements to address constitutional concerns only when it is appropriate to do so as a means of discharging my constitutional responsibilities. In issuing signing statements, I shall adhere to the following principles:

1. The executive branch will take appropriate and timely steps, whenever practicable, to inform the Congress of its constitutional concerns about pending legislation. Such communication should facilitate the efforts of the executive branch and the Congress to work together to address these concerns during the legislative process, thus minimizing the number of occasions on which I am presented with an enrolled bill that may require a signing statement.

2. Because legislation enacted by the Congress comes with a presumption of constitutionality, I will strive to avoid the conclusion that any part of an enrolled bill is unconstitutional. In exercising my responsibility to determine whether a provision of an enrolled bill is unconstitutional, I will act with caution and restraint, based only on interpretations of the Constitution that are well-founded.

3. To promote transparency and accountability, I will ensure that signing statements identify my constitutional concerns about a statutory provision with sufficient specificity to make clear the nature and basis of the constitutional objection.

4. I will announce in signing statements that I will construe a statutory provision in a manner that avoids a constitutional problem only if that construction is a legitimate one.

To ensure that all signing statements previously issued are followed only when consistent with these principles, executive branch departments and agencies are directed to seek the advice of the Attorney General before relying on signing statements issued prior to the date of this memorandum as the basis for disregarding, or otherwise refusing to comply with, any provision of a statute.

Shortly after issuing this Memorandum, President Obama issued a statement upon signing H.R. 2346, the "Supplemental Appropriations Act, 2009," in which he concluded:

> However, provisions of this bill . . . would interfere with my constitutional authority to conduct foreign relations by directing the Executive to take certain positions in negotiations or discussions with international organizations and foreign governments, or by requiring consultation with the Congress prior to such negotiations or discussions. I will not treat these provisions as limiting my ability to engage in foreign diplomacy or negotiations.

Is this signing statement consistent with the above Memorandum? Why or why not?

6. Find and read a recent presidential signing statement. (They are available on the White House website, among other sources. *See* http://www.whitehouse. gov/briefing-room/statements-and-releases.)

7. Much has been written on the use and propriety of presidential signing statements, including Curtis A. Bradley & Eric A. Posner, *Presidential Signing State-*

ments and Executive Power, 23 Const. Comment. 307 (2006), an article referenced in the CRS Report.

8. As discussed above, Presidents unhappy with all or a portion of a bill can sign it and issue a signing statement explaining areas of disagreement. Another alternative, of course, would be to simply veto the bill. Is there a third choice in this context? Perhaps. *See* Ross A. Wilson, Note, *A Third Way: The Presidential Nonsigning Statement*, 96 Cornell L. Rev. 1503 (2011).

B. EXECUTIVE ORDERS AND OTHER PRESIDENTIAL DIRECTIVES

Tara L. Branum

PRESIDENT OR KING? THE USE AND ABUSE OF EXECUTIVE ORDERS IN MODERN-DAY AMERICA

28 J. Legis. 1 (2002)

Although there is no constitutional or statutory definition of "executive order," a congressional study has defined executive orders as "directives or actions by the President" that have the "force and effect of law" when "founded on the authority of the President derived from the Constitution or a statute." While an executive order constitutes perhaps the most widely discussed form in which a presidential directive may be issued, it is not the only type of presidential order. Presidents may also issue proclamations,[16] presidential signing statements,[17] presidential memoranda,[18]

---

16. The primary difference between an executive order and a proclamation is that an executive order is typically an internal order directed at government officials and agencies, while a proclamation is usually directed at those outside the government. However, the lines between the two are often blurred, and the Supreme Court has held that there is no difference between the two in terms of legal effect.

17. Presidential signing statements are usually issued when the President signs legislation, and they may either contain "congratulatory recognitions" to those working on the bill or may express the President's disagreement with certain sections of the bill.

18. Presidential memoranda are often issued at the same time as an executive order and may contain "significant additions to or interpretations of" the provisions in the executive order. Although recent usage of presidential memoranda has most often been in conjunction with executive orders as outlined above, original usage was somewhat different. Until recently, the most prominent use of presidential memoranda was to make findings required by legislation, particularly in the area of foreign policy, or to give formal notice when initiating a process.

or National Security Presidential Directives,[19] among other types of presidential directives. . . .

A system for numbering executive orders was not established until 1907. At that point, all orders then on file were retroactively numbered, beginning with the "first" executive order, an order issued by President Lincoln on October 21, 1862, establishing military courts in Louisiana. Numbering of orders after 1907 remained somewhat informal until the Federal Register Act of 1935 established formal procedures. Today, all new executive orders must be filed with the Division of the Federal Register, which assigns numbers to the executive orders.[24] . . .

The official numbering of executive orders has surpassed 13,000. Due, however, to the large number of executive orders that have never been found or numbered, it is impossible to know exactly how many have been issued since the time of President Washington. In addition, the wide range of presidential action possible — including classified Presidential Decision Directives — makes it difficult to estimate how many orders have actually been issued. . . .

The first twenty-four Presidents issued 1262 executive orders. The last seventeen Presidents (not including the current Bush administration) issued 11,855 orders. . . .

. . . .

From the inception of our republic through 1999, only 253 presidential directives had been modified or revoked, either by Congress or by the courts. . . .

In contrast to the number of presidential directives issued, few challenges have been made. Even when challenges are brought, the most notable contribution of the courts has been its reluctance to get involved. Typically, courts uphold the presidential directive, find that the plaintiff lacks standing, or hold that the dispute revolves around a political question that should not be judicially resolved. On those occasions when a court has modified or revoked a presidential directive, the holding has often been fact-specific or the explanation for the court's action has been brief. The result has been a remarkable dearth of precedent and accountability in this area. . . .

Youngstown Sheet & Tube Co. v. Sawyer
343 U.S. 579 (1952)

MR. JUSTICE BLACK delivered the opinion of the Court.

We are asked to decide whether the President was acting within his constitutional power when he issued [Executive Order 10340] directing the Secretary of

---

19. "National Security Presidential Directives" appears to be the designation that the Bush II administration has given to its directives dealing with foreign policy issues. This type of foreign policy directive has changed names many times over the years. . . . These directives are typically focused on foreign policy issues, but some also have a domestic impact. Many are classified, and Congress may not even be notified of their existence.

24. The Federal Register Act requires that executive orders and proclamations be published. However, no similar requirement exists for other presidential directives, such as presidential memoranda or National Security Presidential Directives.

Commerce to take possession of and operate most of the Nation's steel mills. The mill owners argue that the President's order amounts to lawmaking, a legislative function which the Constitution has expressly confided to the Congress and not to the President. The Government's position is that the order was made on findings of the President that his action was necessary to avert a national catastrophe which would inevitably result from a stoppage of steel production, and that in meeting this grave emergency the President was acting within the aggregate of his constitutional powers as the Nation's Chief Executive and the Commander in Chief of the Armed Forces of the United States. . . .

. . . .

II.

The President's power, if any, to issue the order must stem either from an act of Congress or from the Constitution itself. There is no statute that expressly authorizes the President to take possession of property as he did here. Nor is there any act of Congress to which our attention has been directed from which such a power can fairly be implied. Indeed, we do not understand the Government to rely on statutory authorization for this seizure. . . .

Moreover, the use of the seizure technique to solve labor disputes in order to prevent work stoppages was not only unauthorized by any congressional enactment; prior to this controversy, Congress had refused to adopt that method of settling labor disputes. . . .

It is clear that if the President had authority to issue the order he did, it must be found in some provision of the Constitution. And it is not claimed that express constitutional language grants this power to the President. The contention is that presidential power should be implied from the aggregate of his powers under the Constitution. Particular reliance is placed on provisions in Article II which say that "The executive Power shall be vested in a President"; that "he shall take Care that the Laws be faithfully executed"; and that he "shall be Commander in Chief of the Army and Navy of the United States."

The order cannot properly be sustained as an exercise of the President's military power as Commander in Chief of the Armed Forces. . . .

Nor can the seizure order be sustained because of the several constitutional provisions that grant executive power to the President. In the framework of our Constitution, the President's power to see that the laws are faithfully executed refutes the idea that he is to be a lawmaker. The Constitution limits his functions in the lawmaking process to the recommending of laws he thinks wise and the vetoing of laws he thinks bad. And the Constitution is neither silent nor equivocal about who shall make laws which the President is to execute. The first section of the first article says that "All legislative Powers herein granted shall be vested in a Congress of the United States." After granting many powers to the Congress, Article I goes on to provide that Congress may "make all Laws which shall be necessary and proper for carrying into Execution the foregoing Powers, and all other Powers vested by this Constitution in the Government of the United States, or in any Department or Officer thereof."

The President's order does not direct that a congressional policy be executed in a manner prescribed by Congress — it directs that a presidential policy be executed in a manner prescribed by the President. The preamble of the order itself, like that of many statutes, sets out reasons why the President believes certain policies should be adopted, proclaims these policies as rules of conduct to be followed, and again, like a statute, authorizes a government official to promulgate additional rules and regulations consistent with the policy proclaimed and needed to carry that policy into execution. The power of Congress to adopt such public policies as those proclaimed by the order is beyond question. It can authorize the taking of private property for public use. It can make laws regulating the relationships between employers and employees, prescribing rules designed to settle labor disputes, and fixing wages and working conditions in certain fields of our economy. The Constitution does not subject this lawmaking power of Congress to presidential or military supervision or control.

It is said that other Presidents without congressional authority have taken possession of private business enterprises in order to settle labor disputes. But even if this be true, Congress has not thereby lost its exclusive constitutional authority to make laws necessary and proper to carry out the powers vested by the Constitution "in the Government of the United States, or nay Department or Officer thereof."

The Founders of this Nation entrusted the lawmaking power to the Congress alone in both good and bad times. It would do no good to recall the historical events, the fears of power and the hopes for freedom that lay behind their choice. Such a review would but confirm our holding that this seizure order cannot stand.

. . . .

MR. JUSTICE JACKSON, concurring in the judgment and opinion of the Court.

. . . .

The actual art of governing under our Constitution does not and cannot conform to judicial definitions of the power of any of its branches based on isolated clauses or even single Articles torn from context. While the Constitution diffuses power the better to secure liberty, it also contemplates that practice will integrate the dispersed powers into a workable government. It enjoins upon its branches separateness but interdependence, autonomy but reciprocity. Presidential powers are not fixed but fluctuate, depending upon their disjunction or conjunction with those of Congress. We may well begin by a somewhat over-simplified grouping of practical situations in which a President may doubt, or others may challenge, his powers, and by distinguishing roughly the legal consequences of this factor of relativity.

1. When the President acts pursuant to an express or implied authorization of Congress, his authority is at its maximum, for it includes all that he possesses in his own right plus all that Congress can delegate. In these circumstances, and in these only, may he be said (for what it may be worth) to personify the federal sovereignty. If his act is held unconstitutional under these circumstances, it usually means that the Federal Government as an undivided whole lacks power. A seizure executed by the President pursuant to an Act of Congress would be supported by the strongest of

presumptions and the widest latitude of judicial interpretation, and the burden of persuasion would rest heavily upon any who might attack it.

2. When the President acts in absence of either a congressional grant or denial of authority, he can only rely upon his own independent powers, but there is a zone of twilight in which he and Congress may have concurrent authority, or in which its distribution is uncertain. Therefore, congressional inertia, indifference or quiescence may sometimes, at least as a practical matter, enable, if not invite, measures on independent presidential responsibility. In this area, any actual test of power is likely to depend on the imperatives of events and contemporary imponderables rather than on abstract theories of law.

3. When the President takes measures incompatible with the expressed or implied will of Congress, his power is at its lowest ebb, for then he can rely only upon his own constitutional powers minus any constitutional powers of Congress over the matter. Courts can sustain exclusive presidential control in such a case only by disabling the Congress from acting upon the subject. Presidential claim to a power at once so conclusive and preclusive must be scrutinized with caution, for what is at stake is the equilibrium established by our constitutional system.

Notes and Questions

1. Justice Jackson's opinion, though only a concurrence, has generally become the standard for assessing the propriety of executive orders. What is that standard? *Cf.* Branum, 28 J. LEGIS. at 63-64:

   The end result of *Youngstown* is that, at least nominally, a presidential directive will be valid only if it stems from a statute or from the Constitution itself. If the order does not stem from one of these two sources, then Congress must either ratify the directive or "acquiesce" in the decision before the order will have the force of law. Unless the President has independent constitutional authority, presidential directives are always invalid when they are issued in contradiction to the expressed intent of Congress and Congress does not ratify the policy or acquiesce in the decision promulgated by the order. These standards are probably appropriate, but unfortunately, problems have arisen as a result of Congress's broad delegation of authority, the courts' often cursory examinations of presidents' authority and their broad definition of "acquiesce," as well as the difficulty of enforcing these standards against presidents.

2. Further guidance along this line can be found in Vanessa K. Burrows, *Executive Orders: Issuance and Revocation* (Congressional Research Service Report for Congress, Mar. 25, 2010), in which the author states:

   Just as there is no definition of executive orders and proclamations in the Constitution, there is, likewise, no specific provision authorizing their issuance. As such, authority for the execution and implementation of executive orders stems from implied constitutional and statutory authority. In the constitutional context, presidential power to issue such orders has been derived from Article II, which states that "the executive power shall be vested in a President of the United States," that "the President shall be Commander in Chief of the Army and Navy of the United States," and that the President "shall take Care that the Laws be faithfully executed." The President's power to issue executive orders and proclamations may also derive from express or implied statutory authority. Irrespective of the implied nature of the authority to issue executive orders and proclamations, these instruments have been employed by every President since the inception of the Republic.

Despite the amorphous nature of the authority to issue executive orders, Presidents have not hesitated to wield this power over a wide range of often controversial subjects, such as the suspension of the writ of *habeas corpus*; the establishment of internment camps during World War II; and equality of treatment in the armed services without regard to race, color, religion or national origin. President Obama recently issued an executive order pertaining to the abortion provisions in the new health care law, the Patient Protection and Affordable Care Act.

Id. at 1-2 (footnotes omitted).

3. Burrows further observes that "[t]he controversial nature of many presidential directives . . . raises questions regarding whether and how executive orders may be amended or revoked." *Id.* at 2. The answer to the first question appears to be yes. For one thing, "as long as it is not constitutionally based, Congress may repeal a presidential order, or terminate the underlying authority upon which the action is predicated," and in fact has done so on a number of occasions. *Id.* at 4. Moreover, and "[i]llustrating the fact that executive orders are used to further an administration's policy goals, there are frequent examples of situations in which a sitting President has revoked or amended orders issued by his predecessor." *Id.* at 6.

4. The Federal Register Act, which imposes certain requirements with respect to executive orders, may be found at 44 U.S.C. § 1505 (2012). "Furthermore, executive orders must comply with preparation, presentation and publication requirements established by an executive order issued by President Kennedy. *See* Exec. Order No. 11030, 27 Fed. Reg. 5847 (1962)." Burrows, *supra* note 2, at 1 n.4.

5. Between 1789 and 1995, the fewest executive orders issued by a President serving at least one full term was one, by John Adams; the most was 3522, by Franklin Roosevelt. *See* John Contrubis, *Executive Orders and Proclamations* (Congressional Research Service Report for Congress updated Mar. 9, 1999) table 1.

6. As suggested above, Executive Orders, Presidential Memoranda, and Proclamations issued by the President generally are published in the Federal Register and currently can be found on the official White House website. *See* http:// www.whitehouse.gov/briefing-room/presidential-actions.

C. ADMINISTRATIVE AGENCIES, REGULATIONS, AND THE REGULATORY PROCESS

At the federal level, administrative law represents a broad and important type of law. Administrative law is largely the product of administrative agencies.

Under the Administrative Procedure Act, a major piece of federal legislation governing, in large part, the making of administrative law,* an "agency" is defined generally (and somewhat vaguely) as "each authority of the Government of the United States, whether or not it is within or subject to review by another agency," though not including Congress, the federal courts, or (presumably) the President. 5 U.S.C. § 551(1) (2006). Most federal agencies were created by federal statute.

Conceptually, federal agencies are sometimes divided between "executive" (or "executive branch") agencies, which consist mostly of presidential Cabinet departments (such as the Department of Agriculture), and "independent" agencies, such as the Federal Trade Commission. (A more complete list of the various federal agencies can be found in "The Government of the United States" chart at the conclusion of Chapter 1.) "[I]ndependent agencies are different in structure because the President lacks authority to remove their heads from office except for cause. Thus, these agencies are independent in the sense that the President cannot fire their leaders for political reasons and, consequently, cannot use this ultimate sanction to back up particular policy recommendations." Lisa Schultz Bressman & Robert T. Thompson, *The Future of Agency Independence*, 63 VAND. L. REV. 599, 610 (2010) (footnote omitted). Independent agencies also "are generally run by multi-member commissions or boards, whose members serve fixed, staggered terms, rather than a cabinet secretary or single administrator who serves at the pleasure of the President and thus will likely depart with a change of administration, if not before." *Id.* Moreover, "[i]ndependent agencies are often subject to express bipartisan requirements," such as rules that prevent all commissioners or board members from being from the same political party, and some have more non-governmental sources of funding. *Id.* at 611. In terms of lawmaking ability, though, there is often little distinction between executive and independent agencies, and whatever differences there might be are probably more attributable to the particular agency at issue.

Though agencies engage in a number of activities, from an administrative law perspective, they are best known for their ability to engage in adjudication and rulemaking. Under the APA, "adjudication" is defined as the "agency process for the formulation of an order," and for this purpose, an "order" is "the whole or part of a final disposition, whether affirmative, negative, injunctive, or declaratory in form, of an agency in a matter other than rule making but including licensing." 5 U.S.C. § 551(6)-(7). The general procedure relating to "informal" agency adjudication is

---

* "The Administrative Procedure Act (APA) applies to all executive branch agencies, including so-called independent regulatory agencies. The APA prescribes procedures for agency actions such as rulemaking, as well as standards for judicial review of agency actions." Vanessa K. Burrows & Todd Garvey, *A Brief Overview of Rulemaking and Judicial Review* 1 (Congressional Research Service Report for Congress R41546, Jan. 4, 2011) (footnote omitted).

found in 5 U.S.C. § 554, while "formal" adjudication requires further reference to §§ 556 and 557. Though agency adjudication can differ in many ways from traditional federal court adjudication, there also tend to be many similarities. Thus, because adjudication generally is discussed in detail in Chapter 2, the focus in this Chapter will be on agency rulemaking.

"Rule making" is defined under the APA as the "agency process for formulating, amending, or repealing a rule," and a "rule" is defined (again somewhat vaguely) as

> the whole or part of an agency statement of general or particular applicability and future effect designed to implement, interpret, or prescribe law or policy or describing the organization, procedure, or practice requirements of an agency and includes the approval or prescription for the future of rates, wages, corporate or financial structures or reorganizations thereof, prices, facilities, appliances, services or allowances therefor or of valuations, costs, or accounting, or practices bearing on any of the foregoing.

5 U.S.C. § 551(4)-(5). The general procedure relating to "informal" agency rulemaking is found in 5 U.S.C. § 553, while "formal" rulemaking (like formal adjudication) requires further reference to §§ 556 and 557.

The following excerpt is intended to provide a general understanding of the more common "informal" rulemaking process.

American Bar Association

SECTION OF ADMINISTRATIVE LAW AND REGULATORY PRACTICE

A Blackletter Statement of Federal Administrative Law
Part Two: Informal Rulemaking (2004)

The following summarizes the procedural requirements that must precede the legally effective promulgation, amendment, or repeal of a rule by a federal agency, as imposed by the Administrative Procedure Act (APA), other procedural statutes, and judicial decisions. Certain additional requirements imposed by Executive Order (particularly economic impact analysis, as currently embodied in E.O. 12,866) are also included. Such requirements are not judicially enforceable, may be and often are waived by the relevant executive office, and are particularly subject to change. Economic impact analysis has been required for the last several presidencies in one form or another, and is assumed in much recent reform legislation.

I. APPLICABILITY

A. Definition of a Rule

A "rule" is an agency statement designed to implement, interpret, or prescribe law or policy or describing the organization, procedure, or practice requirements of an agency. Although the definition of "rule" in the APA refers to "an agency statement of general or particular applicability," "rule" is usually understood to refer to a pronouncement that is intended to address a class of situations, rather than a named individual. Certain particularized actions, such as rate-setting or the approval of a corporate reorganization, are explicitly included within the statutory definition. A rule may be prospective, retroactive, or both, but an agency normally may not issue a retroactive rule that is intended to have the force of law unless it has express authorization from Congress.

B. Distinction Between Informal and Formal Rulemaking

The procedures described here apply to "informal" (also known as "notice-and-comment") rulemaking. "Formal rulemaking" requires additional trial-type procedures, not described here but essentially the same as those described for initial licensing in Part One, *supra*. Unless a statute expressly provides for rulemaking "on the record after opportunity for a hearing," or Congress otherwise unequivocally requires formal rulemaking, the requirements for informal rulemaking apply.

Agencies engaged in informal rulemaking may provide additional procedures beyond those established by the APA, other applicable statutes, and the agency's own rules, but courts may not require them to do so.

C. Exemptions

The following types of rules are exempt from all the procedural requirements: rules relating to public property, loans, grants, benefits, and contracts; rules relating to agency management and personnel; and rules that involve a military or foreign affairs function of the United States. However, specific statutes may override these exemptions and agencies may voluntarily forswear them.

The following types of rules are subject to publication and petition requirements, but are exempt from the other procedural requirements set out below: rules regarding agency organization, procedure, and practice; staff manuals; interpretive rules; and general statements of policy. Failure to publish such a rule, either in the Federal Register or as described by 5 U.S.C. § 552(a)(2), denies to the agency any possibility of relying on it to the disadvantage of a private party, unless that party has had actual notice of the agency's position.

An agency may also dispense with notice and comment, and/or may make a rule effective immediately, when it has good cause to do so and explains its reasons at the time of publication. Under time pressure, agencies occasionally adopt "interim final rules" that are both immediately effective and published with an invitation to comment and propose revisions; a subsequent agency revision will treat such a rule as if it were, also, a notice of proposed rulemaking.

II. INITIATING RULEMAKING

A. Means to Initiate Rulemaking

An agency may commence a rulemaking on its own initiative, pursuant to statutory mandate, or in response to an outside petition or to suggestions from other governmental actors. Any interested person has the right to petition for the issuance, amendment, or repeal of any rule. The denial of a petition, which is a reviewable event, should be summarily explained.

B. Developing a Proposed Rule

In developing a proposed rule, and limited in some cases to economically significant rules and/or executive agencies, an agency may be required to evaluate the rule's impacts and prepare appropriate written analyses of (a) environmental impacts and alternatives, (b) overall economic costs and benefits, (c) the extent of new paperwork and information collection requirements, (d) impacts on small businesses, (e) impacts on state, local, and tribal governments and on the private sector, (f) impacts on families, (g) private property rights, (h) the civil justice system, (i) children's health and safety, (j) federalism, and (k) the supply, use, and distribution of energy. Requirements (a) through (e) are imposed by statute; requirements (f) through (k) are imposed exclusively by a series of executive orders. Requirement (b), although now also required by the Unfunded Mandates Reform Act, was first developed by executive orders — currently, E.O. 12,866. In practice the administration of E.O. 12,866 appears to dominate executive branch implementation of all these requirements. Under that executive order, prior to issuing a Notice of Proposed Rulemaking, an executive agency proposing an economically significant rule must provide the Office of Information and Regulatory Affairs (OIRA) in the Office of Management and Budget with an assessment of the proposal's costs and benefits. This analysis may, and typically does, incorporate the analyses required by other statutes and executive orders.

Prior to issuing a Notice of Proposed Rulemaking, an agency may issue and take comments on an Advanced Notice of Proposed Rulemaking and/or establish a negotiated rulemaking committee to negotiate and develop a proposed rule. Under the Negotiated Rulemaking Act, agencies are encouraged to explore the development of consensus proposals for rulemaking with balanced, representative committees under the guidance of a convenor specially appointed for that purpose. Such proposals, if generated, serve as proposed rules under the normal procedure.

C. Semi-Annual Agenda

All rulemaking agencies must semi-annually prepare and publish in the Federal Register a Regulatory Agenda listing all planned regulatory actions that are likely to have a significant economic impact on a substantial number of small entities. Under E.O. 12,866 all rulemaking agencies must prepare an agenda of all regulations under development or consideration. This agenda must include a Regulatory Plan identifying and justifying the most important "significant regulatory actions" the agency expects to issue in proposed or final form in the upcoming fiscal year and must be submitted to OIRA by June 1 of each year. This plan is consolidated with the regulatory agenda for publication purposes.

III. NOTICE OF PROPOSED RULEMAKING AND OPPORTUNITY FOR COMMENT

A. Requirements for a Notice of Proposed Rulemaking

An agency must publish in the Federal Register notice of its intent to promulgate, amend, or repeal a rule. Publication in the Federal Register is not necessary if all persons who will be subject to the rule, if adopted, are named and have actual notice.

The Notice of Proposed Rulemaking must include (1) a statement of the time, place and nature of any public proceedings for consideration of the proposed rule, (2) a reference to the agency's statutory authority for the rule, and (3) the proposed text of the rule, unless a description of the proposal or the subjects and issues involved will suffice to allow meaningful and informed public consideration and comment. Developing caselaw, in the wake of the Freedom of Information Act, has required the agency also to make available in time for comment thereon significant data and studies it knows to be relevant to the proposed rule, including any draft analyses previously made as under II above.

B. Public Comment on Proposed Rule

After publication of a Notice of Proposed Rulemaking, a reasonable time must be allowed for written comments from the public. An agency may, but, unless specifically required to do so by a relevant statute, need not, provide interested parties the opportunity to present oral comments or cross-examine witnesses.

IV. THE RULEMAKING RECORD AND DECISION MAKING PROCESS

A. Record Requirements

The agency must maintain, and allow and facilitate public examination of, a rulemaking file consisting of (1) all notices pertaining to the rulemaking, (2) copies or an index of written factual material, studies, and reports relied on or seriously consulted by agency personnel in formulating the proposed or final rule, (3) all written comments received by the agency, and (4) any other material specifically required by statute, executive order, or agency rule to be made public in connection with the rulemaking.

The obligation to disclose written factual material, studies, and reports relied on or seriously consulted by agency personnel is limited to materials whose disclosure would be required under the Freedom of Information Act. Thus, neither a summary nor a record of predecisional internal agency policy discussions, or like contacts with government officials outside the agency or private consultants, need be included in the rulemaking file. Particular agency statutes or rules, however, may forbid or limit such communications or require that they be logged and made available to the public. The Executive Orders requiring economic impact analysis provoked concern about this issue, and E.O. 12,866 also includes such requirements.

B. Decisional Process

Subject to the obligation to disclose factual material, studies, and reports relied on or seriously consulted, decisionmakers within an agency may freely consult with other agency personnel, government officials outside the agency, and affected persons. Particular statutes or agency regulations may impose logging requirements or other restrictions. A decisionmaker will be disqualified for prejudgment only where the person's mind is unalterably closed.

Under E.O. 12,866 (and under several other impact analysis requirements imposed by statute and/or executive order), a final analysis must be prepared in advance of the final rule; that analysis is generally a part of the rulemaking record. An executive agency may not publish a significant final rule until OIRA has completed, waived, or exceeded the time limit for its review of the rule under E.O. 12,866.

A rulemaking must be completed within a reasonable time, or within the time frame, if any, set by the relevant statute.

V. THE FINAL RULE

A. Publication of Final Rule and the Basis and Purpose of the Rule

The agency must publish the operative text of the final rule. The agency must also provide a statement of basis and purpose that adequately explains the justifications, purposes, and legal authority for the rule and indicates compliance with regulatory analysis requirements imposed by statute. The scope of this explanation depends on the importance and impact of the rule. The Administrative Procedure Act calls for only a "concise general statement of basis and purpose."

However, courts have required that for rules likely to have major economic or other impacts the statement (a) must demonstrate that the agency fully considered significant alternatives to its final rule, important public comments, and relevant information and scientific data and (b) must explain the agency's rejection of any of the foregoing.

After the rule subject to OIRA review has been published, E.O. 12,866 requires that the agency and OIRA disclose specified information pertaining to the review.

If the final rule is not a "logical outgrowth" of the proposed rule, a second round of notice and comment is required.

B. Effective Date

A substantive rule of general applicability is unenforceable unless published in the Federal Register, and cannot ordinarily become effective less than 30 days after its publication (unless it grants an exception or relieves a restriction).

No economically significant rule can take effect (a) until 60 calendar days after the agency has submitted a copy of the rule and a concise general statement relating thereto to both Houses of Congress and the Comptroller General and has submitted additional supporting material to the Comptroller General and made such material available to both Houses of Congress, or (b) if a joint resolution disapproving the rule is enacted. Rules relating to agency management or personnel or agency organization, procedure, or practice are exempt from this 60-day requirement.

Notes and Questions

---

1. The foregoing summary of the informal rulemaking process also can be found at 54 ADMIN. L. REV. 1 (2002). (Notice that this work by the ABA's Section of Administrative Law & Regulatory Practice is part of a broader summary of federal administrative law generally.) For a more detailed summary of the informal rulemaking process, see Curtis W. Copeland, *The Federal Rulemaking Process: An Overview* (Congressional Research Service Report for Congress RL32240, Feb. 22, 2011). For a graphical view of the informal rulemaking process, see "The Reg Map," which can be viewed at http://www.reginfo.gov/public/reginfo/Regmap/index.jsp, and is reproduced below.

The Reg Map

Informal Rulemaking

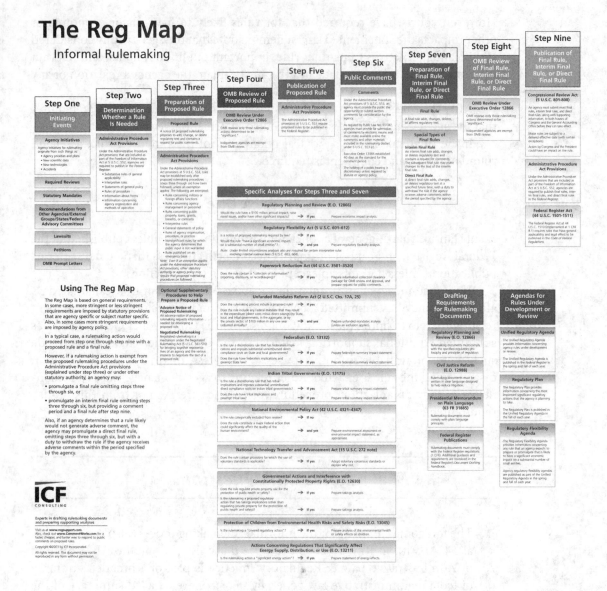

Notice the nine steps in the informal rulemaking process described in the Reg Map.

2. Executive Orders and similar directives also play a role in the rulemaking process. Though a number of such orders and directives have been promulgated over the years, the most important (as well as the most influential) remains President Bill Clinton's Executive Order 12866, "Regulatory Planning and Review," 58 Fed. Reg. 51735 (Oct. 4, 1993). As the "Blackletter Statement" indicates, Executive Order 12866 imposes a number of requirements on agencies during that process.

3. The more significant products of the rulemaking process are published in the *Federal Register* (https://www.federalregister.gov). "Legislative"-type rules typically are "codified" much like federal statutes in the *Code of Federal Regulations* (C.F.R.) (http://www.gpo.gov/fdsys/browse/collectionCfr.action?collectionCode=CFR). As indicated, both are available electronically.

   In some respects, researching federal regulations is similar to researching federal statutes. Most practicing lawyers would first locate the applicable regulation in the *Code*, and then (if desired) trace the regulation back to its entry in the Federal Register. For example, if for some reason one were to wonder whether smoking is permitted at Presidential Libraries (which are generally under the control of the National Archives and Records Administration), one would find that the answer is no. *See* 36 C.F.R. § 1280.24 (citing 65 Fed. Reg. 34978, June 1, 2000).

4. Interpreting regulations can raise many of the same issues associated with the interpretation of statutes. For a recent discussion of this topic, see Kevin M. Stack, *Interpreting Regulations*, 111 MICH. L. REV. 355 (2012).

5. There are a number of excellent books and treatises in the administrative law area. With respect to rulemaking in particular, see CORNELIUS M. KERWIN, RULEMAKING: HOW GOVERNMENT AGENCIES WRITE LAW AND MAKE POLICY (3d ed. 2003), and JEFFREY S. LUBBERS, A GUIDE TO FEDERAL AGENCY RULE-MAKING (4th ed. 2006).

6. *Judicial review of agency action.* Much like the authority of appellate courts to review lower court judgments, federal courts generally have broad authority to review federal agency action. In particular, 5 U.S.C. § 704 (2012) provides in part: "Agency action made reviewable by statute and final agency action for which there is no other adequate remedy in a court are subject to judicial review." Regarding the scope of such review, 5 U.S.C. § 706 (2012) provides:

   > To the extent necessary to decision and when presented, the reviewing court shall decide all relevant questions of law, interpret constitutional and statutory provisions, and determine the meaning or applicability of the terms of an agency action. The reviewing court shall—
   > (1) compel agency action unlawfully withheld or unreasonably delayed; and
   > (2) hold unlawful and set aside agency action, findings, and conclusions found to be—
   > (A) arbitrary, capricious, an abuse of discretion, or otherwise not in accordance with law;
   > (B) contrary to constitutional right, power, privilege, or immunity;
   > (C) in excess of statutory jurisdiction, authority, or limitations, or short of statutory right;
   > (D) without observance of procedure required by law;

(E) unsupported by substantial evidence in a case subject to sections 556 and 557 of this title or otherwise reviewed on the record of an agency hearing provided by statute; or

(F) unwarranted by the facts to the extent that the facts are subject to trial de novo by the reviewing court.

In making the foregoing determinations, the court shall review the whole record or those parts of it cited by a party, and due account shall be taken of the rule of prejudicial error.

D. THE ROLE OF ADMINISTRATIVE AGENCIES IN THE INTERPRETATION OF STATUTES

The interpretation of federal statutes is usually thought of as a *judicial* function, a function that occurs in the context of litigation. Obviously, though, other governmental (as well as non-governmental) actors must, on occasion, interpret statutes as well. This is especially true of administrative agencies, which must interpret and apply statutes — particularly those relating to that agency — on a daily basis. To what extent, if any, must (or may, or should) a court adhere or at least defer to a prior *agency* interpretation of a statute within its ambit? That is the subject of this Part.

1. Historical Beginnings

Skidmore v. Swift & Co.
323 U.S. 134 (1944)

MR. JUSTICE JACKSON delivered the opinion of the Court.

Seven employees of the Swift and Company packing plant at Fort Worth, Texas, brought an action under the Fair Labor Standards Act to recover overtime, liquidated damages, and attorneys' fees, totalling approximately $77,000. The District Court rendered judgment denying this claim wholly, and the Circuit Court of Appeals for the Fifth Circuit affirmed.

. . . .

Congress did not utilize the services of an administrative agency to find facts and to determine in the first instance whether particular cases fall within or without the Act. Instead, it put this responsibility on the courts. But it did create the office of Administrator, impose upon him a variety of duties, endow him with powers to inform himself of conditions in industries and employments subject to the Act, and put on him the duties of bringing injunction actions to restrain violations. Pursuit of his duties has accumulated a considerable experience in the problems of ascertaining working time in employments involving periods of inactivity and a knowledge of the customs prevailing in reference to their solution. From these he is obliged to reach conclusions as to conduct without the law, so that he should seek injunctions to stop it, and that within the law, so that he has no call to interfere. He has set forth his views of the application of the Act under different circumstances in an interpretative bulletin and in informal rulings. They provide a practical guide to employers and employees as to how the office representing the public interest in its enforcement will seek to apply it.

. . . .

There is no statutory provision as to what, if any, deference courts should pay to the Administrator's conclusions. And, while we have given them notice, we have had no occasion to try to prescribe their influence. The rulings of this Administrator are not reached as a result of hearing adversary proceedings in which he finds facts from evidence and reaches conclusions of law from findings of fact. They are not, of course, conclusive, even in the cases with which they directly deal, much less in those to which they apply only by analogy. They do not constitute an interpretation of the Act or a standard for judging factual situations which binds a district court's processes, as an authoritative pronouncement of a higher court might do. But the Administrator's policies are made in pursuance of official duty, based upon more specialized experience and broader investigations and information than is likely to come to a judge in a particular case. They do determine the policy which will guide applications for enforcement by injunction on behalf of the Government. Good administration of the Act and good judicial administration alike require that the standards of public enforcement and those for determining private rights shall be at variance only where justified by very good reasons. The fact that the Administrator's policies and standards are not reached by trial in adversary form does not mean that they are not entitled to respect. This Court has long given considerable and in some cases decisive weight to Treasury Decisions and to interpretative regulations of the Treasury and of other bodies that were not of adversary origin.

We consider that the rulings, interpretations and opinion of the Administrator under this Act, while not controlling upon the courts by reason of their authority, do constitute a body of experience and informed judgment to which courts and litigants may properly resort for guidance. The weight of such a judgment in a particular case will depend upon the thoroughness evident in its consideration, the validity of its reasoning, its consistency with earlier and later pronouncements, and all those factors which give it power to persuade, if lacking power to control.

The courts in the *Armour* case weighed the evidence in the particular case in the light of the Administrator's rulings and reached a result consistent therewith. The evidence in this case in some respects, such as the understanding as to separate compensation for answering alarms, is different. Each case must stand on its own facts. But in this case, although the District Court referred to the Administrator's Bulletin, its evaluation and inquiry were apparently restricted by its notion that waiting time may not be work, an understanding of the law which we hold to be erroneous. Accordingly, the judgment is reversed and the cause remanded for further proceedings consistent herewith.

Notes and Questions

1. Does *Skidmore* provide a clear standard for determining the degree of deference to be given to agency interpretations of federal statutes? Any standard?

2. In *Kasten v. Saint-Gobain Performance Plastics*, 131 S. Ct. 1325 (2011), Justice Scalia criticized the Court's invocation of "so-called *Skidmore* deference," the "doctrine" that "states that agencies' views are 'entitled to respect' to the extent they have 'the power to persuade.'" *Id.* at 1340 (Scalia, J., dissenting) (internal quotation marks omitted).

> In my view this doctrine (if it can be called that) is incoherent, both linguistically and practically. To defer is to subordinate one's own judgment to another's. If one has been persuaded by another, so that one's judgment accords with the other's, there is no room for deferral — only for agreement. Speaking of "*Skidmore* deference" to a persuasive agency position does nothing but confuse.

Id. at 1340 n.6. Not surprisingly, Justice Scalia in *Kasten* concluded that the agencies' views in that case lacked the "power to persuade" him. *See id.* at 1340. Does Justice Scalia nonetheless raise a valid point? (Recall that the concept of "persuasive authority" was discussed in more detail in Chapter 2.)

2. The Modern Standard

Chevron U. S. A. Inc. v. Natural Resources Defense Council, Inc.
467 U.S. 837 (1984)

JUSTICE STEVENS delivered the opinion of the Court.

In the Clean Air Act Amendments of 1977, Pub. L. 95-95, 91 Stat. 685, Congress enacted certain requirements applicable to States that had not achieved the national air quality standards established by the Environmental Protection Agency (EPA) pursuant to earlier legislation. The amended Clean Air Act required these "nonattainment" States to establish a permit program regulating "new or modified major stationary sources" of air pollution. Generally, a permit may not be issued for a new or modified major stationary source unless several stringent conditions are met. The EPA regulations promulgated to implement this permit requirement allows a State to adopt a plantwide definition of the term "stationary source." Under this definition, an existing plant that contains several pollution-emitting devices may install or modify one piece of equipment without meeting the permit conditions if the alteration will not increase the total emissions from the plant. The question presented by these cases is whether EPA's decision to allow States to treat all of the pollution-emitting devices within the same industrial grouping as though they were encased within a single "bubble" is based on a reasonable construction of the statutory term "stationary source."

I

The EPA regulations containing the plantwide definition of the term stationary source were promulgated on October 14, 1981. Respondents filed a timely petition for review in the United States Court of Appeals for the District of Columbia Circuit . . . . The Court of Appeals set aside the regulations.

The court observed that the relevant part of the amended Clear Air Act "does not explicitly define what Congress envisioned as a []stationary source, to which the permit program should apply," and further stated that the precise issue was not "squarely addressed in the legislative history." In light of its conclusion that the legislative history bearing on the question was "at best contradictory," it reasoned that "the purposes of the nonattainment program should guide our decision here." Based on two of its precedents concerning the applicability of the bubble concept to certain Clear Air Act programs, the court stated that the bubble concept was "mandatory" in programs designed merely to maintain existing air quality, but held that it was "inappropriate" in programs enacted to improve air quality. Since the purpose of the permit program — its "*raison d'etre*," in the court's view — was to improve air quality, the court held that the bubble concept was inapplicable in these cases under its prior precedents. It therefore set aside the regulations embodying the bubble concept as contrary to law. We granted certiorari to review that judgment, and we now reverse.

The basic legal error of the Court of Appeals was to adopt a static judicial definition of the term "stationary source" when it had decided that Congress itself had not commanded that definition. Respondents do not defend the legal reasoning of the Court of Appeals.[7] Nevertheless, since this Court reviews judgments, not opinions, we must determine whether the Court of Appeals legal error resulted in an erroneous judgment on the validity of the regulations.

II

When a court reviews an agency's construction of the statute which it administers, it is confronted with two questions. First, always, is the question whether Congress has directly spoken to the precise question at issue. If the intent of Congress is clear, that is the end of the matter; for the court, as well as the agency, must give effect to

---

7. Respondents rely on the arguments rejected by the Court of Appeals in support of the judgment, and may rely on any ground that finds support in the record.

9. The judiciary is the final authority on issues of statutory construction and must reject administrative constructions which are contrary to clear congressional intent. If a court, employing traditional tools of statutory construction, ascertains that Congress had an intention on the precise question at issue, that intention is the law and must be given effect.

the unambiguously expressed intent of Congress.[9] If, however, the court determines Congress has not directly addressed the precise question at issue, the court does not simply impose its own construction on the statute, as would be necessary in the absence of an administrative interpretation. Rather, if the statute is silent or ambiguous with respect to the specific issue, the question for the court is whether the agency's answer is based on a permissible construction of the statute.[11]

"The power of an administrative agency to administer a congressionally created program necessarily requires the formulation of policy and the making of rules to fill any gap left, implicitly or explicitly, by Congress." If Congress has explicitly left a gap for the agency to fill, there is an express delegation of authority to the agency to elucidate a specific provision of the statute by regulation. Such legislative regulations are given controlling weight unless they are arbitrary, capricious, or manifestly contrary to the statute. Sometimes the legislative delegation to an agency on a particular question is implicit rather than explicit. In such a case, a court may not substitute its own construction of a statutory provison [sic] for a reasonable interpretation made by the administrator of an agency.

We have long recognized that considerable weight should be accorded to an executive department's construction of a statutory scheme it is entrusted to administer, and the principle of deference to administrative interpretations

> "has been consistently followed by this Court whenever decision as to the meaning or reach of a statute has involved reconciling conflicting policies, and a full understanding of the force of the statutory policy in the giving situation has depended upon more than ordinary knowledge respecting the matters subjected to agency regulations.
>
> "If this choice represents a reasonable accommodation of conflicting policies that were committed to the agency's care by the statute, we should not disturb it unless it appears from the statute or its legislative history that the accommodation is not one that Congress would have sanctioned."

In light of these well-settled principles it is clear that the Court of Appeals misconceived the nature of its role in reviewing the regulations at issue. Once it determined, after its own examination of the legislation, that Congress did not actually have an intent regarding the applicability of the bubble concept to the permit program, the question before it was not whether in its view the concept is "inappropriate" in the general context of a program designed to improve air quality, but whether the Administrator's view that it is appropriate in the context of this particular program is a reasonable one. Based on the examination of the legislation and its history which follows, we agree with the Court of Appeals that Congress did not have a specific intention on the applicability of the bubble concept in these cases, and conclude that the EPA's use of that concept here is a reasonable policy choice for the agency to make.

. . . .

---

11. The court need not conclude that the agency construction was the only one it permissibly could have adopted to uphold the construction, or even the reading the court would have reached if the question initially had arisen in a judicial proceeding.

VII

. . . .

The arguments over policy that are advanced in the parties' briefs create the impression that respondents are now waging in a judicial forum a specific policy battle which they ultimately lost in the agency and in the 32 jurisdictions opting for the "bubble concept," but one which was never waged in the Congress. Such policy arguments are more properly addressed to legislators or administrators, not to judges.

In these cases the Administrator's interpretation represents a reasonable accommodation of manifestly competing interests and is entitled to deference: the regulatory scheme is technical and complex, the agency considered the matter in a detailed and reasoned fashion, and the decision involves reconciling conflicting policies. Congress intended to accommodate both interests, but did not do so itself on the level of specificity presented by these cases. Perhaps that body consciously desired the Administrator to strike the balance at this level, thinking that those with great expertise and charged with responsibility for administering the provision would be in a better position to do so; perhaps it simply did not consider the question at this level; and perhaps Congress was unable to forge a coalition on either side of the question, and those on each side decided to take their chances with the scheme devised by the agency. For judicial purposes, it matters not which of these things occurred.

Judges are not experts in the field, and are not part of either political branch of the Government. Courts must, in some cases, reconcile competing political interests, but not on the basis of the judges' personal policy preferences. In contrast, an agency to which Congress has delegated policymaking responsibilities may, within the limits of that delegation, properly rely upon the incumbent administration's views of wise policy to inform its judgments. While agencies are not directly accountable to the people, the Chief Executive is, and it is entirely appropriate for this political branch of the Government to make such policy choices — resolving the competing interests which Congress itself either inadvertently did not resolve, or intentionally left to be resolved by the agency charged with the administration of the statute in light of everyday realities.

When a challenge to an agency construction of a statutory provision, fairly conceptualized, really centers on the wisdom of the agency's policy, rather than whether it is a reasonable choice within a gap left open by Congress, the challenge must fail. In such a case, federal judges — who have no constituency — have a duty to respect legitimate policy choices made by those who do. The responsibilities for assessing the wisdom of such policy choices and resolving the struggle between competing views of the public interest are not judicial ones: "Our Constitution vests such responsibilities in the political branches."

We hold that the EPA's definition of the term "source" is a permissible construction of the statute which seeks to accommodate progress in reducing air pollution with economic growth. "The Regulations which the Administrator has adopted provide what the agency could allowably view as an effective reconciliation of these twofold ends."

The judgment of the Court of Appeals is reversed.

Notes and Questions

1. What is the standard of deference to agency interpretations articulated by the *Chevron* Court? Does this standard seem workable and wise? Can you see any problems with this standard? Is this standard nonetheless better than any alternative, or can it be improved upon?

2. The broader holding in *Chevron*, perhaps unintentionally, soon achieved iconic status, leading to what has become known in this area as the "*Chevron* doctrine." For a history of this phenomenon, see Gary Lawson & Stephen Kam, *Making Law Out of Nothing at All: The Origins of the* Chevron *Doctrine*, 65 ADMIN. L. REV. 1 (2013).

3. Back to the Future?

United States v. Mead Corp.
533 U.S. 218 (2001)

JUSTICE SOUTER delivered the opinion of the Court.

The question is whether a tariff classification ruling by the United States Customs Service deserves judicial deference. The Federal Circuit rejected Custom's invocation of *Chevron U. S. A. Inc.* v. *Natural Resources Defense Council, Inc.*, 467 U. S. 837 (1984), in support of such a ruling, to which it gave no deference. We agree that a tariff classification has no claim to judicial deference under *Chevron*, there being no indication that Congress intended such a ruling to carry the force of law, but we hold that under *Skidmore* v. *Swift & Co.*, 323 U. S. 134 (1944), the ruling is eligible to claim respect according to its persuasiveness.

I

A

Imports are taxed under the Harmonized Tariff Schedule of the United States (HTSUS), 19 U. S. C. § 1202. Title 19 U. S. C. § 1500(b) provides that Customs "shall, under rules and regulations prescribed by the Secretary of the Treasury fix the final classification and rate of duty applicable to merchandise" under the HTSUS. Section 1502(a) provides that

> "the Secretary of the Treasury shall establish and promulgate such rules and regulations not inconsistent with the law (including regulations establishing procedures for the issuance of binding rulings prior to the entry of the merchandise concerned), and may disseminate such information as may be necessary to secure a just, impartial, and uniform

appraisement of imported merchandise and the classification and assessment of duties thereon at the various ports of entry."[1]

See also § 1624 (general delegation to Secretary to issue rules and regulations for the admission of goods).

The Secretary provides for tariff rulings before the entry of goods by regulations authorizing "ruling letters" setting tariff classifications for particular imports. 19 CFR § 177.8 (2000). A ruling letter

> "represents the official position of the Customs Service with respect to the particular transaction or issue described therein and is binding on all Customs Service personnel in accordance with the provisions of this section until modified or revoked. In the absence of a change of practice or other modification or revocation which affects the principle of the ruling set forth in the ruling letter, that principle may be cited as authority in the disposition of transactions involving the same circumstances." § 177.9(a).

After the transaction that gives it birth, a ruling letter is to "be applied only with respect to transactions involving articles identical to the sample submitted with the ruling request or to articles whose description is identical to the description set forth in the ruling letter." § 177.9(b)(2). As a general matter, such a letter is "subject to modification or revocation without notice to any person, except the person to whom the letter was addressed," § 177.9(c), and the regulations consequently provide that "no other person should rely on the ruling letter or assume that the principles of that ruling will be applied in connection with any transaction other than the one described in the letter," *ibid*. Since ruling letters respond to transactions of the moment, they are not subject to notice and comment before being issued, may be published but need only be made "available for public inspection," 19 U. S. C. § 1625(a), and, at the time this action arose, could be modified without notice and comment under most circumstances, 19 CFR § 177.10(c) (2000). A broader notice-and-comment requirement for modification of prior rulings was added by statute in 1993, and took effect after this case arose.

Any of the 46 port-of-entry Customs offices may issue ruling letters, and so may the Customs Headquarters Office, in providing "advice or guidance as to the interpretation or proper application of the Customs and related laws with respect to a specific Customs transaction which may be requested by Customs Service field offices at any time, whether the transaction is prospective, current, or completed," 19 CFR § 177.11(a) (2000). Most ruling letters contain little or no reasoning, but simply describe goods and state the appropriate category and tariff. A few letters, like the Headquarters ruling at issue here, set out a rationale in some detail.

B

Respondent, the Mead Corporation, imports "day planners," three-ring binders with pages having room for notes of daily schedules and phone numbers and addresses,

---

1. The statutory term "ruling" is defined by regulation as "a written statement . . . that interprets and applies the provisions of the Customs and related laws to a specific set of facts." 19 CFR § 177.1(d)(1) (2000).

together with a calendar and suchlike. The tariff schedule on point falls under the HTSUS heading for "registers, account books, notebooks, order books, receipt books, letter pads, memorandum pads, diaries and similar articles," HTSUS subheading 4820.10, which comprises two subcategories. Items in the first, "diaries, notebooks and address books, bound; memorandum pads, letter pads and similar articles," were subject to a tariff of 4.0% at the time in controversy. Objects in the second, covering "other" items, were free of duty.

Between 1989 and 1993, Customs repeatedly treated day planners under the "other" HTSUS subheading. In January 1993, however, Customs changed its position, and issued a Headquarters ruling letter classifying Mead's day planners as "Diaries, bound" subject to tariff under subheading 4820.10.20. That letter was short on explanation, but after Mead's protest, Customs Headquarters issued a new letter, carefully reasoned but never published, reaching the same conclusion. This letter considered two definitions of "diary" from the Oxford English Dictionary, the first covering a daily journal of the past day's events, the second a book including " 'printed dates for daily memoranda and jottings; also calendars.' " Customs concluded that "diary" was not confined to the first, in part because the broader definition reflects commercial usage and hence the "commercial identity of these items in the marketplace." As for the definition of "bound," Customs concluded that HTSUS was not referring to "bookbinding," but to a less exact sort of fastening described in the Harmonized Commodity Description and Coding System Explanatory Notes to Heading 4820, which spoke of binding by " 'reinforcements or fittings of metal, plastics, etc.' "

Customs rejected Mead's further protest of the second Headquarters ruling letter, and Mead filed suit in the Court of International Trade (CIT). The CIT granted the Government's motion for summary judgment, adopting Custom's reasoning without saying anything about deference.

Mead then went to the United States Court of Appeals for the Federal Circuit. While the case was pending there this Court decided *United States* v. *Haggar Apparel Co.*, 526 U. S. 380 (1999), holding that Customs regulations receive the deference described in *Chevron*. The appeals court requested briefing on the impact of *Haggar*, and the Government argued that classification rulings, like Customs regulations, deserve *Chevron* deference.

The Federal Circuit, however, reversed the CIT and held that Customs classification rulings should not get *Chevron* deference, owing to differences from the regulations at issue in *Haggar*. Rulings are not preceded by notice and comment as under the Administrative Procedure Act (APA), 5 U. S. C. § 553, they "do not carry the force of law and are not, like regulations, intended to clarify the rights and obligations of importers beyond the specific case under review." The appeals court thought classification rulings had a weaker *Chevron* claim even than Internal Revenue Service interpretive rulings, to which that court gives no deference; unlike rulings by the IRS, Customs rulings issue from many locations and need not be published.

The Court of Appeals accordingly gave no deference at all to the ruling classifying the Mead day planners and rejected the agency's reasoning as to both "diary" and "bound." It thought that planners were not diaries because they had no space for "relatively extensive notations about events, observations, feelings, or thoughts" in the past. And it concluded that diaries "bound" in subheading 4810.10.20 presupposed "unbound" diaries, such that treating ring-fastened diaries as "bound" would leave the "unbound diary" an empty category.

We granted certiorari in order to consider the limits of *Chevron* deference owed to administrative practice in applying a statute. We hold that administrative implementation of a particular statutory provision qualifies for *Chevron* deference when it appears that Congress delegated authority to the agency generally to make rules carrying the force of law, and that the agency interpretation claiming deference was promulgated in the exercise of that authority. Delegation of such authority may be shown in a variety of ways, as by an agency's power to engage in adjudication or notice-and-comment rulemaking, or by some other indication of a comparable congressional intent. The Customs ruling at issue here fails to qualify, although the possibility that it deserves some deference under *Skidmore* leads us to vacate and remand.

II

A

When Congress has "explicitly left a gap for an agency to fill, there is an express delegation of authority to the agency to elucidate a specific provision of the statute by regulation," *Chevron*, 467 U. S., at 843-44, and any ensuing regulation is binding in the courts unless procedurally defective, arbitrary or capricious in substance, or manifestly contrary to the statute. *See id.*, at 844. But whether or not they enjoy any express delegation of authority on a particular question, agencies charged with applying a statute necessarily make all sorts of interpretive choices, and while not all of those choices bind judges to follow them, they certainly may influence courts facing questions the agencies have already answered. "The well-reasoned views of the agencies implementing a statute 'constitute a body of experience and informed judgment to which courts and litigants may properly resort for guidance,'" *Bragdon* v. *Abbott*, 524 U. S. 624, 642 (1998) (quoting *Skidmore*, 323 U. S., at 139-140), and "we have long recognized that considerable weight should be accorded to an executive department's construction of a statutory scheme it is entrusted to administer." *Chevron, supra*, at 844. The fair measure of deference to an agency administering its own statute has been understood to vary with circumstances, and courts have looked to the degree of the agency's care, its consistency, formality, and relative expertness, and to the persuasiveness of the agency's position, see *Skidmore, supra*, at 139-140. The approach has produced a spectrum of judicial responses, from great respect at one end, to near indifference at the other. Justice Jackson summed things up in *Skidmore* v. *Swift & Co.*:

> "The weight accorded to an administrative judgment in a particular case will depend upon the thoroughness evident in its consideration, the validity of its reasoning, its consistency with earlier and later pronouncements, and all those factors which give it power to persuade, if lacking power to control." 323 U. S., at 140.

Since 1984, we have identified a category of interpretive choices distinguished by an additional reason for judicial deference. This Court in *Chevron* recognized that Congress not only engages in express delegation of specific interpretive authority, but that "sometimes the legislative delegation to an agency on a particular question is implicit." 467 U. S., at 844. Congress, that is, may not have expressly delegated authority or responsibility to implement a particular provision or fill a particular gap. Yet it can still be apparent from the agency's generally conferred authority and other statutory circumstances that Congress would expect the agency to be able to speak with the force of law when it addresses ambiguity in the statute or fills a space in the enacted law, even one about which "Congress did not actually have an intent" as to a particular result. *Id.*, at 845. When circumstances implying such an expectation exist, a reviewing court has no business rejecting an agency's exercise of its generally conferred authority to resolve a particular statutory ambiguity simply because the agency's chosen resolution seems unwise, see *id.*, at 845-846, but is obliged to accept the agency's position if Congress has not previously spoken to the point at issue and the agency's interpretation is reasonable, see *id.*, at 842-845; cf. 5 U. S. C. § 706(2) (a reviewing court shall set aside agency action, findings, and conclusions found to be "arbitrary, capricious, an abuse of discretion, or otherwise not in accordance with law").

We have recognized a very good indicator of delegation meriting *Chevron* treatment in express congressional authorizations to engage in the process of rulemaking or adjudication that produces regulations or rulings for which deference is claimed. See, *e. g.*, *EEOC* v. *Arabian American Oil Co.*, 499 U. S. 244, 257 (1991) (no *Chevron* deference to agency guideline where congressional delegation did not include power to " 'promulgate rules or regulations' "). It is fair to assume generally that Congress contemplates administrative action with the effect of law when it provides for a relatively formal administrative procedure tending to foster the fairness and deliberation that should underlie a pronouncement of such force. Thus, the overwhelming number of our cases applying *Chevron* deference have reviewed the fruits of notice-and-comment rulemaking or formal adjudication. That said, and as significant as notice-and-comment is in pointing to *Chevron* authority, the want of that procedure here does not decide the case, for we have sometimes found reasons for *Chevron* deference even when no such administrative formality was required and none was afforded. The fact that the tariff classification here was not a product of such formal process does not alone, therefore, bar the application of *Chevron*.

There are, nonetheless, ample reasons to deny *Chevron* deference here. The authorization for classification rulings, and Customs's practice in making them, present a case far removed not only from notice-and-comment process, but from any other circumstances reasonably suggesting that Congress ever thought of classification rulings as deserving the deference claimed for them here.

B

No matter which angle we choose for viewing the Customs ruling letter in this case, it fails to qualify under *Chevron*. On the face of the statute, to begin with, the terms of the congressional delegation give no indication that Congress meant to delegate authority to Customs to issue classification rulings with the force of law. We are not, of course, here making any global statement about Customs's authority, for it is true that the general rulemaking power conferred on Customs authorizes some regulation with the force of law .... It is true as well that Congress had classification rulings in mind when it explicitly authorized . . . the issuance of "regulations establishing procedures for the issuance of binding rulings prior to the entry of the merchandise concerned." The reference to binding classifications does not, however, bespeak the legislative type of activity that would naturally bind more than the parties to the ruling, once the goods classified are admitted into this country. And though the statute's direction to disseminate "information" necessary to "secure" uniformity seems to assume that a ruling may be precedent in later transactions, precedential value alone does not add up to *Chevron* entitlement; interpretive rules may sometimes function as precedents, and they enjoy no *Chevron* status as a class. In any event, any precedential claim of a classification ruling is counterbalanced by the provision for independent review of Customs classifications by the CIT; the scheme for CIT review includes a provision that treats classification rulings on par with the Secretary's rulings on "valuation, rate of duty, marking, restricted merchandise, entry requirements, drawbacks, vessel repairs, or similar matters." It is hard to imagine a congressional understanding more at odds with the *Chevron* regime.

It is difficult, in fact, to see in the agency practice itself any indication that Customs ever set out with a lawmaking pretense in mind when it undertook to make classifications like these. Customs does not generally engage in notice-and-comment practice when issuing them, and their treatment by the agency makes it clear that a letter's binding character as a ruling stops short of third parties; Customs has regarded a classification as conclusive only as between itself and the importer to whom it was issued, and even then only until Customs has given advance notice of intended change. Other importers are in fact warned against assuming any right of detrimental reliance.

Indeed, to claim that classifications have legal force is to ignore the reality that 46 different Customs offices issue 10,000 to 15,000 of them each year. Any suggestion that rulings intended to have the force of law are being churned out at a rate of 10,000 a year at an agency's 46 scattered offices is simply self-refuting. Although the circumstances are less startling here, with a Headquarters letter in issue, none of the relevant statutes recognizes this category of rulings as separate or different from others; there is thus no indication that a more potent delegation might have been understood as going to Headquarters even when Headquarters provides developed reasoning, as it did in this instance.

Nor do the amendments to the statute made effective after this case arose disturb our conclusion. The new law requires Customs to provide notice-and-comment procedures only when modifying or revoking a prior classification ruling or modifying the treatment accorded to substantially identical transactions; and under its regulations, Customs sees itself obliged to provide notice-and-comment procedures only when "changing a practice" so as to produce a tariff increase, or in the imposition of a restriction or prohibition, or when Customs Headquarters determines that "the matter is of sufficient importance to involve the interests of domestic industry." The statutory changes reveal no new congressional objective of treating classification decisions generally as rulemaking with force of law, nor do they suggest any intent to create a *Chevron* patchwork of classification rulings, some with force of law, some without.

In sum, classification rulings are best treated like "interpretations contained in policy statements, agency manuals, and enforcement guidelines." They are beyond the *Chevron* pale.

C

To agree with the Court of Appeals that Customs ruling letters do not fall within *Chevron* is not, however, to place them outside the pale of any deference whatever. *Chevron* did nothing to eliminate *Skidmore*'s holding that an agency's interpretation may merit some deference whatever its form, given the "specialized experience and broader investigations and information" available to the agency, and given the value of uniformity in its administrative and judicial understandings of what a national law requires.

There is room at least to raise a *Skidmore* claim here, where the regulatory scheme is highly detailed, and Customs can bring the benefit of specialized experience to bear on the subtle questions in this case: whether the daily planner with room for brief daily entries falls under "diaries," when diaries are grouped with "notebooks and address books, bound; memorandum pads, letter pads and similar articles"; and whether a planner with a ring binding should qualify as "bound," when a binding may be typified by a book, but also may have "reinforcements or fittings of metal, plastics, etc." A classification ruling in this situation may therefore at least seek a respect proportional to its "power to persuade." Such a ruling may surely claim the merit of its writer's thoroughness, logic, and expertness, its fit with prior interpretations, and any other sources of weight.

D

Underlying the position we take here, like the position expressed by JUSTICE SCALIA in dissent, is a choice about the best way to deal with an inescapable feature of the body of congressional legislation authorizing administrative action. That feature is the great variety of ways in which the laws invest the Government's administrative arms with discretion, and with procedures for exercising it, in giving meaning to Acts of Congress. Implementation of a statute may occur in formal adjudication or the choice to defend against judicial challenge; it may occur in a central board or office or in dozens of enforcement agencies dotted across the country; its institutional lawmaking may be confined to the resolution of minute detail or extend to legislative rulemaking on matters intentionally left by Congress to be worked out at the agency level.

Although we all accept the position that the Judiciary should defer to at least some of this multifarious administrative action, we have to decide how to take account of the great range of its variety. If the primary objective is to simplify the judicial process of giving or withholding deference, then the diversity of statutes authorizing discretionary administrative action must be declared irrelevant or minimized. If, on the other hand, it is simply implausible that Congress intended such a broad range of statutory authority to produce only two varieties of administrative action, demanding either *Chevron* deference or none at all, then the breadth of the spectrum of possible agency action must be taken into account. JUSTICE SCALIA's first priority over the years has been to limit and simplify. The Court's choice has been to tailor deference to variety. This acceptance of the range of statutory variation has led the

Court to recognize more than one variety of judicial deference, just as the Court has recognized a variety of indicators that Congress would expect *Chevron* deference.[18]

Our respective choices are repeated today. JUSTICE SCALIA would pose the question of deference as an either-or choice. On his view that *Chevron* rendered *Skidmore* anachronistic, when courts owe any deference it is *Chevron* deference that they owe. Whether courts do owe deference in a given case turns, for him, on whether the agency action (if reasonable) is "authoritative." The character of the authoritative derives, in turn, not from breadth of delegation or the agency's procedure in implementing it, but is defined as the "official" position of an agency, and may ultimately be a function of administrative persistence alone.

The Court, on the other hand, said nothing in *Chevron* to eliminate *Skidmore*'s recognition of various justifications for deference depending on statutory circumstances and agency action; *Chevron* was simply a case recognizing that even without express authority to fill a specific statutory gap, circumstances pointing to implicit congressional delegation present a particularly insistent call for deference. Indeed, in holding here that *Chevron* left *Skidmore* intact and applicable where statutory circumstances indicate no intent to delegate general authority to make rules with force of law, or where such authority was not invoked, we hold nothing more than we said last Term in response to the particular statutory circumstances in *Christensen*, to which JUSTICE SCALIA then took exception, just as he does again today.

We think, in sum, that JUSTICE SCALIA's efforts to simplify ultimately run afoul of Congress's indications that different statutes present different reasons for considering respect for the exercise of administrative authority or deference to it. Without being at odds with congressional intent much of the time, we believe that judicial responses to administrative action must continue to differentiate between *Chevron* and *Skidmore*, and that continued recognition of *Skidmore* is necessary for just the reasons Justice Jackson gave when that case was decided.[19]

---

18. It is, of course, true that the limit of *Chevron* deference is not marked by a hard-edged rule. But *Chevron* itself is a good example showing when *Chevron* deference is warranted, while this is a good case showing when it is not. Judges in other, perhaps harder, cases will make reasoned choices between the two examples, the way courts have always done.

19. Surely Justice Jackson's practical criteria, along with *Chevron*'s concern with congressional understanding, provide more reliable guideposts than conclusory references to the "authoritative" or "official." Even if those terms provided a true criterion, there would have to be something wrong with a standard that accorded the status of substantive law to every one of 10,000 "official" customs classifications rulings turned out each year from over 46 offices placed around the country at the Nation's entryways. JUSTICE SCALIA tries to avoid that result by limiting what is "authoritative" or "official" to a pronouncement that expresses the "judgment of central agency management, approved at the highest levels," as distinct from the pronouncements of "underlings." But that analysis would not entitle a Headquarters ruling to *Chevron* deference; the "highest level" at Customs is the source of the regulation at issue in *Haggar*, the Commissioner of Customs with the approval of the Secretary of the Treasury. The Commissioner did not issue the Headquarters ruling. What JUSTICE SCALIA has in mind here is that because the Secretary approved the Government's position in its brief to this Court, *Chevron* deference is due. But if that is so, *Chevron* deference was not called for until sometime after the litigation began, when central management at the highest level decided to defend the ruling, and the deference is not to the classification ruling as such but to the brief. This explains why the Court has not accepted JUSTICE SCALIA's position.

Since the *Skidmore* assessment called for here ought to be made in the first instance by the Court of Appeals for the Federal Circuit or the Court of International Trade, we go no further than to vacate the judgment and remand the case for further proceedings consistent with this opinion.

JUSTICE SCALIA, dissenting.

Today's opinion makes an avulsive change in judicial review of federal administrative action. Whereas previously a reasonable agency application of an ambiguous statutory provision had to be sustained so long as it represented the agency's authoritative interpretation, henceforth such an application can be set aside unless "it appears that Congress delegated authority to the agency generally to make rules carrying the force of law," as by giving an agency "power to engage in adjudication or notice-and-comment rulemaking, or some other procedure indicating comparable congressional intent," and "the agency interpretation claiming deference was promulgated in the exercise of that authority."[1] What was previously a general presumption of authority in agencies to resolve ambiguity in the statutes they have been authorized to enforce has been changed to a presumption of no such authority, which must be overcome by affirmative legislative intent to the contrary. And whereas previously, when agency authority to resolve ambiguity did not exist the court was free to give the statute what it considered the best interpretation, henceforth the court must supposedly give the agency view some indeterminate amount of so-called *Skidmore* deference. We will be sorting out the consequences of the *Mead* doctrine, which has today replaced the *Chevron* doctrine, for years to come. I would adhere to our established jurisprudence, defer to the reasonable interpretation the Customs Service has given to the statute it is charged with enforcing, and reverse the judgment of the Court of Appeals.

I

Only five years ago, the Court described the *Chevron* doctrine as follows: "We accord deference to agencies under *Chevron* because of a presumption that Congress, when it left ambiguity in a statute meant for implementation by an agency, understood that the ambiguity would be resolved, first and foremost, by the agency, and desired the agency (rather than the courts) to possess whatever degree of discretion the ambiguity allows." Today the Court collapses this doctrine, announcing instead a presumption that agency discretion does not exist unless the statute, expressly or impliedly, says so. While the Court disclaims any hard-and-fast rule for determining the existence of discretion-conferring intent, it asserts that "a very good indicator is express congressional authorizations to engage in the process of rulemaking or adjudication that produces regulations or rulings for which deference is claimed." Only when agencies act through "adjudication, notice-and-comment rulemaking, or some

---

1. It is not entirely clear whether the formulation newly minted by the Court today extends to both formal and informal adjudication, or simply the former.

other procedure indicating comparable congressional intent whatever that means" is *Chevron* deference applicable — because these "relatively formal administrative procedures designed to foster fairness and deliberation" bespeak (according to the Court) congressional willingness to have the agency, rather than the courts, resolve statutory ambiguities. Once it is determined that *Chevron* deference is not in order, the uncertainty is not at an end — and indeed is just beginning. Litigants cannot then assume that the statutory question is one for the courts to determine, according to traditional interpretive principles and by their own judicial lights. No, the Court now resurrects, in full force, the pre-*Chevron* doctrine of *Skidmore* deference, whereby "the fair measure of deference to an agency administering its own statute varies with circumstances," including "the degree of the agency's care, its consistency, formality, and relative expertness, and the persuasiveness of the agency's position." The Court has largely replaced *Chevron*, in other words, with that test most beloved by a court unwilling to be held to rules (and most feared by litigants who want to know what to expect); th'ol' "totality of the circumstances" test.

The Court's new doctrine is neither sound in principle nor sustainable in practice.

A

As to principle: The doctrine of *Chevron* — that all *authoritative* agency interpretations of statutes they are charged with administering deserve deference — was rooted in a legal presumption of congressional intent, important to the division of powers between the Second and Third Branches. When, *Chevron* said, Congress leaves an ambiguity in a statute that is to be administered by an executive agency, it is presumed that Congress meant to give the agency discretion, within the limits of reasonable interpretation, as to how the ambiguity is to be resolved. By committing enforcement of the statute to an agency rather than the courts, Congress committed its initial and primary interpretation to that branch as well.

There is some question whether *Chevron* was faithful to the text of the Administrative Procedure Act (APA), which it did not even bother to cite.[2] But it was in accord with the origins of federal-court judicial review. Judicial control of federal executive officers was principally exercised through the prerogative writ of mandamus. That writ generally would not issue unless the executive officer was acting plainly beyond the scope of his authority. . . . Statutory ambiguities, in other words, were left to reasonable resolution by the Executive.

---

2. Title 5 U. S. C. § 706 provides that, in reviewing agency action, the court shall "decide all relevant questions of law" — which would seem to mean that all statutory ambiguities are to be resolved judicially. It could be argued, however, that the legal presumption identified by *Chevron* left as the only "question of law" whether the agency's interpretation had gone beyond the scope of discretion that the statutory ambiguity conferred. Today's opinion, of course, is no more observant of the APA's text than *Chevron* was — and indeed is even more difficult to reconcile with it. Since the opinion relies upon actual congressional intent to suspend § 706, rather than upon a legal presumption against which § 706 was presumably enacted, it runs head-on into the provision of the APA which specifies that the Act's requirements (including the requirement that judges shall "decide all relevant questions of law") cannot be amended except expressly. See § 559.

.... The Court's background rule is contradicted by the origins of judicial review of administrative action. But in addition, the Court's principal criterion of congressional intent to supplant its background rule seems to me quite implausible. There is no necessary connection between the formality of procedure and the power of the entity administering the procedure to resolve authoritatively questions of law. The most formal of the procedures the Court refers to — formal adjudication — is modeled after the process used in trial courts, which of course are not generally accorded deference on questions of law. The purpose of such a procedure is to produce a closed record for determination and review of the facts — which implies nothing about the power of the agency subjected to the procedure to resolve authoritatively questions of law.

As for informal rulemaking: While formal adjudication procedures are *prescribed* (either by statute or by the Constitution), informal rulemaking is more typically *authorized* but not required. Agencies with such authority are free to give guidance through rulemaking, but they may proceed to administer their statute case-by-case, "making law" as they implement their program (not necessarily through formal adjudication). Is it likely — or indeed even plausible — that Congress meant, when such an agency chooses rulemaking, to accord the administrators of that agency, *and their successors*, the flexibility of interpreting the ambiguous statute now one way, and later another; but, when such an agency chooses case-by-case administration, to eliminate all future agency discretion by having that same ambiguity resolved authoritatively (and forever) by the courts? Surely that makes no sense. It is also the case that certain significant categories of rules — those involving grant and benefit programs, for example, are exempt from the requirements of informal rulemaking. Under the Court's novel theory, when an agency takes advantage of that exemption its rules will be deprived of *Chevron* deference, *i. e.*, authoritative effect. Was this either the plausible intent of the APA rulemaking exemption, or the plausible intent of the Congress that established the grant or benefit program?

Some decisions that are neither informal rulemaking nor formal adjudication are required to be made personally by a Cabinet Secretary, without any prescribed procedures. Is it conceivable that decisions specifically committed to these high-level officers are meant to be accorded no deference, while decisions by an administrative law judge left in place without further discretionary agency review are authoritative? This seems to me quite absurd, and not at all in accord with any plausible actual intent of Congress.

B

As for the practical effects of the new rule:

(1)

The principal effect will be protracted confusion. As noted above, the one test for *Chevron* deference that the Court enunciates is wonderfully imprecise: whether "Congress delegated authority to the agency generally to make rules carrying the force of law, as by adjudication, notice-and-comment rulemaking, or some other procedure indicating comparable congressional intent." But even this description does not do justice to the utter flabbiness of the Court's criterion, since, in order to maintain the fiction that the new test is really just the old one, applied consistently throughout our case law, the Court must make a virtually open-ended exception to its already imprecise guidance: In the present case, it tells us, the absence of notice-and-comment rulemaking . . . is not enough to decide the question of *Chevron* deference, "for we have sometimes found reasons for *Chevron* deference even when no such administrative formality was required and none was afforded." The opinion then goes on to consider a grab bag of other factors — including the factor that used to be the sole criterion for *Chevron* deference: whether the interpretation represented the *authoritative* position of the agency. It is hard to know what the lower courts are to make of today's guidance.

(2)

Another practical effect of today's opinion will be an artificially induced increase in informal rulemaking. Buy stock in the GPO. Since informal rulemaking and formal adjudication are the only more-or-less safe harbors from the storm that the Court has unleashed; and since formal adjudication is not an option but must be mandated by statute or constitutional command; informal rulemaking — which the Court was once careful to make voluntary unless required by statute — will now become a virtual necessity. As I have described, the Court's safe harbor requires not merely that the agency have been given rulemaking authority, but also that the agency have *employed* rulemaking as the means of resolving the statutory ambiguity. (It is hard to understand why that should be so. Surely the mere *conferral* of rulemaking authority demonstrates — if one accepts the Court's logic — a congressional intent to allow the agency to resolve ambiguities. And given that intent, what difference does it make that the agency chooses instead to use another perfectly permissible means for that purpose?) Moreover, the majority's approach will have a perverse effect on the rules that do emerge, given the principle (which the Court leaves untouched today) that judges must defer to reasonable agency interpretations of their own regulations. Agencies will now have high incentive to rush out barebones, ambiguous rules construing statutory ambiguities, which they can then in turn further clarify through informal rulings entitled to judicial respect.

(3)

Worst of all, the majority's approach will lead to the ossification of large portions of our statutory law. Where *Chevron* applies, statutory ambiguities remain ambiguities subject to the agency's ongoing clarification. They create a space, so to speak, for the exercise of continuing agency discretion. As *Chevron* itself held, the Environmental Protection Agency can interpret "stationary source" to mean a single smokestack, can later replace that interpretation with the "bubble concept" embracing an entire plant, and if that proves undesirable can return again to the original interpretation. For the indeterminately large number of statutes taken out of *Chevron* by today's decision, however, ambiguity (and hence flexibility) will cease with the first judicial resolution. *Skidmore* deference gives the agency's current position some vague and uncertain amount of respect, but it does not, like *Chevron*, *leave* the matter within the control of the Executive Branch for the future. Once the court has spoken, it becomes *unlawful* for the agency to take a contradictory position; the statute now *says* what the court has prescribed. It will be bad enough when this ossification occurs as a result of judicial determination (under today's new principles) that there is no affirmative indication of congressional intent to "delegate"; but it will be positively bizarre when it occurs simply because of an agency's failure to act by rulemaking (rather than informal adjudication) before the issue is presented to the courts.

One might respond that such ossification would not result if the agency were simply to readopt its interpretation, after a court reviewing it under *Skidmore* had rejected it, by repromulgating it through one of the *Chevron*-eligible procedural formats approved by the Court today. Approving this procedure would be a landmark abdication of judicial power. It is worlds apart from *Chevron* proper, where the court does not *purport* to give the statute a judicial interpretation — except in identifying the scope of the statutory ambiguity, as to which the court's judgment is final and irreversible. (Under *Chevron* proper, when the agency's authoritative interpretation comes within the scope of that ambiguity — and the court therefore approves it — the agency will not be "overruling" the court's decision when it later decides that a different interpretation (still within the scope of the ambiguity) is preferable.) By contrast, under this view, the reviewing court will not be holding the agency's authoritative interpretation within the scope of the ambiguity; but will be holding that the agency has not used the "delegation-conferring" procedures, and that the court must therefore *interpret the statute on its own* — but subject to reversal if and when the agency uses the proper procedures.

One is reminded of Justice Jackson's words in *Chicago & Southern Air Lines, Inc.* v. *Waterman S. S. Corp.*, 333 U. S. 103, 113 (1948):

> "The court below considered that after it reviewed the Board's order its judgment would be submitted to the President, that his power to disapprove would apply after as well as before the court acts, and hence that there would be no chance of a deadlock and no conflict of function. But if the President may completely disregard the judgment of the court, it would be only because it is one the courts were not authorized to render. Judgments within the powers vested in courts by the Judiciary Article of the Constitution may not lawfully be revised, overturned or refused faith and credit by another Department of Government."

I know of no case, in the entire history of the federal courts, in which we have allowed a judicial interpretation of a statute to be set aside by an agency — or have allowed a lower court to render an interpretation of a statute subject to correction by an agency. . . . There is, in short, no way to avoid the ossification of federal law that today's opinion sets in motion. What a court says is the law after according *Skidmore* deference will be the law forever, beyond the power of the agency to change even through rulemaking.

(4)

And finally, the majority's approach compounds the confusion it creates by breathing new life into the anachronism of *Skidmore*, which sets forth a sliding scale of deference owed an agency's interpretation of a statute that is dependent "upon the thoroughness evident in the agency's consideration, the validity of its reasoning, its consistency with earlier and later pronouncements, and all those factors which give it power to persuade, if lacking power to control"; in this way, the appropriate measure of deference will be accorded the "body of experience and informed judgment" that such interpretations often embody. Justice Jackson's eloquence notwithstanding, the rule of *Skidmore* deference is an empty truism and a trifling statement of the obvious: A judge should take into account the well-considered views of expert observers.

It was possible to live with the indeterminacy of *Skidmore* deference in earlier times. But in an era when federal statutory law administered by federal agencies is pervasive, and when the ambiguities (intended or unintended) that those statutes contain are innumerable, totality-of-the-circumstances *Skidmore* deference is a recipe for uncertainty, unpredictability, and endless litigation. To condemn a vast body of agency action to that regime . . . is irresponsible.

. . . .

III

To decide the present case, I would adhere to the original formulation of *Chevron*. " 'The power of an administrative agency to administer a congressionally created program necessarily requires the formulation of policy and the making of rules to fill any gap left, implicitly or explicitly, by Congress.' " We accordingly presume — and our precedents have made clear to Congress that we presume — that, absent some clear textual indication to the contrary, "Congress when it left ambiguity in a statute meant for implementation by an agency, understood that the ambiguity would be resolved, first and foremost, by the agency, and desired the agency (rather than the courts) to possess whatever degree of discretion the ambiguity allows." *Chevron* sets forth an across-the-board presumption, which operates as a background rule of law against which Congress legislates: Ambiguity means Congress intended agency discretion. And resolution of the ambiguity by the administering agency that is authoritative — that represents the official position of the agency — must be accepted by the courts if it is reasonable.

Nothing in the statute at issue here displays an intent to modify the background presumption on which *Chevron* deference is based. The Court points to 28 U. S. C. § 2640(a), which provides that, in reviewing the ruling by the Customs Service, the Court of International Trade (CIT) "shall make its determinations upon the basis of the record made before the court." But records are made to determine facts, not the law. All this provision means is that new evidence may be introduced at the CIT stage; it says nothing about whether the CIT must respect the Customs Service's authoritative interpretation of the law. More significant than § 2640(a), insofar as the CIT's obligation to defer to the Customs Service's legal interpretations is concerned, is § 2639(a)(1), which requires the CIT to accord a "presumption of correctness" to the Customs Service's decision. Another provision cited by the Court is § 2638, which provides that the CIT, "by rule, may consider any new ground in support" of the challenge to the Customs Service's ruling. Once again, it is impossible to see how this has any connection to the degree of deference the CIT must accord the Customs Service's interpretation of its statute. Such "new grounds" may be intervening or newly discovered facts, or some intervening law or regulation that might render the Customs Service's ruling unsound.[5]

There is no doubt that the Customs Service's interpretation represents the authoritative view of the agency. Although the actual ruling letter was signed by only the Director of the Commercial Rulings Branch of Customs Headquarters' Office of Regulations and Rulings, [counsel] represents the position set forth in the ruling letter to be the official position of the Customs Service. No one contends that it is merely a "post hoc rationalization" or an "agency litigating position wholly unsupported by regulations, rulings, or administrative practice," *Bowen* v. *Georgetown Univ. Hospital*, 488 U. S. 204, 212 (1988).[6]

---

5. The Court also states that "it is hard to imagine" that Congress would have intended courts to defer to classification rulings since "the scheme for CIT review includes a provision that treats classification rulings on par with the Secretary's rulings on 'valuation, rate of duty, marking, restricted merchandise, entry requirements, drawbacks, vessel repairs, or similar matters.'" I fail to see why this is hard to imagine at all. If anything, the fact that "the scheme for CIT review treats classification rulings on par with the Secretary's rulings on" such important matters . . . , which often require interpretation of the Nation's customs and tariff statutes, only strengthens the case for according *Chevron* deference to whatever statutory interpretations (as opposed to factual determinations) such rulings embody. In other words, the Court's point is wrong — indeed, the Court's point cuts deeply into its own case — unless the Court believes that the Secretary's *personal* rulings on the legal criteria for imposing particular rates of duty, or for determining restricted merchandise, are entitled to no deference.

6. The Court's parting shot, that "there would have to be something wrong with a standard that accorded the status of substantive law to every one of the 10,000 'official' customs classifications rulings turned out each year from over 46 offices placed around the country at the Nation's entryways," misses the mark. I do not disagree. The "authoritativeness" of an agency interpretation does not turn upon whether it has been enunciated by someone who is actually employed by the agency. It must represent the judgment of central agency management, approved at the highest levels. I would find that condition to have been satisfied when, a ruling having been attacked in court, the general counsel of the agency has determined that it should be defended. If one thinks that that does not impart sufficient authoritativeness, then surely the line has been crossed when, as here, the General Counsel of the agency and the Solicitor General of the United States have assured this Court that the position represents the agency's authoritative view. (Contrary to the Court's suggestion, there would be nothing bizarre about the fact that this latter approach would entitle the ruling to deference here, though it would not have been entitled to deference in the lower courts. Affirmation of the official agency position before this court — if that is thought necessary — is no different from the agency's issuing a new rule after the Court of Appeals determination. It establishes a new legal basis for the decision, which this Court must take into account (or remand for that purpose), even though the Court of Appeals could not. See *Thorpe* v. *Housing Authority of Durham*, 393 U. S. 268, 282 (1969); see also *United States* v. *Schooner Peggy*, 1 Cranch 103 (1801).)

The *authoritativeness* of the agency ruling may not be a bright-line standard — but it is infinitely brighter than the line the Court asks us to draw today . . . . And, most important of all, it is a line that focuses attention on the right question: not whether Congress "affirmatively intended" to delegate interpretive authority (if it entrusted administration of the statute to an agency, it did, because that is how our system works); but whether it is truly the agency's considered view, or just the opinions of some underlings, that are at issue.

There is also no doubt that the Customs Service's interpretation is a reasonable one, whether or not judges would consider it the best. I will not belabor this point, since the Court evidently agrees: An interpretation that was unreasonable would not merit the remand that the Court decrees for consideration of *Skidmore* deference.

IV

Finally, and least importantly, even were I to accept the Court's revised version of *Chevron* as a correct statement of the law, I would still accord deference to the tariff classification ruling at issue in this case. . . .

For the reasons stated, I respectfully dissent from the Court's judgment. I would uphold the Customs Service's construction of Subheading 4820.10.20 of the Harmonized Tariff Schedule of the United States, 19 U. S. C. § 1202, and would reverse the contrary decision of the Court of Appeals. I dissent even more vigorously from the reasoning that produces the Court's judgment, and that makes today's decision one of the most significant opinions ever rendered by the Court dealing with the judicial review of administrative action. Its consequences will be enormous, and almost uniformly bad.

Notes and Questions

---

1. What is the standard of deference to agency interpretations articulated by the Court in *Mead*?

2. Does *Mead* represent a wholesale retreat from *Chevron*, or should *Mead* be confined to the particular type of rulings at issue?

3. Does the *Mead* standard seem wise, even if it is regarded as limited in scope?

4. What are Justice Scalia's criticisms of the Court's approach? Do you agree?

5. To what extent is the disagreement between Justices Souter and Scalia based on a difference in philosophy between the use of bright-line rules as opposed to more flexible standards, and the proper use of discretion by courts in achieving justice?

6. Notice that Justice Scalia, who would have reversed the judgment of the court of appeals, dissented despite the fact that the Court itself vacated the judgment of the court of appeals. Was this appropriate, and if so, does this help highlight one problem with vacatur? (Recall that vacatur was discussed in more detail in Chapter 2.)

Zuni Public School District v. Department of Education

550 U.S. 81 (2007)

JUSTICE BREYER delivered the opinion of the Court.

A federal statute sets forth a method that the Secretary of Education is to use when determining whether a State's public school funding program "equalizes expenditures" throughout the State. The statute instructs the Secretary to calculate the disparity in per-pupil expenditures among local school districts in the State. But, when doing so, the Secretary is to "disregard" school districts "*with per-pupil expenditures above the 95th percentile or below the 5th percentile of such expenditures in the State.*" 20 U.S.C. § 7709(b)(2)(i) (emphasis added).

The question before us is whether the emphasized statutory language permits the Secretary to identify the school districts that should be "disregarded" by looking to the *number of the district's pupils* as well as to the size of the district's expenditures per pupil. We conclude that it does.

I

A

The federal Impact Aid Act provides financial assistance to local school districts whose ability to finance public school education is adversely affected by a federal presence. Federal aid is available to districts, for example, where a significant amount of federal land is exempt from local property taxes, or where a federal presence is responsible for an increase in school-age children (say, of armed forces personnel) whom local schools must educate. The statute typically prohibits a State from offsetting this federal aid by reducing its own state aid to the local district. If applied without exceptions, however, this prohibition might unreasonably interfere with a state program that seeks to equalize per-pupil expenditures throughout the State, for instance, by preventing the state program from taking account of a significant source of federal funding that some local school districts receive. The statute consequently contains an exception that permits a State to compensate for federal impact aid where "the Secretary of Education determines and certifies that the State has in effect a program of State aid that *equalizes* expenditures for free public education among local school districts in the State."

The statute sets out a formula that the Secretary of Education must use to determine whether a state aid program satisfies the federal "equalization" requirement. The formula instructs the Secretary to compare the local school district with the greatest per-pupil expenditures to the school district with the smallest per-pupil expenditures to see whether the former exceeds the latter by more than 25 percent. So long as it does not, the state aid program qualifies as a program that "equalizes expenditures." . . .

The statutory provision goes on to set forth what we shall call the "disregard" instruction. It states that, when "making" this "determination," the "*Secretary shall disregard school districts with per-pupil expenditures above the 95th percentile or below the 5th percentile of such expenditures."* § 7709(b)(2)(i) (emphasis added). . . .

B

This case requires us to decide whether the Secretary's present calculation method is consistent with the federal statute's "disregard" instruction. The method at issue is contained in a set of regulations that the Secretary first promulgated 30 years ago. Those regulations essentially state the following:

When determining whether a state aid program "equalizes expenditures" (thereby permitting the State to reduce its own local funding on account of federal impact aid), the Secretary will first create a list of school districts ranked in order of per-pupil expenditure. The Secretary will then identify the relevant percentile cutoff point on that list on the basis of a specific (95th or 5th) percentile of *student population* — essentially identifying those districts whose students account for the 5 percent of the State's total student population that lies at both the high and low ends of the spending distribution. Finally the Secretary will compare the highest spending and lowest spending school districts of those that remain to see whether they satisfy the statute's requirement that the disparity between them not exceed 25 percent.

. . . .

C

This case concerns the Department of Education's application of the Secretary's regulations to New Mexico's local district aid program in respect to fiscal year 2000. As the regulations require, Department officials listed each of New Mexico's 89 local school districts in order of per-pupil spending. . . . After ranking the districts, Department officials excluded 17 school districts at the top of the list because those districts contained (cumulatively) less than 5 percent of the student population; for the same reason, they excluded an additional 6 schools at the bottom of the list.

The remaining 66 districts accounted for approximately 90 percent of the State's student population. Of those, the highest ranked district spent $3,259 per student; the lowest ranked district spent $2,848 per student. The difference, $411, was less than 25 percent of the lowest per-pupil figure, namely $2,848. Hence, the officials found that New Mexico's local aid program qualifies as a program that "equalizes expenditures." New Mexico was therefore free to offset federal impact aid to individual districts by reducing state aid to those districts.

Two of New Mexico's public school districts, Zuni Public School District and Gallup-McKinley County Public School District (whom we shall collectively call Zuni), sought further agency review of these findings. Zuni conceded that the Department's calculations were correct in terms of the Department's own regulations. Zuni argued, however, that the regulations themselves are inconsistent with the authorizing statute. That statute, in its view, requires the Department to calculate the 95th and 5th percentile cutoffs solely on the basis of the number of school districts (ranked by their per-pupil expenditures), without any consideration of the number of pupils in those districts. If calculated as Zuni urges, only 10 districts (accounting for less than 2 percent of all students) would have been identified as the outliers that the statute instructs the Secretary to disregard. The difference, as a result, between the highest and lowest per-pupil expenditures of the remaining districts (26.9 percent) would exceed 25 percent. Consequently, the statute would forbid New Mexico to take account of federal impact aid as it decides how to equalize school funding across the State.

A Department of Education Administrative Law Judge rejected Zuni's challenge to the regulations. The Secretary of Education did the same. Zuni sought review of the Secretary's decision in the Court of Appeals for the Tenth Circuit. Initially, a Tenth Circuit panel affirmed the Secretary's determination by a split vote (2 to 1). Subsequently, the full Court of Appeals vacated the panel's decision and heard the matter en banc. The 12-member en banc court affirmed the Secretary but by an evenly divided court (6 to 6). Zuni sought certiorari. We agreed to decide the matter.

II

A

Zuni's strongest argument rests upon the literal language of the statute. Zuni concedes, as it must, that if the language of the statute is open or ambiguous — that is, if Congress left a "gap" for the agency to fill — then we must uphold the Secretary's interpretation as long as it is reasonable. See *Chevron U.S.A. Inc. v. Natural Resources Defense Council, Inc.*, 467 U.S. 837, 842-843 (1984). See also *Christensen v. Harris County*, 529 U.S. 576, 589 n. (2000) (Scalia, J., concurring in part and concurring in the judgment). For purposes of exposition, we depart from a normal order of discussion, namely an order that first considers Zuni's statutory language argument. Instead, because of the technical nature of the language in question, we shall first examine the provision's background and basic purposes. That discussion will illuminate our subsequent analysis in Part II-B, *infra*. It will also reveal why Zuni concentrates its argument upon language alone.

Considerations other than language provide us with unusually strong indications that Congress intended to leave the Secretary free to use the calculation method before us and that the Secretary's chosen method is a reasonable one. For one thing, the matter at issue — *i.e.*, the calculation method for determining whether a state aid program "equalizes expenditures" — is the kind of highly technical, specialized interstitial matter that Congress often does not decide itself, but delegates to specialized agencies to decide. See *United States v. Mead Corp.*, 533 U.S. 218, 234 (2001).

For another thing, the history of the statute strongly supports the Secretary. Congress first enacted an impact aid "equalization" exception in 1974. The exception originally provided that the "term 'equalizing expenditures' shall be defined by the Secretary." Soon thereafter, in 1976, the Secretary promulgated the regulation here at issue defining the term "equalizing expenditures" in the manner now before us. As far as we can tell, no Member of Congress has ever criticized the method the 1976 regulation sets forth nor suggested at any time that it be revised or reconsidered.

The present statutory language originated in draft legislation that the Secretary himself sent to Congress in 1994. With one minor change (irrelevant to the present calculation controversy), Congress adopted that language without comment or clarification. No one at the time — no Member of Congress, no Department of Education official, no school district or State — expressed the view that this statutory language (which, after all, was supplied by the Secretary) was intended to require, or did require, the Secretary to change the Department's system of calculation, a system that the Department and school districts across the Nation had followed for nearly 20 years, without (as far as we are told) any adverse effect.

Finally, viewed in terms of the purpose of the statute's disregard instruction, the Secretary's calculation method is reasonable, while the reasonableness of a method based upon the number of districts alone (Zuni's proposed method) is more doubtful. When the Secretary (then Commissioner) of Education considered the matter in 1976, he explained why that is so.

. . . .

Thus, the history and purpose of the disregard instruction indicate that the Secretary's calculation formula is a reasonable method that carries out Congress' likely intent in enacting the statutory provision before us.

B

But what of the provision's literal language? The matter is important, for normally neither the legislative history nor the reasonableness of the Secretary's method would be determinative if the plain language of the statute unambiguously indicated that Congress sought to foreclose the Secretary's interpretation. And Zuni argues that the Secretary's formula could not possibly effectuate Congress' intent since the statute's language literally forbids the Secretary to use such a method. Under this Court's precedents, if the intent of Congress is clear and unambiguously expressed by the statutory language at issue, that would be the end of our analysis. A customs statute that imposes a tariff on "clothing" does not impose a tariff on automobiles, no matter how strong the policy arguments for treating the two kinds of goods alike. But we disagree with Zuni's conclusion, for we believe that the Secretary's method falls within the scope of the statute's plain language.

That language says that, when the Secretary compares (for a specified fiscal year) "the amount of per-pupil expenditures made by" (1) the highest-per-pupil expenditure district and (2) the lowest-per-pupil expenditure district, "the Secretary shall disregard" local school districts "with per-pupil expenditures above the 95th percentile or below the 5th percentile of such expenditures in the State." The word "such" refers to "per-pupil expenditures". . . . The question then is whether the phrase "*above the 95th percentile of per pupil expenditures*" permits the Secretary to calculate percentiles by (1) ranking local districts, (2) noting the student population of each district, and (3) determining the cutoff point on the basis of districts containing 95 percent (or 5 percent) of the State's students.

Our answer is that this phrase, taken with absolute literalness, limits the Secretary to calculation methods that involve "per-pupil expenditures." But it does not tell the Secretary which of several different possible methods the Department must use. Nor does it rule out the present formula, which distributes districts in accordance with per-pupil expenditures, while essentially weighting each district to reflect the number of pupils it contains.

Because the statute uses technical language (*e.g.*, "percentile") and seeks a technical purpose (eliminating uncharacteristic, or outlier, districts), we have examined dictionary definitions of the term "percentile." Those definitions make clear that "percentile" refers to a division of a distribution of *some* population into 100 parts. . . .

These definitions, mainstream and technical, all indicate that, in order to identify the relevant percentile cutoffs, the Secretary must construct a distribution of values. That distribution will consist of a "population" ranked according to a characteristic. That characteristic takes on a "value" for each member of the relevant population. The statute's instruction to identify the 95th and 5th "percentile of such expenditures" makes clear that the relevant *characteristic* for ranking purposes is per-pupil expenditure during a particular year. But the statute does not specify precisely what *population* is to be "distributed" (*i.e.*, ranked according to the relevant characteristic). Nor does it set forth various details as to how precisely the distribution is to be constructed (as long as it is ranked according to the specified characteristic).

But why is Congress' silence in respect to these matters significant? Are there several *different* populations, relevant here, that one might rank according to "per-pupil expenditures" (and thereby determine in several *different* ways a cutoff point such that "*n* percent of that population" falls, say below the percentile cutoff)? We are not experts in statistics, but a statistician is not needed to see what the dictionary does not say. No dictionary definition we have found suggests that there is any *single* logical, mathematical, or statistical link between, on the one hand, the characteristic data (used for ranking purposes) and, on the other hand, the nature of the relevant population or how that population might be weighted for purposes of determining a percentile cutoff.

Here, the Secretary has distributed districts, ranked them according to per-pupil expenditure, but compared only those that account for 90 percent of the State's pupils. Thus, the Secretary has used — as his predecessors had done for a quarter century before him — the State's *students* as the relevant population for calculating the specified percentiles. Another Secretary might have distributed districts, ranked them by per-pupil expenditure, and made no reference to the number of pupils (a method that satisfies the statute's *language* but threatens the problems the Secretary long ago identified). A third Secretary might have distributed districts, ranked them by per-pupil expenditure, but compared only those that account for 90 percent of total pupil expenditures in the State. A fourth Secretary might have distributed districts, ranked then by per-pupil expenditure, but calculated the 95th and 5th percentile cutoffs using the per-pupil expenditures of all the individual *schools* in the State. A fifth Secretary might have distributed districts, ranked them by per-pupil expenditure, but accounted in his disparity calculation for the sometimes significant differences in per-pupil spending at different grade levels.

Each of these methods amounts to a different way of determining which districts fall between the 5th and 95th "percentile of per-pupil expenditures." For purposes of that calculation, they each adopt different populations — students, districts, schools, and grade levels. Yet, linguistically speaking, one may attribute the characteristic of per-pupil expenditure to each member of any such population (though the values of that characteristic may be more or less readily available depending on the chosen population). Hence, the statute's literal language covers any or all of these methods. That language alone does not tell us (or the Secretary of Education), however, which method to use.

Justice Scalia's claim that this interpretation "defies any semblance of normal English" depends upon its own definition of the word "per." That word, according to the dissent, "connotes a single average figure assigned to a unit the composite members of which are individual pupils." In fact, the word "per" simply means "for each" or "for every." Thus, nothing in the English language forbids the Secretary from considering expenditures *for each* individual pupil in a district when instructed to look at a district's "per-pupil expenditures." The remainder of the dissent's argument, colorful language to the side, rests upon a reading of the statutory language that ignores its basic purpose and history.

We find additional evidence for our understanding of the language in the fact that Congress, in other statutes, has clarified the matter here at issue thereby avoiding comparable ambiguity. . . . In these statutes, Congress indicated with greater specificity how a percentile should be determined. . . . In the statute at issue here, however, Congress used more general language (drafted by the Secretary himself), which leaves the Secretary with the authority to resolve such subsidiary matters at the administrative level.

We also find support for our view of the language in the more general circumstance that statutory "ambiguity is a creature not just of definitional possibilities but also of statutory context." That may be so even if statutory language is highly technical. After all, the scope of what seems a precise technical chess instruction, such as "you must place the queen next to the king," varies with context, depending, for example, upon whether the instructor is telling a beginner how to set up the board or telling an advanced player how to checkmate an opponent. . . .

Thus, an instruction to "identify schools with average scholastic aptitude test scores below the 5th percentile of such scores" may vary as to the population to be distributed, depending upon whether the context is one of providing additional counseling and support to *students* at low-performing schools (in which case the relevant population would likely consist of students), or one of identifying unsuccessful learning protocols at low-performing schools (in which case the appropriate population may well be the schools themselves). Context here tells us that the instruction to identify school districts with "per-pupil expenditures" above the 95th percentile "of such expenditures" is similarly ambiguous, because both students and school districts are of concern to the statute. Accordingly, the disregard instruction can include within its scope the distribution of a ranked population that consists of pupils (or of school districts weighted by pupils) and not just a ranked distribution of unweighted school districts alone.

Finally, we draw reassurance from the fact that no group of statisticians, nor any individual statistician, has told us directly in briefs, or indirectly through citation, that the language before us cannot be read as we have read it. This circumstance is significant, for the statutory language is technical, and we are not statisticians. And the views of experts (or their absence) might help us understand (though not control our determination of) what Congress had in mind.

The upshot is that the language of the statute is broad enough to permit the Secretary's reading. That fact requires us to look beyond the language to determine whether the Secretary's interpretation is a reasonable, hence permissible, implementation of the statute. For the reasons set forth in Part II-A, *supra*, we conclude that the Secretary's reading is a reasonable reading. We consequently find the Secretary's method of calculation lawful.

The judgment of the Tenth Circuit is affirmed.
It is so ordered.
. . . .

JUSTICE STEVENS, concurring.

In his oft-cited opinion for the Court in *Griffin v. Oceanic Contractors, Inc.*, then-Justice Rehnquist wisely acknowledged that "in rare cases the literal application of a statute will produce a result demonstrably at odds with the intentions of its drafters, and those intentions must be controlling." And in *United States v. Ron Pair Enterprises, Inc.*, the Court began its analysis of the question of statutory construction by restating the proposition that "in such cases, the intention of the drafters, rather than the strict language, controls." Justice Scalia provided the decisive fifth vote for the majority in that case.

Today he correctly observes that a judicial decision that departs from statutory text may represent "policy-driven interpretation." As long as that driving policy is faithful to the intent of Congress (or, as in this case, aims only to give effect to such intent) — which it must be if it is to override a strict interpretation of the text — the decision is also a correct performance of the judicial function. Justice Scalia's argument today rests on the incorrect premise that every policy-driven interpretation implements a judge's personal view of sound policy, rather than a faithful attempt to carry out the will of the legislature. Quite the contrary is true of the work of the judges with whom I have worked for many years. If we presume that our judges are intellectually honest — as I do — there is no reason to fear "policy-driven interpretations" of Acts of Congress.

In *Chevron*, we acknowledged that when "the intent of Congress is clear from the statutory text, that is the end of the matter." But we also made quite clear that "administrative constructions which are contrary to clear congressional intent" must be rejected. . . . Analysis of legislative history is, of course, a traditional tool of statutory construction. There is no reason why we must confine ourselves to, or begin our analysis with, the statutory text if other tools of statutory construction provide better evidence of congressional intent with respect to the precise point at issue.

As the Court's opinion demonstrates, this is a quintessential example of a case in which the statutory text was obviously enacted to adopt a rule that the Secretary administered both before and after the enactment of the rather confusing language found in 20 U.S.C. § 7709(b)(2)(B)(i). That text is sufficiently ambiguous to justify the Court's exegesis, but my own vote is the product of a more direct route to the Court's patently correct conclusion. This happens to be a case in which the legislative history is pellucidly clear and the statutory text is difficult to fathom.[2] Moreover, it is

---

2. Contrary to Justice Scalia, I find it far more likely that the Congress that voted "without comment or clarification" to adopt the 1994 statutory language relied on the endorsement of its sponsors, who introduced the legislation "on behalf of the administration," and the fact that such language was drafted and proposed by the U.S. Department of Education, rather than a parsing of its obscure statutory text.

Moreover, I assume that, regardless of the statutory language's supposed clarity, any competent counsel challenging the validity of a presumptively valid federal regulation would examine the legislative history of its authorizing statute before filing suit.

a case in which I cannot imagine anyone accusing any Member of the Court of voting one way or the other because of that Justice's own policy preferences.

Given the clarity of the evidence of Congress' "intention on the precise question at issue," I would affirm the judgment of the Court of Appeals even if I thought that petitioner's literal reading of the statutory text was correct.[3] The only "policy" by which I have been driven is that which this Court has endorsed on repeated occasions regarding the importance of remaining faithful to Congress' intent.

JUSTICE KENNEDY, with whom JUSTICE ALITO joins, concurring.

The district courts and courts of appeals, as well as this Court, should follow the framework set forth in *Chevron*, even when departure from that framework might serve purposes of exposition. When considering an administrative agency's interpretation of a statute, a court first determines "whether Congress has directly spoken to the precise question at issue." If so, "that is the end of the matter." Only if "Congress has not directly addressed the precise question at issue" should a court consider "whether the agency's answer is based on a permissible construction of the statute."

In this case, the Court is correct to find that the plain language of the statute is ambiguous. It is proper, therefore, to invoke *Chevron*'s rule of deference. The opinion of the Court, however, inverts *Chevron*'s logical progression. Were the inversion to become systemic, it would create the impression that agency policy concerns, rather than the traditional tools of statutory construction, are shaping the judicial interpretation of statutes. It is our obligation to set a good example; and so, in my view, it would have been preferable, and more faithful to *Chevron*, to arrange the opinion differently. Still, we must give deference to the author of an opinion in matters of exposition; and because the point does not affect the outcome, I join the Court's opinion.

JUSTICE SCALIA, with whom the CHIEF JUSTICE and JUSTICE THOMAS join, and with whom JUSTICE SOUTER joins as to Part I, dissenting.

In *Church of the Holy Trinity*, this Court conceded that a church's act of contracting with a prospective rector fell within the plain meaning of a federal labor statute, but nevertheless did not apply the statute to the church: "It is a familiar rule," the Court pronounced, "that a thing may be within the letter of the statute and yet not within the statute, because not within its spirit, nor within the intention of its makers." That is a judge-empowering proposition if there ever was one, and in the century since, the Court has wisely retreated from it, in words if not always in actions. But today *Church of the Holy Trinity* arises, Phoenix-like, from the ashes. The Court's contrary assertions aside, today's decision is nothing other than the elevation of judge-supposed legislative intent over clear statutory text. The plain language of the federal Impact Aid statute clearly and unambiguously forecloses the Secretary of Education's preferred methodology for determining whether a State's school-funding

---

3. See *Church of Holy Trinity v. United States*, 143 U.S. 457, 459 (1892) ("It is a familiar rule, that a thing may be within the letter of the statute and yet not within the statute, because not within its spirit, nor within the intention of its makers").

system is equalized. Her selection of that methodology is therefore entitled to zero deference under *Chevron*.

I

The very structure of the Court's opinion provides an obvious clue as to what is afoot. The opinion purports to place a premium on the plain text of the Impact Aid statute, but it first takes us instead on a roundabout tour of "considerations *other* than language" — page after page of unenacted congressional intent and judicially perceived statutory purpose. Only after we are shown "why Zuni concentrates its argument upon language alone" are we informed how the statute's plain text does not unambiguously *preclude* the interpretation the Court thinks best. This is a most suspicious order of proceeding, since our case law is full of statements such as "We begin, as always, with the language of the statute," and replete with the affirmation that, when "given a straightforward statutory command, there is no reason to resort to legislative history." Nor is this cart-before-the-horse approach justified by the Court's excuse that the statute before us is, after all, a technical one. This Court, charged with interpreting, among other things, the Internal Revenue Code, the Employee Retirement Income Security Act of 1974, and the Clean Air Act, confronts technical language all the time, but we never see fit to pronounce upon what we think Congress *meant* a statute to say, and what we think sound policy would *counsel* it to say, before considering what it *does* say. As almost a majority of today's majority worries, "were the inversion of inquiry to become systemic, it would create the impression that agency policy concerns, rather than the traditional tools of statutory construction, are shaping the judicial interpretation of statutes." *Ante*, at 107 (Kennedy, J., joined by Alito, J., concurring). True enough — except I see no reason to wait for the distortion to become systemic before concluding that that is precisely what is happening in the present case. For some, policy-driven interpretation is apparently just fine. See *ante*, at 105 (Stevens, J., concurring). But for everyone else, let us return to Statutory Interpretation 101.

We must begin, as we always do, with the text. . . .

The casual observer will notice that the Secretary's implementing regulations do not look much like the statute. The regulations first require the Secretary to rank all of the LEAs [(local educational agencies)] in a State (New Mexico has 89) according to their per-pupil expenditures or revenues. So far so good. But critically here, the Secretary must then "identify those LEAs that fall at the 95th and 5th percentiles *of the total number of pupils in attendance* in the schools of those LEAs." Finally, the Secretary compares the per-pupil figures of *those two* LEAs for the purpose of assessing whether a State exceeds the 25% disparity measure. The majority concludes that this method of calculation, with its focus on student population, is a permissible interpretation of the statute.

It most assuredly is not. To understand why, one first must look beyond the smokescreen that the Court lays down with its repeated apologies for inexperience in statistics, and its endless recitation of technical mathematical definitions of the word "percentile." This case is not a scary math problem; it is a straightforward matter of statutory interpretation. And we do not need the Court's hypothetical cadre of number-crunching *amici* to guide our way.

There is no dispute that for purposes relevant here "'percentile' refers to a division of a distribution of *some* population into 100 parts." And there is further no dispute that the statute concerns the percentile of "per-pupil expenditures or revenues," for that is what the word "such" refers to. The question is: Whose per-pupil expenditures or revenues? Or, in the Court's terminology, what "population" is assigned the "characteristic" "per-pupil expenditure or revenue"? At first blush, second blush, or twenty-second blush, the answer is abundantly clear: local educational agencies. The statute requires the Secretary to "disregard local educational agencies with" certain per-pupil figures above or below specified percentages of those per-pupil figures. The attribute "per-pupil expenditure or revenue" is assigned to LEAs — there is no mention of student population whatsoever. And thus under the statute, "per-pupil expenditures or revenues" are to be arrayed using a population consisting of LEAs, so that percentiles are determined from a list of (in New Mexico) 89 per-pupil expenditures or revenues representing the 89 LEAs in the State. It is just that simple.

. . . .

In sum, the plain language of the Impact Aid statute compels the conclusion that the Secretary's method of calculation is ultra vires. Employing the formula that the statute requires, New Mexico is not equalized.

II

How, then if the text is so clear, are respondents managing to win this case? The answer can only be the return of that miraculous redeemer of lost causes, *Church of the Holy Trinity*. In order to contort the statute's language beyond recognition, the Court must believe Congress's intent so crystalline, the spirit of its legislation so glowingly bright, that the statutory text should simply not be read to say what it says. Justice Stevens is quite candid on the point: He is willing to contradict the text.[3] But Justice Stevens' candor should not make his philosophy seem unassuming. He maintains that it is "a correct performance of the judicial function" to "override a strict interpretation of the text" so long as policy-driven interpretation "is faithful to the intent of Congress." But once one departs from "strict interpretation of the text" (by which Justice Stevens means the actual meaning of the text) fidelity to the intent of Congress is a chancy thing. The only thing we know for certain both Houses of Congress (and the President, if he signed the legislation) agreed upon is the text.

---

3. Like Justice Stevens, respondents themselves were aboveboard when they litigated this case at the administrative level. After hearing argument from the Department of Education, the Administrative Law Judge (ALJ) protested: "The problem is I don't see the ambiguity of the statute." To this the Department's counsel responded: "The only way I can do that is by reference to the statutory purpose." Later in the hearing, the ALJ similarly asked the State of New Mexico how its interpretation was consistent with the statute. The State answered: "Literally, on the face of the words, perhaps not, probably not." Despite his misgivings, the ALJ ultimately decided that he did not possess the authority to invalidate the regulations.

Legislative history can never produce a "pellucidly clear" picture of what a law was "intended" to mean, for the simple reason that it is never voted upon — or ordinarily even seen or heard — by the "intending" lawgiving entity, which consists of both Houses of Congress and the President (if he did not veto the bill). See U.S. Const., Art. I, §§ 1, 7. Thus, what judges believe Congress "meant" (apart from the text) has a disturbing but entirely unsurprising tendency to be whatever judges think Congress *must* have meant, *i.e.*, *should* have meant. In *Church of the Holy Trinity*, every Justice on this Court disregarded the plain language of a statute that forbade the hiring of a clergyman from abroad because, after all (they thought), "this is a Christian nation," so Congress could not have meant what it said. Is there any reason to believe that those Justices were lacking that "intellectual honesty" that Justice Stevens "presumes" all our judges possess? Intellectual honesty does not exclude a blinding intellectual bias. And even if it did, the system of judicial amendatory veto over texts adopted by Congress bears no resemblance to the system of lawmaking set forth in our Constitution.

Justice Stevens takes comfort in the fact that this is a case in which he "cannot imagine anyone accusing any Member of the Court of voting one way or the other because of that Justice's own policy preferences." I can readily imagine it, given that the Court's opinion begins with a lengthy description of why the system its judgment approves is the *better* one. But even assuming that, in this rare case, the Justices' departure from the enacted law has nothing to do with their policy view that it is a bad law, nothing in Justice Stevens' separate opinion limits his approach to such rarities. Why should we suppose that in matters more likely to arouse the judicial libido — voting rights, antidiscrimination laws, or environmental protection, to name only a few — a judge in the School of Textual Subversion would not find it convenient (yea, *righteous!*) to assume that Congress *must* have meant, not what it said, but what he knows to be best?

Lest there be any confusion on the point, I must discuss briefly the two cases Justice Stevens puts forward as demonstrating this Court's recent endorsement of his unorthodox views. *Griffin v. Oceanic Contractors, Inc.* involved a maritime statute that required the master of a vessel to furnish unpaid wages to a seaman within a specified period after the seaman's discharge, and further provided that a master who failed to do so without sufficient cause "'shall pay to the seaman a sum equal to two days' pay for each and every day during which payment is delayed.'" We explained that "Congress intended the statute to mean exactly what its plain language says," and held that the seaman was entitled to double wages for every day during which payment was delayed, even for the period in which he had obtained alternative employment. The result was that the seaman would receive approximately $300,000 for his master's improper withholding of $412.50, even though "it was probably true that Congress did not precisely envision the grossness of the difference between the actual wages withheld and the amount of the award required by the statute." We suggested in dicta that there might be a "rare case" in which the Court could relax its steadfastness to statutory text, but if *Griffin* itself did not qualify, it is hard to imagine what would. The principle Justice Stevens would ascribe to *Griffin* is in fact the one he advocated in dissent. "This is one of the cases in which the exercise of judgment dictates a departure from the literal text in order to be faithful to the legislative will." *Id.* at 586 (Stevens, J., dissenting).

The second case Justice Stevens relies upon, *United States v. Ron Pair Enterprises, Inc.,* is equally inapt. The Court's opinion there (unlike the one here) explained that our analysis "must begin with the language of the statute itself," and concluded that that was "also where the inquiry should end, for where the statute's language is plain, 'the sole function of the courts is to enforce it according to its terms.'" My "fifth vote" in *Ron Pair* was thus only "decisive" in reaffirming this Court's adherence to statutory text, decisively preventing it from falling off the precipice it plunges over today.

Contrary to the Court and Justice Stevens, I do not believe that what we are sure the Legislature *meant* to say can trump what it *did* say. Citizens arrange their affairs not on the basis of their legislators' unexpressed intent, but on the basis of the law as it is written and promulgated. I think it terribly unfair to expect that the two rural school districts who are petitioners here should have pored over some 30 years of regulatory history to divine Congress's "real" objective (and with it the "real" intent that a majority of Justices would find honest and true). To be governed by legislated text rather than legislators' intentions is what it means to be "a Government of laws, not of men." And in the last analysis the opposite approach is no more beneficial to the governors than it is to the governed. By "depriving legislators of the assurance that ordinary terms, used in an ordinary context, will be given a predictable meaning," we deprive Congress of a "sure means by which it may work the people's will."

I do not purport to know what Congress thought it was doing when it amended the Impact Aid program in 1994. But even indulging Justice Stevens' erroneous premise that there exists a "legislative intent" separate and apart from the statutory text, I do not see how the Court can possibly say, with any measure of confidence, that Congress wished one thing rather than another. There is ample evidence, for example, that at the time it amended the Impact Aid statute, Congress knew exactly how to incorporate student population into a disparity calculation. Most prominently, in the *very same* Act that added § 7709(b)(2)(B)(i) to the Impact Aid program, Congress established the Education Finance Incentive Program, known as EFIG. That statute allocates grants to States based on an "equity factor" which requires a disparity calculation similar to that in the Impact Aid statute. In EFIG, however, Congress specifically required the Secretary to take student population into account . . . . And there is more. In EFIG, Congress *expressly provided* that a State would be accorded a favorable "equity factor" rating if it was considered equalized under the Secretary's *Impact Aid regulations*. Congress thus explicitly incorporated the Impact Aid regulations into EFIG, but did no such thing with respect to the Impact Aid statute itself. All this on the very same day.

Nor do I see any significance in the fact that no legislator in 1994 expressed the view that § 7709(b)(2)(B)(i) was designed to upend the Secretary's equalization formula. It is quite plausible — indeed, eminently plausible — that the Members of Congress took the plain meaning of the language *which the Secretary himself had proposed* to be what the Secretary himself had previously been doing. It is bad enough for this Court to consider legislative materials beyond the statutory text in aid of resolving ambiguity, but it is truly unreasonable to *require* such extratextual evidence as a precondition for enforcing an *unambiguous* congressional mandate. The Court points to the fact that "no Member of Congress has ever criticized the method the Secretary's regulations sets forth." But can it really be that this case turns, in the Court's view, on whether a freshman Congressman from New Mexico gave a floor speech that only late-night C-SPAN junkies would witness? The only fair inference from Congress's silence is that Congress had nothing further to say, its statutory text doing all of the talking.

Finally, the Court expresses its belief that Congress must have intended to adopt the Secretary's pre-1994 disparity test because that test is the more reasonable one, better able to account for States with small numbers of large LEAs, or large numbers of small ones. This, to tell the truth, is the core of the opinion. As I have suggested, it is no accident that the countertextual legislative intent judges perceive *invariably* accords with what the judges think best. It seems to me, however, that this Court is no more capable of saying with certainty what is best in this area than it is of saying with certainty (apart from the text) what Congress intended. . . .

. . . .

The only sure indication of what Congress intended is what Congress enacted; and even if there is a difference between the two, the rule of law demands that the latter prevail. This case will live with *Church of the Holy Trinity* as an exemplar of judicial disregard of crystal-clear text. We must interpret the law as Congress has written it, not as we would wish it to be. I would reverse the judgment of the Court of Appeals.

JUSTICE SOUTER, dissenting.

I agree with the Court that Congress probably intended, or at least understood, that the Secretary would continue to follow the methodology devised prior to passage of the current statute in 1994. But for reasons set out in Justice Scalia's dissent, I find the statutory language unambiguous and inapt to authorize that methodology, and I therefore join Part I of his dissenting opinion.

Notes and Questions

1. Does it now appear that *Chevron* is (or remains) the starting point in this area, at least in the eyes of a majority of the members of the Court? If so, then why the disagreement among the Justices? Also, notice that Justice Scalia, though purporting to follow *Chevron*, would not defer to the Secretary's regulation. Why not?

2. Consider again the various opinions in *Zuni*. Which best describes the approach of Justice Breyer (who delivered the opinion of the Court): intentionalist, purposivist, or textualist? What about Justice Stevens? Justice Scalia?

3. In *Talk America, Inc. v. Michigan Bell Tel. Phone Co.*, 131 S. Ct. 2254 (2011), the Supreme Court stated with respect to the interpretation of a *regulation*:

> In the absence of any unambiguous statute or regulation, we turn to the [agency's] interpretation of its regulations in its *amicus* brief. See, *e.g.*, *Chase Bank USA, N. A.* v. *McCoy*, 131 S. Ct. 871, 880 (2011). As we reaffirmed earlier this Term, we defer to an agency's interpretation of its regulations, even in a legal brief, unless the interpretation is " 'plainly erroneous or inconsistent with the regulations' " or there is any other " 'reason to suspect that the interpretation does not reflect the agency's fair and considered judgment on the matter in question.' " *Id.*, at 880, 881 (quoting *Auer* v. *Robbins*, 519 U. S. 452, 461, 462 (1997)).

Id. at 2260-61. But in a concurring opinion, Justice Scalia opined:

> I would reach the same result even without the benefit of the rule that we will defer to an agency's interpretation of its own regulations, a rule in recent years attributed to our opinion in *Auer* v. *Robbins*, 519 U. S. 452, 461 (1997), thought it first appeared in our jurisprudence more than half a century earlier, see *Bowles* v. *Seminole Rock & Sand Co.*, 325 U. S. 410 (1945). . . .
>
> It is comforting to know that I would reach the Court's result even without *Auer*. For while I have in the past uncritically accepted that rule, I have become increasingly doubtful of its validity. On the surface, it seems to be a natural corollary — indeed, an *a fortiori* application — of the rule that we will defer to an agency's interpretation of the statute it is charged with implementing, see *Chevron U. S. A.* v. *Natural Resources Defense Council, Inc.*, 467 U. S. 837 (1984). But it is not. When Congress enacts an imprecise statute that it commits to the implementation of an executive agency, it has no control over that implementation (except, of course, through further, more precise, legislation). The legislative and executive functions are not combined. But when an agency promulgates an imprecise rule, it leaves *to itself* the implementation of that rule, and thus the initial determination of the rule's meaning. And though the adoption of a rule is an exercise of the executive rather than the legislative power, a properly adopted rule has fully the effect of law. It seems contrary to fundamental principles of separation of powers to permit the person who promulgates a law to interpret it as well. "When the legislative and executive powers are united in the same person, or in the same body of magistrates, there can be no liberty; because apprehensions may arise, lest the same monarch or senate should enact tyrannical laws, to execute them in a tyrannical manner." Montesquieu, Spirit of the Laws bk. XI, ch. 6, pp. 151-152 (O. Piest ed., T. Nugent transl. 1949).
>
> Deferring to an agency's interpretation of a statute does not encourage Congress, out of a desire to expand its power, to enact vague statutes; the vagueness effectively cedes power to the Executive. By contrast, deferring to an agency's interpretation of its own rule encourages the agency to enact vague rules which give it the power, in future adjudications, to do what it pleases. This frustrates the notice and predictability purposes of rulemaking, and promotes arbitrary government. The seeming inappropriateness of *Auer* deference is especially evident in cases such as these, involving an agency that has repeatedly been rebuked in its attempts to expand the statute beyond its text, and has repeatedly sought new means to the same ends.
>
> There are undoubted advantages to *Auer* deference. It makes the job of a reviewing court much easier, and since it usually produces affirmance of the agency's view without conflict in the Circuits, it imparts (once the agency has spoken to clarify the regulation) certainty and predictability to the administrative process.

The defects of *Auer* deference, and the alternatives to it, are fully explored in Manning, Constitutional Structure and Judicial Deference to Agency Interpretations of Agency Rules, 96 Colum. L. Rev. 612 (1996). We have not been asked to reconsider *Auer* in the present case. When we are, I will be receptive to doing so.

Id. at 2266 (Scalia, J., concurring). (Justice Scalia recently expanded on these thoughts in *Decker v. Northwest Environmental Defense Center*, 133 S. Ct. 1326, 1339-42 (2013) (Scalia, J., concurring in part and dissenting in part).) What do you think of Justice Scalia's concerns? Does he have a valid point?

4. Though many cases involving the interpretation of statutes by agencies have been decided by the Court since *Chevron* was decided, the "*Chevron* doctrine," for the most part, appears to be quite alive and well. For very recent applications of *Chevron*, see *Holder v. Martinez Gutierrez*, 132 S. Ct. 2011 (2012); *Astrue v. Capato*, 132 S. Ct. 576 (2012); and *Mayo Foundation for Med. Ed. & Research v. United States*, 131 S. Ct. 704 (2011).

4. The Latest Word

City of Arlington v. Federal Communications Commission

133 S. Ct. 1863 (2013)

JUSTICE SCALIA delivered the opinion of the Court.

We consider whether an agency's interpretation of a statutory ambiguity that concerns the scope of its regulatory authority (that is, its jurisdiction) is entitled to deference under *Chevron U. S. A. Inc. v. Natural Resources Defense Council, Inc.*, 467 U. S. 837 (1984).

. . . .

II

A

As this case turns on the scope of the doctrine enshrined in *Chevron*, we begin with a description of that case's now-canonical formulation. "When a court reviews an agency's construction of a statute which it administers, it is confronted with two questions." First, applying the ordinary tools of statutory construction, the court must determine "whether Congress has directly spoken to the precise question at issue. If the intent of Congress is clear, that is the end of the matter; for the court, as well as the agency, must give effect to the unambiguously expressed intent of Congress." But "if the statute is silent or ambiguous with respect to the specific issue, the question for the court is whether the agency's answer is based on a permissible construction of the statute."

Chevron is rooted in a background presumption of congressional intent: namely, "that Congress, when it left ambiguity in a statute" administered by an agency, "understood that the ambiguity would be resolved, first and foremost, by the agency, and desired the agency (rather than the courts) to possess whatever degree of discretion the ambiguity allows." *Chevron* thus provides a stable background rule against which Congress can legislate: Statutory ambiguities will be resolved, within the bounds of reasonable interpretation, not by the courts but by the administering agency. Congress knows to speak in plain terms when it wishes to circumscribe, and in capacious terms when it wishes to enlarge, agency discretion.

B

The question here is whether a court must defer under *Chevron* to an agency's interpretation of a statutory ambiguity that concerns the scope of the agency's statutory authority (that is, its jurisdiction). The argument against deference rests on the premise that there exist two distinct classes of agency interpretations: Some interpretations — the big, important ones, presumably — define the agency's "jurisdiction." Others — humdrum, run-of-the-mill stuff — are simply applications of jurisdiction the agency plainly has. That premise is false, because the distinction between "jurisdictional" and "nonjurisdictional" interpretation is a mirage. No matter how it is framed, the question a court faces when confronted with an agency's interpretation of a statute it administers is always, simply, *whether the agency has stayed within the bounds of its statutory authority.*

The misconception that there are, for *Chevron* purposes, separate "jurisdictional" questions on which no deference is due derives, perhaps, from a reflexive extension to agencies of the very real division between the jurisdictional and nonjurisdictional that is applicable to courts. In the judicial context, there *is* a meaningful line: Whether the court decided *correctly* is a question that has different consequences from the question whether it had the power to decide *at all.* Congress has the power (within limits) to tell the courts what classes of cases they may decide, but not to prescribe or superintend how they decide those cases, see *Plaut v. Spendthrift Farm, Inc.,* 514 U. S. 211, 218-219 (1995). A court's power to decide a case is independent of whether its decision is correct, which is why even an erroneous judgment is entitled to res judicata effect. Put differently, a jurisdictionally proper but substantively incorrect judicial decision is not ultra vires.

That is not so for agencies charged with administering congressional statutes. Both their power to act and how they are to act is authoritatively prescribed by Congress, so that when they act improperly, no less than when they act beyond their jurisdiction, what they do is ultra vires. Because the question — whether framed as an incorrect application of agency authority or an assertion of authority no conferred — is always whether the agency has gone beyond what Congress has permitted it to do, there is no principled basis for carving out some arbitrary subset of such claims as "jurisdictional."

An example will illustrate just how illusory the proposed line between "jurisdictional" and "nonjurisdictional" agency interpretations is. Imagine the following validly-enacted statute:

COMMON CARRIER ACT

SECTION 1. The Agency shall have jurisdiction to prohibit any common carrier from imposing an unreasonable condition upon access to its facilities.

There is no question that this provision — including the terms "common carrier" and "unreasonable condition" — defines the Agency's jurisdiction. Surely, the argument goes, a court must determine *de novo* the scope of that jurisdiction.

Consider, however, this alternative formulation of the statute:

COMMON CARRIER ACT

SECTION 1. No common carrier shall impose an unreasonable condition upon access to its facilities.

SECTION 2. The Agency may prescribe rules and regulations necessary in the public interest to effectuate Section 1 of this Act.

Now imagine that the Agency, invoking its Section 2 authority, promulgates this Rule: "(1) The term 'common carrier' in Section 1 includes Internet Service Providers. (2) The term 'unreasonable condition' in Section 1 includes unreasonably high prices. (3) A monthly fee greater than $25 is an unreasonable condition on access to Internet service." By this Rule, the Agency has claimed for itself jurisdiction that is doubly questionable: Does its authority extend to Internet Service Providers? And does it extend to setting prices? Yet Section 2 makes clear that Congress, in petitioners' words, "conferred interpretive power on the agency" with respect to Section 1. Even under petitioners' theory, then, a court should defer to the Agency's interpretation of the terms "common carrier" and "unreasonable condition" — that is to say, its assertion that its "jurisdiction" extends to regulating Internet Service Providers and setting prices.

In the first case, by contrast, petitioners' theory would accord the agency no deference. The trouble with this is that in both cases, the underlying question is *exactly the same*: Does the statute give the agency authority to regulate Internet Service Providers and cap prices, or not? The reality, laid bare, is that there is *no difference*, insofar as the validity of agency action is concerned, between an agency's exceeding the scope of its authority (its "jurisdiction") and its exceeding authorized application of authority it unquestionably has. "To exceed authorized application is to exceed authority. Virtually any administrative action can be characterized as either the one or the other, depending on how generally one wishes to describe 'authority.'"

. . . .

In sum, judges should not waste their time in the mental acrobatics needed to decide whether an agency's interpretation of a statutory provision is "jurisdictional" or "nonjurisdictional." Once those labels are sheared away, it becomes clear that the question in every case is, simply, whether the statutory text forecloses the agency's assertion of authority, or not. The federal judge as haruspex, sifting the entrails of vast statutory schemes to divine whether a particular agency interpretation qualifies as "jurisdictional," is not engaged in reasoned decisionmaking.

C

Fortunately, then, we have consistently held "that *Chevron* applies to cases in which an agency adopts a construction of a jurisdictional provision of a statute it administers." 1 R. Pierce, Administrative Law Treatise §3.5, p. 187 (2010)....

. . . .

The false dichotomy between "jurisdictional" and "nonjurisdictional" agency interpretations may be no more than a bogeyman, but it is dangerous all the same. Like the Hound of the Baskervilles, it is conjured by those with greater quarry in sight: Make no mistake — the ultimate target here is *Chevron* itself. Savvy challengers of agency action would play the "jurisdictional" card in every case. Some judges would be deceived by the specious, but scary-sounding, "jurisdictional"-"nonjurisdictional" line; others tempted by the prospect of making public policy by prescribing the meaning of ambiguous statutory commands. The effect would be to transfer any number of interpretive decisions — archetypal *Chevron* questions, about how best to construe an ambiguous term in light of competing policy interests — from the agencies that administer the statutes to federal courts.[4] We have cautioned that "judges ought to refrain from substituting their own interstitial lawmaking" for that of an agency. That is precisely what *Chevron* prevents.

III

. . . .

B

A few words in response to the dissent. The question on which we granted certiorari was whether "a court should apply *Chevron* to review an agency's determination of its own jurisdiction." Pet. for Cert. i.[5] Perhaps sensing the incoherence of the "jurisdictional-nonjurisdictional" line, the dissent does not even attempt to defend it, but proposes a much broader scope for *de novo* judicial review: Jurisdictional or not, and even where a rule is at issue and the statute contains a broad grant of rulemaking

---

4. The Chief Justice's discomfort with the growth of agency power is perhaps understandable. But the dissent overstates when it claims that agencies exercise "legislative power" and "judicial power." The former is vested exclusively in Congress, U. S. Const., Art. I, §1, the latter in "one supreme Court" and "such inferior Courts as the Congress may from time to time ordain and establish," Art. III, §1. Agencies make rules ("Private cattle may be grazed on public lands *X, Y,* and *Z* subject to certain conditions") and conduct adjudications ("This rancher's grazing permit is revoked for violation of the conditions") and have done so since the beginning of the Republic. These activities take "legislative" and "judicial" forms, but they are exercises of — indeed, under our constitutional structure they *must* be exercises of — the "executive Power." Art. II, §1, cl. 1.

5. The dissent — apparently with no attempt at irony — accuses us of "misunderstanding" the question presented as one of "jurisdiction." Whatever imprecision inheres in our understanding of the question presented derives solely from our having read it.

authority, the dissent would have a court search provision-by-provision to determine "whether that delegation covers the 'specific provision' and 'particular question' before the court."

The dissent is correct that *United States v. Mead Corp.* requires that, for *Chevron* deference to apply, the agency must have received congressional authority to determine the particular matter at issue in the particular manner adopted. No one disputes that. But *Mead* denied *Chevron* deference to action, by an agency with rulemaking authority, that was not rulemaking. What the dissent needs, and fails to produce, is a single case in which a general conferral of rulemaking or adjudicative authority has been held insufficient to support *Chevron* deference for an exercise of that authority within the agency's substantive field. There is no such case, and what the dissent proposes is a massive revision of our *Chevron* jurisprudence.

Where we differ from the dissent is in its apparent rejection of the theorem that the whole includes all of its parts — its view that a general conferral of rulemaking authority does not validate rules for *all* the matters the agency is charged with administering. Rather, the dissent proposes that even when general rulemaking authority is clear, *every* agency rule must be subjected to a *de novo* judicial determination of whether *the particular issue* was committed to agency discretion. It offers no standards at all to guide this open-ended hunt for congressional intent (that is to say, for evidence of congressional intent more specific that the conferral of general rulemaking authority). It would simply punt that question back to the Court of Appeals, presumably for application of some sort of totality-of-the-circumstances test — which is really, of course, not a test at all but an invitation to make an ad hoc judgment regarding congressional intent. Thirteen Courts of Appeals applying a totality-of-the-circumstances test would render the binding effect of agency rules unpredictable and destroy the whole stabilizing purpose of *Chevron*. The excessive agency power that the dissent fears would be replaced by chaos. There is no need to wade into these murky waters. It suffices to decide this case that the preconditions to deference under *Chevron* are satisfied because Congress has unambiguously vested the FCC with general authority to administer the Communications Act through rulemaking and adjudication, and the agency interpretation at issue was promulgated in the exercise of that authority.

* * * *

Those who assert that applying *Chevron* to "jurisdictional" interpretations "leaves the fox in charge of the henhouse" overlook the reality that a separate category of "jurisdictional" interpretations does not exist. The fox-in-the-henhouse syndrome is to be avoided not by establishing an arbitrary and undefinable category of agency decisionmaking that is accorded no deference, but by taking seriously, and applying rigorously, in all cases, statutory limits on agencies' authority. Where Congress has established a clear line, the agency cannot go beyond it; and where Congress has established an ambiguous line, the agency can go no further than the ambiguity will fairly allow. But in rigorously applying the latter rule, a court need not pause to puzzle over whether the interpretive question presented is "jurisdictional." If "the agency's answer is based on a permissible construction of the statute," that is the end of the matter. *Chevron*, 467 U. S., at 842.

The judgment of the Court of Appeals is affirmed.

Notes and Questions

---

1. After *City of Arlington*, is there any interpretation of a statute by the agency to which it relates that is not governed by *Chevron*? If so, what?

2. Should courts ever defer to agency interpretations of statutes? Is not statutory interpretation the role of the judiciary, at least as it relates to cases and controversies within their jurisdiction?

3. Do you agree that there is a distinction between that which is "jurisdictional" and that which is "nonjurisdictional" that applies to courts, but not agencies?

5. The Effect of Judicial Interpretation on Administrative Interpretation

As you might recall, in *Mead*, Justice Scalia, in dissent, expressed the following concern with respect to the Court's failure to accord *Chevron* deference to the administrative ruling at issue:

> Worst of all, the majority's approach will lead to the ossification of large portions of our statutory law. Where *Chevron* applies, statutory ambiguities remain ambiguities subject to the agency's ongoing clarification. They create a space, so to speak, for the exercise of continuing agency discretion. As *Chevron* itself held, the Environmental Protection Agency can interpret "stationary source" to mean a single smokestack, can later replace that interpretation with the "bubble concept" embracing an entire plant, and if that proves undesirable can return again to the original interpretation. For the indeterminately large number of statutes taken out of *Chevron* by today's decision, however, ambiguity (and hence flexibility) will cease with the first judicial resolution. *Skidmore* deference gives the agency's current position some vague and uncertain amount of respect, but it does not, like *Chevron*, *leave* the matter within the control of the Executive Branch for the future. Once the court has spoken, it becomes *unlawful* for the agency to take a contradictory position; the statute now *says* what the court has prescribed.

United States v. Mead, 533 U.S. 218, 247 (2001) (Scalia, J., dissenting). The argument, in other words, is that a judicial determination that *Chevron* applies allows an agency to possibly alter its position in the future, whereas a determination that *Chevron* does not apply might compel a court to definitively resolve the meaning of the underlying statute, thereby preventing (under stare decisis) an agency from adopting a contrary interpretation. This concern — valid or not — is the subject of the following two cases.

National Cable & Tel. Assn. v. Brand X Internet Services

545 U.S. 967 (2005)

JUSTICE THOMAS delivered the opinion of the Court.

Title II of the Communications Act of 1934, 48 Stat. 1064, as amended, 47 U.S.C. § 151 *et seq.*, subjects all providers of "telecommunications servic[e]" to mandatory common-carrier regulation, § 153(44). In the order under review, the Federal Communications Commission concluded that cable companies that sell broadband Internet service do not provide "telecommunications servic[e]" as the Communications Act defines that term, and hence are exempt from mandatory common-carrier regulation under Title II. We must decide whether that conclusion is a lawful construction of the Communications Act under *Chevron U.S.A. Inc.* v. *Natural Resources Defense Council, Inc.*, 467 U.S. 837 (1984), and the Administrative Procedure Act, 5 U.S.C. § 555 *et seq.* We hold that it is.

I

The traditional means by which consumers in the United States access the network of interconnected computers that make up the Internet is through "dial-up" connections provided over local telephone facilities. Using these connections, consumers access the Internet by making calls with computer modems through the telephone wires owned by local phone companies. Internet service providers (ISPs), in turn, link those calls to the Internet network, not only by providing a physical connection, but also by offering consumers the ability to translate raw Internet data into information they may both view on their personal computers and transmit to other computers connected to the Internet. Technological limitations of local telephone wires, however, retard the speed at which data from the Internet may be transmitted through end users' dial-up connections. Dial-up connections are therefore known as "narrowband," or slower speed, connections.

"Broadband" Internet service, by contrast, transmits data at much higher speeds. There are two principal kinds of broadband Internet service: cable modem service and Digital Subscriber Line (DSL) service. Cable modem service transmits data between the Internet and users' computers via the network of television cable lines owned by cable companies. DSL service provides high-speed access using the local telephone wires owned by local telephone companies. Cable companies and telephone companies can either provide Internet access directly to consumers, thus acting as ISPs themselves, or can lease their transmission facilities to independent ISPs that then use the facilities to provide consumers with Internet access. Other ways of transmitting high-speed Internet data into homes, including terrestrial- and satellite-based wireless networks, are also emerging.

II

At issue in these cases is the proper regulatory classification under the Communications Act of broadband cable Internet service. The Act, as amended by the Telecommunications Act of 1996, 110 Stat. 56, defines two categories of regulated entities relevant to these cases: telecommunications carriers and information-service providers. The Act regulates telecommunications carriers, but not information-service providers, as common carriers. Telecommunications carriers, for example, must charge just and reasonable, nondiscriminatory rates to their customers, design their systems so that other carriers can interconnect with their communications networks, and contribute to the federal "universal service" fund. These provisions are mandatory, but the Commission must forbear from applying them if it determines that the public interest requires it. Information-service providers, by contrast, are not subject to mandatory common-carrier regulation under Title II, though the Commission has jurisdiction to impose additional regulatory obligations under its Title I ancillary jurisdiction to regulate interstate and foreign communications.

. . . .

In September 2000, the Commission initiated a rulemaking proceeding to, among other things, apply these classifications to cable companies that offer broadband Internet service directly to consumers. In March 2002, that rulemaking culminated in the *Declaratory Ruling* under review in these cases. In the *Declaratory Ruling*, the Commission concluded that broadband Internet service provided by cable companies is an "information service" but not a "telecommunications service" under the Act, and therefore not subject to mandatory Title II common-carrier regulation. . . .

. . . .

. . . Numerous parties petitioned for judicial review, challenging the Commission's conclusion that cable modem service was not telecommunications service. By judicial lottery, the Court of Appeals for the Ninth Circuit was selected as the venue for the challenge.

The Court of Appeals granted the petitions in part, vacated the *Declaratory Ruling* in part, and remanded to the Commission for further proceedings. In particular, the Court of Appeals vacated the ruling to the extent it concluded that cable modem service was not "telecommunications service" under the Communications Act. It held that the Commission could not permissibly construe the Communications Act to exempt cable companies providing Internet service from Title II regulation. Rather than analyzing the permissibility of that construction under the deferential framework of *Chevron*, however, the Court of Appeals grounded its holding in the *stare decisis* effect of *AT&T Corp.* v. *Portland*, 216 F.3d 871 (CA9 2000). *Portland* held that cable modem service was a "telecommunications service," though the court in that case was not reviewing an administrative proceeding and the Commission was not a party to the case. Nevertheless, *Portland*'s holding, the Court of Appeals reasoned, overrode the contrary interpretation reached by the Commission in the *Declaratory Ruling*.

We granted certiorari to settle the important questions of federal law that these cases present.

III

We first consider whether we should apply *Chevron*'s framework to the Commission's interpretation of the term "telecommunications service." We conclude that we should. We also conclude that the Court of Appeals should have done the same, instead of following the contrary construction it adopted in *Portland*.

A

In *Chevron*, this Court held that ambiguities in statutes within an agency's jurisdiction to administer are delegations of authority to the agency to fill the statutory gap in reasonable fashion. Filling these gaps, the Court explained, involves difficult policy choices that agencies are better equipped to make than courts. If a statute is ambiguous, and if the implementing agency's construction is reasonable, *Chevron* requires a federal court to accept the agency's construction of the statute, even if the agency's reading differs from what the court believes is the best statutory interpretation.

The *Chevron* framework governs our review of the Commission's construction. Congress has delegated to the Commission the authority to "execute and enforce" the Communications Act, § 151, and to "prescribe such rules and regulations as may be necessary in the public interest to carry out the provisions" of the Act, § 201(b). These provisions give the Commission the authority to promulgate binding legal rules; the Commission issued the order under review in the exercise of that authority; and no one questions that the order is within the Commission's jurisdiction. Hence, as we have in the past, we apply the *Chevron* framework to the Commission's interpretation of the Communications Act.

Some of the respondents dispute this conclusion, on the ground that the Commission's interpretation is inconsistent with its past practice. We reject this argument. Agency inconsistency is not a basis for declining to analyze the agency's interpretation under the *Chevron* framework. Unexplained inconsistency is, at most, a reason for holding an interpretation to be an arbitrary and capricious change from agency practice under the Administrative Procedure Act. See *Motor Vehicle Mfrs. Assn. of United States, Inc.* v. *State Farm Mut. Automobile Ins. Co.*, 463 U.S. 29, 46-57 (1983). For if the agency adequately explains the reasons for a reversal of policy, "change is not invalidating, since the whole point of *Chevron* is to leave the discretion provided by the ambiguities of a statute with the implementing agency." "An initial agency interpretation is not instantly carved in stone. On the contrary, the agency . . . must consider varying interpretations and the wisdom of its policy on a continuing basis," *Chevron*, *supra*, at 863-864, for example, in response to changed factual circumstances, or a change in administrations, see *State Farm*, *supra*, at 59 (Rehnquist, J., concurring in part and dissenting in part). That is no doubt why in *Chevron* itself, this Court deferred to an agency interpretation that was a recent reversal of agency policy. See 467 U.S., at 857-858. We therefore have no difficulty concluding that *Chevron* applies.

B

The Court of Appeals declined to apply *Chevron* because it thought the Commission's interpretation of the Communications Act foreclosed by the conflicting construction of the Act it had adopted in *Portland, supra.* It based that holding on the assumption that *Portland*'s construction overrode the Commission's, regardless of whether *Portland* had held the statute to be unambiguous. That reasoning was incorrect.

A court's prior judicial construction of a statute trumps an agency construction otherwise entitled to *Chevron* deference only if the prior court decision holds that its construction follows from the unambiguous terms of the statute and thus leaves no room for agency discretion. This principle follows from *Chevron* itself. *Chevron* established a "presumption that Congress, when it left ambiguity in a statute meant for implementation by an agency, understood that the ambiguity would be resolved, first and foremost, by the agency, and desired the agency (rather than the courts) to possess whatever degree of discretion the ambiguity allows." Yet allowing a judicial precedent to foreclose an agency from interpreting an ambiguous statute, as the Court of Appeals assumed it could, would allow a court's interpretation to override an agency's. *Chevron*'s premise is that it is for agencies, not courts, to fill statutory gaps. The better rule is to hold judicial interpretations contained in precedents to the same demanding *Chevron* step one standard that applies if the court is reviewing the agency's construction on a blank slate: Only a judicial precedent holding that the statute unambiguously forecloses the agency's interpretation, and therefore contains no gap for the agency to fill, displaces a conflicting agency construction.

A contrary rule would produce anomalous results. It would mean that whether an agency's interpretation of an ambiguous statute is entitled to *Chevron* deference would turn on the order in which the interpretations issue: If the court's construction came first, its construction would prevail, whereas if the agency's came first, the agency's construction would command *Chevron* deference. Yet whether Congress has delegated to an agency the authority to interpret a statute does not depend on the order in which the judicial and administrative constructions occur. The Court of Appeals' rule, moreover, would "lead to the ossification of large portions of our statutory law," *Mead, supra,* at 247 (Scalia, J., dissenting), by precluding agencies from revising unwise judicial constructions of ambiguous statutes. Neither *Chevron* nor the doctrine of *stare decisis* requires these haphazard results.

The dissent answers that allowing an agency to override what a court believes to be the best interpretation of a statute makes "judicial decisions subject to reversal by Executive officers." *Post*, at 13 (opinion of Scalia, J.). It does not. Since *Chevron* teaches that a court's opinion as to the best reading of an ambiguous statute an agency is charged with administering is not authoritative, the agency's decision to construe that statute differently from a court does not say that the court's holding was legally wrong. Instead, the agency may, consistent with the court's holding, choose a different construction, since the agency remains the authoritative interpreter (within the limits of reason) of such statutes. In all other respects, the court's prior ruling remains binding law (for example, as to agency interpretations to which *Chevron* is inapplicable). The precedent has not been "reversed" by the agency, any more than a federal court's interpretation of a State's law can be said to have been "reversed" by a state court that adopts a conflicting (yet authoritative) interpretation of state law.

. . . .

Against this background, the Court of Appeals erred in refusing to apply *Chevron* to the Commission's interpretation of the definition of "telecommunications service."

Its prior decision in *Portland* held only that the *best* reading of § 153(46) was that cable modem service was a "telecommunications service," not that it was the *only permissible* reading of the statute. Nothing in *Portland* held that the Communications Act unambiguously required treating cable Internet providers as telecommunications carriers. Instead, the court noted that it was "not presented with a case involving potential deference to an administrative agency's statutory construction pursuant to the *Chevron* doctrine," and the court invoked no other rule of construction (such as the rule of lenity) requiring it to conclude that the statute was unambiguous to reach its judgment. Before a judicial construction of a statute, whether contained in a precedent or not, may trump an agency's, the court must hold that the statute unambiguously requires the court's construction. *Portland* did not do so.

As the dissent points out, it is not logically necessary for us to reach the question whether the Court of Appeals misapplied *Chevron* for us to decide whether the Commission acted lawfully. Nevertheless, it is no "great mystery" why we are reaching the point here. There is genuine confusion in the lower courts over the interaction between the *Chevron* doctrine and *stare decisis* principles, as the petitioners informed us at the certiorari stage of this litigation. The point has been briefed. And not reaching the point could undermine the purpose of our grant of certiorari: to settle authoritatively whether the Commission's *Declaratory Ruling* is lawful. Were we to uphold the *Declaratory Ruling* without reaching the *Chevron* point, the Court of Appeals could once again strike down the Commission's rule based on its *Portland* decision. *Portland* (at least arguably) could compel the Court of Appeals once again to reverse the Commission despite our decision, since our conclusion that it is *reasonable* to read the Communications Act to classify cable modem service solely as an "information service" leaves untouched *Portland*'s holding that the Commission's interpretation is not the *best* reading of the statute. We have before decided similar questions that were not, strictly speaking, necessary to our disposition. See, *e.g., Agostini* v. *Felton,* 521 U.S. 203, 237 (1997) (requiring the Courts of Appeals to adhere to our directly controlling precedents, even those that rest on reasons rejected in other decisions); *Roper* v. *Simmons,* 543 U.S. 551, 628-629 (2005) (SCALIA, J., dissenting) (criticizing this Court for not reaching the question whether the Missouri Supreme Court erred by failing to follow directly controlling Supreme Court precedent, though that conclusion was not necessary to the Court's decision). It is prudent for us to do so once again today.

IV

We next address whether the Commission's construction of the definition of "telecommunications service" is a permissible reading of the Communications Act under the *Chevron* framework. *Chevron* established a familiar two-step procedure for evaluating whether an agency's interpretation of a statute is lawful. At the first step, we ask whether the statute's plain terms "directly addres[s] the precise question at issue." If the statute is ambiguous on the point, we defer at step two to the agency's interpretation so long as the construction is "a reasonable policy choice for the agency to make." The Commission's interpretation is permissible at both steps.

. . . .

V

Respondent MCI, Inc., urges that the Commission's treatment of cable modem service is inconsistent with its treatment of DSL service, see *supra*, at 3 (describing DSL service), and therefore is an arbitrary and capricious deviation from agency policy. See 5 U.S.C. § 706(2)(A). . . .

We conclude, however, that the Commission provided a reasoned explanation for treating cable modem service differently from DSL service. . . .

. . . We find nothing arbitrary about the Commission's providing a fresh analysis of the problem as applied to the cable industry, which it has never subjected to these rules. This is adequate rational justification for the Commission's conclusions.

. . . .

The questions the Commission resolved in the order under review involve a "subject matter [that] is technical, complex, and dynamic." The Commission is in a far better position to address these questions than we are. Nothing in the Communications Act or the Administrative Procedure Act makes unlawful the Commission's use of its expert policy judgment to resolve these difficult questions. The judgment of the Court of Appeals is reversed, and the cases are remanded for further proceedings consistent with this opinion.

It is so ordered.

JUSTICE STEVENS, concurring.

While I join the Court's opinion in full, I add this caveat concerning Part III-B, which correctly explains why a court of appeals' interpretation of an ambiguous provision in a regulatory statute does not foreclose a contrary reading by the agency. That explanation would not necessarily be applicable to a decision by this Court that would presumably remove any pre-existing ambiguity.

JUSTICE SCALIA, with whom JUSTICE SOUTER and JUSTICE GINSBURG join as to Part I, dissenting.

. . . .

II

In Part III-B of its opinion, the Court continues the administrative-law improvisation project it began four years ago in *United States* v. *Mead Corp.* To the extent it set forth a comprehensible rule,[8] *Mead* drastically limited the categories of agency action that would qualify for deference under *Chevron*. For example, the position taken by an agency before the Supreme Court, with full approval of the agency head, would not qualify. Rather, some unspecified degree of formal process was required — or was at least the only safe harbor.

---

8. For a description of the confusion *Mead* has produced in the D.C. Circuit alone, see Vermeule, *Mead* in the Trenches, 71 Geo. Wash. L. Rev. 347, 361 (2003) (concluding that "the Court has inadvertently sent the lower courts stumbling into a no-man's land").

This meant that many more issues appropriate for agency determination would reach the courts without benefit of an agency position entitled to *Chevron* deference, requiring the courts to rule on these issues *de novo*. As I pointed out in dissent, this in turn meant (under the law as it was understood until today) that many statutory ambiguities that might be resolved in varying fashions by successive agency administrations, would be resolved finally, conclusively, and forever, by federal judges — producing an "ossification of large portions of our statutory law." The Court today moves to solve this problem of its own creation by inventing yet another breathtaking novelty: judicial decisions subject to reversal by Executive officers.

Imagine the following sequence of events: FCC action is challenged as ultra vires under the governing statute; the litigation reaches all the way to the Supreme Court of the United States. The Solicitor General sets forth the FCC's official position (approved by the Commission) regarding interpretation of the statute. Applying *Mead*, however, the Court denies the agency position *Chevron* deference, finds that the *best* interpretation of the statute contradicts the agency's position, and holds the challenged agency action unlawful. The agency promptly conducts a rulemaking, and adopts a rule that comports with its earlier position — in effect disagreeing with the Supreme Court concerning the best interpretation of the statute. According to today's opinion, the agency is thereupon free to take the action that the Supreme Court found unlawful.

This is not only bizarre. It is probably unconstitutional. As we held in *Chicago & Southern Air Lines, Inc.* v. *Waterman S.S. Corp.*, 333 U.S. 103 (1948), Article III courts do not sit to render decisions that can be reversed or ignored by Executive officers. In that case, the Court of Appeals had determined it had jurisdiction to review an order of the Civil Aeronautics Board awarding an overseas air route. By statute such orders were subject to Presidential approval and the order in question had in fact been approved by the President. In order to avoid any conflict with the President's foreign-affairs powers, the Court of Appeals concluded that it would review the board's action "as a regulatory agent of Congress," and the results of that review would remain subject to approval or disapproval by the President. As I noted in my *Mead* dissent, the Court bristled at the suggestion: "Judgments within the powers vested in courts by the Judiciary Article of the Constitution may not lawfully be revised, overturned or refused faith and credit by another Department of Government." That is what today's decision effectively allows. Even when the agency itself is party to the case in which the Court construes a statute, the agency will be able to disregard that construction and seek *Chevron* deference for its contrary construction the next time around.[12]

Of course, like *Mead* itself, today's novelty in belated remediation of *Mead* creates many uncertainties to bedevil the lower courts. A court's interpretation is conclusive,

---

12. The Court contends that no reversal of judicial holdings is involved, because "a court's opinion as to the best reading of an ambiguous statute . . . is not authoritative." That fails to appreciate the difference between a *de novo* construction of a statute and a decision whether to defer to an agency's position, which does not even "*purport* to give the statute a judicial interpretation." *Mead, supra*, at 248 (Scalia, J., dissenting). Once a court has decided upon its *de novo* construction of the statute, there no longer is a "different construction" that is "consistent with the court's holding," and available for adoption by the agency.

the Court says, only if it holds that interpretation to be "the *only permissible* reading of the statute," and not if it merely holds it to be "the *best* reading." Does this mean that in future statutory-construction cases involving agency-administered statutes courts must specify (presumably in dictum) which of the two they are holding? And what of the many cases decided in the past, before this dictum's requirement was established? Apparently, silence on the point means that the court's decision is subject to agency reversal: "Before a judicial construction of a statute, whether contained in a precedent or not, may trump an agency's, the court must hold that the statute unambiguously requires the court's construction." (I have not made, and as far as I know the Court has not made, any calculation of how many hundreds of past statutory decisions are now agency-reversible because of failure to include an "unambiguous" finding. I suspect the number is very large.) How much extra work will it entail for each court confronted with an agency-administered statute to determine whether it has reached, not only the right ("best") result, but "the only permissible" result? Is the standard for "unambiguous" under the Court's new agency-reversal rule the same as the standard for "unambiguous" under step one of *Chevron*? (If so, of course, every case that reaches step two of *Chevron* will be agency-reversible.) Does the "unambiguous" dictum produce *stare decisis* effect even when a court is *affirming*, rather than *reversing*, agency action — so that in the future the agency *must adhere* to that affirmed interpretation? If so, does the victorious agency have the right to appeal a Court of Appeals judgment in its favor, on the ground that the text in question is in fact *not* (as the Court of Appeals held) unambiguous, so the agency should be able to change its view in the future?

It is indeed a wonderful new world that the Court creates, one full of promise for administrative-law professors in need of tenure articles and, of course, for litigators.[14] I would adhere to what has been the rule in the past: When a court interprets a statute without *Chevron* deference to agency views, its interpretation (whether or not asserted to rest upon an unambiguous text) is the law. I might add that it is a great mystery why any of this is relevant here. *Whatever* the *stare decisis* effect of *AT&T Corp.* v. *Portland,* 216 F.3d 871 (CA9 2000), in the Ninth Circuit, it surely does not govern this Court's decision. And — despite the Court's peculiar, self-abnegating suggestion to the contrary — the Ninth Circuit would already be obliged to abandon *Portland's* holding in the face of *this Court's* decision that the Commission's construction of "telecommunications service" is entitled to deference and is reasonable. It is a sadness that the Court should go so far out of its way to make bad law.

I respectfully dissent.

---

14. Further de-ossification may already be on the way, as the Court has hinted that an agency construction unworthy of *Chevron* deference may be able to trump one of our statutory-construction holdings. In *Edelman* v. *Lynchburg College*, 535 U.S. 106, 114 (2002), the Court found "no need to resolve any question of deference" because the Equal Employment Opportunity Commission's rule was "the position we would adopt even if . . . we were interpreting the statute from scratch." It nevertheless refused to say whether the agency's position was "the only one permissible." Justice O'Connor appropriately "doubt[ed] that it is possible to reserve" the question whether a regulation is entitled to *Chevron* deference "while simultaneously maintaining . . . that the agency is free to change its interpretation" in the future. *Id.,* at 122 (opinion concurring in judgment). In response, the Court cryptically said only that "not all deference is deference under *Chevron.*" *Id.,* at 114, n. 8.

Notes and Questions

1. Which opinion do you find more persuasive—the Court's, or the dissent? Why?

2. Review the Court's discussion of the *State Farm* case in part III. A of its opinion. Notice the distinction between a review of agency action under the Administrative Procedure Act (*see supra* at 744)—such as occurred in *State Farm*—which asks, *inter alia*, whether an agency action (or change in agency action) is arbitrary or capricious, and the inquiry under *Chevron*, which asks whether an agency's interpretation of an ambiguous statute is reasonable.

3. Notice Justice Steven's concurrence, in which he argues that a Supreme Court interpretation of a regulatory statute would bind an agency, whereas a court of appeals' interpretation would not. Why? Do you agree?

United States v. Home Concrete & Supply, LLC

132 S. Ct. 1836 (2012)

JUSTICE BREYER delivered the opinion of the Court, except as to Part IV-C.

Ordinarily, the Government must assess a deficiency against a taxpayer within "3 years after the return was filed." 26 U. S. C. §6501(a). The 3-year period is extended to 6 years, however, when a taxpayer "omits from gross income an amount properly includible therein which is in excess of 25 percent of the amount of gross income stated in the return." §6501(e)(1)(A) (emphasis added). The question before us is whether this latter provision applies (and extends the ordinary 3-year limitations period) when the taxpayer overstates his basis in property that he has sold, thereby understating the gain that he received from its sale. Following *Colony, Inc. v. Commissioner,* 357 U. S. 28 (1958), we hold that the provision does not apply to an overstatement of basis. Hence the 6-year period does not apply.

. . . .

In our view, *Colony* determines the outcome in this case. The provision before us is a 1954 reenactment of the 1939 provision that interpreted. The operative language is identical. It would be difficult, perhaps impossible, to give the same language here a different interpretation without effectively overruling *Colony,* a course of action that basic principles of stare decisis wisely counsel us not to take. *John R. Sand & Gravel Co. v. United States,* 552 U. S. 130, 139 (2008) ("[S]tare decisis in respect to statutory interpretation has special force, for Congress remains free to alter what we have done" (internal quotation marks omitted)); *Patterson v. McLean Credit Union,* 491 U. S. 164-173 (1989).

. . . .

IV

A

Finally, the Government points to Treasury Regulation §301.6501(e)-1, which was promulgated in final form in December 2010. The regulation, as relevant here, departs from *Colony* and interprets the operative language of the statute in the Government's favor. The regulation says that "an understated amount of gross income resulting from an overstatement of unrecovered cost or other basis constitutes an omission from gross income." §301.6501(e)-1(a)(1)(iii). In the Government's view this new regulation in effect overturns *Colony*'s interpretation of this statute.

The Government points out that the Treasury Regulation constitutes "an agency's construction of a statute which it administers." *Chevron, U. S. A. Inc. v. Natural Resources Defense Council, Inc.*, 467 U. S. 837, 842 (1984). The Court has written that a "court's prior judicial construction of a statute trumps an agency construction otherwise entitled to *Chevron* deference only if the prior court decision holds that its construction follows from the unambiguous terms of the statute . . . ." *National Cable & Telecommunications Assn. v. Brand X Internet Services*, 545 U. S. 967, 982 (2005) (emphasis added). And, as the Government notes, in *Colony* itself the Court wrote that "it cannot be said that the language is unambiguous." 357 U. S., at 33. Hence, the Government concludes, *Colony* cannot govern the outcome in this case. The question, rather, is whether the agency's construction is a "permissible construction of the statute." *Chevron, supra*, at 843. And, since the Government argues that the regulation embodies a reasonable, hence permissible, construction of the statute, the Government believes it must win.

B

We do not accept this argument. In our view, *Colony* has already interpreted the statute, and there is no longer any different construction that is consistent with *Colony* and available for adoption by the agency.

C

The fatal flaw in the Government's contrary argument is that it overlooks the *reason why Brand X* held that a "prior judicial construction," unless reflecting an "unambiguous" statute, does not trump a different agency construction of that statute. The Court reveals that reason when it points out that "it is for agencies, not courts, to fill statutory gaps." The fact that a statute is unambiguous means that there is "no gap for the agency to fill" and thus "no room for agency discretion."

In so stating, the Court sought to encapsulate what earlier opinions, including *Chevron*, made clear. Those opinions identify the underlying interpretive problem as that of deciding whether, or when, a particular statute in effect delegates to an agency the power to fill a gap, thereby implicitly taking from a court the power to void a reasonable gap-filling interpretation. Thus, in *Chevron* the Court said that, when

> "Congress has explicitly left a gap for the agency to fill, there is an express delegation of authority to the agency to elucidate a specific provision of the statute by regulation. . . . Sometimes the legislative delegation to an agency on a particular question is implicit

rather than explicit. [But in either instance], a court may not substitute its own construction of a statutory provision for a reasonable interpretation made by the administrator of an agency."

Chevron and later cases find in unambiguous language a clear sign that Congress did not delegate gap-filling authority to an agency; and they find in ambiguous language at least a presumptive indication that Congress did delegate that gap-filling authority. Thus, in *Chevron* the Court wrote that a statute's silence or ambiguity as to a particular issue means that Congress has not "directly addressed the precise question at issue" (thus likely delegating gap-filling power to the agency). In *Mead* the Court, describing *Chevron*, explained:

> "Congress . . . may not have expressly delegated authority or responsibility to implement a particular provision or fill a particular gap. Yet it can still be apparent from the agency's generally conferred authority and other statutory circumstances that Congress would expect the agency to be able to speak with the force of law when it addresses ambiguity in the statute or fills a space in the enacted law, even one about which Congress did not actually have an intent as to a particular result."

Chevron added that "[i]f a court, *employing traditional tools of statutory construction*, ascertains that Congress had an intention on the precise question at issue, that intention is the law and must be given effect."

As the Government points out, the Court in *Colony* stated that the statutory language at issue is not "unambiguous." But the Court decided that case nearly 30 years before it decided *Chevron*. There is no reason to believe that the linguistic ambiguity noted by *Colony* reflects a post-*Chevron* conclusion that Congress had delegated gap-filling power to the agency. At the same time, there is every reason to believe that the Court thought that Congress had "directly spoken to the question at hand," and thus left "[no] gap for the agency to fill."

For one thing, the Court said that the taxpayer had the better side of the textual argument. For another, its examination of legislative history led it to believe that Congress had decided the question definitively, leaving no room for the agency to reach a contrary result. It found in that history "persuasive indications" that Congress intended overstatements of basis to fall outside the statute's scope, and it said that it was satisfied that Congress "intended an exception . . . only in the restricted type of situation" it had already described. Further, it thought that the Commissioner's interpretation (the interpretation once again advanced here) would "create a patent incongruity in the tax law." And it reached this conclusion despite the fact that, in the years leading up to *Colony*, the Commissioner had consistently advocated the opposite in the circuit courts. Thus, the Court was aware it was rejecting the expert opinion of the Commissioner of Internal Revenue. And finally, after completing its analysis, *Colony* found its interpretation of the 1939 Code "in harmony with the [now] unambiguous language" of the 1954 Code, which at a minimum suggests that the Court saw nothing in the 1954 Code as inconsistent with its conclusion.

It may be that judges today would use other methods to determine whether Congress left a gap to fill. But that is beside the point. The question is whether the Court in *Colony* concluded that the statute left such a gap. And, in our view, the opinion (written by Justice Harlan for the Court) makes clear that it did not.

Given principles of stare decisis, we must follow that interpretation. And there being no gap to fill, the Government's gap-filling regulation cannot change *Colony*'s interpretation of the statute. We agree with the taxpayer that overstatements of basis, and the resulting understatement of gross income, do not trigger the extended limitations period of §6501(e)(1)(A). The Court of Appeals reached the same conclusion. And its judgment is affirmed.

. . . .

JUSTICE SCALIA, concurring in part and concurring in the judgment.

It would be reasonable, I think, to deny all precedential effect to *Colony, Inc. v. Commissioner*, 357 U. S. 28 (1958) — to overrule its holding as obviously contrary to our later law that agency resolutions of ambiguities are to be accorded deference. Because of justifiable taxpayer reliance I would not take that course — and neither does the Court's opinion, which says that "*Colony* determines the outcome in this case." That should be the end of the matter.

The plurality, however, goes on to address the Government's argument that Treasury Regulation §301.6501(e)-1 effectively overturned *Colony*. In my view, that cannot be: "Once a court has decided upon its *de novo* construction of the statute, there no longer is a different construction that is consistent with the court's holding and available for adoption by the agency." *National Cable & Telecommunications Assn. v. Brand X Internet Services*, 545 U. S. 967, n. 12 (2005) (SCALIA, J., dissenting) (citation and internal quotation marks omitted). That view, of course, did not carry the day in *Brand X*, and the Government quite reasonably relies on the *Brand X* majority's innovative pronouncement that a "court's prior judicial construction of a statute trumps an agency construction otherwise entitled to *Chevron* deference only if the prior court decision holds that its construction follows from the unambiguous terms of the statute."

In cases decided pre-*Brand X*, the Court had no inkling that it must utter the magic words "ambiguous" or "unambiguous" in order to (poof!) expand or abridge executive power, and (poof!) enable or disable administrative contradiction of the Supreme Court. Indeed, the Court was unaware of even the utility (much less the necessity) of making the ambiguous/nonambiguous determination in cases decided pre-*Chevron*, before that opinion made the so-called "Step 1" determination of ambiguity *vel non* a customary (though hardly mandatory[1]) part of judicial-review analysis. For many of those earlier cases, therefore, it will be incredibly difficult to determine whether the decision purported to be giving meaning to an ambiguous, or rather an unambiguous, statute.

---

1. "Step 1" has never been an essential part of *Chevron* analysis. Whether a particular statute is ambiguous makes no difference if the interpretation adopted by the agency is clearly reasonable — and it would be a waste of time to conduct that inquiry. See *Entergy Corp. v. Riverkeeper, Inc.*, 556 U. S. 208 and n. 4 (2009). The same would be true if the agency interpretation is clearly beyond the scope of any conceivable ambiguity. It does not matter whether the word "yellow" is ambiguous when the agency has interpreted it to mean "purple." See Stephenson & Vermeule, *Chevron* Has Only One Step, 95 Va. L. Rev. 597, 599 (2009).

Thus, one would have thought that the *Brand X* majority would breathe a sigh of relief in the present case, involving a pre-*Chevron* opinion that (*mirabile dictu*) makes it inescapably clear that the Court thought the statute ambiguous: "It cannot be said that the language is unambiguous." *Colony, supra*, at 33 (emphasis added). As today's plurality opinion explains, *Colony* "said that the taxpayer had the better side of the textual argument" — not what *Brand X* requires to foreclose administrative revision of our decisions: "the *only permissible* reading of the statute." Thus, having decided to stand by *Colony* and to stand by *Brand X* as well, the plurality should have found — in order to reach the decision it did — that the Treasury Department's current interpretation was unreasonable.

Instead of doing what *Brand X* would require, however, the plurality manages to sustain the justifiable reliance of taxpayers by revising yet again the meaning of *Chevron* — and revising it yet again in a direction that will create confusion and uncertainty. See *United States v. Mead Corp.*, 533 U. S. 218-246 (2001) (SCALIA, J., dissenting); Bressman, How *Mead* Has Muddled Judicial Review of Agency Action, 58 Vand. L. Rev. 1443, 1457-1475 (2005). Of course there is no doubt that, with regard to the Internal Revenue Code, the Treasury Department satisfies the *Mead* requirement of some indication "that Congress delegated authority to the agency generally to make rules carrying the force of law." We have given *Chevron* deference to a Treasury Regulation before. But in order to evade *Brand X* and yet reaffirm *Colony*, the plurality would add yet another lopsided story to the ugly and improbable structure that our law of administrative review has become: To trigger the *Brand X* power of an authorized "gap-filling" agency to give content to an ambiguous text, a pre-*Chevron* determination that language is ambiguous does not alone suffice; the pre-*Chevron* Court must in addition have found that Congress wanted *the particular ambiguity in question* to be resolved by the agency. And here, today's plurality opinion finds, "[t]here is no reason to believe that the linguistic ambiguity noted by *Colony* reflects a post-*Chevron* conclusion that Congress had delegated gap-filling power to the agency." The notion, seemingly, is that post-*Chevron* a finding of ambiguity is accompanied by a finding of agency authority to resolve the ambiguity, but pre-*Chevron* that was not so. The premise is false. Post-*Chevron* cases do not "conclude" that Congress wanted the particular ambiguity resolved by the agency; that is simply the *legal effect* of ambiguity — a legal effect that should obtain whenever the language is in fact (as *Colony* found) ambiguous.

Does the plurality feel that it ought not give effect to *Colony*'s determination of ambiguity because the Court did not know, in that era, the importance of that determination — that it would empower the agency to (in effect) revise the Court's determination of statutory meaning? But as I suggested earlier, that was an ignorance which all of our cases shared not just pre-*Chevron*, but pre-*Brand X*. Before then it did not really matter whether the Court was resolving an ambiguity or setting forth the statute's clear meaning. The opinion might (or might not) advert to that point in the course of its analysis, but either way the Court's interpretation of the statute would be the law. So it is no small number of still-authoritative cases that today's plurality opinion would exile to the Land of Uncertainty.

Perhaps sensing the fragility of its new approach, the plurality opinion then pivots (as the *à la mode* vernacular has it) — from focusing on whether *Colony* concluded that there was gap-filling authority to focusing on whether *Colony* concluded that there was any gap to be filled: "The question is whether the Court in *Colony* concluded that the statute left such a gap. And, in our view, the opinion . . . makes clear that it did not." How does the plurality know this? Because Justice Harlan's opinion "said that the taxpayer had the better side of the textual argument"; because it found that legislative history indicated "that Congress intended overstatements of basis to fall outside the statute's scope"; because it concluded that the Commissioner's interpretation would "create a patent incongruity in the tax law"; and because it found its interpretation "in harmony with the [now] unambiguous language" of the 1954 Code. But these are the sorts of arguments that courts always use in resolving ambiguities. They do not prove that no ambiguity existed, unless one believes that an ambiguity resolved is an ambiguity that never existed in the first place. *Colony* said unambiguously that the text was ambiguous, and that should be an end of the matter — unless one wants simply to deny stare decisis effect to *Colony* as a pre-*Chevron* decision.

Rather than making our judicial-review jurisprudence curiouser and curiouser, the Court should abandon the opinion that produces these contortions, *Brand X.* I join the judgment announced by the Court because it is indisputable that *Colony* resolved the construction of the statutory language at issue here, and that construction must therefore control. And I join the Court's opinion except for Part IV-C.

* * * *

I must add a word about the peroration of the dissent, which asserts that "[o]ur legal system presumes there will be continuing dialogue among the three branches of Government on questions of statutory interpretation and application," and that the "constructive discourse," "'convers[ations],'" and "instructive exchanges" would be "foreclosed by an insistence on adhering to earlier interpretations of a statute even in light of new, relevant statutory amendments." Post, at 7-8 (opinion of KENNEDY, J.). This passage is reminiscent of Professor K. C. Davis's vision that administrative procedure is developed by "a partnership between legislators and judges," who "working [as] partners produce better law than legislators alone could possibly produce."[2] That romantic, judge-empowering image was obliterated by this Court in *Vermont Yankee Nuclear Power Corp. v. Natural Resources Defense Council, Inc.*, 435 U. S. 519 (1978), which held that Congress prescribes and we obey, with no discretion to add to the administrative procedures that Congress has created. It seems to me that the dissent's vision of a troika partnership (legislative-executive-judicial) is a similar mirage. The discourse, conversation, and exchange that the dissent perceives is peculiarly one-sided. Congress prescribes; and where Congress's prescription is ambiguous the Executive can (within the scope of the ambiguity) clarify that prescription; and if the product is constitutional the courts obey. I hardly think it amounts to a "discourse" that Congress or (as this Court would allow in its *Brand X* decision) the Executive can

---

2. 1 K. Davis, Administrative Law Treatise §2.17, p. 138 (1978).

change its prescription so as to render our prior holding irrelevant. What is needed for the system to work is that Congress, the Executive, and the private parties subject to their dispositions, be able to predict the meaning that the courts will give to their instructions. That goal would be obstructed if the judicially established meaning of a technical legal term used in a very specific context could be overturned on the basis of statutory indications as feeble as those asserted here.

JUSTICE KENNEDY, with whom JUSTICE GINSBURG, JUSTICE SOTOMAYOR, and JUSTICE KAGAN join, dissenting.

This case involves a provision of the Internal Revenue Code establishing an extended statute of limitations for tax assessment in cases where substantial income has been omitted from a tax return. The Treasury Department has determined that taxpayers omit income under this section not only when they fail to report a sale of property but also when they overstate their basis in the property sold. The question is whether this otherwise reasonable interpretation is foreclosed by the Court's contrary reading of an earlier version of the statute in *Colony, Inc. v. Commissioner*, 357 U. S. 28 (1958).

In *Colony* there was no need to decide whether the meaning of the provision changed when Congress reenacted it as part of the 1954 revision of the Tax Code. Although the main text of the statute remained the same, Congress added new provisions leading to the permissible conclusion that it would have a different meaning going forward. The *Colony* decision reserved judgment on this issue. In my view, the amended statute leaves room for the Department's reading. A summary of the reasons for concluding the Department's interpretation is permissible, and for this respectful dissent, now follows.

. . . .

II

In the instant case the Court concludes these statutory changes are "too fragile to bear the significant argumentative weight the Government seeks to place upon them." But in this context, the changes are meaningful. *Colony* made clear that the text of the earlier version of the statute could not be described as unambiguous, although it ultimately concluded that an overstatement of basis was not an omission from gross income. The statutory revisions, which were not considered in *Colony*, may not compel the opposite conclusion under the new statute; but they strongly favor it. As a result, there was room for the Treasury Department to interpret the new provision in that manner. See *Chevron U. S. A. Inc. v. Natural Resources Defense Council, Inc.*, 467 U. S. 837-845 (1984).

In an earlier case, and in an unrelated controversy not implicating the Internal Revenue Code, the Court held that a judicial construction of an ambiguous statute did not foreclose an agency's later, inconsistent interpretation of the same provision. *National Cable & Telecommunications Assn. v. Brand X Internet Services*, 545 U. S. 967-983 (2005) ("Only a judicial precedent holding that the statute unambiguously forecloses the agency's interpretation, and therefore contains no gap for the agency to fill, displaces a conflicting agency construction"). This general rule recognizes that filling gaps left by ambiguities in a statute "involves difficult policy choices that agencies are better equipped to make than courts." There has been no opportunity to decide whether the analysis would be any different if an agency sought to interpret an ambiguous statute in a way that was inconsistent with this Court's own, earlier reading of the law. See *id.*, at 1003 (Stevens, J., concurring).

These issues are not implicated here. In *Colony* the Court did interpret the same phrase that must be interpreted in this case. The language was in a predecessor statute, however, and Congress has added new language that, in my view, controls the analysis and should instruct the Court to reach a different outcome today. The Treasury Department's regulations were promulgated in light of these statutory revisions, which were not at issue in *Colony*. There is a serious difficulty to insisting, as the Court does today, that an ambiguous provision must continue to be read the same way even after it has been reenacted with additional language suggesting Congress would permit a different interpretation. Agencies with the responsibility and expertise necessary to administer ongoing regulatory schemes should have the latitude and discretion to implement their interpretation of provisions reenacted in a new statutory framework. And this is especially so when the new language enacted by Congress seems to favor the very interpretation at issue. The approach taken by the Court instead forecloses later interpretations of a law that has changed in relevant ways. Cf. *United States v. Mead Corp.*, 533 U. S. 218, 247 (2001) (SCALIA, J., dissenting) ("Worst of all, the majority's approach will lead to the ossification of large portions of our statutory law. Where *Chevron* applies, statutory ambiguities remain ambiguities subject to the agency's ongoing clarification"). The Court goes too far, in my respectful view, in constricting Congress's ability to leave agencies in charge of filling statutory gaps.

Our legal system presumes there will be continuing dialogue among the three branches of Government on questions of statutory interpretation and application. In some cases Congress will set out a general principle, to be administered in more detail by an agency in the exercise of its discretion. The agency may be in a proper position to evaluate the best means of implementing the statute in its practical application. Where the agency exceeds its authority, of course, courts must invalidate the regulation. And agency interpretations that lead to unjust or unfair consequences can be corrected, much like disfavored judicial interpretations, by congressional action. These instructive exchanges would be foreclosed by an insistence on adhering to earlier interpretations of a statute even in light of new, relevant statutory amendments. Courts instead should be open to an agency's adoption of a different interpretation where, as here, Congress has given new instruction by an amended statute.

Under the circumstances, the Treasury Department had authority to adopt its reasonable interpretation of the new tax provision at issue. This was also the conclusion reached in well-reasoned opinions issued in several cases before the Courts of Appeals.

The Department's clarification of an ambiguous statute, applicable to these taxpayers, did not upset legitimate settled expectations. Given the statutory changes described above, taxpayers had reason to question whether *Colony*'s holding extended to the revised §6501(e)(1). Having worked no change in the law, and instead having interpreted a statutory provision without an established meaning, the Department's regulation does not have an impermissible retroactive effect. It controls in this case.

* * * *

For these reasons, and with respect, I dissent.

Notes and Questions

---

1. Following *Home Concrete*, can you summarize the Court's rule for determining when an agency may interpret a statute in a manner contrary to a prior judicial interpretation? Can anyone?

Table of Cases

14 Penn Plaza LLC v. Pyett, 350
Ada v. Guam Society of Obstetricians and Gynecologists, 664
Adarand Constructors, Inc. v. Mineta, 354
Air Line Pilots Ass'n, Int'l v. O'Neill, 156
Alleyne v. United States, 150, 151
Almendarez-Torres v. United States, 206
American Trucking Ass'ns, Inc. v. Smith, 373
Anastasoff v. United States, 226, 244
Ashcroft v. Iqbal, 80
Asher v. Texas, 202
Ashwander v. TVA, 659
Astrue v. Capato, 736
Austin v. Southwark LBC,151, 152
Awad v. Ziriax, 284
Ayotte v. Planned Parenthood, 660

Bailey v. United States, 512, 517
Bazemore v. Friday, 68
Blanchard v. Bergeron, 547
Bonner v. City of Prichard, 206
Bowen v. Georgetown University Hospital, 621, 623, 639
Bradley v. School Board, 616, 621, 623, 639
Briggs v. Pennsylvania R. Co., 91
Brotherhood of Railroad Trainmen v. Baltimore & Ohio R.R., 523, 524
Brown v. Allen, 100, 215
Brown v. Bd. of Educ., 70
Bullock v. BankChampaign, N.A., 531
Burbank v. Ernst, 64
Bush v. Gore, 67, 80
Bush v. Vera, 68

Cabell v. Markham, 531
Calder v. Bull, 650, 655
Caminetti v. United States, 468, 473, 474
Camreta v. Greene, 225
Caperton v. A.T. Massey Coal Co., Inc., 412, 422
Carducci v. Regan, 340
Carmell v. Texas, 655
Carter v. United States, 524
Chaidez v. United States, 373
Cheney v. United States District Court for the District of Columbia, 411
Cheney v. United States District Court for the District of Columbia, Memorandum of Justice Scalia, 402

Chevron Oil Co. v. Huson, 364
Chevron U. S. A. Inc. v. Natural Resources Defense Council, Inc., 58, 350, 702, 706, 721, 734, 750
Chisom v. Roemer, 530
Christianson v. Colt Industries Operating Corp., 86, 224
Church of the Holy Trinity v. United States, 463, 466, 467, 468, 473, 474
Citizens United v. Federal Election Comm'n, 150
City of Arlington v. Federal Communications Commission, 736, 741
Clinton v. Jones, 659
Commissioner of Internal Revenue v. Estate of Bosch, 101
Conroy v. Aniskoff, 548, 549
Consumer Product Safety Commission v. GTE Sylvania, Inc., 559
Costco Wholesale Corp. v. Omega, S.A., 67

Danforth v. Minnesota, 373
Davis v. United States, 327
Davis v. Wakelee, 95
Day v. McDonough, 318
Dean v. United States, 500
Decker v. Northwest Environmental Defense Center, 736
District of Columbia Court of Appeals v. Feldman, 95

Easley v. Reuss, 92
Eastern Enterprises v. Apfel, 72, 656, 657
Equal Employment Opportunity Commission v. Arabian American Oil Co., 539
Estate of McMorris v. Commissioner of Internal Revenue, 210, 211
Exxon Mobil Corp. v. Allapattah Services, Inc., 551
Exxon Mobil Corp. v. Saudi Basic Industries Corp., 95, 96

FAA v. Cooper, 545
Factors Etc., Inc. v. Pro Arts, Inc., 114
FCC v. WJR, The Goodwill Station, Inc., 288
Forest Grove Sch. Dist. v. T.A., 557

Gonzales v. Thaler, 544
Gozlon-Peretz v. United States, 623, 640
Graham Co. Soil and Water Conservation Dist. v. United States, 549
Graham v. Florida, 279
Granberry v. Greer, 327

Great N. Ry. Co. v. Sunburst Oil & Ref. Co., 355
Green v. Bock Laundry Machine Co., 562
Greene v. Fisher, 373
Greenlaw v. United States, *327*, 350
Gregory v. Ashcroft, 545
Griffin v. Illinois, 355
Griffin v. Oceanic Contractors, Inc., *488*, 498, 499, 500, 562, 577,
Griffith v. Kentucky, 368

Hamilton v. Rathbone, 463
Hanna v. Plumer, 57
Harper v. Virginia Department of Taxation, 373
Harrington v. Richter, 318
Harris v. United States, 150, 151
Hart v. Massanari, 231
Helvering v. Hallock, 151
Henderson v. Shinseki, 56
Hertz v. Woodman, 67
Heydon's Case, 461
Holder v. Martinez Gutierrez, 736
Hollingsworth v. Perry, 456
Hopwood v. Texas, 66
Hutto v. Davis, 100

Illinois Brick Co. v. Illinois, 666
In re Blanchflower, 570
In re Complaint of Judicial Misconduct, 317
In re Korean Air Lines Disaster of September 1, 1983, 101, 152
In re Sanford Fork & Tool Co., 91
In Re Shell Oil Co., 295
In re Winship, 206

Jama v. Immigration and Customs Enforcement, 81
James B. Beam Distilling Co. v. Georgia, 373
Jerman v. Carlisle, McNellie, Rini, Kramer & Ulrich LPA, 558
John R. Sand & Gravel Co. v. United States, 148, 203
Johnson v. New Jersey, 363
Jones v. United States, 206

Kaiser Aluminum & Chemical Corp. v. Bonjourno, 639
Kamen v. Kemper Financial Services, Inc., 327
Kasten v. Saint-Gobain Performance Plastics, 702
Kokkonen v. Guardian Life Ins. Co., 81
Krupski v. Costa Crociere S.p.A., 552

Lampf, Pleva, Lipkind, Prupis, & Petigrow v. Gilberston, 80
Lance v. Dennis, 96
Landgraf v. USI Film Products, *623*, 639, 640, 642, 670
Lawrence v. Texas, 146

Lawson v. FMR LLC, 589
Legal Services Corp. v. Velazquez, 550
Lindh v. Murphy, 642
Linkletter v. Walker, *357*, 363
Lockhart v. Fretwell, 105
Lorillard v. Pons, 557

M'Culloch v. Maryland, 3
Marbury v. Madison, 3, 4
Marks v. United States, 69
Martin v. Coventry Fire Dist., 614
Mayo Foundation for Med. Ed. & Research v. United States, 736
McBoyle v. United States, 569
Medellin v. Texas, 3, 453, 454
Michigan v. Jackson, 148
Milavetz, Gallop & Milavetz, P.A. v. United States, 549
Miller v. Alabama, 279
Mitchell v. W. T. Grant Co., 148
Mohamad v. Palestinian Authority, 525
Montejo v. Louisiana, 148, 149, 150
Morrison v. Nat'l Australia Bank Ltd., 544
Moses H. Cone Memorial Hosp. v. Mercury Constr. Corp., 90
Muscarello v. United States, 517

National Ass'n of Home Builders v. Defenders of Wildlife, 658
National Cable & Tel. Assn. v. Brand X Internet Services, 742
National Federation of Indep. Business v. Sebelius, 663, 664
Neil v. Biggers, 66
New Hampshire v. Maine, 94
New Jersey v. T. L. O., 340
New York Times Co. v. United States, 67
Nix v. Hedden, 526

O'Connor v. Donaldson, 223

Padilla v. Kentucky, 373
Parker v. Ellis, 217
Patterson v. McLean Credit Union, 132
Payne v. Tennessee, 132, *134*, 145
Pegram v. Herdrich, 95
Pension Benefit Guaranty Corp. v. The LTV Corp., 553, 554
Pepper v. Hart, 552
Perez-Llamas v. Utah Court of Appeals, 285
Planned Parenthood of Southeastern Pa. v. Casey, 67, 70, 132, *138*
Plaut v. Spendthrift Farm, Inc., 666, 670
Pub. Serv. Comm'n of Wis. v. Wis. Tel. Co., 317

Quern v. Jordan, 91

Radzanower v. Touche Ross & Co., 657, 658
Railroad Cos. v. Schutte, 79
Reid v. Covert, 453
Republic of the Philippines v. Pimentel, 348
Republican Party v. White, 423, 424
Richards v. United States, 569
Riggs v. Palmer, 575
Rivers v. Roadway Express, Inc., 641, 642
Rodriguez de Quijas v. Shearson/American Express,
    Inc., 203, 204
Rodriguez v. United States, 524
Rogers v. Tennessee, 386
Romer v. Evans, 456
Rooker v. Fidelity Trust Co., 95
Roper v. Simmons, 275
Rubber Co. v. Goodyear, 3

Saint Francis College v. Al-Khazraji, 367
Salve Regina College v. Russell, 106
Schindler Elevator Corp. v. United States ex rel. Kirk,
    500
Schiro v. Indiana, 217
Schwegmann Bros. v. Calvert Distillers Corp., 549, 550
Sears v. Upton, 67
Shady Grove Orthopedic Assoc. v. Allstate Ins. Co., 81
Shannon v. United States, 560, 561
Shreve v. Cheesman, 156
Sibbald v. United States, 91
Singleton v. Commissioner, 212
Singleton v. Wulff, 348, 349
Skidmore v. Swift & Co., 700, 702
Smith v. United States, 500, 522, 529, 530
South Corp. v. United States, 210
St. Mary's Honor Ctr. v. Hicks, 81
Steffel v. Thompson, 105
Stogner v. California, 655
Stovall v. Denno, 363, 364
Sturges v. Crowninshield, 474, 475
Sullivan v. Finkelstein, 559, 560

Talk America, Inc. v. Michigan Bell Tel. Phone Co., 734,
    735, 736
Taniguchi v. Kan Pacific Saipan, Ltd., 531
Taylor v. Louisiana, 370, 371
Taylor v. McKeithen, 296, 297

Teague v. Lane, 370, 371, 372, 373
Tome v. United States, 551, 552
Town of Castle Rock v. Gonzales, 113, 114
Turner Broadcasting System, Inc. v. FCC, 402

*United States Bancorp Mortgage Co. v. Bonner Mall
    Partnership*, 218, 244
United States Nat'l Bank v. Independent Ins. Agents, 450
United States v. American Ry. Exp. Co., 350
United States v. American Trucking Associations, Inc.,
    475, 479, 480, 487
United States v. Bendolph, 325, 327
United States v. Booker, 666
United States v. Carver, 215
United States v. Church of the Holy Trinity, 467
United States v. Dion, 453
United States v. Estate of Romani, 554, 555
United States v. Florida East Coast Railway, 291
United States v. Home Concrete & Supply, LLC, 750
United States v. Juvenile Male, 130
United States v. Kirby, 538
United States v. Locke, 349, 500, 658
United States v. Mead Corp., 706, 721, 741
United States v. Resendiz-Ponce, 57
United States v. Ron Pair Enterprises, Inc., 493, 498, 499,
    500, 562, 577
United States v. Santos, 69
United States v. Seale, 131
United States v. Sec. Indus. Bank, 650
United States v. Verdugo-Urquidez, 218
United States v. Windsor, 525

Vartelas v. Holder, 642

Wal-Mart Stores, Inc. v. Dukes, 552
Watson v. United States, 517, 521, 522
Weisgram v. Marley Co., 342
White v. Murtha, 89
Wilko v. Swan, 204
Wisconsin Public Intervenor v. Mortier, 547, 548
Wisniewski v. United States, 131
Wood v. Milyard, 335
Woods v. Interstate Realty Co., 79
Youngstown Sheet & Tube Co. v. Sawyer, 686

Zuni Public School District v. Department of Education,
    722, 734

Table of Authorities

Michael Abramowicz & Maxwell Stearns, *Defining Dicta*, 57 STAN. L. REV. 953 (2005), 78, 79, 80, 152, 178

RUGGERO J. ALDISERT, OPINION WRITING (2d ed. 2009), 59

Ruggero J. Aldisert *et al.*, *Logic for Law Students: How to Think Like a Lawyer*, 69 U. PITT. L. REV. 1 (2007), 44

Mary G. Algero, *The Sources of Law and the Value of Precedent: A Comparative and Empirical Study of a Civil Law State in a Common Law Nation*, 65 LA. L. REV. 775 (2005), 150

ALI/UNIDROIT Principles of Transnational Civil Procedure (2004), 294, 318, 340, 342, 424

AMERICAN BAR ASSOCIATION, MODEL CODE OF JUDICIAL CONDUCT (2010), 411

American Bar Association, Rule of Law Initiative, http://www.abanet.org/rol/, 18

AMERICAN BAR ASSOCIATION, SECTION OF ADMINISTRATIVE LAW AND REGULATORY PRACTICE, A BLACKLETTER STATEMENT OF FEDERAL ADMINISTRATIVE LAW (2004), 692

AMERICAN BAR ASSOCIATION, TASK FORCE ON PRESIDENTIAL SIGNING STATEMENTS AND THE SEPARATION OF POWERS DOCTRINE, REPORT WITH RECOMMENDATIONS (2006), 682, 683

American Law Institute, *About the American Law Institute*, http://www.ali.org/doc/thisIsALI.pdf, 5

Ellen P. Aprill, *The Law of the Word: Dictionary Shopping in the Supreme Court*, 30 ARIZ. ST. L.J. 275 (1998), 527, 528, 529

B.J. Ard, Comment, *Interpreting by the Book: Legislative Drafting Manuals and Statutory Interpretation*, 120 YALE L.J. 185 (2010), 612

ASSOCIATION OF LEGAL WRITING DIRECTORS & DARBY DICKERSON, ALWD CITATION MANUAL: A PROFESSIONAL SYSTEM OF CITATION (4th ed. 2010), 217

Ballotpedia, http://ballotpedia.org/wiki/index.php/Main_Page, 456

Jennifer M. Bandy, Note, *Interpretive Freedom: A Necessary Component of Article III Judging*, 61 DUKE L.J. 651 (2011), 611

Christopher P. Banks, *Reversals of Precedent and Judicial Policy-Making: How Judicial Conceptions of Stare Decisis in the U.S. Supreme Court Influence Social Change*, 32 AKRON L. REV. 233 (1999), 145

Randy E. Barnett, *Interpretation and Construction*, 34 HARV. J.L. & PUB. POL'Y 65 (2011), 460

Amy Coney Barrett, *Stare Decisis and Due Process*, 74 U. COLO. L. REV. 1011 (2003), 399

Ittai Bar-Simon-Tov, *The Puzzling Resistance to Judicial Review of the Legislative Process*, 91 B.U. L. REV. 1915 (2011), 444

Charles Barzun, *The Forgotten Foundation of Hart and Sachs*, 99 VA. L. REV. 1 (2013), iv

Randy Beck, *Transtemporal Separation of Powers in the Law of Precedent*, 87 NOTRE DAME L. REV. 1405 (2012), 150

Hugh Baxter, *Managing Legal Change: The Transformation of Establishment Clause Law*, 46 U.C.L.A. L. REV. 343 (1998), 84

Aaron S. Bayer, *Home Circuit Rule*, NATL. L.J. 12 (April 27, 2009), 114

Aaron S. Bayer, *Judicial Section Reform: All Over the Map*, NATL. L.J. 10 (June 3, 2013), 424

Bernard W. Bell, *"No Motor Vehicles in the Park": Reviving the Hart-Fuller Debate to Introduce Statutory Construction*, 48 J. LEGAL EDUC. 88 (1998), 2

Ryan C. Black & James F. Spriggs II, *Citation and Depreciation of U.S. Supreme Court Precedent*, 10 J. EMPIR. LEGAL STUDIES 325 (2013), 178

BLACK'S LAW DICTIONARY (10th ed. 2014), 4, 5, 58, 64, 65, 66, 67, 85, 96, 218, 451, 528, 531

Bennett Boskey, *The American Law Institute: A Glimpse At Its Future*, 12 GREEN BAG 2D 255 (2009), 5

Peter Bozzo *et al.*, *Many Voices, One Court: The Origin and Role of Dissent in the Supreme Court*, 36 J. S. CT. HIST. 193 (2011), 72

C. Steven Bradford, *Following Dead Precedent: The Supreme Court's Ill-advised Rejection of Anticipatory Overruling*, 59 FORDHAM L. REV. 39 (1990), 96, 205

Curtis A. Bradley & Eric A. Posner, *Presidential Signing Statements and Executive Power*, 23 CONST. COMMENT. 307 (2006), 684

Tara L. Branum, *President or King? The Use and Abuse of Executive Orders in Modern-Day America*, 28 J. LEGIS. 1 (2002), 685, 689

Lisa Schultz Bressman & Abbe R. Gluck, *Statutory Interpretation from the Inside—An Empirical Study of Congressional Drafting, Delegation, and the Canons: Part II*, 66 STAN. L. REV. 725 (2014), 444

Lisa Schultz Bressman & Robert T. Thompson, *The Future of Agency Independence*, 63 VAND. L. REV. 599 (2010), 691

Stephen Breyer, *On the Uses of Legislative History in Interpreting Statutes*, 65 S. CAL. L. REV. 845 (1992), 550

Myron H. Bright, *The Spoken Word: In Defense of Oral Argument*, 72 IOWA L. REV. 35 (1986), 294

RONALD BENTON BROWN & SHARON JACOBS BROWN, STATUTORY INTERPRETATION: THE SEARCH FOR LEGISLATIVE INTENT (2002), 610

James J. Brudney & Lawrence Baum, *Oasis or Mirage: The Supreme Court's Thirst for Dictionaries in the Rehnquist and Roberts Eras*, 55 WM. & MARY L. REV. 483 (2013), 528

Vanessa K. Burrows, *Executive Orders: Issuance and Revocation* (CRS Report for Congress Mar. 25, 2010), 689, 690

GUIDO CALABRESI, A COMMON LAW FOR THE AGE OF STATUTES (1982), i

Stephen G. Calabresi, *"A Shining City on a Hill": American Exceptionalism and the Supreme Court's Practice of Relying on Foreign Law*, 86 B.U. L. REV. 1335 (2006), 285

Evan H. Caminker, *Why Must Inferior Courts Obey Superior Court Precedents?*, 46 STAN. L. REV. 817 (1994), 97, 99, 100

Richard B. Cappalli, *The Disappearance of Legal Method*, 70 TEMP. L. REV. 393 (1997), ii, 1

ROBERT C. CASAD & KEVIN M. CLERMONT, RES JUDICATA: A HANDBOOK ON ITS THEORY, DOCTRINE, AND PRACTICE (2001), 85

Michael Cavendish, *Diagonal Authority*, 8 FLA. COASTAL L. REV. 133 (2006), 100

Erwin Chemerinsky, *Challenging Direct Democracy*, 2007 MICH. ST. L. REV. 293, 456

Matthew R. Christiansen & William N. Eskridge, Jr., *Congressional Overrides of Supreme Court Interpretation Decisions, 1967-2011*, 92 TEXAS L. REV. 1317 (2014), 666

Cory S. Clement, Comment, *Perception and Persuasion in Legal Argumentation: Using Informal Fallacies and Cognitive Biases to Win the War of Words*, 2013 B.Y.U. L. REV. 319, 57

David R. Cleveland & Steven Wisotsky, *The Decline of Oral Argument in the Federal Courts of Appeals: A Modest Proposal for Reform*, 13 J. APP. PRAC. & PROCESS 119 (2012), 294

CODE OF CONDUCT FOR UNITED STATES JUDGES, *http://www.uscourts.gov/RulesAndPolicies/CodesOfConduct/CodeConductUnitedStatesJudges.aspx*, 411

David S. Cohen, *The Precedent-Based Voting Paradox*, 90 B.U. L. REV. 183 (2010), 72

Mathilde Cohen, *Sincerity and Reason Giving: When May Legal Decisionmakers Lie?*, 59 DEPAUL L. REV. 1091 (2010), 318

RONALD K.L. COLLINS & DAVID SKOVER, ON DISSENT— ITS MEANING IN AMERICA (2013), 72

Jordan Wilder Connors, *Note, Treating Like Subdecisions Alike: The Scope of Stare Decisis as Applied to Judicial Methodologies*, 108 COLUM. L. REV. 681 (2008), 80

John Contrubis, *Executive Orders and Proclamations* (CRS Report for Congress Mar. 9, 1999), 690

Curtis W. Copeland, *The Federal Rulemaking Process: An Overview* (CRS Report for Congress Feb. 22, 2011), 697

John Bernard Corr, *Retroactivity: A Study in Supreme Court Doctrine "As Applied,"* 61 N.C. L. REV. 745 (1983), 362

George Costello, *Statutory Interpretation: General Principles and Recent Trends* (CRS Report for Congress updated March 30, 2006), 610

Sarah M. R. Cravens, *Involved Appellate Judging*, 88 MARQ. L. REV. 251 (2004), 340

THOMAS E. CRONIN, DIRECT DEMOCRACY (1989), 456

FRANK B. CROSS, THE THEORY AND PRACTICE OF STATUTORY INTERPRETATION (1999), 610

Thomas S. Currier, *Time and Change in Judge-Made Law: Prospective Overruling*, 51 VA. L. REV. 201 (1965), 355

ANTHONY D'AMATO, INTRODUCTION TO LAW AND LEGAL THINKING (1996), ii

Jake Dear & Edward W. Jessen, *"Followed Rates" and Leading State Cases, 1940-2005*, 41 U.C. DAVIS L. REV. 683 (2007), 247

REED DICKERSON, THE INTERPRETATION AND APPLICATION OF STATUTES (1975), 457

Jeffrey C. Dobbins, *Structure and Precedent*, 108 MICH. L. REV. 1453 (2010), 100

Michael C. Dorf, *Dicta and Article III*, 142 U. PA. L. REV. 1997 (1994), 74

Michael C. Dorf, *Fallback Law*, 107 COLUM. L. REV. 303 (2007), 666

Tobias A. Dorsey, *Some Reflections on Not Reading the Statutes*, 10 GREEN BAG 2D 283 (2007), 451

Robert B. Dove, *Enactment of a Law* (1997), 444

Michael Downey, *The Delicate Balance of Booting Judges; Clients deserve impartiality, but alleging that a judge can't do the job fairly is a risky undertaking*, NATL. L.J. (online) (Nov. 4, 2013), 411

Martha Dragich, *Uniformity, Inferiority, and the Law of the Circuit Doctrine*, 56 LOYOLA L. REV. 535 (2010), 158

David M. Driesen, *Purposeless Construction*, 48 WAKE FOREST L. REV. 97 (2013), 605

Frank H. Easterbrook, *Statute's Domains*, 50 U. CHI. L. REV. 533 (1983), 614

Suzanne Ehrenberg, *Embracing the Writing-Centered Legal Process*, 89 Iowa L. Rev. 1159 (2004), 295

Eric Eisenberg, Note, *A Divine Comity: Certification (At Last) in North Carolina*, 58 Duke L.J. 69 (2008), 130

William N. Eskridge, Jr., Book Review, *The New Textualism and Normative Canons*, 113 Colum. L. Rev. 531 (2013), 498, 524, 538

William N. Eskridge, Jr., Dynamic Statutory Interpretation (1994), 605

William N. Eskridge, Jr., *Interpreting Legislative Inaction*, 87 Mich. L. Rev. 67 (1988), 553

William N. Eskridge, Jr., *Overriding Supreme Court Statutory Interpretation Decisions*, 101 Yale L.J. 331 (1991), 666

William N. Eskridge, Jr., *The New Textualism*, 37 UCLA L. Rev. 621 (1990), 547

William N. Eskridge, Jr. et al., Cases and Materials on Statutory Interpretation (2012), 444

William N. Eskridge, Jr. & Philip P. Frickey, *An Historical and Critical Introduction to* The Legal Process, *in* Henry M. Hart, Jr. & Albert M. Sacks, The Legal Process: Basic Problems in the Making and Application of Law cii (William N. Eskridge, Jr. & Philip P. Frickey eds., 1994), iii

William N. Eskridge, Jr. & Philip P., Frickey, *Foreword: Law as Equilibrium*, 108 Harv. L. Rev. 26 (1994), iv, 533

William N. Eskridge, Jr. & Phillip P. Frickey, *Quasi-Constitutional Law: Clear Statement Rules as Constitutional Lawmaking*, 45 Vand. L. Rev. 593 (1995), 545

William N. Eskridge, Jr. & Phillip P. Frickey, *Statutory Interpretation as Practical Reasoning*, 42 Stan. L. Rev. 321 (1990), 575

Richard H. Fallon, Jr., *Stare Decisis and the Constitution: An Essay on Constitutional Methodology*, 76 N.Y.U. L. Rev. 570 (2001), 201

David Feldman, Note, *Duck Hunting, Deliberating, and Disqualification:* Cheney v. U.S. District Court *and the Flaws of 28 U.S.C. § 455(A)*, 15 B.U. Pub. Int. L.J. 319 (2006), 411

Jill E. Fisch, *Rewriting History: The Propriety of Eradicating Prior Decisional Law Through Settlement and Vacatur*, 76 Cornell L. Rev. 589 (1991), 224

Chad Flanders, *Toward a Theory of Persuasive Authority*, 62 Okla. L. Rev. 55 (2009), 262, 274

William A. Fletcher, *Dissent*, 39 Golden Gate U. L. Rev. 291 (2009), 72

Sydney Foster, *Should Courts Give Stare Decisis Effect to Statutory Interpretation Methodology?*, 96 Geo. L.J. 1863 (2008), 611

Felix Frankfurter, *Reflections on the Reading of Statutes*, 47 Colum. L. Rev. 527 (1947), 610

Anthony J. Franze & R. Reeves Anderson, *The Supreme Court's reliance on amicus curiae in the 2011-12 term*, Natl. L.J. 18 (2012), 342

David C. Fredrick, The Art of Oral Advocacy (2003), 294

Monroe H. Freedman, *Duck-Blind Justice: Justice Scalia's Memorandum in the* Cheney *Case*, 18 Geo. J. Legal Ethics 229 (2004), 411

Barry Friedman, *The Wages of Stealth Overruling (With Particular Attention to* Miranda v. Arizona*)*, 99 Geo. L.J. 1 (2010), 205

Amanda Frost, *Certifying Questions to Congress*, 101 Nw. U. L. Rev. 1 (2007), 131

Amanda Frost, *The Limits of Advocacy*, 59 Duke L.J. 447 (2009), 85, 340, 341, 610, 611

Lon L. Fuller, *Positism and Fidelity to Law—A Reply to Professor Hart*, 71 Harv. L. Rev. 630 (1958), 2

Lon L. Fuller, *The Case of the Speluncean Explorers*, 112 Harv. L. Rev. 1851 (1999), 609

Lon L. Fuller, *The Forms and Limits of Adjudication*, 92 Harv. L. Rev. 353 (1978), 27

Lon L. Fuller, The Morality of Law (1964), 43

James A. Gardner, Legal Argument: The Structure and Language of Effective Advocacy (2d ed. 2007), 57

Bryan A. Garner, *A Text on Textualism, Part 2*, ABA J. 27 (Nov. 2012), 538

Bryan A. Garner, *Outtakes from a Treatise*, ABA J. 22 (Oct. 2012), 538

Rafael Gely, *Of Sinking and Escalating: A (Somewhat) New Look at Stare Decisis*, 60 U. Pitt. L. Rev. 89 (1998), 148

Michael J. Gerhardt, The Power of Precedent (2008), 201

Ruth Bader Ginsburg, *Remarks on Writing Separately*, 65 Wash. L. Rev. 133 (1990), 72

Timothy J. Goodson, Comment, *Duck, Duck, Goose: Hunting for Better Recusal Practices in the United States Supreme Court in Light of* Cheney v. United States District Court, 84 N.C. L. Rev. 181 (2005), 411

Brianne J. Gorod, *The Adversarial Myth: Appellate Court Extra-Record Factfinding*, 61 Duke L.J. 101 (2011), 401

Abbe R. Gluck, *Statutory Interpretation Methodology as "Law": Oregon's Path-Breaking Interpretive Framework and its Lessons for the Nation*, 47 Willamette L. Rev. 539 (2011), 611

Abbe R. Gluck, *The States as Laboratories of Statutory Interpretation: Methodological Consensus and the New Modified Textualism*, 119 Yale L.J. 1750 (2010), 611, 613

Abbe R. Gluck & Lisa Schultz Bressman, *Statutory Interpretation from the Inside—An Empirical Study of Congressional Drafting, Delegation, and the Canons: Part I*, 65 STAN. L. REV. 901 (2013), 444

Gil Grantmore, *The Headnote*, 5 GREEN BAG 2D 157 (2002), 59

Kent Greenawalt, *Reflections on Holding and Dictum*, 39 J. LEGAL EDUC. 431 (1989), 82

KENT GREENAWALT, STATUTORY INTERPRETATION: 20 QUESTIONS (1999), 609

EUGENE GRESSMAN ET AL., SUPREME COURT PRACTICE (9th ed. 2007), 131, 294

T.J. Halstead, *Presidential Signing Statements: Constitutional and Institutional Implications* (CRS Report for Congress Sept. 17, 2007), 672, 682

John Harrington, Note, *Amici Curiae in the Federal Courts of Appeals: How Friendly Are They?*, 55 CASE WESTERN RES. L. REV. 667 (2005), 342

HENRY M. HART, JR. & ALBERT M. SACKS, THE LEGAL PROCESS: BASIC PROBLEMS IN THE MAKING AND APPLICATION OF LAW (tentative ed. 1958), iv

HENRY M. HART, JR. & ALBERT M. SACKS, THE LEGAL PROCESS: BASIC PROBLEMS IN THE MAKING AND APPLICATION OF LAW (William N. Eskridge, Jr. & Philip P. Frickey eds., 1994), i, 25, 44, 159, 318, 355, 386, 400, 480, 487, 528, 532, 544, 545, 546, 555, 578, 611

H.L.A. Hart, *Positism and the Separation of Law and Morals*, 71 HARV. L. REV. 593 (1958), 2

John J. Hasko, *Persuasion in the Court: Nonlegal Materials in U.S. Supreme Court Opinions*, 94 LAW LIBR. J. 427 (2002), 247

John W. Head, *Codes, Cultures, Chaos, and Champions: Common Features of Legal Codification Experiences in China, Europe, and North America*, 13 DUKE COMP. & INTL. L. 1 (2003), 451

Jon G. Heintz, Note, *Sustained Dissent and the Extended Deliberative Process*, 88 NOTRE DAME L. REV. 1939 (2013), 72

M. Todd Henderson, *From Seriatim to Consensus and Back Again: A Theory of Dissent*, 2007 S. CT. REV. 283, 72

Kristen L. Henke, Comment, *If It's Not Broke, Don't Fix It: Ignoring Criticisms of Supreme Court Recusals*, 57 ST. LOUIS U. L.J. 521 (2013), 425

OLIVER WENDELL HOLMES, COLLECTED LEGAL PAPERS (1920), 475

Oliver Wendell Holmes, *The Path of the Law*, 10 HARV. L. REV. 457 (1897), 148

C. HUGHES, THE SUPREME COURT OF THE UNITED STATES (1928), 4

J.D. Hyman, *Constitutional Jurisprudence and the Teaching of Constitutional Law*, 28 STAN. L. REV. 1271 (1976), iv

INITIATIVE & REFERENDUM INSTITUTE AT THE UNIVERSITY OF SOUTHERN CALIFORNIA, http://iandrinstitute.org/, 455

Vicki C. Jackson, *Constitutional Comparisons: Convergence, Resistance, Engagement*, 119 HARV. L REV. 109 (2005), 285

Arthur J. Jacobson, *Publishing Dissent*, 62 WASH. & LEE L. REV. 1607 (2005), 70, 73

Linda D. Jellum, *"Which Is To Be Master," the Judiciary or the Legislature? When Statutory Directives Violate Separation of Powers*, 56 UCLA L. REV. 837 (2009), 611

MARGARET Z. JOHNS & REX R. PERSCHBACHER, THE UNITED STATES LEGAL SYSTEM: AN INTRODUCTION (2002), 6

Judicial Business of the United States Court, 2011 Annual Report of the Director, www.uscourts.gov/uscourts/statistics/JudicialBusiness/2011/JudicialBusiness2011.pdf, 243, 294

Joseph D. Kearney & Thomas W. Merrill, *The Influence of Amicus Curiae Briefs on the Supreme Court*, 148 U. PA. L. REV. 743 (2000), 342

Orin S. Kerr, *How to Read a Legal Opinion: A Guide for New Law Students*, 11 GREEN BAG 2D 51 (2007), 59

CORNELIUS M. KERWIN, RULEMAKING: HOW GOVERNMENT AGENCIES WRITE LAW AND MAKE POLICY (3d ed. 2003), 699

Vesan Kesavan, *The Three Tiers of Federal Law*, 100 NW. U. L. REV. 1479 (2006), 3

Jeffrey L. Kirchmeier & Samuel A. Thumma, *Scaling the Lexicon Fortress: The United States Supreme Court's Use of Dictionaries in the Twenty-First Century*, 94 MARQ. L. REV. 77 (2010), 528

David Klein & Neal Devins, *Dicta, Schmicta: Theory Versus Practice in Lower Court Decision Making*, 54 WM. & MARY L. REV. 2021 (2013), 82

Donald J. Kochan, *The "Reason-Giving Lawyer: An Ethical, Practical, and Pedagogical Perspective*, 26 GEO. J. OF LEGAL ETHICS 261 (2013), 318

Steven Kochevar, Comment, *Amici Curiae in Civil Law Jurisdictions*, 122 YALE L.J. 1653 (2013), 342

Randy J. Kozel, *Precedent and Reliance*, 62 EMORY L.J. 1459 (2013), 150

Randy J. Kozel, Stare Decisis *as Judicial Doctrine*, 67 WASH. & LEE L. REV. 411 (2010), 150

Mark R. Kravitz, *Written and Oral Persuasion in the United States Courts: A District Judge's Perspective on Their History, Function, and Future*, 10 J. APP. PRAC. & PROCESS 247 (2009), 294

Samuel Krislov, *The Amicus Curiae Brief: From Friendship to Advocacy*, 72 YALE L.J. 694 (1963), 342

Allison Larsen, *Confronting Supreme Court Fact Finding*, 98 VA. L. REV. 1255 (2012), 341, 402

Allison Orr Larsen, *Factual Precedents*, 162 U. PA. L. REV. 59 (2013), 80

Mitchel de S. –O. –L'E. Lasser, Judicial
  Deliberations: A Comparative Analysis of
  Judicial Transparency and Legitimacy (2004), 74

Gary Lawson, *Mostly Unconstitutional: The Case Against
  Precedent Revisited*, 5 Ave Maria L. Rev. 1 (2007), 179

Gary Lawson, *Stipulating the Law*, 109 Mich. L. Rev.
  1191 (2011), 340

Gary Lawson & Stephen Kam, *Making Law Out of
  Nothing at All: The Origins of the* Chevron *Doctrine*,
  65 Admin. L. Rev. 1 (2013), 706

Pierre N. Leval, *Judging Under the Constitution: Dicta
  About Dicta*, 81 N.Y.U. L. Rev. 1249 (2006), 81

Laurie L. Levenson, *Retroactivity of cases on criminal
  defendants' rights; Of the past term's decisions, it's
  clear that one is not retroactive, another will allow for
  collateral attach of convictions*, Natl. L.J. 26 (Aug. 13,
  2012), 373

Hillel Y. Levin, *A Reliance Approach to Precedent*, 47 Ga.
  L. Rev. 1035 (2013), 150

Hillel Y. Levin, *The Food Stays in the Kitchen: Everything
  I Needed to Know About Statutory Interpretation I
  Learned by the Time I Was Nine*, 12 Green Bag 2d
  337 (2009), 605

Mark I. Levy, *Changes in Law*, Natl. L.J. at 13 (Dec. 3,
  2007), 354

Douglas Lind, Logic and Legal Reasoning (2001),
  57

Peter Linzer, *The Meaning of Certiorari Denials*, 79
  Colum. L. Rev. 1227 (1979), 212, 215

Justin R. Long, *Against Certification*, 78 Geo. Wash. R.
  Rev. 114 (2009), 128, 129, 130

Jeffrey S. Lubbers, A Guide to Federal Agency
  Rulemaking (4th ed. 2006), 699

David B. Mableby, Direct Legislation (1984), 456

John F. Manning, *Clear Statement Rules and the
  Constitution*, 110 Colum. L. Rev. 399 (2010), 545

John F. Manning, *Federalism and the Generality Problem
  in Constitutional Interpretation*, 122 Harv. L. Rev.
  2003 (2009), 615

John F. Manning, *Textualism and Legislative Intent*, 91
  Va. L. Rev. 419 (2005), 579

John F. Manning, *The Absurdity Doctrine*, 116 Harv. L.
  Rev. 2387 (2003), 567, 568

John F. Manning, *The New Purposivism*, 2011 S. Ct. Rev.
  113, 605

John F. Manning, *What Divides Textualists From
  Purposivists?*, 106 Colum. L. Rev. 70
  (2006), 590

Justin Marceau, *Plurality Decisions: Upward-Flowing
  Precedent and Acoustic Separation*, 45 Conn. L. Rev.
  933 (2013), 69

Richard L. Marcus, *Conflicts Among Circuits and
  Transfers Within the Federal Judicial System*, 93 Yale
  L.J. 677 (1984), 156, 157

James Markham, Note, *Against Individually Signed
  Judicial Opinions*, 56 Duke L.J. 923 (2006), 68

Robert J. Martineau, Appellate Justice in England
  and the United States: A Comparative Analysis
  (1990), 295

Robert J. Martineau, *Considering New Issues on Appeal:
  The General Rule and the Gorilla Rule*, 40
  Vand. L. Rev. 1023 (1987), 350

Robert J. Martineau, *The Value of Appellate Oral
  Argument: A Challenge to the Conventional Wisdom*,
  72 Iowa L. Rev. 1 (1986), 294

Tony Mauro, *Justices Kagan, Alito Recusals Adding Up in
  New Court Term*, Natl. L.J. 17 (Oct. 21, 2013), 425

Tony Mauro, *Typically Quiet, Justices Open Up About
  Denials; Seven nondecision opinions issued this term-
  so far*, Natl. L.J. 1 (Nov. 25, 2013), 218

John O. McGinnis, *Foreign to Our Constitution*, 100 Nw.
  U. L. Rev. 303 (2006), 285

Joseph W. Mead, *Stare Decisis in the Inferior Courts of
  the United States*, 12 Nev. L.J. 787 (2012), 158

Jason C. Miller & Hannah B. Murray, *Wikipedia in
  Court: When and How Citing Wikipedia and Other
  Consensus Websites Is Appropriate*, 84 St. John's L.
  Rev. 633 (2010), 247

Max Minzner, *Saving Stare Decisis: Preclusion, Precedent,
  and Procedural Due Process*, 2010 BYU L. Rev. 597,
  399

James Wm. Moore, Moore's Federal Practice
  (3d ed. 2008), 92, 95, 100, 102, 105, 130, 157, 158,
  202

Jonathan Remy Nash, *Examining the Power of Federal
  Courts to Certify Questions of State Law*, 88 Cornell
  L. Rev. 1672 (2003), 123, 127

Jonathan Remy Nash, *Resuscitating Deference to Lower
  Federal Court Judges' Interpretations of State Law*, 77
  S. Cal. L. Rev. 975 (2004), 114

Jonathan Remy Nash, *The Uneasy Case for
  Transjurisdictional Adjudication*, 94 Va. L. Rev. 1869
  (2008), 120

National Conference of Commissioners on Uniform
  State Laws, *Drafting Rules* (2006), 524

National. Survey of State Laws (Richard A. Leiter
  ed., 6th ed. 2008), 451

Note, *Litigating the Defense of Marriage Act: The Next
  Battleground for Same-Sex Marriage*, 117 Harv. L.
  Rev. 2684 (2004), 575

Note, *Looking It Up: Dictionaries and Statutory
  Interpretation*, 107 Harv. L. Rev. 1437 (1994), 527

Note, *Securing Uniformity in National Law: A Proposal
  for National Stare Decisis in the Courts of Appeals*, 87
  Yale L.J. 1219 (1978), 157

Victoria Nourse, *A Decision Theory of Statutory
  Interpretation: Legislative History by the Rules*, 122
  Yale L.J. 70 (2012), 551

Barack Obama, Memorandum for the Heads of Executive Departments and Agencies on Presidential Signing Statements, 74 Fed. Reg. 10669, 683, 684

Gary E. O'Connor, *Restatement (First) of Statutory Interpretation*, 7 N.Y.U. J. Legis. & Pub. Pol'y 333 (2004), 610

Office of the Legislative Counsel, U.S. House of Representatives, House Legislative Counsel's Manual on Drafting Style (1995), 612

Chad M. Oldfather, *Writing, Cognition, and the Nature of the Judicial Function*, 96 Geo. L.J. 1283 (2008), 317

Edwin W. Patterson, *The Interpretation and Construction of Contracts*, 64 Colum. L. Rev. 833 (1964), 460

Michael Stokes Paulsen, *Abrogating Stare Decisis by Statute: May Congress Remove the Precedential Effect of* Roe *and* Casey?, 109 Yale L.J. 1535 (2000), 201

Michael Stokes Paulsen, *Does the Supreme Court's Current Doctrine of Stare Decisis Require Adherence to the Supreme Court's Current Doctrine of Stare Decisis?*, 86 N.C. L. Rev. 1165 (2008), 187

Lee Petherbridge & David L. Schwartz, *An Empirical Assessment of the Supreme Court's Use of Legal Scholarship*, 106 Nw. U. L. Rev. 995 (2012), 247

Practice Direction: Citation of Authorities (2012), 244

Prefatory Note, 1996 Uniform Law Commissioners' Model Punitive Damages Act, 14 Uniform Laws Annotated 315 (2005), 5

Jeanne Frazier Price, *Wagging, Not Barking: Statutory Definitions*, 60 Cleve. St. L. Rev. 999 (2013), 526

Daniel Purcell, *The Public Right to Precedent: A Theory and Rejection of Vacatur*, 85 Cal. L. Rev. 867 (1997), 224

Laura Krugman Ray, *Circumstance and Strategy: Jointly Authored Supreme Court Opinions*, 12 Nev. L.J. 727 (2012), 70

Laura Krugman Ray, *The Road to* Bush v. Gore: *The History of the Supreme Court's Use of the Per Curiam Opinion*, 79 Neb. L. Rev. 517 (2000), 68

Laura Krugman Ray, *The Justices Write Separately: Uses of the Concurrence by the Rehnquist Court*, 23 U.C. Davis L. Rev. 777 (1990), 71

Ira P. Robbins, *Hiding Behind the Cloak of Invisibility: The Supreme Court and Per Curiam Opinions*, 86 Tul. L. Rev. 1197 (2012), 68

Nicholas Quinn Rosenkranz, *Federal Rules of Statutory Interpretation*, 115 Harv. L. Rev. 2085 (2002), 610

Jeffrey S. Rosenthal & Albert H. Yoon, *Judicial Ghostwriting: Authorship on the Supreme Court*, 96 Cornell L. Rev. 1307 (2011), 72

Phillip A. Rubin, Note, *War of the Words: How Courts Can Use Dictionaries Consistent with Textualist Principles*, 60 Duke L.J. 167 (2010), 531

James Sample et al., Fair Courts: Setting Recusal Standards (Brennan Center for Justice 2008), 425

James Sample, *Supreme Court Recusal: From* Marbury *to the Modern Day*, 26 Geo. J. Legal Ethics 95 (2013), 425

Antonin Scalia, A Matter of Interpretation (1997), 568, 610

Antonin Scalia, *The Rule of Law as a Law of Rules*, 56 U. Chi. L. Rev. 1175 (1989), 80

Antonin Scalia & Bryan A. Garner, Making Your Case: The Art of Persuading Judges (2008), 55, 245, 292

Antonin Scalia & Bryan A. Garner, Reading Law: The Interpretation of Legal Texts (2012), 460, 531, 537

Walter V. Schaefer, *Reducing Circuit Conflicts*, 69 ABA J. 452 (April 1983), 157

Frederick Schauer, *A Critical Guide to Vehicles in the Park*, 83 N.Y.U. L. Rev. 1109 (2008), 2

Frederick Schauer, *Authority and Authorities*, 94 Va. L. Rev. 1931 (2008), 247

Frederick Schauer, *Giving Reasons*, 47 Stan. L. Rev. 633 (1995), 298

Frederick Schauer, *Has Precedent Ever Really Mattered in the Supreme Court?*, 24 Ga. St. U. L. Rev. 381 (2007), 201

Frederick Schauer, *Precedent*, 39 Stan. L. Rev. 571 (1987), 161

Frederick Schauer, Thinking Like a Lawyer: A New Introduction to Legal Reasoning (2009), 178

Jacob Scott, *Codified Canons and the Common Law of Interpretation*, 98 Geo. L.J. 341 (2010), 538

Section of Administrative Law and Regulatory practice, American Bar Association, A Blackletter Statement of Federal Administrative Law (2004), 692

Bruce M. Selya, *Certified Madness: Ask a Silly Question . . .* , 29 Suffolk U. L. Rev. 677 (1995), 131

Bradley Scott Shannon, *May Stare Decisis Be Abrogated by Rule?*, 67 Ohio St. L.J. 645 (2006), 201, 244

Bradley Scott Shannon, *Overruling by Implication*, 33 Seattle U. L. Rev. 151 (2009), 203, 205

Bradley Scott Shannon, *Responding to Summary Judgment*, 91 Marq. L. Rev. 815 (2008), 83

Bradley Scott Shannon, *Some Concerns About Sua Sponte*, 73 Ohio St. L.J. Furthermore 27 (2012), 341

Bradley Scott Shannon, *The Retroactive and Prospective Application of Judicial Decisions*, 26 Harv. J.L. & Pub. Pol'y 811 (2003), 24, 355

Martin Shapiro, *The Giving Reasons Requirement*, 1992 U. Chi. Legal Forum 179, 318

Jarrod Shobe, *Intertemporal Statutory Interpretation and the Evolution of Legislative Drafting*, 114 COLUM. L. REV. 807 (2014), 428, 444, 498

Linda Sandstrom Simard, *An Empirical Study of Amici Curiae in Federal Courts: A Fine Balance of Access, Efficiency, and Adversarialism*, 27 REV. LIT. 669 (2008), 342

MICHAEL SINCLAIR, GUIDE TO STATUTORY INTERPRETATION 85 (2000), 459, 590

NORMAN J. SINGER, STATUTES AND STATUTORY CONSTRUCTION (6th ed. 2002), 427, 523, 525

Amy E. Sloan, *The Dog That Didn't Bark: Stealth Procedures and the Erosion of Stare Decisis in the Federal Courts of Appeals*, 78 FORDHAM L. REV. 713 (2009), 158

Lawrence Solan, *When Judges Use the Dictionary*, 68 AM. SPEECH 50 (1993), 531

Lawrence B. Solum, *The Interpretation-Construction Distinction*, 27 CONST. COMMENT. 95 (2010), 460

Mark Spottswood, *Live Hearings and Paper Trials*, 38 FL. ST. U. L. REV. 827 (2011), 294

James F. Spriggs II & David R. Stras, *Explaining Plurality Decisions*, 99 GEO. L.J. 515 (2011), 72

Kevin M. Stack, *Interpreting Regulations*, 111 MICH. L. REV. 355 (2012), 699

Kevin M. Stack, Note, *The Practice of Dissent in the Supreme Court*, 105 YALE L.J. 2235 (1996), 72

Kevin M. Stack, *The Divergence of Constitutional and Statutory Interpretation*, 75 U. COLO. L. REV. 1 (2004), 460

Adam N. Steinman, *The Irrepressible Myth of* Celotex: *Reconsidering Summary Judgment Burdens Twenty Years after the Trilogy*, 63 WASH. & LEE L. REV. 81 (2006), 82

Joan Steinman, *Appellate Courts as First Responders: The Constitutionality and Propriety of Appellate Courts' Resolving Issues in the First Instance*, 87 NOTRE DAME L. REV. 1521 (2012), 354

Bezalel Stern, *Nonlegal Citations and the Failure of Law: A Case Study of the Supreme Court 2010-11 Term*, 35 WHITTIER L. REV. 75 (2103), 247

ROBERT L. STERN, APPELLATE PRACTICE IN THE UNITED STATES (1981), 294

Judith M. Stinson, *Why Dicta Becomes Holding and Why It Matters*, 76 BROOK. L. REV. 219 (2010), 81

PETER L. STRAUSS, LEGISLATION: UNDERSTANDING AND USING STATUTES (2006), 610

Charles A. Sullivan, *On Vacation*, 43 HOUS. L. REV. 1143 (2006), 224, 225

John V. Sullivan, *How Our Laws Are Made* (2007), 429

CASS SUNSTEIN, WHY SOCIETIES NEED DISSENT (2003), 72

Symposium, 44 ARIZ. ST. L.J. 1017 (2012), 69

Symposium, 36 ARIZ. ST. L.J. 493 (2004), 69

Symposium, *The State of Recusal: Judicial Disqualification, Due Process, and the Public's Post-Caperton Perception of the Integrity of the Judicial System*, 58 DRAKE L. REV. 657 (2010), 425

Brian Z. Tamanaha, *A Concise Guide to the Rule of Law*, in RELOCATING THE RULE OF LAW (G. Palombella & N. Walker eds., 2009), 7

Brian Z. Tamanaha, ON THE RULE OF LAW: HISTORY, POLITICS, THEORY (2004), 18

Joseph T. Thai & Andrew M. Coats, *The Case for Oral Argument in the Supreme Court of Oklahoma*, 62 OKLA. L. REV. 695 (2008), 294

THE BLUEBOOK: A UNIFORM SYSTEM OF CITATION 101 (19th ed. 2010), 217

The Reg Map, http://www.reginfo.gov/public/reginfo/ Regmap/index.jsp, 697, 698

Samuel A. Thumma & Jeffrey L. Kirchmeier, *The Lexicon Has Become a Fortress: The United States Supreme Court's Use of Dictionaries*, 47 BUFF. L. REV. 227 (1999), 528

Mark Alan Thurmon, Note, *When the Court Divides: Reconsidering the Precedential Value of Supreme Court Plurality Decisions*, 42 DUKE L.J. 419 (1992), 69

Jeff Todd, *Undead Precedent: The Curse of a Holding "Limited to Its Facts,"* 40 TEX. TECH L. REV. 67 (2007), 81

William Michael Treanor & Gene B. Sperling, *Prospective Overruling and the Revival of "Unconstitutional" Statutes*, 93 COLUM. L. REV. 1902 (1993), 665

Will Tress, *Lost Laws: What We Can't Find in the United States Code*, 40 GOLDEN GATE U. L. REV. 129 (2010), 450

Daniel E. Troy, *Toward a Definition and Critique of Retroactivity*, 51 ALA. L. REV. 1329 (2000), 657

Frank Tuerkheimer, *A Short Essay on the Editing of Cases in Casebooks*, 58 J. LEGAL ED. 531 (2008), iv

Charles C. Turner et al., *Beginning to Write Separately: The Origins and Development of Concurring Judicial Opinions*, 35 J. SUP. CT. HIST. 93 (2010), 71

Amanda L. Tyler, *Setting the Supreme Court's Agenda: Is There a Place for Certification?*, 78 GEO. WASH. L. REV. 1310 (2010), 131

Uniform Certification of Questions of Law Act, 12 U.L.A. 67 (1996), 130

UNIFORM STATUTE AND RULE CONSTRUCTION ACT (1995), 610

United States House of Representatives, The Legislative Process, http://www.house.gov/content/learn/ legislative_process/, 444

Carlos Manual Vazquez, *Treaties As Law of the Land: The Supremacy Clause and the Judicial Enforcement of Treaties*, 122 HARV. L. REV. 599 (2008), 454

Louis J. Virelli III, *The (Un)Constitutionality of Supreme Court Recusal Standards*, 2011 WIS. L. REV. 1181, 425

Fred M. Vinson, *Work of the Federal Courts*, 69 S. Ct. v (1949), 71

Eugene Volokh, *Foreign Law in American Courts*, 66 OKLA. L. REV. 219 (2014), 285

Hanah Metchis Volokh, *A Read-the-Bill Rule for Congress*, 76 MO. L. REV. 135 (2011), 444

Jeremy Waldron, *Five to Four: Why Do Bare Majorities Rule on Courts?*, 123 YALE L.J. 1692 (2014), 72

Jeremy Waldron, *Stare Decisis and the Rule of Law: A Layered Approach*, 111 MICH. L. REV. 1 (2012), 201

Jeremy Waldron, *The Concept and the Rule of Law*, 43 GA. L. REV. 1 (2009), 20

Mark Walsh, *Frequent Filers: It was another big term for amicus briefs at the high court*, ABA J. 16 (Sept. 2013), 342

Stephen L. Wasby, *The Per Curiam Opinion: Its Nature and Functions*, 76 JUDICATURE 29 (1992), 68

Stephen L. Wasby, *Why Sit En Banc?*, 63 HASTINGS L.J. 747 (2012), 94

M. DANE WATERS, INITIATIVES AND REFERENDUM ALMANAC (2003), 456

WEBSTER'S THIRD NEW INTERNATIONAL DICTIONARY (1961), 528, 529, 531

Herbert Wechsler, *The Courts and the Constitution*, 65 COLUM. L. REV. 1001 (1965), 24

ANTHONY WESTON, A RULEBOOK FOR ARGUMENTS (4th ed. 2009), 57

Mary Whisner, *Other Uses of Legislative History*, 105 LAW LIBR. J. 243 (2013), 552

Mary Whisner, *There Oughta Be a Law—A Model Law*, 106 LAW LIBR. J. 125 (2014), 5

Mary Whisner, *The* United States Code, *Prima Facie Evidence, and Positive Law*, 101 LAW LIBR. J. 545 (2009), 445

James J. White, Ex Proprio Vigore, 89 MICH. L. REV. 2096 (1991), 5

Ross A. Wilson, Note, *A Third Way: The Presidential Nonsigning Statement*, 96 CORNELL L. REV. 1503 (2011), 685

WORLD JUSTICE PROJECT, http://worldjusticeproject. org/, 18, 19

CHARLES ALAN WRIGHT ET AL., FEDERAL PRACTICE AND PROCEDURE, 90, 91, 92, 94

Stephen Yeazell, *When and How U.S. Courts Should Cite Foreign Law*, 26 CONST. COMMENT. 59 (2009), 279

Donald H. Zeigler, *Gazing Into the Crystal Ball: Reflections on the Standards State Judges Should Use to Ascertain Federal Law*, 40 WM. & MARY L. REV. 1143 (1999), 103, 104, 105

Table of Constitutional Provisions, Statutes, Rules, Regulations, and Executive Orders

United States Constitution

U.S. Const. art. I 2, 650, 682
U.S. Const. art. II 2
U.S. Const. art. III 2
U.S. Const. art. VI 3, 427

Federal Statutes

1 U.S.C. §§ 1-6 525
1 U.S.C. § 7 525
1 U.S.C. § 8 525
1 U.S.C. § 109 640
1 U.S.C. § 112 450
1 U.S.C. § 204 . . . . 449, 450
5 U.S.C. § 551 . . . . 691, 692
5 U.S.C. § 553 692
5 U.S.C. § 554 692
5 U.S.C. § 556 692
5 U.S.C. § 557 692
5 U.S.C. § 704 699
5 U.S.C. § 706 699
8 U.S.C. § 1326 . . . . 205, 206
16 U.S.C. § 1531 524
18 U.S.C. § 924 . . . . 512, 517, 522
18 U.S.C. § 2312 570
18 U.S.C. § 2421 474
28 U.S.C. § 1 66
28 U.S.C. § 46 66
28 U.S.C. § 455 . . . . 410, 411, 422
28 U.S.C. § 1254 131
28 U.S.C. § 1257 131
28 U.S.C. § 1369 526
28 U.S.C. § 1391 . . . . 452, 545
28 U.S.C. § 1652 658
28 U.S.C. § 1920 531
28 U.S.C. § 2072 . . . . 3, 659
28 U.S.C. § 2106 . . . . 223, 348
28 U.S.C. § 2254 373
28 U.S.C. § 2255 373
42 U.S.C. § 2000e 544
43 U.S.C. § 1744 500

44 U.S.C. § 1505 690
E-Government Act of 2002, Pub. L. No. 107-347,
116 Stat. 2899 243
Federal Courts Jurisdiction and Venue
Clarification Act of 2011, Pub. L. No.
112-63, 125 Stat. 763 487
Fraud Enforcement & Recovery Act of 2009,
Pub. L. No. 111-21, 123 Stat. 1617 650

State Statutes

Fla. Code § 794.011 568
Fla. Code § 794.05 568
RSA 458:7 574
Tenn. Code §§ 47-25-1103 120
Tenn. Code §§ 47-25-1104 120

Federal Rules of Appellate Procedure

Fed. R. App. P. 32.1 . . . . 242, 243, 244
Fed. R. App. P. 34 290

Federal Rules of Civil Procedure

Fed. R. Civ. P. 44.1 284
Fed. R. Civ. P. 50 348
Fed. R. Civ. P. 52 318
Fed. R. Civ. P. 54 90
Fed. R. Civ. P. 56 . . . . 318, 341
Fed. R. Civ. P. 78 290
Fed. R. Civ. P. 86 . . . . 642, 659

Federal Rules of Evidence

Fed. R. Evid. 403 567
Fed. R. Evid. 609 567
Fed. R. Evid. 801 551

Supreme Court and Circuit Rules

S. Ct. R. 19 131
S. Ct. R. 28 291

S. Ct. R. 37 342
Ninth Cir. R. 36-3 243

Federal Regulations

36 C.F.R. § 1280.24 699

Federal Executive Orders

Executive Order 12988, 61 Fed. Reg. 4729
(1996) 612, 613, 698
Executive Order 11030, 27 Fed. Reg. 5847
(1962) 690

Index

Absurdity doctrine, 562-68
Adjudicative process
    forms and limits, 27-43
    in general, 25-44
Administrative agencies
    in general, 691-92
    role in statutory interpretation, 700-58
Administrative Procedure Act, 691-92
Administrative rulemaking
    in general, 692-700
    judicial review of, 699-700
Amicus curiae practice, 341-42

Binding effect of prior decisions in related proceedings
    in general, 85-96
    law of the case, 83-92
    preclusion, 83
    precedent, 83
Borrowed statutes, 560-61

Canons of construction, 517, 532-38
Case law
    common law, 23
    interpretation of, 82-83
    interpretive, 23
    terminology, 84
Certification
    abstention contrasted, 121-23
    availability, 130
    certiorari contrasted, 121-23
    costs and benefits, 125-30
    in general, 120-31
    questions of state law, 120-30
    questions of federal law, 131
    procedure, 124-25
    Uniform Certification of Questions of Law
        Act, 130
Clear statement rules, 538-45
Codification, 443, 445-53
Concurring opinion (or concurrence), 65-66, 70-71
Conflicts of laws, 6-7

Deciding issues for the first time on appeal
    appellee exception, 349-50
    changes in law, relation to, 354
    generally, 342-54
    problems with, 353

Decisional methodology
    as part of holding, 79-80
    as to doctrine of stare decisis, 146
    as to methods of statutory interpretation, 610-11
    in general, 79-80
Dicta
    as part of judicial decision, 58
    holding contrasted, 74-82
Dictionaries, use of, 526-31
Dissenting opinion (or dissent), 66, 71-72

Election of judges, 422-24
Executive branch, 2, 671-758
Executive orders, 685-90, 698

Federal courts
    functions, 24-25
Federal system of government, 2
Foreign law, use by United States courts, 274-85

Government of the United States
    diagram, 21

Headnotes, 58-64
Hearings
    oral argument, relation to, 285-91
    meaning of, 285-91
Holdings
    alternative, 78-79
    as part of judicial decision, 58
    decisional methodology as, 79-80
    defined, 74-76, 78-79
    dicta contrasted, 74-82
    factual findings as, 80
    Marks rule, 69
    scope, 81
Horizontal stare decisis. *See* Stare decisis

Impartiality, judicial, 402-25
Initiatives and referendums, 454-57
Intentionalism, 466, 576, 579-90

Judicial branch, 2, 23-425
Judicial estoppel, 94-95
Judgment
    appellate, form, 69
    in general, 58-59, 69

Judicial decisions. *See also* Opinions
    citation, 57, 59
    dicta, 58
    headnotes, 58-64
    holding, 58
    judgment, 58-59
    opinion, 58-59
    parts of, 57-64
    retroactive and prospective effect, 354-99
    syllabus, 58-64
    title, 57, 59

Law of the case, 85-92
    as to coordinate courts, 91-92
    mandate rule, 91
    rationale for, 90
    rule for, 90
    test for, 89-90
    various forms of doctrine, 90-92
Lead opinion, 65
Legal process
    defined, 1
Legislative branch, 2, 427-670
Legislative history, 498-99, 546-53
Legislative inaction, 522, 553-58
Legislative process, 428-44, 452-53
Legislative versus adjudicative facts, 401-02
Legislative versus judicial resolution, 399-402
Logic
    analogy, 52-53
    deductive reasoning, 45-51, 54-57
    inductive reasoning, 51-52
    role in judicial decisions, 44-57

Majority opinion, 64, 72
"Mischief" rule, 463

Opinions. *See also* Judicial decisions
    authorship and delivery, 67, 72
    concurring, 65-66, 70-71
    delivery types, 69-70
    dissenting, 66, 71-72
    foreign judicial systems contrasted, 73-74
    individually signed, 70
    in general, 58-59
    lead, 65
    majority, 64, 72
    per curiam, 67-68
    persuasive effect of, 64-66
    plurality, 65, 72
    various types, 64-74
Opinion writing, 59
Oral argument
    disadvantages, 293-94
    purpose and value, 291-95
    use in England, 296
Overruling
    by implication, 202-06
    generally, 202

Per curiam opinion, 67-68
Persuasive authority
    factors affecting persuasiveness, 246
    in general, 245-74
    sources and ranking, 246, 265
    use by courts, 247
"Plain meaning" rule, 474
Plurality opinion, 65, 72
Precedent. *See also* Stare decisis
    adoption by newly created courts, 206-12
    avoiding, 201-02
    distinguishing, 201
    equally divided court, effect, 66-67
    following, 201
    overruling, 202
Presidential directives
    amendment and revocation, 690
    executive orders, 685-90, 698
    memoranda, 685
    proclamations, 685
    propriety, 686-90
    publication, 690
Presidential signing statements, 672-85
Primary authorities
    case law, 3-4
    Constitution, 3
    federal system, 3-4
    in general, 3-4
    procedural rules, 3
    state systems, 4
    statutes, 3
    regulations, 3
Priority of authorities, 3-6
    case law, 3-4
    Constitution, 3
    federal system, 3-4
    procedural rules, 3
    state systems, 4
    statutes, 3
    regulations, 3
Purposivism, 480, 576-77, 590-605

Reasoned elaboration, 44
Reasons for decisions
    generally, 295-318
    reasons not to give reasons, 317
Reconsideration. *See* Law of the case
Rehearing and rehearing en banc, 92-94

Relative institutional competence, 401-02
Retroactivity and prospectivity
  congressional attempts to reopen federal court
    judgments, 666-70
  constitutional limitations to retroactivity, 386-99,
    650-57
  defined, 354-55
  federal procedural rules, effect, 642
  habeas corpus, 370-73
  judicial decisions, effect, 354-99
  state courts, 373
  statutes, effect, 615-57
  terminology, 356
Rooker-Feldman doctrine, 95-96
Rule of law
  American Bar Association Initiative, 18
  benefits of, 11-14
  defined, 8, 18-19
  elements in establishing, 14-16
  functions of, 8-11
  Index, World Justice Project, 19-20
  in general, 7-20
  noncore aspects, 16-17
  reasons to be wary of, 17-18

Scrivener's errors, 562-68
Secondary authorities
  articles, 6
  books, 6
  case law from other jurisdictions, 4
  in general, 4-6
  model acts, 5
  Restatements, 4-5
  treatises, 5-6
  uniform acts, 5
Stare decisis. *See also* Precedent
  abrogating, 201
  applied as to doctrine of stare decisis, 187-200
  civil law view, 150, 152
  deference to other federal courts, 105-120
  defined, 96
  English view, 151-52
  horizontal, 132-201
  federal law in state courts, effect of, 103-105
  in court of appeals, 152-58
  in district courts, 158
  in state courts, 100
  intermediate appellate court decisions, effect of, 100-01
  in theory, 159-201
  overruling doctrine itself, 201
  reasons for denying further review, 215-16
  relationship to "unpublished" decisions, 225-44
  significance of denials of further review, 212-18

state law in federal courts, effect of, 101-02
state law in other state courts, effect of, 105
state practice, 150
unconstitutionality, 179-87
vacatur, effect of, 69, 218-25
vertical, 96-101
State systems of government, 2
Statutes
  as positive law, 443, 445-50
  as prima facie evidence of the law, 443, 445-50
  codification, 443, 445-53
  conflicts between, 657-59
  effective dates, 639-40
  importance, 427
  in civil law countries, 451-52
  official and unofficial codes, 451
  repeal, effect of, 640
  retroactive and prospective application of, 615-57
  state codes, 451
  unconstitutional, effect, 659-66
Statutory construction, 460
Statutory definitions, 524-26
Statutory history, 498-99, 545-46
Statutory interpretation
  absurdity doctrine, 562-68
  acquiescence rule, 555-57
  ambiguity, 460
  as textual interpretation, 460
  basic concepts, 457-59
  borrowed statutes, 560-61
  canons of construction, 517, 532-38
  clear statement rules, 538-45
  dictionaries, use of, 526-31
  effect of judicial interpretation on administrative
    interpretation, 741-58
  Executive Order 12988, 612-13
  historical development, 460-87
  in general, 457-615
  in state courts, 613
  intentionalism, 466, 576, 579-90
  legislative drafting manuals, 611-12
  legislative history, 498-99, 546-53
  legislative inaction, 522, 553-58
  "mischief" rule, 463
  modern standard, 487-500
  parts of a statute, 523-24
  "plain meaning" rule, 474
  purposivism, 480, 576-77, 590-605
  reenactment rule, 557-58
  rejected proposal rule, 553-55
  role of administrative agencies, 700-58
  scrivener's errors, 562-68
  statutory construction contrasted, 460

Statutory interpretation (*Cont'd*)
    statutory definitions, 524-26
    statutory history, 498-99, 545-46
    subsequent legislative history, 559-60
    summaries, 610
    textualism, 498, 577-78, 579-605
    theories of, 575-615
    unforeseen problems, 569-75
    vagueness, 460
Sua sponte decisionmaking
    in general, 318-41
    problems with, 321-31, 338-41

Subsequent legislative history, 559-60
Syllabus, 58-64

Textualism, 498, 577-78, 579-605
Treaties, 453-54

"Unpublished" opinions
    in general, 225-44
    practice in England, 244

Vacatur, 69, 218-25
Vertical stare decisis. *See* Stare decisis